FAMILY LAW IN THE TWENTIETH CENTURY: A HISTORY

D1460063

Family Law in the Twentieth Century

A History

STEPHEN CRETNEY

OXFORD

UNIVERSITY PRESS

OXFORD
UNIVERSITY PRESS

Great Clarendon Street, Oxford OX2 6DP

Oxford University Press is a department of the University of Oxford.
It furthers the University's objective of excellence in research, scholarship,
and education by publishing worldwide in

Oxford New York

Auckland Cape Town Dar es Salaam Hong Kong Karachi
Kuala Lumpur Madrid Melbourne Mexico City Nairobi
New Delhi Shanghai Taipei Toronto

With offices in
Argentina Austria Brazil Chile Czech Republic France Greece
Guatemala Hungary Italy Japan South Korea Poland Portugal
Singapore Switzerland Thailand Turkey Ukraine Vietnam

Published in the United States
by Oxford University Press Inc., New York

British Library Cataloguing in Publication Data
Data available

Library of Congress Cataloging in Publication Data
Data available
ISBN 0–19–826899–8 (Hbk.)
ISBN 0–19–928091–6 (Pbk.)

1 3 5 7 9 10 8 6 4 2

Typeset by Hope Services (Abingdon) Ltd.
Printed in Great Britain
on acid-free paper by
Biddles Ltd., King's Lynn

Dedication

This book is dedicated to the memory of my father

Fred Cretney

Born: Barnsley, Yorkshire, 30 January 1902
Employed, for more than 50 years in the City of Manchester,
from 1915 to 1968
Died: Sherborne, Dorset, 16 February 1980

Prefatory Note to the Paperback Edition

This is essentially a reprint of the hardback edition published in 2003: no significant revision or up-dating has been undertaken, but the opportunity has been taken to correct some errors in the text. I am particularly grateful to Mr James Buckley, Professor Sir Guenter Treitel, and Professor Nigel Lowe for help in this respect.

Stephen Cretney

25 August 2004

Preface

There are many possible ways of approaching the history of the law and the family. This book is a study of the development of legal doctrine as embodied in English statute and case law and of the processes which led to change in the law in the twentieth century. It is not a study of the social and economic forces which govern the distribution of power in society and ultimately influence attitudes towards legislation and legal practice, nor is it a study of the impact which the law has on individual behaviour.

I believe that studies of the process of law reform can be revealing; and the reader will find many examples—the enactment of the Matrimonial Homes Act 1967 and its subsequent history may be one—in which what are sometimes dismissed as technical details influence the development of law and policy. Those who work away from the public gaze (notably officials in the government departments concerned and, perhaps most of all, the parliamentary counsel) have a greater influence in this respect than is often realised. Again, the fact that legislation in a democracy is almost always to a greater or lesser extent the outcome of a compromise between different interests is frequently not appreciated, whilst the tactics of those who wish to promote or resist change often influence developments (sometimes in an unforeseen way). The long history of the attempt to reform the divorce law in the period between the two World Wars and from 1945 to the enactment of the Divorce Reform Act in 1969 is an obvious example; but the struggle to provide some legal redress for the disinherited is less well known. A study of these processes may also throw some light on the development of what have come to be regarded as fundamental characteristics of English family law, notably the commitment (puzzling to some lawyers within the United Kingdom as well as to those elsewhere in the European Union) to allowing a wide judicial discretion to determine the arrangements to be made following marital breakdown.

I have made use not only of published sources but also of unpublished official papers and other archival sources. This is not a work of empirical research, but I have drawn heavily on studies of the working of the legal system, notably those conducted or inspired by the late Lord McGregor of Durris. It would be difficult to exaggerate his contribution to bringing about a change of attitude to the way in which the community regards the family justice system. I have also drawn on the valuable empirical studies made at a somewhat later period by my former colleagues at Bristol University, Professors Gwynn Davis and Mervyn Murch.

The book focusses on the twentieth century; but goes further back in time when necessary for an understanding of legal developments in the century. It is not a textbook on family law as it is today, and for that reason developments in the last 15 or 20 years of the century are dealt with comparatively briefly.

I intend the book to reflect the importance which issues seemed to have for contemporaries rather than the importance they have for observers at the end of the twentieth century; and it is this which accounts for the comparative brevity of my treatment of domestic violence and of the family outside marriage. But even a book as substantial as this inevitably has gaps: I am, for example, conscious that a lot could be said about the internationalisation of family law from before the Maintenance Orders (Facilities for Enforcement) Act 1920, through the Child Abduction legislation of the 1980s, to the Human Rights Act 1998. I am also conscious that the book (notwithstanding its title) contains no substantial treatment of the law of Scotland. A comparative study of the family justice systems on both sides of the Tweed would make a fascinating study, but this book is not the place for it.

Many remarkable but often today little remembered individuals have played a vital part in the developments with which this book is concerned; and I hope the biographical notes which I have provided will be helpful to an understanding of their roles.

This book is more extensively footnoted than is today the fashion; and for indulgence in this respect I am greatly indebted to the Oxford University Press. Lawyers are trained to give authority for the propositions they advance, and the footnote is the traditional (and much the best) way of doing so. But in a book which I hope will also be of interest to non-lawyers it seemed to be best to deal with the more abstruse legal technicalities in notes which can be consulted by those who wish to do so but can be ignored by others. Many of the footnotes reflect my belief that a writer's own words—particularly the words of such masters of the English language as were (in their different ways) Lord Denning and Sir Claud Schuster—give a far more vivid impression than could be conveyed in any other way. Perhaps readers should treat the footnotes as an 'extra', to be consulted according to personal taste and interest, separately from the text to which they are attached.

The Oxford University Press has throughout given unstinted support for all aspects of this project. I am especially grateful to Deborah Hey for her careful copy-editing of the text. I have incurred many other debts. Rebecca Probert, now of the Warwick University School of Law, most generously offered assistance and support at a time when it was greatly needed; and drafted a most valuable research paper, the scope of which is only inadequately apparent from the use I have made of a part of it in Chapter 13 of this book. For nearly a decade I have been able to enjoy the matchless research environment of All Souls College, Oxford. Without that, neither this book (nor its predecessor *Law, Law Reform and the Family*, on which I have to some extent drawn in the present text) could have been written. Many colleagues at All Souls have given me the benefit of their experience and specialist knowledge, but I owe especial thanks to Professor Andrew Ashworth, Dr Paul Brand, Professor Rees Davies, Dr Anne Davies, Dr Jane Humphries, Professor Roger Hood, Dr John Landers, Professor Jane Lewis, the late Sir Patrick Reilly, and Dr Charles Webster.

I have of course drawn a great deal on the work of other scholars. I must give special acknowledgment to Dr Cordelia Moyse. Her Cambridge University doctoral thesis *Reform of Marriage and Divorce Law in England and Wales 1909–37* is invaluable to anyone working in this field. I am grateful for help freely given over many years by my friend Leo Abse. His mastery of parliamentary procedures and commitment to social justice not only brought about the passage of the Divorce Reform Act 1969 but many other important reforms. Alastair Service provided a wealth of documentary material about the passage of the 1969 Act in an agreeably hospitable setting. Sir Edward Caldwell QC (sometime First Parliamentary Counsel) provided much helpful background information; Sir Peter North QC helped me to avoid error; and His Honour Judge the Lord Meston QC helped me in tracing the final years of the Divorce Law Reform Union. Sir Nicholas Wilson drew on his long experience at the divorce bar to clarify my understanding and direct me to sources I had overlooked. District Judge Roger Bird was, as always, an unfailing guide on practice and procedural questions. David Burrows, solicitor of Bristol, kindly helped me on some Legal Aid matters. Edwin Mullins and Dr Ann Dally helped me with information about their father, Claud Mullins, and his writings.

Scholars in the humanities are dependent on libraries, and this book could not have been written without the resources provided by the Bodleian Library and the Bodleian Law Library in Oxford, the British Library Newspaper Library at Colindale, the Codrington Library at All Souls College, the Oxford University History Faculty Library, Lambeth Palace Library, the Millicent Fawcett Library (now renamed the Women's Library) London Guildhall University, the Law Society's Library, the National Library of Wales Aberystwyth, the libraries of Rhodes House and Nuffield College Oxford, and the library of the Oxford and Cambridge Club London. Staff in the Bodleian Library Official Papers Room and the Bodleian Law Library have been especially helpful, and I would like to place on record how indebted I am to the Bodleian Law Library for its collection of supplanted but authoritative editions of legal texts. The extent to which I have drawn on the admirable facilities of the Public Record Office at Kew will be apparent from even the most cursory glance at the pages which follow.

I am grateful to the publishers for arranging the preparation of the Index and Tables.

Finally, I wish to record my gratitude to my wife Antonia (now Rector of the United Benefice of Beedon, Peasemore, West Ilsley and Farnborough, Berkshire) who for nearly thirty years has unfailingly provided cheerful and devoted support to me and to our family.

Stephen Cretney
The Feast of St Cyprian, Bishop of Carthage, 26 September 2002.

Acknowledgments

Parliamentary copyright material from Bills before Parliament, the Official Reports of Proceedings in Parliament, Select Committee Reports and other parliamentary material is reproduced with the permission of the Controller of Her Majesty's Stationery Office on behalf of Parliament. Crown copyright material is reproduced with the permission of the Controller of Her Majesty's Stationery Office.

Extracts from the *Law Reports* are published by permission of the Incorporated Council of Law Reporting; extracts from the All England Law Reports by permission of Butterworths (a division of Reed Elsevier (UK) Ltd) and extracts from the *Family Law Reports* by permission of Jordan Publishing Limited, Bristol.

Extracts from *Putting Asunder: A Divorce Law for Contemporary Society* published by S.P.C.K. in 1966 are reproduced by permission of the publishers. Extracts from *Private Member* (1973) and from *When Salem came to the Boro* (1988) are reproduced by permission of the authors, Mr Leo Abse and Mr Stuart Bell MP respectively. Professor George Behlmer of the University of Washington has allowed me to draw on his *Child Abuse and Moral Reform in England, 1870–1908* (1982) and his *Friends of the Family, The English Home and its Guardians. 1850–1940* (1998) both published by the Stanford University Press. Extracts from *A Child in Trust, The Report of the Panel of Inquiry into the Circumstances surrounding the Death of Jasmine Beckford* (1985) are reproduced by permission of Sir Louis Blom-Cooper QC and Brent Council; and extracts from *A Child in Mind: Protection of Children in a Responsible Society (The Report of the Commission of Inquiry into the circumstances surrounding the death of Kimberley Carlile)* (1987) by permission of Sir Louis Blom-Cooper QC, Greenwich Council and South East London Health Authority. The extract from E Grierson's *Storm Bird, The Strange Life of Georgina Weldon*, published by Chatto & Windus, is reprinted by permission of The Random House Group Ltd. Sir Crispin Tickell GCMG KCVO, grandson of ESP Haynes and the owner of the copyright of his writings, gave me permission to use extracts from Haynes' published works. I have drawn extensively on Professor BH Lee's study of the background to the Divorce Reform Act 1969, *Divorce Law Reform in England* published by Peter Owen Ltd (1974). Mr Adam Pallant has kindly allowed me to quote from *Effie in Venice* and from *Millais and the Ruskins* both by M Lutyens and published by John Murray in 1965 and 1967 respectively. Lady McGregor of Durris gave me much valuable help; and in particular has given permission for the use of extracts from Professor McGregor's *Divorce in England* (1957). Extracts from *Separated Spouses, A Study of the matrimonial jurisdiction of magistrates' courts* (1970) are reproduced by permission of Lady

McGregor, Sir Louis Blom-Cooper QC and Colin Gibson. Extracts from Professor Lawrence Stone's *Road to Divorce: England 1530–1987* (1990) and his *Uncertain Unions: Marriage in England 1660–1753* (1992) are reprinted by permission of Oxford University Press. Extracts from *A Handful of Dust* (Copyright © Evelyn Waugh 1934) are reproduced by permission of PFD on behalf of the Evelyn Waugh Trust. An extract from *Moments of Being* published by Hogarth Press is used by permission of the executors of the Virginia Woolf Estate and The Random House Group Limited.

I have drawn on the archives of the late Baroness White (Mrs Eirene White MP) and Mr Leo Abse in the possession of the National Library of Wales, Aberystwyth, on the official papers of Archbishop Michael Ramsey preserved in the Lambeth Palace Library, on the papers of Mrs Eva Hubback, Helena Normanton KC, Lady Helen Nutting, the Married Women's Association, the National Union of Societies for Equal Citizenship and the Divorce Law Reform Union preserved in the Women's Library, London Guildhall University, on the papers of Lord Denning of Whitchurch in the Hampshire Record Office Winchester; and on the papers of the third Lord Gorrell, the first Viscount Monckton of Brenchley, the first Viscount Simon, and those of Lord Somervell of Harrow (all preserved in the Bodleian Library Oxford).

The author acknowledges the interest of the Church of England in the papers of the Archbishop's Group on the Reform of Divorce and the interest of the editors and publishers of the *Denning Law Review*, the *Law Quarterly Review* and of the *Child and Family Law Quarterly* in respect of material first published in those journals; and the interest of the Oxford University Press in respect of the author's *Law, Law Reform and the Famly* published in 1998. Every effort has been made to identify those entitled to copyright material and to obtain appropriate permissions. The author and publishers will take appropriate action in the event of any unwitting infringement being drawn to their attention.

Contents

Table of Cases

Table of Statutes

Table of Statutory Instruments

An Explanatory Note on Parliamentary Procedures

Much of this book is concerned with the process whereby legislation is enacted. The following brief explanation of relevant parliamentary procedures may be useful to some readers.

COMPOSITION AND MEETINGS OF PARLIAMENT

The Monarch in Parliament is the sovereign legislature for the United Kingdom. Acts of the United Kingdom Parliament declare that they are enacted 'by the Queen's Most Excellent Majesty, by and with the advice and consent of the Lords Spiritual and Temporal, and Commons, in this present Parliament assembled, and by the authority of the same'. The House of Lords is a non-elected body. The House of Commons is elected at General Elections; and the Monarch summons the new Parliament to meet thereafter. Parliament is today normally opened by the Monarch in person; and the Monarch's speech made from the throne on that occasion sets out Ministers' legislative plans for the immediate future. The Monarch's speech is written by Ministers in accordance with the convention that, save in a number of matters not directly relevant to the topics dealt with in this book, the Monarch acts and only acts on the advice of Ministers who have the confidence of a majority in the House of Commons.

Each Parliament is divided into *Sessions*. The parliamentary session is brought to an end by the Monarch, on the advice of Ministers, *proroguing* Parliament. At the beginning of the twentieth century it was the practice for Parliament to be in session from February to July or August; but in 1930 it was decided that Sessions should normally last from September or October of one year to the following September or October. These Sessions are adjourned for short periods at Christmas, Easter, etc. and for a longer period (usually from July until October) in the Summer. Prorogation brings all the business of a Session to an end; and, under the procedure applicable in the period covered by this book, Bills which had not completed all their parliamentary stages fell. This explains why in recent years prorogation has often been delayed until November: the time is needed to complete the government's legislative programme for the Session. A Bill which had fallen at the end of a Session had to be reintroduced and the whole process repeated. This helps to account for the difficulty experienced by individual members of either House in promoting legislation to which the Government is hostile or indifferent: time is simply not available for debate in all the stages of the legislative process (see below).

The Parliament Act 1911 stipulates that a Parliament is *dissolved* five years from the day on which it was first appointed to meet; but the Monarch (in practice acting on the advice of the Prime Minister) may dissolve Parliament at any earlier time, and in modern times no Parliament has run its full term. The Prime Minister normally advises dissolution at what is judged to be a propitious time for an election, but on occasions the advice follows inevitably from the failure of a Government to retain its voting control of the House of Commons.

The Legislative Process is complex. To become law a Bill has to be passed by both Houses of Parliament (although since 1911 the House of Commons has had power, in certain circumstances, to override the House of Lords) and, finally, receive the Royal Assent. The broad principle in the House of Commons is that Bills are introduced and given a First Reading (a purely formal process in which the Bill's Long Title is announced) and then a Second Reading. The Second Reading is the occasion for a discussion of general principle. If the Second Reading is carried, the Bill is sent for what is usually a detailed clause by clause consideration in the Committee Stage. In practice for the kind of legislation considered in this book the Bill will normally be committed to a so-called Standing Committee consisting of up to 50 members appointed to reflect party strength in the House. The Bill is then Reported; and a Third Reading takes place. If the Bill is passed, it is sent to the House of Lords, where there is a similar process. If the House of Lords makes amendments these have then to be considered by the Commons.

Bills may be (and often are) introduced in the House of Lords, and the procedure described above then takes place effectively in reverse. There are many possible variants of the process; and there are conventions and usages determining what may or may not be done in debate on each stage of the process.

To become law, a Bill passed by the two Houses of Parliament must receive the Royal Assent. For most of the twentieth century it has been assumed that (in accordance with the Convention that the Monarch will always follow the advice of Ministers) the Monarch will not withhold the Royal Assent from legislation passed by both Houses of Parliament. No Monarch has done so since 1712. However, at the time of the 1914 Irish Home Rule crisis there were some who suggested that the power of veto had not fallen into desuetude.

Although in most cases complex and lengthy, the legislative process can with the collaboration of those concerned be extremely rapid: in exceptional circumstances urgent Bills can pass all their stages in a single day. But the normal procedure gives time for those involved to engage in much behind the scenes negotiation on matters of detail; and also allows the officials concerned with the Bill and Parliamentary Counsel to attempt to meet technical points which came to light after the Bill had first been drafted and debated. Many examples of this will be found in the text.

THE GOVERNMENT AND PARLIAMENT: CONTROL OVER LEGISLATION

Executive power is in this country in theory vested in the Crown. But in practice executive power is exercised by, or on the advice of, Ministers appointed by the Monarch on the advice of the Prime Minister. Those Ministers constitute the Government, and it is axiomatic that they can only retain office if they can control the Legislature (if for no other reason than to vote the funds needed for the conduct of Government). Thus, a Government defeated on an explicit vote of confidence (as was the Callaghan Labour administration on 28 March 1979) or on an issue which can be regarded as equivalent thereto (as was the minority MacDonald Labour administration on 8 October 1924 on a vote criticising the decision not to pursue a prosecution instituted against the editor of the *Worker's Weekly*) will have no alternative but to ask the Monarch to dissolve Parliament. If Ministers failed to do so, thereby prejudicing orderly administration and conduct of affairs, the Monarch would no doubt dismiss them.

Ministers are answerable to Parliament for the conduct of the officials employed in their Departments and for the discharge of the Department's responsibilities; and this is one of the reasons why in this country Ministers (members of the Executive) are almost invariably themselves Members of one of the two Houses of Parliament (and thereby also part of the Legislature). Although a greatly increased part of the activities of Government consists of administration, it is the dependence of governments on Parliament for the passage of legislation which is of most importance in the context of the matters dealt with in this book.

In modern times, there is a heavy load of legislation which the Government believes should be enacted; and it will use its power and influence over those who have been elected as its supporters to ensure that it is able to carry its legislation through the process outlined above. This is done through the medium of the 'Whips'. In the House of Commons the Government Chief Whip holds ministerial office as Parliamentary Secretary to the Treasury and in the House of Lords as Captain of the Gentlemen at Arms; and in each House there are a number of Assistant Whips. But the Whips not only exercise disciplinary functions: they also (under the term 'the usual channels') are responsible for a great deal of inter-party negotiation over the conduct of parliamentary business.

Much the largest part of Parliament's legislative activity is concerned with Government Bills and the demands of the legislative process are such that in modern times there has always been pressure on the parliamentary timetable. There is competition between Ministers for 'slots' in the Government's legislative timetable (and it is often said that for this reason difficulty has been found in securing the enactment of supposedly uncontroversial law reform Bills recommended by the Law Commission). But this does not mean that the ordinary (or 'back-bench') Member cannot influence events by promoting legislation. There are various procedures (notably the so-called Ten Minute Rule in the

House of Commons) under which Members may publicly urge the desirability of legislation. These procedures may be valuable in creating pressure for action (for example, John Parker MP used them extensively in his campaign for reform of the law relating to legitimacy). But generally they are ineffective in getting legislation onto the statute book: the Government may (and often does) decide to 'block' a Bill introduced by an MP. In any case lack of time will often prove fatal.

A limited amount of time is made available in the House of Commons for debate of Bills introduced by Members successful in drawing a high place in the ballot held at the beginning of each Session. These Bills, if uncontroversial, may complete all their stages and become law. (In fact the Whips often ask a favourably placed MP to take up a Bill—the Intestates Estates Act 1952 was one such—for which there is no time in the Government's legislative programme).[1] But controversial and opposed Bills will not usually succeed unless—as happened with the divorce reform legislation in both 1937 and 1969—the Government is prepared to make Government time available, necessarily at the expense of the time available for its own business. Members of the House of Lords may find it less difficult than MPs to bring a Bill forward; but even if a Bill passed through all its stages in the House of Lords it would then have to go through the usual stages in the House of Commons. This rarely happens.

---

[1] The Divorce Reform Act 1969 is an unusual case. The Bill was in theory a Private Member's Bill and the Government continued to assert that it was such: but the Bill had been drafted by Parliamentary Counsel on the authority of a Cabinet decision that a Bill should be prepared and handed to a Private Member successful in the ballot, and Ministers took a close interest in the Bill's detailed provisions: see p. 369, below.

Introduction

The first part of the book deals with Marriage and the Legal Family. Although at the beginning of the twentieth century people undoubtedly had intimate relationships outside marriage, marriage was the only socially approved basis for the creation of the family unit. Chapter 1 explains how the State had begun to exercise greater control over the procedures for creating marriage, recognising the claims of the Church of England to special treatment but also gradually making concessions to the claims of Nonconformists. The State also created (with remarkably little enthusiasm) a procedure for marriage to be contracted in a purely secular form. The result of seeking to meet many conflicting pressures was to create a complex body of law; but the reform and simplification which was widely agreed to be desirable proved very difficult to obtain. At the end of the century, the business of providing wedding facilities was (with very little publicity) opened up to competition and commercial exploitation, subject to the condition (not easy to understand without knowledge of how the law had developed) that such wedding ceremonies were to contain no hint of a religious element.

Chapter 2 is concerned with the development of the rules determining eligibility for marriage: should the law allow marriages between people related, if only by marriage? At what age should people be allowed to marry? Should parental consent be a pre-condition to marriage, and so on. And medical and scientific developments were, in this as in other areas dealt with in this book, to present many challenges to traditional understandings of the law.

Chapters 3 and 4 deal with the legal consequences of marriage. The question of the effect of marriage on a couple's property entitlement had been controversial for much of the nineteenth century, and after the end of World War II it became clear that the Married Women's Property Act of 1882 had solved one problem only to create (in the economic conditions prevailing in the second half of the twentieth century) others. But there was to be no systematic reform. The notion—said by one Law Lord to have been inconceivable to public opinion in 1882—that the judiciary should be given an almost unfettered discretion to adjust or vary property rights when marriages broke down seemed to provide a solution acceptable to a sufficiently wide section of opinion to destroy any prospects of achieving more structured and principled reform.

Marriage had also had an important effect on the legal position of husband and wife in other respects. For example, was a man to be allowed physically to control or coerce his wife? Should a husband be entitled to compensation from a man with whom the wife fell in love? The way in which these issues were resolved is dealt with in Chapter 4 of this book.

The second part of the book deals with the legal termination of marriage by divorce—a highly controversial matter for at least the first two-thirds of the century. It may have been possible to wed with little supervision or inquiry by the State or anyone else, but ending the marriage was a different matter. Marriage might be created simply by the parties' agreement; but the notion that marriage could be ended in the same way was for long anathema. Indeed, for the first 60 or so years of the century the fact that a couple were agreed that their marriage should be ended could be a reason for denying them the divorce they both sought. And even at the end of the century it still seemed axiomatic that the State had such a vital interest in marriage that it should require complex procedures, in form at least judicial, to bring the legal status to an end. Chapters 5, 6 and 7 trace the long history of the struggle for reform; and Chapter 9 examines the way in which the reform movement seemed finally to have achieved success by the passing of the Divorce Reform Act 1969. But the 1969 Act did not achieve all the results which its promoters had claimed would follow, and at the end of the century the imperfections of the law had come to be widely recognised. An attempt at reform was made in 1996 but at the end of the century the future direction of the law was not clear.

Procedural issues have, throughout the twentieth century, had a considerable impact, not only on the effect of the law on the consumer but on its development. At the beginning of the century it had been assumed that the majesty of the law could and should be used to promote the notion that marriage was a matter of great public concern; but it began to be realised that, in a world of increasing demand for legal release from the marriage tie, solemnity and dignity were in practice not easy to attain. And a constant concern had been how to make family justice available equally to rich and poor. For long, magistrates exercising what was called a 'summary' jurisdiction provided the only forum for dealing with the family problems of wage-earners; and in the 1930s many of the ideas subsequently to be generally influential in helping to define the respective roles of the law and the social services were discussed in the context of those courts. But the introduction of public funding under the Legal Aid and Advice Act to enable those without adequate financial resources to seek divorce dramatically changed the situation; and the impact of legal procedures on public finance began to be a dominant factor. Chapter 8 of this book interposes an account of these influences on the Family Justice process down to the introduction of divorce founded on irretrievable breakdown.

At the beginning of the twentieth century, much of the expressed concern about divorce focussed on the need for stability; but over the years more practical concerns—especially about money and property—came to prominence. The common law imposed on a man the duty to maintain his wife; but what was to happen if there was a divorce? Did it matter who was the 'innocent' and who the 'guilty' party? And what was to happen if the abandoned wife had to be supported by the Poor Law (supplanted in 1948 by a wider range of welfare benefits)? The introduction of 'no-fault' divorce under the 1969 legislation had only been made politically possible by extending the courts' powers to readjust the parties' finances; but it soon became apparent that the consequences of doing so had not been fully appreciated. Public finance again became an important factor: should husband and wife be allowed to use the availability of welfare benefits (or indeed the intricacies of the tax system) to increase the resources available for their families? And suppose men failed to meet the obligations to support their families which the law imposed on them? The cost to the community of family breakdown became a major concern. These issues are the subject of Chapters 10 and 11 of the book.

For most of the century far more marriages were ended by death than by divorce. Should a man or woman be allowed to disinherit spouse and children by exercising the so-called right of freedom of testation? And suppose no will had been made: was it right to allow a widow to be forced out of the family home so that it could be sold and much of the proceeds given to others—perhaps her husband's children by a previous marriage? These topics, for long controversial, are the subject of Chapter 12. Chapter 13 sketches in developments in the legal position of those who lived together as if they were husband and wife but without in law being so; and outlines the very tentative attempts to give some redress to those who have been married 'in all but name'.

At the beginning of the twentieth century the legal family may have been created exclusively by marriage, but what was the position of children? Suppose there were doubt about a child's true parentage? Science eventually found an answer to the problem of fixing the identity of the child's genetic parents; but science also greatly complicated matters by developing procedures destroying any easy assumption that a baby's social parents would also be his or her genetic parents. The issues of legal parentage are considered in Chapter 14. Chapter 15 deals with the situation where the child's parents are not married to one another and traces the development of the law from the situation in which the child could almost accurately be described as *filius nullius* (no one's child) to the situation in which for many purposes the child's legal position does not depend on whether the parents have or have not been married. Chapter 16 traces the development of the law governing the nature and extent of a parent's legal authority over the child; and the campaign (not wholly successful until 1973) to recognise the child's mother as being in the same legal position as the father. Once again, the question of how far the law should be allowed to intervene in family life was a major concern.

Before easy and reliable contraception became available in the 1960s many children were born to mothers who did not want to (or were unable to) provide care for them; but there were also those who, with little treatment available for infertility, were anxious to bring up a child as their own. The legal institution of adoption came into being to meet the need for a legal regime which could give all concerned a measure of security in taking someone else's child into the home; but it soon became apparent that the Adoption of Children Act 1926 gave opportunity for abuse. Gradually an increased measure of State control was imposed on adoption; but for the first half of the century it remained an institution which largely catered for arranging the care of very young children born to an unmarried woman and taken into the home of a childless couple who would care for the child as if the couple were the child's true parents. Chapter 17 deals with developments down to 1973. Thereafter adoption is best seen as one of the techniques available to public authorities to provide legal security for children who, for whatever reason, are in need.

The remaining three Chapters of Part III (Chapters 18, 19, and 20) explore the legal relationships between State agencies, children, and their parents. For centuries, the Poor Law had had a dominant (indeed a virtually exclusive) role in providing for the needy child; but by the beginning of the twentieth century what came to be called the 'voluntary sector' was playing a significant part (at a time when sectarianism was widespread, very often as much in concern for the child's soul as for material needs). But it soon became all too clear that children were often in need for reasons other than destitution, and that sometimes they most needed protection from their parents. Chapter 18 deals with developments—including the two so-called 'childrens' charters' of 1908 and 1932—down to the outbreak of World War II in 1939. Many of the issues which have remained problematic began to surface in public discussion and governmental response during this period (notably the question of how the delinquent child should be treated, and the circumstances in which the State could justifiably remove a child from the parents).

World War II introduced one novel factor: large numbers of young children were 'evacuated' from their homes to supposedly safe areas. At one level, the impact of this experience provided a great deal of helpful evidence to the professionals increasingly building up specialist expertise in child welfare. At another level it presented what was seen as a major administrative problem: what was to happen when the emergency ended and children would have been expected to return home? The outcome was the enactment—to some extent also influenced by the publicity given to a serious case of child abuse—of the Children Act 1948. Chapter 19 deals with the noble vision, in many ways typical of the pragmatic idealism of the post-World War II world, in which the Community would provide not only material assistance but also personal sympathy and human understanding for the needy child. By 1968 this seemed a fatally simplistic notion; and the Local Authority Social Services Act 1970 reflected the belief that the future lay in skilled professional service provision to be achieved by newly created Local Authority Social Services Departments.

Chapter 19 deals with the period after 1969. The issues of the relationship between the delinquent and the needy were again controversial, as was the extent to which a child's birth parents should be regarded as having a position entitled to special protection from the law. In 1975 the Children Act (to some extent influenced by another emotively publicised child abuse case, that of Maria Colwell) marked what appeared to be a decisive shift in favour of State provision; but economic factors delayed implementation of many of the Act's more important provisions. By the 1980s the law governing the relationship between Child, State and Parents had become confused in terms both of policy and procedure. Happily, a careful and thorough review was undertaken by the Law Commission and the Government; and—its progress facilitated by the storm of public concern prompted by other child abuse cases and culminating in the Butler-Sloss Inquiry into Sexual Abuse in Cleveland— the Children Act 1989 created what, at least in terms of legislative technique, is an outstandingly successful construct. But, as will appear, that did not mean that solutions had been found to all the social problems with which the legal system increasingly accepted it had to deal.

The final chapter of the book deals with reform of the Family Justice system. How far should the legal system seek to encourage a couple whose relationship is fragile to remain together? How far should it provide facilities for what has been called conciliation but is at the end of the century legislatively recognised as mediation? And how far can court structures—perhaps the creation of a 'Family Court'—improve the processing of cases involving family relationships? There have in the course of the twentieth century certainly been massive changes both in institutions and in ideologies; and yet there remain at the millennium many issues still to be resolved.

PART I

THE LEGAL FAMILY: MARRIAGE

1

Weddings

From the perspective of the twenty-first century, the Victorian era is often seen as a period of stability for marriage and the family home—if not quite the 'place of Peace; the shelter not only from all injury, but from terror, doubt and division . . . a vestal temple, a temple of the hearth watched over by Household Gods' described by John Ruskin[1] in the rather high-flown language of the time. But in fact Queen Victoria's reign was to see the creation of the divorce court and the passing of legislation giving magistrates the power to grant separation orders to the working classes. It also saw married women's property legislation, which not only ended the legal fiction that marriage made a man and a woman one flesh, but also gave the married woman the same remedies 'against all persons whomsoever, including her husband' in respect of her property as if she had never been married.[2] The legal system was increasingly expected to provide some protection to the victims of family life, and much of this book is concerned with such developments. However, one aspect of the Victorian era is often overlooked. Eleven days after the young Queen came to the throne,[3] legislation ended the long-standing monopoly of the Church over marriage, and paved the way for the secularisation of the marriage rite. At the same time the State, by creating a system for the compulsory registration of marriages (as well as births and deaths) and scrutinising the qualifications of those who wanted to marry, assumed an important role in seeking to control marriage and indeed family life.

---

[1] The celebrated critic and man of letters: *Sesame and Lilies* (1864) Lecture II, 'Of Queens' Gardens'. In fact Ruskin's own married life was not a model of domestic felicity: see below, Chapter 2.

[2] Married Women's Property Act 1882, s. 1.

[3] The Marriage Act and the Births and Deaths Registration Act were both passed in 1836 and each provided for commencement on 1 March 1837; but the task of training the officials involved and setting up the requisite administrative arrangements proved more time-consuming than had been anticipated; and the Registration of Births, etc, Act 1837 had to be passed to postpone the coming into force of the legislation until 1 July 1837.

(1) 1753: Lord Hardwickes' Act creates an Anglican monopoly

The law had traditionally left the regulation of marriage to the Church. It was the Church which—save for a brief period in the mid-seventeenth century inter-regnum[4]—decided who could marry whom; it was the Church which laid down the rules about how marriages could be solemnised and which kept Registers of the marriages which took place in Church;[5] it was the ecclesiastical courts which dealt with disputes about such matters.[6] The Church (which after the Reformation for these purposes means the Church of England)[7] tolerated[8] an extreme degree of informality: a valid marriage could be contracted simply by the mutual consent of the parties—the *sponsalia per verba de praesenti*. Provided a couple agreed to take one another as husband and wife, using words in the present tense,[9] then husband and wife they became,[10] wherever the words

---

[4] In 1653 Parliament had enacted legislation providing for civil marriage to be contracted before a Justice of the Peace; but with the restoration of King Charles II in 1660 the position of the Church was restored: see RB Outhwaite, *Clandestine Marriage in England, 1500–1850* (1995) p. 12.

[5] But record keeping was a matter in which the State had long had an interest: legislation dating back as far as 1562 had tried (with only limited success) to secure the reliability of Parish Registers; and the Marriage without Banns Act 1695 had required the clergy, on pain of penalties, to keep records of all persons married, buried or baptised in the parish.

[6] See F Pollock and FW Maitland, *The History of English Law* (2nd ed., 1898, reissued 1968); J Jackson, *The Formation and Annulment of Marriage* (2nd ed., 1989). An accessible account of the background is given in L Stone, *Road to Divorce, England 1530–1987* (1990) whilst the same author's *Uncertain Unions, Marriage in England 1660–1753* (1992) contains detailed case studies derived from the Process Books of the Court of Arches and other sources.

[7] In 1563 the Council of Trent laid down Rules requiring the presence of a priest and independent witnesses at weddings. The post-Reformation Church of England did not accept those Rules, and the mediaeval canon law for long continued to govern marriage in England.

[8] The Church had its own rules of ecclesiastical discipline and imposed sanctions on those participating in 'irregular' marriages. But breach did not invalidate the marriage; and the huge seventeenth and eighteenth century growth in the number of clandestine marriages celebrated by disreputable and often disgraced clergy in or near the Fleet Prison in London caused scandal which was a factor leading to the reform eventually made by the Clandestine Marriages Act 1753, below.

[9] Promises to marry at some time in the future did not create a marriage, but if the parties subsequently had sexual intercourse the *sponsalia per verba de futuro*, implying 'such a present consent at the time of the sexual intercourse as to complete the marriage in substance' would be effective to create a legal marriage, having 'equal validity with the contract *de praesenti*': T Poynter, *A Concise View of the Doctrine and Practice of the Ecclesiastical Courts . . .* (2nd ed., 1824) p. 14.

[10] Two qualifications need to be made. First, the fact that an informal marriage was valid did not mean that it would have all the legal consequences attaching at common law to the status of marriage. In particular, the Common Law courts denied a woman the right to dower out of her husband's estate unless the marriage had been solemnised *in facie ecclesiae*, ie in the body of the Church: see J Jackson, *The Formation and Annulment of Marriage* (2nd ed., 1969) p. 15. Secondly, in 1844 the House of Lords held that, for the purpose of rendering a person subsequently contracting another marriage guilty of the crime of bigamy, a 'marriage' was not valid unless an episcopally ordained priest was present at the first ceremony: see *R v. Millis* (1844) 10 Cl&Fin 534. But although loyally followed by the House of Lords in the nineteenth century (see *Beamish v. Beamish* (1861) 9 HLC 274) the *Millis* decision cannot be regarded as a correct statement of the law and, in the improbable event of the issue being litigated at the present day, would probably be overruled (under

were exchanged and irrespective of the presence or absence of witnesses. This allowed a large business in 'informal' marriages and there was no shortage of suppliers to meet the demand: it has been suggested that 'Fleet' marriages—celebrated by clergy imprisoned for debt and other disreputable characters in or near the Fleet Prison—constituted three-quarters of all the marriages in London by 1740.[11]

Informal marriages were evidently popular with those who wanted a quick and easy marriage ceremony. But it was not only the tidy-minded who thought the approach to clandestine and other informal marriages taken by English law was excessively lax. In particular, there was always the risk[12] that a formal and publicly recognised 'marriage' would be attacked, perhaps many years later, by someone who stood to gain by having it set aside as bigamous. A man's indiscreet words breathed under the influence of passion and quickly forgotten by him might destroy the legal rights of the person whom he had later married—as in *Cochrane v. Campbell*,[13] where a woman was left penniless and her children bastardised after the death of the man she believed she had married in church 30 years previously. Unfortunately for her, another woman was able to convince the courts that she had previously contracted a secret marriage with the deceased, that she was thus his lawful spouse, and that accordingly the marriage to the 'widow' was bigamous and void.

The case for reform may seem obvious;[14] but in fact Lord Chancellor Hardwicke had to deploy all his skills[15] to get the legislation onto the statute book.[16] In 1753, after a long struggle, he succeeded.

the power which the House of Lords has enjoyed since 1966) or at least confined within narrow limits: see R Cross and JW Harris, *The English Doctrine of Precedent* (4th ed., 1991). The *Millis* decision, apart from anything else, cast doubt on the validity of Jewish and Quaker marriages but the Marriages of Jews and Quakers Act 1847 retrospectively validated marriages to which both parties were Jews or Quakers.

[11] RB Outhwaite, *Clandestine Marriage in England, 1500–1850* (1995) p. 35; and see generally L Stone, *Uncertain Unions, Marriage in England 1660–1753* (1992) for excellent and entertaining accounts of Fleet and other informal marriages.

[12] For this and other reasons (as Professor Stone has put it) a 'very large number of perfectly respectable people . . . could never be quite sure whether they were married or not': L Stone, *Uncertain Unions, Marriage in England 1660–1753* (1992) p. 3.

[13] (1753) 1 Paton's Cases 519 (HL Scot); and see also *Dalrymple v. Dalrymple* (1811) 2 Hag. Con. 54, (1814) 2 Hag. Con. 137n.

[14] For an interesting if controversial analysis of the motives of the various interests, see S Parker, *Informal Marriage, Cohabitation and the Law* (1990).

[15] See generally L Stone, *Road to Divorce, England 1530–1987* (1990), particularly at pp. 122–124; and for a detailed study RB Outhwaite, *Clandestine Marriage in England, 1500–1850* (1995), Chap. 4.

[16] Hardwicke 'personally master-minded [the Bill's] passage through both Houses of Parliament, in the face of some fierce opposition, by the use of rhetoric, logic, cajolery, and behind-the-scenes threats, deals and lobbying. He bought off the peers by allowing [the Archbishop of Canterbury] to retain the right to issue special licences for noblemen to be married, how, where, and when they pleased. He satisfied the middling sort by allowing the surrogates to continue to sell ordinary licenses to dispense with banns. . . . He tried to satisfy the parish clergy by arguing that the suppression of clandestine marriages would drive the poor into getting married in church, thus augmenting clerical incomes generally. He bought off the Scots by omitting Scotland from the

The Clandestine Marriages Act 1753 gave the Church of England a virtual monopoly over marriages.[17] Banns[18] had to be called in the Parish Church on three successive Sundays; and the marriage had to be solemnised in the presence of two or more credible witnesses[19] in the church where the banns had been called.[20] Details of the calling of banns and of weddings were to be recorded in a proper Register, 'to be carefully kept and preserved for public use'.[21] The Act imposed draconian penalties for breach: a provision,[22] avowedly directed at Fleet and other similar marriages made anyone solemnising a marriage without banns or a proper licence or in a place other than the church in which banns had been called guilty of felony and liable to be transported for 14 years. And anyone falsifying a licence or an entry in the Register was to be executed as a felon.[23]

bill. . . . He bought the support of the squires by offering them the one thing they really wanted, which was a legal veto power over the marriages of their children up to the age of 21. He kept all the lawyers in both Houses lined up solidly behind the bill, partly by persuasion, partly by exploiting their desire to clip the wings of the ecclesiastical courts, partly by appealing to their exasperation at the problems of legal proof of marriage raised by the existing situation. When all else failed, he made it clear that any opponent of the bill would be punished by being excluded from the lord chancellor's extensive patronage': L Stone, *Road to Divorce, England 1530–1987* (1990), pp. 122–123.

[17] See generally R Probert, 'The Judicial Interpretation of Lord Hardwicke's Act 1753' Legal History, Vol 23 (2002) p. 129. The Act did not extend to the marriages of Quakers and Jews: Clandestine Marriages Act 1753, s. 18; and they were thus able to solemnise marriages according to their traditions. Nor did it extend to the marriages 'of any of the Royal family': s. 17. This latter provision has been retained in all subsequent legislation governing the solemnisation of marriage; and accordingly it is apparently possible for members of the Royal Family (an expression not defined) to contract a valid marriage in private and without licence or the calling of banns. It is true that in certain situations the priest could be subject to ecclesiastical sanction, that the provisions of the Royal Marriage Act 1772 (making the consent of the Sovereign in Council necessary) would have to be met, and that in some cases at least convention would require that the approval of the Cabinet be given: see generally V Bogdanor, *The Monarchy and the Constitution* (1995).

[18] The Act did not take away the Archbishop of Canterbury's power to grant a special licence allowing a marriage at any convenient time or place: s. 6. But such licences were supposedly only granted to those 'distinguished by birth and wealth'; and, although there was a substantial proportionate increase in the number of special licences granted immediately after the enactment of the Clandestine Marriages Act, the Church speedily formulated fresh guidelines and the number of licences granted each year soon fell back to single figures. A century later the *Royal Commission on the Laws of Marriage*, 1868, BPP 1867–1868 vol. 32, noted that only 12 special licences were granted each year, and that the fees were such as to confine this procedure to those in 'very affluent circumstances'. The Clandestine Marriages Act did attempt to check the abuse of so-called 'common licences' previously often sold in blank by Bishops' Registrars to surrogates or other clergy and then issued for a fee but without enquiry to parties wishing to avoid the calling of banns. First, the Act (s. 4) provided that no such licence could be granted for a marriage elsewhere than in the Parish in which one or both parties had resided for four weeks; secondly surrogates were required (s. 7) to take an oath of office and to provide financial security for the proper discharge of their duties; and thirdly marriages by licence in which one or both parties were under 21 were declared to be invalid unless parental consent had in fact been given: s. 11. See generally RB Outhwaite, *Clandestine Marriage in England, 1500–1850* (1995) p. 125.

[19] s. 15.
[20] Clandestine Marriages Act 1753, s. 1. The priest was empowered to require the parties to give him seven days' notice 'of their true Christian and surnames' and of their places of abode and how long they had lived there: s. 2. The text ignores complications such as arose where the parties lived in different parishes.
[21] ss. 14, 15.   [22] s. 8.
[23] s. 16. For accounts of the enforcement of the Act's provisions (effectively making the point 'that the ruling elite at last meant business') see L Stone, *Road to Divorce, England 1530–1987* (1990) pp. 128–9.

Breach of the Act's provisions could also be disastrous for the parties: even an innocent[24] mistake in the banns (for example, about the parties' names)[25] invalidated the marriage.

The hardship caused by the provisions avoiding marriages because of formal defect in the preliminaries was one of the factors prompting the next round of legislation: the outcome, in general terms,[26] was that after 1 November 1823 a marriage would only be automatically void if the parties had 'knowingly and wilfully' contravened the statutory provisions.[27] No longer would it be possible for a couple tired of one another to escape from the marriage by finding some technical defect;[28] whilst the provisions about issuing marriage licences were tightened up.

[24] In contrast, a false statement of either parties' residence in banns or a licence did not invalidate a marriage: s. 10. A marriage after licence of persons either of whom was under 21 was void if parental consent had not been given; but in contrast a marriage after the publication of banns was invalidated only if a parent had made an open and public declaration of dissent at the calling of the banns: ss. 3 and 12.

[25] For example, in *R v. Inhabitants of Tibshelf* (1830) 1 B&Ad 190 a couple went through an apparently valid marriage in 1817. The clergyman thought he should call the banns in the surname which appeared for the bride in the Parish Baptismal Register. The Court held that since she had never been known by that name (apparently entered by mistake in the Register) there had been no publication of the banns and the marriage was void. It was immaterial that there was no fraud or intent to deceive since that would only be relevant in cases in which there was a merely partial variation of the name (such as the alteration of letters, the suppression of one Christian name, or the use of a name by which the parties had been known in the locality). No doubt, observed the Chief Justice, the result was a 'great hardship upon these innocent persons . . . but it would be a much greater inconvenience . . . to alter the settled rules upon this subject . . .'.

[26] Three Acts were passed between 1822 and 1833. The 1822 Act (3 Geo 4, c. 75) imposed further restrictions on the grant of licences and required all applicants for a licence to swear an affidavit in support, but it was defective in a number of respects not least in cases where title to property depended on legitimacy. The Act was hurriedly repealed in March 1823. The March Act was itself repealed in July by the Marriage Act 1823 (4 Geo 4, c. 76) which effectively reformulated many of the provisions of Lord Hardwicke's Act and added the provisions mentioned in the text about the effect of formal irregularities as well as making further amendments (for example, providing for the forfeiture of property acquired in consequence of an under-age marriage without parental consent). The reports of the Parliamentary Debates—not at the time verbatim—do not provide wholly satisfactory explanations of what occurred; but a clear account is given by RB Outhwaite, *Clandestine Marriage in England, 1500–1850* (1995) p. 152.

[27] So that (for example) a misstatement of the parties' names in the Banns of Marriage would—in contrast to the situation under the Clandestine Marriages Act as exemplified in *R v. Inhabitants of Tibshelf* above—only invalidate the marriage if the parties had intended thereby to conceal the truth: contrast *Chipcase v. Chipcase* [1942] P 37 (banns called in wife's maiden name; she described herself as widow in order to conceal fact that she was a divorced woman; marriage void) and *Dancer v. Dancer* [1949] P 147 (wife's birth registered as 'Knight', but from age three known by name of mother's cohabitant, Roberts; advised by Vicar to have banns called in name of Roberts as the name by which she had always been known in Parish, husband's subsequent attack on validity of marriage failed because there had been no intention to deceive).

[28] The fact that even the smallest mistake would serve to invalidate the marriage has been said to have 'opened up a new avenue for self-divorce': L Stone, *Road to Divorce, England 1530–1987* (1990) p. 132.

(2) Nonconformists and demographers

The 1823 legislation dealt with technicalities; but it did not attempt to deal with the increasingly vocal complaints[29] of Nonconformists and Roman Catholics who could only marry in this country in an Anglican church by an Anglican rite.[30] Nor did tinkering with the rules about licences and church registers do anything to improve the machinery of fact collection that informed opinion was coming to see as essential to the rational development of an advanced society.[31] In 1836, however, Lord Melbourne's Administration succeeded in getting onto the statute book[32] the legislation which established the system for solemnising marriage still, in essence, in force at the end of the twentieth century. The Births Deaths and Marriages Registration Act established the office of Registrar-General,[33] and set up an ambitious scheme for state registration under the Registrar-General's direction. The Births Deaths and Marriages Registration Act did away with the need to rely on parochial and other local Registers. At the same time (and in parallel to the Registration Act) Parliament passed the Marriage Act 1836 which laid down the formalities for creating a marriage.

---

[29] See RB Outhwaite, *Clandestine Marriage in England, 1500–1850* (1995), Chapter 7.

[30] See the speech of the Home Secretary Lord John Russell, introducing what became the Marriage Act 1836, *Hansard's Parliamentary Debates* (3rd Series) 12 February 1836, vol. 31, col. 373: the law 'compelled persons wishing to contract a legal marriage, to go into a Church which they were not members of, and to have the ceremony performed by a clergyman in whose religious opinions they did not agree, and whose doctrines they did not follow, and many of whose religious opinions they might not be willing to receive or listen to'. It was said that many Roman Catholics went through ceremonies in their own churches, that many of the poorer amongst them neglected the legally necessary second (Parish Church) ceremony 'on account principally of the expense', and that in consequence the 'marriage' was void and 'parishes were, after a few years, burdened with numbers of illegitimate children': *Hansard's Parliamentary Debates* (3rd Series) 12 February 1836, vol. 31, col. 384.

[31] Towards the end of the eighteenth century the question whether the population was increasing at an excessive rate began to engage public interest; and Thomas Malthus (author of *An Essay on the Principles of Population* (1798)) was one of those pressing for a census. The first census in fact took place in 1801; and an interesting feature of the background to the 1836 Marriage Act is the way in which various groups with interests in demography (for example, Friendly Societies and others concerned with the provision of life insurance needing accurate information in order to improve the mortality tables essential to writing policies) came together with the ideologically motivated religious groups: see RB Outhwaite, *Clandestine Marriage in England, 1500–1850* (1995), Chapter 7.

[32] In 1835 Sir Robert Peel had brought forward a Bill providing for marriage before a magistrate but requiring Nonconformists to treat the marriage as a 'mere civil compact'. This qualification appeared to suggest that Nonconformists' marriages were somehow second class: *Hansard's Parliamentary Debates* (3rd Series) 12 February 1836, vol. 31, col. 384.

[33] Russell's brother-in-law was appointed the first Registrar-General, prompting allegations of nepotism from disappointed applicants: see M Nissel, *People Count, A History of the General Register Office* (1987) a book which gives an interesting general history. The history of the Registration Service is also summarised in *Registration: A Modern Service* (1988, Cm. 531) Chapter 1.

(3) Defining the State's interest

The 1836 Act was based on a very clear analysis of the respective interests of Church and State in marriage. The State had a proper interest in preventing clandestine marriages and in being able to determine whether or not a person was married, with all the legal consequences which followed from that status;[34] and the State was therefore entitled to insist on a universal and efficient system for the registration of marriages.[35] But so far as the actual celebration of the marriage, the State's concern was limited to ensuring that the ceremony be recognised by both parties as binding.[36]

For the purpose of this analysis there were three elements in the marriage process. First, there were the preliminaries intended to publicise the parties' intentions and thus 'excite the vigilance' of parents and others—perhaps a person claiming to be already married to one of those concerned—and thereby 'afford them fit opportunities of protecting' their legal rights.[37] Secondly, there was the wedding itself. Finally, there were the administrative procedures for registering and giving notice of the married couple's new status.

Lord John Russell's original intention[38] had been that whilst the first and third stages should be the preserve of the State the second should in principle be a matter of choice for the parties—whether a religious service in the Church of England or in a Roman Catholic church or Nonconformist chapel or even a simple civil ceremony before an official of the State. But the Church of England successfully opposed[39] losing its exclusive right to administer its own preliminaries to marriage; and a Church of England wedding could (and still, at the beginning

---

[34] The State should also be able to 'acquire a general knowledge of the state of the population of the country': see Lord John Russell's speech, *Hansard's Parliamentary Debates* (3rd Series) 12 February 1836, vol. 31, col. 368.

[35] *Hansard's Parliamentary Debates* (3rd Series) 12 February 1836, vol. 31, cols. 368, 372.

[36] 'If they once ascertained the parties had given due notice for the purpose, and that the marriage was settled, and that the contract was such as would be binding on the conscience of the parties . . . they had obtained all that it was necessary for the State to know': *Hansard's Parliamentary Debates* (3rd Series) 12 February 1836, vol. 31, col. 372.

[37] T Poynter, *A Concise View of the Doctrine and Practice of the Ecclesiastical Courts* . . . (2nd ed., 1824) p. 27.

[38] See his speech in *Hansard's Parliamentary Debates* (3rd Series) 12 February 1836, vol. 31, cols. 375–376.

[39] The Archbishop of Canterbury and the Bishops were outspoken in the House of Lords, the Bishop of Exeter going so far as to claim that the Marriage Bill as presented by Russell invited members of the Church of England to dispense with any religious ceremony: see *Hansard's Parliamentary Debates* (3rd Series) 21 July 1836, vol. 35, col. 376. Russell and others regarded the changes made to the Bill by the House of Lords in response to pressure by the Church as seriously damaging but accepted them on the basis that the Act should be allowed to establish a principle and that an opportunity to bring the whole of the original plan into effect would be found at some future time: see *Hansard's Parliamentary Debates* (3rd Series) 11 August 1836, vol. 31, cols. 1122–1123. The Marriage Act 1836, s. 1, therefore expressly preserved the right of the Archbishop to grant licences to marry 'at any convenient time and place' and left unrepealed the provisions of the Marriage Act 1823 dealing with the publication of banns and the grant of common licences.

of the twenty-first century can) take place[40] after the calling of banns, or on the authority of a so-called common licence granted by the Church or on the authority of the Archbishop of Canterbury's Special Licence.[41]

In all other cases, notice of an intended marriage in the prescribed form had to be given to the Superintendent Registrar for the district where the parties lived.[42] The notice was to be entered in the Registrar's Notice book (open to public inspection) for the stipulated period of 21 days (or seven if a higher fee were paid for the Registrar to issue a licence).[43] Once these formalities had been completed the wedding could then take place in a registered[44] place of religious worship[45] with 'open doors' and in the presence of two witnesses according to 'such Form and Ceremony' as the parties saw fit to adopt,[46] provided that each of the parties at some stage made a declaration in prescribed form that there was no impediment to the marriage and uttered prescribed words whereby the one took the other 'to be my lawful wedded wife [or husband]'.[47] The marriage had then to be registered, and a copy of the registration documents sent to the General Register Office.

---

[40] In only one limited respect did the Act require the Church of England to accept the civil system of preliminaries to marriage: an Anglican marriage could take place on the authority of a Superintendent Registrar's Certificate that the prescribed notice had been duly given. For many years this provision was effectively a dead letter but it has at the turn of the twenty-first century been increasingly used in cases where a clergyman does not wish to attract the publicity sometimes attendant on the calling of banns for the marriage of a divorced person.

[41] Once those formalities are completed the marriage can be solemnised—in the case of a marriage by Special Licence in the place named in the Licence, but otherwise in the appropriate Parish church or other church or chapel licensed by the Bishop: Marriage Act 1836, s. 26. The form of Anglican weddings is entirely in the hands of the Church, although the Marriage Act 1836, s. 1 provided that all 'the Rules prescribed by the Rubrick concerning the solemnizing of Marriages shall continue to be duly observed'.

[42] If they lived in different districts, notice had to be given in both.

[43] Marriage Act 1836, s. 7. In addition to paying the then substantial fee of £3 (perhaps £180 or more in year 2000 values) applicants for a Registrar's Licence had to comply with additional formalities (eg the swearing of an oath that there was no impediment to the marriage and that any requisite parental consent had been given).

[44] The Toleration Act 1688, s. 19 and the Places of Religious Worship Act 1812 required congregations or assemblies for worship to be certified to quarter sessions or certified to the bishop or archdeacon and registered in the ecclesiastical court or at quarter sessions. Subsequently, the Registration of Protestant Dissenters' Churches Act 1852 and the Places of Religious Worship Act 1855 (which is still in force: see below) substituted a requirement of registration by the Registrar-General and required him to publish lists of the places so registered.

[45] Marriage Act 1836, s. 18. The church or building in which the wedding was to take place had to be specified in the notice given to the Registrar: Marriage Act 1836, s. 4. The 1836 Act specified that the building be 'separate'; but in 1837 this provision was removed so far as Roman Catholic churches were concerned (apparently on the ground that the church often had a priest's house attached): *Registration: A Modern Service* (1988, Cm. 531) para. 1.16.

[46] The Marriage Act 1836 preserved the right of Quakers and Jews to celebrate weddings in their own form and in places of their choosing but prior notice has to be given to the Superintendent Registrar and the Registration formalities have to be observed.

[47] Marriage Act 1836, s. 20. But the solemnisation had to take place between 8am and noon.

(4) Marriage Act 1836 still leaves Nonconformists and Roman Catholics separate and unequal

This registration requirement accounts for the fact that Nonconformist and Roman Catholic weddings were in one very important respect treated unfavourably compared with weddings in the Established Church. The Government assumed (incorrectly, as experience was to prove) that the Clergy of the Established Church would be able to carry out the registration functions correctly and accurately. At least (as Lord John Russell told the House of Commons)[48] the Anglican priest was 'well known, and . . . his designation and habitation were fixed' and there was accordingly 'great security as to proper care being used in performing the marriage ceremony'. But Nonconformists were different: Nonconformist ministers and Roman Catholic priests did not have the legal status attaching to incumbents of the Established Church, and it was said that there were a great many ministers, and men who frequently 'for a time became the minister of a Dissenting congregation, and afterwards laid down his charge'. The 1836 Act therefore provided that a Registrar had to be present at weddings in registered places of religious worship and a fee paid to the Registrar for his services.[49] It was thought that in the absence of a special provision of this kind for the registration of non-Anglican marriages 'there would be great uncertainty and vagueness'.

(5) The secular marriage

The Marriage Act 1836 also provided for a purely civil wedding for those—it was thought the class would be 'certainly not very numerous'[50]—who believed that marriage was a purely civil matter: anyone who objected[51] to the religious form of marriage could give the necessary notice and then marry in the Office of the Superintendent Registrar by making the prescribed declaration.[52] There could in that case at least be no doubt that the Registration requirements would be properly observed.

[48] *Hansard's Parliamentary Debates* (3rd Series) 12 February 1836, vol. 31, col. 376.

[49] Marriage Act 1836, s. 22.

[50] Lord John Russell: *Hansard's Parliamentary Debates* (3rd Series) 12 February 1836, vol. 31, col. 377.

[51] The Marriage Act 1836, s. 21, provided that any person who 'shall object' to marriage in a registered place of worship was to be allowed to marry before the Registrar; and some Anglicans attached importance to requiring those who wanted an alternative form of wedding to make a declaration that they objected to the form of service used in the Established Church.

[52] The wedding had to take place between 8am and 12 noon, with open doors, in the presence of the Superintendent Registrar and a District Registrar: s. 21.

THE MARRIAGE ACT 1836—BRILLIANT COMPROMISE—AT A PRICE?

The fact that the main structure of the marriage law established by the 1836 Act remains intact after more than one and a half centuries of great social change is in itself a tribute to the skill with which it struck an acceptable balance between various competing interests. Russell bought off the Anglican Church[53] by allowing the Church to continue to solemnise legally valid marriages without the intervention of any State official. He conceded[54] that the Church could continue to operate the system of banns and ecclesiastical Licences as legally effective preliminaries to marriage and Anglicans were exempted from the requirements of prior notification to and certification by a State-appointed Registrar. Russell also managed to get the support of Nonconformists who were to be allowed to hold their own services, albeit in the presence of the Registrar. For much the same reason the Bill had the support of Roman Catholics;[55] whilst Jews and Quakers were allowed to retain their traditional privileges. Although there were a few[56] who feared that the provisions for purely civil marriage would give 'false pretenders to religious scruples' the means of evading the law, the Bill was generally warmly welcomed. Certainly English marriage law allowed for a considerable diversity of forms; but although the procedure by which marriage can be created may vary widely, the result is in all cases the same. To the law, there is only one contract of marriage.[57]

[53] The Act provided that marriages under the other forms which it recognised were to be 'good and cognizable' in the same way as Anglican marriages: s. 21.

[54] He had always intended to allow the Archbishop of Canterbury to retain his power of licensing the solemnisation of marriages at any time or place. But this concession was not sufficient for the Church, which particularly opposed the provisions included in the Bill as originally presented which would have made the calling of banns legally ineffective: see eg the speech of the Bishop of Exeter and the Archbishop of Canterbury *Hansard's Parliamentary Debates* (3rd Series) 11 July 1836, vol. 35, col. 82.

[55] Daniel O'Connell said that 'the relief which [the Bill] would give Roman Catholics from many of their inconveniences and annoyances' was considerable: *Hansard's Parliamentary Debates* (3rd Series) 12 February 1836, vol. 31, col. 384.

[56] See Sir Robert Peel, *Hansard's Parliamentary Debates* (3rd Series) 12 February 1836, vol. 31, cols. 382–387. Peel in fact hoped that many dissenters—'particularly the female portion of them'— would still opt for a wedding in the Parish Church. There were no doubt some who could (in the words of a female correspondent in the *Bradford Observer* of 17 August 1837 and quoted in M Nissel, *People Count, A History of the General Register Office* (1987) p. 16) never 'fancy [a woman] really married unless the knot were tied by a Minister in a surplice'; and this may account for the fact that Nonconformists did not take advantage of the facility of marriage in their own chapels 'in a degree proportionate to their number': *Report of the Select Committee on Nonconformist Marriages (Attendance of Registrars)* (1893) para. 6; see below. But in fact the *Observer's* correspondent was impressed by her sister's chapel wedding and reported the view of her local grocer that it would be necessary for 'the vicar to advertise his old concern, or the new shop . . . will be likely to run away with the trade'.

[57] *R v. Dibdin, ex parte Thompson* [1910] P 57, 114, *per* Fletcher Moulton LJ.

The grievance: 'Workhouse marriages' for all except Anglicans

It was not long before it became apparent that the Russell Act had concealed, rather than solved, a number of problems. The Act was supposed to minimise discrimination against Nonconformists and others unwilling to be married by the Anglican rite; and this involved providing for a State-administered registration service. But who was to provide this service?[58] True, the Registrar-General would exercise overall control over the system from the General Register Office, but who would actually carry out the registrars' functions[59] locally?

The answer was found in the radical reforms of the administration of the Poor Law effected two years earlier.[60] By the time the new marriage and registration laws were to come into force, the Boards of Guardians responsible for local administration of the Poor Law would also be in place and able to take responsibility for local management of the registration legislation,[61] dividing the Union which they controlled into Districts. Register Offices were to be provided;[62] and (although the Registrar-General would make rules[63] for the conduct of officers and had the ultimate sanction of dismissing Registrars) it would be the Poor Law Guardians who would appoint[64] the Superintendent Registrar (in practice, normally their Clerk)[65] for each district.[66]

This no doubt seemed attractive as the basis for an efficiently managed public service;[67] but in fact a provision inserted into the legislation made the role of

[58] Earlier attempts to reform the marriage laws had foundered on the problem of identifying those who were to perform the requisite registration duties. One suggestion had been that tax surveyors would undertake the work but (as Russell explained) it had been found that many were not competent to undertake registration and that in many cases it would have been necessary to 'employ persons of a superior class, and to give them additional remuneration, which would entail a very considerable expense . . .': *Hansard's Parliamentary Debates* (3rd Series) 12 February 1836, vol. 31, col. 369.

[59] Including the potentially onerous task of collecting information about births and deaths, and transmitting reliable information to the General Register Office: see below.

[60] Poor Law Amendment Act 1834.

[61] See Russell's speech, *Hansard's Parliamentary Debates* (3rd Series) 12 February 1836, vol. 31, col. 369.

[62] Births Deaths and Marriages Registration Act 1836, s. 9.

[63] Under the direction of a Secretary of State: Births Deaths and Marriages Registration Act 1836, s. 5.

[64] The Births and Deaths Registration Act 1837 was passed 'to explain and amend' the administrative structure set up by the 1836 Act in a number of respects.

[65] Births Deaths and Marriages Registration Act 1836, s. 7 (giving the Clerk the right of first refusal). In some populous areas it seems that the office of Superintendent Registrar could be expected to be one of considerable profit: see the account in M Nissel, *People Count, A History of the General Register Office* (1987) p. 16 of the competition for appointments in St. Marylebone, West London.

[66] The primary function of the Register Office was to provide a physically secure base for the Registers of Births Marriages and Deaths. It was envisaged that the Registrar would operate from his own home, and that a notice would be displayed on each Registrar's house: Births Deaths and Marriages Registration Act 1836, s. 16.

[67] There were however difficulties, not least that the legislation distinguished between the offices of Registrar of Marriages on the one hand and Registrar of Births and Deaths on the other. Although the Superintendent Registrar appointed the Marriage Registrars, the Board of Guardians appointed the Registrar of Births and Deaths.

the Guardians equivocal, and tainted marriages outside the Church of England with the machinery of the Poor Law and the Workhouse. This was because it was appreciated that simply having notices of intended marriage open to public inspection in a Marriage Notice Book[68] was not likely to achieve much effective publicity; and a provision[69] was therefore inserted requiring not only that the notices be given to the Poor Law Guardians but also (on the analogy of banns) that the notice should be read out to them at three successive weekly meetings. Only then could the Registrar issue the necessary[70] certificate for marriage.

It seems improbable that this was an effective way of publicising the intended marriage, but that of itself might not cause much discontent. What did become a real grievance was that whereas Anglicans could arrange their own preliminaries with banns or licence, Nonconformists (and indeed Roman Catholics) had to make do with the 'workhouse marriage' notified to the Poor Law Guardians. And things were not improved by the fact that in practice it would be a Poor Law official who would attend the marriage to ensure that all was done according to the rules. As *The Times* commented[71] highly respectable Nonconformists might well prefer not to have a daughter's 'marriage party or procession proceed to chapel under the escort of the [Poor Law] overseer or relieving officer . . . after the fashion of the old pauper wedding . . .'.

Removing the taint of the Poor Law

In the 1850s Bills intended to end this discrimination foundered on opposition from the Church of England;[72] but eventually, there was a compromise. The Marriage and Registration Acts Amendment Act 1856 retained the requirement that marriage notices be displayed in the Register Office[73] but abolished the need for them to be read out at meetings of the Poor Law Guardians.[74] The Act turned to the criminal law to provide sanctions against marriage without parental consent and other improprieties: those giving notice of intended marriage had to make a solemn declaration of the truth of the contents of the notice and of the absence of legal impediment—such as the fact that the couple were within the prohibited degrees or that one of them was already married to someone else—to the marriage. Knowingly making a false declaration was to be a criminal offence akin to perjury.[75]

---

[68] Marriage Act 1836, s. 5.   [69] Marriage Act 1836, s. 6.

[70] After seven days from giving notice, the Registrar could issue a licence for the marriage to take place; and in this way—although the Poor Law guardians had still to be informed—the marriage could go ahead without repeated readings to the Guardians: Marriage Act 1836, ss. 6 and 7.

[71] 15 February 1836, as quoted in M Nissel, *People Count, A History of the General Register Office* (1987) p. 16. See also *Hansard's Parliamentary Debates* (3rd Series) 12 February 1836, vol. 31, col. 1123.

[72] Apparently focussing on the fact that Anglican Priests might be required to marry parishioners on the strength of a Registrar's certificate: *Hansard's Parliamentary Debates* (3rd Series) 6 March 1856, vol. 140, cols. 1928–1930.

[73] Marriage and Registration Acts Amendment Act 1856, s. 4.

[74] Marriage and Registration Acts Amendment Act 1856, s. 1.

[75] Marriage and Registration Acts Amendment Act 1856, s. 2.

The 1856 Act also drew a clearer distinction between the role of Church and State in the actual marriage ceremony. The law still insisted that there should be no religious service in any Register Office ceremony[76] but henceforth it allowed a religious marriage service to be held (provided the priest or minister agreed) afterwards, in a church or chapel. In this way it was intended to allow Nonconformists and others to have the religious service they wanted without any 'official' presence.[77] At the same time, the Church of England's control over marriages in Anglican churches was reinforced:[78] only Anglican clergy were to be allowed to officiate, and no rite other than that laid down in the Book of Common Prayer was to be used.[79] In contrast, the Nonconformist and Roman Catholic churches retained the right to conduct marriages with such form of service as they wished.[80]

In this way the 1856 Act reduced if it did not altogether remove[81] the Poor Law taint from Nonconformist weddings, but discrimination remained. The Anglican clergy were masters in their own churches, but the Nonconformist and Roman Catholic wedding ceremonies were only *legally* effective if a Registrar were present. This discrimination was not to be ended until 1898.[82]

The 1868 Chelmsford Royal Commission

Discrimination against Nonconformists caused resentment; but from a practical point of view it was the radical differences between the marriage laws applied in Scotland, Ireland, and in England and Wales which caused real problems— problems made all the greater by the increased mobility of the population made possible by the development of the railway system. In 1868 the government

---

[76] Marriage and Registration Acts Amendment Act 1856, s. 12.

[77] Marriage and Registration Acts Amendment Act 1856, s. 12. The Act makes it quite clear that the religious service is essentially one of blessing rather than a wedding: it specifically provides that nothing in the 'Reading or Celebration of such service shall be held to supersede or invalidate [the Register Office wedding]; nor shall such Reading or Celebration be entered as a Marriage' in the Parish Register.

[78] For the modern Anglican law and its evolution, see RDH Bursell, *Liturgy, Order and the Law* (1996).

[79] Marriage and Registration Acts Amendment Act 1856, s. 11.

[80] Marriage Act 1836, s. 20 (see above, note 47). The Marriage and Registration Acts Amendment Act 1856, s. 11 made it clear that the minister or other responsible person had to consent to the marriage taking place in the registered building concerned.

[81] In spite of the changes made by the 1856 Act the link between the registration service and the Poor Law remained significant in practice: in 1893 the *Select Committee on Nonconformist Marriages (Attendance of Registrars)* (HC 368, 1893, BPP 1893–94, vol. 13, p. 57) reported that notices of marriage were still frequently displayed at the Workhouse. The Poor Law link was not finally broken until 1929 when the Guardian's remaining functions in respect of appointments were transferred to local authorities. The Local Government Act of that year also brought to an end the system under which Registration Officers were remunerated by fees: the Act provided that Officers appointed after the Act came into force should be salaried officials. But the status of Registration Officers remained and remains confused: see below.

[82] Marriage Act 1898: see below.

responded to complaints by setting up a Royal Commission chaired by Lord Chelmsford.[83] The Commission duly concluded that uniformity of the marriage law throughout the United Kingdom was 'highly desirable'; and claimed that the difficulties in the way of achieving such uniformity were 'not insuperable'.[84] But carrying out the Commission's brief to construct a uniform code of law for the whole of the United Kingdom necessarily involved going back to first principles and asking what purpose the marriage laws should serve and how those purposes could best be achieved.

Thus, the Commission accepted[85] that calling banns was totally ineffective in preventing improvident clandestine and unlawful marriage. The affluent simply paid the fee for an ecclesiastical licence.[86] But the poor also valued privacy: for example, a young workman might be embarrassed because he could not afford to 'treat' his mates in the customary style, and domestic servants and farm labourers often feared their employers would not approve of the marriage.[87] Sometimes this distaste for publicity was strong enough to put a couple off the idea of marriage altogether.[88] More commonly the couple, paying at best token regard to the requirement that the banns be called in their home parish, would arrange for the banns to be called in a large city. In the large ecclesiastical marriage factories of the industrial north, the great number of banns called (apparently 'some hundreds' every Sunday in Manchester Cathedral)[89] of itself prevented any publicity being given to the intended marriage. The Chelmsford

---

[83] The Commission's terms of reference included 'the state and operation of the various laws now in force in the different parts of the United Kingdom of Great Britain and Ireland, with respect to the constitution and proof of the Contract of Marriage, and the Registration and other means of preserving evidence thereof'. For Lord Chelmsford, see Biographical Notes.

[84] *Report of the Royal Commission on the Laws of Marriage* (1868, BPP 1867–1868 vol. 32) p. 24.

[85] Even in 1836 Lord John Russell had told the House of Commons that in 'populous parishes . . . where not one-tenth or one-twentieth of the population could attend, there was merely a huddled list of names read over, and this was done in the most careless manner; and clergymen had told him that it often occurred in an interval of the most solemn part of the service, and caused a most unpleasant and an almost indecent interruption of the service': *Hansard's Parliamentary Debates* (3rd Series) 12 February 1836, vol. 31, col. 375.

[86] The *Royal Commission on the Laws of Marriage* (1868, BPP 1867–1868 vol. 32 p. 6) reported that the great majority of marriages in England and Wales were solemnised in the Church of England; and that five sevenths of those—'chiefly those of persons belonging to the poorer classes'— were after the calling of banns.

[87] The Archdeacon of Gloucester reported 'a very general feeling among the poor of wishing to keep their marriages secret' *Report of the Royal Commission on the Laws of Marriage* (1868, BPP 1867–1868 vol. 32), Appendix, q. 1407; and see the Memorandum by the Bishop of Rochester, Memo No 21, and the evidence of the Dean of Chichester.

[88] *Report of the Royal Commission on the Laws of Marriage* (1868, BPP 1867–1868 vol. 32) p. 6. One witness told the Commission that the 1836 Act had made people fearful of making 'painful family secrets' (presumably illegitimate birth etc) public knowledge.

[89] One witness told the Chelmsford Commission that a high proportion of the intended marriages involved young men and women defying the requirement of parental consent. He attributed this tendency to the 'precocious independence' of Lancashire cotton workers: *Report of the Royal Commission on the Laws of Marriage* (1868, BPP 1867–1868 vol. 32).

Commission concluded that the requirement to have banns called 'promoted rather than prevented' clandestinity.[90]

The obvious solution to this problem would be to insist on the need for a uniform system of obligatory civil preliminaries, but the Church of England continued to stand firm against being deprived of its right to deal with the preliminaries to marriages in its own Churches.[91] The Chelmsford Commission preferred a different solution, at the same time more radical and more subtle, to the problem. The Commission believed that the person who was to officiate at the wedding—whether religious or civil—would be the person best placed to detect irregularities and evasions, and that the community could safely rely on the sense of duty and responsibility of the clergy and Registrars[92] to carry out the task of doing so carefully and conscientiously. Notice of intended marriage should therefore be given to the clergyman or to the Registrar of the district where the parties lived; and that person should have statutory power to make enquiry about such matters as the date of a former spouse's death. Where one of the parties was under 21, the necessary parental consent should be given in writing. Although notices were to be filed and open to inspection there was to be no public display. Under this scheme, the calling of banns would no longer be relevant to the validity of marriage, but this would not prevent the Church continuing to follow the practice as a matter of tradition.

The Commission was equally radical about the legal requirements for the wedding itself. The Commission emphasised that it attached 'great value' to the principle of 'strengthening and consecrating the civil tie . . . by the sanctions of organised religion'[93] but nonetheless insisted that, from the State's perspective, marriage was a purely civil contract. Logic might therefore have driven the Commission to advocate the introduction of the system adopted in most West European states (where marriages have to be contracted before a Public Official). It would then be for the parties to decide whether or not they wanted subsequently to have a religious ceremony in order to impress the 'seal of religion on that union which has already received the seal of the law'.[94] But in spite of the fact that the evidence demonstrated that adopting such a system had not in fact affected the popularity of religious marriage services in continental Europe[95] the Commission drew back. They thought that the introduction of

[90] *Report of the Royal Commission on the Laws of Marriage* (1868, BPP 1867–1868 vol. 32) p. 42. And witnesses agreed that the calling of large numbers of banns caused an 'inconvenient and unseemly interruption to divine service'.
[91] It appears that there was sometimes personal antagonism between the clergy of the Established Church and the Marriage Registrars: the Dean of Chichester told the *Royal Commission on the Laws of Marriage* that the Registrars were often 'jacks in office, taken from the lower classes of society' and that they rendered 'themselves obnoxious to the clergy': Appendix, Memorandum No. 19.
[92] *Report of the Royal Commission on the Laws of Marriage* (1868, BPP 1867–1868 vol. 32) p. 40.
[93] *Report of the Royal Commission on the Laws of Marriage* (1868, BPP 1867–1868 vol. 32) p. 35.
[94] *Report of the Royal Commission on the Laws of Marriage* (1868, BPP 1867–1868 vol. 32) Appendix, p. 202, where the words are attributed to Napoleon.
[95] The Commission was told by the Foreign Office that a church ceremony followed the civil marriage in all but 5% of French weddings: Appendix, p. 202.

what was essentially a foreign system would be 'opposed to the habits and feelings of the great majority of the people of Great Britain and Ireland . . .'.[96]

Who then should have the privilege of formally witnessing the contract of marriage? For the Chelmsford Commission the criterion was simply whether those concerned could be relied on to administer the system efficiently.[97] Registrars would of course be adequately supervised by the State, which effectively employed them. In the case of ministers of religion the test should be whether the position they held made them 'amenable to public responsibility, and to the censure and discipline of their own religious communities'.[98] Hence, the clergy of the Church of England would automatically qualify,[99] as would Roman Catholic priests and the ministers actively involved in the service of most Nonconformist communities. But peripatetic missioners would be excluded. The Commission believed there was not the slightest justification for requiring the presence of a Registrar at Nonconformist weddings but not at weddings in the Church of England.[100]

The Commission took an equally radical stance on other issues. For example, the law allowed marriages to be solemnised only between 8am and 12 noon—a provision, aimed at 'secret' weddings,[101] which obviously created difficulties for working men and women. The Commission recommended[102] simply that the rule be scrapped. The question of whether a marriage should be celebrated at

---

[96] *Report of the Royal Commission on the Laws of Marriage* (1868, BPP 1867–1868 vol. 32) p. 35.

[97] See *Report of the Royal Commission on the Laws of Marriage* (1868, BPP 1867–1868 vol. 32) p. 35.

[98] *Report of the Royal Commission on the Laws of Marriage* (1868, BPP 1867–1868 vol. 32) pp. 35–37. It was because Nonconformist ministers were, in contrast to the clergy of the Established Church, often birds of passage that the 1836 Act had required the presence of a Registrar: see above. The Chelmsford Commission also noted difficulties in identifying the appropriate person to be responsible for the registration of Jewish marriages.

[99] In fact, the incompetence of the clergy in performing the Registration functions required by the 1836 Act has been a recurrent theme of evidence given by the Registrar-General to official enquiries over the years: in 1867 the Registrar-General told the Royal Commission that the clergy were 'bad registrars, and [that] the numerous and extraordinary mistakes they made' were 'marvellous' to behold (*Report of the Royal Commission on the Laws of Marriage* (1868, BPP 1867–1868 vol. 32, Appendix, p. 41) whilst a quarter of a century later the *Select Committee on Nonconformist Marriages* (*Attendance of Registrars*) contrasted the 'highly satisfactory' registration arrangements in registered places of religious worship with the 'considerable irregularities and numerous defects' observed in Anglican ceremonies: see (1893–4) BPP vol. 13, pp. 6–9. The Registrar-General attributed these failings to the fact that registration of Anglican weddings was not 'effected by a civil officer who [could] be made to follow certain simple rules . . .': *op. cit.* q. 124. But the Royal Commission evidently did not share the Registrar-General's doubts about the capacity of ministers of religion to administer a system of registration.

[100] *Report of the Royal Commission on the Laws of Marriage* (1868, BPP 1867–1868 vol. 32) pp. 37–38.

[101] Marriage Act 1823, s. 21 gave statutory force to the canonical prohibition of marriage before 8am or after 12 noon. It has been said that 'historically an early hour was prescribed in order that mass could be celebrated afterwards': Law Commission *Published Working Paper* No. 35, *Solemnisation of Marriage* (1971) p. 74, note 8.

[102] *Report of the Royal Commission on the Laws of Marriage* (1868, BPP 1867–1868 vol. 32) p. 36.

(say) 5pm or even 8pm could be left to the good sense of the clergy or Registrar. And the Commission would even have abandoned the requirements that a pre-scribed formula should be used at some stage in the proceedings and that the wedding should take place in a specified building: once again, these matters could be left to the good sense of those whom the State allowed to discharge the function of witnessing and registering marriages.

Radicalism rejected: reform deferred

These conclusions were certainly what the increasingly well organised Nonconformist groups wanted to hear. But the Chelmsford recommendations were intended to apply to the whole of the United Kingdom. They were all too easily seen as an attempt to achieve uniformity by the imposition of Englishmen's will on the other nations making up the United Kingdom; and the Scots soon made it clear that they were not prepared to see the end of the infor-mal marriage which, although proscribed in England since 1753, continued to flourish in Scotland. This opposition effectively destroyed any prospect of achieving a United Kingdom marriage law;[103] and throughout the twentieth century the United Kingdom continued to enjoy the luxury[104] of three distinc-tive marriage codes. Of course, in logic, the fact that there were no prospects of enacting a uniform law applicable to the whole of the United Kingdom should not have precluded the Government seeking to apply the Chelmsford Commission's ruthless logic to the law of England and Wales; but in fact progress was limited to meeting the expressed grievances of Nonconformists and others, and even then it was painfully slow.

Piecemeal reform

In 1886 Parliament took the hardly daring step of extending the permitted hours for marriage to 3pm,[105] but other changes were more difficult to bring about. In particular, Bills to remedy the long-standing grievance of the law requiring a Registrar to attend marriages in Nonconformist and other registered places of religious worship[106] were brought forward but failed to make progress. Eventually, in 1893, the House of Commons set up a Select Committee specifically to look into this matter. The Committee's Report left no room for

---

[103] The formalities for marriage in Scotland were eventually modernised by the Marriage (Scotland) Act 1977 along lines recommended by a Royal Commission chaired by Lord Kilbrandon, *The Marriage Laws of Scotland* (1969, Cmnd. 4011) pp. 8–9 of which contains a succinct historical account of the development of the law.

[104] Or absurdity: as J Jackson QC, an eminent authority on this subject (see Biographical Notes) put it in a paper 'The Right to Marry' addressed to the Law Commission in 1966, a uniform mar-riage law within the United Kingdom ought to be a priority for reform; but it has never been attained: PRO BC3/374; and see below.

[105] Marriage Act 1886.

[106] *Report of the Select Committee on Nonconformist Marriages (Attendance of Registrars)* (1893–4) BPP vol. 13, p. 57 (hereafter '*1893 Select Committee*').

doubt that dissatisfaction was widespread. Some of the dissatisfaction was founded on matters of principle: the Nonconformist laity regarded this continued discrimination to be 'a serious indignity' whilst Nonconformist ministers regarded the law as 'derogatory to their ministerial character'.[107] But the most telling evidence was that of practical failings in the system: the comparatively small number of registrars meant that it was often difficult to arrange a wedding at a time which would suit all those involved. Even worse, Registrars were often late and sometimes—whether 'by reason of weather, accident, illness, forgetfulness or other causes'—failed to appear at all. It needs little imagination[108] to appreciate the distress caused to the couple and their friends and relatives as the clock moved towards 3pm yet nothing could be done because the Registrar had not arrived and (at a period when there was no telephone or motor transport) could not be found.

The Select Committee accepted the Nonconformist case and was notably unimpressed by the Registrar-General's objections (a combination of high principle—the clergy were incapable of operating an efficient registration system— and financial self-interest, for reform would mean Registrars losing the fees for attendance at chapel weddings). Legislation followed with unusual speed: the Marriage Act 1898 empowered the governing body[109] of registered buildings to authorise persons in whose presence marriages in that building could be solemnised[110] without the attendance of any Registrar.[111] The parties still had to give notice to the Registrar, who would in due course issue the necessary certificate,[112] but the wedding and consequential registration formalities would be dealt with by the 'authorised person'. In the first eight months[113] the governing bodies of 1,262 registered buildings appointed authorised persons to solemnise weddings.

The state of the marriage laws 1900–1960

Marriage was popular at the turn of the century: in 1900, the Registrar General reported the highest number of marriages for a quarter of a century with a marriage rate of 16.5 marriages per thousand of the population, and the eclectic approach of English law seemed to provide an acceptable procedure for people of all religions and none. The Church of England continued to provide the

---

[107] *1893 Select Committee*, para. 8.

[108] The *1893 Select Committee* Report contains many horror stories: see eg qs. 769 and 1022.

[109] In the case of Roman Catholic buildings this expression included the Bishop of the diocese: Marriage Act 1898, s. 1(3).

[110] Marriage Act 1898, s. 6.

[111] Marriage Act 1898, s. 4. Provision was made to protect district registrars from loss of fees: ss. 9 and 17.

[112] The Act preserved the parties' legal right to insist on the presence of the district registrar (s. 10) and Roman Catholics did not take advantage of the Act's provisions (apparently on the basis that it is not for their clergy to perform what is an essentially secular function).

[113] *Sixty-Second Annual Report of the Registrar-General* (1900, Cd. 323). The Act had come into force on 1 April 1899 and the figures relate to the year 1899.

setting for the majority of marriages—67.8% of the total. Nonconformist marriages made up 12.4% of the total; whilst Roman Catholic churches accounted for 4.1%. 'Civil' marriages in the Register Office—15% of the total—were much commoner than had been predicted in 1836[114] notwithstanding the stigma which apparently still attached in some circles to secular marriage.[115]

The Marriage Act 1898 can in retrospect be seen as completing the reforms of the law begun by Peel and Russell 60 years before. It is true that the need to satisfy the conflicting interests of the Church of England and other religious groups made the law formidably complex; and from time to time Parliament had retrospectively to validate marriages which were (or might be) void by reason of some technical defect.[116] It is also true that marriages contracted outside England and Wales continued to cause difficulties.[117] But by and large[118] the system worked; and to judge by the statute book, the first half of the twentieth century must have been a period of almost universal content with the rules governing the formalities for marriage. In 1934 Parliament decided that it would not do any harm to extend the hours for marriage from 3pm to 6pm;[119] but, apart

---

[114] *Sixty-Second Annual Report of the Registrar-General* (1900, Cd. 323).

[115] In one extraordinary case—the subject of a parliamentary question by the celebrated secularist Charles Bradlaugh: *Hansard's Parliamentary Debates* (3rd Series) 26 March 1886, vol. 304, col. 13—an Anglican priest disregarded a Register Office wedding between the beadle and the pew-opener and 'married' the couple on a common licence. The priest claimed not to be aware of the legislation, said he had no intention of contravening the law but wished only 'to superadd the sanction of the Church to the secular ceremony'. For his part, the husband stated that his reason for going to the Register Office was 'his desire to avoid any public or general notice'. The Attorney-General commented that 'seeing that he was about to marry his fourth wife, and that his wife was about to marry her third husband, perhaps their modesty was not unnatural'.

[116] For example, the Coatham Marriage Validity Act 1856 was passed to deal with the unfortunate fact that marriages had been celebrated and registered in a church built in 1854 which was not the Parish Church and which had not been licensed by the Bishop under Marriage Act 1836, s. 26 as a place in which marriages could be solemnised. The Provisional Order (Marriages) Act 1905 provided a streamlined legislative procedure for validating marriages in such circumstances, and the Marriages Validity (Provisional Orders) Act 1924 extended the scope of the legislation (the use of which, however, diminished in the years following World War II: see Law Commission *Published Working Paper* No. 35, *Solemnisation of Marriage* (1971) p. 96, note 62).

[117] For the legislation on this subject, see J Jackson, *The Formation and Annulment of Marriage* (2nd ed., 1989).

[118] This is an important qualification: the complexity of the law meant that the Registrar-General's office had to devote a good deal of time to giving advice and rulings on a wide range of problems, ranging from the not infrequent cases in which the wedding had taken place outside the permitted hours (see eg PRO RG48/249) or in a church which had not been licensed to a bizarre case in which a Priest of the Church of England, shocked to discover that two Gypsies presenting their baby to him for baptism were unmarried, 'married' the couple at once. Since no banns had been published the 'marriage' was void, and the couple had to go through a ceremony after banns had been duly published: see PRO RG48/251.

[119] Marriage (Extension of Hours) Act 1934. In 1936 MR Aubrey, General Secretary of the Baptist Union of Great Britain and Ireland, raised the question of further extension 'so that humble parties might have their friends, if they wished to be married in the evening'. But he thought that to save marriages being 'turned into "cocktail parties"' the extended hours should only apply to religious weddings: Memorandum recording a meeting with the Registrar General 1 May 1936, PRO RG48/2327. Not surprisingly nothing more was heard of this proposal.

from that, legislation in the inter-war years was confined to improving the procedure for remedying the unfortunate procedural errors which occasionally invalidated marriages contracted in good faith[120] and to dealing with the arcane (but important) subjects of marriages in foreign countries[121] and marriages in ships of the Royal Navy and in Naval, Military and Air Force Chapels.[122]

But the absence of additions to the statute book is not a safe test of public satisfaction; and in fact the Nonconformist churches continued to feel aggrieved by a law which left them in a position inferior to that of the Established Church.[123] In 1936, there were 'personal and unofficial' discussions between the Baptist Union and the Registrar-General;[124] and apparently a Bill was drafted to gather together and modernise the law, bringing the Free Church (ie Nonconformist) procedures into line with those of the Church of England. But nothing happened—possibly because the furore over reform of divorce law in 1937 made the Government reluctant to introduce legislation which would almost certainly provoke the Bishops (or some of them). Again, Christianity was not the only religion which had its Nonconformists; and at the turn of the century the Registrar-General was involved in a (sometimes acrimonious) correspondence stemming from the growth of Reform and Liberal movements in Judaism.[125] The Chief Rabbi did not collaborate with these 'Nonconformist' synagogues and attempts to resolve the difficulties in the framework of the existing legislation were unsuccessful.[126] Only in 1959 was the nettle grasped.[127]

[120] Marriages Validity (Provisional Orders) Act 1924: see above, p. 21, note 116.

[121] This ranged from legislation relating to a single country (eg the Marriage in Japan (Validity) Act 1912, and the Marriage Act 1939 (which, in spite of the short title, was concerned solely with the implications for marriage of constitutional changes in the Irish Free State) through general provisions designed to facilitate marriage in cases in which a party lived outside the United Kingdom but in a British dominion (see the Marriage of British Subjects (Facilities) Act 1915) to cases in which a British subject wanted to marry a foreigner abroad whilst having the assurance that the marriage would be recognised here (see the Marriage with Foreigners Act 1906).

[122] See the Naval Marriages Act 1908 and the Marriage (Naval, Military, and Air Force Chapels) Act 1932.

[123] This remained a sensitive area for many years; and in the context of the marriage law the long debate about legalising marriage with a deceased wife's sister (see Chapter 2, below) evidently to some extent polarised opinion, being supported by Nonconformists but opposed by many Anglicans.

[124] Memorandum by MR Aubrey, General Secretary of the Baptist Union of Great Britain and Ireland, recording a meeting with the Registrar General 1 May 1936, PRO RG48/2327.

[125] For the background, see the Evidence given to the Joint Committee on Consolidation Bills: *Report* (1948–49, HL 29-v, BPP 1948–49, vol. 6, p. 783). The Liberal Jewish Synagogue complained that the Orthodox disapproved of men and women sitting together, the use of English in services, and the failure of some members of the congregation to wear hats.

[126] See PRO RG48/190. Two synagogues sought to deal with the problem by registering as places of religious worship and seeking the appointment of an 'authorised person' under the Marriage Act 1898; but, as the Registrar-General pointed out, s. 13 of that Act specifically provided that nothing in the Act should affect marriages solemnised in accordance with the usages of persons professing the Jewish religion. In 1949, the Joint Committee on Consolidation Bills declined to accept an amendment to the consolidating Marriage Bill on the ground that it would involve a 'substantial' change in the law: see the Committee's *Report* (1948–49, HL 29-v, BPP 1948–49, vol. 6, p. 783).

[127] Marriage (Secretaries of Synagogues) Act 1959. The rules are set out in J Jackson, *The Formation and Annulment of Marriage* (2nd ed., 1949) p. 201.

Nor were complaints about the law always based on religious allegiance. Nothing, for example, could be clearer as a matter of legal doctrine than the principle that marriage was a public act, to be solemnised publicly rather than in secret. But in fact people continued to be embarrassed. According to one Superintendent Registrar,[128] newspapers employed reporters to do nothing else except go to Register Offices, inspect the Notice Book, and copy out addresses so that they could visit the couple.[129]

The outbreak of World War II in 1939 prevented any further consideration being given to issues of policy; and the Registrar-General's pre-War plans for a rationalisation of the law came to nothing. Nonconformists continued to feel aggrieved at their distinctly unequal treatment under the marriage laws; but, in an increasingly secular age, little attention seems to have been given to those grievances.[130] Somehow, it seemed, the law could be adapted to the needs of a changing society without the need for legislation amending the substantive law. But there was strong bureaucratic pressure to put the law into a more accessible form. In 1949, the Lord Chancellor told the Cabinet's Legislation Committee[131] (with slight, but no doubt pardonable, exaggeration) that the

'law relating to marriage is contained in about 40 enactments dating from 1540 and is almost unintelligible owing to the number and complexity of the enactments. Yet the law has to be interpreted and observed by large numbers of clergymen and registrars; and it is, therefore, very desirable to get the law into as simple and intelligible a form as is practicable. [But] if one were to consolidate the law as it stands it would be full of anomalies and ambiguities . . .'

The situation was just what the recently enacted Consolidation of Enactments (Procedure) Act 1949, allowing 'minor improvements' to be made in consolidation legislation without full debate in both Houses of Parliament (with all the attendant opportunities for trouble-making), was intended to deal with; and the Marriage Act 1949 was one of the first measures to make use of

---

[128] St. Giles, London.

[129] He cited the case of Harry Relph (professionally known on the Music Hall stage as 'Little Tich'—'without doubt a man of highly strung nervous temperament') whose fiancée was visited in the early morning at home by nine reporters. The Registrar colluded with Mr Relph to keep the press away from the wedding; but in response to this and other complaints the Registrar-General ruled that he had no power to stop newspapermen or others from taking notes from the contents of the notice book or indeed publishing the names and addresses of the parties. The Registrar-General did however confirm that Superintendent Registrars acted properly in suggesting to journalists that they refrain from publishing information about cases in which this would cause personal suffering with no corresponding public advantage: Vivian to Stokes, 17 July 1931, PRO RG 48/141.

[130] But they were referred to by Sir Cyril Black MP in the House of Commons debate on the Bill which became the Marriage (Registrar-General's Licence) Act 1970: *Official Report* (HC), 13 February 1970, vol. 795, col. 1613.

[131] May 1949, HOC 49(44), PRO LCO2/6674.

this relaxation in the law.[132] The 1949 Act put the legislation in more user-friendly form, without making any changes of substance[133] to the content.

REFORM DEFERRED, 1960–1994

The intellectual and moral upheavals of the 1960s had their impact on the gradualist approach to the reform of the marriage laws. MPs began to introduce Bills[134] to deal with specific problems they had identified; and behind the scenes the Registrar-General's Office set to work in identifying a number of proposals 'for bringing this branch of the law into line with modern circumstances'.[135] But

---

[132] One of the 'minor improvements' proposed was to abolish the requirement that the certificate for the registration of a building under the Marriage Act should be on 'parchment or vellum'; but unfortunately the Attorney-General told the House of Commons that the reason for this change was that the parchment industry was 'dead or dying', a statement to which Messrs Band & Co, Manufacturers of Parchment and Binding Vellum, took exception. They offered to supply 'an almost unlimited amount of parchment or vellum'. However, the draftsman convinced the Joint Committee that the change in question was one that could properly be made. Curiously, even under an avowedly modernising 21st century government, representations by the vellum and parchment industry were successful in securing the dropping of a proposal that the Queen's Speech at the opening of Parliament be no longer recorded on vellum. *The Times* (11 November 2002) recorded Mr Robin Cook, Leader of the House of Commons, as declaring 'I back the goat'.

[133] The 'minor improvements' included one change of considerable significance: the Act allowed the form of certificates to be prescribed by delegated legislation, and under that power important changes have been made. The procedure was also used to make it clear that the rubric to the Book of Common Prayer was to determine the point at which Banns of Marriage had to be read; and to abolish the provisions for forfeiture of property acquired by a husband by virtue of a marriage without parental consent. The requirement imposed by the 1836 Act on those wanting to marry in the Register Office to declare that they objected to marriage in a place of worship also disappeared from the statute book, s. 44 of the 1949 Act simply requiring the parties to say they wish to be married in a register office. There appears to be no mention of this last change in the *travaux préparatoires* leading to the enactment of the 1949 Act but perhaps the draftsman, unaware of the historical background, assumed that no change of substance was involved.

[134] In 1965 Sir Spencer Summers MP (1902–1976, Conservative MP for Aylesbury) presented a Bill to eliminate the residential requirements imposed on those seeking to marry by common licence: *Official Report* (HC), 8 December 1970, vol. 722, col. 34, Bill No. 34; but in the face of opposition from the Church he was persuaded to withdraw it: see Rooke-Matthews to Cartwright-Sharp 23 April 1968, PRO BC3/374. In 1970, another back-bencher, Victor Goodhew MP successfully piloted through Parliament (with Government assistance) the Marriage (Registrar-General's Licence) Act 1970 to allow the terminally ill to marry in hospital and elsewhere: see below, p. 28.

[135] The General Register Office (GRO) produced a 30-page Memorandum which suggested the abandonment of reliance on publicity as the means of ensuring that those with a legitimate interest in whether or not a marriage could take place were able to have their views properly taken into account. The practice of displaying notices of intended marriage in the Register Office should cease, and more proactive procedures should be introduced on matters such as the giving of parental consent to the marriage of minors. It appears that Ministers had agreed on the GRO making an approach to the Church of England with a view to substituting a system of uniform civil preliminaries for the diversity of existing procedures: PRO BC3/374, Jenkins to Cartwright-Sharp, 5 September 1968; GRO memorandum 29 July 1969. The Church was itself formally considering its relationship with the State, and issues about the marriage laws (for example, the obligation to solemnise marriages irrespective of the parties' religious belief) arose in that context: see *Church and State*, Report of the Archbishop's Committee, 1970 reprinted 1984, at eg para. 200; and the question of the marriage laws was more specifically addressed by the Report *Marriage, Divorce and the Church* (1971).

the commitment of the Law Commission, set up by Harold Wilson's Government in 1965 with the objective of carrying out systematic law reform,[136] to codification of the law eventually prompted a comprehensive and published review of the law and practice.[137]

In December 1969, after some delicate jousting between the various official agencies involved,[138] the Commission set up a Joint Working Party[139] 'to enquire into the formal requirements for the solemnisation and registration of marriages in England and Wales and to propose what changes are desirable'.[140] The Working Party made a full analysis of the purposes of the law of marriage, set out the present law and practice in some detail, discussed the problems and difficulties which had arisen, and made proposals for reform. Only the rules governing marriages of members of the Royal Family were omitted from the survey.[141] The Working Party's ideas were put out to public consultation;[142] and in 1973 the Working Party reported to the Law

---

[136] Law Commissions Act 1965. See further SM Cretney, *Law, Law Reform and the Family* (1998) Chapter 1.

[137] Additional stimulus was provided by the publication in 1969 of the Report of the Departmental Committee appointed to inquire into the Law of Scotland relating to the constitution of Marriage, *The Marriage Law of Scotland* (The 'Kilbrandon' Report) Cmnd. 4011. The Report was closely scrutinised by the Law Commission (see PRO BC3/376) and the Chairman of the Law Commission, Sir Leslie Scarman, opined that this Report could be expected to 'create pressure from public opinion for a similar modernisation of the law' here': Scarman to the Registrar-General, 24 July 1969, PRO BC3/374. Again the publication of the (Latey) *Report on the Age of Majority* (Cmnd. 3342) in 1967 had directed public attention to the issue of the appropriate age for 'free marriage', ie marriage of the young without parental consent: see below.

[138] The Law Commission first broached the matter with the Church and the Registrar-General in 1968, and an informal meeting took place at the Athenaeum on 27 June: PRO BC3/374.

[139] The Working Party was chaired by the Chairman of the Law Commission, Sir Leslie Scarman, and its membership consisted of one representative of the General Register Office, one from the Home Office, and three (including LCB Gower: see Biographical Notes) from the Law Commission. The Law Commission also provided the secretariat: PWP 35, para. 2. The Working Party reported to the Law Commission: see below.

[140] Law Commission Published Working Paper No. 35, *The Solemnisation of Marriage* (1971) (hereafter cited as 'PWP 35').

[141] The Home Secretary, James Callaghan, had on 24 April 1968 (see PRO BC3/415) personally warned the Law Commission's chairman, Sir Leslie Scarman, against making any reference to the provisions of the Royal Marriage Act 1772 (which imposes restrictions on the marriage of descendants of George II) in the course of the Commission's work on the Nullity of Marriage: Callaghan pointed out that any proposal for change would entail obtaining the concurrence of Commonwealth countries, and to 'raise these issues at Westminster might well give rise to controversy; and certainly it would be a great pity to have to bring up at the present time any discussion of the 1772 Act in, for example, the Canadian Parliament'. The Home Secretary also said that this legislation 'was considered in some detail at the time of Lord Harewood's divorce and remarriage' [in July 1967]. At its first meeting, the Working Party agreed that 'in view of the many difficulties involved' no reference should be made to this topic: PRO BC3/374, 4 December 1969.

[142] PWP 35 was given a wide circulation; and comments from those with an interest in this area of the law were invited and taken into account. Unusually, the Law Commission did not publish a list of those who responded to the Paper.

Commission[143] (which on the whole[144] endorsed the Working Party's conclusions).

The Working Party considered that the law fell 'woefully short . . . particularly perhaps as regards simplicity and intelligibility' of the criteria for a good marriage law.[145] The proliferation of procedures meant that the law was not understood by members of the public

'or even by all those who administer it. To make matters worse, there is a bewildering diversity in the consequences of a failure properly to comply with the rules. . . . Whether the marriage is effective or not may depend on the knowledge of the parties regarding the failure. Nor can it be said that the sacrifice of simplicity and intelligibility has enabled the other objectives to be achieved; on the contrary, the system, if such it can be called, manifestly does not promote the uniform or effective investigation of capacity and consents by trained personnel and does not afford an adequate opportunity for objections to be declared and considered. . . . Rationalisation is clearly long overdue and should be attainable . . .'[146]

The 'simplest and most effective' solution would be to enact that civil marriage should—on the Continental model—be the only legally effective way of creating marriage. But in the end this radical solution was rejected:[147] it would be likely to arouse strong opposition both from the churches and from the general public.[148] Evidently opinion had not changed much since the Chelmsford

---

[143] The Working Party's Final Report was published as an Annex to the Law Commission's *Report on Solemnisation of Marriage in England and Wales* (Law Com. No. 53, 1973) hereafter cited as 'Law Com. No. 53'.

[144] The Commissioners were not able to reach agreement amongst themselves on some of the Working Party's recommendations, notably those assimilating the proposals for registration of buildings so that Quakers and Jewish marriages would lose their long-standing privileges: Law Com. No. 53, para. 22.

[145] Defined by the Working Party (WP 35 para. 3; Law Com. No. 53, Annex, para. 4.) as being to 'ensure that marriages are solemnised only in respect of those who are free to marry and have freely agreed to do so and that the status of those who marry shall be established with certainty so that doubts do not arise, either in the minds of the parties or in the community, about who is married and who is not. To this end, it appears to us to be necessary that there should be proper opportunity for the investigation of capacity (and, in the case of minors, parental consent) before the marriage and that the investigation should be carried out, uniformly for parties to all marriages, by persons trained to perform this function. We suggest that the law should guard against clandestine marriages, that there should be proper opportunity for those who may know of a lawful impediment to a marriage to declare it, that all marriages should be publicly solemnised and that the marriage should be duly recorded in official registers. At the same time we recognise that a marriage ceremony is an important family and social occasion and we feel that unnecessary and irksome restrictions on its celebration should be avoided. . . . [S]ince marriage created a status which vitally concerns the public, the law of marriage should be as simple and easily understood as possible . . .'.

[146] PWP 35 para. 5; Law Com. No. 53, Annex, para. 6.

[147] PWP 35 para. 70; cf. Law Com. No. 53, Annex, para. 72. At the beginning of the exercise the General Register Office, albeit 'reluctant to put it forward as their own proposal', had favoured the radical course: PRO BC3/374, Minutes of First Meeting of Working Party, 4 December 1969. So, it appears, had the Law Commission's chairman, Sir Leslie Scarman: see *The Times* 9 December 1969.

[148] It was also suggested that if all the marriages celebrated in churches, chapels and registered buildings had to be channelled into Register Offices 'their accommodation would be inadequate and some increase of staff would also be essential': PWP 35 para. 70; Law Com. No. 53, Annex.

Royal Commission had reached the same conclusion a century earlier.[149] So the Commission put forward a less ambitious policy for rationalisation. This was that there should be uniform civil preliminaries for all marriages regardless of where they were to be celebrated.[150] Indeed, the Working Party claimed that reform of the existing unsatisfactory system would be impossible unless uniform civil preliminaries were made compulsory for all marriages.[151] Detailed proposals were put forward for improving the effectiveness of the procedures: parents consenting to a child's marriage should be required either to attend personally at the Register Office or have their signature witnessed by 'a person of standing';[152] there should be provision for the lodging of objections at the General Register Office;[153] and it should no longer be possible to shorten the period of notice required simply by paying a fee for a licence.[154]

The Law Commission made few recommendations for substantial change in the law governing the places in which marriages can be solemnised and rejected out of hand[155] suggestions that secular venues should be licensed. There was (so it was claimed) no support for setting up commercial 'marriage parlours',[156] and the answer to complaints about the facilities available and the standard of amenity in some Register Offices[157] was to intensify the efforts of the Registrar General and the Association of Local Authorities to raise standards.[158] But diversity was still to have its place: people who wanted their marriage associated with a particular religion should still be allowed to have the appropriate ceremony.[159] Only minor changes in the procedures for solemnising religious

[149] See above. In the latter part of the twentieth century a body of opinion emerged within the Church of England favouring universal civil marriage and so relieving the Church of its obligation to marry all comers. But this never beceame the majority view: see *An Honourable Estate* (1988) para. 159.

[150] PWP 35 para. 3; Law Com. No. 53, Annex, paras. 17–23.

[151] PWP 35 para. 16; Law Com. No. 53, Annex, para. 17.

[152] PWP 35 para. 38; Law Com. No. 53, Annex, para. 50.

[153] Rather than supposing that those wishing to object would easily be able to identify the Register Office or Church where the notice of intended marriage had been given: PWP 35 para. 39; Law Com. No. 53, Annex, para. 52.

[154] In cases of hardship the Registrar-General would have a discretion to allow a marriage after a shorter interval than the stipulated 15 days: PWP 35 paras. 21–22; Law Com. No. 53, Annex, para. 34).

[155] PWP 35 para. 3; Law Com. No. 53, Annex, paras. 76–80.

[156] PWP 35 para. 72.

[157] In the debate on the Bill for the Marriage (Registrar-General's Licence) Act 1970, *Official Report* (HC), 13 February 1970, vol. 795, col. 1610, Mr John Fraser drew attention to the fact that the Register Office in the populous Lambeth area of South London was a converted house surrounded by redevelopment; and that two rooms (divided by a public lavatory and a staircase) were available there for weddings, the larger of which measured 20 feet by 12 feet. Things seem to have been even worse in Manchester where the Register Office Marriage Chamber was also used as a divorce court: col. 1646.

[158] PWP 35 para. 76.

[159] The GRO considered that the requirement that a building could only be registered for marriages if it was a place of religious *worship* as distinct from religious *observance* caused difficulties for Unitarians and some others: see the GRO 1969 Memorandum: PRO BC3/374, para. 45 ff. However, this statement is somewhat difficult to understand since nearly 200 Unitarian buildings were registered at the time: *Marriage and Divorce Statistics 1975*, Government Statistical Service, Series FM2, no. 2 (1978) Tables 3.12b. In the event the Working Party found itself unable to formulate any improved definition: PWP 35 para. 75; Law Com. No. 53, Annex, paras. 76–77.

weddings were recommended—for example, whatever the form of service, the parties should be made clearly to understand that a marriage celebrated in this country by Islamic or other rites was monogamous;[160] whilst the Registrar-General should have greater control[161] over the 'authorised persons' conducting marriages in registered buildings. The Commission's Report ended with a range of proposals for clarifying the legal effect of irregularities; and for rationalising the criminal offences for breaches of the law.[162]

Nobody disputed the Law Commission's view that a new and comprehensive Marriage Act was essential. But by the end of the century nothing of substance to that end had been done. Indeed the incoherence of the law was increased by piecemeal changes dictated by the pressures of the moment.[163] No doubt there are many reasons for the failure of successive governments to act. As the Law Commission put it in 1973, 'reform in this particular field is a topic on which personal views and religious opinions influence decisions';[164] and it does seem that the fact that almost any comprehensive measure would inevitably involve change in the legal position of the Church of England seems to have been particularly important. This was made clear in 1988 by a Working Party established by the Standing Committee of the General Synod of the Church of England.[165] To accept a uniform system of civil preliminaries 'could be interpreted [as a] diminution of the centuries old responsibilities of the Church' in relation to marriage,[166] whilst the notion that the Church of England should be placed in the same position as other churches (involving, as it necessarily would, the end of publication of banns as a legally recognised procedure) was rejected as removing pastoral opportunities for marriage preparation.[167]

Arguments such as these might not seem particularly powerful to people outside the Church of England or indeed to a Government as impatient of inefficiency and committed to rationalisation and cost-effectiveness as was that led by Mrs Margaret Thatcher between 1979 and 1990. The Thatcher Government did look at the question of the marriage laws from what appeared

[160] PWP 35 paras. 92–95; Law Com. No. 53, Annex, paras. 96–99.

[161] For example, by being empowered to reject nominations made by the management of the building, and to require management to cancel appointments and make another nomination or have weddings attended by a registrar: PWP 35 para. 90; Law Com. No. 53, Annex, para. 95.

[162] See PWP 35 Chapters 5 and 6; Law Com. No. 53, paras. 30–32 and Annex, paras. 135–140.

[163] In 1970 the Marriage (Registrar-General's Licence) Act 1970 introduced a civil equivalent of the Archbishop's Special Licence to enable the terminally ill to marry at home or in hospital; and in 1983 the Marriage Act (to some extent overlapping the 1970 Act but not repealing it) allowed persons house-bound by reason of illness or disability or detained in prison or under mental health legislation to marry at home or in their place of detention. (It appears that the 1983 Act was a response to fears that denial of the right to marry to prisoners would be held incompatible with the European Convention on Human Rights.) For the more significant reforms made by the Marriage Act 1994 and the Immigration and Asylum Act 1999 see below.

[164] Law Com. No. 53, para. 34. It seems the Commission realised that it was unlikely their proposals would be enacted since they did not follow their usual practice of drafting the legislation which would be required.

[165] Published as *An Honourable Estate* (1988).   [166] *An Honourable Estate* (1988) para. 188.

[167] *An Honourable Estate* (1988) para. 168.

to be a new perspective, setting up an Efficiency Scrutiny of the Registration Service led by a Marks and Spencer executive, Sir Derek Rayner.[168] The Scrutiny Report[169] duly obliged with accounts of the incompetence of the clergy in discharging their registration duties and the ineffectiveness of marriage notices as a means of achieving publicity for intended marriage. (The Report discovered that notices displayed in Register Offices were used not only by journalists but by photographers, florists and salesmen of 'insurance, babywear and marital aids' seeking out potential customers).[170] The Efficiency Scrutiny made many proposals for streamlining procedures and adapting them to the 'needs of the larger, more mobile and more anonymous' population than had existed in Queen Victoria's time.

The Government adopted a cautious approach. It published a timid Green Paper[171] for consultation which seemed to accept that opposition to the introduction of uniform civil preliminaries from within the Church of England[172] precluded the Government from reopening the question. Even more surprisingly the Thatcher Government refused to alter its view in the face of pressure from the large numbers who claimed that uniformity would result in 'a better quality of registration and would allow for a greater use of new technology'. For its part, the Government believed that there were 'many factors other than administrative advantage' to be taken into account in this area;[173] and that a 'a wider consensus' was needed before 'such fundamental changes' could be contemplated. Instead, the Government announced that it would concentrate on streamlining the structure of the Registration Service and the procedure for registering buildings for marriages, and on making some (comparatively minor) changes in the procedure for civil marriage.

It did not require much management expertise to see that the Registration Service is beset by anomalies.[174] Local Authorities seemed to have responsibility without power: registration officers were paid by Local Authorities but not employed by them: indeed they have no legal employer, and they carry out their work on the instructions of the Registrar-General (who is the only person who can dismiss them). The 'rigid lines of demarcation' embodied in statute between Superintendent Registrars, Registrars of Births and Deaths and Assistant Registrars (each 'Principal Officer' being personally responsible for his own work which could only be delegated to a named deputy) were scarcely compatible with the notions of efficient public service management fashionable in the last two decades of the twentieth century. It was indeed easy enough to make

---

[168] See Biographical Notes.

[169] *Report of the Efficiency Scrutiny of the Registration Service* (1985).

[170] *Report of the Efficiency Scrutiny of the Registration Service* (1985) para. 41.1.

[171] *Registration: A Modern Service* (1988, Cm. 531).

[172] In *An Honourable Estate* (1988).

[173] *Registration: Proposals for Change* (1990, Cm. 939), para. 3.2–3.

[174] Generally on the constitutional position of the officials and the historical evolution of the registration service see *Miles v. Wakefield Metropolitan District Council* [1897] AC 539, HL.

ambitious proposals[175] for restructuring and placing responsibility and management of the service firmly on Local Authorities, but attempts to put them into practice for long made little progress. The 'early legislation' promised for reform of the service never appeared.[176]

(1) Consumerism and the marriage ceremony

Administrative efficiency was only one aspect of the Thatcher Government's approach to the provision of public services. There was an underlying belief in exposing public services to the pressures of consumer demand, competition and market forces; and this led the Government to propose giving the public a greater choice of marriage ceremony. Local authorities should be made to compete with one another to provide more attractive facilities than the stark and unappealing ambience of many Register Offices. The 1990 White Paper[177] accordingly proposed giving people the freedom to choose any Register Office they wanted as a venue for their wedding;[178] whilst local authorities would be allowed to offer:

'Further facilities for those who want them and to charge appropriately for these. . . . For example, different buildings will command different fees and the fee will also vary with the amount of time for which the marriage party wishes to use the premises. . . . Video or photography facilities may be required, and the local authority may wish to make these available in conjunction with the private sector.'[179]

But the consumers' choice of venue for a civil wedding was not to be restricted to Register Offices. The public (so the White Paper declared)[180] were 'enthusiastic about the prospect of civil marriages being able to take place' in other buildings such as hotels and stately homes; and local authorities should be allowed to offer such facilities.[181]

The Government provided facilities for Mr Gyles Brandreth[182] to bring forward the Bill which became the Marriage Act 1994 and this reflected a subtle but

---

[175] See especially *Registration: Proposals for Change* (1990, Cm. 939), Part I.

[176] In 1999 the Blair Government announced yet another review of the legislation *Supporting Families—Summary of Responses to the Consultation Document* (1999) para. 4.13. After long delays, a White Paper, *Civil Registration: Vital Change* Cm. 5355 was published in 2002, see p. 37, below.

[177] *Registration: Proposals for Change* (1990, Cm. 939).

[178] Rather than being required to use the Register Office serving their place of residence.

[179] *Registration: Proposals for Change* (1990, Cm. 939), para. 3.22. The requirement that a party reside in the registration district was removed by Marriage Act 1994, s. 2(1).

[180] *Registration: Proposals for Change* (1990, Cm. 939), para. 3.17. Evidently opinion had changed since the 1970s when the Working Party found no evidence of demand for such facilities: see p. 27, above.

[181] *Registration: Proposals for Change* (1990, Cm. 939), para. 3.17–21; and Summary of recommendations, para. 28.

[182] Mr Brandreth's Westminster Diaries 1990–1997, *Breaking the Code* give surprisingly little prominence to his piloting this Bill through Parliament, but he has subsequently stated that he would like to be remembered for having introduced the Bill: *The Times*, 21 January 2003.

important change of emphasis. Under the Act, it is the private entrepreneur who is to take the initiative and offer the service, and the local authority's role is merely to 'approve' premises for the solemnisation of civil marriages.[183] A huge business developed whereby the owners of hotels, stately homes and other venues—ranging from football grounds to decommissioned warships[184]—offer wedding packages for a fee;[185] and it is clear that the legislation has met a previously unsatisfied demand: in 1999 37,709 weddings—nearly 15% of all weddings and a quarter of all civil weddings—took place in approved premises.[186]

In some ways, therefore, it can be said that the 1994 Act privatised marriage; but it is important to note that the Act was carefully drafted so as to be restricted to *civil* marriage: the premises must have no recent or continuing connection with any religion, religious practice or religious persuasion, no religious service is to be used, any reading, music, words of performance forming part of the ceremony must be secular in character.[187] In this way conflict with the Church of England[188] (and perhaps other religious bodies) was avoided; but the outcome

---

[183] The Marriage (Approved Premises) Regulations 1995 lay down rules intended to ensure that premises provide a 'seemly and dignified venue for the solemnization of marriages'. A Registrar and Superintendent Registrar have to attend to deal with the registration requirements.

[184] According to *The Times* newspaper (11 May 2001) the owners of the London Eye hope that their '£1,700 service will attract thousands of couples'. For their money, it appears that the 'wedding party gets a personal waiter and a pod filled with flowers that contains up to 20 guests. For an extra £299, another 25 guests can watch the ceremony from an adjacent capsule'. At the wedding (presumably to comply with the statutory requirements) 'two members of staff (one on the ground and one in the wedding pod) carried two way radios so that anyone rushing to object at the appropriate time could make their views heard'.

[185] The debates on the Marriage Act 1994 evidence the fact that some MPs consider the proposals did not go far enough, and that marriages should be permitted in the open air; whilst some regrets at the fact that marriages under the Act had to be purely secular were also expressed: see eg *Official Report* (HC) 15 July 1964, vol. 246, col. 1327; and the debate in Standing Committee C, 6 July 1996.

[186] The use made of approved premises marriages are analysed by J Haskey, 'Marriages in Approved Premises . . .' (2002) 107 *Population Trends* 35.

[187] See the detailed regulations made by the Marriages (Approved Premises) Regulations 1995, SI 1995 No. 510.

[188] But the ability of the Church of England to respond to the evident demand for an impressive setting for weddings may have been affected by the rule that normally one or both parties must reside in the parish in which the wedding is to take place: for a full and lucid account of the relevant rules see RDH Bursell, *Liturgy, Order and the Law* (1996) pp. 164–193. This rule makes it difficult for couples—particularly the many who have in fact established their own joint residence elsewhere— wishing to marry in a church in their parents' parish. It is true that the Church has greatly relaxed its attitude to the grant of a Special Licence: at the beginning of the twentieth century the number of such licences granted each year barely rose to double figures and even in 1971—when the Law Commission reported that such licences were granted only in 'exceptional circumstances or grave emergency'—on average only some 250 licences were granted each year: PWP 53, para. 13; but by 1993 the number of Marriages by Special Licence had risen to 2,810. In 1998 (possibly as a result of a shift to Authorised Premises weddings) the number fell back to 1,878 (or 3% of all Anglican weddings): see *Marriage and Divorce Statistics 1993*, Government Statistical Service, Series FM2, no. 21 (1995) Table 3.10; *Marriage, divorce and adoption statistics 1998* Office for National Statistics, Series FM2, no. 26 (2000) Table 3.34). For the Church's rules on the grant of Special Licences, see Bursell, cited above, p. 170.

has been a significant switch from religious weddings to civil marriages in approved premises.[189]

(2) The immigration dimension

The Immigration and Asylum Act 1999 gave effect to some of the proposals made by the Law Commission nearly 30 years earlier:[190] no longer was it to be possible to contract a civil marriage after only a day by paying an extra fee for a certificate with licence, whilst the parties are now required not only to make a solemn declaration that the information they gave on these matters was correct but also to produce evidence of matters such as the parties' age, marital status, residence and nationality if required to do so.[191] The fact that these changes were made by an Immigration and Asylum Act (not to say the provision requiring superintendent registrars to report cases which give rise to suspicion to the Home Office Immigration Department)[192] perhaps furnish sufficient evidence that the Government's motivation was not primarily the simplification and modernisation of the law.[193] The fact that the changes were made by adding clauses to a hotly controversial Bill meant that there was virtually no public discussion of their impact on the marriage laws; and the fact that the new provisions created yet more anomalies[194] apparently passed unnoticed.

MARRIAGE AND THE MARRIAGE LAWS AT THE END
OF THE TWENTIETH CENTURY

Marriage was a popular institution at the beginning of the twentieth century: in 1899 there were 262,334 marriages, that is to say 16.5 per thousand of the population (or, perhaps more meaningfully, 57.5 per thousand unmarried men aged 16 and over).[195] Marriage remained popular for the first 70 years of the century; and in 1972 the number of marriages peaked at 426, 241 (17.4 per thousand of the population 84.4 per thousand unmarried men aged 16 and over).[196] It was at this period that it became part of the conventional wisdom that growth in

[189] See J Haskey in 'Marriages in Approved Premises . . .' (2002) 107 *Population Trends* 35.

[190] *Report on Solemnisation of Marriage in England and Wales* (Law Com. No. 53, 1973). Some of these proposals echoed those of the 1868 Chelmsford Royal Commission: see p. 15 above.

[191] Immigration and Asylum Act 1999, ss. 160, 161.

[192] Immigration and Asylum Act 1999, s. 24; Reporting of Suspicious Marriages and Registration of Births Deaths and Marriages (Miscellaneous Amendments) Regulations 2000, SI 2000 No. 3164.

[193] cf. Law Commissions Act 1965, s. 3(1).

[194] For example, the new provisions do not apply to Anglican marriages, for which there are now shorter periods of notice etc than for marriage after Registrar's notice.

[195] *Sixty Second Report of the Registrar-General* (1900, Cd. 323).

[196] *Marriage and Divorce Statistics 1975*, Government Statistical Service, Series FM2, no. 2 (1978) Table 2.1.

divorce rates did not indicate a rejection of the institution of marriage, since marriage remained popular and had become an almost universal experience.[197] But no sooner had that belief been generally accepted than the situation changed: in the 1980s, both the number of marriages and the marriage rate began to fall;[198] and this trend continued to the end of the century. In 1999, there were only 263,515 marriages (10 per thousand of the population, and 28.1 per thousand unmarried men aged 16 and over).[199] And these figures relate to all marriages: whereas at the beginning of the twentieth century more than 90% of marriages were first marriages for both parties (and only 353 divorced people remarried)[200] at the end of the century 40% of marriages were remarriages for one or both parties.[201]

These figures demonstrate a striking decline in marriage but not a lack of interest in family life (or at least in intimate relationships). There has been a substantial increase in the incidence of cohabitation outside marriage,[202] and a substantial increase in the mean age of marriage: at the beginning of the century the mean age for marriage was 26 for bachelors and 24 for spinsters, but by 1999 the comparable figures were 30 and 28 respectively. (The mean age for all marriages had risen to 34 for men and 31 for women.[203])

The decline of religious weddings

At the beginning of the century, the great majority of marriages involved a religious ceremony: only 15% of marriages took place in the Register Office.[204] By the end of the century, the situation was dramatically different: only 38% of the marriages solemnised in 1999 were in a church or place of religious worship.[205]

[197] *Report of the Committee on One-Parent Families*, Cmnd. 5629, para. 2.4; and generally the statistical analysis in Part 3, Section 2.

[198] By 1993 the number of marriages fell to 299,197 (11.6 per thousand of the population, 37.3 per thousand unmarried men aged 16 and over). This was the first year since the end of World War I in which the number of marriages had fallen below 300,000: *Marriage and Divorce Statistics 1993*, Government Statistical Service, Series FM2, no. 21 (1995) Table 2.1.

[199] J Haskey, 'Marriages in Approved Premises . . .' (2000) 107 *Population Trends* 83.

[200] *Sixty Second Report of the Registrar-General* (1900, Cd. 323).

[201] J Haskey, 'Marriages in Approved Premises . . .' (2000) 107 *Population Trends* 83.

[202] See Chapter 13 below. 71% of those marrying in 1998 gave identical residential addresses (although the proportion was only 51% where the marriage was religious: *Marriage, divorce and adoption statistics 1998*, Office for National Statistics, Series FM2, no. 26 (2000) Table 3.348).

[203] J Haskey, 'Marriages in Approved Premises . . .' (2000) 107 *Population Trends* 83.

[204] *Sixty Second Report of the Registrar-General* (1900, Cd. 323). There is no way of telling what proportion of these were followed by a religious service under the provisions of the Marriage and Registration Acts Amendment Act 1856, above p. 15; but the proportion of Register Office marriages—only 1% of the total in 1838—had risen from 4% of the total in 1851 to 7% in 1861. By 1871 the proportion of civil marriages was 10% of the total, and by the turn of the century it had risen to 16%: see J Haskey, 'Trends in marriage and divorce in England and Wales: 1837–1987' 48 *Population Trends* (1987) p. 11, Table 1.

[205] It is true that the number of religious weddings would probably be substantially higher were it not for the reluctance of some churches to remarry the divorced. In 1999, 11% of Anglican weddings (as compared with rather less than 7% of Roman Catholic weddings) involved a divorced person. In the same year slightly more than half of Methodist marriages (ie some 60%) involved a

English law is unusual in insisting on drawing this sharp distinction—affirmed, as recently as 1994, by the statutory provision that no religious service be used at an approved premises marriage and that the premises should have no religious association[206]—and the application of this distinction can cause difficulties. The law can certainly be made to appear ridiculous when it attempts to define 'religious worship':

In *R v. Registrar-General ex parte Segerdal*[207] the Church of Scientology sought judicial review of the Registrar-General's refusal to register their East Grinstead chapel as a place of meeting for religious worship under the 1855 Act. The courts refused to override the refusal. The Court of Appeal evidently found some embarrassment[208] in defining 'religion' in terms of belief in a God or supreme being, not least because such a definition would perhaps exclude Buddhism. But the Court was able to hold that the combined expression 'religious worship' did necessarily involve a humbling in reverence veneration and recognition of the dominant power and control of a deity or some outside entity or being; and the applicants were held not to satisfy that test.

The difficulty of defining religion has an impact at a more routine level. For example, it has been reported that one Registrar refused to allow an extract from Charles Dickens' *Great Expectations* to be read at a Register Office wedding because the chosen passage included a reference to a church; whilst in the parliamentary debates on 'authorised premises' weddings it was suggested that to play Bach's 'Sheep may Safely Graze' would infringe the prohibition on the use of any music or words not secular in nature.

Minority religions

Challenges of a different kind were presented by large scale immigration (particularly from the Indian sub-continent). When the Marriage Act was passed in 1836 only places of *Christian* worship could (it seems) be registered for solem-

---

divorced person: see *Marriage and Divorce Statistics 1999*, Table 3.31. Just over half the couples marrying *for the first time* in 1999 chose a religious ceremony. But even within this group there has been a marked decline in the popularity of church weddings: see J Haskey, 'Marriages in Approved Premises . . .' (2000) 107 *Population Trends* 83.

[206] See above, p. 31. In practice it may sometimes be difficult to uphold this principle: the author has heard of a case in which a Bishop of the Church of England, invited as a guest to an authorised premises wedding, responded positively to an invitation from the bride's father at the conclusion of the proceedings to give an episcopal benediction.

[207] [1970] 2 QB 697, CA. If scientology is not a religion does it follow that the premises could qualify for approval under the Marriage Act 1994?

[208] See in particular the judgment of Winn LJ.

nising marriages;[209] but a subsequent technical redrafting of the legislation[210] meant that any place of worship could be registered, irrespective of the religion concerned. But it took some time for Muslims and others to realise that mosques and other places of worship could be registered: as recently as 1975 only 36 Sikh temples, 18 mosques and 81 'other bodies'' buildings were registered.[211] Failure to register caused problems:

In 1956, a man and a woman went through a marriage ceremony conducted in accordance with Sikh custom and religion in the Sikh temple in West Kensington. Thirty seven years later, the husband died. The wife's claim for widow's benefit was rejected by the authorities on the ground that, the temple not having at the time been registered, the 'marriage' was void.[212]

It can of course be argued that the need to comply with the registration requirements is today better recognised and that the fact that English law provides facilities for people of all religious faiths to celebrate weddings according to their own rites can be seen as a desirable recognition of the needs of a plural and diverse society. But, although it appears that in 1999 109 mosques and 137 Sikh temples were registered for the solemnisation of marriage, the fact that only 189 Islamic and 926 Sikh marriages were recorded[213] in that year may raise questions.

What are weddings for?

Identifying the purpose to be served by a marriage ceremony had become more difficult than it had been in 1900. In 1900 'married respectability'[214] was well-understood; and it seems difficult to believe that the clergy of the Church of

---

[209] This is because s. 18 of the Act required the building in question to be 'certified according to Law as a place of Religious Worship'; and at the time the provisions of the Toleration Act 1688 and the Places of Religious Worship Act 1812 made specific provision only for the registration of protestant assemblies. The marriages of Jews were exempted from the provisions of the 1836 Act: see above, p. 12.

[210] The Places of Religious Worship Registration Act 1855 extended the Registration provisions to 'any . . . denomination of persons'.

[211] *Marriage and Divorce Statistics 1975* (Government Statistical Service, Series FM2, no. 2, 1978) Tables 3.12a and b.

[212] *Chief Adjudication Officer v. Bath* [2000] 1 FLR 8, CA. The Court of Appeal held that the refusal to award the pension was wrong: the claimant and her husband had intended to marry and were unaware of the fact that the temple was unregistered. The courts are reluctant to invalidate 'marriages' merely because of lack of compliance with the prescribed formalities and have been prepared (on evidence that the couple had cohabited for such a length of time and in such circumstances as to acquire the reputation of being husband and wife) to presume that a marriage ceremony complying with the necessary formalities has taken place: see *Mahadervan v. Mahadervan* [1964] P 233; *Pazpena de Vire v. Pazpena de Vire* [2001] 1 FLR 460; *A-M v. A-M (Divorce: Jurisdiction: Validity of Marriage)* [2001] 2 FLR 6; but compare *Gereis v. Yagoub* [1997] 1 FLR 854.

[213] See *Marriage and Divorce Statistics* 1998 (Office for National Statistics Series FM2, no 26, 2000) Tables 3.40 and 3.43.

[214] *An Honourable Estate* (1988) para. 70.

England (or the Parish clerks who in practice seem to have handled much of the administration of the Anglican wedding system)[215] would have had either the time or the inclination to advise the crowds[216] seeking the publication of banns about the purposes of marriage, much less about how those concerned could qualify themselves for their marital roles. But there seems to have been mounting concern (especially in the period after World War II) about the apparent decline in respect for the institution of marriage as a lifelong union; and, in response to suggestions made by the *Committee on Procedure in Matrimonial Causes*[217] Registrars began the practice of reminding couples of the 'solemn and binding character of the vows you are about to take' and that 'marriage, according to the law of this country is the union of one man with one woman, voluntarily entered into, for life, to the exclusion of all others'.[218] The clergy seem increasingly to have regarded the preliminaries to marriage as a pastoral opportunity; and in 1988 *An Honourable Estate* claimed[219] that any clergyman asked to officiate at a marriage would 'wish to bring the couple to a sensitive and profound Christian understanding of what they are about'. These concerns about family values seem to have reached a climax at the time of the passage through Parliament of the Family Law Act 1996, which would not only have made radical changes to the procedure for obtaining a divorce, but provided[220] that those exercising functions under the Act in connection with divorce, separation, legal aid, and mediation should have regard to a number of general principles including the principle that the institution of marriage was to be supported.

The Blair Government, returned with a large majority in May 1997, took up the provision of marriage support with much enthusiasm. The Government committed itself to the belief that marriage provides a strong foundation for stable relationships, the most reliable framework for raising children, and provides millions of people with a strong and stable basis for bringing up children in a rapidly changing world.[221] Although the Government denied that it wanted to make people marry, or to criticise or penalise those who chose not to do so,[222] it did believe that families wanted support: 'advice on relationships; help with overcoming difficulties; support with parenting; and, should the couple's relationship break down irretrievably, a system of divorce which avoids aggra-

---

[215] Some contemporary light is thrown on the practice by Thomas Hardy's novel *Tess of the D'Urbervilles* (1891). This shows the preliminaries to an Anglican marriage at the end of the nineteenth century as being largely formal, and conducted entirely by the clerk.

[216] See p. 16 above.   [217] 1947, Cmd. 7024.

[218] In view of the fact that more than half of all Register Office marriages involve at least one divorced person the making of this allocution may sometimes seem inappropriate. The same wording is given prominence on the prescribed forms of Notice for Marriage.

[219] p. 168.

[220] Family Law Act 1996, s. 1 (a) and (b). This provision of the Act was brought into force on 21 March 1997. In contrast, the provisions of the Act dealing with the projected reformed divorce procedure have not been brought into force: see Chapter 9, below.

[221] *Supporting Families, a Consultation Document* (1998) paras. 4.3 and 4.6.

[222] *Ibid.*, para. 4.3.

vating conflict within the family'.[223] To this end, it proposed 'measures to strengthen the institution of marriage, including an enhanced role for marriage registrars'.[224] These proposals included providing couples intending to marry with a clear statement of what their new status meant in terms of extra rights and also extra responsibilities; whilst improved arrangements to help people prepare for marriage would include a 'wider role for registrars to give better support to marrying couples; allowing couples more time to reflect before they marry; and requiring both partners to attend the register office to make the first arrangements before marriage' and enhancing and modernising 'the service provided by registrars, who now perform the majority of marriages in Britain'.[225]

The more specific of these proposals[226] were hardly novel; and were hurriedly passed into law in the Immigration and Asylum Act 1999; but proposals to enhance the role of Registrars by enabling them to provide 'more information and support to couples in preparing for marriage (including providing information in register offices in the form of marriage preparation packs, and giving couples information on pre-marriage support services)' evidently proved more difficult.[227] A White Paper, *Civil Registration: Vital Change*[228] was eventually published in 2002; and it appears that the Church of England is prepared to abandon its opposition to the abolition of banns as a legally effective preliminary to church weddings and also to make its own (rather restrictive) rules about where a marriage may be celebrated somewhat more flexible.[229] But, at the end of the twentieth century, no one could claim that the marriage law of England and Wales was either simple or easy to understand. Although there was evidently strong support for reform, a great deal of detailed work remained to be done to translate well-intentioned policies into legislation; whilst some difficult issues of policy—what, for example, is the role of the State in providing ideological support for the institution of marriage, how can such support be given in practice, and how far should couples be free to choose their own form of expressing commitment even if they wish to include some religious element principle?—remain to be solved.

---

[223] *Ibid.*, para. 4.2.   [224] *Ibid.*, para. 4.4.   [225] *Ibid.*, para. 4.12.

[226] For example, requiring both parties to give notice of intended marriage, lengthening the time which has to elapse between giving notice and the marriage taking place: similar proposals had been made by the Law Commission more than a quarter of a century earlier: see above, p. 26.

[227] See *Just Cause or Impediment? A Report from the Review of Aspects of Marriage Law Working Group* (General Synod of the Church of England, 2001), para. 11.

[228] 2002, Cm. 5355.

[229] A debate took place in the General Synod in July 2002.

2

Marriage: Eligibility

INTRODUCTION: THE ENGLISH LAW OF NULLITY OF MARRIAGE

The law lays down rules about the *formalities* necessary to create the status of marriage, but there are also rules about who can marry whom. All developed societies impose certain restrictions on entry into marriage—for example, English law has insisted that marriage is a union between a man and a woman, that it is monogamous, that this union is voluntary and only to be entered into between a couple who wish to be married, and so on. Lawyers classify such rules as rules of *capacity*: a man and a woman must have legal capacity to marry; and unless they do so no marriage ceremony can create the status of marriage between them.

Historically,[1] these matters were left largely in the hands of the ecclesiastical courts; and if, for example, a purported marriage was shown to be bigamous the court would grant a decree declaring it 'to have been and to be absolutely null and void to all intents and purposes whatsoever'.[2] But the matter was not as simple as that. The readiness of the ecclesiastical courts to pronounce that a marriage had never existed (for example, because the couple were closely related) was a threat to the security of property, and this threat was all the more serious because the pre-Reformation ecclesiastical courts would annul a marriage 'even after the death of the parties, after the death of both, or of one only'.[3] The Common Law courts disliked this practice; and in the seventeenth century it became settled that they would in certain circumstances prohibit the ecclesiastical courts from impeaching the validity of marriage once either party had died. In this way, the distinction between marriages *void ab initio* (the validity of which could be attacked by any person at any time, even after the death of one of both of the parties) and those which were merely *voidable* (vulnerable to attack during the parties' joint lives, but only on the application of one of them) became established.[4] It has been said[5] that the effect of this was to allow:

---

[1] The best modern account from a lawyer's perspective is J Jackson, *The Formation and Annulment of Marriage* (2nd ed., 1969) Chapters 1 to 5.

[2] *De Reneville v. De Reneville* [1948] P 100.

[3] *Ray v. Sherwood* (1836) 1 Curt. 173, 199, *per* Sir Herbert Jenner.

[4] The history is complex: see Jackson, *The Formation and Annulment of Marriage* (2nd ed., 1969) pp. 54–59; FH Newark (1945) 8 MLR 203; EJ Cohn (1948) 64 LQR 324; D Tolstoy (1964) 27 MLR 385.

[5] Jackson, *op. cit.* p. 54. By the beginning of the nineteenth century the dividing line between the circumstances in which a marriage would be held to be void and those in which a defect would render it voidable had become well-settled; but the *justification* for allotting different categories of defect to one category or the other was less clear. In both the nineteenth and the twentieth century

'certain of these spineless marriages to acquire posthumous backbones: if these associations could escape being examined by the courts while the parties to them were alive and living together in what, from the premises, were sinful unions, then the common law courts, in any case which came before them, would bury the past simultaneously with the interment of one or both of the spouses so-called, and would give to them as a parting gift at the grave the unimpeachable and retrospective reputation, valid in England and Wales at any rate, of having lived together in holy wedlock.'

In this way, the common law had an important impact on the *consequences* of breaking the rules defining eligibility for marriage. But when the Matrimonial Causes Act 1857[6] transferred the jurisdiction of the Ecclesiastical Courts in respect of nullity of marriage to the newly created Court for Divorce and Matrimonial Causes, it directed the Court to 'proceed and act and give relief on principles and rules which . . . shall be as nearly as may be conformable to the principles and rules on which the Ecclesiastical Courts have heretofore acted and given relief'.[7] Accordingly the canon law of Western Christendom remained the conceptual basis for the content of the English law of nullity[8] until the Nullity of Marriage Act 1971 codified the law.

Nullity, sexual incompatibility, and divorce

One additional complication has to be mentioned. This stems from the fact that until 1857 English law did not provide for judicial divorce. Nullity was the only way to get legally free from a marriage which had become intolerable. In these circumstances it is not surprising that (as the matrimonial history of King Henry VIII demonstrates) the temptation to widen the circumstances in which a decree of nullity could be obtained (in King Henry's case for alleged infringement of the rules about the prohibited degrees) was sometimes strong. But by the beginning of the twentieth century (albeit there was very strong pressure to change the rules to allow a widower to marry his sister-in-law) the law relating to the prohibited degrees (and the other grounds for annulment) was well understood. The law was seen primarily as *prohibiting* marriage, not as a way of escaping from a marriage; and there were comparatively few petitions[9] alleging that a

statute there was some reclassification: in 1835, marriages between persons within the prohibited degrees of relationship were declared to be void (rather than voidable); and in 1971 marriages affected by duress or lack of consent were declared to be voidable rather than void: Marriage Act 1835 ('Lord Lyndhurst's Act'); Nullity of Marriage Act 1971, s. 1: see below.

[6] ss. 2, 6. [7] s. 22.

[8] Over the years, statute made a few changes—notably the amendments of the rules defining the prohibited degrees for marriage and the minimum age for marriage—to the rules: see below. The Matrimonial Causes Act 1937—on one view, inconsistently with the traditional conceptual basis of the law—made one party's wilful refusal to consummate the marriage a ground for annulment: see below.

[9] The statistical tables in Appendix II to the *Report of the Royal Commission on Marriage and Divorce* (1956, Cmd. 9678) suggest that at the beginning of the twentieth century there were no more than two or three nullity petitions each year founded on bigamy, prohibited degrees, non-age, or failure to comply with the rules relating to formalities.

'marriage' which had in fact taken place should be annulled because the parties were related or indeed was invalid because it was bigamous, or that one of the parties was under age or had not truly consented to the marriage, or that the prescribed formalities had not been observed.

But there was one case in which the law of nullity did serve as a kind of divorce in the modern sense. This arose from the fact that the Church, whilst accepting that marriage was created simply by the consent of the parties, regarded it as implicit in the marriage contract that both parties should have the physical capacity to consummate the marriage: a capacity to perform 'the duties of marriage' was necessary to make the marriage valid.[10] For this reason, the ecclesiastical courts were prepared to annul a marriage on the ground that either party was, at the date of the marriage, incapable of consummating it; and in this way some sexually incompatible couples were able to free themselves from the legal marriage tie. The case of the writer and art critic John Ruskin[11] is a well known example.

After his marriage in 1848 Ruskin gave his wife Effie[12] various reasons for his disinclination to have sex. For her part, she had 'never been told the duties of married persons to each other and knew little or nothing about their relations in the closest union on earth';[13] but she became more and more troubled. Ruskin admitted that he had married her 'to have a companion—not for passion's sake'. Eventually he told her that he 'had imagined women were quite different from what he saw [she] was', and that he was disgusted with her person.[14] Mrs Ruskin instituted proceedings in the Ecclesiastical Court,[15] medical reports were obtained confirming that there were 'no impediments on her part to a proper consummation of the marriage' and on 15 July 1854—Ruskin having provided no evidence to refute the inference from all the facts that he was incapable of consummating the marriage—the court pronounced a sentence of annulment thus freeing Effie (after six years) from what she described as a 'hateful and loathsome Cont[r]act'. She promptly married her husband's friend John Everett Millais, by whom she was to have eight children.

To the lay person, it might well seem that Mrs Ruskin had divorced her husband because of his behaviour towards her[16] and there certainly seems little doubt that under the 'breakdown of marriage' ground for divorce introduced in 1969 she would have been able to do so with little of the unpleasantness—for example, the need for medical inspections—attached to nullity suits on the

[10] *Greenstreet v. Cumyns* (1812) 2 Phill. Ecc. 10, *per* Sir John Nicholl; and see *Dickinson v. Dickinson* [1913] P 198, 205.

[11] 1819–1900.   [12] Euphemia Chalmers Gray.

[13] Mrs Ruskin to her father 7 March 1854, as cited in M Lutyens, *Millais and the Ruskins* (1967) p. 156.

[14] According to M Lutyens, *Effie in Venice* (1965) p. 21 Ruskin had not realised that women had pubic hair and suffered traumatic shock when he discovered this fact.

[15] The Consistory Court of Surrey.

[16] But she seems to have suffered some of the stigma then born by the divorced; and in particular Queen Victoria refused to receive her: see M Lutyens, *Millais and the Ruskins* (1967).

ground of sexual incapacity.[17] But in theory there was a great conceptual difference between formally annulling a marriage which, by reason of some vitiating element, had never come into existence on the one hand,[18] and dissolving a valid marriage because of some supervening matter (one party's adultery, for example) on the other. The Church[19] would accept annulment; but it for long refused to accept the legal termination of a valid marriage; and it was to 'escape the onslaught of ecclesiastics' opposed to divorce that over the years, reformers saw advantage in tucking up as much 'divorce law reform into nullity as possible'[20] and that some Christian groups were attracted to the idea of extending the use of nullity in situations of marital breakdown.[21] But in fact these attempts to extend nullity as a remedy to terminate an unsuccessful relationship turned out not to be of great moment, and statistically nullity remained insignificant as a means of obtaining legal release from an unhappy marriage.[22] The fact that nullity allowed a small number of people each year to get what was, so far as they were concerned and for most practical purposes, a divorce should not obscure the fact that in a much larger number of cases the rules prevented marriages taking place. The long and bitter campaign for reform of the law about marriage between relatives demonstrates that the rules were seen to have an impact on many people's lives,[23] and they remain important as effectively defining the law's concept of marriage. The text first discusses how the rules operated to define marriage, and then discusses the extent to which legislation and case law have altered the rules in the course of the twentieth century.

THE PROHIBITION ON MARRIAGE WITH RELATIONS[24]

The Old Testament[25] contains a number of prohibitions (not easy for the modern reader to understand) against sexual relationships between people who are

[17] See the testimony of Sir Ellis William Hume-Williams KC cited at note 275, below.

[18] 'Nullity, in its very nature, presupposes a cause existing at the date of the marriage': *Napier v. Napier* [1915] P 184, 192–193, *per* Warrington LJ.

[19] Protestant churches often adopted a more flexible approach, but in this respect the Church of England continued to uphold pre-Reformation teaching.

[20] Helena Normanton writing to Mrs E Hubback, 12 February 1936, *Normanton Papers*, HN 5; and see Biographical Notes.

[21] See notably *The Church and the Law of Nullity of Marriage* (1955); and, for a critical view of the Church's influence, OR McGregor, *Divorce in England, A Centenary Study* (1957) pp. 41, 112.

[22] In 1900 there were only 18 nullity decrees based on incapacity. In 1931 the total number of nullity decrees rose for the first time above 100. In 1999 there were 495 decrees. Throughout the century divorce was much commoner: in 1900 there were 494 decrees nisi of divorce; in 1931, 3,958 and in 1999 143,106: *Report of the Royal Commission on Marriage and Divorce*, 1956, Cmnd. 9678, Appendix II, Table 2, *Judicial Statistics, Annual Report 1999*, p. 57.

[23] The *Royal Commission into the Law of Marriage as relating to the Prohibited Degrees of Affinity* . . . (1848) BPP 1847–8, Vol. 28 (hereafter '*The 1848 Royal Commission*') p. 233, attempted to estimate how many people were prevented from marrying by the prohibited degrees rules, but the methodology employed was unsatisfactory.

[24] See generally S Wolfram, *In-Laws and Outlaws, Kinship and Marriage in England* (1987).

[25] *Leviticus*, chap. 18.

'near in kin'. These prohibitions extend not only to blood relations (relationships of consanguinity) such as parent and child and brother and sister but also to 'in-law' relationships created by marriage. For the church, marriage made husband and wife one flesh; so if it is wrong to marry my sister it must equally be wrong for me to marry my wife's sister, my sister-in-law.[26] After the turmoil caused by the attempts to resolve Henry VIII's marital problems[27] the prohibitions were codified in what became known as Archbishop Parker's Table of Kindred and Affinity.[28] This table[29] was given canonical authority in the Church of England,[30] and the Table was customarily printed at the end of the *Book of Common Prayer*.[31] The Canons declared that marriages within these prohibited degrees were 'incestuous and unlawful and consequently . . . void from the beginning'.

But this was one of the areas in which the common law, as explained above, modified the rigour of the ecclesiastical law. For the common lawyers, the policy of the canon law was simply to separate those who were cohabiting in a relationship prohibited by divine law and to inflict penance for this wrong-doing. After the cohabitation had been brought to an end by the death of one of the

---

[26] The canonists extended this principle to persons who had sexual intercourse outside marriage; and even in the nineteenth century it could be argued that this principle had remained part of English law. But in *Wing v. Taylor* (1861) 2 Sw&Tr 278 the court refused to annul the marriage of a man who claimed that he had, prior thereto, had intercourse with his bride's mother in the Constable Arms, a public house she owned at Hedon, Yorkshire.

[27] See generally J Scarisbrick, *Henry VIII* (2nd ed., 1997) Chapters 7 and 8, and foreword pp. x–xiii. The King's first marriage to Catherine of Aragon could be impugned on the ground that she was his brother's widow, but the Pope had granted a dispensation. His second marriage to Anne Boleyn could be impugned because the King had had intercourse with her sister, and the Canon law of the time regarded that as putting the sister's relatives within the prohibited degrees: see above and *Roger Donington's Case* 2 Co. Inst. 684 (where the fact that the husband had previously had intercourse with his wife's third cousin invalidated the marriage). The King's marriage to Catherine Howard was vulnerable because she was a cousin of Anne Boleyn. Three statutes were passed to define the prohibited degrees in the King's interest. The Succession to the Crown Act 1533 (25 Hen 8 c. 22) and Succession to the Crown Act 1536 (28 Hen 8 c.7) were repealed in Tudor times but the third Act (the Marriage Act 1540, 32 Hen 8, c. 38) remained on the statute book until 1949. A full account of the complex legislation of the Tudor period can be found in *Wing v. Taylor* (1861) 2 Sw&Tr 278.

[28] Matthew Parker (1504–1575), Archbishop of Canterbury 1559–1575 under Elizabeth I.

[29] First published in 1563.

[30] By Canon 99 (1603). The Code of Canons of 1604 declared marriages in breach of the Parker Table to be 'incestuous and unlawful and consequently shall be dissolved as void from the beginning'.

[31] From the reign of Elizabeth I until 1949 no statute attempted to enumerate the prohibited degrees; and the Marriage Act 1540 simply referred to persons prohibited 'by God's law to marry' without providing any definition or explanation. Nineteenth century case law had adopted the view that Archbishop Parker's table governed the matter: see *R v. Chadwick* (1848) 11 QB 173 (man who had married deceased wife's sister held to be not guilty of bigamy in marrying again); *Wing v. Taylor* (1861) 2 Sw&Tr 278; and see also *R v. Dibdin, ex parte Thompson* [1910] P 57. The draftsman of the consolidating Marriage Act 1949 therefore took the view that to incorporate the Parker table (subject to the amendments made by the Deceased Wife's Sister's Marriage Act 1907, the Deceased Brother's Widow's Marriage Act 1921 and the Marriage (Prohibited Degrees of Relationship) Act 1931) would not change the law: Evidence of Mrs BJ Johnston to the *Joint Select Committee on Consolidation Bills*, 19 July 1949, BPP 1948/49, vol. 6, pp. 26–27.

parties no court order could 'tend to the reformation of the parties' and accordingly the court would no longer assume jurisdiction to declare that a marriage within the prohibited degrees had been invalid. In other words, the marriage was to be classified as voidable: it could not be attacked after the death of either party, and only the parties could question it during their joint lifetimes.[32]

This was just as well. The rules prohibiting marriages between affines began to conflict with social need. A wife died leaving her husband with young children to bring up. Help was urgently needed. Often the wife's sister was the only available source of care for the children. Physical propinquity led to emotional involvement. What could be more natural than marriage?[33] And it was not only the working-classes who found the rigid rules a barrier to their attaining emotional fulfilment.[34]

In those countries which had retained their religious allegiance to Rome such cases could be dealt with by obtaining a dispensation from the application of the rules to a particular case, but this was no longer possible in post-Reformation England.[35] Even so, the problem was for many years not regarded as too serious and many couples were prepared to ignore the prohibition, either relying on the reluctance of anyone undertaking the 'invidious task of disuniting them'[36] or by taking protective legal action.[37]

In 1835 however Lord Lyndhurst's Act dramatically changed the position. Although it declared marriages already celebrated within the prohibited degrees of affinity to be inviolate it also provided that all marriages celebrated in the future between persons within the prohibited degrees of consanguinity or affinity should be 'absolutely null and void to all intents and purposes whatsoever'. The legal effect of the Act was clear—and disastrous. In the words of a Home Office official writing half a century later:[38]

---

[32] Blackstone, *Commentaries on the Laws of England* (4th ed., 1770, Vol. 1 p. 434); *Elliott v. Gurr* (1812) 2 Phil. Ecc. 16, 19; *A v. B* (1868) LR 1 P&D 559; *Harthan v. Harthan* [1949] P 115, 131–2, CA. In *A v. B* the decision was based not only on the doctrine that a decree would no longer serve its purpose after the death of one of the parties but also on the view that incapacity was a ground of personal complaint which should only be put in issue by the party who had suffered.

[33] *The 1848 Royal Commission,* p. x. The evidence presented to the Commission is of great interest.

[34] The case which precipitated the enactment of Lord Lyndhurst's Act in 1835 involved the marriage of the 7th Duke of Beaufort to the half-sister of his deceased wife: see E Buttner, *The Deceased Wife's Sister Debate (1835–1907)* (unpublished M Juris dissertation, Oxford, 1996) p. 11.

[35] On the canon law, see JC Barry (ed.) *William Hay's Lectures on Marriage,* p. 221, ff; and generally see *Brook v. Brook* (1861) 9 HLC 193, 206–207, *per* Lord Campbell LC.

[36] A Hayward, *Remarks regarding marriage with the sister of a deceased wife* (1845) p. 6.

[37] According to a detailed memorandum prepared in the Home Office in 1888, persons 'wishing to contract marriages within the prohibited degrees could protect themselves by instituting a suit against one of the parties himself in the Ecclesiastical Court. It was not competent for anyone to institute a second suit while the first was pending, and thus the parties could make themselves completely safe during their lifetime; and they were protected by the decisions in the Common Law courts . . . as regards the status of their children'. PRO HO45/10064/B2853, 10 April 1888, p. 33.

[38] PRO HO45/10064/B2853, 10 April 1888, p. 34.

'What had before been a somewhat loose and uncertain prohibition became part of the regular law of the land. The English law became at once the most rigid in respect of such prohibitions in force in any civilized country. At a time when many churches relaxed their rule by dispensations, and most countries had allowed wide liberty in this matter, the Canon Law of the English Church was made of binding force even over members of persuasions which tolerated these connections, or approved them.'

It seems, however, that it took some time for the impact of Lord Lyndhurst's Act to be appreciated, and that for some years the Act failed to attain its object of preventing marriages between a man and his deceased wife's sister or niece.[39] Such people continued to go through marriage ceremonies[40] in this country, always illegally and sometimes fraudulently;[41] and the affluent middle and upper classes would travel abroad[42] to contract the marriage in a country whose law permitted marriage with the deceased wife's sister or niece believing that the marriage would be recognised in England.[43] But in 1861 the House of Lords made it clear that this belief was not well founded.[44] In *Brook v. Brook*[45]

William Leigh Brook of Melthain Hall Yorkshire was widowed in 1847 and left with two young children. In 1850 he travelled to Denmark with his wife's sister

[39] *The 1848 Royal Commission*, p. ix. The Commission reported that marriages with a deceased wife's sister were 'by far the most frequent of marriages contracted within the prohibited degrees': p. vi. A survey was made for the Commission in 'a comparatively small portion of England' and found that in the decade since the enactment of Lord Lyndhurst's Act 1,364 'marriages' within the prohibited degrees had been solemnised in the areas covered by the survey. Of these 90% were between a man and his deceased wife's sister. The survey also claimed that only 88 marriages had been prevented by Lord Lyndhurst's Act, and that in 32 of those the intended parties openly cohabited without any form of marriage. The methodology used in this survey is seriously defective (see generally Buttner, *The Deceased Wife's Sister Debate* (1835–1907) (unpublished M Juris dissertation, Oxford, 1996) pp. 17–21) but its conclusion is supported by a Home Office official writing in 1888: 'many such marriages were contracted, and remained valid because no suit was instituted against the parties from a hostile quarter'. PRO HO45/10064/B2853, 10 April 1888, p. 33.

[40] An alternative apparently used by many who realized they were prohibited from marriage by the Lyndhurst Act was simply to live 'together in concubinage': PRO HO45/10064/B2853, 10 April 1888, p. 35.

[41] After 1856 a person giving notice for marriage who knowingly and falsely stated that there was no lawful impediment to the celebration of a marriage within the prohibited degrees would have been liable to severe criminal sanctions: Marriage and Registration Acts Amendment Act 1856. But if the marriage were solemnised in the Church of England after the publication of banns no such notice had to be given; and the main problem was that if the couple subsequently became disenchanted the man could simply repudiate the marriage and leave the 'wife' destitute: see A Hayward, *Remarks regarding marriage with the sister of a deceased wife* (1845) p. 8.

[42] Altona in Schleswig Holstein (then part of Denmark, subsequently annexed to Prussia and in 1937 annexed to the City of Hamburg) was a popular venue. A solicitor gave evidence to the 1848 Royal Commission that it was common for couples to resort there, and the Marriage Law Reform Association published advertisements advising couples to marry there: see *The 1848 Royal Commission*, Evidence, q. 873.

[43] Hayward, note 36 above, p. 7, states the 'better opinion as being that the validity of such marriages would be upheld'.

[44] It seems that the effect of this ruling was for long not appreciated: for example, in *R v. Dibdin, ex parte Thompson* [1910] P 57 it appears that a man went to Canada with his deceased wife's sister evidently believing that a marriage contracted on a short visit there would be recognised in England.

[45] (1861) 9 HLC 193.

and there was a wedding ceremony in the Lutheran church at Wandsbeck near Altona. Mrs Brook bore him three children, but then died in a cholera outbreak only to be followed by her husband two days later. An action was brought over the administration of Mr Brook's estate. The House of Lords held that the legal capacity of someone domiciled in England to contract a marriage remained governed by English law[46] wherever the marriage took place. Accordingly, although the Danish marriage was perfectly lawful and valid in Denmark, as a matter of English law it was void. Accordingly the three children were illegitimate.

The issue became one of great public controversy.[47] Pressure groups[48] were established; petitions were presented to the Crown and to Parliament,[49] and Bills (some more restrictive than others)[50] were presented to Parliament. These Bills often got through the House of Commons, but (even when the promoters tried to buy off clerical opposition by inserting a provision that the Anglican clergy need not celebrate such marriages)[51] the House of Lords could be relied on[52] to ensure that no reforming Bill reached the statute book.[53]

At the turn of the century there seemed to be no likelihood of any imminent change in the law. No doubt the theological arguments which had once seemed so pressing were now advanced with less enthusiasm; but (in addition to a general concern about the impact of any change in the marriage laws) there remained an underlying argument based on social policy: the prohibition was

[46] The law of the place where the wedding took place did govern the question whether the *formalities* necessary to create a marriage had been observed. Hence, a couple domiciled in England could marry in Scotland without parental consent (that being regarded as a matter of form) and without observing any of the formalities (for example the calling of banns) required by English law: see eg *Dalrymple v. Dalrymple* (1811) 2 Hag. Con. 54.

[47] The campaigning had started well before the *Brooks* case. In 1841 Lord Wharncliffe had presented a petition praying that Lord Lyndhurst's Act be amended so as to allow marriage between persons not connected by consanguinity or lineal affinity; and in 1847 pressure for reform led to the appointment of *The 1848 Royal Commission* (whose considerable labours led to the rather limp conclusion that, although Lord Lyndhurst's Act had failed in its objectives and indeed caused great evil, the matter should be left to the wisdom of the legislature).

[48] The Marriage Law Reform Association advocated reform; the Marriage Law Defence Union opposed.

[49] In 1892, for example, (according to *The Times* 8 February 1892) a petition presented to the Queen by the Marriage Law Reform Association was supported by 450 out of the total of 600 Mayors and former Mayors in England and Wales.

[50] The first Bills would have permitted marriage between a man and his deceased wife's sister or her niece; latterly it became the practice to confine the relaxation to permit marriage with a deceased wife's sister: see PRO HO45/10064/B2853, 10 April 1888.

[51] This was first done in 1890; and the Deceased Wife's Sister's Marriage Act 1907 contained such a provision.

[52] Even when, on one occasion, the Prince of Wales presented Petitions and spoke in favour of changing the law: see PRO HO45/10064/B2853, 10 April 1888, p. 40. In spite of the opposition in the House of Lords to change in the law it was often suggested that the campaign for the deceased wife's sister legislation was for the benefit of the upper classes and was brought by those who had broken the law and knew it.

[53] See the detailed account given on HO45/10064/B2853. Bills on the subject were described in Gilbert and Sullivan's *Iolanthe* as 'that annual blister'.

necessary to exclude disturbing sexual feelings from the family group.[54] As Gladstone had put it,[55] the 'purity of sisterly love itself . . . was threatened to be tainted by the invasion of possible jealousies'. In this view,[56] although the family was fundamental to society and natural affection was the cement of the family, sexual attraction was different. To permit sexual attractions within the intimate family circle would 'confuse the two relationships and unsettle the whole basis of society'.

All this sounded very well; but the difficulty facing the retentionists was that other societies—Denmark and Germany to take two examples—seemed to get along perfectly well without the prohibition on marriage with a deceased wife's sister. But the decisive fact seems to have been that when Australians who had married in Australia under local legislation[57] permitting marriage with a deceased wife's sister[58] came to England they were not regarded as living in lawful wedlock and their children were considered illegitimate.[59] In 1904, the Australian Prime Minister made a formal protest:[60]

[54] There is also a general argument against any change, still put forward towards the end of the twentieth century in submissions to a Church commission, that family tradition is vital for society as a whole, both economically and psychologically, but that 'many factors were undermining it. An alteration in the laws relating to the impediments on marriage between affines would be one more such assault on the family and its effect would perhaps be to destroy what was left and to increase breakdown, precipitating any one of a number of possible personal and social aberrations': *No Just Cause* (see note 79 below) para. 57.

[55] *Hansard's Parliamentary Debates* (3rd Series) 20 June 1849, vol. 106, col. 630.

[56] This is a paraphrase of an Internal Minute dated 4 March 1949 by the Registrar-General, JM Ross, PRO LCO2/3163. The same general point was put in somewhat highly coloured language by the nineteenth century philosopher Jeremy Bentham: 'If some insurmountable barrier were not erected between near relations fated to live together in the closest intimacy, the frequency of their contact, the many opportunities that offer, their very affection and innocent caresses, might kindle a fatal passion. The family—that retreat wherein repose should be found in the bosom of order, and the soul, disturbed by the bustle of the outer world, should be at rest—. . . would itself become a prey to all the turbulence of rivalry, all the fires of love . . .': *Theory of Legislation* (ed. CM Atkinson, 1914), pp. 286–287.

[57] As the Australian Prime Minister GH Reid pointed out to the Governor-General on 4 November 1904, this legislation had been 'submitted to, and approved by the Crown' and those contracting such marriages could therefore fairly claim that they had done so with the sanction of the Imperial Government: PRO HO45/10064/B2853, 24118.

[58] The point that the conflict between laws applicable to persons of the 'same race, religion and government' not only caused hardship to individuals but was inconsistent with the policy of fostering closer bonds of union between the various parts of the Empire had already been seized upon by the Marriage Law Reform Association: Petition to the Crown dated 7 February 1898, PRO HO45/10064/B2853, 24118.

[59] In fact this reflected a misunderstanding of the law since if both parties to the marriage were at the time domiciled in Australia the marriage should have been recognised as valid but it appears that this was not widely understood. The only legal disadvantage in such a case was that the rule in *Birtwhistle v. Vardill* (1840) 7 Cl & Fin 895, HL, would prevent the child of such a marriage inheriting land in England as his father's heir at law or succeeding to his father's hereditary peerage. But it seems that this was the foundation for the widespread distress caused to those who believed themselves to be under what Winston Churchill (at the time Under Secretary of State for the Colonies) described as a 'social and almost a moral stigma' in this country: *Hansard's Parliamentary Debates* (4th Series) 30 July 1906, vol. 162, col. 583. In 1907 Lord Heneage told the House of Lords that at a banquet for visiting Colonial Prime Ministers he had discovered that three Premiers were married to a deceased wife's sister, and believed their wives were not recognised in England, one going so far

'I am strongly of opinion that it is unjust to Australian citizens that the full recognition accorded to their marriage . . . in Australia should be taken from them when they remove to another part of the Empire. . . . [T]he consolidation of the peoples of the various countries of the Empire who are of the same race should be made as complete as possible. . . . [T]he anomaly is seriously regarded in Australia, and [the Australian] Government most earnestly desires that the grave hardships and the personal degradation arising from the existing conflict between British and Colonial law in this respect should be removed by Imperial legislation.'

The Government did legislate to remove the particular grievance of people domiciled in parts of the Empire where such marriages were valid;[61] but this made it all the more difficult to resist legislation applying to people domiciled in this country. Whatever the Government might say, the 1906 Act was easily represented as sanctioning the belief that marriage with a deceased wife's sister was harmless or even desirable.[62]

In 1907 the respected Liberal landowner MP Sir Brampton Gurdon[63] presented yet another Bill, and on this occasion the Liberal government gave way. The 'last ditch' objections were mostly of the 'floodgates' variety familiar in almost all law reform debates:[64] society may accept marriage with a deceased wife's sister, but where will the process stop?[65] If society tolerates marriage with the wife's sister, why not marriage with her daughter?[66] But the Government

as to say that if he chose to leave his wife she would have to go to the workhouse and he could marry anyone else he chose in this country: *Hansard's Parliamentary Debates* (4th Series) 20 August 1907, vol. 181, col. 392.

[60] Reid to Governor-General, 4 November 1904, PRO HO45/10064/B2853, 24118.

[61] The Colonial Marriage and Divorce (Deceased Wife's Sister) Act 1906 provided, for the removal of doubt, that a marriage in a British Possession in which both parties were domiciled between a man and his deceased wife's sister should be deemed legal for all purposes including the right of succession to real estate etc. The true effect of the Act was therefore simply to make it clear that the rule in *Birtwhistle v. Vardill* (1840) 7 Cl & Fin 895, HL (above) would no longer apply and Government spokesmen in the House of Lords sought to emphasise that the Bill was really concerned with the law of succession rather than the law of marriage. But Churchill's speech to the House of Commons was somewhat unclear on the point: see *Hansard's Parliamentary Debates* (4th Series) 15 May 1906, vol. 157, col. 316 (HL), 30 July 1906, vol. 162, col. 583.

[62] This was the view which Archbishop Davidson unsuccessfully put to the House of Lords in the debate on the 1906 legislation: *Hansard's Parliamentary Debates* (4th Series) 15 May 1906, vol. 157, col. 324.

[63] See Biographical Notes.

[64] The young Liberal MP Herbert Samuel sat through the all-night third reading debate and claimed privately that the opposition came from 17 'narrow-minded, short sighted, but long-winded bigots': B Wasserstein, *Herbert Samuel, A Political Life* (1992) p. 101.

[65] In 1921, Lord Chancellor Birkenhead recalled his experience of being kept walking through the House of Commons division lobbies 'all night long until a summer dawn', with the result that eloquent pleas about the effect of permitting marriage with a deceased wife's sister would have on the country's morals—'progress down a steep slope comparable to that of the Gadarene swine'—were branded on his ears. Experience, he claimed, had absolutely falsified all those prophecies: see the debate on the Second Reading of the Deceased Brother's Widow's Marriage Bill, *Official Report* (HC) 28 June 1921, vol. 45, col. 824.

[66] Precisely this argument was used 14 years later by Archbishop Randall Davidson in resisting relaxation of the rule prohibiting a woman from marrying her deceased husband's brother: *Official Report* (HL) 28 June 1921, vol. 45, col. 817.

eventually took over the Bill[67] and made success certain. The Deceased Wife's Sister's Marriage Act 1907 provided[68] that no marriage[69] between a man and his deceased wife's sister should be void or voidable 'as a civil contract'[70] by reason only of such affinity. The long fought battle seemed, at last, to have been won.[71]

But it soon became clear that the Act had not resolved all the problems. As a Home Office official had presciently observed in 1888:[72]

'There is no reason why, if a man marry his wife's sister, he should not marry his father's mother's wife and his mother's brother's wife; nor his wife's aunt, nor his nephew's wife, nor his niece by affinity. None of these marriages are now allowed. A man should also be allowed to marry his deceased brother's wife . . .'

The 1907 Act only dealt with the single case of the deceased wife's sister; and the fact that a woman was not allowed to marry her deceased husband's brother was not only an example of the sexual discrimination which increasingly irritated the burgeoning feminist movement[73] but caused hardship on a significant

[67] A possibly jaundiced, but none the less revealing account is given by the High Church Tory Lord Hugh Cecil in *All the Way* (1949), p. 106: 'For some time past there had been a majority in both Houses in favour of the change. In the Lords this was mainly due to the influence of certain highly placed personages in the "smart set". In the Commons it was keenly desired by the militant non-conformists—partly perhaps because the Church took the other view. There was, besides, a considerable body of opinion that the change was socially desirable. Whatever may have been the determining reason, the new Government [in fact it had been in office for more than a year] gratified their nonconformist supporters by making it a government measure. I had no very strong opinion on it, but some of my most respected friends and relations had, and I therefore joined in opposing it. The Government decided to force it through [according to one MP, Laurence Hardy, practically without notice and late at night: *Hansard's Parliamentary Debates* (4th Series) 14 August 1907, vol. 180, col. 1432] and insisted that the Committee or Report stage should be completed in an all-night sitting. There is no more preposterous legislative device than this. As the night goes on, the sense of the House gets less. . . . Curiously some elderly gentlemen rather enjoyed [this strange exhibition of primeval barbarism]; it was for them a kind of "middle-aged lark". Thus was the Bill passed. I have never heard whether it has proved beneficial or disastrous to married life.'
[68] s. 1.
[69] Whether contracted before or after the Act. The Act contains complex provisions to protect persons affected and transactions carried out in reliance on the provisions of Lord Lyndhurst's Act: see s. 2.
[70] These words were held by the Court of Appeal in *R v. Dibdin, ex parte Thompson* [1910] P 57 not to restrict the meaning of the words declaring such marriages valid. It seems probable that they were added as one of a number of provisions intended to mollify the feelings of some Anglican clergy: a proviso to s. 1 made it clear that the clergy were not obliged to solemnise marriage with a deceased wife's sister, whilst s. 4 provided that the Church might still prohibit its clergy from themselves contracting such a marriage. The issue continued to arouse deep feelings in some quarters. For example, in *Dibdin's* case a priest repelled a widower who had married his wife's sister from Holy Communion on the ground that the couple were 'notorious and open evil livers'. The courts held he had acted improperly since the marriage was valid.
[71] It appears to be a coincidence that in 1908 Parliament also made it (for the first time) a criminal offence for a man to have sexual intercourse with certain blood relatives, ie his granddaughter, daughter, sister (including his half-sister) or brother: Punishment of Incest Act 1908. The enactment appears to have been precipitated by concern that incest—said often to result in the birth of severely defective offspring—had become rife amongst the working classes: see PRO HO45/1035/152169.
[72] PRO HO45/10064/B2853.
[73] As early as 1888 the Southport Women's Liberal Association had protested against the great wrong which would be done by violating in this way the principle of equality between men and women: PRO HO45/10064/B2853, 24118.

scale when women widowed in the first World War found themselves debarred from marrying the man of their choice.[74] The Deceased Brother's Widow's Marriage Act 1921 passed through Parliament in the wave of equal treatment legislation which followed World War I[75] but other anomalies remained. For example, the 1907 Act allowed a man to marry his wife's sister, but it did not allow him to marry the sister's daughter:

A constable in the Kent Constabulary was left with three young children on his wife's death. The wife's sister moved in with her husband to help care for the children, but the arrangement was not a success. A friendship developed between the constable and the sister's daughter; and the Chief Constable (having, he said, consulted a Priest of the Church of England) gave the man permission to marry. Everyone was deeply embarrassed when it became apparent that such a marriage would be illegal.

Once again, Bills were introduced to remove such anomalies; once again they died because of opposition.[76] But it was difficult to find any principle to justify resistance and doctrinal opposition from within the Church of England seemed to be crumbling.[77] In 1931 the Marriage (Prohibited Degrees of Relationship) Act 1931 allowing men and women to marry a nephew or niece by marriage[78] was neither opposed nor actively supported by the Church of England or by the Government. The Church of England eventually followed: in 1936 the four Houses of Convocation each urged revision of the Parker Table; and in 1937 Archbishop Cosmo Gordon Lang set up a Commission to carry out an Inquiry. The Commission's Report[79] was undogmatic: and in 1946 the Church of

[74] Or as Lord Newton put it in the debates on the 1921 legislation (see below) the man 'in whose charge their husbands had left them': *Official Report* (HL) 28 June 1921, vol. 45, col. 809.

[75] It did not escape unnoticed that since marriage terminated a widow's entitlement to a service pension it was in the state's economic interest for her to be encouraged to marry: *Official Report* (HC) 8 March 1921, vol. 139, col. 223.

[76] It seems that ten Bills were introduced between 1922 and 1931. In 1924 and 1927 Bills were given Second Readings in the House of Commons, but failed. It appears that the Home Office provided drafting assistance to the later Bills: *Official Report* (HC) 21 November 1930, vol. 245, col. 858.

[77] Modern Biblical scholarship had begun to throw doubt on some of the certainties of former times, whilst at a more practical level missionaries had become unwilling to enforce prohibitions in the face of cultural traditions very different from those of Reformation England. In 1956, Archbishop Fisher blandly told the *Royal Commission on Marriage and Divorce* (1956) Cmnd. 9678 that a spouse released from marriage by death could 'legitimately and without any threat to the family stability and in accordance with the Church's canon law seek to marry the deceased partner's brother or sister' passing in silence over the views powerfully expressed by the Church in the Debates leading up to the 1907 Act.

[78] The Act in fact added eight specified relationships—eg a man's deceased wife's sister's daughter: s. 1(1)—to those excepted from the prohibited degrees by the combined effect of the 1907 and 1921 Acts.

[79] *Kindred and Affinity as Impediments to Marriage* (1940). It appears that the Commission was 'intended to inform the thinking of the Anglican communion as a whole', and to be available for the information of a Lambeth Conference in 1940. The Second World War caused the conference to be postponed to 1948, and by then interest in these questions seems to have receded, since the record of the proceedings, including ten pages of Committee report on the *Church's Discipline in Marriage*, makes no reference to the 1940 study: *No Just Cause, The Law of Affinity in England*

England amended its canons to remove from the Table of Prohibited Degrees those marriages which the 1907, 1921 and 1931 Acts had permitted 'as civil contracts'.

But the issue of who should be allowed to marry whom was still far from finally settled. Suppose, for example, that the 'in-law' relationship had been created by a marriage which ended, not by death, but by divorce:

A soldier divorces the wife who has committed adultery whilst he was serving King and Country. The child is left in the care of the wife's sister. The soldier meets her for the first time on a visit to see the child. A relationship develops and the couple wish to marry.[80]

The law, quite deliberately, did not allow such marriages.[81] The arguments about the risks of doing so were easy to state[82] whilst the possibility that a man might be tempted to set out to seduce his wife's sister if he thought he could eventually marry her prompted particularly strong feeling.[83] But all this was essentially speculation. The reality was that there was pressure from men and women who wanted to marry: Registrars got as many as 200 enquiries every year about the possibility of marriage in cases where the marriage creating the 'in-law' relationship had ended in divorce.

Ministerial response to Parliamentary questions did not hold out even the remotest prospect of change.[84] But in 1947 RAW Stevenson decided not to accept the situation. He sought to introduce a Personal Bill to enable him to

and Wales: Some Suggestions for Change (1984) (hereafter '*No Just Cause*') (see note 101 below) p. 2 note 2. The passion expressed by the Church over so many years seems to have been largely (but not entirely) spent.

[80] A similar case influenced Lord Mancroft to campaign for change in the law: *Official Report* (HL) 26 January 1960, vol. 220, col. 652. The *Royal Commission on Marriage and Divorce* accepted that this was a not uncommon scenario: see (1956) Cmnd. 9678, para. 1166.

[81] The three Acts of Parliament relaxing the prohibitions on marriage with affinal relatives had contained specific provisions to that end: Deceased Wife's Sister's Marriage Act 1907, s. 3(2); Deceased Brother's Widow's Marriage Act 1921, s. 1(2); Marriage (Prohibited Degrees of Relationship) Act 1931, s. 2 (amending the provisions of Supreme Court of Judicature (Consolidation) Act, s. 184, which had consolidated the earlier provisions).

[82] Archbishop Fisher told the 1956 *Royal Commission on Marriage and Divorce* (Cmnd. 9678; Paper No. 16, Appendix B) that since divorce was always possible, the affections of a man to his sister-in-law instead of being 'suppressed as improper and incapable of fulfilment' might 'cease to be regarded as altogether improper' and might be allowed to 'develop instead of being suppressed. . . . Even the remote possibility of being able to marry an "in-law" brother or sister . . .' by bringing about a divorce might be enough to create suspicions and uneasiness and to jeopardise a marriage, especially under the 'unnatural strains' caused when young married couples had to live in the home of an 'in-law' (as they frequently did during the post-World War II housing shortage).

[83] 'Could I be so disloyal to my brother as to make love to his wife, or seduce her and take her away to live with me? It is a monstrous idea . . .' *Official Report* (HL) 3 February 1986, vol. 470, col. 936.

[84] On 9 May 1947 G Coldstream minuted that there had been two such questions during the last six months and that on each occasion the Home Secretary had stated that it was 'not the intention of the Government to introduce legislation to permit such a marriage. . . . The matter has certainly not been considered by the Cabinet . . . and it seems unlikely in the extreme that they would be willing to introduced legislation on such a topic in the present circumstances': PRO LCO2/3163, Coldstream to Napier.

marry his divorced brother's wife during the brother's lifetime: he argued that the marriage would promote the welfare of the 11 year old daughter of the divorced couple; and relied on the fact that the policy of the 1857 Divorce Act had been that after divorce it should be lawful for the parties to marry again 'as if the prior marriage had been dissolved by death'.[85] The Personal Bills Committee accepted the Home Secretary's view[86] that the circumstances of the case were not so exceptional as to justify giving one individual the right to contract a marriage which would still be forbidden to other citizens;[87] and at one level, therefore, Stevenson had failed. But the case had attracted attention; and in January 1949 the Conservative Peer Lord Mancroft[88] introduced a Private Member's Bill which would have permitted a man[89] to marry his former wife's sister unless he had been found in the divorce proceedings to have committed adultery with her. The Government declined to co-operate,[90] but the debate had demonstrated that times had changed and so had opinions. As the former Lord Chancellor Simon pointed[91] out, the strongly felt arguments about the potentially disastrous impact of reform were exactly those used in 1907 against permitting marriage with a deceased wife's sister and experience suggested they had been unfounded.

The idea of reform did not seem as shocking as would once have been the case; and it was eventually decided to include a specific mention of the prohibited degrees of marriage in the terms of Reference of the 1956 *Royal Commission on Marriage and Divorce*.[92] Surprisingly in view of the Commission's generally intensely conservative stance the Commission concluded[93] that the time had come to remove prohibitions arising solely from the fact that a marriage had been ended by divorce rather than death.[94] In 1965 Lord

[85] Matrimonial Causes Act 1857, s. 57. The scope of this provision had been deliberately restricted when Parliament for the first time allowed marriage with 'in-law' relatives after a spouse's death: see Supreme Court of Judicature Act 1925, s. 184(1), proviso.

[86] *Report to the Personal Bills Committee*, 13 May 1947, PRO LCO2/3163.

[87] The basis on which Personal Bill legislation should be permitted, and the role of Lord Chancellor in connection with such Bills, is discussed in Coldstream to Napier, 9 May 1947, PRO LCO2/3163. Coldstream's view was that there was a strong onus on the petitioner in such cases to show reasons why an exception should be made in his case.

[88] (1914–1987), see Biographical Notes.   [89] Corresponding provision was made for women.

[90] See HPC(49) 8 March 1949. Lord Addison, Lord Privy Seal, found it difficult to think of any ground of reason, morality or eugenics against the legislation; but none the less thought that in view of the absence of serious public demand and the likelihood that the Church would oppose the Bill they should suggest Mancroft withdraw it.

[91] *Official Report* (HL) vol. 161, col. 725. Note also the speech of Lord Schuster.

[92] Cmd. 9678.

[93] There were three dissentients, including the Commission's chairman, Lord Morton.

[94] The Commission thought there was a 'substantial number' of cases in which 'the parties desire to marry from the best of motives' but were debarred from doing so by the present prohibition. The Commission pointed out that the hardship caused by the prohibition was a demonstrable fact; whereas the possibility that removal would 'create temptation within the family' was necessarily based on conjecture. The Commission doubted whether the presence or absence of a legal prohibition could influence the matter to any appreciable extent: *Royal Commission on Marriage and Divorce*, Cmd. 9678, para. 1167. In this respect it echoed the views expressed a century earlier by the 1848 Royal Commission.

Mancroft again introduced a Bill[95] and the Government did not oppose it.[96] The Marriage (Enabling) Act 1960 provided that no marriage between a man[97] and the sister, aunt or niece of a former wife of his 'whether living or not' should thenceforth be held voidable as being within the prohibited degrees.

Yet once again, the change did not adequately meet changing social and demographic circumstances: the 1956 Royal Commission acknowledged suggestions made by 'a few witnesses' for the abolition of all prohibitions on marriage with relations by marriage. The Commission noted that this would mean that a woman would be free to marry her step-son, or her father- or son-in-law; and did not see any reason to recommend such a change.[98] And no doubt the possibility that a man might be allowed to marry his step-daughter would at first sight seem abhorrent to many. If the traditional argument about the need to exclude incestuous courtship from the family circle means anything it is surely particularly relevant to the parent–child relationship. A man should not be allowed to look on a young girl as the object of his sexual attentions even as a potential bride when his true social role is that of a father concerned to protect the child against damaging sexual involvement.[99]

Once again, demographic changes seemed to suggest a rather different perspective.[100] The 1970s saw a dramatic increase in divorce and remarriage:

[95] There was no provision (such as had appeared in Lord Mancroft's 1949 Bill) debarring a person found in the divorce proceedings to have committed the adultery on the basis of which the decree had been granted. Lord Mancroft admitted in evidence that he had inserted this provision in the Bill in an attempt to diminish clerical opposition, and that he did not in fact favour such a bar. As the *Royal Commission* pointed out, there were powerful arguments against provisions of this kind: *Royal Commission on Marriage and Divorce*, Cmd. 9678, para. 1167.

[96] *Official Report* (HL) 26 January 1960, vol. 220, col. 665. In fact the Government provided drafting assistance: *Official Report* (HL) 26 January 1960, vol. 221, col. 150.

[97] Corresponding provision was made for women: see Marriage (Enabling) Act 1960, s. 1(1).

[98] *Royal Commission on Marriage and Divorce*, Cmd. 9678, paras. 1159, 1170. In the debates on a Bill seeking to legalise marriage with a nephew or niece by affinity Archbishop Cosmo Gordon Lang had suggested that such legislation—in fact enacted in 1931—would inevitably lead to demands to legalise marriage with a step-daughter: *Official Report* (HL) 1 August 1928, vol. 71, col. 1526.

[99] These arguments were powerfully advanced in the parliamentary debates of the 1980s. In 1981, the parents of some 160,000 children aged 16 or under divorced; and the great majority of these would live with their mother. Some of these children would be brought up by a lone parent, but perhaps one half (80,000 or more) would be cared for by their mother and the man she subsequently married. To allow the possibility of marriage would expose more of these children to the risk of sexual abuse: see eg the speeches of Lord Denning (*Official Report* (HL) 9 December 1985, vol. 469, col. 47); Lord Mishcon (at col. 54) the Bishop of Birmingham (*Official Report* (HL) 3 February 1986, vol. 470, col. 950) and Lord Simon of Glaisdale (*Official Report* (HL) 3 February 1986, vol. 470, col. 953); and see also *No Just Cause* (note 79 above) pp. 20–23 and pp. 96–99. Provided the step-daughter is over 16, her step-father commits no criminal offence if he has sexual intercourse with her with her consent; but for discussion of broadening the ambit of the criminal law, see the Home Office Consultation Paper, *Setting the Boundaries* (2000) and the subsequent White Paper, *Protecting the Public*, Cm. 5668, 2002.

[100] There was some doubt about the extent to which the law caused real problems. In the debates on a Marriage (Enabling) Bill in 1981, a Home Office Minister stated that over the 15 years to 1981 the authorities had come to know of 25 cases in which a couple wishing to marry were debarred from doing so by the prohibitions on marriage with affinal relatives. But, in the absence of any adequate demographic survey, it is impossible to assess the scale of the problem; and (as *No Just Cause*, note 101 below put it at para. 193) it is reasonable to suppose that some couples who would wish to

whereas in 1961 15% of marriages in Great Britain were remarriages for one (or both) partners, 20 years later the proportion had more than doubled and more than one third of all marriages were remarriages.[101] This put in question the validity of the stereotype step-father step-daughter relationship as necessarily involving a paternal or any other familial relationship. Each marriage creates its own family, and each remarriage means—as a Review established by the Archbishop of Canterbury[102] put it in 1984[103]—that a

'new set of affines is acquired. Step-relationships increase; children acquire step-parents and may acquire step-grandparents; and parents of remarried spouses may acquire step-grandchildren. The marrying partners acquire parents-in-law where their spouse's parents are living . . .'

These 'reconstituted' families may well be completely independent of the others and sometimes unaware even that the other exists. Suppose that a man had married a divorced woman (or for that matter a widow) whose own daughter was an adult, perhaps living on the other side of the world. Suppose that the wife died, and that thereafter the man met his step-daughter for the first time. Should he necessarily be debarred from marrying her? Was it right that if he lived with the woman he loved but could not marry their children should be illegitimate?[104]

In 1979 the debate was fuelled by the sociologist Lady Wootton of Abinger.[105] She introduced Bills into the House of Lords intended to remove all prohibitions based on affinity. But the parliamentary debates[106] again demonstrated the strength of feeling that it would be wrong to do anything which could introduce

marry may cohabit, perhaps coming 'to terms with their circumstances but presumably not without some anxiety or distress. Other couples may prefer not to live "in sin" but are equally distressed by their inability to contract a lawful marriage'. Enquiries of journalists dealing with family and personal problems suggested there was a significant number of enquiries from people about affinity.

[101] Figures for the period 1961 to 1981 were given in the Report of a Group Appointed by the Archbishop of Canterbury, *No Just Cause, The Law of Affinity in England and Wales: Some Suggestions for Change* (1984) ('*No Just Cause*'). By the turn of the century it seems that more than 40% of all the marriages solemnised in England and Wales are remarriages for one or both partners: see *Population Trends* (2001) Tables 2.1.

[102] *No Just Cause.*　　　　　　　　[103] *No Just Cause*, para. 181.

[104] Lady Wootton (see below) referred to a case in which on her sister's death a woman took over the running of her step-father's household and the care of the children of his marriage. Being denied the possibility of marriage the couple had lived together as man and wife for more than 20 years: *Official Report* (HL) 13 February 1979, vol. 398, col. 1111.

[105] (1897–1997): see Biographical Notes.

[106] The Marriage (Enabling) Bill passed the Second Reading and Committee Stages in the House of Lords (see *Official Report* (HL) 13 February 1979, vol. 398, col. 1107; *Official Report* (HL) 15 March 1979, vol. 399, col. 797) but it was lost with the dissolution of Parliament in April 1979. An identical Bill was defeated in the House of Lords on a Second Reading: *Official Report* (HL) 14 June 1979, vol. 400, col. 801. When Lady Wootton introduced the Bill for a third time and notwithstanding the fact that concessions were made, it attracted substantial opposition from the Bishops of the Church of England (amongst others) and was defeated on a third reading in the House of Lords: *Official Report* (HL) 20 April 1981, vol. 419, col. 1237. In 1982 Lord Lloyd of Kilgerran introduced the Marriage (Step-parents and Step-children) Bill which, as the short title indicates, had a more restricted scope: it would have given the courts discretionary power to authorise marriages between a step-parent and step-child. Although given a Second Reading (*Official Report* (HL) 22 February 1982, vol. 427, col. 783, the Bill made no further progress: see below.

disturbing sexual overtones and a further element of uncertainty into the difficult relationship between step-parent and step-child. Once again no one could show for a certainty that relaxing the law would have any of these consequences; whilst it was easy to demonstrate the reality of the hardship caused by denying the right to contract a marriage. For example:

In 1943 Edward married a 36 year old widow who had borne four children by her first husband. The eldest of those children (a daughter, Doris) had herself married shortly before her mother's marriage to Edward, worked as an auxiliary nurse in the British Army, and had never lived in the same household as her mother and Edward. Doris's husband was killed in an accident after a 22 year marriage; and her mother died in 1977. Doris (aged 58) and Edward (aged 62) then formed the wish to marry; but they were advised that, being in law stepfather and step-daughter, they could not do so. They lived apart, and did not wish to live as man and wife unless they were permitted to be, and were, married to each other.

There was a happy ending for Edward and Doris. Their solicitor[107] happened to be one of the small number of solicitors practising as a parliamentary agent and he was thus aware of the Personal Bill procedure. The barrister Lord Lloyd of Kilgerran introduced the Edward Berry and Doris Eileen Ward (Marriage Enabling) Bill which provided that the couple's relationship should not constitute a bar to their marrying. The Bill passed through Parliament without opposition to the particular marriage[108] and received the Royal Assent.

The success of the Berry Bill gave publicity to the problem (already highlighted by the Wootton Bills) and there were fears that the Private Bill procedure would be invoked in a large number of cases.[109] Something simpler ought to be available to deal with such cases.[110] Although the Bishops had opposed the Wootton Bills the Church of England accepted that there was a problem and that it needed to be solved. Archbishop Runcie invited a Group[111] to review the

---

[107] Leslie Calder of Rees and Freres.

[108] The fact that such Bills were debated in public was one of the matters which was thought to make them unsatisfactory as a means of identifying meritorious cases: see *Official Report* (HL) 22 May 1980, vol. 409, col. 1037. *No Just Cause* summarised other objections to the Personal Bill procedure: (i) it was little known; (ii) the cost involved would be substantial—somewhere between £5,000 and £7,000 in year 2000 values—and legal aid would not be available; (iii) the statements made by the applicants for a Personal Bill cannot easily or effectively be tested or challenged; (iv) it is not easy to see how opponents of a Personal Bill could set out to challenge it; and if the Bill were opposed by a Peer the applicants would have no opportunity of speaking in their own defence; (v) the Personal Bill procedure is an inappropriate use of parliamentary time. For uncertainty about the criteria employed by the Personal Bill Committee see GP Coldstream's Minute, 9 May 1947, PRO LCO2/3163.

[109] In fact, only two comparable Personal Acts were introduced and passed: the John Francis Dare and Gillian Loder Dare (Marriage Enabling) Act 1982 and the Hugh Small and Norma Small (Marriage Enabling) Act 1982. A summary of the facts in these cases is given in *No Just Cause*, Appendix II. The same solicitor acted in all three cases.

[110] See *per* Lord Hailsham LC, *Official Report* (HL) 22 May 1980, vol. 409, cols. 1059–1060.

[111] For the Group's membership, see Biographical Notes, Part B.

working of the law,[112] to consider 'whether any general modifications were called for and/or whether exceptions should be allowed in particular cases and, if so, according to what criteria and by what procedure these should be authorized'.

The Group was unanimous in considering the law (and especially the procedure for obtaining dispensation by means of a Private Act of Parliament) to be unsatisfactory; but disagreed about how extensive the relaxation of the law should be.[113] In 1986, the barrister Lord Meston[114] introduced what he described[115] as a 'short and simple Bill' to give effect to the recommendations on which the Group had agreed: the prohibition on marriage between a man and step-daughter[116] was to be removed provided both parties were 18[117] or older and the younger had not during minority been a 'child of the family'[118] in relation to the other party.[119] During the course of the Bill's passage through the

---

[112] The Commission was specifically directed to take account of the practice in other States, and Chapter 7 of *No Just Cause* is an admirable survey. As often happens, however, the only conclusion from such a survey is that practice differs widely.

[113] The majority (Seear, Baker, Dunstan, Finnegan, Mattinson, and Rubinstein) would have allowed marriage without restriction between affinal relatives both of whom were over 21. The majority would also have allowed marriage between step-parent and step-child if both parties were over 18, and the younger had at no time been a 'child of the family'—see below—in relation to the older): *No Just Cause*, para. 220. The minority (Hart, Hook and O'Donovan) were not prepared to allow marriage between step-parent and step-child where the relationship of 'child of the family' had existed at any time; and would not have allowed marriage between parent- and child-in law in any circumstances: para. 276).

[114] (1950–): see Biographical Notes.

[115] *Official Report* (HL) 19 December 1985, vol. 469, col. 39. The Government's attitude was one of 'benevolent neutrality': *Official Report* (HL) 24 February 1986, vol. 471, col. 889. The Anglican Bishops approved of the Bill as originally introduced by a majority of 59 to 2 and (as the Archbishop of York, formerly an opponent of change (see above), guilelessly admitted) 'did not feel it right to let the [Church's] General Synod loose' on what he described as a 'technical matter' since it was 'best to keep discussion in the hands of those who already have some knowledge': *Official Report* (HL) 19 December 1985, vol. 469, col. 43. The Roman Catholic Duke of Norfolk also supported the Bill as introduced on the basis that it merely applied to cases in which the Roman Catholic Bishops would have been prepared to grant a dispensation to permit the marriage in question: see at col. 46. These factors no doubt explain why the Bill was allowed to pass through all its stages in the House of Commons on a single day without any debate: *Official Report* (HC) 16 May 1986, vol. 97, col. 1029.

[116] Or his step-granddaughter. Corresponding relaxations applied to marriage by a woman and her step-son or step-grandson.

[117] The age of 21 was substituted, in response to criticism, at 3rd Reading: *Official Report* (HL) 24 March 1986, vol. 472, col. 1253.

[118] ie a child who has lived in the man's household and been treated as a child of the family by him: Marriage (Prohibited Degrees of Relationship) Act 1986, Sch. 1, para. 7. In the Parliamentary Debates Lord Denning argued that the exception would produce anomalies, instancing the case in which a man had two step-daughters the one 17 and the other 21: *Official Report* (HL) 9 December 1985, vol. 469, col. 47.

[119] Provision was made in an attempt to ensure that proper enquiry was made about the ages of the parties and the other conditions for relaxation: no such marriage may be solemnised after publication of banns: Marriage (Prohibited Degrees of Relationship) Act 1986, Sch. 1, para. 3, and those responsible for preliminaries to a marriage between persons who would previously have been within the prohibited degrees are required to obtain appropriate evidence: Marriage (Prohibited Degrees of Relationship) Act 1986, Sch. 1, paras. 4, 5.

House of Lords[120] the prohibition on marriage with a parent- or child-in law was—contrary to the views of the minority of the Archbishop's Group—relaxed;[121] and whatever else this relaxation may have achieved it certainly greatly complicated and lengthened the Bill. However, there appears to be, at the turn of the century, no evidence that the change in the law has encouraged men more frequently to look on their mothers-in-law with lustful eyes.[122] Nor is there any evidence of pressure to follow the example set by Australia and abolish all legal restrictions on marriage between 'in-laws'.[123]

Adoption and the prohibited degrees

If marriage created legal relationships where none had previously existed, what should be the effect of legal adoption, introduced into English law in 1926? As will be seen elsewhere in this book, the 1926 Act (based on the Report of a Committee chaired by Tomlin J) took a robust line.[124] The 'blood tie cannot be severed' and accordingly the adopted child should remain debarred from marriage to his birth parents and other relatives. But the Committee considered that it would be 'repugnant to common sense' to allow 'a purely artificial relationship' to operate as a bar to marriage;[125] and the 1926 Act made no provision at all about the effect of adoption on the prohibited degrees. Not until 1949 did legislation debar an adopted child from marrying his or her adoptive parent;[126] and neither that Act nor any subsequent legislation has imposed a bar on marriage between an adopted child and his or her adoptive brother or sister.[127] Although justification for prohibitions of marriage with relatives (other than blood rela-

[120] Amendments were introduced at the Report and 3rd Reading stages in the light of the points raised in debate see *Official Report* (HL) 24 February 1986, vol. 471, col. 883, and 24 March 1986, vol. 472, col. 1253.

[121] It appears (see *Official Report* (HL) 24 February 1986, vol. 471, col. 886) that Personal Bills intended to permit such marriages were pending, and this may well have influenced the outcome. The amendments made to the Bill would only allow such a marriage where both parties were 21 or over and both 'connecting spouses'—in the case of a marriage between a man and his daughter-in-law, for example, the son and the son's mother—were dead: Marriage (Prohibited Degrees of Relationship) Act 1986, s. 1(4). The drafting of this amendment—not opposed by the Church of England: *Official Report* (HL) 24 February 1986, vol. 471, col. 886—was intended to meet the objection that to allow such marriages would encourage the development of an erotic relationship between the two, but its aptness in this context has been convincingly criticised: see the Scottish Law Commission's *Report on Family Law* (Scot Law Com. No. 135, 1992) para. 8.9.

[122] It may be plausibly argued that the law has been made so complex that it is difficult to imagine its principles being generally understood. For a case in which a couple within the prohibited degrees cohabited and apparently intended to marry see *Smith v. Clerical Medical and General Life Assurance Society* [1993] 1 FLR 47 (where the fact is not remarked upon).

[123] Family Law Act 1975. It seems that this enactment did not result in any great number of marriages between those formerly within the prohibited degrees: *No Just Cause*, para. 149.

[124] The Child Adoption Committee, which produced three Reports (Cmd. 2401, Cmd. 2469, and Cmd. 2711) between 1924 and 1926: see further Chapter 17, below.

[125] *The Tomlin Report*, para. 20.

[126] Adoption of Children Act, 1949, s.11(1) (the Act expressly preserves the validity of any such marriages solemnised before commencement): see Chapter 17.

[127] See below.

tives) has increasingly been based on the feeling that it is wrong to give any encouragement to the development of erotic feelings within the nuclear family the law has not gone so far as to seek to extend control to people who are *in fact* living in a relationship.[128] No one has, for example, suggested that a genetically unrelated boy and girl brought up by foster-parents in the same household should be debarred from marrying.

THE MINIMUM AGE FOR MARRIAGE

Should the age of the parties affect the validity of a marriage? There are three separate, if related, issues. First, marriage is a relationship created by the consent of the parties and youth or old age[129] may well affect the intellectual capacity of a man or a woman to give that consent. Secondly, it is implicit in the contract of marriage that the parties should be capable of consummating the union;[130] and a relationship in which one or both parties had not reached the age of puberty may for that reason be vulnerable. Finally, most legal systems allow parents to forbid the marriage of their children (usually subject to a power in the courts or other state agencies to override a refusal);[131] and English law follows this pattern. Lord Hardwicke's Act fixed the age for 'free marriage'—the age at which marriage could be contracted without any parental or other third party consent[132]—at 21;[133] and so it remained until the Family Law Reform Act 1969 reduced the age to 18.

Child marriages?

At the beginning of the twentieth century no statute laid down any minimum age for marriage. It seems that the Common Law applied a presumption that a boy under 14 and a girl under 12 were not capable of marriage; but the rule was

---

[128] The Home Office Consultation Paper, *Setting the Boundaries* (2000) (followed by a White Paper, *Protecting the Public*, 2002, Cm. 5668), might be thought to go some way towards this; whilst the Government seems unconcerned by the prospect that young people who will be eligible to marry one another should be liable to prosecution if they engage in sexual activity whilst they are under 16 which can be classified as 'manipulative': see *Protecting the Public*, para. 52.

[129] The possibility that an elderly person no longer in possession of his or her mental faculties might be persuaded to go through a marriage ceremony with someone more interested in the proprietary than the personal consequences of marriage has been highlighted by a number of recent cases: see eg *Re Davey* [1981] 1 WLR 164 (marriage of 92-year-old spinster to employee of the nursing home in which she resided); and *Re Park* [1954] P 112.

[130] The age of puberty varies from area to area and from time to time: see further note 143 below.

[131] *Report of the Committee on the Age of Majority*, Chairman the Hon. Mr Justice Latey, 1967, Cmnd. 3342 (hereinafter 'the Latey Report') Appendix 7 contains a useful tabular statement of the legal consequences of youth on legal capacity (including capacity to marry and to contract a 'free marriage') in a large number of States as at that time; and see the *Report of the Select Committee on the Age of Marriage Bill* (HL 90, 66, BPP 1928–29, vol. 5).

[132] This convenient expression was used by the *Latey Report*.

[133] Clandestine Marriages Act 1753, s. 3.

not absolute. In particular, if a couple married below this 'age of discretion' the marriage[134] would be treated as valid if the couple had in fact remained together thereafter. (It is possible that this was because the original marriage was voidable rather than void; but the better view is that in such a case the couple would be deemed to have *ratified* the union.[135])

Whatever the strict legal position may have been, there is little evidence[136] that at the beginning of the twentieth century young teenagers were taking advantage of the freedom to contract marriages. It is true that the 1868 Chelmsford *Royal Commission on the Laws of Marriage*[137] had been pressed with testimony (drawing on the 1861 Census Returns) that youthful marriage was particularly common in the cotton districts of Lancashire;[138] but in the first years of the twentieth century only very rarely is any marriage involving a person under 16 recorded. (The year 1903 is exceptional in that two such marriages were recorded.[139]) There were fewer than ten marriages each year involving a 16-year-old, and some 60 or 70 in which one or both parties was 17. Only at age 18 did marriage become numerically at all significant: at the beginning of the century there were some 600 marriages involving an 18-year-old. But that was a tiny proportion (0.2%) of all marriages. Only one in 20 men marrying were under 21 (although the proportion of 'infant' brides was more than three times as great).[140]

The 1868 Royal Commission rejected suggestions that the minimum age for marriage should be raised. The Commission accepted that the law (apparently based on the principle that marriage between people capable of becoming parents should not be made legally impossible) permitted marriage much earlier than was prudent or desirable, but concluded that to raise the minimum age without giving the young people concerned any effective guardianship or oversight would 'hardly be conducive to their moral improvement'. And the figures

---

[134] See W Macpherson, *Law Relating to Infants* (1841) p. 168; Shelford, *The Law of Marriage and Divorce* (1841) p. 282. The authorities agree that any espousal under the age of seven was absolutely void; and that marriages contracted between that age and 12 or 14 were 'inchoate and imperfect'.

[135] Blackstone, *Commentaries on the Laws of England* (4th ed., 1770, Vol. 1 p. 436); and note that the eminent ecclesiastical lawyer Sir Lewis Dibdin declined to accept that under-age unions were voidable: *Select Committee on the Age of Marriage Bill* (HL 90, 66, BPP 1928–29, vol. 5). See further the discussion in the Law Commission's *Report on Nullity of Marriage* (1970) Law Com. No. 33, para. 16.

[136] The forms of marriage registration prescribed under the 1836 Act did not require the exact age of the parties to be given, and it was usual for parties to be described as 'of full age' or 'minor' as appropriate. By the 1850s the exact age was given in about half of all entries; and by 1900 virtually all ages at marriage were recorded: *Marriage and Divorce Statistics 1873–1983*, Series FM2 No. 16 (OPCS, 1990) (hereafter 'OPCS Historical Statistics') p. 1.

[137] 1868, BPP 1867–1868 vol. 32, p. 6 at Appendix, p. 27.

[138] A witness claimed that in Bolton there were 45 households in which the husband was under 16 and 175 in which the wife was under that age. The comparable figures for Burnley were 51 and 147 and for Stockport 59 and 179. The witness noted the 'precocious independence' of the young cotton operatives: *ibid*.

[139] *OPCS Historical Statistics*, Table 3.2(a).

[140] *Sixty Second Annual Report of the Registrar General* (1900, Cd. 323) pp. 10–12.

given above might be thought to vindicate the Commission's judgment: the problem of the 'child' marriage in this country seemed to have solved itself. So why did Parliament act in 1929, passing the Age of Marriage Act which rendered any 'marriage' to which either party was under 16 void?

There seems to have been no extensive prior campaigning, speech-making or article writing to prepare the way; and there was certainly no evidence that the problem had become in numerical terms significant.[141] The fact that this Act got onto the statute book when it did seems almost entirely attributable to the crusading zeal and determination of the former Liberal Lord Chancellor, Lord Buckmaster.[142] He relied on three main arguments. First, he claimed that the 'age of maturity'[143] was much higher than it had been in the Middle Ages when the rules permitting marriage at so young an age had been formulated.[144] Secondly, he argued that a low age for marriage facilitated the work of traffickers in young women (the so-called white slave trade): young girls were persuaded to leave home, country and parents by the promise of marriage.[145] Finally, he claimed that the law enabled the policy of the Criminal Law Amendment Act 1885 to be defeated. That Act[146] (passed after an emotional campaign against child brothels and trafficking in young girls)[147] made it a criminal offence for a man to have intercourse with a female under 16, and it was immaterial that she had consented. Buckmaster[148] claimed that it was absurd to

---

[141] According to the Government Spokesman the Lord Privy Seal (the Fourth Marquess of Salisbury, 1861–1947) in the previous 12 years only three 13-year-old girls, 28 14-year-olds, and 318 15-year-olds had married in this country: *Official Report* (HL) 19 February 1929, vol. 72, col. 968. Evidence to the *Select Committee on the Age of Marriage Bill* (1928–29, HL 90, 66, BPP vol. 5) confirmed that in the previous five years fewer than 50 couples a year would have been affected by the intended prohibition. In the great majority of these cases the wife was 15.

[142] Stanley Owen Buckmaster (1861–1934): see Biographical Notes.

[143] Buckmaster made no attempt to clarify the meaning of this expression. If 'age of maturity' is used as a euphemism or synonym for the 'age of puberty' scientific evidence makes it clear that the age has been falling over recent years: see the *Latey Report*, para. 174 (and see also paras. 142–145). But 'maturity' may be used in a more general sense as indicating the degree of understanding and intelligence required to be capable of taking the decision in question; and it has been argued that earlier physical maturity does not connote any change in *psychological* maturity: see the Dissenting Report by Geoffrey Howe and John Stebbings published as Part VIII of the *Latey Report*.

[144] There were many references to Shakespeare's 13-year-old Juliet, advised by her mother to 'think of marriage now. Younger than you Here in Verona, ladies of esteem, Are made already mothers. By my count, I was your mother much upon these years That you are now a maid . . .': *Romeo and Juliet,* Act I, Scene 3.

[145] *Official Report* (HL) 19 February 1929, vol. 72, col. 963.

[146] s. 5. It was a defence that the person charged had reasonable cause to believe that the girl was of or above the age of 16.

[147] Associated in its later stages with the activities of the journalist and author WT Stead (1840–1912, a victim of the *Titanic* disaster). Stead demonstrated the inadequacy of the existing law and was imprisoned for what he did to this end. Stead's *Pall Mall Gazette* published full accounts of the activities of procurers and others engaged in the traffic in young girls: see *The Maiden Tribute of Modern Babylon—the Report of the Pall Mall Gazette's Secret Commission* (1885) and for a modern account, C Terrot, *The Maiden Tribute* (1959). However, the Act was strongly opposed, much of the opposition based on fears that no man with young sons would be able safely to employ girls under 16 as domestic servants: see the prolonged debates reported in *Hansard's Parliamentary Debates* (3rd Series) vol. 300.

[148] *Official Report* (HL) 19 February 1929, vol. 72, col. 962.

make a 15-year-old legally incapable of consenting to a single act of sexual intercourse whilst at the same time allowing her, by agreeing to marry, to submit to intercourse in perpetuity. He also claimed that the marriage law was being used to enable men to escape prosecution under the 1885 Act for defiling a girl of 13, 14, or 15: a man would induce the 'little creature against whom he had perpetrated this unforgivable wrong' to marry him and thereby disqualify herself from giving evidence against him.[149]

The Second Reading Debate went well for Buckmaster, and the Government announced that it would not oppose the Bill.[150] But in the Committee stage all went disastrously wrong: influential voices argued that it would be wrong to make an important change to the marriage law without much fuller consideration. Buckmaster must have realised that a Bill opposed by the Archbishop of Canterbury,[151] a leading Roman Catholic peer,[152] a Privy Councillor who had been the senior puisne judge of the King's Bench Division,[153] the Master of the Rolls,[154] and a former Director of Public Prosecutions[155] was not going to get any further[156] unless something could be done to placate the opponents and the hesitant.

But Buckmaster would not accept defeat. He agreed to the Bill being committed to a Select Committee chaired by Lord Ernle.[157] The Committee interviewed witnesses from the Mothers' Union and a number of representatives of the Women's Movement, all of whom favoured the Buckmaster Bill. The Home Office representative[158] told the Committee the Government considered the existing law indefensible.[159] Even better, the Committee managed to high-

---

[149] *Official Report* (HL) 19 February 1929, vol. 72, col. 964. At that time a wife could not be compelled to give evidence against her husband. The law was changed and under the Police and Criminal Evidence Act 1984, s. 80, one spouse is a compellable witness against the other in cases of assault and sexual offences against a person under the age of 16.

[150] Salisbury in his speech was one of the very few speakers on this subject who was prepared to say that the young women involved also had feelings: *Official Report* (HL) 19 February 1929, vol. 72, col. 968.

[151] Randall Davidson (1848–1930: see Biographical Notes): a conservative in matters relating to family life he was one of those who thought the issues should be examined more thoroughly: *Official Report* (HL) 12 March 1929, vol. 73, col. 424.

[152] Viscount FitzAlan of Derwent (1855–1947).

[153] Charles John Darling (1849–1936). His speeches opposing the Bill made no attempt to conceal his dislike of both Bill and Promoter: see eg *Official Report* (HL) 21 February 1929, vol. 72, col. 1030.

[154] Viscount Hanworth (1861–1936).

[155] The 5th Earl of Desart (1848–1934, sometime Treasury Solicitor, King's Proctor, and Director of Public Prosecutions).

[156] It appears that the Government put the Whips on to force an adjournment of the debate: *Official Report* (HL) 12 March 1929, vol. 73, col. 402.

[157] *Select Committee on the Age of Marriage Bill* (1928–29, HL 90, 66, BPP vol. 5). For Lord Ernle (1851–1937) see Biographical Notes.

[158] Sidney West Harris (1876–1962): see Biographical Notes.

[159] The Committee also found that the number of cases in which a girl under 16 exercised real freedom of choice in deciding to marry was small. In the great majority of cases the girls were subjected to pressure (by reason of their own pregnancy, their partner's fear of prosecution, their parents' concern to avoid scandal) which destroyed their ability to exercise a free choice: *Select Committee on the Age of Marriage Bill*, col. iv.

light[160] an issue which suggested that the existing law damaged British interests. The League of Nations was seeking to increase the effectiveness of child protection measures, and was in particular concerned to eradicate arranged child marriage from India and a number of other Asian countries; and the Ernle Committee found that the state of English law impaired the influence of the United Kingdom in these discussions. In this way, what had appeared to be the obsession of an eccentric back-bench peer became a contribution to national prestige.[161] The Committee therefore agreed that the minimum age for marriage should be raised to 16;[162] and that a marriage under that age should be void (as distinct from merely voidable).[163] The Leader of the House of Lords[164] warned that any further discussion would be fatal to the Bill's prospects. The Bill passed the Lords accordingly and went through all its stages in the House of Commons on a single day without a word of debate.[165] It is impossible to assess the impact (if any) of the Age of Marriage Act in achieving its promoters' objectives.

The issue of the age of marriage was revisited between 1965 and 1970 by three[166] official inquiries. Although there was some support in the 1960s for raising[167] the minimum age for marriage[168] none of the inquiries recommended any

---

[160] The difficulty of leading world opinion when English law was 'on a par with that of Siam and Venezuela' had already been mentioned by the Bishop of Southwark in the House of Lords debates; but the Select Committee gave prominence to it and in this way was able to suggest that the nation would benefit from the change Buckmaster had proposed.

[161] The Committee also pointed out that under the Legitimacy Act 1926 any child born to the couple would be legitimated by their subsequent marriage thereby destroying the argument (much used by opponents of reform) that the Bill would bastardise innocent children. (There were in fact very few children—in 1927, only 27—born to couples married when one of them was under 16.)

[162] The Committee rejected the compromise of allowing marriage at 15 (an age at which significant numbers of marriages did take place) on the ground that it would be wrong to pronounce capable of entering on the intimate relations and reciprocal duties and responsibilities of married life those whom the criminal law regarded as too immature and irresponsible to consent to an isolated act of indecency. It rejected proposals that the minimum age at which males could marry be raised to 17 or 18 because of fears that such a law would enable youths to seduce girls on the promise of marriage which they would then be free to repudiate. The Committee recommended two minor amendments to the Buckmaster Bill: first, that it should be a sufficient defence to a charge of indecent assault or of unlawful sexual intercourse under s. 5(1) Criminal Law Amendment Act 1885 to prove that the accused had at the time reasonable cause to believe the victim was his wife: see Age of Marriage Act 1929, s. 1(1); secondly that a woman should be entitled to take proceedings for maintenance in respect of the child born to her in such a void marriage: see Age of Marriage Act 1929, s. 2.

[163] There are plausible arguments (advanced by, for example, Lord Hanworth MR in the Lords' debate) against this view; but the Committee considered that these were outweighed by the advantages of clarity and simplicity implicit in declaring such marriages to be void.

[164] Lord Salisbury.

[165] *Official Report* (HC) 3 May 1929, vol. 227, col. 1918. A week later Parliament was dissolved.

[166] *Report of the Committee on the Age of Majority*, Chairman the Hon. Mr Justice Latey, 1967, Cmnd. 3342; the *Report of the Departmental Committee . . . to inquire into the Law of Scotland relating to Marriage*, Chairman the Rt. Hon. Lord Kilbrandon, 1969, Cmnd. 4011; and by the Law Commission, *Report on Nullity of Marriage* (1970) Law Com. No. 33.

[167] In contrast, there was no support at all for lowering the age: in an attitude survey carried out by the Government Social Survey in 1966 half of those questioned considered that 16 was not the right minimum age for marriage; but virtually no one favoured reducing the age. The majority preference was for 18 or 21: *Latey Report*, Appendix 9, p. 203.

[168] See in particular the *Latey Report*, para. 102.

change in the law[169] and no change was made. The reality is that the 'problem' of youthful marriage had solved itself: whereas as recently as 1966 nearly a third of all brides married when they were still teenagers, by 1991 the proportion had fallen to less than one in twelve[170] and at the turn of the century only 3% of brides were under 21.[171] The problem which became one of increasing concern was not so much that young people were marrying but rather that they were (notwithstanding the provisions of the criminal law)[172] having sex and conceiving and bearing children. It has been estimated that more than a quarter of boys and nearly a fifth of girls under 16 are sexually active; and in 1999 405 girls under the age of 14, 1,866 14-year-olds, and 5,673 15-year-old girls conceived. (Slightly more than half those pregnancies were terminated legally under the provisions of the Abortion Act 1967.[173]) Confident statements made by official bodies in the late 1960s—for example, that the trend then observed to earlier marriage would continue, and that because boys and girls become sexually mature at an earlier age than their parents it followed, not only that they would feel 'sexual desire and be sexually at risk at an earlier age' but also that because of this 'more of them are likely to decide to get married'[174]—have been completely falsified by events. All that can be said with confidence is that the extent to which the law influences sexual behaviour is a controversial matter.[175]

[169] The question whether an under-age marriage should be void (rather than voidable, ie valid unless and until either party took action to avoid it or ratifiable (ie void unless and until the parties affirmed it after both had attained the prescribed age) is in theory one of some difficulty particularly in cases in which the parties married genuinely believing themselves to be of marriageable age and *a fortiori* where they were born in countries with no adequate system of birth registration.

[170] See *Population Trends* (No. 103, 2001) Table 9.1. The proportion of brides marrying at young ages was smaller—10% in 1966 and 2.1% in 1991: *ibid*. The mean age for single men marrying in the year 1999 was 29 and for single women 27: *Social Trends* (No. 32, 2002) p. 44.

[171] 8,957 women marrying in England and Wales in 1998 out of a total of 267,303 were under 20. 108 of these had managed to be divorced before re-marrying: *Marriage, divorce and adoption statistics 1998* (Office for National Statistics, Series FM2 no. 26) Table 3.26. Only 2,233 men under 21 (of whom 24 were divorced) married in that year: Table 3.25.

[172] Since 1885 it has been unlawful for a man to have sexual intercourse with a girl under 16 whether or not she consents: see above (and now Sexual Offences Act 1956, s. 6). In practice, the police are reluctant to prosecute teenage boys for this offence in cases where the girl is a willing party: see *R v. Commissioner of Police of the Metropolis, ex parte Blackburn* [1968] 2 QB 118, 139, *per* Salmon LJ, and generally the number of prosecutions has fallen significantly in the last decade of the twentieth century: see the Home Office's Consultation Paper, *Setting the Boundaries* (2000) para. 3.2, and 3.5 (which asserts that the 'present age of sixteen is well established, well understood and well supported' and recommends that 'as a matter of public policy, the age of legal consent should remain at sixteen').

[173] 'Conceptions in England and Wales, 1999', *Population Trends* (No. 103, 2001), p. 86. Governments have launched programmes intended to reduce the number of teenage pregnancies (see the Report of the Social Exclusion Unit on *Teenage Pregnancies* (1999)) and it appears that in the period 1994–1999 there has been some reduction in the under-age conception rate: *ibid*.

[174] These examples are taken from the *Latey Report* paras. 139 and 145. The *Latey Report* also expressed the view that the Judges of the Chancery Division were wrong in believing that marriage had ceased to be a permanent institution because the 'divorce rate is about 10 per cent—which means that 90 per cent of marriages are lasting': see para. 146.

[175] As evidenced by the strongly held views voiced in the debates on the Sexual Offences (Amendment) Act 2000 which reduced the 'age of consent' for homosexual acts to 16. The Government eventually used the provisions of the Parliament Act 1949 to overcome opposition in the House of Lords to this change.

The age for free marriage: consent of parents or the court[176]

Before 1735 English law did not require either party to a marriage to obtain parental consent; but Lord Hardwicke's Act effectively[177] required that parental consent be given to the marriage of any 'infant' (that is, a person under the age[178] of 21).[179] The parent could enforce this right by making the child a ward of court.[180] A ward was automatically debarred from marrying without the leave of the court; and the court would and could make specific orders (breach of which might be punished by imprisonment)[181] forbidding contact between the ward and a named person.

---

[176] The requisite consent may be that of a guardian or other person standing in the position of a parent to the child; and the law in this respect has been rationalised by Children Act 1989 Sch. 12, para. 5.

[177] A marriage by licence was declared to be void in the absence of parental consent if either party was under 21. A parent or guardian had the right to make an open and public declaration of dissent to a marriage after publication of banns but in the absence of such a declaration the marriage would not be invalidated by the fact that a parent did not consent. In the case of marriages by superintendent registrar's certificate (whether or not by licence) the Marriage Act 1836 established procedures whereby any person could enter a caveat against the issue of a certificate or licence and any person whose consent was required to the marriage could forbid the issue of a certificate by writing the word 'forbidden' opposite the relevant entry in the marriage notice book.

[178] At common law a person attained a particular age at the beginning of the day preceding the anniversary of the date of birth: *Re Shurey* [1918] 1 Ch 263. The Family Law Reform Act 1969, s. 9 (giving effect to a recommendation in the *Latey Report*: see paras. 511–515) provided that thenceforth the time at which a person attained a particular age should be the commencement of the relevant anniversary of the date of his birth. It appears that persons born on 29 February attain ages on that day in a leap year, but not until 1 March in other years, such being said to be the effect of the common law as stated in *R v. Worminghall (Inhabitants)* (1817) 6 M&S 530.

[179] The law of Scotland imposed no requirement of parental consent to the marriage of an infant, and until 1856 it was possible for English couples easily to defeat a refusal of parental consent by travelling to Scotland—Gretna Green being the traditional venue—where they could immediately contract a valid marriage. The Marriage (Scotland) Act 1856 imposed a requirement of three weeks' residence in Scotland prior to marriage and the number of marriages celebrated at Gretna Green fell sharply; but Scotland remained a haven for defiant young people. In 1954 for example the 20-year-old James Goldsmith, wishing to marry the 18-year-old Bolivian heiress Isabel Patino against the wishes of her parents, apparently consulted the leading London lawyers Withers & Co and then eloped with her to Scotland. Notwithstanding legal action by Isabel's father in Scotland he was able to do so, the law of Scotland not recognising the father's right to prohibit the marriage: see I Fallon, *Billionaire, The Life and Times of Sir James Goldsmith* (1991) p. 94; *The Times* 5 to 8 January 1954. Cases such as this became a source of concern, and following recommendations made in the *Report of the Departmental Committee . . . to inquire into the Law of Scotland relating to Marriage,* Chairman the Rt. Hon. Lord Kilbrandon, 1969, Cmnd. 4011 the Marriage (Scotland) Act 1977, s. 3(5) sought to restrict the freedom of young persons of foreign domicile to marry in Scotland. English parents might invoke the wardship jurisdiction to prevent children travelling to Scotland to marry: see below.

[180] See generally NV Lowe and RAH White, *Wards of Court* (2nd ed., 1986); and Chapter 16, below.

[181] See *Re H's Settlement* [1909] 2 Ch 260; and for modern examples, *Re Elwes (No. 1)* (1958) *The Times* 30 July; *Re Dowsett* (1959) *The Times,* 3 October (man's imprisonment for 11 weeks said to be 'thoroughly deserved') and *Re B (JA)(an infant)* [1965] Ch 1112 where parents, who objected to their young daughter associating with a 42-year-old married man obtained an order restraining the man from communicating with the girl pending the court hearing.

The court could of course override the parents' refusal to consent; and when considering the suitability of a particular marriage it would normally be concerned that there should be a 'fair equality of rank and fortune' between the couple and that a proper settlement of the girl's property was to be made.[182] Property was generally the first consideration, and this was perhaps reasonable so long as the effect of marriage was to give the husband substantial entitlements to the property of the woman he married. For example:

In *Bolton v. Bolton*[183] the 19-year-old Evelina Mary Bolton was entitled under her grandfather's will to a considerable fortune expectant on the death of her father. The will was being administered by the court and Miss Bolton thus became a ward.[184] In 1889 Miss Bolton became engaged to a Mr Frank Russell, a commercial traveller in a good position earning some £300 a year (possibly £18,000 in year 2000 values). Mr Russell swore an affidavit in which he formally undertook that, if the court saw fit to permit him to visit and pay his addresses to Miss Bolton he would do so as became a gentlemen and an honourable man and to abide by the directions of the court. Miss Bolton decided that she would like to help her husband financially by providing capital to help him set up his own business. She was advised by solicitors to wait until her 21st birthday, since otherwise the court would insist on all her property being put into a settlement which would prevent her from assisting her husband. The couple decided to marry six days after her birthday; but her father apparently did not like what was happening. Two days before the date set for the marriage the court made an order[185] restraining the couple from marrying.

At the beginning of the twentieth century there were still cases in which parents invoked the wardship jurisdiction in an attempt to discipline their children;[186] and even in the second half of the century, imprisonment was still sometimes used as a sanction. For example, in 1958:

The parents of Miss Tessa Kennedy disapproved of her relationship with Mr Dominic Elwes and instituted wardship proceedings. On 3 December 1957 Roxburgh J made an order restraining him from associating with her, and a week later on evidence that he was still seeing her ordered his committal to prison. Elwes was not apprehended, however, and three months later in New York he married Miss Kennedy. He then, having notified the authorities, returned to this country and was duly conveyed to Brixton prison. The Judge accepted that he loved his wife, but commented that every parent knew that love was not readily convertible into bread and butter for the support of a wife and

---

[182] WP Eversley, *The Law of Domestic Relations* (1896) p. 786.   [183] [1891] 3 Ch 270.

[184] In fact in this case the ward's father approved of the intended marriage, but the court's approval was still necessary.

[185] The Court of Appeal subsequently held that the order had been made without jurisdiction: the court could no longer restrain a ward who had attained the age of majority.

[186] *Re H's Settlement* [1909] 2 Ch 260 (the facts of which are given at p. 585) is a particularly striking example.

family.[187] The judge described the case as an especially serious one, but ordered Elwes' release on the basis that his fortnight in prison was sufficiently long to deter like-minded youths from imitating his foolish escapade. However, he ordered that Mrs Elwes—who had been a willing collaborator—remain a ward, observing that her runaway marriage made the court's supervision all the more important.

Wardship was until the 1960s[188] still largely the preserve of the propertied classes but statute[189] provided a remedy for the offspring of the less affluent. If a parent[190] refused to agree to a marriage the court could, on application by one of the parties, consent to the marriage and such consent would have the same effect as if it had been given by the parent. By the second half of the twentieth century the number of applications to the court (usually[191] the magistrates' court) to overrule a parental refusal of consent had risen substantially; and between 1958 and 1965 there were as many as 500 to 600 applications to the magistrates' courts each year, of which perhaps half were granted.[192] In practice the magistrates' courts were concerned with far more cases than were dealt with in wardship, but almost nothing is known about how such cases were handled.[193] No doubt in the period of rapid social change which followed World War II the whole idea of a young person having to apply to the court—whether the magistrates' or the wardship court—for permission to marry increasingly seemed rather outdated, even by some of those administering the law.[194] But there is no evidence of any particular sense of outrage about the law or that it caused many problems.

The Latey Report on the Age of Majority, 1967

In contrast, there was a great deal of evidence that the inability of 'infants' to make legally binding contracts caused difficulties for young people seeking

---

[187] The judge's gloomy prognostications sadly proved to have been justified. Dominic Elwes appears to have been a man with a talent to amuse and a wide knowledge of architecture and decorating, but he was affected by depression. His marriage broke down, and in 1975 he committed suicide—John Aspinall commenting in a tribute that Elwes' business affairs were never as successful as he believed was his due; see *The Times* 13 September 1975, 26 and 30 November 1975.

[188] For the increased recourse to wardship in the 1950s, see Chapter 16.

[189] Originally the Marriage Act 1823, ss. 16 and 17; but the law—onto which further provisions were grafted by the Marriage Act 1836 and the Guardianship of Infants Act 1886—was left in a confused state: see *Re Queskey* [1946] Ch 250. The Guardianship of Infants Act 1925 did identify the persons whose consent was required to marriage.

[190] Or other person whose consent was required (eg a child's legal guardian).

[191] The High Court, county court and magistrates' courts all had jurisdiction, but it seems that in practice applications were almost invariably made to the magistrates' court. Applications to the magistrates' court were classed as 'domestic proceedings' by the Summary Procedure (Domestic Proceedings) Act 1937 which thereby gave a measure of protection from publicity.

[192] See the figures quoted in the *Latey Report*, para. 570.

[193] There was no appeal against the magistrates' decision (*Re Queskey* [1946] Ch. 250) and accordingly no reported case law.

[194] See for example the evidence of the High Court judges summarised in the *Latey Report*, paras. 77–79.

tenancies and effectively prevented even those who could afford the deposit necessary for house purchase from obtaining a mortgage; and it was complaints to
Members of Parliament about these problems[195] which in 1965 prompted the
newly elected Labour Government to set up a Committee on the Age of
Majority chaired by a Judge of the Probate Divorce and Admiralty Division,
Sir William Latey,[196] with wide terms of reference[197] about the impact of the
private law on young persons.

The majority of the Committee[198] (believing that the historical causes for setting the age of majority at 21 were not relevant to contemporary society and that
young people in 1967 matured earlier than in the past and were ready for the
rights and responsibilities of adult life) concluded[199] that in the areas within
their terms of reference the age of full legal capacity should be lowered to 18;[200]
and that the age of free marriage should be reduced accordingly. The
Committee took a pessimistic view of the influence of the legal rules on family
relationships: 'in this field at least the law is useless as a strengthener of family
ties, and indeed by the friction it causes between the generations may well help
to wear them through.'[201] But the Committee did not agree with those who

---

[195] PRO LCO17/1: Minutes of the First Meeting of the Latey Committee, 27 September 1965. The
Government subsequently denied that pressure from commercial interests had led to the decision to
set up an Inquiry: see *Official Report* (HL) 22 November 1967, vol. 286, col. 1047.

[196] See Biographical Notes.

[197] The Committee's terms of reference were to 'consider whether any changes are desirable in
the law relating to contracts made by persons under 21 and to their power to hold and dispose of
property, and in the law relating to marriage by such persons and to the power to make them wards
of court'. The right to vote, to become a Member of Parliament, to serve on a jury, to hold public
office, as well as criminal law and practice were excluded from the Committee's consideration
(although the Committee did make some comments on these matters: see *Latey Report*, para. 23).

[198] Two members of the Committee (Sir Geoffrey Howe QC and the solicitor John Stebbings)
opposed the majority's recommendations on the reduction of the age for free marriage and wardship:
their persuasively written reasons are hereafter referred to as the *Latey Minority Report*. But the
Committee was unanimous on 44 out of a total of 52 recommendations: *Latey Report*, paras. 518–519.

[199] The Committee received a great deal of evidence, and written submissions preserved in the
Public Record Office are of great interest. PRO LCO17/10 contains a, perhaps revealing, note of the
Chairman's impressions gathered at a visit to Poplar Youth Club: the young people 'are full of basic
practical commonsense. They are better equipped to cope with life than their contemporaries from
more affluent walks of life. There is no cloudy or airy-fairy philosophy about them, which is not to
say that they haven't plenty of idealism but of a practical down to earth kind'. The general approach
of the majority is summarised in the section of the *Latey Report* entitled 'Young People Today',
paras. 58–94.

[200] *Latey Report*, para. 134.

[201] *Latey Report*, para. 106. The Committee was influenced by the experience of newspaper
advice columnists: Mrs. Marjorie Proops of the *Daily Mirror*, for example, concluded from her
experience of advising girls aged between 14 and 20 that to reduce the age would contribute to
reducing the trend towards defiance of authority (PRO LCO17/10, Memorandum of 11 March
1966); whilst the *News of the World's* John Hilton Bureau suggested that parents' views were not
always dispassionate and disinterested: 'Mothers forbid marriages which remove their useful
daughters from home, fathers have their vision clouded by differences of accent or length of hair;
even the wisest and kindest of parents may be, by the very nature of their close personal involvement
with their children, in a poor position to know what their children's deep psychological needs really
are. Sometimes unacknowledged problems in the parents' own marriage entirely distort their judgement': *Latey Report*, para. 152.

thought the requirement of parental consent should be wholly removed:[202] nobody (the Committee claimed) considered that many young people were 'mature' at age 16, and the requirement of parental consent for 16 and 17-year-olds often corresponded with the factual reality in which children were still dependent on their parents materially and psychologically.[203] The Committee did not seem to attach much weight[204] to the fact that the Attitude Survey they commissioned indicated that a substantial majority[205] of young people thought that 21 was the right age for 'free marriage'.

The decision to legislate: the Family Law Reform Act 1969 and its impact

The Government did not immediately express any view about the *Latey Report's* recommendations, but made time available for debates in both Houses of Parliament[206] on the issues to which it gave rise. Although these debates confirmed the widespread feeling that there had been no widespread pressure for change on issues such as the age for free marriage[207] the Government concluded that the *Report* and the publicity and discussion which it had prompted had brought about a consensus that change was desirable.[208] The Family Law Act 1969[209] was therefore introduced as a government Bill. It provided that a person becomes of full age on attaining the age of 18 rather than 21[210] and also

---

[202] The arguments in favour of abolition of any requirement of parental consent are cogently summarised in the Law Commission's Working Paper on Solemnisation of Marriage: PWP No. 35 (1971), para. 35.

[203] These arguments may be difficult to defend on intellectually convincing grounds. The *Latey Minority Report* concluded that parental or court consent to marriage should continue to be necessary until the age of 21, on the basis that 'young people still deserve protection from the consequences of hasty and possibly immature courtships; that society should thus continue to "lean against" young marriage; that the system of requiring parental consent is more discriminating and civilised than any conceivable alternative; and that the system is buttressed rather than embittered by the law': para. 580.

[204] Admitting that the preponderant view (by some 2 to 1) was in favour of the retention of 21 as the age for full legal capacity, the *Latey Report* states that this result 'relates to the whole age group, many of whom would not have been directly concerned with the issues at the time . . .; that had an interested sample been specially interviewed results might have been different; and, perhaps most importantly, that most of those interviewed were not living away from home but with their parents': para. 91(3). Not surprisingly, the *Latey Minority Report* relied on the survey to support the view that there was no substantial demand for change: paras. 523–527, 560(a).

[205] 62% of those aged between 16 and 20; 65% of those aged 21 to 24: *Latey Report*, p. 202.

[206] *Official Report* (HL) 22 November 1967, vol. 286, col. 1047: *Official Report* (HC) 20 November 1967, vol. 754, col. 956.

[207] Except perhaps as a general manifestation of the discontent also evident in the student protests and other events of the late 1960s (and especially 1968): see Lord Henley, *Official Report* (HL) 22 November 1967, vol. 286, col. 1054. Far and away the most youthful speaker in either House—the 22-year-old Sixth Baron Feversham—spoke against acceptance of the *Latey Report's* proposals for change: see *op. cit.* col. 1104.

[208] Lord Gardiner LC, *Official Report* (HL) 22 November 1967, vol. 286, col. 1076.

[209] ss. 1 and 2.

[210] s. 1. The House of Commons disagreed with a House of Lords amendment substituting 20 for 21 as the age of majority. Changes in the age of eligibility to vote and in the law relating to minors' contracts were made subsequently.

reduced the age for 'free marriage' to 18.[211] The Act retained the power of the courts to override the refusal of a parent or guardian to consent to the marriage of 16 or 17-year-olds; but in fact applications for such consent became rare.[212]

Effect of the Family Law Reform Act 1969

It is impossible to assess the effect of the 1969 Act. The *Latey Report* accepted that 'people today are marrying younger';[213] but at almost the same time as the Committee was submitting its Report the trend went into reverse: as already pointed out, since the mid-1960s the mean age for marriage has been rising,[214] and the number of marriages involving a teenager has fallen.[215] It would be difficult to find a clearer illustration of the dangers of assuming that demographic trends are likely to continue unaltered.

MARRIAGE: THE UNION OF A MAN AND A WOMAN

In 1967, a prominent Queen's Counsel and distinguished scholar wrote:

'The requirement, if one may so state it, that the two persons should be two persons of different sexes would appear to be axiomatic. If two persons of the same sex contrive to go through a ceremony of marriage, the ceremony is not matrimonial at all . . .'[216]

It is certainly true that judicial statements about marriage (not least the oft repeated description[217] by Lord Penzance in the 1866 English divorce case of

---

[211] The Act also provided that the courts' inherent jurisdiction over minors should cease to be exercisable in respect of persons aged 18 or more.

[212] In the first six months of 1983 there were only 30 applications to magistrates' courts. The majority appear to have been withdrawn, and only three were refused: *Home Office Statistical Bulletin 1/84*, Table 2. In the years before 1969, there were some 600 applications a year: see above.

[213] *The Latey Minority Report*, accepting the undoubted fact that teenage marriages had recently become more popular, summarised the majority position as being 'It's happening anyway . . . so why not let it rip?'. The Minority thought that the 'growing shortage of girls in each age cohort' was a factor explaining the increase: if 'they are to avoid being left "on the shelf", the young men are obliged to hunt younger partners': para. 562.

[214] In 1967 the median age of marriage for a spinster was 21.18; by 1998 it had risen to 26.97: *OPCS Historical Statistics*, Table 3.4; *Marriage, divorce and adoption statistics 1998* (National Statistics, Series FM2 no. 26) Table 3.15.

[215] In 1965 151,452 brides—nearly 41% of the total—were under 21: *Latey Report*, para. 139, and Appendix 8, p. 197. In 1998 the comparable figures were 15,065 and 5.6%: see *Marriage, divorce and adoption statistics 1998* (National Statistics, Series FM2 no. 26) Table 3.19.

[216] J Jackson, *The Formation and Annulment of Marriage* (2nd ed., 1969) p. 131. The author goes on to say that such a union is 'certainly not a void marriage': see further below.

[217] Although often treated as an attempt to define marriage, the context makes it clear that Lord Penzance was only addressing the issue before him: could the English divorce court properly entertain a divorce petition in respect of a marriage which was potentially (albeit not actually) polygamous? The answer to that question was that 'the matrimonial law of this country is adapted to the Christian marriage, and is wholly inapplicable to polygamy' with the result that the parties to such a relationship were 'not entitled to the remedies, the adjudication, or the relief of the matrimonial law of England'. The court did not decide that the 'marriage' had no legal consequences as between the parties, and the courts have subsequently accorded a substantial measure of recognition to such

Hyde v. Hyde[218] of marriage as 'the voluntary union for life of one man to one woman to the exclusion of all others') have been couched in terms of a relationship between a man and a woman. It is also true that the words of the Book of Common Prayer seem from beginning[219] to end to contemplate only such a relationship. The various statutory formulae used in civil weddings and in marriages in registered buildings are in this respect no different.[220] It is true that some historians have suggested the Church had in the past developed rituals recognising relationships between people of the same sex, and even that such unions 'most likely signified a marriage in the eyes of most ordinary Christians'.[221] But there is no evidence that in this country[222] in the twentieth century either Church or State recognised such relationships as constituting 'marriage'.[223] Sexual relationships between persons of the same sex were, until 1967, severely penalised by the criminal law;[224] and there is no reported case in which anyone in this country tried to persuade a court that a relationship between persons of the same sex was capable of constituting a 'marriage'.[225]

relationships provided that the parties have the legal capacity by their personal law—the law of the domicile—to contract such a marriage: see Cheshire and North's *Private International Law* (13th ed., 1999, by P North and JJ Fawcett) pp. 742–764.

[218] (1866) LR 1 P&M 130, 133.

[219] 'We are gathered together . . . to join together *this Man and this Woman* in Holy Matrimony.'

[220] For the most recent example of gender specific language in this context the Marriage Ceremony (Prescribed Words) Act 1996 under which the parties take one another as 'husband' and 'wife'. See also *Fitzpatrick v. Sterling Housing Association* [2001] 1 AC 27, HL.

[221] J Boswell, *The Marriage of Likeness* (1995), p. 191.

[222] The situation is different in parts of the Commonwealth: see *Quilter v. Attorney-General* [1998] 1 NZLR 523 where however the Court unanimously rejected a claim that the New Zealand marriage legislation accommodated marriages between persons of the same sex, and also held (with one dissentient) that the enactment of the New Zealand Bill of Rights Act 1990 had not affected the matter. In the United States the question whether restricting marriage to persons of different sexes is compatible with constitutional guarantees became much litigated in the closing years of the century: see eg JA Barron, 'The Constitutionalization of American Family Law' in SN Katz, J Eekelaar and M Maclean, *Cross Currents* (2000) Chap. 12. For a discussion of policy, see R Wintermute and M Andenas, *Legal Recognition of Same Sex Relationships* (2001).

[223] The classical definition of marriage emphasised that marriage was 'a contract according to the law of nature, antecedent to civil institution, . . . which may take place to all intents and purposes, wherever two persons of different sexes [*sic*] engage, by mutual contracts to live together . . .': *Lindo v. Belisario* (1795) 1 Hag Con 216, 230–231, *per* Sir William Stowell. In 1947 the House of Lords repudiated the view (sometimes advanced as a rationalisation of the doctrine that there can be no marriage between persons of the same sex) that the primary purpose of marriage was the procreation of children (see *Baxter v. Baxter* [1948] AC 274); but this did not prompt claims that marriage had thereby become open to persons of the same sex. On the relevance of the traditional status view of marriage at the end of the twentieth century, see the dicta of Thorpe LJ in *Bellinger v. Bellinger (Attorney-General Intervening)* [2002] Fam 150.

[224] Sodomy had long been an offence, and the Criminal Law Amendment Act 1885 penalised acts of 'gross indecency' between men (but not between women). The Sexual Offences Act 1967 began the process of decriminalising homosexual acts; and the Sexual Offences Amendment Act 2000 finally removed criminal sanctions in most circumstances.

[225] Contrast claims that a same-sex couple can qualify to make claims under legislation conferring rights on persons 'living together as husband and wife': see *Fitzpatrick v. Sterling Housing Association* [2001] 1 AC 27, HL (where the House of Lords eventually rejected a man's claim to be entitled to succeed as a matter of legal right to his deceased male partner's statutory tenancy under legislation conferring such a right on a person who had lived with the tenant 'as his or her wife or husband').

Whether or not same sex unions were recognised in earlier times seems to be irrelevant to the modern law; and in the circumstances, it might (to cite the words of Mr. Joseph Jackson again) be thought otiose to multiply authority for the simple proposition stated at the outset. However, increases in medical knowledge, and in particular, recognition of the phenomenon of transsexualism (a condition in which people apparently belonging to one sex feel that they belong to the other) and the use of gender reassignment therapy (hormone treatment and surgery intended to bring the physical characteristics into harmony with the patient's psychological nature) in such cases sometimes made the matter more complex.

The legal significance of transsexualism for the law of marriage was first considered by the English courts in 1969:

In *Corbett v. Corbett*[226] April Ashley had undergone what was then described as a sex change operation, had lived as a woman, and worked successfully as a female model. She had also been recognised as a woman for national insurance and passport purposes. But the trial judge held that for the purpose of capacity to marry the question depended on April Ashley's biological sex: marriage was about sex, not gender. And a person born with male genitalia and a male chromosomal structure remained a 'man' for the purpose of the marriage laws, notwithstanding the fact that the patient had, after the reassignment therapy, lived and been accepted as a woman, possessed the external attributes of a woman and in most ways had become philosophically, psychologically and socially a woman.

At the time of the *Corbett* decision, consideration was being given[227] to the codification of the largely case law based law of nullity, and in 1971 the Nullity of Marriage Act[228] declared that a marriage taking place after the commencement of the Act should be void on certain specified grounds only. A clause was inserted that one of those grounds should be that 'the parties are not respectively male and female'. That express provision makes it clear beyond any doubt—as

---

[226] [1971] P 83. The practical importance of the case was whether in cases of purported marriage between persons of the same sex the court should grant a decree of nullity (in which case the parties would be entitled to seek the exercise of the court's discretion to make financial provision and property adjustment orders: see Chapter 10 below) or whether the appropriate procedure was simply to make a declaration that the parties were not husband and wife, in which case no such application could be made. The fact that the court has jurisdiction to hear a financial application does not mean that the court will in the exercise of its discretion feel it appropriate to make such an order: see *S-T (formerly J) v. J* [1998] Fam 103, CA.

[227] By the Law Commission: see *Report on Nullity of Marriage* (1970, Law Com. No. 33) paras. 30–32. The Commission was not able to give any extended consideration to the impact of the *Corbett* case; but considered that the appropriate relief in such cases would be a declaration that the purported marriage was not valid rather than a decree of nullity (thereby disqualifying the parties from seeking financial orders). But Parliament did not accept this view: see below.

[228] s. 1(c); subsequently consolidated in Matrimonial Causes Act 1973, s. 11(c).

the courts have recognised—that English law will not recognise a same sex relationship as a marriage.[229]

But what of the situation where there is some uncertainty or ambivalence about whether one or both parties is 'male' or 'female'? The courts came under pressure over the years to modify the *Corbett* doctrine that a person's sex is fixed for all time at birth,[230] and that the only relevant criteria are biological; but these were uniformly unsuccessful.[231]

It has been officially estimated that there are between 1,300 and 2,000 male to female and 250 female to male transsexual people in the United Kingdom; and the hardship which the law causes for them is considerable.[232] At the start of the millennium an official Working Party[233] recommended some change in the law, but no Government action followed.[234] Further attempts will no doubt be made

---

[229] In *Corbett v. Corbett* [1971] P 86, 106 itself the judge had made clear his view that marriage 'is and always has been recognised as the union of man and woman' and that whilst 'marriage has many characteristics other than the capacity for natural heterosexual intercourse' the characteristic which distinguishes marriage 'from all other relationships can only be met by two persons of opposite sex'. A Lord Justice of Appeal (Ward LJ) has asserted that 'single sex unions remain proscribed as fundamentally abhorrent to' the classical understanding of marriage as the voluntary union for life of one man and one woman, to the exclusion of all others: *S-T (formerly J) v. J* [1998] Fam 103, 141; and see also *per* Potter LJ at p. 146. The House of Lords has accepted that the words 'wife' and 'husband' are gender specific: *Fitzpatrick v. Sterling Housing Association Ltd.* [2001] 1 AC 27. It seems clear from the Parliamentary Debates on the relevant provision of the Nullity of Marriage Act 1971 that the Promoters did not intend to give even the recognition implicit in granting a decree of nullity to relationships between persons who were, and knew themselves to be, unequivocally of the same sex: see *Official Report* (HC) 2 April 1971, vol. 814, col. 1838 (Mr. Leo Abse); and *Official Report* (HL) 22 April 1971, vol. 317, col. 816–7 (Lord Chancellor Hailsham). But cf *Bellinger v. Bellinger* [2002] Fam 150, 186–187, *per* Thorpe LJ.

[230] In contrast, it has been held that where a person is affected by partial androgen insensitivity (resulting in what is sometimes called 'physical inter-sex') the entry in the Birth Register is not conclusive and the court will assess the evidence to classify the person concerned at the relevant time (eg the date of a wedding): *W v. W (Physical Inter-sex)* [2001] Fam 111.

[231] The development of the law is reviewed in *Bellinger v. Bellinger* [2002] Fam 150. One of the three Lords Justice of Appeal (Thorpe LJ) delivered a powerful dissenting judgment urging that medical and social developments since the *Corbett* case had destroyed the view of the law to which it gave effect. Arguments that English law was inconsistent with the provisions of the European Convention on Human Rights also failed (as they had previously done before the European Court on Human Rights, the court accepting that the right to marry protected by the Convention is a right to contract a traditional marriage between persons of opposite biological sex: *X, Y and Z v. UK* [1997] 2 FLR 892, ECHR, *Horsham v. The United Kingdom* (1998) 27 EHRR 163, ECHR). However, the European Court's jurisprudence is continuously developing: in *Goodwin v. United Kingdom* [2002] 2 FLR 487 the Court held that English law was incompatible with Articles 8 and 12 of the Convention. And the House of Lords has given leave to appeal in the *Bellinger* case.

[232] It can be argued that English law prevents transsexuals from forming any legally recognised marital relationship: they are treated as men for the purpose of determining whether a union with a man can constitute a valid marriage; and the treatment which they have undergone may make it legally impossible for them to contract a marriage with a woman, because they will be unable to consummate such a marriage: see *Goodwin v. United Kingdom* [2002] 2 FLR 487.

[233] *Report of the Interdepartmental Working Group on Transsexual People* (Home Office, April 2000).

[234] See the critical assessments in both majority and minority judgments in *Bellinger v. Bellinger* [2002] Fam 150.

to remedy injustice to transsexuals; but there seemed no reason to suppose that English law would abandon its insistence that marriage[235] involved a relationship between one party who can be classified as a 'man' and another party who can be classified as a 'woman'. In that respect the underlying principle of the law remains the same at the close of the twentieth century as it was at the beginning.

MARRIAGE MONOGAMOUS: THE UNION OF ONE MAN AND ONE WOMAN

English law has consistently held to the principle that marriage is monogamous. The Nullity of Marriage Act 1971,[236] providing that a 'marriage' is void if either party was at the time lawfully married, gives effect to this fundamental principle. For example:

In *Whiston v. Whiston*[237] Mr Whiston married a woman from the Phillipines. Sixteen years later the couple (who had had two children) separated, and divorce proceedings were started. The fact that the 'marriage' was bigamous came to light and the court granted a decree of nullity.

So insistent was the law that at the beginning of the twentieth century it asserted its support of monogamy by refusing to allow a party to a marriage which was even *potentially* polygamous[238] any redress in the English divorce court:

In *Hyde v. Hyde*[239] an English Mormon married a Mormon woman in Utah. After three years together the man renounced his beliefs and returned to England where he became the Minister of a nonconformist chapel. Mrs Hyde (by whom he had had children) married another man by Mormon rites in Utah and Mr Hyde sued her for divorce. The court refused to adjudicate: the matrimonial laws of England (said Lord Penzance)[240] are adapted to Christian marriage and are inapplicable to polygamy. Accordingly the parties to a marriage actually or potentially polygamous were 'not entitled to the remedies, the adjudication, or the relief of the matrimonial law of England'.

But large scale immigration into this country from countries where Islam or other systems permitting polygamy governed marriage meant that such a rule

---

[235] In 2002 the House of Lords gave a Second Reading to a Civil Partnerships Bill, intended to allow unmarried partners (whether of the same sex or not) to register their relationship and thereby attach certain legal consequences to it. But such legislation in fact recognises that a same-sex relationship is not a marriage.

[236] s. 1 (b).

[237] [1995] Fam 198, CA. In that case the substantial question was whether the court would exercise its powers to make financial orders in favour of Mrs Whiston (who had in fact known that her prior marriage was still in existence and had lied about this to Mr Whiston and others). It declined to do so on the basis that no one is allowed to benefit by his or her own wrongful action (in that case, knowingly contracting a bigamous marriage).

[238] By the law of the place where it was celebrated.

[239] (1866) LR 1 P&M 130, 133.   [240] (1866) LR 1 P&M 130, 138.

caused severe hardship, and involved considerable cost to the taxpayer (since a wife left destitute could not claim maintenance from her husband, and would often become correspondingly dependent on welfare benefits). Over the years, statute[241] and case law[242] transformed the situation. It is true that any valid[243] wedding in this country creates a monogamous marriage, wherever the parties are domiciled, but the law will now generally recognise a polygamous marriage contracted overseas and make orders in respect of such marriages. The subject is a complex one but it can fairly be said that the 'balance of definition has tipped from defining those instances where, exceptionally, such a marriage will be recognised to defining those few instances where it may not'.[244]

Most cases where bigamy[245] is an issue lack any of the exotic associations traditionally associated with polygamy. In the days before divorce became readily available (and, perhaps, women were less ready to cohabit outside marriage) men might take a chance and not disclose their marital history; and some such cases ended with the man being imprisoned for the criminal offence of bigamy.[246] Difficulties could arise because it was known that a party to a marriage had been previously married, but there was no evidence as to whether the wife or husband was alive at the date of the later ceremony. The law applied a presumption of death if there was no evidence that throughout a continuous period of seven years he was alive;[247] but if this presumption turned out to be incorrect any later marriage would be void. In 1937 statute created a procedure whereby the court could, if satisfied that there were reasonable grounds to presume death, grant a decree of presumption of death and dissolution of marriage. Such a decree would terminate the marriage even if the other party were still alive, and made it possible for the applicant to remarry safe from any fear about the validity of the remarriage.

[241] Notably the Matrimonial Proceedings (Polygamous Marriages) Act 1972 (now Matrimonial Causes Act 1973, s. 47).
[242] Notably the *Sinha Peerage Case* (1939) [1946] 1 All ER 348 and *Baindail v. Baindail* [1946] P 122 in both of which the English courts recognised the validity of marriages polygamous by the law of the place of celebration.
[243] This qualification is necessary because if a ceremony in this country does not purport to be a marriage under the Marriage Acts and is 'nothing like a marriage' the court will not treat it as even a void marriage: see *A-M v. A-M* (*Divorce: Jurisdiction: Validity of Marriage*) [2001] 2 FLR 6 (ceremony in couple's London flat by Islamic Mufti. The ceremony involved the exchange of rings and the taking of vows. Friends attended and the woman wore a wedding dress, hat and veil. A printed document entitled 'Certificate of Marriage' was signed by both parties, expressly as 'bridegroom' and 'bride'. *Held:* the court could not grant a decree of nullity).
[244] Cheshire and North's *Private International Law* (13th ed., 1999, by P North and JJ Fawcett) p. 755 (where the subject is reviewed, lucidly and in detail).
[245] See J Jackson, *The Formation and Annulment of Marriage* (2nd ed., 1969) pp. 144–156.
[246] Offences against the Person Act 1861, s. 57. The offence is punishable by imprisonment for up to seven years. There are statutory defences, notably that the accused's spouse had been continuously absent for seven years or more and the accused did not know that he or she was living within that time.
[247] See *Chard v. Chard* [1956] P 259.

Understanding the marriage contract[248]

Marriage was (and is) a consensual relationship, as we have seen; and if it can be shown that either party was mentally incapable, at the time of the wedding, of understanding the nature of the contract and of the duties and responsibilities which it creates there can, whatever the magnificence of the outward show, be no marriage. At the beginning of the century this was a matter of some practical importance:

In *Cannon v. Smalley (otherwise Cannon)*[249] the wife suffered from melancholia (or depression). Within days of the wedding she tried to commit suicide, and she became violent, suffered delusions, and was admitted to an asylum. The prospect of recovery was small. But the court held that the husband had failed to establish that, at the time of the wedding, she was incapable of understanding the nature of marriage and its incidents. Accordingly, the husband remained for the rest of his natural life married to a woman confined, without any prospect of cure, in a lunatic asylum.

It was exceedingly difficult to establish that a person, however troubled,[250] lacked sufficient understanding. The principle to be applied was that:

'the contract of marriage is a very simple one which it does not require a high degree of intelligence to comprehend. It is an engagement between a man and woman to live together, and love one another as husband and wife, to the exclusion of all others. This is expanded in the promises of the marriage ceremony by words having reference to the natural relations which spring from that engagement. . . . [A] mere comprehension of the words of the promises exchanged is not sufficient. The mind of one of the parties may be capable of understanding the language used, but may yet be affected by such delusions, or other symptoms of insanity, as may satisfy the tribunal that there was not a real appreciation of the engagement apparently entered into . . .'[251]

---

[248] It is sometimes alleged that a spouse's apparent consent to marriage was not a real consent by reason of (for example) mistake or duress.

[249] (1885) 10 PD 96.

[250] However, a nullity petition might succeed if the person concerned was so affected by morbid delusions as not to know and appreciate what was taking place: see *Hunter v. Edney otherwise Hunter* (1881) 10 PD 93 (where the wife was labouring under insane delusions that she was a wicked woman guilty of crimes such as to make her unfit to marry an honest man. On the morning after the wedding she asked her husband to cut her throat).

[251] *Durham v. Durham* (1885) 10 PD 80, where the Earl of Durham unsuccessfully petitioned for the annulment of his 1882 marriage to the granddaughter of the Archbishop of Armagh. The wife was said to be a 'person of low intellectual powers' who had nevertheless been 'capable of receiving the ordinary education of young ladies of her class. She acquired some accomplishments, and took part in private theatricals'. The Archbishop of York also gave evidence that, although she was a shy girl, there was nothing prior to the marriage which marked her manner out from that of others. Sir James Hannen P concluded that her bashful muteness did not constitute imbecility or insanity and that there was no evidence of the onset prior to the marriage of the insanity which subsequently struck her down.

The difficulty of making out a case of lack of mental capacity is exemplified by a case decided midway through the twentieth century:

In *Park v. Park*[252] a lonely 79-year-old widower went through a ceremony of marriage with the cashier at his club. Immediately after the wedding he made a Will in which he left his wife only a comparatively small part of his estate. She subsequently claimed that he lacked the necessary mental capacity to make the Will, and the evidence showed that the arterio-sclerosis from which he suffered affected his mental faculties—it was claimed that he would, for example, walk about his flat with his trousers down to his ankles, start to go out when dressed only in his underclothes, and sit down to breakfast with shaving lather on his face. A jury agreed that he had not been 'of sufficiently sound mind memory and understanding' to make that will; and the wife no doubt expected to receive a substantial sum on his intestacy. But Mr Park's relatives then claimed that if he was not sane enough to make a Will he equally lacked capacity to marry, and that accordingly they were entitled under an earlier Will. The Court of Appeal—applying the 'marriage is in essence simple' doctrine[253]—upheld the trial judge's finding in favour of the validity of the marriage.

The will overborne

If mental incapacity attributable to 'natural weakness of the intellect'[254] sufficed to found a nullity decree, should the result be different if the petitioner's 'consent' had been extracted by force or fear—the classic case being that of the so-called shot-gun marriage where if there had not been a wedding there would have been a funeral?[255] The courts held there was no difference in principle between the two cases: if either party was 'actually in a state of mental incompetence to resist pressure improperly brought to bear' there was no consent, and the courts would annul the marriage. For example:

In *Scott v. Sebright*[256] a 22-year-old heiress fell into the clutches of a man who (amongst a 'long series of misdeeds perpetrated against a defenceless girl')[257] induced her to accept Bills of Exchange to the value (in year 2000 values) of some £50,000. The holders of the Bills wrote (as she put it) 'such rude letters' to her and issued writs to enforce their rights. The man told her that she would be made bankrupt if she did not marry him, and she, reduced to a state of 'bodily and mental prostration' and also no doubt influenced by his threat to shoot her if she declined, went through a marriage ceremony in the South Audley Street register office. The marriage was never consummated, and the couple separated immediately after the ceremony. The court, accepting her plea that she had been induced to go through with the ceremony not of her own free will but through fear and terror of the respondent, granted her a decree of nullity.

---

[252] [1954] P 112.   [253] *Durham v. Durham* (1885) 10 PD 81.
[254] *Scott v. Sebright* (1886) 12 PD 21, 24, *per* Butt J.   [255] *Lee v. Lee* 3 SW 2d 672 (1928).
[256] (1886) 12 PD 21.   [257] *Per* Butt J at p. 28.

But (as the judge remarked in *Scott v. Sebright*) public policy required that marriages should not be lightly set aside;[258] and it was difficult to apply the general principle to the facts of particular cases.[259] There were few petitions (although at the height of the Cold War the courts did sometimes annul on this ground marriages contracted to facilitate emigration from totalitatian countries[260] and in recent years the courts have been readier than in the past to accept that young women from ethnic minority communities may be totally dominated by their parents so as to make an apparent consent to a forced marriage ineffective).[261] One thing was clear: misrepresentation fraud or deceit was not a basis on which a marriage could be avoided.

The application of this principle caused hardship:

In June 1896 a young woman pressed the petitioner (a groom to whom she had been engaged for a year or so) to fix a date for their marriage. Immediately after the wedding on 29 September the petitioner began to suspect that the woman he had married was pregnant. The couple separated and a child was born on 17 October. Several witnesses stated that they had no reason to suspect that she was pregnant at the time of the marriage, and the President accepted that the groom did not know of her condition and that he had no grounds for making any inquiry as to her character. But the fact that she was pregnant by someone else, and that she had deceived the husband about her condition, were not grounds on which the marriage could be annulled, and the couple remained bound to one another until death terminated the marriage.[262]

Physical capacity

The Church regarded it as implicit in the marriage contract that both parties should have the physical capacity to consummate the marriage and the ecclesiastical courts would annul a marriage on the ground that either party was, at the

[258] A similarly severe policy was adopted in cases in which it was claimed that the petitioner's mistake was sufficient to avoid the marriage: the courts reluctantly allowed such pleas in cases in which the petitioner was under a misapprehension about the nature of the ceremony. See for example, *Hall v. Hall* (1908) 24 TLR 756 where the court accepted a woman's evidence that she believed that marriages could only be celebrated in church and that her wedding in Kensington Register Office was merely to register her name; and *Mehta v. Mehta* [1945] 2 All ER 690 where the wife believed that a ceremony (conducted in Hindi) was solely to mark her conversion to Hinduism; and see generally J Jackson, *The Formation and Annulment of Marriage* (2nd ed., 1969) pp. 290–298. The courts however refused to accept pleas that mistake as to the legal consequences under Soviet law of having married—for example, the fact that they would not be allowed to live together—would suffice as grounds upon which marriages contracted in the Soviet Union during or immediately after World War II could be annulled: see *Way v. Way* [1950] P 71. These cases had considerable diplomatic repercussions.
[259] *Per* Butt J at p. 24.
[260] See eg *H v. H* [1954] P 258; *Szechter v. Szechter* [1971] P 286; and see generally J Jackson, *The Formation and Annulment of Marriage* (2nd ed., 1969) pp. 282–290. The reasoning in these cases is somewhat questionable: far from their will being overborne the parties wanted to marry precisely to enjoy the legal consequences of that status.
[261] *Hirani v. Hirani* (1982) 4 FLR 232.   [262] *Moss v. Moss* [1897] P 263.

date of the marriage, incapable of consummating it.[263] The provisions in the Matrimonial Causes Act 1857 directing the Divorce Court to 'proceed and act and give relief on principles and rules which . . . shall be as nearly as may be conformable to the principles on which the Ecclesiastical Courts have heretofore acted and given relief'[264] meant that the courts continued[265] to apply doctrines about the sexual implications of marriage developed in the nineteenth century and earlier.

The principle was that (at least in the case of young persons) marriage presupposed 'the power, present or to come, of sexual intercourse'; for 'without that power neither of two principal ends of matrimony can be attained, namely, a lawful indulgence of the passions to prevent licentiousness, and the procreation of children, according to the evident design of Divine Providence'. But applying this general principle in contested cases (and even, given the court's inquisitorial role,[266] in undefended cases) could be much more difficult. What, for example, does the term 'sexual intercourse' actually mean? Dr Lushington (the most prominent ecclesiastical lawyer of his time) provided a definition: sexual intercourse was:

'ordinary and complete intercourse . . . not partial and imperfect intercourse: yet, I cannot go the length of saying that every degree of imperfection would deprive it of its essential character. There must be degrees difficult to deal with; but if so imperfect as scarcely to be natural, I should not hesitate to say that, legally speaking, it is no intercourse at all. I can never think that the true interest of society would be advanced by retaining within the marriage bonds parties driven to such disgusting practices. Certainly it would not tend to the prevention of adulterous intercourse, one of the greatest evils to be avoided.'[267]

It came to be accepted that what was required was the ability for the man to have an erection and for the female organ to be apt to be penetrated for a reasonable length of time.[268] The fact that the wife had no uterus, or that for any other reason there was no possibility that children would be born was irrelevant. But even if the criteria to be applied were clear, the judges still had to make the 'most disgusting and painful' enquiries often causing great distress to the people concerned. For example:

---

[263] Note 10 above.   [264] Matrimonial Causes Act 1857, ss. 2, 22.

[265] But the numbers were small. The number of decrees granted on the ground of physical incapacity only rose to 30 in 1920. But in each of the years 1934 to 1938 (ie immediately before divorce became more readily available in consequence of the coming into force of the Matrimonial Causes Act 1937) there were more than a hundred incapacity decrees: see *Report of the Royal Commission on Marriage and Divorce*, 1956, Cmd. 9678, Appendix II, Table 2.

[266] See Chapter 5, below.

[267] *D-e v. A-g (falsely calling herself D-e)* (1845) 1 Rob Ecc 279, 281, *per* Dr. Lushington. A full account of the case law is given by J Jackson, *The Formation and Annulment of Marriage* (2nd ed., 1969) Chapter 7.

[268] There was a difference of opinion about whether the man's ability to ejaculate was an essential component of what was called *vera copula*: see J Jackson, *The Formation and Annulment of Marriage* (2nd ed., 1969).

In *D-e v. A-g (falsely calling herself D-e)*[269] a man complained that 'the parts of generation and sexual or seminal organs of the said Maria A. otherwise D. were and are not such or in the same state as are the same parts and organs in women capable of having connexion with or of being carnally known by a man, but were and are naturally in a different state, and that by reason of such the natural malconformation thereof, and her other natural bodily defects, she the said Maria A. otherwise D. was and is incapable of having connexion with or of being carnally known by man'. In fact Maria had no uterus; but the fact that she was therefore incapable of having children did not mean that she was incapable of intercourse.[270]

Developments over the years in gynaecological knowledge and techniques meant that what might at one time have been regarded as an incurable impediment could be remedied; but even in the second half of the twentieth century this did not always make things easier for a couple convinced of their incompatibility:

In 1962, after 16 years of frequent but unsuccessful attempts at intercourse, a husband petitioned for the annulment of his marriage on the ground of the wife's incapacity. Six days before the hearing of the petition she underwent surgery; and the Court of Appeal held[271] that the case should have been adjourned for further evidence to be tendered about the effects of the operation. To some this seemed reminiscent of the old ecclesiastical courts' practice of requiring the parties to make further attempts before the court would reach a decision.

It was, of course, for the petitioner to prove the case.[272] At one time the issues were left to the judgment of a 'jury of matrons', but by the twentieth century the parties were required to submit to medical examination; and the doctors' report would state whether or not the parties were physically capable and if not whether the incapacity was incurable. But the courts also depended on the evidence of the parties: statute[273] required the petitioner to file an affidavit in support of the petition and to attend to be examined or cross examined.[274] This was often a profoundly distressing experience: one leading divorce barrister[275] testified that the cases were:

---

[269] (1845) 1 Rob Ecc 279.
[270] Further evidence about the wife's condition was obtained, and a decree granted.
[271] *S v. S* [1963] P 162, CA.
[272] See eg the allegations in *Brown v. Brown* (1828) 1 Hagg. Ecc. 523, 524. However, incapacity might be presumed if the parties had cohabited for three years or more and had not succeeded in having intercourse during that time; but where there was specific evidence the courts would not insist on the parties waiting for this period: *Briggs v. Morgan* (1820) 3 Phil Ecc 325.
[273] Matrimonial Causes Act 1857, s. 41.   [274] Matrimonial Causes Act 1857, s. 43.
[275] Sir Ellis William Hume-Williams KC, giving evidence to the *Select Committee on the Matrimonial Causes (Regulation of Reports) Bill* (1923) HC 118, BPP 1923, vii, q. 674.

'most revolting in their details. The abortive attempts of sexual intercourse are horrible in their details and are most distressing to hear, because the people who give evidence are greatly distressed at having to give evidence of these horrible things, which go to the most secret events of their lives.'[276]

It is true that the ecclesiastical courts had been prepared to accept that incapacity was not confined to cases of physical malformation;[277] and the courts did grant annulments on the basis that impotence could often have a psychological (rather than a physiological) cause.[278] In one late Victorian case,[279] for example, the wife's account was that:

'on the afternoon of the marriage apartments were engaged at a certain hotel, and then at respondent's desire, who stated that he wished to see the town, we walked about for nearly three hours, and returned to the hotel about eight pm. During the remainder of the evening the respondent became and continued to be very dull and abstracted and silent, which he had not been previously, or at any former period of my acquaintance with him. . . . [H]e shewed and expressed reluctance to retire to our bedroom, which adjoined, and consequently we were very late in going to bed, and when at length he followed me into the bedroom, and I was in bed, he dawdled for a long time about the room before he came into bed. When we were in bed together the respondent caressed me, but with a total absence of that warmth of manner which he had theretofore shewn towards me, and then expressed his desire that we should not have any sexual intercourse for three months or so, and alleged as his reason, that it would be better to defer it, because in case we should have any family at an early period, it might be said that there had been intimacy between us before our marriage, or, to that effect; but the respondent afterwards, during that night, endeavoured to have sexual intercourse with me, but entirely failed in so doing, owing, as I believe, to his total want of power for that purpose. . . . [Subsequently] we went to the respondent's house in the country, where he on several occasions renewed his attempts but failed, and on such failures would shed tears and become silent and depressed.'

It remained the law that there not only had to be a genuine incapacity (as distinct from mere disinclination) but also that this should have existed at the date of the marriage. To hold otherwise would be in effect to allow the legal dissolution of a valid marriage on the ground of events occurring after the marriage; and the application of this principle sometimes caused difficulties. What, for

---

[276] Lord Birkenhead LC justified the insistence on proof because the charge against the respondent 'though physical and not moral, is nevertheless a grave and wounding imputation that the respondent is lacking . . . in the power of reproducing his species, a power which is commonly and rightly considered to be the most characteristic quality of manhood': *C v. C* [1921] P 339, 400.

[277] 'A person need not be a profound psychologist to know how rarely the structure of the body is deficient for the purposes of our nature. Malformation is not common in our sex, and perhaps is still more uncommon in the other, and where it does exist, and is known to the parties, it naturally deters them from contracting marriage': *Briggs v. Morgan* (1820) 3 Phil Ecc 325, 327, *per* Sir William Stowell.

[278] In *Wise v. Wise* [1944] P 56, 57, Hodson J (perhaps the judge most experienced in post World War I matrimonial practice) stated that the number of cases in which there was no evidence of physical incapacity 'far outnumbers' those where there is such evidence.

[279] *F (falsely called D) v. F* (1865) 4 Sw&Tr 86, 87.

example, should the courts do when faced with a case like *Dickinson v. Dickinson*:[280]

The wife told her husband that she would never live with him 'as man and wife' because she did not want to have children and thought sexual intercourse to be 'unnecessary, vulgar, rude and disgusting'. She claimed that she had hinted as plainly as possible what her intentions were when they first became engaged and had no reason to suppose he had not understood her meaning, and she repudiated the notion that she was to blame for his seeking consolation in the heavy drinking of intoxicants or for the nervous breakdown which he claimed to have suffered.

One solution would have been to infer incapacity from the fact that intercourse simply did not occur;[281] and by the beginning of the twentieth century the courts would often be prepared to find that the husband was and always had been incapable of consummating his marriage and grant the decree even when there was little evidence beyond a straightforward refusal. In 1913 the President of the Probate Divorce and Admiralty Division sought to bring the law into conformity with modern ideas by recognising that a simple refusal to consummate the marriage (not a 'mere temporary unwillingness due to a passing phase, or the result of coyness, a feeling of delicacy, affected or real, or a nervous ignorance which might be got rid of or cured by patient forbearance, care and kindness; but a wilful, determined, and steadfast refusal to perform the obligations and to carry out the duties which the matrimonial contract involves') was of itself a sufficient basis on which the court could justify granting a decree of nullity.[282] This (so it was argued) would be consistent with the true basis of annulment: in the same way that the contract of marriage implied the ability to consummate it so it also implied the willingness to consummate it; and that to deny such a remedy would be to frustrate the fundamental purposes of marriage.[283]

But this attempt at judicial rationalisation did not survive scrutiny in the Court of Appeal; and in 1915 that court reasserted the traditional doctrine that nullity 'in its very nature, presupposes a cause existing at the date of the marriage' (whereas wilful and persistent refusal to consummate necessarily arose after the marriage). For the courts to accept wilful refusal as a ground of relief would come perilously close to allowing divorce for sexual incompatibility, and this could not be done by judicial law-making and legal fiction.[284] The furthest the courts were prepared to go was to hold that 'invincible repugnance' to sexual intercourse could constitute incapacity, and to accept that the wife who had

---

[280] [1913] P 198.

[281] *S v. A (otherwise S)* (1878) 3 PD 72: 'Recent cases . . . establish . . . that where a woman is shewn not to have had intercourse with her husband after a reasonable time for consummation of the marriage, if it appears that she has abstained from intercourse, and resisted her husband's attempts, the Court will draw the inference that that refusal on her part arises from incapacity'.

[282] *Dickinson v. Dickinson* [1913] P 198, 204, *per* Sir Samuel Evans P.   [283] *Ibid.*

[284] *Napier v. Napier* [1915] P 184, 192–193 CA; cf. *Dickinson v. Dickinson* [1913] P 198, *per* Sir Samuel Evans P.

a hysterical aversion to intercourse was as incapable of consummation as one suffering from some physical malformation. But the aversion had to be total (unlike the case where the evidence showed that a man could consummate a relationship if he were 'encouraged and had plenty of time and was not nervous, and if a little champagne were given him beforehand').[285] In particular, a rational decision not to have intercourse did not ground the making of a decree:[286]

In 1971 the Court of Appeal refused an annulment to a 17-year-old Sikh girl who had reluctantly gone through a marriage ceremony arranged by her parents with a man she had not previously met. She never 'submitted to the physical embraces of the husband. . . . Having taken the view . . . that she did not want to be married to him, it is understandable that she did not want to have sexual intercourse with him; but that . . . seems to be a very long way from an invincible repugnance'.[287]

The distinction between incapacity and lack of inclination may have been logical; but the outcome appeared arbitrary and harsh. As Sir Samuel Evans put it in *Dickinson v. Dickinson*:[288] to deny relief to a spouse whose partner totally refused to consummate the marriage meant that they remained 'bound by the matrimonial tie, until one of them committed the matrimonial offences which are necessary to enable the Court to dissolve it, and the other invokes the aid of the Court for that purpose'. No doubt in some cases the aggrieved spouse would commit adultery and thus provide the ground for divorce, but it did not of course follow that the 'innocent' spouse would petition.

TWENTIETH CENTURY STATUTORY CHANGES

The theory of nullity is that the law having defined the conditions necessary to create a valid marriage necessarily provides procedures whereby the court declares that a wedding has not created the legal status of marriage between the parties. But often (especially where the ground related to the parties' sexual relationship) the petition could more realistically be seen as providing legal relief from an unsatisfactory marriage. There is a long-standing tension between these two aspects of the law. Changes in the law made in the course of the twentieth century which do primarily affect whether people of certain descriptions—the young, or close relatives for example— are to be allowed to marry have already been dealt with; it remains to deal with changes made by statutes which primarily relate to the role of nullity as providing a means of escape from a

---

[285] *G v. M* (1885) 10 App Cas 171, 176 (where however a decree was granted since the evidence established that the husband was genuinely incapable of consummating his relationship with his wife: impotence *quoad hanc* suffices).
[286] See *Singh v. Singh* [1971] P 226.   [287] *Singh v. Singh* [1971] P 226, 232.
[288] [1913] P 198, 202.

relationship (rather than on the classical role of preventing couples from getting married in the first place).

The 1912 Royal Commission recommends extension of the grounds for annulment; the Matrimonial Causes Act 1937 gives effect to that recommendation

The Gorell Royal Commission of 1912[289] was sympathetically disposed to removing some of the features of the law which caused evident hardship. But the Commission was also faced with a tactical dilemma. It was of course well aware of the fundamental distinction[290] between, on the one hand, annulling a marriage because of the existence *at the time of the marriage* of some fundamental vitiating factor and dissolving it because of some *subsequent* event. But it had become clear that three of the Commissioners, whilst adamantly opposed to any extension of the grounds for divorce[291] were prepared to be flexible about extending the grounds upon which a decree of nullity could be granted. The outcome was that the Commission unanimously recommended significant extensions to the law of nullity. The Commission had received much evidence about eugenics, and was evidently concerned about the risk of 'deterioration of the stock' and favoured measures which would prevent marriages between 'persons unfit to marry';[292] and it was comparatively easy to move from that starting point to recommending that if such a couple did marry the courts should be empowered to annul the marriage. Thus, the Commission thought that annulment should be available where one party was sane enough to have consented to the marriage taking place but was not sane enough to be married and to procreate children. It recommended that the court be empowered to annul a marriage on the grounds that one party to a marriage suffered from 'unsoundness of mind existing at the time of marriage' and even that he or she was 'in a state of incipient mental unsoundness, which becomes definite within six months after marriage'. But attempts had to be made to preserve the principle that annulment was only to be available when a condition vitiated the marriage from the outset. Hence, the suit would have to be instituted within one year of the marriage, and the petitioner would have to prove that he was at the time of the marriage

---

[289] *Report of the Royal Commission on Divorce and Matrimonial Causes*, 1912, Cd. 6478.

[290] See the speech of Lord Atkin in the debates on the Matrimonial Causes Act 1937—one of the very few references at that time to the provisions which eventually gave effect to the Royal Commission's recommendations on nullity: *Official Report* (HL) 7 July 1937, vol. 106, col. 177.

[291] See below, Chapter 6.

[292] The Commission had been pressed to recommend public health procedures (such as obligatory testing for venereal disease and tight control on the marriage of the mentally ill) but dismissed the suggestions made to it as impracticable: *Report of the Royal Commission on Divorce and Matrimonial Causes*, 1912, Cd. 6478, para. 352.

ignorant of the other's condition and that no marital intercourse had taken place after the discovery of the 'defect'.[293]

In the same way, the notion that certain conditions made a person unfit for marriage led the Commission to recommend (subject to similar conditions) that epilepsy or recurrent insanity should be a ground for nullity. The Commission also heard 'compelling evidence' of the prevalence of syphilis and gonorrhoea, and of the 'dire effects' which these infections had upon innocent spouses and the terrible consequences for any children;[294] and there was no difficulty in concluding that to permit annulment in cases where one spouse was suffering at the time of the marriage from a venereal disease in a communicable form would 'promote the interests of morality and also aid the complainant in being able to avoid being subjected to the possibility of contamination'.[295] But the Commission had no wish to appear to be opening the door too wide and drew the line at accepting misrepresentation by itself as a ground for annulment:[296] to allow such a ground would be likely to engender a 'flood of litigation'.[297] Even so the facts of *Moss v. Moss*[298] seemed to demonstrate that there was a need for some reform in cases in which a woman had concealed the fact that she was pregnant by a third party. This was conduct of 'such a gross and fraudulent character' as to make it reasonable to allow annulment; and the Commission recommended that the court should be empowered to annul a marriage if the wife were 'found to be pregnant at the time of her marriage, her condition being due to intercourse with some man other than her husband, and such condition has not been disclosed by her'.

In one respect the Commission can be accused of having ignored the fundamental principle that annulment is a remedy for a condition existing at the time of the marriage: it accepted—with hardly any discussion—a proposal that wilful refusal to consummate the marriage should become a ground for annulment.[299] This is surprising in view of the Commission's concern to be seen to accept the boundary between annulment and divorce. What is even more surprising is that the minority—notwithstanding their general commitment to the

---

[293] *Report of the Royal Commission on Divorce and Matrimonial Causes*, 1912, Cd. 6478, paras. 353(a), 528 6(i). Not everyone thought that in these respects the Commission had kept within the traditional boundaries of nullity; and, for example, Sir Boyd Merriman, President of the Probate Divorce and Admiralty Division told the Lord Chancellor in 1936 that the new mental illness, venereal disease and pregnancy grounds recommended by the Royal Commission were 'debatable grounds for divorce' rather than grounds for annulment: Merriman to Hailsham, 21 April 1936, PRO LCO2/1195.

[294] *op. cit.* para. 354. The Commission was particularly impressed by the evidence of Dr. JA Bloxham: *Evidence taken before the Royal Commission*, 1912, Cd. 6479–82 BPP 1912–13, vol. 20, p. 389.

[295] Provided that the complainant was ignorant of the facts at the time of the marriage, and subject to the suit being instituted within a year of the wedding and to there having been no intercourse after he or she learned of the infection: *Report of the Royal Commission on Divorce and Matrimonial Causes*, 1912, Cd. 6478, para. 528 6(iii).

[296] *Op. cit.*, para. 351.   [297] *Ibid.*   [298] [1897] P 263, CA.   [299] *Op. cit.*, para. 327.

doctrines of the established Church—should (again, without giving reasons) have concurred in this recommendation.[300]

The Matrimonial Causes Act 1937 eventually gave effect to the substance of these recommendations; and the saga of the struggle to get divorce legislation onto the statute book is told at length elsewhere in this book. It is perhaps surprising that when the Bill for the Matrimonial Causes Act 1937 was going through Parliament there should have been virtually no discussion of the new grounds[301] for nullity;[302] and the Bill's sponsor (AP Herbert) certainly appreciated how fortunate it was that no one publicly criticised the inclusion of wilful refusal as a ground for annulment:[303]

'It is very strange how those who strain at a gnat of divorce will swallow eagerly a camel of nullity. Nobody in either House ever whispered a word against the first new ground for declaring a marriage to be null and void—"that the marriage has not been consummated owing to the wilful refusal of the respondent to consummate the marriage". No time-limit applies to this provision: the petition can be made six weeks or (I believe) six years after the marriage. It is not less tempting to persons determined on "collusion" . . . than, say, a divorce for desertion. The grievance is not in substance much different from that of the wife who after, say, one bridal week-end is deserted for life. But the same people who hotly fought against relieving the second victim . . . had not a word to say about the much more easy relief of the first. But in politics the unexpected seems to happen as often as it does in cricket . . .'

Herbert and his colleagues were fortunate that this change to the law passed unnoticed; and the acceptance of wilful refusal as a ground on which annulments could be granted evidently met a need. During World War II the number of annulments for non-consummation increased markedly.[304]

Wilful refusal and willingness to have children: a restrictive approach in the House of Lords

The addition of the new 'wilful refusal' ground for annulment presented the courts with a problem: it was necessary to return to the question of what,

---

[300] *Op. cit.*, p. 190.

[301] Enacted as Matrimonial Causes Act 1937, s. 7. The authorities were well aware of the erosion of the traditional dividing line between divorce and nullity. The President of the Probate Divorce and Admiralty Division wrote to the Lord Chancellor on 21 April 1936 protesting that the provision introducing new grounds for annulment LCO2/1195 involved a confusion 'between nullity and divorce . . . [It] is true that mere wilful refusal is not a ground for nullity. But in practice, if refusal is unexplained, the Court almost necessarily infers incapacity . . .' PRO LCO2/1195. This was reinforced by advice from the Permanent Secretary questioning whether the new grounds were appropriate as grounds for annulment rather than divorce: Schuster to Hailsham 24 November 1936.

[302] But see note 290 above. Lord Atkin's intervention was prompted by the moving of an amendment which would have extended the circumstances in which mental illness could be the basis of a nullity petition so as to cover cases such as *Durham v. Durham* (1885) 10 PD 80—to which Viscount Cecil of Chelwood seems to be referring in his speech: *Official Report* (HL) 7 July 1937, vol. 106, col. 175.

[303] AP Herbert, *The Ayes Have it, The Story of the Marriage Bill* (1937) pp. 140–141.

[304] See *Report of the Royal Commission on Divorce and Matrimonial Causes*, 1912, Cd. 6478, Appendix II, Table 2. In 1946 these numbers peaked at 1,423 (of which 920 were refusal cases).

precisely, constituted 'consummation'. Specifically, did a spouse who refused to allow intercourse unless a condom were used[305] refuse to consummate the marriage? Behind this linguistic dispute there lay a more difficult and controversial issue:[306] was the primary purpose of marriage the procreation of children (a view which appealed to those concerned about apparently declining birth rates) or was it to be accepted that for many married people having children was no part of the marriage contract?

In a number of cases the courts accepted dicta which emphasised the procreation of children as the 'primary and most legitimate object' of marriage. On this basis they held that annulments could be granted for wilful refusal where there was insistence on the use of a condom. Perhaps as a result[307] the number of wilful refusal decrees surged to 920 in 1947.[308] But in 1947 the House of Lords slammed on the brakes:

In *Baxter v. Baxter*[309] the wife, from the time of the marriage in 1934 until the husband left her ten years later, refused to allow intercourse unless he wore a condom. He sought an annulment based on her wilful refusal to consummate the marriage. The House of Lords held that its task was to construe the language used in a statute passed in 1937: what did the expression 'consummation of marriage' mean at that time? Their Lordships had no doubt that it extended to cases in which the couple used a condom. Lord Jowitt LC declared it to be wrong to say that a marriage was not consummated unless children were procreated; and equally wrong to say that the procreation of children was the principal end of marriage.

The effect of the decision was to preserve the empty shell of marriages which had long since broken down, and on that ground it was severely criticised.[310] The number of wilful refusal annulments fell back sharply.[311]

1956: The Morton Royal Commission tries to put the clock back

The grounds for annulment were within the terms of reference of the Royal Commission which deliberated on Marriage and Divorce between 1951 and

[305] At this time condoms were used primarily as a birth control technique (although they were also distributed to service personnel in an attempt to minimise the spread of sexually transmitted disease).

[306] This was one of the issues which prompted the setting up of the *Royal Commission on Population* in 1944. For an indication of the nature of the controversy see EM Hubback, *The Population of Britain* (1947).

[307] The July 1945 decision of the Court of Appeal in *Cowen v. Cowen* [1946] P 36 no doubt drew the attention of the legal profession to the possibility.

[308] *Report of the Royal Commission on Divorce and Matrimonial Causes*, 1912, Cd. 6478, Appendix II, Table 2. It does not follow that over the years annulment petitions increased as a proportion of all matrimonial decrees: see OR McGregor, *Divorce in England, A Centenary Study* (1957) pp. 40–42.

[309] [1948] AC 274, HL.   [310] See eg LCB Gower (1948) 11 MLR 176.

[311] *Report of the Royal Commission on Divorce and Matrimonial Causes*, 1912, Cd. 6478, Appendix II, Table 2.

1956.[312] The Morton Commission's general stance was conservative and (in the view of some) legalistic; and it accepted that nullity should be confined to cases of defect or incapacity existing at the date of the marriage. Wilful refusal was 'something that happens after the marriage' and the Commission accordingly recommended that wilful refusal should cease to be a ground for annulment but instead become a ground for divorce.[313] The Commission also rejected suggestions that there should be a general and comprehensive ground of nullity based on the concealment of material facts,[314] and refused to accept any of the proposals[315] put forward to minimise the hardship—highlighted by the *Baxter* decision[316]—suffered by spouses denied the possibility of having a child. All that the Commission was prepared to recommend was some up-dating of the terminology used in relation to mental illness[317] and allowing some flexibility in the application of the rule requiring nullity petitions on certain grounds to be presented within one year of the marriage.[318] None of these recommendations was taken up.

1971: Codifying the law of nullity

The law inherited from the ecclesiastical courts in 1857 had never been codified;[319] and was thus a prime target for the attentions of the Law Commission.[320] It soon became apparent that no such review could be carried out without the danger of arousing controversy; and at this stage in its history the Commission was concerned to present itself as a dispassionate body of experts advising primarily on matters of technical feasibility.[321] The

[312] *Report of the Royal Commission on Marriage and Divorce*, 1956, Cmd. 9678.

[313] The Commission was evidently also impressed by evidence from the Bar which wanted not only to uphold the sanctity of the marriage tie and restore the logic of the law of nullity but also to 'avoid the danger (inherent in the absence of a medical examination) of collusion, and false evidence being given upon matters incapable of satisfactory proof': *op. cit.*, para. 77. *Minutes of Evidence taken before the Royal Commission on Marriage and Divorce, 1952–1954*, Paper No. 4.

[314] *Report of the Royal Commission on Marriage and Divorce*, 1956, Cmd. 9678, paras. 267–272.

[315] These included making wilful refusal to have a child a ground for divorce (see para. 80) and making the fact that one party had before the marriage been sterilised a specific ground for annulment (see para. 271).

[316] See above, p. 85.

[317] *Report of the Royal Commission on Marriage and Divorce*, 1956, Cmd. 9678, paras. 276–282.

[318] *Ibid.*, paras. 284–285.

[319] The Matrimonial Causes Act 1937 had simply provided that in 'addition to any other grounds on which a marriage is by law void or voidable' a marriage should be voidable on the four new grounds introduced by that Act.

[320] The Law Commissions Act 1965, s. 1 required the Commission to review the law with a view to its systematic development and reform, including in particular codification of the law: see generally SM Cretney, *Law, Law Reform and the Family* (1998) Chapter 1. The Law Commission had already committed itself to a comprehensive review of family law with a view to its eventual codification: *Second Programme of Law Reform*, Item XIX.

[321] SM Cretney, *Law, Law Reform and the Family* (1998) p. 27. The Commission's role in relation to the enactment of the Divorce Reform Act 1969 demonstrates the falsity of this image (*op. cit.* Chap. 2) but may also account for the Commission's apparent concern to avoid controversy in relation to the codification of nullity.

Commissioners[322] did not encourage radical suggestions even those emanating from the Commission's own legal staff.[323] The Commission's *Report on Nullity of Marriage*[324] emphasised that its primary concern was to take the opportunity to state comprehensively the circumstances in which a nullity decree would be granted;[325] and the Commission accepted that the traditional distinction between valid, void and voidable marriages 'corresponded to factual differences in the situation of the parties'[326] and recommended that the substance of the law should remain substantially unchanged. In particular, the distinction between void and voidable marriages should be retained, wilful refusal should continue to be a ground for nullity rather than divorce, under-age marriages should continue to be void (rather than voidable or ratifiable) and no additional grounds for annulment (such as sterility) should be introduced. The only change of any substance which the Commission recommended was that marriages to which either party had not validly consented should be transferred from the category of the void to that of the voidable; and it seems doubtful whether the Commission appreciated what a vast conceptual change[327] this involved. Minor modifications (such as removing epilepsy as a discrete ground for annulment,[328] for example and modifying the language used in the 'mental illness' ground for

---

[322] There were differences of attitude: LCB Gower (who was formally the Commissioner primarily responsible) favoured a 'bolder approach' than that adopted by one of his colleagues (whose views were described as 'altogether too conventional and hidebound') and on 20 December 1967 Gower minuted that the 'New Year Resolution of the Family Law Team should be that we will drag the law kicking and screaming into the twentieth century sometime before the century is over': PRO BC3/415.

[323] See eg the reaction to a paper dated 3 October 1967 prepared by Mrs Ruth Deech (see Biographical Notes). The Commissioner primarily responsible for the matter (LCB Gower) 'adamantly opposed' Mrs Deech's suggestion that voidable marriage be equated with divorce, and even had doubts about the wisdom of examining the rules governing the prohibited degrees for marriage because of misgivings about 'stirring up this particular mess': PRO BC3/415.

[324] Law Com. No. 33 (1970). This had been preceded in 1968 by the publication of a consultative *Working Paper* (No. 20).

[325] *Report on Nullity of Marriage* (Law Com. No. 33, 1970), para. 96. In fact this objective was only attained after negotiation between Parliamentary Counsel (Henry de Waal) whose first draft merely legislated for the changes in the law which the Commission recommended. The suggestion that all the grounds upon which a marriage could be annulled should be stated comprehensively came from the leader of the Commission's legal team, Dimitry Tolstoy QC.

[326] para. 3.

[327] 'The result [of the change] is that a person who does not understand what he or she is doing may become legally bound to a relationship whose whole juridical basis is the consent of both parties. Moreover . . . a man—such as an attendant in a nursing home—may go through a marriage ceremony with a rich elderly woman who is so severely demented that she has no idea what is happening; and such a "marriage" will effectively revoke the will she had made . . . in favour of her family . . . and her "husband" will have extensive succession rights on her death intestate': SM Cretney and JM Masson, *Principles of Family Law* (6th ed., 1998) p. 68. For a full critical analysis of the Law Commission's recommendations and of the Nullity of Marriage Act 1971 see SM Cretney, *Principles of Family Law* (4th ed., 1984) pp. 45–87.

[328] The Law Commission's consultation process had revealed a consensus in favour of abolishing the stigmatisation of epilepsy, not least because epilepsy often had a physical cause rather than being a symptom of mental illness.

annulment) were recommended; whilst significant (but minor)[329] changes were made to the bars to the grounds for annulment introduced in 1937.[330]

In spite of the Law Commission's efforts to avoid controversy, a determined effort was made—possibly inspired by the Church of England which was concerned that the law applied in the secular courts should not be inconsistent with its own doctrines[331]—to remove wilful refusal from the grounds for annulment.[332] But Lord Chancellor Hailsham refused to budge;[333] and at the turn of the century wilful refusal remained a ground on which the courts could grant an annulment. It appears still to be of some utility in cases of arranged marriages:

In *Kaur v. Singh*[334] a marriage was arranged between two Sikhs. The two parties went through a Register Office ceremony. But—as both parties were well aware—by Sikkh law and custom it was the husband's duty thereafter to arrange a religious solemnisation. The husband refused to do so. The court held that he had thereby refused to consummate the marriage (and it seems that the result would have been the same even if he had tried to have intercourse with the

---

[329] For example, knowledge at the time of the marriage that the respondent was mentally ill was no longer to be a bar, nor was the fact that the couple had had intercourse after the existence of one of those grounds had become known, whilst the time limit within which petitions on certain grounds had to be brought was to be extended from one to three years. These modifications (all of which shifted the emphasis from nullity as identifying a defect existing at the time of the marriage to providing a remedy for a situation which developed thereafter) caused considerable difficulty within the Law Commission: PRO BC3/418, notably Tolstoy's minute of 5 March 1970 and the subsequent discussions.

[330] The Law Commission also recommended that there should be a clearly defined statutory bar applicable to all forms of voidable marriage to replace the ill-defined case law bar of 'approbation': see *Report on Nullity of Marriage* (Law Com. No. 33, 1970), paras. 39–45. The Commission recommended the abolition of the rule that a nullity decree operated retrospectively so that the parties were deemed never to have been married; instead, a decree annulling a voidable marriage should operate to terminate a voidable marriage with the same consequences in law as if it had been ended by a divorce decree. But the application of this rule proved capable of producing unsatisfactory results: see eg *Ward v. Secretary of State for Social Services* [1990] 1 FLR 119; SM Cretney and JM Masson, *Principles of Family Law* (6th ed., 1998) p. 72.

[331] As set out in *The Church and the Law of Nullity of Marriage* (1955), for example.

[332] The Bishop of Exeter assured the House of Lords that there 'cannot be any doubt that wilful refusal is not and cannot be a ground for nullity but must be a ground for divorce': *Official Report* (HL) 11 May 1971, vol. 318, col. 945. A former President of the Probate Divorce and Admiralty Division revealed that in the official consultation carried out amongst the judges of the Division (and also in consultation with Lords Justice of Appeal experienced in this area) there was unanimity that wilful refusal was not properly a ground for annulment: *Official Report* (HL) 22 April 1971, vol. 317, col. 810. But the most experienced of all divorce judges—Lord Hodson—had in fact told the Law Commission that, whilst 'obviously' wilful refusal should strictly be a ground for divorce rather than nullity he would for practical reasons favour retaining the law as established in 1937: Note dated 29 July 1968, BC3/417.

[333] *Official Report* (HL) 11 May 1971, vol. 318, col. 941. The Bill was in form a Private Member's Bill but in fact the Government was entirely responsible for its contents: see *Official Report* (HL) 22 April 1971, vol. 317, col. 798 (Lord Gardiner). The Government relied on the fact that wilful refusal had been accepted as a ground for annulment for 34 years to everyone's satisfaction, and that Parliament should leave well alone: see *Official Report* (HC) 17 February 1971, Standing Committee C, cols. 22–23.

[334] [1972] 1 WLR 105, CA.

wife but she refused to permit him to do so until the religious ceremony had taken place).

But the truth of the matter is that divorce has become so easily obtainable (and increasingly acceptable to some at least of the clergy of the Church of England and to the nonconformist churches) that few people[335] today feel the need to seek annulments. As one judge[336] put it in dealing with a case raising similar issues to *Kaur v. Singh*:

'Nullity proceedings are nowadays rare, though not wholly extinct. It is unfortunate that these had to be fought out, for the simple fact is that the couple have never lived together, not even for a week. They have lived apart since their civil wedding which was over two years ago. The marriage had irretrievably broken down, indeed has never started up, so there would have been no difficulty in pronouncing mutual decrees nisi, dissolving the marriage, if the necessary consent had been forthcoming . . .'

[335] In 1998 only 474 nullity decrees nisi were granted (compared with 143,879 decrees nisi of divorce): *Marriage, divorce and adoption statistics 1998* (2000), Table 4.23.

[336] Anthony Lincoln J, *A v. J (Nullity Proceedings)* [1989] 1 FLR 110, 111.

3

The Legal Consequences of Marriage: Property Regimes

INTRODUCTION: LEGAL STATUS

Marriage creates a legal status.[1] By marriage a couple acquire legal rights and duties, and, broadly speaking, the law refuses to allow them to vary those rights or escape from those duties however much they might want to do so.[2] These rights and duties were particularly significant in relation to entitlement to property and rights of financial support. But marriage was also of great significance because the fact that a child's parents were married conferred on the child the status of legitimacy, a status from which again certain legal consequences flowed.

THE UNITY THEORY AND ITS EFFECT AT COMMON LAW

The starting point for any discussion of the legal effect of marriage is the common law doctrine that marriage makes husband and wife one person in law.[3] In Blackstone's classic summary:[4]

---

[1] ie 'the condition of belonging to a class in society to which the law ascribes peculiar rights and duties, capacities and incapacities': *The Ampthill Peerage* [1977] AC 547, 577, *per* Lord Simon of Glaisdale; and see *Salvesen v. Administrator of Austrian Property* [1927] AC 641, 653, *per* Lord Haldane.

[2] The classic statement of this doctrine is by an American judge, Appleton CJ, in the case of *Adams v. Palmer* (1863) 51 Maine 480, 483:

'When the contracting parties have entered into the married state, they have not so much entered into a contract as into a new relation, the rights, duties and obligations of which rest, not upon their agreement, but upon the general law of the State, statutory or common, which defines and prescribes those rights, duties and obligations. They are of law, not of contract. It was of contract that the relation should be established, but, being established, the power of the parties, as to its extent or duration, is at an end, their rights under it are determined by the will of the sovereign as evidenced by law. They can neither be modified nor changed by any agreement of parties. . . . The reciprocal rights arising from this relation, as long as it continues, are such as the law determines from time to time, and none other.'

Even in the light of the social and scientific changes of the past 150 years it remains true that marriage affects status upon which depend entitlements benefits and obligations, although entry into marriage and (especially) exit from it have become more a matter of choice than was true at the beginning of the century: cf. *Bellinger v. Bellinger (Attorney-General Intervening)* [2002] Fam 150, 184, *per* Thorpe LJ.

[3] The doctrine seems to originate in Genesis, 2.24 ('therefore shall a man leave his father and his mother and shall cleave unto his wife, and they shall be one flesh') and see also Matthew 19.5–6; but (as Oliver J pointed out in *Midland Bank Trust Co Ltd v. Green (No. 3)* [1979] Ch 496, 514) this strictlybiblical notion became confused with, if not overtaken by, the equally fictitious concept of a predominating masculine will. After the fall, the woman's will was subject to her husband's, he was to rule

'the very being or legal existence of the woman is suspended during the marriage, or at least is incorporated and consolidated into that of the husband: under whose wing, protection, and *cover*, she performs every thing; and is therefore called in our law-french a *feme-covert, femina viro co-operta*; is said to be *covert-baron* or under the protection and influence of her husband, her baron, or lord; and her condition during her marriage is called her *coverture*. Upon this principle, of an union of person in husband and wife, depend almost all the legal rights, duties, and disabilities, that either of them acquire by the marriage.'

From this doctrine of the unity of husband and wife, it was said to follow that in principle a married woman could not own property; and that all the personal property[5] which she had owned before marriage, all her earnings after the marriage, and any savings she made out of them vested in the husband.[6]

Effect of unity theory not restricted to property

The unity theory did not only affect property rights. Since the wife effectively lacked any distinct legal personality of her own she could not sue in her own name, and she could not in principle make an enforceable contract; whilst her husband had to be joined in any legal action against her (and was liable to pay any damages awarded against her) and he was also liable for her pre-marital debts, contracts, and torts. It is not a great exaggeration to say that the common law robbed the married woman of full human personality.[7]

This chapter is primarily concerned with reform of the rules relating to married women's property rights; but, as will be seen, the way in which reform was carried out meant that the consequences of the unity theory remained relevant for many years. Not until the second half of the twentieth century could it confidently be said that the doctrine of unity and its ramifications was dead and had been buried and that the law recognised husband and wife as two individuals equally capable of acquiring and holding property, entering into contracts, and equally responsible for their own wrongs.[8]

over her, and the law disabled her from making any 'grant, contract, or bargain, without the allowance or consent of her husband': *Manby v. Scott* (1663) 1 Mod 124, 126, *per* Sir Robert Hyde.

  [4] *Commentaries on the Laws of England* (4th ed., 1770) Vol. 1, p. 442.

  [5] But the doctrine of unity was not applied so remorselessly to the wife's real property: the husband was only entitled to the rents and profits during the parties' joint lives (and this was extended to a full life interest if a child capable of inheriting were born alive): see generally the summary given by RE Megarry and HWR Wade, *The Law of Real Property* (3rd ed., 1966) 986; and the fuller account by CS Kenny, *History of the Law of England as to the effects of Marriage on Property* (1879). Conversely, the wife was entitled at common law to dower (effectively a life interest in a third) out of the husband's realty: see Megarry and Wade *op. cit.* p. 522.

  [6] But it should not be supposed that the effect of marriage was totally one-sided: at common law the married woman has a right to be supported by her husband 'according to his estate and condition'. However, for most middle class wives, this 'right' was not of great utility: see p. 393, n 1, below) and generally *Lush on the Law of Husband and Wife* (4th ed., by SN Grant-Bailey), Chapter 12.

  [7] *Barber v. Pigden* [1937] 1 KB 664, 678, *per* Scott LJ.

  [8] *Midland Bank Trust Co Ltd v. Green (No 3)* [1982] Ch. 529, 538, *per* Lord Denning MR at p. 538; and upholding *Midland Bank Trust Co Ltd v. Green (No 3)* [1979] Ch 496, Oliver J.

ENTITLEMENT TO PROPERTY: EQUITABLE INTERVENTION

The first limitation on the proprietary consequences of the common law doctrine dates back to the eighteenth century when the courts of equity rejected the notion that a woman lost her legal personality by marriage. Equity (it was said):[9]

'devised the doctrine of "*separate use*". [The Court of Chancery] could not interfere with legal interests in property, but when that legal interest was transferred to trustees upon trust to deal with it in a certain way, the Court of Equity compelled the trustees to act in accordance with the trust. In this way when the beneficial or equitable interest . . . in property was limited to the separate use of a woman, whether before or after marriage, she could enjoy it independently of her husband and he could not get control of it against her will. Property so settled was called her "*separate property*". After the first quarter of the eighteenth century the Court of Equity went even further and adopted the practice of protecting as her separate property any property given to her for her separate use even without the intervention of trustees. In such a case, the husband (to whom the legal title in the property passed) was regarded as a trustee of the property for the wife.'

Marriage settlements

For this reason, prudent parents in the wealthy and middle classes would insist on a proper settlement being made on a daughter's marriage to ensure that her property[10] was held for her separate use; and in this way family capital could be protected against appropriation by the husband (and his creditors), whilst the wife could be assured a level of financial independence. The result (according to Dicey)[11] was that although the 'daughters of the rich enjoyed . . . the considerate protection of equity, the daughters of the poor suffered under the severity and injustice of the common law'.

The limits of equitable protection: the campaign for reform

Equity did not protect women who had married without a settlement; nor could it adequately protect a married women (whether or not she had a settlement)

---

[9] In the words of the Law Revision Committee's *Fourth Interim Report* (1934 Cmd. 4770) para. 8. For an account of the development of equitable principles, see RE Megarry and P V Baker (eds.) *Snell's Principles of Equity* (27th ed., 1973) pp. 513–517.

[10] A settlement could not in terms bind so-called after-acquired property (for example, a legacy left to a married woman under a will taking effect after the marriage). But conveyancers developed techniques (recognised by the courts of equity) whereby a wife's covenant in a marriage settlement to bring such property into the settlement was effective to impose the trusts of the settlement on it as soon as the wife became entitled, and in this way the husband was deprived of the beneficial interest to which the common law would have entitled him: see J McGhee (ed.) *Snell's Principles of Equity* (30th ed., 2000) paras. 7.42–54.

[11] AV Dicey, *Lectures on the Relation between Law and Public Opinion in England During the Nineteenth Century* (2nd ed. with preface by ECS Wade, 1962) p. 383.

against the exercise of her husband's common law right to seize her *earnings* and any savings she made out of them. It was this latter gap which seems to have been most influential in creating pressure for reform of the law. Although the upper and middle classes would usually have settlements, the great majority of married women did not have substantial family capital and thus the fact that they either did not have a marriage settlement, or had a settlement which produced only a tiny income,[12] did not greatly affect them. But (to quote Dicey again) the number of women who could as 'teachers, musicians, actresses, or authoresses, gain large emoluments by their professional skill had, since the beginning of the nineteenth century, greatly increased, and . . . this body of accomplished women had obtained the means of making known to the public through the press every case of injustice done to any one of them'.[13]

The pressure which these articulate high earners[14] could bring to bear through pamphleteering,[15] meetings and pressure groups was formidable; but it seems to have been the plight of the woman deserted by a drunken labourer and compelled to keep herself by working as a seamstress or laundress which really struck home. Such women would often find the tiny savings they had deposited for safety in a Co-operative Society or Savings Bank seized by the husband in the exercise of his common law rights.[16] Few of even the most conservative Members of the (then exclusively male) Parliament felt able to defend the way in which the law worked, not least because the lack of legal security for savings may have deterred some deserted wives from even trying to become self-sufficient.[17]

These factors eventually had a decisive influence not only on Parliament's acceptance that something should be done to remedy a 'monstrous injustice to the working classes'; but also on the content of the reforming Married Women's Property Acts 1870[18] and 1882; and the way in which these statutory reforms

---

[12] Law Revision Committee *Fourth Interim Report*, (1934, Cmd. 4770) para. 10.

[13] See generally L Holcombe, *Wives and Property* (1983), especially Chapter 4; ML Shanley, *Feminism, Marriage, and the Law in Victorian England 1850–1895*.

[14] In the 1870s George Eliot, for example, had a total annual income from her literary activities of £5,000 per annum (equal to the salary of a High Court Judge, and the equivalent of perhaps £300,000 per annum in year 2000 values). Women writers catering for the more popular market (such as Mrs Henry Wood, author of *East Lynne* and Mary Elizabeth Braddon, author of *Lady Audley's Secret*) no doubt earned substantially more: see KT Hoppen, *The Mid-Victorian Generation 1846–1886* (1998) pp. 378–388.

[15] The tone of some of this work is indicated by Francis Power Cobbe's *Criminals, Idiots, Women and Minors. Is the Classification Sound?* (1869). The bibliography by OR McGregor, 'The Social Position of Women in England 1850–1914' (1955) *British Journal of Sociology*, vol. 6, p. 48 is invaluable (although much further research has subsequently been published).

[16] See the evidence given by (for example) the Rector of Bethnal Green to the Select Committee on the Married Women's Property Bill, BPP 1867–1868, vii, 415.

[17] See the speech made by Mr Russell Gurney MP introducing the Married Women's Property Bill, 18 May 1870, *Hansard's Parliamentary Debates* (3rd Series) vol. 201, col. 878.

[18] The House of Lords effectively redrafted the Bill, the scope of which was restricted to securing for married women the benefit of any property earned by their industry or talents (with limited extension of the same principle to sums received on intestacy, small legacies, and savings deposits): see *per* Lord Penzance, *Hansard's Parliamentary Debates* (3rd Series) 18 July 1870, vol. 203, col. 395.

were carried out in turn had a strong influence on the development of family property law in the twentieth century.[19] A brief summary of developments in the second half of the nineteenth century is therefore essential to an understanding of later developments.

(i) The Matrimonial Causes Act 1857

In 1857 the Palmerston government decided to legislate for judicial divorce (for which there seemed to be comparatively little demand) and rejected pleas to legislate on married women's property (for which there was a great deal of demand).[20] But the divorce debates did provide an excellent opportunity to publicise the injustices of the law governing married women's property; and this criticism did not come exclusively from radicals. The former Tory Lord Chancellor, Lyndhurst[21] was, for example, prominent amongst the campaigners and claimed to know of countless cases where a man married, dissipated his wife's money, abandoned her, and only reappeared when she got a legacy or had accumulated earnings and would then 'act the old part over again, until, the money being spent, he finally abandoned her.

If the coming into existence of a marriage had given the husband a right to the wife's property it would perhaps have been logical for that property to be returned when the marriage was dissolved,[22] or at least to give the court a discretion to order that it be returned. But the 1857 Divorce Act did not deal coherently even with the implications of divorce for property entitlement. The Act did seek to deter the adulterer[23] by giving the court power to order a wife divorced for adultery to settle some or all of her separate property for the benefit of the innocent party and the children of the marriage. But the Act was silent about the much commoner case in which property had been settled in a marriage settlement;[24] and in 1859 legislation was hurriedly introduced to prevent the adulter-

---

[19] See below.   [20] See pp. 164–165, below.   [21] See Biographical Notes.

[22] On the relationship between property and divorce law reform at this period see pp. 164–165, below; ML Shanley, '"One must ride behind": Married Women's Rights and the Divorce Act of 1857' *Victorian Studies*, 25 (1982), 361.

[23] See Lord Penzance's words in *March v. March and Palumbo* (1867) LR 1 P&D 440, quoted at p. 398 below, which continued to be quoted with apparent relish almost a century later: *Compton v. Compton and Hussey* [1960] P. 201.

[24] As Lord Merrivale P. put it in *Bosworthick v. Bosworthick* [1926] P 159, 163 'it was something of a surprise to some people when the Divorce Act of 1857 came into operation to find that although the marriage of parties had been dissolved pecuniary interests of which the basis was their marriage remained in being . . . [The Act] made no provision with regard to settlements the basis of which had gone, and no other provision than that empowering the court to deal with the property of an unfaithful wife. It was very soon realized that although a marriage had been dissolved, the marriage settlement continued in force, with the result that the guilty party in divorce might remain entitled to funds settled upon him or her in the capacity of husband or wife, either for the gratification of that party or even for the maintenance of a second husband or a second wife . . .'.

ous wife from living 'with the adulterer upon that income which she had received from the generosity' of her husband.[25]

In these respects the divorce legislation seemed concerned to protect the interests of cuckolded men rather than to remedy the injustices highlighted by Lyndhurst and others; but one concession was made to the working wife. The 1857 Divorce Act gave courts (including magistrates' courts) power to make a so-called *'protection order'* on the application[26] of a deserted wife who could prove that she was 'maintaining herself by her own industry or separate property'. Such an order 'protected' money or property acquired after the desertion by the wife's 'own lawful industry' (as well as any other property acquired by her, for example by inheritance or gift) by declaring that the property in question was to belong to the wife as if she were a *feme sole*. But, notwithstanding the considerable trouble taken in drafting the clause[27] experience demonstrated that it was in many respects defective,[28] and the Protection Order procedure remained largely a dead letter.[29] As we shall see, the reforms of the 1870s and 1880s made the protection order redundant in the context of matrimonial property, whilst the need to protect the vulnerable against domestic violence remained a major problem over the years.

---

[25] *Hansard's Parliamentary Debates* (3rd Series) 11 August 1859, vol. 155, col. 1378 (Mr Edwin James MP). Matrimonial Causes Act 1859, s. 5, gave the court power to vary marriage settlements in the interests of either party and the children; and an order extinguishing any interest of the wife, at least in the funds derived from the husband or his family, was for long regarded as 'ordinary and proper': see *Maxwell v. Maxwell and Rognor* [1951] P 212, 215, *per* Wallington J.

[26] It appears that the Government accepted the need to legislate on this narrow basis in order to avoid the much more extensive reforms proposed by Sir Erskine Perry and others: see p. 165, below and L Holcombe, *Wives and Property* (1983) pp. 102–103.

[27] See the remarks of the Attorney-General, *Hansard's Parliamentary Debates* (3rd Series), 7 August 1857, vol. 147, col. 1235; the final version was only moved on the Report stage in the House of Commons on 20 August 1857.

[28] The main problems were that:

(1) women of means might well prefer to seek judicial separation (available after two years' desertion) rather than the very limited protection afforded by Matrimonial Causes Act 1857, s. 21;

(2) working class women, who might have found a protection order effective in some cases, did not know that the law provided a means of protection and did not have easy access to legal advice;

(3) the court could only make orders in cases of desertion, and protection was not available where (for example) the wife left because of her husband's cruelty; and

(4) there was no power to make an order where the husband simply lived on the wife's earnings perhaps leaving her from time to time but returning to seize her wages and savings.

Amending legislation was introduced in 1858 and 1864: see Matrimonial Causes Acts of those years, ss. 6 and 8 and s. 1 respectively.

[29] According to the evidence of J Westlake, GW Hastings and JS Mansfield, *Report of the Married Women's Property Bill Committee*, BPP 1867–1868, vii, 365, at pp. 375 and 379 only 14 orders were made by the police court over a six-month period in the populous Marylebone district of London; and generally very few orders were ever made. But apparently there was a 'popular superstition' that the legislation gave magistrates' courts a wide jurisdiction to protect spouses from assault, and requests for 'a protection' were often made in the informal surroundings of the Metropolitan Police Courts: see p. 290, below.

The 1857 Act did make express provision dealing with the effects of a decree of judicial separation (for otherwise the wife would have remained subject to all her legal disabilities and would, for example, have no right to make contracts in her own name). The Act provided[30] that a judicially separated woman should be considered a *feme sole* in relation to any property she subsequently acquired, and also for the purposes of contracts, torts, and legal actions.[31]

(ii) The Married Women's Property Act 1870

The publication of John Stuart Mill's *The Subjection of Women* in 1869 gave powerful intellectual stimulus to the reform movement. Bills were introduced in 1868 and 1869; and the debates (as well as the evidence given to the Select Committees which reported on the Bills)[32] exposed the hardship and injustice caused by the unreformed law.[33] Eventually the Married Women's Property Act 1870 was passed; but drastic amendment in the House of Lords[34] made it a pale shadow of what even the most moderate reformers had wanted. As Lord Penzance[35] put it, the Bill presented to the Commons had been a Bill to separate husbands' and wives' property; the Act which emerged after the House of Lords had made amendments did little[36] more than give the married woman the legal right to property earned by her own industry or talents[37] and to keep sums received on intestacy, small legacies,[38] and savings deposits.[39] Agitation contin-

[30] ss. 25, 26.

[31] It is possible that this provision was modelled on the Married Women's Property Bill introduced by Sir Erskine Perry on 14 May 1857: see *Hansard's Parliamentary Debates*, vol. 144. Perry also tried unsuccessfully to amend the Government's divorce bill to give married women protection in respect of their property interests: see further L Holcombe, *Wives and Property* (1983), p. 102.

[32] See *Report of the Married Women's Property Bill Committee*, BPP 1867–1868, vii, 339; *Report of the Married Women's Property Bill Committee*, BPP 1868–1869, viii, 769.

[33] For the campaign, see L Holcombe, *Wives and Property* (1983), Chapters 7 and 8.

[34] The amendments were put forward in the *Report of the House of Lords Select Committee on the Married Women's Property Bill*: BPP 1870, HL No. 196, vol. 8, p. 1. The extent of the House of Lords' amendments can best be appreciated from the print of the Bill as amended BPP 1870, ii, 663.

[35] *Hansard's Parliamentary Debates* (3rd Series),18 July 1870 vol. 203, col. 396.

[36] But it was also provided that a married woman with separate property should be liable under the Poor Law for the maintenance of her husband and their children: ss. 13–14. Until 1870 the common law duty to maintain a spouse was confined to the husband.

[37] The Act provided that a married woman's wages, earnings, and money acquired through the exercise of any literary, artistic or scientific skill (and investments of the income from these sources) should be her separate property: s. 1.

[38] Up to a limit of £200: s. 7. Monies received on intestacy were (irrespective of the amount) to be separate property as were the rents and profits from real property which she had inherited as heiress under the common law rules of devolution. AV Dicey considered these rules demonstrated the 'utter indifference of Parliament to any fixed principle of fairness': AV Dicey, *Lectures on the Relation between Law and Public Opinion in England During the Nineteenth Century* (2nd ed. with preface by ECS Wade, 1962) p. 90.

[39] Married Women's Property Act 1870, ss. 2–5 (containing complex provisions giving the wife the right to apply for her holdings to be registered as separate property). The Act also included provisions intended to prevent the manipulation of property in fraud of the husband's creditors.

ued, and eventually Lord Chancellor Selborne was persuaded to introduce the Bill which became the Married Women's Property Act 1882.[40]

(iii) The Married Women's Property Act 1882

It would have been possible to meet the objectives of the reformers by a simple legislative provision,[41] to the effect that no person should 'by marriage acquire any interest in the property of the person whom he or she marries, nor become incapable of doing any act in respect of his or her own property, which he or she could have done if unmarried'.[42] But this was not the technique used in the 1882 Act. Instead, the Act[43] gave the married woman[44] the right to hold all the property belonging to her at the time of the marriage or acquired by her thereafter as her *separate property*. In this way the Act not only avoided the alien connotations of the community of property regimes in force in most of continental Europe but could be defended as doing 'no more than [to] give to every married woman nearly the same rights as every English gentleman had for generations past secured under a marriage settlement for his daughter on her marriage'.[45]

These tactics may have been politically astute since even those who disagreed with the notion of equal rights for the sexes were often prepared to concede the case for separate property.[46] The passage of the 1882 Act seemed (at least in the short term) to remedy the grievances against which women had for so long protested; and it is understandable that the groups at the forefront of the

---

[40] For a detailed study of the events between 1870 and 1882 see L Holcombe, *Wives and Property* (1983), Chapter 9.

[41] Such as that in the Indian Succession Act 1865, s. 4.

[42] Or by following the wording used in Matrimonial Causes Act 1857, s. 26, to define the consequences of judicial separation: see above. As the Law Revision Committee *Fourth Interim Report,* (1934, Cmd. 4770) para. 11 pointed out, had 'this simple course been adopted a woman on marriage would not have changed her status as regards capacity to contract, to hold property and to sue and be sued' but instead 'Parliament took a much more indirect course, with the result that the Married Women's Property Act of 1882 was a very complicated measure of 27 sections, [which] has given rise to much difficult litigation'.

[43] s. 2. The Act did effectively confer legal personality on the married woman by giving her the right to sue in contract and tort 'in all respects as if she were a feme sole': s. 1(2). For a dramatic illustration of the use to which this provision could be put see *Weldon v. de Bathe* (1884) 14 QBD 339; and Chapter 4, below.

[44] The old rules continued to apply to women married before 18 August 1882 (the date of Royal Assent to the Act). However, a wife could sue for torts committed before the Act: *Weldon v. Winslow* (1883) 13 QBD 784.

[45] AV Dicey, *Lectures on the Relation between Law and Public Opinion in England During the Nineteenth Century* (2nd ed. with preface by ECS Wade, 1962) p. 389. CS Kenny, *History of the Law of England as to the effects of Marriage on Property* (1879) p. 16 described the effects of a regime of separate property in more picturesque language: the reform merely afforded to 'the mangle, the teapot and the sewing machine the same protection which diamonds and consols had always purchased for themselves in the teeth of the law'.

[46] See eg L Stephen, *Liberty, Equality and Fraternity* (1873) Chapter V. And this policy could be said to be consistent with the principles of the Judicature Acts (enacted at the same period), ie that law and equity should be administered in a single Supreme Court, and that in case of conflict between the two systems the Rules of Equity should prevail: Judicature Act 1875, s. 10(11).

campaign should have talked of a 'bloodless and beneficent revolution' and a 'great victory of the principle of human equality over the unjust privilege of Sex'.[47] Indeed, Dicey[48] saw the Act as reinforcing the belief that women ought to stand substantially on an equality with men in the eye of the law and thus encouraging further legislative moves towards equality. But at a technical level the 1882 Act had serious disadvantages.

THE PRICE PAID FOR THE MARRIED WOMEN'S PROPERTY ACT 1882

The High Court judge who claimed that the 1882 Act left nothing but 'confusion, obscurity and inconsistency'[49] was exaggerating; but the drafting technique of extending (and, in 1882, universalising) separate property did lead to misunderstanding[50] and the legislation had unforeseen incidental effects.[51] Many problems remained to be resolved over the years to come.[52] For example:

---

[47] *Final Report of the Married Women's Property Committee* as quoted in L Holcombe, *Wives and Property* (1983), p. 205.

[48] AV Dicey, *Lectures on the Relation between Law and Public Opinion in England During the Nineteenth Century* (2nd ed. with preface by ECS Wade, 1962) p. 44. Dicey's thesis was that the 1857 divorce reforms—which he believed to have given 'national sanction to the contractual view of marriage, and propagated the belief that the marriage contract, like every other agreement, ought to be capable of dissolution when it fails to attain its end'—together with the 1870 and 1882 Married Women's Property Act 'deeply affected not only the legislative but also the social opinion of the country as to the position of women . . .'.

[49] *Gottliffe v. Edelston* [1930] 2 KB 378, 392, *per* McCardie J.

[50] For example, s. 17 of the 1882 Act—still, as slightly amended, in force in the year 2000—provided that the court should, on the application of either party or of any company in which either held investments, make such order as it thought fit in respect of the title to or possession of property. This provision had its origins in s. 9 of the 1870 Act, which was restricted to the resolution of questions 'between husband and wife as to property declared by this Act to be the separate property of the wife'; and it seems likely that s. 9 was intended to be used in resolving questions about whether a particular asset could be said to represent the fruit of the wife's earnings (in which case it would be deemed to be her separate property) or merely the product of careful housekeeping (in which case it would not). But for many years this context was overlooked; and it was assumed that the 1882 Act gave the court a wide discretion to apply 'palm tree justice' in relation to matrimonial property: see below.

[51] For example, s. 11 of the 1882 Act (replacing a comparable provision in ss. 10 and 11 of the 1870 Act) provided that a policy of assurance on a man's life expressed to be for the benefit of his wife created a trust in her favour and that the policy moneys should not form part of his estate. It seems clear that this was intended simply to establish that the wife was to be entitled to take the proceeds of such a policy without risk of claims from the husband's creditors; but in the early 1960s such policies were (often in conjunction with annuities) widely used as part of ingenious schemes to achieve substantial savings of estate duty on the husband's death by reason of the fact that the husband had never had an interest in the proceeds and that accordingly these were not aggregable with his other assets (even though he had paid all the premiums).

[52] The following list is incomplete and does not attempt to deal with the complexities and ramifications of the law (for example, in relation to the husband's liability in respect of his wife's pre-marital torts and contracts). Full discussion can be found in SN Grant-Bailey (ed.) *Lush on the Law of Husband and Wife* (1933).

(i) At common law, a married woman lacked the single woman's capacity to make contracts;[53] but equity made her liable to the extent of her separate property. The 1882 Act did not reverse the common law rule, but did provide[54] that a married woman was capable of entering into, and *to the extent of her separate property* rendering herself liable on, any contract. A contract could only be enforced against her, therefore, if the plaintiff could prove that at the time of making the contract she had separate property. Otherwise she could not be rendered liable, irrespective of how much property she had acquired after making the contract.[55]

(ii) At common law the husband was liable for the wife's torts; and the 1882 Act did not (so a majority of the House of Lords held)[56] reverse this rule.

(iii) The Act did not reverse the general rule of the common law prohibiting spouses from suing one another in tort. The Act provided[57] that a wife could sue her husband 'for the *protection and security of her own separate property*'; and the interpretation of this provision caused considerable difficulty.

(iv) The wife's liability in tort and contract was not personal but proprietary and limited *to the extent of her separate property*. Accordingly, even if she were held liable, the judgment could not[58] be enforced by committal to prison under the Debtors Act 1869.[59]

(v) The Act did not prevent a married woman's property being made subject to *restraint on anticipation*.[60] A restraint prevented the wife from anticipating her entitlement (for example by assigning her interest in the property) and prevented a creditor from enforcing judgments against the property.[61]

---

[53] For an admirable succinct survey of liability in tort and contract, see Chapters 5 and 6 (by CA Morrison) in RH Graveson and FR Crane (eds.) *A Century of Family Law 1857–1957* (1957).

[54] s. 1(2).

[55] The Married Women's Property Act 1893 was passed to remedy this particular defect; and the Married Women's Property Act 1907 remedied a number of other technical defects.

[56] *Edwards v. Porter* [1925] AC 1.

[57] s. 12.

[58] *Scott v. Morley* (1887) 20 QBD 120. The 1882 Act (s. 1(5)) made a married woman carrying on a trade separately from her husband subject to bankruptcy (but only in respect of her separate property). The Bankruptcy Act 1914, s. 125 made a married woman carrying on a trade or business (whether or not separately from her husband) liable in bankruptcy as if she were a *feme sole*.

[59] s. 5.

[60] Devised by Lord Chancellor Thurlow in the late eighteenth century to protect a married woman against being persuaded to alienate her separate property by the husband's 'kicks or kisses': see *Tullett v. Armstrong* (1838) 1 Beav 1, 22 (and also against the risk that she might yield to her own 'extravagance, generosity, [or] speculations': Law Revision Committee, *Fourth Interim Report* (1934, Cmd. 4770) para. 20.

[61] As the Law Revision Committee's *Fourth Interim Report* (1934, Cmd. 4770) para. 20, put it: 'The way in which [the restraint] protects her from her creditors is that if they obtain a judgement against her, they cannot enforce it against so much of her property as is subject to a "*restraint*", either by causing the capital to be seized or by attaching the income before it reaches her hands. From one point of view this may be called protection against creditors; from another it appears to be a not very creditable means of defeating creditors'.

All except the last of these problems arose because the law was framed in terms of grafting special rules onto the concept of the wife's 'separate property' as it had been developed by the Court of Chancery.[62] In the years up to the beginning of World War II the courts were much occupied in clarifying the meaning of this concept, whilst legislation culminating in the Law Reform (Married Women and Tortfeasors) Act 1935 focussed largely on remedying the problems which experience had revealed.

Unravelling the consequences of the separate property regime

The concept of separate property had developed in the context of trusts and settlements; but the 1882 Act used it much more broadly. For example:

In *Ralston v. Ralston*[63] a wife, for many years separated from her husband, brought a libel action against him alleging that the gravestone he had erected in memory of his 'dearly beloved wife' implied that the deceased had been (and the plaintiff was not) lawfully married. She claimed that she was entitled to pursue the action, (notwithstanding the general rule that spouses were debarred from suing one another in tort) because the 1882 Act allowed a married women to bring such actions in order to protect her 'separate property'[64] and that since the libel would damage the goodwill attaching to her substantial business as a garage proprietor her claim fell within that exception. The claim failed.

A much commoner situation was where a man's negligent driving injured the woman he subsequently married. Could she, after the marriage, sue him (or in reality his insurance company)?

In *Gottliffe v. Edelston*[65] a man negligently drove his car into a horse and cart and the injuries caused his companion to lose her sight in one eye. At the time of the accident they were in what the judge described as 'the glamour of that period which precedes the romantic severity of a formal engagement'; but they subsequently married. The wife claimed that the action she brought against her husband was for the protection of her separate property. In a lengthy and scholarly

---

[62] As the Law Revision Committee pointed out in its *Fourth Interim Report* (1934, Cmd. 4770) para. 12 the decision to adopt the equitable notion of separate property was 'in itself . . . harmless enough and the expression was no doubt a convenient way of referring to such property of a married woman as was to be hers and not her husband's. It was one that would be readily understood by those acquainted with the equitable doctrine of the "separate use". But unfortunately . . . the legislature not only adopted the name by which the Court of Chancery had designated such property, but attached to this statutory separate property many of the other qualities with which the Court of Chancery had endowed it'.

[63] [1930] 2 KB 238.

[64] See Married Women's Property Act 1882, s. 12. In *Shipman v. Shipman* [1924] 2 Ch 140 the Court of Appeal held that the court's powers to protect a married woman's separate property extended to granting the plaintiff an interim injunction excluding her (drunken and violent) husband from the matrimonial home, which she owned. In contrast, a married man could not by action in tort exclude his wife from the matrimonial home; and this fact was for a time thought to be the foundation of the so-called deserted wife's equity: see further p. 109, below.

[65] [1930] 2 KB 378.

judgment McCardie J held that, taking into account the 'scheme and wording' of the 1882 Act the right of action vested in her before the marriage could not be described as her 'separate property'; and accordingly the claim failed. However, in 1948 the Court of Appeal[66] overruled the decision, on the basis that the wife's cause of action constituted a 'chose in action' which the 1882 Act specifically brought within the expression 'separate property'.

Married Women's Property Act unfair to married men?

The 1882 Act had been intended to remedy the inequities which married women suffered in relation to property rights; but grafting a separation regime onto the common law unity doctrine was soon found to put married men at a disadvantage. The Act was admittedly a Married Woman's Property Act and not a Married Man's Relief Act;[67] but some men thought the process had been taken too far. In *Gottliffe v. Edelston*[68] McCardie J[69] made it clear that he took this view:[70]

'Married women, however 'wealthy of purse or independent of character, possess powers and privileges which are wholly denied to husbands. Husbands are placed under burdens from which wives are free. Thus a husband living with his wife is liable to pay income tax upon her income,[71] even though she may refuse to contribute anything to the household expenses. . . . Again, a husband is liable for any tort his wife may commit provided it is not connected with a contract. . . . It matters not whether the tort be negligence, slander, trespass or assault. Thus she may be driving a motor car against his express request. She may, by her negligence, cause damage to a third person to the extent of thousands of pounds. For this damage the husband can be sued. . . . Judgment may be given against him for the damages, and upon that judgment he may be made bankrupt. He has no right whatever to claim any part of the damages from his wife, even though she be possessed

---

[66] *Curtis v. Wilcox* [1948] 2 KB 474. However, this decision created a further anomaly since a husband remained debarred from suing his wife for an ante-nuptial tort: *Baylis v. Blackwell* [1952] 1 KB 154 (in which McNair J stated that the anomaly was too firmly established to be removed save by legislation).

[67] *Per* Lord Sumner, *Edwards v. Porter* [1925] AC 1, 38.   [68] [1930] 2 KB 378.

[69] See Biographical Notes.

[70] The language of PM Winfield's leading *Textbook of the Law of Tort* (6th ed., 1954) p. 124, suggests that he too shared that view: '. . . it might well be less expensive for a man to keep a dog with a savage temper than to marry a wife with a venomous tongue; he could kill the animal, he could not even lock up the woman, and while he was not liable for the dog's bites unless he knew of its evil disposition, ignorance of his wife's vices was no excuse'.

[71] The rule whereby the income of husband and wife was aggregated for tax purposes (and the husband in principle liable to make returns of his wife's income and liable to tax on it) was a particular grievance in the 1930s; and the Law Revision Committee's *Fourth Interim Report* (1934, Cmd. 4770) suggested that if a married woman was to be placed in respect of her property in the same position as a single woman it was 'at least worthy of consideration whether the hardship, which in some cases now falls upon a husband in respect of his wife's income' should not be obviated by repealing the aggregation rule. In the event the aggregation rule was only finally abolished in 1990 in the first tranche of reforms carried through by Chancellor Nigel Lawson: Finance Act 1988, s. 32.

of a large private fortune of her own. A wife, on the contrary, is not liable for her husband's tort, unless she authorized or joined in it. Nay more, if the wife threatens to commit a tort which may inflict a heavy burden on a husband he has no right whatever to apply to the Court to prevent her from doing the wrongful act. The husband is helpless. . . . Again, if a husband wrongfully converts to his own use the goods of his wife she may bring an ordinary action against him for public trial in the courts. . . . But if a wife wrongfully converts to her own use the goods of her husband the only remedy of the husband, so far as he has any remedy at all, is to apply to the Court under the special[72] provisions of s. 17 of the Married Women's Property Act, 1882 . . .'[73]

But whatever the injustices suffered by married men, it was feminists who continued public agitation[74] for further reform, and full legal equality was only attained half a century later after four statutes and a mass of hotly disputed case law.

REMOVING THE LAST 'BARBAROUS RELICS' OF THE WIFE'S SERVITUDE[75]

(i) The Law Reform (Married Women and Tortfeasors) Act 1935

In 1934 the continuing agitation for further reform bore fruit: Lord Sankey[76] referred the liability of spouses in tort and contract[77] to his newly established

---

[72] The question of how far husband and wife were confined to seeking relief under s. 17 (which, at this time, was thought to empower the court to administer a kind of 'palm tree justice' disregarding legal rights) caused difficulties. In *Larner v. Larner* [1905] 2 KB 539 the Court of Appeal rejected the argument that questions about title to property were to be resolved exclusively by application under s. 17 of the 1882 Act and allowed the wife to sue her husband in the tort of detinue for the recovery of chattels.

[73] As Holcombe *(Wives and Property*, 1983, p. 219) points out, McCardie was a bachelor: see Biographical Notes.

[74] In the words of Sir Arthur Underhill, Senior Conveyancing Counsel of the Court (and father of Evelyn Underhill, the once well-known author of *Mysticism* (1911) and other books on religious subjects) in *The Law Reform (Married Women & Tortfeasors) Act, 1935* (1936) p. 20, for 'some years past an agitation has been carried on in feminist circles for legislation placing married women with regard to status, including their rights of property and liability for contracts, debts and other obligations, on the same plane as men, maidens or widows. Apart from sentiment this has been quite altruistic in effect; for under the Act of 1882 married women were placed in several respects in a better position than men'.

[75] The phrase used by Lord Denning MR to describe the rule (based on the unity doctrine) whereby a married woman automatically acquired and retained her husband's domicile: *Gray v. Formosa* [1963] P 259, 267. The rule was eventually abolished by Domicile and Matrimonial Proceedings Act 1973.

[76] See Biographical Notes.

[77] The matter referred to the Committee was 'the liability of a husband for the torts of the wife and the liability of a married woman in tort and contract . . .'—words which seem to have been carefully drafted to exclude the question of the liability in tort of one spouse to the other; and the Committee's Report simply records at the end of its Report and in a discussion of consequential provisions that whilst 'some might think it desirable' to remove the statutory restriction embodied in Married Women's Property Act 1882 on tort actions between spouses this matter 'does not appear to us to be within our terms of reference': *Fourth Interim Report* (1934, Cmd. 4770) para. 23. It is

Law Revision Committee;[78] and the Committee evidently took the view that this remit necessarily required an examination of the concept of 'separate property' central to the 1882 Act. The Committee's recommendations were radical; and it has been said[79] that the Law Reform (Married Women and Tortfeasors) Act 1935 (which gave effect to them) constituted a 'frontal attack' on some of the fundamental problems of the English law of husband and wife.

The Law Revision Committee's starting point was breathtakingly simple:

'Women nowadays, whether married or single, engage in almost all professions, trades and businesses and are eligible to hold and do in general hold every sort of public and official post and exercise every right and franchise[80] just as much as men.[81] There seems no reason, once it is established that they are no longer debarred by the law from holding property independently of their husbands, why they should not do so with all the corresponding rights and liabilities like everyone else.'[82]

On that basis, the Committee could see no reason for treating property owned by a married woman in any way differently from that of any other woman or any man. There was no good reason for keeping alive the idea of *'separate property'*; and if a married woman incurred a debt the judgment against her should be personal (rather than merely proprietary) and in the same form and with the same legal consequences as would apply in the case of a spinster, a widow, or a man. In short, the conception of the wife's separate property should be abolished; and the married woman exposed to the rigours of bankruptcy and debt enforcement in the same way as were others.[83]

In one respect, however, the Committee was unwilling to recommend radical action. At a surprisingly late stage in its deliberations,[84] the Committee realised that in some—perhaps many—cases the reason why a creditor was unable to enforce a judgment was not because the married woman debtor had no separate property, but because that property was subject to a *restraint on*

---

thus surprising that the Committee took in contrast a generous view of its remit in relation to property matters (particularly since the Committee's distinguished membership was not overweighted with Chancery lawyers).

[78] Subsequently to be renamed the Law Reform Committee. At the time, the Committee was made up of six judges (including the future Lord Chief Justice, Goddard) four barristers, two professors of law, one solicitor, and the Lord Chancellor's redoubtable Permanent Secretary Sir Claud Schuster: see Biographical Notes.

[79] By O Kahn-Freund, 'Inconsistencies and Injustices in the Law of Husband and Wife' (1952) 15 MLR 133.

[80] The Sex Disqualification (Removal) Act 1919 had removed most of the disabilities to which women were subject in public law: see generally N.St.J Stevas, 'Women in Public Law' in RH Graveson and FR Crane (eds.), *A Century of Family Law, 1857–1957.*

[81] This language is similar to that used 40 years later by Lord Denning MR in *Midland Bank Trust Co Ltd v. Green (No 3)* [1982] Ch 529, 538.

[82] *Fourth Interim Report* (1934, Cmd. 4770) para. 16.

[83] *Fourth Interim Report* (1934, Cmd. 4770) paras. 16–18.

[84] The matter was discussed at a meeting on 14 November, and only dealt with in the fourth draft of the Committee's Report: see PRO LCO2/1969.

anticipation[85]—a provision almost routinely inserted into marriage and other settlements[86] which effectively prevented creditors from seizing the capital or attaching the income derived from the property in question;[87] and the Committee therefore had to consider whether restraints should continue to be recognised. It concluded that to retain the institution would be incompatible with the 'present position of married women, to whom alone it applies'; but (mindful of the political difficulties which might arise in respect of legislation which could be said to be retrospective)[88] the Committee drew back from proposing outright abolition. Instead it recommended[89] that, whilst no restraints upon anticipation should be created in the future the provisions of existing settlements should remain unaffected. As we shall see, a decade later this topic was to provoke more parliamentary discussion and acrimonious debate than any other twentieth century legislation dealing with matrimonial property.

Sankey evidently appreciated the sensitivity of legislation dealing with the relations between the sexes, and was well aware that the Committee's proposals significantly improved the legal position of married men,[90] and in practical terms did very little for married women. He therefore took particular care to gain the support of women MPs[91] for the changes. In fact the Law Reform

[85] The fact that the Committee only came to consider this matter at such a late stage is no doubt attributable to the fact that its terms of reference apparently focussed on the law of tort and contract. Property law had been brought in only consequentially. In the event, the tail wagged the dog.

[86] 'a matter of common form', as Sir Hartley Shawcross A-G told the House of Commons in 1949: *Official Report* (HC) 7 November 1949, vol. 469, col. 898.

[87] In fact women had campaigned against the continued recognition of the restraint on anticipation since such provisions prevented a significant number of married women from having the same rights over their property as would a man or an unmarried woman. In particular, a married middle-class woman with property she was debarred from 'anticipating' might find this made it impossible for her to raise capital (as a single woman or man similarly circumstanced would do) by charging the property to start or help her in the trade profession or business in which it was increasingly likely she would want to engage: *Fourth Interim Report* (1934, Cmd. 4770) para. 20.

[88] This caution was well founded: note Underhill's criticism of the 'astonishing' decision (based on 'some fanciful argument that all distinctions between "men's property" and "women's property" ought to be abolished') to prohibit future restraints: *The Law Reform (Married Women & Tortfeasors) Act, 1935* (1936) p. 8.

[89] *Fourth Interim Report* (1934, Cmd. 4770) paras. 21–23. The Committee pointed out that the court had powers in certain circumstances to lift restraints (but it did not point out that the court exercised a cautious attitude to applications for the exercise of these powers).

[90] Much of the evidence submitted to the Law Revision Committee was from Trade Protection Societies (complaining about the complexity of the law) and from firms of solicitors focussing on the hardship caused to husbands by their liability to pay damages in respect of their wives' torts: see PRO LCO2/1969. In the House of Lords, Lord Listowel (a youthful peer of progressive outlook: see Biographical Notes) spoke of the great relief the measure would bring to married men and criticised the rule whereby the husband was liable for tax on his wife's income and for 'careless and thoughtless extravagance' on her part: see *Official Report* (HL) 5 June 1935, vol. 97, col. 304.

[91] Papers on PRO file LCO2/1977 show that Sir Claud Schuster evidently used Miss Marjorie Graves (Conservative MP for South Hackney, 1931–1935) as a source of contact and information. She informed him that the so-called 'Advanced Women' (a group including Lady Astor and Eleanor Rathbone: see Biographical Notes) were determined to seek enlargement of the Law Revision Committee's proposals; and that some of this Group's more prominent members were concerned more with theory rather than practical reforms and were hence 'beyond all argument'. Sankey

(Married Women and Tortfeasors) Act 1935 passed through Parliament with little opposition or hostile criticism; and in retrospect it can be seen that the Act—by abolishing the special regime applicable to 'separate property' and equating for the future the legal position of married and unmarried women in contract and tort—made a fundamental change in the law.[92] It deserved the title Law Reform (Status of Married Women) Act that at one stage was intended for it.[93]

(ii) The Married Women (Restraint on Anticipation) Act 1949

The 1935 compromise on Restraints on Anticipation[94] did give rise to controversy.[95] On the one side it was said that recognition of existing restraints implied that married women were irresponsible; and that to prevent women from dealing with their property as they wished was not in accordance with human dignity. On the other side it was claimed that the refusal to allow restraints to be imposed in the future merely evidenced a preference for naive ideology as against recognition of the legitimate interests of property owners in protecting their womenfolk against exploitation and abuse.[96]

But that was largely theory. The war-time and post-war increases in the rates of tax on income (to as much as 97.5%) were facts. The spending power of many married women of independent means was dramatically reduced; whilst the existence of a restraint made it virtually impossible to take the measures open to the well advised to minimise the tax system's worst burdens. The Married

nevertheless decided to meet all the women MPs who wished to attend and in the event only the Duchess of Atholl, Lady Astor and Megan Lloyd George stayed away. Schuster recorded that they all showed 'a very reasonable spirit' no doubt accepting the argument that the price of getting the Bill into the Government's programme was that the Whips had to be convinced it would 'not arouse controversy or take up time': Schuster to Hanworth (Chairman of the Law Revision Committee), LCO2/1977, 20 February 1935.

[92] The Government was exceedingly cautious about the restraint on anticipation: the Act accepted the principle that whilst existing restraints should remain effective it should not be possible to create restraints in the future; but the Law Reform (Married Women and Tortfeasors) Act 1935, s. 2(3) preserved the validity of restraints imposed by the wills of those dying within the next ten years (ie before 31 December 1945).

[93] The draftsman, Sir Granville Ram, could not conceal the irritation he experienced when members of the Law Revision Committee bombarded him with comments on successive drafts. He suggested that it would be better if they were to draft the complete Bill rather than making isolated comments.

[94] It was no longer possible to impose fresh restraints on anticipation but existing restraints remained effective: see above.

[95] According to Lord Jowitt LC, *Official Report* (HL) 5 July 1949, vol. 163, col. 894.

[96] AV Dicey, *Lectures on the Relation between Law and Public Opinion in England During the Nineteenth Century* (2nd ed. with preface by ECS Wade, 1962) p. 389 had claimed that 'most English gentlemen thought and still think [the restraint] necessary for the protection of a married woman against her own weakness or the moral authority of her husband . . .'; and Sir Arthur Underhill *The Law Reform (Married Women & Tortfeasors) Act, 1935* (1936) pp. 8, 40–43 took a similar view. (He also made suggestions as to how protective or discretionary trusts could achieve a similar result.) The leading solicitor Sir John Withers had noted that the restriction on imposing restraints was almost epoch making from 'the ordinary practising lawyer's point of view': *Official Report* (HC) vol. 304, col. 123.

Women (Restraint on Anticipation) Act, passed in 1949, seemed to bring the progress of assimilating the property rights of married men and married women to a triumphant conclusion. The Act[97] proclaimed that no 'restriction upon anticipation or alienation attached . . . to the enjoyment of any property by a woman which could not have been attached to the enjoyment of that property by a man shall be of any effect . . .'; and thus seemed neatly to assert the principle that, whilst conveyancing techniques[98] intended to protect beneficiaries from their own misfortune or extravagance could still be used, inequality between the sexes was not to be tolerated.

That was indeed the outcome. But in fact it was the pressing need to escape from an embarrassing political situation rather than any concern for removing sex discrimination which explained the Government's decision to legislate. In March 1949, the Attorney-General, Sir Hartley Shawcross told an MP who had taken up the case of a constituent suffering hardship that there was 'no prospect' of amending legislation;[99] yet three months later (even though the Government was faced with the possibility of a back-bench rebellion against what was seen by some as a 'rich-man's tax dodging scheme')[100] it had decided to act.

This dramatic change in policy was precipitated[101] by the case of the Countess Mountbatten of Burma, the heiress wife of the former Viceroy of India. Her pre-war income of £110,000—approaching three million pounds in modern values—from her grandfather's[102] 1920 will, had been reduced by taxation etc to a mere £4,500; and the financial burden of carrying out the public duties the Mountbattens had assumed after the death on active service of the King's brother and the 'great and necessary personal expense' the Mountbattens incurred whilst in India left Lady Mountbatten 'financially embarrassed'.[103] She was therefore advised to present a private Bill to

[97] s. 1(1).

[98] Such as discretionary or protective trusts (of which a statutory form is provided in Trustee Act 1925, s. 33).

[99] Shawcross to Davies, PRO LCO2/3601.

[100] See the paper dated 4 July 1949 sent by Dr Stephen Taylor (MP for Barnet 1945–1950) to the Lord President (Herbert Morrison): PRO LCO2/3204.

[101] This is not to cast doubt on Lord Chancellor Jowitt's explanation that he had been convinced the restraint operated as a 'hardship in practically every case where it applies': *Official Report* (HL) 5 July 1949, vol. 163, col. 894.

[102] Sir Ernest Cassell (to whom academic lawyers owe a debt of gratitude for his having endowed the chair of Commercial Law bearing his name at the London School of Economics, held by Lord Chorley of Kendal, LCB Gower, Lord Wedderburn of Charlton and other distinguished scholars).

[103] These facts are taken from the Statement of Reasons filed on behalf of Lady Mountbatten and investigated by the Lords' Committee. It had become a convention that Personal Bills investigated and passed by the Lords in this way were not questioned in the House of Commons, and the action of Conservative MPs led by Sir John Mellor was thus thought by some to be embarrassing.

Parliament,[104] the effect of which would have been to remove the restraint in her case, and thus give her the unfettered right of dealing as she wished with her interest under the will.[105] The Bill passed through the elaborate Private Bill procedure in the House of Lords; but the Mountbattens had enemies.[106] Backbench Opposition MPs put down a notice of a motion in the Commons declining to give a second reading 'to a personal Bill promoted to secure an amendment of the law which, if justifiable, should be made by Public Act for the benefit of all whom it may concern'. The Government, after some vacillation, decided to accept the principle underlying the motion; and (after a stormy passage)[107] the Married Women (Restraint on Anticipation) Act consigned the Restraint to history. Of course, the 1949 Act benefited the many 'ordinary little

---

[104] P Ziegler, *Mountbatten* (Fontana Paperback ed., 1990) p. 488 cites evidence from the Mountbatten archives, suggesting that Lord Mountbatten had been acting on the advice of Sir Walter Monckton KC (see Biographical Notes) and in the summer of 1948 had launched a 'full-blooded campaign' involving the King, the Prime Minister, and the Chancellor of the Exchequer to win support for the Private Bill. It appears that at first Monckton had advised applications to the court under Law of Property Act 1925, s. 169 as and when funds were needed; but the Mountbattens were outraged at the prospect of a series of annual applications: J Morgan, *Edwina Mountbatten, A Life of her Own* (1991) p. 445.

[105] Freed from the restraint, Lady Mountbatten could have sold her interest to an insurance company which (being liable to taxation on the income at a lower rate) would have been able to offer a substantial sum of capital which she could then have reinvested in an annuity or otherwise; or she could have borrowed money by mortgaging her interest under the settlement (and at that time tax relief would have been available to her on interest paid on the sum borrowed). Lady Mountbatten's solicitors told the Lord Chancellor's Office that it was not her intention to engage in a transaction with an insurance company; but nothing was said about her intentions with regard to another tax saving possibility—dividing the capital between herself and the remainderman—which could often be a more financially attractive proposition. The Lord Chancellor's Office investigated the tax avoidance schemes and were told that the maximum loss to the Treasury would be £45,000; but such assurances were not sufficient to allay the concern of Lord Simon who, in the House of Lords debate on the Government's Bill said that 'as a former Chancellor of the Exchequer' (not to say as someone who, lacking inherited wealth, had never had a marriage settlement) he was 'not prepared to remain silent . . . as to the effect upon the Revenue of this wholesale cancellation of a provision in past marriage settlements': *Official Report* (HL) 19 July 1949, vol. 164, col. 182. For Simon, see Biographical Notes.

[106] Not least the proprietor of the *Daily Express*, Lord Beaverbrook, who conducted a persistent vendetta against Mountbatten: see P. Ziegler, *Mountbatten* (Fontana Paperback ed., 1990), particularly at p. 488. Some Conservative backbenchers were also personally hostile to Lord Mountbatten on account of his supposed left-wing sympathies and attitudes to Indian independence; and Woodrow Wyatt (at the time a Labour MP) claimed that the 'despicable, underhand action' was founded on personal and political animosity against a man believed to have betrayed his class: *Official Report* (HC) 7 November 1949, vol. 469, col. 1003.

[107] The Commons debate on the Government's Bill occupies some 60 pages of Hansard and 47 Conservatives voted against it, whilst the debate in the House of Lords is notable for a particularly bitter attack by Lord Simon on Jowitt and others. (Simon's wrecking amendment was only defeated by 28 votes to 23: *Official Report* (HL) 14 July 1949, vol. 163, col. 1346.) Simon did however have good points—not least that that the Bill would release one kind of person from a restraint imposed in a settlement whilst leaving others subject to the same practical consequences by reason of the property being held on protective trusts. Only in 1958 did Parliament, in enacting the Variation of Trusts Act, allow all such provisions to be removed.

people'[108] affected by restraints (such as a teacher's wife left an inheritance of
£5,000) whose plight was feelingly depicted by Sir Hartley Shawcross[109] in the
Debates; but it was the need to remedy[110] the financial embarrassment suffered
by a woman who needed 19 domestic staff (including three cooks, a valet, a butler and two housemaids) and 'a minimum of two high-class secretaries and two
or three stenographers' to support the public work from which she would otherwise have had to withdraw[111] which was directly responsible for a socialist
government's decision to legislate.

(iii) The Law Reform (Husband and Wife) Act 1962

The common law would not countenance actions in tort between husband and
wife. This rule had had to be modified[112] so that a married woman could sue her
husband (for example, in detinue or conversion) for the protection of her property. But the modification gave added weight to the view that the bar on tort
actions was both anomalous and unjust;[113] and the sense of injustice was
increased as more and more spouses, injured by their partner's negligent driving,
found themselves debarred from recovering compensation from the insurance
company.[114] It seemed insulting that a wife seriously injured in this way should be
able to get compensation for the damage done to the dress she was wearing,[115] but

---

[108] Lady Pakenham (subsequently Longford, wife of Jowitt's ministerial colleague, Minister for
Civil Aviation) was one of those who had made representations: see her letter of 6 February 1949 to
the Lord Chancellor's Private Secretary asking that the Lord Chancellor should know 'how interested we both are'. This letter was circulated to the Attorney-General and others so that they would
be 'aware of the amount of pressure which is being brought to bear': Rieu to Read, 8 June 1949: PRO
LCO2/2304.

[109] *Official Report* (HC) 7 November 1949, vol. 469, col. 905.

[110] However, according to J Morgan, *Edwina Mountbatten, A Life of her Own* (1991) p. 445,
four more years of negotiations with the trustees—presumably about the terms on which the capital
should be divided—were necessary before the Mountbattens were again 'in funds'.

[111] Statement by Lady Mountbatten's solicitors, as reported in *The Times*, 8 May 1949.

[112] Married Women's Property Act 1882, s. 12 (amended by Law Reform (Married Women) and
Tortfeasors Act 1935 to remove the restriction to actions for the protection of her 'separate' property).

[113] Law Reform Committee, *Ninth Report* (1961, Cmnd. 1268), para. 3. 'It is anomalous that
. . . a husband should be in a worse position than his wife in regard to the right of action in tort. This
anomaly is accentuated by the fact that there is no restriction on a wife's right to sue her husband
for a tort committed before marriage (*Curtis v. Wilcox . . .*) though he cannot sue her for an ante-
nuptial tort (*Baylis v. Blackwell . . .*). The law is unjust in its effect on the spouses themselves as well
as on third parties. The fact that the wife's right of action is limited to the protection of her property means that in no circumstances can she sue her husband for personal injury inflicted on her
however grievous . . .' The injustice to third parties was exemplified in the rule (see *Chant v. Read*
[1939] 2 KB 346) denying a person jointly liable with a husband for the wife's death in an accident
any claim to contribution from the husband: *op. cit.* para. 16.

[114] This is because a typical motor insurance policy provides an *indemnity* against the driver's liabilities. The rule would not affect claims under a policy which specifically provided cover for personal injuries suffered by the policy holder's family.

[115] On the basis that s. 12 Married Women's Property Act permitted a wife to sue in tort for
injury to her property: see above.

not for her (perhaps seriously disabling) personal injuries.[116] The combination of powerful academic criticism,[117] evidence of practical hardship, and lack of any opposition from major insurance interests,[118] suggested that it should not be difficult to bring about reform; and in March 1959 Lord Chancellor Kilmuir[119] referred the matter to the Law Reform Committee.

The Committee found the problem rather more difficult than had been assumed. The rule had its origins in the common law doctrine that husband and wife became one person,[120] but however unrealistic the legal unity of husband and wife might have become, there was still 'a genuine unity of the household which should be protected against anything likely to undermine it'.[121] More generally, there were fears that litigation between husband and wife would be 'unseemly, distressing and embittering'.[122] As the Committee put it—

'We think that to allow complete freedom of action in tort would be undesirable as a matter of general social policy. The strains which are liable to be set up and the troubles which are liable to arise when two people are living together in the constant close proximity of marriage produce a situation that should not be regarded merely from a narrow legal point of view. If either spouse were able without let or hindrance to bring an action in tort against the other in respect of injuries of a personal nature, it might easily lead to harmful results. Litigation in respect of petty acts of negligence in the domestic sphere would certainly not be conducive to the continuance of the marriage and would, we think, do nothing but harm.'[123]

Other, apparently more technical, difficulties surfaced. For example the protection given to a wife against being evicted by her husband from the matrimonial home was sometimes[124] attributed to the fact that he could not sue her in trespass after he had terminated her licence to remain. If that were

---

[116] The illustration given by Professor CJ Hamson in a letter to DW Dobson, Secretary of the Law Reform Committee, 18 April 1959, PRO LCO2/7383.

[117] Notably O Kahn-Freund, 'Inconsistencies and Injustices in the Law of Husband and Wife' (1952) 15 MLR 133; G Williams, 'The Legal Unity of Husband and Wife' (1947) 10 MLR 16.

[118] The Law Reform Committee was given to understand that the insurance industry would not oppose change in the law (the implication being that any increase in claims would be met simply by an increase in premiums).

[119] See Biographical Notes.

[120] See eg *Phillips v. Barnet* (1876) 1 QBD 436, 438, *per* Blackburn J; *Edwards v. Porter* [1925] AC 1, 9, *per* Lord Cave.

[121] Law Reform Committee, *Ninth Report* (1961, Cmnd. 1268) para. 7 reflecting the view of McCardie J that marriage created a 'substantial identity of social and other interests between husband and wife' and that accordingly there was 'a sound sociological basis for the view . . . that in certain respects there should be a presumption of modified unity between husband and wife': *Gottliffe v. Edelston* [1930] 2 KB 378, 385; and the view put forward in evidence by Professor CJ Hamson that the law should reconcile the recognition that husband and wife had separate *identities* with a recognition that they had a *common establishment*: PRO LCO2/7384, 18 April 1959.

[122] *Gottliffe v. Edelston* [1930] 2 KB 378, 392, *per* McCardie J.

[123] Law Reform Committee, *Ninth Report* (1961, Cmnd. 1268) para. 9.

[124] Originating in dicta by Goddard LJ: *Bramwell v. Bramwell* [1942] 1 KB 370.

correct,[125] to allow spouses an unrestricted right to sue one another in tort would have disastrous consequences. More generally, the Committee was impressed[126] by the fact that the court exercised a wide and flexible discretion[127] in dealing in private with applications raising issues of title to or possession of property under s. 17 of the Married Women's Property Act 1882; and it was reluctant to allow questions of the parties' rights to property—'notoriously difficult to disentangle . . . and . . . not really capable of being satisfactorily decided by the application of strict rules of law'[128]—to be dealt with in the same way as disputes between strangers.

The supposed technicalities concealed central issues about matrimonial property, answered by case law and legislation only many years later.[129] Not surprisingly, the Committee was for long divided;[130] and the Secretary feared that it would be impossible to produce a unanimous Report.[131] But eventually a compromise was agreed:

1. In the case of torts not affecting the title to or possession of property, either spouse should be able to sue the other as if they were unmarried.[132] But this should be 'without prejudice to' any right which a deserted wife may have to remain in the matrimonial home;[133] and the wife should lose the right given her by the Married Women's Property Act 1882 to sue her husband in tort for the protection of her separate property.[134]
2. All disputes relating to title to or possession of property should be dealt with under s. 17 of the Married Women's Property Act 1882.[135]
3. In order to minimise the risk of the courts being used to air petty grievances between husband and wife,[136] the court should have power to stay an action if, having regard to all the circumstances including the conduct of the parties and the nature of the matter complained of, the judge was satisfied that the

---

[125] It had for long been considered doubtful whether it was: see *Pargeter v. Pargeter* [1946] 1 KB 370; and papers on PRO LCO2/7386 (particularly Newman to Dobson 5 July 1961) make it clear that the Law Reform Committee's secretariat accepted that the protection accorded to the wife was a consequence of the husband's common law duty to maintain her (a view developed by Denning LJ and subsequently accepted by the House of Lords in *National Provincial Bank Ltd v. Ainsworth* [1965] AC 1175, HL, see further below).

[126] And evidently influenced by a powerfully argued memorandum by Professor O Kahn-Freund. This urged that the court should have a discretion in inter-spouse tort actions relating to property: see PRO LCO2/7383.

[127] See below p. 122.

[128] Law Reform Committee, *Ninth Report* (1961, Cmnd. 1268) para. 14.

[129] See p. 123 below.

[130] John Foster QC and the future Labour Lord Chancellor Gerald Gardiner QC (who on this occasion found himself in the surprising position of sharing the views expressed in evidence by the Inns of Court Conservative and Unionist Association) wanted to confine the right to sue to cases involving a claim to property or compensation for motoring accidents; whereas Professor Hughes Parry and Ashworth J favoured the abolition of all restriction: see the minutes on PRO LCO2/7384.

[131] Dobson to Jenkins, PRO LCO2/7385, 27 July 1960.

[132] Law Reform Committee, *Ninth Report* (1961, Cmnd. 1268) para. 11.

[133] *Ibid.*, para. 15.   [134] *Ibid.*, para. 14.   [135] *Ibid.*   [136] *Ibid.*, para. 15.

complaint lacked substance or that it was not in the interests of the parties for the action to proceed.[137]

Translating these recommendations into the language of an Act of Parliament proved remarkably difficult. For example, everyone agreed that there must be some fetter[138] on the right of aggrieved spouses to bring their petty grievances before the court[139] but there was little agreement on what the fetter should be.[140] The Law Reform Committee had proposed giving the court power to stay actions, but to require a court to decide whether it would be 'in the best interests of the parties' to allow the action to go ahead (as the Law Reform Committee had recommended)[141] might require it[142] to 'assess the future prospects of the parties' marriage' and even to require the court to act as a kind of reconciliation tribunal.[143] In the end it was decided that the court should be empowered to stay proceedings if 'no substantial benefit would accrue to either party from the continuation of the proceedings'.[144] The reader may feel that this was not really[145] 'much narrower and more precise'[146] than the criterion put forward by the Committee, and it is impossible not to sympathise with the draftsman who engagingly admitted that he and the officials 'don't quite know what we do mean' but had simply to do their best.

At what is apparently a more technical level, the Government refused to accept the Committee's recommendation that disputes about title and possession of property be brought exclusively under the (supposedly discretionary)

---

[137] *Ibid.*, para. 11.

[138] Some shared the views of J Foster and G Gardiner (note 130 above) and thought the right to sue should be restricted to cases of personal injury: see eg RT Paget MP, *Official Report* (HC) 18 May 1962, vol. 659, col. 1713.

[139] The precise basis for this policy was never entirely clear: was it intended to protect the courts or the parties? And no one seems ever to have answered Professor Glanville Williams' point (Memorandum to the Law Reform Committee, PRO LCO2/7383) that the law did not impose fetters on the right of one spouse to launch a private prosecution of the other intended to lead to conviction and imprisonment—action which might seem just as likely to engender distress and bitterness as an action in tort for damages.

[140] Sir Reginald Manningham Buller AG pointed out that if the restriction took the form of a stay, substantial costs would inevitably be run up in preparing for the hearing: PRO LCO2/7386 (Home Affairs Committee, 20 July 1961); but the Law Reform Committee had considered and specifically rejected the alternative of prohibiting actions unless the court first gave leave, in part because such a requirement might suggest that the theory underlying the common law rule remained valid: *op. cit.* para. 10. Eventually it was agreed that the rules should provide for the court to consider the question of imposing a stay at an early stage of the proceedings: Law Reform (Husband and Wife) Act 1962, s. 1(3).

[141] See above.   [142] *Official Report* (HL) 2 July 1962, vol. 241, col. 1112.

[143] See the comments of the draftsman, Sir Noel Hutton, on suggestions made by Sir Jocelyn Simon SG: PRO LCO2/7386, 7 November 1961.

[144] Law Reform (Husband and Wife) Act 1962, s. 1(2)(a). Officials considered that this test would make it possible to stay proceedings where the amount claimed was trivial or 'where as may not infrequently be the case' proceedings are brought against the 'only breadwinner in the family', thereby risking the 'impoverishment of the family as a whole': Departmental Brief for Second Reading in House of Commons, PRO LCO2/7387.

[145] See Hutton to Dobson, PRO LCO2/7387, 15 February 1962.

[146] *Official Report* (HL) 2 July 1962, vol. 241, col. 1112, *per* Viscount Kilmuir LC.

Married Women's Property Act 1882, s. 17.[147] Instead the Act gave the court a discretionary power to stay tort proceedings if the questions in issue could 'more conveniently be disposed of' on a s. 17 application.

At one level these disputes may be thought to demonstrate the futility of much of the enormous volume of skilled bureaucratic effort put into the legislative process: there is overwhelming (if only anecdotal) evidence that actions in tort between husband and wife are only brought in cases where the real defendant is an insurance company, and most solicitors and district judges cannot recall ever having been faced with threats of action in any other circumstances. But before dismissing the lengthy discussions on the precise terminology of the 1962 Act as a time-wasting irrelevance, it should be noted that in the United States tort actions—and especially actions for intentionally inflicting emotional distress[148]—between husband and wife have become common, often in an attempt to secure the financial benefits denied by the courts' refusal to take matrimonial conduct into account in settling the financial outcome of marital breakdown.[149]

The unity doctrine a long time dying

In 1937[150] the Court of Appeal declared that the Law Reform (Married Women and Tortfeasors) Act 1935 made a 'clean sweep of the old fiction of our common law that a woman on marrying became merged in the personality of her husband and ceased to be a fully qualified and separate human person'. But in truth this was far from the case. Even after the 1962 Act had been put onto the statute book further statutory reform (notably the Domicile and Matrimonial Proceedings Act 1973,[151] providing[152] that a married woman's domicile should no longer automatically be the same as her husband's but rather should be 'ascertained by reference to the same factors as in the case of any other individual capable of having an independent domicile') was needed to effect a total

---

[147] This was because the question of what constituted a dispute about 'title or possession' might be difficult to answer.

[148] For the position in England see *Wilkinson v. Downton* [1897] 2 QB 57; and *Janvier v. Sweeney* [1919] 2 KB 316.

[149] See HD Krause, 'On the danger of Allowing Marital Fault to Re-emerge . . .' (1998) 73 Notre Dame L Rev 1355. See RE Spector, 'Marital Torts: The Current Legal Landscape' (1999) 33 FLQ 745.

[150] *Barber v. Pigden* [1937] 1 KB 664, 678 *per* Scott LJ.

[151] Other landmarks were the Law Reform (Miscellaneous Provisions) Act 1970 (which abolished the right to sue for enticement and harbouring and the claim for damages for adultery: see Chapter 8 below) and the Administration of Justice Act 1982 (which abolished the husband's right to sue a person whose negligence had caused the loss of the services which at common law the wife was bound to render him).

[152] s. 1(2). Some evidence of the movement of opinion may be found in the fact that 21 years earlier the Private International Law Committee's *First Report* on *Domicile* (1954, Cmd. 9068) was not willing to go beyond recommending that a woman separated from her husband by court order should be capable of acquiring a separate domicile. At much the same period the *Royal Commission on the Taxation of Profits and Income* (Second Report, Cmd. 9105, paras. 117–134) had denied that the rule aggregating spouses' incomes (see below) embodied an 'outmoded or an unworthy conception of the relations of man and woman in marriage'.

juristic severance between spouses; whilst the much criticised[153] rule[154] aggregating the spouses' income for income tax purposes[155] lingered on until 1990.[156] But the final quietus for the unity doctrine was given by the courts in litigation (appropriately 'bidding fair to rival in time and money the story of *Jarndyce v. Jarndyce*')[157] stemming from the breakdown of relationships between parent and child. There was an action for conspiracy; and the courts rejected a defence that for this purpose husband and wife had to be treated as one person and thus could not be guilty of a tort[158] based on the collaboration of two or more. Oliver J declined[159]

'. . . to apply . . . a medieval axiom which was never wholly accurate and which appears to me now to be as ill-adapted to the society in which we live as it is repugnant to common sense'

and in the Court of Appeal Lord Denning spoke eloquently of the contrast between mediaeval and contemporary England. The maxim that husband and wife are one was (he said)

'a fiction then. It is a fiction now. . . . Nowadays, both in law and in fact, husband and wife are two persons, not one. They are partners—equal partners—in a joint enterprise, the enterprise of maintaining a home and bringing up children. Outside that joint enterprise they live their own lives and go their own ways—always, we hope, in consultation one with the other, in complete loyalty one with the other, each maintaining and deserving the trust and confidence of the other. They can and do own property jointly or

---

[153] And, latterly, much misunderstood. In fact, special relief was given in respect of a wife's earned income, and as a result a married couple with modest earnings would pay less tax on their incomes than two single people. Application of the aggregation rule only increased liability where a spouse had significant investment income or earned income attracting surtax: see the detailed explanation in SM Cretney, *Principles of Family Law* (3rd ed., 1979) pp. 399–403.

[154] The Rule had been criticised in the Law Revision Committee's *Fourth Interim Report* (1934, Cmd. 4770). The Royal Commission on Marriage and Divorce (1956, Cmnd. 9678, paras. 717–8) noted the strength of the criticism but, being very doubtful whether the matter was within its terms of reference, expressed no view on the issue. Even a quarter of a century later, a Government Consultation Paper, *The Taxation of Husband and Wife* (1980, Cmnd. 1980) did not lead to any immediate reform initiative.

[155] The impact of the rule at a period in which women's liberation had become an issue was sharpened by the practice of the Revenue—only abandoned in 1979: see [1979] BTR 481—in addressing correspondence about the wife's affairs to her husband.

[156] Finance Act 1988, s. 32.

[157] *Midland Bank Trust Co Ltd v. Green* [1980] Ch 496, 622, *per* Lord Denning MR.

[158] It remains the case that they cannot be convicted of the *crime* of conspiracy: Criminal Law Act 1977, s. 2(2)(a); and in *Mawji v. R* [1957] AC 126 the Judicial Committee of the Privy Council held that the same rule applied in cases where the marriage was polygamous. Hence a rule based on the fiction that husband and wife are one was extended to a case in which they might be five (or even more). In *Midland Bank Trust Co Ltd v. Green (No 3)* [1979] Ch 496, Oliver J adopted the view that the criminal law rule was based not on unity (for it would be an absurdity after 1882 to hold that a married woman was capable of entering into a commercial contract with her husband but incapable of agreeing with him to commit a crime) but rather on 'a public policy which, for the preservation of the sanctity of marriage, accords an immunity from prosecution to spouses who have done no more than agree between themselves in circumstances which would lay them open, if unmarried, to a charge of conspiracy'.

[159] [1979] Ch 496, 527.

severally or jointly and severally. . . . They can and do enter into contracts with others
. . ., and can be made liable for breaches just as any other contractors can be. They can
and do commit crimes jointly or severally and can be punished severally for them. They
can and do commit wrongs jointly or severally and can be made liable jointly or severally just as any other wrong-doers. The severance in all respects is so complete that I
would say that the doctrine of unity and its ramifications should be discarded altogether,
except in so far as it is retained by judicial decision or by Act of Parliament.'[160]

And so the doctrine of unity passed into history. The doctrine of separation
of property was firmly established. The Victorian campaigners' reform had
achieved what they wanted.

It is impossible to deny that this outcome better reflects the twentieth century
personal relationship of husband and wife. As a High Court judge[161] had put it
in 1930:

'Husbands and wives have their individual outlooks. They may belong to different political parties, to different schools of thought. A wife may be counsel in the courts against
her husband. A husband may be counsel against his wife. Each has a separate intellectual
life and activities. Moreover . . . the modern notion is that it is one's right to assert one's
own individuality. . . . We are probably completing the transition from the family to the
personal epoch of woman.'

THE CONSEQUENCES OF SEPARATION OF PROPERTY REAPPRAISED: INSTITUTIONALISED INEQUALITY?

So far, so good. But husband and wife still normally lived together, under the
same roof. How well did separation of property reflect their expectations? In
1952 the eminent comparative lawyer, Otto Kahn-Freund[162] sounded a cautionary note:

'. . . husband and wife face each other in matters of property like strangers. The fact that
they are husband and wife has no effect on their property. Nothing is by law 'theirs';
everything . . . is in the absence of express agreement to the contrary, either 'his' or 'hers'.
Sociologists must decide whether this legal rule reflects the *mores* and ideas of the
people.'[163]

That separation of property would not achieve justice for married women in
the conditions prevalent in the second half of the twentieth century had already

---

[160] [1982] Ch 529, 538.   [161] McCardie J., in *Gottliffe v. Edelston* [1930] 2 KB 378, 385.
[162] 'Inconsistencies and Injustices in the Law of Husband and Wife' (1952) 15 MLR 133. For
Kahn-Freund, see the Biographical Notes.
[163] Note Dicey's comment (*Lectures on the Relation between Law and Public Opinion in England
during the Nineteenth Century* (2nd ed with preface by ECS Wade, 1962) p. 387 note 2) that it
'would have been possible [in 1882] to place husband and wife, as under French law, in something
like the position of partners as regards each other's property. An innovation . . . of this kind would
have been radically opposed to English habits. It has not . . . been advocated either in or out of
Parliament'.

begun to appear during World War II. As Professor OR McGregor[164] was to put it:[165] the nineteenth century reforms had

'unintentionally institutionalised inequality in the economic relations of husbands and wives. By preventing husbands getting their hands on their wives' money, the statute denied wives rights in their husband's money. And in the real world, it was mostly the husbands who had the money'.

The beginning of the move for further reform of family property law—or at least of official notice being recorded of dissatisfaction with the consequences of the separation doctrine—can be dated precisely. On 6 May 1943 Judge Hirst, sitting in the Oxford County Court, gave judgment for Mr John Blackwell[166] in his claim for the £103.50 which his wife had deposited in her account with the Oxford Co-operative Society. The law (said the Judge) was quite clear: if a wife made savings (as Mrs Blackwell had done) from a housekeeping allowance the savings and any articles bought with them belonged in law to the husband unless it could be proved that he had intended the money as a gift.[167]

Perhaps Mr Blackwell was surprised to find his case reported in *The Times* and other newspapers; and he would certainly have been surprised to find it taken up by Dr Edith Summerskill[168] and others as exemplifying the law's injustice to married women, and even more surprised to find that a quarter of a century later his claim was used in the House of Commons by a Conservative MP[169] to illustrate the need for wide-ranging reform of the law of family property.[170] The case was taken to the Court of Appeal;[171] but the efforts of the two women barristers instructed by the woman solicitor acting for the wife[172] failed

[164] See Biographical Notes.

[165] In a debate on the Law Commission's proposals for co-ownership of the matrimonial home: *Official Report* (HL) 18 July 1979, vol. 401, col. 1437.

[166] Of Cranham Street, Jericho, Oxford—then an area of working class housing as immortalised in Thomas Hardy's *Jude the Obscure*. Half a century later a typical house in that street may fetch more than a quarter of a million pounds. Such escalation of property values is relevant to the legal doctrines discussed in this chapter: see below.

[167] The basis of the rule (according to the *Royal Commission on Marriage and Divorce* (1956, Cmd. 9678, para. 699) was that a wife was to be considered as her husband's agent in disposing of the money he had provided.

[168] See Biographical Notes.   [169] Dame Joan Vickers: see Biographical Notes.

[170] *Official Report* (HC) 24 January 1969, vol. 776, col. 848.

[171] The Court of Appeal's judgments are reported in [1943] 2 All ER 579. An application was made for leave to appeal to the House of Lords—a development which caused embarrassment in the Lord Chancellor's Department since Viscount Simon felt he had to retract his agreement to receive a women's organisation deputation: 'I must not . . . and will not . . . contribute in any way to a possible confusion between my judicial duty and my duty as a Minister who has to advise about proposed amendments to the law. You will, I am sure, appreciate why I am punctilious in such a matter' [PRO LCO2/2777]. In the event, the case went no further; and the deputation had to be satisfied with an interview with Sir Claud Schuster and the Attorney-General.

[172] In addition, Miss Venetia Stephenson held a watching brief for the Married Women's Association: *The Times*, 28 October; and it appears that the Association may have organised the Appeal: see the speech of Dame Joan Vickers in the debate on the Matrimonial Property Bill 1969, *Official Report* (HC) 24 January 1969, vol. 776, col. 848.

to convince any of the three (male) judges that the law was other than totally clear[173] and in the husband's favour.

A 'novel and dangerous element in matrimonial relations'?[174]

This ruling prompted Dr Summerskill and the Married Women's Association to start a campaign of meetings[175] letters[176] and parliamentary questions.[177] Eventually, the Association put forward its Equal Partnership Bill giving spouses the right to an equal share of the family income in recognition of their mutual services to the family; and the Bill conferred a wide jurisdiction on the court to decide how the family income should be allocated 'for the necessary domestic expenditure'.

The Government[178] was evidently appalled[179] by the extent of what was proposed; and preferred to concede, at least in private,[180] the case for measures

---

[173] The same point arose subsequently in *Hoddinott v. Hoddinott* [1949] 2 KB 406, (wife had no interest in football pool winnings because stake taken from housekeeping—note Denning LJ's dissent on ground that the winnings were the product of wife's skill and that she was accordingly entitled to share in the fruits of the joint effort).

[174] G Coldstream to Schuster, commenting on a Parliamentary Question put down by Dr Edith Summerskill which was thought to be based on the assumption that a 'wife who is a hard worker and an efficient manager is entitled to be rewarded on a cash basis': PRO LCO2/2777, May 1943.

[175] On 8 November 1943 the Married Women's Association passed a resolution declaring that the decision in *Blackwell* 'had made a mockery of the marriage vows' and asserting that a housewife should have the right to an equal share of the family income 'in recognition of her services in the home and in the community': *The Times*, 9 November 1943.

[176] PRO file LCO2/2777 records that the Lord Chancellor's Office had received a 'great number of letters'. Officials were worried that the campaign might make some impact on other ministers (notably Ernest Bevin, the Minister of Labour) not least because Bevin 'might not realize how many are the legal difficulties which are involved in it, and . . . we might find ourselves committed to a course of action which we might subsequently regret': Schuster to Somervell, 6 December 1943. However, Somervell's explanation of the 'difficulties' convinced Bevin, who recorded that the more he thought about it the more he became convinced that they should not attempt to deal with the matter 'unless we are forced to do so'. If it became impossible to resist pressures a Bill providing for equal division of savings would be the 'neatest way out of an awkward position': Bevin to Somervell, 29 December 1943. (This was in fact the solution eventually enacted 21 years later.)

[177] Mr SS Hammersley, Unionist MP for East Willesden had also been active, pointing out the difficulties arising from the inability of magistrates' courts to deal with the allocation of furniture and other matrimonial property in maintenance proceedings. However, the Home Secretary refused to set up an inquiry: see *Official Report* (HC) 29 July 1943, vol. 391, col. 1764.

[178] As represented by the Attorney-General, Sir Donald Somervell, and Sir Claud Schuster: see Biographical Notes.

[179] Although Lord Chancellor Simon believed that demand by married women for 'some pecuniary recognition of their services in the home is strong' and likely to grow, and that in the post-War world change would come about, not everyone agreed. Mrs Marjorie Bourne, for example, in a letter published in *The Times* 2 November 1943 and claiming to speak 'for many of my contemporaries now serving their country in uniform and waiting to set up their homes' thought it 'nauseating if love for husband and children is in the future to be regarded as a professional service for which one is entitled to receive payment'.

[180] The Married Women's Association was told that enquiries would be made about the experience in other countries. The enquiries extended to asking JG Foster (see Biographical Notes) about the situation in France; but his detailed reply suggested that French married women were more disadvantaged than were the English.

confined to equal entitlement to the household savings and furniture. But no action was taken; and paradoxically the return of a Labour Government in 1945 seems to have brought Government involvement in the issue to an end,[181] possibly because Edith Summerskill (the campaign's most persistent parliamentary voice) accepted ministerial office and thereby disqualified herself from public campaigning.

Labour ministers certainly showed little sympathy for the women's cause when the issue resurfaced in 1951; and the Cabinet's Legislation Committee reacted with apparent hilarity[182] to the Deserted Wives Bill introduced by Mrs Irene Ward[183] and others. This would have given the court power to transfer statutory tenancies and to apportion chattels between the spouses if (but only if) the applicant had obtained a magistrates' maintenance order on the ground of desertion. But the Lord Chancellor's officials were much more sympathetic than the Ministers they had to serve: the Bill (they thought) might have been prompted by a real grievance.[184] The Attorney-General advised that the Bill should be condemned 'with faint praise' but not rejected entirely;[185] and the Lord Chancellor's officials made sure that the terms of reference of the Royal Commission on Marriage and Divorce (eventually set up in September 1951) extended to the law relating to 'the property rights of husband and wife, both during marriage and after its termination'.[186] Time had been successfully bought. But the fact that English law did not recognise the household as a unit for the ownership of property increasingly seemed to be a defect, rather than a virtue. As Sir Leslie Scarman[187] was to put it in 1971, 'Married women are not single women. They live with and for their husbands and children in a unit known as the family, which it is the policy of the law to cherish and support'.[188]

[181] The last entry on PRO LCO2/2777 is a copy of a general review carried out by the Haldane Society. This recommended, amongst other things, joint ownership of the family home and furniture.

[182] Ministers—who thought the Bill was 'rather a joke'—apparently believed that the principle of *in*equality of the sexes had been allowed to go too far, with the result that the husband was in danger of becoming his wife's chattel: RL Rieu (a Senior Legal Assistant in the Lord Chancellor's Office) to Shawcross, PRO LCO2/4851, 22 January 1951.

[183] See Biographical Notes. The Bill's sponsor was another Conservative woman MP, Mrs Eveline Hill.

[184] The Lord Chancellor's officials sought the views of a County Court judge, and tried to encourage the Home Office to make enquiries amongst social workers.

[185] The Bill was refused a second reading on a division in the House of Commons: *Official Report* (HC) 26 January 1951, vol. 483, col. 535. The Government spokesman did offer to enter into discussions with the promoters, but declined to give any undertaking about future legislation. Women's Disabilities Bills—somewhat broader in scope than the 1951 Bill—were introduced in 1952 and 1953 but made no progress. The criticisms made of the Bills are summarised in the *Report of the Royal Commission on Marriage and Divorce* (1956, Cmd. 9678, paras. 641–642).

[186] 'except by death': *Royal Commission on Marriage and Divorce* (1956, Cmd. 9678, p. iii).

[187] See Biographical Notes.   [188] *Women and Equality before the Law* (1971).

Changing economic conditions

The feeling that something had to be done was reinforced by court decisions which exposed the law's failure to deal with changed economic conditions. The war-time and post-war housing shortages were particularly significant. Nearly one in three houses had been destroyed or damaged during World War II and virtually none had been built. There were stringent controls intended to protect tenants—and in the late 1930s very few workers' houses were owner occupied[189]—from exploitation. In effect, the statutory tenant's rent could not be increased nor could his tenancy be terminated. The result, paradoxically, was to make it very difficult for a wife forced to leave her husband to find anywhere to live: property owners increasingly found letting houses an unattractive proposition and there was a dramatic fall in the availability of accommodation to rent.[190] In 1939 court ordered periodical payments would have enabled a wife to rehouse herself in leasehold property. In 1945 that was no longer true.[191]

The shift in preference to buying rather than renting, combined with the scarcity caused by the lack of new building, no doubt contributed to the inflation in owner occupied house prices. This of course brought windfall gains for people who had bought houses before the war,[192] but very often the wife found that the title to the property was in the husband's sole name (perhaps because it was 'common knowledge' that a building society would at that time be 'more inclined . . . to have the husband as the mortgagor than the wife')[193] so that she had no share in the gain. If the marriage broke down, the court had no

---

[189] Less than one fifth: see generally R McKibbin, *Classes and Cultures, England 1918–1951,* (1998) p. 73.

[190] The shift away from private renting towards owner occupation continued (and accelerated) in the post-War period. Whereas in 1950 44% of the country's housing stock was rented from private owners (as against 30% owner-occupied) by 1961 the percentages were 16% and 50% respectively. Between 1961 and 1994 the proportion of owner occupied properties doubled and the proportion of privately rented halved: *Social Trends* (1970 and 1994) Table 89 and p. 110 respectively. It should not be forgotten that a major contribution to working class housing was at this time made by Local Authorities: a million 'council houses' were built between 1919 and 1939, and in 1950 such houses constituted nearly a fifth of the total housing stock: see *Social Trends* (1970) Table 89, and generally R McKibbin, *Classes and Cultures, England 1918–1951,* (1998) p. 188 ff. Until the enactment of the Housing Act 1980 council tenants had few legal rights (so that, in the days before Judicial Review, few if any cases involving the right to live in such property came before the courts); but the Authorities usually managed their estates in a benevolent if paternalistic way, and would often re-allocate tenancies on marital breakdown so as to protect the wife and children: see *Davis v. Johnson* [1979] AC 264, 343, *per* Lord Salmon.

[191] This point was forcefully put by Mr H Lightman QC for the wife in *National Provincial Bank Ltd v. Ainsworth* [1965] AC 1175, HC; and its validity was accepted by Lord Wilberforce and others. As shown below, the case went against the wife, but made the pressure for legislation irresistible.

[192] See eg *per* Lord Evershed MR, *Rimmer v. Rimmer* [1953] 1 QB 63, 68: house bought in 1935—deposit of £29 paid in cash, balance of £460 purchase price borrowed from Building Society—sold in 1952 for £2,117.

[193] *Per* Lord Evershed MR, *Rimmer v. Rimmer* [1953] 1 QB 63, 68.

power to order a transfer of the house (or any other capital).[194] As Lord Wilberforce was to recognise in *National Provincial Bank Ltd v. Ainsworth*,[195] once the wife lost possession of a house, the process of acquiring another place to live could be painful and prolonged.

Judicial activism? Three legal issues

Three main issues came before the courts. First, what was to happen if a deserting husband left his wife in the home of which he was a statutory tenant? This was quickly and satisfactorily resolved. In 1950[196] the Court of Appeal unanimously held that the wife continued the occupancy protected by the Rent Acts, and that neither the husband nor the landlord could turn her out provided that she continued to pay the rent and to comply with the other terms of the tenancy.[197]

The second issue was how far similar protection was available if the deserting husband owned the house. The courts had little difficulty in deciding that a husband could not legally turn an innocent wife out of the home[198] (although the identification of the legal principle upon which this protection could be

---

[194] It was occasionally possible to treat the house as being subject to a marriage settlement, the trusts of which could be varied.

[195] [1965] AC 1175, 1241, HL.   [196] *Middleton v. Baldock* [1950] 1 KB 657.

[197] The statutory protection was dependent on the husband's remaining in occupation; and in holding that the husband remained in occupation by virtue of the wife's still being there the court had to accept that there was still a 'special relationship' recognised and regulated by the law between them even though they were no longer one person in law.

[198] The principle seems to have been first stated by Denning J in *Hutchinson v. Hutchinson* [1947] 2 All ER 792 (reported at somewhat greater length *sub nom. H v. H* (1947) 63 TLR 645). In *Bendall v. McWhirter* [1952] 2 QB 466, 475, Denning LJ gave a full description of the wife's rights: 'A wife is no longer her husband's chattel. She is beginning to be regarded by the law as a partner in all affairs which are their common concern. Thus the husband can no longer turn her out of the matrimonial home. She has as much right as he to stay there even though the house does stand in his name. This has only been decided in the last ten years. It started in 1942 . . . see *Bramwell v. Bramwell* [1942] 1 KB 374 . . . [The wife's right] to stay in the matrimonial home proceeds out of an irrevocable authority which the husband is presumed in law to have conferred on her. . . . The authority . . . is . . . to stay in the house until the court orders her to go out. This authority flows from the status of marriage, coupled with the fact of separation owing to the husband's misconduct. . . . The authority is . . . purely personal to her. She alone can exercise it. She cannot assign it. It does not give her any legal interest in the land. . . . Her possession is not always exclusive. If the husband has only been guilty of desertion and nothing else he is entitled to come back at any time asking to be forgiven, and she is then bound to receive him. She cannot then keep him out of his house. But if he has, in addition to desertion, been guilty of cruelty or adultery, she is not bound to take him back. She can keep him out of the house. . . . Her occupation is comparable with that of a contractual licensee, the only difference being that a contractual licence is revocable in accordance with the terms of the contract, whereas her licence is not revocable except by an order of the court . . .'.

based proved much more troublesome).[199] But there was a long controversy about whether her right to remain in occupation—the so-called 'deserted wife's equity'—was capable of binding a third party (such as a mortgagee to whom the husband had charged the property). Here Lord Justice Denning's view that the rights of a wife in possession or actual occupation[200] were binding on anyone dealing with the husband was doctrinally much less securely founded, and was seen by conveyancing lawyers as a threat to the security of property transactions.[201] For many years the law remained uncertain.[202]

---

[199] In *Bendall v. McWhirter* (above) Denning LJ astutely sought to attribute the origin of the doctrine to a decision of Lord Chief Justice Goddard (an extremely able lawyer whom none could describe as radical or even progressive: see Biographical Notes). Goddard had in *Bramwell v. Bramwell* [1942] 1 KB 374 based his ruling on (i) the belief that an action of ejectment was an action in tort, which one spouse could not bring against the other; and (ii) that it therefore followed that the husband's only redress was to take proceedings under s. 17 of the Married Women's Property Act 1882 (which at the time was thought to give the court a very wide discretion in resolving the question before the court). This explanation was apparently accepted by the *Royal Commission on Marriage and Divorce* (1956, Cmnd. 9678, para. 604) but is of doubtful historical accuracy not least because the plaintiff in a common law action for ejectment would not have been the husband but the fictitious John Doe; and in any event equity (whose doctrines prevailed) would not have debarred a spouse from suing to protect property: see the argument of Mr E Goulding QC in *National Provincial Bank Ltd v. Ainsworth* (above). Had the Goddard view been correct the abolition of the spouses' immunity from suit in tort effected by the 1962 Law Reform (Husband and Wife) Act would have caused severe embarrassment not least because that Act did not contain any provision giving effect to the Law Reform Committee's recommendation that the ending of the immunity should be without prejudice to the deserted wife's rights in the home. But by that time officials in the Lord Chancellor's Office had become convinced (see Newman to Dobson, PRO LCO2/7386, 5 July 1961) that the basis of the wife's right was not immunity from suit in tort, but (as explained by Denning LJ in *Bendall v. McWhirter*) flowed from the status of marriage coupled with the fact of separation owing to the husband's misconduct. This view was never challenged by any decision of the courts—a decade after the 1962 Act, Denning LJ felt able to say that his view had become 'so well established that it is not open to question': *National Provincial Bank Ltd v. Hastings Car Mart Ltd* [1964] Ch 665, 684—and in this respect the House of Lords in *National Provincial Bank Ltd v. Ainsworth* [1965] AC 1175 broadly accepted this rationalisation of the nature of the wife's rights: see *per* Lord Hodson at p. 1220, *per* Lord Upjohn at p. 1229, and *per* Lord Wilberforce at p. 1247.

[200] And, perhaps, provided that the husband's common law duty to maintain the wife had not been terminated, for example by her committing adultery: see the dissenting judgment of Devlin LJ in *Short v. Short* [1960] 1 WLR 833; and note the concern expressed by RE Megarry ('The Deserted Wife's Right to Occupy the Matrimonial Home' (1952) 68 LQR 379) and echoed in the speeches in *Ainsworth* that purchasers and lenders might, to avoid being fixed with notice of the wife's entitlement to remain in the home, be compelled to make enquiries into what Lord Upjohn in that case described as the 'delicate and possibly uncertain and fluctuating state of affairs between a couple whose marriage is going wrong'.

[201] RE Megarry, 'The Deserted Wife's Right to Occupy the Matrimonial Home' (1952) 68 LQR 379, was particularly influential. The threat to mortgage lenders was however reduced by Upjohn J's decision in *Lloyds Bank Ltd v. Oliver's Trustee* [1953] 1 WLR 1460 that the wife's rights only arose at the moment when the husband deserted her, and that accordingly the mortgagee's right would usually have priority over hers.

[202] The *Report of the Royal Commission on Marriage and Divorce* (1956, Cmd. 9678, para. 612) judiciously summarised the state of the law in 1956: (i) the wife could apply under s. 17 of the Married Women's Property Act 1882 for an order restraining the husband from selling or otherwise disposing of the house: *Lee v. Lee* [1952] 2 QB 489; (ii) the wife's right to remain in occupation could be enforced (subject to the court's discretion) against a purchaser who had knowledge of her occupation, and a purchaser who failed to make reasonable enquiries would be deemed to have notice of her rights. However, this doctrine 'must be applied to the case of a deserted wife with great caution, since

The third and fundamental issue only came to prominence rather later; and a former President of the Probate Divorce and Admiralty Division[203] was to use a telling[204] and much quoted metaphor[205] to describe the problem:

'The wife spends her youth and early middle age in bearing and rearing children and in tending the home; the husband is thus freed for his economic activities. Unless the wife plays her part, the husband cannot play his. The cock bird can feather his nest precisely because he is not required to spend most of his time sitting on it.'

In 1943, it was this division of function which led the Married Women's Association to claim the right to an equal share of the family *income* in recognition of the wife's services in the home and the community. A decade later it was clear that the claim could not be confined to income: the real injustice was that the wife often had no share in the *capital* invested in the family home.

The first reported case[206] demonstrating the nature of the problem was *Rimmer v. Rimmer*[207] which came to court in 1952:

In 1934 husband and wife bought a house for £460. The wife paid the deposit of £29 required by the Building Society, but the legal title was taken (apparently as the Building Society required) in the husband's sole name. The husband paid £151 off the mortgage debt before the outbreak of war in 1939. Thereafter, whilst he was away serving in the merchant navy, the wife paid off the rest of the loan (£280) out of her earnings. In 1951 they separated. The house was sold for £2,117 (some £38,000 in year 2000 values); and the question the court had to answer on the wife's application under s. 17 of the Married Women's Property Act 1882 was how that should be divided. The County Court judge held that the wife should get 29/460 of the proceeds (ie the proportion which the deposit she had paid bore to the total purchase price) plus

---

normally it would not be reasonable for an intending purchaser or lender to have to enquire into the relationship of husband and wife. Lastly, since the wife's right is a mere equity, it will not be allowed to prevail against a *bona fide* purchase for value without knowledge of her occupation'.

[203] Lord Simon of Glaisdale: see Biographical Notes.

[204] *With all my worldly goods . . .* (1964).

[205] See eg *Pettitt v. Pettitt* [1970] AC 777, 811, *per* Lord Hodson; *Wachtel v. Wachtel* [1973] Fam 72, 92, *per* Lord Denning MR: *Dart v. Dart* [1996] 2 FLR 304, *per* Butler-Sloss LJ.

[206] The view that the law of implied resulting and constructive trusts might found a claim that the legal title did not accurately reflect the parties' beneficial interests was slow to develop. As late as 1952 it apparently did not occur to any of those appearing in *Bendall v. McWhirter* [1952] 2 QB 466, to suggest that the fact the legal title to the house was in the husband's name was not conclusive; whilst the *Report of the Royal Commission on Marriage and Divorce* (1956, Cmd. 9678, Part IX) scarcely mentions the possible relevance of trust law. Only in 1970 was it finally settled that claims to share in 'family assets' had to be based on the law of trusts, and that there was no special regime (whether statutory or otherwise) allowing the court to do what Lord Denning and others had done, and put on one side the 'question of contract, gift, or trust': see eg *Fribance v. Fribance* [1957] 1 All ER 357, 359.

[207] [1953] 1 QB 63.

the £280 which she had paid off the mortgage debt,[208] and the husband should have the rest.[209]

The fact that over the years house prices[210] have risen much more than inflation[211] would have caused serious injustice to the married women who had no legal entitlement to any share; but the injustice was all the more dramatic because house purchase was in the years after World War I usually financed by borrowing; and in the rising markets prevalent since the end of World War II the effect of what is called 'gearing'[212] is dramatic. The Rimmers put up £29 in cash, and (if they had not reduced the mortgage) would have got back £1,686[213] when the house was sold. Their £29 'investment' had thus appreciated by a factor of nearly 60, 12 times the increase in value of the house (and more than 20 times the increase in retail prices).

The injustice of holding that the whole of such a gain should belong to the husband was obvious,[214] but for many years it was mitigated by the exercise of the power given to the court by s. 17 of the Married Women's Property Act

---

[208] ie £413 (or some £7,000 in year 2000 values).

[209] The Court of Appeal, on the basis that s. 17 of the Married Women's Property Act 1882 gave the court a discretion to do what would be just between the parties held that the proceeds should be divided equally: see below.

[210] In 1961, the average price of a new house in the United Kingdom mortgaged to a building society was £2,810: *Social Trends 1970*, Table 98. In 2000, the price of the average dwelling in England and Wales was £110,200: *Social Trends* 32 (2002) p. 176.

[211] Whereas house prices between 1961 and 2000 may have appreciated by a factor of 39 (see above) the Retail Price Index over the same period rose by a factor of 12. In this respect the warning given by Lord Evershed in *Rimmer* that the 'great rise in values in house properties' might not be sustained has been proved unwarranted.

[212] ie, an asset (in this case a house) is bought with the aid of a loan, the amount of which is not affected by changes in the value of the property acquired. If that value increases, the purchaser/borrower's 'equity' increases disproportionately. Conversely, if the value falls, the 'equity' is reduced, correspondingly sharply. See for example the illustration given in the *Nationwide Building Society's Housing Finance Review* July 1995, p. 4: 'A borrower buying a house worth £40,000 with a 90 per cent mortgage starts off with a loan of £36,000 and an equity stake of £4,000. If prices rise by 10 per cent the property will be worth £44,000 but the borrower's equity will increase to £8,000, so that a 10 per cent increase in prices produces a doubling in the value of the equity'. Gearing can lead to dramatic outcomes if the investment is volatile (as is often the case with share, commodity, and financial derivatives dealings): see for example the facts of *CIBC Mortgages v. Pitt* [1994] 1 AC 200, HL: Mr Pitt borrowed £130,000 on the security of the family home and used the money to speculate on the stock exchange. Initially he was successful, and by buying shares and in turn using them to provide security for further deals, he became a millionaire; but when the stock exchange crashed in 1987 this borrowing exceeded the value of his assets, the lenders called in the loan, and Mr Pitt was unable to pay.

[213] ie Sale Proceeds (£2,117) less amount borrowed (£460 – £29 = £431).

[214] 'A married woman may spend years of her life looking after and improving the home. Yet often the house and its furniture are the sole property of the husband and he may dispose of them without her consent or he may leave them by will to someone else. The woman may have been earning an independent livelihood before marriage and had she remained single could have set up her own home. If, on marriage, she gives up her paid work in order to devote herself to caring for her husband and children, it is an unwarrantable hardship when in consequence she finds herself in the end with nothing she can call her own': *Royal Commission on Marriage and Divorce* (1956, Cmd. 9678, para. 647, Views of those members who support the introduction of some form of community of property).

1882 to make 'such order as it thinks fit' on an application to determine questions of title to or the possession of property. The courts, aware of changing economic factors, did not simply[215] give effect to the parties' strict legal rights;[216] but were prepared to apply what Lord Evershed in the *Rimmer* case called palm tree justice. In each case, he said,[217] 'the question is . . . what is the fair and just answer to be given to the question posed, having regard not merely to what occurred at the time when the property was originally purchased but also having regard to the light which the conduct of the husband and wife throws on their relationship as contributors to the acquisition of the property which was their joint matrimonial home'. Moreover, 'the old established doctrine' that equity leans towards equality was peculiarly relevant in resolving disputes between spouses. Accordingly in *Rimmer* the right solution would be to divide the proceeds of sale equally between the parties (rather than seeking to apply the conventional understanding of a resulting trust and dividing the proceeds between the parties in proportion to their contributions to the purchase price—an exercise all the more artificial and difficult in cases in which a large part of that sum has been borrowed from an outside source).

STATUTORY REFORM NEEDED?

(i) The Report of the Royal Commission on Marriage and Divorce (1956)[218]

The law was evidently uncertain and, as we have seen, the subject of matrimonial property rights was in 1951 deliberately included in the terms of reference of the Royal Commission on Marriage and Divorce (set up in 1951). The Commission was taking evidence[219] when the *Rimmer* decision was made; and

---

[215] This interpretation was not only accepted in case law (see below) but was regarded as not controversial both by officials and by the Government spokesman in parliamentary debates, for example on the Law Reform (Husband and Wife) Act 1962. The departmental briefing note stated that '. . . the respective rights of husband and wife in matrimonial property are notoriously difficult to disentangle; and their determination is therefore best left to a judicial discretion' (PRO LCO2/7387). The Solicitor General also emphasised the width of the court's discretion: *Official Report* (HC) 18 May 1962, vol. 659, col. 1702.

[216] This approach was not taken until the Second World War. Thus in *Kelner v. Kelner* [1939] P 411 the court was asked to decide who was entitled to £1,000 given to the parties jointly as dower in accordance with Jewish custom. The court held that the question to be answered was 'Whose property is this? Is it the husband's, or is it the wife's, or does it belong to them both jointly?' The court affirmed that this question differed 'by the whole breadth of heaven from the procedure for variation of settlements' available in divorce proceedings.

[217] [1953] 1 QB 63, 71.   [218] Cmd. 9678.

[219] In addition to receiving evidence from bodies as diverse as The Trade Union Congress, the Married Women's Association and the National Federation of Business and Professional Women's Clubs the Commission itself sought the views of certain bodies whose experience qualified them to express an opinion but who had not done so: see *Royal Commission on Marriage and Divorce* (1956, Cmd. 9678) paras. 625, 708, and App. Part II.

the majority of witnesses thought the law was unfair to the wife.[220] But the Commission's attitude was, in this as in other respects, conservative. It concluded that the law did not always sufficiently recognise the importance of the wife's contribution to the joint family undertaking, and that 'real hardship' could occur.[221] The Commission therefore accepted the necessity for some amendment of the law but in deciding on appropriate remedies thought it 'essential' to 'keep in mind, first, the practical limitations of any attempt to legislate in a matter of social policy, . . . secondly, the vital consideration that so far as possible the law should be kept out of the intimate life of the family', and thirdly the need 'to guard against the risk that substantial injustice may be done to husbands as a result of measures designed to alleviate the hardship which some wives may suffer'.

This scarcely sounds like a prelude to proposals for radical reform.[222] The Commission did recommend that savings from housekeeping money should be deemed to belong to husband and wife equally, and made a number of other proposals for minor reform.[223] But a majority of the members rejected proposals for any statutory community of property regime[224] (even in a limited form,

[220] There were two distinct lines of criticism in the evidence given to the Commission. The first focussed on the status of the wife in the marriage partnership: the wife had no right to a sufficient allowance on which to run the home or for personal expenses, and she did not even have the right to find out what the husband earned. Any savings she made from the housekeeping belonged to the husband. She had no right to a share in the house and furniture unless she could prove she had contributed to the cost out of her own separate income, and she had no right to share in the profits of her husband's business even if she worked in it without pay. The second focussed on the hardship a wife might suffer on the breakdown of the marriage. A woman would often put up with gross ill-treatment because she feared the loss of the home; and even if she got a separation order she might find nowhere else to live and be forced to return to the husband. She might also find herself without furniture; and a husband who left the wife could return at any time (perhaps even bringing another woman with him): *Royal Commission on Marriage and Divorce* (1956, Cmd. 9678) paras. 626–629.

[221] 'There are husbands who look on their income as their own to spend freely on themselves and grudgingly dole out small sums to their wives. But it is when the marriage breaks down that the wife who has given all her energy to her work in the home may have to face the situation that she has nothing she can call her own; even money she has saved over the years from the housekeeping allowance belongs in law to her husband': *Royal Commission on Marriage and Divorce* (1956, Cmd. 9678) para. 645.

[222] The Commission unanimously rejected proposals to give the wife a legal right to a definite part of her husband's income (paras. 654–655) and to give each spouse a right to information about the other's earnings and other resources: paras. 706–711.

[223] eg that s. 17 of the Married Women's Property Act 1882 be amended to allow the court to order one spouse to pay the other a sum of money in compensation for the loss of an interest in property to which the other had established title, and to order a sale of the property in issue if that would be the only reasonable solution to the dispute—thus negating the decision of the Court of Appeal in *Tunstall v. Tunstall* [1953] 1 WLR 770: para. 705. A recommendation which had more significance than the Commission seems to have appreciated would allow a divorced wife to use her husband's contribution record under the National Insurance scheme to qualify in her own right for the state retirement pension: para. 713.

[224] The majority considered (i) there was no general desire for community of property, not least because husband and wife were always free to opt for joint ownership if they wished; (ii) a community regime would be 'extremely complicated'; and would (iii) often be unjust (as for example where a wife who had by hard work and thrift managed to buy a house found herself compelled to yield half its value to a 'lazy and improvident' husband. See *Report of the Royal Commission on Marriage and Divorce* (1956, Cmd. 9678) para. 651.

confined to the matrimonial home and furniture).[225] The Commission did however recommend giving a spouse a statutory right of occupation of the family home which could be protected[226] against third parties subsequently dealing with the property; and it recommended that the divorce court should have extended powers to deal with occupation rights[227] and to prohibit dealings with the matrimonial home.

(ii) The impact of case law, 1956–1971

The immediate public (and parliamentary) response to the Royal Commission's report focussed on possible reform of the ground for divorce; and although Ministers wanted to avoid being exposed to criticism for leaving the work of such bodies 'for too long unattended' the Lord Chancellor's Officials quickly found that there was no quick fix in the Commission's recommendations about property rights of husband and wife. The subject in general, and in particular the Royal Commission's recommendations about the rights of a deserted wife in the matrimonial home',[228] bristled with difficulties; and little of substance was done to prepare legislative solutions.[229]

Three decisions of the House of Lords delivered in the years between 1965 and 1970 demonstrated not only the unsatisfactory state of the law but also that

[225] Three members of the Commission favoured a full community of property regime. Relying in part on Scandinavian experience, they thought the difficulties in the operation of community of property had been exaggerated. The group thought contracting out should be allowed (wholly or partially—as for example where one spouse was running an independent business), that the community property should be administered by husband and wife acting together, and that on divorce the court should have power to deal with the distribution of furniture and the right to occupy the home. Another three members favoured a community regime restricted to the matrimonial home and its contents, whilst one favoured an even more restricted regime applying only to the contents of the home.

[226] By registration of a land charge.

[227] The Commission envisaged that the divorce court might order the husband to leave the home, and thought this would be merely a 'different way of making provision for the wife. In one case, the court may order the husband to pay to the wife a sum of money so that she can buy a home; in another, it may order him to allow her the use of the home'.

[228] Minute by G Dobson to Sir G Coldstream, PRO LCO2/6139, 16 March 1956.

[229] The only exception was the Married Women's Property Act 1964. The *Report of the Royal Commission on Marriage and Divorce* (1956, Cmd. 9678) para. 701 had recommended that savings made from money contributed by either the husband or the wife or by both for the purpose of meeting housekeeping expenses (and any investments or purchases made from such savings) should be deemed to belong to husband and wife in equal shares unless they had otherwise agreed. Dr Edith Summerskill (see Biographical Notes) had continued to campaign on this subject, and eventually she got Government assistance in drafting a Bill (more restricted than the Royal Commission proposal insofar as it only applied to cases of allowances made *by the husband*). Even then, the Bill was blocked in the House of Commons on numerous occasions before finally getting through 'on the nod': *Official Report* (HC) 6 March 1964, vol. 690, col. 1796. The Act would have remedied the situation revealed in 1943 by the *Blackwell* case (see above) but by 1964 the campaign for reform had become much more ambitious, and in practice the 1964 Act seems to have had little impact. For a detailed analysis see the Law Commission's *Published Working Paper No. 90, Transfer of Money between Spouses* (PWP 90, 1985); and for the Law Commission's proposals for more extensive reform in this area—notwithstanding its finding (para. 2.7) that opinions were 'sharply divided' as to whether there was a need for further reform—see *Report: Family Property* (Law Com. No. 175, 1988).

legislation would be necessary to bring about any significant change. First, in *National Provincial Bank Ltd v. Ainsworth*[230] the House of Lords unanimously and convincingly held that rights to *occupy the matrimonial home* flowing from the status of marriage were purely personal and could not, as a matter of law, bind third parties.[231] This decision vindicated, after almost a decade, the Royal Commission's view that protection of the wife's rights could not confidently be left to the courts, and that it would be necessary to lay down in a statute the circumstances in which a wife should have the right to stay in the matrimonial home.[232] Secondly, in *Pettitt v. Pettitt*[233] the House of Lords unanimously held[234] that s. 17 of the Married Women's Property Act 1882 was purely procedural in scope. Issues of beneficial entitlement between husband and wife had to be determined 'on the general principles of law applicable to the settlement of claims between those not so related, whilst making full allowances in view of that relationship';[235] and the court had no power to vary[236] spouses' existing property rights.[237] Finally, in *Gissing v. Gissing*,[238] the House of Lords held that a wife who had divorced her husband on the ground of his adultery after a 25-year marriage was not entitled to any beneficial interest in the former matrimonial home. Such cases were governed by the doctrines of implied, resulting and constructive trust, and 'family assets' were not a special class of property to which special rules for determining title applied. On the facts of the

---

[230] [1965] AC 1175.

[231] *National Provincial Bank Ltd v. Ainsworth* [1965] AC 1175, *per* Lord Upjohn at p. 1223.

[232] There had been strong support amongst property lawyers for legislation if only to avoid the courts providing 'an easy path of transition whereby a wife's general matrimonial rights *in personam* to be protected against her husband is transformed into a right *in rem* adhering to the matrimonial home and its contents': RE Megarry, 'The Deserted Wife's Right to Occupy the Matrimonial Home' (1952) 68 LQR 379, 389.

[233] [1970] AC 777. The facts of the case were unusual in that the claim was made by a husband divorced by his wife for cruelty to share the value of her house by reason of improvements he had made to it which he believed had increased its value. The House of Lords decision meant that he was entitled to nothing.

[234] This ruling had been anticipated in dicta in *National Provincial Bank Ltd v. Ainsworth* [1965] AC 1175: see eg *per* Lord Upjohn at p. 1229 and *per* Lord Wilberforce at p. 1246. But these did not form part of the *ratio decidendi* of that case and the Court of Appeal in *Pettitt* held itself still bound (see *per* Willmer LJ at [1968] 1 All ER 1053, *per* Russell LJ at p. 1060, and *per* Danckwerts LJ at p. 1063) to follow the earlier decision of that court in *Appleton v. Appleton* [1965] 1 WLR 25 (in which Lord Denning had asserted that the court could simply ask what order would be 'reasonable and fair in the circumstances as they have developed') notwithstanding the fact they considered it to be wrong.

[235] [1970] AC 777, 813, *per* Lord Upjohn.

[236] As already explained the view that the court did have a discretion to do what seemed to be fair in all the circumstances at the time of the hearing was for many years part of the orthodoxy. But Lord Denning went further than others: and *Hine v. Hine* [1962] 1 WLR 1124, 1127 represents the high water mark of his view that s. 17 gave the court an overriding discretion to reallocate 'family assets' transcending 'all rights legal or equitable'.

[237] It had to be accepted that s. 17 gave the court power to restrict enforcement of the parties' property rights—so that, for example, the court might refuse to order the wife to give up possession of the husband's house until he had provided her with suitable alternative accommodation: *Lee v. Lee* [1952] 2 QB 489—but the discretion was limited to the terms of the order giving effect to the rights of the parties (rather than determining what those rights were).

[238] [1971] AC 886.

case, the wife failed because she could not prove that it was ever intended she should own a share of the home.[239] The fact that it was the wife who had persuaded her employer to give the husband his job and that it was the employer who (possibly influenced by the wife's faithful services over 20 years) gave the husband a loan which made the purchase possible[240] were not relevant.

The effect of these decisions was to confine the courts to resolving what Lord Denning[241] had described as the 'cold legal question' of property entitlement. But the Law Lords had repeatedly emphasised the 'urgent need' for 'comprehensive legislation'[242] and in the long term these three decisions can be seen as a decisive influence for progress, even if that progress was achieved by techniques[243] different from those for which reformers had campaigned.

(iii) The Matrimonial Homes Act 1967

The House of Lords gave judgment in the *Ainsworth* case on 13 May 1965, seven months after the return of a Labour Government[244] committed to modernisation and reform. One of the first fruits of that commitment came with the creation of a body professionally committed to systematic law reform: the Law Commissions Act received Royal Assent on 15 June 1965.[245] Lady Summerskill had extracted a promise[246] from the incoming Lord Chancellor, Gerald Gardiner that he would co-operate in providing a draft Matrimonial Bill; and he invited the Law Commission to assist.[247]

---

[239] The House of Lords did impose a stay on the sale of the house to give the wife an opportunity to apply for further financial relief in the divorce proceedings; and Lord Dilhorne cited a dictum of Lord Denning's to the effect that the divorce court had power to do whatever was fair and reasonable having regard to the parties' conduct. In the event, the Matrimonial Proceedings and Property Act 1970 (conferring extensive powers on the divorce court to make financial provision and property adjustment orders) had received Royal Assent on 29 May, some five weeks before the opinions in *Gissing* were delivered on 7 July 1970.

[240] See the facts as set out in the judgments in the Court of Appeal: [1969] 1 All ER 1043. The House of Lords decision is based in part on there being 'no suggestion' that the wife's efforts or her earnings made it possible for the husband to raise the loan—contrast the approach of Phillimore LJ in the Court of Appeal at pp. 1054–1055.

[241] In *Gissing v. Gissing* [1969] 2 Ch at 93.

[242] See *per* Lord Reid, *Pettitt v. Pettitt* [1970] AC 777, 797.

[243] ie by giving the court in matrimonial proceedings a discretion to adjust the parties' beneficial entitlements rather than by the introduction of a community regime.

[244] At the General Election on 15 October 1964 Labour had an overall majority of only four seats in the House of Commons. In the circumstances it was less difficult than is sometimes the case to find space in the legislative programme for technical and apparently uncontroversial matters of law reform.

[245] On the background to the Law Commissions Act 1965 see SM Cretney, *Law, Law Reform and the Family* (1998) Chapter 1.

[246] Dobson to Lawson, PRO BC3/423, 16 September 1965.

[247] *Ibid.* The Law Commission had already, in its *First Programme* (Law Com. No. 1, 1965, Item X(b)) announced that it intended to examine the impact of the *Ainsworth* decision; and the Bill was drafted by Mrs EA Eadie (a Parliamentary Counsel attached to the Law Commission: see Biographical Notes) The Instructions to Counsel were agreed between the Commission and the Lord Chancellor's Department; but it appears that the Department later assumed exclusive responsibility when it became necessary to deal with some 'fairly substantial points raised by the Ministry

Unfortunately, it soon became apparent that there were serious problems to be resolved in translating the Royal Commission's recommendations into detailed legislation. For example: should protection of the wife's right to occupy be restricted to cases where the husband had deserted her? Should it depend on her having first obtained a court order? Was it practicable to give the wife protection against third parties given that any such measure would inevitably provoke what one of the Law Commissioners[248] described as 'screams from the highly organised hire-purchase finance industry'?[249] Again, the Building Societies could be expected to be highly critical of any suggestion that the wife be substituted for the husband as the person liable to make the mortgage payments; whilst the Royal Commission's recommendation that the court be empowered to transfer Rent Act tenancies from one spouse to the other involved interfering with a highly complex and technical part of the statute book—in order to gain only a very limited benefit.

On these and many other points there was what was tactfully described[250] as 'a measure of disagreement' between the Law Commission and the Lord Chancellor's Department; and the Law Commission was careful to distance itself, both in public[251] and in private,[252] from the Bill which was eventually[253] ready for Lady Summerskill to introduce.

of Housing': Gardiner to Simon, PRO BC3/423, 3 March 1966. The division of responsibility for the Bill evidently became a source of increasing tension: see below.

[248] LCB Gower: see Biographical Notes.

[249] Memorandum by LCB Gower, PRO BC3/423, 2 November 1965. Gower took the lead in the Law Commission's work on this subject; but at a Commissioner's Meeting on 3 November 1965 expressed anxiety at the prospect of the Law Commission being pressed into making proposals too quickly, and 'added that he was becoming increasingly worried' in the light of the discussions between the Law Commission's team and the Lord Chancellor's Office: PRO BC3/1.

[250] By LCB Gower: PRO BC3/423, note dated 2 November 1965.

[251] The Commission's *First Annual Report, 1965–66* para. 81 stated that it had 'become apparent that we could not in so short a time complete full consultations with the many interests concerned and formulate comprehensive proposals. We agreed, however, to assist with the drafting of a Bill which would give immediate protection to the spouse while avoiding the practical conveyancing difficulties adverted to in the *Ainsworth* case'. The Commission's involvement was not at first revealed, and the failure to disclose the terms of its advice was strongly criticised by the former Lord Chancellor Viscount Dilhorne: *Official Report* (HL) 7 July 1966, vol. 275, col. 1198.

[252] Gower was careful to explain to Professor FR Crane (of the Society of Public Teachers of Law) that Lady Summerskill's Bill was not a Law Commission bill 'although we have had a certain amount to do with its gestation'; whilst on 17 December 1965 the Chairman of the Law Commission had told the Lord Chancellor that the Bill 'should not be regarded as a Law Commission proposal as it does not pretend to cover all the ground that needs to be covered if a final and scientific solution to this problem is to be achieved. Nor have there been the consultations with the legal and other interests concerned which will be essential for a complete solution. All we have attempted is a stop-gap measure, dealing with the pressing hardship arising from the *Ainsworth* Case, of a sort which Lady Summerskill may care to sponsor, which will not handicap the future development of the law in the light of the fuller investigation that the Commission is undertaking': PRO BC3/423, Scarman to Gardiner. In his turn, Gardiner (in a manuscript addition to a letter dated 2 March 1966 to the President of the Probate Divorce and Admiralty Division) admitted that the Bill was '*not* an attempt at a radical reform such as you and I would like. It is simply an attempt to restore the pre-*Ainsworth* position. This in itself has proved to be a lot more complicated than we anticipated'.

[253] She had continued to exercise pressure on the draftsman: see Eadie to Gower, PRO BC3/423, note of telephone call, 17 November 1965.

It can be argued that the differences and difficulties had a positive outcome; and that exposure to what has been described[254] as 'the testing and refining process of argument' greatly improved the Royal Commission's proposals. Certainly the opening words of the Matrimonial Homes Act strike a positive note somewhat unusual in English statutory drafting. A spouse (and not only a wife) who has no proprietary interest in a matrimonial home none the less has 'a right not to be evicted or excluded from the dwelling house or any part thereof by the other spouse except with the leave of the court';[255] and these rights of occupation constitute a charge on the other's interest easily protected by registration against anyone subsequently dealing with the property. There is no need to prove that the other spouse is in desertion or has been guilty of any other specific wrong; and the court is given a wide adjustive power to extend the rights of occupation in cases of divorce or death[256] and to make such order about the occupation of the home (and also such matters as payment of outgoings and liability for repairs) as it 'thinks just and reasonable having regard to the conduct of the spouses in relation to each other and otherwise, to their respective needs and financial resources, to the needs of any children and to all the circumstances of the case'.[257]

There was of course scope for argument about whether the Act correctly struck the balance between on the one hand protecting the wife's rights and on the other hand ensuring that the efficiency of the property transfer system was not impaired. In this context, a crucial issue was (and, at the turn of the century, remained) whether registration should be necessary to make the spouse's rights bind a third party;[258] but the fears voiced by some speakers[259] in the debates that the legislation would impose a fetter on ordinary dealings with the family home have been proved unfounded.[260] The Act, with many additional

---

[254] By Megarry J, *Cordell v. Second Clanfield Properties, Ltd* [1969] 2 Ch 9, 17.

[255] A spouse who is not in occupation has a similar right with leave to 'enter into and occupy the' home: Matrimonial Homes Act 1967, s. 1(1)(b).

[256] Matrimonial Homes Act 1967, s. 2(2).   [257] Matrimonial Homes Act 1967, s. 1(3).

[258] The 'registration requirement' was, and remained, controversial: see Lord Denning's speech *Official Report* (HL) 14 June 1966, vol. 273, col. 43 for his fears that 'the poor ignorant wife' would not know about registration (a fear repeated in his judgment in *Williams & Glyn's Bank Ltd v. Boland* [1979] Ch 312, 328)—the wife still living at home in peace with her husband 'would never have heard of a . . . charge: and she would not have understood it if she had'. The Law Commission in its *Report on the Implications of Williams & Glyn's Bank Ltd v. Boland* (1982, Law Com. No. 115) considered the advantages and disadvantages of a registration requirement at some length; but pointed out that there was no evidence of any general reluctance to register: see paras. 78, 81. There were some 17,000 charges registered under the Act in 1977–78.

[259] Notably by Lord Wilberforce: see *Official Report* (HL) 14 June 1966, vol. 273, col. 29.

[260] It is undoubtedly true (as pointed out by Ormrod LJ in *Williams & Glyn's Bank Ltd v. Boland* [1979] Ch 312, 339) that registration may be seen as a 'hostile' step, and since registration of a spouse's rights may in practice make it difficult for the other to sell the property (see eg *Wroth v. Tyler* [1974] Ch 30) one spouse may be tempted to register to pressure the other into a favourable financial settlement on breakdown. But it is a misuse of the legislation to act in this way: see *Barnett v. Hassett* [1981] 1 WLR 138.

refinements[261] introduced over the years in the light of experience, continues[262] to provide a comprehensive legal framework protecting the rights of a vulnerable wife. In only one respect did the 1967 Act not go as far as the 1956 Royal Commission would have wished: the technical problems encountered in giving any protection in respect of the furniture and other goods proved intractable, and the Bill in the end did not attempt to do so. The much needed reform in this area was only effected in 1996.[263]

The 1967 Act has provided practical relief for countless families over the years. Historically the importance of the Act is that, through the medium of the legal right of occupation which it created, it gave formal recognition to the claims of the family to a secure home as against commercial claims founded on traditional property rights. The Chairman of the Law Commission may have thought the 1967 Act was only a 'stop-gap measure';[264] but in reality it established a principle from which it was impossible subsequently to retreat.

In one sense, therefore, the 1967 Act can be seen as exemplifying all that is best in one model of law reform—the growing recognition of a social problem, the determined efforts of well-placed individuals to bring about legislative action, the collaboration of experts such as the Parliamentary Counsel, the officials in the Lord Chancellor's Office, and (in this case) the Law Commission. But it could also be taken as an exemplar of the defects of this process. A mass of technical problems (which could and should have been brought out by detailed prior consultation with experts in property transactions) had to be dealt with in great haste, and at one stage it appeared that the Bill would have to be abandoned because of difficulty in dealing with the problems which were raised. What, for example, were the duties of a solicitor acting on a house purchase in advising the wife[265] about registering a charge?[266] Was Lord Denning

---

[261] For defects which were exposed in litigation and by analysis, see the Law Commission's *Published Working Paper No. 42, Family Property Law* (1971) and Book Two of the Commission's *Third Report on Family Property: The Matrimonial Home (Co-ownership and Occupation Rights) and Household Goods* (Law Com. No. 86, 1978). The 1967 Act was much amended—notably by the Matrimonial Homes and Property Act 1981, giving effect to many of the Commission's recommendations—and the legislation was consolidated in the Matrimonial Homes Act 1983. That Act in its turn was repealed by the Family Law Act 1996, Sch. 10, and the 1996 Act now provides a comprehensive codification of the law governing the occupation of the family home and the remedies available against molestation.

[262] The provisions of the 1967 Act, although now repealed, still provide the basis of the comprehensive code of protection embodied in Part IV of the Family Law Act 1996.

[263] See Family Law Act 1996, s. 40(1)(c)(d) and (e).

[264] Scarman to Gardiner, PRO BC3/423, 17 December 1965.

[265] Examples in the text take the common case in which it is the wife who has need of protection; but remedies under the Matrimonial Homes legislation are equally available to husbands.

[266] See the attempt by D Dobson, in a 12-page letter, to allay the Law Society's fears: PRO BC3/423. This led to a meeting on 9 January 1967, and the Law Society was responsible for putting forward amendments 'designed to reduce the practical difficulties to a minimum': see 64 Law Soc. Gaz. 544. The debates in House of Commons Standing Committee D and on 3rd Reading (see *Official Report* (HC) 21 July 1967, vol. 750, cols. 2707–2737) was dominated by discussion of these matters.

right in suggesting[267] that registration should be routine, whether or not there was any ground for suspecting that it would be necessary? What was to happen if a purchaser discovered the existence of a registered charge after agreeing to buy the property?[268] And the Law Society, using the expertise of its members, was able to point to a host of even more technical difficulties: would the creation of a charge give rise to liability for betterment levy (a now long forgotten tax intended to secure the benefit of increases in value for the community)? Should the wife's rights affect the amount of compensation paid for property compulsorily acquired by a local authority?[269] The original four short clauses rapidly grew to eight, and the Matrimonial Homes Act as it came into force was a much more complex measure than the Bill originally introduced.

Rethinking and redrafting did not resolve all the problems. The Act gave rise to considerable difficulty[270] (and hardship[271] to the innocent); and in 1974 a High Court judge called for action to remove the

'cumbersome uncertainties that the Act of 1967 has produced, to the peril of all, and not least to those of modest means. . . . [S]omething better than the Act of 1967—much better—must be possible.'[272]

It took 14 years for the worst of the technical defects in the 1967 legislation to be removed; and the realisation that legislation in this area is inevitably a complex and technically difficult matter may well have deterred Government and the legal profession from accepting the much more ambitious proposals for community of property put forward by the Law Commission in 1979.[273] The story of what happened in the course of putting the 1967 Act on the statute book and in the sequel vividly demonstrates how legal technicality may present obstacles to achieving social policy objectives which can only be overcome by the most careful and thorough planning and research.

[267] *Official Report* (HL) 14 June 1966, vol. 273, col. 45. The suggested practice was not adopted.

[268] A provision was eventually inserted (s. 4) whereby a vendor was obliged to procure the removal of any charge registered at the date of the contract for sale; but there remained problems when the charge was registered after completion: see *Wroth v. Tyler* [1974] Ch 30 (in which the husband became liable to pay heavy damages to a contracting purchaser because of his inability to convey the property free of the wife's rights).

[269] Both these matters were raised by a Solicitor MP Mr Graham Page who effectively put forward the problems which the Law Society had uncovered and sought valiantly to remedy them: *Official Report* (HC) 21 July 1967, vol. 750, col. 2710.

[270] See the discussion in the Law Commission's *Third Report on Family Property: The Matrimonial Home (Co-ownership and Occupation Rights) and Household Goods* (Law Com. No. 86, 1978) pp. 241–272. The recommendations in the Law Commission's Report were supported by the (Finer) *Report of the Committee on One-Parent Families* (1974, Cmnd. 5629), para. 6.43 (although implementation of the Commission's proposals by the Matrimonial Homes and Property Act 1981 did nothing to deal with what Finer described as the 'very high (and, in our view most undesirable) level of technical intricacy'.

[271] See notably *Wroth v. Tyler* [1974] Ch 30.   [272] *Wroth v. Tyler* [1974] Ch 30, 64.

[273] See below.

Entitlement or discretion: the campaign for fair sharing of the family assets

The Matrimonial Homes Act established an important principle; but it was of only limited scope. It certainly did little if anything to solve the underlying grievances about the effects of the separate property regime established by the Married Women's Property Acts[274] in the changed economic circumstances (notably the emergence of what Lord Diplock called[275] a 'real-property-mortgaged-to-a-building-society-owning . . . democracy') of the post-World War II world.[276] The decision of the House of Lords in the *Pettitt* case,[277] handed down on April 23 1969 and denying the courts any jurisdiction to deal with family property entitlements simply on the basis of what would be reasonable and fair in the circumstances[278] brought matters to a head.

Women's groups had a powerful, and for long not fully exploited, weapon. The unfairness of the law existed however idyllically happy the marriage might be; but it often only threatened to cause practical economic hardship if the marriage broke down. In that situation, a wife innocent of any matrimonial offence could simply refuse to petition for divorce,[279] perhaps seeking a judicial separation; and there is evidence that many wronged women did precisely that.[280] In many cases the husband, denied the possibility of remarriage, would be condemned to live in what came to be called a 'stable illicit union'; and the growth in numbers of such relationships was the single most important factor in the campaign to liberalise the ground for divorce. By 1966 that campaign seemed to be close to success. 'Informed opinion' (as represented by the Archbishop of Canterbury's *Putting Asunder* group and by the Law Commission) was well disposed to making divorce available where the marriage had irretrievably broken down. But it was also reluctant to allow divorce to be forced on an 'innocent' wife if the ending of the marriage would cause her serious economic deprivation, for example, by the loss of the matrimonial home or of her rights under a

---

[274] 1870 and 1882.   [275] *Pettitt v. Pettitt* [1970] AC 777, 824.

[276] For the impact of rising property values, see p. 121 above.

[277] *Pettitt v. Pettitt* [1970] AC 777, HL.

[278] cf. the view expressed by Lord Denning MR in *Appleton v. Appleton* [1965] 1 WLR 25, 28.

[279] In some cases, a wife might agree to petition if, but only if, the husband made an appropriate financial settlement in her favour ((although until 1963, when the Matrimonial Causes Act 1963, s. 4, transformed collusion from an absolute into a discretionary bar to the grant of a divorce) such a 'deal' if discovered might lead to dismissal of any divorce petition: see eg *H v. H* (1947) 63 TLR 645, *per* Denning J—husband's offer to allow wife to have the house if she would petition for divorce tainted with collusion).

[280] The courts held that a wife was entitled to seek judicial separation notwithstanding the fact that the marriage had irretrievably broken down, and irrespective of the fact that the husband was prepared to make adequate financial provision on divorce: *Sansom v. Sansom* [1966] P 52. It seems that Mrs Ainsworth petitioned for judicial separation rather than divorce in the belief that as a separated (rather than a divorced) wife she would keep her right to stay in her home: see *National Provincial Bank Ltd v. Hastings Car Mart* [1964] Ch 665, 680, *per* Lord Denning MR. This was true, but unfortunately for her, the House of Lords held that her right was a purely personal one which did not bind third parties (such as the bank in whose favour the husband had charged the property): *National Provincial Bank Ltd v. Ainsworth* [1965] AC 1175, HL.

pension scheme.[281] Reform of property law thus became in effect the price to be paid for liberalising the divorce law. As the *Putting Asunder* group put it:

'. . . it would be intolerable to allow the party responsible for the breakdown so long as the economic and financial rights of the other party . . . were not fully protected, and our recommendation of the principle of breakdown is therefore conditional on that protection being assured'.[282]

And the Group stated[283] their belief 'that the establishment of community of property in some form would do much to prevent injustice'. In their turn the Law Commission accepted that reforms 'far more radical' than those contained in the 1967 Matrimonial Homes Act were needed in the law relating to the family property if divorced wives were not to suffer.[284]

In this way, both those opposed in principle to 'easier' divorce and those merely seeking to remove the injustices of family property law were given a powerful weapon and a strong incentive to unite and vote down divorce for irretrievable breakdown unless something was done to improve the property rights of married women. Lady Summerskill, for one, made her position pellucidly clear:[285]

'Few men can afford to support two wives—so I have called [the Divorce Reform Bill] a Casanova's charter . . . [But] if they introduce an amendment offering community of property, I would accept the Bill.'

The way in which the issues were finally resolved has had a profound impact on the development of English family law; and this can best be seen by looking at events chronologically.

Reform of divorce law, the economic position of married women: Edward Bishop's Matrimonial Property Bill, 1969

On 17 December 1968[286] the House of Commons gave a second reading to a Bill providing for 'irretrievable breakdown' divorce after a prolonged debate in the course of which much was made of the Casanova's Charter. But just before that Bill was due to go into Committee[287] the House (against the strong advice of the Government)[288] gave a Second Reading[289] to Mr Edward Bishop's Matrimonial Property Bill.[290] This Bill was intended to introduce an element of community of

[281] Law Commission *Report on Reform of the Grounds of Divorce, The Field of Choice* (1966) Cmnd. 3123, para. 39.
[282] *Putting Asunder* (1966) para. 64.   [283] *Ibid.*
[284] *Report on Reform of the Grounds of Divorce, The Field of Choice* (1966) Cmnd. 3123, para. 39.
[285] From a leaflet by the Humanist lobby as quoted in BH Lee, *Divorce Law Reform in England* (1974) p. 201. Note also the remarks of Mrs Juanita Francis, Chairman of the Married Women's Association, 'I oppose this Bill completely, but I'm not asking for protection, I'm asking for legal rights in hard cash . . .': *ibid.*
[286] See Chapter 9, below.   [287] On 29 January 1969.
[288] See *Official Report* (HC) 24 January 1969, vol. 776, col. 831.
[289] On a division, by 86 votes to 32: *Official Report* (HC) 24 January 1969, vol. 776, col. 894.
[290] Bill No. 23, ordered to be printed 27 November 1968. For Mr Bishop, see Biographical Notes.

property into English law, not least by requiring the court on divorce to divide up the couple's 'matrimonial property';[291] and Mr Bishop admitted[292] that he would not have brought the Bill before the House at the time had it not been for the progress of the divorce legislation. The debate on the Bishop Bill was punctuated by repeated attempts on the part of Leo Abse[293] to convince the House that the Government was in effect committed to putting through in the next session a measure on 'matrimonial relief, which could [sic] include property matters'.[294]

The Bishop Group had the backers of divorce reform in a tactically dangerous position, for the Group could almost certainly have stopped the Divorce Bill had they wanted to. Capitalising on the Second Reading success, Bishop and others met the Lord Chancellor and the Law Commissioners on 20 February, and were given undertakings that in return for his withdrawing the Matrimonial Property Bill the Government would not bring the new divorce law into effect until legislation giving effect to the Law Commission's promised report on matrimonial financial relief had been introduced.[295]

Limited scope of Matrimonial Proceedings and Property Act 1970: a 'confidence trick'?

The Lord Chancellor's undertaking was less generous than members of the Bishop group may have thought. The Law Commission had never disguised the fact that it was engaged on *two* separate studies, and that the Report (promised for the summer of 1969, and in fact published in July of that year[296] just as the Divorce Bill was going through its final stages in the House of Lords) was concerned solely with the orders courts could make in divorce and other matrimonial proceedings. The 1970 Report did not pretend to be what the Law Commission had called a 'root-and-branch reform of family property' (which as

---

[291] The Bill was technically defective in many ways: see eg the speech by the Solicitor General: *Official Report* (HC) 24 January 1969, vol. 776, col. 831; and SM Cretney, 'The Community of Property' (1969) 113 SJ 116.

[292] *Official Report* (HC) 24 January 1969, vol. 776, col. 807.

[293] The principal tactician progressing the Divorce Bill: see Biographical Notes.

[294] *Official Report* (HC) 24 January 1969, vol. 776, col. 877, and see also at cols. 824, 825, 889. Leo Abse has candidly recorded that 'with the connivance of those in authority' he had planned to rebuke the sponsors of the Bill for its weakness, 'praise extravagantly its good intentions, and demand that the government meet the well-founded concern to its sponsors by undertaking to implement these minor but not unimportant proposals . . . the sponsors of Bishop's Bill could withdraw their Bill believing they have wrested out of the Government real concessions, and the women's organizations would believe Bishop and his sponsors had been gallant fighters. And meantime the way to the conclusion of the Divorce Bill would be clear': *Private Member* (1973) p. 199. However, as Abse admits, things did not go entirely as planned.

[295] *Official Report* (HC) 28 January 1970, vol. 794, col. 1596.

[296] The Report (*Financial Provision in Matrimonial Proceedings*, Law Com. No. 25) is dated 23 July and was ordered by the House of Commons to be printed on 24 July 1969. No doubt by a coincidence the Report Stage of the Divorce Bill in the House of Lords also took place on 24 July; but the summer adjournment meant that the Bill did not complete its passage through the Lords until 13 October.

the Commission rightly said) would be a 'far more intractable problem . . .'.[297] The recommendations in the 1969 Report were implemented by the Matrimonial Proceedings and Property Act 1970, and the Divorce Reform Act 1969 and the 1970 Act came into force on 1 January 1971.[298] But the essence of the 1970 Bill was no more than a rationalisation and extension of the courts' powers to make discretionary financial awards in divorce proceedings.[299] The Act did indeed extend the court's powers in those respects, and the guidance which the Act gave to the court about the exercise of its discretion to make financial orders on divorce did include a specific reference to the contributions made by the parties to the welfare of the family including contributions made by looking after the home or caring for the family.[300] It is true that those provisions enabled the courts to move away from an exclusive concern with maintenance and towards a pattern of equitable redistribution of the family assets on the breakdown of marriage,[301] and that neither the Law Commission nor the Lord Chancellor had ever in terms suggested that the 1970 Act would go any further. But it may be that they did not go out of their way to remove misconceptions; and the truth is that the 1970 Act did almost[302] nothing to meet what the Law Commission had previously identified as 'the fundamental cause of the present dissatisfaction' with the law. This was summed up by the women who ('with considerable male support') said: 'We are no longer content with a system whereby a wife's rights in family assets depend on the whim of her husband or on the discretion of a judge. We demand definite property rights, not possible discretionary benefits'.[303]

---

[297] *Financial Provision in Matrimonial Proceedings*, Law Com. No. 25, para. 2.

[298] The Bill as passed by the House of Commons contained a provision for it to be brought into force by order; but the House of Lords at Report stage substituted a provision that it come into force on 1 January 1971: Divorce Reform Act 1969, s. 11(3). The Matrimonial Proceedings and Property Act 1970, s. 43(2) provided the same commencement date for the relevant provisions.

[299] In the debate on the Bishop Bill Leo Abse had (perhaps with knowledge of the Law Commission's discussions) given an indication of how these powers could be used 'to divide up the family property': *Official Report* (HC) 24 January 1969, vol. 776, cols. 824–825.

[300] Matrimonial Proceedings and Property Act 1970, s. 5(1)(f) (subsequently Matrimonial Causes Act 1973, s. 25(1)(f)).

[301] The courts have made extensive use of the power to reallocate property between divorcing spouses: see Chapter 10, below. But this does not alter the fact that such powers only arise when the marriage has broken down, and are in any case discretionary: see below.

[302] The qualification is necessary because the Commission had recommended that doubts caused by the decision of the House of Lords in *Pettitt v. Pettitt* [1970] AC 777 about the extent to which contributions made after the acquisition of property to its improvement could give rise to a beneficial proprietary interest: see the discussion in the Commission's *Report on Financial Provision in Matrimonial Proceedings*, Law Com. No. 25, paras. 55–58. The Matrimonial Proceedings and Property Act 1970, s. 37 gave effect to this recommendation—which the Commission admitted gave the court 'something in the nature of a discretion, but a very limited one exercisable only in circumstances where a discretion is inevitable because of the informality of family arrangements': para. 58—and seems now to be rarely invoked: see SM Cretney and JM Masson, *Principles of Family Law* (6th ed., 1997) pp. 181–183. The Act also included two other minor reforms of property law: see the Commission's *Report, op. cit.*, paras. 59–62.

[303] Law Commission *Published Working Paper No. 42, Family Property Law* (1971) para. 0.22.

In the circumstances it is not surprising that Lady Summerskill should claim[304] the 'rather miserable little Bill' leaving everything to the secret exercise of a judicial discretion was no more than 'a confidence trick against the women of this country'. She would certainly have been reinforced in that view if she had known that the Law Commission's internal files recorded[305] the Law Commission's aim as being ' to achieve liberalization of the grounds of divorce on the basis of [the Commission's recommendations relating to financial orders on divorce] *without the need to wait for the overhaul of family property'*.

A GENUINE LAW OF FAMILY PROPERTY? THE REFORM WHICH NEVER HAPPENED

The divorce reformers' strategy had certainly succeeded; but what was now to happen about the unfinished business—should there be legislation for what the Commission called[306] a 'genuine law of family property'? In fact, the 1970 Bishop Bill has its place as a significant historical landmark: it is the last Bill seeking to establish the principle of community over the whole range of matrimonial property ever to be fully debated in either House of Parliament. The story of how and why the struggle for community came to be quietly abandoned can be told quite briefly.

In September 1970 the Law Commission presented a preliminary draft Working Paper to a seminar held in Manchester; and the discussion[307] seems to have very much set the agenda for subsequent Law Commission work on the subject. A year later the Commission published its definitive (and lengthy) *Working Paper on Family Property Law*.[308] This, whilst acknowledging that any community system would inevitably be 'complex', made a powerful case for the introduction of a rights (as distinct from discretion) based system:[309]

'In the last resort, the main question to be decided is whether it would lead to a greater measure of justice to give effect to the idea that marriage is a partnership, by sharing the assets acquired during the marriage, regardless of which spouse contributed financially to their acquisition. This question cannot be avoided on the ground that community is too difficult.

There is, of course, a case for saying that discretionary powers are all that is needed when a marriage ends in divorce, nullity or judicial separation. But the relative advan-

---

[304] *Official Report* (HL) 6 November 1970, vol. 305, col. 500.

[305] PRO BC3/400, 24 February 1967, (italics supplied) recording the final discussions on the draft of what became the Commission's *Working Paper No. 9, Matrimonial and Related Proceedings—Financial Relief*.

[306] Published Working Paper No. 42, *Family Property Law* (1971), para. 0.2.

[307] Papers were presented by Professor L Neville Brown (who urged caution against an uncritical acceptance of ideas drawn from other societies) Professor Roger Crane with Mrs Jennifer Levin (who drew attention to the difficulties arising from the existing law) and Dr Olive Stone (who underlined the difficulties and injustice caused by the law). A transcript of the discussions is on PRO BC3/600.

[308] Published Working Paper No. 42, *Family Property Law* (1971).

[309] *Ibid.*, paras. 5.85–5.86.

tages and disadvantages of a system of fixed shares, such as community, and a system of discretionary powers should not be considered only in legal terms. It is important not to forget the advantages of security and status which a community system would give to the spouse who, because of marital and family ties, is unable to acquire an interest in the assets by a financial contribution. Instead of being, as now, regarded as a dependant, who must apply to the court, such a spouse would become an equal partner in marriage, entitled at the end of the marriage to claim an equal share in the net assets acquired during the marriage. The pattern of social development in the future may be that on the end of a marriage an able bodied spouse would be expected to become self-reliant and independent as soon as possible, rather than to look to the former marriage partner as a source of support for life. A system of sharing on fixed principles may be more in harmony with this idea than the present system of separate property, reinforced, in certain situations, by the enforcement, possibly over a long period, of maintenance obligations determined with regard to discretionary factors. These are matters on which many will have views . . .'

The Law Commission's Compromise: community of property restricted to matrimonial home

Some two years later, the Law Commission (now differently composed)[310] published its *First Report on Family Property: A New Approach*.[311] The Commission stated that it had been assisted in reaching its conclusions by an 'exceptionally wide' consultation.[312] Although there had been some opposition to the introduction of any kind of fixed property rights between husband and wife on the grounds that this was 'unnecessary and . . . objectionable'[313] the 'great majority' regarded it as 'essential in the interests of justice and certainty to introduce a new principle upon which the property rights of husband and wife would be determined in accordance with fixed principles' and

---

[310] Norman Marsh QC was the only one of the Comissioners originally appointed in 1965 still in post to sign the Commission's *First Report on Family Property: A New Approach* on 9 April 1973; the others (Sir Leslie Scarman, Mr Neil Lawson QC and Professor Andrew Martin QC) had demitted office between 1970 and 1973.

[311] Law Com. No. 52.

[312] *First Report on Family Property: A New Approach* (1973, Law Com. No. 52) paras. 3–7. The Commission relied in part on (i) the result of an attitude survey carried out by the Office of Population Censuses and Surveys (JE Todd and LM Jones, *Matrimonial Property* (1972)); (ii) an analysis of 300 replies to a questionnaire published in the *Sun* newspaper in 1972 carried out by KJ Gray and other Cambridge undergraduates, and (iii) the traditional input from meetings, conferences and written comments on the Working Paper. The General Appendix to the Commission's *Third Report on Family Property: The Matrimonial Home (Co-ownership and Occupation Rights) and Household Goods* (1978 Law Com. No. 86) lists 65 individuals—three judges, eleven practitioners and fifteen academic lawyers—as well as groups (eight lawyers' organisations, nineteen interest groups, three representatives of property interests, three government departments, and the Church of England's Board for Social Responsibility) who had made comments, but suggests that 'many' other members of the public had commented on the proposals.

[313] Para. 10.

'overwhelmingly' favoured co-ownership of the matrimonial home.[314] But the Commission also concluded[315] that if the co-ownership principle were applied to the home,[316] much of what was regarded as unsatisfactory or unfair would be eliminated, the marriage partnership would be recognised by family property law in this 'very important context' and it would not be necessary to introduce a system of community applying to any other asset.

In making a recommendation restricted in this way the Commission was heavily influenced[317] by decisions of the courts (notably *Wachtel v. Wachtel*)[318] evidencing the courts' readiness to exercise the discretionary powers on divorce conferred by the Matrimonial Proceedings and Property Act 1970[319] on a 'broad and generous basis' resulting in the spouses being given equal interests in the matrimonial home in many cases.[320] But the Commission concluded that the 'difference between the rules applied to married couples and those applied on divorce can no longer be regarded as acceptable',[321] and that accordingly a principle of co-ownership under which the matrimonial home would be shared equally should be introduced.

The Law Commission then set up a Working Party[322] to give advice about the conveyancing and other legal problems to which the adoption of the principle of

[314] Para. 11. Co-ownership would be subject to a contrary agreement by the parties, and the court would retain its power in matrimonial proceedings to make orders varying the fixed community shares in cases where such an allocation did not produce a 'just result in the circumstances': para. 56.

[315] Para. 59.

[316] Such a regime had been supported by three members of the *Report of the Royal Commission on Marriage and Divorce* (1956, Cmd. 9678, para. 652) on the basis of securing justice to women at risk of finding themselves left with nothing they could call their own. A further three members had favoured a more general community regime, and one had favoured a community restricted to household contents.

[317] However, the Law Commission's first Chairman (Sir Leslie Scarman) had recorded in 1970 that he did not expect any reform of matrimonial property law to extend to a statutory community regime. He anticipated that community would emerge in practice as a result of judicial discretion; but thought that the Commission 'owed it to those who had supported [Mr Edward Bishop's Bill: see above] to give community a reasonable run with the public': PRO BC3/600, Minute dated 30 September 1970. It is not possible, from the materials currently in the public domain, to assess the attitudes of the other Commissioners.

[318] [1973] Fam 72.   [319] Consolidated in the Matrimonial Causes Act 1973.

[320] *First Report on Family Property: A New Approach* (Law Com. No. 52, 1973) para. 20.

[321] The principles applicable in cases about beneficial entitlement where the adjustive discretion of the divorce court was not available had been settled by the House of Lords in *Pettitt v. Pettitt* [1970] AC 777 and *Gissing v. Gissing* [1971] AC 886 and their effect had been dramatically illustrated by the first instance decision in *Cowcher v. Cowcher* [1972] 1 WLR 425 in which (in the words of the Law Commission) Bagnall J had 'decided the issues by applying strictly the equitable principles governing the formation and continuance of trusts; he expressly disregarded the fact that the parties were married or that the home was a family asset. He was not required to consider what would be fair and reasonable between the spouses; any contribution by either party, other than a strictly financial contribution, was irrelevant'. Accordingly, a wife who nine years earlier had contributed one third of the price of the matrimonial home was only entitled (subject to equitable accounting) to one third of the ultimate sale proceeds.

[322] Chaired by Mr Claud Bicknell, formerly a practising solicitor, appointed a Law Commissioner in 1970. The majority of the other members were associated with the Law Commission: see *First Report on Family Property: A New Approach* (1973, Law Com. No. 52), Appendix 1.

joint ownership would give rise. It soon became clear that the task of putting even the restricted form of co-ownership favoured by the Commission into statutory form was more complex than anyone had anticipated. The Commission had intended to submit a Report with draft legislation 'during the course of 1973' but in fact the Report—a densely reasoned document extending over more than a hundred printed pages—together with a 34-clause draft Bill was only finally submitted five years later.

This delay proved fatal[323] to the prospects for implementing the Commission's proposals. By the time the co-ownership Report was presented the complaints (stimulated by pressure groups such as the Campaign for Justice in Divorce and given extensive media coverage) which burdened MPs' postbags were no longer about the injustice done to wives by the legal system but rather about the allegedly harsh and unfair consequences of divorce for men. It was all very well for seasoned community campaigners (such as Lord McGregor of Durris and Lord Simon of Glaisdale) to urge that the 'the law governing matrimonial property in part reflects and in part helps to shape the community's attitudes to the family and to relationships within it'[324] and that the 1882 separation regime has 'institutionalised inequality', but the campaigners were on distinctly thin ice in claiming[325] that the public wanted change and that this had been 'demonstrated over and over again during the last dozen or so years'.[326] As Lord Chancellor Hailsham put it:

'I must tell [those who make this claim] absolutely flatly that they could not sit for a week in the Lord Chancellor's office and believe that there was any popular demand for statutory co-ownership of the matrimonial home.'

What people did want, according to Lord Hailsham, was reform of the adjustive jurisdiction following divorce, a topic on which he had had 'literally hundreds of letters', and which he regarded as a legislative priority. As will be seen, in 1984 Lord Hailsham was successful in getting a place in the legislative timetable for the Bill which became the Matrimonial and Family Proceedings

---

[323] The issue of matrimonial property reform was brought before the House of Lords on three occasions between 1979 and 1982. First, in 1979 Lord Simon of Glaisdale moved a motion calling for papers on the Commission's *Third Report on Family Property*: see *Official Report* (HL) 18 July 1979, vol. 401, col. 1431. Secondly, in 1980 Lord Simon introduced the Law Commission's Matrimonial Homes (Co-ownership) Bill *Official Report* (HL) 12 February 1980, vol. 405, col. 112, to be met with a negative response from the Lord Chancellor who (in addition to pointing to the pressure for reform of a different kind from the Campaign for Justice in Divorce: see below) pointed out that in the growing number of second marriages with step-children co-ownership did not necessarily produce a socially just outcome, and saying his misgivings had for that reason increased. Thirdly, in 1982, Lord Simon again initiated a debate calling for papers in response to the Law Commission's *Report on the Implications of Williams & Glyn's Bank Ltd v. Boland* (1982) Law Com. No. 115 (which had repeated its support for a scheme of equal co-ownership of the matrimonial home); and on this occasion Lord Chancellor Hailsham made it clear that there could be no immediate prospects for implementing statutory co-ownership.

[324] *Official Report* (HL) 18 July 1979, vol. 401, col. 1437.

[325] Made by Lord McGregor, *Official Report* (HL) 15 December 1982, vol. 437, col. 654.

[326] This is presumably a reference to the Survey evidence used by the Law Commission: see above.

Act 1984; and although as the century drew to a close there were suggestions that the guidelines structuring the court's discretion in exercising its powers to make financial orders needed revision[327] to give greater precision and predictability, it seems clear that the preference dating from 1970 for dealing with the consequences of marital breakdown by the exercise of a broad discretion had, by the end of the twentieth century, now become firmly established. Reform of matrimonial property law seemed to be a lost cause.[328]

Much of the pressure for reform was removed because the practice of having the matrimonial home vested in husband and wife jointly[329] (a trend which may have been influenced by the readiness of mortgage lenders to take the income of both husband and wife into account in assessing the maximum amount of the loan they would advance in joint purchase cases) became almost universal. Again, although the House of Lords continued to assert that as a matter of law informally created proprietary interests in the matrimonial home and other property could only be established under the rules of implied resulting and constructive trusts,[330] in practice the task of doing so seems to have become much easier. In particular, it seems that creditors and others have become much readier to accept (without any need for litigation) that each spouse had an equal share in the property,[331] whilst a decision of the House of Lords in 1980[332] meant that any such interest would be likely to bind a purchaser or lender unless the spouse had agreed to defer his or her interest to that of the lender. In fact, lenders adopted the almost universal practice of seeking such a waiver from

[327] See Chapter 10, below.

[328] In 1988 the Law Commission's *Report on Family Law: Matrimonial Property* (Law Com. No. 175) made a spirited defence of its previous proposals for the introduction of a community regime (see in particular para. 1.4) and recommended that property purchased or transferred to spouses for their joint use should be jointly owned; but the Commission (remarkably) now suggested that the matrimonial home (and certain other assets) should be excluded from this principle: see para. 4.5. These recommendations have not been implemented.

[329] The survey of *Matrimonial Property* by JE Todd and LM Jones established as long ago as 1972 that more than 90% of those interviewed believed that the home and its contents should be legally jointly owned, and in the intervening years that belief seems to have been translated into routine practice. By 1984 76% of respondents to the *General Household Survey* in the United Kingdom were joint owners (and this may underestimate the proportion of joint owners in England and Wales): see the Law Commission's *Report on Family Law: Matrimonial Property* (Law Com. No. 175) p. 13 note 4.

[330] In *Lloyds Bank plc v. Rosset* [1991] 1 AC 107 the House of Lords adopted a strictly traditional approach. However, there are some indications that (at least once it has been established that the wife has a valid claim to *some* beneficial interest) the courts are prepared to adopt a somewhat more flexible approach to determining the extent of that interest: see SM Cretney and JM Masson, *Principles of Family Law* (6th ed., 1997) Chapter 5.

[331] In *Williams & Glyn's Bank Ltd v. Boland* [1981] AC 487, HL, for example, the Bank (seeking to enforce its security against a husband in whose sole name the title was registered) did not dispute the wife's claim that as against the husband she was entitled to a property interest. The Bank did claim that it took free from the wife's interest, but the House of Lords held that the wife's interests constituted an overriding interest and under the provisions of the Land Registration Act 1925, s. 70(1)(g) bound a person who had not made enquiries. Again a research project into the effect of insolvency on the matrimonial home carried out in Bristol in 1989 confirmed that most trustees in bankruptcy would in practice concede that a wife was entitled to a beneficial interest.

[332] *Williams & Glyn's Bank Ltd v. Boland* [1981] AC 487; see above.

wives and other residents in the family home; and the courts increasingly became concerned with the validity of such waivers[333] rather than with the question whether the parties were entitled to any beneficial interest in the property. Community of property had become yesterday's reform.

PROPERTY ENTITLEMENTS ON DEATH

All the property[334] which a man or woman owns vests, on his or her death, in the personal representatives. It is for the personal representatives to distribute the assets to those entitled, whether under the deceased's will or under the rules governing intestate succession. The personal representatives must, therefore, first determine what property the deceased did own. They will accordingly have to determine whether a deceased had a property interest[335] in the former family home under the rules discussed above, notwithstanding the fact that the deceased's spouse (or cohabitant) was the sole legal owner. Having decided what assets the deceased did own, the personal representatives will have to identify the persons entitled to take the property as a result of the deceased's death; and in so doing the question whether the deceased was married or not will (especially if the deceased died wholly or partially intestate) be highly relevant. The development of the law governing these matters is explained in Part III of this book (Ending relationships: the legal consequences).

---

[333] Following the landmark decision of the House of Lords in *Barclays Bank plc v. O'Brien and Another* [1994] 1 AC 180 these and other security transactions were frequently attacked on the ground that the waiver had been obtained by misrepresentation or undue influence on the part of the husband: see generally B Fehlberg, *Sexually Transmitted Debt* (1997).

[334] Including real property (which, before 1925, had vested automatically in the heir at law): Administration of Estates Act 1925, s. 1.

[335] The right to occupy the former matrimonial home under the Matrimonial Homes Act 1967 and subsequent legislation ends on death: see Family Law Act 1996, s. 33(5); *O'Malley v. O'Malley* [1982] 1 WLR 244.

4

Other Legal Consequences of Marriage: Conjugal Rights and Remedies

INTRODUCTION

In 1857, as we shall see, the Matrimonial Causes Act established a procedure whereby the Court for Divorce and Matrimonial Causes could grant divorce decrees, thereby terminating the parties' marital status, and permitting them to remarry. Divorce came to dominate the Court's caseload;[1] but the Court was concerned not only with divorce but also with the other 'matrimonial causes' (nullity of marriage, restitution of conjugal rights, judicial separation, and jactitation of marriage) previously dealt with in the Ecclesiastical Courts.[2] In addition, the 1857 Act gave the Court for Divorce and Matrimonial Causes[3] power to award a husband damages against the man with whom his wife had committed adultery; and statute[4] gave the Court power to make orders for the protection of the wife's property.

Notwithstanding the dominance of divorce, these other 'matrimonial causes' should not be overlooked. The law of nullity has been dealt with elsewhere in this book.[5] Petitions for jactitation of marriage—seeking a decree of perpetual silence against a person falsely boasting that he or she is married to the petitioner—became so rare that no more than a footnote explanation is

---

[1] Figures are given in the *Report of the Royal Commission on Marriage and Divorce* (1956, Cmd. 9678) (subsequently 'the *Morton Report*') App. 2. In 1900 there were 609 divorce petitions and the court granted 494 decrees nisi (81%); and in 1925 the comparable figures were 2,973 and 2,657 (89 %). The comparable figures for judicial separation are: 1900, 89 petitions and 19 decrees (21%); 1925, 115 petitions and 36 decrees (31%). For nullity, in 1900 there were 26 petitions and 23 decrees (88%); in 1925 there were 81 petitions and 58 decrees (72%). Statistics for restitution petitions are given at note 29, below. No statistics are available in respect of proceedings for jactitation of marriage, but these were virtually obsolete: see note 6 below. There were a significant number of damages claims, but no statistics are available.

[2] Matrimonial Causes Act 1857, ss. 2, 3.

[3] This replaced the common law action for criminal conversation: Matrimonial Causes Act 1857, s. 33.

[4] The Matrimonial Causes Act 1857, s. 21 had given magistrates power to make such orders; and the Matrimonial Causes Act 1858, s. 6 gave the same power to the Judge Ordinary. The procedure was misleadingly named, and was in practice of little use: see p. 95, above.

[5] Chapter 2, above.

required.[6] But the remedies of restitution, separation, and damages for adultery have considerable conceptual importance: they all reflect the fact that in 1857 marriage was still seen as a legal relationship which gave rise to legally enforceable rights and duties. In the latter part of the twentieth century this approach increasingly seemed outdated; and the legislative response betokens a changed view of the relationship between the family and the law. Less summary treatment of restitution, separation and damages for adultery therefore seems appropriate.

ENFORCING THE OBLIGATION TO LIVE TOGETHER:
RESTITUTION OF CONJUGAL RIGHTS

The Ecclesiastical Courts had been concerned to enforce the obligations of matrimony, which included the duty of husband and wife to 'live together after God's ordinance'.[7] This they did by making decrees directing the husband[8] to take his wife home 'and receive her as his wife'.[9] Originally the pastoral role of the church was emphasised: excommunication was the ultimate sanction for failure to comply with such an order. But in 1813 the Ecclesiastical Courts Act substituted committal to prison for excommunication as the ultimate sanction, and occasionally men and women were imprisoned for disobedience to such an order.[10] In 1857 the newly established Court for Divorce and Matrimonial Causes[11] inherited this jurisdiction from the Ecclesiastical Court;[12] and each

---

[6] See generally *Declarations in Family Matters* (Law Com. No. 132, 1984, Part IV; J Jackson, *Formation and Annulment of Marriage* (2nd ed., 1969) p. 87. In 1900 it was said that the remedy of jactitation had 'fallen into disuse' (see *Cowley v. Cowley* [1900] P 305, 313) but very occasionally—there appear to have been six instances in the course of the twentieth century—a jactitation suit was used to get a declaration as to the validity of a foreign divorce decree or because the petitioner was embarrassed by repetition of a falsehood: *Declarations in Family Matters* (Law Com. No. 132, 1984, para. 4.5). The *Morton Report,* paras. 525–526, declined to recommend abolition, taking the view that such petitions could 'on occasion still be useful' in cases where the respondent was actively claiming a false relationship; but the Family Law Act 1986, s. 61, gave effect to the Law Commission's recommendation that the right to petition for jactitation should be abolished.

[7] And to love honour and keep each other in sickness and in health, forsaking all other—the form of words used in the Book of Common Prayer which was, until the enactment of the Marriage Act 1836, prescribed for use in all save Jewish and Quaker marriages.

[8] Either party could petition, and both husbands and wives did so; but the published statistics suggest that far more women than men petitioned: *Morton Report,* Appendix II, Table 1.

[9] The form of the order in *Weldon v. Weldon* (1883) 9 PD 52; see below.

[10] See eg *Barlee v. Barlee* (1822) 1 Add 304 (the Court of Arches expressed its sincere commiseration with a wife's situation but refused to order her release from Ipswich gaol, where she was 'reduced to the gaol allowance of bread and water, and a small amount of cheese'). The court was more merciful in *Lakin v. Lakin* (1854) 1 Sp Ecc & Ad 274, ordering the release of a husband who had been in prison for three years.

[11] See Chapter 5, below.

[12] Matrimonial Causes Act 1857, ss. 17, 22. The 1857 Act also gave jurisdiction to order Restitution of Conjugal Rights to all Assize judges, but that provision was repealed by the Matrimonial Causes Act 1858, s. 19.

year, the Divorce Court made a handful of decrees.[13] It seems reasonable to suppose that few petitioners believed they could in this way actually compel an errant spouse to return and that they were motivated more by the prospect of the Court exercising its power[14] to make 'such order for the payment by the husband of alimony to the wife' as it thought just.[15] But in 1882 Mrs Georgina Weldon[16] earned her place in the history of law reform:

Mrs Weldon, acting in person, petitioned for Restitution of Conjugal Rights. Her husband at first resisted her claim on the ground that she had committed adultery; but this defence was eventually dropped. The court accordingly granted Mrs Weldon the decree to which she was entitled.[17] The husband—a figure of some prominence in London society[18]—accepted his obligation to support her: he made monthly payments of £500 (perhaps £30,000 in year 2000 values), rented Acton House in Acton Middlesex (at the time a no doubt agreeable West London village) for her to live in, and engaged two servants to attend on her. But, not unreasonably[19] believing that 'living together again could only entail certain misery on both of us', he rejected her entreaties[20] that they should

---

[13] An average of four decrees were granted annually in the decade 1868 to 1878: *Morton Report*, Appendix II, Table 2(iv).

[14] Matrimonial Causes Act 1857, s. 17.

[15] In *Marshall v. Marshall* (1879) 5 PD 19, 23, Sir James Hannen remarked that he had never known of restitution proceedings being started for any purpose other than to enforce a money demand. But he was soon to be enlightened.

[16] Georgina Weldon (who gave her profession as 'composer and singer') was, to put it mildly, a flamboyant character. She took advantage of the enactment of the Married Women's Property Act 1882 to bring a large number of tort and other legal actions in her own name (as that Act permitted) mostly to seek redress against those she believed to be responsible for her incarceration (at the instance of her husband) in a private lunatic asylum. At least one of those cases—*Weldon v. de Bathe* (1884) 14 QBD 339—was important as demonstrating that the effect of the 1882 Act was to deprive the husband of the right to decide who should be allowed into the wife's house and remains of importance for its discussion of the respective legal rights of spouses to have visitors in the matrimonial home. Mrs Weldon's colourful career has attracted the attention of a number of writers: see eg P Treherne, *A Plaintiff in Person* (1923); E Grierson, *Storm Bird, The Strange Life of Georgina Weldon* (1959); JR Walkowitz, *City of Dreadful Delight: narratives of sexual danger in late-Victorian London* (1992); and B Thompson, *A Monkey among Crocodiles, The Lives, Loves and Lawsuits of Mrs Georgina Weldon* (2000). None gives an entirely satisfactory account of her litigious career, but the first two listed are of value in this respect.

[17] An account of her behaviour in court is given in E Grierson, *op.cit.*, p. 197.

[18] Henry William Weldon, an officer in the 18th Hussars at the time of his disastrous marriage, subsequently inherited a substantial fortune. Long interested in heraldry, he became Rouge Dragon in 1869 and Windsor Herald in 1880. Once the threat of imprisonment for defying the Restitution decree was lifted his career again flourished. In 1902 he acted as Deputy Garter King of Arms at the coronation of King Edward VII, and was appointed CVO. In 1904 he became Secretary to the Earl Marshal and was knighted in 1919, the year of his death. But he was only able to remarry after Georgina Weldon's death in 1914.

[19] Especially since she had at the same time as serving the restitution decree on her husband also served him with a writ for libel.

[20] 'Now, my dear Harry, believe me. Bow to the inevitable; you married me—and I want a home and I am determined to have one. The law gives me the only reparation it *can* give a married woman . . . Separated I won't be. I do not like single life and I think I shall like you all the better now, as you must be getting older now and want a little taking care of.' Apparently on the day she obtained the decree she had written him a letter beginning 'My darling old Poompsey Keat' and proceeding

once again live together under the same roof. Mrs Weldon then applied to the court for a writ of attachment committing the husband to prison for disobedience to the court order. The President of the Probate Divorce and Admiralty Division of the High Court[21] accepted her argument that a man was legally bound to live with his wife and that his marital obligations were not satisfied by providing a house, servants and financial support for her. The President held that he had no alternative but to issue the writ for the husband's imprisonment although he made it clear that he felt such a sanction inappropriate.[22]

The Government responds: imprisonment not to be used to enforce obligation to live together

The government reacted swiftly.[23] The Matrimonial Causes Act 1884 was passed through both Houses of Parliament without debate or even an explanatory Government statement and received the Royal Assent on 14 August 1884. The Act abolished the sanction of imprisonment for failure to comply with a restitution decree, and substituted a power for the court to make financial orders.[24] Mr Weldon was thus spared the necessity of leaving the country to save himself from imprisonment;[25] but for the history of the divorce law the most important feature of the Act was that it gave the wife the right immediately to petition for divorce if her husband had not only committed adultery but also failed to comply with a restitution decree.[26] In this way the 'Weldon Relief Act' (as it was apparently called)[27] enabled women to circumvent the policy of the Matrimonial Causes Act 1857 Act[28] and get a speedy divorce against husbands who had done no more than set up house with another woman.

---

through a dozen or so lines of mixed insults and endearments to the signature, 'Your ever loving Tatkin and wife.': E Grierson, *Storm Bird, The Strange Life of Georgina Weldon* (1959) pp. 197–199.

  [21] Sir James Hannen (1821–1894).

  [22] *Weldon v. Weldon* (1883) 9 PD 52.

  [23] Judgment in *Weldon v. Weldon* was given on 22 November 1883; and Royal Assent was given to the Matrimonial Causes Act 1884 on 14 August 1884. But Mr Weldon must have spent an anxious time awaiting the tipstaff's call in the nine months during which the writ of attachment might have been enforced.

  [24] In the case of a husband respondent, periodical payments (including secured periodical payments): s. 2. Where the wife failed to comply with an order the court was given power to order her to make periodical payments out of any trade profits or earnings and to order a settlement of her property: s. 3.

  [25] E Grierson, *Storm Bird, The Strange Life of Georgina Weldon* (1959) p. 199.

  [26] Matrimonial Causes Act 1884, s. 5, provided that failure to comply with a restitution decree constituted desertion, and that a suit for judicial separation could be started immediately (rather than after desertion for a continuous period of two years). The Act also expressly provided that a wife whose husband did not comply with a restitution decree could immediately petition for divorce on the ground of adultery coupled with desertion.

  [27] See P Treherne, *A Plaintiff in Person* (1923).

  [28] ie that divorce should only be available to a wife who could prove her husband had not only committed adultery but also some other aggravating offence: see Chapter 5, below.

In fact, it seems to have taken a surprisingly long time[29] for solicitors[30] to appreciate this, but by 1912 the Gorrell Royal Commission acknowledged that the device of obtaining a Restitution decree had become 'an understood means of enabling a woman to obtain a divorce on the grounds of her husband's adultery alone', and that the decree had become in those circumstances 'something of a sham'.[31]

Enforcing a restitution decree by self-help: the courts respond

The 1884 Act thus gave effect to the policy that it was oppressive and unnecessary[32] to imprison those who preferred to live apart from their spouses. But the extent to which the courts were prepared to recognise the existence of legally enforceable 'rights' in the family context remained unclear. Only a few years later, a sensational case illustrated the difficulty:

In *R v. Jackson*[33] a husband applied for and obtained a decree for restitution against his newly married wife, and set about enforcing it. Assisted by two young men (one a solicitor's articled clerk) he seized her as she was leaving church in the Lancashire town of Clitheroe and forced her into a carriage, claiming to have used no more force than was absolutely necessary to separate her from the sister he believed to be responsible for what had happened. Mrs Jackson was kept in the husband's house in Blackburn in charge of her sister and a nurse and she was visited by a doctor. The husband claimed that he showed her every kindness and consideration and that she had the free run of the house,

---

[29] In the ten years 1872–1882 there were on average 19 restitution petitions a year, and the annual average for the ten years 1884–1894 was only 22. The number of petitions by wives increased significantly in the first decade of the twentieth century: there were 67 in 1910. The end of World War I was marked by a very large increase (130 wife petitions in 1914, 491 in 1919). In 1924 (after the coming into force of the Matrimonial Causes Act 1923, giving the wife the right to petition for divorce on the ground of her husband's adultery) the number of wife petitions fell to 52: see the statistics in *Morton Report,* Appendix II, Table 1.

[30] Before filing a petition, the petitioner had to make 'a written demand' for restitution of cohabitation and conjugal rights; but case law established that this had to be in conciliatory terms: see *Elliott v. Elliott* (1901) 85 LT 648 (where the letter, although somewhat peremptory, was judged sufficient). It appears that '. . . the drafting of the letter in suitable terms was left to a member of the legal profession—in the best cases it would be settled by counsel—and it was copied out and signed by the petitioner. . . . It is certain that not one petitioner in a hundred can ever have intended or hoped that the letter in conciliatory terms would produce any effect on the husband, so the whole thing was a mockery . . .': C Binney, *The Divorce Court* (1957) p. 25. But there is a celebrated fictional account of a case in which the husband did return, to the extreme discomfiture of the wife and her advisers: J Galsworthy, *The Forsyte Chronicles, In Chancery* (Penguin ed. 1978, p. 553).

[31] *Report of the Royal Commission on Divorce and Matrimonial Causes,* 1912, Cd. 6478, paras. 102 and 376. The Commission accepted the evidence of Sir George Lewis, the prominent divorce lawyer, that the 1884 Act had led to collusion between husband and wife each anxious for divorce: the wife wrote a letter asking him to return, he (as both had agreed) refused, and a divorce could be obtained without embarking on the disagreeable task of giving evidence of the husband's cruelty etc. Note also the view of Bargrave Dean J that the 'statutory desertion' provisions of the 1884 Act should be repealed: *Evidence taken before the Royal Commission,* 1912, Cd. 6479–82, Vols. I–III, 26 February 1910, q. 848.

[32] *R v. Jackson* [1891] 1 QB 671, 684, *per* Lord Esher.   [33] [1891] 1 QB 671.

'doing just as she pleased, save leaving the house'; and that he 'had offered several times to take her for a drive, but she had declined to go'. The wife's relatives instituted *habeas corpus* proceedings; and the Court of Appeal[34] rejected the husband's argument that a husband had the right to enforce the 'general dominion' he had over his wife[35] by imprisoning her if she refused him the conjugal rights to which a court had declared him entitled. Lord Esher MR[36] regarded the 1884 Act as the 'strongest possible evidence to shew that the legislature had no idea that a power would remain in the husband to imprison the wife for himself', not least because to accept this view would result in his being allowed to act[37] as party judge and executioner.[38]

The *Jackson* decision was at the time unpopular in some quarters,[39] and it was certainly widely misunderstood.[40] But it is a landmark in family law: the decision recognises that the 'rights' which exist between husband and wife are of a different order than (say) the rights of the parties to a commercial contract. But the question of 'how different' remained difficult.

The lingering death of Restitution of Conjugal Rights

The Matrimonial Causes Act 1923 enabled a wife to divorce her husband on the ground of his adultery; and it was no longer necessary for a wife to seek a decree of restitution (no doubt devoutly hoping that it would not be obeyed)[41] to free herself of her marriage to an adulterous husband. Until 1950, a wife might be advised to seek a restitution decree because the court would then be able to

---

[34] Reversing the decision of the Queen's Bench Division.

[35] *In re Cochrane* (1840) 8 Dowl. 630.   [36] At p. 684.   [37] *per* Fry LJ at p. 686.

[38] But the judgments give some support for the view that a husband retained the right to restrain his wife from flagrant misconduct (for example eloping with her lover): see *per* Halsbury LC at p. 679. The right of a married woman to complete domestic autonomy may be thought to have been finally established by the controversial ruling of the House of Lords that a husband is not exempt from criminal liability for raping his wife: *R v. R* [1992] 1 AC 599, HL (and note that statute subsequently confirmed and clarified the position: Criminal Justice and Public Order Act 1994, s. 142).

[39] In one view, 'marriage, as hitherto understood in England, was suddenly abolished one fine morning last month'; and it has been said that the Court of Appeal's decision caused a 'deep shock of surprise and indignation' to thrill through the country: Eliza Lynn Linton, 'The Judicial Shock to Marriage' (1891) *Nineteenth Century* 691 as quoted in D Rubinstein, *Before the Suffragettes: Women's Emancipation in the 1890s* (1986) pp. 54–58. *The Times* predicted that the *Jackson* decision would be unpopular in Blackburn 'where somewhat primitive ideas prevail as to the rights of man and the duties of women'. There were riots, Mrs Jackson had to be protected against the mob by police and her sisters' house was stoned: see the full account in Rubinstein, *op. cit.*

[40] Including by some who were responsible for the administration of the law. Lord Esher (one of the judges involved) said in the House of Lords that it had been 'more misunderstood than any judgment I recollect': *Hansard's Parliamentary Debates* (3rd Series) 16 April 1891, vol. 352, col. 642; and it was reported that magistrates mistakenly believed that the effect of the *Jackson* case was to render unenforceable the orders which they had power to make under the legislation shortly to be consolidated as the Summary Jurisdiction (Married Women) Act 1895: see the account in *Hansard's Parliamentary Debates* (3rd Series) 16 April 1891, vol. 352, col. 641 also fully reported in *The Times*, 17 April 1891.

[41] For a fictional account of a case where the husband did comply, see J Galsworthy, *The Forsyte Chronicles, In Chancery* (Penguin ed. 1978, p. 553) and note 30 above.

make a maintenance order in her favour;[42] but the Matrimonial Causes Act 1950[43] gave her the right to seek a maintenance order simply on the ground of the husband's wilful neglect to provide reasonable maintenance for her or the children. After that, it was not easy to see what useful purpose a restitution decree could serve;[44] and the 1956 *Morton Report* accepted that there were no steps which the court could take 'to enforce its order that conjugal rights be rendered' and accepted that the order was in fact rarely obeyed.[45] But the conservatively minded Commission declined to recommend abolition.[46] Unhappily, case law was to show that, even in the second half of the twentieth century, by no means everyone appreciated the limited effect of the decree:[47]

In *Nanda v. Nanda*,[48] a couple married in their native India and lived together there for a few weeks before the husband left to pursue his profession as a dental surgeon in England. Shortly after arriving here he began living with another woman and had children by her. Mrs Nanda then came to England, obtained a decree of restitution of conjugal rights and sought to enforce it by her own means, which included turning up at the husband's home and surgery, insulting his partner, and eventually moving into the house. It was held that the husband was entitled to an order restraining his wife from even visiting the house. History does not record Mrs Nanda's reaction to this refusal to give effect to what she could reasonably (but erroneously) regard as her legal rights. As the Judge remarked, anyone might misunderstand the form and effect of a decree of restitution of conjugal rights and it was all the more likely that a woman brought up in India would have been misled.

This case (like *R v. Jackson*) provides a convincing demonstration of the way in which the retention of legal forms dating from an earlier age may be mis-

---

[42] A wife could have applied to a magistrates' court for a maintenance order, but the maximum amount which the magistrates could order was limited: see Chapter 11 below.

[43] s. 23.

[44] The *Morton Report*, para. 324, noted that the number of petitions (which had risen to a peak of 70 in 1948) decreased by one half in the first year in which High Court wilful neglect proceedings could be taken; and that thereafter 'the number of petitions filed, though small, has remained at a fairly steady figure' (in fact some 30 a year: see Appendix II, Table 2(iv)).

[45] para. 324. An experienced divorce practitioner (Geoffrey Crispin) had told the Royal Commission that only on one occasion had he ever known a restitution decree to have been obeyed: *Minutes of Evidence taken before the Royal Commission on Marriage and Divorce (1952–1954)* Paper No. 56.

[46] The Commission thought there might still be some financial advantages to a spouse in obtaining a decree (see para. 323) and noted that 'it was said to be useful that a spouse can obtain a finding of the court which puts on record the circumstances of the separation, if these are not altogether clear'. It noted that if 'opinion had been unanimous against the retention of the remedy, we might have come to the conclusion that there was no justification for keeping it': para. 92.

[47] As Payne J explained in *Nanda v. Nanda* (below) the decree gave the wife 'the right to financial provision, the right to petition for a judicial separation and in due course, if she wishes, the right to petition for a dissolution of the marriage on the grounds of desertion. She cannot enforce the restitution decree by imprisonment of her husband, and she has no more right than any other separated wife to trespass in a new home established by the husband with another woman'.

[48] [1968] P 351, Payne J.

understood by those not professionally trained in the law's arcane mysteries. Only in 1970 was the right to seek a decree for restitution of conjugal rights abolished[49] after a Law Commission report[50] had convincingly demonstrated that retention would serve no useful purpose.

THE DECREE OF JUDICIAL SEPARATION: COURT-ORDERED SEPARATION?

The Matrimonial Causes Act 1857 gave the Court power to grant decrees of judicial separation. But this was more a change of vocabulary, done 'for the sake of simplicity, and to mark it the more clearly from proper divorce',[51] than substance. The Act provided that the grounds on which the decree could be granted were to be the same as those in the Ecclesiastical Courts for a decree of *divorce a mensa et thoro*,[52] and that a judicial separation should have 'the same force and the same consequence as a divorce a mensa et thoro'.[53] Not until 1937 did legislation spell out in English that the effect of a decree was to make it 'no longer obligatory for the petitioner to cohabit with the respondent.[54] Only in 1969[55] was the reference to the grounds for making a decree of *divorce a mensa et thoro* before 1857 finally removed from the legislation. In some respects, however, the 1857 Act did improve the position of the wife who obtained a decree: the Court could (unlike the Ecclesiastical Court)[56] make orders for the custody, maintenance and education of the children;[57] the Court had more extensive powers in relation to the award of alimony[58] than had the Ecclesiastical Court, whilst the Act[59] gave the judicially separated wife the legal status of a *feme sole* in respect of after acquired property and and also gave her capacity to sue in contract and tort.[60]

A judicial separation was in some ways the counterpart of the decree for restitution of conjugal rights, and the name was equally misleading. For a judicial

---

[49] By the Matrimonial Proceedings and Property Act 1970, s. 20.

[50] *Proposal for the Abolition of the Matrimonial Remedy of Restitution of Conjugal Rights* Law Com. No. 23 (1969). The Law Commission's consultation revealed 'overwhelming support' for abolition (although one solicitor told the Commission that he had been involved in a case in which the petitioner's motive had been a genuine wish to save the marriage; and petitions were occasionally filed in order to resolve the question of which of the two parties was in desertion): PRO BC3/422.

[51] *MacQueen on the Law of Divorce* (2nd ed., 1860) p. 277.

[52] 'from the table and the bed'. The effect of the 1857 Act was that a decree could be granted on the grounds of adultery, cruelty, desertion for two years, and sodomy or bestiality and attempts thereat: ss. 7, 16, 22.

[53] Matrimonial Causes Act 1857, s. 7.   [54] Matrimonial Causes Act 1937, s. 5.

[55] Divorce Reform Act 1969, s. 8.

[56] *MacQueen on the Law of Divorce* (2nd ed., 1860) p. 277 states that the Ecclesiastical Court left children to their fate, and that 'great injury to families consequently arose, where parents were unreasonable, or where one of them obstinately refused to come to a voluntary arrangement, calculated to save exposure and obviate the evils of litigation'; and in such a case the Chancery wardship jurisdiction could have been invoked.

[57] Matrimonial Causes Act 1857, s. 35.   [58] Matrimonial Causes Act 1857, s. 24.

[59] Matrimonial Causes Act 1857, ss. 25, 26.

[60] In 1857 the legal status of a separated wife was still that of a wife, and she accordingly lacked legal capacity to sue in her own name. Only in 1882 did the Married Women's Property Act give all married women capacity to sue: see above, Chapter 3.

separation decree did not order the parties to separate; it merely terminated the legal duty to live together and in effect put a stamp of legal approval on the ending of any factual relationship between husband and wife.

Cruelty was long the ground most often relied on by petitioners,[61] but the Ecclesiastical Courts had been reluctant to countenance separation, and since the end of the eighteenth century,[62] had consistently held that the courts should interpret cruelty narrowly and that the duty of the court was to apply an 'extremely strict' criterion.[63] Marriage was a lifelong obligation, for better or worse; and only behaviour which showed 'an absolute impossibility that the duties of the married life could be discharged' was to be sufficient ground for giving the parties the legal right to live separate and apart:

'Mere austerity of temper, petulance of manners, rudeness of language, a want of civil accommodation, even occasional sallies of passion, if they do not threaten bodily harm, do not amount to legal cruelty: they are high moral offences in the marriage-state undoubtedly . . . but still they are not that cruelty against which the law can relieve. Under such misconduct . . . the suffering party must bear in some degree the consequences of an injudicious connection; must subdue by decent resistance or by prudent conciliation.'[64]

The effect of this policy can be illustrated by decided cases which give some indication of what marriage meant in Victorian England:

In *Smallwood v. Smallwood*[65] the husband, suspecting his wife had committed adultery, seized her by the throat, shook her and threw her to the ground. But no marks were left on her body. The Court rejected her petition: one violent act committed under excitement did not justify a finding that she could not safely live with her husband.

However, the test produced rather different results where the husband was the victim of an assault by his wife:

In *Forth v. Forth*[66] the wife threw a pie and a bowl of milk at the husband, scratched his face, and constantly abused him and did things she knew would

---

[61] For an account of the reality of some Victorian marriages, see the *Report of the Committee on One-Parent Families,* (Chairman: Sir M Finer) (1974, Cmnd. 5629), Vol. 2, pp. 104–105; and generally on the phenomenon of wife battering, see ME Doggett, *Marriage, Wife-Beating and the Law in Victorian England* (1992).

[62] *Evans v. Evans* (1790) 1 Hag. Con. 35, 37, *per* Sir William Scott.

[63] MacQueen claimed that these principles 'adapted to a former state of things, but ill fitted for the present day, especially in a Protestant community, come from the dark ages . . . when the priesthood . . . condemned to the strictest celibacy themselves were thought the only proper judges of disputes between husband and wife': *MacQueen on the Law of Divorce* (2nd ed., 1860) p. vii.

[64] *Evans v. Evans* (1790) 1 Hag. Con. 35, 38, *per* Sir William Scott.

[65] (1861) 2 Sw&Tr 397.

[66] (1867) 16 LT 574, adopting the principles set out in *Prichard v. Prichard* (1864) 3 Sw&Tr 523 by the Judge Ordinary, Sir James Wilde: if 'the physical effects of violence by the wife are less, the moral results are immeasurably greater. How is it possible that submission, which is the wife's lot in marriage, can be maintained by the husband if she becomes his assailant'?

annoy him. The Court held he was entitled to a decree because he might, in defending himself, be tempted to retaliate. A man had to put up with the ill-humour of the woman he had married, but the moment she stepped beyond that mark and lifted her hand to her husband and subjected him to violence the court would accept that cohabitation was impossible.

In 1869, however, the Court did accept that wife abuse could be moral as well as physical:

In *Kelly v. Kelly*[67] the husband, a clergyman, became convinced that his wife was plotting and conspiring against him. He refused to sit next to her at meals, insisted on occupying a separate bedroom, and forbade her to visit the poor. The wife became ill, losing her sense of taste and smell. Her doctor advised her to leave home to prevent a further deterioration in her health. The court held that the husband's abuse had broken her health and that the law could properly allow her to live apart from him. The Full Court rejected the husband's appeal against the trial judge's decision to grant Mrs Kelly a decree of Judicial Separation.

And in the course of the twentieth century there developed a much less demanding approach to what spouses could be expected to tolerate.[68]

However, the main significance of the history of judicial separation is that it constitutes the counterpart of the history of divorce. Critics claimed that a judicial separation was 'in fact, a permanent divorce, though an imperfect one';[69] and in 1912 the *Royal Commission on Divorce and Matrimonial Causes* chaired by Lord Gorell[70] reported that judicial separation

'places the parties in a position in which, while remained married, they are subjected to enforced celibacy. Such separation . . . [is] productive of immorality, and misery to the parties, both the innocent and the guilty, and detrimental to the interests of the children'.[71]

Those who took this view naturally favoured extending the grounds for divorce so as to allow the parties to remarry. At the very least, they favoured restricting the courts' power to grant judicial separation in cases in which it was clear that

---

[67] (1870) LR 2 P&D 59.

[68] But the courts still expected a couple to tolerate the 'ordinary wear and tear of married life': see *Buchler v. Buchler* [1947] P 25 and Chapter 7, below.

[69] It was also said that 'a husband who chooses to quarrel with his wife, or a wife who chooses to quarrel with her husband, let the grounds be ever so slight, has only to draw up a short petition, make an affidavit, and walk to Doctors' Commons, where the legislature has established an office for the uncontrolled issue of matrimonial citations . . . litigation becomes inevitable; the husband and wife prepare for combat. Friends, relations, and peradventure witnesses, share in the humiliation'. In this view, judicial separation proceedings rarely served any useful purpose, but merely provided a public forum for the ventilation of the 'vulgar matrimonial squabbles' which would far better be resolved by agreement: *MacQueen on the Law of Divorce* (2nd ed., 1860) pp. iv–v.

[70] 1912, Cd. 6478; see below.

[71] *Report of the Royal Commission on Divorce and Matrimonial Causes* (1912, Cd. 6478).

the marriage had irretrievably broken down. Thus, the *Gorell Report*[72] favoured giving the court power, on application by the respondent, to grant a divorce instead of a judicial separation; but 40 years later the *Morton Report* regarded the fact that this would mean granting divorces against an applicant who had committed no recognised matrimonial offence as a conclusive objection to the proposal.[73] The *Morton Report* recognised that judicial separation could impose 'undue hardship'[74] but nevertheless believed it 'necessary' to retain it[75]

'In order to provide relief, where sufficient and appropriate grounds exist, for those who have religious or conscientious objections to divorce. We also consider it desirable that a remedy should be available for an injured spouse which, at the same time, keeps open the door for the possibility of subsequent reconciliation'.

Only the enactment of the Divorce Reform Act 1969 resolved the conflict of values:[76] thereafter either party to a marriage, whether 'guilty' or 'innocent', could be confident that sooner or later he would be able successfully to petition for divorce; and judicial separation was retained primarily as a remedy in cases in which neither spouse wanted to divorce but did wish to have the legal effects of separation (for example, in relation to the upbringing of children and financial matters) formalised and in those few cases where divorce was not immediately available.[77]

Two further points need to be made. First, as we have seen, a judicial separation decree is an order that the petitioner and respondent be no longer obliged to cohabit, rather than an order that the respondent cease to live with the petitioner.[78] It followed that the courts would not necessarily exclude the respondent from the matrimonial home; and it was not until the last quarter of the twentieth century that the legal system, against the background of increasing concern about the extent of domestic violence, finally recognised that effective remedies had to be found in legislation specifically directed at molestation and harassment[79] rather than in any increased recourse to judicial separation

---

[72] By a majority: see Cd. 6478, paras. 391–392.   [73] *Morton Report*, para. 310.

[74] 'a spouse in electing to obtain a judicial separation instead of a divorce may be moved by unworthy motives, yet the effect is that he or she is entitled to keep the other spouse tied for life and at the same time to refuse a genuine offer by the other spouse to resume married life': *Morton Report*, para. 304.

[75] *Morton Report*, para. 303. The Commission considered but rejected a number of proposals limiting the scope or permanence of the decree: these included giving either party the right to apply for the conversion of a judicial separation into divorce: *Morton Report*, para. 304.

[76] See Chapter 9, below.

[77] For example, because the requisite periods of 'living apart' had not elapsed.

[78] *Montgomery v. Montgomery* [1965] P 46.

[79] See Chapter 21, below. In the year 2000 the courts, under the codified legislation dealing with family violence and occupation of the matrimonial home, were making more than 18,000 non-molestation orders and more than 7,700 orders specifically dealing with the occupation of the family home. A significant proportion of these orders were accompanied by orders empowering the police to arrest a person reasonably suspected of being in breach: see *Judicial Statistics, Annual Review 2000*, Table 5.9 and Chapter 21, below.

and that appropriate police and social work provision was necessary if these remedies were to be effective.

For many years only a small number of separation decrees were made: at the beginning of World War II there were under 30 a year, and thereafter for many years the number was well below a hundred each year. But there was a dramatic increase in the late 1970s.[80] It is not easy to explain this, but it seems that the desire to obtain orders from the divorce court on financial matters and child upbringing was a powerful influence.[81]

COMPENSATION FOR INTERFERENCE WITH MARITAL RELATIONSHIPS: DAMAGES FOR ADULTERY

At common law, a cuckolded husband was entitled to claim damages in an action for so-called criminal conversation. By 1857 this form of action had become discredited.[82] But there remained a feeling that sanctions of some kind should be imposed upon adulterers;[83] and the Government accepted amendments[84] to its Divorce Bill. The Matrimonial Causes Act 1857 abolished the

[80] In 1980, for example, 5,423 petitions were filed and 2,560 decrees granted: *Judicial Statistics Annual Report 1980,* Table D 8. Three years later these (already historically high) figures had risen to 7,430 and 4,854 respectively: *Judicial Statistics Annual Report 1983,* Tables 4.5–6.

[81] See S Maidment, *Judicial Separation, A Research Study* (1982); and P Garlick, 'Judicial Separation: A Research Study' (1983) 46 MLR 719.

[82] See L Stone, *Road to Divorce, England 1530–1987* (1990), especially at pp. 21–22. In some cases the action was used as a necessary preliminary to a petition for Parliamentary divorce (see Chapter 5, below) and in this context a particular source of criticism was that the action was often collusive: see the *First Report of the Royal Commissioners into the Law of Divorce* (1852–1853, C. 1604, para. 45 note 9): 'In the majority of actions which are brought against adulterers, judgment is allowed to go by default. This admits the defendant's guilt; and it only remains for the plaintiff shortly to prove the facts before the sheriff and a common jury. . . . In these cases it usually happens that no counsel appears for the defendant. The facts, therefore, sworn to, are admitted without inquiry; the witnesses are subject to no cross-examination; the cause is heard *ex parte.* What security against fraud is afforded by such a proceeding? If the parties are anxious to collude, what is to prevent the plaintiff from receiving the damages with his right hand, and then as soon as the Bill of Divorce has passed, returning them with his left?'; and see further Stone, *op.cit.* p. 302.

[83] Traditionally English law had regarded adultery as a sin rather than a crime. The church might impose penance on the offender, but the Ecclesiastical Courts never assumed a jurisdiction to order the payment of financial compensation. There was a long history of pressure to make the commission of adultery a criminal offence, punishable as such. The *Reformatio legum Ecclesiasticarum* published in the reign of Edward VI had proposed that adultery be punished by perpetual imprisonment or transportation for life: *Campbell Royal Commission* para. 12. But this proposal—said by L Stone to be 'the work of a small minority of protestant zealots' (L Stone, *Road to Divorce, England 1530–1987* (1990) p. 302)—never became law. Various attempts—all unsuccessful—were made in the late eighteenth and early nineteenth century to criminalise adultery: see *Hansard's Parliamentary Debates* (3rd Series) 17 August 1857, vol. 147, cols. 1740–1744. Even in 1912 there were those who thought adultery should be a criminal offence, but the Gorell *Royal Commission on Divorce and Matrimonial Causes* (1912, Cd. 6478, para. 306) thought this question to be outside their terms of reference.

[84] The relevant amendment was only introduced on 19 August 1857: *Hansard's Parliamentary Debates* (3rd Series) vol. 147, col. 1868. The decision was influenced by the need to defeat attempts to make adultery a criminal offence.

right to sue for criminal conversation;[85] and provided[86] instead that a husband
could claim a sum of money from any person who had committed adultery with
his wife and that such claims were to be heard[87] and tried on the same principles
that had governed criminal conversation actions in the common law courts.[88]
The Act also gave the court[89] specific power to order a guilty co-respondent[90] to
pay the whole or any part of the costs[91] of the proceedings.

[85] Matrimonial Causes Act 1857, s. 59.

[86] The claim could be made either in a petition for divorce or judicial separation or in a petition
confined to a claim for damages; and it was apparently considered that a man might wish to punish
or obtain compensation from an adulterer without being obliged to divorce his wife: see *Hansard's
Parliamentary Debates* (3rd Series) 19 August 1857, vol. 146, cols. 1869–1870.

[87] The 1857 Act stipulated that damages should in all cases be ascertained by the verdict of a jury:
see s. 33. But the behaviour of juries in the assessment of damages was sometimes cavalier: for example, in *Beckett v. Beckett* [1901] P 85 the jury awarded £400 (perhaps £24,000 in year 2000 values)
which was more than the sum claimed; and in *Izard v. Izard and Leslie* (1889) 14 PD 45 the jury
awarded £5,000 (more than a quarter of a million pounds in year 2000) to an actress's husband
against the lessee of the theatre at which she was performing, apparently disregarding the judge's
direction that in cases in which the parties had previously separated the husband's loss would be
adequately 'compensated by the smallest amount of damages'. Following criticism by the *Royal
Commission on Divorce and Matrimonial Causes* (1912, Cd. 6478, paras. 397–405) the right to
claim jury trial was abolished by the Supreme Court of Judicature (Consolidation) Act 1925, Sch. 6:
see *Rugg-Gunn v. Rugg-Gunn and Archer* [1931] P 147, CA.

[88] Matrmonial Causes Act 1857, s. 33. In *Bell v. Bell and Marquess of Anglesey* (1858) 1 Sw&Tr
565 the Court accepted that the 1857 Act had (notwithstanding the 'great objection' which had been
taken to the action for criminal conversation) left the substance of the law governing the award of
damages. According to Lord Brougham LC (*Hansard's Parliamentary Debates* (3rd Series) 23 June
1857, vol. 146, cols. 209–210) the intention was to provide redress, especially for working men suffering 'serious pecuniary evil' from the loss of the wife's 'superintendence of the family and management of the household'. It seems also to have been thought that married women working in
factories were vulnerable to seduction by the employer 'who obviously would have opportunities,
which it would be difficult if not impossible to guard against'. One MP told of a married woman
'possessing very great personal attractions, [who] was employed in a mill, and by her earnings was
enabled to support a sick husband and two young children . . . [T]he overlooker in the mill . . . made
dishonourable proposals to her, which she at first rejected, but afterwards, overcome by his impor-
tunities, and with the alternative of starvation for her children and husband, she permitted herself
to break her marriage vow': *Hansard's Parliamentary Debates* (3rd Series) 19 August 1857, vol. 146,
col. 1869.

[89] Matrimonial Causes Act 1857, s. 34.

[90] The fact that the adulterer was not aware that the woman was married did not prevent his
being held liable to pay damages (although it was material to the amount of any award): *Lord v.
Lord and Lambert* [1900] P 297. But it became the practice not to order costs against a co-
respondent who was unaware that the woman was married: *Badcock v. Badcock and Chamberlain*
(1858) 1 Sw&Tr 687; *Lord v. Lord and Lambert* [1900] P 297. But this was not an absolute rule: in
Langrick v. Langrick and Funnell [1920] P 90 Sir H Duke P awarded costs on the basis that the co-
respondent ought to have known that the woman was married whilst in *Smith v. Smith and Reed*
[1922] P 1 he ordered the manager of a cinema to pay costs in respect of his adultery with a maid
whom the respondent knew only as 'Florrie' apparently because the co-respondent was a man of
'superior condition' who 'committed adultery with the wife of a soldier' not pausing to consider
whether she was married or not.

[91] It was immaterial that the court refused the petitioner the divorce or other decree he sought:
see *Waudby v. Waudby and Bowland* [1902] P 85 (where a divorce was refused because the petitioner had condoned the wife's adultery, but the co-respondent was nevertheless ordered to pay the
costs of proving his adultery in a trial and re-trial); *Quartermaine v. Quartermaine and Glenister*
[1911] P 180 (where the co-respondent was ordered to pay costs notwithstanding the fact that the
decree was rescinded after the spouses' reconciliation).

In one important respect the 1857 Act introduced a new principle. The successful husband was to have no absolute right[92] to claim the damages for his own benefit; and the Act[93] empowered the court to direct that all or part of the damages be settled for the benefit of the children of the marriage[94] or even as a provision for the seduced wife's maintenance.[95]

Assessment of damages for adultery

The courts gradually developed principles for the assessment of damages for adultery.[96] It was settled that damages were not intended to be exemplary or punitive but compensatory: the husband was 'entitled to compensation for the loss of his wife and for the injury to his feeling and the hurt to his family life'. Factors to be taken into account in assessing the value of the loss of the wife were her fortune, her assistance in the husband's business, her capacity as a housekeeper and her ability in the home, and her character and conduct generally'.[97] In assessing the injury to the husband's feelings the courts for long took account of 'the resentment of a poor man whose wife has been seduced by means of the adulterer's wealth'.[98]

---

[92] The distinctive nature of an award of damages under the 1857 Act is exemplified by *Brydges v. Brydges and Wood* [1909] P 187, CA (unsuccessful attempt to recover damages from deceased co-respondent's estate).

[93] s. 33.

[94] See *Mozley Stark v. Mozley Stark* [1910] P 190, CA, where it appears that the cost of educating the teenage daughter of the marriage and maintaining her was 'substantially provided for out of the damages paid by the co-respondent'.

[95] Thus, in *Meyern v. Meyern and Myers* (1876) LR 2 PD 254 the court directed that one quarter of the £5,000 (more than a quarter of a million pounds in year 2000 values) damages be allotted to the husband (a bank clerk earning £450—£27,000 in year 2000—a year), a quarter for the maintenance of the youngest child of the marriage, and the remainder in buying an annuity to support the wife for so long as she lived chastely and did not marry the co-respondent.

[96] The text draws on the summary given in the 1956 *Morton Report*, para. 430. There is no evidence to suggest that the principles applied were any different in the early years of the Divorce Court's existence.

[97] Sometimes this factor does not seem to have been given a great deal of weight. In *Evans v. Evans and Platts* [1899] P 195 the wife had violently snatched the husband's watch chain and scarf-pin, scratched his face and hands, kicked him violently in the stomach, threw his belongings into the garden and subsequently barred the door in his face. She committed adultery with the solicitor whom she rather surprisingly retained to bring an action for Restitution of Conjugal Rights against the husband. The court awarded £500 (£30,000 in year 2000 values) damages against the solicitor.

[98] *Ibid.* Although logically 'the only question is what damage the petitioner has sustained, and the damage he has sustained is the same whether the co-respondent is a rich man or a poor man' (*Keyse v. Keyse* (1886) 11 PD 100, 102, *per* Sir J Hannen P) it seems that the way in which the co-respondent used his wealth in gaining his end were for long taken into account: *Butterworth v. Butterworth and Englefield* [1920] P 126, McCardie J—a factor perhaps relevant in the jury's award of £10,000 (more than half a million pounds in year 2000 values) against the Marquess of Anglesey who had taken advantage of the prestige of his rank in 'making a vain woman false to her duty to her husband': *Bell v. Bell and Marquess of Anglesey* (1858) 1 Sw&Tr 565. By 1967 however a Lord Justice of Appeal found it 'impossible to accept that, in these egalitarian and materialistic days, the feelings and pride of a reasonable man are more affronted if his wife commits adultery with an opulent baronet rather than with an impoverished dustman, with a young Adonis rather than an elderly Caliban. The lower the material and physical attractions of his supplanter, the more wounding the comparison, and the greater the blow to his own self-esteem': *Pritchard v. Pritchard and Sims* [1967]

From the perspective of the twenty-first century the notion that a wife should be considered her husband's property and that her worth is to be quantified in money seems indeed 'repugnant to modern and sensible ideas';[99] and even before World War I the Gorell Commission[100] recommended that the adulterer should be made to settle property or make maintenance payments for the woman he had seduced rather than paying damages to the husband. But in 1956 the *Morton Report* (whilst accepting that the wife should also be given the right to claim damages from an adulteress) recommended that in all other respects the existing law should be retained. (The Commission believed that the compensatory nature of damages coupled with the fact that 'the court has a complete discretion in directing the application of the sum awarded ensures that a claim by a husband is kept within reasonable bounds'.).[101] Although free-standing claims[102] for damages had become rare[103] claims in divorce petitions remained by no means uncommon, and there were still those who considered that the law had a cogent moral foundation[104] and—perhaps fearful of a world in which rich philanderers would be able to cruise past the factory gates in leather upholstered Rolls Royces importuning with diamonds the prettiest wife at the works[105]— favoured retention of the remedy in some form. However, the view that the action for damages for adultery rested on social assumptions which were no longer valid,[106] and that a claim frequently brought great bitterness into a divorce action, eventually carried the day;[107] and in 1970[108] the Law Reform (Miscellaneous Provisions) Act abolished the right to claim damages for

P 195, 213, *per* Diplock LJ (who also thought that compensation for injured feelings required the court to consider the unreal concept of the 'reasonable cuckold').

[99] See *Pritchard v. Pritchard and Sims* [1967] P 195, *per* Diplock LJ. He favoured the award of a 'modest conventional figure' in respect of adultery; but compare the views of Willmer LJ at p. 207.

[100] *Royal Commission on Divorce and Matrimonial Causes* (1912, Cd. 6478) paras. 393–396.

[101] *Morton Report*, paras. 429–435. There appears to be no available information about the proportion of cases in which settlements for the benefit of the children or for the wife's maintenance were in fact ordered.

[102] ie, not made in a divorce petition.

[103] Law Commission *Published Working Paper No. 9* (1967) para. 128.

[104] *Butterworth v. Butterworth and Englefield* [1920] P 126, 133, *per* McCardie J.

[105] As Leo Abse MP put it in *Official Report (Standing Committee C)* 11 February 1970, col. 38.

[106] The Law Commission's *Published Working Paper No. 9* (1967) para. 132 asserted that the 'rather barbarous theoretical basis' of the action for damages was simply to compensate a man for the fact that the defendant had had sexual intercourse with his wife; and believed that the action encouraged blackmail by collusion between husband and wife and perjury if the wife and her seducer were in collusion, and that such claims increased and perpetuated bitterness between the parties.

[107] The Law Commission recognised that the question was a social one on which opinion was likely to be divided, but (whilst accepting that the Commission was not qualified to give a final answer on this issue) concluded that damages for adultery should be abolished: Law Com. No. 25, para. 99.

[108] Law Reform (Miscellaneous Provisions) Act 1970, s. 4, giving effect to the Law Commission's proposal: *Report on Financial Provision in Matrimonial Proceedings*, Law Com. No. 25, paras. 99–102; and Published Working Paper No. 9, paras. 128–142 (where the competing arguments are fully explored).

adultery.[109] The Act also abolished the action for breach of promise of marriage,[110] actions for the seduction of a child, and enticement or harbouring a spouse or child.[111] Family life was thus further distanced from the world of commercial bargains and property deals.

[109] The Court of Appeal spoke the last appellate word on the subject in *Pritchard v. Pritchard and Sims* [1967] P 195, reducing to £2,000 (some £18,000 in year 2000 values) an award (which it considered 'plainly wrong') of £7,500 (£67,000) damages against the 70-year-old co-respondent proprietor of an electrical business who had used his money consciously and intentionally to secure the wife—a good housekeeper and virtuous woman—for himself, thereby deliberately breaking up a 21-year marriage. In the course of argument, Scarman LJ had given examples from his 'own personal records' of awards in his court including an agreed award of £4,000 (£42,000) in the 'serious case' of *Connor v. Connor and Harrison* (1962) *The Times*, 3 March (in which the co-respondent had flaunted his wealth); and £2,500 (£26,000) in *Richards v. Richards and Bagnall* (1963) *The Times*, 7 May where a 'prosperous and attractive barrister' (Kenneth Bagnall, later a QC), had wooed the wife of a £1,500 pa scientific civil servant (whose failure to pass his BSc examinations had disappointed her).

[110] Giving effect to recommendations by the Law Commission in *Breach of Promise of Marriage*, Law Com. No. 26, 1969; see SM Cretney (1970) 33 MLR 534.

[111] Implementing recommendations in the Law Reform Committee's 11th Report (1963, Cmnd. 2017) and see also the Law Commission's *Published Working Paper No. 19, The Action for Loss of Services, Loss of Consortium, Seduction and Enticement* (1968).

PART II

THE ENDING OF MARRIAGE: DIVORCE

5

Ending Marriage by Judicial Divorce under the Matrimonial Causes Act 1857

INTRODUCTION

The Catholic Church's view of marriage was that it could not be dissolved: those whom God had joined together were not to be put asunder by any human act. But after the Reformation English law no longer entirely reflected this doctrine. It is true that divorce by decree of the civil courts was only introduced into the law in 1857 by the Matrimonial Causes Act of that year. But it is not true to say that there was no divorce in England before that Act came into force on 1 January 1858.[1] A man could have his marriage dissolved before as well as after the 1857 Act if he could establish that his wife had committed adultery,[2] that he himself had not done so, and that there was no connivance or collusion between the parties.[3]

What the 1857 reforms did do was greatly to simplify *procedures*. Before the 1857 Act a man seeking divorce had first to obtain a divorce *a mensa et thoro* (an order permitting husband and wife to live separate and apart) from the Ecclesiastical Court. Then he had to obtain judgment in a common law action for 'criminal conversation' (that is, adultery). Finally he had to secure the enactment of a private Act of Parliament definitively dissolving the marriage and permitting him to remarry.[4] As has been aptly said, 'Whom God had joined

---

[1] Matrimonial Causes Act 1857, s. 1.

[2] A wife had to show not merely that her husband had committed adultery but that there were aggravating circumstances: see below.

[3] The husband would also have to meet the costs involved in the necessary procedures.

[4] The process was ironically described by Maule J in sentencing a man convicted of bigamy: 'You ought to have brought an action for criminal conversation; that action would have been tried by one of Her Majesty's judges at the Assizes; you would probably have recovered damages; and then you should have instituted a suit in the ecclesiastical court for divorce *a mensa et thoro*. Having got that divorce, you should have petitioned the House of Lords for a divorce *a vinculo*, and should have appeared by counsel at the bar of their Lordships' House. Then, if the Bill passed, it would have gone down to the House of Commons; the same evidence would possibly be repeated there; and if the Royal Assent had been given after that, you might have married again. The whole proceeding would not have cost you more than £1,000' (or perhaps £60,000 in year 2000 values). The prisoner is said to have replied that he was never worth so much as a thousand pence in all his life. There are several versions of this story (see J Jackson, *The Formation and Annulment of Marriage*, 1969) but that used in the text, taken from RH Graveson and FR Crane, *A Century of Family Law 1857–1957* (1957) p. 8 whilst possibly less accurate is shorter than some.

together, Englishmen had contrived a painful and labourious method of allowing to be sundered'[5] but sundered they were.

Why then was the 1857 Act passed? Its origins certainly do not lie in any concern for abstract justice. Rather they lie in the pressing need, highlighted by the growth in personal wealth associated with industrialisation, to get rid of the ramshackle probate jurisdiction exercised by 350 or so[6] ecclesiastical authorities[7] and to replace it with a more efficient system of dealing with deceaseds' property.[8] That was done by creating the Court of Probate.[9] But proposals to strip the ecclesiastical courts of their probate jurisdiction inevitably raised the question of what should be done with their other non-doctrinal jurisdiction, that is the law of 'matrimonial causes'; and in 1852 the Government had appointed a Royal Commission[10] to examine in particular 'the mode of obtaining a Divorce *a vinculo matrimonii* in this country'.

The Royal Commission did not see itself as proposing a legal revolution. On the contrary, it asserted that the *principles* of the existing law were founded 'on the securest wisdom' and ought to be retained.[11] The Commission simply wanted a modernised secular[12] *procedure* to provide more efficiently the

---

[5] By MK Woodhouse, 'The Marriage and Divorce Bill of 1857' (1959) 3 *American Journal of Legal History* 260. A full account of what could be involved in the pre-1858 divorce process is given in L Stone, *Road to Divorce, England 1530–1987* (1990), Chapters 8 to 11; whilst reference should also be made to S Wolfram, 'Divorce in England 1700–1857' (1987) 5 OJLS 155 and S Anderson, 'Legislative Divorce: Law for the Aristocracy?' in GR Rubin and D Sugarman (eds.), *Law and Society 1750–1914: Essays in the History of English Law* (1984) for analysis of the social and economic circumstances of those resorting to the Private Bill procedure.

[6] *The Business of the Courts Committee* (Chairman, Lord Hanworth MR) *Second Interim Report* (1933, Cmd. 4471) para. 8.

[7] *The Reports of the Commissioners . . . into the . . . Ecclesiastical Courts . . .* (HL Sessional Papers 1831–32 vol. 302) run to some 600 pages. After considerable dispute, the Court of Probate Act 1857 (abolishing the voluntary and contentious Jurisdiction and Authority of all Ecclesiastical, Royal Peculiar, Peculiar, Manorial, and other Courts and Persons) was enacted. Those concerned were compensated (often substantially) for the pecuniary loss suffered (the Registrar of the Prerogative Court of Canterbury being granted an annuity of £8,000 per annum, or nearly half a million pounds in year 2000 values): see A Horstman, *Victorian Divorce* (1985) p. 76. Thenceforth all jurisdiction in relation to probate was exercised in the name of the Crown by one court—the Court of Probate—with one judge (paid £4,000 per annum and holding rank and Precedence with the Puisne Judges of the Superior Courts of Common Law at Westminster), a secretary (£300 per annum) and an Usher (£150 per annum). The buildings and site of Doctors' Commons (the ecclesiastical lawyer's college in London) were sold to the Metropolitan Board of Works in 1865 to facilitate the building of Queen Victoria Street, and the proceeds of sale were divided amongst the members. Doctors' Commons (whose charter is now held in the Codrington Library, All Souls College, Oxford: see GD Squibb, *Doctors' Commons* (1977) pp. 105–109) continued its legal existence as a corporation until the death of the last surviving member, Dr Tristram, on 8 March 1912.

[8] *Reports of the Commissioners . . . into the . . . Ecclesiastical Courts . . .* (HL Sessional Papers 1831–32 vol. 302). It appears that probate administration was the most lucrative of the work done by the ecclesiastical courts, and for this reason (it has been said) 'appealed to greedy country lawyers': A Horstman, *Victorian Divorce* (1985) p. 72.

[9] Court of Probate Act 1857.

[10] *Report of the Commissioners . . . into the Law of Divorce* (1852–3) BPP vol. 40, p. 249.

[11] *ibid.*, para. 4.

[12] This aspect of the case for reform is clearly demonstrated by A Horstman, *Victorian Divorce* (1985) Chapter 4; whilst MK Woodhouse, 'The Marriage and Divorce Bill of 1857' (1959) 3 *American Journal of Legal History* 260 quotes to good effect the views of many churchmen on the issue.

results which had been available for more than 200 years to those with sufficient means and motivation. To achieve this, the matrimonial jurisdiction of the ecclesiastical courts would be abolished.[13] Instead, the jurisdiction in divorce (and other matrimonial causes) would be exercised 'in the name of Her Majesty' in a Court of Record called[14] the Court for Divorce and Matrimonial Causes.[15] True this would increase the role of the State at the expense of the Church but this was the price to be paid for increasing the efficiency of the court system.[16] And it was as a simple measure of rationalisation that the Bill was presented to Parliament.[17]

MORE EFFICIENT DIVORCE LIKELY TO INCREASE APPETITE FOR DIVORCE?

The difficulty with this approach was that making the divorce process more 'efficient' could also be seen as making divorce 'easier', and inevitably increasing the appetite for divorce and threatening the stability of family life.[18] And the proposed legislation had implications in another sensitive area: the Act would continue to discriminate against women,[19] thereby outraging the group of

---

[13] Matrimonial Causes Act 1857, s. 2. However, the Act also provided that the newly established court should act and give relief on principles and rules 'as nearly as may be conformable to the principles and rules on which the Ecclesiastical Courts have heretofore acted' (save in dissolution suits); and this had a powerful influence in leading the Divorce Court to assert that its jurisdiction was essentially inquisitorial (rather than, as was the traditional common law jurisdiction of the common law courts, accusatorial) and echoes of this approach were still heard at the close of the twentieth century: see below.

[14] The 1857 Act retained links between the different jurisdictions: it provided that the Judge of the Court of Probate was to be the Judge Ordinary of the Court for Divorce and Matrimonial Causes: s. 9; and the Court of Probate Act envisaged that the same person would hold the office of Judge of the Court of Admiralty. For the judicial heads of the Divorce Court since 1857, see Biographical Notes, C.

[15] Matrimonial Causes Act 1857, s. 6. In 1854 the Government had proposed simply to transfer the ecclesiastical courts' matrimonial jurisdiction to the Court of Chancery; but in the end the Campbell Commission's view that it was undesirable to place the burden of deciding whether a marriage should be dissolved onto a single judge carried the day, if only for a short time: see below.

[16] The 1857 Act did nothing to affect the sovereignty of Parliament, and Private Bills continued to be passed—for example to grant divorces to those domiciled in Ireland. And in the 1980s Private Bills were used to permit the marriage of persons within the prohibited degrees: see eg the Edward Berry and Doris Eileen Ward (Marriage Enabling) Act 1980: see above, Chapter 2.

[17] The Bill embodied no new principle, but gave a 'judicial habitation' to 'doctrines which for centuries had been recognized as the law of the land', Sir Richard Bethell AG as recorded in the *Annual Register* 1857, p. 163.

[18] WE Gladstone was for this and other reasons a determined and vigorous opponent of the Bill both in Parliament (a filibustering speech on 4 August 1857 occupying, it seems, some six hours: HCG Matthew (ed.), *The Gladstone Diaries* vol. 5, entry for 4 August 1857) and in print: see generally R Shannon, *Gladstone, Peel's Inheritor 1809–1865* (1999) pp. 340–346. Gladstone continued to believe that remarriage was not admissible under any circumstances whatsoever; and towards the end of his life recorded his view that there had been a perceptible decline in the standard of conjugal morality at least amongst the higher classes since the 1857 Act. But he accepted that 'other disintegrating causes have [also] been at work': *Gladstone Diaries* vol. 12, p. 240, note 8.

[19] See below. For an analysis of the reasons underlying the acceptance of the double standard embodied in this and other areas of the law see K Thomas, 'The Double Standard' (1959) *Journal*

women writers[20] and their supporters[21] campaigning for improvements to the legal position of women. So the Government's supposed 'rationalisation' drew fire not only from those who, in the interests of morality and family stability, opposed any move towards 'easier divorce' but also from the women's groups who thought the government's proposed legislation did not go anything like far enough.[22]

In these circumstances, the Government could not have expected (and certainly did not get) an easy ride. Parliament had to be kept in session 'for an unprecedented time into the summer, forcing members to endure the burden of debating from noon to two in the morning every day in the broiling heat of one of the hottest summers in living memory'.[23] But the Government was determined. Palmerston had a simple message for recalcitrant (and uncomfortable) MPs:[24] 'we shall sit here [he threatened] day by day, and night by night, until this Bill be concluded'. Even though apparently many MPs did drift away to the cool and peace of their country seats[25] the Government's placemen did their duty and the Bill eventually reached the statute book on 28 August 1857 with only 54 MPs and some 80 peers voting in the final divisions.

Quite why Palmerston's Government persisted in driving the 1857 Bill through to Royal Assent in the face of numerous objections and amendments is not really clear.[26] Lawyers[27] have tended to accept growing public conscious-

of the History of Ideas 20, p. 195. See also R Probert, 'The Double Standard of Morality in the Divorce and Matrimonial Causes Act 1857' (1999) 28 Anglo-American Law Review 73.

[20] The treatment of marriage failure by contemporary novelists, male and female, is illuminatingly noted by R Probert, 'The Double Standard of Morality in the Divorce and Matrimonial Causes Act 1857' (1999) 28 Anglo-American Law Review 73. In this context the account of the marital situation of Charles Dickens' character Stephen Blackpool in *Hard Times* (1854) is particularly striking.

[21] In particular, they were deployed by the 84-year-old former Lord Chancellor, Lord Lyndhurst, who accepted that 'men make the laws and women are the victims': for his role, see L Stone, *Road to Divorce, England 1530–1987* (1990) pp. 378–382.

[22] The main topics discussed in the course of the parliamentary debates were the circumstances in which women (who had rarely obtained divorces under the Private Bill procedure) could seek divorce, and whether a wife divorced for adultery should be allowed to remarry: see L Stone, *Road to Divorce, England 1530–1987* (1990) pp. 378–382, whilst MK Woodhouse, 'The Marriage and Divorce Bill of 1857' (1959) 3 *American Journal of Legal History* 260 gives a vivid account of what she aptly describes as the 'exciting almost erotic discussion'. The remarriage question involved the relationship between Church and State: a clergyman of the Church of England was legally obliged to solemnise the marriage of any person resident in his parish, and it was claimed that many would have conscientious objections to marrying divorced adulterers. Eventually, the legislation embodied a compromise: the clergy were not obliged to marry such persons, but they were required to permit another clergyman to solemnise the marriage: Matrimonial Causes Act 1857, ss. 57, 58. This became a major grievance of the clergy.

[23] L Stone, *Road to Divorce, England 1530–1987* (1990) p. 378. The accuracy of this assessment can be verified by reference to the quotations taken from the debates by MK Woodhouse, 'The Marriage and Divorce Bill of 1857' (1959) 3 *American Journal of Legal History* 260.

[24] *Hansard's Parliamentary Debates* (3rd Series) 13 August 1857, vol. 147, col. 1642.

[25] *Hansard's Parliamentary Debates* (3rd Series) 13 August 1857, vol. 147, col. 1021.

[26] Three earlier Bills introduced between 1854 and 1857 failed to make progress.

[27] See Lord Evershed in RH Graveson and FR Crane (eds.), *A Century of Family Law 1857–1957* (1957), p. x (referring to the 'clear and vivid' explanation given by Professor RH Graveson at *op. cit.* pp. 6–8).

ness of the injustices of the old law and in particular its harshness to women[28] as the explanation; but there is little evidence of pressure for reform of the *divorce* law. (In contrast, there was very strong and well organised pressure for reform of family *property* law.[29]) Perhaps the explanation is to be found in other factors (including the desire of an assertive Prime Minister to demonstrate his political power).[30]

The prolonged debates certainly had little impact on the substance of the Act;[31] and it is not easy to deny the accuracy, as a matter of strict analysis, of the assessment made of the Act made by Professor OR McGregor[32] a hundred years after its enactment: the 'main and only important purpose of the Act . . . was to make the civil system of divorce established by the House of Lords in 1697 more widely available. It altered the procedure for obtaining divorce but introduced no new principles'. But this view does not reflect the true impact of the Act. As has happened over and over again, changes in procedure did affect perceptions of the law. (Indeed it could be argued that, in relation to divorce, procedural change has over the years often had more impact than changes in the substantive law.) The question is not so much what the Act did as a matter of law as what it was believed to have done and what impact the popular belief of its effect had on behaviour.

[28] L Stone, *Road to Divorce, England 1530–1987* (1990) p. 374, states that it is 'today widely believed that divorce was forced on to the political agenda in the middle of the nineteenth century by major changes in the economic conditions of the labouring poor. The argument runs that a strain was put on the working-class family system by the growth in the number of wives earning a wage in factories outside the home . . .'. But as Stone points out, there is 'nothing in the Parliamentary debates of the 1850s which shows the slightest awareness of these problems . . .'.

[29] Sir Erskine Perry (a distinguished lawyer MP: see Biographical Notes) pointed out that not a single petition demanding reform of the divorce law had been addressed to the Commons and claimed that there was no popular demand for divorce law reform. Seeking leave to bring in a Bill to amend the law of property as it affected married women, he expressed astonishment that the Government should prefer to legislate on divorce rather than accepting 'the wise and comprehensive reform of matrimonial property' urged in a petition supported by no less than 25,000 signatures including the most distinguished names in literature art and society. In his view, reform of matrimonial property law would remove 'all demand or necessity for tampering with the indissolubility of marriage': *Hansard's Parliamentary Debates* (3rd Series) 14 May 1857, vol. 145, cols. 267–268.

[30] See A Horstman, *Victorian Divorce* (1985), p. 77 for the view that Palmerston, who had won a large parliamentary majority in the election of March 1857 'set out to demonstrate his strength, to friends and foes, by pushing the Divorce Bill' through a House of Commons against the opposition of Gladstone, Disraeli and others. In this context, Horstman cites a telling observation from *The Times* that the Bill 'offers one of those occasional instances in which a large majority furnishes the best answer to ingenious and plausible arguments'.

[31] L Stone claims that the Bill as enacted 'bore very little relation to the bill first introduced by the government two years before' and that 59 of the 73 clauses in the Bill were either new or had been altered: *Road to Divorce, England 1530–1987* (1990) p. 382; but compare Woodhouse's view that the 'bill as passed was essentially the same as presented': MK Woodhouse, 'The Marriage and Divorce Bill of 1857' (1959) 3 *American Journal of Legal History* 260, 274. Both statements are correct: there were indeed large numbers of drafting amendments, and some novelties—notably the provisions seeking to improve the protection of married women's financial interests—but the underlying scheme of the Act remained as it had been originally: see below.

[32] *Divorce in England, A Centenary Study* (1957) p. 18.

In any event, whatever the truth about the motives underlying the introduction and enactment of the Matrimonial Causes Act, it unquestionably constitutes a landmark in legal history[33] not least because it remained in its essentials[34] the basis of the substantive English law of divorce[35] for 80 years, and was increasingly used to provide what lawyers call 'relief' to the unhappily married. We need, therefore, to examine how in fact the Court for Divorce and Matrimonial Causes dealt with cases under the Matrimonial Causes Act 1857 after the new Act had come into force on 1 January 1858.[36]

THE OBJECTIVE OF THE LAW: TO PROMOTE REVERENCE FOR THE NUPTIAL TIE

The declared policy of the 1857 legislation (as expressed by the Campbell Royal Commission)[37] was very clear. The need to protect the 'reverence accorded to the nuptial tie' required that the causes of divorce be limited to a 'few extreme and specific provocations'. Accordingly divorce should only be available if it was established 'by the strictest proof' that adultery had been committed; that there had been no contrivance by which the parties were endeavouring to escape from their solemn obligations to themselves and their children, that the husband and wife could not discharge their mutual duties by continuing any longer to cohabit with each other, and that the party complaining was free from guilt.

---

[33] L Stone, *Road to Divorce, England 1530–1987* (1990) p. 382, points out that the 1857 Act made the first significant change in English divorce law since the sixteenth century.

[34] The qualification is necessary because experience of the working of the 1857 Act exposed many defects and technical difficulties which had to be remedied by amending legislation in each of the three following years: Matrimonial Causes Acts 1858, 1859 and 1860. Some of these amendments dealt with the judicial machinery established in 1857 (for example, the Matrimonial Causes Act 1860, s. 1 gave the Judge Ordinary power to act alone in all cases, thus making it less difficult for the court to deal with the 200 and more divorce petitions required by the 1857 Act to be heard by a bench of three judges of the court); others attempted to deal with the unsatisfactory protection of earnings orders introduced by s. 21 of the 1857 Act; whilst yet others filled in gaps in the Court's financial powers. The most significant amendment for the future development of the law was the attempt to minimise the risk of divorce being obtained collusively by establishing the machinery for the Queen's Proctor to enquire into suspicions of collusion and providing for him to intervene in a case to show cause against the *decree nisi* granted after the hearing being made absolute. There were over the years other comparatively minor changes in the substantive law: for example, the circumstances in which a wife could divorce her husband were slightly extended whilst a largely ineffective procedure was introduced in an attempt to protect married women's property and earnings.

[35] The 'Court for Divorce and Matrimonial Causes' also inherited the jurisdiction formerly exercised by the Ecclesiastical Courts to grant 'divorce *a mensa et thoro*' (renamed judicial separation: Matrimonial Causes Act 1857, s. 6) nullity of marriage and restitution of conjugal rights: Matrimonial Causes Act 1857, s. 6. In exercising its powers in these respects the Court was to 'proceed and act and give relief on principles and rules which . . . shall be as nearly as may be conformable to the principles and rules on which the Ecclesiastical Courts have heretofore acted and given relief' save in so far as statute provided otherwise: s. 22.

[36] Matrimonial Causes Act 1857, s. 1. Late nineteenth century and twentieth century material is used where this provides the best illustration of the working of the legislation.

[37] *Report of the Commissioners . . . into the Law of Divorce* (1852–3) BPP vol. 40, p. 249, para. IV.

'Extreme and specific provocation': adultery a pre-requisite to dissolution

The Royal Commission accordingly recommended that dissolution of marriage should 'be allowed for adultery, and for adultery only'.[38] This was to follow the historical precedent of the Private Bill procedure: to allow divorce for adultery provided some protection for the 'unhappy husband whose bed had been violated' against the risk of having illegitimate children foisted on him;[39] whilst any scriptural justification for divorce was usually based on the fact that Christ appeared to contemplate the validity of divorce for adultery.[40]

The 1857 Act[41] gave effect to the policy that only this most serious of marital crimes should be sufficient ground for divorce[42] and for the next 80 years[43] a husband could divorce his wife in this country[44] only if he[45] could prove that she had committed adultery.

Additional requirement imposed on wife petitioners: proof that case one of 'aggravated enormity'

Wives were treated rather differently. There had been those who wanted to debar a wife from divorce save in a few cases (apparently to be determined on a discretionary case-by-case basis[46] as the House of Lords was said to have done

---

[38] The Commission assumed that divorce by mutual consent would be wholly unacceptable, and this has remained the policy of English law down to the present day.

[39] *Mr Lewkenor's Case* 13 State Trials 1308. The 1853 Commission thought the reason for allowing divorce to a husband on the ground of adultery was that this offence 'destroys altogether the primary object of the married state, by introducing, in some instances, a confusion of offspring; by cutting off, in others, all hope of succession; and by diverting, in all, the affections and feelings into strange channels, which reason and religion forbid them to flow in'. In all other cases the Commission considered the door of reconciliation remained open: para. 39.

[40] See the discussion in the *Report of the Royal Commission on Divorce and Matrimonial Causes*, 1912, Cd. 6478.

[41] s. 27, s. 31.

[42] The position where the wife was the petitioner was slightly different: see below.

[43] ie until the Matrimonial Causes Act 1937 added desertion, cruelty and some other grounds: see below.

[44] It goes without saying that English law did not recognise extra-judicial divorces: see for example the remarkable case of *Whitworth v. Whitworth and Thomasson* [1893] P 85 in which a 'stupid man' in a 'humble rank of life' accepted the advice of a friend that it would be foolish to spend money on a divorce and that he and his wife could simply sign an agreement for divorce which would be effective. The husband in reliance on this advice then went through a marriage ceremony and subsequently had to ask the Divorce Court to exercise its discretion in respect of the adultery committed by having intercourse with the 'wife'.

[45] The 1857 Act (again giving effect to the 1853 Commission's view that a wife should only be eligible to divorce her husband in cases of 'aggravated enormity': paras. 40 and 51) imposed additional requirements on wives seeking divorce: see below.

[46] The success of a Private Act Petition depended on the vote of peers, who (it seems) were sometimes influenced by personal connection with those concerned: see L Stone, *Road to Divorce, England 1530–1987* (1990) p. 361.

when considering petitions for Private Acts of Parliament)[47] 'extraordinary in their enormity'.[48] But in the end it was accepted that statute should set out a list[49] of the matters which would entitle the wife to divorce.[50] Simple (even if repeated) adultery was not to be sufficient: the Act[51] required a wife petitioner to prove not only that her husband had committed adultery but also that the adultery was incestuous[52] or that he was guilty of bigamy or of cruelty to the wife or that he had deserted the wife for two years or more.[53] The Act also

[47] According to the 1853 Campbell Commission, there were only four cases in which wives had succeeded in obtaining divorce by Private Act of Parliament; and in those cases 'the husbands were guilty of other offences besides adultery. . . . In two the adultery was incestuous. In the third there was profligacy, deceit, abandonment, and the grossest injury done to the woman which villainy could inflict. In the fourth, there was bigamy. . . . The applications which have been made on the ground of adultery, and that alone, have always failed . . .': *Report of the Commissioners . . . into the Law of Divorce* (1852–3) BPP vol. 40, p. 249, para. XL. It may be that the case of Mrs Moffatt, whose petition for divorce was rejected in 1832, is an extreme example of the difficulty of satisfying the requirement of 'enormity': in the words of L Stone, *Road to Divorce, England 1530–1987* (1990) pp. 360–361, 'Mr Moffat had been unfaithful to [his wife] on their wedding night, had debauched all the maidservants in the house, had given the wife venereal disease, and was constantly drunk. . . . At the time of the [petition to the House of Lords] Mr Moffatt was in the King's Bench prison, living there with a woman who maintained them both from her earnings as a common prostitute in Drury Lane'.

[48] See *Report of the Commissioners . . . into the Law of Divorce* (1852–3) BPP vol. 40, p. 249, para. 40.

[49] The question of what marital crimes should be specified in the legislation was a matter extensively discussed in Parliament: see L Stone, *Road to Divorce, England 1530–1987* (1990) pp. 379–80; and R Probert, 'The Double Standard of Morality in the Divorce and Matrimonial Causes Act 1857' (1999) 28 Anglo-American Law Review 73.

[50] The view that the Divorce Court had any residual discretion to withhold a decree in circumstances other than those specified by statute was categorically rejected by the House of Lords in *Mordaunt v. Moncrieffe* (1874) LR 2 Sc&Div 374. In that case the question was whether the fact that the wife's mental illness made her unable to answer the petition could prevent the husband from proceeding; and the House of Lords' ruling that he was entitled to go ahead was based on the fact that the Act had (in Lord Chelmsford's words) given a petitioner 'a right not previously existing to obtain the dissolution of a marriage for adultery, by the decree of a newly-created Court of Law, and from its provisions alone we must learn the conditions upon which the jurisdiction is to be exercised . . . [And] by s. 31 the petitioner is absolutely entitled to a decree . . . unless any of the Acts mentioned in the proviso are proved against him'. This (so Lord Chelmsford thought) was a 'great hardship and misfortune' but such was the law. The case in question was perhaps the most sensational of all Victorian divorce cases, including an appearance of the Prince of Wales—subsequently King Edward VII—to deny that he had committed adultery with the wife; and it has been the subject of a number of detailed accounts: see most recently E Hamilton, *The Warwickshire Scandal* (1999). Curiously, the view that the court should have a wide discretion as to whether or not to grant a divorce was put forward by the President of the Probate Divorce and Admiralty Division when reform was under consideration in 1936: see Merriman to Hailsham, 21 April 1936, PRO LCO2/1195.

[51] s. 27.

[52] Defined as adultery with a woman who would, if the wife were dead, be within the prohibited degrees of marriage: Matrimonial Causes Act 1857, s. 27.

[53] Various justifications were advanced for the double standard. It was said that a wife's adultery involved the risk that spurious offspring would be introduced into the family (whereas, as Dr Johnson put it, a man imposes no bastards upon his wife), that to allow both husband and wife to petition on the ground of simple adultery would increase the number of collusive divorces, and that a wife's adultery might result in her husband being infected with venereal disease. But these seem to have been essentially rationalisations of Dr Johnson's general view (as quoted in the Campbell Report, para. 40—the Commissioners also relied on the views of eminent foreign jurists such as

treated rape, sodomy and bestiality as sufficient evidence of a man's depravity to justify the court granting his wife a divorce.[54] It seems remarkable that, in spite of these restrictive grounds, 40% of divorce petitioners[55] in the period between 1858 and the end of the century were wives.[56]

Proof necessary

The Ecclesiastical Courts had insisted that proof of the adultery (which they regarded as akin to a crime)[57] should be 'strict, satisfactory and conclusive'.[58] But as the leading textbook on divorce law[59] was to put it, 'it is rarely indeed that parties are surprised in the direct fact of adultery; and such evidence is apt

Pothier and Montesquieu) that 'the difference between the adultery of the husband and wife is . . . boundless'; and that it was 'possible for a wife to pardon a husband who had committed adultery, but it was hardly possible for a husband ever really to pardon the wife': see Lord Chancellor Cranworth's speech on the second reading of the Matrimonial Causes Bill 1857, *Hansard's Parliamentary Debates* (3rd Series), 19 May 1857, vol. 145, col. 490. As R Probert points out, the fact that these arguments are unappealing to the modern mind does not mean that they were so in the middle of the nineteenth century: 'The Double Standard of Morality in the Divorce and Matrimonial Causes Act 1857' (1999) 28 Anglo-American Law Review 73. For a full and perceptive analysis of 'The Double Standard' see K Thomas in *Journal of the History of Ideas* (1959) 20 p. 195 (concluding that 'the desire of men for absolute property in women, a desire which cannot be satisfied if the man has reason to believe that the woman has once been possessed by another man, no matter how momentarily and involuntarily and no matter how slight the consequences' is a more convincing explanation than the traditional 'pollution of the blood' argument).

[54] Matrimonial Causes Act 1857, s. 27. Since at that time a man could not be guilty of rape on his wife, rape by him necessarily involved the commission of adultery; but sodomy or bestiality on his part did not.

[55] Wives had at this time one considerable advantage in the Divorce Court. A husband was under a common law duty to provide the cost of necessaries (including legal advice and representation) supplied to the wife, and the Divorce Rules No. 158 and 159 accordingly stipulated that a husband should provide not only for his own costs but also for those of his wife. The wife had a right to have her costs paid 'from day to day'; and when the petition was set down for hearing the wife's solicitor was entitled to be given security by the husband for all future costs of the action: see *Evans v. Evans and Robinson* (1858) 1 Sw&Tr 328 where the husband was ordered to pay £73 immediately and give security for £700—more than £40,000 in modern values. Although the husband succeeded in divorcing his wife, it appears that the co-respondent did not comply with the court's order that he pay the whole of the costs, which accordingly were paid out of the security fund provided by the husband. From the earliest days it was recognised that requiring a man to provide security for the costs of legal proceedings against him could lead to abuse (as the *Report of the Royal Commission on Divorce and Matrimonial Causes*, 1912, Cd. 6478, para. 407 noted). This was especially so in cases in which the wife in fact had means and was not dependent on her husband.

[56] L Stone, *Road to Divorce, England 1530–1987* (1990) Table 13.2 p. 437. The number of wives' petitions worried some contemporary observers: see Horstman, *Victorian Divorce*, p. 86; but modern commentators have tended to share Stone's view that the 1857 Act gave wives previously effectively debarred from divorce the freedom to remarry.

[57] This doctrine was still being applied after World War II: see *Ginesi v. Ginesi* [1948] P 179: see p. 254, note 26, below.

[58] *Rix v. Rix* (1777) 3 Hag. Ecc. 74, *per* Sir George Hay. The 1853 Campbell Commission proposed a number of procedural safeguards intended to reinforce this principle, few of which were specifically enacted: see *Report of the Commissioners . . . into the Law of Divorce* (1852–3) BPP vol. 40, p. 249, paras. 45–47.

[59] *Rayden on Practice and Law in the Divorce Division* (1st ed., 1910) p. 63.

to be disbelieved'. Even so, some of the early reported cases suggest that the Divorce Court could have provided rich pickings for a theatrical farce:

In *Alexander v. Alexander and Amos*[60] a groom employed by the husband claimed to have climbed a ladder to a bedroom window, and seen the wife in the act of adultery with another groom. But the court did not regard this testimony as sufficient. The court refused to believe that such a woman—it seems to have been thought relevant that she was a person of humble origin and of scarcely any education—would 'at once, without any preparation, [have] condescended to disgrace herself with a groom who had been about two months in her husband's service; with so little regard for decency, with so little regard as to whether she was discovered or not, that she was guilty of acts of adultery with him in the face of day, without taking the precaution of pulling down a window-blind, or closing a washhouse door'. The judges were prepared to admit that there would from time to time be 'cases in which passion amounting to insanity may lead a person to forget all sense of duty, all regard for decency and all fear of detection' but 'the most cogent testimony' would be necessary to convince the court.

Sometimes the suspicious would use the services of professional private detectives in order to gather evidence; but, at least in the early days, the court[61] was extremely suspicious of testimony from such persons:

In *Sopwith v. Sopwith*[62] the wife of a Tunbridge Wells surgeon and her parents agreed that the explanation for the husband's unfriendly behaviour was probably that he had taken a lover. They sought the professional services of a private detective. The detective gave evidence that, by peering through a keyhole, he had been able to see the husband kissing the maid and that immediately afterwards he had seen the shadows of two figures undressing in the husband's bedroom. The Judge Ordinary (dismissing the petition)[63] contrasted the position of the private detective with that of constables in the police force. The latter were 'employed in a government establishment, they are responsible to an official superior, they have no pecuniary interest in the result of their investigations' whereas 'when a man sets up as a hired discoverer of supposed delinquencies, when the amount of his pay depends upon the extent of his employment, and the

---

[60] (1860) 2 Sw&Tr 95, 101–102.

[61] Since adultery was regarded as akin to a criminal offence it is not surprising that the 1857 Act provided that an alleged adulterer could insist on trial by jury: s. 28. In 1912, the Gorrell Royal Commission (in spite of evidence from lawyers who argued that the jury understood the people who came to the Divorce Court better than did the judges: see eg the evidence of J C Priestley KC: 7 March 1910, p. 549, *Evidence taken before the Royal Commission*, 1912, Vols. I–III, Cd. 6479–82) recommended abolition of jury trial in matrimonial cases. But, in spite of erosion of the right to jury trial effected by the Administration of Justice Act 1925, s. 27 (making the question of mode of trial a matter to be determined by Rules of Court) the editor of *Rayden and Jackson on Divorce and Family Matters* (16th ed., 1991, p. 2009) recorded that he had participated in a fully contested divorce trial before a judge and jury as recently as 1953.

[62] (1859) 4 Sw&Tr 243.

[63] However, in accordance with the usual practice, the husband was required to pay the wife's costs in bringing the suit as well as those he had incurred in defending himself: see note 55 above.

extent of his employment depends upon the discoveries he is able to make, then that man becomes a most dangerous instrument'.

Adultery usually inferred from evidence of inclination and opportunity

In the absence of 'ocular proof' the best that the court could do was to look to evidence of the parties' adulterous inclination and the opportunity they had had to commit adultery. The court would usually be prepared to infer that a spouse had committed adultery if there was evidence that he or she had engaged in what were described as 'indecent familiarities' and that there had been an opportunity to succumb to temptation:

In *Wales v. Wales and Cullen*[64] a barman gave evidence that he had seen the wife kissing the co-respondent,[65] and that he had subsequently seen the wife sitting in her underwear on a bed whilst the co-respondent was sitting in a chair in the same bedroom with his boots off. The court granted the husband a decree on the ground that his wife had committed adultery.

Confessions viewed with suspicion

Would it be sufficient if the wife admitted her adultery? The courts treated such confessions with the utmost circumspection and caution. To accept uncorroborated confessions would encourage collusion and make it far too easy to get a divorce merely because both parties wanted to escape from the marriage. And the courts hinted that 'other sinister motives' might lead a frustrated woman to admit to a relationship existing only in her fevered imagination.[66] For these reasons, the general rule was that a confession would only be accepted as sufficient if corroborated by other evidence.

---

[64] [1900] P 63.

[65] The person with whom the wife was alleged to have committed adultery had to be made a co-respondent with the wife except in special circumstances: Matrimonial Causes Act 1857, s. 28.

[66] See for example *Robinson v. Robinson and Lane* (1859) 1 Sw&Tr 362 where a husband unsuccessfully relied on the contents of the wife's diary. According to Cockburn CJ the diary demonstrated that she was a woman 'of more than ordinary intelligence and of no inconsiderable attainments, but in whom sound sense and judgment were wanting to correct a too vivid imagination and too ardent passions. This is more particularly the case in all that relates to her intercourse with the opposite sex; the most commonplace attentions are invested by her flighty imagination with the character of romance and passion, to be followed in more sober moods by complaints of disappointment and confessions of her own folly in thus dwelling on delusions and dreams'. The diary certainly gives a vivid picture of a woman confined in a marriage in which 'nothing goes on but gloom, sullenness, silence or fault-finding'. It is not surprising that she got some pleasure from walks in Whiteknights (then 'a fine park' and today the campus of the University of Reading Law Faculty) with the co-respondent who (notwithstanding his feeling of being undervalued because he 'was not a University man') was able to engage her in discussion about sculpture, painting, and the works of Shelley, Rousseau and Goethe not to mention more mundane subjects such as women's dress and what behaviour could be regarded as 'becoming or suitable'. This presumably would have extended to the 'passionate kisses, and whispered words' as she leaned back against some 'firm dry heather bushes' and made no opposition to 'what she had often dreamed of'.

Cogent evidence or guesswork?

The courts' suspicions about the reliability of uncorroborated confessions may have been justified; but at least a confession was some kind of evidence. In many defended divorce cases, the need for the court to decide whether the facts which had been proved justified it in inferring that a spouse had committed adultery drove it to making dubious value judgments. This problem never went away, and the best illustration of how haphazard the process could be is to be found in a case[67] which came before the courts after nearly a century's experience of determining allegations of adultery:

A distinguished British diplomat whose marriage had broken down many years previously wanted to remarry. He made no secret of his adultery, but his wife refused to petition. He therefore started proceedings alleging that the wife had committed adultery with one Francisco de Amat y Torre. The most telling evidence against the wife and Señor de Amat y Torre was found in letters dating back to 1936; but the trial judge found that these contained nothing inconsistent with a wholly innocent relationship. However, in the Court of Appeal Tucker LJ confidently pronounced that the letters 'were those of a lover, and a satisfied lover, who had been spending a week with the woman he loved'. A decree was awarded to the husband.[68]

Birth of a child?

There were, in contrast, cases in which the evidence was compelling. For example the fact that a wife had borne a child of whom the husband could not possibly be the father was virtually conclusive evidence[69] that she had committed

---

[67] *Cavendish-Bendick v. Cavendish-Bendick*, *The Times* (1947) 28 March, Hodson J; (1947) November 7 (Court of Appeal). The court papers are lodged in the Public Record office, file J77/3965.

[68] The wife was given leave to appeal to the House of Lords; but in April 1948 it was announced (according to the husband's biographer) that her appeal had been withdrawn because satisfactory financial arrangements had been made: P Howarth, *Intelligence Chief Extraordinary, The Life of the Ninth Duke of Portland*. Although the husband—who many years later succeeded as a distant collateral relative to the Dukedom of Portland—was enabled to remarry, the public revelation that he had committed adultery led to his summary dismissal from the Diplomatic Service and the forfeiture of his substantial pension rights. The fact that such a harsh penalty could be inflicted on a man who had rendered outstanding service to his country (not least as Chairman of the Joint Intelligence Committee during World War II) may give an indication of the stigma at the time associated with being the guilty party in divorce proceedings.

[69] Birth of a child was often relied on as evidence by members of the armed forces serving for long periods overseas during the two twentieth century World Wars. In *Fearn v. Fearn* [1948] 1 All ER 459, for example, husband and wife were married in November 1940. In August 1941 the husband was ordered abroad on active service. He did not return until September 1945. The child was born on 12 August 1944 and it was accepted that the husband could not possibly be the father. The wife admitted that in August 1943 she had been to a party and after having two or three drinks had committed adultery. (The point for decision was whether the husband was debarred from divorcing her by having written—extremely moving—letters saying that he had forgiven her: see below.)

adultery.[70] But the law presumed that a husband was the father of any child born to his wife during the marriage, and a husband seeking to rebut this presumption and convict his wife of adultery on the basis of the birth of a child had to show that it was virtually *impossible* for him to have been the father.[71] The task was complicated by technical rules about the admissibility of evidence[72] which often prevented the courts from hearing material which most people would have regarded as highly relevant:

The sensational case of *Russell v. Russell*[73]—a desperate struggle between 'a great English family fighting to the last for the honour of its name, and . . . a woman doing battle for her own honour and that of the little child'[74]—vividly exemplifies the difficulties of establishing the truth in these circumstances. The essence of the husband's case was that the wife had born a child and that the husband could not be the father because he 'had had no connection with her at any time which could have produced conception at the time conception in fact took place'.[75] The husband therefore invited the jury to infer that his wife must have committed adultery (perhaps with one of the 30 or more men she claimed

---

[70] Proof that one spouse had contracted a sexually transmitted disease (otherwise than from the other) was also sufficient proof that he or she had committed adultery: see eg *Gleen v. Gleen* (1900) 17 TLR 62 (where evidence that Sergeant Gleen of the Coldstream Guards had been admitted to hospital suffering 'from a certain illness' was accepted as proof of his adultery, and—the wife proving his cruelty—was granted a divorce).

[71] In *Preston-Jones v. Preston-Jones* [1951] AC 391, HL the trial judge held that a husband who had gone abroad 360 days before his wife gave birth to an 8.25 pound apparently normally developed child only returning 186 days before the birth had not discharged the burden of proving that he could not have been the child's father. The wife denied that she had committed adultery and (according to Lord Normand at p. 404) there was no evidence that she wife had had 'any suspicious relations' with any other man or that she had been guilty of any looseness of conduct, nor did anything appear to suggest that she was other than a respectable hard-working woman. A 3–2 majority in the House of Lords held that the husband was entitled to a decree: the issue was whether there was clear and satisfactory evidence of the adultery going beyond a mere balance of probabilities, and that on this basis the evidence should have satisfied the judge. But the question of the standard of proof remained difficult.

[72] There were two rules which caused especial difficulty. First, statute (latterly the Evidence (Further Amendment) Act 1869, s. 3)—reflecting the view that witnesses should be protected against self-incrimination—provided that although that parties and their spouses should be *competent* to give evidence in proceedings instituted in consequence of adultery neither they (nor any other witness) should be 'liable to be asked or bound to answer any question tending to show that he or she has been guilty of adultery, unless such witness shall have already given evidence in the same proceeding in disproof of his or her alleged adultery'. This rule caused problems and was strongly criticised: see notably the *Report of the Royal Commission on Divorce and Matrimonial Causes*, 1912, Cd. 6478, para. 101 recommending abolition on the ground that the rule made it easier for a petitioner to conceal the fact that he had himself committed adultery. But the rule survived until 1968: Civil Evidence Act 1968, s. 16(5). Secondly, the House of Lords in *Russell v. Russell* [1924] AC 687, held that neither spouse could give evidence as to whether or not sexual intercourse had taken place: see further below.

[73] [1924] AC 687, HL. A fuller account of this sensational case and its impact is given in SM Cretney, *Law, Law Reform and the Family*, (1999) Chapter 4.

[74] In the words of E Marjoribanks, *The Life of Sir Edward Marshall Hall* (1929) p. 429.

[75] *per* Lord Sterndale MR, *Russell v. Russell* [1924] P 1, 8, CA.

had been in love with her)[76] from the fact that he had never had intercourse with her.[77] The child was produced for inspection by the jury in support of the wife's claim that there was a physical resemblance to the husband (who, when in the witness box, was invited by counsel to move his head so that his ears—the formation of which was evidently thought to be strikingly similar to that of the child—were clearly visible to the jury). After an eight-day trial, the jury could not agree. After an 11-day retrial, another jury (perhaps swayed by counsel's emotional plea[78] that they should give the husband[79] his freedom) found the wife guilty of adultery with an unknown man; and the judge pronounced a decree nisi. However, this was not the end of the family's troubles: the wife successfully appealed to the House of Lords[80] which held that, in the interests of public decency, spouses should not be allowed to give evidence about whether or not sexual intercourse had taken place. Accordingly there had been no admissible evidence to rebut the presumption that a husband is father of the child his wife had born, and, in the absence of any other sufficient evidence of adultery against the wife, the decree nisi obtained by the husband[81] was

[76] The wife told the court that she was not in love with her husband; and she had married him because it would 'be nice to be no longer pestered by men to marry them. I thought it would be peaceful . . .'.

[77] Both husband and wife admitted to having indulged in 'hunnish practices': the husband 'had been in use to lie between her legs with the male organ in more or less proximity to the orifice of the vagina, and to proceed to emission; but he . . . specifically denied that there had been these practices during the relevant period, though he admitted that he was in bed with her on at least two nights' during the same time: *Russell v. Russell* [1924] AC 687, 721, *per* Lord Dunedin. This could have led to the wife (albeit *virgo intacta*) conceiving, and she claimed that the husband was the only person with whom she had had such relations. However, to cite Lord Dunedin again, 'the jury . . . came to the conclusion that she had been fecundated ab extra by another man unknown' and he had no doubt that fecundation ab extra by a third party constituted adultery. (Some 30 years later the Court of Appeal held that penetration *was* a necessary element of adultery: *Dennis v. Dennis* [1955] P 33, CA. Lord Dunedin's dictum in the *Russell* cases was not cited and the Court of Appeal distinguished Lord Birkenhead's similarly unequivocal view in the earlier case of *Rutherford v. Richardson* [1923] AC 1, 11, in a somewhat unconvincing way. But if the Court of Appeal was right in its 1955 decision, Mrs Russell could not have been guilty of the adultery with which she was charged and the issue should never have been left to the jury.)

[78] 'I ask you to find a verdict in favour of John Russell, and free him from the tie which he once hoped would be a tie of love, but which is now a rusty chain that burns into his soul': E Marjoribanks, *The Life of Sir Edward Marshall Hall* (1929) p. 428.

[79] Patrick Hastings KC for the wife accepted in his closing speech that the husband had given his evidence 'like an English gentleman', suggested that there were still prospects for reconciliation between the parties, and made an emotional speech about the 'little chap' who would be rendered fatherless by a verdict against the wife. Hastings' biographer, H Montgomery Hyde, confirms that the husband made a favourable impression on the jury at the first trial: he 'gave his evidence admirably' and was 'simple, manly, and quite obviously speaking what he believed to be the truth': *Sir Patrick Hastings: His Life and Cases* (1960) p. 90.

[80] *Russell v. Russell* [1924] AC 687. This so-called rule in *Russell v. Russell* (which caused administrative difficulties in the kind of wartime divorce referred to at note 69 above, since documentary evidence that the husband had been abroad at all relevant times had to be produced from service records) was eventually abolished by the Law Reform (Miscellaneous Provisions) Act 1949, s. 7.

[81] The husband succeeded to the peerage on the death of his father in 1935. He remarried in 1937 but there were no children of that marriage. A year after his second wife's death in 1948 he again remarried, and by his third marriage had a daughter and a son, John Hugo Trenchard Russell born on 13 October 1950. JHT Russell's claim to be entitled to succeed to the Ampthill peerage as his

rescinded; and the High Court made a declaration that the child was the legitimate child of the marriage.[82] John and Christabel Russell were thus required to remain husband and wife for a decade after their marriage had broken down beyond repair.[83]

Legal requirement for proof not understood by public

One of the reasons for insisting on a high standard of proof of adultery was to protect the innocent against being found guilty of adultery, with all the stigma which at that time would follow. But it was not only the husband and wife who might find that an appearance in the Divorce Court left a stigma:

In 1885 a Scottish lawyer, Donald Cameron, petitioned for divorce on the ground of his 22-year-old wife's adultery with Sir Charles Dilke, a successful Liberal politician with a claim to succeed Gladstone as party leader. The wife confessed, and since the confession was in part corroborated the trial judge accepted it as sufficient proof that the wife had committed adultery and he granted the husband a decree. But since there was nothing in the corroborative evidence to implicate Dilke the judge dismissed him from the suit and ordered the petitioning husband to pay his costs. As Dilke's biographer[84] has put it, the verdict seemed in the popular mind to be that Mrs Cameron had committed adultery with Dilke, but that he had not done so with her. Because of the potentially disastrous effect of the case on his reputation and standing Dilke did not discourage an intervention by the Queen's Proctor;[85] but the court would only set aside the decree if the Queen's Proctor could establish that Mrs Cameron had *not* committed adultery with Dilke, and this he failed to do. The decree stood; and Dilke's political career was destroyed.[86]

father's only legitimate son was rejected by the Committee of Privileges: the Committee held that the Declaration obtained in 1926 was conclusive: *The Ampthill Peerage* [1977] AC 547.

[82] *Russell (GDE) (By his guardian) v. The Attorney-General* (1926) *The Times*, 29 July, Swift J. This case dramatically illustrates the limitations of the legal process as a means of influencing personal behaviour: notwithstanding the solemn court declaration, the husband refused throughout his life to recognise the child as his lawful son and heir, and declined to meet him or have any contact with him or to provide any financial support for him except in so far as he was legally compelled to do so. Notwithstanding the presumably traumatic experiences to which he had been subjected, the child had a long and successful career, serving in the Irish Guards in World War II and thereafter active as a Director of Companies. Following the decision of the Committee of Privileges, he took his seat in the House of Lords as the fourth Baron Ampthill, served as a Chairman of Committees, was appointed CBE in 1986, called to the Privy Council in 1995, and remained a member of the House of Lords notwithstanding the abolition of the right of hereditary peers to sit by virtue of House of Lords Act 1999, s. 2.

[83] In *Baroness Ampthill v. Baron Ampthill* (1935) *The Times* 26 November the husband did not contest the wife's petition alleging that he had committed adultery with a woman named Doris Jones at a London hotel in 1931.

[84] Roy Jenkins, *Dilke, A Victorian Tragedy* (reprinted 1996)—a brilliant account of the trial and its consequences.

[85] For the functions of the Queen's Proctor, see below.

[86] The case is a striking illustration of the difficulty of communicating to non-lawyers the nature of legal proof.

As a matter of law, there was no finding against Dilke: the court had found only that Mrs Cameron had committed adultery with *someone*. True, the court had not found that Mrs Cameron had *not* committed adultery with Dilke, but it is notoriously difficult to establish a negative. These subtleties were not understood by the public.

Hotel cases

Cases such as those described above may have provided good copy for the newspapers[87] but they give a misleading impression of the typical divorce. From the beginning, the great majority of divorce cases were undefended; and, in many, husband and wife were both anxious to bring their marriage legally to an end. Hence, the practice developed[88] of one party providing the other with evidence (in the form of a confession) that he had committed adultery. To satisfy the requirement that a confession needed to be corroborated if any weight was to be given to it, the confession statement would be accompanied by a hotel bill and other details such as would allow witnesses to be summoned from the hotel in question. But for many years, such evidence was likely to make the court suspicious not only that there might have been collusion[89] between the parties but that the 'evidence' might have been concocted. This was particularly the case if the adultery in question was alleged to have taken place in a hotel with an unnamed woman. In the 1930s the 'hotel divorce' became a matter of major concern, and this was a factor in the movement which eventually led to the Matrimonial Causes Act 1937, discussed at Chapter 6 below.

PETITIONER MUST HAVE 'CLEAN HANDS':[90] THE BARS TO DIVORCE

The assumption underlying the 1857 divorce law was that marriage was no ordinary contract but a matter in which the State had a vital interest, trans-

---

[87] Publication of intimate details of husband wife relations was regarded as distasteful in some quarters, and the Judicial Proceedings (Publication of Reports) Act 1926 (still in force at the turn of the century) placed severe restrictions on the publication of information about divorce cases: see SM Cretney, *Law, Law Reform and the Family* (1999) Chapter 4.

[88] The fashionable nineteenth century divorce lawyer Sir George Lewis was notably taciturn in dealing with a question about the prevalence of 'hotel adultery' divorces in *Evidence taken before the Royal Commission,* 1912, Vols. I–III, Cd. 6479–82 26 February 1910.

[89] See below; and note *Todd v. Todd* (1866) LR 1 P&D 121.

[90] If ever there was a court in which it was 'incumbent to hold up the maxim that a man who seeks relief should come with clean hands it is undoubtedly the Court of Divorce': *Gipps v. Gipps and Hume* (1864) 11 HLC 1, *per* Lord Westbury, LC; and the 'clean hands' doctrine was expressly accepted by the Judge Ordinary in *Clarke v. Clarke and Clarke* (1865) 34 LJ (PA&M) 94 (a case in which a single act of adultery, apparently with a prostitute, after the wife had left the husband was held to debar him from obtaining a decree founded on the wife's incestuous adultery).

cending and operating independently of the will of the parties.[91] Public policy was an important factor in determining the circumstances in which dissolution should be permitted: hence, although a petitioner had to prove that there were grounds for divorce it did not automatically follow that the court would on such proof automatically grant the decree sought. The Matrimonial Causes Act 1857 established two kinds of 'bar' to the grant of the relief sought in the petition. First, there were the so-called absolute (or 'peremptory') bars. The court was bound[92] to dismiss a petition if the petitioner had been accessory to or had connived at (or had condoned) the respondent's adultery or if the petition had been presented in collusion with the respondent.[93] Secondly, there were the 'discretionary' bars. The court was not bound to grant a decree[94] if the petitioner had 'during the marriage been guilty of adultery' or if he had been 'guilty of unreasonable delay in presenting or prosecuting' the petition, or of having 'deserted or wilfully separated himself or herself from the other party before the adultery complained of, and without reasonable excuse, or of such wilful neglect or misconduct as [had] conduced to the adultery'.[95]

COURT'S INQUISITORIAL ROLE

The belief that the dissolution of their marriage was not a matter to be left to the parties led not only to the creation of special bars to the grant of decrees but also to the court being given a distinctive role. The Court for Divorce and Matrimonial Causes was not to adopt the accusatorial system of justice of the common law courts (in which the court's function was to listen to the evidence which the parties choose, in accordance with the rules of evidence, to put before it and decide the case solely on the basis of that evidence).[96] Rather, the Court

---

[91] Marriage was an institution 'subject in all countries to general laws which dictate and control its obligations and incidents, independently of the volition of those who enter upon it': *Mordaunt v. Mordaunt* (1870) LR 2 P&M 109, 126, *per* Lord Penzance. Accordingly there was a 'profound difference . . . between the permitted liberty of procedure in ordinary civil litigation inter partes and the statutory conditions which prevent dissatisfied spouses from dealing as they will with their marital relationship. . . . The Court must direct its attention not only to the facts alleged but to the questions whether the petitioner was accessory to or conniving in the adultery alleged, or has condoned it. If the affirmative is shown the petition must be dismissed . . .': *Apted v. Apted and Bliss* [1930] P 240, 260–261 *per* Lord Merrivale P (asserting the 'consistent legislative view as to marriage and divorce during [the] upwards of seventy years' since the enactment of the Matrimonial Causes Act 1857).

[92] Matrimonial Causes Act 1857, s. 30.

[93] Matrimonial Causes Act 1857, s. 30 refers to petitions presented in collusion 'with either of the respondents' thus debarring the court from dissolving the marriage if (for example) there had been collusion with the alleged adulterer.

[94] But there was no *general* discretion to withhold a decree. If the court was satisfied of the matters referred to in the statute the petitioner was entitled to a divorce whatever view the court might take of the rights and wrongs of the case: see *Mordaunt v. Moncrieffe* (1874) LR 2Sc&Div 374, HL.

[95] Matrimonial Causes Act 1857, s. 31.

[96] A vivid description of the common law accusatorial process is given by Denning LJ in *Jones v. National Coal Board* [1957] 2 QB 55, 63.

was to adopt the inquisitorial approach of the Ecclesiastical Courts.[97] It was not to restrict itself to a consideration of the material the parties put before it, but had a duty 'to satisfy itself, so far as it reasonably can', not only as to the truth or the facts alleged in the petition, but also whether or not the petitioner had 'during the marriage been accessory to or conniving at the adultery, or [had] condoned the same' and the court was also required to inquire into any counter-charge made against the petitioner.[98] In discharging these duties the court was assisted[99] by secret investigators working for the Queen's Proctor.

For these reasons the divorce process had a distinctive character[100] until well after the end of World War II. The text first explains the machinery established in an attempt to enable the court to carry out the investigative functions which statute laid on it. It then gives an account of the three absolute bars to divorce (connivance, condonation and collusion) and the three discretionary bars (adultery on the part of the petitioner, delay and conduct conducing).

The inquisitorial role, the practice: the role of the Queen's Proctor[101]

It was all very well to require the court to satisfy itself about the various matters referred to in the Statute and to inquire into the facts of the case, but the 1857 Act provided no machinery to enable the court to discharge these duties. This soon became all too apparent;[102] and in 1861 the Government introduced two amendments to the 1857 Act intended in particular to minimise the horrifying risk that couples might be getting divorces by agreement.[103] First, the making of a divorce decree was to become a two-stage process. The court would initially grant a decree *nisi*;[104] which would only be made absolute after an interval of six months.[105] It was provided that during that time, any person could intervene in the proceedings 'to show cause why the . . . decree should not be made absolute by reason of the

---

[97] See Matrimonial Causes Act 1857, s. 22.   [98] Matrimonial Causes Act 1857, s. 29.

[99] After the enactment of Matrimonial Causes Act 1860, s. 7: see below.

[100] See the description by Sir Harold Kent of the posture appropriate for a divorce petitioner quoted at p. 269, below.

[101] Contrary to the assumption apparently made by GL Savage, 'The Divorce Court and the Queen's/King's Proctor: Legal Patriarchy and the Sanctity of Marriage in England, 1861–1937' (1989) *Historical Papers, Quebec* 210, this office was not 'created' by the Matrimonial Causes Act 1861 but is of some antiquity.

[102] See JF Macqueen, *A Practical Treatise on The Law of Marriage, Divorce and Legitimacy . . .* (2nd ed., 1860) for a strong expression of the view that 'to look behind the scene is an imperative duty cast upon the court . . . but one of the greatest difficulty in undefended cases'. Macqueen believed that the judges were the last to hear of collusion, that the legislation provided hardly any security against the frauds practised by parties acting in collusion, and that (barring accidents) such conspiracies were bound to succeed.

[103] For the background, see GL Savage, 'The Divorce Court and the Queen's/King's Proctor: Legal Patriarchy and the Sanctity of Marriage in England, 1861–1937' (1989) *Historical Papers, Quebec* 210, 212–213.

[104] 'unless'.

[105] Matrimonial Causes Act 1860, s. 7 provided a minimum delay of three months; but Matrimonial Causes Act 1866 extended the period.

same having been obtained by collusion or by reason of material facts not brought before the court'.[106] Secondly, the Act[107] provided that individuals could give information to the Queen's Proctor at any stage before the decree had been made absolute; and if 'from any such information or otherwise the said Proctor shall suspect that the parties to the suit are or have been acting in collusion for the purpose of obtaining a decree contrary to the justice of the case' the Proctor could intervene in the suit, retaining counsel and subpoenaing witnesses.[108]

Under the powers given by this legislation, what one hostile critic described as an 'elaborate machinery of espionage' was said to have been constructed[109] at the expense of the taxpayer in an attempt to prevent divorces being obtained by consent or divorces being granted to petitioners who had themselves committed adultery.[110] The Proctor's office would examine[111] every undefended case in which a decree *nisi* had been granted,[112] and make further investigations

[106] The court could dismiss the intervention, rescind the decree, or require the Queen's Proctor to carry out further inquiries: s. 7. The couple remained married until decree absolute: see below. Over the years the notion that their marriage subsisted in fact (as distinct from in law) increasingly strained credulity, as was recognised by the House of Lords in *Fender v. St. John Mildmay* [1938] AC 1 (promise to marry made to a third party not illegal by reason of fact that man 'married'; cf. *Wilson v. Carnley* [1908] 1 KB 729).

[107] s. 7.

[108] The Act also (s. 5) empowered the court to direct that the papers in any undefended case be sent to the Queen's Proctor who would instruct counsel to appear and argue any point which the court considered relevant. This power was frequently exercised in cases in which the evidence suggested the possibility of collusion or condonation.

[109] It is not clear how large this 'army' was: according to the Earl of Dysart (who had held the Office of King's Proctor for nearly 15 years) very careful instructions were given to the Proctor's Officers in London (who reported and took instructions almost every day) and the 'greatest possible care' was taken to conduct an 'efficient enquiry' guarding against the risk of injury being done to the characters of the innocent: *Evidence taken before the Royal Commission, 1912.* In the country it appears that local agents (often, it seems, solicitors) were instructed: see the evidence of F Rowland, below.

[110] ESP Haynes, *A Lawyer's Notebook* (1936) p. 238. In fact interventions based on collusion were very rare (possibly only one or two each year) and the majority of interventions were based on the petitioner's failure to reveal his or her own misconduct: see the evidence of Sir John Bigham P *Evidence taken before the Royal Commission* q. 590, also suggesting that non-disclosure was often influenced by the reluctance of the court to exercise its discretion in favour of an adulterer: see below and Lord Alverstone's *Evidence taken before the Royal Commission,* q. 15,496 to q. 15,506. Lord Alverstone (who, as Attorney-General for more than 12 years, had been responsible for the final decision whether to intervene) could not understand why anyone wished to 'do away with the office of King's Proctor altogether' since if 'you remove some officer who is to have the power of intervening in cases in which there has been an abuse of the court, by divorce being obtained when it ought not to be obtained, you will enormously increase the temptation to perjury': q. 15,506. The Divorce Law Reform Union however took the view that 'two or three stiff sentences for perjury' would do all the good the King's Proctor could do in 20 years: WG Ramsay Fairfax, *Evidence taken before the Royal Commission,* q. 5,124.

[111] In evidence to the Gorell Royal Commission the Earl of Dysart said that at that time an 'enormous number' of cases were investigated ('it varies from 306 to 631'): *Evidence taken before the Royal Commission,* q. 16,002.

[112] It appears from *Hyman v. Hyman and Goldman (The Kings's Proctor showing cause)* [1904] P 403 that an intervention would be prosecuted even if the parties admitted that they had become reconciled and resumed cohabitation for the sake of the children and did not intend to apply for the decree to be made absolute. In *Hyman's* case, it was held that the Proctor's intervention was justified, and that the decree *nisi* and award of damages against the co-respondent must be set

if 'anything attracted attention'.[113] It is true that these investigations were often ineffective[114] and only rarely led to an intervention[115]—there was a policy that the Proctor would only intervene if success was certain[116]—but the knowledge that a neighbour or jealous rival might tell the Proctor[117] that the petitioner had committed adultery[118] (or even that he was still doing so)[119] must have made life very uncomfortable for many spouses anxious for what would later be called a 'civilised' divorce:

A solicitor practising in Accrington Lancashire told the 1912 Royal Commission[120] of a case in which a woman, deserted by her husband and left without means, took a position as housekeeper to a publican. Some years later the publican died and the housekeeper received some money under an insurance policy. This enabled her to instruct a solicitor to obtain a divorce, but the deceased's daughter considered that she should have had the insurance money and (falsely and maliciously) informed the King's Proctor that her father had repeatedly committed adultery with the housekeeper. The King's Proctor duly intervened; and the housekeeper, who had insufficient funds to travel to London, was unable to defend herself. The decree was rescinded; and eventually the King's Proctor issued execution for his costs. The housekeeper's goods 'were actually sold, lock, stock, and barrel, and she was thrown into the street'.[121]

aside. However, the court considered the co-respondent entirely responsible for what had occurred and ordered him to indemnify the husband against any liability for the King's Proctor's costs of the intervention.

[113] Earl of Dysart, *Evidence taken before the Royal Commission*, 1912, Vol. II, 1 June 1910, q. 15,778.

[114] Lord Alverstone CJ told the Gorrell Royal Commission that the Proctor's Office as then constituted could not find out 'one-tenth of the cases in which there has been misconduct of the petitioner, and . . . he can only find out a small proportion of the cases in which there has been collusion'. He also said that the means of getting information was 'utterly insufficient'. *Evidence taken before the Royal Commission*, 1912, Vols. I–III, Cd. 6479–82 1 June 1910, q. 15,493, q. 15,495.

[115] There were on average fewer than 30 interventions a year. Almost all resulted in the decree *nisi* being reversed: *Report of the Royal Commission on Divorce and Matrimonial Causes*, 1912, Cd. 6478, para. 99.

[116] Lord Alverstone CJ, *Evidence taken before the Royal Commission*, 1912, Vols. I–III, Cd. 6479–82, q. 15,493. Alverstone claimed that no intervention which he had authorised had been unsuccessful, but that officials in the Queen's Proctor's Office thought he was unduly strict in deciding whether to allow an intervention.

[117] In 1937 the Lord Chancellor's Department noted that 'publication of the decree nisi leads members of the public to give information upon which the King's Proctor can act': Memorandum PRO LCO2/1195 p. 6; and there were cases in which an individual exercised the right conferred by statute to intervene personally: see eg *Stuart v. Stuart and Holden (Moon showing cause)* [1930] P 77 where the petitioner was found (notwithstanding his denials) to have committed adultery and Hill J refused to exercise discretion; and, for a case in which a private citizen by exercising the statutory right to intervene in a divorce case, exacerbated a serious constitutional crisis, see *Simpson, W v. Simpson, EA (Application by the King's Proctor for Directions)* (1937) *The Times* March 20, p. 233, below.

[118] See eg *Wyke v. Wyke (The King's Proctor showing cause)* [1904] P. 149.

[119] Particular hardship might be caused by the fact that adultery committed after decree *nisi* was adultery committed during the marriage.

[120] F Rowland, *Evidence taken before the Royal Commission*, 1912, Vols. I–III, Cd. 6479–82, q. 17,592.

[121] This was no doubt the kind of case which the Earl of Dysart had in mind when he confessed that he had felt 'over and over again . . . that my intervention has done more harm than good': *Evidence taken before the Royal Commission*.

The fact that it was the normal practice for the King's Proctor to 'put his sleuths on to' undefended divorce cases[122] seems to have entered into the popular consciousness; but it was some time before the apparatus of 'anonymous letters, back-door espionage, . . . cross-examination of cooks, . . . bribery of maids and porters, the searching of hotel registers, the watching of windows, the tracking of taxi cabs, [and] the exploitation of malicious gossip and interested malignity' all 'done in the King's name to preserve the sanctity of the home'[123] began to be questioned.

THE INQUISITORIAL ROLE, THE SUBSTANTIVE LAW: ABSOLUTE BARS TO DIVORCE

(i) Connivance etc

The Matrimonial Causes Act 1857[124] required the court to satisfy itself 'whether or not the petitioner has been in any manner accessory to or conniving at the adultery' and if the court found that the petitioner had done so it was required to dismiss the petition.[125]

The word 'connivance' is derived from the Latin *connivere*, meaning 'to wink at'; and in its simplest form the bar of connivance gave clear effect to the 'clean hands' principle: it would be 'monstrous' to allow a man who had, for example, driven his wife to prostitution and lived on her earnings to divorce her and marry again.[126] Another explanation would see connivance as an application of the principle (usually discussed in connection with personal injury claims) that *volenti non fit injuria*,[127] that is to say that one cannot complain of something to which one has freely consented. But the divorce court gave the word an exceptionally wide meaning.[128] A man was expected to take adequate care of his

---

[122] Sir Harold Kent *In on the Act* (1979) p. 70.

[123] As AP Herbert was to describe it in *Holy Deadlock* (1934).   [124] s. 29.   [125] s. 30.

[126] *Gipps v. Gipps and Hume* (1864) 11 HLC 1, 25, *per* Lord Wensleydale at p. 22.

[127] *Gipps v. Gipps and Hume* (1864) 11 HLC 1, 25, *per* Lord Westbury at p. 22. The 1833 Royal Commission regarded this as the governing principle (referring to *Rogers v. Rogers* ((1830) 3 Hagg. Ecc. 58) and the principle that a 'guilty acquiescence in . . . crime can receive no favour': *First Report of the Commissioners . . . into the Law of Divorce . . .* (1853) p. 17, note 1. But the doctrine could be applied in cases where the husband was unquestionably a victim. More than a hundred years after the passing of the 1857 Act a man returned home having had 'a certain amount to drink' to find the wife and co-respondent embracing each other. 'He was angry and said "If you two want to go to bed together, why the hell don't you?"'. They did. The following morning he 'thought better of it and turned out the co-respondent'. The House of Lords held that he had connived at the adultery, that the connivance could not be regarded as having been 'spent' and that accordingly he was debarred from obtaining a divorce from her: *Godfrey v. Godfrey* [1965] AC 444, HL.

[128] See the authoritative *Practical Treatise on the Law of Marriage, Divorce, and Legitimacy*, by JF Macqueen (2nd ed., 1860), p. 78: the conniver was typically a man who gave his wife 'the opportunity without appearing to do so. He looks up at the ceiling or out at the window; he feigns deep intoxication or profound sleep, and affects to snore while his dishonour is being completed'.

property, and therefore he should 'exact a due purity on the part of his wife'.[129] Failure to do so would debar him from subsequently complaining about the consequences:

In *Robinson v. Robinson and Dearden*[130] the husband left his home to look for work. On his return he found his friend Dearden installed as a lodger. Dearden became increasingly intimate with Mrs Robinson, and the two paid no respect to the husband and sneered at him. The rest of the 'short and simple story' is best told in the judge's[131] words: the 'petitioner allowed this state of affairs to go on. Matters got worse and worse, as one would naturally expect, until, on June 1, the petitioner found his wife and [Dearden] coming up to bed after he himself had retired for the night. That ought to have aroused his suspicions. On another occasion the petitioner says that he saw his wife and [Dearden] embracing and kissing each other. What did he do? He merely went down and talked to [Dearden] and threatened to turn him out. . . . On another occasion the petitioner says he saw his wife leaning on [Dearden] in an indecent or improper manner. What did he do then? Nothing. On June 15 the petitioner comes home and finds them in a bedroom together, but he appears to have accepted the ridiculous excuse that [Dearden] was going to wash his hands. It is too absurd and ridiculous for a man to accept such excuses under such circumstances. . . . I come to the conclusion that the petitioner by tacit acquiescence, allowed his wife so to carry on and conduct herself . . . that adultery has resulted'. Mr Robinson was refused a divorce.[132]

But there were limits to the scope of the doctrine. A husband could perfectly reasonably seek evidence of his wife's adultery without warning her of what he was doing;[133] and the fact that a husband simply tolerated the continuance of an

---

[129] *Gipps v. Gipps and Hume* (1864) 11 HLC 1, 22, *per* Lord Westbury LC. For this reason a presumption of connivance would also arise if a deed of separation contained what could be construed as a licence to commit adultery (perhaps a clause that the wife might reside at such places and with such persons as she thought fit: see *King v. King and Evans* (1929) 142 LT 162) and the petitioner would have to rebut this presumption if he could: see *Thomas v. Thomas* (1860) 2 Sw&Tr 113.

[130] [1903] P 155.   [131] Bucknill J.

[132] Once a husband had allowed his wife to succumb to the blandishments of one man, he could not complain that the fallen woman thereafter committed adultery with another lover: 'Can a man, consenting to adultery with A, but not . . . with B . . . say "Non omnibus dormio"? This is language not to be endured'. *Lovering v. Lovering* (1792) 3 Hagg. Ecc. 85, 87, *per* Sir William Scott.

[133] But a post-World War II decision demonstrates how narrow was the dividing line between seeking evidence on the one hand and, on the other, lulling the wife into a false sense of security and failing to stop an intimate friendship developing into an adulterous one. In *Manning v. Manning* [1950] 1 All ER 602 a man and woman, suspecting their spouses to be guilty of adultery, placed a microphone in the drawing room piano and hid in the garage. Hearing a conversation of a 'highly indecent nature', they entered the drawing room 'but only found that the appearance of Mrs Manning was rather dishevelled'. They pretended to believe the explanation that the couple had fallen asleep while looking at some photographs; but subsequently the two observers gave the couple every possible opportunity to commit adultery. Eventually, having let the couple believe they would be away, they again installed themselves (on this occasion in the company of some of Mr Manning's police colleagues) in the garage, and found the couple in the act of adultery. The court held their behaviour constituted connivance.

adulterous relationship about which he had at first been ignorant did not necessarily make him guilty of connivance.[134]

(ii) **Condonation**[135]

'Condonation' means forgiveness and it is hardly surprising that a law based on the matrimonial offence should refuse to allow a man who had forgiven his wife's lapses subsequently to claim the right to cast her aside. But the word 'forgiveness' was used, not in the sense in which a moral philosopher or theologian would understand it,[136] but rather as reflecting the legal principle that one may not at the same time approbate and reprobate.[137] By waiving his or her right to take matrimonial proceedings the injured spouse was debarred from relying on the offence which had been condoned. But over the years the courts found it necessary[138] to elaborate what had been an essentially simple principle. The case law came to establish a number of propositions.

Mere verbal forgiveness insufficient

In *Keats v. Keats and Montezuma*[139] Mrs Keats eloped with a Spanish musician, Don Pedro de Montezuma. Her husband[140] sought a reconciliation, and agreed to say that he had forgiven her for the wrongs she had done him. But he subsequently changed his mind and successfully sought a divorce. The Court accepted that mere words of forgiveness[141] could never constitute condonation.

[134] But the courts might regard tolerance of a continuing relationship as evidence that the man had from the outset been prepared to wink at his wife's infidelity: *Crewe v. Crewe* (1800) 3 Hagg. Ecc. 123.

[135] Matrimonial Causes Act 1857, ss. 29, 30.

[136] 'The doctrine of condonation is peculiar in its origin, peculiar in its features, but perhaps most peculiar in its notion of forgiveness. It seems to me to be vital to remember that the forgiveness of condonation may be a wholly different thing to the forgiveness spoken of by ordinary men and women': *Cramp v. Cramp* [1920] P 158, 162–163, *per* McCardie J. Hence, it was 'no good a husband whose wife has been reinstated showing that he had never forgiven his wife, that he had showed no affection to her, that he still deeply resented her adultery, that the motive for the resumption of cohabitation was economic, or for the sake of the children, or to conceal from the world that the marriage had run into trouble, or that their life together was uneasy and painful, full of animosity and unhappiness': SM Cretney, *Principles of Family Law* (2nd ed., 1976), p. 113, omitting references.

[137] 'or in the more homely expression, blow hot and cold': *per* Sir J Simon P, *Howard v. Howard* [1965] P 65, 73. For other illuminating discussions of the relationship between the Divorce Court notion of condonation and common law doctrines such as estoppel and remedies for breach of contract see *Inglis v. Inglis and Baxter* [1968] P 639; *Quinn v. Quinn* [1969] 1 WLR 1394, 1410, *per* Phillimore LJ; *Hearn v. Hearn* [1969] 1 WLR 1832.

[138] JF Macqueen, *A Practical Treatise on the Law of Marriage, Divorce, and Legitimacy* (2nd ed., 1860), p. 56 claimed that the concept of condonation had caused little difficulty to the Ecclesiastical Courts dealing with applications for divorce *a mensa et thoro* and that the meaning of the term was thought to be thoroughly understood. However, the 1857 Act made it necessary to define condonation when summing up the issues to a jury and this led to extensive exegisis.

[139] (1859) 1 Sw&Tr 334.

[140] High Sheriff for London and Middlesex and a partner in Fortnum & Mason, the high class Piccadilly provision merchants.

[141] Contrast an *agreement* whereby the offence was forgiven: compare *Rose v. Rose* (1883) 8 PD 98 (separation agreement) and *Fearn v. Fearn* [1948] 1 All ER 459 (no agreement, but simply 'plain words of absolute forgiveness' and hence no condonation).

Lord Chelmsford conjured up a picture in which every 'species of artifice or influence' would be used 'to extort from the injured party the healing words which are to be of such powerful and uncontrollable efficacy. The strong and sudden impulse of recollected affection, the importunity of friends, or the surprise of weakness, each of these might produce a hasty expression of forgiveness which, when once uttered would be irrevocable. How naturally, too, compassion for a guilty creature, associated with the remembrance of former days of happiness, would find vent in such an expression. Those who felt that perpetual separation must be the inevitable consequence of the unpardonable fault, might still anxiously desire to lighten the load of despair by some kind words of consolation and peace'. Such was not the forgiveness which amounted to condonation; on the contrary it was that 'which declares it to be impossible . . .'. The true view of condonation (a 'blotting out of the offence) involved the offending party being reinstated in the same position he or she occupied before the offence was committed'.

Reinstatement in former matrimonial position required

It did not follow from this that the guilty but forgiven wife must be kept in the style to which she had been accustomed before her fall from grace. By her infidelity the wife had 'forfeited all her title to be regarded as a wife' and the fact that the husband required her to live 'as a degraded wife' would not prevent the court holding the adultery to have been condoned[142] so that neither husband nor degraded wife could remarry.

Relevance of sexual intercourse

Condonation, then, involved reinstatement; but over the years the courts developed the doctrine that a man who, knowing that the wife had committed adultery, had sexual intercourse with her was thereby deemed conclusively to have condoned that adultery unless it could be shown that the intercourse was induced by the wife making a fraudulent misstatement of fact.[143] Thus:

In *Henderson v. Henderson and Crellin*[144] the husband told the wife that she must break completely all acquaintance with her lover. She agreed to do so. That night, at the wife's suggestion, husband and wife had sexual intercourse; but the next morning the wife said she had changed her mind and did not see why she should not go on seeing the other man. The husband immediately left, and never saw her again. The House of Lords held that he had condoned her adultery.

But the rule was not so inflexible where the question was whether *a wife* had condoned *her husband's* adultery by having intercourse with him. The law

---

[142] *Keats v. Keats and Montezuma* (1859) 1 Sw&Tr 334, 357, *per* Lord Chelmsford LC.
[143] For example, that she was not pregnant: *Roberts v. Roberts and Temple* (1917) 117 LT 157.
[144] [1944] AC 49 HL.

would *presume* that a wife who allowed her husband to have intercourse thereby condoned his adultery, but this presumption could be rebutted by evidence that she had not intended to forgive the offence. The reason for drawing this distinction between the sexes was said to be that it might 'be difficult for a wife immediately to break off relations with her husband'[145] and that a wife would suffer 'extreme prejudice' if she became pregnant as the result of the intercourse.[146]

Conditional forgiveness: revival of the condoned offence

The law presumed that the innocent spouse had told the guilty 'you shall not only abstain from adultery but shall in future treat me . . . with conjugal kindness; on this condition I will overlook the past injuries you have done me'[147] and accordingly implied[148] a condition that the guilty spouse would in the future[149] be true to the marriage vows.[150] It followed from this that the condoned offence would be revived if the guilty party either committed adultery or at any time in the future[151] committed an offence—such as cruelty, or desertion for however short a period—which would have founded the making by the Ecclesiastical Courts of a decree of divorce *a mensa et thoro*.[152] In effect, the bar of condonation continued 'only so long as the matrimonial conduct of the repentant spouse [remained] such as the divorce court [could] accept as

---

[145] *Report of the Royal Commission on Marriage and Divorce* (1956, Cmd. 9678) para. 237.

[146] *Tilley v. Tilley* [1948] 2 All ER 1113, 1123, *per* Denning LJ; *Fearn v. Fearn* [1948] 1 All ER 459 (condonation depended on guilty party being prejudiced, and sexual intercourse with wife (*per* Bucknill LJ, at p. 464) an 'extreme illustration of such prejudice').

[147] *Durant v. Durant* (1825) 1 Hagg. Ecc. 733, 762, *per* Sir John Nicholl; and see *Palmer v. Palmer* (1860) 2 Sw&Tr 61.

[148] A spouse condoning the other's adultery could impose an *express* condition; and the law allowed the parties by express agreement to exclude the possibility of revival of the condoned offence. At a time when divorce and the publicity attached to it could have very serious social and business consequences it was common for couples to make separation agreements dealing with the financial consequences of the breakdown of their relationship, and such agreements would often contain what was called a *Rose v. Rose* clause whereby the parties undertook not to take proceedings in respect of any existing cause of complaint and that all matrimonial offences committed by either party were to be treated as condoned. In *Rose v. Rose* (1883) 8 PD 98 the Court of Appeal held that in such a case the husband's subsequent adultery did not revive matrimonial offences committed by him before the separation agreement.

[149] There was also an implied condition that the guilty spouse had made a full disclosure of his guilt; and if there had been no proper disclosure, the condoned offence would be revived when the undisclosed offences came to light: *Dempster v. Dempster* (1861) 2 Sw&Tr 438.

[150] *Newsome v. Newsome* (1871) LR2P&D 306, 312, *per* Lord Penzance.

[151] Only in 1950 did the Court of Appeal question whether the 'probationary period' was lifelong so that a wife would be entitled to say that adultery condoned seven years previously was 'revived because on one occasion [the husband] has slapped her face': *Richardson v. Richardson* [1950] P 16; *Beale v. Beale* [1950] 2 All ER 539.

[152] It was often said that the effect of condonation was to 'blot out' the offence in question; and as Greer LJ put it in *Statham JT v. Statham JC* [1929] P 131, 146, CA, 'the condonation may itself be blotted out, and the right to complain of the condoned offence may be revived if after a condonation a new matrimonial offence, such as cruelty, is committed'.

consistent with matrimonial duty'.[153] The guilty spouse remained, in effect, on probation for many years.[154]

(iii) Collusion

The underlying concern of the legislature in making 'collusion' into an absolute bar to divorce[155] was primarily to ensure that divorce by mutual consent should remain 'remote from the contemplation of English law'. It was also intended to ensure that no material fact was kept from the court[156] and minimise the risk of parties manipulating the divorce process to achieve objectives inconsistent with public policy; and the courts emphasised the duty laid upon them of eliciting the whole truth so that they could be confident in the light of the true facts of the justice of the decision.[157] But the Act failed to provide any definition of collusion[158] and the meaning had to be worked out by the courts. They analysed the concept of collusion under a number of heads.[159]

The first type of collusion involved the parties agreeing to put forward a false case in order to obtain the divorce which they wanted.[160] The classic example of this kind of collusion was the bogus hotel case: the parties would agree that the husband should provide evidence of adultery which in fact was never committed.

In the second type of collusion the parties agreed to suppress a possible defence to the petition. For example, the fact that the petitioner had himself committed adultery was a discretionary bar to the grant of a divorce decree, and the court was for long unlikely to grant a decree in such a case. The temptation for a couple both anxious to remarry not to reveal the fact that each had

---

[153] *Beard v. Beard* [1946] P 8, 22, *per* Scott LJ.

[154] Note, however, the view that the doctrine of revival 'eased the task of wives seeking divorce' as for example in *Newsome v. Newsome* (1871) LR 2P&D 306, where a wife condoned her husband's incestuous adultery which was subsequently revived by his non-incestuous adultery (at the time not of itself sufficient to found a divorce petition by a wife): see R Probert, 'The controversy of equality and the Matrimonial Causes Act 1923' [1999] CFLQ 33, 36.

[155] See *First Report of the Commissioners . . . into the Law of Divorce . . .* (1853), para. XLVI.

[156] *Laidler v. Laidler* (1920) 36 TLR 510 (where merely asking the husband to provide evidence of the adultery he admitted was held not to constitute collusion).

[157] *Churchward v. Churchward and Holliday* [1895] P 7. The Matrimonial Causes Act 1860 was intended to provide the means whereby the court could carry out this duty: see above.

[158] The word has unpleasant overtones of fraud, conspiracy, and deceit; but it seems that it was often broadly interpreted by practitioners concerned that any discussion of the future might be regarded as collusive and thus debar the client from divorce: see below.

[159] See JF Macqueen, *A Practical Treatise on The Law of Marriage, Divorce and Legitimacy . . .* (2nd ed., 1860), p. 67; and (for a full statement of the developed case law) *Rayden's Practice and Law in the Divorce Division* (3rd ed., 1932, by C Mortimer and HHH Coates) pp. 117–120. *Churchward v. Churchward and Holliday (The Queen's Proctor intervening)* [1895] P 7, CA; and *Laidler v. Laidler* (1920) 36 TLR 510 are the most helpful judicial discussions of the concept and its early development.

[160] 'An agreement between the parties for one to commit or appear to commit an act of adultery in order that the other may obtain a remedy at law as for a real injury': *Crewe v. Crewe* (1800) 3 Hag. Ecc. 123, 130.

committed adultery was often not resisted;[161] but it was to be many years before the legislature was prepared to face the question whether it was really in the public interest to preserve the legal relationship of husband and wife between couples whose marriages had so completely broken down that both parties had established homes with other partners and had children with them.

The third type of collusion was often much more difficult to identify. The principle was that the court would withhold a decree from a petitioner if the facts on which he relied had been 'corruptly and fraudulently preconcerted'.[162] Thus:

In *Todd v. Todd*[163] the parties separated after living together for only six months; and the husband (owner of an Indian tea estate) promised his wife and her father that as soon as he was richer he would 'let her be honestly divorced'. His solicitor gave the wife's enquiry agent details of various addresses in France and Belgium where he intended staying, and the husband eventually wrote to the wife saying that he had 'performed his promise'. The wife petitioned; but the Judge Ordinary held that the husband had gone to Paris with the wife's consent for the express purpose of committing adultery and of being detected and that accordingly the court could not grant a divorce. The fact that the husband had had good motives[164] was irrelevant.

This type of collusion caused great difficulty because it raised the question of how far the parties could go in agreeing the consequences of ending their marriage. A wife might, for example, be reluctant to take proceedings unless her financial position was first secured. But if the court found that there had been a bargain between the parties (for example that the wife would petition on the basis of the husband's admitted adultery if, but only if, he paid her a lump sum and met all her legal expenses; or if he agreed that she should have custody of the children)[165] the court might well label the agreement collusive and reject the petition. The leading case, decided in 1895, was *Churchward v. Churchward and Holliday (The Queen's Proctor intervening)*:[166]

Husband and wife agreed that he would petition for divorce in order to allow the wife to marry the co-respondent. He was not to claim damages against the

---

[161] As Lord Merrivale P was to put it in *Apted v. Apted and Bliss* [1930] P 246, 262, there is an 'inevitable tendency to collusion' where both petitioner and respondent are guilty. The President reminded litigants that knowingly putting forward a false case constituted a contempt of court punishable by imprisonment.

[162] JF Macqueen, *A Practical Treatise on The Law of Marriage, Divorce and Legitimacy . . .* (2nd ed., 1860), p. 67, giving the example of a wife undertaking to pay the husband £1,000 in cash and an annuity of £600 in exchange for his sharing a bedroom at night with a woman expressly selected for the purpose of providing evidence.

[163] (1865) LR 1P&D 121.

[164] It appears that he had persuaded the wife to marry against the wishes of her family, and that the relationship had never been happy.

[165] *Irving v. Irving (King's Proctor showing cause)* (1931) *The Times* 4 November.

[166] [1895] P 7.

co-respondent;[167] and she agreed to settle capital on the child of the marriage, to pay the costs of the proceedings, and not to defend the petition. All this was disclosed to the President when the case came on for hearing, and he referred the papers to the Queen's Proctor, who intervened. The petition was rejected: the court held that it was bound to reject a petition whenever the initiation of a divorce suit had been procured, or its conduct determined by agreement (especially an agreement not to defend). It was immaterial that no specific fact had been falsely dealt with or withheld. The underlying principle was that a petitioner had to appear before the court 'in the character of an injured [spouse] seeking relief from an intolerable wrong'. The fact that the petitioner was acting in concert with the respondent cast doubt on whether that was so.

This wide interpretation of collusion undoubtedly discouraged couples from even discussing the financial arrangements and the upbringing of their children until they had actually been divorced; but it was many years before this became a matter of expressed concern.

DISCRETIONARY BARS TO DIVORCE

(i) Petitioner's adultery

The Campbell Royal Commission recommended that a petitioner who had committed adultery should be debarred from obtaining a divorce. If both parties were guilty neither should be able to 'claim the vindication of a law which each has broken, nor reasonably complain of the breach of a contract which each has violated'.[168] But if both husband and wife had demonstrated their unworthiness as spouses might there not be a case for no longer seeking to hold them within the solemn estate of matrimony?

The 1857 Act[169] appeared to compromise between these two views: it provided that the court 'should not be bound to pronounce' a decree of divorce if it found the petitioner to have been guilty but that it should have a discretion to do so. In practice, for many years the courts (believing their role to be to 'promote virtue and morality and to discourage vice and immorality')[170] would exercise this discretion only in cases of an exceptional character.[171] The pattern

---

[167] See Chapter 4, above.

[168] *First Report of the Commissioners . . . into the Law of Divorce . . .* (1853), para. XLI, BPP 1852–3 vol. 40 p. 249.

[169] s. 31.

[170] *Constantinidi v. Constantinidi and Lance* [1905] P 253, 278, *per* Stirling LJ.

[171] In the extraordinary case of *Lautour v. Her Majesty's Proctor* (1864) 10 HLC 685 (where the petitioner, General Lautour failed to disclose the fact that for 25 years he had been 'cohabiting with a female and habitually committing adultery with her') Lord Westbury LC seems almost to say that the discretion to grant a decree should never be exercised.

was set in 1865 by the Judge Ordinary's decision in *Clarke v. Clarke and Clarke*:[172]

The wife left her husband (apparently without cause or reason) in 1862. Although the husband said he never expected to see her again, she returned after eight or nine months. But the reconciliation did not last long. In March 1864 she eloped with her husband's brother and was still living with him at the time of the hearing. The husband petitioned for divorce, and the wife did not defend. He disclosed the fact that on one occasion after his wife had deserted him he had committed adultery with a woman he had never seen before or since; and his counsel argued that his case was one 'in which, if ever, the discretion of the Court ought to be exercised' in his favour. The Court disagreed.

Again:

In *Wyke v. Wyke (The King's Proctor showing cause)*[173] the husband committed adultery and was often cruel to his wife (the mother of three children). She left, got a job as a barmaid, and over three years saved up the money necessary to petition for divorce. She was granted a decree *nisi*; but the King's Proctor found out that after the decree *nisi* she had gone to live with another man and intervened. She explained that she had been ill, lost her job, and was not able to find another situation because she was no longer capable of hard manual work; and that 'this young gentleman asked me to go and live with him, it was the only thing left for me to do, as I had expended all my earnings, which I had saved up, on the decree, to get what I wanted, so that I could marry again'. The decree was set aside. The judge said that 'no feeling of sympathy . . . on behalf of an ill-treated woman . . . can be entertained; nor may I listen to the appeal that she made to me, that if she can obtain her divorce today, another man is ready to marry her and take her child'.

The Divorce Court believed itself to be a court of morals. In *Evans v. Evans and Elford*[174] for example:

The five-year marriage of a butler broke down because (he alleged) of his wife's drunken and dissipated habits. He paid her 12/-[175]weekly maintenance and furnished a home for her (although he claimed that she had continued her drunken habits, on several occasions selling up the home in order to procure drink). In 1902 he petitioned for divorce on the ground of her adultery; but the King's Proctor (having discovered that two years after the separation the husband had started a relationship with a cook as a result of which two children were born) successfully intervened. In 1905 the husband found out that his wife had again committed adultery, and he again petitioned for divorce, seeking the exercise of the court's discretion in respect of his admitted adultery with the cook (which, he claimed, had ceased). Sir Gorrell Barnes P predictably held that it would 'not

---

[172] (1865) 34 LJ(PA&M) 94.   [173] [1904] P 149, Bucknill J.   [174] [1906] P 125.
[175] 60 pence—some £35 in year 2000 values.

be in the interests of society and public morality and purity' to grant a decree in such circumstances. It was (said the President) the husband's case that his wife was 'a drunken and immoral woman, but he himself has been guilty of gross immorality. After he separated from his wife, he debauched his fellow-servant—a serious offence in a household, especially having regard to the risks and temptations to which female servants are exposed owing to the necessary continued proximity in which they are placed with others. It is an offence which may have disastrous consequences to the woman, both as regards character and employment. His intercourse with her extended over a lengthy period, and resulted in the birth of two illegitimate children. He now says[176] this was caused by his wife's misconduct. How this can really be so I fail to see. It is true that the cause of the separation was . . . his wife's conduct; but how can this justify his own immorality? . . . [I]s it to be said that every case [in which husband and wife have to live apart, he or she] is to be at liberty to commit adultery, and that if he or she is in a position to prove adultery against the other party . . . his or her own adultery is to be excused if the separation is due to the conduct of the other?'

The principle to be applied was clear:

A 'loose and unfettered discretion . . . upon matters of such grave import, is a dangerous weapon to entrust to any court, still more so to a single judge. Its exercise is likely to be the refuge of vagueness in decision, and the harbour of half-formed thought . . . the result is apt to be coloured with the general prejudices, favourable or otherwise' to the person concerned. Accordingly where the petitioner's adultery had no special circumstances attending it, and no special features placing it in some category capable of distinct statement and recognition, there would be great mischief in this Court assuming to itself a right to grant or withhold a divorce 'merely because the adultery could be seen as more or less pardonable or excusable'.[177]

Yet the Act did envisage that there would be some cases in which there was such 'palliation of matrimonial infidelity by a petitioner . . . that public morality will not be outraged by the exercise of judicial discretion';[178] and in those cases a decree could be granted notwithstanding that the petitioner had himself been guilty of adultery. The court's approach to the exercise of this discretion was highly restrictive, and there were only three situations in which the court accepted that it could be proper to exercise discretion to dissolve a marriage at the instance of the adulterous spouse. First, there was so-called 'innocent adultery':[179] the courts accepted that it would not seriously damage the 'spirit of

---

[176] It is tempting to think that this may have been prompted by his lawyers' explanation of the 'causal responsibility' principle, explained below.

[177] *Morgan v. Morgan and Porter* (1869) LR 1P&M 644, 647, *per* Lord Penzance.

[178] *Evans v. Evans and Alford* [1906] P 125, 127, *per* Sir Gorell Barnes P.

[179] This is the terminology employed by Sir William Jowitt AG *arguendo* in *Apted v. Apted and Bliss* [1930] P 246, a decision which marked a much more flexible approach to the exercise of the discretion: see below.

public morality'[180] underlying the 1857 Act to allow divorce to a man who had 'married' after his wife's conduct had led him to believe that she was dead.[181]

Secondly, there was 'unwilling adultery': the court would not withhold a decree from a woman whose husband had literally driven her to prostitution:

In the 1866 case of *Coleman v. Coleman*[182] the husband began to batter his wife within three weeks of their marriage, frequently beating her, knocking her down, and even threatening to kill her. He refused to find work, sold all the furniture which the wife had bought, and then deserted her for a period of two years. During this time, the wife made a living by needlework and dressmaking; but when the husband came back he told her that she must (in her words) 'go on the streets, and get money for him by prostitution. I refused to go. He insisted that I should go. I begged and entreated him to get work, and to help me to get a living, but he would not. . . . He said there was nothing left for it but my going on the streets, and he would murder me if I did not. We were in great want, and the landlord had threatened to seize for rent. He took me out into the streets, and waited till I had received money from gentlemen, and took the money away from me, and I went home. He saw me crying, and laughed at me. . . . He took me into the streets day after day. . . . He used to spend the money I gave him in drinking and gambling. . . . I was not a consenting party to this mode of life. It was forced on me by his violence. I was in constant terror of him . . . '. The Judge Ordinary referred to the presumption in the criminal law (as it was at the time) that a wife was acting under the influence of her husband and should thus be excused from criminal liability for her acts, and held that a similar principle could 'very reasonably be called in aid to solve any difficulty that may seem to arise . . ., and to guide the discretion of the court'. The wife was accordingly granted a decree by reason of the husband's cruelty and of the adultery he was proved to have committed after the final separation.

Thirdly and lastly, there was 'condoned adultery': the court might allow a husband a decree notwithstanding his own adultery[183] if the wife had condoned that adultery and the husband was able to convince the court[184] that his behaviour

---

[180] *Constantinidi v. Constantinidi and Lance* [1905] P 253, 278, *per* Stirling LJ.

[181] *Joseph v. Joseph and Wenzell* (1865) LJPM&A 96.   [182] (1866) LR 1 P&D 81.

[183] Some judges, recognising the 'weakness of the female sex' (see *per* Bargrave Dean J, *Pretty v. Pretty* [1911] P. 83, 89) were markedly readier to exercise discretion in favour of a wife petitioner; and in *Habra v. Habra and Habal* [1914] P 100 Bargrave Dean J stated that he had never previously exercised his discretion in favour of an adulterous husband but had 'always distinguished between the weakness of women and the weakness of men in such cases'. On the facts of that case, however, he did grant the petitioner husband a decree: the husband had made a full disclosure of his adultery, which had in any event been condoned and could be attributed to the wife's repeated refusal to live with him; whilst the wife, who had become a common prostitute in Damascus, had been guilty of 'continual and promiscuous adultery'.

[184] The doctrine of causal responsibility was never wholly accepted: see *Evans v. Evans and Alford* [1906] P 125, 126–127; *Apted v. Apted and Bliss* [1930] P 246.

had in no way been responsible for the wife's subsequent breach of her marital obligations.[185]

Even in these three exceptional cases, the petitioner would usually fail unless the person seeking the exercise of the court's discretion had made a full and frank disclosure of his or her adultery. Even here, however, broad considerations of public policy sometimes allowed departures from principle:

In the remarkable case of *Pretty v. Pretty (The King's Proctor shewing cause)*[186] the petitioner wife, the daughter of 'respectable parents' was seduced by a groom in her father's employ and then 'finding herself pregnant by him, secretly went off and, when little more than a child' married him. . . . In due course her child was born, and she experienced at the hands of her husband the grossest cruelty, and, apart from actual assaults, the most odious conduct; and, eventually, he also committed adultery. The judge concluded that she 'was practically forced to leave her husband's home'. But she had made the acquaintance of one Halfpenny (a cab-driver employed by her husband) and—'her moral calibre' long gone—travelled to New Zealand with him. The jury, notwithstanding her denials on oath under cross-examination, found[187] that she had committed adultery with Halfpenny. In deciding that it would be proper to exercise the discretion to grant a decree in favour of a petitioner guilty of perjury, the judge seems to have been strongly influenced by the view that 'the woman is the weaker vessel: . . . her habits of thought and feminine weaknesses are different from those of the man: and . . . what may perhaps be excusable in the case of the woman would not be excusable in the case of the man'. More specifically, to rescind the decree (and thereby tie her for the rest of her life to the man who had seduced her and whose vile treatment made their living together impossible) would result in 'absolute ruin' for a young woman of 21 whose life had been 'fairly described as a tragedy'; whereas to allow the decree to stand would allow her to marry the 'gentleman in her own original sphere of life' who had fallen in love with her and would 'lift her up out of the slough of misery and distress and despair into which, through her husband, she has fallen'.

[185] This seems to have been the situation envisaged by the Judge Ordinary in *Clarke v. Clarke and Clarke* (1865) 34 LJ(PA&M) 94: 'a case may arise where a husband many years before his wife's adultery may have fallen a victim to some sudden impulse and may have committed an act of adultery, which has been followed by long cohabitation with his wife; and in such a case the Court might hold that he was entitled to relief, notwithstanding his misconduct'. But the test of causal responsibility (apparently founded on two decisions of Sir Francis Jeune P at first instance: *Symons v. Symons (The Queen's Proctor Intervening)* [1897] P 167, and *Constantinidi v. Constantinidi* [1903] P 246) produced some striking decisions: see for example *McCord v. McCord* (1875) LR 1 P&D 237, Sir James Hannen P (an actress's husband had on a single occasion during the marriage committed adultery. His wife forgave this lapse, and the couple continued to cohabit. But the President refused to exercise discretion in the husband's favour, saying that it was 'in the highest degree probable that his conduct tended to weaken [the wife's] sense of obligation of the marriage contract, and so conduced to her guilt').

[186] [1911] P 83.

[187] And the judge stated that he agreed and that the jury could not properly have come to any other conclusion: see at p. 85.

This was obviously an unusual case; and the statistics confirm that it was wholly exceptional for the courts to exercise discretion in favour of an adulterous petitioner: in only 64 cases in the first 50 years of the divorce court's existence[188] did petitioners even ask for the exercise of the court's discretion in their favour; and the facts of some of the cases in which the exercise of the discretion was sought but refused make the apparent reluctance entirely understandable.[189]

(ii) Other discretionary bars to divorce

There were two other 'discretionary bars' to divorce. Both reflected the policy that a petitioner should be an innocent person labouring under an intolerable grievance. The first appears to have been a statutory codification of the bar known in the Ecclesiastical Courts as 'recrimination'. The court was not bound to grant a decree to a petitioner guilty of cruelty to the other party, or to a petitioner who had 'deserted or wilfully separated himself or herself from the other party before the adultery complained of, or to a petitioner guilty of such "wilful neglect or misconduct" as had conduced to the adultery'.[190] In these cases, in effect, the petitioner had brought the problem on himself:

In *Baylis v. Baylis*[191] a young man (in the Judge Ordinary's words) married a woman of loose character, with whom he had lived for nine months previously.[192] They disagreed about money. He accused her of extravagance, and she him of parsimony. At last he broke up the house, sold his furniture, and told his wife she must go and live by herself in the Regent Street chambers he had occupied when a bachelor. As soon as she went there he set a watch over her, and soon detected her in adultery. 'In truth, she made little concealment of it, saying she must have a protector, and would not live alone. The result is this suit. But the court cannot grant the petitioner a divorce . . . [A] husband is at all times bound to accord to his wife the protection of his name, his home, and his society, and is certainly not the less so in cases where the previous life of his wife renders her peculiarly accessible to temptation. No man is justified in turning his wife from his house without reasonable cause, and then claiming a divorce on account of the misconduct to which he has by so doing conduced. And this I am of opinion the petitioner did.'[193] The judge evidently did not consider it

---

[188] *Apted v. Apted and Bliss* [1930] P 246, 254.

[189] Only after the First World War did the courts come to accept that changes in society since 1857 made it essential to formulate new rules to determine the principles upon which the court would be prepared to allow a 'guilty' petitioner to have the divorce which he—and usually his spouse—desired: see below.

[190] Matrimonial Causes Act 1857, s. 31.   [191] (1867) LR 1 P&D 395.

[192] Subsequent cases established that a man who had lived with his wife before their marriage was under an obligation to take especial care of her in view of his knowledge of her propensities: *Hawkins v. Hawkins* (1885) 10 PD 177.

[193] Note that the misconduct must have been directed at the other spouse: a man sent to prison for theft would not be guilty of misconduct conducing to her adultery, even though that adultery was the foreseeable consequence of his incarceration: *Cunnington v. Cunnington* (1859) 1 Sw&Tr 475.

necessary to discuss exercising the discretion to grant the husband a divorce notwithstanding his culpability.

The second of these remaining bars was that the court was not obliged to grant a decree to a petitioner 'guilty of unreasonable delay in presenting or prosecuting' the petition.[194] Such delay might indicate that the petitioner did not find his spouse's behaviour intolerable;[195] but frequently the explanation for the failure to take immediate action was the need to accumulate the substantial funds needed to meet the costs involved.[196] It seems that in practice this bar caused the courts little difficulty.[197]

DIVORCE: THE IMPACT OF THE 1857 ACT

Discussion of the courts' interpretation of the 1857 Act demonstrates (if nothing else) that at the beginning of the twentieth century a restrictively drawn statute was being restrictively interpreted by the courts. But it seems that few of those who petitioned were, in the end, denied the divorce they sought. In the first three years of its existence,[198–199] the Court for Divorce and Matrimonial Causes granted 416 divorce decrees, and rejected a mere 29 petitions;[200] and there is no reason to suppose that the ratio altered very much over the years. But this tells us little if anything about the impact of legal doctrine on practice. On the one hand, skilled legal advisers came to know how to present the law to the client so that the client would be able to give an account of the breakdown emphasising those matters which the law regarded as relevant and perhaps passing over those which the law regarded as irrelevant; on the other hand, there is no way of quantifying the cases in which there was clearly no point in expending time and money on drawing up a petition which would be bound to fail.

In numerical terms, there seems no doubt that there were more petitions under the new legislation than had been expected. Before 1858, there had been a mere handful of parliamentary divorce petitions;[201] but the Court for Divorce and Matrimonial Causes found itself dealing with more than 200 divorce petitions each year.[202] Not for the last time new procedures had to be introduced to

---

[194] Matrimonial Causes Act 1857, s. 31.

[195] See eg *Mason v. Mason and McClure* (1882) 7 PD 233.

[196] See eg *Harrison v. Harrison* (1864) 3 Sw&Tr 362 (separation in 1834, wife took in needlework to provide subsistence, husband a vagabond, of no fixed address, and occasionally employed as drover; wife's petition allowed notwithstanding delay).

[197] *Rayden on Practice and Law in the Divorce Division* (1st ed., 1910) p. 88.

[198–199] Between January 1858 (when the 1857 Act came into force: see s. 1) and July 1861.

[200] *Returns relating to Divorce and Matrimonial Causes* (1862) BPP vol. 44, pp. 503–518.

[201] There had been a total of 22 in the seven years between 1850 and 1857: see Table 10.1 in L Stone, *Road to Divorce, England 1530–1987* (1990) p. 432.

[202] There were between 200 and 250 petitions in each year (save for 1861 when there were 161) between 1858 and 1868: *Report of the Royal Commission on Marriage and Divorce* (1956, Cmd. 9678), Appendix II, Table 1.

enable the court to avoid building up arrears[203] on a scale which would constitute a denial of justice.[204] The number of petitions increased rapidly from the
1870s; and in 1900 the Court made 494 decrees.[205] It was difficult to deny that
divorce had become somewhat[206] more accessible and there were (and are)
those who believe that making divorce 'easier' affects attitudes towards marriage. Lord Redesdale,[207] for example, claimed in 1860 that:

'Everything which had occurred in the Divorce Court since it had been established had
done much to lessen in the country the sanctity of the matrimonial tie . . . [T]he marriage
tie was no longer regarded by the people of this country with the sanctity that had hitherto attached to it. . . . At present divorce was brought within the reach of men of moderate means. The cry would soon be raised to bring it within the reach of men of any
means; and he believed that an attempt would be made to have divorces settled in other
and cheaper courts . . . '

Whatever may be thought about Lord Redesdale's views on the relationship
between the divorce law and popular respect for marriage (and the argument
continues to rage more than a century later) his predictions about the future
were, as we shall see, to be proved remarkably accurate.

[203] According to Lord Lyndhurst (an active supporter of reform) in the first two and a quarter
years of its existence, the court had dealt with 177 of the 509 petitions filed but 232 remained to be
heard: *Hansard's Parliamentary Debates* (3rd Series) 17 April 1860, vol. 157, col. 1877 and see col.
1874.
[204] See *per* Lord Lyndhurst, *Hansard's Parliamentary Debates* (3rd Series) 17 April 1860, vol. 157,
col. 1875.
[205] *Report of the Royal Commission on Marriage and Divorce* (1956, Cmd. 9678) Appendix II,
Table 2.
[206] Note the assessment made by Professor OR McGregor (in *Divorce in England, A Centenary
Study* (1957) p. 22 that the 1857 Act was ineffective in remedying the fact that there was one law for
those who could afford to bring a suit for divorce in London and another for the 'large majority of
the population' who could not.
[207] *Hansard's Parliamentary Debates* (3rd Series) 17 April 1860, vol. 157, cols. 1871–1882.

6

The Campaign for Reform of the Victorian Divorce Law

INTRODUCTION

The Matrimonial Causes Act 1857 may have made divorce somewhat more accessible; but the previous chapter will have made it clear that many people locked into an unhappy marriage could not hope to get the 'relief' which the law offered to some. Sometimes the reason was that they had no legal grounds for divorce; sometimes it was that, although in theory they had such grounds, they lacked the financial resources necessary to bring their case before the Divorce Court.

The expense of bringing matrimonial cases to court was often associated with the fact that divorce suits could be heard only by the court in London; this chapter begins, by way of background to later developments, with a brief outline of the changes made in the structure of the courts dealing with marriage breakdown in the latter part of the nineteenth century. The rest of the chapter deals with the long campaign for reform of the divorce law which eventually led (80 years after the passing of the 1857 Act) to a measure of reform.

THE COURTS

From the Court for Divorce and Matrimonial Causes to the Probate Admiralty and Divorce Division of the High Court

Parliament had taken pains to ensure that the Matrimonial Causes Act 1857 conveyed a very clear message about the importance of divorce: the process of dissolving marriage was to be invested with the full majesty of the law. The Lord Chancellor, the Lord Chief Justice of the Court of Common Pleas, the Lord Chief Justice of the Court of Queen's Bench, the Lord Chief Baron of the Court of Exchequer, and the senior puisne judge of each of the courts of Common Pleas Queen's Bench and Exchequer were all to be judges of the Court[1] along with the Judge Ordinary.[2] The Judge Ordinary sitting alone could exercise the court's jurisdiction to grant separation or restitution decrees; but he had to sit

---

[1] Matrimonial Causes Act 1857, s. 8.

[2] For the evolution of the Judge Ordinary into the President of the Probate, Divorce and Admiralty Division of the High Court, see note 14 and the text thereto, below.

with two of the other judges of the court in divorce and nullity cases.[3] The special and distinctive nature of the Court's jurisdiction was emphasised by requiring it to carry out an inquisition into the facts of every case rather than merely accepting the evidence the parties chose to put before it.

It very soon became clear that these attempts to demonstrate that divorce was 'different' were far too ambitious. In particular, it was found difficult to muster the three judges required to deal with divorce and nullity cases. In 1859 a half-hearted attempt was made[4] to increase judge-power by appointing the judges of the Queen's Bench as judges of the Court for Divorce and Matrimonial Causes. Not surprisingly this failed: those judges (said the Lord Chancellor)[5] were unable to find time to spare. In 1860[6] Parliament agreed to abolish the require-ment[7] that dissolution and nullity petitions should be heard by three judges. But this did not go without a struggle: the Lord Chancellor might claim that to insist on three judges was a 'mere waste of judicial power' and point out that a single judge was allowed to decide issues of life and death, but the opponents of the 1857 legislation could plausibly claim that the legislature would never have agreed to a single judge having the power to dissolve[8] marriage.[9] The 1860 Act allowed the Judge Ordinary to sit alone (although he was given express power to sit with another judge of the court if he deemed it expedient to have such assistance[10] and to direct that cases be heard by the full court of three judges).[11]

The 1860 legislation was of some importance in the development of the fam-ily justice system; but further (and much more significant) change was in the air. The whole court structure had evolved without any rational plan;[12] and the Commissioners appointed to make 'full and diligent inquiry' into the structure of the courts recommended that the Courts of Admiralty Divorce and Probate be consolidated into 'one Chamber or Division of the Supreme Court'.[13] The Supreme Court of Judicature Act 1873 gave effect to this recommendation, and created the Probate, Divorce and Admiralty Division of the High Court and made the Judge Ordinary the President of the Division.[14]

---

[3] Matrimonial Causes Act 1857, s. 9.   [4] Matrimonial Causes Act 1859, s. 1.

[5] Lord Campbell LC, *Hansard's Parliamentary Debates* (3rd Series) 17 April 1860, vol. 157, col. 1874.

[6] Matrimonial Causes Act 1860, s. 1.   [7] Matrimonial Causes Act 1857, s. 10.

[8] It had been thought that a three-judge tribunal would be better able to detect collusion than a single judge; and for this reason the 1860 Act provided machinery for the court to refer cases to the Queen's Proctor.

[9] See *per* Lord St Leonards, *Hansard's Parliamentary Debates* (3rd Series) 17 April 1860, vol. 157, col. 1876 and also *per* Lord Cranworth at col. 1879.

[10] Matrimonial Causes Act 1860, s. 1.   [11] Matrimonial Causes Act 1860, s. 2.

[12] B Abel-Smith and R Stevens, *Lawyers and the Courts* (1967) p. 48. This book contains the best accessible account of developments in the court system in divorce and other family matters.

[13] *First Report of the Commissioners* (1869) BPP 1868–1869 vol. 25, p. 9.

[14] Supreme Court of Judicature Act 1873, ss. 3, 31(5). The Supreme Court of Judicature Act 1884, s. 3, gave the President of the Division the rank and precedence of a Lord Justice of Appeal; and the Administration of Justice Act 1920 gave the President precedence next after the Master of the Rolls. This was (according to Lord Chancellor Birkenhead) intended to give formal recognition to the President's responsibility for 'vast interests and . . . a considerable patronage': *Points of View* (1922) p. 44. Even so, it remained difficult to find suitably qualified lawyers prepared to serve as President: see below.

Wives, wills and wrecks: unhappy bedfellows

This amalgamation of three apparently so different types of work ('wives, wills and wrecks' as AP Herbert was to describe the business of the Division) was not self-evidently rational. It is true that there was a genuine historical link between probate and matrimonial work: both classes of work had been dealt with in the Ecclesiastical Courts, and the specialists who practised[15] in those courts developed a knowledge of both subjects;[16] and the fact that the 1857 Act constituted the same person Judge of the Court of Probate and Judge Ordinary of the Court for Divorce and Matrimonial Causes[17] evidenced this historical association. The modern reader might also find a justification for putting Probate and Matrimonial work into the one Division of the High Court in the fact that both types of work have to do with the family and its functioning. But the decision to transfer the jurisdiction of the High Court of Admiralty[18] to the same Division is much more difficult to justify. The argument that admiralty law is also to some extent derived from the Civil Law carries little conviction: there really is 'no likeness between . . . a collision at sea or a salvage operation . . . and a petition for the severance of the marriage tie'.[19]

This mismatch was not simply an academic problem of classification. The decision to use the admiralty jurisdiction as a make-weight[20] in the structural rationalisation of the 1870s soon caused practical problems. In particular, it proved difficult to find lawyers able and willing[21] to undertake both admiralty

---

[15] 'The jurisdiction of the newly constituted Probate, Divorce and Admiralty Division was by nature and origin unfamiliar to the old common law and chancery courts. The lawyers who had practised in the old ecclesiastical courts were specialists, doctors and proctors and even had their own Inn, known as Doctors' Commons . . .': Lord Gardiner LC moving the Second Reading of the Administration of Justice Bill, *Official Report* (HL) 4 December 1969, vol. 306, col. 197. Lord Gardiner invited peers to refresh their memories of the account of Doctors' Commons given by Charles Dickens in *David Copperfield* (1849–50) Chapter 23; and reference may also be made to Dickens' *Sketches by Boz* (1836) Chapter 8. A scholarly account is to be found in GD Squibb, *Doctors' Commons* (1977); and see p. 162, note 7, above.

[16] *Report of the Royal Commission on the Despatch of Business at Common Law 1934–6*, (Chairman: Earl Peel) (1936, Cmd. 5065) BPP 1935–6, xi, 105, para. 169.

[17] Matrimonial Causes Act 1857, s. 9.

[18] A court of great antiquity but limited jurisdiction, made a court of record by the Admiralty Court Act 1861, s. 14.

[19] *Report of the Royal Commission on the Despatch of Business at Common Law 1934–6* (Chairman: Earl Peel) (1936, Cmd. 5065) BPP 1935–6, xi, 105, para. 169.

[20] In 1969, Lord Gardiner LC, moving the Second Reading of the Administration of Justice Bill (which abolished the Probate Divorce and Admiralty Division and created the Family Division of the High Court) claimed that in the 1870s 'there was so little matrimonial business that no one would have dreamt of constituting a Division of the High Court especially to deal with it': *Official Report* (HL) 4 December 1969, vol. 306, col. 197.

[21] At that time, many Roman Catholics were not prepared to accept appointment to the bench if this would involve their pronouncing divorce decrees; and in 1920 Lord Phillimore (who favoured the abolition of the Divorce division) pointed out that the two leading advocates then practising in admiralty were Roman Catholics and 'would feel unable to accept office in a Division in which more than half of their work would be in Divorce cases'. Phillimore thought that such persons would, in contrast, be prepared to take such work as it came if it were merely an incident in their case-load 'just as a vacation judge does now': Memorandum dated 11 June 1920 by Lord Phillimore: PRO LCO2/460.

and divorce work or even to accept office as President of the Probate Divorce and Admiralty Division[22] and the standing of the Division was to suffer. As we shall see, this made it all the more difficult to justify restricting the power to grant divorces to a single Court sitting exclusively in London, with all the implications for expense which that entailed.

Courts for the working classes: the domestic jurisdiction of magistrates

None of this really affected the problem of access to the courts: the working classes often could not afford the expense of travelling to London and paying their witnesses travelling expenses. One answer, suggested in the debates on the 1857 Act, would have been to allow the county courts (originally established in 1844 and by the 1870s well established as a nationwide system of local, professional[23] adjudication of civil claims)[24] to deal with at any rate certain categories of divorce. But the Government had found no difficulty in discovering plausible objections to such a notion in 1857;[25] and it only began to be advocated again after the beginning of the twentieth century.

Such matters were controversial, and certainly proposals to set up the Divorce Court in 1857 had attracted debate and discussion. Surprisingly, therefore, there was virtually no debate or discussion of the creation in the last quarter of the nineteenth century of a parallel system of matrimonial justice administered in what has, somewhat emotively, been described as 'inferior tribunals, given over to the criminal process, and universally known, because of their close association with the police, as "police courts"'. How this happened was explained by Professor McGregor and Sir Morris Finer a century later:[26]

---

[22] This remained a problem. As late as 1933, Sir Claud Schuster told the *Business of the Courts Committee* (Chairman: Lord Hanworth) that '. . . difficult as it has been from time to time to find puisne Judges for the Division, the difficulty of finding Presidents has been greater still. The President of the Division must necessarily be a man of eminence in the profession . . . but men of eminence have shrunk from accepting the position. Thus, on the death of Sir Samuel Evans [in 1918], Lord Sterndale . . . was only persuaded to accept the position upon a representation being made to him that it was his duty to do so on patriotic grounds, regard being had to the difficult duties still to be discharged by the President during the War. Similarly, upon the translation of Lord Sterndale to the Mastership of the Rolls, direct and vehement pressure was needed to induce Lord Merrivale to accept the position. Both these eminent Judges regarded the change as most distasteful to themselves, as taking them away from work which they enjoyed, and as compelling them to devote themselves to an extremely laborious and, in many respects, repulsive occupation'. And it appeared that solicitors with shipping practices were not prepared to take the risk of cases coming before a judge unskilled in admiralty law.

[23] County court judges had to be barristers of seven years standing: for the refusal to extend eligibility to solicitors, see B Abel-Smith and R Stevens, *Lawyers and the Courts* (1967) pp. 34–36.

[24] See generally P Polden, *A History of the County Court 1846–1971* (1999).

[25] See B Abel-Smith and R Stevens, *Lawyers and the Courts* (1967) p. 42.

[26] *Report of the Committee on One-Parent Families*, Appendix 5, pp. 104–105 Chairman: Sir M Finer (1974, Cmnd. 5629). On the phenomenon of wife battering, see ME Doggett, *Marriage, Wife-Beating and the Law in Victorian England* (1992) and generally on the attempts made in the last quarter of the twentieth century to provide effective remedies for victims see Chapter 21, below.

'By the early 1870s, the spread of crimes of violence had become a much agitated "law and order" issue, and lawyers and politicians were drawing particular attention to the ill-usage and sufferings of working-class wives. The evil was described and a remedy proposed in Frances Power Cobbe's pamphlet, *Wife Torture* . . . In 1878, Parliament adopted Miss Cobbe's proposals. Lord Penzance had a bill before the House of Lords dealing with the costs of the Queen's Proctor. He tacked on a clause which gave the magistrates' courts power to grant a separation order . . .'

The Matrimonial Causes Act 1878 empowered magistrates to make orders that a wife be no longer bound to cohabit with a husband who had been convicted of assaulting her. Under the 1878 Act this power was only exercisable in narrowly defined circumstances;[27] but by the end of the century the scope of the magistrates' courts' powers was considerably extended. In 1886 the Married Women (Maintenance in Cases of Desertion) Act gave a wife who had been deserted by her husband a direct financial remedy against him.[28] Instead of being compelled to enter the workhouse[29] until the Poor Law authorities were able to take action against her husband to compel him to meet his obligation to maintain her,[30] she could take out a summons. If the court was satisfied that she had been deserted and that the husband was able wholly or in part to maintain her but had wilfully refused or neglected to do so it could order him to pay her a weekly sum not exceeding £2. The Summary Jurisdiction (Married Women) Act 1895 tidied up the legislation;[31] and the code thus cre-

---

[27] The court had to be satisfied that the wife's future safety was in peril; and it has been suggested that this gave magistrates an excuse to avoid interfering with patriarchal prerogative, 'even when marital authority has been enforced by the breaking of arms or jaw, by throttling to well-nigh strangulation, by cutting with knives, by biting, kicking, and striking with clenched fist, [and] by dragging upstairs and downstairs by the hair'. But if made the order had effect in all respects as a decree of judicial separation granted on the ground of cruelty: Matrimonial Causes Act 1878, s. 4; see *Dodd v. Dodd* [1906] P 189, 200, *per* Sir Gorrell Barnes.

[28] The Bill as introduced would have allowed the magistrates also to make separation and custody orders based solely on desertion, but the Government opposed this as going 'much too far': see *Official Report* (HC) 24 March 1886, vol. 303, col. 1770; 5 May 1886, vol. 305, col. 344; and 16 June 1886 vol. 306, col. 1672.

[29] A Metropolitan Magistrate told the Gorrell Commission that although a deserted working class woman in Bermondsey could 'sometimes drag along with the aid of friends' she would often be 'driven to the workhouse in a week or a fortnight'. It appears that the Poor Law authorities were reluctant to allow married women claiming to have been deserted so-called 'outdoor relief' for fears that they were acting in collusion with their husbands: see *Report of the Committee on One-Parent Families* (Chairman, the Hon. Sir M Finer) (1974, Cmnd. 5629) Appendix 5 paras. 68–69.

[30] The Poor Law authorities had a right to reimbursement from the husband of the cost of any relief given to a married woman or his children: see Poor Law Amendment Act 1868, s. 33 (the relevant provisions being subsequently consolidated in Poor Law Act 1927, ss. 41 and 43) and generally LN Brown (1955)18 MLR 110, 112–116.

[31] The Bill's promoter (EW Byrne) stated that it was intended to get 'rid of some of the anomalies which exist in the civil law and the criminal law in cases of aggravated assaults on wives by husbands and . . . to give similar relief in cases of persistent cruelty by a husband towards a wife as now exists in cases of aggravated assault': *Official Report* (HC) (4th Series) 22 May 1895, vol. 34, col. 62. Apart from that the Bill seems to have passed through both Houses of Parliament with little discussion.

ated[32] remained the basis for the magistrates' matrimonial jurisdiction[33] for more than 70 years.[34]

Divorce for the working classes?

In one respect, the magistrates' matrimonial jurisdiction was extremely successful. By the beginning of the twentieth century far more orders were made by magistrates' courts than by the Divorce Court: in 1900, the Divorce Court granted 494 divorce decrees and 19 judicial separations[35] but magistrates were at the same period making more than 5,000 orders each year. Most of these magistrates' orders included the provision (originally intended to deal with husbands convicted of violence) that the parties be no longer bound to cohabit, and had precisely the same effect as a decree of judicial separation. 'Relief' for matrimonial problems could therefore be obtained from the magistrates, but that relief did not extend to the right to remarry; and thousands of unhappy men and women, unable to afford the cost of petitioning in the High Court for divorce, were condemned in this way to what had been eloquently described as the 'living death of separation'. The fact that English law accommodated two separate—and distinctly unequal—systems of family justice became an important element in the campaign for reform which built up in the early years of the twentieth century, but the question of extending jurisdiction to grant divorces to other, more accessible, courts became interlinked with the question of the ground for divorce and was (for most of the first half of the twentieth century) treated as a matter of less importance.

---

[32] The following were the grounds of complaint under the 1895 Act:

(a) husband convicted of aggravated assault contrary to Offences against the Persons Act 1861, s. 43;

(b) husband convicted on indictment of assault and sentenced to a fine of more than £5 or a prison term exceeding two months;

(c) husband deserted wife;

(d) husband guilty of persistent cruelty, or wilful neglect to provide reasonable maintenance, provided that the cruelty or neglect had caused her to leave and live separately and apart from him.

Summary Jurisdiction (Married Women) Act 1895, s. 4. The adulterous wife lost her rights unless the husband had condoned, connived at or by wilful neglect or misconduct conduced to the adultery: ss. 6, 7.

[33] On proof of any of the prescribed grounds, the court had power to make a non-cohabitation order, a custody order giving the wife custody of children of the marriage so long as they were under 16, maintenance at a rate not exceeding £2 weekly, and costs: s. 5. The 1895 Act blurred the distinction between cases involving the wife's safety and those in which the sole issue was financial: see *Dodd v. Dodd* [1906] P 189, *per* Gorell J at p. 198. For the difficulties caused by the courts making non-cohabitation orders in inappropriate circumstances, see below.

[34] The Licensing Act 1902 added habitual drunkenness (by either husband or wife) to the grounds on which an order could be made.

[35] *Report of the Royal Commission on Marriage and Divorce* (Cmd. 9678, 1956) App. 2.

LIBERALISING THE GROUND FOR DIVORCE

The Matrimonial Causes Act 1857 (as explained above) did not in fact significantly alter the substance (as distinct from the procedures) of the law governing the availability of divorce. By the beginning of the twentieth century the hardship and injustice of the law was widely appreciated, whilst the fact that the law seemed to enshrine a double standard of morality—a man could divorce his wife if she committed adultery; a wife could only divorce her husband if she could prove some specified factor aggravating the husband's adultery[36]—was an easy target for the increasingly vocal[37] feminist movement. And yet the nineteenth century saw little institutional campaigning for change. Only in 1892[38] was the issue of reform of the ground for divorce formally debated in Parliament.

THE BEGINNINGS OF THE MOVEMENT FOR REFORM

The 1892 Hunter Bill

In 1892 Dr William Hunter,[39] a Scottish Professor of Roman Law, had introduced into Parliament a Bill to extend the ground for divorce. But Hunter did not put the case for reform on any strong appeal to considerations of equality and justice. Rather he argued that intermarriage between the English and the Scots was so common that it would be sensible for the law[40] of the two countries to be the same. But his claim that Scots law[41] (which allowed divorce for simple adul-

---

[36] After 1884 wives could in practice often circumvent the requirement of an additional 'aggravating factor' by obtaining a decree for Restitution of Conjugal Rights against an adulterous husband: see Chapter 4, above.

[37] However, as shown by R Probert, 'The controversy of equality and the Matrimonial Causes Act 1923' [1999] CFLQ 33, 35, there were many different attitudes towards the double standard in divorce amongst women's groups at the turn of the century, and 'even the groups which were in favour of reform did not at that time play an active role in promoting changes to the law. There was no campaign equivalent to those mounted in other areas of the law in which women suffered disadvantage'. But the emergence of the National Union of Societies for Equal Citizenship, doctrinally committed by Rule II of its Constitution to 'real equality of . . . status . . . between men and women' put the dual standard firmly on to the reform agenda: see below.

[38] On 26 April 1892: see *Hansard's Parliamentary Debates* (4th Series), vol. 3, col. 1438. Hunter had first introduced his Bill in 1889 (when it was described simply and economically as a 'Bill to Assimilate the Law of Divorce in England and Scotland'); and that it attracted somewhat ambivalent support from the Moral Reform Union and the Women's Liberal Foundation: R Probert, 'The controversy of equality and the Matrimonial Causes Act 1923' [1999] CFLQ 33, 35.

[39] See Biographical Notes.

[40] The *Report of the (Chelmsford) Royal Commission on the Laws of Marriage* (1868), dealing with the formation of marriage, had been inspired by the same philosophy: see Chapter 1, above.

[41] The Westminster Confession of 1643 accepted by the Church of Scotland recognised adultery and 'such wilful desertion as can no way be remedied by the church or civil magistrate' as sufficient cause for dissolving the bond of marriage; and Scots law thereafter allowed divorce for adultery or desertion for four years.

tery by either spouse or for desertion) had stood the test of 300 years' experience and would not lead to any great increase in the divorce rate did not convince the Attorney-General.[42] The Hunter Bill was lost on a division by 71 votes to 40.

The 1902 Russell Bill

The Hunter Bill was presented dispassionately with calm appeals to reason. But the next, and historically much more significant, attempt at reform was a very different matter not least because the Bill's promoter (the Second Earl Russell)[43] made no secret of the fact that his interest in matrimonial law was intensely personal. The complex story of his first marriage and its ending is worth recording, if only to indicate the corrosive potential of litigation in family matters:

Earl Russell's marriage to Mabel Edith Scott broke down within three months. Thereafter (according to the Earl) Mabel and her mother started a relentless persecution designed to extract money from him, filing a judicial separation petition alleging cruelty constituted by his committing an 'odious crime' with a young man. That petition was dismissed; but two years later she sought an order for Restitution of Conjugal Rights. The Earl riposted with a petition for judicial separation alleging that her repeatedly and publicly making allegations which she knew to be false constituted cruelty. After a trial before a jury, the Earl was granted a decree. Mabel appealed. The Court of Appeal set aside the judicial separation decree on the ground that the conduct alleged against her was not legally capable of constituting cruelty, but the Court refused the wife's Restitution application because it considered that Earl Russell had reasonable grounds for refusing to live with her.[44] The Earl then instigated a prosecution of Mabel's mother for criminal libel, and she was sentenced to eight months' imprisonment. The Earl appealed to the House of Lords against the Court of Appeal's ruling on what was capable of constituting cruelty, and the wife appealed against the Court's refusal to grant her the Restitution decree she had sought. The House of Lords by a majority upheld the ruling on cruelty;[45] and the wife abandoned her own appeal. The Earl employed detectives in the hope of obtaining proof of the adultery which he believed Mabel was habitually committing at Bray-on-Thames, Berkshire but he was advised that the evidence thus obtained would be insufficient to convince a jury. The Earl and Mabel remained, in law, married.

Whilst fighting an election to the London County Council, the Earl met a Miss Mollie Cooke and wanted to marry her. He could not do so because English law

[42] Sir Richard Webster: see Biographical Notes. He expressed the conventional view that to allow divorce for desertion would in reality be to allow collusive divorce by consent.

[43] See Biographical Notes.

[44] [1895] P 315. The Court's ruling was based on the view that the Matrimonial Causes Act 1884 (see p. 145, above) had given the court power to refuse a Restitution petition if the effect of the decree would be to compel the court to treat a spouse as being in desertion, contrary to the real justice of the case. This view was subsequently followed: see *Brooking Phillips v. Brooking Phillips* [1913] P 80, CA.

[45] *Russell v. Russell* [1897] AC 395.

did not allow him to divorce his wife, whilst his wife had no grounds upon which she might divorce him even if she wished to do so. The Earl, disenchanted with what he sarcastically described as the 'beauties of our English law', agreed with Mollie that they would marry in the United States after obtaining an American divorce notwithstanding the fact that they knew such a marriage would not be valid in English law. They travelled to Nevada where a court granted the Earl a divorce; and he went through a form of marriage with Mollie at the Riverside Hotel, Reno. On returning to this country he was arrested, charged with bigamy, tried for that offence by his peers,[46] and sentenced to three months' imprisonment as an Offender of the First Division in Holloway Prison.[47] He served his sentence in conditions of some comfort;[48] and Mabel was eventually persuaded[49] to divorce him on the grounds that he had been guilty of bigamy and adultery.

It is not surprising that his experiences converted the Earl into a dedicated campaigner for reform of the divorce laws. But the very fact that he had been involved in such a notorious case was a handicap to the cause of reform. Only six months after his release from Holloway he introduced what was in fact a very workmanlike Bill into the House of Lords. This would have allowed divorce to either spouse on the ground of adultery, cruelty, living apart for three years, living apart for a year if both husband and wife agreed on divorce, sentence of penal servitude of three years or longer, and incurable insanity. The Bill would also have made divorce more accessible to those of modest means by giving the county court jurisdiction if the parties' income were £500 a year[50] or less.

These proposals were not strikingly dissimilar[51] to those subsequently recommended by the Gorell Royal Commission ten years later and eventually made law in 1937. But, not surprisingly, few of his peers seemed to accept Russell's claim that his motives were entirely disinterested. The 78-year-old Lord Chancellor Halsbury ('dancing with rage' according to Russell)[52]

[46] The Earl had not understood that bigamy is one of the (at the time, few) crimes which can be prosecuted in England even if committed abroad. For that reason he pleaded guilty, but urged in mitigation that he had believed the Nevada divorce to be valid.

[47] Apparently Halsbury (who advised the peers that a sentence of imprisonment would be appropriate because the Earl had defied the law) believed the indictment to be defective since it did not allege that the accused was a British subject. He considered that, had the point been taken, the indictment would have had to be quashed: RFV Heuston, *Lives of the Lord Chancellors 1885–1940* (1964) p. 76.

[48] The text draws primarily on the account given in the Earl's autobiography, *My Life and Adventures* (1923) p. 283.

[49] She was (according to the Earl's autobiography, p. 279) paid £5,000 (some £300,000 in year 2000 values).

[50] Something over £30,000 in year 2000 values.

[51] Apart from allowing consensual divorce after a year's separation. In 1990 the Law Commission recommended that divorce should be available 12 months after filing a notice of intent (whether or not the parties had separated): see Chapter 21, below.

[52] *My Life and Adventures* (1923) p. 324. Halsbury described Russell to his daughter as 'an impudent cad', but believed that he had 'squashed him' in the debate: RVF Heuston, *Lives of the Lord Chancellors 1885–1940* (1964) p. 77. Home Office officials noted that Halsbury had given Russell a 'dressing down': Note dated 26 September 1902 PRO HO45/15006.

denounced the Bill as an 'outrage' on the House and claimed it would effectively abolish marriage.[53] Their Lordships evidently agreed, and formally rejected the Bill (rather than taking the more conventional and gentlemanly course of 'deferring' the second reading). The following year Russell tried again[54] and again was unsuccessful.

Russell none the less has a secure place in the history of divorce reform: in 1902 he had set up the Society for Promoting Reforms in Marriage and Divorce Laws in England,[55] and the Society held public meetings[56] and promoted discussion of the issue. In May 1906 ESP Haynes (a practising solicitor)[57] engineered a merger of the Russell Society with the Divorce Law Reform Association[58] to form the Divorce Law Reform Union. The Union played an important part in the reform movement over the next half century.

[53] *Hansard's Parliamentary Debates* (4th Series), 1 May 1902, vol. 107, col. 408.

[54] *Hansard's Parliamentary Debates* (4th Series), 23 June 1903, vol. 124, col. 202. In 1905 Russell unsuccessfully presented another (more limited) Bill following the pattern of Hunter's 1892 Bill; and in 1908—encouraged by the judgment of Gorell Barnes P in *Dodd v. Dodd* [1906] P 189 and hoping that a Liberal government would be more sympathetic to the cause of reform—did so again; but the only success he could claim was that in 1908 he persuaded other peers to vote with him. Even so the House refused the Bill a Second Reading by 61 votes to 2: *Hansard's Parliamentary Debates* (4th Series), vol. 193, col. 4. Russell continued to take an active interest in divorce reform and spoke in most of the Parliamentary debates down to and including the debates on the Matrimonial Causes Act 1923 (favouring much more radical reform, he sardonically described the 1923 Bill as a 'thoroughly bad and inadequate Bill' which it was nevertheless practically impossible to oppose: *Official Report* (HL) 26 June 1923, vol. 54, col. 575).

[55] The objects of the Society were to extend the grounds for divorce to cases in which the home was destroyed by desertion for three years or more, permanent lunacy, or long sentences of imprisonment, to give women the same rights in relation to divorce as men had, and to confer jurisdiction on the county court to deal with people of moderate means: Earl Russell's *Evidence* to the Royal Commission on Divorce and Matrimonial Causes, 19 December 1910 (1912, vol. 3, Cd. 6480, p. 453).

[56] Attendance at the Society's meetings seems in fact to have been sparse—ESP Haynes recorded that only five people attended the Society's General Meeting in July 1905—but Russell apparently had more success at public lectures and claimed to have addressed audiences of a thousand or more: *Minutes of Evidence taken before the Royal Commission on Divorce and Matrimonial Causes* 19 December 1910 (1912, vol. 3, Cd. 6480, p. 453).

[57] Haynes, who had acted as Secretary to the Divorce Law Reform Association, was described by Russell as a 'very active and intelligent gentleman': *Minutes of Evidence taken before the Royal Commission on Divorce and Matrimonial Causes* 19 December 1910 (1912, vol. 3, Cd. 6480, p. 453). Haynes practised in the family firm Hunter and Haynes in New Square Lincoln's Inn and saw the harshness of the divorce laws at first hand. He was a considerable publicist and man of letters, author of *Divorce Problems of Today* (1912) and many other books and articles: see Biographical Notes. His influence was considerable, and AP Herbert appropriately dedicated his autobiographical account of the passing of the 1937 Matrimonial Causes Act (*The Ayes Have It* (1937)) to 'ESP Haynes and all the veterans'.

[58] According to Haynes, this was done in part because persons such as Sir Frederick Pollock and Professor A V Dicey 'objected to the society being run by a man who had been in prison for bigamy. I did not sympathise with their objections, but Lord Russell agreed that he might as well take up another favourite reform, namely that of the police force. I fear he did not attain much success': ESP Haynes, *The Lawyer, A Conversation Piece, selected from the Lawyer's Notebooks and other writings by ESPH 1877–1949*, with an autobiographical introduction and a memoir by Renée Haynes (1951) p. xxviii.

THE DIVORCE LAW REFORM UNION; AND THE PRESIDENT OF THE PROBATE DIVORCE AND ADMIRALTY DIVISION

The Divorce Law Reform Union's declared objective was precise, specific, and moderate:[59] it was to press for the appointment of a Royal Commission to investigate the working of the law and the options for reform. Over the years, this eminently respectable body[60] played a major role in eventually achieving reform of the divorce process.[61] But it was the outspoken support for reform voiced by the country's senior divorce judge Sir John Gorell Barnes[62] which transformed the situation.

Gorell Barnes had first publicly revealed his support for reform in April 1906—coincidentally, a few days before the foundation of the Divorce Law Reform Union—in giving judgment in the case of *Dodd v. Dodd*:[63]

Mr Dodd, a Manchester grocer, took to drink, stopped working, and lived off his wife. The wife then left him, went to her mother, and a few weeks later got a magistrates' order[64] based on his neglect to maintain her. The order provided that the husband pay her ten shillings weekly[65] and included the usual[66] provision that she be no longer obliged to cohabit with him. The husband failed to make the stipulated payments; and nine years later the wife (having found evidence that the husband was committing adultery) petitioned for divorce on the basis of his adultery coupled with desertion. On the facts of the case the husband was not in desertion: he had not the slightest intention of repudiating the marriage or the wife because the wife was in fact keeping him. But in any case, as a matter of law, a judicial separation (and thus a non-cohabitation order) relieved the spouses of the duty of living together, and thus immediately terminated desertion (in this case long before the period of two years necessary in divorce proceedings had elapsed). The fact that the legislation[67] provided that an order

[59] As Russell put it, the Divorce Law Reform Union (DLRU) took over all the Russell Society's funds and literature and the 'vast masses of correspondence from distressed people all over the country' in its archives: *Minutes of Evidence taken before the Royal Commission on Divorce and Matrimonial Causes* 19 December 1910 (1912, vol. 3, Cd. 6480, p. 453). It appears that a German Air Raid during World War II destroyed the DLRU offices and all its records (*An Appreciation*, Mrs May Louise Seaton-Tiedeman (1948), *Eirene White Papers*) but some of the early DLRU publications have been preserved in the Fawcett Library.

[60] The Union had some 300 or 400 members at this period, including some whom Lord Gorell described as 'some persons of position': *Minutes of Evidence taken before the Royal Commission on Divorce and Matrimonial Causes* 8 March 1910 (1912, vol. 3, Cd. 6480, p. 212). It seems that members of the 'lower classes' were rather rarer: *ibid*. Over the years it sought to gain influence by inviting distinguished public figures to accept office: see below.

[61] The DLRU has been fairly described as 'the single most important pressure group' in the campaign for reform: see CA Moyse: *Reform of Marriage and Divorce Law in England and Wales 1909–37* (Cambridge University, unpublished PhD thesis, 1996) p. 49.

[62] A judge of the Probate Divorce and Admiralty Division since 1892 and President since 1905: see Biographical Notes.

[63] [1906] P 189.   [64] Under Summary Jurisdiction (Married Women) Act 1895: see above.

[65] Ie 50 pence—perhaps £25 in year 2000 values.   [66] See p. 201 above.

[67] Summary Jurisdiction (Married Women) Act 1895, s. 5(a).

containing a non-cohabitation clause should 'have the same force and effect in all respects as a decree of judicial separation on the ground of cruelty' did not mean that the husband was to be treated as if he were guilty of cruelty; and it was not true that a woman who obtained a magistrates' non-cohabitation order against an adulterous husband could then successfully petition for divorce on the grounds of his adultery and cruelty.

The decision was important enough in its own right. Magistrates habitually made non-cohabitation orders without considering the consequences; and the President's judgment warned them that in so doing they might well deprive the wife of any right to divorce.[68] But the President's judgment is historically remarkable[69] for its sustained indictment of the failings of the law. As we have seen the great majority of matrimonial cases were dealt with by magistrates under the 1895 Act rather than by the High Court under its divorce jurisdiction; and Barnes stated in the plainest terms his belief that the 'direct tendency' of magistrates' separation orders was to encourage immorality.[70] Moreover, magistrates' orders were usually ineffective:

'rather than pay the allowance ordered, the man goes elsewhere, whether to another town, or to America, or to the Colonies, and forms other ties almost as a matter of course'.

Barnes did not merely point out that the petitioning wife would have succeeded if her case could have been brought in Scotland or most other civilised countries and express his conviction (founded on 14 years' experience on the bench) that permanent separation without divorce was an unsatisfactory remedy to apply to the evils it was supposed to prevent.[71] He denounced the whole of the English law of separation and divorce as 'full of inconsistencies, anomalies, and inequalities amounting almost to absurdities'. But Barnes was more cautious in putting forward a specific remedy:

'Whether any, and what, remedy should be applied raises extremely difficult questions, the importance of which can hardly be over-estimated, for they touch the basis on which society rests, the principle of marriage being the fundamental basis upon which this and other civilized nations have built up their social systems; and it would be most detrimental to the best interests of family life, society, and the State to permit of divorces being lightly and easily obtained, or to allow any law which was wide enough to militate by its laxity against the principles of marriage. It is not necessary for me now to express a formal and final opinion upon these serious questions but the consideration of what I have found it necessary to deal with in the judgment brings prominently forward the

[68] Because the order would terminate the husband's desertion.

[69] Gorell's younger son wrote that his father had become convinced that the law was full of injustices and anomalies, and that the judgment was given 'of set intent and after most anxious consideration': Introduction to JEG de Montmorency, *John Gorell Barnes, First Lord Gorell (1848–1913)* (1920), p. 11.

[70] 'Bearing in mind that human nature is what it is, and the classes of person with whom the magistrates usually have to deal . . .': *Dodd v. Dodd* [1906] P 189, 205.

[71] *Dodd v. Dodd* [1906] P 189, 207.

question whether, assuming that divorce is to be allowed at all . . . any reform would be effective and adequate which did not abolish permanent separation, as distinguished from divorce, place the sexes on an equality as regards offence and relief, and permit a decree being obtained for such definite grave causes of offence as render future cohabitation impracticable and frustrate the object of marriage; and whether such reform would not largely tend to greater propriety and enhance that respect for the sanctity of the marriage tie which is so essential in the best interests of society and the State. It is sufficient at present to say that . . . there appears to be good reason for reform, and that probably it would be found that it should be in the direction above indicated . . .'

ESP Haynes[72] correctly summed up the effect of Barnes' 'fearless utterances' in the *Dodd* judgment as having played a large part in overcoming the fierce taboo which (as the debates on the Russell bills suggest) had surrounded discussion of the divorce law. Barnes himself modestly accepted that he had 'set the ball rolling';[73] and, although reluctant to be seen[74] as a campaigner, he was in truth an extremely effective one.

1906: THE TIME RIPE FOR REFORM

The political situation in 1906 was propitious for reform. The general election held at the beginning of the year had seen a landslide in favour of the Liberals,[75] and Barnes was known[76] to represent what his biographer described as 'the best thinking of the old school of liberal thought'.[77] It was not therefore surprising that he should have been appointed to chair an official inquiry into the division of jurisdiction between the High Court and the county court.[78] But coinciden-

[72] ESP Haynes, *Divorce Problems of Today* (1912).

[73] ESP Haynes, *The Lawyer,* (1951) p. 64. Haynes had drawn Gorell's attention to the existence of the DLRU, and records that Gorell was 'always interested to hear what was going on': p. 65.

[74] At least in the public eye. Gorell's younger son recorded at the time that his father meant 'to do a tremendous deal and become a really big figure in other fields than the purely legal': *Gorell Diaries* 17 January 1909.

[75] According to *British Political Facts 1900–2000* by D Butler and G Butler (8th ed., 2000) p. 234 the Liberals had 400 seats in the House of Commons, Labour 30, and Conservatives 157.

[76] In 1909 Lord Chancellor Loreburn told Prime Minister Asquith that Barnes was 'a very liberal minded man, whatever his party may be': RFV Heuston, *Lives of the Lord Chancellors 1885–1940* (1964) p. 149. On 6 February 1909 the *Law Journal*, welcoming his elevation to the peerage, commented that Barnes had displayed the 'true spirit of a law reformer'; and the *Journal* expressed the hope that he would be able 'to promote those great alterations in our judicial system of which he is known to be one of the strongest advocates'.

[77] JEG de Montmorency (author of *John Gorell Barnes, First Lord Gorell (1848–1913)* with an introduction by Ronald, Third Lord Gorell (1920)). The quotation is taken from de Montmorency's memoir in the *Dictionary of National Biography 1912–1921*, p. 31.

[78] The *Committee appointed by the Lord Chancellor to inquire into certain matters relating to County Court Procedure* was appointed in July 1908 and reported in 1909, BPP vol. 72, p. 311. The Committee did not recommend radical reforms in relation to common law suits (see P Polden, *A History of the County Court, 1846–1971* (1999) pp. 106–109) but the Committee recorded that there was still in relation to divorce 'practically one law for those who can afford to bring a suit in the Divorce Courts and another for those who cannot, and the latter embraces a very large portion of the population . . .': p. 23.

tally it happened that the Government felt the need to increase the number of judges able to sit in House of Lords appeals.[79] Barnes was offered a peerage[80] which (after some hesitation) he accepted. The Government had intended the peerage simply to allow him to sit judicially on appeals, but the newly elevated Lord Gorell now also had a voice in Parliament,[81] and he soon exploited the opportunities which this gave. Within a few months of taking his seat he moved a motion in the House of Lords seeking support for giving the County Court jurisdiction to deal with poor persons' divorce cases;[82] and in the ensuing debate both the Lord President[83] and the Lord Chancellor[84] accepted the strength of the case for a further enquiry into the whole subject of divorce[85] and its administration. The appointment of a Royal Commission on Divorce and Matrimonial Causes was announced at the end of October 1909.

THE GORELL COMMISSION 1909–1912

The Royal Commission's terms of reference required it to 'inquire into the present state of the law and the administration thereof in Divorce and Matrimonial Causes, and Applications for Separation Orders, especially with regard to the position of the poorer classes in relation thereto'.[86] This was exactly what the Divorce Law Reform Union had wanted. It was also precisely what Gorell's

---

[79] The problem had arisen because there were no vacancies for (stipendiary) Lords of Appeal in Ordinary: see RFV Heuston, *Lives of the Lord Chancellors 1885–1940* (1964) p.149.

[80] ie a hereditary peerage, as distinct from a life peerage under the provisions of the Appellate Jurisdiction Act 1886. Although (as Loreburn had wryly remarked) 'a full peerage is I suppose more desirable than a life Peerage: at all events it is more desiderated', the offer (at the time unprecedented) was—as Gorell's younger son recorded in his diary—'not all roses' since there was no machinery to make any payment to Gorell and the judicial pension of £3,500 to which he became entitled on vacating the office of President was substantially less than the £5,000 salary to which he had been entitled as President. Although Gorell warned his family that to accept the offer might involve their having to sell their country home, his son records that the offer had been put on grounds of duty, and could not be refused. Moreover, 'the greatest and best work of which father is capable is offered to him—international arbitrations, legal reforms and great decisions. England has need of him, he must go': *Gorell Diaries* 11 January 1909; and see generally JEG de Montmorency, *John Gorell Barnes, First Lord Gorell (1848–1913)* (1920) pp. 142–143.

[81] Since he had ceased to hold judicial office he could speak on controversial issues without restraint: Introduction by Gorell's younger son to JEG de Montmorency, *John Gorell Barnes, First Lord Gorell (1848–1913)* (1920) p. 13. The Lord Chancellor had specifically referred to the fact that as a peer Gorell would have the opportunity to advance 'whatever views you think best in Law Reform and to render public service on such work as International Arbitrations or Royal Commissions': Loreburn to Barnes, 1 January 1909, as copied in *Gorell Diaries*.

[82] See *Hansard's Parliamentary Debates* (5th Series)(HL) 14 July 1909, vol. 2, col. 473. According to the *Daily Mail*, 15 July 1909, Gorell's 'striking personality' and lawyer-like precision in putting the case for cheap divorce 'dominated the House of Lords'.

[83] Viscount Wolverhampton.   [84] Loreburn.

[85] In addition to the public support of these two highly placed Cabinet Ministers the Prime Minister, HH Asquith, was sympathetic to reform and had acted as one of the sponsors of the 1889 and 1890 Hunter Bills.

[86] The Commission was also to examine the subject of the publication of reports of such causes and applications: see below.

judgment in *Dodd* had suggested. And it was Gorell whom the Government chose to chair the Commission.[87]

There was no doubt where Gorell's sympathies lay.[88] But the other members were to some extent representative of particular social groups or interests[89] and it was less easy to predict how they would respond to the problems with which the Commission was to be concerned for more than two years.[90]

The Gorell Commission sat on 71 occasions, 56 of which were devoted to taking evidence.[91] Much of this related to the cost of divorce proceedings and painted a clear picture of the poor being excluded from the remedy which the 1857 Act in theory provided. This can hardly have come as a surprise.[92] Everyone agreed that no one ought to be deprived of his legal rights merely by poverty;[93] but finding an appropriate remedy for the injustice which had been identified was a different matter.

[87] Gorell's elder son (who had served him as Secretary to the President of the Probate Divorce and Admiralty Division from 1906) was appointed Secretary to the Commission. His younger son Ronald recorded in his diary that the 'family will run the whole thing' (*Gorell Diaries* 19 September 1909) and it is clear that both father and son worked effectively in providing detailed memoranda to the Commission and marshalling the copious evidence. Further input was provided by the Assistant Secretary, JEG de Montmorency (1866–1934): see Biographical Notes. Gorell's two sons each played an active part in promoting legislation to give effect to the Royal Commission's recommendations: see below.

[88] The question whether an official inquiry should best consist of those without known views on the subject matter (or even any particular knowledge or interest in it) or alternatively consist of representatives of opposing viewpoints is interesting and controversial; see SM Cretney, *Law, Law Reform and the Family* (1998) pp. 40–42. As shown by CA Moyse in Chapter 3 of *Reform of Marriage and Divorce Law in England and Wales 1909–37* (Cambridge University, unpublished PhD thesis, 1996), the Church of England was insistent on its right to representation on the Gorell Commission and this was eventually conceded notwithstanding the initial opposition of Prime Minister Asquith (who was particularly opposed to the appointment of Cosmo Gordon Lang, Archbishop of York): see generally Moyse, *op. cit.* pp. 160–161.

[89] For the Commission's membership, see pp. 814–815, below. Gorell's younger son recorded that there were some 'very good names on [the Committee] and as [Gorell had] asked, ladies, for the first time I believe'.: *Gorell Diaries*, 29 October 1909.

[90] But some poor people did obtain divorces, particularly those who lived within easy reach of London or had saved up for many years.

[91] For the evidence, see *Minutes of Evidence taken before the Royal Commission on Divorce and Matrimonial Causes* in three volumes (1912, Cd. 6480). The usual practice was for witnesses to submit a written memorandum which was then treated as a 'proof' of evidence, on which they were subjected to oral questioning at the public hearings. Gorell attached great importance to the taking of evidence in public: JEG de Montmorency, *John Gorell Barnes, First Lord Gorell (1848–1913)* (1920).

[92] In the 1909 debate on Gorell's motion to give divorce jurisdiction to the county court Lord Chancellor Loreburn had claimed that 'the poorer the people . . . the harder are the consequences of matrimonial misconduct. When a man has children and no one to look after them, and is obliged to bring up those children in destitution, in a miserable hovel, he suffers more than a man in affluent circumstances':*Hansard's Parliamentary Debates* (5th Series)(HL) 14 July 1909, vol. 2, col. 505.

[93] *Report of the Royal Commission on Divorce and Matrimonial Causes, Minority Report* (1912, Cd. 6478) (subsequently cited as '*Minority Report*') p. 171.

The Gorell Commission fails to agree

The Majority Report

Gorell struggled hard to achieve a consensus.[94] But his efforts were unavailing: the Archbishop of York, Sir William Anson and Sir Lewis Dibdin dissented from the Majority's main recommendation. The majority of the Commissioners could not accept that it would be sufficient merely to provide a more accessible tribunal to administer the law established by the 1857 Act. The Majority Report repeated the message given by Barnes in the *Dodd* case: the law led to immorality;[95] and the Report gave repeated illustrations of the practical consequences of making it virtually impossible for the respectable working class to divorce and remarry. For example:

'. . . a working man whose wife leaves him to live with another man, is practically compelled to take a housekeeper to look after his children and home, and the accommodation therein is such that . . . immoral relations almost inevitably result. So again, in the case of a woman, whose husband leaves her and fails to provide for her, she endeavours to support herself and her children by letting lodgings, and the evidence shows how frequently this results in an irregular union with a lodger . . .'.

'. . . the husband turned out to be drunken and unfaithful; the wife went back into domestic service, never saw her husband again, and did not know whether he was alive or dead. She now lives with an engineer's labourer and has two children. The house is clean and comfortable, and to all outward appearances satisfactory'.

A drunken, unfaithful, and cruel gas stoker, having three children by his wife. The wife left him seven years ago and is now living with another man, by whom she has two children, well cared for but legally bastards. They will have to labour under that 'horrible disability' all their lives.

The majority[96] asked why divorce should be impossible where the husband had simply disappeared, perhaps to the United States or the colonies? Why should it be denied where one spouse was confined for many years in a lunatic asylum or was serving a long sentence of imprisonment?

For the majority, there was only one answer. The marriage tie should not be seen as 'necessarily indissoluble in its nature, or as dissoluble only on the ground of adultery; but . . . [should] allow other grave causes'—desertion for three years

---

[94] Gorell's son records that his father set the 'greatest store by friendly relations' with all the Commissioners; and it is apparent that Gorell's own immensely thorough analysis of the religious aspect of divorce (reproduced as Appendix 1 to JEG de Montmorency, *John Gorell Barnes, First Lord Gorell (1848–1913)* (1920)) was intended to make it possible for the Church of England to accept a wider basis for divorce. But the Archbishop, Dibdin and Anson stood firm. Gorell appears to have had a depressive temperament, and suffered a number of health breakdowns in the course of his career: see the Third Lord Gorell's Introduction to de Montmorency, above.

[95] ESP Haynes, as a member of a deputation to the Prime Minister in 1924, claimed that Government research in connection with the National Registration Act of 1916 revealed a 'vast number of people living without any kind of matrimonial arrangements . . .': PRO PREM1/38, p. 11.

[96] *Report of the Royal Commission on Divorce and Matrimonial Causes* (1912, Cd. 6478) (subsequently cited as '*Gorell Report*') para. 48.

and upwards, cruelty, incurable insanity after five years' confinement, habitual and incurable drunkenness, and imprisonment under a commuted death sentence[97]—as sufficient grounds for divorce.[98]

The Minority Report

The Majority Report clearly established that the existing law caused hardship; but the minority seized on the absence from the Majority Report of any underlying principle which could justify the changes the majority recommended. In this view, the majority were simply accepting that divorce should be allowed 'when it is clear that the parties have irreparably lost affection for each other, or . . . when either party has become permanently alienated from the other'. But (so the minority argued) this was really an argument for divorce by consent or on the ground of mutual aversion—divorce because the 'parties have grown tired, and mutually desire to make an end'. The minority claimed that the only reason why the Majority Report did not go so far was that the majority realised that public opinion did not at the time support such an extension. But the danger was that acceptance of the majority's proposals would make a major breach in the *principle* that marriage was indissoluble. This would inevitably create a 'habit of mind in the people'[99] that divorce was simply a matter for mutual arrangement and would thus:

'lead the nation to a downward incline on which it would be vain to expect to be able to stop half way. It is idle to imagine that in a matter where great forces of human passion must always be pressing with all their might against whatever barriers are set up, those barriers can be permanently maintained in a position arbitrarily chosen, with no better reason to support them than the supposed condition of public opinion as the moment of their erection . . . [The result of accepting the majority view] would be practically to abrogate the principle of monogamous life-long union'.[100]

This (said the minority) was what had happened in the United States and other countries which had relaxed their laws. The illustrations given by the Majority Report of hardship caused by restricting divorce really proved too much, and (according to the minority) established a logical case for allowing

[97] *Gorell Report*, Summary, p. 163.
[98] The Majority Report was somewhat equivocal on the question of the bars to divorce. In many of the illustrations of hardship given in the Majority Report the prospective petitioner would, as the law then stood (see p. 188, above) have been refused divorce even if she had been able to establish the ground prescribed by law because she too was guilty of adultery. The majority did recommend that in these circumstances the 'court should exercise its discretion to pronounce a decree according to the circumstances of the case' but the conscientious administration of such a bar would inevitably be difficult and to some extent unpredictable.
[99] Minority Report, p. 185.
[100] The Minority Report placed substantial reliance on the testimony of the Mother's Union (described in the Report, p. 176, as consisting of 278,500 wives and mothers 'almost entirely of the working classes') that there was no demand in such quarters for extension of the ground for divorce and that to extend the ground upon which divorce could be granted would be 'to lessen the sense of the binding character of marriage amongst the poor'.

divorce whenever the marriage has broken down. The minority believed that to accept the majority recommendations would open the floodgates and lead inevitably to the divorce by consent or for 'mere incompatibility'.

The Royal Commission report pigeon-holed?

The fact that the Royal Commission was divided on the issue of fundamental principle furnished the Government with more than adequate grounds for refusing to introduce legislation;[101] but it also served to divert attention from the fact that the Commission had been unanimous in recommending many specific reforms, including equality between the sexes in respect of the ground for divorce, restricting the powers of magistrates to make lifelong separation orders, the introduction of divorce on presumption of death, and the extension of nullity to certain cases of mental illness, epilepsy, venereal disease and pregnancy by a third party.

The reformers were faced with a dilemma: should they, at least as a first step, accept the recommendations on which the whole Commission was agreed or should they push for nothing less than implementation of all the recommendations of the Majority Report? Some believed that a limited reform would be a step on the way to eventual acceptance of the whole Majority Report package; others thought that limited reform would take the steam out of the campaign and make it difficult if not impossible to get legislation extending the ground for divorce in the way the Majority Report had recommended. Disagreement on this central tactical issue was skilfully exploited by opponents of reform.

The effectiveness of opposition to reform was soon to be demonstrated. The first Lord Gorell had died in 1913,[102] but in July 1914 his son (who had succeeded to the title) introduced a Bill[103] to give effect to the recommendations on which Majority and Minority Reports concurred. The debate provoked predictable opposition from Roman Catholic sources;[104] but the Church of

---

[101] The Government made it clear that there were no prospects of the Government bringing forward legislation to give effect even to the recommendations of the Royal Commission, and that implementation was to be a matter for private initiative: *Hansard's Parliamentary Debates* (5th Series)(HL) 28 July 1914, vol. 17, col. 190.

[102] His younger son attributed his father's premature death in part to the strain of presiding over the Commission: Introduction to JEG de Montmorency, *John Gorell Barnes, First Lord Gorell (1848–1913)* (1920) p. 2.

[103] On 8 July 1913 Sir David Brynmor Jones KC had introduced a Bill (No. 242) into the House of Commons, but Home Office officials advised that 'a private member's Bill on so important a subject and on such a scale ought not to be allowed to pass unopposed while the Government is still considering what action should be taken on the Report of the Commission': Minute dated 25 July 1913. The Bill made no progress (and when it was re-introduced in the summer of 1914 the Home Office arranged for it to be blocked). The Home Office had also blocked a Bill introduced by Mr Annan Bryce which would simply have allowed both men and women to divorce on the ground of adultery: such an important point of principle should not 'slip through late at night' without further discussion: Minute dated 11 April 1913: PRO HO45/15006.

[104] *Hansard's Parliamentary Debates* (5th Series)(HL) 28 July 1914, vol. 17, col. 202, Lord Braye (see Biographical Notes).

England was prepared (albeit 'with the greatest possible reluctance')[105] to support the Bill. Even more significant was the support given by Lord Chancellor Haldane for what he described as a Bill representing the full agreement of all the members of a Royal Commission of 'great authority and great weight'. To give the Bill a Second Reading would demonstrate approval for what was really a 'very moderate and substantially non-controversial measure of reform'.[106] But nothing to do with divorce could be described as uncontroversial; and Gorell evidently thought it best to withdraw the motion for a Second Reading[107] in return for the Roman Catholic Braye doing the same with his wrecking amendment.

Inter armes, silent leges?

A week later, Britain and Germany were at war. There was no time for further debate about divorce reform. The Second Lord Gorell was one of the millions killed in action.[108] Many marriages failed to survive the strains of war. In 1914 there were just over a thousand divorce petitions; in 1919 (the first year of peace) there were five times as many.[109] As one member of the Gorell Commission rather sourly noted:[110] had 'the recommendations of the Report, been embodied in a Bill which might have passed both Houses, it would certainly have been said, that the great increase of late years of divorces was due to the changes in the Laws'.

PRESSURE FOR REFORM CONTINUES: THE ROLE OF THE
DIVORCE LAW REFORM UNION

The War may have destroyed any prospect of immediate legislation; but it did nothing to restrict the build up of pressure for reform. In particular, the Divorce Law Reform Union,[111] whose objectives had originally been confined to getting

---

[105] *Hansard's Parliamentary Debates* (5th Series)(HL) 28 July 1914, vol. 17, col. 207, Archbishop Cosmo Gordon Lang (see Biographical Notes). Lang, a signatory of the Minority Report believed that judicial divorce had done more harm than good to the social and moral fabric of the country; but (foreshadowing the official attitude of the Church of England at the time of the 1937 and 1969 divorce reforms) believed that as a citizen he was 'bound to do what I can to see that the operation of that law is so far as possible not antagonistic to the morals of the country, and . . . where it has revealed abuses those abuses ought to be remedied'.

[106] *Hansard's Parliamentary Debates* (5th Series)(HL) 28 July 1914, vol. 17, col. 206.

[107] It was too late in the Session for there to be any chance of the Bill becoming law that year.

[108] The Second Lord Gorell was killed near Ypres on 16 January 1917. The title passed to his younger brother, Ronald, who for some years continued the family involvement in divorce reform: see below.

[109] The figures are: 1914: 1,075; 1919: 5,085. The proportion of these petitions brought by men sharply increased from 56% to 80%: *Report of the Royal Commission on Marriage and Divorce* (1956, Cmd. 9678) Table 1.

[110] Lady Frances Balfour, in *Ne Obliviscaris*, (1930) vol. I, p. 425.

[111] Which (symptomatically of its changing status) was incorporated as a company limited by guarantee in 1914. Again, perhaps symbolically, seven years after the enactment of the Divorce Reform Act 1969, in 1976 the DLRU was dissolved and the file in the Companies Registry has been destroyed.

a Royal Commission established to investigate the situation,[112] now vigorously committed itself to securing the implementation of the 1912 Majority Report.[113] Henceforth[114] its objectives were to press 'by every means in its power, for legislation to give effect to the recommendations of the Royal Commission . . . and to break up the system of permanent separation without the power to remarry'.[115] To this end, the Union employed a small paid staff, who with its officers,[116] produced pamphlets urging reform, organised public meetings and ran an advisory service;[117] and the Union appointed Parliamentary Representatives.[118] The irrepressible ESP Haynes[119] acted as Honorary Solicitor to the Union and continued to draft Bills.[120]

[112] The Union's then Honorary Secretary, RT Gates, had assured the Royal Commission that its whole object had been to press for the appointment of a Commission and that 'practically speaking' the object of the Union had been brought to an end: *Gorell Report*, Minutes of Evidence, 8 March 1910, q. 5151; but the membership evidently did not agree.

[113] See generally CA Moyse, *Reform of Marriage and Divorce Law in England and Wales 1909–37* (subsequently referred to as 'Moyse')(Cambridge University, unpublished PhD thesis, 1996) pp. 49–61. The text of this part is heavily indebted to that work.

[114] As early as 1910 a General Meeting held at the Inns of Court Hotel had resolved that the Union's objects should be to 'promote the reform and amendment of the laws relating to divorce and separation': *The Work of the Divorce Law Reform Union* (1911).

[115] Editorial in the Unions *Journal* 1 May 1919, as quoted in Moyse, p. 52.

[116] Notably the Union's 'colourful and indefatigable' Secretary, Mrs May Louise Seaton-Tiedeman (1858–1948): see Biographical Notes.

[117] This was latterly run by the solicitor Sir George Fowler. Fowler, dissatisfied with the cautious policies of the DLRU, eventually formed the Marriage Law Reform League which (unlike the DLRU) was prepared to advocate divorce by consent: see Moyse, p. 368. The DLRU regarded this commitment as being likely to delay reform.

[118] Edward Shortt KC MP was appointed in 1915 to 'present the Union's Bill as soon as possible': *DLRU Annual Report 1914–1915*. Shortt was succeeded for a short time by Henry Snell (subsequently Leader of the Labour Party in the House of Lords). Other MPs who represented the Union's views in the House of Commons were Sir F Acland, Sir Frederick Low, and Athelstan Rendall. In 1926 the dominance of Liberal/Labour MPs was broken by the appointment of the conservative James Cassell: see the relevant entries in Biographical Notes. Later in that decade a paid Parliamentary Agent was also appointed. In 1917 interested MPs and Peers set up an inter-party Marriage Law Reform Committee: Moyse, p. 56.

[119] Haynes personally favoured divorce by consent, a policy which was extremely controversial and was never that of the Union.

[120] Haynes also assisted the Union financially, guaranteeing a loan of £50 made to the Union to finance its reorganisation at the time when its objectives were widened: *The Work of the Divorce Law Reform Union* (1911). A financial guarantee also enabled the Union to have a draft Bill professionally settled: *Divorce Law Reform Union Annual Report 1912/13*. This Bill was introduced into the House of Commons by Sir David Brynmor Jones KC; and the same Bill was introduced by James Chuter Ede in 1931, and by GW Holford Knight KC in 1933: see Biographical Notes. But Lord Buckmaster appears to have drafted the Bill he introduced in 1920 without the Union's assistance; whilst Lord Gorell's attempted compromise of 1922 was based on a draft which his elder brother (Secretary of the Royal Commission) had drafted. AP Herbert used a DLRU Bill as a starting point for his parliamentary campaign but made many changes both of substance and drafting before introducing his own Bill in 1936, and he recorded that the DLRU in general (and Mrs Seaton-Tiedeman in particular) disliked many of the changes he made: *The Ayes Have It* (1937) p. 73. Nonetheless, as Moyse points out (p. 77), the Union 'performed the valuable service of acting as a memory bank and a depository of Bills for other campaigners'.

The DLRU's membership increased rapidly from the pre-War 400 to perhaps 1,700 in 1919.[121] It may be that these were (as the Union's *Journal* claimed)[122] simply 'sufferers and sympathisers of all creeds and parties'; but the Union's commitment to the eminently reputable Gorell proposals enabled it to obtain a 'respectability that its origins and members lacked'.[123] This image was reinforced by the practice the Union adopted of appointing well-known public figures to titular office.[124]

The Union described[125] its activities as 'patient and progressive toil' publishing pamphlets, organising 'drawing rooms' in Kensington and elsewhere, providing speakers for meetings, continually striving to 'disseminate its views more widely throughout the country and to educate Public opinion to the more perfect understanding of the need for a reformed divorce law'. The Union's lobbying was discreet:[126] it may be an exaggeration to say that the Union was highly invisible but it was certainly 'highly influential'.

PRESSURE FOR REFORM: LORD BUCKMASTER TAKES THE LEAD

Organised pressure groups can be highly effective in creating a climate of opinion favourable to reform. But the charismatic or enthusiastic individual also has a part to play; and the former Lord Chancellor, Lord Buckmaster[127] (one of the most brilliant orators of a period when oratory was fashionable and appreciated) made an important contribution to the campaign for divorce reform. Buckmaster's passionate support for reform was not confined to speeches in the House of Lords.[128] He also wrote articles in the popular

---

[121] For an analysis of the membership, see Moyse, p. 63.   [122] *ibid.*, p. 60.

[123] *Ibid.*, p. 57. This is not to say that the Union kept narrowly to reform of the ground for divorce or that it always expressed its policies in moderate language: see for an example of an outspoken attack on the policy adopted by the Labour Party DLRU pamphlet No. 22 *Scandalous Illegitimacy Bills.* This claimed that it was 'amazing' for the Labour Party to put forward a Bill which (by restricting legitimation by subsequent marriage to the children of unmarried parents) would 'penalise thousands of children of the workers, who are the people most affected by permanent separation . . . [W]hat explanation have they to offer for a measure which . . . would fix a permanent disability on many thousands of workers in the country'?

[124] The President of the Union was originally the businessman W Ramsay Fairfax; but in 1909 the author of the Sherlock Holmes tales, Sir Arthur Conan Doyle, became President, to be succeeded in 1922 by the former Lord Chancellor Lord Birkenhead: Moyse, p. 61. A large number of other distinguished public figures (such as Professor Gilbert Murray, the distinguished classical scholar and the writer Thomas Hardy, whose novels *The Woodlanders* and *Jude the Obscure* sought to depict the reality of the divorce process, particularly for working class men and women) became Vice-Presidents.

[125] *Annual Report, 1911–1912.*

[126] The suggestion that it should start a 'militant campaign of public meetings and parliamentary activity' (made in the 1911–1912 Report) seems never to have become a reality, possibly because of the lack of funds which plagued the Union.

[127] See Biographical Notes.

[128] Buckmaster's most important parliamentary speeches on divorce reform are collected in James Johnson (ed.), *An Orator of Justice, A Speech Biography of Viscount Buckmaster* (1932).

press[129] and letters to *The Times*[130] expressly drawing on his own judicial experience. In 1922, for example, he described in a letter to *The Times* the experience of trying undefended divorces earlier that year:

'In no case that I tried did there appear to me the faintest chance of reconciliation; the marriage tie had been broken beyond repair and its sanctity utterly defiled; nor . . . though I watched with extreme vigilance, was there any single case where collusion could be suggested . . . Our divorce laws have been condemned by the most competent authority as immoral and unjust . . . Common sense—but for respect to my adversaries I should have added common decency—rejects the existing law. Is it asking too much to entreat the Government to afford a chance to Parliament to cleanse our laws from this disgrace'?[131]

The battle of the Bills 1918–1924

Buckmaster had an advantage denied to others: as a member of the House of Lords he had the right to introduce Bills and he wasted no time in doing so. On the day after the armistice,[132] Buckmaster moved the Second Reading of a Bill to allow divorce on the basis of five years' desertion or separation under a court

---

[129] In the week before the election held on 15 November 1922 the *Daily Mail* published three articles by Buckmaster entitled 'Married Misery' in which he urged that candidates be compelled to answer the 'plain question': 'Are you satisfied with the justice and morality of our marriage laws'. These articles were reprinted as a book entitled *'Married Misery' and its Scandinavian Solution* by HG Bechman (1923).

[130] *The Times*, 11 October 1922. The letter was reprinted by the DLRU and issued as its Pamphlet No. 21.

[131] Buckmaster's letter published in *The Times* on 22 October 1922 asserted that every judge with experience of trying undefended divorces favoured an alteration of the law, and that the only reason why the demand for reform was not universal was that the facts were not known and that false modesty prevented their disclosure. Plain facts needed plain speech, and he gave examples based on the cases which had come before him:

'A woman marries a man, and is at once infected by him with syphilis . . . the law politely bows her out of Court and makes her pay the cost of her struggle for liberty. . . . Another woman had been made the victim of the unspeakable savagery of brutal and perverted lust. She also must have remained bound by the bonds of matrimony, enforced by violence. . . . A third was deserted, after a week, by a soldier who went to the American continent, where he might have lived unmolested for ever in a life of peaceful adultery, but as he violated two children he . . . was discovered, and she was able to be free . . . [In another case] the husband who had first insulted and then deserted his wife, left the country in a ship with the woman with his affection for whom he had often taunted his wife, but, of course, that did not constitute legal proof of adultery, but merely companionship. I was, of course, faced with the question as to what is cruelty, which, we are informed, is so difficult that you want the King's Proctor as an expert in cruelty to keep the law steady. [But however brutal and repeated cruelty may be it alone does not and must not suffice as a ground for divorce] or we shall Americanize our institutions and soil the sanctity of English homes.'

Buckmaster's *Daily Mail* articles also refer to the much publicised case of Mrs Rutherford:

'A man commits adultery, murder and robbery. He is found not to be too insane to plead and to be responsible for the action which he has committed; but after the trial he is found to be of unsound mind and is sent to a criminal lunatic asylum. Even that accumulated catalogue of wrong would not enable the woman to be free [although if he had been guilty of cruelty to his wife as well as his victim] liberty would have been within her grasp.' Mrs Rutherford appealed to the House of Lords against the refusal to grant her a divorce; and Lord Birkenhead took the opportunity to include in his opinion a call for statutory reform: 'the true remedy lies with Parliament . . . to end a state of things which in a civilised community and in the name of morality, imposes such an intolerable hardship upon innocent men and women': *Rutherford v. Richardson* [1923] AC 1, 12.

[132] *Hansard's Parliamentary Debates* (5th Series)(HL) 12 November 1918, vol. 31, col. 1184.

order.[133] On that occasion the House of Lords refused to give his Bill a Second Reading;[134] but in 1920 another Bill, based on the Royal Commission *Majority Report*[135] and supported (in a particularly powerful speech) by Lord Chancellor Birkenhead,[136] passed through all its stages in the House of Lords.[137] But neither that Bill, nor any of the other Bills attempting comprehensive[138] reform introduced between 1920 and 1924,[139] became law; and it was not until 1937 that the

[133] The Bill would also have allowed the county court to deal with divorce petitions where the parties had only small means.

[134] By 39 votes to 29. This Bill did not follow the recommendations of either the *Majority* or *Minority Reports* of the Royal Commission and, for example, appeared to remove the discretionary bars to divorce, thereby horrifying those particularly concerned at the possibility of agreed divorce: see the speech of the Third Lord Gorell, opposing Buckmaster's Bill whilst asserting the 'real and vital need for reform' and specifically for equality of treatment between the sexes: *Hansard's Parliamentary Debates* (5th Series)(HL) 12 November 1918, vol. 31, col. 1226.

[135] *Official Report* (HL) 24 March 1920, vol. 39, col. 663 (Second Reading); 20 April 1920, vol. 39, col. 817; 27 April 1920, vol. 39, col. 1035; 4 May 1920, vol. 40, col. 63; 11 May 1920, vol. 40, col. 234 (Committee); 8 June 1920, vol. 40, col. 489 (Report); 22 June 1920, vol. 40, col. 693 (Third Reading and Passed). The 1920 Buckmaster Bill prompted a flurry of detailed memoranda from Officials in the Lord Chancellor's Office, and they made considerable efforts to improve the drafting of the Bill. A detailed printed memorandum (see PRO LCO2/460) was submitted to the President of the Probate Divorce and Admiralty Division who responded incisively to the suggestions of an Advisory Committee established by the Lord Chancellor's officials and chaired by the experienced solicitor JT Withers (see Biographical Notes). Parliamentary Counsel drafted amendments to give jurisdiction to the Assize Judges (rather than the county court), but in the event this reform was carried out by the Administration of Justice Act 1920: see p. 277, below.

[136] See Biographical Notes. Birkenhead's support was not limited to making speeches on the floor of the House of Lords. He had in public stated that the Coalition Government (of which he was a Member) 'would be taking a prodigious responsibility' if it refused facilities for a Bill to be debated in the House of Commons: *Official Report* (HL), 10 March 1921, vol. 44, col. 495; and he urged the Cabinet to 'push on, as soon as possible' with the Bill in the Commons, claiming that some of its provisions were uncontroversial and could be passed into law without delay. But the Cabinet rejected this plea, ostensibly because several important measures had already had to be dropped: see meeting of 19 November 1920 63(2) PRO CAB 23/23. The Lord Privy Seal told the House of Commons that the Government's legislative programme would take the whole of the time available in that Session of Parliament and that accordingly he saw no prospect of the Bill being further advanced: *Official Report* (HC) 19 October 1920 vol. 133, col. 772.

[137] According to Buckmaster, the attendance on the last reading of the 1920 Bill was 'the largest attendance that I have known since I have been a member of the House of Lords': Note of Deputation to Prime Minister, 24 March 1924, PRO PREM 1/38, p. 2.

[138] As distinct from the limited reform effected by the Matrimonial Causes Act 1923.

[139] The parliamentary history can be summarised as follows.

(i) In 1918 Lord Buckmaster introduced a Bill which did not receive a Second Reading: see above.

(ii) In 1920, Buckmaster introduced a Bill to give effect to the Royal Commission Majority Report. It passed all its stages in the House of Lords: see above.

(iii) In April 1920 Athelstan Rendall moved a motion in the House of Commons asserting that it was desirable that legislative effect should be given without delay to the recommendations of the majority of the Gorell Commission. On a division (134–91) the House rejected the introduction of wider grounds for divorce, but asserted that it would be desirable to place the sexes on a footing of equality in regard to divorce: *Official Report* (HC) 14 April 1920, vol. 127, col. 1805.

(iv) In March 1921 Lord Gorell introduced a Bill in the House of Lords which would have given effect to the recommendations on which the Royal Commissioners were agreed. The Bill passed all its stages in the House of Lords, but made no further progress: *Official Report*

reforms recommended by the 1912 Royal Commission Majority Report were adopted.

The explanation for this long delay seems to lie in three factors. First, both the Roman Catholic church and the Church of England remained doctrinally opposed[140] to implementation of the Royal Commission Majority Report; and this opposition still carried weight.[141] Secondly, the issue of divorce reform was

(HL) 10 March 1921, vol. 44, col. 453; 12 April 1921, vol. 44, col. 884; 21 April 1921, vol. 44, col. 1077; 28 April 1921, vol. 45, col. 102; see below, p. 220.

(v) On 11 March 1924, Lord Buckmaster reintroduced the 1920 Bill into the House of Lords. The Bill was given a Second Reading (*Official Report* (HL) vol. 56, col. 636) by 88 votes to 51 but made no further progress.

Thereafter no bill seeking comprehensive reform was debated until 1930. In 1923, however, Major Cyril Entwistle, MP (Liberal) for South-West Hull introduced a Bill restricted to removing the distinction between the grounds for divorce available to men and women into the House of Commons, and this became the Matrimonial Causes Act 1923.

[140] The opposition of the Roman Catholics was undeviating; but the Church of England also remained strongly opposed to divorce: in 1888 the Lambeth Conference had resolved (Resolution 4A) that '. . . inasmuch as Our Lord's words expressly forbid Divorce, except in the case of fornication or adultery, the Christian Church cannot recognise divorce in any other than the excepted case . . .' and the 1920 Lambeth Conference reiterated the view that marriage was a lifelong and indissoluble union: see R Davidson, *The Six Lambeth Conferences 1867–1920* (1929); GKA Bell, *Randall Davidson, Archbishop of Canterbury* (3rd ed., 1952) Chapter 51; Moyse, Chapter 3. and generally PA Welsby, *A History of the Church of England* (1984) pp. 226–234; GIT Machin, *Churches and Social Issues in Twentieth-Century Britain* (1998) and 'Marriage and the Churches in the 1930s . . .' (1991) *Journal of Ecclesiastical History* vol. 42, p. 68. Other protestant churches were less rigid in their approach and the nonconformist members of the Gorell Royal Commission signed the Majority Report. The [Anglican] Mothers' Union was particularly active in opposing divorce reform: see the Evidence of Mrs Evelyn Hubbard and Mrs E Steinthal to the Royal Commission, *Gorell Report*, Minutes of Evidence, 7 June 1910, and generally Moyse, Chapters 2 and 3. It is difficult to know how far the Mothers' Union and the Church of England truly reflected the views of their members in particular or public opinion in general. M Pugh, *Women and the Women's Movement in Britain 1914–1959* (1992) provides convincing evidence drawn from women's magazines in the 1930s that at the time divorce was often presented as being contrary to women's best interests: readers were often counselled against regarding divorce as a solution to marital problems (with eg *Woman's Own* repeatedly printing 'I wish I hadn't divorced my husband' and 'Dragooned into Divorce' stories).

[141] Lady Frances Balfour, a member of the Gorell Commission writing in 1930, regarded the opposition of the Church to the *Majority Report* as being an 'insuperable barrier' to reform: *Ne Obliviscaris*, (1930) vol. I, p. 425. The Church of England did have a special and legitimate interest in the ground for divorce since the law required clergy to marry any parishioner free to marry by the law of the land. It is true that the Matrimonial Causes Act 1857 had provided that a clergyman could not be required to solemnise the marriage of the guilty party to a divorce suit, but a clergyman who refused was required to allow any other priest entitled to minister in the diocese to perform the marriage ceremony. This compromise was not regarded as satisfactory by the Church but the situation would become intolerable to some if the grounds for divorce were extended to admit divorce based on desertion or on other grounds which the Church of England had never accepted as being compatible with the principles laid down in the Gospels. (In the debates on Buckmaster's 1920 Bill Archbishop Davidson moved an amendment which would have prohibited the marriage of any divorced person (whether innocent or guilty) in an Anglican church so long as the other party to the dissolved marriage was alive, and this was only defeated by one vote: *Official Report* (HL) 4 May 1920, vol. 40, col. 126.)

not one on which any of the major political parties had a particular stance[142] and support for reform tended to cut across traditional party divisions. In particular, the presence of large numbers of Roman Catholic Liberal and Labour voters in the industrial cities was (and remained for many years)[143] an important impediment to extension of the grounds for divorce.[144] Thirdly, the Reformers were (as already noted) divided amongst themselves; and this division between those prepared to compromise by supporting a Bill to implement the recommendations on which the Royal Commission had been unanimous and those who believed this would fatally damage the prospects for really effective reform was exploited by opponents of reform and notably by the Archbishop of Canterbury, Randall Davidson.

THE CHURCH MILITANT

In January 1921 Davidson wrote to the younger son of the Royal Commission's Chairman, now the Third Lord Gorell,[145] 'most earnestly hoping' that he would introduce a Divorce Bill 'immediately the new Session starts'.[146] But this was no Damascus Road conversion to the cause of divorce reform.[147] On the contrary, Davidson realised that legislation making access to the Divorce Court somewhat easier for people of moderate means and allowing women to petition on the same grounds as men (changing the administration rather than the principles of the law as he put it)[148] would cut away much of the support which a Bill extending the grounds for divorce would otherwise have.[149] And the Reformers obligingly

---

[142] See the speech of Lord Birkenhead LC attempting to explain why the 1920 Bill had failed to make progress. He urged those seeking implementation of the Majority Recommendations to 'concentrate upon the organisation of supporters' and to explore and develop every means by which the 'strong and growing volume of opinion in the country can be made effective in the House of Commons. [The opponents] are very well organised . . . [and] every form of organised appeal that would be brought to bear [on MPs] was so brought to bear': *Official Report* (HL) 10 March 1921, vol. 44, col. 492.

[143] In 1937, according to AP Herbert, 'Lord Snell, Labour's able and well-liked leader in the Lords' was ready and willing to sponsor Herbert's Bill in its passage through the House of Lords 'but his own Party thought it would be better for the Bill to be born on the other side of the House': *The Ayes Have It* (1937) p. 170.

[144] The DLRU was well aware of the fact that MPs representing working class areas could not necessarily be relied on to support reform. No doubt in an attempt to overcome fears that to vote for reform would be to lose election votes the Divorce Law Reform Union presented a petition to the Home Secretary in 1920 signed by over 100,000 persons, the great majority 'poor workers': see PREM1/18, p. 8 (Mrs Seaton-Tiedeman).

[145] See Biographical Notes.

[146] *Gorell Diaries*, 6 January 1921. The Archbishop followed this approach by dining with Gorell in February 1921.

[147] Gorell wrote: '. . . York, Salisbury, Canterbury, it is really rather funny. I don't much like being used to pull the chestnuts out of the fire for the Church but if I do introduce the Bill I shall certainly not oppose an amendment giving desertion à la Scotland': *ibid*.

[148] *Official Report* (HL), 12 April 1921, vol. 44, col. 856.

[149] The belief that limited reform would remove the steam from the campaign to extend the ground for divorce had been publicly acknowledged: see eg the speech by the Unionist MP RJ McNeill in the debate on the 1920 Rendall motion. This was also the reason given in 1923 by

stepped into the trap which had been laid for them. When Gorell brought his Bill to give effect to the recommendations on which *Minority* and *Majority* Royal Commission Reports were agreed before the House of Lords in March 1921,[150] the radicals[151] insisted[152] on amending it to allow desertion as a ground for divorce. The Bill did not get off the ground in the House of Commons.

Worse was to come. In 1922 the Coalition Government fell, to be replaced by a Conservative Administration; and there were no prospects for comprehensive reform with a Government in which in which the outspoken opponent of divorce reform Bridgeman[153] was Home Secretary and the only slightly more liberal Cave[154] was Lord Chancellor. In 1923, the National Union of Societies for Equal Citizenship, committed to achieving equality of status between men and women,[155] procured the introduction of a Bill[156] allowing women to petition for divorce on the ground of the husband's adultery. It was difficult if not impossible to find any plausible ground on the merits[157] for resistance; and the

the right wing Conservative Home Secretary, WO Bridgeman for not opposing the Bill to put men and women on the same footing in terms of the ground for divorce: see *Official Report* (HC), 2 March 1923, vol. 160, col. 2360.

[150] Gorell acknowledged that the defeat of the Rendall motion in April 1920 (see note 139(iii) above) had made it difficult to suppose that the House of Commons would agree to extension of the ground for divorce. It is difficult to know whether he genuinely believed that his Bill would be uncontroversial: *Official Report* (HL), 10 March 1921, vol. 44, col. 458.

[151] As represented by Buckmaster and Earl Russell (who moved an amendment that the House was not prepared to disregard the findings of the Royal Commission at the bidding of ecclesiastical tradition; and that it declined to proceed further with a Bill which provided 'illusory remedies for real hardship': *Official Report* (HL), 10 March 1921, vol. 44, col. 462). Eventually Russell withdrew his amendment on the basis that 'more valuable cargo' would be packed into the Bill at a later stage.

[152] Buckmaster claimed that the Gorell Bill was not the gist of the Royal Commission recommendations but rather the residue: 'I cannot assent to the passage of a Bill which will condemn to a life of shame and loneliness and misery those people . . . who have looked to your Lordship's House with unspeakable gratitude for the effort which was made last session . . ., and who still look with pathetic hope to your Lordship's House to afford them redemption from their distress': *Official Report* (HL), 10 March 1921, vol. 44, col. 468. In 1924 Buckmaster told the Prime Minister that he could not allow a Bill to go to the Commons containing no extended ground of divorce because to do so would suggest the House of Lords thought that to be a 'satisfactory measure of matrimonial reform'. Buckmaster explained that he had taken charge of the amended Bill, 'the fight became fierce again, and again we beat them off after a very stubborn debate on the third reading . . .': PRO PREM 1/ 38, p. 3.

[153] See Biographical Notes.   [154] *Ibid.*

[155] On NUSEC's role, see generally Moyse, p. 106 ff.

[156] The Bill was introduced in the House of Commons by Major Cyril F Entwistle (1887–1974): see Biographical Notes. For an account of the Bill and one view of the background to it see R Probert, 'The controversy of equality and the Matrimonial Causes Act 1923' [1999] CFLQ 33. The Bill was poorly drafted and (in theory at least) put women at an advantage since a wife could petition on the ground that her husband had been guilty of rape, sodomy or bestiality as well as on the ground that he had committed adultery: see Matrimonial Causes Act 1923, s. 1 and Matrimonial Causes Act 1857, s. 27 as amended by the Schedule to the 1923 Act.

[157] But there were those who opposed even this reform, claiming that they were not opposed to equal treatment of men and women but were opposed to this particular reform since to allow divorce on the basis of simple adultery would facilitate sham and collusive divorces: see eg Dennis Herbert MP, *Official Report* (HC) 26 June 1923, vol. 53, col. 2365. In the debates on the AP Herbert Bill in 1936 and 1937 it was repeatedly and widely claimed that the 1923 Act had greatly increased the incidence of collusive divorces: people married on the basis that if a couple found themselves incompatible the husband would 'do the decent thing' and provide evidence of adultery: see

radical reformers (from whom NUSEC had been careful to distance themselves) did not oppose what Earl Russell described[158] as a 'thoroughly bad and inadequate Bill'. Even Bridgeman, the strongly conservative Home Secretary[159] accepted equal treatment of the sexes;[160] and on the Second Reading Division in the House of Commons 257 MPs voted in favour and only 26 against.[161] The Matrimonial Causes Act duly became law on 18 July 1923. The strong feminist pressure for equality ceased to be a factor in the move for further divorce reform;[162] and, although the Reformers put on a brave face,[163] there seems little doubt that their cause had been significantly damaged.

The extent of the damage was soon to be demonstrated. At the end of 1923 the Conservatives were defeated at a General Election, to be replaced by Britain's first Labour Government.[164] Early in 1924 Buckmaster took the opportunity to reintroduce what was in substance[165] his 1920 Bill. Once again, he made a powerfully emotional speech: the Bill (he said) had one purpose and one purpose only, the relief of human agony. But the Archbishop of Canterbury[166] was now able to make effective debating points. The reformers had got equal treatment for wives. They had got cheaper divorce.[167] What evidence (the

eg *Standing Committee A Official Report*, 8 December 1936, col. 11. This is certainly the assumption underlying the descriptions of hotel divorces in *Holy Deadlock* and other works: see p. 231, below; and the statistics (see *Report of the Royal Commission on Marriage and Divorce*, 1956, Cmd. 9678, Table 1) indicate a marked growth in the proportion of petitions filed by wives between 1924 and 1939 (in which latter year wartime conditions may account for the upsurge in the proportion of petitions by husbands).

[158] *Official Report* (HL) 26 June 1923, vol. 54, col. 602.   [159] See Biographical Notes.

[160] Whilst making it clear that the 'abominable proposals' in Buckmaster's 1920 Bill would be in a wholly different category.

[161] The remaining stages in the Commons were—notwithstanding some opposition—completed on 8 June 1923, *Official Report* (HC) vol. 164, col. 2660. This Bill was given a Second Reading in the House of Lords on 26 June 1923 by a majority of 95 to 8 (*Official Report* (HL) vol. 54, col. 573) and passed its remaining stages without debate.

[162] This was accepted by Entwistle in introducing the Bill: *Official Report* (HC) 2 March 1923, vol. 160, col. 2360; and it is certainly the case that NUSEC had been ambivalent about supporting extension of the ground for divorce, an issue on which its membership was, at this time, divided: see M Pugh, *Women and the Women's Movement in Britain 1914–1959* (1992) p. 246 and note the opposition of Lady Astor founded on her belief (based on experience in the United States) that easier divorce had not been in the interests of women: *Official Report* (HC) 14 April 1920, vol. 5, col. 1794. In the House of Lords Buckmaster (who had the carriage of the Bill) made it quite clear that to move amendments to the Bill would be seen to be an attempt to destroy it: *Official Report* (HL) 26 June 1923, vol. 53, col. 575.

[163] See the address given by Mrs Francis Acland under DLRU auspices on 10 December 1925 (*Eirene White Papers*): 1923 Act 'a distinct gain for morality' but insignificant 'compared with the total objectives of our Union'.

[164] But the Labour Party held only 191 out of the 625 seats in the House of Commons.

[165] There were some changes: for example, Buckmaster had restored imprisonment under a commuted death sentence as a ground for divorce and the Bill equated homosexual acts—'surely one of the darkest of all shadows that blackens the face of man'—with adultery as a ground on which the court could dissolve a marriage.

[166] *Official Report* (HL) 11 March 1924, vol. 56, col. 636.

[167] The Administration of Justice Act 1920 allowed cases to be tried in the provinces by the Assize judge: see p. 277 below.

Archbishop asked) was there of any demand for further change?[168] After all, the Mothers' Union continued to fill MPs' mail bags with expressions of resolute disapproval of further erosion of the principle that marriage was, and should remain, indissoluble. Where would it all end? With divorce by consent whenever couples grew tired of their relationship?

Buckmaster and his supporters needed to answer that; and Buckmaster believed he could do so if the Labour Government would agree to find the time necessary to allow a Bill to be fully debated in the Commons. But Lord Chancellor Haldane[169] was not encouraging.[170] The Government's electoral position was weak. Public opinion was divided. So was opinion within the Government.[171] Faced with Haldane's refusal to promise facilities for the Bill, Buckmaster quickly arranged for an impressive delegation[172] to see the Prime Minister, Ramsay MacDonald.[173] There was (he said) no point in simply repeating what had happened in earlier years. Would the Government introduce a Bill which would not include any extension of the grounds for divorce, but which would have a long title sufficiently broad to allow amendments made by the Commons of its own free will?

[168] Buckmaster subsequently pointed out to the Prime Minister that this question was 'unwise'. 'You cannot expect to get big popular demonstrations by men who have been unhappily married. It is the one thing that men would desire to conceal. You cannot help these people unless outsiders are impressed with the sense of the wrong they suffer and the injustice of their position, and are prepared to champion their cause without expecting that it is going to receive popular applause'. Buckmaster pointed to the majorities in the House of Lords for reform as the 'surest warrant that enlightened public opinion' supported reform: PRO PREM 1/38, p. 6.

[169] See Biographical Notes.

[170] It is interesting to compare Haldane's discouraging attitude as Lord Chancellor in a Labour Administration to that which he had taken in 1914 as Liberal Lord Chancellor. It may be that the explanation for the change in attitude is that the Labour Cabinet was much more reluctant to be associated with divorce reform proposals: see below.

[171] According to Sir Claud Schuster (Permanent Secretary to the Lord Chancellor, 1915–1944) the 'matter of divorce reform was considered on two or three separate occasions by both the first [1924] and the second [1929–1931] Labour Governments, and on each occasion the majority of the Cabinet were directly opposed on merits to any change in the law': Schuster to Sir Geoffrey Fry (Private Secretary to Stanley Baldwin), 26 February 1934, PRO LCO2/1194. And although the Labour Party Annual Conference had passed a resolution in 1913 supporting the Royal Commission majority report electoral considerations pointed away from the Government associating itself with divorce reform.

[172] The official record of the meeting (PRO PREM1/38) describes the deputation as being from the 'Divorce Law Reform Union and other interests'. The Union's Vice-Chairman (Hon. Gilbert Coleridge, son of a former Lord Chief Justice of England, sometime Assistant Master in the Crown Office) Secretary (Mrs Seaton-Tiedeman) and Honorary Solicitor (ESP Haynes) were members. There were three persons active in Liberal politics (The Rt. Hon. Sir FD Acland, MP for North Cornwall, Mr Silas Hocking, a successful author, previously Methodist Minister and unsuccessful parliamentary candidate—both long term active supporters of the DLRU—and Hay Morgan KC, Liberal MP for Truro 1906–1918, formerly Elementary School Teacher and Pastor of the Baptist Church Woodberry Down London), as well as the Liberal journalist JA Spender, a member of the Gorell Royal Commission. The other delegates were Dr Ethel Bentham (who had given evidence to the Royal Commission, and was a member of the Labour Party National Executive, later MP for East Islington) and Cecil Chapman (the Metropolitan Police Magistrate for Tower Bridge 1899 to 1924, and sometime a Conservative member of the LCC).

[173] The meeting took place at 10 Downing Street on 24 March 1924. A full note, taken by Treasury Reporters, is on PRO file PREM 1/38.

MacDonald's response was (in spite of his protestations of personal support and sympathy) profoundly depressing.[174] The Government, lacking a majority in the Commons, could not compel the closure of debate; and their control of the House (and thus the legislative timetable) was 'more moral than numerical'. There was not 'the ghost of a chance' of the Government being able to give time for so controversial a measure as a divorce Bill. MacDonald refused to give even the 'word of hope' for the future which the Divorce Law Reform Union asked for on behalf of the 'sufferers' it represented.[175] But in the event the question was academic: the Labour Government fell[176] and there was a Conservative land-slide[177] at the election on 29 October 1924. Prospects for support from a Government in which Lord Cave was Lord Chancellor and the leading Evangelical churchman Sir William Joynson-Hicks Home Secretary were once again virtually non-existent. No one seems even to have tried directly to persuade the Government (which remained in office until 1929) to provide any help for the reform movement. No one even bothered to introduce a Bill.

PARLIAMENTARY BATTLES RESUME, 1930

There may have been little parliamentary activity whilst the Conservatives remained in power, but the Divorce Law Reform Union continued to campaign.[178] At the election held on 30 May 1929—the first in which women had the

[174] 'Sincere but somewhat depressing' as Buckmaster put it: PRO file PREM 1/38, p. 17.

[175] See Mrs Seaton-Tiedeman's question at PRO PREM1/38, p. 20. Instead, MacDonald launched into an extraordinary outburst against ministerial statements being quoted out of context: 'I would like to answer [the question whether there was any prospect of legislation in the next Session], but you know that next Session is next Session, and it would be exceedingly awkward if I went and said something to you to-day which would be taken out of its context and conditions and used for other purposes . . . I am perfectly appalled at the dishonest use that is made of statements sincerely made—perfectly appalled by it. I have found it is impossible to say a word about anything but it is turned into some extraordinary pledge, if you can call it so, and both—all the Parties are just lying like cats watching for the twist of a mouse's whisker in order to pounce upon it; and until there is some more decency in Party life, I think you will find that some of us will say nothing at all. . . . But I am sick of the whole thing. I give you my personal feelings in the matter, and if I could do anything, I would do it. The point today is *this Session*, and if I could see my way, I would not say what I have said, but you know the terrible trouble' (PRO PREM 1/38, pp. 19–20).

[176] It had been defeated in the House of Commons on 8 October 1924 by 364 votes to 198 on motions arising out of the decision to halt the prosecution of the editor of the *Workers' Weekly* under the Incitement to Mutiny Act 1797 in respect of an article calling on soldiers to let it be known that neither in the class war nor in a military war would they turn their guns on their fellow workers.

[177] In the new Parliament the Conservatives held 419 seats, as against 151 held by Labour (and 40 by the Liberals).

[178] See for example the thoughtful address given by Mrs Francis Acland under DLRU auspices on 10 December 1925 (*Eirene White Papers*) seeking to establish that divorce reform would foster morality in the face of a perfect spate of literature setting forth the advantages, pleasures, and naturalness of 'free love . . . [T]he choice before society today is not between the Sanctity of Marriage and Divorce Law Reform but rather between Divorce Law Reform and a great increase of unregulated unsanctioned indulgence of the tremendous force of sexual desire'.

vote on the same terms as men—there was a sharp swing to Labour. For the first time, Labour was the largest party in the House of Commons, and Ramsay MacDonald became Prime Minister for the second time. This did not necessarily mean that his Government would be any more prepared than its Conservative predecessor to risk losing votes by itself becoming identified with divorce law reform;[179] but the election did bring into the Commons a number of new Members who were prepared to take action. Of these, the most significant was the lawyer Labour member for South Nottingham, GW Holford Knight KC.[180]

Divorce as a remedy for national degeneracy?

Holford Knight[181] seems to have identified one area in which several traditionally opposing groups might perhaps be brought together. The plight of the spouses of the incurably insane[182]—in 1921 it was estimated that as many as 17,000 married men and women had been confined in lunatic asylums for more than five years[183]—was easy to depict in moving terms;[184] and the Gorell Royal Commission had accepted that incurable insanity was more effective in destroying the marriage relationship than any of the other causes which might be put

---

[179] The majority of the cabinet was opposed to any change in the law: Schuster to Fry (Private Secretary to Stanley Baldwin), 26 February 1934, PRO LCO2/1194; see note 171 above.

[180] See Biographical Notes.

[181] It may be that pressure from the DLRU Parliamentary Representative James Cassell influenced this view. It is arguable that insanity was the most controversial of the Royal Commission's proposals involving a definite breach of the principle that spouses are to hold to one another 'in sickness and in health'. But there were considerations pointing in favour of a single insanity ground bill: see below.

[182] It is important to remember that, before the development of modern drug therapy, the prospects for recovery from mental illness were poor: the *Gorell Report* had estimated that there were some 150,000 registered insane persons in the United Kingdom of whom 60,000 or more were married; and noted that two-thirds of the inhabitants of lunatic asylums—'kept in close and compulsory confinement'—could be regarded as incurable. The *Report* cited evidence that the large number of hopelessly insane spouses had no interest in life, were quite incapable of caring for themselves or managing their affairs, their affection for their relations was perverted or dead, they were incapable of deriving any comfort from the visits of friends, and regarded their spouses as strangers: para. 286.

[183] *Official Report* (HC) 26 February 1930, vol. 235, col. 2265.

[184] The *Gorell Report* said that the spouse of an incurably insane person was 'not only denied the enjoyments and advantages of married life, but is condemned—often whilst still young—to a compulsory celibacy which may extend to the end of his or her days. The sane spouse is unable to add healthy legitimate children to the State and continue the family name. The poor man, whose wife is in an asylum for life, must find a housekeeper to manage his home, and take care of his children. The woman, who is deprived of her husband, loses a protector and supporter. As a result, irregular unions, immorality, and the production of illegitimate children are inevitable. The wife may in some instances be driven to prostitution, the children of the legitimate union are apt to be neglected, and the economic troubles incident to the support of two families may be acute. There is no doubt that the hardships which are inevitable when a husband or wife is confined for life to an asylum, tell more hardly upon the poor than upon the rich, and that the demand for relief in a large series of cases is very pressing' (para. 288).

forward as ground for dissolution.[185] The Commission had accordingly recommended that incurable insanity should, subject to certain limitations[186] be a
ground for divorce.[187]

There was another factor which influenced the move to allow divorce of the
insane. The Eugenic movement,[188] committed to the belief that moral as well as
physical characteristics were inherited, was at the time powerful and influential.
It wanted to improve the physical and mental health of the population by
encouraging the fit to have children and to prevent the propagation of a degen-
erate race by preventing the unfit from doing so.[189] The result of denying the
possibility of remarriage to men and women whose marriages had effectively
ceased to exist meant (as Lord Birkenhead put it[190] in the debates on the 1920
Buckmaster Bill) that thousands of English men and women

'in the prime of their lives, who ought to be contributing to the child-strength of the
Empire at a moment when the very future of the Empire may depend upon the sufficiency
of a virile population'

—were debarred from remarrying and bearing children. It was necessary to control the fertility of the unfit and encourage the fertility of the fit; and considerations such as these had influenced countries such as New Zealand to allow
divorce for incurable insanity.[191]

[185] *Gorell Report*, para. 268. The Report took the view that in cases of incurable insanity the
married relationship ends as if the insane person were dead, and the objects for which the marriage
was formed have become wholly frustrated. In a passage of great importance for the future development of the law the Report stated that 'persons marrying cannot reasonably be supposed to contemplate the continuance of the relationship becoming impossible, the joint life determined, and the
objects . . . wholly frustrated by reason of misconduct *or otherwise*' (italics supplied): *ibid*.

[186] ie that the insane person should be certified as incurable, that he should have been continuously confined for not less than five years, and that he should not be over 50 (or, if a man, 60)—this
last provision being intended to exclude cases of senile dementia and cases where there would be 'no
reasonable ground for dissolving the marriage, having regard to the to the age of the parties': *Gorell
Report*, para. 292. The Commission also recommended a number of special procedural requirements intended to protect the person alleged to be insane.

[187] *Gorell Report*, para. 289. It was to be a defence that the petitioner's conduct had brought
about the respondent's insanity: para. 296.

[188] See generally 'Divorce and the eugenics movement' in R Phillips, *Putting Asunder, A history
of divorce in Western society* (1988) pp. 507–512; and generally on this topic (uncomfortable for the
post-World War II reader) D Knowles, *In the name of Eugenics* (1986).

[189] A considerable body of evidence on the principles of eugenics and its application to the law
of marriage and divorce was given to the Gorell Royal Commission: see *Gorell Report*, para. 297,
and (eg) the evidence of MH Crackanthorpe KC, *Gorell Report*, Minutes of Evidence, 2 November
1910. The Commission noted that some witnesses were disappointed that the scope of enquiry did
not include questions relating to the 'marriage of persons with an extremely bad mental and nervous
heredity, with criminality, and with positive signs of degeneration, and the prevention of fatherhood
and motherhood on the part of those almost certain to produce a diseased and bad stock of citizens
in the future'. These witnesses felt that 'the prevention of mental disease and of imbecility would
also imply the prevention of much vice, criminality and ineffectiveness' amongst citizens. But the
Commission noted that matters relating to the formation of marriage were not within the
Commission's terms of reference: *Gorell Report*, para. 297.

[190] *Official Report* (HL), 10 March 1920, vol. 39, col. 672.

[191] 'We have got to guard this colony against the fertility of the unfit . . . What is to become of
the future peoples of this dominion if we allow either a man or a woman who has been certified as
a lunatic to come back and resume cohabitation, resulting in the breeding of a race . . . unfortunate

Holford Knight had a limited success. In 1930 (putting at the forefront of his argument the 'pitiful cases of spouses who have been in asylums for many years' as evidencing the need for relief from a 'sorely felt grievance')[192] he got leave[193] to introduce a Bill which would have allowed divorce where the respondent was incurably insane and had been a certified lunatic for a continuous period of at least five years. But the Government refused to give facilities for the Bill. The 'present state of Parliamentary Business' was given as the reason[194] but the truth (as we now know)[195] is that a majority of the Cabinet were opposed to extension of the ground for divorce.[196] Twice Holford Knight repeated the attempt to get an incurable insanity Bill through the Commons,[197] and twice he failed.

Getting the Government to recognise its responsibility

Holford Knight explained that the reason for restricting the Bills which he introduced to this single reform[198] (rather than taking on the whole of the Gorell Report) was that 'a Bill of that character, making drastic and far-reaching changes in the law should be undertaken only by the Government itself'.[199] But the only response was negative.[200] Eventually, in February 1934 Holford Knight

in every sense of the word': a New Zealand MP quoted in Phillips, *Putting Asunder, A History of divorce in Western Society* p. 510.

[192] The previous year the DLRU had reprinted and circulated an address by JS Risien Russell, 'Insanity as a ground for Divorce', claiming that divorce was one means of putting a check on the transmission of 'vices of all descriptions' (including 'cheating, stealing and murder'). The problem he identified was that husbands frequently demanded the release of an insane wife from an asylum so that she 'could look after him and the home', and a short period of cohabitation before her return led to conception of a child. It was claimed that such children were often born in the asylums to which the wives were quickly forced to return.

[193] *Official Report* (HC) 26 February 1930, vol. 235, col. 2263. Leave was given on a division by 210 to 102.

[194] *Official Report* (HC) 30 June 1930, vol. 240, col. 1602.

[195] The question whether the DLRU should seek to achieve piecemeal reform (rather than the comprehensive measure to which it had become committed) had been put to a vote in 1926, and three quarters of the membership favoured the introduction of one clause Bills. The most favoured ground to be added by such a Bill was desertion (favoured by twice as many as insanity): Moyse, p. 59.

[196] Schuster to Fry, 26 February 1934, see note 171, above.

[197] On the first of these occasions he failed (by 148 votes to 114) even to get leave to introduce the Bill: *Official Report* (HC) 28 January 1931, vol. 247, col. 975. On the second occasion (after the General Election on 27 October 1931 had returned a huge majority for the 'National' (ie coalition) Government formed by MacDonald on 24 August 1931) the House did give leave by 96 votes to 42: *Official Report* (HC) 30 November 1932, vol. 272, col. 823; but the House was then twice counted out and the Bill made no further progress: see *Official Report* (HC) 5 May and 12 May 1933, vol. 277, cols. 1194, 1872. To complete the saga, it should be recorded that James Chuter Ede and others introduced a Bill (No. 106) to give effect to the whole of the Gorell recommendations on 4 March 1931, but this was not even debated.

[198] However, the long title—a Bill to amend the law of Matrimonial Causes—was wide enough to allow members of either house to move much more far-reaching amendments.

[199] *Official Report* (HC) 30 November 1932, vol. 272, col. 824.

[200] On two occasions in 1932 Ministers in the National Government, responding to parliamentary questions, refused to introduce legislation: see *Official Report* (HC) 24 February 1932, vol. 262, col. 386; 10 March 1936, vol. 263, col. 274.

did bring forward a Bill to implement all the Gorell recommendations. He repeated that it was his view that such a Bill should be undertaken by a responsible Government:

but unfortunately 'it is the case that no responsible Government is in sight, as far as I can see, which will undertake this task, and such is the accumulation of private and public mischief as the result of not proceeding with this reform that I have undertaken this task in the hope that the Government may be persuaded to respond to the general opinion, not only in this House but in the country, that this matter should be brought under close discussion'.[201]

Yet once again, the Bill failed to make progress: shortage of parliamentary time[202] gave those opposed to divorce reform[203] the opportunity they needed, and the Bill was lost.

Public opinion?

Holford Knight and his supporters must have been bitterly disappointed by the repeated failure to make progress, whilst the many who remained legally bound to a spouse with whom they had ceased to have any real relationship found it difficult to restrain themselves from expressing their bitter feelings. But, as Sir Claud Schuster[204] pointed out:

'It would be impossible for a Bill to be again and again talked out in the Commons if there were not a very considerable body of responsible opinion averse to the proposal . . .'

and he went on to point out the strength of the opposition to extension of the grounds for divorce. In addition to the Roman Catholics, the:

'whole body of Anglicans—I mean by Anglicans those whose primary interest in life is bound up with the body of doctrine of the Anglican Church—take the same view. They have sympathisers also among those of the laity, who, though not ardent churchmen, are very unwilling to see a further schism between the law of the land and the law of the Church. . . . Furthermore, objection may be taken to many of the proposals by people who do not share the religious convictions referred to above. . . . On every one of [the proposed new grounds for divorce] a very powerful argument can be constructed adverse

---

[201] *Official Report* (HC) 2 February 1934, vol. 285, col. 748.

[202] It was effectively talked out: see *Official Report* (HC) 3 February 1934, vol. 285, col. 772 and col. 806.

[203] Dr WJ O'Donovan, an Irish Roman Catholic consultant dermatologist practising from Harley Street and returned at the 1931 election as the Conservative Member for Stepney, Mile End, persistently and effectively opposed divorce reform. Although he operated within the permitted constitutional conventions his actions were resented by those who considered legislation should be properly considered by Parliament. It could be claimed that his defeat by a Labour candidate in the General Election on 13 November 1935 made possible the passage of the Matrimonial Causes Act 1937.

[204] Schuster to Sir Geoffrey Fry Bt. (Baldwin's Private Secretary) 26 February 1936, PRO LCO2/2294 (note 171 above) commenting on the case of a prominent Conservative politician.

to the proposal. . . . [I]t is impossible to say . . . that there is a unanimous, or nearly unanimous, body of public opinion outside the religious bodies in favour of the change . . . I should like to add that, so far as I am concerned, I do not share the religious views, to which I have alluded above, and that I have very little sympathy with any objection taken to divorce . . . on religious grounds. I do think, on the other hand, that the very grave social considerations which arise upon the proposals of the [Holford Knight 1934 Bill] require a very much greater and more extensive survey than they have yet received before Parliament ought to pass them into law. I think that the proposals lend themselves to all the evils of the present system (which are many and great) and introduce fresh occasions for scandal and hardship, and it is hardly possible to foresee what their effect might be upon the structure of English society . . .'

And yet within four years the proposals had become part of English law. What explanation can be given for this transformation?

Ridicule more powerful than outrage? Perceptions of the divorce law in practice

There seems little doubt that 'public opinion' (an expression which, before the development of scientific attitude surveys is difficult satisfactorily to define) was changing, and in part this may be attributable to a change of approach on the part of those urging reform. No doubt the hardship caused by the law remained a factor, but a strong sense that the existing law was ridiculous and almost corrupt seems to have developed. A law which was supposed to promote (or at least safeguard) morality was in reality encouraging either immorality or perjury:[205] people who recognised that their marriage was in fact at an end could usually get the freedom to remarry but only by either committing adultery or pretending that they had done so. The result was that the wrong people—the immoral and the untruthful—got the divorce they wanted; the right people—those who took their marriage vows seriously and were not prepared to lie to get their freedom— could not do so.[206] A particular problem was the so-called 'hotel divorce'.

Hotel divorces: law held up to ridicule and contempt?

In 1934, the publication of two novels brought the absurdity of the divorce laws forcefully into the consciousness of people who were perhaps not usually particularly interested in what so often appeared as the boring obsession of the well-meaning or personally involved:

[205] In 1931 the NUSEC Executive Committee rejected its former policy of not advocating extension to the ground for divorce and voted overwhelmingly for the implementation of the Royal Commission recommendations because under the existing law 'morality was being attacked by people committing or pretending to commit adultery in order to get divorce': Moyse, p. 110. But the *Normanton Papers* (Helena Normanton KC, Millicent Fawcett Library (now the Women's Library, London Guildhall University)) reveal continuing difficulties within NUSEC, particularly on the question of how best to give financial protection to the divorced wife.
[206] AP Herbert, moving the second reading of the Marriage Bill, *Official Report* (HC), 20 November 1936, vol. 317, col. 2082.

In *A Handful of Dust*[207] Evelyn Waugh[208] described the legal process whereby a man, spurned by his wife in favour of another, is persuaded to allow himself to be divorced on the ground of adultery (which he has never committed). A week-end was 'fixed for [his] infidelity' ; and his solicitors engaged rooms at a Brighton hotel where the servants were 'well accustomed to giving evidence'. However, the solicitors stopped short of 'selecting a partner' because (although they had 'on occasions been instrumental in accommodating clients') there had also been complaints. Indeed they had had one recent case 'involving a man of very rigid morality and a certain diffidence' which was only resolved by his own wife going with him (admittedly wearing a red wig) and 'supplying the evidence'. Eventually, the husband finds a night-club hostess who 'knew how to behave at a hotel'. Unfortunately, the hostess's child care arrangements for her eight-year-old daughter break down, and the child accompanies her mother and the husband to the hotel thereby greatly increasing the stress of the procedures. As one of the private detectives (worried about his firm getting mixed up with the King's Proctor) remarked, 'bringing a kid into it' set a 'nasty note'. But the necessary procedures were followed, and the case was 'regular and complete'.[209]

Although Evelyn Waugh had had personal experience of the working of the English divorce laws his novel was not a polemic. In contrast, AP Herbert was happily married[210] and appears to have been animated only by a keen sense of

---

[207] Quotations (reproduced by permission) do not reflect Waugh's personal experience.

[208] Waugh himself had divorced his wife after a marriage lasting only a year on the ground of her adultery. ESP Haynes acted as Waugh's solicitor: *The Times*, 18 January 1930 and Waugh subsequently recalled that Haynes had given him 'far more in oysters and hock . . . than he charged me in fees': C Sykes, *Evelyn Waugh, A Biography* (1975) p. 95. It seems not improbable that Waugh's account of collusion in *A Handful of Dust* owed something to his talks with Haynes.

[209] In the end the husband, outraged by the financial demands made on his wife's behalf, decides not to proceed with the divorce. In reality, the 'regular' procedure was more demanding: see C Mortimer and HHH Coates (eds.), *Rayden's Practice and Law in the Divorce Division* (3rd ed., 1932), pp. 140–141: a 'wife's petition . . . frequently has its origin in a letter written by the husband to the wife enclosing an hotel bill and inviting the wife to institute proceedings for divorce. The solicitor consulted in circumstances of this kind should first satisfy himself that there has been between his client and her husband no discussion or arrangement which has brought about the sending of such evidence. He should then make inquiries at the hotel in question, and ascertain whether the proposed respondent has signed the hotel register, and whether evidence of the fact that he and a woman, not his wife, stayed there is available from the persons who attended him. . . . The next step will be to write a letter to the proposed respondent, stating that divorce proceedings are contemplated, and inviting him to furnish the full name and address of the woman with whom he stayed at the hotel. Upon compliance with this request it will be possible to state the name of the woman in the petition, and this should always be done where practicable. But if there is refusal by the husband to disclose the woman's name, further enquires should be made. . . . But where the respondent is firm in his refusal to disclose the name and inquiries fail to elicit any evidence of his association with a woman who can be identified, the charge in the petition can be confined to the adultery with the woman unknown . . .'.

[210] In his speech introducing the Bill for the Matrimonial Causes Act 1937 Herbert was able to point out that he had been married for 22 years and had four children and one grandchild: *Official Report* (HC) 20 November 1936, vol. 317, col. 2079.

the absurdities of many aspects of English law[211] and the cruelty which it could cause. His novel *Holy Deadlock* (aptly described by his biographer[212] as 'a tract for the times presented as fiction') brilliantly satirised the absurdities of the divorce process:

A husband agreed to 'behave like a gentleman' and provide the evidence needed for the divorce which his wife wanted. Normally in such cases (as Herbert put it) 'good lawyers were engaged, a good many pennies had to be put in the slot, but the divorce emerged from the machine at least as easily as a motor licence, and rather more easily than a passport'; and—although his solicitor refused to provide direct assistance[213]—the husband duly found a 'secretarial agency' which provided the services of a 'well-trained expert, discreetly doing her job, no more'. (The 'expert' portrayed in the novel is able to keep her blind father and five siblings on the proceeds of this work.) Evidence was duly provided, but following a hilarious series of accidents involving an intervention by the King's Proctor (whose agent's activities in prowling the corridors of a large hotel 'in the King's name and a dressing gown' are described with relish) husband and wife are denied the divorce which they both want.

Some years later, a distinguished solicitor[214] was to describe how the so-called hotel divorce had come to be used even by well-intentioned and basically law-abiding people:[215]

'The husband and wife have tried to make a success of the marriage but have found it impossible and breaking point is reached at last. They probably have a frank discussion as a result of which the husband leaves and promises to supply his wife with evidence for a divorce. He finds a lady who is willing and takes her to a hotel where they occupy a double room. Adultery may or may not take place . . . but . . . adultery will appear to have taken place. He then writes to his wife a pathetic letter indicating that he has fallen in love with another woman who he believes will make him happy and he encloses the hotel bill

---

[211] See Biographical Notes; and generally AP Herbert, *Independent Member* (1950) and R Pound, *AP Herbert, A Biography* (1976).

[212] R Pound, *AP Herbert, A Biography* (1976), p. 115. Similar language was used in the review appearing in *The Times Literary Supplement* on 5 April 1934 which correctly stated that the 'subject of the novel is a simple conflict with a young couple in the sympathetic role and the divorce law which keeps them bound to one another as the villain'.

[213] The book does evidence the concern expressed by the divorce judges about collusive divorce: 'when a man behaves like a gentleman with a woman who is not quite a lady it looks like a fishy case, and that old President is very hot': p. 43. Thus, the rule whereby in principle all hotel cases were to be heard by a High Court judge sitting in London is noted; as is the courts' increasing reluctance to accept evidence of adultery unless there were also corroborative evidence of what were described as adulterous tendencies.

[214] Professor LCB Gower, addressing an Anglo-French Legal Conference in Paris in 1949: *Report of the Royal Commission on Marriage and Divorce 1956*, Minutes of Evidence p. 17. There is no reason to suppose that the practice had changed very much in the previous decade.

[215] It was widely believed that even in the years after World War II 'there were firms of solicitors who provided a service including the booking of the room, the presence of the lady and no doubt careful briefing of the chambermaid': R Dunn, *Sword and Wig, Memoirs of a Lord Justice* (1993) p. 140. However, the belief that the evidence of a chambermaid was essential to success was not well founded.

in case she decides to take any action. The wife consults her solicitor, tells him a discreet version of the story carefully avoiding any mention of the discussion which took place on their parting and produces the bill. The solicitor obtains the necessary evidence from the hotel and in a few weeks they are divorced.'

Even the judiciary were prepared to accept that cases such as this did occur,[216] and were concerned about the effect of publicity. From this perspective, what was important was not so much what did in fact happen but what the public were led to believe happened. As the President of the Probate Divorce and Admiralty Division wrote to the Lord Chancellor's Permanent Secretary in 1936:[217]

'There always has been, and no doubt there always will be, a certain amount of collusion in connection with divorce. The danger is not that some individuals should present collusive suits, but that it should become notorious that the presentation of a collusive suit is the recognised way to obtain a divorce . . . [The judges] all think that the scandal is limited to about 5%, or possibly a little more, of the undefended cases heard in London, while the rest are perfectly clear, straightforward cases, which give us no anxiety at all. But unfortunately this comparatively small percentage of cases includes those which are most talked about in general society and there are definite signs that the example they set is spreading. Already in the press . . . in novels, and on the stage, it is assumed that this class of case is the normal. That is bad enough, but it would be disastrous to the respect for the law if this assumption became increasingly true.'

Herbert's book sold 90,000 copies.[218] His exposé of the reality of the divorce process struck home. In June 1934 the Scottish Unionist MP Frederick Macquisten KC gave Herbert's book some gratuitous publicity. He put down a Parliamentary Question asking whether the authorities' attention had been drawn to *Holy Deadlock*, a book 'wherein His Majesty's Judges and courts and the legal system they administer in matrimonial causes are held up to public ridicule and contempt'.[219] The Attorney's reply that allegations in a work of fiction were not something requiring action merely prompted the rejoinder that the book did recount 'pretty much what is happening in the courts just now', and the Attorney's denial did not altogether carry conviction.

---

[216] The judges had viewed such cases with suspicion; and in 1928 Lord Merrivale P had begun to refuse decrees where the only evidence was that the respondent had spent one night in a hotel with someone not his wife: *Aylward v. Aylward* (1928) 44 TLR 456. But in *Woolf v. Woolf* [1931] P 134 the Court of Appeal had held that the President (apparently influenced by the absence of any evidence of previous adulterous tendencies on the husband's part and by his refusal to name the woman concerned) had been wrong to withhold a decree against a husband proved to have registered at a hotel with a woman not his wife and to have been seen by a chambermaid in bed with her on two successive nights. This may have marked the turning of the tide in favour of a less restrictive approach: see CP Harvey QC, 'On the State of the Divorce Market' (1953) 16 MLR 129, 131. Examples of the routine use of 'hotel evidence' can be found in case papers filed in the Public Record Office: see eg PRO J77/3896 (decree dissolving marriage of parties separated for 11 years founded on evidence of adultery in Charing Cross Hotel provided by the husband).

[217] Merriman to Schuster, 16 November 1936, pp. 2–3, PRO LCO2/1195.

[218] R Pound, *AP Herbert, A Biography* (1976), p. 115.

[219] *Official Report* (HC) 4 June and 13 June 1934, vol. 290, cols. 566 and 1690.

Hotel divorces: the abdication crisis

The most dramatic apparent confirmation of the belief that Herbert's description of the divorce process reflected the reality came two years later shortly after King Edward VIII had succeeded to the throne:

The King had met Mrs Wallis Warfield Simpson in 1931, and a close relationship had developed between the two.[220] In October 1936, a judge sitting at Suffolk Assizes had, on her undefended petition, granted Mrs Simpson a decree nisi of divorce on the ground that her husband had committed adultery at a hotel in the Thames Valley with a woman whose name was not given in court. As and when Mrs Simpson's decree was made absolute she would be free to remarry; and on 16 November the King told the Prime Minister that he did intend to marry her. The possibility that the King's marriage would put on the throne as Queen a woman with two former husbands living precipitated a constitutional crisis; and on 11 December the King abdicated. It was apparently widely believed that the decree nisi had been obtained by collusion and so for that and other reasons it should not have been granted.[221] One writer[222] has said that it was generally assumed that *Holy Deadlock* had been used as a procedural handbook in the case.

All these matters no doubt contributed to a gradual shift of opinion; but divorce reform was still a topic which none of the political parties was anxious to espouse. The general election held on 14 November 1935 was dominated by foreign policy issues and the problem of mass unemployment; but it turned out to be very significant for the future of divorce reform.

ENTER AP HERBERT MP

The reason why the 1935 election was of such moment for the history of divorce reform stems from the fact that at that time[223] university graduates were

[220] An excellent account of the Abdication crisis and the events leading up to it is given in P Ziegler, *King Edward VIII, The Official Biography* (1990), Chapters 13 to 18. The legal implications of the Simpson divorce are explored in SM Cretney, 'The King and the King's Proctor: the Abdication Crisis and the Divorce Laws 1936–1937' (2000) 116 LQR 583.

[221] There were four matters which gave rise to comment. First, the case was based on adultery allegedly committed at a hotel and proved by evidence of the hotel staff; and such cases were (as noted above) increasingly viewed with suspicion. Secondly, there were rumours suggesting collusion between the parties. Thirdly, Mrs Simpson had not asked for the exercise of the court's discretion in her favour, yet the closeness of the relationship between her and the King had led some to think it had been adulterous. Finally, the decree had been granted at Ipswich Assizes (rather than by a judge of the Probate Divorce and Admiralty Division sitting in London); and it was suggested that Mrs Simpson lacked the necessary residential qualifications to justify a hearing outside London. Enquiries made by the King's Proctor found no evidence such as would justify the court in setting the decree nisi aside: see *Simpson, W v. Simpson, EA (Application by the King's Proctor for Directions)* (1937) *The Times* March 20.

[222] B Inglis, *Abdication* (1966) p. 352.

[223] The University Franchise was abolished by the Representation of the People Act 1948.

allowed to vote for an MP in the constituencies in which they lived and also to vote in their own special university constituencies. Herbert[224] decided to stand as an Independent Candidate for one of the two Oxford University[225] seats. His manifesto[226] affirmed that Governments had shamefully neglected Home Affairs, and he specifically committed himself to working for reform in a number of areas[227] including the law of divorce.[228] Herbert was elected. Since the University's electors (who, as Herbert was fond of pointing out, included more clergymen than any other English constituency) also returned the anti-divorce Lord Hugh Cecil[229] with more votes than Herbert the result can hardly be seen as a massive endorsement of the cause of divorce reform; but Herbert may well have been right in identifying a movement of opinion[230] in favour of the cautious reforms[231] he advocated.

[224] Apparently (see AP Herbert, *The Ayes Have It* (1937) p. 5) at the urging of the Hon. Frank Pakenham, then a History Tutor at Christ Church, subsequently (as Baron Pakenham) a Minister in the 1945 Labour Cabinet and later (as the Seventh Earl Longford) a prominent campaigner on penal policy and other issues of social policy.

[225] The two Members were elected by the single transferable vote system. The other candidates were the Labour philosopher Professor JL Stocks, the Conservative Lord Hugh Cecil (a sitting member, passionately opposed to extending the grounds for divorce) and CRMF Cruttwell, Principal of Hertford College and a well-regarded historian of the First World War, in which he had served with distinction. By a coincidence, Cruttwell had antagonised the undergraduate Evelyn Waugh who revenged himself by attaching Cruttwell's name to 'a series of shady or absurd characters in his early novels'—in *A Handful of Dust* to a bone-setter (or osteopath) with a fashionable practice particularly amongst Society ladies: see M Davie (ed.), *The Diaries of Evelyn Waugh* (1976) p. 153.

[226] *Letter to the Electors of Oxford University from AP Herbert, New College 1910–1914, Independent National Candidate.*

[227] Other commitments were an overhaul of the laws governing the sale of alcohol, the betting law, road safety and Law Revision.

[228] ESP Haynes, an Oxford graduate of Balliol College, was one of Herbert's 12 nominators: *The Ayes Have it* (1937) p. 12.

[229] The fact that Cecil had been a Member for the University since 1910 was no doubt a factor contributing to the large number of votes cast for him. Cecil believed the only argument for more divorce to be 'the hardship of indissoluble marriage, but this is no argument for it assumes a right of happiness. There is no such right. The path of virtue may often lead to unspeakable misery. It was hard in the War to stay in the front line places, it was hard to be wounded, mutilated and maimed for life, it was hard to be scourged and crucified. Is any unhappy marriage worse? If not the Christian must endure as his Lord endured': quoted in *Official Report* (HC) 20 November 1936, vol. 317, col. 2117. He responded to a letter from Herbert congratulating him on the poll with the statement that sincerity obliged him to say that, on 'public grounds' he 'deeply and keenly' regretted Herbert's election. In the event, Cecil took no part in the debates on the Bill Herbert introduced.

[230] Herbert believed that the majority of churchmen were 'ready and even eager for a reasonable reform' (*The Ayes Have It* (1937) p. 9) and noted that the Lord Chief Justice had written a newspaper article concluding that reform of the substantive law was inevitable: *op. cit.* p. 62.

[231] His election address said that he would wish to make the divorce process more 'humane, direct and honest' but that he did not contemplate hasty or 'Hollywood' divorce, and he affirmed his belief in the 'wholesome safeguard of delay'. Herbert was throughout careful to foster the support of those Anglicans prepared to contemplate reform, and insisted on his concern to save savable marriages: he specifically applauded the 'efforts of Mr Claud Mullins to secure that the court shall endeavour to conciliate before it separates' and Lord Merrivale's proposals to the same end.

Once elected, Herbert[232] wasted no time.[233] With the assistance of a former Parliamentary Draftsman[234] and advice from a number of sources,[235] a divorce reform Bill was drafted and presented.[236] But it was not a case of first time lucky. Herbert was unsuccessful in the ballot for Private Members' Bills;[237] and the Prime Minister responded with heavy sarcasm to Herbert's suggestion that the Government should set aside a day for discussion of his proposals.[238]

Herbert was not the only MP who thought that the time had come for the question of divorce reform to be brought into the open: in the 1936 Session Rupert de la Bere, a Conservative MP of impeccable background and credentials,[239] drew a high[240] place in the ballot. He agreed to take up the Bill which Herbert had drafted: de la Bere did not (he said)[241] object to conscientious opposition to change in the law, but he did object to apathy or even cowardice on the part of MPs fearful of electoral damage in their constituencies. What was needed was honesty and courage.

Herbert's strategy: 'selling' divorce reform

Herbert believed the Gorell Royal Commission had stood the test of time and the recommendations of the Majority Report were to be the 'flesh, bones and blood' of his own Bill. But he was a realist:

[232] Herbert's *The Ayes Have It* (1937) is an invaluable (and entertaining) account of the passage of the Matrimonial Causes Act 1937. *The Birth of an Act* (1956) (Sterling Library, University of London) is a unique handsomely bound collection of documents (including the texts used by Herbert during the Bill's passage) with a manuscript introduction by Herbert, and notes (some in typescript—often derived from *The Ayes Have It*—others in manuscript) by him relating to the Bill and its parliamentary history.

[233] The day after the new Parliament first met, disregarding the convention that an MP's maiden speech should be non-controversial, Herbert made a witty speech of protest at the Government's decision (apparently agreed with the official Opposition) not to make any time for Private Member's Bills before the House rose for Christmas: he claimed to have a suitable Bill—in fact it was a copy of the last Holford Knight Bill—in his hand and swore that it would be passed 'before this Parliament is over'. His action in forcing a division on this issue earned him a solemn rebuke from *The Times'* leader writer on 5 December 1935. Winston Churchill, encountering him afterwards, told Herbert that his speech had been a 'brazen hussy' rather than a 'maiden' speech: see *The Birth of an Act* (1956) f. 4; *The Ayes Have It* (1937) p. 48. Herbert's action in putting down two other Bills on the first possible day in 1936—one of which would simply have assimilated the laws of England and Wales relating to the supply of refreshments and drink to those of France—earned him 'frowns of frivolity': *The Birth of an Act* (1956) f. 17; and his reputation as a person to be taken seriously had to be restored.

[234] Lord Kilbracken, CB, KC (1877–1950): see Biographical Notes.

[235] Notably Claud Mullins: see below.

[236] *Official Report* (HC) 7 February 1936, vol. 308, col. 505. The Cabinet Conclusions merely state that there was little risk of the Bill being debated; but (according to Sir Claud Schuster) 'a view was expressed that the Government would not like it to have a Second Reading': Schuster to Mold, 23 April 1936, PRO LCO2/1195.

[237] *The Ayes Have It* (1937) p. 69.

[238] Baldwin said that if Herbert would give an undertaking that a Bill would be uncontroversial he would be happy to consider having a Government Bill prepared: *Official Report* (HC) 20 May 1936, vol. 312, col. 1191.

[239] (1893–1978): see Biographical Notes.   [240] Second place: *The Ayes Have It* (1937) p. 83.

[241] *Official Report* (HC) 20 November 1936, vol. 317, col. 2081.

'the stark fact remained that, for one reason or another, Parliament has not accepted the proposals of the Royal Commission; and it was not my habit to close my ears to new ideas'.[242]

Hence, the 'Gorell picture' needed to be put into a new frame, hung in a better light—and sold.[243] The Divorce Law Reform Union and other pressure groups[244] had done a lot to create a climate of opinion favourable to reform; but in order to 'sell' the Bill Herbert realised he needed not only to compromise with the opponents of reform[245] but (if at all possible) get the Government, with its power to control the legislative timetable, to collaborate.

Re-packaging Gorell

The message which Herbert wanted to get over was that his Bill would 'strengthen the institution of marriage and increase respect for the law';[246] and this was made explicit in the Bill's preamble (unmistakably in Herbert's own words). It was 'expedient for the true support of marriage, the protection of children, the removal of hardship, the reduction of illicit unions and unseemly litigation, the relief of conscience among the clergy, and the restoration of due respect for the law' to amend the law.

For this reason, the provisions of the Bill Herbert introduced were significantly different[247] from those of earlier attempts at reform.[248] First, there were new provisions intended to mitigate the evils of collusion and perjury which he believed infected the existing law. Secondly, Herbert wanted to make it clear that his Bill would facilitate 'humane and honest divorce in the genuine hard case', but would do nothing to make divorce 'too easy for the merely irresponsible and foolish'.[249] Hence, the Bill which Herbert and his supporters presented[250] provided that no divorce should be possible until five years had

---

[242] *The Ayes Have It* (1937) p. 59.   [243] *Ibid.*

[244] The Union engaged in extensive lobbying the expense of which caused it considerable problems: *Thirtieth Annual Report 1937*. Greater difficulty was experienced in attracting the unequivocal support of NUSEC and other women's groups: Herbert did negotiate with Mrs Eva Hubback: NUSEC Secretary to Normanton 2 March 1937, *Normanton Papers* HN5/2. But the NUSEC leadership really wanted its own comprehensive legislation focussing more specifically on achieving equal status for women, and the *Normanton Papers* make it clear that Herbert's claim to have the support of NUSEC was controversial.

[245] See S Redmayne, 'The Matrimonial Causes Act 1937: A Lesson in the Art of Compromise' (1993) 13 OJLS 183.

[246] *Memorandum* to the Marriage Bill ordered to be printed on 6 November 1936 (Bill No. 5).

[247] Not least the Bill's short title, which was originally the Marriage Act. (At a late stage Herbert unwillingly acceded to the advice of Parliamentary Counsel that precedent required the legislation to be contained in a Matrimonial Causes Act: see *The Ayes Have It* (1937) p. 187.)

[248] Herbert relied on the drafting skills of Lord Kilbracken, and received advice from ESP Haynes and Claud Mullins: see Biographical Notes.

[249] *The Ayes Have It* (1937) p. 65.

[250] The statement made in 1980 by the Law Commission in para. 6 of its Working Paper *Time Restrictions on Presentation of Divorce and Nullity Petitions* (Working Paper No. 76) that the 'Bill leading to the Act, introduced by Sir Alan Herbert . . . did not originally contain a time restriction' is incorrect.

elapsed from the date of the wedding. Reckless marriage and reckless divorce were to be discouraged, and no one was to think of divorce until they had been married for at least five years.[251] In this way Herbert hoped to win the support of the Church of England (which had come to accept the possibility of amendment to the secular law of divorce 'provided that any . . . amendment does not tend to make marriage a temporary alliance or to undermine the foundations of family life').[252] Thirdly, he included a provision specifically aimed at the Church: the clergy were to be free to refuse the use of a church for the marriage of a divorced person (whether innocent or guilty) whose former spouse was still alive.[253] Fourthly, the Bill would 'introduce the machinery of conciliation' into the Divorce Court.[254] Finally the Bill included provisions allowing the dissolution of marriages which had 'irreparably collapsed'.[255] Desertion for three years or more, cruelty, incurable insanity, habitual drunkenness, and imprisonment under a commuted death sentence[256] were (almost, it was made to seem, as an afterthought) added to the grounds for divorce.

Herbert's strategy was eventually successful. The Matrimonial Causes Act 1937 provided new grounds for divorce, and in fact most of the provisions grafted on to the Gorell proposals in order to placate potential opponents disappeared along the way.[257] The 1937 Act was little different from Buckmaster's Bill almost two decades previously. How was this achieved?

[251] *Official Report, Standing Committee A*, 8 December 1936, cols. 7, 25. Herbert believed that marriage (rather than divorce) should be made more difficult; and his Bill as originally drafted contained a provision requiring a couple to give three months' notice of an intended marriage. It was pointed out that in some parts of the country 'walking-out couples' traditionally put off marriage until they were 'sure they could procreate' and Herbert, not wishing to 'condemn a child to illegitimacy' dropped the clause: AP Herbert, *The Birth of an Act* (1956) f. 12.

[252] Resolution of the Upper House of the Convocation of Canterbury as quoted in *The Ayes Have It* (1937) p. 65.

[253] At a somewhat more technical level, Herbert refused to accept a provision (giving effect to one of the Gorell Commission recommendations) whereby a court considering a petition for judicial separation could instead grant a divorce: he considered it wrong to impose dissolution of the marriage on an innocent spouse who did not agree to divorce. Herbert records that this decision 'had a profound influence on the passage of the Bill': *The Ayes Have It* (1937) p. 55. Herbert tried to give effect to Gorell's underlying objective—that it was wrong to impose a permanent separation on someone wishing to remarry—by giving the court a discretionary power to convert a judicial separation into a divorce decree after it had been in force for two years; but he felt obliged to drop this in Committee. However, Sir John Withers successfully moved an amendment (see Matrimonial Causes Act 1937, s. 9) allowing a respondent against whom a decree nisi of divorce had been granted himself to apply for the decree to be made absolute. The amendment was intended to prevent 'the greedy wife' from using the machinery of the decree nisi for purposes of blackmail—for example, by 'refusing to apply for the decree absolute until her husband had coughed up another motor-car or yacht': *The Birth of an Act* (1956) f. 40. Conceptually this provision created a breach in the principle that it was solely for the innocent party to determine whether or not to obtain a dissolution.

[254] *Memorandum* to the Marriage Bill ordered to be printed on 6 November 1936 (Bill No. 5). The word 'conciliation' at the time was understood as meaning what at the end of the twentieth century is more often described as 'reconciliation'; and the relevant provisions were included at the suggestion of the reforming Metropolitan Magistrate, Claud Mullins.

[255] *Ibid.*   [256] Clause 2 of the Marriage Bill ordered to be printed on 6 November 1936.

[257] See below p. 241.

Getting the Government on side

Herbert's Bill was given a Second Reading in the House of Commons on 20 November.[258] Whilst only 78 MPs voted in favour[259] very few MPs were prepared to make reasoned speeches against.[260] The Attorney-General, Sir Donald Somervell,[261] recorded:[262]

'The smallness of the vote against the Bill . . . indicates . . . not only a change in public opinion but also very definitely resulted from the form of the Bill. In the first place, the Bill is a conservative measure in that it preserves the basic structure of our divorce law in its prohibition of collusive divorce and in other important respects. In addition to proposing the extended grounds recommended by the [Gorell] Royal Commission it contains two provisions which are acceptable to many of those who would oppose a Bill which contained the extended grounds and nothing else. In the first place, the provisions . . . which preclude a decree within the first five years. Secondly, [the clause permitting the clergy to refuse to celebrate, or allow the use of their churches for the marriage of divorced spouses] to which, I understand, considerable importance is attached by the clergy. Although I think there are some provisions in the Bill which definitely ought to go it may well afford a good opportunity to deal with this very difficult subject.'

It is difficult to imagine clearer evidence of the success of Herbert's strategy. There were of course Ministers (of whom the Lord Chancellor, Hailsham, was certainly one)[263] who strongly disapproved of the Bill; but it appears that there was no support in Cabinet for attempting to block it.[264] The question which Herbert had to answer was how should he deal with objections to specific provisions found unacceptable by Ministers, the Judges and Officials? The question for the Government was how far it should allow itself to become involved?

These issues were inter-related. The Home Secretary, Sir John Simon,[265] persuaded the Cabinet not to cold-shoulder the Bill, but to adopt a policy of

---

[258] Sir Claud Schuster, the Lord Chancellor's Permanent Secretary had noted that there had been a 'change in the general opinion of the House [of Commons] and that it was not improbable' that the Bill would get a Second Reading, although at that stage he did not think there was any 'substantial risk' that it would get through all its stages in the House of Commons: Schuster to Merriman, 20 November 1936, PRO LCO2/1195.

[259] Only 12 voted against: *Official Report* (HC) 20 November 1936, vol. 317, col. 2079.

[260] Notwithstanding the fact that the Mothers' Union had circulated MPs claiming that 100,000 Union members were opposed to extending the availability of divorce: *Official Report* (HC) 20 November 1936, vol. 317, col. 2125; and see HS Kent, *In on the Act* (1979) p. 83.

[261] See Biographical Notes.

[262] 'Memorandum on the Marriage Bill' PRO LCO2/1195, undated, initialled DBS.

[263] See eg Schuster to Merriman 20 November 1936; Schuster to Hailsham 24 November 1936, PRO LCO2/1195. Hailsham had suffered a stroke and was at the time unable to attend Cabinets and other meetings in London and for this reason his influence was perhaps less than would otherwise have been the case. The Foreign Secretary, Lord Halifax, in fact voted against the Bill, but (as Herbert gratefully acknowledged: *The Ayes Have It* (1937) p. 127) neither he nor Hailsham spoke in public against the Bill.

[264] The fact that the Attorney-General advised that the Second Reading was likely to be carried seems to have been influential: Cabinet 66(36) 18 November 1936, Conclusion 12, PRO CAB 23/86.

[265] Herbert believed Simon to have been impressed not only by the fact that the Bill had been given a Second Reading with so little apparent opposition but also by the moderation with which it had been presented: *The Birth of an Act* (1956) f. 25.

neutrality, neither of approbation nor disapprobation.[266] The Cabinet[267] accepted this advice, and decided that a Law Officer would 'be available to help' at the Committee Stage of the Bill, not indicating any view on policy[268] but rather assisting with the technicalities. The Government also agreed to make the services of Parliamentary Counsel available.[269]

[266] Cabinet 66(36) 18 November 1936, Conclusion 12, PRO CAB 23/86.

[267] The Cabinet was chaired by the pro-Reform MacDonald (rather than the Prime Minister Baldwin, who was at best equivocal on the subject); and this fact may have had some influence on the outcome. The main force within the Cabinet in favour of reform seems to have been the Home Secretary, Sir John Simon whose powerful arguments in favour of allowing Government time to complete the passage of the Bill were of decisive importance. Herbert himself recorded that 'Sir John seldom seems to receive due credit for anything he does; so let me say here that he, too, . . . within the limits of his authority did all he could for us throughout the year: and though I know no Cabinet Secrets believe it was not his fault that the Government did not come out more strongly' in favour of reform: *In on the Act* (1937) p. 96. Herbert also records that after the Second Reading the Conservative Chief Whip, Captain Margesson, did 'all he could to help us; and that was very much': p. 95.

[268] Sir John Simon had pointed out to the Cabinet that 'it would hardly be possible for [the Attorney-General] to abstain from indicating a personal view on some of the questions which would arise, and that there were other matters on which a personal view from the Attorney General would certainly be expected'; and he urged the Cabinet to authorise the Attorney to 'express, where necessary, his personal view on points as they arose, making it clear that he was not stating any Government conclusions but merely assisting the Committee to reach a conclusion as to the best form in which the proposals should be embodied. He also suggested that the Attorney (who was not in the Cabinet) should be placed in the same position as other Ministers outside the Cabinet and be allowed to vote. The Cabinet did not agree: the Attorney should 'avoid expressing his personal view . . . and should content himself with explaining the consequences which would arise on one side or the other from the proposals in the Bill': Cabinet 2 December 1936 69(36) Conclusion 11. Somervell found this direction 'very embarrassing': Schuster to Hailsham, 16 December 1936, PRO LCO2/1195. In particular, he found difficulty in dealing with some of the Bill's procedural provisions—for example, those dealing with 'conciliation'—without giving a personal view on policy. An appeal by Schuster to Hailsham was unavailing; and in the end Somervell obtained written guidance from the Home Secretary on how to avoid transgressing his instructions: Simon to Somervell, 11 January 1937, PRO HO45/17102. Somervell concealed his sympathies throughout most of the parliamentary debates but came close to revealing his own support for reform in the debate on what became the Matrimonial Causes Act 1937, s. 4: see below.

[269] There were two opposing views on Government involvement. On the one hand, Sir Claud Schuster initially took the view that 'Parliament ought not to make substantial alterations in the present law except upon the proposals of the Government. The subject has not been examined in any serious way since the Report of [the Gorell Commission] for the debate which took place on Lord Buckmaster's Bill were of a very unreal character and no one then believed that the Bill could possibly pass. Since then [various changes had been made] and it would seem only right that [these] should be discussed publicly by some responsible body and not depend . . . upon the somewhat unsatisfactory proceedings of the Committee of the House of Commons upstairs': Schuster to Merriman 20 November 1936, PRO LCO2/1195. On the other hand (Schuster wrote) both the Home Secretary (Sir John Simon) and the Attorney-General 'think that some amendment of the existing law is inevitable in the near future and that it would be less embarrassing if that amendment should be effected by a Bill introduced by a Private Member than if the Government were themselves forced to introduce legislation . . .': Schuster to Hailsham 24 November 1936, PRO LCO2/1195. The Simon/Somervell view prevailed.

Government assistance

The Government's offer of 'private advice and aid'[270] was far more valuable than Herbert at first appreciated.[271] Although in theory[272] those concerned[273] were merely to offer help with the technicalities, in reality they were all supporters of reforming legislation and had no hesitation in giving advice not only about how to win over those opposed to legislation[274] but also about how to deal with the overriding problem of the parliamentary timetable. As the Parliamentary draftsman explained:

'. . . there was no promise of Government time, and time was of the essence . . . [N]o one doubted that we should get [the Bill] through the Committee stage. The crunch would come at the Report stage on the floor of the House, which we would have to get through in five short hours on a Friday afternoon in late spring. Our hope of doing this lay in streamlining the Bill in Committee by cutting out any unimportant provisions on which people could talk, and trying to get as much agreement on the main provisions as possi-

---

[270] As Sir John Simon described it at a meeting with Herbert: *The Birth of an Act* (1956) f. 25.

[271] *The Ayes Have It* (1937) p. 103. The clearest example of this is that the Treasury Solicitor's office provided Herbert with briefing notes (mostly drafted by Kent) which are indistinguishable from those provided to Ministers introducing Government Bills. The notes—some of which are collected in *The Birth of an Act* (1956) f. 24—go far beyond technicality and (for example) suggest how amendments put down by other MPs should be handled.

[272] At the start of the Committee stage the Attorney-General emphasised that the Government had not taken a position on the policy of the Bill and that it was for the Committee to decide policy. He emphasised that the Law Officers should not be asked to give opinions on matters of policy: *Official Report, Standing Committee A*, 8 December 1936, col. 19. But by the last day of the Committee stage the Attorney told the Committee that 'it would necessarily very much determine the attitude which His Majesty's Government might have to take towards this Bill' if the grounds for divorce were extended with no compensating power for the court to inquire into abuses: *Official Report, Standing Committee A*, 9 February 1937, col. 321.

[273] ie the Attorney-General (Sir Donald Somervell), the Solicitor-General (Sir Terence O'Connor), the Treasury Solicitor and King's Proctor (Sir Thomas Barnes), his predecessor Sir Maurice Gwyer (at the time First Parliamentary Counsel), and Harold S Kent of the Parliamentary Draftsman's office: see Biographical Notes. Herbert had the friendliest of relationships with the Law Officers: 'both Oxford men of my own time . . . Both were delightful, courteous, and indefatigable allies, to say nothing of their learning and ability. They passed like sun and moon alternately across our sky, and, contrary to the course of nature, were equal providers of light and warmth': *The Ayes Have It* (1937) p. 118. Herbert described Barnes—who had at their first meeting given it as his opinion that the Bill would go through, and was as 'keen as' Herbert 'that the thing should happen'—as 'one of the most human and charming of all the tribe of Whitehall, and it was a great privilege and pleasure to work with this most able and industrious public servant . . . without his constructive and tireless toil—and much of it I must not mention—I doubt if there would be an Act . . .': *op. cit.* p. 105. Gwyer was 'a man of great stature, massive mind, colossal calm. Talking to him, one cannot imagine the possibility of disturbance or error. It is always a pleasure to watch a master at his craft . . . smooth as an off-drive, the long amendment would flow from his pen. And, perceiving then how numerous were the gaps to be filled, the traps to be avoided, we were thankful indeed to know that we were to have the best practitioners in the country behind us': *op. cit.* p. 106. Kent was simply described as 'the brilliant young Treasury draftsman': *op. cit.* p. 118. These assessments may seem fulsome, but there is ample evidence to corroborate the view that at this period the Government was served by legal advisers of the highest calibre.

[274] In particular the views of the chronically conservative legal profession and those who 'wanted something done about the collusive divorce, which brought the law into contempt': HS Kent, *In on the Act* (1979) p. 81.

ble, so that the Bill would emerge from Committee in a comparatively uncontroversial state. Even if we ran out of time on the Report stage, the feeling of the House would be an important factor in the Government's decision whether to rescue us or not'.[275]

The best as enemy of the good?

Herbert and his supporters were prepared to be ruthless in order to gain support or kill opposition. For this reason they dropped provisions (notably the attempt to introduce 'the machinery of conciliation' into the Divorce Court[276] and the abolition of the two-stage decree nisi/decree absolute procedure) which they

[275] HS Kent, *In on the Act* (1979) p. 81. For a brief explanation of relevant parliamentary procedures see 'An Explanatory Note on Parliamentary Procedures', p. xv, above.

[276] The Bill as originally presented contained a provision drafted by Claud Mullins and reflecting his view that it was entirely wrong for the Divorce Court to be solely concerned with the law when what was often needed was 'conciliation' and advice. Mullins believed that the techniques which he had applied in the South West London Magistrates' Court could and should be available to working class families who wanted divorce; and that (as he wrote to the Attorney-General Sir Donald Somervell on 21 November 1936) the 'great need' of people of modest means was that 'their divorce cases shall somehow or other begin in Magistrates' Courts and thus come automatically within our social services': Simon Papers, Bodleian Library MS Simon 84. Herbert was sympathetic to Mullins' ideas (see *The Ayes Have It* (1937) pp. 57–63) and told Standing Committee A that he still believed in the 'spirit and intention' of the clause providing a procedure whereby the conciliation services provided in at least some magistrates' courts would be made available to those seeking divorce. But Herbert accepted that the procedure envisaged (which would involve the magistrates' court hearing the evidence and the Divorce Court pronouncing the decision) contributed to the 'singularly unanimous condemnation' of the clause by lawyers. Sir Claud Schuster had described the clause as 'a confused mass of muddled thinking by that mischievous creature Mullins' (see Schuster to Maxwell, 9 April 1937, PRO LCO2/1195) the Home Office considered the provision 'wholly fallacious' (PRO HO45/17102) whilst HS Kent described it (comparatively mildly) as a 'frightful clause': *In on the Act* (1979), p. 82. Herbert agreed to drop the clause without debate. Mullins believed that Herbert had 'found it impossible to stay the course' and that dropping the provision would be 'a serious blow to the masses of the people' and would lead to 'wholesale divorces that could have been prevented' and he continued to lobby for his 'conciliation' procedure: see Mullins to Maxwell, 8 February 1937, PRO HO45/17102. At a late stage, faced with the possibility of the 'conciliation' provision being reintroduced in the House of Lords by a Bishop, Schuster (who must have thought that the Church would have been satisfied by an explanation given by Simon to the Archbishop of Canterbury on 15 April: PRO HO45/17102) asked Barnes to 'make it clear to the promoters that we really cannot have this and that it is their job to prevent such a catastrophe as the House accepting this clause'. He added that if the clause were reinstated the Lord Chancellor would oppose the passage of the Bill: Schuster to Barnes, 6 July 1937, PRO LCO2/1195. For a fuller account, see S Redmayne, 'The Matrimonial Causes Act 1937: A Lesson in the Art of Compromise' (1993) 13 OJLS 183, 193–195, 198–200; and note that the idea that magistrates should have jurisdiction to grant divorce was put forward as long ago as 1892: PRO HO45/15006, Memorandum by RB Moore, Birkenhead. The 1937 Act did add adultery to the grounds on which magistrates' courts could make separation and maintenance orders (s. 11); and Herbert apparently continued to believe that adultery cases were thereby brought 'into the area of conciliation provided by the Social Services of the Magistrates' courts': *The Birth of an Act* (1956) f. 41. A provision of potentially great significance permitting the Divorce Court to accept a magistrates' order founded on adultery, desertion, or cruelty as 'sufficient proof' of those matters (although the Divorce Court was still required to hear evidence from the petitioner) also survived: Matrimonial Causes Act 1937, s. 6.

knew the Government would oppose.[277] They also dropped other provisions (notably the proposed new 'habitual drunkenness'[278] and 'imprisonment under commuted death sentence'[279] grounds for divorce) which seemed likely to provoke 'amendments and orations' jeopardising the timetable for the Bill.[280]

[277] Sir Alexander Maxwell, the Permanent Under Secretary of State at the Home Office (see Biographical Notes) had composed a magisterial critique for the Home Secretary: 8 December 1936, PRO HO45/17102, which was circulated to Somervell and Barnes. Barnes recorded that they all thought the conciliation clause should come out of the Bill 'but the difficulty is to decide how best to effect this end': Barnes to Scott, 19 December 1936. But in fact Herbert was easily convinced that 'the continued presence' of the provisions in question 'might militate (in diplomatic language) against the continuance of Government neutrality' and he had accordingly 'let it be known that we should not be stubborn about hanging out odd flags that were repugnant to the Admiral, though we should not surrender the ship [ie reform of the grounds for divorce] to anyone. For I never thought that we were likely to come through without escort: and even then I have one eye on the distant date when we might have to ask for Government time': Herbert, *The Ayes Have it* (1937) p. 104. Both provisions were dropped at the Committee stage because (Herbert admitted) the decree proposal would 'be repugnant to Her Majesty's Government' whilst there was not the 'remotest chance' of the conciliation proposal getting past 'legal and other barriers': *Official Report, Standing Committee A*, 2 February 1937, col. 265.

[278] The provision (based on a recommendation of the Gorell Commission) included in the Bill as originally presented would have required a petitioner to prove that the respondent (a) was an habitual drunkard (as defined), (b) that the condition was incurable, (c) that in consequence of habitual drunkenness the parties had been separated for at least three years. It was pointed out that this would be difficult and expensive for a poor spouse to prove (particularly after an absence of three years) and it was claimed that to include such a provision might remove any incentive for rehabilitation: *Official Report, Standing Committee A*, 15 December 1936. Herbert discovered that a comparable (but less demanding) ground in the magistrates' matrimonial jurisdiction was rarely used; whilst it was likely that anyone who could satisfy the proposed conditions would be able to establish cruelty or desertion (actual or constructive). Herbert believed that the Committee would probably have rejected the clause had he pressed the matter to a division: *The Ayes Have It* (1937) pp. 121–125.

[279] Following the recommendation—consistently subjected over the years to powerful criticism—of the Gorell Commission. As Sir Boyd Merriman P pointed out: 'The death sentence (apart from treason and military offences) can only be imposed for murder. The commutation of a death sentence implies that there are extenuating circumstances. Why make such a sentence the condition for divorce and ignore sentences of penal servitude for other crimes which may be far more detrimental to the marriage?': Merriman to Schuster, 21 April 1936, PRO LCO2/1195. Home Office officials also pointed out the illogicality of making the origin of the detention a relevant consideration: sometimes reprieved murderers were released after two or three years and in some cases after only two or three months: PRO HO45/17102 note on clause 2 of the Bill. Herbert himself pointed out (see *The Ayes Have It* (1937) p. 125) that of the comparatively small number of imprisoned murderers (74 in 1934, not all of them married) many 'were, and always are, poor women who have killed their babies. These, though convicted of murder, are often released after a short period, and it was thought to be hard if in that short space an unfeeling husband were to be enabled to whip in a petition for divorce': see *In on the Act* (1979) pp. 81–82). Once again, as Herbert admitted, underlying the decision was 'the strategic desire to reduce the area of controversy, in the certain knowledge that we should be pressed for time. There would, I am sure, have been protracted debate . . . at each successive stage': *The Ayes Have It* (1937) p. 125.

[280] The Act (unlike the Bill originally presented, and presumably on the advice of Parliamentary Counsel) preserved the anomaly created in 1923 whereby a wife could petition on the ground that her husband had, since the celebration of the marriage, committed rape, sodomy or bestiality: Matrimonial Causes Act 1937, s. 2. Many other 'technical' provisions (not least the removal of the definitions of 'desertion' and 'cruelty' contained in the original Bill and most of its predecessors) were dropped, sometimes without explanation. The provision of the Bill equating 'any unnatural or grossly indecent offence' with adultery for the purpose of divorce proceedings was also dropped, and an amendment moved by the eminent physician Lord Dawson of Penn to add 'the practice of homosexuality' as an additional ground for divorce was successfully resisted: *Official Report* (HL) 7 July 1937, vol. 106, col. 140.

Although Herbert's readiness to compromise brought complaints from both inside[281] and outside[282] Parliament that his 'anxiety to placate his opponents, and more especially his episcopal opponents' had done 'grave injury' to the Bill and 'thoroughly let down' his supporters, Herbert himself perceived very clearly that failure to make concessions would result in yet another failed divorce Bill.

Doing something about the 'scandal' of collusion

Herbert was willing to go further than jettisoning provisions included in the Bill originally presented, and was prepared to go a long way to accept suggestions for additions genuinely intended to improve the law. He thus not only reiterated that the Bill did nothing even to open the door to divorce by consent[283] but accepted[284] that some additional provision should be included to minimise what was widely believed[285] to be the 'scandal of collusion'.[286] Something therefore

[281] See *Official Report, Standing Committee A*, 9 February 1937, col. 324.

[282] Notably from Claud Mullins who claimed that the removal of the 'conciliation' provision made the Bill a 'dangerous measure': see Herbert, *The Ayes Have It* (1937) p. 58. Herbert claimed that Mullins 'became a public enemy [of the Bill], I will not say stabbing, but bullying us in the back. Twice, just before a critical debate (this, no doubt, was an accident), he made public utterances hostile to the Bill': *The Times*, 10 September 1937. Herbert complained that it was wrong for a judge who would have to administer the law to criticise its provisions in public before it was even in force (as distinct from giving private advice during the passage of the Bill); and his resentment at the behaviour of 'one who was a helpful collaborator, if only so long as he had his own way' is apparent.

[283] Herbert's personal view was that there was 'much that can be said for . . . divorce by mutual consent subject to the wholesome safeguard of delay, to certain time limits and age limits, and . . . the absence of children. But whatever my private opinions may be, it would have been unforgivable folly . . . to have added to my already explosive cargo the smallest packet of divorce by consent . . . We could not in one breath boast (as we were always doing) the tremendous backing of the Royal Commission, and in the next challenge its fundamental principles. Somebody, maybe, will do that later; but we were content to ride one horse at a time': see *The Ayes Have It* (1937) pp. 128–129.

[284] Herbert believed that it was the fact that the law confined the ground for divorce to adultery which drove people 'into the odious paths of collusion, perjury and contempt for the law' and that once 'reasonable new grounds'—especially desertion—were admitted 'the temptation to concoct bogus adultery cases would depart, and at least the worst scandals would come to an end': *The Ayes Have It* (1937) pp. 129–130. But he was forced to accept that others did not agree. In fact, the President wanted the Court to be given a general discretion to look at the 'reality of the matter' and withhold a decree if it suspected that there had been collusion or connivance rather than being obliged to grant a decree on proof of a single act of adultery.

[285] No doubt the views of the President of the Probate Divorce and Admiralty Division were influential: 'My colleagues and I feel very strongly how grave is the danger involved to the respect for the law in the Divorce Law as it stands and is administered to-day. The Divorce Law touches the lives of the people much closer than do the laws relating to motoring or drink, and things may easily reach a stage where they have here the same effect on the public attitude to the law generally as had Bootlegging in the United States. We are convinced that if an attempt is to be made to stop the rot it must be now or never': Merriman to Schuster, 16 November 1936, PRO LCO2/1195; and see p. 229, above.

[286] The Roman Catholic Lord Fitzalan of Derwent opposing the Bill in the House of Lords (*Official Report* (HL) 24 June 1937, vol. 105, col. 733) claimed that collusion was one of the 'gravest scandals of the day' and similar sentiments were voiced by many of those who favoured reform. In 1938 the Church of England, by Resolutions of the Convocations of York and Canterbury, stated that it was 'urgently desirable that every care should be taken to enforce and, if necessary, to strengthen the safeguards against the employment of collusion and perjury in seeking to secure decrees of divorce': see AF Smethurst and HR Wilson (eds.), *Acts of the Convocations of Canterbury and York* (1961) pp. 90–93.

had to be done to meet the promise stated in the Bill's preamble that it would restore 'due respect for the law';[287] but what?

There was much behind-the-scenes negotiation[288] and discussion.[289] Eventually,[290] Parliamentary Counsel was able to draft and negotiate a clause which all parties were prepared to accept. What became section 4 of the Matrimonial Causes Act 1937 was intended to reverse the onus of proof: it was to be for the petitioner to satisfy the court that there had been no collusion or connivance; and if the court was left with any real suspicion it would be entitled to withhold the decree.[291] Herbert regarded the agreement on this issue as the

[287] In fact Herbert himself believed collusion was an evil: '. . . once it is admitted that to secure a divorce the party must prove an offence before a court of law, it follows that the offence must be a genuine offence sincerely complained of; for, if it is not, the Court is being deceived and mocked, and individuals become accustomed to a low valuation of the truth, and of the law of England': AP Herbert, *The Ayes Have It*, (1937) p. 129.

[288] A much more radical proposal to defeat collusion was that divorce based on adultery should be confined to cases where the petitioner could prove 'persistent' adultery. Herbert stood firm against this attempt to eradicate the 'hotel' divorce and an amendment was defeated by 24 votes to 8. The Attorney-General undertook to give careful consideration to 'any amendments put down with a view to remedying evils which have arisen under the present system': *Official Report, Standing Committee A*, 8 December 1936, col. 34, 39 . However, the issue was particularly sensitive because on that day the abdication crisis was at its height, and the decree nisi granted to Mrs Simpson (subsequently the Duchess of Windsor) was founded on evidence of adultery from hotel staff . Herbert's biographer writes that Herbert 'had moments of agonising anxiety about the possible effect on the Bill's proposals of the . . . King's intimacy with Mrs Simpson': see R Pound, *AP Herbert, A Biography* (1976) p. 145; and see generally SM Cretney, 'The King and the King's Proctor . . .' (2000) 116 LQR 583.

[289] Such off-the-record negotiations and discussions can be of vital importance, especially in the case of a Private Member's Bill. Herbert gives a vivid picture of the process after the Bill had passed to the House of Lords: 'Now, again, began the conferences, the composing of "whips", the drafting of amendments and counter-amendments. There grew, as in the Commons, an eager and active little group, a General Staff, round the Bill; Lord Gorell, Lord Droghreda (a practising barrister in divorce) and the wise Lord Roche—with Sir Thomas Barnes still working and willing on the wing. In the background, too, Lord Maugham, Lord Wright, and Lord Atkin were devoting their lucid minds and long experience to the improvement of the measure. And greatly they did improve it . . .': *The Ayes Have It* (1937) p. 171.

[290] Herbert records that the clause was 'the cause of interminable misunderstandings, and consultations, and doubts' which were all the more distressing to him because the original provision was a 'proposal of my own, which was loathed by the enemy and little liked by my friends': *The Ayes Have It* (1937) p. 135. Matters were not improved by what HS Kent describes as 'terrible sessions in the President's room . . . after the President ("an obstinate and difficult man") had risen for the day and was tired and irritable'. Eventually the President 'was good enough to say that he was reasonably happy with the latest version and, as [the main opponent of the Bill in the House of Commons] was too, we were home and dry': *In on the Act* (1979) p. 82. There was, none the less, impressive criticism of the provisions of what became s. 4 of the Act in the House of Lords: see for references S Redmayne, 'The Matrimonial Causes Act 1937: A Lesson in the Art of Compromise' (1993) 13 OJLS 183, 196–197.

[291] The interpretation of the new clause caused difficulty both for the draftsman and (subsequently) the courts: see the discussion in *The Ayes Have It* (1937) pp. 131–135. The 4th edition of the standard practitioner's textbook, *Rayden's Practice in the Divorce Division* (4th ed., 1942) p. 126 reflects the view stated in the text that the provision of s. 4 required the petitioner to prove a negative (ie that he had not been guilty of collusion etc) and suggested that the courts would be entitled to dismiss a petition if the facts raised a mere *suspicion* that there had been collusion (and in 1937 the Lord Chancellor had warned the Cabinet that the 'substantial alteration in the duty . . . imposed upon the court when considering a petition', 'additional and stricter' than the duty imposed by the

'turning point';[292] and it appears that his success in that respect contributed to[293] the Government's decision to allow time for the Bill to complete its passage.

No divorce within the first five years of marriage?

The provision in the Bill providing that no divorce petition be presented within five years of the wedding[294] caused little real trouble in the House of Commons. The clause had (as Sir Claud Schuster told the Lord Chancellor)[295]

'been inserted with the idea of propitiating both the Church of England and the Roman Catholics. It is understood that the Archbishop of Canterbury regards it as an important concession, and it seems to be the case that he is prepared to accept the Bill if this provision is retained'.

—and this assessment at first seemed correct. Herbert himself believed that Catholic MPs[296] would have been 'much more combative' had this provision

existing law', would necessitate provision of more resources: CP98(37) 18 March 1937). However, after a series of decisions between 1938 and 1949 (notably *Emmanuel v. Emmanuel* [1946] P 115, Denning J, *Churchman v. Churchman* [1945] P 44, CA, and *Tilley v. Tilley* [1949] P 240, CA) it was accepted that, although the onus of proof did lie on the petitioner it would initially be discharged by presuming the petitioner's innocence: *Rayden's Practice in the Divorce Division* (5th ed., 1949) p. 130. Accordingly the section (to which so much effort had been devoted) had little practical effect.

[292] *The Ayes Have It* (1937) p. 131.

[293] The question arose critically after the Bill had completed its Committee stage in the House of Commons. On 24 March 1937, the Cabinet was told that 'there was some evidence of a change of attitude towards the Bill in the House of Commons owing to changes that had been made in the Committee stage, and there was a possibility that it might be rejected on the report stage'. Sir John Simon's Minute, CP97(37) 18 March 1937 urging that the Government should not let the Bill lapse 'merely for want of supplying a little more time if that was all that was needed to get it through by a substantial majority' seems however to have been influential; and on 5 May 1937 the Cabinet eventually decided to make a limited amount of government time available 'to enable the House of Commons to reach a decision on the Bill' (that form of words being substituted in the Cabinet Conclusions for the Secretariat's original 'improving the passage of the Bill through Parliament'): PRO CAB 20(37) Conclusion 7. But the Bill did not complete its Report stage in the House of Commons within the allotted time (see for a dramatic account HS Kent, *In on the Act* (1979) p. 83) and the possibility that there would have to be further protracted debate remained a worry to the promoters.

[294] The insertion of this clause had apparently been suggested by Claud Mullins: see AP Herbert, *The Ayes Have It* (1937) p. 64. But the view that a time restriction of this kind would constitute a safeguard 'against divorce being too hasty [and] widespread' had a long ancestry and was supported by many reformers (including ESP Haynes: see *The New Separation Bill*, not dated but probably 1918).

[295] Schuster's Minute of 24 November 1936, PRO LCO2/1195.

[296] In fact there appear to have been only three Roman Catholic members of the 60-strong Standing Committee, described by Herbert as 'Sir Patrick Hannon, courtly and lovable, as round and genial as the sun; Anthony Crossley, intellectual, eloquent, and earnest; Commander Bower, tall, bold, and blunt. They disliked everything except the Five Years' Clause . . . I had expected the most bitter antagonism [from the Roman Catholics] but in fact we were much more harassed by the Anglicans. The Catholics expressed their faith sincerely but shortly, and when they saw defeat magnanimously accepted it'.: AP Herbert, *The Ayes Have It* (1937) pp. 112–113.

not been included in the Bill[297] and that the clause contributed much to the harmony of the proceedings in the House of Commons (and especially in the Standing Committee).[298]

The clause may well thus have served an important purpose in helping the Bill through the House of Commons, but from the outset it had caused concern amongst lawyers. The President 'disapproved entirely' of the proposed bar;[299] Sir Claud Schuster regarded it as 'extremely cruel and as likely to lead both to very great hardship and to the aggravation of those social evils which the Bill professes to cure';[300] whilst the experienced and respected solicitor Sir John Withers had pointed out that few petitions were in fact presented within the first five years of a marriage and that petitions filed within that time were normally cases of real hardship. But Herbert felt that to allow the clause to be 'whittled away'[301] would be a breach of faith to many of those who had supported the Bill from the beginning.[302]

In the House of Lords, however, there was an eruption. The Law Lords (and especially Lord Atkin)[303] eloquently and cogently denounced the time bar, whilst few peers spoke in support.[304] Herbert and his friends once again saw the

---

[297] *The Ayes have It* (1937) p. 181.

[298] But the solicitor Sir John Withers had given warning of the difficulties, moving an amendment to reduce the period from five years to three. (Alternatively, he would have been content with a five-year period provided the court were given a dispensing power in cases of hardship). But he withdrew these proposed amendments: see *Official Report, Standing Committee A*, 8 December 1936, col. 6; AP Herbert, *The Ayes Have It* (1937) pp. 180–181.

[299] Merriman to Hailsham, 21 April 1936, PRO LCO2/1195. He subsequently accepted that he had expressed his disapproval 'in too unqualified manner'. He felt very strongly that no such bar should apply in cases of rape, sodomy etc, insanity, or imprisonment, whilst in a considerable number of cases the ordinary grounds of divorce were of 'so glaring a character as to make any attempt to reconstruct the marriage impossible'. But subject to 'provision being made for specific exceptions of this character I think there is a good deal to be said for having a five year period of trial and error, particularly if the grounds on which the Court might be permitted to pronounce a decree of divorce were more extensive': Merriman to Hailsham, 23 April 1936, PRO LCO2/1195.

[300] It 'seems to me that to say to a party to a marriage whose spouse has . . . committed adultery with a third party within a year of the marriage, that he or she must remain bound during perhaps the five most important and fruitful years of his or her life is an impossibility. It can only lead to both parties forming irregular unions. For I cannot believe that either a man or a woman of the age of, say, 25 will remain celibate for five years. . . . Furthermore, it seems to me to bear very hardly on women. . . . The result of this Clause would be that a woman married at the age of 25 or 26 [then the average age] . . . will have to wait till somewhere about 32 or 33 before she bears her first child; and I do not believe that either the parties or public opinion will tolerate such a state of things when the result is realised': Schuster's Minute of 24 November 1936, PRO LCO2/1195. Those who supported the clause on the basis that victims of serious violence or other marital misbehaviour could always get a decree of judicial separation (or an order from the magistrates' court) had no answer to Schuster's argument (and it has to be remembered that a child born to a separated married woman would not only be born illegitimate but, as the law then stood, would not be legitimated by her subsequent marriage to the father: see Chapter 15, below).

[301] *Official Report, Standing Committee A*, 8 December 1936, col. 7.

[302] *The Ayes Have It* (1937) p. 182.

[303] *Official Report* (HL), 24 June 1937, vol. 105, col. 758.

[304] Note in particular the reservations of Lord Reading (*Official Report* (HL), 24 June 1937, vol. 105 col. 778), the Bishop of Birmingham (col. 817), Lord Dawson of Penn (col. 826), and Lord Gorell (col. 847).

need for compromise.[305] The Bill was amended to provide that whilst in principle no divorce petition could be filed within the first *three* years of marriage, the court would have power in cases of exceptional hardship suffered by the petitioner or exceptional depravity on the part of the respondent to give leave to present a petition within the three-year period; and it was provided that the Act did not in any event prohibit the presentation of a petition based upon matters which occurred before the expiration of the three-year period.[306] Even so the debate was long and bitter. But the main spokesman for the Bill had been carefully chosen[307] and was able convincingly to argue that the amendment would represent 'a large measure of agreement between its promoters and those who were at first its most severe critics'.

Herbert recorded that the time bar provision gave more trouble than anything else in the Bill;[308] and for a time the Bill seemed likely to founder. But Lord Gorell[309] was able to remind the House that time was the enemy of the Private Member's Bill and warned Peers that if the House spent a great deal of time trying to make the Bill a perfect instrument 'then you must weigh very carefully in your minds . . . whether that perfect instrument will be used'. His plea that the Lords should 'not lose this chance after a quarter of a century of passing into law reforms upon which, with almost no exceptions' they were all 'heartily in

---

[305] *The Ayes Have It* (1937) pp. 182–185. There were in fact two divisions in the House of Lords on the time bar; but it appears that the matter was largely dealt with by informal behind-the-scenes negotiations.

[306] Matrimonial Causes Act 1937, s. 1. It appears that the version finally put forward was an amalgam of proposals by three eminent Law Lords, Lords Atkin, Maugham and Wright: *The Ayes Have It* (1937) pp. 184–185.

[307] The Labour Party was unwilling to allow a Labour peer to sponsor the Bill: see note 143 above, and in any event as Sir Claud Schuster wrote to Herbert on 1 June 1937 'there are advantages both from your point of view and from ours [*sic*] being conducted by someone on the Government side of the House'. Schuster put forward two names of suitable Conservative peers. Lord Brocket, the 33-year-old former MP for Wavertree—'full of life and vigour and anxious to make his mark' in the House of Lords—may have been rejected because Schuster regarded him as 'somewhat extreme Right Wing in outlook' or perhaps because his interest in ecclesiastical affairs was (rather surprisingly) evidently much greater than Schuster had appreciated. In any event Schuster's second suggestion—Lord Eltisley, formerly MP for Cambridge Borough, Chairman of Cambridgeshire County Council, High Sheriff, and Assistant Secretary (unpaid) to the Ministry of Reconstruction from 1917–1919 for which work he had been made KBE in 1919 and, although a peer of first creation, possessed of impeccable antecedents as the grandson of an earl, substantial landowner and country gentleman—was preferred. Schuster admitted that he did not know about Eltisley's 'theological views' but surmised that having been educated at Eton and Trinity he was probably 'not an active anti-Churchman'. Eltisley made a good impression on Herbert, who wrote: Lord Eltisley 'was experienced, industrious, able and tactful . . . [His] big subject was agriculture; and at that date, I believe, he knew as little of my subject as I knew of his. But he went at it like a tiger . . . [W]ithin a week or two he was talking like a lawyer': *The Ayes Have It* (1937) p. 171.

[308] The clause 'gave more trouble than anything else in the Bill': HS Kent, *In on the Act* (1979) p. 65. The provision allowing divorce on the basis that the respondent was incurably of unsound mind was also controversial and caused difficulty even at the last stages of the Bill's passage through the House of Lords: see *Official Report* (HL) 15 July 1937, vol. 106.

[309] Gorell would have seemed an obvious choice to have the carriage of the Bill in the House of Lords, but Herbert remarks that there 'were equally obvious reasons against saddling him with the entire burden, which, I am sure, he himself perceived. But he was . . . one of the Bill's most powerful aids . . .': *The Ayes Have It* (1937) p. 170.

agreement' seems to have struck home. Opposition to the Bill from the Church of England was muted:[310] only one Bishop[311] voted against the Bill and the Archbishop of Canterbury conceded that the Bill had 'real merits within the sphere of State law'.[312]

The Lords sat late at night to conclude the Bill's passage; and it received the Royal Assent on 30 July.[313] AP Herbert entertained a party (including the draftsman Harold Kent and the King's Proctor Sir Thomas Barnes) to a celebratory performance at the Adelphi theatre of his Review *Home and Beauty*. Kent recalled[314] that this included a sketch written specially for the occasion

'about a new nursery game in which the dolls consisted of the petitioner, the respondent, the co-respondent and, of course, the King's Proctor . . . Binnie Hale played the whole thing at Tommy Barnes in the stage box, and he responded manfully, and gradually the audience woke up to the fact that the King's Proctor, then a mysterious and sinister figure, was actually joining in an impromptu rag . . .'.

There was indeed something to celebrate: Herbert's achievement as a private (and Independent) MP in getting such complex legislation[315] on so controversial

---

[310] In contrast, the Roman Catholic Viscount Fitzalan of Derwent was outspoken in his opposition to the Bill which (he said) treated 'marriage as a question of convenience and sentiment': *Official Report* (HL) 24 June 1937, vol. 105, col. 739. Again, the only one of the Law Lords to oppose reform was the Roman Catholic, Lord Russell of Killowen: *The Ayes Have It* (1937) p. 170.

[311] The Bishop of St Albans. In contrast, the Bishop of Durham (Hensley Henson) was a longstanding supporter of reform and made a powerful speech on Second Reading, urging that the enactment would 'rebuild a great many broken homes, and shall once more enable many children to have strength and comfort in an ordered domestic life' and that to deal with the 'dark, menacing and apparently insoluble' population question in this way would be to 'strengthen the state by helping to rebuild it': *Official Report* (HL) 24 June 1937, vol. 105, col. 742. Henson's attitude on these matters is illuminated by O Chadwick, *Hensley Henson, A Study in the friction between Church and State* (1983).

[312] *Official Report* (HL) 24 June 1937, vol. 105, col. 774. The Church of England, whilst affirming a strict view of the indissolubility of marriage for its own members, had come to accept that 'while convinced that Christ's principle of a lifelong and exclusive personal union provides the only sure ground on which to base the relations of man and woman in marriage, and that the Church should therefore commend that principle as the true foundation for legislation by the State, . . . nevertheless recognises that its full legal enactment may not always be possible in a State which comprises all sorts and kinds of people, including many who do not accept the Christian way of life or the means of grace which the Church offers to its members': Resolutions of the Convocations of York and Canterbury, June 1938; *The Church and Marriage being the Report of the Joint Committees of the Convocations of York and Canterbury 1935* (1935). Generally on this issue reference should be made to CA Moyse, *Reform of Marriage and Divorce Law in England and Wales 1909–37* (Cambridge University, unpublished PhD thesis, 1996) Chapter 3; and GIT Machin, 'Marriage and the Churches in the 1930s: Royal Abdication and Divorce Reform, 1936–7' *Journal of Ecclesiastical History*, Vol. 42, 1991, p. 68.

[313] The Act (s. 14(2)) provided that it should come into operation on 1 January 1938 thus giving time for the necessary court rules to be settled.

[314] *In on the Act* (1979) p. 84.

[315] The Herbert Act also modified the law of nullity of marriage (in accordance with the unanimous recommendations of the Gorell Commission) to allow a marriage to be annulled on the grounds of the respondent's wilful refusal to consummate; being at the time of the marriage an epileptic, mental defective or of unsound mind; suffering from a venereal disease in a communicable form, or pregnant by a third party. Various restrictions applied to these grounds: see

a subject on to the statute book was remarkable[316] and seems unparalleled in modern times.[317] Those who worked with him no doubt shared Kent's 'pleasure and satisfaction'[318] at what had been accomplished. Informed opinion could be satisfied that the Matrimonial Causes Act 1937 'settled the problem of divorce reform for a generation'.[319]

Matrimonial Causes Act 1937, s. 7. The Act (again following the unanimous Gorell recommendations) introduced a procedure whereby the court could presume that a spouse had died and make a decree which would dissolve the marriage even if that presumption were subsequently rebutted: s. 8. And it allowed the English courts to assume jurisdiction to hear a petition by a wife notwithstanding the fact that her husband had deserted her and acquired a domicile abroad: s. 13, see p. 102, note 75, above.

[316] *Official Report* (HC) 26 July 1937, vol. 326, col. 2632. The Herbert Bill is generally regarded by students of the political process as being a remarkable (if only because so unusually effective) a use of the Private Members' Bill procedure (on which see generally PA Bromhead, *Private Members' Bills in the British Parliament* (1956) and PG Richards, *Parliament and Conscience* (1970)). However, Professor HJ Laski (who believed the Private Members' procedure to be an anachronism) claimed that the Herbert Bill was a 'truncated measure' which had been drastically amended and thus been 'in high degree' narrowed in scope: *Parliamentary Government in England* (1938) p. 166; but this assessment is difficult to accept. In contrast, Laski's view that the Herbert Bill would 'probably prevent the serious rationalisation of the marriage laws for many years to come' is somewhat easier to defend.

[317] The Divorce Reform Act 1969 was also a Private Members' Bill, and the achievement of Mr Leo Abse and its other promoters is also truly remarkable. But the Government of the time was much more collaborative (both in preparing the way for legislation and in making it possible) than the 1937 National Government had been: see further below p. 369.

[318] *In on the Act* (1979) p. 84.

[319] This assessment by Kent (who attributes the same view to Barnes) also reflects the attitude of Sir John Simon (see his Minute, CP97(37) 18 March 1937) and no doubt other pro-Reform ministers.

7

The Ground for Divorce under the Matrimonial Causes Act 1937

INTRODUCTION

The Matrimonial Causes Act 1937 extended the grounds for divorce;[1] and with effect from 1 January 1938, either party to a marriage could petition for divorce on the grounds that the other:

(a) had since the celebration of the marriage committed adultery; or
(b) deserted the petitioner without cause for a period of at least three years immediately preceding the presentation of the petition; or
(c) since the celebration of the marriage treated the petitioner with cruelty.[2]
(d) A spouse could also petition on the ground that the other was incurably of unsound mind and had been continuously under care and treatment for a period of at least five years immediately preceding the presentation of the petition.[3]

The Act also amended the law about the application of the bars to divorce[4] originally laid down in the 1857 Act; and provided[5] that no petition for divorce should be presented within the first three years of marriage unless the court gave leave on specified 'exceptional' grounds to do so.

[1] The Act also introduced a procedure whereby the court could make a decree of presumption of death and dissolution of marriage: Matrimonial Causes Act 1937, s. 8; and it added adultery to the grounds upon which magistrates could make orders under the provisions of the Summary Jurisdiction (Separation and Maintenance) Acts 1895 to 1925. The Act also amended the law of nullity of marriage.
[2] Matrimonial Causes Act 1937, s. 6(2) provided that the court could treat a magistrates' matrimonial order or a decree of judicial separation as sufficient proof of the adultery, desertion, or other ground upon which it was based. But this provision was restrictively interpreted by the courts (see *Kara v. Kara and Holman* [1948] P 287, CA) and was apparently little relied on in practice.
[3] Matrimonial Causes Act 1937, s. 2. The Act retained a wife's right to petition on the ground that her husband had, since the celebration of the marriage, been guilty of rape, sodomy or bestiality; but it came to be accepted that, although sodomy on the wife was a ground for divorce as much as sodomy with a third party, the wife could not petition if she had genuinely consented to the act or had condoned it: see *Statham v. Statham* [1929] P 131; *Bampton v. Bampton* [1959] 2 All ER 766; *T v. T* [1963] 2 All ER 746.
[4] The 1937 Act, s. 4, extended the bars of unreasonable delay and the petitioner's own cruelty (Matrimonial Causes Act 1857, s. 31) to divorce petitions brought on any ground. The petitioner's desertion or wilful separation was applied to petitions founded on adultery or cruelty, whilst the petitioner's 'wilful neglect or misconduct conducing' to the respondent's adultery, unsoundness of mind or desertion was extended to petitions based on those grounds. The same section also dealt with the burden of proof in relation to the bars to divorce: see below.
[5] s. 1.

These provisions remained virtually unamended for 20 years[6] and the 'Herbert Act' (as it was often called) constituted the statutory framework governing the availability of divorce in this country for more than 30 years.[7] The present chapter seeks to give an account of the working of the reformed law.[8] But the administration of the law was (once again) greatly affected by the increase in demand for divorce associated with the Second World War; and changes in the structure of the courts dealing with matrimonial matters, with procedures, and with the funding of access to the courts are dealt with separately in the following chapter of this book.[9]

THE POLICY OF THE MATRIMONIAL CAUSES ACT 1937

AP Herbert's genius (it has been well said)[10] lay in presenting[11] the reforms made by the 1937 Act 'not as a force for social disorder but as a source of stability'. He sought to make it clear that the Act would not introduce Reno-style[12] 'quickie' divorce in this country; and that the introduction of extended grounds for divorce would not alter the basic principle of the law. Marriage was to remain the voluntary union for life of one man and one woman to the exclusion of all others.[13] But for a spouse to commit one of the specified 'matrimonial offences'[14] would be 'fundamentally incompatible with the undertakings given at marriage'; and accordingly the other spouse was given the right (provided that he or she was innocent of wrongdoing) to have the marriage terminated by a judicial decree of divorce.

---

[6] ie until the changes made by the Divorce (Insanity and Desertion) Act 1958, see below. The statutory provisions were twice consolidated, by the Matrimonial Causes Acts 1950 and 1965.

[7] ie until the coming into force of the Divorce Reform Act on 1 January 1971.

[8] Because the 1937 Act remained for so long the foundation of the law, illustrations in the text are not confined to judicial decisions in the early years whilst comments on the working of the law made (for example in the *Report of the Royal Commission on Marriage and Divorce*, 1956, Cmd. 9678—hereafter 'the *Morton Report*') are included wherever relevant.

[9] See Chapter 8, below.

[10] By CA Moyse, *Reform of Marriage and Divorce Law in England and Wales 1909-37* (Cambridge University, unpublished PhD thesis, 1996) p. 382.

[11] ie 'by harnessing the fear of collusion, the desire to improve the quality of marital relationships and enhance respect for marriage'.

[12] Herbert clearly wanted to avoid any suggestion that divorce would be available on demand (as was popularly believed to be the case in Nevada USA): see above, pp. 236–237. Herbert had also been anxious to avoid being associated with the radical views of bodies such as the World League for Sexual Freedom and writers such as HG Wells. In 1930 Wells had published an article 'Divorce is Inhuman' in the *Daily Express* (subsequently collected with others, including one by Bertrand Russell, in *Divorce as I See It* (1930)). The general approach was that an adult's sexual conduct was 'his or her own affair as far as it does not affect the collective welfare' and was no more than part of the individual's 'peculiar personal mental moral and physical hygiene'.

[13] *Hyde v. Hyde* (1866) LR 1 P&D 130, 133, *per* Lord Penzance.

[14] In 1956 the *Morton Report* claimed that all the grounds for divorce constituted conduct of a grave nature which cut at the root of marriage: para. 56. But the *Morton Report* had to accept that insanity (a ground for divorce under the 1937 Act) was not an offence but rather a misfortune; and the Report claimed that 'special considerations' applied in that case.

Divorce remains a daunting legal process

The change in the law did not alter the fact that to obtain a divorce decree was an often daunting legal process involving a high degree of formality. Striking evidence of what petitioning for divorce meant in practical terms is provided by the documentation[15] sent out by The Law Society during World War II specifying the information which soldiers and others seeking public funding for divorce proceedings had to provide:

First of all the applicant had to supply the marriage certificate to prove that there was a marriage to be dissolved. He also had to submit certified copies of any previous court orders with notes of evidence, photographs of the spouses 'and any third party concerned' and any relevant letters or other documents. But most important was the applicant's statement. This had to contain a 'full story of the matrimonial history, which should not necessarily exclude hearsay evidence', together with relevant correspondence and documents. But the focal point of the statement would be the allegations necessary as the legal basis for dissolving the marriage. For example, if the petition was to be based on adultery[16]—still much the commonest ground—the applicant had to give 'all known details with dates and addresses, together with the sources of applicant's information, and the names and addresses of known or possible witnesses who are willing to give statements and to appear in Court if required. If the spouse has confessed adultery, full circumstances and as full details as possible of the conversation and the names and addresses of any witness present should be given. If the Co-Respondent [ie the allegedly guilty third party] was present, this should be stated . . .' and so on.

The need for evidence and proof

This information was not required to satisfy the prurient interest of bureaucrats. On the contrary, it was necessary to enable the divorce process to be

---

[15] Form HMF 2: this information is derived from PRO LCO2/4621.

[16] Where the petition was to be based on desertion (the most widely used of the new grounds introduced by the Herbert Act) the information required was even more comprehensive: '. . . the facts leading up to the separation must be given in detail, with particulars of quarrels and any allegations made by the spouse against the applicant, together with the applicant's explanation thereof. Full particulars of the actual parting should be given, together with as full an account as possible of any relevant conversation between the parties. It is essential that the date, or at least the month and year, of the final parting be given and the address from which the spouse deserted. All offers by either party to resume cohabitation and the replies thereto must be set out in detail giving addresses and dates. If it is asserted that the applicant has been driven from home by the conduct of the other party, particulars of that conduct must be given. . . . The names and addresses of relatives or independent persons who can corroborate the applicant's story should be given': Form HMF 2 para. 7(vi).

brought, smoothly and quickly, to a successful conclusion. If the case was well organised by a competent and experienced legal team this would not usually cause any difficulty, at least in those cases (the great majority) in which the other spouse did not resist legal dissolution of a relationship both accepted to be broken beyond repair. The husband would prove (by production of a birth certificate)[17] the birth of a child whilst he was on military service overseas[18] of whom he could not be the father;[19] or the wife would swear that she recognised the signature in a hotel register as being in her husband's hand, and private detectives[20] and hotel staff[21] would give evidence[22] that the husband had stayed at the hotel with a woman who was not the wife.[23] If all this were done with

[17] It was considered necessary for the petitioner (or a witness able to identify the wife's signature) to attend at the Register of Births and inspect the original register so as to be able to give evidence that the signature of the informant was that of the wife: see Form HMF 2, para. 9(iv).

[18] Proof of such absence could be provided by reference to service records. It was also considered desirable that the witness should be able to testify that the wife was in England at the material times: HMF 2, para. 9(iv).

[19] See eg *Fearn v. Fearn* [1948] 1 All ER 459, CA.

[20] The evidence of the Federation of British Detectives to the Royal Commission (*Morton Report, Minutes of Evidence* p. 780) reflects the concern of some employed in this capacity about unprofessional behaviour by others. Note that the fictional private detective Parkis, sympathetically portrayed in Graham Greene's novel *The End of the Affair* (1951) felt that the judiciary were 'often prejudiced against the profession'.

[21] Traditionally evidence was given by a chambermaid who had served early morning tea to the couple in bed. One King's Bench judge who made no secret of the fact that he detested having to hear undefended divorce cases on circuit recorded that the production of this evidence by a 'chambermaid of superhuman powers of observation and memory, who recalls that a man and woman spent a night in a bedroom a year or two ago, that she took morning tea to them in bed, that a blurred snapshot produced to her is a portrait of the man, and that the Petitioner-wife who has just left the box was not the woman' was 'obviously incredible' but part of the 'absurd ritual': FD MacKinnon, *On Circuit 1924–1937* (1940) p. 113; and note also Professor LCB Gower claimed (see *Morton Report, Minutes of Evidence* p. 17 footnote 16) that the evidence of a chambermaid had 'become such a feature of divorce that many members of the lay public erroneously believe it to be a *sine qua non*'. In one case (he claimed) a husband, discovered 'by his wife and her enquiry agent naked in the wardrobe of another woman's bedroom, exclaimed triumphantly "You can't do anything; there's no chamber-maid"'.

[22] Evidence to the (Denning) *Committee on Procedure in Matrimonial Causes* (1947, Cmd. 7024) suggested that some hotels would not give evidence save under sub-poena: PRO LCO2/3948, Littlewood to Skyrme, 8 July 1946. Other hotels seem to have acquired a special reputation as being co-operative: the prominent London Solicitor Sir David Napley records a case in which the staff of a prestigious West End hotel which did not like to be involved in divorce cases suffered from collective amnesia about the remarkable stay of his client (who subsequently found the Strand Palace Hotel 'marginally more amenable'): *Not Without Prejudice* (1982) p. 31). In any event the procedure could be expensive: LCB Gower told the Committee that one large Russell Square hotel charged four guineas (something approaching £100 in year 2000 values) as an initial fee for searching their records, and that it was usually necessary to give the manager a substantial gratuity in addition. He claimed that a 'professional class of witnesses' was growing up and this situation 'is getting so bad . . . that you cannot get evidence out of the hotel unless you tip lavishly, and if you tip lavishly enough you are getting to the point when you will get the evidence you want': Minutes of Evidence, 17 December 1946, p. 21.

[23] As in the successful petition of Mrs Wallis Simpson (subsequently Duchess of Windsor): see *Simpson, W v. Simpson, EA (Application by the King's Proctor for Directions)* (1937) *The Times* 20 March; and SM Cretney, 'The King and the King's Proctor . . .' (2000) 116 LQR 583.

professional efficiency the court would rapidly infer that the respondent had[24] committed adultery. Of course, if the allegation were contested,[25] or the necessary evidence had not been collected, matters would be much more difficult. In the case of petitions founded on adultery the courts still[26] insisted that the court had (as with a criminal prosecution, and in contrast to what was required in other civil proceedings) to be satisfied of the respondent's guilt 'beyond reasonable doubt'. In cases of alleged cruelty the petitioner would have to list specific acts in chronological order; and the court would have to ask itself whether it was satisfied that they had in reality occurred and that taken together they were sufficient to constitute the matrimonial offence of cruelty. These requirements often led to protracted trials engendering much bitterness. Sometimes the result was to preserve intact the legal shell of a marriage which had long since ceased to exist as a functioning relationship.

JUDGES DECIDE WHAT IS ACCEPTABLE MARITAL CONDUCT

The question whether the facts proved constituted a relevant matrimonial offence was classified as a question of law. The effect of this was to make the judiciary the arbiters of what were the limits of acceptable marital behaviour. A considerable body of complex doctrine developed.

Adultery

In the case of adultery the courts had to decide precisely what degree of sexual intimacy was sufficient to constitute the offence. They held that mutual masturbation and other indecencies were insufficient[27] and that there had to be some penetration of the female genitalia by the male organ.[28] Again, inter-

---

[24] No doubt in some of these cases adultery had not in fact taken place: a solicitor of 20 years' standing told the House of Commons on 18 July 1950 that this was so in 'a large number' of undefended cases: Ronald Mackay, Labour MP for Hull NW, *Official Report* (HC) vol. 477, col. 2,197.

[25] As in *Russell v. Russell* [1924] AC 687, above p. 173, and *Cavendish-Bentinck v. Cavendish-Bentinck* (1947) *The Times* 28 March, Hodson J; (1947) 7 November (Court of Appeal).

[26] It was for long common to describe adultery as a 'quasi-criminal offence': see eg *Ginesi v. Ginesi* [1948] P 179, CA; and although this analogy came to be regarded with disfavour it remained true that the courts regarded adultery as a very serious matter and that accordingly a high standard of proof was required: see *Blyth v. Blyth and Pugh* [1966] AC 643 and *Bastable v. Bastable and Sanders* [1968] 1 WLR 1684, 1687, CA. It seems that the criminal analogy for long influenced the courts' approach—for example, in relation to the importance of evidence being coroborrated: see eg *Galler v. Galler* [1954] P 252, CA (sole evidence of adultery statements given by children's nurse employed by husband for two years claiming that she had frequently committed adultery with him; husband's appeal allowed because judge had failed to warn himself of danger of acting on uncorroborated evidence of accomplice). But in 1966 dicta in the House of Lords cast doubt on the validity of the criminal analogy: *Blyth v. Blyth and Pugh* [1966] AC 643.

[27] *Sapsford v. Sapsford and Furtado* [1954] P 394.

[28] *Dennis v. Dennis* [1955] P 33, CA—a decision which seems difficult to reconcile with the House of Lords' decision in *Russell v. Russell*: see in particular [1924] AC 687, 721, *per* Lord Dunedin. The question whether a wife's voluntarily submitting to AID treatment without her husband's consent

course had to be consensual if it was to constitute adultery. This meant that a woman who had been raped was not guilty of adultery,[29] but did it mean that a person who had intercourse whilst drunk or under the influence of drugs could escape? The courts found this a difficult question but generally managed to reach what no doubt seemed an acceptable moral compromise: if drink or other substances have been taken in the knowledge that their effect was likely to inflame the passions the mere fact that the person concerned had no recollection of the incident would not prevent the court from finding adultery proved.[30]

In relation to adultery it was the finding of the necessary facts which caused the main problems; and the courts' definitional role was limited. However, it was very different with desertion and cruelty (which became distinct grounds for divorce under the Herbert Act).

Desertion

The Matrimonial Causes Act 1857[31] provided that either party to a marriage might petition for a decree of judicial separation on the ground of desertion without cause for two years and upwards;[32] whilst magistrates' courts had since 1886[33] had power to make orders against a husband guilty of deserting his wife for any period. The courts thus had long experience of the concept of desertion (which had been elaborately defined by the Ecclesiastical Courts[34] before 1857) and it might have been thought that they would find little difficulty in interpreting the provision of the Herbert Act[35] making desertion a ground for divorce. Indeed, it was because desertion was a well-settled legal concept that Herbert

---

constituted adultery on her part was never the subject of a reported decision of the English courts: cf. *Maclennan v. Maclennan* 1958 SLT 12 (not adultery in Scotland) and *Orford v. Orford* (1921) 58 DLR 251 (AID did constitute adultery in Ontario).

[29] *Redpath v. Redpath* [1950] 1 All ER 600, CA.

[30] *Goshawk v. Goshawk* (1965) 109 SJ 290; and see *Hanbury v. Hanbury* (1892) 8 TLR 559, and, in relation to the effect of drugs, *Benton v. Benton* [1958] P 12, CA (where the question was whether the heavily tranquillized husband's acts constituted condonation of his wife's adultery rather than whether those acts performed with another partner would have constituted adultery).

[31] s. 16.

[32] As noted in Chapter 4, above, under the Matrimonial Causes Act 1884, s. 5, a respondent guilty of failure to comply with a decree for restitution of conjugal rights was deemed to be guilty of desertion without cause; and the petitioner could seek a judicial separation immediately notwithstanding the fact that two years had not elapsed. It followed that a wife whose husband failed to comply with a restitution decree could, if she could prove that he had committed adultery, petition for divorce; and the principle that a wife could only obtain a divorce if the husband were guilty of adultery with aggravating circumstances was significantly eroded.

[33] Married Women (Maintenance in Case of Desertion) Act 1886; Summary Jurisdiction (Married Women) Act 1895.

[34] The Matrimonial Causes Act 1857, s. 22 provided that the divorce court should act on the principles theretofore applied by the Ecclesiastical Courts.

[35] Matrimonial Causes Act 1937, s. 2.

agreed to the removal of the statutory definition which he had included in the first draft of the Bill.[36]

But quite how well-settled *was* the law? No doubt everyone accepted that there had to be a separation against the petitioner's will, and no doubt the petitioner had to be able to persuade the court that the respondent intended to bring the married life to an end without any sufficient cause; but the courts had refused to attempt any comprehensive definition, and there were difficulties even in deciding what 'separation' meant. There could, of course, be no doubt that the men who had emigrated to the colonies and United States were 'separated' from the wives whose plight had so much concerned the Gorell Commission, but other cases were not so simple. In wartime Britain and for long afterwards there was an acute housing shortage.[37] Was the law to deny a divorce to a couple who wanted nothing to do with each other but could not find anywhere else to live? In 1949 the Court of Appeal decided that a husband who shut himself up in one or two rooms of the house and ceased to have anything to do with his wife was (as Denning LJ put it)[38]

'living separately and apart from her as effectively as if they were separated by the outer door of a flat. They may meet on the stairs or in the passageway, but so they might if they each had separate flats in one building. If that separation is brought about by his fault, why is that not desertion? He has forsaken and abandoned his wife as effectively as if he had gone into lodgings. The converse is equally true. If the wife ceases to have anything to do with, or for, the husband and he is left to look after himself in his own rooms, why is not that desertion? She has forsaken and abandoned him as effectively as if she had gone to live with her relatives'.

So the requirement of 'separation' was satisfied provided that there was a complete separation of *households*. But this criterion would only be met if there was no sharing of any aspect of domestic life.[39] In particular, the mere fact that

[36] Clause 16 originally provided that 'desertion' meant 'desertion without the consent or against the will of the other party to the marriage, and without reasonable cause, and, where there has been no actual desertion, wilful and persistent refusal to permit marital intercourse shall be treated as equivalent to desertion'. It was removed by Standing Committee A: see *Minutes of Proceedings on the Marriage Bill*, HC 40, p. 6.

[37] In 1953 CP Harvey QC wrote that 'at one time it seemed that housing shortages were going to lead to a serious slump in divorce for desertion, but the situation was saved by the humane discovery [in October 1939] that desertion is by no means inconsistent with the parties having continued to live under the same roof': 'On the State of the Divorce Market' (1953) 16 MLR 129, 130. Thirty years later a judge with extensive experience of divorce practice said that the doctrine derived from *Hopes* (see below) 'was invented by a succession of judges to get over the impossible position where a couple had ceased to communicate altogether but neither could leave because they had no alternative accommodation; and a certain amount of stretching of the law had to be done': *Adeoso v. Adeoso* [1980] 1 WLR 1535, 1537, *per* Ormrod LJ.

[38] *Hopes v. Hopes* [1949] P 227, 235, CA.

[39] In *Le Brocq v. Le Brocq* [1964] 1 WLR 1085, CA, a wife shut her husband out of the matrimonial bedroom by putting a bolt on the inside of the door and had as little to do with him as possible. But she did continue to cook meals for him; and he paid her a weekly housekeeping allowance. This 'separation of bedrooms, separation of hearts, [and] separation of speaking' was insufficient: the court held that there had still been only a single household.

one spouse refused the other any sexual relationship[40] was insufficient as the basis for a finding of desertion:[41]

In *Weatherley v. Weatherley*[42] a 22-year-old RAF sergeant married a 30-year-old spinster in 1941. On the three occasions on which the husband had short periods of leave the couple had intercourse in the wife's flat; but in November 1941 the wife told him that 'she thought this sex business was horrid, and beastly and she did not want any more of it'. Thereafter they slept in separate rooms, but otherwise lived as a normal married couple. Eventually the husband petitioned for divorce. He was unsuccessful both at first instance and on appeal up to the House of Lords.[43]

The difficulty of deciding whether there was a sufficient factual separation to allow the court to make a finding of desertion paled into insignificance compared with the 'metaphysical niceties'[44] to be applied in interpreting the requisite mental element. Again the policy was clear: the law was not to allow a marriage to be dissolved merely because the parties had been separated for some years; and if the parties had agreed to separate there could be no desertion. The vital difference between a consensual separation and a separation which had

[40] The Matrimonial Causes Act 1937, s. 7 made the respondent's wilful refusal to consummate the marriage grounds for annulment. The (subsequently withdrawn) definition clause (16) in the first draft of the Herbert Bill had in terms provided that wilful and persistent refusal constituted desertion.

[41] More accurately, to provide the *factual basis* of the separation necessary to constitute desertion. Some years later the courts held that if a wife unreasonably refused to allow the other sexual intercourse, and the husband then left, the wife would be guilty of *constructive* desertion: *Slon v. Slon* [1969] P 122, CA. Eventually, following the House of Lords' 1963 decisions in *Gollins v. Gollins* [1964] AC 644 and *Williams v. Williams* [1964] AC 698 (minimising the necessity of showing the one spouse had intended to injure or inflict misery on the other) the courts would accept persistent refusal to have sexual intercourse as the basis for a divorce petition founded on cruelty provided that the refusal caused grave injury to the petitioner's health, and that allowances were made 'for any excuses' which might account for the refusal 'such as ill-health, or time of life, or even psychological infirmity': *Sheldon v. Sheldon* [1969] P 62, *per* Lord Denning MR.

[42] [1947] AC 628, HL.

[43] The Book of Common Prayer stated that 'the procreation of children' was one of the causes for which matrimony was ordained; and this led some judges to believe that the mutual right of sexual intercourse was therefore fundamental to the marriage state and that denial constituted a repudiation of the obligations of marriage sufficient to constitute desertion. But the House of Lords would have none of this 'dangerous and fallacious' argument: 'the fact is that the law of the land cannot be co-extensive with the law of morals, nor can the civil consequences of marriage be identical with its religious consequences. What marriage means to different persons will depend on their upbringing, their outlook and their religious belief'. The answer to the questions which came before the courts was to depend 'not on a consideration of the Christian doctrine of marriage . . . but on the true construction of the relevant Acts of Parliament': *Weatherley v. Weatherley* [1947] AC 628, HL, *per* Lord Jowitt LC. The difficulties of those who regarded procreation as the basis of marriage were increased when the House of Lords held that a wife who refused to permit intercourse unless her husband used a condom was not refusing to consummate the marriage: *Baxter v. Baxter* [1948] AC 274. In the result, a single act of intercourse using a condom sufficed to consummate the marriage and the refusal subsequently to permit intercourse did not give any basis for a petition founded on desertion.

[44] *Hall v. Hall* [1962] 1 WLR 1246, 1254, *per* Diplock LJ.

been caused by one party deserting the other had to be maintained.[45] The petitioner had to show the respondent had intended to break the marriage up for good and that the petitioner had not agreed to this.[46]

But this was not as straightforward as it might seem. Of course, there were cases in which it was possible to argue that an apparent consent was not in reality a consent to separation at all.[47] But it was the statutory requirement that desertion had to be 'for a period of three years immediately preceding the petition' which had the most striking impact. As the Master of the Rolls[48] put it in 1952:[49]

'. . . desertion as a ground for divorce differs from the statutory grounds of adultery and cruelty in one important respect. The offence founding the cause of action is not complete—is (as it were) inchoate—until the action is constituted. If one spouse has committed adultery or has treated the other with cruelty, the latter has an accrued right to petition for divorce. He or she may repudiate the marriage and is no longer bound to affirm it and reinstate the offending spouse. The deserted spouse has no such right, no such election. If the deserting spouse genuinely desires to return, his or her partner cannot refuse reinstatement.'

This has an undeniable logic, but led to a good deal of tactical manoeuvring. First, a spouse in desertion could provide himself with a defence by the simple device of making a so-called 'bona fide offer to return'.[50] Secondly, if the offer was refused without reasonable cause the person to whom the offer had been made became the deserter (a fact which was of considerable significance at a time when a spouse in desertion had no right to financial support from the other).[51] Not surprisingly, astute divorce lawyers became adept at drafting such offers:

In *Price v. Price*[52] the wife left and took the children with her. Husband and wife each petitioned for divorce. The judge held that 'neither of this ill-assorted couple' had succeeded in establishing a case of cruelty against the other.[53] The wife's solicitor subsequently drafted a letter saying that the wife felt 'good will and a bona fide desire by both parties to forget and forgive might save the

[45] *Morton Report*, para. 150(ii).

[46] In the military parlance at the time widely understood, the distinction was between being guilty of desertion or merely absent without leave: *Herod v. Herod* [1939] P 11, 33, *per* Lord Merriman P.

[47] The court had rejected a husband's claim that his wife's anguished 'Go if you like, and when you are sick of her, come back to me' constituted an agreement on her part to a separation: *Haviland v. Haviland* (1863) 32 LJPM&A 65.

[48] Sir Raymond Evershed. [49] In *Perry v. Perry* [1952] P 203, CA.

[50] See J Tiley, 'Desertion and the Bona Fide offer to Return' (1967) 83 LQR 89.

[51] The onus of establishing that an offer to return was not genuine was best discharged by accepting it and (in effect) calling the offeror's bluff: see *Pike v. Pike* [1954] P 81, CA.

[52] [1951] P 513, CA.

[53] Notwithstanding the fact that the husband had used physical violence against the wife, injuring her jaw. It appears that the judge took the view that she might, by irritating her husband, have been the victim of her own misfortune.

marriage'; and she offered to return to the matrimonial home provided only that neither mother-in-law visited them there. The judge found that, although the wife hated the husband and had hated him for some time before she left him, she was none the less willing to return to the home so that her husband could support her financially there. The court held that by leaving the husband the wife had put herself in desertion, but that her offer to return was genuine in the sense that 'she was willing to implement it, although not anxious to do so' and would have much preferred for him simply to pay her an allowance. The result was that the husband became the party in desertion. Accordingly he either had to take the wife back and maintain her under his own roof as his wife or provide financial support for her to live somewhere else.

A well-drafted letter could be useful in other situations too. A couple might drift apart, recognise that their marriage had broken down, and want to regain their single status. Could anything be done if the man did 'not like the idea of taking some strange female to a hotel'?[54] The answer was that the husband could write his wife a letter drafted so as to make it appear that he had in law deserted her, and then she would (in spite of the fact that the separation was in reality entirely consensual) be able to petition for divorce after they had lived apart for three years on the ground of desertion.[55] And, for those who did not want to wait for three years, it seems that a skilfully drafted letter written after the separation[56] could be made to operate retrospectively[57] and form the basis for an immediate divorce. In short, the appearance of desertion could be manufactured (albeit not so easily as was possible with adultery).

[54] In order to provide his wife with the evidence necessary for a divorce founded on adultery: see *Morton Report, Minutes of Evidence* p. 21, q. 192 (Professor LCB Gower).

[55] *Ibid.*, and *Morton Report, Minutes of Evidence* p. 25 (Professor LCB Gower).

[56] For an early example of what may be such an exchange, see the correspondence on the basis of which Mrs Walter Sickert was able to prove that her husband (the celebrated artist) had been guilty not only of persistent adultery but of desertion, notwithstanding the fact that the separation appears to have been in the beginning consensual: *Sickert v. Sickert* [1899] P 278, 281.

[57] For example, by the wife writing in terms that she had throughout been anxious that her husband should return to her. In his evidence, Professor Gower claimed that he had personally advised a friend in these terms: 'She and her husband had been separated for a number of years. She showed me all the correspondence. It was perfectly clear to me that there was no desertion, they had obviously drifted apart . . . I took some pains to prepare a letter, and I said, "Now, if you send this letter to your husband, and after a month or so there is no reply, I should then go to a solicitor and you may get a divorce". . . . [A] few months later she went to her solicitor. The solicitor went through all the correspondence and said, "There is no hope here". Then he came to this particular letter, and he said, "This puts an entirely different complexion on it, I think we might get a divorce on the basis of three years' desertion in view of this letter".' A decree was granted on the grounds of desertion, and Professor Gower claimed that without 'the letter there would have been no divorce. As a result of the letter the court was satisfied that there had been desertion for the past three years'. (He had to admit that he could be said to have assisted the petitioner successfully to deceive the court.): *Morton Report, Minutes of Evidence*, qs. 283–4. No other witness to the Commission was as specific as Gower had been about the incidence of 'manufactured' divorce, and the reliability of his evidence was attacked by legal members of the Commission with what Professor OR McGregor described in *Divorce in England* (1957) p. 139 as 'hostility and rudeness'. Some corroboration of the accuracy of Gower's account is to be found in 'On the State of the Divorce Market' (1953) 16 MLR 129 by the eminently respectable, albeit keenly reformist, barrister CP Harvey QC.

But it was the law's insistence that a factual separation could only constitute desertion if it were 'without cause' (words specifically included in the statutory definition of the ground for divorce) which gave rise to most forensic difficulty. Once again, the courts had to define the limits of what one spouse could be expected to tolerate, and the answer was: quite a lot. True, if one spouse had committed one of the traditional matrimonial offences (most commonly adultery or cruelty)[58] the other could not be expected to continue to share a home with him or her. But the courts were reluctant to allow anything else to relieve a spouse of the duty to cohabit. 'The ordinary wear and tear of married life', such as every spouse bargained to accept when taking the other 'for better or worse',[59] was not to be sufficient justification for breaking up the family home.[60] Only 'grave and weighty' conduct making 'the continuance of the matrimonial cohabitation virtually impossible' would suffice:[61]

In *Timmins v. Timmins*[62] the trial judge found that the husband was overbearing, domineering, had a hasty temper, habitually expressed himself in rapid unmeasured terms, and was insistent on maintaining his rights as a husband. The trial judge held that such behaviour did not justify the wife's leaving. Rejecting the wife's divorce petition founded on alleged cruelty the judge granted the husband a decree of restitution of conjugal rights.[63]

The courts' restrictive approach was influenced by the development of the concept of so-called *'constructive' desertion*. It had long been accepted that the person who actually left the home was not necessarily the one who was respon-

---

[58] Although cruelty by itself had only been made a ground for divorce under the provisions of Matrimonial Causes Act 1937 it had been a ground for judicial separation since 1857 and was a concept—albeit described as *saevitia*—familiar to the Ecclesiastical Courts.

[59] *Buchler v. Buchler* [1947] P 25, *per* Asquith LJ (the son of Prime Minister HH Asquith and step-son of the legendary Lady Margot—a strong character, described by her Memorialist in the *Dictionary of National Biography* as a 'woman of unrestrained candour' who could never bring herself to believe 'that truth could wound' and thus perhaps likely to have given her son ample opportunity to witness the strains of married life).

[60] 'Irritating idiosyncrasies' which get on a wife's nerves are 'part of the lottery in which every spouse engages on marrying': *Lang v. Lang* [1955] AC 402, 417–418 (Privy Council).

[61] *Young v. Young* [1964] P 152, Sir J Simon P. In effect, conduct sufficient to justify separation had to be sufficiently serious to constitute cruelty and only failed to do so because some element of that offence (usually, that the innocent spouse's health be affected) could not be made out: see for example *Russell v. Russell* [1897] AC 395, HL, [1895] P 315, where the wife's conduct in persisting in making charges of homosexual conduct against her husband after she had ceased to believe they were true was held by the Court of Appeal to justify his refusing to live with her even though his health had not been adversely affected by her conduct.

[62] [1953] 1 WLR 757.

[63] The Court of Appeal subsequently, by a majority, held that—whilst the trial judge had correctly found that the matters proved against the husband did not constitute cruelty such as would entitle her to a divorce on that ground—the judge should have refused to decree restitution. In a later case, it was held that the only reason why the charge of cruelty had failed was because the husband's behaviour had not been motivated by a desire to injure or distress the wife: *Young v. Young* [1964] P 152, Sir J Simon P. It will be apparent that the case law is not easy to reconcile: see the full analysis in *Rayden and Jackson's Law and Practice in Divorce and Family Matters* (15th ed., 1988) para. 88.

sible for disrupting the home and breaking up the marriage. If one spouse (say the wife) had in reality been driven out by conduct making it 'unbearable for a wife with reasonable self-respect, or powers of endurance, to stay' the husband could be said to have *constructively* deserted her.[64] Three years later the wife would be entitled to petition on that ground.

The courts were concerned that a liberal interpretation of this concept might 'run wild'[65] and lead to the creation of a new ground for divorce—in effect, mere incompatibility of temperament and unhappiness—not prescribed by statute.[66] Judges protested[67] against cases in which the wife left the matrimonial home merely because she was unhappy about her husband's behaviour, refused his offers to return on the ground that his behaviour justified her living apart from him, and then promptly charged him with constructive desertion.

It became clear that no charge of constructive desertion could succeed unless the judge would think that the husband's conduct went beyond the 'ordinary wear and tear of married life'.[68] Otherwise, as we have seen, there would be no justification for leaving the home, much less making that the basis of a divorce petition. But what did that mean in reality? Inevitably different judges applied different standards:

In *Hall v. Hall*[69] a Lancashire couple had been married for 21 years, but the marriage was unhappy and the husband's drinking habits appeared to be the

---

[64] *Lang v. Lang* [1955] AC 402 (Privy Council).

[65] *Pike v. Pike* [1954] P 81, 88, *per* Denning LJ. The classic example of constructive desertion dated from the time when a wife petitioner had not only to prove that her husband had committed adultery, but also that there was an additional aggravating factor. Hence a wife could not be expected to tolerate a situation in which her husband refused to sack the housemaid with whom he was committing adultery (see eg *Koch v. Koch* [1899] P 221) or installed his mistress in the matrimonial home; and accordingly the husband would be guilty of constructive desertion if she left.

[66] *Buchler v. Buchler* [1947] P 25, *per* Lord Greene MR; and see *Leng v. Leng* [1946] 2 All ER 590 (danger of allowing one spouse's neurotic condition to become ground for other petitioning for divorce).

[67] *Pike v. Pike* [1954] P 81, 88, *per* Denning LJ.

[68] *Buchler v. Buchler* [1947] P 25. In that case, the wife left the husband (a farmer) because she objected to the close friendship which her husband had formed with a male pigman employed by him on the farm. Although the judge found that the friendship was a 'perfectly clean one' and not of a 'homosexual or other degrading character' there was gossip amongst the villagers and other servants about the husband's close relationship—involving visits to the theatre, to the Motor Show, and to the launching of the *Queen Mary* as well as playing darts and ping-pong in public houses—with a 'man of little education' so obviously his social inferior. The wife felt humiliated and that she had been displaced in her husband's affection. She repeatedly asked him to give up the association, but the husband refused to do so, telling her that if the wife did not like his behaviour she could 'clear out' and go to live with her mother. Although the Court of Appeal thought that 'a man of refined susceptibilities' would have done what his wife asked, regardless of the sacrifice to himself, they were quite clear that the husband's conduct was not of sufficient gravity to justify the trial judge's finding the husband guilty of constructive desertion. Since the wife had no cause to live apart from her husband it was in fact she who was guilty of desertion, and it was he rather than she who was entitled to a decree of divorce. But contrast *Winnan v. Winnan* [1949] P 174, CA (where the wife kept 25 or more cats in the matrimonial home; their excretions smelt very badly, and the court accepted that the wife's preference for the cats as against her husband was a sufficient basis for a finding that she had constructively deserted him) and note that the actual decision on the facts in *Buchler* has been doubted: see eg *Hall v. Hall* [1962] 1 WLR 1246, *per* Danckwerts LJ.

[69] [1962] 1 WLR 1246 CA.

cause of the trouble. He would go out most evenings of the week, return home drunk in the early hours of the morning, and cause disturbance by banging and shouting, depriving his wife and teenage children of their sleep and peace of mind. Notwithstanding the fact that he was never violent to the wife and that there was no evidence of 'any disgusting behaviour such as vomiting or being unable to control his bladder' the local magistrates[70] found his behaviour to be in excess of what any decent spouse could be expected to endure and that it was equivalent to expelling the wife from the matrimonial home. The husband successfully appealed to the Divisional Court,[71] where the President of the Probate Divorce and Admiralty Division of the High Court[72] accepted the argument put forward on the husband's behalf that although his conduct was undoubtedly unpleasant 'it was such as was unfortunately required to be suffered by wives on many occasions', and that it would be 'impossible' to hold that the husband's conduct was serious enough to justify the wife leaving. The Court of Appeal was more sympathetic to the wife's plight. Although the question whether conduct was capable of constituting constructive desertion was a matter of law, cases such as this fell into a 'no-man's land' where the question was one of fact and the magistrates were best able to assess the gravity of a spouse's conduct 'in the light of the social environment of the parties and the local mores with which they would have a particular familiarity'.

The most serious conceptual difficulty in determining the scope of constructive desertion lay in defining the mental element necessary on the part of the alleged offender. In some cases, no doubt, malicious motivation or an actual intention to injure would make it clear that the husband intended the wife to leave. But suppose that the husband simply did not know that his conduct would, if persisted in, in all probability result in her leaving? Or suppose that the husband, whilst appreciating that his wife might leave, none the less desired that she should stay?

There was an acute conflict on this. Some said that, however bad the husband's behaviour, he could not be held guilty of constructive desertion if the facts showed that the last thing he desired was that the wife should leave him;[73] but others thought that, since a man is presumed to intend the natural and probable consequences of his acts, a man would be held to have the necessary intention to found a charge of constructive desertion if he must have known that his conduct

---

[70] The wife had gone to live with her brother, and the question was whether the husband was liable to maintain her or whether he was exempt from the liability to do so because she was in desertion.

[71] [1962] 2 All ER 129. [72] Sir Jocelyn Simon P (with whom Cairns J agreed).

[73] See eg *Boyd v. Boyd* [1938] 4 All ER 181.

would cause her to leave, however passionately he might desire or request that she remain.[74] The correct answer to the question remained doubtful.[75]

The question of intention also caused difficulty in cases in which one party was suffering from mental illness. Suppose, for example that a wife had delusions about her husband's behaviour and believed that he was frequently committing adultery with his secretary. The courts held that since desertion involves an intention to repudiate the obligations of marriage the situation should be assessed as she believed it to be. A wife would have had good cause to live apart from an adulterous husband, and accordingly the deluded wife could not be guilty of desertion. But supposing that a deeply religious woman believed her husband to have been guilty of 'grave sins' which did not however constitute a recognised matrimonial offence? The courts held that such conduct would not justify her in living apart from him, and that she could accordingly be held to have deserted him.[76]

Use of desertion as a ground for divorce

The need to perform such intellectual gymnastics may suggest that the 1937 Act had not been conspicuously successful in making the divorce process more 'humane, direct and honest' and thereby increasing respect for the law. But it seems that the legal profession learned how to manipulate the technicalities in their clients' interests. In 1938 over a third of divorce petitions were founded on desertion; and in the years after 1949 desertion even overtook adultery as the most favoured ground alleged in petitions.[77] What is perhaps more remarkable is the substantial increase in the proportion of petitions alleging cruelty in the years after World War II.

Cruelty

Although cruelty only became a ground for dissolving a marriage in 1937, the legal concept had long been familiar. The leading authorities dated back to the

---

[74] See eg *Sickert v. Sickert* [1899] P 278. The two views are discussed in *Hosegood v. Hosegood* (1950) 66 (pt 1) TLR 735, 738, and by the Privy Council in *Lang v. Lang* [1955] P 81, where the Privy Council took the view that a man who knew that the probable result of his acts would be that his wife would leave could be held to have the necessary intention since his 'intention was to act as he did, whatever the consequences, though he may hope and desire that [his acts] will not produce their probable effect'. See also the discussion in the *Morton Report* paras. 151–156.

[75] See eg *Saunders v. Saunders* [1965] P 449. Over the years, the trend of decisions was towards the latter view: see eg *Gollins v. Gollins* [1964] AC 644 (especially the opinion of Lord Reid at p. 666; and *Hall v. Hall* [1962] 1 WLR 1246: '*This* husband must have known that *this* wife would in all probability not continue to endure his conduct if he persisted in it', *per* Diplock LJ, at p. 1256).

[76] See *Kacmarz v. Kacmarz* [1967] 1 WLR 317.

[77] In 1938, 38.8% of husband's petitions and 37.6% of wives' petitions were founded on desertion. By 1945, the proportion of desertion petitions had dropped to 25%, but rose again to a peak of 42.5% in 1953: OR McGregor, *Divorce in England* (1957) Tables IX and X (and note the author's justification for his belief that reference to divorce petitions is to be preferred to reference to the number and declared grounds for divorce decrees).

Ecclesiastical Courts' decisions on divorce *a mensa et thoro*;[78] since 1857 cruelty had been a ground for judicial separation and one of the possible aggravating elements in a wife's divorce petition, while since 1895[79] magistrates' courts up and down the country had frequently had to adjudicate on complaints that a husband had been guilty of persistent cruelty to his wife.[80] Not surprisingly, therefore, Herbert agreed to drop the elaborate definition of 'cruelty' included in the Bill first presented to Parliament;[81] and the House of Commons was content to leave it to the courts to interpret the provision that either husband or wife could petition for divorce on the ground that the respondent had since the celebration of the marriage treated the petitioner with cruelty.[82]

Evidence of specific facts required

The starting point in any cruelty case was always the need for evidence of the facts on which the petitioner relied. The petitioner's solicitor would translate the complaints elicited from his client's statement into the formal language of legal pleadings.[83] The details of each incident (including the date when and the address at which it had occurred) would need to be set out. Evidence of witnesses would have to be obtained. Finally the court would have to be convinced of the truth of the petitioner's allegations; but provided the judge made clear

[78] And since 1857 the Divorce Court had had power to grant decrees of judicial separation on the same ground: Matrimonial Causes Act 1857, s. 16.

[79] Summary Jurisdiction (Married Women) Act 1895.

[80] The Divisional Court, hearing appeals, frequently gave guidance on the correct interpretation of the law: see JM Biggs, *The Concept of Matrimonial Cruelty* (1962); L Rosen, *Matrimonial Offences* (3rd ed., 1975); and for a consideration of the reality behind the legal doctrine, AJ Hammerton, *Cruelty and Companionship Conflict in nineteenth-century married life* (1992).

[81] Clause 16 of the Bill (removed by Standing Committee A: see *Minutes of Proceedings on the Marriage Bill*, HC 40, p. 6), reproducing a similar clause in the Holford Knight Bill, defined cruelty as 'such conduct by one married person to another as makes it unsafe, having regard to the risk to life, limb, or health, bodily or mental, for the latter to continue to live with the former, or as is calculated to cause and has caused the latter prolonged and unnecessary mental distress, and the following facts: (a) that one party to a marriage has knowingly or negligently infected the other with venereal disease; and (b) that a husband has compelled his wife to submit herself to prostitution; shall, without prejudice to the generality of the forgoing definition of cruelty, be treated as equivalent to cruelty'.

[82] Matrimonial Causes Act 1937, s. 4. In the first case reported on the meaning of cruelty in the 1937 Act the court unequivocally held that the legislature had 'without doubt . . . intended the word to have the meaning assigned to it by the courts in many earlier matrimonial cases . . .': *Horton v. Horton* [1940] P 187. (In that case the husband left the wife after more than 30 years of marriage because he found it impossible to live with the woman who in jealous spite deliberately scratched the lens of his spectacles, damaged his masonic regalia, kicked and otherwise assaulted him and perpetually nagged him about his absence from home on Masonic business. She also made unfounded allegations about his relations with other women. The judge held that this 'good husband and father, fond of his home, fond of his children and fond of his dog' was driven from the home by his wife's conduct and that his 'miserable existence' had caused him to suffer from neurasthenia; and that accordingly the wife was guilty of legal cruelty.)

[83] See for example the complaint taken from a 1945 file preserved in the Public Record Office (J77/3965) against a husband said to have been 'bad tempered, rude, sulky and irritable with [the wife] . . . has not given her the sympathy and protection which she was entitled to as his wife but . . . has tried to push her into the arms of any man who attempted to pay her any attention and has continually taunted her'.

findings based on the evidence presented to him the Appeal Courts would be reluctant to upset his decision.[84]

The question of whether the facts proved constituted 'cruelty' for the purposes of the divorce law was a question of law; and once again there were difficult conceptual issues lurking not far beneath the surface. If one party could plausibly claim that the judge had misdirected himself there could be an appeal to the Court of Appeal or even to the House of Lords;[85] and over the years significant changes in policy came about as a result of decisions on such appeals.

On 1 January 1938,[86] however, the law seemed clear. The courts had since the eighteenth century insisted that only behaviour which showed 'an absolute impossibility that the duties of the married life could be discharged' was to be sufficient.[87] For this reason, if one spouse's behaviour were to be held to amount to legal cruelty there had to be proof of 'grave and weighty conduct' on the respondent's part; and the petitioner had also to prove, as a distinct matter, that this conduct had caused 'danger to life, limb or health or a reasonable apprehension' of such injury.[88] *Russell v. Russell*[89] illustrates this:

The wife's conduct (variously described as abominable, atrocious and scandalous) in repeatedly and publicly making allegations which she knew to be false that her husband had been guilty of unnatural crimes (ie homosexual acts) could at that time certainly be said to deserve the description 'cruel' in the ordinary sense of that word; but that was insufficient to 'measure up to the standard set by the ecclesiastical courts in that no physical harm was found to have been inflicted or was reasonably to be apprehended'.[90] Hence the husband's petition[91] had to be dismissed.[92]

---

[84] 'These are pure questions of fact—questions on which the demeanour of the parties in the witness box is . . . highly important, and often decisive . . .': *King v. King* [1953] AC 124, *per* Lord Asquith of Bishopstone.

[85] Such appeals were often brought because of the impact of a finding of guilt on the parties' maintenance expectations rather than because either party wanted to keep the marriage in existence.

[86] When the Matrimonial Causes Act 1937 came into force: s. 14(2).

[87] See the dicta in *Evans v. Evans* (1790) 1 Hag. Con. 35, 38, *per* Sir William Scott, cited at p. 150, above.

[88] *Russell v. Russell* [1897] AC 395. But it sufficed if the conduct damaged the petitioner's mental and emotional health; and the courts came to accept that 'mental cruelty' of sufficient gravity sufficed: see *Lauder v. Lauder* [1949] P 277, CA (where an army officer of 'somewhat peculiar temperament' had moods or fits of depression, remaining morose and sullen to his 'extremely affectionate' wife whilst 'being jolly with other people if they happened to be there' and would not speak to his wife for periods as long as a week or ten days. This had a 'serious effect on the wife's nervous and emotional stability'. The Court of Appeal (by a 2–1 majority) held that she was entitled to a divorce on the ground of cruelty. But the need to show some injury to health was a grievance to those women who could say 'I was too strong to have a nervous breakdown, so my cruelty case failed': *Official Report* (HC) 9 March 1951, vol. 485, col. 934 (Mrs Eirene White).

[89] [1897] AC 395.   [90] *Gollins v. Gollins* [1964] AC 644, *per* Lord Hodson.

[91] For Judicial Separation.

[92] If the parties separated, conduct (such as that in the *Russell* case) which would have constituted legal cruelty if the petitioner's health had been affected by it might be the basis on which a successful case of constructive desertion could be founded: see above.

It was necessary to prove that the respondent had been guilty of grave and weighty conduct, but it was not *sufficient* to do so. Because of their concern about 'the possibility of divorce being granted for incompatibility of temperament'[93] the courts at this time insisted that some element of intention underlying the respondent's behaviour be demonstrated. Although it was not necessary to show that the one spouse had actually intended to injure the other, it was necessary to show that the conduct in question had (so it was said) been 'aimed at' him or her. Both the requirement that the conduct be 'grave and weighty' and that it should have been 'aimed at' the petitioner caused the courts considerable difficulty.

There is no need to burden the reader with a long account of court decisions on what constituted sufficiently 'grave and weighty' conduct. The content of the test (however difficult it might be to apply to particular facts) was well-settled: it was the same as that applied in cases of constructive desertion:[94] the conduct had to transcend 'the ordinary wear and tear of married life'[95] and be such as to make future cohabitation impossible. True, there could be differences of opinion about what one spouse could be said to have bargained to accept in marriage,[96] and (as one case demonstrates) even appeal judges sometimes differed amongst themselves:

In *Bravery v. Bravery*[97] the wife's petition alleged that 'during the year 1938 . . . the husband without consulting the wife who had often expressed her desire to have more children informed the wife that he . . . had arranged for sterilisation which operation subsequently was performed, thereby causing the wife to suffer great anguish'. The Court of Appeal, by a 2–1 majority, dismissed her appeal against the trial judge's decision that since she had consented to the operation the husband's conduct could not be described as 'cruel'. But Denning LJ considered that vasectomy done 'to enable a man to have the pleasure of sexual intercourse without the responsibilities attaching to it' was illegal, and that in the circumstances the husband had been guilty of cruelty even if the wife had consented.

Sometimes these differences of opinion caused great anguish to those involved:

In *King v. King*[98] the husband petitioned for divorce on the ground of his wife's cruelty. He claimed that his wife had not only twice committed acts of physical violence against him[99] but that her constant nagging allegations about his

---

[93] *Morton Report*, para. 123.					[94] See above.

[95] Or (as the trial judge in *Bravery v. Bravery* (above) put it) the 'ordinary ups and downs and unpleasantnesses which accompany married life'.

[96] For example, was a judge right to hold that a husband's untidiness, dirty and distasteful domestic habits, excessive interest in art and music, meanness, distasteful domestic habits, excessive interest in art music and Indian philosophy, burning incense in front of idols and playing Indian music at all hours of the day and night were not sufficiently serious to be classified as cruelty?: see *Bravery v. Bravery* [1954] 1 WLR 1169.

[97] [1954] 1 WLR 1169, CA.					[98] [1953] AC 124, HL.

[99] All the reported judgments however regard these as being unimportant.

alleged adultery had damaged his health. At the conclusion of a five-day trial, the judge found that her behaviour constituted legal cruelty, and granted the husband a decree of divorce. But the Court of Appeal (by a majority of 2–1) held he had been wrong; and the House of Lords (after a six-day hearing, and by a majority of 3–2) upheld the Court of Appeal's decision. The parties remained married.

The question whether the respondent had to be shown to *intend* harm or injury to the other was one which the courts found extremely difficult. Of course, the fact that there was an 'element of malignity' in the respondent's conduct would always be a relevant fact;[100] and if one spouse deliberately set out to hurt the other and thereby caused injury to the other's health he or she would properly be found guilty of cruelty. But what of the case in which the respondent claimed that he or she had never intended to harm the other spouse? What of the situation in which the conduct complained of was attributable to mental (or physical) ill-health?[101]

For long these issues troubled the courts and the position was far from clear.[102] But in 1963 (a quarter of a century after the coming into force of the 1937 Act) the House of Lords significantly restricted the relevance of intention in determining whether cruelty had been established:

In *Gollins v. Gollins*[103] the husband was 'incorrigibly and inexcusably lazy'. He failed to work or provide any support for his wife, and he was constantly being

---

[100] See eg *Squire v. Squire* [1949] P 51; *Gollins v. Gollins* [1964] AC 644.

[101] As in *Squire v. Squire* [1949] P 51, CA, where an invalid wife systematically and persistently prevented her husband from sleeping and demanded that he read to or talk with her. If her entreaties failed, she would demand that he perform various menial services for her, or she would strip the clothes from his bed, move furniture around the room or switch the lights on and off. The husband, a 'man of honour with a high sense of duty' ultimately 'broke under the strain' and petitioned for divorce on the ground of the wife's cruelty. The trial judge dismissed his petition because he considered that it was necessary to establish that 'cruelty must be deliberate, malignant and intended'; but the Court of Appeal (by a 2–1 majority) held that he had been wrong to do so: an intent to injure was not an essential element in cruelty.

[102] The *Morton Report*, para. 124, commenting in 1956 on the most recent appellate decisions laying down that to constitute legal cruelty the conduct in question must be in some way 'aimed by one person at the other' gave as clear an analysis of the then understanding of the law as is likely to be found: conduct 'aimed at' a spouse 'consists of actions or words (i) which are actually or physically directed at that spouse, or (ii) which, though not actually or physically directed at that spouse, are done or said with intent to injure him or to inflict misery on him. Conduct coming within the first category need not be accompanied by an intent to injure and will include nagging, sulking, and excessive demands by one spouse on the time and attention of the other. The second category may include such conduct as, for instance, arises from an addiction to drink, gambling or crime. Conduct of that sort, which clearly results from a defect of temperament, will not be regarded as legal cruelty unless an intent to injure is proved to exist. If, however, it is shown that the spouse knew the consequences which would result from a persistence in his conduct but nevertheless continued in it, heedless of the effect on the other spouse, the court may presume the existence of an intent to injure that other spouse or to inflict misery on him. . . . Moreover, the very nature of the conduct may be such as to lead the court to hold that the respondent must have known the effect which it would have on the other spouse'. The Commission refused to recommend statutory amendment of the law.

[103] [1964] AC 644, HL.

dunned by creditors. The wife, in contrast, was a capable, well-balanced woman who made a success of running a guest house for elderly people. But she was 'worried to death' by calls from bailiffs and others trying to extract money from her husband. Eventually she was reduced to headaches, agitation, unexplained fits of weeping, and other symptoms of a moderately severe anxiety state. The House of Lords (by a 3–2 majority) held that the husband had been persistently cruel to the wife.[104] The majority cast doubt on whether intention was truly a necessary element in cruelty;[105] and preferred to ask the simple question: 'were the acts in question "cruel" in the ordinary sense of that word?' The minority thought that in the present case they could not properly be so described.

In *Williams v. Williams*[106] the husband (a miner who had been certified as insane under the legislation then in force) heard voices telling him that there were men in the loft of the family home and that his wife was committing adultery. He followed her around the house and repeatedly made unfounded allegations of adultery against her; and his behaviour damaged her health. Although he knew what he was doing he did not know that it was wrong; and in such a case he would under the so-called McNaughten rules have had a defence in a criminal prosecution. The question was whether his insanity equally provided a defence to her petition for divorce on the basis of his cruelty. The House of Lords, by a 3–2 majority, held that his insanity provided no defence.[107] The question was simply whether, taking all the relevant facts into account, his conduct could properly and objectively be described as cruel.

These two cases marked a decisive shift in the law: the emphasis moved strongly towards asking simply whether the facts established that the petitioner needed protection. Was 'the conduct complained of and its consequences so bad that the petitioner must have a remedy'?[108] Considerations of culpability became less dominant than was once the case; and divorce was no longer to be restricted to cases where the respondent could be found to be the 'guilty' party. Moreover, the question whether the marriage was in any sense still viable seems to have became of greater relevance. But the law still failed to give relief in the many cases in which both parties recognised that their relationship had ceased to be a functioning marriage and wished their legal status to recognise that fact:

[104] And that accordingly magistrates had properly made an order against him under the Matrimonial Proceedings (Magistrates' Courts) Act 1960.

[105] There were, of course, cases in which the presence of an intention to injure could convert acts otherwise cruel into sufficiently grave and weighty matters as to found a divorce decree: 'a blow speaks for itself, [but] insults, humiliation, meannesses, impositions, deprivations, and the like may need the interpretation of underlying intention for an assessment of their fullest significance. And that interpretation may . . . turn the scale': *Gollins v. Gollins* [1964] AC 644, 696.

[106] [1964] AC 698.

[107] However, in cases where the need for protection was more marginal, a divorce petition might still fail by reason of the respondent's inability to form an intention to injure: *Jamieson v. Jamieson* [1952] AC 525, 535, *per* Lord Normand.

[108] *Gollins v. Gollins* [1964] AC 644, 666–667, *per* Lord Reid.

In *Le Brocq v. Le Brocq*[109] the marriage between a submissive and retiring bank clerk and his volatile and lively wife[110] had completely broken down. For seven years they had hardly spoken to one another. But the Court of Appeal held that the husband's taciturn, unsociable and submissive withdrawal into his shell did not constitute cruelty as that term was used in the divorce law, and rejected the wife's petition for divorce. The Court of Appeal also rejected the husband's cross-petition alleging that his wife had deserted him.[111] The marriage, in law, survived.

BARS TO DIVORCE UNDER THE HERBERT ACT: A CONSERVATIVE POLICY

Even if the petitioner proved that there were grounds for divorce it did not necessarily follow that the marriage would be dissolved. 'The posture of a petitioner for divorce had' (the draftsman of the Herbert Act has written)[112] 'to be that of an innocent party willing to perform his or her side of the contract, neither conniving at nor condoning the wickedness of the other party, and above all seeking no deal or understanding . . . to let the divorce go through'. The Herbert Act (as we have seen) not only retained all the existing bars to divorce but reformulated the relevant statutory provisions[113] in an attempt to make it more difficult for a couple to collude in getting a divorce.

In fact, the reformulation seems to have had remarkably little effect. The courts were uneasy about requiring petitioners to prove affirmatively that they had not been guilty of collusion and whilst the Herbert Act also imposed a specific duty of enquiry[114] on the court, in reality the court had no means of carrying out an enquiry (save by sending the papers to the King's Proctor).[115] But although it is clear that the Herbert Act was intended to be a conservative measure in relation to the bars to divorce, case law soon brought about a radical change in the way in which the court exercised its discretion in those cases where the petitioner admitted his or her own adultery.

The attitude of the Victorian judges had, as we have seen[116] been only to exercise the discretion to grant a divorce to a petitioner guilty of adultery in the most

---

[109] [1964] 1 WLR 1085.

[110] who liked 'a bit of a dispute and perhaps a certain amount of a row occasionally, as many married people do . . .': *per* Harman LJ at p. 1090.

[111] Because the court concluded that there had been no sufficient factual separation: see note 39, above.

[112] HS Kent, *In on the Act* (1979) p. 81.   [113] Matrimonial Causes Act 1937, s. 4.

[114] The statement made by the *Matrimonial Causes Procedure Committee Consultation Paper*, 1983, para. 1.10 that the duty to inquire could be traced back 'almost word for word' to the 1857 Act ignores the change of wording made in 1937. But it is true that the Divorce Court from its inception claimed that its procedures were inquisitorial.

[115] Supreme Court of Judicature (Consolidation) Act 1925, s. 181. In theory, the court could have called before it witnesses whose evidence it thought might be relevant, but this seems rarely if ever to have been done.

[116] See pp. 188–193, above.

exceptional circumstances; but after World War I this practice came under pressure. It may be that the fact that many divorce cases were now handled by judges from outside the Probate, Divorce and Admiralty Division led not only to some lack of consistency[117] but also to a greater readiness to accept that the public interest was not always served by keeping legally in existence a marriage which had in fact completely ceased to exist. In 1930, the President delivered what was intended to be seen as authoritative guidance:[118] on the one hand, the governing consideration was the 'interest of the community at large in maintaining the sanctions of honest matrimony' and thus a 'strong affirmative case' would have to be made out to justify the court overriding the 'conditional prohibition' imposed by the legislation against granting a decree to an adulterous petitioner.[119] On the other hand the President's emphasis on the public interest (as against a narrow interpretation of exceptional categories already defined by case law) as the most important factor in deciding on how the discretion should be exercised in any particular case gave the courts much greater flexibility. But the real turning point[120] came with a decision of the House of Lords in 1943.[121] The House declared that in deciding whether or not to exercise discretion in favour of a petitioner guilty of a matrimonial offence the court should regard it as of primary importance to consider the interest of the community at large in maintaining a 'true balance between respect for the binding sanctity of marriage and the social considerations which make it contrary to public policy to insist on the maintenance of a union which has utterly broken down'. In practice, (in spite of occasional protests from members of the judiciary)[122] the fact the marriage had truly broken down became so strong an element in the matter that the court's discretion came to be exercised in all but the most flagrant[123] cases. Certainly the court would no longer withhold a decree (as was routinely done at the beginning of the century) simply because, after the breakdown of the marriage, the petitioner as well as the respondent had established another stable relationship.[124] It is also possible that the increased readiness of the courts to overlook the petitioner's own misconduct reduced the temptation to present a false case. Be that as it may, the *Blunt* decision of the House of Lords (in the words of the Finer Report)[125] put 'the seal of highest authority' to giving

---

[117] *Apted v. Apted and Bliss* [1930] P 246, 254.   [118] *Ibid.*

[119] *Apted v. Apted and Bliss* [1930] P 246, 259.

[120] *Moor v. Moor* [1954] 2 All ER 458, CA, *per* Denning LJ.

[121] *Blunt v. Blunt* [1943] AC 517.

[122] *Moor v. Moor* [1954] 2 All ER 458, CA, cited with approval in the *Morton Report*, para. 226.

[123] *Moor v. Moor* [1954] 2 All ER 458, CA, *per* Sir Raymond Evershed, MR; *Morton Report*, para. 225.

[124] Thus, in 1965 the court's discretion was exercised in 3,850 cases in the Principal Divorce Registry (out of a total of 11,221) and refused in only three. Even when the adultery had not been disclosed by the petitioner but came to light as the result of the Queen's Proctor's investigations the court usually exercised its discretion: in 1965, the Court heard and allowed 54 interventions by the Proctor, but exercised its discretion in favour of the petitioner in 34 of those cases: *The Field of Choice* (1966, Cmnd. 3123) p. 12, notes 30, 32, 33.

[125] *Report of the Committee on One-Parent Families* (1974, Cmnd. 5629) para. 4.35.

'great importance to the fact of breakdown. There was nothing to be found about breakdown in the grounds of divorce as enacted by Parliament. But the reality was that thousands passing through the divorce courts were obtaining consensual decrees under a
system in which they were theoretically prohibited.'

But although the fact of breakdown may increasingly have been seen as relevant
to allowing the marriage to be dissolved in law as well as in fact if both parties
were agreed it did nothing to allow divorce where one party refused, whilst the
bar of collusion could still operate as a deterrent to a divorce in which the financial and other consequences were agreed between the couple concerned.

BARS INHIBIT ATTEMPTS AT RECONCILIATION AND SETTLEMENT
OF CONSEQUENCES OF BREAKDOWN

There were two particular problems. First, the law was widely agreed to be confusing[126] and to inhibit the making of sensible arrangements for the future. As
the *Morton Report* put it[127] in 1956:

It 'is natural that husband and wife would wish to make early arrangements for the
future of the children, and that a wife would wish to have some assurance about the
provision to be made for her maintenance and for the division of the home, and, sometimes, for the payment of the costs of the proceedings. Yet, as the law stands at present,
the parties must be advised that such arrangements will have to be left until after the
divorce, for fear that the court will regard the proceedings as collusive. Moreover, a
spouse may be deterred from approaching the other spouse with a view to reconciliation because proceedings for divorce following on the failure of the attempted reconciliation might be regarded as collusive'.

Secondly, the courts had held that a husband who had sexual intercourse with
an adulterous wife, with knowledge of her adultery[128] was to be conclusively

---

[126] In 1947 the *Final Report of the Committee on Procedure in Matrimonial Causes,* (Chairman,
Denning J) (1947, Cmd. 7024) para. 29(xi) claimed that the 'law as to collusion does not need
amendment but needs to be better understood. It does not forbid discussion with a view to reconciliation. If reconciliation is impossible, it does not forbid discussions as to the future of the children,
the house and furniture, the provision of maintenance and necessaries for the wife or costs. It only
forbids the parties to concoct a false case in order that it may appear as genuine, or to create by
arrangement between themselves the grounds for divorce, or to bribe one or the other in order to get
a divorce'. But solicitors lacked the confidence to follow the Committee's advice that 'lawyers
should cease to advise their clients to have nothing to do with one another, but should point out that
the law favours reconciliation and that any overtures to that end will not prejudice the case'; and
nine years later the *Morton Report* (para. 234), accepting that there was still uncertainty as to the
bounds of the law, recommended that collusion be defined by statute. The definition should make
it clear that such discussions were permissible, but that a petitioner who had been bribed to take proceedings or had extracted a price for so doing would still be denied a divorce.
[127] Para. 231.
[128] Or with knowledge of the fact she was guilty of cruelty. In the case of desertion, condonation
was not in this sense a bar; but any resumption of cohabitation would terminate the desertion: *Perry
v. Perry* [1952] P 203, CA. If the attempted reconciliation was ended by the guilty spouse again leaving, the injured spouse would have to wait for another three years before petitioning.

deemed to have condoned the offence unless it could be shown that the inter-course was induced by the wife making a fraudulent misstatement of fact.[129] The fact that a single act of intercourse would cancel out his right to petition[130] might well deter a man from agreeing to any attempt at reconciliation.

These refinements did little to suggest that the Herbert Act had been success-ful in reducing the incidence of 'unseemly litigation' and it seems improbable that they did much to restore 'due respect for the law'.[131]

DIVORCE IN THE EARLY YEARS OF MARRIAGE

However clear it may have been that one spouse had committed a matrimonial offence, the innocent party had no right to file a petition until three years had passed since the date of the marriage.[132] But as we have seen, the Act gave judges of the High Court[133] a discretion to allow a petition to be presented before the three-year period if the case was one 'of exceptional hardship suffered by the petitioner or exceptional depravity on the part of the respondent'. What impact did this provision have?

For many years there were comparatively few applications for leave to pre-sent a petition within the three-year period on the ground that the case was 'exceptional' in terms of the statutory language;[134] and the courts adopted a restrictive approach to the meaning of those terms. As Denning LJ put it in 1949:[135]

'If there is nothing more than adultery with one person within the first three years of mar-riage that may be considered ordinary depravity. There is, I am sorry to say, nothing

---

[129] *Henderson v. Henderson and Crellin* [1944] AC 49. Where a wife had intercourse with her husband the presumption of condonation was rebuttable.

[130] And equally a wife with grounds for divorce might be 'reluctant to make any approach to her husband because the fact that they have come together, if only for a few days or weeks, will deprive her of the remedy of divorce if the court holds that the matrimonial offence has thereby been con-doned': *Morton Report*, para. 238.

[131] Cf. the terms of the preamble to Matrimonial Causes Act 1937; p. 236, above.   [132] s. 1.

[133] Section 1 of the Act specifically referred to the High Court, and would thus seem to have excluded commissioners who might try divorce cases on assize from its scope: see *Ambler v. Ambler* [1951] 1 All ER 980.

[134] It does not follow that the time bar had any significant impact in deterring recourse to divorce: see the Law Commission's *Working Paper, Time Restrictions on Presentation of Divorce and Nullity Petitions* (WP No. 76, 1980, paras. 44, 48).

[135] *Bowman v. Bowman* [1949] P 353. This attempt to lay down general guidelines was subse-quently criticised by the Court of Appeal: *Blackwell v. Blackwell* (1973) 117 SJ 939; and, 30 years after the *Bowman* decision another Lord Justice said that it was 'unlikely' that the meaning of the terms depravity and exceptional depravity given by Denning LJ would 'find much support today': *C v. C (Divorce: Exceptional Hardship)* [1980] Fam 23, *per* Ormrod LJ. Two years later, however, the House of Lords emphasised the significance of the word 'exceptional' in the statute, but refused to attempt more precise definition, arguing that the imprecision of these concepts with the resultant impossibility of definition must have been deliberately accepted as appropriate by the legislature and as itself an indication that the determination of what is exceptional is essentially a matter for the judge of first instance to decide: *Fay v. Fay* [1982] AC 835, 842, *per* Lord Scarman.

exceptional about that situation, and it does not involve exceptional hardship on the innocent spouse. . . . The distress that it causes is one which many have to endure . . . [But] the husband who commits adultery within a few weeks of marriage, or who commits adultery promiscuously with more than one woman or with his wife's sister, or with a servant in the house, may probably be labelled as exceptionally depraved. . . . Cruelty again, by itself, is, I fear, not exceptional, but, if it is coupled with aggravating circumstances, as, for instance, drunkenness and neglect, or if it is exceptionally brutal or dangerous to health then . . . it does . . . cause exceptional hardship to the applicant. If it is coupled with perverted lust, it shows exceptional depravity on the part of the proposed respondent.'

The Herbert Act[136] expressly required the judge hearing an application for leave to 'have regard to the interests of any children of the marriage and to the question whether there is reasonable probability of reconciliation between the parties'. But it seems that in the great majority of cases there could be no serious likelihood of a reconciliation;[137] and in this way, once more, experience underlined the significance of whether or not the marriage had truly broken down in determining whether it should be dissolved.

THE CASE FOR FURTHER REFORM

The Herbert Act (as interpreted by the courts) did in these ways significantly shift the emphasis of the law so as to make the question whether a marriage had or had not irretrievably broken down of greater significance. But the Act did not (and did not pretend to) provide a legal mechanism for the dissolution in law of all those marriages which were, in terms of the parties' personal relationship, completely dead. This led to another long campaign for reform of the ground for divorce. But it was not only the substance of the law which seemed manifestly imperfect. From the beginning of the century there had been problems with the structure of the courts dealing with matrimonial cases and with the procedures which the courts used. The Herbert Act had only a very minor impact on these matters; but they were of great importance for the working of the family justice system, as the next chapter demonstrates.

---

[136] s. 1(2).

[137] In *Bowman v. Bowman* Denning LJ emphasised the importance of this provision and suggested that applicants should always state in detail what steps (if any) they had taken to explore the prospects of reconciliation, for example by consulting the Probation Service. The specific statutory reference to the relevance of reconciliation was the basis on which an experiment was started in 1971 whereby in cases in the London area applications for leave would be referred to a Court Welfare Officer to explore the prospects. The fact that this initiative—founded on the belief that the court's duty to consider the prospects of reconciliation could not otherwise be realistically performed—was justified by the statutory reference in the Herbert Act deserves to be remembered in the light of the subsequent burgeoning of interest in institutionalised conciliation and reconciliation.

8

The Family Justice Process
1900–1970

INTRODUCTION

Divorce seemed popular at the beginning of the twentieth century (to some, shockingly so). In 1875, the three judges of the newly created Probate Divorce and Admiralty Division of the High Court had to deal with fewer than 400 divorce petitions.[1] But 30 years later the number of petitions had almost doubled;[2] and by 1914 there were for the first time more than a thousand.[3] And worse was to come: in 1919, in the aftermath of World War I, an unprecedented 5,085 divorce petitions were filed.[4] At one level the danger was that the Divorce Court would simply not be able to cope and would collapse under the pressure. But there was another worrying factor. In spite of the increase in the number of cases it had become clear that matrimonial justice was still not equally available to rich and poor. The fact that hearings took place only in London effectively put judicial divorce 'beyond the reach of numbers of the poorer classes'[5] and indeed beyond the reach of the less affluent (or perhaps less thrifty) members of the middle class. It is true, as we have seen,[6] that magistrates' courts were available to administer a form of justice to ill-treated or deserted wives; but the 'relief' available in such proceedings to the 5,000 or so applicants did not extend to allowing them to remarry, whilst the procedures of the 'police courts'[7] often

---

[1] 362 divorce petitions were filed in that year, 400 in 1876: *Report of the Royal Commission on Marriage and Divorce,* Cmd. 9678, Appendix II, Table 1.

[2] 752 petitions were filed in 1905: *ibid.*   [3] 1,075 petitions were filed in 1914: *ibid.*

[4] *Ibid.*

[5] The fullest analysis of the problem of expense is to be found in the *Report of the Royal Commission on Divorce and Matrimonial Causes,* 1912, Cd. 6478, paras. 50–77; and see also the *Report of the Committee appointed by the Lord Chancellor to inquire into certain matters relating to County Court Procedure* (1909) BPP vol. 72, p. 311, para. 6. GK Behlmer, *Friends of the Family, The English Home and its Guardians, 1850–1940* (1998) p. 190 estimates that an uncontested divorce case cost about the equivalent of 30 weeks' pay for the average male wage-earner in the Edwardian period (and about 93 weeks' pay for a contested case). If these multipliers are applied to the year 2000 average earnings of a male manual worker the figures are £10,500 and £32,500 respectively.

[6] See pp. 199–201, above.

[7] The terms 'police courts' and 'police magistrates' ceased to be used in legislation following criticisms made in the *Report of the Departmental Committee on Courts of Summary Jurisdiction in the Metropolitan Area* (Chairman, Sir A Maxwell (1937), HMSO, p. 28) but Sir M Finer and Professor OR McGregor (Appendix 5 to *Report of the Committee on One-Parent Families,* 1974, Cmnd. 5629, p. 105) suggest that the courts remained 'universally known, because of their close association with the police, as "police courts"'.

seemed more suitable to dealing with petty criminals than with the difficulties associated with family breakdown. Reform of the substantive law of divorce was only a partial solution to the fact that the legal system was not truly available to all those who needed a legal remedy for family problems.

One factor contributing to the heavy expense of divorce proceedings was the expense for the petitioner and witnesses of travelling to London; and this chapter first considers the question whether divorce should still only be available in the High Court sitting in London. It then outlines the attempts made to improve the procedures for dealing with domestic cases in the magistrates' courts. However, the most effective way of making the courts truly open to all was the introduction in the aftermath of World War II of a measure of public financial support for those who would otherwise be denied the remedies which the law in theory provided. The Legal Aid Act 1949 has a claim to being the most significant of all the various influences on the development of the family justice system in this country; and it is the subject of the final part of this chapter. The chapter ends on the eve of the coming into force of the Divorce Reform Act: the fact that divorce under this legislation was no longer to be based on the commission of a matrimonial offence but (in theory at least) on the fact that the marriage had irretrievably broken down raised a range of issues about process in divorce and other family cases; and these are best discussed[8] after the evolution of the new substantive law has been explained.

THE FORUM FOR DIVORCE

The 1908 *County Court Procedure Committee*[9] chaired by the President of the Probate Divorce and Admiralty Division Sir John Gorell Barnes,[10] stated the problem of access to divorce very clearly:

'There is still practically one law for those who can afford to bring a suit in the divorce court and another for those who cannot, and the latter embraces a very large portion of the population who cannot afford even the moderate expense of a suit in the present court. . . . The great proportion of the cases are undefended, but proof of the facts before the judge is necessary; and even in these cases, poor people very frequently cannot find the money to commence and proceed with these suits and bring their witnesses from a distance to London, nor can they find the time or leave their employments for sufficient time, either to file their petitions in London . . . or to attend a hearing in London. . . . Without doubt there is a practical denial of justice in this matter to numbers of people.'

Three years later the Royal Commission on Divorce chaired by Lord Gorell (as he had become) agreed that 'beyond all doubt' divorce was 'beyond the reach

---

[8] See Chapter 21, below.

[9] *Report of the Committee appointed by the Lord Chancellor to inquire into certain matters relating to County Court Procedure* (1909) BPP vol. 72, p. 311: see pp. 208–209, above.

[10] See Biographical Notes.

of the poor';[11] and it was difficult for the fair-minded to disagree with the Royal Commission's view[12] that if 'there is to be a law of divorce . . . there can be neither justice nor common sense in not opening [the] courts to the suitor, who claims the benefit of that law, and cannot otherwise enforce his claim'.

How then could the problem be solved? An obvious solution would have been to allow the county courts to deal with at any rate certain categories of divorce; and in view of the fact that Lord Gorell, the Chairman of the 1912 Royal Commission, had already urged this in the House of Lords[13] it might have been assumed that the Commission would make a formal recommendation to this effect. But, although the Royal Commission's *Report*[14] accepted that an influential body of opinion favoured extending jurisdiction to the county court[15] and rejected the principal objections[16] to so doing, it none the less concluded[17] that some objections to allowing county court divorce were valid. One of these[18] apparently weighed heavily with the Commission.[19] It was that:

'the gravity of divorce and other matrimonial cases, affecting as they do the family life, the status of the parties, the interests of their children, and the interest of the State in the moral and social well-being of its citizens, makes it desirable to provide, if possible, that, even for the poorest persons, these cases should be determined by the superior courts of the country assisted by the attendance of the Bar, which we regard as of high importance

---

[11] *Report of the Royal Commission on Divorce and Matrimonial Causes* (1912, Cd. 6478) para. 77; and a modern scholar has written that by stipulating that all divorce suits had to be brought before a single, specialised Divorce Court in London, the 1857 Act had 'built an economic fence that only the most determined working-class suitor could scale': GK Behlmer, *Friends of the Family, The English Home and its Guardians, 1850–1940* (1998) p. 190. Note that some law-makers had been well aware that the 1857 Act would not bring divorce within the reach of the poorest classes in society, and they had correctly predicted that an attempt would be made to have cases heard in cheaper courts: see p. 195, above.

[12] *Report of the Royal Commission on Divorce and Matrimonial Causes* (1912, Cd. 6478) para. 78.

[13] See p. 209, above.

[14] *Report of the Royal Commission on Divorce and Matrimonial Causes* (1912, Cd. 6478) para. 95.

[15] Because 'of the great convenience which these courts afford to suitors, owing to the sittings being held at a large number of places throughout the country, also because the procedure is speedy, simple and economical, and generally because. . . these courts are suited to the needs of those who resort to them, and are competent to deal with the suggested additional jurisdiction'.

[16] '. . . that divorce ought not to be made too easy, and that to give the county courts jurisdiction would have this effect; that uniformity of decision is desirable, and would not be obtained if the jurisdiction were entrusted to the county court judges, who number 55; and that there would be more opportunity for collusion than if the trial of cases were confined to London': *Report of the Royal Commission on Divorce and Matrimonial Causes* (1912, Cd. 6478) para. 96.

[17] *Report of the Royal Commission on Divorce and Matrimonial Causes* (1912, Cd. 6478) paras. 105–106.

[18] Other arguments accepted by the Gorell Commission were (i) the large number of county court judges (some of whom might be Roman Catholics or have objections to divorce); (ii) the association of the county courts with recovery of small debts; (iii) the fact that divorce often involved a foreign element, with which the county courts were not well fitted to deal: see para. 106.

[19] This argument was accepted by official bodies for many years: see the *Report of the Matrimonial Causes (Trial in the Provinces) Committee* (Chairman: Sir R Wedgewood, Bart) (1943, Cmd. 6480): see para. 28. The passage in the text was quoted by, and expressly adopted by, the Denning Committee on Matrimonial Causes Procedure in 1946: see below.

in divorce and matrimonial cases, both in the interests of the parties and in the public interest.'[20]

Accordingly, the Commission rejected the proposal to confer jurisdiction on the county court as such. Instead, it recommended that the High Court should hold divorce sittings at local centres throughout the country, and county court judges would be appointed Commissioners to sit at these Assize centres.[21] The Commissioners would have all the powers of a judge of the High Court in relation to divorce although only petitioners of modest[22] means would be eligible to have their cases dealt with locally in this way.

There was no immediate response to even this modest proposal and the fact that the Commission had adopted what seemed (particularly when compared with its quite bold approach to the issue of the ground for divorce) to be a conservative and cautious approach to proposals to extend the courts' jurisdiction meant that those who had agitated for reform were disinclined to devote much effort to what seemed to many to be a secondary issue. But with the wartime upsurge in divorce petitions the situation became critical and the Ministers and officials responsible for the functioning of the court system took emergency action[23] to deal with the backlog of cases. After the War, the Administration of Justice Act 1920 was intended to provide a long-term solution dealing[24] both with the inadequacy of judge power to meet demand and the fact that centralisation of divorce work in London greatly increased the costs of divorce.

The 1920 Act followed the Royal Commission proposal up to a point by adapting the assize system (the practice, dating back to the twelfth century, of sending out judges round the shires to hold an assize in every county at least

[20] It was also thought that to confer jurisdiction on the county court would cause problems in relation to the administrative and interlocutory work: the 'vast majority of the [County Court] Registrars are only part-time officials being in the remainder of their time practising solicitors carrying on business in the district. Their client's affairs, or the affairs of their competitors' clients would constantly come before them for judicial purposes. This is a considerable evil in the present County Court system. It would be a much larger evil if this system were extended so as to bring within their purview all the very delicate matters which are necessarily involved in a matrimonial cause': Official Memorandum dated 10 March 1920 on the Bill introduced in that year by Lord Buckmaster, PRO LCO2/460, p. 3.

[21] Eight or ten selected county court judges would be appointed as Commissioners of Assize, each taking the divorce and matrimonial cases for his district.

[22] Ie those whose joint capital and income did not exceed £250 and £300 per annum (approximately £14,000 and £16,500 respectively in year 2000 values): see *Report of the Royal Commission on Divorce and Matrimonial Causes* (1912, Cd. 6478) para. 117. This was a tactically unwise proposal since the poor would be forced to take their matrimonial grievances to a tribunal inferior to that available to the more affluent: see Birkenhead, *Points of View* (1922) p. 42.

[23] Lord Chancellor Birkenhead and other Law Lords (such as Lord Buckmaster: see Biographical Notes) Lords Justice of Appeal and King's Bench judges came to the relief of the judges of the Probate Divorce and Admiralty Division; and in one term 1,261 undefended and 220 defended divorce cases were dealt with. As Birkenhead's biographer remarks this was 'magnificent but it was war': J Campbell, *FE Smith, First Earl of Birkenhead* (1923) p. 482; and see the memorandum by G Coldstream, 5 January 1946, PRO LCO2/4197.

[24] This was only done after intensive debate in Whitehall: see the Minute dated 20 March 1920 on PRO LCO2/460.

twice a year)[25] to accommodate some divorce work. But the 1920 Act did not follow the Royal Commission in restricting the cases to be dealt with in this way to those of the poor. It went much further. The Assize judges[26] were given jurisdiction to process not only petitions brought under the special poor persons' procedure[27] but also all undefended petitions.[28]

This change attracted little discussion[29] or comment at the time, and for some years the 1920 Act evidently worked well enough at a practical level.[30] But it seems to have passed unnoticed[31] that allowing a large number of judges with no special knowledge or experience to administer divorce law was completely inconsistent with the philosophy upon which the 1857 Act had been founded.[32] For it was in undefended cases that the risk of collusion was greatest and it was in those cases that the respondent was least likely to be represented by experienced (or any) counsel; and it had always been argued that the need for specialist knowledge and experience from bench and bar was most pressing.[33] Yet it

---

[25] The assize system was abolished—to the regret of some, who attached importance to the ceremonial whereby the judge had been conducted by coach, surrounded by pikemen and trumpeters, from the lodgings to the court building—by the Courts Act 1971.

[26] Ie not only the King's Bench judges but also any 'commissioner acting under a commission of assize'. The Supreme Court of Judicature (Consolidation) Act 1925, s. 70(3) (replacing a somewhat ambiguous provision in the Supreme Court of Judicature Act 1873, s. 29) made it clear that the commission could include not only serving and retired High Court or Court of Appeal judges but also county court judges and King's Counsel. In 1920 the Lord Chancellor's officials had doubted whether barristers would be willing to serve as commissioners (see PRO LCO2/460, 10 March 1920) but in fact it proved possible to make extensive use of the procedure: see below.

[27] The poor persons' procedure was only available to those with assets of £50 (perhaps £1,250 in year 2000 values): see p. 306, below.

[28] The Administration of Justice Act 1920, s.1 conferred power on the Assize judges to try matrimonial causes of any class prescribed by the Lord Chancellor (with the concurrence of the Lord Chief Justice and the President).

[29] The parliamentary debate on the Act was sparse (the 'exceptional course' of taking all the Bill's stages in the House of Commons on a single day was taken no doubt to get the Bill on the statute book before prorogation on 23 December 1920: see *Official Report* (HC) 20 December 1920, vol. 136, col. 1481); but the Committee stage debate in the House of Lords was notable both for the public warning given by the Lord Chief Justice against making any assumption that King's Bench judges would accept the imposition of a duty to deal with divorce and for the Lord Chancellor's assurance that the requirement for the concurrence of the Lord Chief Justice was a substantial one rather than a formality: *Official Report* (HL) 9 December 1920, vol. 43, cols. 8–13.

[30] In the years immediately before the Second World War it appears that petitions could often be heard on Assize within a few weeks whereas in London there were often long delays: *Simpson, W v. Simpson, EA (Application by the King's Proctor for Directions)* (1937) *The Times* 20 March.

[31] The *Business of the Courts Committee* (Chairman, Lord Hanworth MR), *Second Interim Report* (1933, Cmd. 4471, BPP 1933/4, xi. 1), para. 13 recorded that the 1920 Act had 'probably unwittingly' effected a fundamental change.

[32] Memorandum by Lord Gorell (1896) as cited in the Second Interim Report of *The Business of the Courts Committee* (Chairman, Lord Hanworth MR) (1933, Cmd. 4471, BPP 1933/4, xi. 1), para. 15.

[33] 'To look behind the scene is an imperative duty cast upon the Court—a duty of the greatest importance, but in undefended cases of the greatest difficulty': JF Macqueen, *A Practical Treatise on the Law of Marriage, Divorce, and Legitimacy* (2nd ed., 1860) p. viii. But the reality of dealing with undefended divorce was often rather different: for a vivid description of the monotony of trying such cases see the speech by Clement Davies KC, *Official Report* (HC) 8 November 1937, vol. 328, col. 1449: '. . . an undefended divorce now takes five minutes, or less than 10 minutes. This is what takes place: There is no speech by counsel. He merely gets up . . . and he says: "Your

was these cases which the 1920 legislation transferred[34] to the jurisdiction of the
common law judges on circuit. In this way, the notion that the trial of divorce
cases required the special expertise of a small and select priesthood became
increasingly difficult to sustain. The truth was that a large proportion of divorce
work was to be discharged, not by the Division specially maintained in London
for that purpose, but by common law[35] judges on circuit sitting in isolation up
and down the country.[36] By definition, those judges lacked the knowledge[37]and
experience[38] in the trial of divorce 'postulated by the very existence of this special Division'. The transfer of undefended divorces to non-specialist judges
effected by the Administration of Justice Act 1920 was quite inconsistent with
the objective of preserving judicial uniformity in the exercise of the wide discre-

Lordship, this is a wife's petition. Mrs—whatever her name is—will you go into the box?" He then
asks her about 12 or 15 questions, and asks her to identify a photograph. She then walks out of the
box, and ready to walk into the box is the agent who served the papers on the husband. He goes in
and identifies the photograph, and says he found the husband living with another woman. "That is
my case, my lord", says counsel; "I ask for a decree". The judge nods his head and says "So be it",
and it is finished. There is a queue all nicely arranged by the usher so that no time is wasted'. Davies
quoted the evidence given by Langton J who had told the Peel Commission that he did not think that
'any one with anything approaching a first-class intelligence would be content to spend his whole
judicial life in the unrelieved study of divorce' and that he should doubt the 'complete sanity after
five years of divorce of any man who spent his entire time in that way'. Even President Merriman
described the prospect of hearing hundreds of undefended divorces as 'appalling': Merriman to
Simon, 31 January 1945, PRO LCO2/4197.

[34] Because of pressure of public opinion, according to the Hanworth Committee, para. 15. This
evidently overcame the objections to extending the Assize jurisdiction to matrimonial cases of any
description cogently put forward by the *Report of the Committee appointed by the Lord Chancellor
to inquire into certain matters relating to County Court Procedure* (Chairman: Lord Gorell) (1909)
BPP vol. 72, p. 311, at para. 6.

[35] Legislation provided that every judge of the Probate Divorce and Admiralty Division should
share with the other judges the duty of holding sittings of assize, provided that the state of business
should permit this, and until the number of PDA judges was increased in 1944 it never did: *Report
of the Matrimonial Causes (Trial in the Provinces) Committee* (Chairman Sir R Wedgewood, Bart.
(1943, Cmd. 6480) para. 5.

[36] Divorce petitions came to outnumber other actions tried on circuit. *Report of the Royal
Commission on the Despatch of Business at Common Law 1934–6*, (Chairman: Earl Peel) (1936,
Cmd. 5065, BPP 1935–6, xi, 105) para. 174 (1,716 matrimonial causes and 1,400 other actions dis-
posed of on circuit).

[37] As the Lord Chief Justice told the Peel Committee, *Report of the Royal Commission on the
Despatch of Business at Common Law 1934–6*, (Chairman: Earl Peel) 1936, Cmd. 5065. BPP 1935–6,
xi, 105, para. 175, an Assize judge might well have said 'I do not know anything about discretion,
and I do not want to know anything about it'.

[38] Although the majority of the King's Bench judges (in public at least) loyally undertook the
entirely new and unexpected burden of dealing with divorce on circuit there was at least one conspicuous exception: in *On Circuit 1924–1937* (1940) at pp. 112–113 Sir FD MacKinnon recorded that
undefended divorce cases were 'the only form of judicial work that I have always detested. And I have
resented having to do it. . . . Not only is it repulsive to have to sit and listen to repeated tales of adultery, but the actual work involved would be degrading to the meanest intellect. The text-books about
divorce purport to set forth principles that are said to have been laid down, e.g. as to the exercise of
judicial discretion in favour of a petitioner who confesses to have himself, or herself, committed adultery. I have never been able to discover that there really are any principles at all: I believe you could
find some authority for anything you thought fit to do. So I used to sit, in savage boredom, listening
to the sordid stories . . . I cannot conceive why these cases cannot be heard in the County Court, and
by its Registrar. It would still be hard on that capable official; for in fact they would not tax the powers of the stupidest man who was ever an acting-deputy-Registrar of a County Court'.

tion conferred in divorce work; and it was certainly no longer possible for the judges concerned to 'be able to take counsel together'.[39] And the fact that defending a petition would[40] result in it being tried in London with all the consequential expense in terms of paying for the travel and accommodation of witnesses meant not only that justice might be denied to those who were marginally above the poverty line[41] but that the risks of collusion were increased.[42] Would an innocent but unhappily married man wrongly accused of adultery by his wife be prepared to fight—at considerable financial cost—when he could come to a convenient arrangement by which the divorce would go through undefended, perhaps on the basis that he would not be liable to make any payments of maintenance?

The 1920 Act was thus far more significant in the development of divorce law than is often realised; and it is one of the ironies of history that the Act allowed[43] the most highly publicised of all twentieth century divorce cases (that of Mrs Wallis Simpson) to be dealt with by a King's Bench judge sitting in the Assize court at Ipswich rather than by a judge of the Probate Divorce and Admiralty Division sitting in London.

The 1920 Act made the separate existence of the Probate Divorce and Admiralty Division seem increasingly anomalous; and it is not surprising that a movement developed to rationalise the situation by abolishing the Division and transferring divorce work to the King's Bench Division (perhaps with a nominated judge[44] to exercise a general supervision).[45] But the forces of inertia or reac-

---

[39] See the Second Interim Report of *The Business of the Courts Committee* (Chairman, Lord Hanworth MR) (1933, Cmd. 4471, BPP 1933/4, xi. 1), paras. 15–17. The Committee noted that the King's Bench judges trying divorce at assizes 'may, and in some cases do, hold divergent views from the judges of the Divorce Division, and the grounds on which the discretion is to be exercised cannot be formulated and limited with precision': para. 15.

[40] For all apart from the really poor, whose petitions under the Poor Persons Rules were dealt with, whether defended or not, on assize.

[41] The 1920 Act did nothing to deal with the injustice suffered by husbands of modest means (who under the rules then in force usually had to pay the wife's costs in any event) and who were effectively compelled to allow a divorce petition to go undefended because of the expense which would otherwise be involved.

[42] See Clement Davies KC, *Official Report* (HC) 8 November 1937, vol. 328, cols. 1450–1451.

[43] Because Mrs Simpson's petition was undefended: *Simpson, W v. Simpson, EA (Application by the King's Proctor for Directions)* (1937) *The Times* 20 March. It appears that experienced divorce lawyers would advise clients on where to institute an undefended suit to ensure the minimum delay. In his judgment in the *Simpson* case the President emphasised that the allocation of undefended cases to a particular venue was a matter to be decided by the Registrar, rather than a matter for the parties' unrestricted choice.

[44] An alternative proposal was that 'a special Divorce Commissioner should be appointed to discharge on circuit the severe and sometimes distasteful burden now imposed on the King's Bench judges': *Report of the Royal Commission on the Despatch of Business at Common Law 1934–6*, (Chairman: Earl Peel) (1936, Cmd. 5065, BPP 1935–6, xi, 105) para. 169. But the Peel Committee considered it would be wrong for the status of the person entrusted with dissolving marriages ('a task of such importance not only to the individual but to the state') to appear in any way inferior to that of a High Court judge.

[45] This was the reform advocated in the Second Interim Report of *The Business of the Courts Committee* (Chairman, Lord Hanworth MR) (1933, Cmd. 4471, BPP 1933/4, xi. 1). The Hanworth Committee accepted that uniformity in exercise of discretion was an 'important desideratum' which

tion were too strong. The Divorce Division remained in existence, and in 1937 the number of its judges was increased.[46]

The Second World War brought another crisis. Yet again there was a huge increase in the number of divorce petitions, from 8,517 in 1939, to 14,887 in 1943 and 24,857 in 1945.[47] And worse was to come. On 3 September 1945[48] Lord Jowitt, Lord Chancellor in the recently elected Labour Government,[49] informed the Cabinet that the judicial system was barely able to cope with the number of divorce petitions currently being entered[50] and was likely to collapse under the avalanche of cases expected to be entered for trial in the near future. It was clear that the palliative action taken during the War—increasing the number of judges in the Probate Divorce and Admiralty Division,[51] sending those judges out on circuit,[52] and allowing defended (as well as undefended) cases to be heard at Assize[53]—were hopelessly inadequate.[54] There were long delays and complaints of

should be 'once more established and maintained'. The Committee (see para. 17) considered that this could only be done 'by co-ordinating all those who are charged with the trial of divorce cases into one unity, wherein after consultation inter se all the judges may resolve upon a line of common action'. On this basis, divorce work would become 'an integral part of the work of the King's Bench Division'. However, the proposals prompted much adverse criticism and were not put into effect: *Report of the Royal Commission on the Despatch of Business at Common Law 1934–6*, (Chairman: Earl Peel) (1936, Cmd. 5065, BPP 1935–6, xi, 105) para. 179. The Peel Commission accepted that the abolition of the Probate, Divorce and Admiralty Division might well be the ultimate solution of the difficulties and anomalies with which the High Court was beset; but the majority—there is a powerful dissent by Clement Davies KC—declined to make a recommendation because they felt that to do so would be outside their terms of reference.

[46] In 1937 the Government introduced legislation permanently increasing the number of PDA judges to three to cope with the increase in work expected to follow the extension of the grounds for divorce introduced by the Matrimonial Causes Act 1937 whilst the appointment of a fourth judge was intended to be a short-term measure: Supreme Court of Justice (Amendment) Act 1938, s. 1(2); *Official Report* (HC) 8 November 1937, vol. 328, col. 1438. In fact further increases in the number of Probate Divorce and Admiralty Division Judges proved necessary.

[47] These are the figures given in Appendix II, Table 1, of the Report of the *Royal Commission on Marriage and Divorce* (Chairman: Lord Morton of Henryton) (1956, Cmd. 9678).

[48] Lord Chancellor's Memorandum to the Cabinet, CP 45, 3 September 1945, PRO LCO2/4197.

[49] The divorce problem—which continued to cause Jowitt the 'greatest worry' *Official Report* (HL) 13 November 1946, vol. 144, col. 67—had also weighed heavily on Jowitt's predecessor as Lord Chancellor, Lord Simon; and three of the five matters to which Simon drew his successor's attention as needing attention were related to divorce and its administration—the other two were apparently trivial personal matters: see 'Memorandum to my Successor', July 1945, LCO2/4197.

[50] There was a large back-log of cases—Jowitt estimated as many as 25,000. These had accumulated because the system of Legal Aid for the Armed Forces had collapsed. A very large number of cases would therefore come into the court system once the problems of personnel (and in particular the shortage of copy-typists, in part accounted for—according to Ernest Bevin, Minister of Labour, Bevin to Simon 23 March 1945, LCO2/4197—by the reluctance of women to deal with the sordid subject matter) had been remedied.

[51] Supreme Court of Judicature (Amendment) Act 1944 permitted the appointment of three additional puisne judges (one of whom was Denning J).

[52] Judges of the Probate Divorce and Admiralty Division went circuit for the first time in the summer of 1944.

[53] These reforms followed the *Report of the Matrimonial Causes (Trial in the Provinces) Committee* (Chairman Sir R Wedgewood, Bart. (1943, Cmd. 6480).

'chaotic and indecorous conditions' as the judges tried to deal with a mass of cases. The scenes outside the courts in one assize town were described[55] as 'more reminiscent of Epsom Downs than a court of justice'. Yet again, something had to be done.[56]

It might have been thought that the Labour Government, returned to office in 1945 with a large majority[57] would be prepared to take a more radical view. After all, it was widely known that some[58] influential ministers[59] (not least the two law officers)[60] advocated the transfer of divorce work to the county

[54] Lord Chancellor Simon had submitted a memorandum to the War Cabinet on 1 March 1945 arguing that the judges could not hope to deal with the anticipated volume of cases, that it would be a pity to wait for public outcry before taking steps to meet the situation, and that an appropriate solution would be to confer jurisdiction on the Registrars of the Divorce Court to try undefended divorces both in London and the provinces: see WP(45) 127, copied on LCO2/4197. The War Cabinet agreed to a Bill being drafted; but the Archbishop of Canterbury came to hear of what was afoot and threatened that the Church would 'oppose it with all its might' and did not seem to be wholly mollified by a lengthy (and superbly unctuous) explanation by the Lord Chancellor: see Simon to Fisher, 12 April 1945, PRO LCO2/4197. Although Simon's successor in the incoming Labour administration recommended the introduction of such legislation as a temporary measure the Cabinet decided not to proceed. As Lord Chancellor Jowitt wrote to President Merriman: '. . . the strong balance of opinion was against proceeding with the Bill and to this opinion I had no option but to bow. On the one hand there was the view that in a matter affecting the status of the citizen it was not fitting that anybody, save a Judge of the High Court, should have the right to pronounce a decision. On the other hand, the view was expressed that the matter was one which might safely be entrusted to the County Court': see Jowitt to Merriman, 20 September 1945, PRO LCO2/4197. Eventually the Government set up the Committee on Procedure in Matrimonial Causes (Chairman: the Hon. Mr Justice Denning, and subsequently described as the Denning Committee) to consider this and other issues: see below.
[55] In the Second Interim Report of the Denning Committee (1946, Cmd. 6945) para. 6(i).
[56] See the Second Interim Report of the Denning Committee (1946, Cmd. 6945) para. 6 for the Committee's views on the various measures taken during the War.
[57] According to the Table in D Butler and G Butler, *British Political Facts 1900–2000* (8th ed., 2000) pp. 236, 393 Labour MPs were returned giving Labour a majority over all other parties of 146 members.
[58] But not the Lord Chancellor, Jowitt. He warned the Cabinet that to confer jurisdiction on the county courts would 'give rise to acute differences of opinion and to violent controversy. . . . The more extreme controversialists would regard the proposal to confer jurisdiction on the County Courts as only the first step on a slippery slope. The next step, they would say, would be to confer jurisdiction on the magistrates, and the last step would be the institution of a system under which parties could go and buy a divorce at the Post Office. . . . The President of the Divorce Division would, I feel sure, be strongly opposed to the grant of such complete jurisdiction to the County Courts and would feel bound to voice his objections in the House of Lords': Memorandum by the Lord Chancellor, 3 September 1945, PRO CP (45) copied on LCO2/4197.
[59] Including the powerful Lord President of the Council, Herbert Morrison, who as Home Secretary in the wartime coalition had made it clear he considered the county court to be the appropriate forum for divorce.
[60] Sir Hartley Shawcross A-G and Sir Frank Soskice S-G: see their joint memorandum to the Lord Chancellor, 29 August 1945, PRO LCO2/4197. Shawcross in particular was something of a radical in divorce matters and subsequently told the Lord Chancellor 'I do feel . . . that the administration of the divorce law in this country has become something of a racket and I look forward to the day when the PD and A Division will go altogether. Specialisation by the Divorce Bar has tended to give them a vested interest in what should be (and in truth is) a very simple branch of the law and they are able to make very substantial incomes at the cost of litigants by doing cases which take only two or three minutes and require no study or thought at all'. Shawcross to Jowitt, 5 January 1951, PRO LCO2/6163.

court;[61] and the records show the Law Officers warned Ministers that opinion in the Labour Party would not support anything short of this.[62]

But the Radicals did not carry the day. The Lord Chancellor, Jowitt, gave the traditional response to 'thorny and difficult problems'.[63] A Committee was established,[64] chaired by a High Court judge (Denning J),[65] to examine 'the present system governing the administration of divorce and nullity of marriage . . . with special reference to the Courts in which such suits should proceed'.[66]

The Denning Committee: a 'brilliant compromise'?

Notwithstanding the prominence given to the question in the Denning Committee's terms of reference, the Committee did not waste much time in discussing the merits of conferring divorce jurisdiction on the county court. The Committee's Report set out the Gorell Commission's view that divorce should continue to be 'determined by the Superior Courts of the country, assisted by the attendance of the Bar', stated that it had heard further evidence and had considered it, and asserted that it re-affirmed the Gorell Commission's view.[67] The only additional justification advanced by the Denning Committee was that it believed

'. . . the attitude of the community towards the status of marriage is much influenced by the way in which divorce is effected. If there is a careful and dignified proceeding such as obtains in the High Court for the undoing of a marriage, then quite unconsciously the people will have a much more respectful view of the marriage tie and of the marriage status than they would if divorce were effected informally in an inferior court'.

---

[61] In preference to the proposal which Jowitt had taken over from the wartime coalition of delegating jurisdiction to the Divorce Registrars. The joint memorandum submitted by Shawcross and Soskice to the Lord Chancellor claimed that conferring jurisdiction on the county court would better achieve the objectives of ensuring petitions were tried by persons known to and commanding the confidence of the public and with due dignity than would the Jowitt/Simon plan: Memorandum by the Law Officers, 29 August 1945, LCO2/4197.

[62] See in particular Shawcross to Jowitt, 18 September 1945, PRO LCO2/4197 warning Jowitt that in the absence of radical proposals 'it is not impossible that some of the lawyers may divide the House' against a government Bill which could be said to do nothing to deal with 'the inevitably long delay of the present procedure and the intolerably high costs'.

[63] Jowitt complained that his colleagues were 'reluctant to get their hands scratched': Jowitt to Merriman, 20 September 1945, PRO LCO2/4197.

[64] Some of the background is described in SM Cretney, *Law, Law Reform and the Family* (1998), Chapter 6.

[65] See Biographical Notes. Denning J had recently been translated to the King's Bench.

[66] For the Committee's full terms of reference, see note 205, below. The Committee's recommendations on proposals to extend jurisdiction in divorce to the County Court are discussed below; its proposals for procedures to protect the children of divorcing parents are discussed at p. 578, below whilst the Committee's recommendations on concilation procedures are considered at pp. 302–304, below.

[67] Second Interim Report of the Denning Committee (1946, Cmd. 6945) para.4.

The Committee saw the real difficulty as being how to 'maintain that principle' in the face of the increase in divorce petitions;[68] and in particular, what could be done about the lack of the judge power in the High Court necessary to process the petitions. The answer given by the Denning Committee was that it did not follow from the fact that only the High Court had jurisdiction to grant divorces that the judges dealing with these cases should necessarily be High Court judges. After all, the law had long recognised that 'commissioners' could exercise the functions of the High Court judge, and there was no reason why *all* the county court judges of England and Wales should not be appointed commissioners for matrimonial causes with power to hear both defended and undefended cases. These judges (the Committee thought) would handle matrimonial cases 'with efficiency and a full sense of responsibility';[69] and they would be 'accorded all the dignity of a High Court judge', be addressed as a High Court judge, be paid at the same rate as a High Court judge for the days on which they sat as commissioners, and sit in courts 'commensurate with the dignity of the High Court'.[70]

Thus was born what Lord Chancellor Gardiner[71] subsequently described[72] as 'the usual brilliant English compromise': divorce cases were in fact to be tried by county court judges but these judges were to be dressed up for the day as High Court judges and treated as such until, like Cinderella, they returned to reality as the clock struck midnight.

[68] Lord Chancellor Jowitt told the Lord Chief Justice of England that he hoped and believed the large number of divorces would 'prove to be largely a temporary problem, unless it be the fact that the idea of Christian marriage has gone. It is a squalid business . . .': Jowitt to Goddard, 7 November 1946, PRO LCO2/3951; and in fact the number of petitions filed fell back to 29,096 in 1950. But the Denning Committee was correct in predicting that, whilst the increase had 'been influenced considerably by the conditions produced by the recent war, nevertheless the numbers are likely to remain higher in the future than they have been in the past': see (1946, Cmd. 6945) para. 5. Never again did the number of divorce petitions fall significantly below 30,000 a year.
[69] *Second Interim Report of the Committee on Procedure in Matrimonial Causes* (Chairman: the Hon. Mr Justice Denning) (1946, Cmd. 6945) para. 7(ii).
[70] In reality the shortage of suitable accommodation continued to be a problem, and PRO file LCO2/6163 notes that one judge had to try civil cases in a small room where, if the windows were open, there was a nauseating smell of fried fish and sprouts from the British Restaurant below and a deafening noise from the traffic outside, and with the windows closed there was no ventilation at all and everybody went to sleep: Goddard to Simonds, 26 March 1952; whilst, in announcing the decision taken in 1966 to confer jurisdiction on the county court the Lord Chancellor admitted that commissioners hearing divorce cases in London sat in army huts, converted jury rooms, and even in a room measuring no more than seven yards each way: *Official Report* (HL) 23 November 1966, vol. 278, col. 265. Lord Gardiner subsequently pointed out that the designers of the Law Courts in the Strand (opened in 1882) 'no doubt thought that they were providing for all future time in providing for four divorce courts' in that building at a time when the Probate Divorce and Admiralty Division consisted of the President and one puisne judge (as compared with 17 puisnes in 1969): *Official Report* (HL) 4 December 1969, vol. 306, col. 197.
[71] See Biographical Notes.
[72] *Official Report* (HL) 14 February 1967, vol. 280, col. 169; see also *Official Report* (HL) 23 November 1966, vol. 278, col. 256.

The Denning Committee: a squalid conspiracy?

With the benefit of hindsight it is difficult to take seriously the arguments[73] which apparently convinced the Denning Committee; and it is particularly striking that the Denning report does not discuss at any length the fact that preserving the exclusive (if nominal) jurisdiction of the High Court would prevent solicitors from appearing as advocates for their clients. Anyone sympathetic to conspiracy theories will find no difficulty in believing that the judges[74] (universally ex-barristers)[75] and barristers so dominant in the Denning Committee and amongst the Lord Chancellor's advisers[76] were strongly (and perhaps even primarily) motivated by the desire that the Bar's monopoly of divorce advocacy remain sacrosanct.[77] And there is certainly no way of telling whether the divorcing population was impressed by the fact that the court in which they were making a (usually brief)[78] appearance was the High Court rather than the county court. But it is today difficult to appreciate the horror which the notion that divorces might be obtained by consent aroused amongst the right-thinking people who sat on the Denning Committee and other similar enquiries, and it is impossible to dismiss as wholly unrealistic the argument that a solicitor faced with the loss of a valued client might be prepared to suppress the fact that there had been collusion.[79] Perhaps it is true that a barrister retained for a single case would be less likely to know that the application was collusive (although whether the fact that the advocate put forward a case in ignorance of the fact that it was collusive better advanced the cause of justice than allowing such a case to be put forward by

[73] A recurrent theme—convincing Lord Chancellors from Birkenhead (see his *Points of View* (1922) pp. 41–42) to Simon (see his memorandum to the War Cabinet, PRO WP (45) 127, 1 March 1945)—was that to confer jurisdiction on the county court would result in a great variation in practice, and that preservation of the exclusively High Court jurisdiction was essential to preserve a 'common standard'; but it is not easy to see how this problem would be avoided simply by giving the county court judges the temporary status of the High Court bench.

[74] President Merriman told Lord Chancellor Simon that the 'traditions which govern the Bar in the presentation of divorce cases are of inestimable value to the Court' PRO LCO2/4197, 31 January 1945) and Merriman continued to insist on the need for the exclusive right of audience of the bar to be strictly maintained: see Merriman to Jowitt, 19 November 1946, PRO LCO2/3951.

[75] Although it cannot be said that President Merriman was wholly ignorant of the solicitors' profession since he had served articles of clerkship before deciding to read for the Bar.

[76] See p. 813, below. At a meeting in the Lord Chancellor's department on 14 February 1945 it was agreed that the right of audience in undefended divorces should continue to be restricted to the Bar (who 'by reason of their peculiar position' were far more able to deal with the difficulties caused by a client's reluctance to disclose material matters than were solicitors) but that it would be better to avoid express reference to this fact in putting proposals forward: PRO LCO2/4197.

[77] See B Abel-Smith and R Stevens, *In Search of Justice* (1968) p. 32.

[78] For what appears to be an accurate account of the hearing of a typical undefended divorce case see the description by Clement Davies KC quoted in note 33 above.

[79] President Merriman—who was not wholly ignorant of the practices of the solicitors' profession—was (according to the Permanent Secretary in the Lord Chancellor's Department) opposed to extending the right of audience to solicitors because he thought they could not be trusted not to suppress evidence of collusion: see Napier to Dobson, 11 January 1951, PRO LCO/26131. (It is wrong to say that Merriman was 'naturally reluctant to express [this view] in public' since he had in fact done so: see *Official Report* (HL) 28 November 1946, vol. 144, cols. 480–482.)

someone who did have such knowledge and was prepared to take the risk of professional sanctions if this were discovered seems debatable).

The Government acts

Whatever the motives of those concerned, the Denning Committee's recommendation was exactly what the Lord Chancellor's officials wanted. The
Government accepted what Denning had proposed and officials took the necessary action.[80] For the next 20 years 'High Court' divorce was in practice largely
administered by county court judges[81] sitting as Special Commissioners in
Divorce.[82] But the *principle* that divorce should be exclusively a matter for the
High Court had been upheld, whatever might be the reality.

MONEY TALKS: THE COST OF 'HIGH COURT' DIVORCE

In 1956 the Morton Royal Commission,[83] consistently with its conservative
approach to divorce tried to make the practice reflect the principle: it urged that
steps be taken as soon as possible to enable all divorce cases to be tried by judges
of the High Court. But the system of trial by Commissioners had enabled the
court system to deal adequately with the demand[84] for judicial divorce; and the

[80] The Government's intention to implement the scheme for divorce commissioners was
announced on 13 November 1946 and put into effect on 1 January 1947: see *Official Report* (HL) 28
November 1946, vol. 144, col. 472. PRO file LCO2/3955 indicates that the Lord Chancellor's
officials (led by Sir George Coldstream, subsequently Permanent Secretary 1954–1968) had to work
'night and day' on implementation, and there is a great deal of correspondence on such matters as
textbooks (the Lord Chancellor wished *Rayden on Divorce* to be the 'official textbook' although
some difficulty was experienced in supplying sufficient copies) and robes (the Lord Chancellor letting it be known that the judges should wear a black gown and not, in any circumstances, the purple robes of a county court judge, and that he also wished them to wear a court black coat and
waistcoat for which clothing coupons were not to be required). Coldstream reported that the results
of the new procedure 'entirely justified the views of the Denning Committee, and incidentally, the
confidence of the Lord Chancellor in the County Court Judges and in the County Court administrative system': Coldstream to Shawcross, April 1947, LCO2/3958.
[81] Some King's Counsel were also appointed as Special Commissioners. The suggestion made in
the Official Memorandum dated 10 March 1920 on the Bill introduced in that year by Lord
Buckmaster, PRO LCO2/460, p. 4, that there would be difficulty in finding counsel prepared to
accept appointments (a 'busy practitioner cannot be expected to accept such a position which offers
no permanence or any particular prospect of advancement and cannot be remunerated on a scale
commensurate with the fees which he can earn') was evidently falsified.
[82] In 1966, for example, county court judges dealt with 34,000 out of the 38,000 undefended
divorces, and with 894 'short defended' divorces.
[83] *Report of the Royal Commission on Marriage and Divorce* (Chairman: Lord Morton of
Henryton) (1956, Cmd. 9678) paras. 736–760.
[84] Although the 1947 peak of 48,501 divorce and nullity petitions was not reached again until
1967 (when there were more than 50,000 petitions) Jowitt's hopes that the appetite for divorce
would slacken were not well founded: in 1950 there were 29,729 petitions, in 1960 28,542, and in
1970 (the last year before the Divorce Reform Act 1969 substituted irretrievable breakdown as the
sole ground for divorce) there were 71,662 petitions. Since 1970 there has been no year in which
fewer than 110,000 divorce petitions were filed. (These figures are extracted from *Reform of the
Grounds of Divorce, The Field of Choice* (1966, Cmnd. 3123) Appendix D, and *Marriage and
Divorce Statistics 1975* (OPCS, 1978, Table 4.8).)

notion that money would be found to appoint the 15 additional High Court judges necessary to do the work being undertaken by commissioners was far-fetched. Cost became a dominant concern. For it had soon became clear that the Denning scheme was not going to save money. The largest part of the public funding provided by Legal Aid[85] was consumed by divorce cases; and the ever increasing cost bore on the privately funded litigant as well.[86] True, young barristers could make substantial incomes by appearing in a series of brief undefended divorce cases; but that of itself was not regarded as an adequate justification. Financial considerations soon began to influence a shift in opinion within the Lord Chancellor's Department: in 1951 a senior official[87] minuted: 'The truth is that if we are determined to reduce the cost of divorce it can only be done by transferring the jurisdiction to the county court' and urged that experience showed 'conclusively that costs will never be reduced to any significant extent so long as they remain on the High Court scale'. But it took more than a decade for this advice to be heeded.[88] Eventually, Lord Dilhorne[89] (Lord Chancellor in Sir Alec-Douglas-Home's 1963/4 administration) accepted that the time had come to confer divorce jurisdiction on the county court;[90] and in 1967 the Labour Government introduced legislation providing for all divorce proceedings to be started in the county court and transferred to the High Court only if they were defended.[91] The Church was no longer doctrinally opposed to change;[92] whilst opposition from the Bar[93] was seen off in an outstanding piece of parliamentary advocacy by Lord Chancellor Gardiner.[94] Procedural reform

[85] See below. In 1965/6 legal aid cost £5.5 million out of which divorce proceedings took £3.25 million: *Official Report* (HL) 14 February 1967, vol. 280, col. 172.

[86] It appears that the average cost of undefended divorce to the legal aid fund was some £120—perhaps £1,200 in year 2000 values: see *Official Report* (HL) 14 February 1967, vol. 280, col. 183.

[87] D Dobson (subsequently Permanent Secretary 1968–1977) to Napier, 10 January 1951.

[88] Notwithstanding the fact that this had been accepted by both major political parties: *Official Report* (HL) 14 February 1967, vol. 280, col. 173.

[89] See Biographical Notes.   [90] See *Official Report* (HL) 14 February 1967, vol. 280, col. 183.

[91] Matrimonial Causes Act 1967, s. 1. Only county courts designated as 'divorce county courts' (now under Matrimonial and Family Proceedings Act 1984, s. 33) have divorce jurisdiction; but at the turn of the century some 160 courts were so designated.

[92] In 1945 Archbishop Fisher had warned Lord Chancellor Simon that 'the Church would certainly wish to oppose . . . with all its might' any proposals to remove divorce jurisdiction from the High Court: Fisher to Simon, 24 March 1945, LCO2/4197; but by 1967 the Church of England was prepared to accept quite radical change to the procedures for granting divorce: see below. The Bishop of Exeter (who had chaired the influential Archbishop's Group) said he was not desperately opposed to the proposal to allow the county courts divorce jurisdiction since it would not make an 'enormous amount of difference': *Official Report* (HL) 14 February 1967, vol. 280, col. 182.

[93] The Government encountered much more difficulty in the House of Commons not only from the Bar but from those who urged that the Government should have introduced much more radical measures such as a Family Court: see *Official Report* (HC) 4 April 1967, vol. 744, col. 82.

[94] Having dealt with the misconceptions held by some churchmen ('my clerical friend') Gardiner concluded: 'Finally, with regard to my barrister friend, he goes on about the need to uphold the status and dignity of matrimony, and then he says what a terrible thing it would be if solicitors handled cases in the courts on their own, as one cannot trust a solicitor as one can a barrister. But, of course, I have known him for a long time, and I simply say, "Come off it, George! The fear of the Bar is simply that they are going to lose a certain amount of work to the solicitors, and you

had ceased to arouse passion; and could be welcomed (even by those who would have preferred to see changes in substantive law as well as in procedures) as stripping away a little of the 'humbug and hypocrisy' surrounding divorce. People did not change their characters by switching from a purple robe (worn by county court judges) to a black robe (worn by county court judges when hearing divorce).[95] Nor was it true that cases tried in the 'High Court' were necessarily heard 'in a superior-looking kind of court, and the proceedings . . . conducted with every formality, whereas if . . . the case is tried in the county court, it will be tried in some grubby place in between half a dozen judgment summonses and actions about hire-purchase'. Gardiner was able convincingly to show[96] that this was 'nothing like what happens'.

Nobody pretended that the Government's main motive in insisting on giving divorce jurisdiction to the county court[97] was other than financial: costs (particularly cost to the legal aid fund) had to be controlled. In particular, the Government expected that solicitors[98] would exercise their right of audience to appear for petitioners in perhaps a quarter of the undefended divorce cases coming to the courts rather than instructing counsel. But in fact (whether because of inflation, or because solicitors still found it more economical to instruct counsel —who might well be appearing in several cases in succession on the same day— than to appear themselves for a single petition or because any reduction in the costs incurred in dissolving the marriage were more than outweighed by increasing expenditure on investigation into financial and child-related matters) no long term reduction of public expenditure was achieved.[99]

remember the language you used when there was that demarcation dispute between the shipwrights and the boiler-makers". That is really all it is'. *Official Report* (HL) 14 February 1967, vol. 280, col. 176.

[95] See *per* Leo Abse MP, *Official Report* (HC) 4 April 1967, vol. 744, col. 82.

[96] *Official Report* (HL) 23 November 1966, vol. 278, col. 255.

[97] The final step of giving the county court jurisdiction to hear *defended* divorces was only taken in 1984: Matrimonial and Family Proceedings Act 1984, s. 33; but by that time the judicial role in dealing with undefended divorces had been reduced to vanishing point by requiring most of them to be dealt with under a so-called 'special procedure' involving no open court hearing at all: see pp. 381–383, below.

[98] The Law Society's Divorce Department was kept in existence and handled a significant case load. But experience suggested that the cost of cases handled by that Department was higher than that of cases dealt with by solicitors in private practice (see 8th *Legal Aid Annual Report 1957/1958*, para. 38); and in 1961 it was decided to wind up the Department.

[99] According to the 25th *Legal Aid Annual Report 1974/1975*, para. 7, the 'hopes that were entertained of achieving a tangible reduction in cost through . . . transfer to the county court have been belied through the effects of inflation. There has been some development of self-help in simple cases, but the number of such cases appears to be smaller than some expected. The experience of area secretaries is that it is rarely practicable to discriminate between those cases in which professional assistance is, or may be, essential and those in which it is sufficiently clear that this could be dispensed with. Matrimonial break-down is a primary source of frustration and distress and, so long as it is the function of the law to deal with it, the demand for legal aid in that field is bound to dominate the legal aid work-load'.

THE ROLE OF THE MAGISTRATES IN THE FAMILY JUSTICE SYSTEM 1900–1970

The 1912 Royal Commission had received a mass of evidence about the hardship caused by judicially prescribed separations and of the immorality to which such orders gave rise; and since the Commission's chairman had in giving judgment in *Dodd v. Dodd*[100] vigorously criticised the law it is perhaps not surprising that the Commission unanimously recommended the abolition of the power of magistrates' courts to make orders having the permanent[101] effect of a decree of judicial separation. The Commission urged that the decision whether to make a separation order required

'the deliberate consideration of a superior court. The ready opportunity for applications for orders of this character to a court of summary jurisdiction is undoubtedly likely to lead to hasty and ill-considered action by applicants . . . [The] courts are the 'ordinary petty sessional courts presided over by magistrates who . . . are, in general, laymen possessed of no legal training or qualifications, assisted by a clerk, who may or may not be a competent solicitor or clerk. Moreover, these courts form part of the judicial system for administering the criminal law in the case of petty offences. We think there is a serious objection to a court, whose main duties are of a criminal character, entertaining applications which, if granted, may produce the practical although not the legal dissolution of the marriage tie. The evidence satisfies us that the general administration of the Acts is not satisfactory where these cases are dealt with by lay magistrates . . . [In some parts of the country] orders are made too easily and on too slender materials, and in others are too difficult to obtain . . .'.[102]

But it was to be more than 60 years before the magistrates' power to make separation orders was abolished; and, although the modest degree of localisation brought about by the Administration of Justice Act 1920 may have made it marginally less difficult for some people of modest means to get before the Divorce Court, magistrates' courts continued for many years to deal with the great bulk of working class litigation relating to domestic matters.[103] Efforts at reform were directed primarily towards civilising the procedures of the magistrates' courts; whilst some campaigners sought to transform the magistrates' courts into agencies for saving marriages and for administering social aid to the distressed. Although those campaigns were unsuccessful in achieving their main

---

[100] [1906] P 189.

[101] As Lord Gorrell had observed in *Dodd v. Dodd* [1906] P 189, 199, the legislation contained no provision expressly empowering magistrates to make orders for temporary separation, or orders of a probationary character, with such conditions and restrictions as might be useful, though such orders might meet the needs of many cases in which 'time for reflection and amendment might end the trouble'.

[102] Paras. 140–142. The Commission recommended that orders should be effective for a maximum of two years.

[103] For an excellent study, based in part on detailed research into the work of the courts in South-West London, see GK Behlmer, *Friends of the Family, The English Home and its Guardians, 1850–1940* (1998) especially Chapter 4 'Summary Justice and Working-Class Marriage'.

objectives they had a significant long term effect on the development of the English family justice system.[104]

The magistrates' courts: courts or advice centres?

In twenty-first century England, magistrates' courts do not seem different in kind from other courts. True, their sentencing powers are restricted, whilst neither the magistrates (who in the twentieth century were not usually professional lawyers) nor the advocates appearing in the courts wear robes or other distinctive dress. But it seems improbable that a woman needing help with a family problem (for example, because her partner had left her without support) would regard any court as her first port of call; and, even if she did, she would almost certainly seek help from one of the surviving agencies traditionally associated with the welfare state (such as a Citizens' Advice Bureau, a Refuge, or the offices of the Department of Social Security). It requires some effort to envisage a society in which none of these agencies existed and in which the functions now usually performed by paid and trained professionals were performed by voluntary organisations, doctors, the clergy and neighbours;[105] and it requires an even greater effort to envisage a time when the magistrates' courts were regarded as a source of advice and assistance.

Yet there is evidence that at the beginning of the twentieth century some magistrates' courts at least were regarded in this way, and that in London and some other inner cities poor men and women would 'pop in' on the magistrate[106] 'asking his advice in a friendly way'.[107] One writer[108] claimed that

'Day by day, year in and year out, men and women unburden their minds and expose their difficulties and sorrows to the magistrate; and though many of them know before they come that the magistrate cannot solve their difficulties or remove their sorrows, still they come, well knowing that they will be patiently listened to, and that kind words will be spoken to them. And scores of them go away comforted with the thought that they have been listened to, and in their turn have heard kind words spoken to them. . . . The poor battered wife comes and tells the story of her sufferings, is listened to, garrulous though she sometimes be, and is advised either to take out a summons or to "look over it this time" . . . every kind of domestic difficulty is laid before the magistrate . . .'.

---

[104] A full, dispassionate and scholarly account of the magistracy and the evolution of the court system is given by Sir Thomas Skyrme in *History of the Justices of the Peace* (2nd ed., 1994), Chapter 14.

[105] *R v. City of Birmingham District Council, ex parte O* [1982] 2 All ER 356, 361, *per* Donaldson LJ.

[106] In London the magistrate would be a qualified lawyer appointed under the Metropolitan Police Courts Act 1839 to serve as stipendiary magistrates in the Metropolitan Police. Stipendiary magistrates were appointed in some other areas under Stipendiary Magistrates Act 1863.

[107] *Daily News*, 11 February 1873, and *Saturday Review*, 15 February 1873, both as quoted by G Behlmer, 'Summary Justice and Working-Class Marriage in England, 1870–1940' (1994) 12 Law and History Review 229, 232.

[108] T Holmes, *Pictures and Problems from London Police Courts* (1911) pp. 43–44.

It may be questioned whether this roseate vision could ever[109] have reflected the reality;[110] but research[111] supports the view that in the second half of the nineteenth century London's working class did look to the courts for advice and arbitration (and even financial assistance)[112] in a wide variety of circumstances. In particular, it seems that the Metropolitan Police Magistrates did offer a wide range of advice to their predominantly working class clientele, and that the Metropolitan Police Courts became centres of advice and charity for the working class.

This image of a court is far distant from that current in the latter part of the century of a body standing above the parties to disputes—the subjects of rights and not the objects of assistance, as the Finer Report put it in 1974[113]—and adjudicating impartially on the issues raised in accordance with the law. And whatever may have been happening in the Metropolitan Police Courts, the 'official' view of the proper role of a court is clearly evident from an early Home Office file dealing with conciliation:[114]

The Administrator of the Given Wilson Institute in Plaistow—evidently an organisation with many activities ranging from an Education Department through a National Kitchen for the Poor to a Toy Mission—urged[115] the establishment of 'Domestic Courts to be managed on the lines of a Children's Court'[116] with a Stipendiary Magistrate giving 'invaluable advice to poor married people who cannot get on together, or who would get on if they had the advantage of wise trained advice and guidance'. But Home Office officials would have none of this. A note in bold ink by HB Simpson[117] riposted:

'what is wanted is not a Court at all in the ordinary sense but someone to give advice on domestic problems arising between husband and wife—not the only kind of domestic problem on which many are in great need of good advice! This could be much better supplied by voluntary agencies than through official channels.'

[109] A number of factors (including the emergence of alternative sources of advice and problem resolution) tended to reduce reliance on the magistrates' courts towards the end of the nineteenth century: see J Davis, 'A Poor Man's System of Justice: The London Police Courts in the Second Half of the Nineteenth Century' (1984) 27 *Historical Journal* 309, 333–334 but Behlmer, 'Summary Justice and Working-Class Marriage in England, 1870–1940' (1994) 12 Law and History Review 229, 238 emphasises the continuing importance of the magistrates' role in working class communities.

[110] As Behlmer points out at p. 244, there is 'no such thing as a "typical" English police court'.

[111] See J Davis, 'A Poor Man's System of Justice: The London Police Courts in the Second Half of the Nineteenth Century' (1984) 27 *Historical Journal* 309, 321.

[112] A factor in encouraging recourse to the magistrates was traditionally the availability of financial assistance from the 'poor box'—in reality sometimes a substantial endowment: see Davis *op. cit.* at pp. 325–326 and Behlmer *op. cit.* at p. 236; and note the claim by the sometime Chief Magistrate Sir Chartres Biron (*The Times*, 6 January 1939) that 'with the assistance of the poor box the work done out of court was almost as important as the legal routine'.

[113] *Report of the Committee on One-Parent Families*, (Chairman: Sir M Finer) (1974, Cmnd. 5629) para. 4.285.

[114] PRO HO45/15719.   [115] By letter dated 15 April 1919.

[116] Juvenile Courts had been created by the Children Act 1908, and their apparent success in dealing with problems of juvenile delinquency was a source of much favourable comment: see below, Chapter 18.

[117] See Biographical Notes.

Preserving the family or enforcing rights?

HB Simpson may have reflected official orthodoxy, but even the most orthodox magistrates accepted that the magistrates' matrimonial jurisdiction was not to be handled in the same way as other business coming before the courts. For example, if statute conferred a right on an individual to recover damages from a neighbour it would have been a bold judge who advised the plaintiff that he or she should not enforce that right because to do so would be inconsistent with future neighbourly relationships; but magistrates did not hesitate to express the view that in domestic cases the courts should (in the words of the Chief Magistrate,[118] giving evidence to a Parliamentary Select Committee in 1922) seek

'to keep people out of court if possible. You cannot expect an ideal home in Hoxton any more than perhaps you can in Mayfair, but you want to get the thing on a reasonable basis, and what we always tried to do was to get together the people if possible. Before granting any summons I always went very carefully into the cases and a great many were obviously frivolous applications. . . . The whole object in all these matters dealing with women and children and husbands was at all costs, even at some sacrifice of the individual, to keep the homes together, because we were always firmly persuaded that it was very much better for people to live together even under circumstances of some discomfort and with occasional outbreaks . . .'.[119]

The technique used was based on the assumption[120] that the grant of a summons was a matter of discretion. An applicant under the Summary Jurisdiction (Married Women) Act 1895[121] had to appear before the court to make formal application, and magistrates assumed they were entitled not to issue a summons (or at least not to do so unless and until the applicant had first seen a Missionary or Probation Officer). Of course, an applicant who insisted on the issue of a summons without more ado would usually succeed; but in practice such determined litigants were not often found. Those concerned rarely had any kind of legal representation and were often in a state of shock, numbed by personal and financial difficulties, and almost always ignorant of the law and their rights.[122]

[118] Sir Chartres Biron (1868–1920): see Biographical Notes.
[119] *Joint Select Committee on the Guardianship of Infants Bill, Minutes of Evidence*, 19 July 1922, q. 9.
[120] See the statement by Sir C Biron cited above. There is no doubt that an applicant who could demonstrate a prima facie case had a legal right to have a summons issued: see LM Pugh, *Matrimonial Proceedings before Magistrates* (2nd ed., 1966) p. 31; but it is more doubtful whether a magistrate could properly refuse to grant a summons because he considered the applicant had failed to make out a prima facie case: see OR McGregor, L Blom-Cooper and C Gibson, *Separated Spouses* (1970) p. 54.
[121] Or subsequent legislation.
[122] See OR McGregor, L Blom-Cooper and C Gibson, *Separated Spouses* (1970) p. 54. In the circumstances there could be a great deal of informality: as Sir Chartres Biron told the *Joint Select Committee on the Guardianship of Infants Bill* (*Minutes of Evidence*, July 19 1922, q. 22): 'In our courts when people come, especially women, to ask for these summonses and when these cases are tried they talk a great deal, and they tell us everything that is in their mind . . .'.

As the *Departmental Committee on the Social Services in Courts of Summary Jurisdiction*[123] put it in 1936

'There is reason to believe that many persons go to a Court with the intention of making an application who are seen by the Clerks, probation officers and other officials of the Court . . . [But a large] number decide not to proceed with their application because a reconciliation has been effected or because they have been led rightly or wrongly to believe that an application will be fruitless'.[124]

Even if a summons was issued and the case did formally come before a magistrate[125] he might well decide to refer the parties to a court missionary or probation officer.[126] The Lord Chancellor explained to the House of Lords[127]

'. . . before the case comes into court, [the probation officer is asked] to interview the parties, and experience shows that he is frequently able to bring the disputants to a better frame of mind and to guide them to a settlement. Often the parties are young people and the quarrel is due to inexperience and ignorance. In such cases and in many others it is possible for a mediator of experience to remove misunderstandings, to show how difficulties may be overcome and to bring about a permanent reconciliation . . .'.

Finding a better procedure for domestic cases

It is clear that the practice of seeking to divert cases from formal adjudication was widespread;[128] and probation officers might sometimes stop cases coming into court. But what of those which were not diverted in this way? The staple

---

[123] 1936, Cmd. 5122.

[124] *Report of the Departmental Committee on the Social Services in Courts of Summary Jurisdiction* (1936, Cmd. 5122) (chaired by SW Harris—as to whom see Biographical Notes—and hereafter cited as the 'Harris Committee') para. 6.

[125] A survey carried out 30 years after the Harris Committee had reported revealed a general consensus amongst the clerks who advise magistrates that 'conciliation' was a permissible function for court officials 'from the moment that a complainant approaches the court' but that courts interpreted their powers in this respect in diverse ways. In particular, whilst few courts deliberately held up the application for a summons in order to promote conciliation, some did do so: see OR McGregor, L Blom-Cooper and C Gibson, *Separated Spouses* (1970) p. 55.

[126] Voluntary missionaries (as to whose role see GK Behlmer, *Friends of the Family, The English Home and its Guardians, 1850–1940* (1998) pp. 208–213) were, after the coming into force of the Probation of Offenders Act 1907, gradually replaced by professional probation officers: see generally the Harris Report, paras. 133–180.

[127] In the debate on the Summary Jurisdiction (Domestic Procedure) Bill introduced by Lord Listowel: *Official Report* (HL), 15 May 1934, vol. 92, col. 382 (Lord Sankey).

[128] The Harris Report carried out a survey which indicated that 3,152 out of 6,222 persons approaching a sample of 60 courts in connection with a matrimonial dispute over a three-month period had been seen in the first instance by probation officers or missionaries, 1,704 by the warrant officer or other court official, and 1,335 by the clerk or an assistant: para. 10. It was claimed that as many as 'two-thirds of the attempts to effect a reconciliation' appear to be successful': para. 13. Even if the case got as far as a formal hearing by the court it appears that often no order was made: see Harris Report, p. 155 (order made in only 914 of the 1,766 cases heard by the courts surveyed).

business of the magistrates' courts was dealing with petty crime; and one of the metropolitan magistrates, Claud Mullins[129] claimed that

cases sometimes involving the inmost secrets of married life 'were dealt with precisely in the same way as the other work of the court. The wife . . . stood in the witness box, like a policeman prosecuting a criminal. The husband stood in front of the dock, like a motorist accused of having driven contrary to law. Later the husband, like the motorist, came into the witness box to tell his story. . . . There was no restriction on the attendance of the public, so that gossiping neighbours could come and hear the cases; and there was no restriction on reports in the newspapers. . . . In addition to all this, the parties had to be invited to cross-examine each other, a procedure that sometimes threatened to develop into a brawl . . .'.[130]

The courts' role: therapy or adjudication?

There was little dispute that the procedures for dealing with cases in the magistrates' courts needed improvement. But Mullins and some others wanted to go much further than merely removing the criminal overtones of the courts' procedures. In Mullins' view, the magistrates' courts' family jurisdiction should and could be transformed.[131] No longer should the courts treat husband and wife disputes 'solely as matters of law'.[132] Rather, magistrates trained in the causes of marital disharmony[133] should ensure that some 'form of social help' (extending in appropriate cases to advice from 'sex experts')[134] would be made available to those involved.[135] For Mullins, the problem was that couples coming to the courts under the existing procedure 'did not understand what was wrong in their relations with their partners' and 'prolonged unhappiness and discontent had made it impossible [for a husband or wife] even to consider' whether they might not have some responsibility for the difficulties in the relationship.[136] In this view, the very least the magistrates could do was to ensure that the couple under-

---

[129] Claud Mullins (1887–1968) was untypical of the metropolitan magistracy, not least in his zeal for reform: see Biographical Notes and generally GK Behlmer, *Friends of the Family, The English Home and its Guardians, 1850–1940* (1998) pp. 213–229; and SM Cretney, 'Marriage Saving and the Role of the Courts, Claud Mullins and the Early Days of Conciliation' in *Law, Law Reform and the Family* (1988).

[130] *Marriage Failures and the Children*, by Claud Mullins (1954) p. 15 (in part a quotation from the same author's earlier writings.

[131] Claud Mullins was a prolific author and lecturer, and it is his recorded views which are summarised in the text. There are useful references in GK Behlmer, *Friends of the Family, The English Home and its Guardians, 1850–1940* (1998) and see the Bibliography thereto at p. 424.

[132] C Mullins, *Marriage Failures and the Children* (1954) p. 16.

[133] C Mullins, Memorandum on Home Office file PRO HO45/21034 'for private circulation only' commenting on the *Report of the Committee on Social Services in Magistrates' Courts* (1936, Cmd. 5122).

[134] See C Mullins, *One Man's Furrow* (1963) pp. 104–108.

[135] C Mullins, *Marriage Failures and the Children* (1954) p. 11.

[136] 'even to consider the existence of the "beam that is in thine own eye"': C Mullins, *Marriage Failures and the Children* (1954) p. 18.

stood the consequences of a court order both for themselves and for their children before legal steps were taken to break up the marriage.[137]

The Summary Procedure (Domestic Proceedings) Bill 1934: the 'conciliation summons'

Mullins was an enthusiastic missionary for the causes in which he believed. It seems that he drafted a Bill[138] and persuaded the young Earl of Listowel[139] to introduce it into the House of Lords.[140] The Bill was intended[141] to found the resolution of matrimonial differences 'on the principle of conciliation instead of that of litigation'. Amongst other things, the Listowel Bill would have allowed magistrates to conduct cases according to a special 'domestic procedure' in which the rules of evidence would not apply,[142] there would be no right of cross-examination,[143] and statements to the court would not be made under oath unless the court specifically directed otherwise.[144] Yet more remarkably, provision was made[145] for husband or wife to apply for a 'conciliation summons' which the court could grant if the family's circumstances threatened to give rise to an application for a separation, maintenance, or custody order or even if the circumstances were 'detrimental to the happiness of the parties'. The court would then investigate the matter, and 'advise or admonish' the parties.[146] The court was not to make a separation, financial or custody order unless it had 'failed to achieve a reconciliation' or was satisfied that reconciliation was impossible.[147]

It was not necessary to share the contempt which the Chief Magistrate[148] had expressed for 'social workers' and other 'do-gooders'[149] to be concerned about the Listowel Bill. Its objective seemed to be nothing less than to transform the court's function from adjudication to social case work. It is true that Press comment on the Bill was generally favourable;[150] but this was almost irrelevant given the powerful criticisms, forcefully expressed, of those responsible for the administration of the family justice system. Lord Merrivale[151] (the recently

---

[137] C Mullins, *Fifteen Years Hard Labour* (1948) p. 134.

[138] The Summary Procedure (Domestic Proceedings) Bill 1934 (HL Bill 60, 1933/34).

[139] See Biographical Notes.

[140] Mullins' book *Wife v. Husband in the Courts* (1935) is dedicated to the Earl of Listowel 'whose speech in the House of Lords on May 15 1934 when introducing the Summary Jurisdiction (Domestic Procedure) Bill (drafted by the author) directed the attention of public opinion to the urgency of the matters discussed in this book'.

[141] In the words of the *Explanatory Memorandum*.   [142] Clause 4(5).

[143] Clause 4(5)(b).   [144] Clause 4(4).   [145] Clause 5.   [146] Clause 6.

[147] Clause 6.   [148] Sir Chartres Biron.

[149] In fairness, it should be said that he was, as already indicated, a strong supporter of the work of the police court missionaries in their dealings with marital problems.

[150] See GK Behlmer, *Friends of the Family, The English Home and its Guardians, 1850–1940* (1998) p. 217. Mullins himself recorded that the Bill had had 'vast' publicity and a 'very good press indeed'— a fact which as he recorded was surprising in view of the fact that the Bill would have imposed significant restrictions on press reporting: C Mullins, *Fifteen Years Hard Labour* (1948) p. 138.

[151] See Biographical Notes.

retired former President of the Divorce division) not only described the procedure envisaged by the Bill as a 'burlesque'[152] but went so far as to put down an amendment asserting that the Bill subverted 'the established principles and methods of administration of justice'.[153] The notion that the court should itself investigate the parties' private lives and give advice would (said the Lord Chancellor)[154] be to

'confer upon a court of law functions of a non-judicial, advisory and patriarchal character which are difficult to reconcile with the purposes for which a court exists. That in matrimonial disputes such functions can often be usefully exercised by some unofficial person or body of persons is admitted, but they are not functions of a court of law . . .'.

Not surprisingly the Bill failed to make progress. And it seemed that Listowel's initiative had done harm. The ambitious notion of transforming the functions of the courts had failed; and the discussion seemed to have defined the courts' role in a very restrictive way. But in fact the publicity did something to make the Government accept that reform of the magistrates' domestic jurisdiction was overdue.

The Harris Committee and the Summary Procedure (Domestic Jurisdiction) Act 1937

It would have been possible to meet some of the reformers' more modest objectives by administrative means.[155] But the Government, influenced by progressively minded civil servants in the Home Office, decided to go further. Coincidentally, the Government had already decided to set up a Departmental

---

[152] *Hansard* (5th Series), (HL), 15 May 1934, vol. 92, col. 371. Strongly critical comments were made inside the Government machine (Sir Claude Schuster, Permanent Secretary in the Lord Chancellor's office describing the Bill to a Home Office colleague on 19 April 1934, PRO file HO45/15719 as 'ridiculous'). Feelings amongst Mullins' magisterial brethren (who unanimously voted to inform the Home Secretary that the Bill was 'objectionable in many respects and would wholly fail to attain the ends it professed to serve') were also roused. Privately some used strong language: RA Powell, the Metropolitan Police Magistrate at Westminster, wrote on 1 May 1934 to a Home Office official complaining that the Bill was 'clearly a propaganda stunt and one that is misleading and mischievous and calculated to bring the stipendiaries' courts into disrepute'. Powell continued that 'it is all the more obnoxious when a Metropolitan magistrate gives this agitation his open support . . . I wish he [Mullins] could be muzzled!'.

[153] However, Merrivale was strongly in favour of improving the magistrates' procedure and of encouraging settlement, and he introduced his own Matrimonial Causes (Amended Procedure) Bill (HL Bill No 7, 1934/5). This Bill (which received a Second Reading—see *Official Report* (HL), 7 November 1934, vol. 94, col. 173—and with amendment passed all its stages in the House of Lords) provided for proceedings to be started by a deposition, required the court to consider 'whether it will be well to hear the parties in private with a view to settlement by mutual consent of the matters in question', permitted it to hear the views of any person with knowledge of the parties' relationship, and empowered the court to make consent orders. Had the Merrivale Bill been enacted it would have transferred much of the work of conciliation then being performed by probation officers to the magistrates themselves: see *Report of the Departmental Committee on the Social Services in Courts of Summary Jurisdiction*, (1936, Cmd. 5122), para. 18; *Hansard* (5th Series), (HL), 15 May 1934, vol. 92, col. 366.

[154] *Hansard* (5th Series), (HL), 15 May 1934, vol. 92, col. 382.

[155] See Lord Sankey LC, *Hansard* (5th Series), (HL), 15 May 1934, vol. 93, col. 384.

Committee to investigate the long-standing problems of the management of the probation service; and it decided to broaden this Committee's terms of reference to cover the wider questions of the procedure and constitution of the magistrates' courts in the exercise of their matrimonial jurisdiction.[156]

The *Report of the Departmental Committee on the Social Services in Courts of Summary Jurisdiction* (chaired by the progressive Home Office administrator, Sidney Harris)[157] laid down a clear starting point for reform: there should be a 'marked distinction in the atmosphere of the Court when it hears matrimonial cases from that when it hears criminal cases';[158] and that principle was the basis for the Summary Procedure (Domestic Jurisdiction) Act 1937. The Act provided that the hearing of domestic proceedings[159] be separated from hearings of other types of case;[160] and envisaged adapting the courts' procedures so as to enable unrepresented parties to 'tell their story in their own words'[161] (so that, for example, the court would where necessary itself put appropriate questions by way of examination or cross-examination).[162] Moreover, if the parties had seen a probation officer,[163] he or she was to draft a statement of the allegations made by the parties. This would give the court the means itself to enquire into the case[164] and avoid making husband and wife attempt to explain their grievances in a perhaps daunting atmosphere. Finally, to avoid the parties being intimidated by a large number of justices sitting on the bench, it was provided that not more than three justices (including both a

---

[156] See the *Report of the Departmental Committee on the Social Services in Courts of Summary Jurisdiction* (Chairman: SW Harris)(1936, Cmd. 5122) pp. vi–viii (the 'Harris Report'). Perhaps because of the remit originally intended, the Committee's membership was dominated by persons with an established interest in probation work, and this factor may have had some influence on the Report's recommendations about the proper division of function between courts and social services.

[157] See Biographical Notes.   [158] Harris Report, para. 28.

[159] The Government—believing that the support of those categorised by Lord Chancellor Hailsham as 'sentimentalists and socialists' would be insufficient to overcome the powerful advocacy of Lord Atkin and others (see Hailsham to Hoare, 14 June 1937, PRO HO45/15719) conceded that bastardy proceedings should be excluded from the scope of the Act; and they remained outside the definition of 'domestic proceedings' until 1978: Domestic Proceedings and Magistrates' Courts Act 1978, s. 79(1)(f).

[160] Summary Procedure (Domestic Proceedings) Act 1937, s. 2(1) (now Magistrates' Courts Act 1980, s. 69(1)).

[161] Harris Report, *Summary of Recommendations*, 15.

[162] Summary Procedure (Domestic Proceedings) Act 1937, s. 6 (now Magistrates' Courts Act 1980, s. 73).

[163] Under the conciliation schemes operating in many magistrates' courts.

[164] s. 4. The Report of the *Departmental Committee on the Probation Service* (1962, Cmnd. 1650) paras. 128–129 concluded that this provision was ineffective and that any report on conciliation should be limited to a statement whether the attempt had been successful or not; and in 1976 the Law Commission (in its *Report on Matrimonial Proceedings in Magistrates' Courts* (Law Com. No. 77, para. 4.140)) endorsed this view: see now Domestic Proceedings and Magistrates' Courts Act 1978, s. 26(2). The 1937 Act also empowered probation officers to report to the court about the parties' financial means: s. 5 (see now Magistrates' Courts Act 1980, s. 72); whilst it was provided that conciliation was to be regarded as a proper part of the functions of the probation service: s. 7.

man and a woman)[165] should hear domestic cases.[166] The 1937 Act also provided that only those with a legitimate interest in the case should be present at the hearing,[167] whilst press reporting was restricted.[168]

The 1937 Act[169] thus went some way to meet the objective, stated by Claud Mullins, of providing 'decent conditions . . . for hearing the matrimonial troubles of wage-earners' and Mullins claimed[170] to be 'immensely pleased' that the Harris Report went 'far beyond' his own 'most optimistic expectations'. But in reality the Report was a cautious document[171] and the 1937 Act can be seen as an essentially conservative measure.

Conciliation and the courts

The Harris Report (contradicting not only Mullins' strongly held view but also that embodied in the Bill drafted by the former President of the Divorce Division) concluded without qualification that the task of conciliation was not one for the court itself to undertake.[172] This was because the Committee believed that for the courts to be directly involved in conciliation attempts would be to blur the distinction between adjudication and social work. For this reason, the court's functions in relation to conciliation should be restricted to identifying the cases in which conciliation might (with the agreement of the parties)[173] usefully be attempted, deciding who should make those attempts, and exercising such general supervision over the process 'as may be consistent with the judicial functions which [the court] may be called upon to exercise at a later stage'.[174] This analysis of the respective functions of the court and others involved in dealing with the consequences of marriage breakdown was to prove extremely influential.

[165] Summary Procedure (Domestic Proceedings) Act 1937, s. 1 (now Magistrates' Courts Act 1980, s. 66(1)); but—paradoxically in view of the fact that much of the agitation had focussed on the unsatisfactory procedures in London—the Government refused to override opposition from the majority of the metropolitan magistrates and the new provisions were not extended to the metropolis until the enactment of the Administration of Justice Act 1964.

[166] In this and some other respects the legislation was evidently influenced by what was then seen as the success of specialist juvenile courts.

[167] Summary Procedure (Domestic Proceedings) Act 1937, s. 2(2)–(6) (now Magistrates' Courts Act 1980, s. 69(2)–(6)).

[168] Summary Procedure (Domestic Proceedings) Act 1937, s. 3 (now Magistrates' Courts Act 1980, s. 71). Comparable provisions had governed reporting of cases in the Divorce Court since 1926: Judicial Proceedings (Regulation of Reports) Act 1926, for the background to which see SM Cretney, *Law, Law Reform and the Family* (1988) Chapter 4.

[169] Some improvements were also made by administrative measures.

[170] Mullins to Harris, 6 April 1936, PRO HO45/17152.

[171] Note for example the Report's statement that the success of conciliation had 'clearly been substantial and even if it were not so marked as is sometimes claimed, any failure cannot ordinarily be attributed to want of effort': para. 14.

[172] Harris Report, paras. 16–18 and *Summary of Recommendations*, para. 3.

[173] Anything like forced conciliation might not only appear to be depriving the parties of their legal rights, 'but also may in the end aggravate the situation. Successful conciliation can only be arrived at by the consent and co-operation of both parties': Harris Report, para. 20.

[174] Harris Report, para. 18.

The danger that conciliation may constitute denial of justice

The Harris Report insisted on the importance of preserving spouses' rights of direct access to adjudication by the courts. It saw a 'real risk that conciliation (by which it meant persuading the parties to drop the contemplated proceedings) could be carried too far'[175] and might indeed lead to some 'denial of justice'.[176] True, 'some machinery for conciliation [was] an essential part of the administration of the Acts relating to matrimonial disputes'[177] and well-qualified probation officers could and should provide a valuable and constructive service in seeking to remove the causes of disputes.[178] But the Committee warned of the strong temptation for the zealous probation officer (particularly a probation officer actuated by 'personal convictions as to the sanctity of the marriage tie')[179] to settle as many cases as possible out of court. The Committee urged that probation officers' work be closely supervised to ensure both that undue pressure was not used and that conciliation procedures were not carried out in a perfunctory manner.[180]

No statutory obligation to provide conciliation

The Harris Committee was 'strongly of the opinion' that no statutory obligation should be imposed on the courts to provide conciliation.[181] It was sufficient that magistrates were alive to the social implications of matrimonial disputes, were well aware of the need where possible to uphold the permanence of the marriage contract and of the effect[182] of breaking up the home. Because of this, magistrates had built up their own procedures 'based on the good sense of the Justices or their Clerks and on the facilities available to them';[183] and that tradition should be respected. But the Harris Report and the 1937 Act had affirmed a principle which Mullins and other campaigners emphatically rejected. Conciliation (in the 'marriage-saving' sense) was not an appropriate

---

[175] Harris Report, para. 16. This certainly occurred in the case of Mrs Esther Gough who dropped an application for an order founded on her husband's cruelty; two years later her husband was convicted of manslaughter of their foster child, Dennis O'Neill, and Mrs Gough was convicted of neglect: see generally SM Cretney, *Law, Law Reform and the Family* (1998) at p. 212, ff.

[176] GK Behlmer, 'Summary Justice and Working-Class Marriage in England, 1870–1940' (1994) 12 Law and History Review 229, 238 suggests that in the inter-war years 'for every person who actually saw a marital complaint through to trial, perhaps three more sought relief of some kind without invoking the formal machinery of justice'; and concludes that the conciliators sought to persuade applicants for separation orders that they should cease legal action; and see generally GK Behlmer, *Friends of the Family, The English Home and its Guardians, 1850–1940* (1998) pp. 213–229 ('Claud Mullins and Coercive Conciliation').

[177] Harris Report, para. 13.   [178] Harris Report, paras. 19–24.
[179] Harris Report, para. 16.   [180] Harris Report, para. 24.
[181] Harris Report, para. 14.
[182] 'often . . . disastrous to the children of the marriage if not to the parties themselves'.
[183] Para. 8.

function for the courts. As the Law Commission put it in 1976[184] in a passage echoing Lord Chancellor Sankey's words more than 40 years earlier:

'The primary function of any court is adjudication and, while that certainly does not exhaust its functions, a careful limit must be set to any functions going beyond adjudication.'

The fact that the courts' formal role was firmly defined as adjudication did not of course mean that 'conciliation' was not to be undertaken; but the notion that magistrates should themselves provide help and social work seemed to have gone beyond recall.

The impact of the Harris Report: the role of conciliation in the family justice system

In this informal way 'conciliation facilities' came to be offered in many magistrates' courts; and in 1946 Lord Merriman, President of the Probate Divorce and Admiralty Division[185] regarded it as a source of reproach that, whereas in every 'properly conducted' magistrates' court the probation officer would 'have a shot at effecting conciliation'; and adjournment for reconciliation was 'the common practice' in the magistrates' courts and 'often achieves its object'[186] no such facilities were then available in the Divorce Court.[187] He decided[188] to remedy this omission and put forward a scheme to bring an 'element of reconciliation' into divorce procedure. Merriman believed that such a scheme would 'take some of the pressure off the courts and would also tend to arrest the laxity of public opinion about Divorce'.[189]

CONCILIATION IN DIVORCE: THE PRESIDENT'S SCHEME FOR STATUTORY CONCILIATION AND INQUIRY TRIBUNALS, 1946

The Merriman scheme was ambitious. Commissions of Conciliation and Inquiry would be established by statute, and would work through tribunals con-

---

[184] *Report on Matrimonial Proceedings in Magistrates' Courts* (Law Com. No. 77, 1976) para. 4.12.

[185] See Biographical Notes.

[186] *Ibid*; and Evidence of Sir Boyd Merriman P to the (Denning) *Committee on Procedure in Matrimonial Causes*.

[187] The Denning *Committee on Procedure in Matrimonial Causes* believed that the reason for this was that the social stigma attaching to divorce in pre-War Britain was such that only cases in which reconciliation was out of the question ever reached the courts: *Final Report* (1947, Cmd. 7024) para. 10. And it is certainly true that the law relating to collusion discouraged attempts to agree on the consequences of divorce.

[188] Lord Chancellor Jowitt actively encouraged Merriman: see Jowitt to Merriman, 5 February 1946, PRO LCO2/3928.

[189] Merriman to Jowitt, 9 January 1946, PRO LCO2/3927.

sisting of a lawyer and welfare worker or probation officer.[190] All undefended divorce cases would be referred to one of the tribunals which would first consider the possibilities of effecting a reconciliation between the parties. If there was no reconciliation[191] the tribunal would, by consent, deal with financial and custody issues. Eventually, the case would be remitted to the court;[192] and, in the absence of any objection, a decree (including relevant ancillary orders)[193] would be pronounced. The role of lawyers (with their potential for engaging in 'unhelpful recrimination')[194] would thus be greatly reduced.[195]

The Merriman scheme[196] attracted the unanimous approval of the divorce judges[197] and of the Archbishops[198]—a fact which (as Lord Chancellor Jowitt informed his colleagues) was 'very valuable politically'[199]—whilst Jowitt[200]

---

[190] The question of the qualifications of those lay people to be involved remained troublesome. The work of probation officers in the matrimonial jurisdiction of the magistrates' courts was well established; but the Denning Committee was apparently concerned that 'better class parties would not readily turn to probation officers or a state service' and it considered the employment of 'voluntary workers of superior class': see the note of a discussion between the Assistant Secretary in charge of the Probation Department in the Home Office and the Secretary of the Denning Committee (TG Skyrme: see Biographical Notes) on PRO file HO45/25202.

[191] Merriman accepted that attempts at reconciliation would be unsuccessful in many, perhaps most, cases; but considered, first, that it was 'the successes that matter, as in the Parable of the Lost Sheep' and secondly 'that if the scheme as a whole appeals to the public imagination the educative effect of the reconciliatory procedure may be a great, if imponderable gain': see his further letter to Jowitt, 8 February 1946, LCO2/3928.

[192] One of the matters upon which Merriman and others felt strongly was that the dissolution of a marriage should under no circumstances be allowed to become an administrative (as distinct from a judicial) act, and he attached importance to the fact that his proposals would avoid this: Merriman to Jowitt, 8 February 1946, LCO2/3928.

[193] There would be no separate ancillary relief proceedings, but a single 'comprehensive but informal' investigation: Merriman to Jowitt, 9 January 1946, LCO2/3927.

[194] Merriman to Jowitt, 8 February 1946, LCO2/3928.

[195] Merriman explained to Jowitt that it was essential that the hearing should be in camera and informal; and although he 'would not preclude the attendance of legal advisers' the tribunal should be able to insist on a private interview with either party or with both: Merriman to Jowitt, 8 February 1946, LCO2/3928.

[196] Minimising the risk of collusion was a major pre-occupation: Merriman to Jowitt, 9 January 1946, LCO2/3927. The need to establish that charges made in the petition were true created obvious difficulties—was a spouse, contrary to a 'long established principle of the law' (as Jowitt put it to Merriman on 5 February 1946) to be asked questions tending to show the commission of a matrimonial offence, for example? Merriman's robust view was that the Government should give priority to the 'enormous body of cases in which the facts are plain and in which the Respondent is at least as anxious as the Petitioner for a divorce and, very often, has said so . . .': Merriman to Jowitt, 8 February 1946, LCO2/3927. The notion that divorce should be available by consent was, at this time, anathema.

[197] Merriman to Jowitt, 17 January 1946, LCO2/3927.

[198] The Archbishop of Canterbury wrote to Jowitt on 19 April 1946 (PRO LCO2/3928) urging that Merriman's scheme 'does something to deal with the social questions involved and would really help to stem the tide of divorce by enabling people primarily interested in reconciliation to meet both parties . . .'.

[199] As Jowitt told his colleagues: Minutes of the Committee on Reform of Legal Procedure, 5 April 1946, RLP(46) 3rd meeting, LCO2/3928.

[200] Jowitt thought the scheme would bring the parties together in private, and that this was the only way in which attempts at reconciliation had any prospect of success: Minutes of the Committee on Reform of Legal Procedure, 4 February 1946, RLP(46) 2nd meeting, LCO2/3927.

told Merriman that he personally thought Merriman had 'hit upon a really great idea, which may do very much to reform our marriage laws'.

Opposition to the Merriman scheme

The Law Officers[201] did not agree. They did not think the Merriman scheme would achieve reconciliations, simplify machinery or reduce costs.[202] Presented with this united and hostile front against Merriman's scheme the Government decided to reserve its position. It established a 'strong but small committee'[203]— the Denning Committee[204]—to consider how divorce cases might be tried 'with special reference to reconciliation, costs, expedition, and the general interests of the parties'.[205]

The Denning Committee: State to promote conciliation, but conciliation not a proper function of courts

The Denning Committee's Report[206] expressed itself enthusiastically in favour of reconciliation procedures: the 'preservation of the marriage tie is of the highest importance in the interests of society' as well as to the parties and their children, and accordingly 'reconciliation should be attempted in every case where there is a prospect of success'. So important was this that 'the State itself should

---

[201] Other lawyers on the relevant Cabinet Committee shared these doubts about whether Merriman's scheme could be made to work: Jowitt to Merriman, 5 February 1946, PRO LCO2/3928.

[202] Jowitt to Merriman, 5 February 1946, PRO LCO2/3928.

[203] PRO LCO2/3928, Committee on Reform of Legal Procedure, Minutes of Meeting on 5 April 1946.

[204] For the appointment of the Committee, see pp. 283, 813. The Cabinet Committee on Reform of Legal Procedure had noted the view that since the committee would have to consider 'social' issues as well as technical subjects such as costs and procedure it would probably be better not to have a legal chairman. But in the event, although the name of Lord Lindsay, Master of Balliol College Oxford, was considered as chairman it was decided to approach Denning (recently translated from the Divorce Court to the King's Bench Division). Although Lord Denning has recorded his distaste for divorce work ('sordid in the extreme': *The Due Process of Law* (1980) p. 189) his work there was admired by Jowitt (who told Denning in 1949 that he congratulated himself on realising that 'sitting in the Divorce Court you used to be wasting your sweetness on the desert air': LCO2/4617); whilst Lord Uthwatt had on 28 April 1945 told the Permanent Secretary that Denning was wasted in the Divorce Court, notwithstanding the fact that he was the only judge there who gave proper consideration to the children's welfare.

[205] The Committee's full terms of reference were: 'to examine the present system governing the administration of divorce and nullity of marriage in England and Wales; and, on the assumption that the grounds upon which marriages may now be dissolved remain unchanged, to consider and report upon what procedural reforms ought to be introduced in the general interests of litigants, with special reference to expediting the hearing of suits and reducing costs and to the Courts in which such suits should proceed; and in particular whether any (and if so, what) machinery should be made available for the purpose of attempting a reconciliation between the parties, whether before or after proceedings have been commenced'.

[206] *Final Report of the Committee on Procedure in Matrimonial Causes* (1947, Cmd. 7024) para. 3. The Committee had published two interim reports (on the period between decree nisi and absolute (1946, Cmd. 6881) and on the courts which should have jurisdiction (1946, Cmd. 6945).

do all it can to assist reconciliation'.[207] But the Denning Committee, with a lack of sensitivity in handling personal relationships which may have had important and damaging long term effects,[208] rejected the Merriman scheme for a Commission of Conciliation and Inquiry for two reasons it believed to be 'conclusive'. First, it pointed out that work towards a reconciliation would not begin under the Merriman scheme until after proceedings had been started, whereas the Denning Committee believed that if reconciliation were to have any prospects of success it had to be attempted 'long before proceedings are begun'.[209] Secondly, the Denning Committee believed that

'. . . the work of reconciliation is . . . necessarily a personal task for those who undertake it, and if it is to appeal to the Englishman's character must be removed as far as possible from any suspicion of official supervision or interference in the private affairs of individuals . . . [T]he work of welfare officers as proposed in the [Merriman] scheme would be prejudiced from the outset by their status as members of the Tribunal'.[210]

In effect, the Denning Committee drew a sharp distinction between the judicial role[211] on the one hand and what Denning believed to be the essentially social work task of providing treatment (and hopefully cures) for marriages which seemed to have failed on the other. The Denning Committee firmly believed that there should be no direct State intervention in the private realm of married life. Certainly the State should 'assist' in reconciliation; but that assistance should be at one remove from the parties to a particular relationship. What was required was a

'Marriage Welfare Service to afford help and guidance both in preparation for marriage and also in difficulties after marriage. It should be sponsored by the State but should not be a State institution. . . . It should not be combined with the judicial procedure for divorce but should function quite separately from it'.[212]

The judicial system was thus to be adapted to facilitate reconciliation so far as practicable; but the business of the courts was to remain adjudication. The provision of services for reconciliation was a matter for others, and above all for

---

[207] Para. 28(1).

[208] See SM Cretney, *Law, Law Reform and the Family* (1998) p. 146 ff. Lord Merriman felt that he had been treated discourteously by the Committee which had failed to consult him. The Lord Chancellor agreed that Merriman had not been 'treated with that consideration which he might have expected. . .': Jowitt to Goddard, 7 November 1946, PRO LCO2/3951. In his autobiography, *The Due Process of Law* (1980, at p. 192) Lord Denning subsequently recorded: Merriman 'felt very strongly. . . . He never forgave me. When I happened to go to his room afterwards on another matter, he said to me: "You are a blackguard". . .'.

[209] Para. 25.   [210] Para. 25.

[211] The Committee in effect accepted the view put forward by the Treasury Solicitor that the Merriman scheme mixed up 'two things. You are having divorce by more or less an administrative machine with a sort of rubber stamp of the Court put upon it' (Minutes of Evidence, 17 July, LCO2/3948). Note also the view put forward in evidence by Sir Hartley Shawcross AG that people with an established legal right to a divorce should not be compelled to submit their private affairs to enquiries by strangers, and that the legal system should not tolerate secret inquisitions at which adultery would have to be disclosed.

[212] Para. 28(iii).

voluntary action.[213] The Denning Committee thus reinforced in the context of the Divorce Court the division of function upon which the Harris Committee into magistrates' procedures[214] had insisted a decade previously.[215]

The Morton Royal Commission on Marriage and Divorce (1956)

The Denning Committee's backing for marriage guidance did give a considerable stimulus to the National Marriage Guidance Council[216] and other organisations concerned with the provision of support for troubled marriages and with education for marriage; and ten years later the Morton Report[217] gave further support to the work of conciliation agencies.[218] The Morton Report supported expanded provision of skilled counselling to help husband and wife 'overcome their difficulties' and to achieve a reconciliation;[219] and it recommended that State financial support for agencies engaged in matrimonial conciliation be improved[220] and that solicitors should inform clients at the earliest possible stage of suitable marriage guidance agencies.[221] More generally, it

---

[213] See the remarks of Archbishop Fisher in the debate on the *Denning Report's* reconciliation procedure recommendations, *Official Report* (HL) 27 March 1947, vol. 146, col. 890; whilst Jowitt declared himself 'absolutely satisfied—good Socialist though I am—that it would be completely disastrous if the State were to try to undertake this task':*Official Report* (HL) 27 March 1947, vol. 146, col. 914. After some inter-departmental manoeuvring, it was accepted that marriage guidance was a matter for the Home Office; and a *Departmental Committee on Grants for the Development of Marriage Guidance* was established under a retired senior Home Office official, Sir Sidney Harris (see Biographical Notes). The Harris Marriage Guidance Committee's Report (1948, Cmd. 7566) recommended that certain agencies should be funded and made a number of other proposals. (Relevant papers are to be found in LCO2/3963—'Financial Assistance to enable the Marriage Guidance Council to carry on their work'—and on Home Office files HO45/25202.)

[214] The Harris Report; see Chapter 8, above.

[215] In one respect a welfare function became closely associated with the courts. The Denning Committee recommended that Court Welfare Officers be appointed in the Divorce Court, in part to give guidance to litigants and those contemplating proceedings, and in part to discharge special functions in cases involving children where (the Committee considered) skilled advice was often needed both by parents and children, and by the court which had to adjudicate on the questions that arise: *Committee on Procedure in Matrimonial Causes, Final Report* (1947, Cmd. 7024) para. 33. In 1950, a probation officer was appointed to the Divorce Division in London on an experimental basis to assist the court by investigating and reporting in accordance with the court's directions; and in 1956 the Morton Report recommended that this arrangement should be expanded, and that a court welfare officer should be appointed for every town where divorce cases were tried. From this modest start, a Divorce Court Welfare Service, with staff seconded from the Probation Service, gradually emerged, receiving formal recognition as the Divorce Court Welfare Service in 1959.

[216] See J Lewis, D Clark and DHJ Morgan, *'Whom God hath joined together' The Work of Marriage Guidance* (1992) is an indispensable if controversial study of the work of Relate National Marriage Guidance.

[217] *Royal Commission on Marriage and Divorce* (1956, Cmd. 9678) Part IV.

[218] But the Commission insisted that the State's role should be to give every encouragement to conciliation agencies rather than setting up an official conciliation service: Morton Report, para. 341.

[219] *Ibid.*, para. 339.   [220] *Ibid.*, para. 349.

[221] *Ibid.*, para. 353. The Commission also recommended that what was disclosed to a marriage guidance counsellor in the course of conciliation work should not be admissible in evidence in any subsequent matrimonial proceedings between the spouses: para. 358.

advocated the development of education calculated to combat 'false standards of value and of behaviour in marriage'.[222] But in many ways the Morton Report's most significant recommendation for the development of social services in the Divorce Court was its proposal for the expansion of what was to become the court welfare service.[222a]

Conciliation and reconciliation

What precisely was the objective of the 'conciliation' which seems to have commanded universal support? The Denning Report and the Morton Report[223] clearly envisaged that the terms 'conciliation' and 'reconciliation' were synonyms; and for many years the primary focus for 'conciliation' was on education for marriage and on 'saving' marriages which had run into difficulties. This was certainly the sense in which the word 'conciliation' was used in statute,[224] whilst official guidance on the conduct of conciliation by probation officers makes it fairly clear that the primary task of the conciliator was to reunite couples who were estranged.[225] For nearly 20 years, nothing happened

---

[222] *Ibid.*, para. 330. The Commission also advocated provision of 'specific instruction for those about to enter marriage', and recorded its belief that 'more needed to be done' to prevent 'hasty and ill-considered marriages'. Believing that the matter fell outside the Commission's Terms of Reference, the Report recommended that the Government should 'at an early date set up a suitably qualified body to review the marriage law and the existing arrangements for pre-marital education and training'.

[222a] See note 215, above.

[223] The Morton Report did emphasise the need to encourage 'experiment and diversity of method and technique' on the basis that it was 'only through a wide experience gained from a variety of sources that the best form and method of approach' was 'likely to emerge'.

[224] Magistrates' Courts Act 1952, s. 59, made provision for a probation officer to report to the court in cases in which he had been asked to 'attempt to effect a conciliation between the parties' but the attempt had 'proved unsuccessful'. As the (Finer) *Report of the Committee on One-Parent Families* (1974, Cmnd. 5629, see below) was to accept, it is evident that the word conciliation is employed in this provision 'at least primarily, in the sense we are giving to "reconciliation"'.

[225] Guidance published by the Home Office in 1948 (*Memorandum on the Principles and Practices in the Work of Matrimonial Conciliation in Magistrates' Courts, produced for the use of Probation Officers*) by a committee of Probation Officers and Probation Inspectors, December 1948, (copy on PRO LCO2/6135) pp. 8–9, gives a very clear picture of what was seen as the objective of conciliation. The probation officer, having seen the parties separately, should ask himself 'How did this couple come to marry, what brought them together, and what has since gone wrong?' He should take them through their engagement and early married life. 'Bit by bit the story unfolds and the conciliator tries to see it as both see it. He watches, too, for any sparks of affection that could be rekindled, any common interests that can be revived and at the same time for the mistakes which were made and which should be avoided if the marriage is to be rebuilt. Now diagnosis begins to merge into mediation. . . . The conciliator points out where he sees goodwill and constructive factors and also where he sees mistakes. . . . Then comes consideration of what can be done. If the causes are agreed, are the couple prepared to try to remedy them and rebuild from the start with the help of the conciliator or a specialist, or do they feel the rift has grown too great? If so' the couple will need to consider the impact of separation for the children, and the 'economics of keeping two homes must also be discussed. Sometimes the realisation of these dilemmas will bring the two back to a fresh consideration of a way out, back to the possibilities of conciliation. . . . Conciliation in the true sense of the word can be achieved only where there remains some affection between the two. There is then a desire to make the readjustment necessary to regain the respect and affection of the other, and it is the purpose of the conciliator to show how this can be done . . .'.

to alter this understanding (although the emphasis given to different aspects of the process did differ from time to time[226] and between individuals).[227] Only in 1974 did the Finer Committee on One Parent Families[228] redefine the word; and conciliation (or mediation) came to be a key concept in proposals for reform of the family justice system for the rest of the century. But by then the Divorce Reform Act 1969 had introduced what was believed to be an entirely new basis for divorce; and discussion of the role of conciliation will be resumed in Chapter 21.

PUBLIC FUNDING: THE LEGAL AID AND ADVICE ACT 1949

Before Legal Aid: the Poor Persons' Procedure

Legislation dating back to 1495[229] had provided for the poor to be exempt from payment of court fees[230] and conferred other privileges. In theory, it should have been possible for anyone, however poor, to start civil proceedings, but the reality was very different.[231] In part this was because court fees were not the only expense which had to be met by the litigant. In divorce cases, the petitioner had to be present in court in London to give evidence as had the witnesses the peti-

---

[226] See the discussion in *Marriage Matters* (a consultative document issued in 1979 by the Working Party on Marriage Guidance set up by the Home Office in consultation with the DHSS).

[227] For example, Claud Mullins (see Biographical Notes) originally placed the emphasis on achieving reconciliation but later came to attach more weight to ensuring the parties understand the process being put in motion, and then adjusting to the consequences of breakdown. Thus in *Marriage Failures and the Children* (1954) p. 26 he wrote 'the word "conciliation" has now a definite meaning. It involves a patient hearing of the married partner or partners in difficulty by someone with wide social experience who has studied marriage problems, the laying of emphasis on the best interests of the children of the marriage, the offering of suggested means of improving the situation, and, where necessary, an explanation of the different remedies provided by law. . . . If a wife or husband is really determined, after careful consideration of all the relevant issues, to break up the marriage and to apply for legal relief, conciliation does not stand in the way'; and see also *Fifteen Years Hard Labour* (1948) pp. 134–135.

[228] *Report of the Committee on One-Parent Families*, Chairman: Sir M Finer (1974, Cmnd. 5629); see p. 756 ff., below.

[229] The Suing in forma pauperis Act, 1495, 11 Hen 7 c.12. This Act was only finally removed from the statute book by the Statute Law (Repeals) Act 1973.

[230] This fact may be regarded as providing some support for the notion that unimpeded access to the courts is a common law constitutional right: see *R v. Secretary of State for the Home Department, ex parte Leech* [1994] QB 198, 210, *per* Lord Steyn; and *R v. Lord Chancellor, ex parte Witham* [1998] QB 575 (order made by Lord Chancellor under statutory powers removing exemption accorded to recipients of income support from liability for court fees declared to be unlawful).

[231] The most accessible brief account of the common law *in forma pauperis* procedure is now RI Morgan, 'The Introduction of Civil Legal Aid in England and Wales' (1994) *Twentieth Century British History*, Vol. 5, pp. 38–76, although earlier works (notably RE Egerton, *Legal Aid* (1945)) remain useful. A succinct account of the historical and other background to the Legal Aid legislation is given in EJT Matthews and ADM Oulton, *Legal Aid and Advice under the Legal Aid Acts 1949 to 1964* (1971). As an overall conspectus of the provision of legal services, B Abel-Smith and R Stevens, *Lawyers and the Courts* (1967) remains unequalled, with Chapters 6 and 12 being of particular relevance to the topics dealt with in this book.

tioner would require to prove the case. Another important factor was lack of proper administrative machinery for the practical execution of the poor persons' procedure; whilst stringent conditions were imposed on prospective litigants (for example, counsel's opinion had to be obtained about the merits of a claim). The result was that the procedure remained 'practically inoperative'.[232] In the early years of the twentieth century only about 15 divorce cases under the *in forma pauperis* procedure were heard each year.[233]

In 1914, in response to criticism[234] and agitation for change,[235] a reformed 'Poor Persons' Procedure' was introduced.[236] Its main features were:

(a) The Poor Persons' Department of the High Court would refer a poor person's[237] application to a 'reporting solicitor'.[238] On receiving the solicitor's report, the court could admit the applicant as a 'Poor Person'.

(b) A 'Poor Person' was exempt from payment of any court fees; and the Poor Persons' Department would assign the case to a (different) solicitor and to counsel whose names were taken from a list of volunteers. These lawyers would have the actual conduct of the case. They were not allowed to take any fee, profit or reward for their work; and the court would not make any award of costs in favour of or against the applicant.[239]

In spite of these severe limitations, the 1914 scheme did play a significant part in providing a response to the demand for divorce associated with World War I: in 1918, 1,014 divorce petitions[240] (out of a total of 2,323)[241] were brought under

---

[232] EJT Matthews and ADM Oulton, *Legal Aid and Advice under the Legal Aid Acts 1949 to 1964* (1971), p. 12 (and note the references to other relevant literature).

[233] *Royal Commission on Divorce and Matrimonial Causes* (1912, Cd. 6478) para. 73. The Royal Commission heard a great deal of evidence about the problems facing poor people wishing to have their marriages dissolved. Although it recommended some amendments to the poor persons' procedure, it considered that implementation of its proposed scheme for the local trial of divorce cases would be 'to reduce the cost of proceedings in the smaller class of cases so materially that it would be found that recourse to proceedings *in forma pauperis* would not be very extensively needed': para. 123. The Commission did not accept the imaginative suggestion made by B Fossett Lock (the barrister chairman of the Charity Organisation Society) that unclaimed funds in court should be used to fund impecunious litigants' travel expenses.

[234] Including criticism by the 1912 *Royal Commission*: see para. 409 ff.

[235] See RI Morgan, 'The Introduction of Civil Legal Aid in England and Wales' (1994) *Twentieth Century British History*, Vol. 5, p. 38, at pp. 41–42.

[236] Rules of the Supreme Court (Poor Persons) 1913, substituting new O. XVI rr. 22–32.

[237] Ie one whose assets (excluding clothes, household goods, tools of the applicant's trade etc) did not exceed £50 (perhaps £2,800 in year 2000 values).

[238] The Reporting Solicitor was to provide his services without charge; but in 1925 the *Report of the Committee to Enquire into the Poor Persons' Rules*, paras. 24–28, noted that some solicitors did not comply with this rule.

[239] Save in exceptional circumstances.

[240] *Report of the Committee on Legal Aid and Legal Advice in England and Wales* (Chairman, Lord Rushcliffe)(1945, Cmd. 6641) para. 10.

[241] *Royal Commission on Marriage and Divorce* (Chairman: Lord Morton of Henryton) (1956, Cmd. 9678) App. II, Table 1.

the Poor Persons' Procedure, and demand grew rapidly.[242] However, the scheme made no provision for any reimbursement of the out-of-pocket expenses (for example, in meeting witnesses' travelling expenses or obtaining the necessary evidence of adultery)[243] necessarily incurred in prosecuting a case and, largely for that reason, the hopes raised by the success of an application to proceed as a poor person were often dashed by inability to bring the case to its conclusion. As many as half the cases accepted[244] as eligible for the Poor Persons' Procedure did not go to trial.

In 1919 a Committee recommended changes designed to improve matters. However, these changes[245] (which stopped well short of the radical step advocated by some of transferring the conduct of such cases to a salaried government official)[246] were largely ineffective.

The Law Society takes over administration of the Poor Persons' Scheme

In 1924 another enquiry was set up.[247] It attributed the difficulties which continued to be experienced entirely to lack of an adequate number of solicitors willing to undertake the conduct of poor person divorce cases;[248] and (in a passage which will read strangely to some in the post-Thatcher era) assumed that the legal profession had a 'moral obligation' to render 'gratuitous legal assistance . . . in return for the monopoly in the practice of the law which it

---

[242] There were no fewer than 4,101 divorce applications to the Poor Persons Department (2,215 of which were granted) leading the *Committee to Enquire into the Poor Persons Rules* (Chairman: PO Lawrence J)(1919, Cmd. 430) to talk of a 'vast influx' and a 'glut'. There were in contrast far fewer applications (eg 193 to bring actions in the King's Bench Division) relating to other forms of civil litigation.

[243] Although solicitors were not allowed to charge professional fees they were allowed to charge for copying and other out-of-pocket disbursements; and it appears that in practice these 'office expenses' did sometimes include an element in respect of clerks' time and overheads. Sir Claud Schuster believed this constituted 'an inducement to a certain type of solicitor to undertake' poor person cases: PRO LCO2/644.

[244] Which constituted approximately half of those in which application had been made: see above. Decrees were granted in all but a tiny number (15 in 1918) of the cases which did proceed to trial.

[245] The Committee proposed that applicants should at the outset deposit a sum of £5 (estimated to cover typical out-of-pocket expenses) and that they show not only that they satisfied the £50 capital qualification but also that their usual weekly income was less than £2 (in special circumstances £4). (These figures should be multiplied by 25 to give some indication of year 2000 equivalents.) The Committee also proposed further restrictions on payments to solicitors, notably that no payment was to be made in respect of 'office expenses'.

[246] The Committee thought it would be 'highly objectionable to create an official to conduct private litigation': para. 49.

[247] *Report of the Poor Persons Rules Committee* (Chairman, PO Lawrence J)(Cmd. 2358).

[248] This should hardly have come as a surprise. The 1919 changes to the scheme had deprived the lawyers involved of the possibility of recovering even a contribution to overhead expenses; and the 1919 *Committee to Enquire into the Poor Persons Rules*, para. 21 had reported that in London (where the bulk of the work was concentrated) there were only about 68 solicitors prepared to act in poor persons' cases (as compared with 790 who would act for fee paying clients). The 1924 Lawrence Committee also noted that there were factors other than the narrowly financial which deterred some solicitors from participating in the Poor Persons' Procedure, not least the need to receive uneducated, ignorant, ill-dressed and sometimes ill-mannered people.

enjoys'.[249] The Committee, reporting in 1925, believed that solicitors would more readily respond to appeals to participate in the scheme[250] coming from members of their own profession 'themselves bearing their full share of the burden' than to similar appeals coming from civil servants. Hence, the organisation and routine administration of the Poor Persons' Scheme should be transferred from the Court Poor Persons' Department to the solicitors' profession acting through Committees appointed by The Law Society and by the provincial Law Societies and approved by the Lord Chancellor.[251] Government involvement would be restricted to the making of a financial contribution to the Committees' office premises and clerical staff.[252]

The Law Society accepted the Committee's proposal;[253] and in effect the solicitors' profession took over control[254] of the arrangements for making divorce available to the poor.[255] The amount of State funding involved was tiny in modern terms[256] but sufficed to establish the structural foundations for the legal aid system subsequently established in 1949.

The burden on the legal profession

The Poor Persons' Scheme provided help at considerable cost to solicitors[257] and the barristers they instructed. For the barrister (as Lord Chancellor

[249] The Committee accepted that no undue burden should be cast upon any individual members of the profession.

[250] For the repeated appeals made by the Law Society, see RE Egerton, *Legal Aid* (1945) pp. 14–16.

[251] For the Committees' functions etc see Appendix 3 to the Lawrence Committee's Report. It was entirely up to the Local Committee to decide whether an applicant was within the financial limits to qualify for assistance and whether an applicant had a *prima facie* case; and there was no appeal against the Committee's decision.

[252] However, in recommendations designed in part to equalise the burden between solicitors in different parts of the country, poor person divorces were to be dealt with on assize and interlocutory matters could be dealt with locally in High Court District Registries. Extension of divorce jurisdiction to the county court was rejected.

[253] The Committee had prudently taken steps to win the Law Society's assent to the scheme before submitting its report. A factor in the discussions was that the Law Society was highly susceptible to suggestions that failure by the profession to respond would inevitably lead to the establishment of a central government department conducting litigation, and that any such expansion of State involvement would jeopardise solicitors' prosperity. On the negotiations between The Law Society, the Committee and the Lord Chancellor's officials see further RI Morgan, 'The Introduction of Civil Legal Aid in England and Wales' (1994) *Twentieth Century British History*, Vol. 5, p. 38, at pp. 47–50; B Abel-Smith and R Stevens, *Lawyers and the Courts* (1967) pp. 144–148.

[254] It also took over the personnel and offices of the existing Poor Persons' Department.

[255] B Abel-Smith and R Stevens, *Lawyers and the Courts* (1967) p. 148, comment that a 'professional association had been entrusted with the task of running a statutory public service. There was no precedent for such a step'.

[256] The initial grant from government funds for the expenses of administering the scheme was £3,000; and by 1944–45 this had risen to £14,500 (something over £300,000 in year 2000 values): *Report of the Committee on Legal Aid and Legal Advice in England and Wales* (Chairman, Lord Rushcliffe)(1945, Cmd. 6641) para. 19. In 1996/7 the amount disbursed in legal aid on matrimonial work was £182 million: Legal Aid Board Annual Report 1996/7 Table 12.

[257] The *Report of the Poor Persons (Divorce Jurisdiction) Committee* (1929, Cmd. 3375) Chairman, Sir Claud Schuster, pays warm tribute to the solicitors undertaking work under the Poor Persons' Procedure.

Gardiner was subsequently to recount)[258] it 'was not just a matter that you did not get any fee; if you had a two-day poor person case at Derby Assizes, you had to pay your own train fare and hotel bill. We all did it because it was the thing to do . . .'. In the same way solicitors (who had offices to run and staff to pay) found[259] that every poor person's case represented a substantial financial burden[260] whilst the solicitors who served on the local committees administering the scheme gave many hours of service without any direct return.[261] But the legal profession's participation in the Poor Persons' Procedure was not entirely altruistic.[262] In return for co-operation, the profession escaped direct State interference in the relationship between solicitor and client, and some attached great importance to this.[263] But quite how the balance between concern to provide a service to the community and the claims of professional self interest should be struck is a matter on which different views can properly be held.

Cracking under the strain

The reformed Poor Persons' Procedure appears to have worked tolerably well until the late 1930s.[264] The scheme certainly permitted many who would not otherwise have been able to meet the inevitable expense to obtain the freedom to remarry. In 1937 nearly half of all divorce cases were dealt with under the Poor Persons' Procedure. By 1939 there were more than 10,000 applications (of

---

[258] *Official Report* (HL) 15 June 1976, vol. 371, col. 1231.

[259] In the words of the *Report of the Committee on Legal Aid and Legal Advice in England and Wales* (Chairman, Lord Rushcliffe)(1945, Cmd. 6641) para. 69. The Committee added its own tribute to 'that frequently paid by the Judges but too little appreciated by the public' to the barristers and solicitors involved.

[260] The eminent London solicitor Sir John Withers estimated that each poor person's case represented a financial contribution of £20 by the conducting solicitor: see RE Egerton, *Legal Aid* (1945) p. 16.

[261] The honorary secretaries of the local committees in practice had to help with applications, and the burden falling on them has been described as 'enormous': RE Egerton, *Legal Aid* (1945) p. 16.

[262] B Abel-Smith and R Stevens, *Lawyers and the Courts* (1967) were evidently not over impressed by suggestions that the legal profession was capable of altruism. Even those directly involved with the scheme were often confused. The Law Society's annual reports emphasised the charitable nature of the scheme but repeatedly complained of the ingratitude of clients who assumed the £5 deposit was full payment of the normal fee (or alternatively that the solicitor received state funding)—a 'perfectly logical response from the point of view of many of those helped under the scheme, for whom £5 represented more than two weeks' wages': RI Morgan, 'The Introduction of Civil Legal Aid in England and Wales' (1994) *Twentieth Century British History*, Vol. 5, pp. 38, 53.

[263] *Final Report of the Committee on Legal Aid for the Poor* (Chairman, The Hon. Mr Justice Finlay)(1928, Cmd. 3016) para. 18. This Committee (which also produced a *First Report* (1926, Cmd. 2638) was primarily concerned with the question of extension of legal aid to the county court (which a majority opposed).

[264] *Report of the Committee on Legal Aid and Legal Advice in England and Wales* (Chairman, Lord Rushcliffe)(1945, Cmd. 6641) para. 22.

which 5,760 were granted).[265] But this increased demand for divorce (fuelled in part by the extended grounds introduced by the Matrimonial Causes Act 1937) placed the system under strain.[266] In some parts of the country solicitors refused to take on poor persons' divorces.[267]

The Second World War made radical change inevitable. More than half the country's solicitors left their practices to serve the war effort.[268] An 'almost intolerable burden' was put on those who remained:[269] a small number of hard-pressed solicitors had to cope with a remorselessly increasing demand for divorce.

War-time solutions

The authorities acted decisively in an attempt to minimise damage to morale, especially in the Armed Forces. First, all service personnel up to the rank of sergeant were brought within the category of persons entitled to bring proceedings under the Poor Persons' rules. Secondly, the Forces established Legal Advice Bureaux which in practice undertook the formidable[270] burden of collecting the information on which the divorce petition would be based.[271] Thirdly, the Law Society established a 'Services Divorce Department' under the supervision of a paid, whole-time, solicitor[272] to deal with service divorces and also civilian poor persons' cases in which the local committee had been unable to find a solicitor to act gratuitously.

---

[265] See RE Egerton, *Legal Aid* (1945) p. x. RI Morgan, 'The Introduction of Civil Legal Aid in England and Wales' (1994) *Twentieth Century British History*, Vol. 5, pp. 38, 52 provides a useful chart showing the proportion of divorces brought under the Poor Persons' Procedure.

[266] *Report of the Committee on Legal Aid and Legal Advice in England and Wales* (Chairman, Lord Rushcliffe)(1945, Cmd. 6641) para. 22. B Abel-Smith and R Stevens headline their account, 'The system collapses' in *Lawyers and the Courts* (1967) p. 158.

[267] Notably in Wales. The Welsh Associated Law Society formally boycotted the scheme and did not yield to urgent pleas from The Law Society. As Morgan notes, the poor persons' cases were 'particularly unpopular in areas. . . where, because of low wages and poor social conditions, a particularly large proportion of the population qualified for help under the scheme's stringent means tests'. A considerable burden was placed on solicitors in such areas: 'The Introduction of Civil Legal Aid in England and Wales' (1994) *Twentieth Century British History*, Vol. 5, pp. 38, 55.

[268] *Report of the Committee on Legal Aid and Legal Advice in England and Wales* (Chairman, Lord Rushcliffe)(1945, Cmd. 6641) para. 23. An even higher proportion of the clerks often bearing the main burden of divorce work abandoned private practice.

[269] It became 'almost impossible for them to find time to attend to the gratuitous work involved in undertaking Poor Persons' cases': *ibid*.

[270] The Law Society's Instructions on Applications for Legal Aid in Service Divorce Cases (Form HFM 2) covers two densely printed foolscap pages: see p. 252, above.

[271] The bureaux also played a pioneering role in developing conciliation procedures: see *Final Report of the Committee on Procedure in Matrimonial Causes* (Chairman: Sir AT Denning)(1947, Cmd. 7024) paras. 17–18. The bureaux employed 'all legitimate arguments towards reconciliation' and soldiers were not allowed to take steps to formalise marital breakdown without the conciliation machinery having first been put in motion.

[272] Eulalie Spicer (1906–1997), a formidable character: see Biographical Notes.

By 1945 the Law Society's Services Divorce Department[273] (funded by the allocation[274] of a flat payment of three guineas[275] taken out of the £5 deposit made by all 'poor person' litigants)[276] had a staff of over a hundred including eight qualified solicitors; and processed over 4,000 cases a year. It would clearly be impossible to return to the haphazard pre-war arrangements, which had in any event been on the verge of breakdown.[277] Accordingly in May 1944 Lord Simon (Lord Chancellor in the wartime coalition Government) set up a powerful committee[278] chaired by Lord Rushcliffe[279] to enquire into the facilities available for giving legal advice and assistance to poor persons and to make recommendations.

THE RUSHCLIFFE REPORT ON LEGAL AID AND ADVICE

The Report of the Rushcliffe Committee, published in May 1945,[280] led to the enactment of the Legal Aid and Advice Act 1949. Only a brief and highly selective account of the Committee's recommendations can be given here.[281]

Legal Aid no longer to depend on gratuitous provision by the legal profession

The Rushcliffe Committee[282] thought it impossible to expect any extension of gratuitous professional services. Rather, legal aid should be available at State expense in all courts in such manner as would enable everyone in need to have access to professional help. Legal Aid Centres should be set up throughout the country; and the barristers and solicitors involved should receive adequate remuneration for their services. In effect, the burden of providing legal services for those who could not afford them was to be shifted from the collective charity of lawyers to the State.

---

[273] Its organisation is described in the *Rushcliffe Report* (see note 280, below) paras. 71–81.

[274] This change in practice was made by amendment to the Rules of Court in 1941; and as GP Coldstream minuted in a full account of the arrangements for dealing with service divorce cases dated 28 November 1944, it 'was part of the bargain made with the Law Society by the Lord Chancellor's Office. (It is doubtful whether the sum of three guineas has proved adequate in the circumstances so far as the Law Society are concerned)'. PRO LCO2/4197.

[275] Perhaps £80 in year 2000 values.   [276] See note 245 above.

[277] In 1939, on the request of the Law Society, a Committee, chaired by Hodson J and given wide terms of reference had been appointed, but it had to abandon its work on the outbreak of war.

[278] See Biographical Notes, Part B.

[279] Henry Bucknall Betterton, Baron Rushcliffe GBE (1872–1949): see Biographical Notes.

[280] May 1945, Cmd. 6641. The evidence given to the Committee is in PRO LCO2/3899–3891.

[281] See generally RI Morgan, 'The Introduction of Civil Legal Aid in England and Wales' (1994) *Twentieth Century British History*, Vol. 5, pp. 38–76; and B Abel-Smith and R Stevens, *Lawyers and the Courts* (1967) Chap. 12. EJT Matthews and ADM Oulton, *Legal Aid and Advice under the Legal Aid Acts 1949 to 1964* (1971) contains a useful account of the background and a detailed account of the scheme established by the 1949 Act as it operated in its maturity.

[282] As Abel-Smith and Stevens point out, *op. cit.* p. 319, the Rushcliffe Committee consisted of 14 lawyers and five laymen.

Scheme to be administered by the legal profession

The Committee rejected proposals for a State scheme or a scheme administered by local authorities, in part because of the constitutional doctrine that the administration of justice should be independent of the Executive,[283] in part because local authorities were themselves often interested parties in some types of litigation, and in part because the many years' experience gained by the Law Society in administering the Poor Persons' System would be of 'inestimable value' in administering the proposed new scheme.[284] Local committees of solicitors would assess whether the applicant had reasonable grounds for bringing the proceedings in question.

Suggestions for lay or consumer involvement in the administration of the scheme were not viewed favourably[285] (although the Lord Chancellor, to whom the Law Society would be answerable[286] for the administration of the scheme, was to be advised on matters of general policy by an Advisory Committee).[287]

Scheme not to be confined to the 'poor'

The Rushcliffe Report recommended that the term 'assisted person' be used in place of 'poor person'. This was far more than a merely cosmetic change in terminology. The basis of the scheme was to be that all people of moderate means were entitled to help, contributing what they could afford[288] to the costs involved.[289]

---

[283] Napier to Bridges, 6 June 1945, PRO LCO2/3902.

[284] *Report of the Committee on Legal Aid and Legal Advice in England and Wales* (Chairman, Lord Rushcliffe) (1945, Cmd. 6641).

[285] The Haldane Society (representing socialist lawyers) subsequently advocated that a social worker be appointed to each of the local committees charged with detailed administration of the scheme; but Lord Chancellor's Office officials, noting the difficulty experienced in getting support from the provincial Law Societies, opined that those Societies would 'certainly withdraw if lay people were to be appointed', 2 January 1946, PRO LCO2/3902.

[286] The Treasury was concerned about accountability for the large sums of public money which would be involved; and Treasury officials could draw on a wealth of experience in these matters (for example, the 'gentleman sent to Spain by the British Council who went chamois hunting': PRO LCO2/3902). The Lord Chancellor's officials considered that the Law Society was so anxious to run the scheme they would not object to any reasonable proposals for control: PRO LCO2//3902, note of discussion on 21 June 1945.

[287] A note on PRO LCO2/3902 records that 'there was considerable divergence of opinion among Members of our committee' about the composition and functions of this body.

[288] The assessment of means was to be done by the independent and expert National Assistance Board.

[289] The details of the Report's proposals on financial eligibility are given at paras. 141–156. An applicant would only be disqualified from entitlement to legal aid if his annual income were more than £420 per annum; and it has been said that the 'overwhelming majority' of the population would be eligible: RI Morgan, 'The Introduction of Civil Legal Aid in England and Wales' (1994) *Twentieth Century British History*, Vol. 5, p. 67. But the Committee thought that a man involved in litigation could properly be expected to exhaust his *capital* before requiring public aid (para. 151) and the rules reflected this approach.

Scheme not to affect lawyer/client professional relationship

It was fundamental to the Rushcliffe Committee's thinking that a person financially assisted by legal aid was not thereby to be stigmatised or disadvantaged. Immediately a solicitor accepted a client the relationship of solicitor and client was to be established between them and the solicitor would proceed with the conduct of the case in exactly the same way as if the client were not an assisted person.[290] However (perhaps because there were signs of some fall off in the number of applications from Forces personnel, with the consequent danger of underemployment or even redundancy amongst those working in the Law Society's Services Divorce Department) the Committee recommended that divorce cases should continue to be dealt with by the Law Society's salaried solicitors.[291]

Effect of Legal Aid scheme on liability for costs

Under the Poor Persons' Procedure, the claimant was not only relieved from liability for payment of court fees, but was not liable to make any payment (apart from the £5 deposit for expenses) in respect of his own lawyers' costs. No order for costs would normally[292] be made against the poor person.[293] Equally the court would not normally[294] make an order for costs against the other party.

The Rushcliffe Committee had no difficulty in deciding that the blanket exemption from court fees would be inappropriate in a scheme providing assistance not only to the poor but also to people who had the means to make some contribution to the costs of litigation. The Committee accordingly recommended that full court fees should be payable and included as a disbursement in computing the assisted person's costs bill. But the Committee evidently found much more difficulty in deciding how far the ordinary costs rules (effectively, in ordinary civil litigation, that 'costs follow the event') should apply in cases in

[290] *Rushcliffe Report*, para. 171(16). However, only counsel who had placed their names on the appropriate panel could be instructed.

[291] See *Rushcliffe Report*, para. 171(23).

[292] Where a substantial amount was recovered by a poor person the court might order that such costs should be allowed to his or her solicitor as would have been recovered if the solicitor had been acting in the normal way.

[293] The effect of these rules in personal injury and other damages cases was to give solicitors an incentive to agree to act outside the poor person rules on a contingency basis since if the case were strong—and it would only be pursued if it appeared to be so—normal profit costs would eventually be recovered either on a settlement or from the loser at the end of litigation. To act in this way was entirely contrary to the recognised rules of professional practice, but it appears that not all solicitors resisted temptation. The costs rules did not have this effect in divorce litigation: see RI Morgan, 'The Introduction of Civil Legal Aid in England and Wales' (1994) *Twentieth Century British History*, Vol. 5, particularly at pp. 53–54, 68–69; Abel-Smith and Stevens, *op. cit.* particularly at pp. 138–139.

[294] The court might do so if the other party had acted unreasonably in prosecuting or defending the action; and in such a case the poor person's solicitor would be entitled to costs in the usual way.

which one or both parties was legally aided. Eventually it recommended that the ordinary rule should apply where an assisted person succeeded against an unassisted person, but that where a legally aided person was unsuccessful any award of costs should be limited to such amount as the Judge, having regard to the assisted person's finances, might direct. In divorce cases, the principle should be that costs recoverable by one spouse from another were not to exceed that party's legal aid contribution.[295]

The Committee would make the Legal Aid authorities effectively the assisted person's banker: all money recovered should be paid to the authorities who would then pay over to the assisted person 'any balance remaining on his account after all costs of the action have been met'.[296] This recommendation eventually took effect as the so-called statutory charge[297] and gave rise to considerable problems over the years.[298]

Provision to be made for giving of legal advice

The Rushcliffe Committee was required to consider not only *legal aid* ('assistance in conducting or defending proceedings in the courts') but also *legal advice* ('advice on legal matters, drafting of simple documents, and negotiations apart from the conduct of litigation . . .');[299] and the Committee received a great deal of evidence. Although the extent of the work undertaken by voluntary organisations (such as Poor Man's Lawyers and latterly the Citizens' Advice Bureaux)[300] was not widely understood, the Committee had no doubt that the existing facilities needed extending. There were large parts of the country without any provision for working people to get legal advice, and even where facilities existed and were well organised there was too much work for the volunteers.

---

[295] *Rushcliffe Report*, para. 173. Special provision had to be made about two other aspects of costs in divorce cases. Firstly, the Rushcliffe Committee thought it undesirable that 'public money should be employed in speculative enquiries into the conduct of individuals with a view to civil litigation, particularly in matrimonial cases': para. 159. Accordingly no public money was to be spent on preliminary enquiries (eg the cost of employing an enquiry agent to seek evidence of adultery). Secondly (and of greater long term importance) the traditional practice, flowing from the principle that a man was under a legal obligation to support his wife's requirements for 'necessaries', was that a husband would be required to give security for his wife's costs (see the account of this practice in *Povey v. Povey* [1972] Fam 40, CA, *per* Sir J Simon P); and Rushcliffe proposed therefore that legal aid should only be available to a wife down to the time when she could get an order for security. However, if the husband were also granted legal aid he would be treated as having satisfied the order to give security.

[296] *Rushcliffe Report*, para. 173.

[297] The fact that the Legal Aid authorities were given a 'charge' over the property recovered or preserved conferred advantages in enforcing the obligation, particularly when a house or other land was involved. The notion that there should be a charge in respect of costs liabilities seems to have been influenced by the fact that solicitors are traditionally entitled to security by way of a lien in respect of their unpaid costs: see generally *Hanlon v. The Law Society* [1981] AC 124, HL.

[298] See p. 437, below.

[299] The definitions are taken from the *Rushcliffe Report*, para. 5.

[300] There is a useful summary of the services then available in Part IV of the Rushcliffe Report; and see further note 309, below.

The Committee proposed that legal advice from whole-time paid solicitors should be made available throughout the country. Each of the ten Legal Aid Area Offices should have an office open during all reasonable hours (including on occasion in the evening to allow working people to attend); and in addition branch offices should be established wherever need could be shown, whilst solicitors would also be sent out from time to time to other areas. The legal advice scheme was not to be formally means tested; and in principle every applicant should pay a fee of half-a-crown[301] but even this modest charge could be remitted in suitable cases. Conversely legal advice could be refused if it was apparent that the applicant was able to pay the costs in the ordinary way.

The Legal Aid and Advice Act 1949: Bliss it was in that dawn . . .

The Rushcliffe Committee's report provides what is in many ways a classic example of post-War consensus reform. There is, for example, the sense of continuity with the structure of the local solicitors' committees established under the Poor Persons' Procedure. There is the collaboration between potentially hostile groups (notably the Law Society on the one hand, representing to extremely good effect the interests of the solicitors' profession, and on the other a Labour Party committed to massive reform and not yet exposed to the constraints of peace-time government).[302] And finally there is the sympathetic approach of officials in the Government Department primarily concerned. They no doubt welcomed a solution in which the Lord Chancellor's Department retained overall control but could delegate responsibility for the actual running of the scheme to others.

The Government accepted most of the Rushcliffe recommendations; and the Attorney-General was able to describe the Legal Aid and Advice Bill[303] as 'the charter of the little man to the British courts of justice . . . without regard to the question of their wealth or ability to pay'. But it soon became apparent that by no means everything was going to plan. Circumstances prevented the Government introducing the Bill until 1948.[304] By then serious economic

---

[301] 12.5 pence, perhaps £2.50 in year 2000 values.

[302] Most of the suggestions for 'improvement' to the Rushcliffe scheme came from the Socialist Haldane Society; and Lord Chancellor Jowitt received a delegation from the Society on 4 February 1946: PRO LCO2/3902.

[303] *Official Report* (HC) 15 December 1948, vol. 459, col. 1221.

[304] There were administrative difficulties in ensuring that the legal profession would not be swamped by implementation of the Act, but the main reason for delay seems to have been the acute pressure on Parliamentary time in the session 1947/8. The Government authorised an approach to the Opposition to seek an expedited passage for the Bill (Jowitt wrote to Sir David Maxwell Fyfe that even when lawyers 'approve a Scheme' they are apt to speak at some length to show their approval' but Maxwell Fyfe's response on 19 June 1947 was studiously non-committal: PRO LCO2/3902). By this time the Law Society was pressing for action lest their members lose their enthusiasm and the personnel of the Service Divorce Department drift away.

difficulties[305] had to be faced. Lord Gardiner's account[306] a quarter of a century later vividly encapsulates how events appeared to sympathetic contemporaries:

'The Act received the Royal Assent in July 1949. Being not impartial in these matters, I thought what a splendid Government this was; they had the wisdom and courage to give independence to India, Burma and Ceylon; gone was the great fear of most of our people: what was to happen about paying fees if they were ill? Gone, for that matter, was the worry of the doctors in dunning their patients to try to squeeze out the money which the patients could not really afford. There was the National Health Service. There was this legal aid scheme.

Then came September, devaluation, crisis, cuts all round. The Lord Chancellor was told, "You cannot do any of this now". . .'

The most important consequence for legal aid of this economic crisis was that, although the scheme for assistance to finance *proceedings* (including divorce proceedings) in the High Court was implemented in October 1950,[307] more than a decade passed before legal aid was made available for representation in family proceedings in magistrates' courts.[308] Perhaps even more seriously, the provisions for making legal *advice* available were never brought into force in the form originally envisaged.[309] On one view, the result was that the Legal Aid scheme encouraged premature litigation; and the availability of legal aid encouraged divorce when in reality the breakdown of the relationship (or at least recourse to contested litigation) might have been avoided by well-timed counselling or conciliation.[310]

---

[305] Culminating in the devaluation of the pound on 18 September 1949. It is difficult today to recapture the atmosphere of a society in which strict food controls were maintained—not only by rationing, but by restricting even the grandest restaurants to a maximum charge for food to 25 pence and to an allocation of 17/280ths of an ounce of cheese for each diner. On the day on which the Legal Aid and Advice Bill was introduced into the House of Commons Members were concerning themselves with such matters as the shortage of marmalade and boiled sweets: *Official Report* (HC) 15 December 1948, vol. 459, col. 1214.

[306] *Official Report* (HL) 15 June 1976, vol. 371, col. 1232.

[307] EJT Matthews and ADM Oulton, *Legal Aid and Advice under the Legal Aid Acts 1949 to 1964* (1971) pp. 16–19 gives a detailed account of the phased implementation of the Act.

[308] On 8 May 1961. Legal Aid and Advice Act 1949 (Commencement No. 10) Order 1961. Care proceedings (which came to impose a heavy burden on legal aid) did not become eligible for legal aid until 1965: Legal Aid (General)(Amendment) Regulations 1964, reg. 2.

[309] A more economical scheme, whereby legal advice would be given by solicitors in their own offices, was put forward by the Law Society in 1958, and this was brought into operation in 1959: Legal Aid and Advice (Commencement No. 6) Order 1959. Legal advice was made available from solicitors under the so-called 'green form' scheme (technically, 'legal advice and assistance' under Legal Aid Act 1988, Part III); and advice was also sometimes available from other sources, notably Citizens' Advice Bureaux and Law Centres. For a valuable conspectus, see Smith Bailey and Gunn's *The Modern English Legal System* (4th ed. by SH Bailey and MJ Gunn, 2001) Chapter 9.

[310] Note the concern expressed by the Bishop of Norwich, *Official Report* (HL) 27 June 1949, vol. 163, col. 328. Claud Mullins was particularly critical of the fact that the 'state-assisted road to divorce' diverted unhappy wives and husbands from the 'high-powered system in conciliation that has been developed in Magistrates' Courts in all of our larger cities . . .' Lord Chancellor Jowitt recorded (in a letter to the Lord President of the Council, Herbert Morrison, PRO LCO2/3902, 21 June 1947) that he was being 'pressed, and I think rightly pressed, to adopt some conciliation procedure to stop this vast number of divorce cases' and opined that 'This Rushcliffe scheme does give me a real chance of dealing with this problem [presumably by making advice available] and trying to introduce some reconciliation process before the thing has definitely got into the lawyers' hands'.

Legal Aid scheme victim of its success

In some ways, the legal aid scheme[311] became the victim of its own success: in
the first 40 years[312] some 2.3 million people were given help, and more than £588
million was paid out to the lawyers involved.[313] In 1995/6 over 140,000 applications for legal aid were made, and some 80% of those applications led to the
funding of proceedings.[314] And the availability of legal aid had a particular
impact on divorce and other family litigation, which consumed a disproportionate share of legal aid expenditure. By 1966, divorce cost the legal aid fund
£3.25 million out of a total legal aid expenditure of £5.5 million. By 1976 the
total expenditure had (notwithstanding economy measures) risen to £34 million; and by 1996/7 the net expenditure on civil legal aid had risen to no less than
£429 million of which matrimonial and child related cases absorbed more than
60%.[315] Over the years attempts to reduce (or at least to control) legal aid
expenditure have had a profound impact on family law and on procedures.[316]
But they were less effective in financial terms and in 1997 New Labour took radical action. The Lord Chancellor stated that 'legal aid has run out of control';[317]
and the Access to Justice Act 1999 abolished the scheme set up in 1949. Instead,
a Legal Services Commission was established; and a Community Legal Service
fund replaced the Legal Aid Fund. The Lord Chancellor is empowered to give
the Commission directions and guidance about how it should exercise its functions. It is too early to say whether the declared intention[318] of developing a 'network of legal service providers of assured quality, offering the widest possible
access to information and advice about the law, and assistance with legal problems' will be achieved.

[311] The text deals exclusively with *civil* legal aid. Legal aid in criminal matters (which is granted
in many more cases) is covered by different procedures.
[312] The year 1988/9 is chosen since that was when the administration of the scheme was transferred from the Law Society to the newly created Legal Aid Board.
[313] Legal Aid Board Annual Reports 1989–90, p. 3. In 1987 the Government still claimed that
legal aid covered 70% of households, but made it clear that it did not intend this proportion to rise.
In fact it seems clear that the proportion of the population eligible for assistance has fallen dramatically over the years: see B Abel-Smith and R Stevens, *Lawyers and the Courts* (1967) pp. 335–348;
C Glasser (1988) 85(10) *Law Soc Gaz* 11.
[314] Legal Aid Board, Annual Report, 1995/6, Civil 3.
[315] Legal Aid Board Annual Report 1996/7, Tables 4 and 12.
[316] Notably the creation of the 'special procedure' in divorce; and the determined encouragement
of mediation in preference to litigation. The impact of the statutory charge has also been considerable: see p. 437.
[317] Lord Irvine of Lairg, 'How I'll give the law back to the people', *The Times*, 18 October 1997.
[318] In the words of the *Explanatory Notes* to the Access to Justice Bill as introduced in the House
of Lords on 2 December 1998.

9

Irretrievable Breakdown as the Ground for Divorce: The Divorce Reform Act 1969

INTRODUCTION

The explanatory Memorandum to AP Herbert's Bill had stated its purpose as being 'to strengthen the institution of marriage and increase respect for the law'; and Herbert evidently believed that the Matrimonial Causes Act 1937 had worked well in practice. True, the divorce rate increased, but (as he wrote in 1945)[1] 'we have no statistics of the number of divorces which are followed by happy and fruitful second marriages'. But it was soon realised that the Act was not a panacea;[2] and by 1945 Herbert was receiving 'innumerable sad letters from citizens' separated but still unable to divorce.[3] For another quarter of a century the question whether the law should refuse to allow divorce save on the basis of proven matrimonial default remained highly controversial.

Some of the defects of the law can be illustrated from the author's personal recollection:[4]

'In 1953, during the school holidays, I attended a three day trial in open court at Manchester Assizes of a wife's petition for the dissolution of her thirty year marriage on the ground of the adultery which (she alleged) the husband had committed with an unknown woman in one of the dark alleyways in that part of Manchester subsequently romanticised in the television soap, "Coronation Street". Under intensive and skilled cross-examination the husband admitted most of the allegations made against him by the

---

[1] See his *Letter to the Electors of Oxford University*. Herbert was again returned in the 1945 election (demonstrating his independence by expressing his support for 'our great Prime Minister' Winston Churchill whilst also affirming his view that 'the much maligned Mr Chamberlain' had been right in his policy of appeasement, intended to 'preserve peace by Christian dealing' and taking pride in the fact that this country 'suffered so much provocation so long, and tried, in Christian fashion, not to believe the worst of others').

[2] In 1937 the Divorce Law Reform Union commented in its *Thirtieth Annual Report* that the only criticism of the 1937 Act was that it had not gone far enough.

[3] A particular problem, highlighted by the DLRU at this period (see eg Mrs Seaton-Tiedeman's article, 'Prisoners of Broken Marriage' in the *Sunday Pictorial*, 16 April 1939) related to the legal consequences of separation deeds. Such deeds were often used to regulate the financial affairs of middle-class couples who did not wish to 'face the publicity and difficulty of a divorce case in the courts'. But since a separation deed terminated desertion the effect was to make it impossible to divorce on that ground should one party subsequently wish to remarry.

[4] Taken from 'Divorce Reform in England—Humbug and Hypocrisy, or a smooth transition?' in MDA Freeman (ed.), *Divorce, Where Next?* (1996).

private detective and other witnesses but denied that he had succeeded in having intercourse with the woman concerned. The judge directed himself on the serious nature of
an allegation of adultery, held that the wife had not discharged the onus of proving
beyond reasonable doubt that adultery had taken place and accordingly dismissed her
petition. But that was not the end of the matter. The husband had retaliated by cross-
petitioning on the ground of his wife's cruelty; and the greater part of the hearing was
devoted to a meticulous examination of his complaints. Again, most of the allegations of
conjugal unkindness and other wifely failings were not denied, but the judge concluded
that, as a matter of law, these incidents did not cross the dividing line between the "ordinary wear and tear of conjugal life" on the one hand and cruelty in its legal sense on the
other. Those whom the law had made one flesh were thus to remain legally yoked
together; and the public interest in upholding the institution of marriage had been triumphantly asserted.'[5]

Such cases, in which both parties agreed that the marriage should be ended
but were not prepared to allow the other a court-room victory, were both
unusual and untypical. Far more common was the case where the 'innocent'
party refused to take proceedings; and the fact that one spouse could both deny
the other the liberty to remarry whilst still asserting (through the remedy of judicial separation)[6] the right to enforce alimony payments was a source of considerable grievance, particularly to middle-class men.[7] And it was not only adults
who suffered. This was because the refusal of the innocent party to petition
resulted (as the Law Commission was to put it in 1966) in a 'large number of
illicit unions which cannot be regularised and a still larger number of bastard
children who cannot be legitimised'; but the law seemed indifferent to this. For
example:

In *Pigott v. Piggott*[8] a Roman Catholic wife refused to divorce the husband from
whom she had been separated for 17 years. She applied for maintenance, but the
trial judge made a much smaller order than would otherwise have been appropriate because he thought it wrong to keep in existence the legal shell of a marriage which had irretrievably broken down particularly since this meant that
children born to the husband and his partner would be illegitimate. But the
Court of Appeal held the judge had been wrong to take the fact that the wife

---

[5] Footnotes in the original text are not reproduced.

[6] The Gorell Commission had been strongly critical of permanent separation orders; but in 1937
AP Herbert thought it prudent to drop a provision empowering the court to convert such an order
into divorce after two years: see p. 237, note 253, above.

[7] Wage earners may have been equally aggrieved, but the financial cost of supporting the recalcitrant wife would usually be less, and probably it was more difficult in practice to enforce payment of
a court order against a manual worker than against a salaried employee.

[8] [1958] P 1, CA (but the text draws on the fuller version of the judgments given by Sir J Simon P
in *Sansom v. Sansom* [1966] P 52, another case in which a husband failed to persuade the court that
the fact his wife had out of malice petitioned for judicial separation rather than a divorce, with the
result that he had been 'forced' to live in adultery with another woman by whom he fathered an illegitimate child was of any relevance in determining the amount of maintenance which he should pay
her. The husband also failed to persuade the court that the wife should not be entitled to share in
the large increases in his income which had come about after the separation).

could have petitioned for divorce had she been so minded into account as a factor reducing the wife's claim for financial support against the man who was still her husband.

'Progressive opinion' increasingly came to accept that while the 1937 Act had provided an 'easy escape from the bond of matrimony for those . . . minded to take it'[9] the time had come to provide for divorce in cases where the marriage had broken down completely, irrespective of whether or not a matrimonial offence had been committed and (if it had) by whom. But as one highly experienced divorce judge[10] put it:

'The history of divorce is one of conflict between those who believe that divorce is an evil thing, destructive of family life and accordingly of the life of the community—and those who take the "humanitarian" view that when a marriage has irretrievably broken down it should be dissolved.'

Legislation would be necessary to give effect to the humanitarian view; and the Labour Government which took office in 1945 had (notwithstanding its large majority)[11] not the slightest desire to get 'embroiled' at the beginning of its term of office in controversy about the ground for divorce—a topic which in no way concerned the distinctive outlook of the Labour party. The Government certainly had to deal with the threatened collapse of the court system under the pressure of the unprecedented number of divorce petitions;[12] and so it had set

---

[9] There were however some (for example doctors and the clergy, who faced automatic loss of their living if found guilty of adultery: see Clergy Discipline Act 1892, s. 1) for whom consensual divorce on that ground was not in practice an option: see eg the case cited by Colonel Lipton, *Official Report* (HC) 31 October 1950, vol. 480, col. 84. But statistically such cases were probably not significant; and nine members of the 1956 Royal Commission accepted that consensual divorce was in practice readily available on the basis of desertion for three years and that 'for those who wish a speedier release, the commission of adultery, is all that is needed'. But as this group put it, for those 'not prepared to resort to such expedients [*sic*]—and we believe the number is by no means negligible—there is . . . no relief. We think it may be said that the law of divorce as it at present exists is indeed weighted in favour of the least scrupulous, the least honourable and the least sensitive; and that nobody who is ready to provide a ground of divorce, who is careful to avoid any suggestion of connivance or collusion and who has a co-operative spouse, has any difficulty in securing a dissolution of the marriage': *Royal Commission on Marriage and Divorce* (Chairman: Lord Morton of Henryton) *Report 1951–1955* (1956, Cmd. 9678) (subsequently cited as the *Morton Report*) para. 70(v)–(vii).

[10] Sir Charlton [Charles] Hodson in evidence to the *Royal Commission on Marriage and Divorce*, 1956, *Minutes of Evidence*, p. 771.

[11] Elected with a majority of 146 over all other parties.

[12] The Committee described the increase as 'deplorable', but noted that the war had greatly increased the 'external difficulties which strain . . . marriage. It has removed men and women from their accustomed environment, separated them for long periods, and subjected them to severe physical and emotional strains. There is a housing shortage which often prevents married couples from living together; or huddles families so closely together that the strain of constant association becomes almost intolerable; or subjects young couples to the interference of relatives. The mere mechanics of every day life have become so exhausting for women as to have an immeasurable effect, through sheer weariness, on married happiness'. The Committee thought that many of these difficulties would be removed as war conditions passed, but warned that no step should be taken which would 'accelerate the process': *Committee on Procedure in Matrimonial Causes, Final Report* (1957, Cmd. 7024) (hereafter '*Denning Report*') para. 7.

up the Denning Committee[13] to examine the *administration* of the law of divorce'; but the Committee's terms of reference were carefully drafted[14] to exclude any consideration of the grounds for divorce from the Committee's remit.[15]

THE DENNING COMMITTEE

The fact that the grounds for divorce were clearly off limits did not altogether inhibit the Committee from expressing its rather conservative views. The *Denning Report* expressed concern about the 'deplorable increase' in the number of divorces[16] and took the opportunity to assert its belief that the preservation of the marriage tie was of the 'highest importance in the interests of society'[17] and that the 'institution of marriage itself needs to be anchored by effective public opinion, sound moral teaching, and careful administration of the law'.[18] It emphasised the importance of seeking reconciliation for estranged couples;[19] and (accepting that the 'basic causes of marriage failure were to be found in false ideas and unsound emotional attitudes developed before marriage, in youth and even in childhood')[20] favoured greatly extended facilities for education for marriage, parenthood, and family living.[21]

The narrow terms of reference could not however stop witnesses from volunteering 'many suggestions' for reforms in the substantive law to the Denning Committee; and in fact (rather than simply ignoring them) the Committee did (under the heading 'Suggestions Received')[22] record[23] that there appeared to be 'a large number of cases where husband and wife have been separated for many

---

[13] The *Committee on Procedure in Matrimonial Causes* (Chairman, Sir AT Denning) (subsequently referred to as the Denning Committee). For the Committee's terms of reference etc. see p. 302, note 205, above.

[14] See SM Cretney, *Law, Law Reform and the Family* (1998) Chapter 6.

[15] The Committee was specifically required to assume that the 'grounds upon which marriages may now be dissolved remain unchanged'.

[16] *Denning Report*, para. 8.   [17] *Ibid.*, para. 4.   [18] *Ibid.*, para. 9.

[19] But the prohibition on recommending changes in the substantive law prevented the Committee from considering the commonly made claim that the law of condonation hampered the making of attempts at reconciliation: *Denning Report*, para. 86(i).

[20] *Ibid.*, para. 5.

[21] The Committee favoured the development of a 'carefully graded system of' education on these matters available to all young people 'through the enlightened co-operation of their parents, teachers and pastors; and in addition specific marriage preparation of engaged couples to give them instruction and guidance to ensure the success of their marriage': *Denning Report*, para. 5.

[22] The fact that it did so was said by supporters of reform to demonstrate that the facts 'were obviously' of a compelling character: see *Official Report* (HC) 31 October 1950, vol. 480, col. 81 (Colonel Marcus Lipton).

[23] *Denning Report*, para. 86(iii). The Committee also noted as one of the 'principal suggestions' made to it the possibility that the law of condonation inhibited reconciliation (para. 86(i)); and the view that the restrictions on the court's power to allow a divorce petition to be presented within three years of the marriage should be altered to permit leave to be given whenever the judge was satisfied that there were no prospect of reconciliation: *Denning Report*, para. 86(ii).

years and there is no possibility of their ever coming together again, but a divorce cannot be obtained because the separation was by mutual consent and did not amount to desertion'. And the Government's reluctance to get embroiled in the controversy about changing the ground for divorce did nothing to inhibit people from joining lobbying groups or from writing to their MPs.[24] Parliamentary pressure built up.

PARLIAMENTARY PRESSURE FOR REFORM OF THE GROUND FOR DIVORCE: 1949 ONWARDS

In 1949, the Labour MP Colonel Marcus Lipton[25] put down an amendment to the Law Reform (Miscellaneous Provisions) Bill which would have added seven years' separation to the grounds for divorce. 200 MPs signed a Motion in support.

After the February 1950 election 120 MPs asked the Government to consider the appointment of a Royal Commission to investigate the state of the marriage laws.[26] The Government resisted;[27] but pressure grew.[28] Within the governing

---

[24] AP Herbert was not the only MP to receive 'innumerable letters': Mrs Eirene White (see Biographical Notes) told the 1956 Royal Commission that in 1950 (following the announcement that she intended to introduce a Private Member's Bill) she had received between 2,000 and 3,000 letters; whilst Colonel Lipton said that in 12 months he had received some 4,000 letters from every part of the country: *Official Report* (HC) 31 October 1950, vol. 480, col. 83. In the debate on the 1951 White Bill, even opponents of reform accepted these often revealed 'untold unhappiness, degradation, and . . . great danger both for the wife and children' from the continuance of the marriage: *Official Report* (HC) 9 March 1951, vol. 485, col. 942 (Hon Richard Wood, Conservative MP for Bridlington, younger son of the Lord Halifax whose strong Anglo-catholic sympathies had made him a powerful, if publicly silent, opponent of the 1937 legislation). Many of these letters told of long separations (one of 33 years), others from old age pensioners wishing no longer to 'live in sin' but to be able to be 'respectably married': *op. cit.* col. 961, Mrs CS Ganley JP. But letters were also received from women concerned that to allow divorce in such cases would jeopardise their pension entitlements: *op. cit.* col. 931, Mrs Eirene White (who asked herself whether such women were 'really married to a man or to an old age pension?').

[25] See Biographical Notes.

[26] *Official Report* (HC) 31 October 1950, vol. 480, col. 80 (Colonel Lipton).

[27] The Lord Chancellor refused to see a deputation on the ground that no useful purpose would be served by his doing so; and the Prime Minister rejected the request for investigation by a Royal Commission: *ibid.*

[28] The speech by Lt-Col. Marcus Lipton JP in the Debate on the Loyal Address (*Official Report* (HC) 31 October 1950, vol. 480, col. 79) urging the need for an enquiry seems to have been particularly influential. On 23 November 1951 Lord Mancroft (an active campaigner for a change in the law so as to permit marriage between a man and his former wife's sister) initiated a debate in the House of Lords on a motion to ask the Government to appoint a Royal Commission to inquire into the 'confused state of the law' of marriage and divorce—a tactic evidently deliberately intended to move the focus of attention from the notoriously contentious subject of the ground for divorce. The Lord Chancellor agreed with the view that marriage laws should be 'altered as seldom as possible, and then only at considerable intervals of time' and perhaps that 30 years should be allowed to elapse before assessing the impact of the Herbert Act. He drew attention to the need to take into account the impact of the recent introduction of Legal Aid and doubted whether he would derive much help from a Royal Commission on the main issue of policy. But he seemed not wholly to rule out the eventual appointment of a Commission: see *Official Report* (HL) 23 November 1951, vol. 169, col. 510.

Labour Party[29] there was a group of MPs committed to reform,[30] and when in November 1950 the newly elected Labour MP Mrs Eirene White[31] drew fifth place in the ballot for private member's Bills[32] she was persuaded to introduce a Matrimonial Causes Bill.

THE 1951 EIRENE WHITE BILL: BREAKDOWN OF MARRIAGE THE NEW PRINCIPLE

Mrs White's Bill[33] was avowedly intended 'to deal with marriages in which the spouses have lived separately for seven years, but in which no hitherto recognised ground for divorce exists or in which one partner, having grounds for action, declines to take it and keeps the other partner tied against his or her will, generally for life'. Mrs White believed that to allow separation divorce was unlikely significantly to increase recourse to divorce, and made the point that the 'passage of time also has the great advantage of being beyond the capricious, angry or spiteful control of the parties'.[34] But she also recognised the strength of the view that the law failed to protect the large number of women[35] who had no career except that of a housewife against the financial hardship which might flow from divorce.[36]

[29] The Government's majority had been reduced to a mere five seats at the February 1950 general election. This is no doubt one of the factors influencing it towards a cautious policy on an issue thought to be likely to lose votes.

[30] And there was support for divorce reform in the other political parties: Colonel Lipton was able to claim that the signatories of the Commons motions came from all political parties and from 'every important religious denomination': *Official Report* (HC) 31 October 1950, vol. 480, col. 80; and note the efforts successfully made to present the Bill as an all-party initiative: see below. Some indication that 'breakdown' had become recognised as a possible solution to the problem of divorce is given by a lengthy and thoughtful article in *The Economist* 19 August 1950, which concluded that it was time to consider whether the courts should not be given the power to dissolve a marriage which was beyond doubt at an end as a fact, and yet where the cause of that ending did not fit into any of the categories that parliamentary skill had laid down. By 1959 Mrs White was claiming (at any rate in the popular press) simply that her Bill had been intended to provide for divorce on the ground of irretrievable breakdown: *Sunday Dispatch* 5 July 1959.

[31] See Biographical Notes.

[32] See on the private member's Bill procedure generally JAG Griffith and M Ryle with MAJ Wheeler-Booth, *Parliament, Functions, Practice and Procedures* (1989) Chapter 10; PA Bromhead, *Private Members' Bills in the British Parliament* (1956); and on the use of this procedure in the context of divorce legislation PG Richards, *Parliament and Conscience* (1970).

[33] The Matrimonial Causes Bill, Bill No. 22, 1950/51. The Debate is reported in *Official Report* (HC) 9 March 1951, vol. 485, col. 926.

[34] Draft letter to *The Times*, 22 March 1951: *Eirene White Papers*.

[35] This was an issue which the reformers had to handle with some care: on the one hand the fact that a large number of men (some 3,000 each year) were prepared to go to prison rather than comply with magistrates' maintenance orders could be presented as indicating the extent of bitterness felt by people subject to a gross injustice: see Colonel Lipton's speech, *Official Report* (HC) 31 October 1950, vol. 480, col. 82. On the other hand it could be said to demonstrate the ineffectiveness of the legal system in compelling men to meet their responsibilities. Mrs White and others favoured the introduction of attachment of wages to provide effective redress.

[36] It has been claimed that at this period rather more than half of all women aged between 16 and 60 were housewives, wholly occupied in the care of their homes and families. The interests of such women had been vigorously promoted by a number of groups, notably the Married Women's Association: see below.

Mrs White's Bill invoked 'a new principle, in that it looks to the breakdown of the marriage as the ground for divorce'[37] (whilst not prejudicing the right of an injured party to seek divorce under the existing matrimonial offence provisions); and effect was to be given to this policy by simply adding seven years' separation to the existing grounds for divorce and requiring the court to be satisfied that there was no reasonable prospect of cohabitation being resumed.[38] But the Bill went further. In an attempt to ensure that a divorced wife should be no worse off (and might even be better off)[39] financially as a result of divorce the court was to have power to withhold a decree unless satisfied that a petitioning husband had made adequate provision for his family's maintenance.[40]

These contrasting provisions of the Bill encapsulated the main issues of the debate which was to take place about divorce for the next 20 years: few lay people[41] were prepared to dissent (at least in public) from the principle that a marriage which had irretrievably broken down should be dissolved, but there was a great deal of concern about the damage (particularly the financial damage) which divorce might do to married women in general and 'innocent' wives in particular.

The Government's difficulty

The Government was in a difficulty. The Lord Chancellor's officials warned him that the Bill had a 'good deal of support among all parties'.[42] But another

---

[37] This and the following quotations are taken from the Explanatory Memorandum to Mrs White's Bill: the Bill itself did not mention breakdown as a ground for divorce or otherwise.

[38] Clause 1 of the Bill.

[39] *Official Report* (HC) 9 March 1951, vol. 485, col. 929. Mrs White's claim that a husband could not 'even claim to have his petition heard unless he can satisfy the court that he has fulfilled his financial obligations towards the family' slightly exaggerated the effect of the provision which was merely to give the court a *discretion* to withhold a decree.

[40] In correspondence with the solicitor and long-time supporter of divorce reform Ambrose Appelbe (see Biographical Notes) Mrs White accepted that her Bill would make unilateral 'what is now in fact divorce by mutual consent in about 90% at least of the ordinary cases and putting the ageing and less physically attractive woman at a further disadvantage in what is so frequently a sex trouble' and that her Bill would take away the bargaining power of the middle-class married woman who could as the law then stood insist as the price of divorce on terms such as the transfer of most of the family assets. Mrs White responded that she had intended to introduce a clause to try to meet this problem and had forborne from doing so in the Bill originally presented in the interests of keeping it brief and straightforward. She hoped that the Royal Commission would be able to make better provision than could be done by moving amendments in the House of Commons: see letters of 9 March and 4 April 1951, *Eirene White Papers*.

[41] The Roman Catholic Hierarchy continued to deny the validity of any secular divorce; whilst within the Church of England the Mothers Union continued to oppose any extension of the ground for divorce. Rosamond Fisher (Central President of the Union and wife of the then Archbishop of Canterbury) initiated a vigorous correspondence in *The Times* with a letter on 6 March 1951 urging rejection of the White Bill.

[42] Dobson to Jowitt, 5 March 1951, PRO LCO2/4854. The promoters of the White Bill devoted considerable effort to emphasising the all-party nature of the support for reform—not least by the choice of the Scottish Tory Laird, Martin Lindsay of Dowhill ('22nd in derivation from Sir William Lindsay, 1st of Dowhill, 1398') and war hero (CO 1st Battalion The Gordon Highlanders, wounded on active service, DSO) to second the motion for a Second Reading. Mr Lindsay

general election could not be long away. Legislation, even by Private Member's Bill,[43] could have serious electoral implications for the Labour Party[44] (and all the more so if the White Bill were amended to shorten the prescribed seven-year period of separation to five years or even two,[45] or if the protection Mrs White's Bill sought to provide for the 'innocent' were eroded). In the past, the Government had rejected calls for a Royal Commission to investigate the whole subject; but faced with a choice between a Commission and the possibility of immediate (and perhaps electorally damaging) legislation the Government did not hesitate for very long. It would try to get the White Bill thrown out (or withdrawn) by agreeing to set up a Royal Commission.[46] In this way the Government would have bought time, even though it believed a Commission was unlikely to produce a unanimous report.[47]

In the Second Reading debate the Attorney-General, Sir Hartley Shawcross,[48] tried desperately[49] to persuade the Commons to accept the Government's advice

followed the precedent of others initiating legislation on this subject by asserting that his long and happy marriage meant that he would not seek relief from the Bill or any other; but in fact his first marriage was dissolved in 1967. Two other Conservatives were amongst the Bill's sponsors: Mrs Eveline Hill (1898–1973) MP for Manchester, Wythenshawe; and the right-wing Ulster born Unionist MP (since 1925) for Ayr Burghs, Lt Col Sir Thomas Moore (who also—greatly to the surprise of Dr Edith Summerskill—supported her Women's Disability Bill in 1952: see *A Woman's World* , 1967 p. 150). Liberal backing came from the MP for Camarthen, Hopkin Morris KC. The other sponsors were all Labour MPs: Colonel Lipton (see above); Ian Mikardo (1908–1993) the left-wing MP for Reading South; John Paton (former General Secretary of the Independent Labour Party, author of two revealing volumes of autobiography—*Proletarian Pilgrimage* (1935) and *Left Turn* (1936)—about his career as a left-wing socialist); the newly elected MP for Coventry South Miss Elaine Burton (1904–1991, an accomplished athlete, ennobled in 1962); Mrs Caroline Ganley JP (1879–1966, MP for Battersea South).

[43] The Attorney-General asserted the then accepted constitutional usage that it had 'long been a necessary tradition of our affairs that in matters such as this the Government does not seek to impose any collective view upon the House, nor can they usefully express a collective voice': *Official Report* (HC) 9 March 1951, vol. 485, col. 999.

[44] Much of the Labour Party's electoral strength was at this time concentrated in areas in which the Roman Catholic church had a strong influence.

[45] As JES Simon KC (subsequently President of the Probate Divorce and Admiralty Division of the High Court) pointed out in a powerful letter to *The Times* on 9 March 1951 opposing the 'fundamentally new principle' which the White Bill embodied, once a marriage had irretrievably broken down it could plausibly be argued that the sooner 'the farce was ended' the better, and that seven years might seem an intolerably long period to wait. In evidence to the 1956 Morton Royal Commission Mrs Eirene White admitted that the period of seven years was chosen because it had been mentioned as a 'possible period by the Denning Committee, and it was felt that it would be advisable . . . to have the implied support [*sic*] of a body of some standing which considered that such a matter should at least be worthy of consideration'. Mrs White went on to say that provided the various economic sanctions which she regarded as essential were fully enforced a 'somewhat shorter period' would be advisable: *Morton Report Evidence*, q. 13.

[46] The Lord Chancellor admitted this to the Archbishop of Canterbury: Jowitt to Fisher: see PRO LCO2/6131.

[47] Cabinet Conclusions, 8 March 1951, CM (50) 11th Conclusions, Minute 3, copied on LCO2/4854.

[48] See Biographical Notes.

[49] Some MPs claimed that the Attorney had tried to intimidate MPs in the Division Lobby: *Official Report* (HC) 9 March 1951, vol. 485, cols. 1016–1018.

not to attempt to deal 'piecemeal' with a single aspect of a very wide problem but rather to allow a Royal Commission to study and report on the 'whole field' of the marriage laws. On this occasion, however, his usually persuasive advocacy[50] failed to convince. Mrs White and her friends refused to accept his plea not to take the Bill to a division because to do so would 'inevitably gravely prejudice any subsequent inquiry by a Royal Commission';[51] and the Bill was given a Second Reading by 131 votes to 60.[52] It is perhaps significant that a hundred more MPs were prepared to reveal their position to the public than had done so by voting on the Second Reading of the Herbert Bill in 1936 (when only 90 MPs voted).

The decision to establish a Royal Commission on Marriage and Divorce

In fact it was highly unlikely that the promoters could have got a Bill through all its stages in both Houses of Parliament in the six months (or less) which remained of the current Session;[53] but by this time it only had a tiny majority in the Commons and did not want to have the anxiety of votes on a Divorce Bill raising passions and interfering with the legislative programme. For this reason (notwithstanding the Attorney's threats[54] that if the White Bill were taken to a division there would be no Royal Commission) the Government agreed to go ahead with the appointment of a Commission;[55] and Mrs White withdrew her

---

[50] Shawcross's catalogue (see *Official Report* (HC) 9 March 1951, vol. 485, cols. 1001–1004) of the 'other problems' requiring consideration at the same time as the ground for divorce ranged from 'uncertainty of the law as to non-consummation and nullity', the rules prescribing the prohibited degrees for marriage, and the legal consequences of artificial insemination, through other questions about divorce (the role of the King's Proctor—'a very important matter'; the bars to divorce; damages for adultery, whether the law of maintenance was satisfactory, the rules about jurisdiction in cases with a foreign element) to the topic he regarded as the foremost amongst them: the 'problem of dealing with the unhappy children of these unhappy marriages'. This latter matter had already been the subject of a debate in the House of Lords on 14 February 1951.

[51] *Official Report* (HC) 9 March 1951, vol. 485, col. 1004.

[52] *Official Report* (HC), 9 March 1951, vol. 485, col. 1020.

[53] This point was made by the Conservative MP (and opponent of the Bill) Lord Winterton: *Official Report* (HC), 9 March 1951, vol. 485, col. 1006. The small Government majority meant that the situation in the Commons was unusually volatile, and the Whips had to resort to unpopular tactics in order to prevent the Government being defeated: see *The Times*, March 1951, *passim*.

[54] 'If the House rejected the view which I have ventured to commend to it, that we should not seek to prejudice the inquiries by a Royal Commission, we should, of course, have to reconsider whether the establishment of a Royal Commission would serve such a useful purpose . . . I am saying that . . . it would be very unwise to take a vote upon this matter if the House agrees that the proper course is to submit it to a Royal Commission': *Official Report* (HC), 9 March 1951, vol. 485, col. 1006. Notwithstanding the Attorney's repeated assertions that he was not seeking to make the offer to establish a Royal Commission conditional on the sponsors withdrawing the Bill without going to a division the note of menace is apparent in his remarks. After the vote he repeated that the Government would reconsider the proposal to set up a Royal Commission: see col. 1020.

[55] The decision was announced by the Prime Minister on 14 March 1951: *Official Report* (HC), 14 March 1951, vol. 485, col. 1536; but publication of the terms of reference and membership were delayed: see below.

Bill,[56] agreeing (in public at least)[57] that the complexity of the issues pointed to this approach to reform.[58] Ministers and Officials settled down to the task of settling the Commission's precise terms of reference and choosing its members.

THE ROYAL COMMISSION

Terms of reference

Agreeing the Royal Commission's terms of reference proved to be comparatively straightforward. The Government had justified opposition to the White Bill by asserting the wide scope of the problems to which reform would give rise and their complexity; and so it was decided that the Commission's investigations should not only cover divorce and matrimonial causes, the domestic jurisdiction of magistrates,[59] and the law governing the prohibited degrees for marriage but also the law relating to property rights of husband and wife during marriage and after its termination 'having in mind the need to promote and maintain healthy and happy married life and to safeguard the interests and well-being of children'.[60-61]

---

[56] To the annoyance of some of her supporters such as Colonel Lipton and Douglas Houghton. Mrs White's motion that Standing Committee B should not proceed with the Bill was carried on a division by 20 votes to 8, the minority including some of the strongest supporters of reform.

[57] On 14 March 1951 Mrs White asked the Prime Minister for assurances that the terms of reference would be wide enough to cover cognate matters such as pensions, insurance and marriage guidance and advice so that people could be 'helped to avoid' broken marriage; but on 21 March *The Times* published a letter from her saying that the complexity of the issues pointed to a Royal Commission investigation as the basis for reform, and in evidence to the Morton Commission she stated that she was 'extremely glad' the Government decided to appoint a Royal Commission because the complex factors involved 'could not have been adequately dealt with . . . by the process of taking a Bill through the Committee Stage in the House of Commons: *Morton Report Evidence*, q. 3. However, BH Lee, *Divorce Law Reform in England* (1974) p. 26 suggests that Mrs White had been unable to resist 'mounting pressure from the Government' to accept their preferred solution.

[58] See her speech in Standing Committee B, *Official Report*, 17 April 1951: she pointed out that the prospects of the Bill reaching the statute book were 'so remote as to be negligible' (col. 3); but she also conceded—to the evident annoyance of some who had supported the Bill—that the introduction of the new breakdown principle for divorce would make it necessary to have prolonged deliberations and consultation on appropriate safeguards, and that this was a task for which a Royal Commission was better fitted than the House of Commons.

[59] The terms of reference extended to the administration of the law as well as its content.

[60-61] The draft terms of reference had originally contained a reference to the desirability of increasing public regard for the sanctity of marriage; but this was eventually removed, perhaps because of the Lord Chancellor's officials' view that the phrase was 'somewhat propagandist' or because of the view of the newly appointed Attorney-General (Sir Frank Soskice) that the reference suggested bias and would be seized upon by those, particularly in the Labour Party 'who feel that there should be rather more freedom of approach': Soskice to Jowitt, 3 May 1951: PRO LCO2/6131.

Membership

The selection of Members was a much more difficult exercise. The task of chairing the Commission was first offered to the Tory aristocrat and educationalist Lord Eustace Percy.[62] However, his enthusiastic letter of acceptance[63] revealed that he held 'the strictest views about the indissolubility of marriage and also about the evil of dissociating religious principle from the marriage law of England'. The Government had to extricate itself[64] and find someone apparently more open-minded: eventually[65] the name of Fergus Morton[66] (an eminent Chancery Judge, appointed Lord of Appeal in Ordinary in 1947, and known to the Lord Chancellor's Department for his 'safe' handling in the previous year of the *Committee on the Law of Intestate Succession*)[67] emerged instead.[68]

The selection of Members to serve on the Commission required a decision on an issue of principle: should they be seen as in some sense representative of particular interests (and here the claims of religious bodies were particularly strongly pressed)[69] or should the Government try to appoint people with broad and open minds on the issue? The Attorney-General had told the House of Commons that he preferred the latter solution;[70] and the Government favoured a balanced and impartial membership made up primarily of 'ordinary men and women'.[71] But in practice this objective was easier to state than to achieve.

[62] See Biographical Notes.   [63] 5 April 1951, PRO LCO2/6131.

[64] The decision to offer the Chair to Percy is all the more remarkable since it appears that his deep religious convictions were widely known.

[65] Other names put forward for the Chair had included Lord Beveridge ('too old'), the Marquess of Reading (long-standing interest in family matters did not outweigh the fact that he was 'not a Christian') and a woman medical consultant (there were doubts about her being involved in a 'possible irregular relationship'): see PRO LCO2/6131.

[66] See Biographical Notes.   [67] 1951, Cmd. 8310.

[68] After some initial hesitation caused in part by concern about his health, Morton accepted with enthusiasm the prospect of a 'job which is so vitally important' on 2 June 1951: PRO LCO2/6131. His appointment and the Commission's terms of reference were announced on 10 June: *Official Report* (HC) vol. 490, col. 204.

[69] There was disagreement amongst Ministers about whether the churches should be represented on the Commission or merely invited to give evidence to it. The Lord Chancellor, whilst favouring the appointment of those without preconceived views realised that 'it may be impossible to avoid having a churchman': note by D Dobson, PRO LCO2/6131, 16 March 1951. Presumably to provide for this eventuality Jowitt had asked Archbishop Fisher for the names of suitable churchmen; but his suggestion that he and the Archbishop should meet 'quite privately' from time to time was apparently vetoed by his ministerial colleagues (see Jowitt to Fisher, 28 May 1951, PRO LCO2/ 1362) and would in any event have been frustrated by the defeat of the Labour Government in the 1951 General Election. The Government eventually decided to exclude clergy from the Commission, and were severely criticised by the Archbishop of York for so doing: *The Times*, 20 September 1951.

[70] *Official Report* (HC) 9 March 1951, vol. 485, col. 1005.

[71] In an undated pencilled note (PRO LCO2/6132) Lord Chancellor Jowitt minuted Dobson that the list he had put forward to the Cabinet (presumably at the first meeting to discuss the matter, held on 3 May 1951) had been 'very badly received' and criticised as consisting exclusively of 'bourgeois nonentities'. Officials plaintively recorded that the Cabinet considered the 'common man and woman' should be appointed, but 'how the common man is to be selected I do not know': Dobson to RMJ Harris, 4 May 1951, PRO LCO2/6132. Ministers were invited to suggest names of possible Commissioners: and eventually the list ran to ten foolscap pages. Three Heads or former Heads of

The membership of the Commission was not finally announced for some six months.[72] There can be no answer to the charge[73] that in terms of social composition the Commissioners were overwhelmingly upper and middle class. Nor can it be denied that the legal profession was numerically over-represented.[74] Nine of the nineteen signatories of the Commission's Report were legally qualified,[75] giving the clear impression that the Commission was to be concerned with a primarily legal, rather than a primarily social, issue. There was no representative of institutional religion; but equally there was nobody qualified to give any professional input from the social sciences. Six of the Report's nineteen signatories were women.[76]

The Royal Commission at work

The Commission set to work in the then traditional manner. It invited submissions from interested bodies, received written submissions, invited some of

Boys' Public Schools were named, as were the novelist and Labour publicist JB Priestley (but he was rejected perhaps because Sir John Maud, then Permanent Secretary at the Ministry of Education, considered he was 'not good on committees'), the actress Celia Johnson (possibly thought suitable because of her sensitive portrayal in the 1945 film *Brief Encounter* of a middle-class housewife seized by romantic passion for a doctor played by Trevor Howard) and John Fulton (the philosopher Principal of University College Swansea, subsequently Vice-Chancellor of the University of Wales and Chairman of the Committee on the Civil Service, 1966–68). The Minister of Defence, Emmanuel Shinwell, doubted the wisdom of having 'too many women on the Commission': 11 May 1951.

[72] For the membership, see p. 817, below.

[73] Made by OR McGregor, *Divorce in England* (1957) p. 179. The only commissioner with any obvious claim to represent the working classes was Ethel Brace (formerly Mayor of East Ham); although Sir Frederick Burrows had served in the ranks of the Grenadier Guards in World War I and had been President of the National Union of Railwaymen during World War II.

[74] In contrast, only one member of the Commission (Sir Walter Russell Brain) was medically qualified. Other Commissioners (Rosemary Portal, May Baird, Alice Bragg, Kate Jones-Roberts and Dr Violet MC Roberton (Deputy Chairman of the Corporation of the City of Glasgow and Member of Scottish Central Probation Council)) seem to have been actively concerned with Health or Social Service Management; whilst education was also well represented—by HLO Flecker, Headmaster of Christ's Hospital, and Robert Beloe, Chief Education Officer, Surrey County Council as well as George Brown (Hamilton Crescent Junior Secondary School).

[75] *viz*, Morton (Lord of Appeal), Keith (Appointed Lord of Appeal, 1955), Holroyd Pearce (High Court Judge—Divorce Division to 1953, thereafter Queen's Bench), Walker (Scottish Judge), Young (Sheriff), Mace (Liverpool solicitor) Jones-Roberts (woman barrister), Maddocks (Stipendiary Magistrate) and Lawrence (QC, subsequently High Court judge). This preponderance is all the more striking since at the outset Jowitt had thought it better not to have a judge on the Commission: LCO2/6131, note by Dobson, 16 March 1951. Professor McGregor claimed that the 'only apparent principle' in the choice of members of the Commission 'appears to have been the importance of securing a preponderance of lawyers': *op. cit.* p. 179.

[76] Viscountess Portal (Chairman of the Hampshire Children's Committee), Lady Bragg (WVS Administrator, sometime Mayor of Cambridge), Kate Jones-Roberts (barrister and Member of Advisory Council on Child Care and the Welsh Regional Hospital Board), Margaret Allen (Journalist and President of Watford Co-operative Society), May Baird (Chairman of the North-East Regional Board for Hospitals), Ethel Brace (sometime Mayor of East Ham).

those who had written[77] to give oral evidence,[78] and made enquiries about the law and practice in the Commonwealth, the United States, and a number of European states.[79] The Commission collected a considerable amount of statistical material about divorce rates, the number of divorce petitions and decrees, and so on.[80]

What did the Commission learn from the thousands of pages of written evidence and from the oral testimony given by 48 individual witnesses and the representatives of 67 organisations in the course of the Commission's 102 meetings?[81]

The case for and against breakdown as the ground for divorce

On the main issue of the ground upon which divorce should be obtainable the battle lines were quite clearly drawn in the first two days of oral evidence. Mrs Eirene White[82] made a powerful case for the principle of recognising the *de facto* breakdown of a marriage with no prospect of reconciliation as a sufficient ground for legal dissolution; but she was adamant that the economic sanctions against breaking up a home should be made more effective, that the court should have a discretion to refuse a divorce when there had been a failure to maintain, and that effective enforcement of maintenance obligations was the key to other reforms. As already noted, Professor LCB Gower[83] greatly irritated some of the lawyer members of the Commission[84] by his claim that many divorces (over half, he claimed, among the upper income groups) were collusive or based on bogus evidence. Gower said there was never any difficulty in getting a divorce if the parties were agreed; but this fact not only enabled one party to extort unduly favourable financial terms as the price of agreement but also often involved the parties in the degrading business of actual or pretended adultery

---

[77] The Commission received over 2,000 letters, statements and other written material. *The Morton Report*, para. 5, explains: 'The letters [from private individuals], which we found very helpful, generally contained accounts of the personal histories of the individuals concerned, and against that background the writers argued for or against various changes in the law. It would have been impracticable to ask all these correspondents to amplify their statements by oral evidence and in most cases we considered it unnecessary to do so. . . . As regards the memoranda, in some cases we did not ask those concerned to supplement their written evidence by oral testimony, either because their memoranda were complete in themselves, or had only an indirect bearing on our terms of reference, or because it was evident that the hearing of evidence would have involved substantial repetition of views on which evidence had already been given by others, or because they themselves did not wish to give oral testimony'.

[78] The Memoranda submitted to the Commission together with a verbatim record of the oral testimony given by 113 witnesses were indexed and published: see the *Morton Report, Minutes of Evidence*.

[79] Published in *Morton Report*, Appendix III.

[80] Published in *Morton Report*, Appendix II.   [81] *Morton Report*, para. 7.

[82] *Morton Report, Minutes of Evidence* p. 1.   [83] (1913–1997). See Biographical Notes.

[84] See *Morton Report, Minutes of Evidence* pp. 20–26; Professor McGregor's characterisation (in *Divorce in England* (1957) p. 139) of these passages as 'hostile and rude' is difficult to controvert. The accuracy of Gower's evidence was also denied in forceful language by the Bar Council's witnesses: *Morton Report, Minutes of Evidence* p. 46.

and always involved them deceiving the court. Gower accordingly favoured introducing divorce by consent (which would 'merely allow the parties to do openly what they now do clandestinely')[85] and (in the absence of consent) divorce based on a period of separation.[86]

The submissions made the next day on behalf of the General Council of the Bar were in sharp contrast. To introduce divorce by consent or on the unilateral demand of one spouse would (said the Bar's representatives) 'strike a disastrous blow at family life . . . [and] basically alter' attitudes towards marriage, whilst to accept the White Bill principle of breakdown would 'dangerously undermine marriage and family life'.[87] True, withholding divorce might lead to the formation of illicit unions, but that consideration was 'heavily outweighed by the protection and reinforcement of marriage and the family provided by limited grounds for divorce and the principle that if husband or wife commits a matrimonial wrong and breaks up the marriage he or she does not thereby establish a vested right to his or her freedom'.[88] 'The Bar's representatives claimed that it was their experience[89] of great numbers of divorce suits which convinced them that for many marriage had become a temporary affair with no degree of permanency. The cure was to call a halt to easier, cheaper and quicker divorce. In the circumstances it was hardly necessary to wait for the Roman Catholic[90] and Anglican churches[91] to denounce proposals inevitably making divorce more

[85] *Morton Report, Minutes of Evidence* p. 16.

[86] 'When the parties have been apart for seven years and the court is satisfied that there is no possibility of a reconciliation, to talk about preserving "the sanctity of marriage" appears to me to be casuistry': *Morton Report, Minutes of Evidence* p. 16.

[87] *Morton Report, Minutes of Evidence* pp. 28–29. The Bar Council was prepared to consider the recognition of additional matrimonial offences, but (believing that the utmost caution should be exercised in approaching any suggestion for extending the grounds for divorce) apparently did not favour any change beyond marginal amendment of the definition of 'incurable insanity'.

[88] *Morton Report, Minutes of Evidence* p. 29.

[89] Critics of the Royal Commission's Report (such as Lord Chorley: *Official Report* (HL) 24 October 1956, vol. 199, col. 983) were to point out that the experience of the Bar was much narrower than that of solicitors who routinely came into close contact with the parties to matrimonial proceedings; and it is certainly true that the evidence of the Law Society (see *Morton Report, Minutes of Evidence* p. 741) was much less hostile to reform proposals—favouring the abolition of Judicial Separation, for example because of its use for vindictive reasons or as a means of extortion, and the abolition of the bar of collusion—than that of the Bar.

[90] The Roman Catholic position had at least the merit of being straightforward and unequivocal: it 'is the firm belief of Catholics that according to the law of God himself there is no power on earth, ecclesiastical or civil, which can dissolve the bond of a valid and consummated marriage between two baptised persons'; and marriage even where the parties were not baptised Christians was 'essentially indissoluble according to the natural law: for it is of the very nature of marriage that it exists primarily for the procreation, education and welfare of offspring': Evidence of the Catholic Union of Great Britain 'with the approval of the Catholic Hierarchy of England and Wales': *Morton Report, Minutes of Evidence* p. 428.

[91] The Memorandum submitted by the Archbishop of Canterbury on behalf of the Church of England did accept that the law of the State could not be based solely on Christian Doctrine; but claimed that on social grounds the national standards and habit should approximate so far as possible to the Christian standard. The Memorandum claimed that, although divorce after seven years' separation had 'so easy an appeal as a remedy for hard cases' its acceptance would 'destroy the hitherto accepted principle of marriage, . . . be ethically unsound and . . . capable of causing great social mischief': *Morton Report, Minutes of Evidence* p. 137.

readily available, but the churches[92] duly did so. At least no one claimed that the churches'[93] opposition to change was motivated by financial self interest.

The rest of the evidence did not take matters much further. On the fundamental issue of the ground for divorce most of those who favoured significant change (as distinct from changes of detail on such matters as the definition of 'incurable insanity') would probably have accepted the position taken by the Haldane Society (of socialist lawyers):

'The law cannot make people love one another, or make them live together if they do not do so of their own free will . . . It should be recognised that the law can only do the following things for [couples unable to achieve or maintain a good marriage]: (a) decide whether they should have the legal status of being married; (b) protect a party who does not desire cohabitation against the attentions of one who does; (c) make and enforce orders as to the custody of children; (d) make and enforce financial arrangements. There can be genuine disputes about (c) and (d), and such disputes can be fit subjects for decision by the court. In the case of (a) and (b), the function of the law should be mainly declaratory—to give public recognition to an already accomplished change in the private relations of the parties.'

In effect the Haldane Society accepted the functional notion of the divorce law first articulated in the Gorell Royal Commission 40 years previously.

Divorce by consent?

There was a significant division within the pro-reform group between (on the one hand) those who would take the 'breakdown' concept to its logical conclusion by allowing the parties themselves to decide that their marriage should be legally terminated, and those (on the other) who continued to regard consensual divorce as inherently objectionable. This latter group would only allow divorce if the breakdown were evidenced by some objective fact (most obviously a period of separation, but perhaps also the commission of one or other of the traditional matrimonial offences) or perhaps by a judicial inquiry.

---

[92] Nonconformist opinion was much less dogmatically opposed to divorce; and the Methodist Church of Great Britain regarded the 1937 Act as a 'reform long due' alleviating hardship and removing grave scandal without impairing the Christian ideal of marriage: *Morton Report, Minutes of Evidence* p. 63. Even within the Church of England, the Modern Churchman's Union claimed that a large number of Anglican clergy and the majority of the laity did not support the 'rigorist' approach to divorce taken by the Archbishop of Canterbury, but would wish to recognise divorce as 'necessary and permissible as being the lesser of two evils' in certain cases. However, the Union concluded that the provisions introduced in 1937 (which it considered to have been on the whole beneficial) had made the grounds for divorce sufficiently wide and (with the possible exception of the introduction of habitual drunkenness as an additional ground) it did not favour further change. The Union was particularly outspoken in its opposition to divorce by consent; and expressed regret at the increased readiness of the courts to allow divorce to a petitioner guilty of adultery: *Morton Report, Minutes of Evidence* p. 507, and q. 4307.

[93] Compare the passage in McGregor's *Divorce in England* (1957) pp. 140–141 in which it seems to be suggested that this was a motive for the Bar's attitude.

The Marriage Law Reform Society[94] represents the first point of view. The Society's lengthy[95] and closely argued paper claimed that an 'honest and rational divorce law' would (despite a probable increase in the number of divorces) help morality and promote stability for the institutions of marriage and the family. In contrast, the existing law invited contempt and thus damaged those very institutions.[96] The Society believed that the State should provide simple and quick relief where the purpose of marriage had been frustrated. Couples should not have to break the law and to practise deceit and subterfuge in order to get a divorce.[97] The Society favoured not only divorce after a period of separation[98] but (believing that if 'two responsible persons together freely and knowledgeably decide that their marriage is ended, the State should, subject to certain precautions,[99] recognise this agreement') advocated allowing divorce by consent.[100] The Society realistically noted that suggestions for express legislative recognition of divorce by consent sometimes prompted 'violent' reaction; and felt it necessary to try and refute the argument that such a change would make English law comparable to that in force in the Soviet Union.[101]

The Divorce Law Reform Union in contrast rejected divorce by consent[102] and generally put forward a much less radical case in a notably deferential

---

[94] The Society, formed in 1946, claimed to have some 1,400 members, 'mostly sufferers from the present law': *Morton Report, Minutes of Evidence*, q. 1825. It had an influential list of sponsors (including Gerald Gardiner KC, the actor Michael Redgrave, the writers Leonard Woolf and J Middleton Murry, the popular journalist Hannen Swaffer, the leading academic lawyer Glanville Williams, and the philosophers Bertrand Russell and CEM Joad, the latter best known for his appearances in the BBC Radio Programme *The Brains Trust*). Like other pressure groups it suffered from lack of funds—having no office of its own and not even its own telephone number: see its newssheet, *Just Cause* No. 16. A dominant and effective contribution to the Society's activities (not least in writing serious and well informed articles for the quality press: see for example *The Contemporary Review* January 1951) was played by its Chairman, solicitor Robert Pollard, who had supplied Mrs White with a great deal of background material in connection with her 1951 Bill and also advised her about publicising the cause of divorce reform: see *Eirene White Papers*. Pollard's experience as chairman of a Magistrates' Domestic Court was of considerable value in advancing the case for reform.

[95] The Written Memorandum was 255 pages in length, with nine appendices in addition.

[96] The Society was equally outspoken in its condemnation of the bars of collusion and adultery. The Society claimed that ordinary people saw collusion as 'a silly legal device' to prevent divorce in cases where it was obviously appropriate. The court became involved in 'subterfuge and deceit'; and the provisions introduced by s. 4 of the Herbert Act had been of 'little or no avail', and encouraged lying and perjury. A bad law, unsupported by public opinion, was constantly disregarded: *Morton Report, Minutes of Evidence*, p. 225.

[97] *Morton Report, Minutes of Evidence*, p. 222.

[98] Initially it suggested that two years should suffice, but in oral evidence accepted that so short a period was an 'unrealistic' proposal put forward 'in a flush of enthusiasm' and substituted five years: *Morton Report, Minutes of Evidence*, q. 1840.

[99] For example, it was 'imperative' that such cases be dealt with by a court which would hear from the two spouses in person: Memorandum, para. 45, *Morton Report, Minutes of Evidence*, p. 234.

[100] The 'most intelligent and the most decent way of getting a divorce': Memorandum, para. 45, *Morton Report, Minutes of Evidence*, p. 234.

[101] Memorandum, para. 49, *Morton Report, Minutes of Evidence*, p. 235.

[102] *Morton Report, Minutes of Evidence*, q. 1599.

manner.[103] It should be possible (after time for careful reflection) for the court to terminate[104] marriages which existed in name only. For this purpose, five years' separation would be an adequate criterion.[105] The Union emphasised its wholehearted support for procedures to encourage reconciliation and for the protection of divorced wives and their children. There are signs of some tension[106] between the long established Union and the perhaps rather brash (and by this time much larger)[107] Marriage Law Reform Society.

The Morton Report: marital breakdown caused by failure to take 'proper view of marriage obligations'

The Royal Commission deliberated for four years. Its Report, published on Tuesday 20 March 1956, was suffused by 'grave anxiety' about what the Commissioners believed to be the fact that marriages were breaking up which in the past would have held together.[108] Some of the factors which had led to this 'disturbing situation' were (the Commission accepted) 'in themselves socially desirable and, in their other aspects, of benefit to the community'.[109] But the

[103] By Mrs EM Watson, and the barrister former Army Officer the second Lord Meston (who answered one question from Lord Morton 'I think it is a very good point [he] has made and I only wish we had been more helpful': *Morton Report, Minutes of Evidence*, q. 1569).

[104] Memorandum, para. 20, *Morton Report, Minutes of Evidence*, p. 194.

[105] It also advocated adding the following grounds for divorce:

(i) Refusal without just cause to have children. (The decision of the House of Lords in *Baxter v. Baxter* [1948] AC 274, denying a nullity decree to a man whose wife for ten years refused to allow intercourse unless he used a contraceptive sheath, had given some prominence to this issue.)

(ii) Respondent sentenced to five years or longer imprisonment.

(iii) Recurrent insanity (on the basis that the existing 'incurable insanity' ground was ineffective in many cases in which the 'continuation of the marriage is undesirable and procreation of children a positive danger').

(iv) 'Gross and frequent' drug taking or drunkenness.

In all cases, the husband's wilful refusal to support was to be a discretionary bar: Memorandum, para. 2 ff, *Morton Report, Minutes of Evidence*, p. 194.

[106] Lord Meston did not respond to a question about the relationship between the two bodies: *Morton Report, Minutes of Evidence*, q. 1562.

[107] DLRU membership was about 100 compared to the MLRS's 1,400: *Morton Report, Minutes of Evidence*, q. 1559, 1825. Much of the fire seems to have gone out of the DLRU with the enactment of the Herbert Act, which had given it much of what it had for so many years advocated. The death of many of its most prominent and active supporters—notably Mrs May Seaton-Tiedeman (who died at the age of 84 in 1948) and ESP Haynes (who died, aged 71, in 1949 having suffered the indignity of being struck off the roll of Solicitors the previous year) may have been a contributory factor.

[108] *Morton Report*, para. 42.

[109] One of these was that 'greater demands are now made of marriage, consequent on the spread of education, higher standards of living and the social and economic emancipation of women. The last is probably the most important. Women are no longer content to endure the treatment which in past times their inferior position obliged them to suffer. They expect of marriage that it shall be an equal partnership; and rightly so. But the working out of this ideal exposes marriage to new strains. Some husbands find it difficult to accept the changed position of women: some wives do not appreciate that their new rights do not release them from the obligations arising out of marriage itself and, indeed, bring in their train certain new responsibilities': *Morton Report*, para. 45.

root of the problem of increasing marriage breakdown was the tendency 'more dangerous, because more insidious in its effects, than any of the others'[110]

'to take the duties and responsibilities of marriage less seriously than formerly. Yet if, as we have said, more is now asked of marriage, it follows that more, not less, should be put into it. The result of this outlook is that there is less disposition to overcome difficulties and to put up with the rubs of daily life and, in consequence, there is an increasing disposition to regard divorce, not as the last resort, but as the obvious way out when things begin to go wrong. In other words, remedies which were intended for the relief of real hardship are used in cases where relief should be unnecessary if a proper view of their marriage obligations were taken by husband and wife'.

The cure: an increased sense of duty and obligation

What was to be done? Some of the Commissioners evidently believed that if the tendency to resort 'too readily and too lightly to divorce' were not checked it might 'become necessary to consider whether the community as a whole would not be happier and more stable if it abolished divorce altogether and accepted the inevitable individual hardships that this would entail'.[111] But the Report drew back from suggesting that divorce be made more difficult. Rather, the remedy lay

'. . . in fostering in the individual the will to do his duty by the community; in strengthening his resolution to make marriage a union for life; in inculcating a proper sense of his responsibility towards his children. These objectives can only be achieved by education in the widest sense, by specific instruction before marriage, and by providing facilities for guidance after marriage and for conciliation if breakdown threatens'.

Given this somewhat bleak and heavily 'obligation' focussed outlook, it is hardly surprising that the Commission did not look favourably on anything which could be seen as making divorce easier. Indeed, five[112] of the Commissioners doubted whether the introduction in 1937 of divorce for desertion had been of benefit to the community.[113] And the Commission was hope-

---

[110] *Morton Report,* para. 47. Amongst the other factors which the Report identified were the 'rapid and far-reaching social changes' which had taken place in the previous 40 years, and the consequent weakening of 'old restraints' before 'new ideals to take their place' had been fully formed. The Commission thought it was 'perhaps inevitable that at such a time there should be a tendency to regard the assertion of one's own individuality as a right, and to pursue one's personal satisfaction, reckless of the consequences to others. The teaching of modern psychology has been widely interpreted as laying emphasis on self-expression and the harmfulness of repression, with the consequent assumption that much that had previously held sexual licence in check could be jettisoned. The wider spread of knowledge in matters of sex is of great value but may have produced in the popular mind an undue emphasis on the overriding importance of a satisfactory sex relationship without a similar emphasis on the other stable and enduring factors of a lasting marriage': para. 46.

[111] *Morton Report,* para. 54.

[112] Lord Morton, Sir Frederick Burrows, Geoffrey Lawrence, David Mace, and Lord Walker. With the exception of Lord Walker (see below) these Commissioners all rejected the introduction of divorce on the ground of breakdown.

[113] The fact that nearly half of all divorce petitions were based on desertion suggested 'that this ground may often provide an easy way out for those who fail to take their marital responsibilities seriously and to show the proper spirit of give and take in married life'.: *Morton Report,* para. 139.

lessly divided on the main issue of what it should recommend in relation to the ground for divorce.[114] There were three different views.

A Commission divided

(1) Lord Walker's views

Only one member of the Commission, the Scottish judge Lord Walker, was prepared to take his stand on the ground of principle that the law should allow the dissolution of marriages which had broken down, irrespective of the 'guilt' or 'innocence' of the petitioner; and that accordingly divorce should be available to a spouse who had lived apart from the other for at least three years and could establish that the facts and circumstances were such as to make it improbable that husband and wife would ever resume cohabitation.[115]

But Lord Walker's position is often misunderstood. Far from being liberal or permissive he only supported abolition of the matrimonial-offence-based divorce law because he thought 'lax interpretation' had transformed it into a 'technical cause of action without a real cause for complaint'. True, Lord Walker thought that breakdown should become the ground for divorce but he insisted that the court would need to be satisfied *by proper evidence* that the alleged breakdown was indeed irretrievable. He certainly did not favour a permissive approach to the granting of divorce:[116] divorce by consent would 'destroy the concept of marriage as a life-long union';[117] and if (contrary to his preference) the offence principle survived he insisted that the letter of the law be followed 'as closely as may be' and without the addition of any separation ground.

---

[114] The Commission did unanimously recommend some minor additions to the grounds of divorce:

(i) wife accepting artificial insemination by a donor without her husband's consent: *Morton Report*, para. 90;
(ii) spouse mentally defective with violent or dangerous propensities and institutionalised for at least five years: para. 92;
(iii) sodomy and bestiality by a wife (equally as by a husband): para. 210.

The Commission also recommended that wilful refusal to consummate should cease to be a ground for nullity, and become a ground for divorce: para. 88. In relation to the bars to divorce, the Commissioners recommended a statutory definition of collusion, making it clear that the making of reasonable arrangements about child upbringing and financial matters should not be a ground for withholding a decree: *Morton Report*, paras. 234–235. The Commission also suggested minor amendments to the law of nullity of marriage: *Morton Report*, pp. 312–313. It was divided on a proposal to amend the law of condonation to encourage attempts at reconciliation: para. 241–3. The Commission made 81 other recommendations for change in the law and practice.

[115] 'Statement of his Views by Lord Walker': *Morton Report*, pp. 340–341, paras. 4, 7.

[116] Note his reservations about divorce for desertion: see note 112, above.

[117] Para. 3.

(2) The hard-liners: divorce only as relief for a proven matrimonial offence

The remaining 18 Commissioners fell into two groups, each of nine people. First, there were those[118] who simply rejected the introduction of the doctrine of breakdown of marriage in any form, and remained convinced that the matrimonial offence should remain 'the determining principle of the divorce law'.[119] True, there was an element of artificiality in supposing that all the right was on one side of the case and all the wrong on the other. But the offence doctrine none the less provided a 'clear and intelligible principle'.[120] The law helped men and women to strengthen their good impulses and weaken the bad,[121] and people needed the 'external buttress of a system of law' which specified the circumstances in which an individual had the right to seek the dissolution of marriage. The fact that a husband or wife tempted to be unfaithful would never be certain that he or she would be able to marry the lover and have legitimate children was a 'strong deterrent' to setting up an illicit union.

For this group, to allow divorce by consent would be a change 'disastrous to the nation' encouraging people to 'abandon their marriages on the flimsiest provocation';[122] whilst to allow divorce simply on the basis of a period of separation 'would have even more damaging consequences for the institution of marriage . . . it would mean that either spouse would be free to terminate the marriage at pleasure . . . [and] people would enter marriage knowing that no matter what they did or how their partners felt, they could always get free'.[123] For these nine members, the proper function of the law was to give relief where a wrong had been done, not to provide a dignified and honourable means of release from a broken marriage.[124]

(3) The 'liberals': divorce permissible after long separation in some circumstances

The second group of nine recognised that matrimonial offences were in many cases merely symptomatic of the breakdown of the marriage; and accepted the principle that the law should make provision for divorce in some circumstances of irretrievable breakdown even if there were no matrimonial offence.[125] These nine Commissioners favoured allowing divorce when the fact of breakdown had been demonstrated by the spouses having lived apart for seven years or more. But five[126] of this group would have refused divorce for separation if either party

---

[118] ie Lord Morton, Robert Beloe, Lady Bragg, Sir Russell Brain, Sir Frederick Burrows, Henry Flecker, Geoffrey Lawrence, David Mace, and Mr Justice Pearce. Four of these were practising lawyers.
[119] *Morton Report*, para. 69 (xxxvi).   [120] *Morton Report*, para. 69 (xxxvi).
[121] *Morton Report*, para. 69 (xxxvii).   [122] *Morton Report*, para. 69 (viii).
[123] *Morton Report*, para. 69 (xiii).   [124] *Morton Report*, para. 69 (xiii).
[125] *Morton Report*, para. 70 (vii).
[126] ie Margaret Allen, Ethel Brace, Henry Maddocks, Viscountess Portal and Sheriff Young. Two of these were lawyers.

objected;[127] and even the four[128] prepared to accept separation-divorce against the will of one spouse would have insisted on an applicant in such a case demonstrating that the separation was attributable to 'unreasonable conduct of the other spouse'.

One thing is abundantly clear. Sir Hartley Shawcross had been quite wrong to fear that a Commons vote in favour of the White Bill would in some way tie the hands of a Royal Commission. Far from feeling bound by the House of Commons vote for 'breakdown' divorce[129] the Commission seems to have given it no weight whatsoever. Only four of the Commission's 19 members were prepared to support the reform for which an impressive majority of the House of Commons had voted in March 1951. 'Informed opinion' had been decisively— almost offensively—rejected.

REACTIONS TO THE *MORTON REPORT*

Reaction to the Royal Commission's massive 405-page document with its 149 recommendations on detailed matters of law and practice[130] was at first curiously muted. This may have been in part because those who had for so long campaigned for more liberal divorce did not quite know how to respond to the rejection of their case.[131] Rather surprisingly, perhaps, the immediate response from within Whitehall seems to have been that the support of nine members for a proposal 'somewhat on the lines of Mrs Eirene White's Bill' would 'set off a strong demand for the adoption of a proposal of this kind'.[132] The Conservative Government[133] was sensitive to the charge[134] that Royal Commissions were a 'recognised and timely method of shelving inconvenient questions' and decided that the Lord Chancellor[135] should announce the Government's intention to take 'all possible steps by means of subordinate legislation, amendment of the

---

[127] *Morton Report*, para. 70 (viii).

[128] Dr May Baird, George Brown, Kate Jones-Roberts, and Lord Keith of Avonholm (the only one of the four engaged full time in the profession of the law).

[129] Lord Morton suggested the vote was influenced by party political considerations: *Official Report* (HL) 24 October 1956, vol. 199, col. 983.

[130] For legislation prompted by recommendations in the *Morton Report*, see pp. 344–345, below.

[131] The Marriage Law Reform Society was predictably dismissive, rejecting the Report as 'of little social value': *The Times*, 21 March 1956. Robert Pollard appeared on a BBC TV *Panorama* programme six days after publication of the Commission's Report and condemned the Report as the work of 'rigid, timorous English lawyers' only to prompt the response from *Marriage Guidance* (May 1956, p. 16) that his 'vigorous and unreasonable attack [on, amongst other things, the Commission's emphasis on marriage guidance] secured widespread sympathy for the responsible outlook of the Marriage Guidance movement'.

[132] Minute by Dennis Dobson, PRO LCO2/6139, 16 March 1956.

[133] Returned, at a General Election held on 26 May 1955 with an increased overall majority of 58 seats. The Conservatives remained in power until October 1964.

[134] Which was indeed made by the Labour Lawyer Peer Lord Silkin (see Biographical Notes) in a House of Lords debate he initiated in October: see *Official Report* (HL) 24 October 1956, vol. 199, col. 972.

[135] Viscount Kilmuir: see Biographical Notes.

rules of court, administrative and Private Members' Bills'[136] to give effect to
those recommendations of the Royal Commission which they accepted and
which were susceptible to this treatment'.[137] But there could be no prospect of
finding time in the immediate future for Government sponsored primary legislation, even on widely supported recommendations (such as improved facilities
for Marriage Guidance[138] and the proposal that the court should not allow a
decree nisi to be made absolute unless and until it was satisfied that proper
arrangements had been made for the care and upbringing of children). As for the
ground for divorce itself, in the light of the divergent views put forward in the
Morton Report no one could 'possibly expect' any Government to introduce
legislation permitting divorce (even by consent) after a separation of seven
years.[139] Any kind of official support for legislation permitting a 'man who had
gone off leaving a guiltless wife for seven years [to] come back and divorce her
against her will'[140] seemed even less likely to be forthcoming.

The case against the *Morton Report*

The reformers may have been slow to voice their bitter disappointment at the
Royal Commissions's rejection of the case for major change in the ground for
divorce but the publication in 1957 of *Divorce in England, A Centenary Study*
by the distinguished social historian, Professor OR McGregor[141] left no room

[136] Kilmuir had obtained Cabinet approval to his saying that the Government would entertain
proposals for Private Members' Bills and hinting that the assistance of parliamentary draftsmen
might be made available in appropriate cases: LCO2/6139, HP(56) 22 October 1956.

[137] As Lord Mancroft (who had given evidence to the Royal Commission in favour of relaxation
of the prohibited degrees of marriage, but had entered the Government as Under-Secretary of State
at the Home Office and thereby had responsibility for policy in this area) put it in a minute to Dennis
Dobson in the Lord Chancellor's Department: the Home Affairs Committee felt 'we must do all we
can to enhance such jam as we have wrapped round the pill' (PRO LCO2/6139, undated).

[138] Peers seemed to have curious views about this topic. Lord Silkin evidently believed that it
would include giving engaged women cookery lessons so that their husbands would not have to
share this task: *Official Report* (HL) 24 October 1956, vol. 199, col. 975. There were also somewhat
bad tempered exchanges suggesting that the Royal Commission had been overweighted with those
engaged in Marriage Guidance: *Official Report* (HL) 24 October 1956, vol. 199, col. 1014.

[139] The Government's approach was first indicated in answer to a question put by Colonel Lipton
to the Attorney-General (Sir Reginald Manningham Buller, who subsequently, as Lord Chancellor
in 1963 was one of the main facilitators of the moves leading eventually to the Divorce Reform Act
1969: see p. 353 below): *Official Report* (HC) 4 June 1956, vol. 553, col. 681. Lipton suggested that
unless there were legislation in the following Session many people would regard the Royal
Commission as having been 'rather a waste of time and money' but this evidently did not weigh with
the Government: see Kilmuir's speech in the debate on the Report initiated by Lord Silkin: *Official
Report* (HL) 24 October 1956, vol. 199, col. 1058. Although Kilmuir had told the Cabinet's Home
Affairs Committee that 'he proposed to say no more than that the Government had no present intention of introducing legislation' permitting separation divorce (PRO LCO2/6139, HP(56) 22 October
1956) he used much stronger language in the Debate.

[140] Lord Morton claimed in the debate that 'not a single member of the Commission' had supported such legislation: *Official Report* (HL) 24 October 1956, vol. 199, col. 983. But it appears that
Lord Walker would have been prepared to allow divorce in such circumstances. Where he differed
from the White proposals was that he favoured breakdown established by separation as the *sole*
ground for divorce.

[141] See Biographical Notes.

for doubt. McGregor's brilliantly written text, supported by a wealth of statistical, demographic and historical material, claimed that the Morton Report 'contributed nothing to . . . knowledge', suggested that the Commission was 'intellectually the worst' and its Report the most 'unreadable and confused' Royal Commission report of the twentieth century. Professor McGregor concluded that the Report was no more than a 'device for obfuscating a socially urgent but politically inconvenient issue'.

McGregor's book has been influential in creating an enduring and strongly unfavourable perception of the Morton Commission. Criticism has focussed on three main issues.

(i) Failure to use statistical information

The first, and most powerful, criticism of the *Morton Report*[142] was that the Commission did not obtain adequate statistical information, and that it made inadequate use of the information which it did collect.[143] This criticism is not easy to refute. For example, the Commission seems to have made no attempt to quantify the number of what came to be called 'stable illicit unions' in spite of the fact that it had been uncertainty[144] about the scale of this problem and about how far the law of divorce was responsible for the phenomenon which had powerfully influenced the decision to establish a Royal Commission. And yet it is by no means certain that such evidence would really have been material to the issue of principle facing the Commission. No one disputed that the denial of divorce caused hardship to many, but the question was how far that hardship had to be tolerated in the interest of preserving the principle that marriage is to be seen as a life-long relationship. In any event, the belief that evidence[145] from

[142] See Lord Chorley's speech, *Official Report* (HL) 24 October 1956, vol. 199, col. 1013; and for a balanced critique O Kahn-Freund, 'Divorce Law Reform?' (1956) 19 MLR 573.

[143] Professor OR McGregor in *Divorce in England* (1957), pp. 186–187 states: the Commission 'obtained, but did not publish as evidence, compilations from the Registrar-General. Thirteen tables and two diagrams are printed without discussion or explanation of their meaning in a forlorn appendix to the Report which makes, significantly, hardly any reference to them. The statistics of divorce are notoriously scanty and uninformative yet the Commission made no suggestions for their improvement . . . [Without collecting information about] the incidence of divorce amongst town and country dwellers, or by occupational and income groups . . . Commissioners could not pass from the contemplation of unsupported conjectures to the study of reality. As the Commissioners decided not to collect social evidence and obtained none from witnesses, their Report is a soufflé of whipped conjectures'.

[144] Mrs White had made unsuccessful attempts to ascertain the numbers from official sources; but it was pointed out that legislation would be required to require the parents of an illegitimate child to reveal whether or not they were free to marry; and the official view was that Parliament might be unwilling (as was apparently the case with the Population (Statistics) Bill in 1937) to give such a power: Blenkinsop to White, 6 March 1951, *Eirene White Papers*.

[145] McGregor believed that a research secretariat could have provided the Commission with (a) an analysis of statistical data with suggestions for improvement; (b) empirical investigations designed to test witness' assertions about attitudes to marriage and other matters; (c) an analysis of divorce petitions 'in order to make a study of the changing incidence of divorce by social class during the last half-century'; (d) provision of 'socially relevant information' about the use of magistrates' separation and maintenance orders; (e) a factual study of the consequences of their parents' divorces for a representative sample of children: *Divorce in England*, p. 187.

social scientists could (as McGregor claimed)[146] really have provided 'actual knowledge of the types of divorce law most likely to promote marital and familial stability' may be met with a certain scepticism. For example, the most expert social scientists have been shown to be unreliable even in predicting the future extent of recourse to divorce. McGregor dismissed almost with contempt fears that 60,000-odd decrees absolute 'would become the community's normal divorce habit'; 40 years later as many as 140,000 divorce petitions each year had become the norm. Looking back from the year 2000 it can be seen that the earlier prophecies were indeed false, but only in *under*estimating the long term future trend in recourse to divorce.

(ii) Commission dominated by lawyers and lawyers' concerns

Critics claimed that the Morton Commission was dominated by lawyers and their concerns. Even the terms of reference were couched in 'legalistic terms'; and this was said to have led the Commissioners to adopt an approach based on legal procedures, and to give inadequate attention to family breakdown as a matter of social policy.[147] The statistical over-representation of lawyers cannot be denied, and this no doubt is one of the factors which led critics[148] to see a heavy bias 'towards upper- and middle-class outlooks' amongst the Commissioners.

(iii) Commission lacked vision

Finally, and most subjectively, critics claimed that the Commissioners lacked vision[149] and failed to give the clear lead which was their responsibility on the major issues of controversy.[150] The reader must decide whether Lord Morton's riposte[151] that the Commissioners were an 'average cross-section of reasonably intelligent and hard-working people' and that the division on the main issue of policy probably reflected public opinion is adequate. But it is certainly true that the Morton Commission's concentration on the views of those involved in the legal system about its operation and impact, and the views of lawyers and others about the effects of the divorce law[152] made it an easy target for hostile

---

[146] *Divorce in England*, p. 192.

[147] See O Kahn-Freund, 'Divorce Law Reform?' (1956) 19 MLR 573. Similar criticisms of the Commission's composition were made by Lord Chorley (who, as Lord Kilmuir could not resist pointing out, had actually been a member of the Government which established the Commission): *Official Report* (HL) 24 October 1956, vol. 199, col. 1013.

[148] OR McGregor, *Divorce in England* (1957) p. 179.

[149] O Kahn-Freund, 'Divorce Law Reform?' (1956) 19 MLR 573, 600.

[150] A criticism made by the Home Office Minister Lord Mancroft: *Official Report* (HL) 24 October 1956, vol. 199, col. 994.

[151] *Official Report* (HL) 24 October 1956, vol. 199, col. 985.

[152] McGregor was critical of the Commission's apparent hostility to the evidence of Moya Woodside, a Research Psychiatric Social Worker at Guy's Hospital; but it is not surprising that evidence suggesting that 'many' of the parents in 114 'unhappy' homes (out of a total sample of 400 working class men and women in London 1943–1946) were 'severely maladjusted or psychopathic individuals, quite unsuited to bring up their own children' should have been greeted with incredulity by a group such as the Morton Commission.

criticism;[153] and that this factor influenced future developments. In particular, the need for any inquiry into marriage and the family to have an input from the social sciences became part of the conventional wisdom.

THE IMPACT OF THE *MORTON REPORT*: NO MORE THAN A 'RIPPLE ON THE SURFACE' OF THE TIDE[154]

In 1956 it must have appeared (as the *Finer Report* on one-parent families was to put it in 1974)[155] that the 'Morton Commission . . . had . . . put the quietus on divorce law reform for many years to come';[156] and Professor McGregor had in 1957 stated[157] that it was a 'safe prediction' that divorce reform 'would take a long, long time'. But within 15 years the Divorce Reform Act 1969 gave this country 'the most radical measure in the history' of English divorce law.[158] In the context of reform of the ground for divorce, Finer could (with only a little exaggeration) describe the *Morton Report* as 'little more than a ripple on the surface of a tide that was moving strongly in the other direction'.[159] How did this remarkable transformation come about?

---

[153] McGregor claimed that the hostility which he believed Lord Morton and his colleagues displayed to the social sciences led to their being 'unable to penetrate to the heart of the problems set before them'. At p. 199 of *Divorce in England* McGregor invoked a verse written by AP Herbert (*Punch* (1934), vol. 186, p. 708) satirising the methods used by an imaginary *Royal Commission on Kissing* to describe the unscientific approach he believed had been adopted by Morton: the imaginary Commission

'. . . collected evidence, but carefully dismissed
The opinion of anyone who actually kissed;
We summoned social workers from the cities of the North,
Good magistrates from Monmouth, Nonconformists from the Forth;
We summoned all the Bishops who were over sixty-one
And asked if they were kissed and, if they were, how it was done.
They answered in the negative and said there was abundant
Support for the opinion that the practice was redundant—
And that took a long, long, time.'

[154] *Report of the Committee on One-Parent Families* (1974, Cmnd. 5629) (Chairman: the Hon. Sir Maurice Finer) (hereafter referred to as *Finer Report*) para. 4.32.

[155] *Ibid.*

[156] The *Finer Report* allotted an equal share of the responsibility to the Church of England, which the Report—in this respect mirroring the strongly anti-clerical stance adopted by McGregor in his *Divorce in England* (1957)—regarded as 'the most influential opponent of change in the matrimonial law': *Finer Report*, para. 4.31.

[157] *Divorce in England* (1957) p. 199.   [158] *Finer Report*, para. 4.42.

[159] *Finer Report*, para. 4.32.

IMPLEMENTATION OF MORTON'S 'LEGALISTIC' REFORMS KEEPS
THE ISSUE OF REFORM ON THE AGENDA

The Conservative governments which remained in office until 1964 never departed from the decision[160] not to introduce legislation and not to support any Private Member's Bill[161] extending the grounds for divorce. But the Government did show itself ready and willing to take action on the Commission's other recommendations. The Cabinet's Home Affairs Committee set up a Committee of Civil Servants to 'consider the extent to which effect could be given to the [Morton] recommendations by means short of Government legislation'. This Committee carried out a meticulous examination of what could and could not be done. The 35-page tabular analysis produced in June 1957[162] showed that most of the Commission's recommendations capable of being implemented by subordinate legislation or administrative measures (mostly, of course, matters of procedural detail)[163] had already been acted on.

The Committee of Civil Servants also recorded that a significant number of Morton's other recommendations would be suitable for Private Members' Bills;[164]

---

[160] See *Report of Official Committee appointed to examine recommendations of Royal Commission on Marriage and Divorce*, 18 June 1957, PRO LCO2/6140, para. 3. But, whilst Lord Chancellor Kilmuir certainly agreed with this policy, his successor, Lord Dilhorne (Lord Chancellor July 1962–October 1964) was much more open-minded in his approach to reform, seems to have recognised that reform was inevitable, and took an active if discreet part in the events leading up to the formation in 1964 of the Archbishop's Group: see below.

[161] Note also that Mrs Eirene White told correspondents who had written urging reform in response to an article by her in the *Sunday Dispatch* 5 July 1959 that she had no intention of introducing a Bill since she did not think that 'in the present Parliament it would have any chance of success': *Eirene White Papers*.

[162] *Report of Official Committee appointed to examine recommendations of Royal Commission on Marriage and Divorce*, 18 June 1957, PRO LCO2/6140.

[163] For example, the Matrimonial Causes (Amendment) Rules 1957 gave the court the power which it had lacked to grant an injunction restraining the removal of children from the jurisdiction immediately proceedings were started.

[164] The Committee classified proposals as (a) 'acceptable and suitable for Private Member'; (b) 'suitable for Private Member, but not important'; and (c) 'Private Member should not be encouraged'. These classifications were not necessarily definitive: for example, the Committee classified the *Morton Report's* proposals about the matrimonial home and its contents (pp. 321–322) as 'difficult and controversial' and private members legislation was 'not to be encouraged', but eventually the Private Member's Matrimonial Homes Act 1967 gave effect to the *Morton Report's* proposals. Again, the Committee (fearing that it 'might well be controversial') was reluctant to encourage action on the *Morton Report's* recommendation that the court should declare its satisfaction about the arrangements to be made for the upbringing of children before making a divorce decree absolute; but the Matrimonial Proceedings (Children) Act 1958 dealt fairly comprehensively with the *Morton* recommendations (including extending the court's powers to step-children). The Committee recommended 'further study' in some cases and occasionally there were speedy results (eg the Maintenance Orders Act 1958 dealt with the highly complex topic of enforcing orders as well as the controversial subject of attachment of earnings—a subject on which the *Morton Report* pp. 282–285 had recommended against legislation).

and over the next few years much detailed reform took place[165] with the support of the Conservative Government.[166]

These detailed, and often technical, reforms can fairly be described as 'legalistic'; and the Government certainly did not intend to give any encouragement to those seeking further reform of the ground for divorce. But by keeping the subject of matrimonial litigation on the legislative agenda, these measures kept the possibility of reform in the minds of civil servants, MPs and other informed and concerned people.

LOBBYING AND PARLIAMENTARY ACTION: THE 1962 ABSE BILL

'Keeping reform on the agenda' was not of course enough for the many personally affected by the existing law and unable to take the dispassionate attitude

---

[165] Legislation included:

(a) the Maintenance Agreements Act 1957, empowering the court to vary maintenance agreements;

(b) the Matrimonial Causes (Property and Maintenance) Act 1958 (extending the court's powers to make financial orders, including orders for payments out of a deceased husband's estate);

(c) the Matrimonial Proceedings (Children) Act 1958 (extending the courts' powers to inquire into the post-divorce arrangements proposed to be made for the children);

(d) the Divorce (Insanity and Desertion) Act 1958 (relaxing the conditions under which divorce could be obtained against a spouse suffering from mental illness);

(e) the Legitimacy Act 1959 (permitting the children of void marriages to be treated as legitimate);

(f) the Marriage (Enabling) Act 1960 (permitting a divorced man or woman to marry relatives of his or her former spouse);

(g) the Matrimonial Proceedings (Magistrates' Courts) Act 1960 (changes in the domestic jurisdiction of magistrates: see also the *Report of the Departmental Committee on Matrimonial Proceedings in Magistrates' Courts* (1959, Cmnd. 638);

(h) the Matrimonial Causes Act 1963 which amended the law in an attempt to facilitate reconciliation; and also gave the court power to order one spouse to make a lump sum payment to the other. (This last reform, recommended by the Morton Commission, para. 516, deserves to be noted since it was the precursor of the extensive powers of the court to reallocate capital on divorce now embodied in Matrimonial Causes Act 1973.)

Moreover, the *Morton Report* for the first time highlighted the unsatisfactory position of divorced spouses in respect of pensions and this led to improvements in the conditions governing eligibility for the state retirement and widow's pensions: see the statement by the Minister of Pensions HP (56) 17th Meeting, 22 October 1956, PRO LCO2/ 6139. Finally, the Commission's Report also gave further support to state provision of reconciliation and marital guidance: *ibid.* and the speeches in the House of Lords debate: *Official Report* (HL) 24 October 1956, vol. 199, col. 971 and note that increases of 25% were made in government grants to the relevant voluntary agencies.

[166] The Lord Chancellor Kilmuir recorded his satisfaction at having been able to introduce or support some ten Acts of Parliament recommended in the 'valuable report' of his 'old friend' Lord Morton. There was particular satisfaction at the introduction of a measure intended to ensure the welfare of children 'so far as humanly possible, and mitigate the disaster to them of the failure of their parents' marriage': Kilmuir, *Political Adventure* (1964) p. 300.

appropriate for officials advising Ministers. The lobbying groups[167] continued
their activities. But the decisive step was taken in November 1962 by the Labour
MP and solicitor Leo Abse.[168] He drew a favourable place in the Ballot for Private
Member's Bills and used the opportunity to introduce a Bill[169] which would have
added seven years' separation to the grounds for divorce.[170] Abse took advantage
of the history of technical and legalistic reforms giving effect to Morton recommendations and skilfully presented his Bill (with all party support[171] from MPs of

[167] Although the comparatively newly formed Marriage Law Reform Society seems to have taken
a much more active part in campaigning than the Divorce Law Reform Union, it was apparently the
DLRU which in 1960 arranged for the lobbying of MPs in support of a proposed Matrimonial
Causes (Breakdown of Marriage) Bill allowing divorce for breakdown in cases in which the court
considered it to be fair and reasonable to do so but also giving the courts power to apportion responsibility for the breakdown which would then be taken into account in assessing maintenance etc.
Lord Chancellor Kilmuir (on the advice of his officials) repeated that no Government could be
expected to introduce legislation in the face of the division of opinion evidenced by the Morton
Commission's Report which was thought to reflect a similar division of opinion both in Parliament
and in the country at large. Kilmuir refused to commit the Government in advance to any course of
action should such a Bill be introduced by a Private Member, remarking that the subject 'bristles
with difficulties and would require the most careful consideration': Kilmuir to Brooke, 21 December
1960, PRO LCO2/6157. The papers in this file confirm that the Mothers' Union was actively lobbying MPs against any Bill on this subject; and the Lord Chancellor's officials advised him that the
'small trickle of letters' received since 1956 confirmed that there remained a 'wide cleavage of opinion'. But many informed observers would have agreed with JW Bourne (an official in the Lord
Chancellor's Department; subsequently Permanent Secretary 1977–1982) that the Morton
Commission had 'missed a golden opportunity' to put the law on a more logical footing by substituting the breakdown of marriage principle for that of the matrimonial offence: LCO2/6157.
[168] See Biographical Notes.
[169] The Matrimonial Causes and Reconciliation Bill, Bill 19, as ordered to be printed
21 November 1962. The title of the Bill is further evidence of Abse's wish to focus attention on supporting rather then destroying marriage; but at the Report stage in the House of Lords the
Government insisted that the short title be changed to the more orthodox 'Matrimonial Causes Act'.
[170] However, in defended cases the petitioner would have to satisfy the court the separation was
'in part due to unreasonable conduct of the respondent'; and the Bill also contained provisions
intended to protect the financial position of wife and children by requiring the court to dismiss a
petition by a husband who defaulted on his maintenance obligations to wife or children and requiring the court granting a decree on the basis of separation to take the wife's pension provision into
account in exercising its powers to make financial orders: clause 2(3) and (4).
[171] But one of the difficulties facing the reformers was that opposition to separation divorce was
also all-party. Abse alluded to this in his speech on the Second Reading debate, noting that the MPs
most conservatively minded on this issue might well be found on the Labour benches: *Official
Report* (HC) 8 February 1963, vol. 671, col. 806; and it appears that Labour voters and the unskilled
working class were more likely to be opposed to divorce reform than others: see the findings of the
1967 *Sunday Times* opinion poll as summarised in BH Lee, *Divorce Law Reform in England* (1974)
p. 87. Abse recalled in his memoirs (L Abse, *Private Member* (1973) p. 163) that '. . . a secret all-party
cabal of church and chapel members had been formed to kill the Bill. On the Tory side it was led by
[William] van Straubenzee . . . who became the voice of the bishops; and from the Labour Benches,
Eric Fletcher . . . a low churchman who co-ordinated opposition on the opposition benches. Both
Straubenzee and Fletcher were highly intelligent men, the one incredibly pompous and the other
infinitely dreary'. But the assessment Fletcher made of attitudes on the Labour benches seems to
have been accurate: the Archbishop of Canterbury's Lay Secretary Robert Beloe (see Biographical
Notes) recorded a 'most valuable meeting' with Fletcher who confirmed that, whilst most of the
party's intellectuals strongly favoured reform, there were also many MPs who were Roman
Catholics (or who had Catholic constituencies) and also 'many people in the Labour Party of the
rather inarticulate kind . . . representing Trade Union constituencies . . . [who] were disturbed' by
proposals for reform in this area: *Ramsey Papers*, vol. 43, 22 March 1963; and for Fletcher's own

standing)[172] as being primarily concerned to give effect to Morton's proposals for amending the law of condonation and collusion[173] in order to foster reconciliation and minimise hostility. But there could be no disguising the fact that the Bill would have allowed separation divorce. Abse put the case in a moderate and rational way. By focussing on the hardship caused to children born illegitimate[174] because their parents were unable to marry he was able claim that the Bill was not primarily 'about divorce but about family'[175] and above all about family stability.[176] Abse's speech was calculated to gain the sympathy of many committed to traditional family values; and he was also able to sow the seeds of doubt amongst the more sensitive opponents of separation divorce by claiming (in retrospect with justification) that if nothing were done to meet the plight of those whose legal marriages had long since ceased to exist in fact a far more radical measure would eventually get onto the statute book.[177] In this way Abse was able to suggest that these considerations more than outweighed the fact that to allow a woman to be divorced against her will when she had committed no matrimonial offence would

approach see his memoirs, *Random Reminiscences* (1986). It appears that Harold Wilson, Leader of the Labour Party, had ('possibly in order to quieten the outburst' by Labour reformers) committed the Shadow Cabinet to consider the whole principle of separation divorce: *Ramsey Papers,* vol. 43, note by Beloe 8 May 1963.

[172] Those who joined Abse in presenting the Bill were the barrister Liberal MP for Montgomery Emlyn Hooson (1925–); the Conservatives Joan Vickers (see Biographical Notes), John Foster QC (see Biographical Notes) and Nicholas Ridley (1929–1993; MP for Cirencester, subsequently a Cabinet Minister); and from the Labour Party David Weitzman QC (1893–1987; MP for Hackney North and Stoke Newington), John Morris (1931–; MP for Aberavon, subsequently Attorney-General in the Blair Government), Dick Taverne (1928–; MP for Lincoln—he subsequently resigned his seat and successfully fought a by-election as a 'Democratic Labour' candidate), John Parker (see Biographical Notes), Michael Foot (1913–; MP for Ebbw Vale, subsequently Leader of the Opposition) and Llywelyn Williams (1911–1965, MP for Abertillery, and a Congregational Minister). Abse was also successful in attracting the support in debate of highly respected elder statesmen—notably Captain Walter Elliot MC, Conservative MP for Glasgow Kelvingrove and Cabinet Minister in the pre-War National Government.

[173] By allowing for so-called 'kiss-and-make-up' exceptions to the law of condonation and by amending the law of collusion so as to encourage couples to make proper arrangements for the future before starting divorce proceedings: see *Morton Report,* paras. 230–243. These were not altogether uncontroversial: the 'kiss-and-make-up' recommendation was opposed by five members of the Morton Commission; and the 1957 *Official Committee appointed to examine recommendations of Royal Commission on Marriage and Divorce* had recommended that a Private Member should 'not be encouraged' to introduce a Bill to give effect to the proposal which it considered 'open to objection for reasons given by minority': PRO LCO2/6140.

[174] Abse painted an emotive picture of the '200,000 little ones, born into permanent but illicit unions . . . condemned to be brought up in an atmosphere of guilt and deceit and never to be legitimised': *Official Report* (HC) 3 May 1963, vol. 676, col. 1561. There was no doubt that the plight of such children was seen as an important feature of the case for reform, but estimates of the numbers involved varied: it was claimed that in 1961 37,000 children had been born into stable illicit unions, whilst John Parker MP claimed that as many as 40% of the two million illegitimate children were living with parents who were debarred from marriage.

[175] *Official Report* (HC) 3 May 1963, vol. 676, col. 1561.

[176] He claimed that it was 'misleading to talk of consistently mounting figures for divorce' at a time when marriage had 'never been so popular', and the family 'never . . . more secure': *Official Report* (HC) 8 February 1963, vol. 671, col. 808.

[177] *Official Report* (HC) 8 February 1963, vol. 671, col. 818.

be to make a 'fundamental change in the whole of the English law of divorce'.[178] His tactics appeared remarkably successful: only three MPs[179] spoke against the Bill on the floor of the House of Commons.

But appearances were deceptive. Opposition was being skilfully organised behind the scenes by the Archbishop of Canterbury's Lay Secretary,[180] Robert Beloe (one of the 'hardline' members of the Morton Commission who had rejected any compromise on the introduction of 'breakdown' as a ground for divorce). MPs opposed to separation divorce let it be known that any Bill containing such a provision would be 'talked out'.[181] Faced with this 'formidable opposition'[182] Abse withdrew the clause adding separation to the grounds for divorce in exchange for an agreement[183] that the other provisions in the Bill[184] would reach the statute book.[185]

---

[178] Sir Peter Rawlinson S-G, *Official Report* (HC) 8 February 1963, vol. 671, col. 858.

[179] They were: the Labour MP Eric Fletcher (see above), and the Conservatives Sir Peter Agnew and Charles Doughty (a Solicitor, partner in the leading firm of Withers & Co, whose founder—Sir John Withers—had played a large part in securing the enactment of the 1937 Herbert Act).

[180] For a somewhat fuller account, see SM Cretney, *Law, Law Reform and the Family* (1998) pp. 43–46. Beloe's briefing paper for the Archbishop was prophetically headed 'How to secure rejection of Mr Abse's clause'. In addition to his lobbying amongst members of both Houses of Parliament Beloe secured and publicised a statement by the Archbishops of Canterbury, York and Wales, the Moderator and General Secretary of the Free Church Federal Council and the Roman Catholic Archbishop of Birmingham. This statement (issued on 3 April 1963) declared that the provisions of the Abse Bill would cause injustice to the innocent and introduce into the law the 'dangerous new principle' that a marriage could be terminated by the desire of the parties and thus 'undermine the basic understanding of marriage as a lifelong union'. However, Beloe was unsuccessful in getting Jewish support for this proposition since (it was pointed out) Judaism accepted a measure of divorce by consent. Beloe's skill in obtaining the collaboration of the Free Churches is all the more remarkable in view of their traditionally less hostile attitude to divorce reform.

[181] A note by Beloe records that opponents of separation divorce had met and agreed to put down 'a great many amendments' to ensure this outcome: *Ramsey Papers*, vol. 43, 28 March 1963, and see also Beloe's 'Note on a meeting with Straubenzee on 9 April'—the 'plan was to prevent the Bill reaching the end of the Report stage . . . unless Abse withdrew the offending clause'.

[182] Leo Abse, *Official Report* (HC) 3 May 1963, vol. 676, col. 1557. In a bitter speech, Abse accepted that he had had 'no alternative but to yield to' duress: col. 1562. Opponents of the Bill—in a move said by Abse to be unprecedented—sought (unsuccessfully) to prevent the Bill being Reported: *Standing Committee C, Official Report*, 27 March 1963; L Abse, *Private Member* (1973) pp. 164–166 (which gives a particularly revealing account of the manoeuvring leading up to and during the Bill's Committee stage).

[183] According to a file note by Beloe, Abse had negotiated this with WR van Straubenzee MP, one of the main opponents of separation divorce and a prominent Anglican layman (see Biographical Notes): *Ramsey Papers* vol. 43, 2 May 1963; and see *Official Report* (HC) 3 May 1963, vol. 676, col. 1564. But it appears that Dr Jeremy Bray (1930–; at the time Labour MP for Middlesborough West) acted as an intermediary: see L Abse, *Private Member* (1973) p. 170. Straubenzee's 'immense amount of detailed staff work' in achieving the 'careful co-ordination and organisation' essential to defeating the separation provision was acknowledged in a letter (see *Ramsey Papers* vol. 43, 9 May 1963) to Beloe from David James MBE DSC MP a prominent Roman Catholic layman and director of the English Publishers to the Holy See.

[184] Intended to remove obstacles to reconciliation attempts. The provision empowering the Court to award a capital sum to a divorced spouse also survived.

[185] Abse's detailed account of the manoeuvres is invaluable: L Abse, *Private Member* (1973) pp. 162–171.

In the House of Lords Lord Silkin and others tried to reintroduce the separation divorce provision,[186] but Lady Summerskill[187] passionately and effectively advanced the case (founded primarily on fears of financial hardship to women) against what she described as 'the compulsion clause'. Once more the Church of England was active both in the debate[188] and behind the scenes;[189] and Lord Silkin's amendment was defeated on a division.[190]

Losing a battle, but winning the war?

In a bitter speech Abse had expressed his anger at having no alternative but to 'yield to duress'[191] and drop the separation divorce provision from the Bill. Yet, with the benefit of hindsight, it can be seen that his Bill directly paved the way for the Divorce Reform Act 1969. 'Technicalities' they may have been, but the changes introduced by the 1963 Act made the notion of divorce as a remedy given only to an innocent victim seem increasingly remote from reality. There were two particularly significant provisions.

---

[186] Abse's difficulties had been increased by a division of opinion, emerging publicly in the debate in Standing Committee C on 13 March 1963, about the need for any 'public interest' bar to separation divorce. Mrs Eirene White argued that it would not be right to provide for separation divorce without such a safeguard; and Dick Taverne successfully moved an amendment (modelled on provisions of the Australian Matrimonial Causes Act 1959): see *Official Report, Standing Committee C*, 13 March 1963, cols. 59, 90–91.

[187] *Official Report* (HL) 22 May 1963, vol. 250, col. 401. She claimed that the Bill was a 'husband's Bill, drafted by a man who doubtless means well but has failed to recognise that marriage has different values for men and women'. The argument about economic disadvantage had been raised in House of Commons Standing Committee C, *Official Report*, 6–27 March 1963, and Abse had made determined efforts to meet it by giving the court discretionary powers to withhold a decree. Moreover, the opportunity was taken in the Standing Committee to introduce (as the Morton Commission had recommended) a power for the court to make orders in divorce proceedings for the payment of lump sums—a development of immense importance for the future development of the law: see House of Commons Standing Committee C, *Official Report*, 27 March 1963, col. 157. The Bill was also amended so as to give the High Court power to prohibit transfers of assets intended to defeat an application for financial relief: see Matrimonial Causes Act 1963, s. 6.

[188] This debate on what was clearly the most important issue of principle took place in the Committee stage: *Official Report* (HL) 21 June 1963, vol. 250, col. 1528. Lord Morton spoke in support of the hostile stance to separation divorce taken in the *Morton Report*: see col. 1548; and Archbishop Ramsey (see Biographical Notes) made a particularly powerful speech claiming (i) that the notion of there being an 'honourable respectable way of ending a marriage' constituted a serious threat to the concept of marriage as a lifelong union; (ii) that it was improbable that seven-year separation divorce would reduce the number of illicit unions; and (iii) that legitimising children of such unions would be done at the expense of the father's first wife and the children of that relationship: see col. 1543. Ramsey's biographer (O Chadwick, *Michael Ramsey, A Life* (1990) pp. 150–153) believes the speech to have been an important factor in securing the rejection of seven-year separation divorce. But Ramsey's speech is historically of greater significance for the announcement of a Church Group to consider reform: see below.

[189] Beloe had obtained an assurance of assistance from the Roman Catholic peers, Monsignor Derrick Worlock (then Private Secretary to the Archbishop of Westminster) writing to Beloe on 31 May 1963 that 'our peers will be glad to help on the combined tactics which were so successful when the Bill was in the Commons'.

[190] By 52 votes to 31: *Official Report* (HL) 21 June 1963, vol. 250, col. 1578.

[191] *Official Report* (HC) 3 May 1963, vol. 676, col. 1562.

First, the law of condonation was (as a majority of the Morton Commission had recommended)[192] amended to allow couples to resume cohabitation with a view to reconciliation for one period of up to three months without this constituting condonation.[193] Secondly, and contrary to the recommendation of the Morton Commission,[194] collusion was made into a discretionary (rather than an absolute bar) to divorce.[195] Each of these provisions caused difficulty both as the Bill passed through Parliament[196] and subsequently in the

[192] *Morton Report*, paras. 237–243. The Commission was unanimous in thinking that it should no longer be the law that a man who had intercourse with his wife, knowing that she had committed a matrimonial offence, was irrebuttably to be presumed to have condoned that offence; and all were agreed that the presumption that sexual intercourse implied condonation should be capable of being rebutted by sufficient evidence to the contrary. But five Commissioners would not accept the majority view in favour of what came to be called a 'kiss-and-make-up' provision—ie that spouses should be allowed a trial period to attempt reconciliation and that nothing which happened during that period should amount to condonation. The minority were concerned that a wife might become pregnant during the trial period, and believed that an injured spouse should make up his mind at the outset whether he wished to resume cohabitation even if this involved the risk of his losing the right to divorce if the attempt failed: *Morton Report*, para. 243. The provisions of what became Matrimonial Causes Act 1963, s. 2, were controversial during the Bill's passage through Parliament: see especially the speech of Lady Summerskill (with the support of the Lord Chancellor) on the Committee stage in the House of Lords, *Official Report* (HL) 12 July 1963, vol. 251, col. 1557 asserting that it would be repugnant to any decent minded person for the law thus to provide an opportunity for a man to resume sexual intercourse with his wife for a night, a week-end or three months, and then to proceed with the divorce. But on a division the House voted 42 to 15 in favour of the change.
[193] Matrimonial Causes Act 1963, s. 2. The mischief at which this provision was aimed was said by Abse to be that under the existing law a husband and wife separated for six or 12 months but now experiencing the actual reality and isolation of separation would too often be 'afraid to make another go of it because to try would mean that the period of desertion' had been broken and other matrimonial offences would inevitably have been condoned: *Official Report* (HC) 3 May 1963, vol. 676, col. 811. At a late stage in the Bill's passage Lord Hodson (a consistent opponent of the reforms) successfully moved an amendment (enacted as s. 3 of the Act) to provide that adultery which had once been condoned could no longer be revived (see p. 185 above) thus—as he put it: *Official Report* (HL) 12 July 1963 vol. 251, col. 1591—preventing a hatchet which had once been definitively buried subsequently being unearthed. This amendment took the promoters and the Government by surprise not least because it had not been considered in the *Morton Report*.
[194] The Commission (unanimously) favoured dealing with the admitted problem that the law deterred parties from having discussions about the arrangements necessary for the future by providing a statutory definition which would restrict the operation of the bar to cases in which there had been a conspiracy or corruption: *Morton Report*, paras. 234–235. This was a sensitive topic since almost all commentators were agreed that the 'arranged divorce' should remain anathema. Possibly for this reason, the Committee of Officials (noting that the Senior Divorce Registrar was strongly opposed to the change) considered that Private Member's legislation on this topic should 'not be encouraged': PRO LCO2/6140, p. 4.
[195] Matrimonial Causes Act 1963, s. 4.
[196] The first version of what became Matrimonial Causes Act 1963, s. 2 ('Relief notwithstanding temporary cohabitation with a view to reconciliation') closely followed the majority *Morton Report* recommendation and would have restricted the maximum period of the trial cohabitation to one month. The clause was substantially redrafted not only to deal with technical matters but also to extend the maximum period to three months: see *Official Report, Standing Committee C*, 20 March 1963, col. 101 ff. The first version of s. 4 ('Amendment of law of collusion') provided simply that nothing in the existing legislation was to prevent parties to a matrimonial dispute from making 'any reasonable agreement' about certain specified matters (such as the children of the family and financial matters); and it gave a specific right of application to the court for approval of any agreement made under the section. Eventually, a provision simply converting collusion from an absolute to a discretionary bar was substituted with a rider expressly affirming the court's duty of inquiry and the

courts.[197] But it does seem that the conversion of collusion into a discretionary rather than an absolute bar to divorce was particularly influential (as the authors of the authoritative practitioners' textbook on divorce law[198] and practice put it) in leading to a 'consensual approach to divorce being implemented, since parties could for the first time openly bargain about the grounds of their divorce and the consequent financial arrangements'.[199] In this way apparently technical changes in the law played their part in creating a climate of opinion in which only a few years later legislation allowing divorce for irretrievable breakdown (effectively[200] including divorce by consent) and consigning the doctrines of condonation and collusion to the history books seemed to command general support.[201]

functions of the Queen's Proctor. This was apparently what Abse had wanted from the outset: see *Official Report* (HC) 3 May 1976, vol. 676, col. 815, even though the legislation failed to give any guidance to the court about how the discretion should be exercised. However, Lord Hodson's objection (*Official Report* (HL) 22 May 1963, vol. 250, col. 401) that no court would ever be justified in approving what was in the true sense a collusive agreement had to yield to the more pragmatic approach (adopted by Lord Denning and others) that the existence of a procedure for reference to the court would encourage solicitors to adopt a conciliatory approach in negotiating the consequences of divorce rather than continuing what Abse described (*Official Report* (HC) 8 February 1963, vol. 671, col. 813) as the existing practice of advising against having any 'contact whatsoever with each other, and under no circumstances to talk about future financial arrangements or domestic arrangements for the wife or the children'.

[197] The courts held that the 'kiss-and-make-up' provision only applied in situations in which the parties had acted with a view to effecting a reconciliation, and that it did not apply to cases in which the injured spouse had forgiven the guilty immediately and unconditionally: see *Brown v. Brown* [1967] P 105; *Herridge v. Herridge* [1965] 1 WLR 1506, CA. In *Mulhouse v. Mulhouse* [1966] P 39 the President of the Divorce Division asserted that the conversion of collusion into a discretionary bar did not allow the court to grant a decree in a case in which a substantial defence had been bought off; and accordingly in that case the court refused to sanction an agreement whereby the husband would drop a defence to his wife's allegation of cruelty in exchange for her dropping her claim to financial relief. But a somewhat less strict interpretation was given by other judges, and in *Nash v. Nash* [1965] P 266 Scarman J asserted that a collusive bargain 'which represents an honest negotiation between the parties, which is not intended to deceive the court either by putting forward false evidence or suppressing or withdrawing a good defence and which takes its place in an agreement which is intended to make reasonable provision for its parties according to its subject matter, is a perfectly reputable transaction', and other decisions gave rise to concern that the type of agreement likely to be approved depended as much on the individual judge as on the law and that some courts were allowing divorce by consent to creep through the back door into a law which was still firmly based on the matrimonial offence: see generally N Michaels, 'Collusion as a Discretionary Bar to Divorce' (1966) 29 MLR 241 where the case law is reviewed.

[198] *Rayden & Jackson's Law and Practice in Divorce and Family Matters* (17th ed., 1997) para. 1.22.

[199] From a different perspective it was possible to criticise the Act on the ground that these provisions would lead to a situation in which a couple could obtain a divorce by consent and manipulate the law to their own advantage: see N Michaels, 'Collusion as a Discretionary Bar to Divorce' (1966) 29 MLR 241.

[200] The qualification is important: in theory divorce by consent is not available under the Divorce Reform Act 1969 and would not have been available under the Family Law Act 1996.

[201] *Sutton v. Sutton* [1984] FLR 579; *N v. N (Divorce: Agreement not to Defend)* [1992] 1 FLR 266, 268.

Changes in judicial policy

Judicial decisions in the 1960s reflected (but may also have contributed to the creation of) an attitude favourable to changing the basis of the ground for divorce. Two developments were particularly significant.

First, decisions of the House of Lords in 1964 allowed the courts to grant decrees on the ground of cruelty against a respondent who was in no way morally blameworthy.[202] Increasingly the question became simply whether the factual situation was such that the petitioner could not be expected to tolerate;[203] and this question could easily be paraphrased in terms of whether the marriage had in fact broken down.

Secondly, (as we have seen) the courts' attitude to the exercise of the discretion to withhold a decree had changed dramatically over the years. At the beginning of the century the fact that both parties had established stable adulterous relationships with others would have certainly led to a decree being refused, and after World War I men were habitually 'refused discretion on account of a single weekend at an hotel after the wife had long deserted them'.[204] But after the House of Lords 1943 decision in *Blunt v. Blunt*[205] it became increasingly accepted that no public interest was served by keeping legally in existence a marriage which had in fact broken down.[206]

The effect of these changes should not be exaggerated. The fact that the petitioner had committed adultery remained a bar to divorce, and a petitioner still had to file a discretion statement in support of an application for the exercise of the court's discretion. Even in the year in which the Divorce Reform Act was passed, a respected divorce judge[207] found it necessary to reiterate that solicitors had a duty to ensure that their clients understood both the meaning of the word

---

[202] *Gollins v. Gollins* [1964] AC 644; *Williams v. Williams* [1964] AC 698. Permitting divorce on the ground of incurable insanity (as the Herbert Act did) was also a breach in the matrimonial offence doctrine, although such petitions were in practice comparatively uncommon (238 out of a total of 28,347 or less than 1% in 1954, for example).

[203] A striking feature of the divorce statistics is the great proportionate increase in those founded on cruelty: in 1950 the proportion was 10%; in 1954, 16%; and by 1970 the proportion had risen to 20% of all divorce petitions (and 56% of wives' petitions): *Registrar General's Statistical Review of England and Wales, 1970*; OR McGregor, *Divorce in England* (1957) Table X. McGregor speculates on the reason underlying these trends, claims that there was no evidence of any change in judicial attitude such as would have accounted for the change, and concludes that whilst the explanation remains obscure the growing financial independence of working class wives, the penetration of knowledge about divorce and the availability of legal aid amongst working class women, and perhaps an 'increased habit of "faking" divorce petitions' by working class couples using cruelty in the same way as the middle classes had used adultery were plausible hypotheses: *Divorce in England* (1957) pp. 41–48.

[204] *Masarati v. Masarati* [1969] 1 WLR 393, 396, *per* Sachs LJ.   [205] [1943] AC 517.

[206] *Blunt v. Blunt* [1943] AC 517, HL; *Masarati v. Masarati* [1969] 1 WLR 393, CA; but cf. *Moor v. Moor* [1954] 2 All ER 458, CA; *Bull v. Bull* [1968] P 618 (emphasising the importance of the petitioner having made a full disclosure to the court).

[207] Latey J, in *Pearson v. Pearson* [1971] P 16.

adultery[208] and the absolute obligation to disclose adultery on their part at any stage of the proceedings. The courts apparently expected solicitors to repeat their explanation at each important stage in the proceedings (although it was conceded that 'with a sufficiently well educated and well informed client' it might be sufficient 'for the solicitor to say at the outset, having asked the question "Have you committed adultery?" to say "Be sure that if ever you do so between now and the time when the suit comes to be heard, let me know because the court will have to be informed" '.[209] No doubt many clients were bemused by the requirement to provide what the *Finer Report* described as a 'sexual autobiography';[210] but solicitors found the burden placed on them distasteful.[211] Amongst those professionally involved the social utility of the offence based divorce law came increasingly to be questioned.

Ministers and officials

It was not only in the legal profession that traditional attitudes were changing. Lord Chancellor Dilhorne might speak out in public against the Abse Bill, but his attitude in private was very different.[212] Moreover, the Conservative Party

---

[208] In *Barnacle v. Barnacle* [1948] P 257 the petitioner had not understood the meaning of the word, and Wallington J gave examples of misunderstandings on other occasions: ' "it is not adultery if she is over 50" . . . "I did not think it was adultery during the daytime"; "I thought it meant getting a girl into trouble"; "I thought it meant drinking with men in public houses" '.

[209] *Pearson v. Pearson* (1965) 109 SJ 290, *per* Cairns J. But even the highly educated might have their own vocabulary: the fictional heroine—a First Class graduate in English of Cambridge University—of AS Byatt's *Babel Tower* (1996) petitioning for divorce in 1965 does not tell her solicitor about her relationship because she believes that it was 'not adultery which is serious [but] just sex'.

[210] ' . . . a sexual autobiography in the nature of an inventory of the occasions, with dates, names and places, on which the petitioner had illicitly succumbed to his or her frailties, together with such explanations and excuses, or even expressions of remorse, as the talents of counsel who settled the document might devise. If the variety of illicit experience had been so rich as to defeat itemised recollection, the discretion statement would traditionally begin, "On divers occasions your petitioner has committed adultery at times and places so numerous that your petitioner can no longer give any particulars of the same, save and except that . . .".': *Finer Report*, p. 76, note 4.

[211] ' . . . the distress caused to an already shy female client need not be emphasized': LCB Gower's Memorandum, para. 22, *Morton Report, Minutes of Evidence*, p. 17.

[212] Beloe had told the Archbishop of Canterbury that Dilhorne was a low church Anglican, 'not thought to be very intelligent but [nonetheless] a politician of experience' who (as his officials had told Beloe) was 'contrary to general belief, extremely interested in Reform of the law': *Ramsey Papers*, vol. 43, 21 May 1963. Beloe had also noted (on 19 March 1963) the preference expressed by Dilhorne at a meeting with Ramsey for 'his own more radical proposal' ie a judge considering the 'matter as a whole' and to make a finding as to whether or not the marriage had broken down'. In the House of Lords debate on the Abse Bill Dilhorne had strongly opposed the grafting of a proposition based on breakdown onto the existing law; and he had expressed his wish that the Abse provision be defeated to Archbishop Ramsey: Canterbury to York, 27 March 1963, *Ramsey Papers*, vol. 43. But he was careful to leave open in his speech the possibility of replacing the offence based law by 'another system where divorce would . . . be dependent upon the fact of the breakdown of the marriage': see *Official Report* (HL) 21 June 1963, vol. 250, col. 1566. Some months later Dilhorne wrote to the Archbishop referring to the 'desirability of getting away from the present concept of matrimonial offence': Dilhorne to Ramsey, 16 December 1963, *Ramsey Papers* vol. 43; and subsequently, in evidence to the Archbishop's Group, Dilhorne expressed himself as favouring divorce for breakdown 'with the least possible fuss': *Minutes of the Archbishop's Group on the reform of Divorce*, Lambeth Palace MS 3460, 30 July 1965, p. 100.

was well aware of the need to modernise its 'grouse moor' image;[213] and doctrinal opposition to reform of the divorce law was no longer necessarily to be expected from Conservative politicians.[214] From a somewhat different perspective, the officials who advised Ministers seem increasingly to have favoured moves towards the substitution of breakdown for the matrimonial offence doctrine.[215] But—given the traditional and persistent opposition of the Church of England to divorce reform—nobody could have predicted that it would be a Committee established by the Archbishop of Canterbury[216] which would take the lead in the events which led to radical reform and that a major part in the negotiations would be played by the Archbishop's Lay Secretary[217] (a man with an established record of opposition to reform of the ground for divorce).

The man and woman in the street

The machinations of highly placed individuals within the Government and Ecclesiastical establishment were of great importance, but no reform on so contentious an issue could be carried through without support from a significant body of public opinion. Leo Abse had ensured that the public were well aware of his attempts to achieve reform.[218] After the reverse in 1963, other committed reformers continued to keep divorce reform in the public eye; and in three

---

[213] See SM Cretney, *Law, Law Reform and the Family* (1998) pp. 33–34, and p. 46 note 96.

[214] Home Secretary Henry Brooke (another politician widely thought to be somewhat reactionary on social issues) bluntly warned Beloe at a meeting on 7 October 1963 that the Church had acquired a reputation for hostility to change; and Beloe was concerned that the Conservative Party might see in reform of the divorce law a means of improving its own image. Sir Charles Cunningham, the Permanent Under-Secretary at the Home Office, had warned Beloe in May 1963 that another Bill providing for separation divorce was almost certain to be introduced by a private member the following session: *Ramsey Papers*, vol. 43, note dated 2 May 1963.

[215] This became apparent in the discussions (at the time, focussed on how to ensure the defeat of separation divorce provision in the Abse Bill) which Beloe had had in early 1963.

[216] For a somewhat fuller account of the background, see SM Cretney, *Law, Law Reform and the Family* (1998), Chapter 2 (described as an 'unpublished paper' in J Lewis and P Waller, 'Fault, Breakdown and the Church of England's Involvement in the 1969 Divorce Reform' *Twentieth Century British History*, vol. 11 (2000) p. 308, which covers some of the same ground).

[217] Robert Beloe: see above.

[218] As Abse characteristically put it: 'On television and in articles I dramatized the problems: and above all else repeated and repeated the consequence of the existing divorce laws to the children of estranged and unmarried parents. Never in Britain have we had a wider section of the community taking with high seriousness and concern their obligations as parents: and to them I constantly appealed with calculation. Parliament is a stage and if you want to be heard you don't mumble or lecture. The electorate have a right to histrionics, panache and style: the bugles must blow and the flags and bunting fly. The grey politicians are not worth their money: they are paid to act, to give the great audience a tumultuous catharsis, and if the players lack the principle which alone vitalizes the performance, then they should be compelled to quit the stage. They have failed if, at the end of the show, democracy is given only two cheers, not four': *Private Member*, p. 169.

successive Parliamentary sessions the Labour MP John Parker[219] brought Bills[220] to allow divorce after five years' separation into Parliament. Opinion Polls[221] indicated that a majority of the population supported divorce founded on separation.

THE ARCHBISHOP'S GROUP: 'PUTTING ASUNDER'

In May 1963 the Archbishop's Lay Secretary, Robert Beloe met senior officials[222] from the Home Office and Lord Chancellor's Department. He floated the notion that the Archbishop might set on foot an investigation into marriage and its dissolution. The suggestion that the Archbishop's mediation might be aimed at the possibility of 'substituting for all other grounds the ground that a marriage had come to an end' emerged.[223] Then the Archbishop (using deliberately low key language)[224] announced in the course of his House of Lords speech strongly attacking the Abse separation proposal that he had asked 'some fellow churchmen' to seek to find a 'principle at law of breakdown of marriage . . . free from any trace of the idea of consent, which conserved the point that offences

---

[219] See Biographical Notes.

[220] In each of the sessions 1963/4, 1964/5 and 1965/6 he obtained leave under the Ten Minute Rule to introduce a Bill entitled the Strengthening of Marriage Bill. Such Bills had no prospect of making progress, but on each occasion Parker was able to make a speech—in fact much the same speech on each occasion—and thereby gain a certain amount of publicity for the case for reform: see PG Richards, *Parliament and Conscience* (1970) Chapter 2. The Parker Bills would have enabled a further marriage to be contracted by either spouse when a separation had persisted for five years or more; but there were exceptions if dissolution would be contrary to the public interest or harsh and oppressive to the respondent or if a proper financial settlement had not been made for the wife and children: see eg Bill No. 208 1963/64. On each occasion the Bill was backed by three or four Labour MPs; and Parker's speech made the point that the breakdown principle had been part of Australian law since 1959 and had worked well there, and that the main purpose of extending the ground for divorce in this way was to legitimise the 40% of illegitimate children born in stable families headed by parents who were unable to marry. He claimed that the Church's concern at permitting divorce by consent was irrelevant since divorce could be obtained under the existing law if the parties were prepared to agree; and urged that what was needed was legislation allowing a marriage to be ended without the consent of one party: see eg *Official Report* (HC) 29 July 1964, vol. 699, col. 1453. He pointed out that comparatively few children were involved in divorce compared with the numbers forever illegitimate because their parents were unable to marry.

[221] By 1960, methods of ascertaining public opinion by attitude surveys had been developed and become well established. For Polls on the 1968/9 divorce reforms see the results of two polls given in BH Lee, *Divorce Law Reform in England* (1974) pp. 96–97; and for a historical summary of the different organisations see D Butler and G Butler, *Twentieth-Century British Political Facts 1900–2000* (2000).

[222] Sir Charles Cunningham, the Permanent Under-Secretary of State and RJ Guppy (the Assistant Under-Secretary of State) from the Home Office and Denis Dobson (Deputy Permanent Secretary in the Lord Chancellor's Department). The text draws on *Ramsey Papers*, vol. 43, folio 5, note of meeting on 21 May 1963.

[223] *Ramsey Papers*, vol. 43, folio 5, Beloe's note of meeting on 21 May 1963.

[224] 'if it were possible to find a principle . . . then I would wish to consider it': *Official Report* (HL) 21 June 1963, vol. 250, col. 1547. The unenthusiastic tone no doubt reflects Ramsey's belief that it was 'very doubtful whether [the group he planned to appoint] would be able to produce anything constructive': Canterbury to York, 6 June 1963, *Ramsey Papers* vol. 63.

and not only wishes are the basis of breakdown, and which was protected by a far more thorough insistence on reconciliation procedure first'.

No one hearing these tentative words would have anticipated that this initiative would be particularly significant; but in fact the appointment of what came to be called the 'Archbishop's Group' proved to be of decisive importance. The Group (albeit chaired by the Bishop of Exeter, Robert Mortimer)[225] was very different from the 'group of churchmen' Ramsey had envisaged.[226] This was largely because both the Home Secretary[227] and the Lord Chancellor[228] took an active part[229] in choosing who should (and who should not)[230] be asked to serve;[231] and the selection process came to resemble that traditionally conducted in Whitehall trawls of the 'great and the good'. The criticism of the lack of social science expertise in the Morton Commission made it seem imperative that a 'sociologist' be a member of the Archbishop's Group; and 'slots' were also allocated to particular professions (for example, child psychiatry) and interests (for example, marriage guidance). Again, the Group's Terms of Reference[232] were

[225] See Biographical Notes.

[226] However, the members had to be Christians, at least in a broad sense. For this reason, the eminent Jewish lawyer, Professor Otto Kahn-Freund, was considered not to be a suitable member of the group.

[227] Henry Brooke. Names were discussed at a meeting between Beloe, Brooke, the Joint-Under Secretary CM Woodhouse, and Guppy on 26 August 1963; and the Home Office was responsible for suggesting the names of two of those who served on the group—Viscount Colville of Culross (see Biographical Notes) and EW Short, MP (Labour) for Newcastle upon Tyne Central (who resigned on appointment as Labour Chief Whip in November 1964). In the end Beloe was able to tell Bishop Mortimer that the Home Office thought the composition of the Group was 'all right, or unobjectionable'.

[228] Beloe had consulted Dobson about the names he had in mind on 19 August 1963: *Ramsey Papers* vol. 43; and Dobson replied from his holiday hotel commenting in detail on membership and on the terms of the draft letter of invitation to be sent by the Archbishop. Lord Chancellor Dilhorne told the Archbishop that he favoured the appointment of a judge to sit on the Committee: Dilhorne to Ramsey, 16 December 1963; and the person he suggested (Sir Henry Phillimore—member of a family of distinguished ecclesiastical lawyers, a judge of the Probate Divorce and Admiralty Division from 1959 to 1962 and at the time a judge of the Queen's Bench Division) was duly appointed. The Law Lord, Patrick Devlin was also—notwithstanding reservations about his suitability on the part of the Home Office—invited to join the group, evidently because it was thought politic to have a Roman Catholic on the Committee. But he only attended a single meeting and distanced himself from the recommendations eventually made by the Archbishop's Group for procedural change to enable the court to satisfy itself that there had indeed been an irretrievable breakdown: *Putting Asunder* p. 63, footnote. For Devlin's views on this subject, see his *The Enforcement of Morals* (1965) Chapter IV, particularly at p. 75 ff.

[229] Professor JND Anderson (1908–1994) (see Biographical Notes) was the source of most suggestions.

[230] For example, the Lord Chancellor's office (see *Ramsey Papers*, vol. 62, Beloe to Mortimer 25 March 1964) advised against the appointment of one eminent Queen's Counsel; whilst Professor OR McGregor was rejected as being 'rather too irritating for the sort of calm exchange . . . needed' but in any event (as any reader of *Divorce in England* could testify) he was outspokenly hostile to what he evidently regarded as the pretensions of the Church in relation to family law and otherwise.

[231] For the membership, see Biographical Notes.

[232] To 'review the law of England concerning divorce and, recognising that there is a difference in the attitudes of the Church and State towards the further marriage of a divorced person whose former partner is living, to consider whether the inclusion of any new principle or procedure in the law of the State would be likely to operate (1) more justly and with greater assistance to the stability of

only settled after lengthy discussion with the Lord Chancellor's Department, the Home Office and others in Whitehall.

The Archbishop's Group held its first meeting on 26 May 1964; and a consensus[233] in favour of substituting irretrievable breakdown as the sole ground for divorce soon emerged. The court should have power to dissolve marriage if 'having regard to the interests of society as well as of those immediately affected by its decision, it judged it wrong to maintain the legal existence of a relationship that was beyond all probability of existing again in fact'.[234] This would involve the court giving a judgment on the state of the marriage; and its decree would no longer be 'against' the respondent but rather 'against' further legal recognition of the marriage.[235]

The Group remained adamantly opposed to divorce by consent on the ground that it would reduce marriage to a purely private contract and ignore the interest of the community—a 'grave, indeed overwhelming objection'.[236] Hence, it was to be for the court, representing the community, to decide whether the marriage had really broken down irretrievably;[237] and, although the agreement of the parties in wanting a divorce would not be a bar (and might even count in favour of granting a decree) in no case was it to be sufficient.[238] It was, for the Archbishop's Group, essential that the court should always examine[239] the issue of breakdown according to the evidence.[240] The Group insisted that its recommendation for amendment of the substantive law was conditional upon procedural changes to enable the court to conduct the necessary inquest[241] into the alleged fact and causes of the death of the marriage relationship and to 'get to

marriage and the happiness of all concerned including children than at present; and (2) in such a way as to do nothing to undermine the approach of couples to marriage as a lifelong covenant': *Putting Asunder, A Divorce Law for Contemporary Society* (1966) (henceforth *Putting Asunder*) p. ix.

[233] *Minutes of the Archbishop's Group on the Reform of Divorce*, Lambeth Palace MS 3460, Third Meeting, 5 November 1964. So strong was the pro-Reform sentiment which had developed in the Group that AJ Irvine MP QC (who had been appointed to the Commission in March 1965 in the place of EW Short) felt obliged to resign to avoid having to take any part in the drafting of propositions with which he was out of sympathy: Irvine to Beloe, *Ramsey Papers* vol. 82, 17 November 1965.

[234] *Putting Asunder*, para. 56.   [235] *Putting Asunder*, para. 52.

[236] See Mortimer's speech in the House of Lords debate on *Putting Asunder: Official Report* (HL) 23 November 1966, vol. 278, col. 243.

[237] ie '... declare defunct *de jure* what ... is already defunct *de facto*': *Putting Asunder*, para. 54. The Group agreed in principle on a clause defining the criterion as there being 'no reasonable probability of such a reconciliation as would enable the spouses to live together for their mutual support and comfort as husband and wife': *Minutes of the Archbishop's Group on the Reform of Divorce*, Lambeth Palace MS 3460, 9 April 1965, p. 74.

[238] *Putting Asunder*, para. 59(a).

[239] Possibly aided by counsel representing the public interest and by forensic social workers who would investigate matters about which the court needed to be informed: *Putting Asunder*, para. 89.

[240] *Putting Asunder,* para. 59.

[241] 'It would have to be made possible for the court ... to inquire effectively into what attempts at reconciliation had been made, into the feasibility of further attempts, into the acts, events, and circumstances, alleged to have destroyed the marriage, into the truth of statements made (especially in uncontested cases), and into all matters bearing upon the determination of public interest': *Putting Asunder*, para. 84.

grips with the realities of the matrimonial relationship' instead of having to 'concentrate on superficialities' (as happened under the offence based law).[242]

The Group refused to accept that any of the well rehearsed objections to the breakdown principle outweighed its advantages. No doubt (the Group accepted)[243] critics would point to the economic deprivation caused by divorce; but the solution to that lay primarily in reforms of the law of property, pensions (a topic much discussed) and insurance. But the Group did not see it as part of its remit to prescribe detailed remedies for these problems.

What of the objection that breakdown divorce would allow the guilty to take advantage of their own wrong? The Group thought that the court's judgment could and should be seen as the recognition of a state of affairs and a consequent redefinition of status (rather than as a verdict of guilty after a law suit) and for that reason the maxim would have no general application.[244] But even so, the Group accepted[245] the need for a safeguard: there should be an absolute bar on divorce if on the facts of any particular case considerations of fundamental importance (such as the public interest in justice and in protecting the institution of marriage) outweighed the case for dissolution.[246]

On one matter in particular the Group was adamant: the doctrine of breakdown was to *replace* divorce founded on the matrimonial offence. On no account should breakdown be introduced as an additional ground[247] grafted onto the existing law.[248] Indeed, the Group thought that rather than 'to inject into [the offence based law] a small but virulent dose of incompatible principle'[249] it would be better to keep the law based firmly on the matrimonial offence and to consider how the administration[250] of the law could be improved.

---

[242] *Putting Asunder*, para. 69(b).

[243] *Minutes of the Archbishop's Group on the Reform of Divorce*, Lambeth Palace MS 3460, 23 October 1965, p. 119.

[244] *Putting Asunder*, para. 52.   [245] *Putting Asunder*, para. 53.

[246] *Putting Asunder*, para. 53.

[247] The Minutes of the Group's penultimate meeting record that the Group felt 'most strongly' that if the proposal for divorce founded exclusively on breakdown were rejected, the existing ground for divorce should be preserved: *Minutes of the Archbishop's Group on the Reform of Divorce*, Lambeth Palace MS 3460, 28 February 1966, p. 166. A whole section of *Putting Asunder* (pp. 57–59) is devoted to an exposition of 'why the principle of breakdown must not be introduced into a law based on the matrimonial offence'.

[248] In the House of Lords debate on *Putting Asunder* (*Official Report* (HL) 23 November 1966, vol. 278, col. 245) Bishop Mortimer said that to follow the precedent of the Abse Bill would be to leave the matrimonial offence as the main ground of divorce (not least because people would prefer a speedy way of securing divorce once they had decided the marriage was over) and this would accordingly do nothing to remove the unsatisfactory features of the law.

[249] *Putting Asunder*, para. 69.

[250] The Group noted the decisions of the House of Lords in *Gollins v. Gollins* [1964] AC 644 and *Williams v. Williams* [1964] AC 698 which had emphasised the 'principle of the intolerable situation' (ie the emergence through the respondent's conduct of a situation the petitioner should not be called upon to endure) as the essence of the matrimonial offence of cruelty; and it was evidently concerned that 'if allowed to get out of hand' this might 'transform the doctrine of the matrimonial offence out of all recognition' and turn it 'into something that was neither fish, flesh, nor fowl, but solely a red herring': *Putting Asunder*, paras. 50, 69.

All these points were incorporated into the Group's Report, *Putting Asunder*, eventually published (to the accompaniment of much, generally favourable,[251] radio television and press publicity)[252] on 29 July 1966.

THE LAW COMMISSION AND ITS 'PURELY LEGAL' ADVICE

The 'swinging sixties' are commonly believed to have been a time of great change in social and political attitudes; and certainly the Labour Government which took office in October 1964 (some five months after the appointment of the Archbishop's Group, but before the publication of *Putting Asunder*) was publicly committed to a programme of energetic social and economic reform. The 'white heat' of the scientific revolution (to use a phrase coined by the incoming Prime Minister Harold Wilson)[253] was to be applied to modernising the country and its institutions. The damage done by 'thirteen wasted years' of amateurish Tory misrule was to be reversed by skilled professionalism.

The legal system had been singled out as being particularly in need of radical reform.[254] This was to be carried out through the agency of the Law Commission, one of the new government's first creations,[255] committed by statute[256] to the systematic development, reform, simplification and modernisation of the law. Not surprisingly, family law immediately attracted the newly created Commission's attention;[257] and the Commissioners established a close relationship with the Archbishop's Group. The Commission had advance

---

[251] For example, *The Times'* leading article on 29 July 1966 declared that it 'is doubtful whether there has been published in recent times a more persuasive, thoughtful or constructive plea on behalf of the breakdown of marriage doctrine or a more effective condemnation of the present method of divorce'.

[252] Originally it had been thought that it might be best if the Group's work were kept confidential; and Ramsey (who, further evidencing his wish to distance himself from the Group's recommendation, refused to allow a bound presentation copy of *Putting Asunder* to be embossed with the Arms of the Province of Canterbury) seems to have remained doubtful about the wisdom of publication. But in the event Beloe was able to organise lists of speakers prepared to discuss the Report on publication and there was extensive media coverage: Beloe to Hornby, 20 May 1966, *Ramsey Papers* vol. 102; and note folio 221 commenting that the 'advantages of giving broadcasting organisations ample advance warning and full details of important Church publications have again been demonstrated'. *The Times* and other broadsheet newspapers published favourable comments on the Report on 29 July; as did the *Observer* on 31 July.

[253] See B Pimlott, *Harold Wilson* (1992) p. 304.

[254] The Chapter on 'Family Law' by OM Stone and A Gerard in the influential manifesto *Law Reform NOW* (1963) (edited by Gerald Gardiner QC—appointed Lord Chancellor in Wilson's 1964 Government—and Professor Andrew Martin—appointed by Gardiner as one of the first Law Commissioners) had favoured five years' separation as a ground on which a divorce petition could be presented, although if there were children the court was to have a discretion, 'the sincerity of the efforts at reconciliation made by the petitioner being the touchstone of the matter'.

[255] See generally SM Cretney, *Law, Law Reform and the Family* (1998) Chapter 1.

[256] Law Commissions Act 1965, s. 1.

[257] The Commission's *First Programme* committed it to a preliminary examination of matrimonial law, having regard to the variety of views expressed in and following the Report of the Morton Commission.

knowledge of what *Putting Asunder* was going to say; and seems deliberately to have fanned expectations that the Archbishop's Group's Report would provide the catalysis for divorce reform.[258] As soon as *Putting Asunder* was published, Lord Chancellor Gardiner,[259] a committed advocate of divorce reform, formally referred the document to the Commission for its advice.[260] In this way, what had originally been intended by the Church as a low-key contribution to the debate (probably not even to be published)[261] was moved to the centre of the stage; and it was the Church which for the first time was made to appear to be advocating a reform it had traditionally opposed.

Three months later,[262] on 9 November 1966, the Law Commission's Advice to the Government was published under the title *Reform of the Grounds of Divorce, The Field of Choice*.[263] The Commissioners (of whom a clear majority

[258] The Commission organised a high-level seminar on divorce reform (attended by Mortimer, members of the judiciary, practising and academic lawyers, marriage guidance workers, and others at All Souls College Oxford on 8–9 July 1966, ie some weeks before the publication of *Putting Asunder* on 29 July): for the Record see PRO BC3/592. Statements made to the Press by Scarman about the seminar were widely publicised. The Commission's *First Annual Report 1965–66* (1966) para. 78 also emphasised the importance of the Report: it stated that the Commission would 'make no attempt to formulate views on . . . the grounds for divorce . . . until after the publication of [the Archbishop's Group's Report, which would] be of great value as an indication of the present state of an important and responsible section of public opinion'.

[259] Formerly Gerald Gardiner QC, co-editor with Martin of *Law Reform NOW* and a long-standing member of the Divorce Law Reform Union: BH Lee, *Divorce Law Reform in England* (1974) p. 62.

[260] The reference was in the form of a request to provide advice to the Government under the provisions of Law Commissions Act 1965, s. 3(1)(e). The Commission could, of course, have simply continued with its work under the *First Programme of Law Reform* (above) but this would inevitably have involved delay whilst consultation was carried out and would almost certainly have involved the Commission in abandoning the role it was able to adopt under the reference as a mere purveyor of technical advice about procedural practicability. The Archbishop had sent the Lord Chancellor a typed copy of the Group's Report on 7 April 1966 (almost four months before publication) and Scarman and others had been well aware of the trend of the Group's thinking long before that date: see SM Cretney, *Law, Law Reform and the Family* (1998) pp. 57–58.

[261] Shortly before the Report was formally presented to him on 29 March 1966 Ramsay made it clear to Scarman that he had still not made up his mind whether the document should be published: *Ramsey Papers* vol. 102, 8 March 1966. But Beloe recorded that although his own feeling was in favour of silence about even the existence of the Group, the Home Secretary had told him personally 'that he thought it would do the Church good for it to be known that there was a feeling of compassion towards this problem. The Church had, in his view, been merely in opposition for too long'; and (ii) the existence of the Group was almost certain to become known in some way or other 'and then there might be in say the Daily Express a tremendous news story': Beloe to Hornby, 27 January 1964, *Ramsey Papers* vol. 62.

[262] Even making allowances for the fact that the topic did not come as a novelty to some of those involved, the speed with which the Commissioners and their staff prepared their advice to the Government is remarkable. It appears that on 19 August 1966 (Minutes of Commissioners' Meeting, PRO BC3/2) the Commission's Family Law team had not got beyond preparing a 'preliminary paper' on the ground for divorce; yet the Commission's Report was ready for publication only two months later.

[263] *Report on a Reference under section 3(1)(e) of the Law Commissions Act 1965* (1966), Cmnd. 3123, Law Com. No. 15 (subsequently referred to as *The Field of Choice*).

were already publicly identified as supporters of reform)[264] had decided[265] that the 'form of the [Report] would be factual and not recommendatory, excluding value judgments in so far as that was possible'. Accordingly *The Field of Choice* purported to have a narrow objective:

'It is not [said the Commission] . . . for us but for Parliament to settle such controversial social issues as the advisability of extending the present grounds of divorce. Our function in advising . . . must be to assist the Legislature and the general public in considering these question by pointing out the implications of various possible courses of action. Perhaps the most useful service that we can perform at this stage is to mark out the boundaries of the field of choice . . . We have . . . tried to restrict this Report to a consideration of what appears from a lawyer's point of view to be practicable . . ..'[266]

'Purely practical difficulties' compel rejection of 'Putting Asunder'

The Commission's Press Release was even more modest: the Commission was a 'purely legal body'; and it had therefore considered the Archbishop's Group's proposals solely 'from the point of view of what would be feasible as a matter of legal administration'.[267] This approach led *The Field of Choice* to reject[268] the *Putting Asunder* proposal for 'breakdown with inquest' (notwithstanding its 'undoubted attractions and [the Commission's] sympathy with the principles' underlying the Archbishop's Group's Report). 'Purely practical difficulties' in making the scheme work[269] 'forced' the Commission to this conclusion.

---

[264] Scarman had stated his support for 'breakdown' in a public lecture at Bristol University in March 1966 (*Family Law and Law Reform*, 1966); and he had earlier (in evidence given to the Archbishop's Group on 19 February 1965) stated his belief that breakdown as a ground for divorce would be 'both sensible and viable' (although, unlike the Group, he favoured the retention of the matrimonial offence as an alternative ground for divorce): *Minutes of the Archbishop's Group on the Reform of Divorce*, Lambeth Palace MS 3460, pp. 60–64. Martin had edited *Law Reform NOW* (see above; and see Biographical Notes) Gower's evidence to the 1956 Royal Commission favouring divorce by consent or divorce for separation had been widely publicised and he was a well known member of the Divorce Law Reform Union. It was in fact Gower who had the carriage of the Law Commission's work on *Putting Asunder*. The author has no documentary evidence about the sympathies of the other two Law Commissioners, Norman Marsh QC and Neil Lawson QC (beyond the fact that the latter was a member of what *The Observer* described as 'the very left-wing Haldane Society') although those working in the Commission at the time seem to have had no doubt about the Commissioners' strong personal feelings in favour of reform: see further SM Cretney, *Law, Law Reform and the Family* (1998) p. 58, note 183.
[265] Minutes of Commissioners' Meeting, 20 September 1966, PRO BC3/2.
[266] *Field of Choice*, paras. 2, 3.
[267] However, *The Field of Choice* did contain a significant amount of demographic material and did not hesitate to make predictions about future trends. As one of those involved in the drafting of that Report has subsequently put it, however, 'every prediction made then, on the basis of the figures used, turned out to be not just marginally wrong, but very far off the mark indeed. This is a reflection not on the accuracy of the figures used but rather on the extrapolations made from them': R Deech, 'Divorce Law and Empirical Studies' (1990) 106 LQR 229, 231.
[268] *The Field of Choice*, para. 70.   [269] *Ibid.*

What, then did the Commission propose as an alternative? *The Field of Choice* suggested that two alternatives[270] would 'be practicable'.[271] The first was described as 'breakdown without inquest'. Instead of the court being required to carry out a detailed examination of the alleged fact and causes of the breakdown (a process necessarily 'elaborate, time-consuming and expensive')[272] there would be 'an easier procedure'. On proof of a period of separation the court would (in the absence of evidence to the contrary) presume that the marriage had broken down. This, so the Commission claimed, would 'give effect to the . . . principles'[273] underlying the *Putting Asunder* approach.[274] But the Commission asserted that this form of 'breakdown without inquest' would not be 'feasible' if the requisite period of separation were significantly longer than six months.[275] If the stipulated period were longer, 'intolerable hardship' would, in the Commission's view, be caused to innocent parties currently able to obtain an offence-founded divorce on the grounds of the other's 'outrageous conduct'.[276]

If (said the Commission) so short a period were not acceptable, breakdown (even breakdown without inquest) could not be accepted as the sole ground for divorce. The Commission therefore put forward its second alternative: the 'separation ground'. But because the stipulated period of separation would necessarily[277] be 'substantially longer' than six months the 'separation ground' 'would be practicable only as an addition to the existing grounds based on matrimonial offence'.[278]

---

[270] *The Field of Choice* also discusses divorce by consent and concludes that this would be a 'feasible proposal' if it were restricted to cases where there were no dependent children, other grounds for divorce remained available in all cases, and there were machinery to verify the genuineness of the consent. But even then the Commission considered that unless the consent were accompanied by a period of separation marriages might be dissolved which had not broken down irretrievably. For that reason the main text suggests that divorce by consent be rejected in favour of breakdown for separation, the period required being shorter if there is consent than otherwise: see paras. 84–95. However there were differences of opinion amongst the Commissioners on this issue—Gower continuing to support divorce by consent: Minutes of Commissioners' Meeting, 20 September 1966, PRO BC3/2—and it seems possible that the rather less negative approach to divorce by consent apparent in the Summary and Conclusions to *The Field of Choice*, para. 120 reflects the draftsman's difficulty in coping with these differences under great pressure of time.

[271] In either case, safeguards (for example, to protect the respondent spouse and children: see the summary in *The Field of Choice* para. 120(7)(d)) would be necessary.

[272] *The Field of Choice*, para. 71.   [273] *Ibid.*   [274] *Ibid.*, para. 70.

[275] *Ibid.*, para. 120(6)(a).

[276] *Ibid.*, paras. 75–76. This assertion cannot survive serious examination. Divorce is a procedure whereby the parties are freed to remarry; and there seems no overwhelming case for giving even those who have been the victims of outrageous conduct such a right after a waiting period as short as six months. The Commission made it appear that divorce was a means of *protecting* the victim of outrageous conduct: but it would have been perfectly possible to provide such protection either by means of the traditional remedy of judicial separation or by providing avowedly protective remedies of the kind now found in Part IV of the Family Law Act 1996 (itself in part based on provisions protecting a spouse's right to occupy the family home contained in the Matrimonial Homes Act 1967, then being drafted by the Commission's draftsmen).

[277] Ie because six months had been rejected as an unacceptably short period: see above.

[278] *The Field of Choice*, para. 120(6)(c).

An unbridgeable gulf between Law Commission and Archbishop's Group?

The *Field of Choice* might thus have seemed distinctly unhelpful in building a consensus. The Law Commissioners must have known that the Archbishop's Group would never accept six months' separation as in effect the sole ground for divorce whilst *Putting Asunder* had made it abundantly clear that the Group would have preferred to 'keep the law firmly based on the matrimonial offence'[279] rather than accept the introduction of breakdown as an addition to the grounds for divorce (instead of a substitute for it). And yet when, two weeks after publication of *The Field of Choice*, the House of Lords debated the issue of divorce reform only two or three speakers opposed the principle of reform.[280] Reviewing *The Field of Choice* in the *Modern Law Review*[281] Professor Otto Kahn-Freund was to say that all that could be said on the subject of divorce reform had been said, and that the time for action had arrived. A similar impatience was expressed in the House of Lords by the former Lord Chancellor (and opponent of the Abse 1963 Bill)[282] Lord Dilhorne:[283] there was (he said) general agreement about the serious defects of the existing law; and Dilhorne urged that rather than quarrelling about who was right and who wrong a serious attempt should be made to find ways of making the breakdown principle work satisfactorily.

Creating a consensus

There seems to have been general sympathy for Dilhorne's robust approach; and the Bishop of Exeter was able to oblige. At the end of the debate[284] he revealed that he had arranged to meet the Law Commission[285] the following day; and he was personally 'quite convinced' that the gap between divorce with inquest and divorce without inquest was not wide 'and that in fact we could come to an agreement about a practicable method of working a divorce law which was based wholly on the principle of the breakdown of marriage'. Over the next six months negotiations took place between the two groups.[286]

---

[279] *Putting Asunder*, para. 59.

[280] Lord Hodson, Lord of Appeal in Ordinary (and formerly a judge of the Probate Divorce and Admiralty Division) objected to what he called 'compulsory divorce' of an innocent spouse; whilst Lady Summerskill claimed that breakdown divorce as proposed in *Putting Asunder* would amount to a rejection of a lifelong marriage and the substitution of trial marriage to the great prejudice of married women. Lord Reid (also a Lord of Appeal in Ordinary) opposed any reform which would allow the blameless deserted wife to be divorced against her will.

[281] (1967) 30 MLR 180, 186.

[282] See above, p. 353.   [283] *Official Report* (HL) 23 November 1966, vol. 278, cols. 302–303.

[284] *Official Report* (HL) 23 November 1966, vol. 278, col. 347.

[285] The Chairman (Scarman J) and one other Commissioner (in fact Gower).

[286] For an account, see SM Cretney, *Law, Law Reform and the Family* (1998) pp. 63–68.

The concordat between the Law Commission and the Archbishop's Group

Eventually[287] the terms of a 'concordat'[288] between the Archbishop's Group and the Law Commission were finalised and published.[289] The concordat reiterated that irretrievable 'breakdown should replace matrimonial offence and become the sole and comprehensive ground of divorce'. But in place of the detailed inquest proposed in *Putting Asunder* the court was (in the absence of evidence to the contrary) to infer breakdown 'on proof of the existence of certain matrimonial situations', ie that the parties had lived apart (for two years if the respondent consented to divorce or for five years if there were no consent) or one of several other specified facts akin to the traditional matrimonial offences.

This was all the reformers could have wished. The concordat was favourably received in the Press. On 12 October the Cabinet[290] accepted Gardiner's advice[291] that a Bill to give effect to the concordat should be drafted by Parliamentary Counsel in the Law Commission and handed to a Private Member.[292] The Law Commission settled[293] Instructions to Parliamentary Counsel.[294] On 9 November Mr William Wilson MP[295] drew fourth place in the Ballot for Private Members' Bills, and agreed to take up the Bill. On 29 November the House of Commons ordered the Divorce Reform Bill presented

---

[287] On 2 June 1967: Scarman to Gardiner, 24 July 1967, PRO BC3/377.

[288] Mortimer had reported to Ramsey on 17 May 1967 that the two bodies were 'on the verge of agreement' and that the Commission's proposals and the accompanying notes constituted 'the most satisfactory compromise attainable': *Ramsey Papers*, vol. 117.

[289] The conclusion of the negotiations was publicly announced in the Law Commission's *Second Annual Report* published on 26 July 1967; and the terms of the concordat were attached to a 'press-handout' distributed on that day and published as an appendix to the Law Commission's *Third Annual Report* (1968, Law Com. No. 12). It is reproduced in BH Lee, *Divorce Law Reform in England* (1974) pp. 235–240.

[290] PRO CAB 128/42, CC(7) 59th Conclusions.

[291] Scarman had met the Lord Chancellor to discuss the 'proposed private member's bill on the grounds of divorce': Minutes of Commissioners' Meeting, 17 October, 1967, PRO BC3/3.

[292] In fact Instructions to Counsel had already been drafted: see PRO BC3/378, 25 October 1967.

[293] In addition to the formulation of the bars to divorce (see below) there appears to have been some disagreement within the Commission about the wording of the 'living apart' facts now embodied in Matrimonial Causes Act 1973, s. 1(2)(d) and (e), Scarman pointing out that not all separations evidenced breakdown: Memorandum dated 26 October, PRO BC3/377.

[294] The Law Commission's *Third Annual Report 1967–1968* (July 1968) para. 51 states that the 'Government agreed to provide drafting assistance for Mr Wilson, and the Divorce Reform Bill, now before Parliament, was the result. We for our part have given assistance so as to ensure that the Bill as introduced should accord with the understanding which we reached with the Archbishop's Group'. This appears to understate the Commission's role. In contrast, when *The Times'* commentator criticised the drafting of the Bill (which he attributed to its not having been drafted by Parliamentary Counsel) the Secretary to the Law Commission confirmed that 'although the Law Commission do not give advice on controversial social issues, they have given technical and legal assistance at all stages and on all amendments tabled . . .': *The Times*, 23 June 1969.

[295] See Biographical Notes.

by Mr Wilson[296] to be printed.[297] With one exception, all concerned with *Putting Asunder* seem to have been content with the outcome of their efforts.

The Archbishop dissents

That one exception was significant. It may have been reasonable to suppose that an agreement between the Law Commission and 'the Archbishop's Group' meant that the Archbishop himself accepted the 'concordat'. The *Daily Mirror* went so far as to claim that 'the pacemaking Archbishop' had been converted into a 'powerful ally' of Leo Abse and his fellow campaigners. But in fact Ramsey had consistently distanced himself from the concordat,[298] and refused even to have the document embodying the concordat formally submitted to him;[299] whilst the Law Commission was firmly told by Beloe that the Archbishop had not given his approval to the concordat and that if the Commission were asked whether the Archbishop approved and agreed with it 'the answer should be that he did not agree with everything in it'. Ramsey evidently understood that the concordat departed in important respects from what *Putting Asunder* had proposed; and he wanted (as Beloe recorded) to be 'free to

---

[296] The Bill was formally supported by five Conservative, five Labour and one Liberal MP, viz: *Conservative*: Ian Gilmour (1926–, MP for Norfolk Central, formerly an officer in the Grenadier Guards and Editor of *The Spectator*, subsequently ennobled as Lord Gilmour of Craigmillar), Nicholas Ridley (1929–1993, MP for Cirencester and Tewkesbury, subsequently a Minister in Margaret Thatcher's Cabinet, and later ennobled as Lord Ridley of Liddlesdale), Anthony Royle (1927–, MP for Richmond, formerly an officer in the Life Guards, junior Minister, and at the time a Tory Whip; subsequently ennobled as Baron Fanshawe of Richmond), George Sinclair (1912–, MP for Dorking, formerly Deputy Governor of Cyprus) and Dame Joan Vickers (see Biographical Notes); *Labour:* Leo Abse (see Biographical Notes), Peter Jackson (1928–, MP for High Peak, formerly Lecturer in Sociology, Hull University), Lena Jeger (1915–, MP for Holborn and St. Pancras South, formerly Civil Servant and journalist on the *Guardian*, subsequently ennobled as Baroness Jeger of St. Pancras), Dr David Kerr (1923–, MP for Wandsworth Central, formerly a medical practitioner and LCC Councillor), and John Parker (see Biographical Notes); *Liberal*: Emlyn Hooson. It appears that the names of the sponsors were put forward by Abse and accepted by Wilson: BH Lee, *Divorce Law Reform in England* (1974) p. 93.

[297] See Bill 18; and note the account in Lee *op. cit.* p. 94. The author has not been able to consult the Lord Chancellor's Department records about the passage of the Bill, but the text draws on such of the Law Commission's files as survive.

[298] He had been careful not at the outset to endorse *Putting Asunder*, telling the publisher (see *Ramsey Papers* vol. 102, Ramsey to Davey, 25 May 1966) that he had 'to take great care about the words'used in the Preface to *Putting Asunder* (and note also his refusal to allow the Arms of the See of Canterbury to be put on a presentation copy of the Report: note 252 above. Ramsey's Preface warned that if there were to be legislation as proposed in the Report the 'Churches would still maintain their own pastoral discipline'; and concluded with the less than enthusiastic commendation that the Archbishop hoped the Report would 'lead to a full discussion of the issues which it raises').

[299] So Ramsey put it to Mortimer at a meeting at Lambeth on 24 May 1967. Ramsey wanted to preserve his freedom to 'make such public comment as in due course he may think fit'; and considered that since the document would 'not have been produced by a body appointed by me' a formal presentation could put him 'in a wrong position' and that 'awkward questions might be asked about my place in the matter': Ramsey to Mortimer, 22 May 1967, *Ramsey Papers*, vol. 117. In fact in responding to correspondents Ramsey made it clear that he was 'not in favour of the way in which [breakdown] is approached' in the Law Commission's Bill: see eg Ramsey to National Council of Women, 30 January 1968, *Lady Helen Nutting Papers*.

criticise and seek for amendment of some of the propositions' in the concordat.[300] In particular, Ramsey had always insisted that it was 'of the utmost importance that breakdown should be not an additional ground but a substitute for all existing grounds'.[301]

Was that what the concordat provided, or did it rather use the language of breakdown merely to disguise the addition of separation to the existing grounds for divorce?[302]

Giving effect to the 'consensus': the draftsman's role

The precise terms chosen to translate the general policy expressed in the concordat into language which the courts would interpret were thus of great importance. The draftsman of the Law Commission's Bill[303] had to give effect to instructions that 'divorce should be available upon proof that the marriage [has] irretrievably broken down, and upon no other ground'; but also that 'no marriage should be treated as having broken down irretrievably unless the court was satisfied' that (for example) the respondent had committed adultery and the petitioner found it intolerable to continue or resume cohabitation or that the 'parties to the marriage had lived apart for a continuous period of at least five years'. The dual requirement was necessary to satisfy the members of the Archbishop's Group that the Bill would not simply add the 'separation ground' to variations of the existing matrimonial offence, but rather that the court would have to be satisfied, as a separate matter, that the marriage had truly broken down irretrievably and all possibilities of reconciliation explored.

It was clear enough from this that there could be no divorce in the absence of proof of one of the specified facts (however plain it was that the marriage had

---

[300] Leo Abse claims that Ramsey—a 'wily prelate . . . following the principles of Machiavelli'—was anxious to keep his options open: L Abse, *Private Member* (1973) p. 182.

[301] Ramsey to Mortimer, 22 May 1967, *Ramsey Papers*, vol. 117.

[302] In an important debate in the Church Assembly Professor JND Anderson had warned that pressure of public opinion might lead to 'a period of separation' being 'tacked on' to the matrimonial offence as an additional ground for divorce (as had been the policy of the White and Abse Bills). Anderson claimed that this would be to preserve 'the worst of the present' combined with 'an ease of divorce which does not exist today'. Although Anderson presciently expressed his fear that 'we might get a law which accepts a breakdown of marriage as a fundamental ground, but which accepts the matrimonial offence so blindly as *prima facie* evidence of divorce that in effect we are having the matrimonial offence plus separation' (see *Church Assembly Record of Proceedings*, 16 February 1967, vol. 47 at pp. 241–242) he does not seem to have appreciated that on one view that was precisely the effect of the concordat which he had joined in negotiating. The fact that the Archbishop did not agree with the most prominent lay member of the Archbishop's Group was made all too clear with the publication in the *Sunday Times* on 11 February 1968—two days after the Bill was given a second reading in the House of Commons—of an article by Ramsey under the title 'My Doubts about the Divorce Bill'. This caused something of an uproar in the Law Commission (where it was thought that Ramsey had misunderstood the Bill: see the minutes in PRO BC3/380) and Anderson replied on 18 February objecting to—amongst other matters—the Archbishop's statement that the matrimonial offence would be 'virtually retained'. In retrospect, it appears that on this occasion at least the Archbishop understood the principles of statutory construction better than did the legal experts he had appointed to advise him.

[303] Mrs Ellice A Eadie: see Biographical Notes.

broken down); but what was to happen in the converse situation where there was proof of a fact but possibly some doubt whether the breakdown was truly irretrievable? The terms of the concordat, quoted above, gave no answer. But the draftsman (acting on the instructions of the Law Commission) supplied one. True it is that the Bill[304] (and the Act)[305] began with the resounding statement that 'the sole ground on which a petition for divorce may be presented to the court by either party to the marriage shall be that the marriage has broken down irretrievably'; and the Bill provided that the court was not to hold that a marriage had so broken down unless the petitioner satisfied the court of one of the specified facts.[306] But the Bill (unlike the concordat) went on to provide an answer to what was to happen in the converse situation: once a 'fact' has been proved, the court '*shall*[307] . . . grant a decree' unless it is 'satisfied on all the evidence that the marriage has not broken down irretrievably'. In other words, the court faced, for example, with proof of the adultery 'fact' or the 'fact' that the parties had lived apart for five years would be bound to dissolve the marriage unless the respondent could discharge the almost impossible task of satisfying the court that the marriage had *not* broken down. As the President of the Probate Divorce and Admiralty Division[308] was to put it:

'If even one of the parties adamantly refuses to consider living with the other again, the court is in no position to gainsay him or her. The court cannot say, "I have seen your wife in the witness-box. She wants your marriage to continue. She seems a most charming and blameless person. I cannot believe that the marriage has really broken down". The husband has only to reply, "I'm very sorry; it's not what *you* think about her that matters, it's what *I* think. I am not prepared to live with her any more". He may add for good measure, "What is more, there is another person with whom I prefer to live". The court may think that the husband is behaving wrongly and unreasonably; but how is it to hold that the marriage has not nevertheless irretrievably broken down?'

Not surprisingly, there has been no reported instance of a respondent succeeding in rebutting the presumption that proof of one of the 'facts' establishes breakdown.[309] Mortimer's assumption that the evidence of breakdown would be rebuttable rather than conclusive[310] has thus been falsified. The draftsman's choice of the one word 'shall' inevitably meant that the *effective* ground for divorce under the 1969 Act was not breakdown at all. Rather the effective ground for divorce became either separation for the prescribed period or the commission of any of the three matrimonial offences, adultery, behaviour, or

---

[304] Bill No. 17, Clause 1.   [305] Divorce Reform Act 1969, s. 1.

[306] Bill No. 17, Clause 2(1); Divorce Reform Act 1969, s. 2(1).

[307] Bill No. 17, Clause 2(3); Divorce Reform Act 1969, s. 2(3); italics supplied.

[308] Sir Jocelyn Simon, in a lecture to the Institute of Legal Executives, reprinted in *Rayden on Divorce* (11th ed., 1971) p. 3232.

[309] A typical example is *Le Marchant v. Le Marchant* [1977] 1 WLR 559 (husband granted divorce based on five years' separation notwithstanding wife's plea that she still loved her husband and that the breakdown was not irretrievable). For an account of the case law, see SM Cretney and JM Masson, *Principles of Family Law* (5th ed., 1990) p. 98.

[310] *Official Report* (HL) 30 June 1969, vol. 303, col. 379.

desertion.[311] Anderson's prophesy[312] that 'we might get a law which accepts a breakdown of marriage as a fundamental ground, but which accepts the matrimonial offence so blindly as *prima facie* evidence of divorce that in effect we are having the matrimonial offence plus separation' was fulfilled, not (as Anderson had feared) by legislation deliberately ignoring the *Putting Asunder* principle, but by legislation purporting to be based upon it, following the concordat which Anderson had helped to negotiate. The truth is that the apparent consensus between the Group and the Law Commission was vitiated by a skilful piece of legislative legerdemain.[313]

Mortimer (the Chairman of the Archbishop's Group) evidently continued to believe that 'the great merit of [the Bill supposedly giving effect to the concordat] lies in its first clause' which (he claimed) clearly established the principle that the true ground for divorce is the breakdown of marriage.[314] But a different parliamentary draftsman was soon brutally to demonstrate the reality. The consolidating Matrimonial Causes Act 1973 removed the ringing assertion to which Mortimer referred (presumably on the ground that it had no legal function) and substituted the provision that a divorce petition may be presented 'on the ground that the marriage has broken down irretrievably'.

The Church group was warned how the Bill would be interpreted by the courts:[315] but it appears that people were becoming bored with these niceties.[316] Perhaps readers will have some sympathy with the impatience expressed by Lord Dilhorne and others; but the need for the Law Commission's Bill to *appear* to give effect to the principle that irretrievable breakdown should be the sole

---

[311] The five facts were indeed commonly (albeit incorrectly) referred to as the 'grounds' for divorce; and when the further reform of the divorce law embodied in the Family Law Act 1996 was under discussion many lay commentators erroneously believed that a provision that irretrievable breakdown should be the ground for divorce was a novelty: see below, p. 388.

[312] *Church Assembly Record of Proceedings,* 16 February 1967, vol. 47 at pp. 241–242.

[313] In fairness to those concerned, it ought to be said that the Explanatory Memorandum attached to Mr Wilson's Bill made it quite clear that on 'proof of any of the facts mentioned . . ., the court must grant a decree unless it is satisfied on all the evidence that the marriage has not irretrievably broken down . . .': Bill No. 18 ordered by the Commons to be printed on 29 November 1967.

[314] *Official Report* (HL) 30 June 1969, vol. 303, col. 377.

[315] See Lord Reid's speech: *Official Report* (HL) 26 June 1969, vol. 303, col. 347.

[316] Note Lord Dilhorne's somewhat testy riposte to Reid's speech. Dilhorne urged that the Archbishop should vote for a Second Reading and leave such matters to the committee stage (but he emphasised that he thought a lot more work should be done on the detail of the Bill and that it would be wrong to deal with it under pressure of time: *Official Report* (HL) 26 June 1969, vol. 303, col. 363). It may be significant that the main thrust of the Archbishop's Second Reading speech was not directed to the question whether the Bill truly substituted irretrievable breakdown for the matrimonial offence as the basis for divorce but rather to three 'specific blemishes' he identified and which were for him 'matters of justice and principle': *Official Report* (HL) 30 June 1969, vol. 303, col. 342. The three 'blemishes' Ramsey identified were (i) the short period of separation (two years) required for a divorce on which both parties agreed; (ii) the inadequacy of the court's power (under what became Matrimonial Causes Act 1973, s. 10) to withhold divorce on the grounds that adequate financial provision had not been made; and (iii) the inadequacy of the court's power (under what became Matrimonial Causes Act 1973, s. 5) to withhold a divorce when it would be wrong in all the circumstances to do so. Ramsey doubted whether this corresponded effectively to the 'safeguard for justice for which the authors of *Putting Asunder* pleaded'.

ground for divorce (as so eloquently advocated in *Putting Asunder*) whilst in truth doing no more than adding divorce for separation may have played some part in making the law 'confusing and misleading'[317] and indeed impossible for most lay people to understand. As the Law Commission put it when it returned to reform of the Ground for Divorce in 1990[318] this could 'only lead to . . . lack of respect for the law' and indeed that some might regard what had been done as 'downright dishonest'. This was hardly realised in the parliamentary debates, which focussed on issues less abstract than the philosophical basis of the ground for divorce. But a price had been paid[319] to get the support of one particularly important interest group.

GETTING THE BILL ON TO THE STATUTE BOOK: THE GOVERNMENT'S ROLE

No Bill dealing with the ground for divorce has ever had an uneventful passage through Parliament,[320] and what became the Divorce Reform Act 1969 was no exception. The Bill introduced in 1967 by William Wilson was given a Second Reading by 159 votes to 63 on 9 February 1967; and was debated for nearly 40 hours in Standing Committee; but it was impossible to make time for it to get through all its stages in the House of Lords.[321] So it was necessary to start again in the following (1968/1969) Session; and another MP (Mr Alec Jones) who had drawn a reasonably favourable place in the ballot for Private Members' Bills agreed to sponsor what was in substance the Bill introduced the previous session.[322] The Government had again agreed[323] to consider making Government time available for the Bill 'in the light of the degree of support shown for it on Second Reading'; and the substantial vote in favour of a second reading on the Wilson Bill in the previous Session evidently tipped the scales. The Government

[317] For a recent example (demonstrating that the judiciary may sometimes also be confused) see *Butterworth v. Butterworth* [1997] 2 FLR 336.
[318] *Family Law: The Ground for Divorce* (Law Com. No. 192, 1990) para. 2.8. The Law Commission—differently constituted from the Commission as it had been in 1966—had in 1988 itself accepted that the concordat 'apparently introduced the breakdown principle but in reality created just the sort of dual system deprecated in *Putting Asunder*': *Facing the Future, A Discussion Paper on the Ground for Divorce* (Law Com. No. 170, 1988) para. 3.14.
[319] The Chairman of the Divorce Law Reform Union, W Banks, admitted at the Union's Annual General Meeting on 17 August 1967 that he would have preferred simpler legislation along the lines of Abse's 1963 Bill, but that it would 'be a mistake to engage in controversy as to the means by which successfully agreed means should be attained': *Service Papers*.
[320] The statement in L Stone, *Road to Divorce* (1990) p. 400 that the Herbert Bill 'easily passed both Houses' of Parliament is misleading.
[321] See BH Lee, *Divorce Reform in England* (1974) p. 109, note 27. In fact the Bill did not proceed to the Report and Third Reading stage in the House of Commons.
[322] There were only two changes in the Bill's sponsors: from the Labour side, William Wilson took over the position formerly taken by Dr David Kerr, whilst the Conservative Sir George Sinclair dropped out (apparently because of a desire to concentrate on race relations matters: see Lee *op. cit.* p. 188, note 7) to be replaced by the solicitor and one-time Hussar officer Daniel Awdry, MP for Chippenham.
[323] PRO CAB 128/42, CC(7) 59th Conclusions.

did eventually[324] agree to make time available for the Jones Bill. Given the size of the pro-reform majority in both Houses of Parliament[325] and the skilled and effective management of the Bill by Abse and his supporters[326] this decision can in retrospect be seen to have made it almost certain[327] that the Divorce Reform Bill would become law. Opponents of reform bitterly criticised the decision,[328] but the Government stood firm. Even so, there were anxious moments.

Overcoming the opposition

Opposition[329] to the divorce reform legislation was of three main types. First, there was (as there always had been) opposition of principle to any extension

[324] The decision to make time available seems only to have been finally taken in May 1969. On 4 May 1969 the *Sunday Times* had reported that 'Divorce Reform faces death on a Friday', and in a contemporaneous letter Alastair Service recorded that it was 'becoming obvious' that it was 'by no means certain that the Government would live up to their undertaking to give the Bill time for a decision one way or the other': Service to Abse, 22 May 1969, *Service Papers*. Service collected 108 Labour backbenchers' signatures on a round robin to the Chairman of the Parliamentary Labour Party and 'turned on every pressure we could, direct and indirect, behind the scenes' urging that the Government give time for the Bill's final stages in the House of Commons. Service comments that 'It was all pretty hectic and we were on tenterhooks until it was announced . . . that we had the time, though it was on a Thursday night'. And even after the Government's decision had been taken the supporters of the Bill had to keep MPs in the House of Commons in order to vote and this required considerable effort, particularly on the final all-night sitting. The *Service Papers* are an invaluable source for this aspect of the legislative process.

[325] The Jones Bill was given a Second Reading in the House of Commons on 17 December 1968 by 183 votes to 106: *Official Report* (HC) vol. 775, col. 1132. The size of both pro- and anti-Bill votes had increased considerably, but even so less than half the members of the House of Commons voted at all. For a full analysis of the voting on the Jones Bill see BH Lee, *Divorce Law Reform in England* (1974) Chapter 7.

[326] A particularly important contribution was made by Alastair Service (1933–): see Biographical Notes. The parliamentary lobbying is well covered by Lee, *op. cit.* Chapters 6 and 7; but the *Service Papers* also reveals the skill of Leo Abse in occasionally restraining lobbyists when publicity would have been unhelpful: see eg Abse to Service 2 August 1967.

[327] The qualification is necessary because the Bill might still have failed if its promoters had been unable to persuade sufficient supporters to remain in the House—on one occasion (12/13 June 1969) for an all-night sitting—to secure a majority on any division and to avoid the House being 'counted out'. The promoters engaged in effective 'whipping' of their supporters: see Lee, *op. cit.* at eg pp. 152–156; and the *Service Papers, passim.*

[328] On 12 June 1968 the House of Commons spent nearly two hours debating the propriety of the Government's action in providing facilities for a Bill on the merits of which it professed neutrality: see *Official Report* (HC) vol. 784, col. 1797. In the House of Lords Gardiner was able to point out that in the years from 1948 Governments had given time to Private Members' Bills—some concerned with family law—on 58 occasions, or three times a year on average: *Official Report* (HL) 30 June 1969, vol. 303, col. 316.

[329] The most persistent and effective of those speaking against the Bill in the House of Commons were three Conservative lawyer MPs: Sir Lionel Heald QC (1897–1981) Member for Chertsey since 1950 spoke with the authority of a respected senior member of the Bar and former Attorney-General; Sir Ian Percival QC (1921–), Member for Southport since 1959 was also a respected senior barrister who continued in active practice; however, K Bruce Campbell QC (1916–) who had won Oldham West for the Conservatives at a by-election in June 1968, may have seen the Bill as an opportunity to make his mark on the House, and certainly did so (justifying the assessment by BH Lee, *Divorce Law Reform in England* (1974) p. 117 of him as the 'toughest opponent' of the Bill): see further, Biographical Notes.

of the grounds for divorce.[330] But the Church of England[331] had effectively been bought off by the promise that what was being offered was divorce for irretrievable breakdown, and the Free Churches[332] took the same favourable position. Even the Mothers' Union[333] did not object to the principle of divorce for irretrievable breakdown.[334] Only the Roman Catholics refused to budge[335] from the stand they had taken in the 1950s[336] (and indeed the 1850s): a marriage contract was governed by the law of God which no civil law could change.[337]

Secondly, there was opposition to the Bill based on the financial injustice which would be caused to innocent women divorced against their will; and it was opposition of this kind which at one time threatened the Bill[338] and did lead to its implementation being deferred until legislation dealing with the financial consequences of divorce had been enacted. This is dealt with below.[339]

---

[330] Mrs Jill Knight, the Conservative MP for Birmingham, Edgbaston (1923–, subsequently ennobled as Baroness Knight of Collingtree) had in June 1968 presented a petition claiming that the Wilson Bill was in some respects unjust to women and praying for its rejection: *Official Report* (HC) 27 June 1968, vol. 767, col. 783. Baroness Knight's autobiography, *About the House* (1995) does not seem to refer to her part in opposing divorce reform.

[331] The Church Assembly had, on 16 February 1967, welcomed *Putting Asunder* and approved irretrievable breakdown as the sole ground for divorce. Professor JND Anderson had told the Assembly that he was 'convinced that changes in our law of divorce will come. There is a mounting pressure in many different areas and among many different groups. In the past, the Bishops . . . have stood . . . rather like Canute trying to prevent the tide coming in . . . [W]e should realise that we have a responsibility to the nation not merely to say "No" and then accept whatever law comes, but to make constructive and suitable suggestions': *Church Assembly Report of Proceedings*, vol. 47, p. 239. But some Anglicans—not least the Archbishop of Canterbury, who refused to vote for the Divorce Reform Bill: *Official Report* (HL) 30 June 1969, vol. 303, col. 342— remained unconvinced that the Bill did give effect to this policy; and see the editorial in the *Church Times*, 29 July 1966.

[332] The Methodist Department of Christian Citizenship presented a detailed report (which had been prepared with the benefit of help about 'matters of practicality' from the Law Commission and assistance from Miss Rubinstein, a member of the Archbishop's Group) to the Methodist Conference in July 1967: see PRO BC3/377. The Conference accepted the Law Commission's proposals for breakdown without inquest.

[333] Which at this time still refused full membership to any woman whose marriage had been terminated by divorce: see C Moyse, 'Idolatry and pragmatism: the sanctity of marriage and the Mothers' Union 1876–1976' in A Thatcher (ed.), *Celebrating a Christian Marriage* (2001).

[334] See BH Lee, *Divorce Law Reform in England* (1974) p. 99. Alastair Service (see Biographical Notes) believed the Roman Catholic church arranged lobbying as the Bill progressed through the Commons, and that 'small deputations' of Roman Catholics went to see 'a very large number of MPs in their constituencies' and believed this was 'not just chance, but the result of a direction from on high . . .': Service to Abse, 22 May 1969, *Service Papers*.

[335] See eg the speeches of Lord Longford and Lady Kinloss in the House of Lords debate: *Official Report* (HL) 30 June 1968, vol. 303, col. 369.

[336] See the Evidence given to the Morton Commission, p. 332 above.   [337] *Ibid.*

[338] Notwithstanding the fact that the Long Title of the Bill had been carefully drafted so as to 'restrict the ambit of parliamentary debate . . . we would wish to avoid debate on any question . . . on financial relief and matrimonial property'. The danger that the debates might provide an opportunity for amendments to be moved on these issues had been a major pre-occupation of participants in a meeting attended by the Lord Chancellor, Leo Abse, William Wilson with Officials on 27 November 1967: PRO BC3/378.

[339] And see pp. 132–135, above.

The third type of opposition related to the details of the legislation. Some of the proposals were for largely technical amendments[340] of the kind virtually always found necessary. At the opposite extreme there were proposals clearly designed to destroy the Bill (for example, an amendment which would have restricted the legislation to marriages contracted after its enactment[341] and another amendment which would enable couples to opt for an indissoluble form of marriage).[342] These had to be (and were) defeated. More successful[343] were attempts to change the emphasis of the Law Commission's draft Bill, for example by requiring positive consent to be given to a divorce founded on two years' separation (rather than the mere failure to object which would have sufficed under the Law Commission's draft Bill).[344]

Opposition based primarily on financial detriment to women: Bill a Casanova's Charter?

Opponents[345] of reform knew that a majority of the population seemed to support divorce founded on separation;[346] and for this reason they concentrated their fire on the financial consequences of divorce for the economically vulnerable, and especially the 'innocents' who were likely to suffer financially.[347] Groups such as the National Council of Women of Great Britain expressly made support for breakdown divorce conditional on 'sufficient financial safeguards' being 'simultaneously introduced within the new . . . Divorce Law

[340] For example, the removal of the requirement that adultery constituting a 'fact' on the basis of which irretrievable breakdown could be inferred should have been committed 'since the celebration of the marriage'—a decision which has intrigued text writers: see SM Cretney, *Principles of Family Law* (4th ed., 1984) p. 123.

[341] *Official Report* (HC) 12 June 1969, vol. 784, col. 1797.

[342] *Official Report* (HC) 2 May 1969, vol. 782, col. 182.

[343] But the Bill's promoters successfully resisted proposed amendments which would greatly have increased the difficulty of getting a quick 'civilised' divorce, notably a proposal to remove adultery from the list of facts leading to an inference of irretrievable breakdown: see *Official Report* (HL) 10 July 1969, vol. 303, col. 1206. Another amendment sought to provide that the adultery in question should be the cause of the petitioner finding it intolerable to continue cohabitation: see SM Cretney, *Principles of Family Law* (4th ed., 1984) p. 122.

[344] *Official Report* (HL) 11 July 1969, vol. 303, col. 1313.

[345] The supporters of reform realised that this was a topic on which they were somewhat vulnerable: the Divorce Law Reform Union issued a pamphlet 'Financial Security of Divorced Women' in February 1968 which attempted to meet these concerns; but at that time Leo Abse was reluctant to highlight the question, preferring to treat it 'as if it were a Committee point and not get involved, if at all possible, in too detailed an argument at this stage . . .': Abse to Service, 23 January 1968, *Service Papers*. But the issue refused to go away.

[346] See the results of two polls given in BH Lee, *Divorce Law Reform in England* (1974) pp. 96–97.

[347] This point was well put by the Conservative MP Sir Edward Boyle (1923–1981) in a letter responding to a briefing communication from the Divorce Law Reform Union: 'there is one point which does cause concern—even to those of us who have no social or religious objections to the widening of the divorce laws—what is to happen to the widow's pension for women divorced under the circumstances set out in the Bill? . . . While I am strongly opposed to the notion that a matrimonial offence should be a *sine qua non* for a divorce, I should consider it unjust that a woman, who is deserted by her husband and has herself committed no offence, should be deprived of the right to a widow's pension when the time comes . . .': Boyle to Service, 18 December 1967, as printed in Lee, *Divorce Law Reform in England* (1974) p. 94.

itself'.[348] This view, which can be crudely but effectively caricatured as being that the Law Commission's Bill would constitute a Casanova's Charter,[349] caused the Government and the Bill's sponsors[350] serious embarrassment;[351] but once again the Law Commission was on hand to produce palliative amendments and reassuring but (it has to be said) not always entirely candid[352]

[348] Lee, *op. cit.*, p. 100. The original Wilson Bill contained three relevant provisions, under the following headings. (1) *Decree may be refused if divorce would result in grave financial or other hardship to respondent*: clause 5. This was amended; and the amended version was passed into law as s. 4 of the 1969 Act and remains in force as s. 5 of the consolidating Matrimonial Causes Act 1973. The heading was changed to the (perhaps less informative) *Decree to be refused in certain circumstances* but the amendments—save for expressly defining hardship as including the 'loss of the chance of acquiring any benefit which the respondent might acquire if the marriage were not dissolved'—appear to have been of little effect. (2) *Power to rescind decree nisi in certain cases*: clause 6. This provision applied only to 'two year separation and consent' divorces, and empowered the court to rescind a decree nisi if the petitioner (whether intentionally or unintentionally) misled the respondent about his or her financial position as it would be after the divorce. Slightly broadened in scope (ie by being made applicable where the misconception was about 'any matter which the respondent took into account' in deciding to agree) it became s. 5 of the 1969 Act and is still in force as s. 10(1) of the 1973 Act. It appears to be little invoked in practice: see SM Cretney, *Principles of Family Law* (4th ed., 1984) pp. 159–161. (3) *Financial Protection for Respondent in Certain Cases*: clause 7. This complex provision entitled a respondent to apply to the court if a decree nisi had been pronounced on the basis of two or five years' separation for consideration of his financial position as it will be after divorce; and the court is not to make the decree absolute unless satisfied either (a) that the petitioner should not be required to make any financial provision for the respondent, or (b) that the financial provision made by the petitioner for the respondent is reasonable and fair or the best that can be made in the circumstances. Opponents of reform were quick to point out that 'the best that can be made in the circumstances' was hardly a very attractive guarantee, but the provision passed into law virtually unamended as s. 6 of the 1969 Act and remains in force as s. 10(2) of the Matrimonial Causes Act 1973. Initially there were more than 2,500 applications a year under this provision, but a more accurate understanding of the broad extent of the court's powers to order financial provision under Matrimonial Proceedings and Property Act 1970 led to a sharp falling off in numbers: see SM Cretney, *Principles of Family Law* (4th ed., 1984) pp. 173–175.

[349] An expression coined by Lady Summerskill in an address to the Married Women's Association: BH Lee, *Divorce Law Reform in England* (1974) p. 101; and used to some effect in the Parliamentary debates: see eg *Official Report* (HC) 12 June 1969, vol. 784, col. 2034, *Official Report* (HL) 30 June 1969, vol. 303, cols. 310, 342–344; and subsequently in 1970, Official Report (HC) vol. 794, cols. 1597–1598.

[350] The Divorce Law Reform Union published a pamphlet entitled 'Financial Security of Divorced Women' which claimed that the law already provided 'much help and protection' and that such protection would be '*considerably* increased' by specific provisions of the Jones Bill: *Lady Helen Nutting Papers*, Service to Nutting, 3 December 1968.

[351] Culminating in the Second Reading given (against the Government's advice) to the Matrimonial Property Bill introduced by Mr Edward Bishop (1920–1984): see Biographical Notes. Bishop was persuaded to drop his Bill in return for the Lord Chancellor's undertaking that the Divorce Reform Act would not be brought into force until legislation giving effect to Law Commission reform proposals had been introduced in the next session of Parliament: see pp. 132–135, above.

[352] On 25 June 1969 as the Divorce Reform Bill was nearing the end of its progress through Parliament Sir Leslie Scarman, the chairman of the Law Commission wrote a letter to the Lord Chancellor which the latter read to the House of Lords asserting that the provisions of the Bill 'gave the maximum protection possible' to innocent respondents. At an earlier stage, Scarman had recorded his view that there would need to be research into the financial implications of divorce under the breakdown principle: see PRO BC3/378, 16 May 1968; but there were objections on practical grounds (notably because financial matters might have to be divulged in divorce petitions) and no action appears to have followed an offer from Professor OR McGregor and Louis Blom-Cooper to undertake such research. (The relevant Law Commission files, BC3/29 and 30, are closed until 2003.)

assurances about the scope and effect of the financial provisions which were to be introduced at the same time as the alteration in the ground for divorce took effect. These new provisions (outlined elsewhere in this book)[353] did give the Divorce Court a broad discretion to make financial orders on divorce; but the problem of securing the wife a share in the husband's pension fund (the topic at the forefront of the concerns of those doubtful about reform) was not to be comprehensively tackled until the last year of the twentieth century,[354] whilst the divorced woman's claim for definite and ascertainable property rights rather than the mere possibility of receiving discretionary benefits has to this day never been conceded.[355] The promoters of the Bill gave assurances[356] that re-drafting of the provision requiring the court to refuse a decree if divorce would cause the respondent grave financial or other hardship[357] would greatly increase the protection available to the economically vulnerable partner; but experience of the working of the Act soon demonstrated[358] that there would be very few cases in which the exercise of the power could even be considered. And the Bill which finally passed into law[359] with substantial majorities in both Houses of Parliament[360] contained no general power (such as had been

---

[353] See p. 420, below.   [354] Welfare Reform and Pensions Act 1999.

[355] See Chapter 3, above. The principles upon which the court would exercise its discretion to redistribute the parties' capital on divorce remained unresolved (and controversial) at the end of the century: see *White v. White* [2001] 1 AC 596, HL, *Cowan v. Cowan* [2002] Fam 97, CA, and Chapter 10 below.

[356] See *per* Mr Alec Jones, *Official Report* (HC) 25 April 1969, vol. 782, col. 182. The substitute provision still contained the fatal defect that the court could only exercise the power to withhold a decree on proof that the ending of the legal status of marriage would cause 'grave financial or other hardship' to the respondent. As Lord Chancellor Gardiner had made clear in most cases in which the parties had been living apart for five years the legal dissolution of the marriage would make no difference to the wife's financial position: the wife (unless in possession of adequate resources of her own) would have been in receipt of maintenance under a court order which could continue, or she would have been (and would continue to be) dependent on social security payments: Gardiner to Banks, 25 March 1969, BH Lee, *Divorce Law Reform in England* (1974) p. 150.

[357] The relevant provision of what had been clause 5 of the Wilson Bill became s. 4 of the Divorce Reform Act 1969 and then s. 5 of the Matrimonial Causes Act 1973. In practice, this has rarely been applied and has only had any noticeable effect in cases where middle aged and elderly wives have been faced with loss of pension rights on a scale which makes it unlikely that the loss will be made up by social security benefit: see *Reiterbund v. Reiterbund* [1974] 1 WLR 788. There is no reported case in which the bar has been successfully invoked in cases where the hardship alleged is not financial but (for example) injury to religious susceptibility. For the courts' approach to such cases, see eg *Rukat v. Rukat* [1975] Fam 63.

[358] See for an analysis of the case law, SM Cretney, *Principles of Family Law* (4th ed., 1984) pp. 161–172.

[359] The Wilson Bill had contained a provision empowering the court to dismiss a divorce petition in cases in which the petitioner had attempted to deceive the court. It did not appear in the Jones Bill.

[360] The House of Commons gave a Third Reading to the Jones Bill by 109 votes to 55. The House of Lords gave the Bill a Third Reading without a division, but the Second Reading vote was 122 to 34, whilst most of the Committee majorities for the Bill as it came from the Commons were substantial: see generally BH Lee, *Divorce Law Reform in England* (1974) Chapter 7 (which contains much interesting analysis of the voting).

envisaged in the concordat)[361] permitting the court to withhold a decree in cases in which (to use the Archbishop's Group's words)[362] the petitioner had not only been 'patently responsible for ending the common life but had blatantly flouted the obligations of marriage and treated the other party abominably'.

THE DIVORCE REFORM ACT 1969 ON THE STATUTE BOOK

The Divorce Reform Act received the Royal Assent on 22 October 1969; and came into force on the same date as the Matrimonial Proceedings and Property Act 1970,[363] 1 January 1971.[364] The Divorce Reform Act provided (as already noted) that the sole ground for divorce should be that the marriage had broken down irretrievably;[365] but went on to provide that the court should not hold that there had been such a breakdown unless the petitioner satisfied the court of one or more of the following five facts:[366]

'(a) that the respondent has committed adultery and the petitioner finds it intolerable to live with the respondent;

(b) that the respondent has behaved in such a way that the petitioner cannot reasonably be expected to live with the respondent;

(c) that the respondent has deserted the petitioner for a continuous period of at least two years immediately preceding the presentation of the petition;

(d) that the parties to the marriage have lived apart for a continuous period of at least two years immediately preceding the presentation of the petition . . . and the respondent consents to a decree being granted;

(e) that the parties to the marriage have lived apart for a continuous period of at least five years immediately preceding the presentation of the petition.'

---

[361] Para. 7(b) of the concordat provided that the court should be required to refuse a divorce if satisfied that, 'having regard to the conduct and interests of the parties and the interests of the children and other persons affected, it would be wrong to dissolve the marriage, notwithstanding the public interest in dissolving marriages which have irretrievably broken down'. It is true that the explanatory note to this provision warned that it was 'not intended to make the grant of a divorce discretionary' (since to do so would be 'to introduce an impossibly wide area of uncertainty and would inevitably lead to wide variations of practice'). The note emphasised that the intention was rather to create a '"long stop", requiring the court to refuse a divorce in defended cases if the overall justice of the case, including in particular the interests of the respondent and the children, appears to demand it. Where the interests of the respondent and the children can be properly protected, we do not intend that the court should refuse to dissolve the marriage on the ground that to penalize a petitioner who has shown a contempt for the sanctity of marriage in some way upholds the sanctity of marriage'.

[362] *Putting Asunder*, para. 56.

[363] Ie the Act (based on a Law Commission Report) intended to give the courts the necessary powers to achieve a just financial settlement on divorce: see below, p. 420.

[364] Divorce Reform Act 1969, s. 11(3).   [365] Divorce Reform Act 1969, s. 1.

[366] Divorce Reform Act 1969, s. 2(1).

THE DIVORCE REFORM ACT IN PRACTICE

For some time after the Divorce Reform Act came into force in 1971 it was possible to believe that the 'mechanism for dealing with breakdown'[367] which it had established—'the most radical measure in the history of our divorce law'[368]— had not only 'commended itself to the general conscience long before it succeeded in gaining the statute book'[369] but also that this mechanism had won 'rapid and easy acceptance'[370] not least on the part of the judiciary who had 'proceeded without pause to implement the spirit as well as the letter of the law founded on breakdown'.[371] But this assessment may have been premature.

In the *Field of Choice* the Law Commission had set out, in words much cited in the years ahead, the criteria by which it believed a divorce law should be evaluated. A good divorce law should

'(i) buttress, rather than . . . undermine the stability of marriage; and (ii) when, regrettably, a marriage has irretrievably broken down, . . . enable the empty legal shell to be destroyed with the maximum fairness, and the minimum bitterness, distress and humiliation'.[372]

How far did the 1969 Act achieve these objectives in practice?

Buttressing the stability of marriage?

The Law Commission considered[373] that divorce law could make a positive contribution towards upholding the stability of marriage; and that this was to be done firstly by ensuring that divorce was 'not so easy that the parties are under no inducement to make a success of their marriage and, in particular, to overcome temporary difficulties', and secondly by ensuring that 'every encouragement is afforded to a reconciliation' and that the procedure was not such as to 'inhibit or discourage approaches to that end'.

It soon became apparent that divorce under the new Act was in fact extremely 'easy' if the parties agreed on this outcome. For example, the requirement that a petitioner should not only have to prove that the respondent had committed adultery but also that he or she found it intolerable to live with the respondent[374] was deprived of any impact by judicial decisions denying that there need be any causal link between these two matters.[375] The courts held that it sufficed if the one spouse did genuinely find it intolerable to live with the other whether

---

[367] In the language of the *Report of the Committee on One-Parent Families* (1974, Cmnd. 5629) (Chairman: the Hon. Sir Maurice Finer) (hereafter referred to as *Finer Report*) para. 4.42. In this and the other passages quoted from the *Finer Report* it is tempting to see the pen of Professor OR McGregor (who contributed, jointly with Sir M Finer, a learned but far from dispassionate account of 'The History of the Obligation to Maintain' published as Appendix 5 to the *Finer Report*).

[368] *Ibid.*   [369] *Ibid.*, para. 4.43.   [370] *Ibid.*   [371] *Ibid.*

[372] *The Field of Choice*, para. 15.   [373] *Ibid.*, para. 16.

[374] Divorce Reform Act 1969, s. 2(1)(a).   [375] *Cleary v. Cleary* [1974] 1 WLR 73, CA.

or not the adultery was in any way the cause; and in practice it was extremely difficult to controvert the petitioner's assertion.[376] Solicitors soon learned that an allegation of adultery remained an easy way of obtaining a divorce; and a quarter of all divorce petitions were based on this 'fact'. Again, it was easy enough to make allegations of 'behaviour'; and within a few years,[377] 'behaviour' had become the most often invoked 'fact' on which divorce petitions were based. Comparatively few of those who wanted a divorce were prepared to separate for two years in order to establish the relevant 'fact'.[378] The number of divorce petitions rose dramatically.[379]

The bar on 'hasty' divorce

There was, however, one exceptional case in which there remained a barrier to divorce, however much the parties might wish their marriage to be dissolved. As we have seen, the Herbert Act had forbidden the filing of any divorce petition within the first three years of marriage unless a judge gave leave to do so on the ground that the case was one of exceptional hardship suffered by the petitioner or exceptional depravity on the part of the respondent;[380] and *The Field of Choice*[381] took the view that this provision was a 'useful safeguard against irresponsible or trial marriages and a valuable external buttress to the stability of marriages during the difficult early years'. But experience soon demonstrated that an increasing number of spouses were not willing to stay in a marriage which had become unbearable for them. In 1969 there had only been 177 applications for leave to petition within three years of the marriage, but a decade after the coming into force of the Divorce Reform Act there were nearly 2,000 such applications each year.[382] And although it seemed that most of these were successful, the requirement to demonstrate that a spouse had been guilty of 'exceptional depravity' was hardly consistent with the declared objective of enabling broken marriages to be

---

[376] *Pheasant v. Pheasant* [1972] Fam 202.

[377] In 1974, for the first time, 'behaviour' (28.47% of all petitions) was more commonly relied on than adultery (27.49%). A decade after the new law came into force, behaviour was the ground relied on in almost 40% of all petitions (compared with nearly 28% founded on adultery): see the Statistical Appendix in SM Cretney, *Principles of Family Law* (4th ed., 1984) p. 219.

[378] In no year have divorces based on two years' separation and consent exceeded 25% of the total: *ibid*.

[379] In 1965, 42,070 matrimonial petitions were filed. In 1971, the first year of operation of the Divorce Reform Act, there were 110,017 divorce petitions. Thereafter the number of petitions never fell below 100,000; and in 1990 (when 191,615 petitions were filed) it seemed probable that the 200,000 barrier would be broken before the end of the decade. The number of decrees rose from some 89,000 in 1971 to a peak of 165,018 in 1993, and in the year 2000 there were 141,135 decrees: *Marriage Divorce and Adoption Statistics*, Series FM 2 no. 28. A significant number of petitions (perhaps 15%) do not result in decree absolute. See generally the *Law Commission 1988 Discussion Paper*, Appendix A. Predictions that making divorce available on the basis of five years' separation might be followed by an increase of approximately 4,900 divorces each year (see *The Field of Choice*, para. 67) seem in retrospect remarkably naive.

[380] Matrimonial Causes Act 1937, s. 1; see above p. 245.   [381] Para. 19.

[382] See the Law Commission's Report on *Time Restrictions on the Presentation of Divorce and Nullity Petitions* (1982) Law Com. No. 116 (hereafter '*Time Restrictions Report*').

dissolved with the minimum of bitterness, distress and humiliation. Even if applicants increasingly relied on 'exceptional hardship' they would still wish to demonstrate that this was attributable to their spouse's behaviour. They would be advised[383] to 'set out in detail all the facts, however unpleasant, which could possibly constitute depravity even if the court would in practice usually regard them as going to proof of exceptional hardship'. That judges had to consider whether the applicant's sworn recital of the details of the alleged hardship or depravity was sufficiently cogent to justify giving leave to petition in 2,000 cases a year was a demonstrable fact. Whether the existence of the bar had any impact at all on the stability of marriage was much more questionable;[384] and in 1984 the Government introduced legislation[385] substituting an absolute bar on starting divorce proceedings within one year of the marriage (this period being thought sufficient to constitute the necessary symbolic assertion of the State's interest in upholding the stability and dignity of marriage).

Encouraging reconciliation?

The long title of the 1969 Act[386] claimed that its purposes included facilitating reconciliation; and the Act contained the three specific provisions[387] 'designed to encourage reconciliation'.[388] But these seem to have had virtually no effect.[389]

---

[383] According to the Law Commission's Published Working Paper No. 76, 1980, para. 55. This tendency was reinforced by the House of Lords decision in *Fay v. Fay* [1982] AC 835 emphasising the need for the applicant to show the 'exceptional' nature of the case (for example, by evidence, not restricted to that prescribed by the Rules of Court, 'of ill-health, of nervous sensibility or tension resulting in severe emotional or mental stress or breakdown').

[384] In 1982 the Law Commission's *Time Restrictions Report* noted that no such bar existed in Scotland, and statistical comparisons suggested that the effect of the three-year bar was simply to delay divorce.

[385] Matrimonial and Family Proceedings Act 1984, s. 1. The fact that the change would economise on expenditure of judicial time may well have influenced the Government's decision.

[386] The preamble to the Herbert Act had similarly declared that it was intended to support marriage.

[387] s. 3(1) provided for solicitors to certify whether [*sic*] they had discussed the possibility of reconciliation and given information about relevant agencies. A certificate that no such discussion had taken place was therefore acceptable and apparently often given: see *Report of the Matrimonial Causes Procedure Committee* (Chairman: Dame Margaret Booth, 1985) para. 4.42; and see also the Law Commission's *Facing the Future, A Discussion Paper on the Ground for Divorce* (Law Com. No. 170, 1988) (hereafter '*Law Commission 1988 Discussion Paper*') paras. 3.9–10. It may be thought that the use of the word 'whether' in this context is another example of statutory legerdemain. Secondly, s. 3(2) empowered the court to adjourn proceedings if it considered there was a reasonable prospect of reconciliation; but in practice once cases were dealt with almost entirely on the papers under the 'special procedure' the court would rarely be able to detect any such prospect: *Law Commission 1988 Discussion Paper*, para. 3.9. Thirdly, a 'kiss and make up' provision was intended to encourage trial reconciliation, but there is no information about how effective this provision may have been: *Law Commission 1988 Discussion Paper*, para. 3.9.

[388] The side-heading to Divorce Reform Act 1969, s. 3, so described them; but once again this piece of manifesto writing was consigned to the waste-paper basket by the draftsman of the consolidating Matrimonial Causes Act 1973 who preferred the purely descriptive 'attempts at reconciliation of parties to marriage'.

[389] See the *Law Commission 1988 Discussion Paper*, paras. 3.9–3.11. The Paper concluded that the process of divorce under the 1969 legislation—for example, by forcing a petitioner (especially a petitioner relying on 'behaviour') into an entrenched hostile position from the outset, and by

Destroying the empty legal shell with the maximum fairness, and the minimum bitterness, distress and humiliation?

It seems unnecessary to devote much space to the question whether the 1969 Act facilitated the destruction of the 'empty legal shell' of broken marriages.[390] The statistics[391] are consistent with anecdotal evidence[392] that in 1971 and for several years afterwards a substantial number of persons were able to obtain the divorce which their legal spouse had, perhaps for many years, denied them.[393] Moreover, the fact that the court would sooner or later, in all save the most unusual cases, be bound to grant a decree[394] made the pressure to agree to divorce (whether based on adultery, behaviour, or some other 'fact')[395] in return for acceptable financial and other settlement provisions considerable.

denying the parties any opportunity to reflect—might in fact deter couples from attempting reconciliation and diminish any chance of its success: para. 3.11.

[390] There were of course cases in which one party refused to agree to a divorce; but if the parties had lived apart for five years or more there would rarely be any difficulty in terminating the marriage. It is true that in *Santos v. Santos* [1972] Fam 247, CA, the courts laid down that the parties had not only to be physically separated for the prescribed period, but that a mental element was also required, with the result that the period did not start to run until one at least had recognised that the marriage was at an end. But although in theory perhaps questionable (see SM Cretney, *Principles of Family Law* (4th ed.), 1984 pp. 152–158) this decision seems in practice to have had little impact on the number of petitions.

[391] In 1971 29,911 petitions—nearly 30% of the total—were based on the five-year living apart 'fact'. But by 1982 the proportion of all divorce petitions based on this fact had fallen from the 1991 27% to just under 7%: see SM Cretney, *Principles of Family Law* (4th ed., 1984) pp. 214 and 221. This is consistent with a substantial 'backlog' having been dealt with in the early years of the 1969 Act's regime.

[392] The author has given an impression of a visit to the Divorce Court in 1972: 'A succession of elderly persons of eminently respectable appearance came to the witness box to give the oral testimony then required in support of divorce petitions. All had lived apart from their lawful spouse for more—usually much more—than the stipulated five years. In almost every case the story was essentially the same: the youthful wartime marriage, the long separation in service of "King and Country", the drift apart, the formation of a new relationship, the birth of children, the woman taking the man's name, the passionate desire to legitimize those children and so on. In each case, the decree was granted: in each case the elderly couple's faces reflected happiness and quiet domestic content . . . [O]ne would have to be hardhearted (or highly principled) in the extreme to believe that the law had done harm rather than good in that courtroom that afternoon'.: SM Cretney, 'Divorce Reform in England—Humbug and Hypocrisy, or a smooth transition?', in MDA Freeman (ed.), *Divorce, Where Next?* (1996) p. 41.

[393] Note also the letter thanking Leo Abse for 'creating so much happiness to so many unhappy people' from a man who had lived with a woman outside marriage for 21 years and had just obtained a decree enabling him to marry her: *Abse Papers*, F/h/5 13 November 1971.

[394] Ie because living apart for five years was a fact from which the court would infer breakdown unless the respondent could establish the contrary.

[395] The introduction of the so-called special procedure removed any real likelihood of the court being able to scrutinise the evidence the parties chose to put forward.

Destroyed with the maximum fairness, and the minimum bitterness, distress and humiliation

It seems much more doubtful whether the new divorce law allowed marriages to be dissolved with the maximum fairness and the minimum bitterness, distress and humiliation to those affected. True, section 1 of the 1969 Act declared that the sole ground for divorce was to be irretrievable breakdown. But it soon became clear that in reality the 1969 Act retained fault-based divorce alongside no-fault separation divorce. Contrary to the expectations of the reformers, a comparatively small proportion of divorce petitions were founded on consent after two years' separation;[396] and an increasingly high proportion[397] were founded on 'behaviour'.[398] There was a significant body of evidence[399] suggesting that respondents were often shocked by the allegations made against them in 'behaviour' petitions and resented being stigmatised in this way.[400] The rules required[401] petitioners to set out their complaints in some detail: in one case, reported in 1974[402] the written pleadings in a case founded on 'behaviour'

---

[396] Consensual separation divorces constituted approximately one fifth of the total from 1971 to 1989 and in the year 2000 were slightly less than a quarter of the total: see the Tables in SM Cretney and JM Masson, *Principles of Family Law* (5th ed., 1990) pp. 172–173, the *Law Commission 1988 Discussion Paper*, Appendix B, and *Marriage Divorce and Adoption Statistics,* Series FM 2 no. 28, Table 4.20. As noted above, after the initial 'backlog' of long term separation divorces had been processed in the first three years of the Act's operation the five year living apart fact was comparatively little used.

[397] By 2000, the proportion of behaviour petitions was 44% of all divorce petitions: see *Marriage Divorce and Adoption Statistics,* Series FM 2 no. 28.

[398] The proportion of petitions founded on adultery had remained fairly constant around a quarter of all divorce petitions over the years. In contrast, the proportion of five-year separation petitions fell from the initial 27% to only some 7% of all petitions: see the sources cited above.

[399] See the sources cited in the *Law Commission 1988 Discussion Paper,* paras. 3.25–3.27.

[400] Judges' comments (especially when reported in the press) could also be a source of offence— see for example the case reported as a news item in *The Times* 17 October 1981, in which a wife was reported to have admitted adultery with labourers and lorry drivers in the open air, provoking the judge to remark that although she came from a highly respectable background she seemed 'for all her religious beliefs . . . to have been from time to time a promiscuous woman' gaining sexual gratification from members of the labouring classes in circumstances the judge considered to have something in common with *Lady Chatterley's Lover* and *Tom Jones.*

[401] By the Rules of Court: Matrimonial Causes Rules 1977, App. 2, para. 1(m); but over the years solicitors increasingly became conscious of the damage likely to be done by the making of detailed allegations of conduct (see G Davis and M Murch, *Grounds for Divorce* (1988)); and there were suggestions that some courts were prepared to accept petitions alleging 'behaviour' in the most general terms coupled with a statement that particulars would be provided on request. The *Report of the Matrimonial Causes Procedure Committee* (Chairman: Dame Margaret Booth, 1985) para. 4.25 gave its support to such an approach and recommended that the requirement to give particulars should be abandoned in order to 'shift the emphasis away from the particulars of behaviour and guilt to the fact of the breakdown of marriage'. The rules remained unchanged; but it seems that practice changed. In particular, the Solicitors' Family Law Association *Code of Practice* requires solicitors to consider whether the other party's solicitor should be contacted in advance about the petition, the 'facts' on which it is to be based and the particulars, 'with a view to coming to an agreement and minimising misunderstanding'; and similarly the SFLA Code states that a solicitor should discourage the naming of the 'guilty party' in adultery cases 'unless there are very good reasons to do so'.

[402] *Griffiths v. Griffiths* [1974] 1 WLR 1350. The hearing of the case took 26 days.

covered 66 pages. If the allegations and denials were persisted in, the resultant trials could be degrading, sordid, bitter and hostile. For example:

In *O'Neill v. O'Neill*[403] the wife complained that the husband (amongst other failings) did not have adequate standards of personal hygiene. 'The wife said he hardly ever bathed himself; the husband said he bathed once a week. The judge made a specific finding that he was a reasonably clean man . . .'

In *Mason v. Mason*[404] the husband alleged that the wife's refusal to permit intercourse more than once a week constituted behaviour such as to make it unreasonable to expect him to live with her. The court disagreed.

In *Livingstone-Stallard v. Livingstone-Stallard*[405] the wife alleged that the husband constantly criticised her over petty things (such as her attitude to housework and the efficiency of her methods of washing underwear) adopted a disapproving and boorish attitude to her and retaliated for her supposed failings by sweeping her belongings into cardboard boxes.

The 'special procedure' and its impact

The Divorce Reform Act had carefully preserved[406] the distinctive requirement that the court inquire, so far as it reasonably could, into the facts alleged by the petitioner and into any facts alleged by the respondent; and for some time after the coming into force of the 1969 Act the courts continued[407] to assert that the law required judicial care and scrutiny to ensure that what was described[408] as the stringent test of breakdown had been satisfied and that the court's function was not merely to act as a 'rubber stamp' even in cases in which the parties had come to an agreement.[409] But research carried out in 1973[410] cast serious doubts on whether the typical, necessarily rather perfunctory, hearing of undefended

---

[403] [1975] 1 WLR 1181. Similarly, in *Dady v. Dady* (reported as a news item in the *Daily Telegraph,* 19 November 1981) the wife alleged that the husband would not wash regularly, took a bath only once weekly, had sweaty feet and often smelled stale.

[404] (1980) 11 Fam Law 143, CA. This case was extensively reported in the popular press under headings such as 'once a week is enough, say Law Chiefs'; and three newspapers went so far as to seek interviews with the wives of the Lords Justice concerned: see *Official Report* (HL) vol. 416, col. 409.

[405] [1974] Fam 247, 264.   [406] s. 2(2).

[407] But the courts early refused to get involved in detailed inquests irrelevant to the question whether the statutory requirements for divorce had been met: see eg *Grenfell v. Grenfell* [1978] Fam 128 (cross petitions—wife alleged 'behaviour'; husband denied and alleged five years' separation which it was impossible to deny—court rejected wife's argument that it was obliged to inquire into her complaints about husband's behaviour because divorce was inevitable and her allegations therefore irrelevant—no point in 'conducting enquiry into behaviour merely to satisfy feelings, however genuinely and sincerely held . . . To do so would be a waste of time of the court and . . . would be running counter to the general policy or philosophy of the divorce legislation' which is to dissolve irretrievably broken marriages as quickly and painlessly as possible: see *per* Ormrod LJ at p. 141).

[408] *Pheasant v. Pheasant* [1972] Fam 202, 207, *per* Ormrod LJ.

[409] *Santos v. Santos* [1972] Fam 247, CA.

[410] By E Elston, J Fuller and M Murch (1975) 38 MLR 609.

cases (lasting perhaps ten minutes) commanded petitioners' confidence and respect or served any other useful purpose; and this finding was eagerly seized on by a Government only too conscious that the enormous growth in the number of divorce petitions had made the provision of formal judicial hearings in all cases burdensome in terms of judicial time and expense (much of which would be born by Legal Aid and thus ultimately by the taxpayer).

In 1973 the Conservative Government applied a so-called 'special procedure' to some undefended divorces:[411] divorce was to be granted after an examination of printed forms lodged by the parties carried out by a District Judge in private and without any attendance by the parties; and in 1976[412] the 'special procedure' was applied to all undefended[413] divorce petitions.[414] It was intended in this way to make the grant of a divorce decree so simple that petitioners would not need

[411] Although Lord McGregor of Durris has in his *Social History and Law Reform* (1981) p. 43 described the introduction of the special procedure as 'the only fundamental change in divorce since it ceased to be obtained by private act of parliament' the Government avoided any parliamentary debate on the decision to introduce it. It should, however, be said that the function of the District Judge remains judicial (rather than administrative), and that the Judge may seek further information and has power to adjourn a case for trial in open court; but there is (as the Law Commission pointed out in 1988) 'a dearth of statistical or other information' about the proportion of cases which do not appear to the parties to have been dealt with entirely on the basis of the written statements submitted to the court at the outset: *Facing the Future, A Discussion Paper on the Ground for Divorce*, Law Com. No. 170, 1988, para. 2.8.

[412] The 'special procedure' was first applied—without any parliamentary debate—by the Conservative administration in 1973. It was extended to all undefended divorces by the Labour Government in 1976 and (since in practice virtually all divorce petitions are undefended: the so-called special procedure became the ordinary procedure for dealing with the great majority of divorce cases). For a description of the steps in the special procedure, see *Pounds v. Pounds* [1994] 1 FLR 775, 776, *per* Waite LJ.

[413] For a number of reasons the great majority of divorce petitions are undefended. If either party wants a divorce he or she will today in practice sooner or later be able to obtain one, and a solicitor is therefore likely to advise a client not to oppose the grant of the decree but perhaps rather to bargain for satisfactory financial and other arrangements as the price for not putting the petitioner to the trouble and expense of dealing with a defended case. In any event, the cost of litigation usually makes it 'unrealistic, if not impossible' for most couples to pursue their suits to a fully contested hearing, and if it is clear that the marriage has irretrievably broken down legal aid is not usually available to a respondent to enable him or her to defend a divorce petition. In any event, the courts discourage defended divorce 'not only because of the futility of trying a contention by one party that the marriage has not broken down despite the other party's conviction that it has, but also because of the emotional and financial demands that it makes upon the parties themselves and the possible harmful consequences for the children of the family'.

[414] In 1976 the radical nature of the procedural change was recognised; and in order to make it acceptable to informed public opinion the extension was accompanied by the introduction of the children's appointments system under which the judiciary were given the task of scrutinising and assessing the child raising arrangements which the parties had agreed. The Children's Appointments—which, according to Lord Chancellor Elwyn Jones (*Official Report* (HL) 15 June 1976, vol. 371, col. 1218) would ensure that the divorce law would continue to protect children and to emphasise the importance of the duty placed on the judges of discussing with the parents 'as of course they will' what was to happen—were subsequently found to be ineffective and were abolished by the Children Act 1989: see p. 284, and Chapter 16, below.

legal aid to end their marriages; and legal aid[415] was accordingly withdrawn from undefended divorce.[416]

The savings expected to follow from the introduction of the special procedure were, in the event, never made;[417] but the 'special procedure' can in retrospect be seen to have transformed the whole basis of the divorce law. Unfortunately the transformation seems to have done nothing to minimise the incidence of bitterness, distress and humiliation. Indeed the fact that a respondent was in practice denied the opportunity of answering allegations in the petition which he believed to be exaggerated, one-sided or even untrue apparently often engendered a burning sense of injustice; and it seems that this bitterness then often found expression in proceedings relating to the financial and child-upbringing consequences of divorce (which, reflecting the situation when these issues were subsidiary to the often difficult question of whether a divorce decree would be granted, were still usually dealt with only after the granting of the decree). Litigation after the marriage had been formally dissolved provided the focus for ventilating the grievances which at one time might have been at the heart of the divorce suit itself. Yet these grievances were unlikely to be eradicated when a spouse had to be told that a factor which he or she believed to be of great importance—for example, the relative responsibility of the parties for the breakdown of the marriage—was legally irrelevant to the determination of the financial and other consequences of dissolution.[418]

Protecting the children?

Children have long been seen as the innocent victims of divorce;[419] and in 1958 the Matrimonial Proceedings (Children) Act provided that no decree of divorce

---

[415] However, a limited amount of legal *advice and assistance* could be given by a solicitor under the so-called 'green form' scheme; and it was envisaged that this would cover advice on the proceedings generally, negotiations and conciliation on maintenance, family property, and child upbringing, and help with the preparation of the petition and other court documents.

[416] The Legal Aid Board would not normally grant legal aid to defend divorce proceedings if it considerered that the marriage had irretrievably broken down: see *Legal Aid Handbook* (1995 para. 8-07). This policy was criticised by the Court of Appeal: *McCarney v. McCarney* [1986] 1 FLR 312, CA.

[417] See the analysis in the 32nd *Annual Report of the Law Society on the Operation and Finance of the Legal Aid Scheme* 1981/1982, paras. 77–106. It appears that savings in connection with the process of dissolution were outweighed by greatly increased expenditure in dealing with financial disputes (often 'the areas of real contest between the parties to divorce proceedings today': *per* Lord Elwyn Jones LC, *Official Report* (HL) 15 June 1976, vol. 371, col. 1219).

[418] See below p. 424.

[419] See eg *Morton Report*, para. 361 recording the 'wealth of testimony as to the effects on children of the breakdown of normal family relationships. Where family life breaks down, there is always the risk of a failure to meet fully the child's need for security and affection. If in fact there is such failure, the child may become so emotionally disturbed as to reject the influence of the family, and this may result in anti-social behaviour . . .'. Those Commissioners opposing the introduction of the principle of breakdown as a ground for divorce did so in part because of their deep concern about the effect on children of divorce and their belief that children's suffering would be multiplied if divorce were to become more widespread: *Morton Report*, para. 69(iii).

or nullity should be made absolute unless the court was satisfied that arrangements for the children's upbringing were satisfactory or the best that could be
made in the circumstances. The need to protect these innocent victims became
part of the ritual of debates on the ground for divorce. In 1967 the Law
Commission's *Field of Choice*[420] affirmed that the effect of divorce on children
was one 'of the most serious and disturbing aspects of the' matter; but its
response to the 'major problem'[421] of providing adequate protection for
children was unspecific. The Commission did promise a review of the statutory
provisions; and this review led to some minor changes in the law.[422] But
the Commission clearly considered the legitimising of 200,000 children and
thereafter saving some 19,000 children who would otherwise be condemned to
permanent illegitimacy each year to be a substantial benefit[423] outweighing any
disadvantages in terms of the impact of what it believed would be a small
increase in the divorce rate.

Subsequent events do not make for happy reading. The extension of the 'special procedure' to all undefended divorce petitions meant that something had to
be done to demonstrate the law's concern to protect the children of divorcing
parents;[424] and an elaborate system of judicial 'children's appointments' was
created under which a judge would sit in private to consider what was proposed.
A research project found this, too, to be largely ineffective;[425] and the Children
Act 1989 abolished the appointment system.[426]

Whatever the case for and against these attempts to demonstrate an effective
commitment to mitigating the adverse impact of divorce on children[427] it seems
to be the case that contested litigation about such matters as contact has (perhaps because such litigation provides an officially sanctioned procedure
whereby the parties can seek the emotional release not otherwise available to

---

[420] Para. 47.   [421] *Field of Choice*, para. 120(3)(d).

[422] Matrimonial Proceedings and Property Act 1970, s. 17. In fact the most significant change
made by that Act was to broaden the definition of children in respect of whom the Divorce Court
exercised its powers.

[423] *Field of Choice*, para. 37.

[424] In introducing the extension of the Special Procedure Lord Chancellor Elwyn-Jones said:
'. . . If I thought that there would be anything in my proposals which detracted from such protection
as the law already gives to children in this unhappy situation I should not be putting it forward
today': *Official Report* (HL) 15 June 1976, vol. 371, col. 1218.

[425] 'Undefended Divorce: Should Section 41 of the Matrimonial Causes Act 1973 be Repealed?'
by G Davis, A MacLeod and M Murch (1983) 46 MLR 121. The issue is fully considered in the Law
Commission's Working Paper No. 96, *Review of Child Law: Custody* (1986) pp. 86–110, which concluded at para. 4.10 that the procedure had 'not been successful in any of its declared aims'.

[426] Children Act 1989, s. 108(4) and Sch. 12, para. 31, provided that the court should consider
whether it was necessary to exercise its powers to make orders under that Act in respect of children
of the family; and in certain very restricted circumstances the court could direct that the making of
decree absolute should be postponed.

[427] The political importance of this factor was again demonstrated during the passage of the
Family Law Act 1996, when changes (of uncertain effect) in the court's duties were made (see s. 11
of the Act) in an attempt to still criticism that the law did not provide adequately for children
involved in divorce.

them) escalated dramatically.[428] At the turn of the century, there are contested applications for contact in one in every five divorce cases in which there are children,[429] and the number of court orders had risen by more than 100% over a five-year period. Inevitably, these cases involve precisely the bitterness, distress and humiliation which it was the declared objective of the 1969 legislation to minimise.

Finally, the belief that the new divorce law would reduce the illegitimacy rate has been dramatically falsified: in 1971, there were some 74,000 illegitimate births in the United Kingdom or about 8% of the total; but by 1998 there were no less than 270,000 such births or not far short of 40% of all live births. (It is of course true that these statistics may reflect social change, not least a sharp decline in the proportion of couples who believe that marriage is the only appropriate basis for a long term sexual relationship, which had not been foreseen at all in 1969.)

Further reform needed?

It did not take long for the enthusiastic endorsement of the 1969 Act made in 1974 by the *Finer Report*[430] to be questioned. In 1979 a Law Society Committee gave its weight[431] to the view that the 1969 Act, insofar as it embodied a compromise in which offence based 'facts' were often relied on, had been only partially successful in meeting its promoters' declared objectives.[432] In 1980 the Law Commission itself, noting that the majority of divorce petitions were based on adultery or behaviour, decided to undertake a further review of the law governing the dissolution of marriage.[433] But for some time it became part of the conventional wisdom that the legal *procedures* for dealing with the consequences of breakdown (rather than the substantive law itself) were in part at least responsible for the failure to achieve 'civilised' outcomes.[434] As the Law Commission put it,[435] the adversarial nature of court proceedings seemed to magnify the

---

[428] See the account of a research project conducted by G Davis and others in SM Cretney (ed.), *Family Law—Essays for the New Millennium* (2000).

[429] In 1997 more than 100,000 of the 146,000 divorced parents had children of the family aged under 16: *Annual Abstract of Statistics* (2000 ed.) Table 5.12 , and it seems that the parents of some 150,000 such children divorced.

[430] See p. 376 above.

[431] *A Better Way Out*, a discussion paper prepared by the Family Law Sub-Committee of The Law Society, particularly paras. 33–40.

[432] Further evidence from an official source of the bitterness still engendered by divorce procedures was provided in the *Fifth Annual Report of the Lay Observer appointed under the provisions of the Solicitors Act 1974* (1980).

[433] *Fourteenth Annual Report 1978–1979*, Law Com. No. 97. The Commission's investigation of *Time Restrictions on the Presentation of Divorce and Nullity Petitions* (1982) Law Com. No. 116 had been intended to be the first step in this Review: see above p. 377.

[434] See Chapter 21, below.

[435] Expressed in the Law Commission's Report, *The Financial Consequences of Divorce* (1981) Law Com. No. 112, para. 15.

inevitable unhappiness associated with matrimonial proceedings.[436] There was a great upsurge of interest in mediation and conciliation as substitutes for hostile litigation; and the Government set up a Committee chaired by Dame Margaret Booth (a High Court judge)[437] to examine procedural matters and recommend reforms which might (a) mitigate the intensity of disputes; (b) encourage settlements; and (c) provide further for the welfare of the children of the family.

Although the Booth Committee's terms of reference were confined to procedural matters,[438] the Committee's Report in fact served to draw attention again to the substantive law governing the ground for divorce. The Committee noted that the 1969 Act had not achieved in fact the clear concept of the no-fault irretrievable breakdown of marriage as the only ground for divorce; and that—save in the disappointingly small proportion of divorces based on separation and agreement—the parties were at the outset of proceedings required to think in terms of wrongdoing and blameworthiness in a way which perpetuated the images of the innocent and guilty;[439] and it recorded a 'general consensus of feeling'[440] that 'divorce should be truly and not merely artificially based upon a no-fault ground and that the concepts of guilt and innocence which have ruled our divorce laws . . . since 1857 should no longer have any part to play'.[441]

In 1988 the Law Commission marked the completion of the first stage of the review of the law started nine years previously[442] by publishing a powerfully argued paper, *Facing the Future, A Discussion Paper on the Ground for Divorce*.[443] *Facing the Future* concluded that the law fell 'far short' of the objectives set out in *The Field of Choice*,[444] and canvassed various options for

[436] *The Financial Consequences of Divorce* (1981) Law Com. No. 112, para. 13.

[437] For the Committee's membership, see Biographical Notes.

[438] The Committee made 80 recommendations for procedural change: *Booth Report*, pp. 91–97.

[439] Whereas it was generally accepted that in the majority of divorce proceedings both parties were at fault in varying degrees.

[440] However, the Committee also noted the existence of a 'minority view, strongly held, which supported the retention of the fault concept in relation to divorce' on the basis that to remove it would lead to a denial of justice: *Booth Report*, para. 2.9.

[441] *Ibid.*   [442] *Fourteenth Annual Report* 1978–1979, Law Com. No. 97; see note 433 above.

[443] Law Com. No. 170.

[444] See above, p. 376. The Commission expressed its views at paras. 3.48–3.50 in eloquent language which deserves to be recorded:

'The present law does not, nor could it reasonably be expected to, buttress the stability of marriage by preventing determined parties from obtaining a speedy divorce. Because of the compromise nature of the 1969 Act, the benefits referred to above have been bought at the price of incoherence and increased confusion for litigants. Thus the law is neither understandable nor respected and there is evidence of not inconsiderable consumer dissatisfaction. Attaining the aims of maximum fairness and minimum bitterness has been rendered impossible by the retention of the fault element. The necessity of making allegations in the petition "draws the battle-lines" at the outset. The ensuing hostility makes the divorce more painful, not only for the parties but also for the children, and destroys any chance of reconciliation and may be detrimental to post-divorce relationships. Underlying all these defects is the fact that whether or not the marriage can be dissolved depends principally upon what parties have done in the past. In petitions relying on fault-based facts, the petitioner is encouraged to "dwell on the past" and to recriminate.

At the same time, the present divorce process may not allow sufficient opportunity for the parties to come to terms with what is happening in their lives. A recent study of the process of "uncoupling" points out that one party has usually gone far down that path before the other one discovers this, by which time it may be too late. Once the divorce process has been started it may have a "juggernaut" effect, providing insufficient opportunity for the

reform.[445] Two years later, in 1990, the Commission published its definitive *Report on the Ground for Divorce*.[446] According to this, consultation[447] had 'overwhelmingly endorsed' the Commission's preliminary view that the divorce law was confusing, unjust, and that it fulfilled neither of its original objectives'.[448] Yet—so the Commission reported—there was also 'overwhelming support' for retaining irretrievable breakdown as the 'fundamental basis' of the ground for divorce. Hence, it seems that the complaint was not of the breakdown principle itself but rather of the legal rules and procedures by which that breakdown was established.[449] The Commission accordingly proposed that breakdown should be established by the expiry of a minimum period of one year from the filing by one or both parties of a 'statement of marital breakdown'. This period was intended to be used 'for consideration of the practical consequences which would result from a divorce and reflection on whether the breakdown' was truly irreparable.[450] To help the parties use this period constructively they would be provided with a comprehensive information pack;[451] whilst various steps would be taken to facilitate counselling, reconciliation, conciliation and mediation.[452]

At this stage, the Government, for the first time in the twentieth century, assumed a direct role in deciding on the policy of legislation dealing with the ground for divorce. (Apart from any other considerations, the fact that the extension of mediation as an integral part of the package would have had inevitable consequences for public expenditure made private member's legislation inappropriate.) At first the Government's approach was

---

parties to re-evaluate their positions. Thus, there is little or no scope for reconciliation, conciliation or renegotiation of the relationship. It is clear that both emotionally and financially it is much less costly if ancillary matters can be agreed between the parties. Where antagonism is created or exacerbated by the petition, or their respective bargaining power distorted, the atmosphere is not conducive to calm and sensible negotiations about the future needs of the parties and their children.

Above all, the present law fails to recognise that divorce is not a final product but part of a massive transition for the parties and their children. It is crucial in the interests of the children (as well as the parties) that the transition is as smooth as possible, since it is clear that their short and long-term adjustment depends to a large extent on their parents' adjustment and in particular on the quality of their post-divorce relationship with each parent. Although divorce law itself can do little actively to this end, it can and should ensure that the divorce process is not positively adverse to this adjustment. As Lord Hailsham has said, "though the law could not alter the facts of life, it need not unnecessarily exaggerate the hardships inevitably involved". There seems little doubt that the present law is guilty of just this.'

[445] The Commission thought the 'most realistic' were (a) divorce after a period of separation; and (b) divorce by a 'process over time' ie after a period of transition in which the parties are given time and encouragement to reflect and make the necessary arrangements for the future: para. 6.3. But the Commission eventually rejected the proposal for divorce based on separation. Instead, the formal divorce process would be started simply by filing a written statement asserting that the marriage had broken down, and there would be no requirement for separation or any other objective evidence of breakdown: see below.

[446] *The Ground for Divorce* (1990) Law Com. No. 192.

[447] This was extensive and included public opinion surveys as well as discussion with persons professionally involved in the family justice system and others: see *The Ground for Divorce*, Part I.

[448] *The Ground for Divorce* (1990) Law Com. No. 192, para. 1.5.   [449] Para. 1.7.

[450] Para. 7.2.   [451] Para. 7.15.   [452] Para. 7.15; paras. 7.24–7.28.

tentative[453] no doubt in part because it was well aware that different views on the subject were held in the Conservative Party.[454] But in April 1995, after yet another round of consultation and after another Attitude Survey[455] had been taken, the Government published a White Paper, *Looking to the Future, Mediation and the ground for divorce*,[456] containing proposals for reform of the law and procedures.

The White Paper proposals were broad in scope:[457] they placed considerable emphasis on the need to support the institution of marriage and to promote reconciliation wherever possible, and—as the title of the White Paper itself made apparent[458]—mediation was intended to play an important part in the divorce process. So far as the substantive law of divorce was concerned, irretrievable breakdown was to remain the sole ground, but as the Law Commission had proposed such breakdown was to be inferred (and could only be inferred) from the

---

[453] In December 1993 the Government published a Consultation Paper, *Looking to the Future, Mediation and the ground for divorce*, Cm. 2424, which emphasised (at para. 12.1) that 'No decisions have yet been taken. Divorce is an important and sensitive subject on which many people have strong views and the Government wishes to consult widely about the options for reform . . . The Government will then decide whether to introduce legislation'.

[454] Prime Minister Margaret Thatcher has recorded (in *The Downing Street Years*, 1995, p. 630) that she 'did not accept that we should follow the Law Commission's recommendation . . . that this should just become a process in which fault was not at issue. In some cases—for example where there is violence—I considered that divorce was not just permissible but unavoidable. Yet I also felt strongly that if all the remaining culpability was removed from marital desertion, divorce would be that much more common . . .'. Subsequent events confirmed that on this as on some other occasions Mrs Thatcher's views reflected those of others in her party. Mrs Thatcher's resignation on 28 November 1990 (four weeks after the Law Commission's *Ground for Divorce* had been laid before Parliament) paved the way for subsequent Government action, but others who held similar views and were prepared to express them remained: see below.

[455] The use made of Attitude Surveys by the Law Commission and the Government is somewhat controversial: for example, 84% of the sample interviewed in the Law Commission's survey thought that the present law of divorce was satisfactory because one person could start proceedings at once if the other had committed adultery or behaved intolerably: see *The Ground for Divorce*, Appendix D, para. 1.4, whilst the same percentage thought fault-based divorce to be acceptable. Overall there was an equal division of opinion on whether the law should be changed at all; and it may therefore be questioned whether these findings support recommendations for change involving a compulsory period of delay however intolerable the respondent's behaviour.

[456] Cm. 2799 (1995) hereafter cited as the White Paper.

[457] Lord Mackay of Clashfern (who as Lord Chancellor was responsible for the Family Law Act) took the view that mediation was 'often a better way to achieve agreement on matters of residence, access and the division of assets and maintenance than court procedure'; and he has emphasised that it was intended (i) that divorce should not be 'easier than it was prior to the Bill'; (ii) that 'everything possible should be done to minimise the damaging effect which divorce of their parents has on the children' and 'to allow the relationship of the children with both parents to continue strong and fruitful'; (iii) that divorce reform should be set in the context of support for marriage, and that the divorce process should be 'fitted into a scheme which had as its principal emphasis the support of marriage . . . and the providing of assistance to spouses who got into difficulties to overcome them'; (iv) that the consequences of the first marriage, particularly on the parties' financial position, should be determined before a second marriage was contracted; (v) and that information about the likely effect of divorce might 'help to discourage married persons from taking the final step of divorce': SM Cretney (ed.), *Family Law—Essays for the new Millennium* (2000) p. 11.

[458] It was apparently thought that linking the ground for divorce with the provision of mediation would 'make each more acceptable': B Hale, 'The Family Law Act 1996—Dead Duck or Golden Goose' in SM Cretney (ed.), *Family Law—Essays for the new Millennium* (2000) p. 23.

lodging with the court of a statement of marital breakdown by either or both parties, and the expiration of a period of one year from the lodging of the statement 'for reflection and consideration'.

The rest of the story must be briefly summarised. In the Queen's Speech at the opening of the 1995/1996 Session of Parliament,[459] the Government announced its intention of introducing legislation, and eventually the Family Law Act 1996 received the Royal Assent on 4 July 1996. But the Bill which the Government introduced was different in some important[460] respects[461] from the Bill which the Law Commission had recommended; and strong opposition[462] to the main proposals (seen by some as conveying the message that 'breaking marriage vows does not matter'[463] and as 'making divorce easier') compelled the Government to accept many amendments. The result was an exceedingly complex legislative construct, which may to some extent have reflected conflicting policy objectives.

---

[459] *Official Report* (HL) 15 November 1995, vol. 567, col. 4.

[460] The Law Commissioner primarily responsible for the Law Commission's 1990 Report has said that the Government 'adopted the Law Commission's scheme, but with significant (and ultimately fatal) complications': B Hale, 'The Family Law Act 1996—Dead Duck or Golden Goose' in SM Cretney (ed.), *Family Law—Essays for the new Millennium* (2000) p. 26.

[461] The main changes to the Law Commission's scheme made by the Government in the Bill were as follows. (i) Attendance at an information meeting became a statutory pre-condition to initiating divorce proceedings (whereas the Law Commission had merely recommended the provision of an information pack as part of the routine processing of divorce matters). (ii) Financial and other arrangements had to be finalised before the marriage could be dissolved (whereas under the Law Commission's proposals a divorce would have been automatically granted at the expiration of the 'period for reflection and consideration' although the court would in certain circumstances have had power to defer the dissolution until appropriate arrangements were in place). The fact that many of those attending 'pilot' information meetings indicated that they were, as a result of what they learned, more likely to seek legal advice (rather than relying on mediation) than they had been before the meeting seems to have been a major factor in influencing the Government's 1999 decision to postpone implementation of the new divorce provisions: see below. Further changes were accepted by the Government as the Bill passed through Parliament, notably: (i) the period for reflection and consideration was lengthened, and periods of different lengths were prescribed in a number of situations; (ii) provisions were introduced evidently intended to increase the weight given to the parties' conduct in fixing the terms of financial orders. Dame Brenda Hale has written that in the result a 'simple modernising measure was made well nigh unworkable': 'The Family Law Act 1996—Dead Duck or Golden Goose' in SM Cretney (ed.), *Family Law—Essays for the new Millennium* (2000) p. 23.

[462] The Government allowed a free vote on many of the provisions; but its position was made difficult by the fact that it had only a small overall majority in the House of Commons and by the fact that much of the opposition—in both Houses—came from its own supporters. (For example, as Mrs Jill Knight pointed out, 112 Conservative MPs (including the Home Secretary and four other ministers) voted against the Government on the basic issue of whether a fault-based ground for divorce should be retained: see *Official Report* (HC) 24 April 1996, vol. 276, col. 543.)

[463] See the speech of the Conservative Baroness Young (*Official Report* (HL) 29 February 1996 vol. 569, col. 1638) and note that Baroness Young (see Biographical Notes) claimed (*Official Report* (HL) 30 November 1995, vol. 567, col. 733) that the 'removal of fault undermines individual responsibility. By removing it, the state is actively discouraging any concept of lifelong commitment in marriage, to standards of behaviour, to self-sacrifice, to duty, to any thought for members of the family. It declares that neither party has any responsibility for the breakdown of marriage. Furthermore, it undermines the legal basis of marriage by making the contract meaningless; and it weakens the distinction between marriage and cohabitation. . . . Now, marriage can be ended just on the say-so of one or other, or both, partners'.

The Family Law Act 1996 did envisage a new relationship between the legal process necessary to end the legal status of marriage and various measures of applied social work[464] intended to identify marriages which might be saved, and to minimise the damage done to children by marital breakdown and its consequences. In April 1997 the Government set up an *Advisory Board on Family Law* to advise on issues arising from implementation and operation.[465] The return of a Labour Government at the May 1997 General Election at first put the prospects for implementation of the divorce provisions of the 1996 Act into question;[466] but provisions asserting the general principles to be kept in mind by those carrying out functions under the new divorce law, making provision for marriage support and governing public funding for mediation were brought into force by the incoming Lord Chancellor;[467] and officials in the Lord Chancellor's Department (some of whom had conveyed to observers what seemed to be a strong personal commitment to the ideology of the Act) continued to let it be known that the remaining provisions of the new divorce code would be brought into force in the year 2000.[468] But on 17 June 1999, without any advance warning (and apparently without seeking the views of the Advisory Board or even warning the Board of what was envisaged) the Lord Chancellor announced that 'implementation of the remaining provisions had been deferred';[469] and on 16 January 2001 the Lord Chancellor announced that the Government had decided not to proceed to implementation of the provisions of the 1996 Act dealing with the ground for divorce and that Parliament would be invited to repeal the relevant sections of the Family Law Act once a suitable legislative opportunity arose.[470] Remarkably, no full explanation of the Government's decision has ever been given; but it has been suggested that the failure of couples to opt for mediation in preference to legal representation[471] on the scale apparently expected was significant.[472]

[464] *Relate Marriage Guidance* was amongst organisations which thought the period would only be valuable if couples had access to a trained counsellor and/or mediator during the period. *Relate* considered that divorce reform needed to be set in the context of a wider set of policies which support marriage and prevent its unnecessary breakdown, arguing that 'given adequate funding' *Relate* was well placed to play its part in a new strategy of this kind.

[465] See *Second Annual Report of the Advisory Board on Family Law 1998/1999* (1999) pp. 1–2.

[466] Mr Paul Boateng MP, the Labour Party's main spokesman during the passage of the 1996 legislation, is said to have described it as 'a dog's breakfast': *Law Society Gazette*, 30 May 1996, p. 10.

[467] Family Law (Commencement No. 2) Order 1997, SI No. 1982, 28 July 1997.

[468] Pilot projects to investigate means of conveying information about the divorce process were undertaken and extensively researched (the final report covering 957 pages of single-spaced typescript): *Information Meetings and Associated Provisions within the Family Law Act 1996*, Lord Chancellor's Department, 2001. Key Findings from the Research are summarised in Annex C to the *Fourth Annual Report* of the Advisory Board on Family Law, 2000/2001. Research by a team led by Professor Gwynn Davis into *Monitoring Publicly Funded Family Mediation* was also conducted and the Report published by the Legal Services Commission in December 2000 is available on the Internet. A summary is printed as Annex D to the *Fourth Annual Report* of the Advisory Board on Family Law, 2000/2001. A number of articles by Professor Davis and others summarise the findings and comment on relevant issues: see [2001] Fam Law 110, 186, 265, 378.

[469] *Third Annual Report* of the Advisory Board on Family Law, 1999/2000, para. 2.11.

[470] *Fourth Annual Report* of the Advisory Board on Family Law, 2000/2001, para. 2.13.

[471] *Fourth Annual Report* of the Advisory Board on Family Law, 2000/2001, para. 3.19.

[472] *Fourth Annual Report* of the Advisory Board on Family Law, 2000/2001, Annex C, p. 42.

DIVORCE LAW AT THE MILLENNIUM: REFUSING TO FACE REALITY?

English divorce law is in a state of confusion. The theory of the law remains that divorce is a matter in which the State has a vital interest, and that it is only to be allowed if the marriage can be demonstrated to have irretrievably broken down. But the practical reality is very different: divorce is readily and quickly available if both parties agree, and even if one of them is reluctant he or she will, faced with a divorce petition, almost always accept the inevitable: there is no point in denying that the marriage has broken down if one party firmly asserts that it has.[473] Fifty years ago the notion that a certificate of dissolution of marriage might be issued automatically 'after a reasonable period for reflection' seemed too absurd to contemplate;[474] and yet such was the essence of the Law Commission's 1990 proposals and the basis for the 1996 Family Law Act. Indeed one of those responsible for the proposals could reasonably claim[475] that they constituted no more than a 'simple modernising measure'. But the truth is that at a *conceptual* level the proposals (as the Lord Chancellor's Advisory Board on Family Law[476] recognised) did constitute 'an extremely radical departure from the arrangements for divorce entrenched over the years since 1857'; and the main element in that departure was recognition that the decision whether or not a marriage should be dissolved was one for the parties which the State was not in a position to question.

The parliamentary debates on the Act, and the extremely complex structure of the Act as it emerged from Parliament, make it clear that public opinion as reflected in the two Houses was not ready to accept such a simple truth. One other factor makes the future of divorce law difficult to predict. This is that until 1969 pressure (often extremely strong pressure) for change came primarily from those directly affected by the divorce law and particularly from those who could not remarry because of it. In contrast, in the closing years of the twentieth century the only significant pressure for change in the ground for divorce[477] had come from professionals working (or in the case of mediators, wishing to work) within the system. It is not clear whether such pressure will suffice to bring about what logic might dictate.

---

[473] See p. 379, above.

[474] See the speech by the Marquess of Reading, confidently predicting that any such proposal would be bitterly and successfully opposed: *Official Report* (HL) 28 November 1946, vol. 144, col. 470. Again, in the debate on the 1951 White seven years' separation Bill Sir Hartley Shawcross AG assured the House of Commons that he (and as he thought the majority of people) would reject divorce by consent 'and still more reject the idea that one should be able to obtain a divorce unilaterally by filling in a form and presenting it at the Food Office or wherever it may be': *Official Report* (HC) 9 March 1951, vol. 485, col. 1008.

[475] Dame Brenda Hale: see above p. 389, notes 460, 461.

[476] *Advisory Board on Family Law, Fourth Annual Report 2000/2001*, para. 3.7.

[477] There was significant pressure for change in the law governing the consequences (and especially the financial consequences) of divorce: see Chapter 10 below.

PART III

ENDING RELATIONSHIPS: THE LEGAL CONSEQUENCES

On marriage, a woman's property vested in her husband, and he was thereafter under a common law obligation to maintain his wife.[1] What, then, was to happen if the marriage was dissolved so that she ceased to be a wife? Should it make any difference if she were the guilty party and responsible for the breakdown of the marriage? What was to happen to any property which the equitable doctrine of separate property[2] had allowed her to keep for herself? And what was to happen to property which the spouses' parents or other relatives had put into a marriage settlement?

As we have seen, many unhappy men and women were for long denied the possibility of divorce. What was to happen if a man who had left his wife refused to support her? For the middle and upper classes the answer might lie in judicial separation (and the court would then have powers to make financial orders) but for wage earners the magistrates' courts provided the only possible source of help in compelling him to support the wife. On what principles were the courts to deal with such cases?

Far more marriages ended in death rather than divorce[3] and the question of what was to happen to the deceased spouse's property would have to be answered. Could a husband disinherit his wife? What was to happen if he had not made a Will? And many couples live together without marrying. Does such a relationship give rise to financial rights and duties, during the couple's lifetime or on death? Such are the topics considered in this part of the book.

---

[1] In fact, the common law right was extremely restricted, see generally *Lush on the Law of Husband and Wife* (4th ed., by SN Grant-Bailey) Chapter 12. During cohabitation, fixing an appropriate standard of living was a matter entirely for the husband; and even if his conduct justified the wife in leaving, the methods whereby she could enforce her right of support were not always effective. The fact that the law often failed to provide a remedy for wronged women was commented on in the debates on the 1857 divorce Act: a man who had deserted his wife told his wife that she might occupy a hovel on his land and come to his house for her dinner consisting of scraps to be doled out to her by the woman who had supplanted her: see *Hansard's Parliamentary Debates* (3rd Series) 6 August 1857, vol. 147, col. 1189 (Mr Drummond). But the 1857 Act failed to provide the cheap and easy redress 'either in a County Court or at petty sessions' which Drummond believed appropriate.

[2] See Chapter 3, above.

[3] This was unquestionably true in 1900 and in the year 2000 it is still true that more marriages are ended by death than divorce: cf. *Bellinger v. Bellinger* [2001] 2 FLR 1048, 1082, *per* Thorpe LJ. But demographic projections suggest that divorce may soon terminate more marriages than death.

10

Marital Breakdown: The Financial Consequences

INTRODUCTION

In 1853 the Campbell Royal Commission[1] had pointed out that a husband divorcing his wife by Private Act of Parliament[2] had invariably been required to make some suitable (albeit 'moderate') provision for his former wife;[3] and the Commission recommended[4] that the Divorce Court should be 'intrusted with a large discretion[5] in prescribing whether any and what provision shall be made to the wife,[6] in adjusting the rights which she and her husband may respectively have in each other's property, and in providing for the maintenance of the children'.

In fact the 1857 Matrimonial Causes Act did not go anything like as far as the Campbell Commission had recommended. The Act provided, firstly, that the court might, in its discretion, order the husband to 'secure' to the divorced[7] wife such 'gross sum of money, or such annual sum of money . . . as having regard to her fortune (if any), to the ability of the husband, and to the conduct of the parties' it deemed reasonable. Secondly, the Act provided[8] that the court pronouncing a decree[9] against the wife on the ground of her adultery could order a settlement, for the benefit of the innocent party and the children of any property

---

[1] *First Report of the Royal Commissioners into the Law of Divorce* (1852–1853, C. 1604).

[2] See p. 161 above.

[3] See *Campbell Royal Commission*, para. 31, for an account of the procedure whereby a functionary called the Ladies' Friend took care to ensure that legally enforceable provision was made for the wife before the Bill was allowed to pass through the House of Commons.

[4] Summary of recommendations, p. 22.

[5] The Commission pointed out that there were advantages in the private Bill procedure which entrusted these matters to the discretion of Parliament. Parliament could 'mould and adapt its relief according to the facts and exigencies of the case' whereas a court would in the absence of express provision be bound by rules: see para. 31.

[6] The Commission proposed that the right to divorce should be confined to husbands.

[7] The relevant provision of the 1857 Act (s. 32) is confusingly headed 'alimony'. In fact that term is correctly applied to the periodical and unsecured maintenance which the Ecclesiastical Courts would grant to a separated wife; and other provisions of the 1857 Act (ss. 16, 17, 22, 24) gave statutory recognition to the practice of awarding 'permanent alimony' to a judicially separated wife: see *M v. M* [1928] P 123 *per* Lord Merrivale. In divorce proceedings, the parties remained husband and wife until decree absolute, and the court, exercising its coercive authority to enforce the marital duty to maintain (including providing the means of subsistence and the funds necessary to enable the wife to pursue her claims) would exercise the power, inherited from the Ecclesiastical Court, to make orders for *alimony pending suit* (or *pendente lite*) in her favour.

[8] s. 45.   [9] Of divorce or judicial separation: see Matrimonial Causes Act 1857, s. 45.

to which the wife was entitled whether in possession or reversion. Finally, the Act gave a husband[10] the right to claim damages from the man who had committed adultery with his wife. This cause of action has a different historical origin from the other powers of the Divorce Court and was not dependent on the court making a divorce or judicial separation decree; and has therefore been dealt with in the chapter of this book dealing with conjugal rights and remedies.[11] The present chapter deals with the evolution of the law governing what is called 'ancillary' relief. (This term reflects the fact that the power to make orders only arose on or after making a decree, so that the court's powers in this respect could correctly be regarded as subordinate to the grant of the principal relief afforded by the divorce or other decree.)

ANCILLARY RELIEF UNDER THE MATRIMONIAL CAUSES ACT 1857

The powers given to the courts by the 1857 Act to make orders for family support after divorce were thus narrow in scope. Over the years gaps and obscurities revealed in litigation were spasmodically dealt with by both case law and amending legislation. For example, the courts (albeit at first rather grudgingly) held that the fact that a wife chose to divorce her adulterous husband did not debar her from seeking an order for maintenance against him.[12] But not even a

---

[10] s. 33.   [11] Chapter 4, above.

[12] The argument that there was no such power was founded in part on the wording of s. 32 of the Act (which implied that the husband was the petitioner) and in part on the precedent of parliamentary divorce, in which (according to Sir Cresswell Cresswell in *Fisher v. Fisher* (1861) 2 Sw&Tr 410, 413) no Divorce Bill had ever compelled a husband 'to make provision for a wife, who elected to be divorced from him'. The judge did conclude that Parliament could not have intended a wife to be left destitute by exercising her legal right to seek a divorce, but opined that 'it would not be politic to give to wives any great pecuniary interest in obtaining a dissolution of the marriage tie. The petitioner had no fortune of her own; the husband has some fortune and trading profits, but they are neither large nor certain. Under such circumstances I think I ought not to award more than a maintenance'. However, this niggardly approach was not followed subsequently, and in *Sidney v. Sidney* (1865) 4 Sw&Tr 178, 180, Sir J Wilde pointed out that 'a very large number of the divorce cases since the Act' had been petitions by the wife based on the husband's adultery coupled with cruelty or desertion; and he thought it would be wrong to allow a husband who had grown tired of his wife to part with her 'at the door of the Divorce Court without any obligation to support her, and with full liberty to form a new connection, [for that would make] his triumph over the sacred permanence of marriage complete'. A man should not be allowed to treat marriage as 'a mere temporary arrangement, conterminous with his inclinations, and void of all lasting tie or burden'. Rather, the guilty should be told '"According to your ability you must still support the woman you have first chosen and then discarded. If you are relieved from your matrimonial vows it is for the protection of the woman you have injured, and not for your own sake. And so much of the duty of a husband as consists in the maintenance of his wife may be justly kept alive and enforced upon you in favour of her whom you have driven to relinquish your name and home". If this be to give the wife a pecuniary interest in obtaining divorce, it is also to hold a pecuniary penalty over the head of the husband for the observance of married duty. And if it be wise to repress divorce, it is still wiser to go a step higher and repress that conduct which makes divorce possible. It is the foremost duty of this Court in dispensing the remedy of divorce to uphold the institution of marriage . . . Those for whom shame has no dread, honourable vows no tie, and violence to the weak no sense of degradation, may still be held in check by an appeal to their love of money'.

much bolder approach to statutory interpretation than was acceptable in the latter part of the nineteenth century could overcome the problems caused by the clear statutory words which restricted the courts powers to make orders against a husband for income maintenance to orders for *secured*[13] provision. It followed that the court had no power under the 1857 Act to make any maintenance order against a man who had 'sufficient income from his labour' to support his family but lacked assets[14] on which the periodical payments could be secured.[15] Fifty years had to go by before the Matrimonial Causes Act 1907 gave the court an effective power to order a divorced husband to make *unsecured* weekly or monthly payments[16] for the wife's maintenance and support.[17] In theory at least, the divorced but property-less artisan or clerk[18] could thenceforth be made to support the wife he had betrayed.

The 1857 legislation had thus clearly been framed primarily in the context of the wealthier families who had at least some capital, but it reflected the Victorian belief that capital was to be used to provide income and not to be spent. For this reason, the Act gave the court no power to order a husband to pay or transfer capital to the wife:[19] maintaining the ex-wife was one thing, but dissipating the family capital was quite another.

---

[13] Ie the husband would provide a fund of capital, the income from which would be available to provide the payments. At this period it seems that an order for secured provision was 'not an order to make periodical payments and secure the payments; it is an order to secure and nothing else. Under it the only obligation of the husband is to provide the security; and having done that he is under no further liability. He enters into no covenant to pay and never becomes a debtor in respect of the payments. The wife has the benefit of the security and must look to it alone; if it ceases to yield the expected income she cannot call upon the husband to make good the deficiency': *Shearn v. Shearn* [1931] P 1, 4.

[14] The court, in the exercise of its discretion, would not make an order for secured provision which would require a businessman with capital locked up in trade to pledge it as security if to do so would destroy 'the very means by which the trade is carried on': *Jardine v. Jardine* (1881) 6 PD 213. The courts were also reluctant to require payments to be secured on fluctuating partnership profits, but the same consideration did not apply to cases in which the income was well-defined: see *Hanbury v. Hanbury* [1894] P 102.

[15] *Sidney v. Sidney* (1865) 4 Sw&Tr 178, 182, Sir J Wilde. In 1866 Parliament enacted the Matrimonial Causes Act in an attempt to deal with cases (commonly those of the comparatively poor) where an order for payment from income would be appropriate, but in *Medley v. Medley* (1882) 7 PD 122 it was held the power was restricted to those cases in which the husband had *no* property on which payments could be adequately secured.

[16] Whereas secured payments could be ordered for the wife's lifetime unsecured payments were restricted to the parties' joint lives. On the other hand, an order for secured provision, once made, could not be varied; whereas an order for unsecured periodical payments could be varied if the husband's means changed: see Matrimonial Causes Act 1907, s. 1(2). It appears that the power to vary unsecured periodical payments was initially exercised very cautiously: in *Jardine v. Jardine* (1881) 6 PD 213 Lord Coleridge emphasised that the husband should not assume he could successfully seek a reduction in the award after 'only a short interval'.

[17] Matrimonial Causes Act 1907, s. 1.

[18] But the powers were not restricted to the lower income groups: in *Jardine v. Jardine* (1881) 6 PD 213 the court had made orders for unsecured payments against a diamond and jewel broker who had made annual profits of £18,000 (something over £1 million in year 2000 values).

[19] See *Twentyman v. Twentyman* [1903] P 82: husband had neither business nor other occupation, and for many years his expenditure had exceeded his income. The Registrar concluded that it would be right to order him to pay the wife £8,000 (perhaps £480,000 in year 2000 values) out of his remaining capital; but it was held that the court had no power to do so.

There was, however, one important exception to the principle that the Divorce Court had no powers to adjust[20] the parties' capital entitlements.[21] The 1857 Act clearly saw[22] the typical situation as that of a husband divorcing his adulterous wife who would then remarry; and it seemed intolerable that the property preserved for her by the doctrine of the married woman's separate estate should then pass to the seducer. As Lord Penzance subsequently proclaimed, it would 'be an evil example if this Court were to decide that the entire fortune of a wealthy married woman was to be reckoned as part of the prospects of an adulterer, or the resources of a second home for a guilty woman';[23] and the Act accordingly[24] provided[25] that the court could direct such settlement of an adulterous wife's property as it thought reasonable for the benefit of the husband or children.

Decisions on the exercise of this power required the courts to assess 'the nature and extent of the pecuniary charge operated by the wife's criminality';[26] and over the years the courts discharged this task with some enthusiasm. But a gap in their weaponry soon became apparent. The power to order a settlement of the wife's property could only be exercised over property to which she was beneficially entitled;[27] and did not allow the court to vary the trusts of the mar-

---

[20] However, sometimes spouses tried to invoke the more arcane parts of matrimonial property law in order to achieve what they regarded as justice: for example, in *Tasker v. Tasker and Lowe* [1894] P 1, an exceedingly wealthy husband (his annual income was in excess of £40,000, or nearly £2.5 million in year 2000 values) invoked the 'unfamiliar' doctrine of paraphernalia in an attempt to recover jewellery (worth £0.5 million in modern values) which he claimed to have given his wife solely for her use as a decoration for so long as he chose. The court conceded that if that had been his intention the doctrine would entitle him to recover 'even if [he] had never heard of paraphernalia'; but held on the facts that the gifts had been absolute: some were peace offerings after quarrels, and 'jewellery liable at any moment to be reclaimed would not make a very graceful or grateful offering': p. 6.

[21] As distinct from requiring a husband to provide security for the provision of income maintenance to the wife: see above.

[22] But incorrectly. Experience soon demonstrated that wives also often sought divorce: see above, p. 169.

[23] See *March v. March and Palumbo* (1867) LR 1 P&D 440, 443 (wife of a blameless foreign office clerk with nothing except his salary of £260 went to Italy on account of her health. On her return she confessed that 'she was in the family-way by' Signor Palumbo).

[24] See the discussion about the consequences of adultery in *Hansard's Parliamentary Debates* (3rd Series) 17 August 1857, vol. 147, col. 1738; and note also *Hansard's Parliamentary Debates* (3rd Series) 17 April 1860, vol. 157, col. 1876.

[25] s. 45 (amended by Matrimonial Causes Act 1860, s. 6).

[26] See for a comparatively modern example *Style v. Style and Keiller* [1954] P 209, CA, where the settlement had the effect of virtually doubling the income of the husband of a rich Texan (worth perhaps £8 million in year 2000 values). The court displayed little sympathy for the argument that the husband would not have benefited from her fortune: 'what really broke up this marriage was her adultery with the co-respondent; and it is both idle and futile at this stage, when she is seeking to prevent a settlement of her property, to put this defence forward', *per* Barnard J, at p. 212; and see also *Compton v. Compton and Hussey* [1960] P 201, Marshall J.

[27] Hence, the court had no power under the provisions dealing with settlements of a wife's property to deal with a life interest determinable on attempted alienation: 'the Court can only look and see what is the interest which the wife takes, and such interest as she takes under that instrument is one which the Court cannot interfere with, and cannot enlarge, curtail, or destroy' notwithstanding the fact that it might seem 'perfectly reasonable and right that the Court should have power' to do

riage settlements which governed the financial arrangements of many middle-and upper-class Victorian families. The discovery of this omission was apparently[28] something of a surprise;[29] but the Matrimonial Causes Act 1859[30] hastily conferred power on the court to 'enquire into the existence of ante-nuptial or post-nuptial settlements, and . . . make such orders with reference to the application of the whole or a portion of the property settled whether for the benefit of the children of the marriage, or of their respective parents as to the Court shall seem fit'. This power[31] came to be freely exercised.[32]

Narrow as the Divorce Court's powers to make financial orders were, they remained substantially unamended until 1963; and major statutory reform only came with the acceptance of divorce for irretrievable breakdown of marriage under the Divorce Reform Act 1969.

---

so: *Loraine v. Loraine and Murphy* [1912] P 222, CA *per* Cozens-Hardy MR at p. 228. The courts experienced considerable difficulty in deciding how far they could properly override provisions (notably the so-called restraint on anticipation) designed to protect Victorian wives from yielding their separate property to the husband: see eg *Constaninidi v. Constantinidi No. 2* [1904] P 253, CA; *Churchward v. Churchward* [1910] P 195; *Loraine v. Loraine and Murphy* [1912] P 222, CA; *Morgan v. Morgan and Kirby* [1923] P 1.

[28] *per* Lord Merrivale P, *Bosworthick v. Bosworthick* [1926] P 159.

[29] 'It was very soon realized that although a marriage had been dissolved, the marriage settlement continued in force, with the result that the guilty party in divorce might remain entitled to funds settled upon him or her in the capacity of husband or wife, either for the gratification of that party or even for the maintenance of a second husband or a second wife . . . which seems a little incongruous to common sense': *Bosworthick v. Bosworthick* [1926] P 159, *per* Lord Merrivale P.

[30] s. 5. The clause was introduced into the Bill by Mr Edwin James MP who claimed that it was needed 'to deal with the case of wife with a handsome income settled upon her by her husband at the time of the marriage . . . [If] she were divorced on account of her own adultery, she ought not to be enabled to live with the adulterer upon that income which she had received from the generosity of her husband': *Hansard's Parliamentary Debates* (3rd Series) 11 August 1859, vol. 155, col. 1378. In fact, the power also applied to nullity decrees but not decrees of judicial separation.

[31] The statutory language was amended to allow the power to be exercised even if there were no children of the marriage: Matrimonial Causes Act 1878, s. 3 reversing the effect of *Thomas v. Thomas* (1860) 1 Sw&Tr 926.

[32] '. . . it is common knowledge that this court does exercise the power of overriding the wishes of a living and expostulating settlor if it thinks fit to do so. There is no doubt about that; it constantly happens': *per* Davies J, *Thomson v. Thomson and Whitmer* [1954] P 384. Moreover, over the years the courts gave an increasingly wide interpretation to the expression 'settlement' leading Scrutton LJ to comment that 'the ordinary Chancery barrister' would recoil from the divorce court's lax approach: *Bosworthick v. Bosworthick* [1927] P 64, CA. However, the courts drew the line at regarding an outright payment of cash as a settlement (see *Hubbard v. Hubbard* [1901] P 157; *Prescott (formerly Fellowes) v. Fellowes* [1958] P 260) and insisted that there be some 'nuptial' element in the settlement: the question was whether or not a settlement had been made upon the husband in the character of the husband and/or the wife in the character of a wife; and the essential point was that provision had to be made 'for the financial benefit of one or other or both of the spouses as spouses and with reference to their married state': *per* Hill J, *Prinsep v. Prinsep* [1929] P 225, [1930] P 35 (and see *Hargreaves v. Hargreaves* [1926] P 42—settlement by bachelor containing limitations capable of creating benefits on marriage not within definition; followed in *Burnett v. Burnett* [1935] P 1—settlement by husband whilst married to W1 and providing for his spouse not a nuptial settlement in respect of W2).

The principles upon which the court's powers were exercised

The Matrimonial Causes Act 1857[33] directed the court in taking decisions about the wife's maintenance to have 'regard to her fortune (if any), to the ability of the husband, and to the conduct of the parties' and make such order as it deemed reasonable . . .';[34] and in this way (as judges constantly asserted) Parliament had vested in the judges 'an unfettered discretion' to be exercised 'according to the particular circumstances of each case'.[35]

The existence of a wide discretion to do, within the framework of the law, whatever was just in each case was a characteristic of the Divorce Court and had many obvious advantages in facilitating the resolution of the financial consequences of divorce. It also had obvious disadvantages; but it must be remembered that in the early days of judicial divorce, the law was administered by a handful of men who no doubt developed habits and practices known to the select group of counsel who appeared before them but not necessarily articulated. As Lord Merrivale P put it[36] there were certain 'axiomatic matters' (in that case the expectation that a wife would be awarded one-third of the husband's income) 'which a judge sitting here does not think it necessary to formulate in the presence of counsel of experience in cases of this kind'. For this reason, reported cases may not be as helpful as they might be[37] in assessing the actual practice of the court; whilst the existence of unarticulated assumptions, coupled with a lack of empirical data about the orders which the court did in fact make over the years mean that it is difficult to determine quite what were the principles upon which the court worked and how far those principles changed over the years. The statements of principle which the courts did make are often couched in extremely broad language which raise as many questions as are answered;[38] whilst the application of principles has 'varied from decade

---

[33] s. 32.

[34] In relation to settlements of the wife's property, s. 45 directed the court to order 'such settlement as it shall think reasonable'; while Matrimonial Causes Act 1859, s. 5, empowered the Court to make such variation of a nuptial settlement 'as to the court shall seem fit'.

[35] *Lister v. Lister* (1890) 15 PD 4, CA. It followed that the only question on an appeal was whether the judge had exercised his discretion in a proper manner. As Lindley LJ put it in *Wood v. Wood* [1891] P 272, the Court of Appeal had 'constantly disclaimed its right to fetter the exercise by any judge of a discretion vested by Act of Parliament in him' and would only interfere if the judge had 'apparently been guided by some supposed rule which this Court thinks erroneous, or has overlooked some material fact'.

[36] *Sherwood v. Sherwood* [1928] P 215.

[37] But statements made by experienced judges in cases which are reported are correspondingly likely to reflect their established practice: it is true, for example, that the President of the Probate Divorce and Admiralty Division did not cite any precedents when asserting in 1928 that the court would take into account the position in which a wife would have expected to be had the marriage continued, but it seems inconceivable that he was not aware of, or was mis-stating, the practice of the Division over which he presided: cf. J Eekelaar and M Maclean, *Maintenance after Divorce* (1986) p. 11.

[38] For example, in *Porter v. Porter* [1969] 1 WLR 1155, CA, *per* Sachs LJ at p. 1159, suggesting that the principles governing the exercise of the discretion to make financial orders in divorce had

to decade' since judges take into account the 'human outlook of the period in which they make their decisions'. In the exercise of such a broad discretion, the law (it has been said)[39] 'is a living thing moving with the times and not a creature of dead or moribund ways of thought'. In fact, the breadth of the discretion enabled the courts, applying the same legislation, to make orders in 1957 which would have seemed outrageously wrong a century before.[40]

There were some recurrent questions, two of which merit discussion in some detail. How far should the parties' conduct affect the outcome; and should a wife reasonably expect to be awarded a certain fraction of the husband's income?

The significance of the parties' conduct

Since it took a judicial decision to establish that a wholly blameless wife petitioning for divorce was entitled to claim maintenance from her former husband[41] it is hardly surprising that the question of how the court should deal with cases where there was a dispute about responsibility for the breakdown continued to trouble the courts. The legislation specifically required courts considering maintenance to have regard to the 'conduct of the parties'; and over the years the courts had to grapple with two distinct issues. First, how were they to seek to establish the relevant facts; and secondly, how far were the court's findings to affect the actual outcome in financial terms?

Finding the facts

As we have seen, the Divorce Court (in contrast to the courts of common law)[42] did not follow the adversarial mode traditional in English litigation. Rather, the courts were themselves to inquire into the facts alleged, so that their role (following the traditions of the Ecclesiastical Courts in which historically they had their origins) was essentially inquisitorial. Such being the theoretical basis, it might be thought to follow that the court would develop procedures whereby the statutory obligation to have regard to the parties' conduct could be properly

---

been settled 80 years earlier in the case of *Wood v. Wood* [1891] P 272, 276: the court would take into account '(i) the conduct of the parties; (ii) their position in life, and their ages and their respective means; (iii) the amount of the provision actually made; (iv) the existence or non-existence of children, and who is to have the care and custody of them; (v) any other circumstances which may be important in any particular case'. But how, for example, is it to be decided what circumstances are important and what are not? How significant is a finding that one party has behaved badly and contributed to the breakdown of the marriage?

[39] *Porter v. Porter* [1969] 1 WLR 1155, 1159, CA, *per* Sachs LJ at p. 1159.

[40] See for example the decisions on whether a 'guilty' wife should be awarded maintenance against her former husband: see p. 406, below.

[41] *Fisher v. Fisher* (1861) 2 Sw&Tr 410; see p. 396, and note 12 above.

[42] For a discussion of this principle and its consequences, see *Pounds v. Pounds* [1994] 1 WLR 1535, CA, *per* Waite LJ.

discharged. But in practice the matter was, for two main reasons, much less straightforward.

The first complicating factor was that the court's primary concern in divorce cases was whether it should dissolve the marriage or not. Only if a decree were granted did the court have power to grant what was 'euphemistically'[43] called ancillary relief in the form of periodical payments[44] or orders varying or directing the making of settlements. Thus, the 'auxiliary or supplementary jurisdiction' to make financial orders could only be exercised after decisions had been made on the 'more important'[45] question; and this notion was reinforced by rules of practice which required applications for maintenance and other financial relief to be the subject of a separate petition[46] only to be filed after the decree nisi had been made.[47] Ancillary relief applications were thus dealt with (as the Denning Committee put it in 1947)[48] at what was in effect a separate trial.

The second factor causing difficulty was that the decree itself seemed to conclude the question of who was guilty and who was innocent. The decree conclusively determined that the respondent had committed adultery; and in practice for many years the Divorce Court would decline to grant a divorce to a petitioner who had himself committed adultery. In this way the law reinforced the 'binary concept'[49] that the conduct of a successful petitioner had necessarily been blameless, and that responsibility for the breakdown of the marriage rested exclusively with the unsuccessful respondent.[50] Of course, this had always been a crude simplification of the realities of human relationships and no doubt the conduct of the unsuccessful respondent was quite often much better than that of the successful petitioner,[51] but at least the courts could determine the financial

---

[43] 'Euphemistically' because these were often—at least once divorce had lost much of its stigma—the matters which were 'at the very heart of the real issues with which the parties are concerned' *Porter v. Porter* [1969] 3 All ER 640, 644, CA, *per* Sachs LJ.

[44] The power to order periodical payments for example was only to be exercised 'on' a decree: Matrimonial Causes Act 1857, s. 32. This wording caused many problems over the years, mostly in cases in which the application for maintenance was delayed: see eg *Bradley v. Bradley* (1878) 3 PD 47 (unsuccessfully argued that no jurisdiction to entertain application made a fortnight after decree); and compare *Robertson v. Robertson* (1883) 8 PD 94 and *Scott v. Scott* [1921] P 107 (no order on application made more than a year after decree).

[45] *Sidney v. Sidney* (1867) 36 LJ(P&M) 73, 75, HL, *per* Lord Westbury. It was consistent with this view that, whereas an appeal about whether or not the marriage should be dissolved lay to the House of Lords, there was no such appeal in relation to ancillary matters: *ibid*.

[46] The Denning Committee (*Committee on Procedure in Matrimonial Causes* 1946, Cmd. 6945), para. 16(2).

[47] This rule also caused inconvenience to wives who needed maintenance for living expenses, since any order for alimony pending suit would terminate on decree absolute. In 1937 statute permitted applications to be made at any time after presentation of a divorce petition; but Rules of Court continued to require the application to be made within a short time of the decree: see Matrimonial Causes Act 1937, s. 10(1), and the criticisms made in the *Second Interim Report* of the Denning Committee (1946, Cmd. 6945) para. 93.

[48] *Final Report* of the Denning Committee (1947, Cmd. 7024) para. 36.

[49] *Porter v. Porter* [1971] P 282, 285, *per* Ormrod J.

[50] See JL Barton, 'The Enforcement of Financial Provision' in RH Graveson and FR Crane (eds.), *A Century of Family Law, 1857–1957*, at p. 362.

[51] *Ibid.*

consequences of divorce on the basis of who had been successful in the decree proceedings. However, after the World War I the courts became readier to grant a decree to a petitioner who had to seek the exercise of the court's discretion to his or her own admitted adultery and this more humane approach towards allowing broken marriages to be terminated in law as they had been in fact no doubt considerably reduced the misery suffered by those involved. But it also increased the problems faced by the courts in deciding what financial consequences should flow from the dissolution. By 1950 Denning LJ could say[52] that it was 'common knowledge that, when parties are divorced, you cannot really tell which of the two was to blame merely by asking which of them obtained the decree'.[53]

The difficulty of determining the relevant facts was increased by a curious procedural practice. Since the financial consequences of divorce were in theory of subsidiary importance it made sense to allow them to be handled, not by the judges of the Probate Divorce and Admiralty Division,[54] but by the Court's Registrars[55] (whose jurisdiction in these matters grew steadily over the years).[56]

---

[52] Apparently not entirely accurately, since nearly 20 years later Sachs LJ found it necessary to repeat that 'it is now commonly accepted that a decree based on a matrimonial offence, whilst of course establishing the factum of that offence, is often of little and sometimes of no importance in reaching conclusions as to whose conduct actually broke up the marriage': *Porter v. Porter* [1969] 1 WLR 1155, 1159.

[53] 'I desire to say emphatically that the fact that the husband has obtained this decree does not give a true picture of the conduct of the parties. I agree that the marriage has irretrievably broken down and that it is better dissolved. So let it be dissolved. But when it comes to maintenance . . . then let the truth be seen . . .': *Trestain v. Trestain* [1950] P 198 (where the husband obtained a decree on the ground of his wife's cruelty, the court exercising its discretion in respect of his admitted adultery), but the facts, according to Denning LJ, were that 'the most the wife has been guilty of is abusive and scandalous words and one trifling blow, all done at a time when she had a good deal to put up with from him' whereas the husband had been 'guilty of the grave matrimonial offence of adultery, with, be it noted, a girl twenty years his junior'). In the earlier case of *Sydenham v. Sydenham and Illingworth* [1949] 2 All ER 196, CA, Denning LJ had given another illustration from his own experience of having 'tried several cases where a husband left his wife and, unknown to her, committed adultery. She thereafter, in her loneliness, herself committed adultery. He then obtained a divorce against her for that adultery. She knew she was guilty and did not defend the case, but she did not know that he was equally, and even more, guilty than she was. The innocent-looking request in his petition that the court should use its discretion conveyed nothing to her. Hence she was deprived of maintenance which she ought to have had, or rather she would have been deprived of maintenance if I had not asked her to come to court and explained the position to her . . . There is nothing in the statute to say that a wife against whom a decree has been made cannot be awarded maintenance, and there is nothing in it about discretion being exercised "in favour of" one side or the other or about a "compassionate allowance" '.

[54] It appears that the allocation of responsibility in these matters was a consequence of the inability of the three judges of the Court for Divorce and Matrimonial Causes to cope with the unexpectedly large number of cases: see P Bartrip, 'An Historical Account of the Evolution of the Registrars' Jurisdiction in Matrimonial Cases' in *The Matrimonial Jurisdiction of Registrars*, by W Barrington Baker, J Eekelaar, C Gibson, and S Raikes (1977).

[55] For the developing role of Registrars in the nineteenth century judicial system, see P Bartrip (1984): 'County Court and Superior Court Registrars, 1820–1875: the Making of a Judicial Official', in GR Rubin and D Sugarman (eds.), *Law, Economy and Society, 1750–1914: Essays in the History of English Law* (1984).

[56] For a succinct account, see R Bird, 'The Rise of the District Judge' in SM Cretney (ed.) *Family Law—Essays for the New Millennium* (2000). For one example of the developing role, note that in

In this way the Registrars became powerful judicial figures[57] able to deal with the things that were of real importance to the parties.[58] But not everyone believed this outcome to be satisfactory. In 1947, the Denning Committee[59] thought it wrong to leave such matters to a 'decision in chambers on affidavit when the parties are not present'[60] and also believed that the system of adjudication of financial disputes failed to reflect the gravity of the issues for the parties.[61] The Committee accordingly recommended that the 'procedure in the Divorce court with regard to maintenance should be entirely changed'. The statutory duty imposed on the court to 'have regard not only to the fortune of the wife and of the ability of the husband to pay' but also 'to the conduct of the parties' was one which should be 'tried by a Judge, and not by a Registrar'; and the Committee thought it should 'be tried by the Judge who hears the divorce suit, because he is the person who hears the evidence as to the conduct of the parties and can better have regard to it than a Registrar who has only affidavits before him'. The Committee considered that to have all the issues heard on the same day by the judge on oral evidence with the parties present would give an 'added sense of importance to the whole divorce process';[62] and that to have the assessment of financial matters made by the judge who had tried the divorce suit 'would not only better carry out the intention of the legislature but would also save much time and money' not least because there would only have to be 'one hearing and one attendance necessary for those concerned and not two as at present'.

The Denning Committee's recommendation was not implemented.[63] Indeed, over the years the restrictions on the powers of Registrars—in 1990 transformed into District Judges[64]—to make financial orders were removed; and by the end

---

1865 the Judge Ordinary made Rules (under the power conferred by Matrimonial Causes Act 1857, s. 53) providing that questions relating to maintenance and settlements were to be referred to a Registrar who was to make a written report to the court; but by 1924 the Registrar himself had been given jurisdiction to make periodical payment orders, and the old rule requiring the Registrar to submit a Report to the judge (who would then take the decision) was retained only in relation to orders for the variation of settlements or for the settlement of a guilty wife's property: Matrimonial Causes Rules 1924, rr. 71–72. Another important development was the extension of the jurisdiction exercised by the specialist Registrars in the Divorce Registry in London to the District Registrars of the High Court: note the account in P Bartrip, 'An Historical Account of the Evolution of the Registrars' Jurisdiction in Matrimonial Cases' in *The Matrimonial Jurisdiction of Registrars*, by W Barrington Baker, J Eekelaar, C Gibson, and S Raikes (1977).

[57] P Bartrip, 'An Historical Account of the Evolution of the Registrars' Jurisdiction in Matrimonial Cases' in *The Matrimonial Jurisdiction of Registrars*, by W Barrington Baker, J Eekelaar, C Gibson, and S Raikes (1977) p. 104.

[58] *Final Report of the Denning Committee* (1947, Cmd. 7024) para. 52.

[59] *Ibid.*, para. 36.   [60] *Ibid.*, para. 52.

[61] Maintenance awards often involved 'considerable payments over many years, indeed for the lives of the parties': para. 40.

[62] A matter to which the Committee attached great importance: see p. 283, above.

[63] Lord Justice Denning thought that, in view of this, the judge hearing the divorce should express his view on the conduct of the parties so as to assist the Registrar: *Trestain v. Trestain* [1950] P 198, 203.

[64] Courts and Legal Services Act 1990, s. 74.

of the twentieth century it was they who handled the great bulk of what were still called ancillary relief applications.[65]

The division made between the proceedings leading to the grant of a divorce and the subsequent proceedings about the consequential financial orders exposed another difficult problem. Suppose a man who recognised that the marriage was at an end, and was indeed himself anxious for a divorce[66] so that he could remarry, wanted to produce evidence about his wife's conduct which could possibly affect the decision whether the court should grant the decree. Was he to be allowed to let the divorce petition go undefended and then seek to raise in the ancillary relief proceedings the matters which might have provided a defence to the petition, or did the doctrine of estoppel (or some variant of it) prevent him from doing so? Eventually[67] the courts adopted the view that, whilst it was not permissible to question in the ancillary relief proceedings the basis upon which the divorce had been granted—for example, that the man was in desertion and that his wife's conduct had not given him just cause for leaving[68]—the respondent would be allowed to rely on any other matters (for example, that there were extenuating circumstances which went some way

[65] See R Bird, 'The Rise of the District Judge' in SM Cretney (ed.), *Family Law—Essays for the New Millennium* (2000). In 2000, District Judges sat for 16,947 court days (and Deputies for 2,202 days) to deal with 'private' family law matters. The published statistics (*Judicial Statistics Annual Report 2000*, Table 9.2 and accompanying text) provide no indication of how different types of 'private' family business is divided between the different classes of judge. But it appears that 30,546 lump sum and property orders were made in county courts, and anecdotal evidence suggests that the majority would have been made by District Judges. The published statistics in respect of periodical payment orders do not state how many such orders were made in total.

[66] 'No doubt the husband was anxious for a divorce, as well as his wife': *Mould v. Mould* [1933] P 76, *per* Bateson J (a case in which the husband was allowed to raise 15 sub-paragraphs of conduct allegations in ancillary relief proceedings many of which could have been, but were not, raised in the divorce suit itself as suggesting that there had been 'conduct conducing'); compare *Robinson v. Robinson* [1943] P 43, below.

[67] For an illustration of the strict view, see *Robinson v. Robinson* [1943] P 43, where (although denying that the doctrine of estoppel as traditionally understood had any relevance) Henn Collins J had refused to allow a man to make allegations of adultery against his wife in maintenance proceedings. The issue remained 'constantly recurring and much disputed' (*per* Sachs J, *Hull v. Hull* [1960] P 118) but the courts gradually demonstrated greater flexibility: in *Thompson v. Thompson* [1957] P 19, CA, it was held that the application of the general principle of *estoppel per rem judicatam* could not inhibit the court from carrying out its general duty to enquire into all relevant matters; and in the declining years of the matrimonial offence doctrine, the courts accepted the need for a more robust policy. In *Duchesne v. Duchesne* [1951] P 101 Pearce J sought to reconcile the authorities, and ultimately in *Tumath v. Tumath* [1970] P 78 the Court of Appeal rationalised the law: see particularly *per* Salmon LJ at p. 86: 'Where a marriage has irretrievably broken down and it is obvious that it will be dissolved it seems to me to be wrong that a great deal of public time and money should be spent in deciding which of the parties is to be granted the decree or whether perhaps they should both be granted a decree. Still less is a respondent obliged to spend time and money in calling evidence as to whether or not facts may exist which theoretically entitle the court in its discretion to refuse a decree. Everyone knows that until comparatively recently divorce cases have habitually been hotly contested in public at great expense to the parties or to the legal aid fund solely for the purpose of securing a supposed benefit for one or other of the parties in future maintenance or custody proceedings. This cannot . . . serve any useful purpose and may indeed be properly regarded as contrary to modern concepts of public policy'.

[68] *Hull v. Hull* [1960] P 118.

towards explaining or even justifying his conduct) which could be relevant to determining the financial consequences of the divorce.[69] In this way the courts produced a tolerably satisfactory compromise between the competing considerations of public policy;[70] but the difficulties were only finally removed in the 1970s as a consequence of the courts' developing policy that considerations of conduct and culpability were, under the 'irretrievable breakdown' doctrine introduced by the Divorce Reform Act 1969, rarely relevant.

Effect of findings on the assessment of financial orders

By marriage a wife acquired the right to be supported by her husband for the rest of her life, and the courts soon settled that the object of the legislature in giving her a right to apply for financial provision after divorce was to provide a substitute for the support to which she would have been entitled had the marriage continued.[71] If it was the husband who divorced his adulterous wife she might well be required to settle property to mitigate the damage which had been done to the husband and children. This seemed for many years quite simple, but the question whether a 'guilty' wife should have any claim to continued support from the husband caused far more difficulty.

It certainly seems that in the early days a wife who had committed adultery or deserted her husband could expect no order against him for financial support:[72] after all, she would have forfeited her common law right to be maintained[73] and she had broken the terms implied by law into the marriage contract. But, as has already been pointed out, it had been the practice in the days of parliamentary divorce to ensure some provision for even an adulterous wife; and in 1883 the

---

[69] In *Tumath v. Tumath* (above) Salmon LJ insisted that it was 'well settled' that in maintenance proceedings it was 'of the utmost importance for the court to have regard to the conduct of the parties . . .'; and Edmund Davies LJ drew attention to the fact that the conduct of the parties was the first of the matters listed by Lindley LJ in *Wood v. Wood* [1891] P 272, 276, as being relevant to assessment of maintenance.

[70] See *Porter v. Porter* [1971] P 282, 284, *per* Ormrod J, on the 'conflict between two issues of public policy; on the one hand, the desirability of finality in litigation, which means the very proper and reasonable wish to prevent the same parties litigating the same issues of fact in the suit, and again in chambers on ancillary applications; and, on the other hand, the importance in the interests of justice to the individuals concerned, that the discretionary powers of the court in ancillary matters should be exercised with a full knowledge of all the relevant facts, rather than on a basis, partly of fact and partly of assumptions, arising from such rules as estoppel. It is particularly difficult to do justice in so personal a field as matrimonial cases if the realities of the situation are allowed to be obscured by the application of rules or principle which in other situations assist the cause of justice'.

[71] See *The Financial Consequences of Divorce: The Basic Policy* (1980, Law Com. No. 103) para. 10.

[72] Leading counsel appearing for the husband in *Robertson and Robertson v. Favagrossa* (1883) 9 PD 94, 95, CA, told the court that the Divorce Court had not followed the pre-1857 House of Lords practice and that maintenance 'for a guilty wife has not been ordered except with the consent of the husband or under special circumstances'.

[73] See pp. 91, 393, above.

Court of Appeal doubted[74] whether the courts had been correct in departing from the old parliamentary practice. In 1902 the Court of Appeal (in *Ashcroft v. Ashcroft and Roberts*)[75] finally accepted that the court did have an absolute discretion to make orders in favour of the guilty wife; but the discretion to do so was to be sparingly exercised. In the *Ashcroft* case:

After a three-day trial, the wife of a moderately prosperous[76] Liverpool timber merchant was found guilty of adultery and the court dissolved the 23-year-long marriage (in the course of which the wife had born five children). The wife was absolutely destitute and entirely without means or relatives to whom she could turn for support, whilst her poor health made it impossible for her to earn her own living. The trial judge[77] ordered the husband to 'provide a small maintenance for her, so that she may not be turned out destitute on the streets'; and for this purpose £1 weekly (perhaps £50 in year 2000 values, and a sum significantly less than a manual labourer's weekly wage) was considered sufficient. The husband, relying on the fact that there was no reported case in which the Court had given an allowance to the guilty wife unless there had been some fault on the side of the husband or he had received some financial benefit from the wife,[78] appealed against this order. He was unsuccessful.

The guilty wife was therefore not to be turned out into the streets to starve[79] but she could expect[80] no more than what came to be described as a 'compassionate allowance' to save her from utter destitution.[81] Even if her husband were also guilty and only able to obtain a divorce by the exercise of the court's discretion in his favour the court's approach at the beginning of the twentieth century was that payment of an allowance to the wife could be justified only as a way of making the wife 'reasonably safe from the terrible temptation which might otherwise assail her'.[82]

This approach could not survive the increasing appreciation that divorce decrees often gave a misleading impression about the realities of the parties' conduct and that in any event human behaviour was often more complex than had been appreciated by the divorce judges before the First World War. By the

[74] 'I am not prepared to say on the present occasion that [the practice of not allowing maintenance to the guilty wife unless a special case is shewn] is the correct rule. I am not going to lay down that it is not . . . but it appears to me that . . . the Act has left an absolute discretion in the Court' (*per* Jessell MR, *Robertson and Robertson v. Favagrossa* (1883) 9 PD 94, 96). The Master of the Rolls justified his opinion by the hardship that would otherwise be caused to the wealthier sections of society; for whereas when 'a working man who has married a washerwoman obtains a divorce, she can very well go to washing again' this was not the case with persons of more genteel background.

[75] [1902] P 270, CA.

[76] He drew £500 yearly (£30,000 in year 2000 values) and the firm's stock-in-trade (of which he was entitled to one half) was £3,500 (£210,000).

[77] Gorrell Barnes J.   [78] See the summary of his counsel's argument at [1902] P 270, 274.

[79] *Robertson v. Robertson and Favagrossa* (1883) 8 PD 94, *per* Jessell MR.

[80] Even in 1962 Holroyd Pearce J referred to the 'rare cases' in which a husband would be required to pay maintenance to his adulterous wife: *Slater v. Slater* [1962] P 94, 98.

[81] *Dailey v. Dailey* [1947] 1 All ER 847, 851, *per* Willmer LJ.

[82] *Squire v. Squire* [1905] P 4 (where £1 weekly was ordered).

late 1960s, some judges in the superior courts were able to say that the expression 'compassionate allowance' came 'from a past age' and had 'no place' in the contemporary law of maintenance;[83] and that accordingly even a guilty wife was not to be deprived of her right to maintenance unless her misconduct had been of a 'really serious nature, disruptive, intolerable, and unforgivable'.[84]

But theory as expounded by the higher judiciary and the practice of the courts up and down the country seem often to have been different. For example:

In *Iverson v. Iverson*[85] the husband had deserted his wife. On two occasions after he had left her she committed adultery. Apparently[86] 'those exercising jurisdiction in maintenance matters in Newcastle' shared the husband's erroneous belief that an adulterous wife would not in any circumstances be awarded maintenance.

Even more remarkably:

In *Porter v. Porter*[87] a 42-year-old woman, married for 23 years to a man who had refused to buy clothing for the children and habitually fell into long and morose silences, admitted that she had committed adultery after the marriage had broken down.[88] The County Court judge at Southend told her that she was accordingly in the position of a woman who had never married, and that she would be allowed only five pence a week maintenance. The Court of Appeal held that this was a fundamentally incorrect approach; and said that the judge[89] appeared 'totally unaware' of the modern principles governing the award of maintenance, and that his expressed views were 'decades if not generations out of date'.

Such cases suggest that the superior courts found it difficult to secure any uniformity of approach in relation to the impact of conduct on the assessment of periodical payments;[90] and in practice:

---

[83] *Porter v. Porter* [1969] 3 All ER 640, 644, CA, *per* Sachs LJ.

[84] *Ackerman v. Ackerman* [1972] Fam 1, 6, *per* Sir G Baker P (subsequently reversed by the Court of Appeal, but not so as to cast doubt on the accuracy of this statement of past practice); and note *Porter v. Porter* [1969] 1 WLR 1155, 1160, *per* Sachs LJ (in cases 'where the marriage has lasted some twenty three years, it would be rare, if ever, when she is living on her own . . . for her to get no maintenance at all' . . .).

[85] [1967] P 134.   [86] According to Latey J.   [87] [1969] 1 WLR 1155.

[88] The wife had petitioned on the ground of her husband's cruelty. The 'twenty long paragraphs' alleged that the husband was morose and sullen, was of 'great meanness, had sexual differences, displayed no affection, was a man of temper and . . . was guilty of an assault': [1969] 1 WLR 1161. The wife had sought the exercise of the court's discretion in respect of her admitted adultery (which however occurred only after the marriage had broken down); and the husband relied on that as the ground on which he should be granted a divorce. It was then agreed—'an arrangement of a type which has often been commended by judges of the . . . Divorce . . . Division as one that saves much waste of the court's time and of public money'—that the petition should proceed on the basis of the admitted adultery; but this should not have prejudiced the wife's chances of success in relation to maintenance: *per* Sachs LJ at p. 1157.

[89] Sachs LJ (at p.1158) appreciated 'the difficulties of some county court judges . . . called on to exercise a jurisdiction' which had, until the transfer of undefended divorces to the county court in 1967, been 'vested solely in the judges of the Probate, Divorce and Admiralty Division'.

[90] In relation to the court's power to direct a settlement of the wife's property, the law remained influenced by the need to compensate the family for the loss which the consequential breakdown had

'The notion that a "guilty" wife is virtually disqualified from obtaining an order for maintenance . . . persisted in the fact of strong authority to the contrary . . . [T]his . . . led to bitterly contested divorce cases in which the only real issue has been maintenance . . .'[91]

In short, the judges found it difficult, even in the permissive 1960s, to make 'conduct' go away as a factor influencing divorce practice.

THE QUEST FOR CERTAINTY:

THE ONE-THIRD APPROACH TO MAINTENANCE ASSESSMENT

The Ecclesiastical Court in granting what was called permanent alimony to a wife separated from her husband, would usually quantify the amount so that the wife would have one third of the joint incomes; and the Divorce Court at first was content to follow that precedent.[92] Hence, although there was no hard and fast rule[93] the court would normally[94] allocate to a successful wife petitioner[95]

---

on the family's circumstances: see *Compton v. Compton and Hussey* [1960] P 201; and the exercise of the discretionary power to vary nuptial settlements also seems to have been heavily influenced by considerations of the parties' share of the responsibility for the breakdown of the marriage.

[91] *Wachtel v. Wachtel* [1973] Fam 72, 78, *per* Ormrod J.

[92] '. . . the considerations laid down in section 32 of the Matrimonial Causes Act 1857, in relation to divorce were, in my view, declaratory of the practice of the ecclesiastical courts in their jurisdiction in alimony as to what was a reasonable amount . . .': *Sansom v. Sansom* [1966] P 52, 54. However, little is known about the practice of the Ecclesiastical Courts in this respect but it seems that where there were no children the wife might be allotted up to half the joint income (especially in cases where much of the property from which the income derived had originally been provided by the wife): see *Otway v. Otway* (1813) 2 Phill. 109 (London Consistory Court, Sir J Nicholl), and see also 'The Enforcement of Financial Provision', by JL Barton in RH Graveson and FR Crane (eds.), *A Century of Family Law, 1857–1957* (1957) at pp. 352–355.

[93] See *per* Lord Hanworth MR. *Stibbe v. Stibbe* [1931] P 105, 110, where a one-third allocation is described as a 'sound working rule . . . , yet . . . not an absolute rule . . . [rather] a guide'. The one-third guideline was not applied in cases involving the very rich or very poor: see below.

[94] For an early illustration of the normal proportion and that it was no more than a starting point, see *Louis v. Louis* (1866) LR 1 P&D 230 (permanent alimony for wife fixed at £40 on the basis that Sir John Louis, a lieutenant in Indian Army on leave in England was paid £120. When his pay was subsequently increased to £480 the court accepted the husband's contention that the cost of living in India was much higher than in England and rejected the wife's application for the 'ordinary proportion', allowing her only one quarter, ie £120). See also *Dean v. Dean* [1923] P 172, 176, *per* Sir H Duke P: a quarter of the joint incomes would be the starting point in cases in which the income was liable to fluctuate; and even less would be allowed in a case in which the wife (who was apparently of a less elevated social class than the husband) had 'acquiesced in a much narrower scale of living than her husband . . . could have afforded'. Conversely, the courts in practice rarely awarded more than one-half even where the wife had originally provided most of the capital from which the income was derived: *Haigh v. Haigh* (1869) LR 1 P&D 709.

[95] Although at one time distinctions were sometimes drawn between the scale of provision appropriate in cases of divorce on the one hand and judicial separation on the other (see *Haigh v. Haigh* (1869) LR 1 P&D 709; *Gilbey v. Gilbey* [1927] P 197, *per* Lord Merrivale P: always necessary to remember that the practice as to alimony observed in the Ecclesiastical Courts 'does not govern, as of course [*sic*], the award of maintenance after dissolution of the marriage') it came to be accepted that the material tests were usually identical: see *Schlesinger v. Schlesinger* [1960] P 191.

such a sum as would bring her income up to one-third[96] of the joint incomes.[97]

What was the justification for settling on one-third, rather than one-half or indeed any other fraction? The strongest influence seems simply to have been tradition: one-third was seen as the wife's share in inheritance and other financial matters; but in 1966 the President of the Probate Divorce and Admiralty Division found a justification[98] in the fact that 'in a typical case the court was concerned with three groups of needs—those of the wife, those of the husband and those of children for whose support the husband was liable'.[99]

[96] The Divorce Court also had power, derived originally from the practice of the Ecclesiastical Courts and seen in part as an incident of the husband's common law duty to maintain his wife, to award alimony *pending suit (pendente lite)* 'in order to protect the position of the wife pending trial'; and the normal practice on such applications was to award such a sum as would give the wife *one-fifth* of the joint incomes (averaged over three years): see eg *Goodheim v. Goodheim and Frankinson* (1861) 2 Sw&Tr 250 (where in fact no order was made against a Manchester cap manufacturer earning £100 a year in favour of his wife who was earning substantial sums). Orders for alimony pending suit were made even although the wife 'appears to have little chance of success in her litigation': *per* Pearce J in *Silverstone v. Silverstone* [1953] P 174, 177. And see to the same effect Holroyd Pearce LJ *Slater v. Slater* [1962] P 94: '. . . during the pendency of its litigation wives must be, so far as possible, relieved from necessity, even where it seems probable that they are guilty, until such time as the law formally releases the husband from his matrimonial obligations. In a court concerned amongst other things to prevent collusion it is particularly desirable that wives should not be subject to the pressure of financial stringency pendente lite . . .'.

[97] See *Cobb v. Cobb* [1900] P 294, 295, *per* Sir FH Jeune, 'although not applied with absolute rigidity in this Division' the rule 'nevertheless generally recognised and accepted here as a practical guide in cases of judicial separation . . . where there are no children of the marriage or where, if there are children, the wife has not to support them, [is that] she, if she has no means of her own, shall be allotted one-third of the husband's nett income, or, if she has means apart from her husband, then her income is to be made up to one-third of the joint incomes'. For other cases in which the existence of the one-third principle was accepted see *Theobald v. Theobald* (1889) 15 PD 26; *Hanbury v. Hanbury* [1894] P 102 (where the issue was simply whether the calculation should be based on the husband's drawings—£2,400 or £140,000 in year 2000 values—from his brewing partnership or on the whole of his share of the profits, and the higher figure was taken); *Kettlewell v. Kettlewell* [1898] P 138 (although less than a third was awarded: see the text at pp. 411–412 below); and *Sherwood v. Sherwood* [1928] P 215 where Lord Merrivale P explained that 'the course which is taken and has been taken, at any rate, during the period in which I have had any experience in these matters—has been to allot the . . . wife, about one-third of the expected income of the respondent . . . These are elementary matters here' (ie amongst Judges of the Divorce division, in effect so obvious that they do not need to be justified or mentioned). See also *Powell v. Powell* [1951] P 257, CA, where counsel's arguments all use one-third as a benchmark (although in fact the court ordered a 10% increase to the wife because the maintenance payments to the three children had been artificially depressed for tax reasons); and note that in *Tulip v. Tulip* [1951] P 378, CA, the report refers to the 'customary calculations'.

[98] Or more accurately gave an explanation of the reason why the 'rule of one third' so often worked out 'soundly and fairly': *Sansom v. Sansom* [1966] P 52, 55, *per* Sir Jocelyn Simon P Rather curiously, Simon P had (two years earlier) described the rule as 'discredited': see *Kershaw v. Kershaw* [1966] P 13, 17. Even more curiously the one-third approach 'after a period in which it had been doubted quite strongly' was (briefly) reinstated in the post-Divorce Reform Act 1969 case-law: see *Rodewald v. Rodewald* [1977] 2 All ER 609, CA, *per* Ormrod LJ (referring to *Wachtel v. Wachtel* [1973] Fam 72, CA, in which an attempt was made to justify this fractional starting point on rather different grounds: see below).

[99] And also because after divorce the husband might have remarried and undertaken obligations to another woman (although the President added that he did not say that 'the claims of this group are in all circumstances entitled to rank with, much less before, the claims of a wife petitioner . . . and the children of the marriage'): *Sansom v. Sansom* [1966] P 52, 55, *per* Sir Jocelyn Simon P.

Whatever the justification, the fractional approach continued to influence practice; and in 1947 the Denning Committee[100] described the one-third 'rule of thumb' as 'inveterate'.[101] But such a crude approach did not escape criticism. It was certainly not universally applied;[102] and indeed the superior courts repeatedly denied that the assessment of maintenance had become a matter of arithmetic rather than discretion,[103] and one President of the Probate Divorce and Admiralty Division went so far as to claim that the 'only principle to be observed is that [the court] should follow the statute'.[104]

One-third approach not applicable to the rich or the poor: the emergence of needs and requirements as a criterion

By the beginning of the twentieth century it had become clear that the courts would be reluctant to allocate to the wife an income greatly in excess of the amount needed to support her usual needs and standard of living:

In *Kettlewell v. Kettlewell*[105] husband and wife had enjoyed a lavish standard of living with a joint[106] income of some £20,000 (more than £1 million in year 2000 values). The court awarded the wife an annual sum sufficient to give her an income of £3,000 (£180,000 in year 2000 values). Although (said Sir FH Jeune P)

---

[100] *Final Report of the Denning Committee* (1947, Cmd. 7024) para. 40.

[101] The Committee (which disapproved of delegating adjudication in financial matters to the Registrars) thought that the practice had become so well established 'probably because the procedure before the Registrars enables them to have regard to the means of the parties but is ill suited to enable them to have regard to their conduct': *ibid.* Although 'The Enforcement of Financial Provision', by JL Barton in RH Graveson and FR Crane (eds.), *A Century of Family Law, 1857–1957*, states at p. 361 that 'during the early years of the twentieth century the one-third rule was quietly abandoned [and that the] modern view is that . . . there is not even a prima facie arithmetical rule' it seems improbable that the members of the Denning Committee were unaware of the courts' practice.

[102] Indeed, in *N v. N* (1928) 138 LT 693, 695, Lord Merrivale P claimed that he had 'repeatedly called attention to the fact . . . that, in considering what is the statutory right of a petitioner, whose marriage has been dissolved, to maintenance out of the funds of her former husband, the tribunal, making the award, will be misled if they suppose that these facts are the same as those which gave rise to the practice and the inveterate practice in the Ecclesiastical Courts, whereby a wife who had obtained a divorce *a mensa et thoro* was entitled under normal circumstances to an award of something like a third of her husband's available means'. This may be thought difficult to reconcile with the same judge's defence of the one-third approach in *Sherwood v. Sherwood* [1928] P 215; but the explanation may lie in the fact that *N v. N* was a case of substantial means—the husband's earnings being some £4,500 (perhaps £127,000 in year 2000 values) per annum—and as shown below the courts were reluctant to apply the one-third approach to such cases.

[103] See *Horniman v. Horniman* [1933] P 95, *per* Lord Merriman P.

[104] *Chichester v. Chichester* [1936] P 129, 133, *per* Lord Merriman P.

[105] [1898] P 138. For other similar cases, see *Sykes v. Sykes* [1897] P 306, CA—£3,000 (£180,000 in year 2000) out of income alleged to total £70,000 (or more than £4 million); *Hulton v. Hulton* [1916] P 57 (wife awarded £5,000—nearly £200,000 in year 2000 values—out of income admitted by newspaper baron husband to be £29,000 or rather more than £1 million and alleged by wife to be £70,000 (not far short of £3 million)); *Gilbey v. Gilbey* [1927] P 197 (wife awarded £4,000 (£130,000 in year 2000 values)—husband's income £24,337 (£730,000)).

[106] The wife's income (£1,400) was derived from a settlement the husband had made in her favour.

the ordinary rule would be to allow her a third of the joint income 'no one would suggest' an award of that size in this case. 'It would [said the judge[107]] clearly be too much'.

Hence, in high income cases, the notion that £3,000[108] was the maximum award ever to be made to a wife began to acquire some currency;[109] and the courts applied the practice of fixing a sum which appeared to be 'adequate, having regard to the wife's position in life and necessities'[110]—in effect, what judges towards the close of the twentieth century were describing as the wife's reasonable[111] requirements.[112] At the other end of the social scale[113] the application

[107] [1898] P 138, 140–141.

[108] To put the issue in perspective it is worth recording that at this time—and until 1954—a High Court judge was paid £5,000 per annum.

[109] But note that in *Hulton v. Hulton* [1916] P 57 the Court of Appeal held that there was no hard and fast rule limiting maintenance to this amount.

[110] *Sykes v. Sykes* [1897] P 306, 313 *per* Lord Ludlow LJ. And note *Gilbey v. Gilbey* [1927] P 197 *per* Lord Merrivale P: 'Where the husband's whole income has been expended on the requirements of the matrimonial home, a third of the husband's means may well be required for the wife's maintenance; but where, beyond everything called for by such requirements in the most comprehensive view, the husband possesses an ample fortune, of which he can dispose for external purposes, the amount of his income affords no definite guidance as to what sum is required for personal, domestic, and social expenses, and what sum will supply to his sometime wife the necessaries, comforts and advantages incidental to her station in life.' In *Kettlewell v. Kettlewell* [1898] P 138 the Court (following *Sykes v. Sykes*, above) had suggested that the appropriate approach where substantial assets were involved was to ask what would be an adequate jointure—ie the sum traditionally charged on settled property to support a widow after her husband's death—if the marriage had been ended by death, but this approach seems not to have had much impact, and was ultimately decisively rejected as having any relevance to the post-World War II world: see *Schlesinger v. Schlesinger* [1960] P 191, 200, *per* Sachs J (approach 'originated in the days when a relict was expected to retire quietly either to a dower house or to some other suitable residence, and it continued to be used in the era when to say of a man of substance that he lived on capital might well be defamatory, and when the effect of death duties was not a major factor. Today, when high standards of living can often only be maintained by wealthy men if they use either capital or capital profits, the idea that a millionaire would necessarily or even normally make his sole provision for a good wife by means of some fixed income charged on capital has an element of unreality'). Nevertheless, at that time the court had no power to order a husband to transfer capital to his wife, and an order for £20,000 yearly periodical payments (£225,000 in year 2000 values) was made: the wife was entitled to 'live on a really high standard, to be able to travel, and to be able out of her income to provide such furniture and such car as may be appropriate'. At the time, the salary of a High Court judge was £8,000: Judges' Remuneration Act 1954.

[111] But this word was given a broad interpretation: see *Acworth v. Acworth* [1943] P 21, CA, *per* Scott LJ, maintenance is 'a very wide word, and . . . should be read as covering everything which a wife may in reason want to do with the income which she enjoys. It includes much more than food, lodging, clothes, travelling, and so on. It includes . . . charity and making arrangements for the future, thus incurring various liabilities in her discretion, and it is wrong to limit it to any particular form of expenditure. The figure arrived at by the court in the first instance was not arrived at primarily on the basis of her needs. It is not for the court, when making a maintenance order, to decide, by a close consideration of a wife's needs, how much she ought to spend. I do not say that the needs of a wife should be altogether disregarded, but I do say that that is not the primary consideration'.

[112] The 'reasonable requirements' principle was not confined to cases of the very rich. See *Leslie v. Leslie* [1908] P 99 [1911] P 203 where the wife petitioned for judicial separation but (before the case had been heard) was sentenced to five years' penal servitude for fraud. At the first hearing the court refused to make an order. In divorce and judicial separation cases, the courts looked 'to the means of both parties; we look at the condition of both parties; we look at the surrounding circumstances; and we allot such a sum as we think, considering the conditions of the parties, considering their means, and

of any rigid arithmetical proportion also increasingly seemed unrealistic.[114] More generally, changing economic and fiscal circumstances made the approach of the courts in nineteenth and early twentieth century England seem increasingly irrelevant to conditions after the two World Wars;[115] and from this

in view of all the circumstances, should be paid by the husband to the wife and as will support her in the position of life in which she actually is. This woman is in penal servitude at the cost of the State; she is boarded by the State; she has no opportunities of spending money on amusements; in fact, I cannot conceive any matter upon which it should be necessary that she' should have, so long as she is in prison, alimony allotted to her: *per* Bargrave Dean J at [1908] P 107. The hearing was adjourned and the court subsequently awarded her £3 weekly—£150 in year 2000 values and at the time somewhat more than the average white-collar worker's wage—rather than the £10 (£500) to which she would have been entitled under the 'proportion usually allowed by the court'. (The case is also relevant on the issue of conduct, Sir Samuel Evans P rejecting the husband's argument that he should not be obliged to pay anything. He had indeed been 'most unfortunate in his marriage and in his marital relations . . . [and had] greatly suffered from the financial losses which he has incurred by reason of his wife's extravagant and fraudulent conduct' yet he was still married to her; and she had no means at all. 'If she receives no alimony, she may either have to beg, or to become a burden on the public, or to be driven to vice, or to starve. It may be, and no doubt is, a hardship upon the husband . . .': see [1911] P. 203.)

[113] 'The conventional standard in the divorce court derived from the old jurisdiction of the ecclesiastical courts, by which a wife is not likely to get more than one-third of the joint income, is very difficult to apply to a man earning wages and a woman able to earn money': *Jones v. Jones* (1929) 142 LT *168, per* Lord Merrivale P.

[114] In *Cobb v. Cobb* [1900] P 294 (a case under the magistrates' procedure discussed in Chapter 11, below) a 66-year-old railway porter with weekly earnings of £1-3-0 was ordered to make weekly maintenance payments of £1 and was imprisoned for non-compliance. Sir FH Jeune P had held that magistrates should adopt the one-third principle and the order was reduced to 8/-; but it gradually emerged that this too could result in men being left with resources wholly insufficient for survival. Both divorce and magistrates' courts moved towards seeking to ensure that both husband and wife should have a roughly comparable standard of living: see *Kershaw v. Kershaw* [1966] P 13, *per* Sir J Simon P; *Attwood v. Attwood* [1968] P 591. Another method adopted for achieving what was perceived to be substantial justice in cases where for one reason or another the application of the one-third ratio would not do so was to take a man's expenses 'into account as a relevant circumstance in order to arrive at a just solution' rather than simply making a computation in which they would be a 'matter of strict calculation on one side or other of the account': see *Chichester v. Chichester* [1936] P 129; *Collins v. Collins* [1943] P 106; *Powell v. Powell* [1951] P 257. Similar flexibility came to be applied to the question of the extent to which the courts should regard 'moral' obligations not legally enforceable—such as that to support the husband's cohabitant—as reducing his ability to support his wife: see *Cockburn v. Cockburn* [1957] 1 WLR 1020; *Roberts v. Roberts* [1970] P 1. Lord Merriman strongly criticised continued reliance on a fractional approach and condemned text-book writers for failing to give prominence to his views on the matter: 'I hope that some day textbooks will take note of the fact that it has been repeatedly laid down since 1930 that it is quite absurd to apply automatically—and especially to working-class people—a standard which applied in days when income tax was 1/- in the pound, rent-rolls were £10,000 a year and pin-money was £2,000 or £3,000 a year . . .': *Ward v. Ward* [1948] P 62, 63; see also *Collins v. Collins* [1943] P 106.

[115] In *Schlesinger v. Schlesinger* [1960] P 191, 197, Sachs J (in a case concerning the amount of permanent alimony to be paid to the wife of a man with an income of £110,000 (£1.25 million in year 2000 values) and capital assets of £2 million (or £23 million in year 2000 values) pointed out that the authorities cited to him all concerned 'circumstances in periods before the Second World War' since when 'taxation has risen to heights which the . . . Registrar rightly described as fantastic; the purchasing power of money has decreased enormously; and there has arrived an era in which it is well known that there are rich men who live on capital, very often on capital profits, much more than they do on income. No authority has been cited to me where the combined effect of these changes has been discussed . . .'. At a time when income in excess of £15,000 was taxed at more than 90% it was wrong to place reliance on 'principles' supposedly established at a time when income tax was less than 10%. An order should be made which would meet the cost of a suitable standard of living taking into account the burden of taxation.

dissatisfaction of some of the judges and others professionally involved there emerged a principle originally formulated in the context of the court's powers to require a settlement of an adulterous wife's property or to vary settlements: the court should seek to put the parties in the financial position (or at least to preserve the living standards)[116] which they would have enjoyed had the marriage not been dissolved.[117] As Lord Merrivale put it:[118]

'I conceive that I must take into consideration the position in which the parties were, and the position in which the wife was entitled to expect herself to be and would have been, if her husband had properly discharged his marital obligation . . .'[119]

THE FINANCIAL CONSEQUENCES OF DIVORCE: REFORM, 1963–1984

It is rather curious that, although the question of the grounds upon which a marriage could be dissolved were throughout most of the twentieth century highly controversial, for many years (and certainly throughout the first half of the twentieth century) there was very little public discussion of the financial conse-

---

[116] The principle of supporting the wife 'in the position of life in which she actually is' stated by Bargrave Dean (in the unusual case of *Leslie v. Leslie* [1908] P 99, 107: see note 112 above) was restated in the declining years of the matrimonial offence jurisdiction: see *Kershaw v. Kershaw* [1966] P 13; *Attwood v. Attwood* [1968] P 591; *Porter v. Porter* [1969] 3 All ER 640.

[117] See *March v. March and Palumbo* (1867) LR 1 P&D 440 (objective is to restore 'in a reasonable degree the pecuniary status of the parties before [the] abrupt termination' of the marriage); *Hartopp v. Hartopp* [1899] P 65, 72, *per* Gorrell Barnes J (in a variation of settlement case) 'the guiding principle which will be found running through the cases is, in my opinion, this: Where the breaking up of the family life has been caused by the fault of the respondent, the Court, exercising its powers . . . ought to place the petitioner and the children in a position as nearly as circumstances will permit the same as if the family life had not been broken up'; *Hodgson Roberts v. Hodgson Roberts* [1906] P 142, Gorrell Barnes P ('main object and intent of the Court . . . is to place the parties in the same position as if the marriage had not been put an end to through the fault of one of them'; and see to similar effect *Lorriman v. Lorriman and Clair* [1908] P 282, 289, *per* Bucknill J, and *Compton v. Compton and Hussey* [1960] P 201, Marshall J). It appears that the same principle was adopted in nullity cases: see *Sharpe v. Sharpe* [1909] P 20, 22: aggrieved party 'is to be placed, as far as may be, in the same pecuniary position as she would have enjoyed if the marriage had continued, and no distinction ought to be drawn between cases of nullity and cases of divorce'.

[118] *N v. N* (1928) 138 LT 693 as approved in *J v. J* [1955] P 215, 242 *per* Hodson LJ; and in *Schlesinger v. Schlesinger* [1960] P 191, *per* Sachs J (in both of which cases the court was concerned with preserving a standard of life rather than with a balance sheet of the parties' resources) whilst in *N v. N* itself Lord Merrivale was concerned to restrict the amount of periodical payments which would have been due to the wife under 'the mathematical proportion . . . which would have been assigned by an ecclesiastical court' to a separated wife: see above. J Eekelaar and M Maclean, *Maintenance after Divorce* (1986) p. 11 consider that Lord Merrivale's statement, made 'without citing precedent' was based on a misreading of the case of *Sidney v. Sidney* (1865) 4 Sw&Tr 178; but it will be apparent from the text above that there was a good deal of support in the authorities for the approach he adopted. Moreover, as Lord Merrivale P had pointed out, divorce judges regarded certain matters as too obvious to need explanation: see *Sherwood v. Sherwood* [1928] P 215.

[119] See also *Matheson v. Matheson* [1935] P 171.

quences of divorce.[120] It is true that after World War II the question whether a wife guilty of adultery[121] should ever be entitled to financial support did arouse a certain amount of controversy,[122] and it was sometimes said that the courts were over-reluctant to take a wife's earnings (or, more frequently, her supposed earning capacity)[123] into account in making the necessary adjustments; but broadly speaking none of the official bodies which examined divorce and its procedures before 1956 gave any extended consideration to the *principles* upon which ancillary relief was granted. Such discussion as there was focussed on the desirability of amplifying and rationalising the scope of the courts' powers.[124]

---

[120] As the Law Commission put it in its *Published Working Paper No. 9, Matrimonial and Related Proceedings—Financial Relief* (1967) para. 6, 'more attention has been paid to the law governing the grounds for divorce . . . than to the ancillary relief which may be granted in such a suit, even though the ancillary relief is often at least as important to the parties as the principal relief sought . . .'. However, there were (to quote the Law Commission again) many 'bouts of amending legislation' mostly of a technical kind; and obvious defects—for example, the inability of the court to make an order for unsecured periodical payments—took sometimes many years to be remedied. Even in 1967 there remained 'anomalies, uncertainties and gaps' in the law, which—irrespective of decisions on major issues of policy—required clarification and amendment.

[121] The extent to which other misconduct should be taken into account was also in issue: the *Final Report of the Denning Committee* (1947, Cmd. 7024) para. 40 wanted more effective procedures to be created the better to make reliable judgments on these matters: see p. 404 above; and even the Law Commission's *Published Working Paper No. 9, Matrimonial and Related Proceedings— Financial Relief* (1967) para. 21 stated firmly that 'few would suggest that in awarding maintenance the conduct of the parties should not be an important consideration'.

[122] The *Royal Commission on Marriage and Divorce* (1956, Cmd. 9678) was divided on this issue: the majority (13) of the members thought the existing right of an adulterous wife to ask the court to award her maintenance—under powers which had 'been used sparingly and in cases where the wife would have suffered great hardship if the order had not been made': para. 502—should be preserved; but a minority (six, including the Chairman, Lord Morton) thought that a spouse who had had a decree made against him or her based on the commission of a matrimonial offence should not have any right to apply for maintenance: para. 503. The issue of the adulterous wife's right to seek support was still controversial in 1973 (see in particular the Law Commission's *Published Working Paper No. 53, Matrimonial Proceedings in Magistrates' Courts*) and the issue of the impact of 'conduct' on financial orders remained so at the end of the century.

[123] The *Royal Commission on Marriage and Divorce* (1956, Cmd. 9678) para. 493 felt that 'the dissatisfaction with the present system which the evidence reveals stems for the most part from a feeling that the court does not take into consideration sufficiently, or at all, the fact that a wife may well be able to obtain employment but chooses not to do so'. The Commission unanimously recommended that the court should have regard in every case not only to the wife's actual earnings but to her potential earning capacity; and that it should be made clear that the court had power to make periodical payment orders for limited periods of time (although this would not preclude the court from varying the order at any time during the period for which it was set to run or from making a fresh order at any time after the lapsing of an order).

[124] The *Royal Commission on Divorce and Matrimonial Causes* (1912, Cd. 6478) para. 440 concluded that the powers of the court needed amplification. 'The court should be able to deal more fully in all cases with the property settled on or belonging to the parties, or either of them, and to order payments and security for moneys ordered to be paid, so that the position of the parties and their children, which is changed by virtue of the order of the court, should be dealt with also as regards property, income and payments . . .'. Thirty five years later, the *Final Report of the Denning Committee* (1947, Cmd. 7024) para. 49 stated that this observation was 'as true today as it was then'; whilst the *Royal Commission on Marriage and Divorce* (1956, Cmd. 9678) Part VIII noted deficiencies and anomalies in the law, recommended that on divorce the court 'should have the widest possible discretion as to the kind of financial provision it can order' and also made detailed proposals for rationalisation.

The Morton Commission unwittingly opens Pandora's Box

The 1956 *Report of the Royal Commission on Marriage and Divorce* was a conservative document; but one of its recommendations led albeit indirectly to a decisive change in the approach of the courts, the legislature and the community to divorce. The Commission recommended[125] that the court be given an unrestricted power to order either party to the marriage to make provision by way of capital payment to the other, and the Matrimonial Causes Act 1963[126] gave the court the power on or after[127] granting a decree (whether of divorce, nullity or judicial separation) to order payment of a lump sum, unrestricted in amount.[128] The long-term significance of this provision on perceptions of the nature of the divorce process is considerable: the courts and the legislature began to move away from thinking solely in terms of income maintenance,[129] and towards making provision by way of capital adjustment. Of course, changing economic conditions (notably high rates of income taxation combined with a benign fiscal regime in relation to ownership of capital, and the emergence of the first signs of the inflationary pressures which so dominated English society in the 1960s and 1970s) were important factors in creating a climate of opinion favourable to the creation of a power whose scope would have seemed remarkable to Victorian[130] and Edwardian judges and legislators.

The long-term impact of this extension of the court's powers should not be understated. But initially the courts adopted a cautious and uncertain approach to the exercise of the newly acquired jurisdiction:

---

[125] The Commission's approach to financial issues was surprisingly radical: its starting point was that the 'court should have the widest possible discretion as to the kind of financial provision it can order one spouse to make to the other' (para. 516) and it recommended (for example) that the court should have power to make orders in favour of either party and power to direct what came to be called a 'clean break': see below.

[126] The main provision of the Matrimonial Causes and Reconciliation Bill as presented to the House of Commons by Leo Abse MP would have allowed divorce after seven years' separation. That provision was eventually removed after extensive debate and manoeuvring: see above. In the result, very little attention was given to the other provisions of the Bill.

[127] Under the existing law, the court's power was only exercisable 'on' granting a decree, and this restriction gave rise to difficulties.

[128] The only guidance given by the legislation as consolidated in the Matrimonial Causes Act 1965, s. 16(1) was that the court could, if it thought fit, order the husband to pay the wife 'such lump sum as the court thinks reasonable'; but in *Davis v. Davis* [1967] P 185 the Court of Appeal held that in determining what was reasonable the court should take into account the matters specified in the statute as relevant to the award of secured periodical payments—ie 'her fortune (if any), his ability and the conduct of the parties' (words which originated in Matrimonial Causes Act 1857, s. 32).

[129] Note the vivid historical sketch by Sachs J, *Schlesinger v. Schlesinger* [1960] P 191, 200, and that he suggested there was a need for legislation empowering the court to order the wealthy to make settlements on modern lines.

[130] Note *per* Lord Reid, *Pettitt v. Pettitt* [1970] AC 777, 793. In 1882, 'the certainty and security of rights of property were still generally regarded as of paramount importance and I find it incredible that any Parliament of that era could have intended to put a husband's property at the hazard of the unfettered discretion of a judge (including a county court judge) . . .'.

In *Davis v. Davis*[131] an actress—Dinah Sheridan, star of Genevieve and other now classic films—gave up her career at its peak to marry the exceedingly wealthy[132] Chairman of the Rank Organisation.[133] After 11 years she petitioned for divorce on the ground of her husband's cruelty. The petition was a 'lengthy document setting out a number of grave allegations, some of them of an extremely unpleasant nature';[134] but the husband[135] filed no answer and allowed the case to go undefended. The Registrar (taking a 'reasonably lenient' view of the wife's admitted adultery which had apparently occurred only after the husband's conduct had reduced her to a state of considerable depression) awarded her periodical payments of £8,500[136] (£85,000 in year 2000 values) and a lump sum payment of £10,000 (£100,000). Although satisfied with the periodical payments order[137] the wife appealed on the ground that the lump sum award was much too low, and that she was entitled to such a sum as would suffice to enable her to buy and furnish a house of a standard commensurate with the accommodation she had enjoyed during the marriage. Orr J increased the award to £15,000; and the Court of Appeal—noting that a wife's standard of living was recognised by precedent[138] as a relevant factor—increased it further to £25,000 (a quarter of a million pounds in year 2000 values)[139] compared with the £30,000 which the wife had claimed. The wife's need for suitably furnished

---

[131] [1967] P 185, CA.

[132] And much-married. Willmer LJ (presumably relying on the wife's affidavit) stated that it was the husband's fifth marriage, but his entry in *Who's Who* would suggest it was his fourth, and the husband's obituary indicates uncertainty about the status of some of those with whom he had intimate relationships: see *The Times*, 29 May 1993. For her part, the wife had been married once previously and had two children by that marriage (one of whom, JJ Hanley, became Chairman of the Conservative Party).

[133] In that capacity he was (see *The Times*, 29 May 1993) responsible for establishing the link between Rank and Xerox, thereby effectively bringing mass photocopying to the UK and indirectly vastly increasing the work of the legal profession and the courts.

[134] *per* Willmer LJ [1967] 1 All ER 123, 125 (the Law Reports do not give the verbatim text of this part of the judgment).

[135] Whose character appears to have been somewhat combative: according to *The Times*, 29 May 1993, he was in his business life 'loathed as much as he was admired . . . [was] notorious for the way he bossed around the Rank Organisation's contract film stars and starlets; and for the cold-blooded way in which he axed executives' apparently claiming to 'eat Managing Directors for breakfast'. Notwithstanding his turbulent marital history and controversial business career he was knighted in 1971, appointed CVO in 1985, and from 1973 to 1985 was a trustee of Westminister Abbey's fund-raising appeal committee.

[136] £4,500 of which was to be secured.

[137] Although said by her husband's counsel to be 'very large' the Court of Appeal pointed out that after tax she would be left with a spendable income of only £3,000.

[138] Notably *N v. N* (1928) 138 LT 693; *Schlesinger v. Schlesinger* [1960] P 191.

[139] Calculated by rough approximation to the Index of Retail Prices. But that index does not adequately reflect the considerable additional inflation in house prices (particularly in London) which occurred between 1965 and 2000: advertisements in *The Times*, 11 May 1966, indicate that a 'Superb Family House' in Brompton Square (then and now one of the most prestigious addresses in London) would cost all of £40,000; a three-bedroom freehold in Campden Hill £16,750; whilst £13,500 would suffice to acquire a non-basement bijou house in Chelsea, and as little as £12,750 was then the asking price for a four-bedroom house in Barons Court.

accommodation was the dominant factor[140] which weighed with the Court of Appeal: £15,000 would not 'go very far towards purchasing house property in the sort of neighbourhood where a woman with this background can reasonably expect to live'; and accordingly the Appeal Court was 'bound to interfere'. But the Court expressed the view that the question of making a lump sum order was not likely to arise 'except in relatively rare cases'.

The statement that lump sum awards would only be made in 'exceptional'[141] circumstances was evidently intended merely to reflect the obvious truth that there is no point in making an order to hand over substantial capital unless the husband owns such capital;[142] but although the courts did begin to show a willingness to exercise their lump sum powers in cases involving families of much smaller means in order to achieve specific objectives[143] for a decade the typical scenario continued to involve the very rich, as in the last case on the issue to come before the Court of Appeal prior to the enactment of the Divorce Reform Act in 1969:

In *Brett v. Brett*[144] the husband was an extremely wealthy businessman and underwriting member of Lloyds. He persistently failed to make proper disclosure about his finances, so that it was never clear exactly how wealthy he was. But the case proceeded on the basis that he might well have assets in this country worth half a million pounds (perhaps £5 million in modern values) as well as substantial assets in overseas tax-havens. Certainly in the course of the five and a half months for which the marriage lasted Mr and Mrs Brett lived lavishly, spending a honeymoon in Mexico and the West Indies and three holidays in Switzerland. The 23-year-old wife left the husband complaining of his revolting sexual demands and practices—allegations which he did not deny—and, having established that the case was one of exceptional hardship or exceptional depravity,[145] obtained the leave at that time necessary to present a cruelty petition

---

[140] Although the court also took the view that her misconduct had to be taken into account; and that the award would have been somewhat higher but for that factor.

[141] So described by Willmer LJ in *Hakluytt v. Hackluytt* [1968] 2 All ER 868, 871.

[142] See *Davis v. Davis* [1967] P 185, 192, *per* Willmer LJ; *Hakluytt v. Hackluytt* [1968] 2 All ER 868, 871 *per* Willmer LJ ('I do not feel repentant about that [statement made in *Davis*]: I think that is right. It can only be in relatively rare cases that the question is likely to arise'); *von Mehren v. von Mehren* [1970] 1 All ER 153.

[143] *Hakluytt v. Hakluytt* [1968] 2 All ER 868 (lump sum of £500 awarded to cover cost of repairing wife's house made against husband who had commuted part of naval pension thereby converting income into capital); *von Mehren v. von Mehren* [1970] 1 All ER 153 (husband ordered to pay £4,000 on terms that it would be settled giving wife right to reside in house for her life, then to children, then to husband or his estate); but note *per* Karminski LJ at p. 156: 'cases in which lump sums can be ordered are of necessity relatively rare. I rely only on my own experience in these matters, but I would hazard a guess that it is in only a small minority of cases, in possibly not as much as 5 per cent of the total of maintenance orders, when an order of this kind could possibly be made'. In *Curtis v. Curtis* [1969] 2 All ER 207 a lump sum order was made against a man of substantial means primarily so that it could as the law then stood (cf. *Woodley v. Woodley (No 2)* [1993] 2 FLR 477) be enforced against him in bankruptcy proceedings.

[144] [1969] 1 All ER 1007, CA.   [145] Matrimonial Causes Act 1965, s. 2(2).

notwithstanding the fact that three years had not elapsed since the marriage. The husband's conduct reduced the wife to a severe anxiety state, and (although she had qualified as a solicitor) she was at the time of the hearing unable to work; and would in any event not expect to earn more than about £1,250 a year.[146] She had virtually no capital. The Registrar awarded Mrs Brett a lump sum of £15,000 which, on appeal to the judge, was increased to £25,000. The Court of Appeal rejected the husband's argument that £15,000 would suffice to provide the wife with appropriate housing, and made a lump sum award of £30,000[147] (£300,000 in year 2000 values) together[148] with periodical payments.[149] In reaching that decision, the Court of Appeal applied Lord Merrivale's *N v. N* principle, ie 'the test of taking into consideration the position in which the wife was entitled to expect herself to be, and would have been, if the husband had discharged his marital obligation, the marital obligation being, of course, an obligation to maintain her on the scale appropriate to his station in life'.[150] True it was that the marriage had only lasted a very short time, but, given that it was the husband's conduct which had the effect of driving the wife out, this was not a factor on which the husband could rely.[151]

The Divorce Reform Act 1969 and the effect of divorce on the financial position of women

On one view, the *Brett* decision reflects a judicial perception of a husband's obligation to keep his divorced wife supplied with 'every conceivable luxury';[152] but it was the financial damage which divorce might cause to married women in general and 'innocent' wives in particular which had become an important factor in debates on the ground for divorce. The fact that divorce might deprive a woman of the pension expectations she would have enjoyed as the husband's widow under the (at the time, increasingly common) Occupational Pension Schemes[153]

---

[146] This (perhaps £12,000 in year 2000 values) was a not untypical salary for a young solicitor at the time.

[147] The award to be adjusted in certain circumstances dependent on whether or not the husband delivered to the wife a Get which under Rabbinical law would free the wife to remarry.

[148] Phillimore LJ expressed the view that had no periodical payments been awarded the lump sum would have amounted to at least £50,000 (half a million pounds in year 2000 values).

[149] Of £2,000 (increased to £2,500 if the husband delivered a Get: see note 147 above).

[150] See *per* Willmer LJ at [1969] 1 All ER 1007, 1013.

[151] See *per* Willmer LJ at [1969] 1 All ER 1007, 1011.

[152] See J Eekelaar and M Maclean, *Maintenance after Divorce* (1986) p. 11.

[153] The increase in rates of taxation associated with World War II and its aftermath was a significant influence on the development of occupational pensions, intended (in effect) to spread the employer's earnings over the whole of his adult life rather than confining them to the years in which he was economically active: see the *Report of the Committee on the Taxation Treatment of Provision for Pensions for Retirement* (J Millard Tucker QC, Chairman) (1954, Cmd. 9063). Paras. 47–8 of the Report give a valuable historical conspectus, demonstrating the very small scale of formal pension provision until after the end of World War II. More favourable tax treatment introduced in consequence of the *Millard Tucker Report* was a boost to the use of pension contracts. Whereas in 1956 only 7.9 million employees were members of pension schemes (see *Social Trends* No. 1, 1970, Table 51) by the 1990s the Pension Law Review Committee (Professor Roy Goode,

was a particular grievance,[154] as were the restricted rights which a wife seemed to have in the family home.

The story of how the campaign for reform of the ground for divorce almost foundered in 1969 on opposition from those claiming that the proposed new law would be a 'Casanova's Charter' enabling blameless wives to be repudiated by their husbands and left in penury has been told elsewhere in this book; and we have seen that the Government effectively bought off opposition by giving an undertaking[155] that the new law of divorce would not be brought into force unless and until legislation had been brought in to deal comprehensively with the financial consequences of divorce. We have also seen how the amending legislation was a disappointment to those who sought far-reaching reform of the property rights of married women[156] but the Government decided to call an election, and the Matrimonial Proceedings and Property Bill was hurriedly pushed through the necessary parliamentary stages after only a truncated debate in the House of Commons on 27 May 1970.[157] In this way the issues which could well have proved troublesome were never fully discussed in Parliament.

Financial matters to be a matter of discretionary adjustment rather than entitlement

The Matrimonial Proceedings and Property Act effectively rejected the introduction of community of property between husband and wife into English law. Instead, the court's powers to make orders on divorce, judicial separation and nullity were extended and its discretion accordingly increased. The Act was

---

Chairman) was able to show that over 11 million employees were in occupational schemes and a further 5 million had personal pension policies, and that the aggregate value of occupational pension rights approached that of the wealth stored in housing: see *Consultation Document on the Law and Regulation of Occupational Pension Schemes*.

[154] Note the view of Sir Roger Ormrod (see Biographical Notes) in evidence to the Archbishop's Group that the majority of spouses who refused to divorce their partners were either averse to divorce on religious grounds or determined not to lose their pension rights; and note also the view formed by the then President of the Divorce Division that the Chairman of the Archbishop's Group had when questioned on his advocacy of divorce for breakdown been 'hopelessly embarrassed by the case of the woman who would be deprived of her rights on widowhood by any form of divorce by compulsion': SM Cretney, *Law, Law Reform and the Family*, (1998) p. 53, note 142 and p. 59, note 185.

[155] On 24 January 1969 the House of Commons, against the strong advice of the Government, gave a Second Reading to a Private Member's Bill intended to remedy perceived injustice by the creation of a system of community of property: see p. 132–135 above. For the Government's undertaking see *Official Report* (HC) 28 January 1970, vol. 794, cols. 1560, 1597–1598.

[156] See p. 136, above.

[157] Seven and a half hours were spent in House of Commons Standing Committee J discussing the first five clauses of the Bill. After the decision to dissolve had been announced all the remaining Commons stages were disposed of in less than two and a half hours, and many important amendments were not discussed at all: the Standing Committee was discharged on 26 May, and the Bill taken to a Committee of the Whole House the following day. On 28 May it was pushed through its final stages in the House of Lords on the basis that all controversial provisions had been removed: *Official Report* (HL) 28 May 1970, vol. 310, col. 1180.

based on a Bill drafted in the Law Commission;[158] and the Commission's recommendations on the court's powers in divorce and other matrimonial proceedings[159] fell into two main groups.

First, the Commission recommended rationalising the powers of the court to make orders for financial provision: old fashioned terminology (such as 'alimony') should be modernised; and there should be no distinction between the powers of the courts in relation to husbands and wives or petitioners and respondents.[160] The Commission also recommended 'some extension and a considerable rationalisation'[161] of the court's powers to adjust property entitlements: in addition to the power to order a lump sum payment the court should also have power to order settlements or transfers of property for the benefit of either spouse or any children.[162]

Secondly, the Commission recommended[163] that statute provide 'a uniform and more detailed set of guidelines to which the court should have regard' in exercising its discretion to make financial orders on divorce than existed in the Matrimonial Causes Act 1965 (which in its turn incorporated legislation dating back to 1857). The Commission thought this to be 'requisite especially having regard to the wider and more flexible powers which we have recommended in relation to property adjustments'; but with two exceptions the Report did not discuss the policy to which these guidelines were to give effect. These exceptions were (a) that the guidelines should include[164] a specific reference to the 'extent to which each [spouse] has contributed to the welfare of the family, including not only contributions in money or money's worth ... but also the contributions made (normally by the wife) in looking after the home and family';[165] and (b) the Commission gave it as its 'considered opinion' that the courts should be

---

[158] The Commission had published a wide-ranging 128-page *Working Paper, Matrimonial and Related Proceedings—Financial Relief* in 1967. This provisionally recommended measures of rationalisation (such as harmonising the names given to the various forms of relief available in divorce and other proceedings, and allowing both husbands and wives to apply for them). This consultation paper included an extended (but inconclusive) treatment of the pensions issue, about which the Commission recognised there was 'strong public feeling'. The Government's undertaking to legislate must have put the Commission under strong pressure but it produced a *Report on Financial Provision in Matrimonial Proceedings*, Law Com. No. 25, in July 1969, to which was annexed the draft Matrimonial Proceedings and Property Bill.

[159] The Commission also recommended the enactment of a declaratory provision about the effect of contributions to improvements of property. The Matrimonial Proceedings and Property Act 1970, s. 37 gave effect to this.

[160] Law Com. No. 25, para. 115 contains a 'comprehensive summary' with cross-references.

[161] Law Com. No. 25, para. 64.

[162] Law Com. No. 25, para. 66. The Commission recommended that the category of children be extended to all those treated by either party as a child of the family: see in particular paras. 23–32.

[163] Law Com. No. 25, para. 8.   [164] Law Com. No. 25, para. 69.

[165] The Commission thought that these measures would meet 'the strongest complaint made by married women, and recognised as legitimate by the Morton Commission in 1955, namely that the contribution which wives make towards the acquisition of family assets by performing the domestic chores, thereby releasing their husbands for gainful employment, is at present wholly ignored in determining their rights'.

readier than they had been in the past to make orders for the payment of a lump sum.[166]

In one respect the Commission had to admit defeat: the Bill contained no provisions empowering the court to adjust the parties' pension expectations. The Commission recorded that the 'problem remains unsolved and, after full consideration, we believe it to be incapable of direct and complete solution'.[167]

ANCILLARY RELIEF UNDER 'IRRETRIEVABLE BREAKDOWN' DIVORCE

(1) The court's powers[168]

The Law Commission's Report[169] had talked of 'considerable rationalisation'; but it was soon evident that the powers to make financial provision[170] and property adjustment orders[171] had been widened so as to allow the court to redistribute virtually all the parties' economically valuable resources, whether capital or income, if it considered it appropriate to do so. The decision whether to take a restricted or broad view of how the powers should be exercised was one for the courts to determine in the exercise of the discretion which the Act conferred; and it would have been open to the courts to follow a policy similar

[166] 'We say this because the award of periodical payments very frequently gives rise to difficulties of enforcement and tends to prolong what has proved an unhappy situation between the parties and to exacerbate their hostile feelings. A lump sum, on the other hand, avoids the difficulty of attempting to recover at intervals relatively small periodical payments and, being a judgment debt, can be enforced by bankruptcy proceedings. Furthermore, it enables the parties to start afresh without relics of the past hanging like millstones round their necks. Such an award may also be the best method of compensating the wife for the loss of a possible widow's pension . . . We appreciate . . . that unless there is some capital a lump sum cannot be awarded, But if, for example, the husband owns the matrimonial home we see no reason why, in appropriate circumstances, he should not be ordered to pay a lump sum which he could raise by charging the house': Law Commission *Report on Financial Provision in Matrimonial Proceedings* (Law Com. No. 25, 1969) para. 9.

[167] Law Com. No. 25, para. 112.

[168] Ie under the Matrimonial Proceedings and Property Act 1970. The provisions of this Act discussed in this section were repealed and consolidated in the Matrimonial Causes Act 1973; and references are given to the 1973 consolidation.

[169] Law Com. No. 25, para. 64.

[170] These were orders for periodical payments, secured periodical payments, and (in the light of the use subsequently to be made of the power, rather curiously) lump sum payments. Property Adjustment Orders were orders dealing with property rights, ie orders for the transfer or settlement of property or for the variation of a nuptial settlement: Matrimonial Causes Act 1973, s. 21. The courts gave a generous interpretation to the extent of the powers conferred by the Act; and in *B v. B (Post Nuptial Settlements)(Pension Fund)* [1996] AC 375 the House of Lords held that the funds subject to an occupational pension scheme were capable of constituting an 'ante-nuptial or post-nuptial settlement' the trusts of which the court had power to vary under Matrimonial Causes Act 1973, s. 24(1)(c). The court also had power to make an order for maintenance pending suit, ie periodical payments for the period between the presentation of the petition and ending with the determination of the suit: Matrimonial Causes Act 1973, s. 22.

[171] This formal classification was introduced by the consolidating Matrimonial Causes Act 1973, s. 21, apparently in order to provide a clearer structure for the powers originally contained in Matrimonial Proceedings and Property Act 1970, ss. 2–4. But the 1973 Act did not change the substance of the law.

to that adopted between 1963 and 1970 in respect of the power to make orders for the payment of a lump sum, that is to say that reallocation of capital should only be ordered in exceptional circumstances.[172] In fact (as we shall see) the courts soon decided to adopt a very broad approach in order to achieve whatever result it believed to be fair just and reasonable in the circumstances.[173]

(2) Guidelines for the exercise of the court's powers

The Law Commission's Report[174] recommended that there be substituted for the sparse legislative guidance given in the existing legislation 'a uniform and more detailed set of guidelines to which the court should have regard' in the exercise of these very wide powers. The 1970 Act adopting[175] the draft Bill annexed to the Law Commission's Report, provided that it should be the duty of the court in deciding whether to exercise its powers and, if so, in what manner 'to have regard to all the circumstances of the case' (including a number of matters specifically referred to, such as contributions to the welfare of the family)[176] and 'so to exercise those powers as to place the parties, so far as it is practicable and, having regard to their conduct just to do so, in the financial position in which they would have been if the marriage had not broken down and each had properly discharged his or her financial obligations and responsibilities towards the other'.

It soon became clear that many practitioners found it difficult to give confident advice[177] about how the legislation would be interpreted by the courts, whilst 'divergences of view and of practice between judges'[178] emerged (some taking the view that the new legislation did no more than codify the existing law and practice[179] whilst others favoured a much more radical approach). The situation was not eased by the lack of any extended discussion of principle either in the Law Commission's Report or in parliamentary debate. It was necessary for authoritative guidance to be given, if only to provide a basis upon which lawyers could advise clients as to the likely outcome of any proceedings and thus, in most cases, enable the parties to reach a settlement of the matter rather

---

[172] See *Hakluytt v. Hakluytt* [1968] 2 All ER 868, 871 *per* Willmer LJ; and p. 418 above.

[173] *Walsh v. Corcoran* (1982) 4 FLR 59, 63.   [174] Law Com. No. 25, para. 8.

[175] With only minor, and for present purposes, irrelevant variations.

[176] 'Including any contribution made by looking after the home or caring for the family': Matrimonial Proceedings and Property Act 1970, s. 5(1)(f). The other specified circumstances were (a) the parties' financial resources; (b) their financial needs; (c) the standard of living enjoyed by the family before the breakdown of the marriage; (d) the age of the parties and the duration of the marriage; (e) any physical or mental disability; and (g) the value of any benefit '(for example, a pension) which, by reason of the dissolution . . . of the marriage that party will lose the chance of acquiring'. Neither disability nor (surprisingly) the parties' age and the duration of the marriage were included in the draft legislation put forward by the Law Commission: see Law Com. No. 25, draft clause 5.

[177] *Martin v. Martin* [1977] 3 All ER 764, 769, *per* Ormrod J.

[178] *Wachtel v. Wachtel* [1973] 1 All ER 829, 833, *per* Lord Denning MR. An important piece of empirical research conducted between 1973 and 1975 confirmed this assessment: see W Barrington Baker, J Eekelaar, C Gibson and S Raikes, *The Matrimonial Jurisdiction of Registrars* (1977).

[179] *Ackerman v. Ackerman* [1972] Fam 225, 232, *per* Phillimore LJ.

than being forced into adversarial litigation. In *Wachtel v. Wachtel*[180] the Court
of Appeal set out to lay down authoritative guidance on some of the matters
which had given rise to problems. Of these, a particularly difficult problem was
that of how far the fact that one party to the marriage was to some extent 'at
fault' should influence the decision about the exercise of the court's financial
powers.

Conduct

We have seen that in the declining days of the matrimonial offence doctrine an
assessment of the conduct of the parties was often still a significant factor in the
determination of the financial consequences of divorce; but that there was a difference of opinion about quite what weight such an assessment should have.
Under the Divorce Reform Act, however, the availability of divorce did not
depend on whether one or the other party was 'guilty' or 'innocent' but (in principle at least) on whether or not the marriage had broken down irretrievably;
and the question of the extent to which an assessment of the parties' responsibility for the breakdown or of their conduct in other respects was relevant to
settling the financial consequences of divorce became controversial.

There seems little doubt that the 'breakdown' legislation was put forward on
the basis that conduct should continue to be relevant to the assessment of
financial provision.[181] The Law Commission's 1966 Report on the ground for
divorce[182] accepted that the conduct of the parties 'must remain an important
element in the courts' decisions about financial matters;[183] and the parliamentary
debates on the Matrimonial Proceedings and Property Act 1970, also support the
view that it was assumed that conduct would continue to be relevant to the
assessment of financial provision.[184] But did it follow from this that (as it was put
in one of the early decided cases on the interpretation of the new law):

'if a wife's conduct were found to a given extent to be worse than her husband's she
would be placed in a financial position, compared with the hypothetical position, to that
extent lower than his position, similarly compared?'

The fact that such an approach would be completely inconsistent with the
objectives of the reformed divorce law was soon dramatically exemplified:

---

[180] [1973] Fam 72, CA.
[181] See the discussion in *The Financial Consequences of Divorce; The Basic Policy* (1980, Law
Com. No. 103), paras. 36–38.
[182] *The Field of Choice* (1966, Law Com. No. 15) para. 17.
[183] In 1967 the Commission said in its Working *Paper, Matrimonial and Related Proceedings—
Financial Relief,* that 'few would suggest that in awarding maintenance the conduct of the parties
should not be an important consideration'; and in its *Report on Financial Provision in Matrimonial
Proceedings* (Law Com. No. 25, para. 6) the Commission accepted that payments ordered by way
of ancillary relief would 'depend to some extent on the court's findings regarding the respective conduct of the parties'.
[184] For instance the Solicitor General stated that 'the Bill, in its present form, requires the court
to have regard to the conduct of the parties. There is no doubt about that: it is there as one of the
factors which is to receive consideration'.

In *Ackerman v. Ackerman*[185] the President of the Family Division held that the legislation required the conduct of both parties to be taken into account, at least if it was 'of a really serious nature, falling within the category of the disruptive, the intolerable, the unforgivable' and a contributory cause[186] of the breakdown. The President therefore heard evidence (including evidence from the couple's 17-year-old daughter) over several days. The wife alleged that her husband had assaulted her (and been convicted by a magistrates' court of causing her actual bodily harm) that he had called her a prostitute and a slut, engaged in unusual sexual practices and then lectured her on sex; and that he was wedded to his work and neglected his wife. For his part the husband complained that the wife had confessed to committing adultery in the Spiritualist church in Hitchin, that she was neglectful of the home and family, was obsessively jealous and suspicious, and that she had threatened him on one occasion with a knife. The President concluded that, although hers was not the major responsibility for the breakdown, it was quite impossible for the wife to escape some responsibility for it; and a discount of 25% from the periodical payments which would otherwise have been payable would be justified.[187]

If this approach were correct, the court would have to make an investigation into the responsibility for the breakdown of the marriage[188] in a great many cases, and this would almost inevitably involve a wide-ranging investigation into the parties' conduct. Every item of conjugal unkindness which could be dragged out of the memory would have to be embodied in an affidavit upon which the parties would be subjected to examination and cross-examination. (In one decided case[189] the pleadings occupied 66 pages, the hearing lasted more than a month, and the judge's findings occupied 64 pages of transcript.) The policy of minimising bitterness distress and humiliation was thus in serious danger of being defeated, since questions of fault would merely be transferred from the

---

[185] [1972] Fam 1.

[186] Or in some other manner relevant to the parties' financial position.

[187] On the facts, it was clear that the husband's means were insufficient to meet the wife's needs much less to keep her in the position she would have been in had the marriage not broken down, and in those circumstances the President did not order any reduction because of the wife's conduct. He considered however that the courts should attempt to produce certainty and finality both for the present and future, and to that end made what he called a declaratory judgment stating the 'the percentage by which, having regard to the conduct of the parties and the duration of the marriage, it would be just to reduce the wife's maintenance if, but only if, no other variable factor calls to be considered. The actual discount, if any, to be made at any particular time can then be decided in the circumstances which then prevail. It can never . . . be more than the maximum unless the wife's subsequent conduct is relevant, and that will rarely arise'. The Court of Appeal did not agree with this approach: it accepted that the judge, having heard the evidence, might properly express his view on who had the major responsibility for the breakdown (and no doubt it would be rare for such an assessment subsequently to be questioned) but the court should not seek to make a declaratory judgment intended to be binding for all time. Moreover, the degree of responsibility for breakdown could not properly be expressed by a mathematical formula.

[188] See *Harnett v. Harnett* [1973] Fam 156, 161–162; *Wachtel v. Wachtel* [1973] Fam 72, 79, *per* Ormrod J; and see *Ackerman v. Ackerman* [1972] Fam 1, 5.

[189] *Griffiths v. Griffiths* [1974] 1 WLR 1350.

hearing at which the grant of the decree was in issue to the hearing at which financial and other matters were decided.

In *Wachtel v. Wachtel*[190] the courts firmly decided that this should not be allowed to happen: the notion that there should be a discount or reduction in what a wife was to receive by reason of her 'supposed misconduct, guilt or blame' would (said Lord Denning)[191] in the 'vast majority of cases' be 'repugnant to the principles' underlying the new legislation. Since in most cases both parties had contributed to the breakdown there should be no necessity for the judge to hear the parties' mutual recriminations and go into their petty squabbles, not least because (as Ormrod J had put it at first instance) the forensic process was 'much too clumsy a tool for dissecting the complex inter-actions which go on all the time in a family. Shares in responsibility for breakdown could not be properly assessed without a meticulous examination and understanding of the characters and personalities of the spouses concerned, and the more thorough the investigation the more' likely it was that husband and wife would eventually be found to bear an equal responsibility for what had happened.

In the light of this decision, the trend in practice moved towards ignoring questions of conduct in all but exceptional cases;[192] and this came to be accepted by the courts[193] and the legal profession. However, the courts faced considerable difficulties in defining the 'exceptional' cases in which misconduct might be relevant[194] and also in solving the dilemma of how to resolve that issue without 'costly, indecent, and time-wasting investigation'.[195] Moreover, although the *Wachtel* decision may have satisfied the judges and others concerned with the administration of the law it was much more questionable whether the general public was prepared to accept the removal of blameworthiness from the factors relevant to the assessment of financial orders. Indeed in 1981 the Law Commission[196] reported that many of those involved in divorce proceedings 'felt a considerable sense of injustice because the court had not been prepared to take account of the other spouse's behaviour, especially as this was for the parties the most important single factor in assessing financial provision'. Eventually the Law Commission concluded that the basis upon which the court exercised its financial powers on divorce merited re-examination. But that re-examination was required in part because of controversy about an even more fundamental issue, the underlying objective to which the court should seek to give effect.

---

[190] [1973] Fam 72. [191] At pp. 89–90.

[192] *The Financial Consequences of Divorce; The Basic Policy* (1980, Law Com. No. 103) para. 41.

[193] But not without some resistance: see *The Financial Consequences of Divorce; The Basic Policy* (1980, Law Com. No. 103), para. 138 note 139; SM Cretney, *Principles of Family Law* (4th ed., 1984) pp. 802–806.

[194] *Backhouse v. Backhouse* [1978] 1 All ER 1158, 1166.

[195] See *Campbell v. Campbell* [1976] Fam 347.

[196] *The Financial Consequences of Divorce; The Response . . .* (1981, Law Com. No. 112) para. 36.

ANCILLARY RELIEF: THE POLICY OBJECTIVE?

The Matrimonial Proceedings and Property Act 1970[197] stipulated a two-stage process for dealing with ancillary relief applications. Having considered 'all the circumstances' the court was 'so to exercise its powers as to place the parties, so far as it is practicable and, having regard to their conduct, just to do so, in the financial position in which they would have been if the marriage had not broken down and each had properly discharged his or her financial obligations and responsibilities towards the other'.

But what was this intended to achieve in practice? Surprisingly, the wording was scarcely explained in the Law Commission's Report, and was hardly discussed in the parliamentary debates.[198] It appears that the Law Commission, in putting forward what became known as the 'statutory hypothesis' or 'minimal loss' principle, was intending simply to codify the principle stated by Lord Merrivale in the 1928 case of N v. N;[199] and as we have seen it is clear that in that case Lord Merrivale was seeking merely to discourage application of the so-called one-third principle and to encourage the courts to have regard to what latterly was called the parties' 'reasonable requirements'. However, the literal meaning of the words might suggest that the formula gave effect to the principle that divorce, although terminating the marriage, did not terminate the financial ties which it had created, and that the primary objective of the law was that the parties' financial position should so far as possible be unaffected by the divorce. In 1980 the Law Commission marshalled evidence suggesting that it was rarely possible in practice[200] to give effect to such a requirement;[201] but it seems that the direction—rightly described[202] as an 'elusive concept based on a difficult hypothesis'—was sometimes[203] given the more literal interpretation by the

---

[197] s. 5 (subsequently consolidated as Matrimonial Causes Act 1973, s. 25(1)).

[198] The draft provided by the Law Commission was in fact amended—without much discussion—so that the comparison was to be between the financial position of both parties (rather than simply the party in whose favour the order was made): see *Official Report* (HL) 4 December 1969, vol. 305, col. 267.

[199] (1928) 44 TLR 324, 328; see above; and note the (somewhat bland) explanation given in Law Com. No. 25, draft clause 5, note 2.

[200] And see *Ackerman v. Ackerman* [1972] Fam 1, Sir George Baker P: amount of money available after provision made for children insufficient to place wife in 'anything like the position in which she would have been had the marriage not broken down'.

[201] *The Financial Consequences of Divorce; The Basic Policy* (1980, Law Com. No. 103), paras. 43–44.

[202] See per Bagnall J, *Harnett v. Harnett* [1973] Fam 156, 161.

[203] It was possible to see the formula as still being primarily concerned with the preservation of the wife's *standard of living* (rather than with equating her financial position with that she would have enjoyed if the divorce had never occurred): see *Porter v. Porter* [1969] 1 WLR 1155, *per* Sachs LJ relying on *Kershaw v. Kershaw* [1966] P 13, and *Roberts v. Roberts* [1970] P 1. It was pointed out in *Daubney v. Daubney* [1976] Fam 267 that the Act referred to equating the position of 'the parties' (rather than 'the wife') and Sir George Baker P suggested that 'too often' the position of the husband was disregarded': see *H v. H (Financial Provision: Remarriage)* [1975] Fam 9. See also *Trippas v. Trippas* [1973] Fam 134, CA; *O'D v. O'D* [1976] Fam 83, CA—a case involving a 'rich but not

courts. This was seen by groups claiming to represent the interests of divorced men[204] as creating injustice; and the controversy was fuelled by the ready availability of divorce, the unwillingness of the courts to consider the impact of any save 'gross and obvious' conduct and the greatly increased readiness of the courts to make orders in relation to capital.

This last factor is particularly significant: the question was whether the court's objective was to ensure the wife was adequately maintained, or was it intended to achieve an equitable re-distribution of all the assets to which the two parties were entitled?

Although the 1970 legislation, as a matter of strict economic analysis, did not really extend the court's powers (the true break-through having been made in 1963 when the courts were given power to order a capital payment, unlimited in amount against either party) it could have been plausibly argued that whilst the courts' powers had indeed been rationalised and made more flexible—so that, for example, settlements of the family home (or other property) could be ordered—no great change of policy about the principles on which the amount of awards were to be based could have been intended. After all, it had increasingly been accepted[205] that the rigid demarcation between capital and income traditional before World War I was no longer valid in a world of inflation and high taxation; whilst the explicit reference in the new legislation to the significance of contributions made to the family welfare would have reinforced the trend to order transfers where the 'family capital' consisted of the family home.[206] On this view there was no indication that the courts were to change the traditional view of their function as being concerned with ensuring the family an adequate standard of living rather than focussing on re-distribution of capital. As we have seen, the evidence of the parliamentary debates is that the introduction of what would amount to community of property was specifically rejected at the time.[207]

extremely rich' husband (*per* Ormrod LJ, *Edgar v. Edgar* [1980] 1 WLR 1410) in which the Court favoured a 'reasonable requirements' criterion but did apply the statutory hypothesis to demonstrate that the husband's offer of a £30,000 lump sum and periodical payments of £3,000 was inadequate; *Calderbank v. Calderbank* [1976] Fam 93, CA (husband needed capital; reference to statutory hypothesis justified this, see particularly *per* Cairns LJ); *Hanlon v. Hanlon* [1978] 2 All ER 889, CA; *Scott v. Scott* [1978] 3 All ER 65, CA. *Page v. Page* (1981) 2 FLR 198 (where the statutory hypothesis was applied to a case in which the wife's contributions were not directly related to the business from which the family wealth was derived); *Preston v. Preston* [1982] Fam 17, CA (where again the application of a 'reasonable requirements' test was justified to some extent by reference to the hypothesis). In *Hector v. Hector* [1973] 3 All ER 1070, CA, the statutory hypothesis had been used to justify allowing the wife the right to occupy the house, the husband having a charge for 25% of its eventual sale proceeds, and similar reasoning was employed in *Smith v. Smith* (1973) [1975] 2 All ER 19, CA.

[204] Notably the Campaign for Justice in Divorce.   [205] See above.

[206] The courts had already interpreted the existing statutory power to vary settlements as conferring a power to vary the parties' beneficial interests in the home if it had been purchased in joint names (see *Brown v. Brown* [1959] P 86) or even if it had been purchased in the name of one spouse but the circumstances were such as to justify the imposition of an implied resulting or constructive trust: *Cook v. Cook* [1962] P 235.

[207] See also *per* Bagnall J, *Harnett v. Harnett* [1973] Fam 156, 160 (community of property 'somewhat clumsy continental concept . . . [which] has no place in English property law'; where parties'

Here too, the judgments in *Wachtel v. Wachtel*[208] had a decisive impact. The Court of Appeal,[209] upholding a decision to allocate to the wife a sum sufficient to allow her to fund the purchase of a house for herself,[210] proclaimed that the 1970 Act was not in any sense a merely codifying statute but that it was a 'reforming statute designed to . . . accord to the courts the widest possible powers in readjusting the financial position of the parties and to afford the courts the necessary machinery to that end'; and that it was intended to 'remedy the injustice' whereby a wife's contributions to the welfare of the family[211] were given little recognition in determining entitlement to family property. In the light of that decision, it was even possible for Lord Denning to claim[212] that the court's function on divorce was

to take 'the rights and obligations of the parties all together and put . . . the pieces into a mixed bag. Such pieces are the right to occupy the matrimonial home or have a share in it, the obligation to maintain the wife and children and so forth. The court then takes out the pieces and hands them to the two parties—some to one party and some to the other—so that each can provide for the future with the pieces allocated to him or to her. The court hands them out without paying any too nice a regard to their legal or equitable rights but simply according to what is the fairest provision for the future, for mother and father and the children'.

After the *Wachtel* decision it was clear that the court would use its powers to ensure that the wife and children were adequately housed; and in order to achieve this they would sometimes resort to complex settlements.[213] Moreover,

property rights clearly ascertainable effect to be given to them as they would have existed had there been no breakdown); *Griffiths v. Griffiths* [1973] 3 All ER 1155, *per* Arnold J: it was a question whether the court was engaging in two separate functions—providing maintenance and support and redistributing family assets; but the latter could only become a relevant consideration where the resources available exceeded those required to secure a standard of living commensurate with that obtaining before breakdown. (The Court of Appeal varied the judge's order and disagreed with this statement insofar as it might suggest that capital should only be touched if a just result could not be attained by recourse to income.)

[208] [1973] Fam 72, CA.

[209] Their views had been foreshadowed by the trial judge, Ormrod J, who claimed that the statutory language evidenced an intention by Parliament 'to bring about a shift of emphasis from the old concept of maintenance of the wife and children by the husband to one of redistribution of assets and purchasing power. It was intended that the courts should use their powers of re-allocation so as to do broad justice between the spouses and to reflect in this their real contributions to the welfare of the family . . .'.

[210] Although in fact the Court *reduced* the sum awarded from £10,000—approximately half the value of the equity—to £6,000, paradoxically approximately one-third of the value of the house. As Bagnall J remarked in *Harnett v. Harnett* [1973] Fam 156, 162, *Wachtel* was hailed in the press as a triumph for the cause of divorced wives, but examination of the outcome meant that it was 'at least tinged with Pyrrhic characteristics'.

[211] 'including any contributions made by looking after the home or caring for the family': Matrimonial Proceedings and Property Act 1970, s. 5(1)(f).

[212] In *Hanlon v. The Law Society* [1981] AC 124, 146, CA.

[213] For example, the so-called *Martin* order (see *Martin (BH) v. Martin (BW)* [1978] Fam 12) under which the house is settled on the wife for her life or until her remarriage or her ceasing to reside in the house, and subject thereto for husband and wife in equal shares. In this way, the wife has secure occupation but the husband is not deprived of his capital investment. On this complex subject, see generally SM Cretney and JM Masson, *Principles of Family Law* (6th ed., 1997) p. 489.

there could be no dispute about the extent of the courts' powers; and it soon became accepted that these powers were not to be restricted to so-called 'family assets'[214] and that all the parties' resources[215] were to be taken into account in making the allocation. But in one vital respect the *Wachtel* decision was unclear: it did not give any real guidance about the underlying *principle* to be applied in exercising the court's powers. Indeed, in that case the Court of Appeal had seemed to favour a fractional allocation[216] of both income and capital, at least as a 'flexible starting point'; and for a time the courts tended to fall back (certainly in relation to income payments)[217] on to the one-third principle.[218] But ultimately the courts moved against[219] adopting a fractional approach.[220] So

[214] Ie those things (typically the family home and furnishings) 'which are acquired by one or other or both of the parties, with the intention that they should be continuing provision for them and their children during their joint lives, and used for the benefit of the family as a whole': *Wachtel v. Wachtel* [1970] Fam 72, 90, *per* Lord Denning MR. However, some judges deprecated use of this phrase because 'a great deal of energy is spent in the courts . . . debating whether or not a particular item is properly regarded as a family asset. I would only like to say once and for all that the phrase "family assets" does not occur in the 1973 Act and it has nothing to do at all with s. 25 of that Act . . . It is a convenient phrase that came into existence in the days before the courts had the wide jurisdiction [originally provided in 1970] . . . it is not now a phrase of any particular use': *P v. P (financial provision: lump sum)* [1978] 3 All ER 70, 73, *per* Ormrod LJ.

[215] See eg *Daubney v. Daubney* [1976] Fam 267, CA (where damages awarded in respect of pain and suffering were taken into account as a financial resource).

[216] In cases in which the wife received only capital the Court of Appeal seemed to favour an equal division; but in other cases one-third of assets and joint income was thought appropriate. Lord Denning MR justified this inequality by pointing out that the husband would have to accept a continuing obligation to support his former wife out of future earnings, and he also believed the husband would have greater expenses after the break-up than would the wife: 'When a marriage breaks up, there will thenceforward be two households instead of one. The husband will have to go out to work all day and must get some woman to look after the house—either a wife, if he remarries, or a housekeeper, if he does not. The wife will not usually have so much expense. She may go out to work herself, but she will not usually employ a housekeeper. She will do most of the housework herself, perhaps with some help. Or she may remarry, in which case her new husband will provide for her . . .'.

[217] See *Page v. Page* (1981) 2 FLR 198, 202, CA, *per* Dunn LJ: one-third of joint incomes a useful guide for periodical payments; and to divide the proceeds of the family home so as to give the wife one-third would be appropriate if there were also an order for continuing periodical payments. If no periodical payments were awarded the whole proceeds of sale of the family home would be appropriate. See also *Foley v. Foley* (1981) 2 FLR 215, CA.

[218] Said by Ormrod LJ to have been 'reinstated' by the *Wachtel* decision 'after a period in which it had been doubted quite strongly': *Rodewald v. Rodewald* [1977] Fam 192, 200, CA. That case gave a measure of approval to the use of one-third as a 'starting point' providing a 'base line . . . from which the court can . . . consider the details of the particular case under consideration'; and in *Chamberlain v. Chamberlain* [1974] 1 All ER 33, 36, Scarman LJ tested an order against 'the ordinary practice of calculating a third of the total income as some sort of a guide to what is the appropriate sum for the wife's maintenance . . .'. The one-third fractional approach was said to be useful to practitioners seeking a yardstick by which to advise clients (see *Potter v. Potter* [1982] 1 WLR 1255, 1257, 1260) and there is evidence suggesting that in some parts of the country it was almost universally applied by solicitors: see C Smart, *Interviewing Solicitors . . .* (1981).

[219] In *Ackerman v. Ackerman* [1972] Fam 225, CA, it was held that in assessing periodical payments under the reformed divorce law the proper course was to apply the 'one third rule'; and it was still referred to as the 'one third guideline' *per* Arnold J in *McGrady v. McGrady* (1977) 1 FLR 67. The guideline was still being applied in the Registry in *Sibley v. Sibley* (1979) 2 FLR 121; whilst as recently as 1989 one judge is reported to have spoken of 'a conventional one third of income': *Fisher v. Fisher* [1989] 1 FLR 423, 427, CA. In *Burgess v. Burgess* [1996] 2 FLR 34, CA, Waite LJ says that

what (other than a general notion that the order should be fair and reasonable)[221] was to be put in its place?

There was particular difficulty where the assets had been inherited from one side of the family or the other, or for some other reason there was no clear link between the wife's contributions to the family and the acquisition of the family capital. For example, in *Trippas v. Trippas*:[222]

The husband was a partner in his family's business. A year after the break-down of the marriage there was a take-over bid, and he received £175,000 (perhaps something over £2 million in year 2000 values). The Court of Appeal held that the wife's contributions to the family did not entitle her to 'claim a share in the business as such. She did not give any active help in it. She did not work in it herself. All she did was what a good wife does do. She gave moral support to her husband by looking after the home. If he was depressed or in difficulty, she would encourage him to keep going'. That (said Lord Denning[223] bluntly) does not give her a share.[224]

This and similar cases exemplify the weakness of the two-stage process envisaged in the legislation: no indication was given of the relationship between the court's duty to 'have regard to all the circumstances of the case' and its duty to place the parties in the financial position in which they would have been had the marriage not broken down. One eminent Lord Justice pointed out:[225]

there can be no objection to the court proceeding from some convenient and familiar starting point (such as the two-thirds proportion when assessing income provision or a 50/50 division when dealing with the interests in a matrimonial home).

[220] In *Page v. Page* (1981) 2 FLR 198, CA Ormrod LJ pointed out that 'in many cases where the assets are small relative to the needs and obligations of one party, [the application of a one third principle would produce] a result which is too low and obviously does not accord with the requirements of [the Act]. Where there are substantial assets the rule may yield too high a figure. The effect of applying a "one half rule" [as Bush J had done] is . . . to exaggerate this difference. Moreover, the choice between a denominator of three or two is highly arbitrary as there are no reliable criteria to guide the choice'. The difficulty with judicial statements such as this is that they fail to reveal the basis upon which is held that payments are 'too high' or 'too low': see further below.

[221] See *Cumbers v. Cumbers* [1975] 1 All ER 1, CA, for an early example of a case in which Lord Denning declared that a wife who had 'really played a part in the [18-month] marriage' deserved compensation; and note *Hall v. Hall* [1984] FLR 631, CA, where the recently retired Sir Roger Ormrod admitted that opinions differed about the utility of a one-third starting point but, acknowledging that many judges in practice still made the computation, concluded that in the instant case the one-third approach had done nothing but confuse the issue. Note however that Sir Roger was unable to do more than state that the court should do what was 'fair and reasonable all round'.

[222] *Trippas v. Trippas* [1973] Fam 173.   [223] At p.141.

[224] The court, by reference to the statutory directive to have regard to the value of any benefit which would be lost by reason of divorce, did allocate the wife an enhanced lump sum, but the result was still to leave a substantial disparity between the capital assets of a couple married for 27 years.

[225] Ormrod LJ, in *O'D v. O'D* [1976] Fam 83. In *Dart v. Dart* [1996] 2 FLR 286, CA (a case in which the wife of an exceedingly wealthy businessman, basing her claim in part on the passages in the *Wachtel* decision suggesting a fractional division, claimed on appeal that the judge should have awarded her a payment of £100 million rather than the £9 million in fact awarded). Thorpe LJ said that behind the 'deferential acknowledgments' made to *Wachtel* and its acceptance in the 'essentially typical case of a middle class family that had prospered through a long marriage in an inflationary era' lay 'the reality that it has been consistently rejected as an authority of general

The *Wachtel* case was one of two people starting their married life with 'little or nothing but their earning capacities, and together founding a family and building up by their joint efforts such capital as they were able to save. Typically their main capital asset was the matrimonial home, bought on a mortgage and paid for out of income. These cases are true examples of equal partnership and such expressions as "family assets" and "the wife earning her share" are wholly apposite to them. In other cases the situation is different. One or other, or perhaps both, spouses may bring into the marriage substantial capital assets, or may acquire such assets during the marriage by inheritance or by gift from members of their families . . . In these cases it is necessary to go directly to the terms of [the legislation] for guidance'.

The reality may be that the terms of the legislation did not really provide this guidance; but the cases began to evidence some judicial support for inferring that the objective was no more than to meet[226] the family's 'reasonable needs' or perhaps their 'reasonable requirements'.[227] Towards the end of the twentieth century such an approach increasingly seemed demeaning and unfair, especially to the wives of successful businessmen. But it was discontent on the part of divorced men (and, sometimes, their new partners) which influenced the Law Commission's decision in 1980 to review of the policy of the law. The allegation was that divorce routinely cost the husband his home and children; and resentment was likely to be particularly strong if the husband believed his wife to have been responsible for the breakdown of the marriage, and exacerbated if he believed his wife was capable of working but refused to do so or that she was being supported by a cohabitant.[228] It may be that these allegations were to some extent based on a misunderstanding about the courts' interpretation of the statute; but even a requirement limited to satisfying the wife's 'reasonable

application' (ie to cases outside that 'typical' kind). He regarded Ormrod LJ as the 'real interpreter' of the legislation, and *O'D* as initiating the move towards 'reasonable requirements' as the appropriate criterion in 'big money cases'.

[226] Having calculated the 'net effect' of the order: see *Saunders v. Saunders* (1979) 1 FLR 121, 125 CA, *per* Brandon LJ: the right approach in such cases 'is rather to consider the disposable income of each party apart from any order, and then to see what order will produce a redistribution of the disposable incomes which is fair and just in all circumstances of the case'; and see also *Furniss v. Furniss* (1981) 3 FLR 46, CA.

[227] See eg *Scott v. Scott* [1978] 3 All ER 65, 68, *per* Cumming-Bruce LJ: the court's task 'has nothing to do with fractions and the one-third rule, it is an attempt to deal with the future of the two parties . . . When one comes to the realities of the situation . . . reference to the one-third rule as a starting-point is of no assistance, not of little assistance but of no assistance, because the dominating feature is the necessity of providing for three young children and the requirement of providing a home for them by means of mortgage payments . . .'. In *Preston v. Preston* (1981) 2 FLR 331, CA, Ormrod LJ went so far as to say that it is 'wrong in principle to adopt a purely arithmetical approach'; and see also *Furniss v. Furniss* (1981) 3 FLR 46, CA, for another warning from Ormrod LJ that the one-third approach is not helpful, and that although it may sometimes help in giving a rough idea of the position 'generally it misleads'; whilst finally in *Hall v. Hall* [1984] FLR 631 the recently retired Sir R Ormrod says that feelings vary on whether it is useful to do a third calculation and accepted that many judges still did so, but that in the case before him it had done nothing but to confuse the issue.

[228] The 1970 legislation accepted the Law Commission's recommendation that remarriage should (but unmarried cohabitation should not) automatically terminate an order for periodical payments: *Report on Financial Provision in Matrimonial Proceedings* (Law Com. No. 25, 1969) para. 14.

requirements' would (save in the case of the truly wealthy) often in practice mean that it would be the wife who would have first claim to occupation of what had been the family home. Whatever the truth, the feeling that the 1970 Act gave rise to serious injustice was sufficiently widespread, and articulated in letters to Members of Parliament and the Press, to lead the Law Commission to act.

THE MATRIMONIAL AND FAMILY PROCEEDINGS ACT 1984:
A CHANGE OF EMPHASIS?

The Law Commission's 1980 discussion paper *The Financial Consequences of Divorce: The Basic Policy*[229] was the first attempt by any official body in this country[230] to analyse the principles upon which the financial consequences of divorce should be determined. In 1981 the Commission made recommendations[231] based on the response to the 1980 discussion paper. It appears that there had been a substantial consensus in favour of change; and the vast majority of those who had commented on the matter considered that the direction to 'place the parties in the financial position in which they would have been if the marriage had not broken down' should be removed from the law as being undesirable even in the few cases in which it might be practicable of attainment. The Commission accepted the need to retain a wide discretion but favoured legislation indicating certain changes of emphasis in the way in which the courts exercised that discretion. Specifically, the law should emphasise as a priority the

---

[229] Law Com. No. 103, 1980.

[230] At much the same time, the Scottish Law Commission was considering reform of the law of Scotland; and subsequently the Family Law (Scotland) Act 1985 gave effect to the Scottish Law Commission's recommendations. Under that Act the court is to be guided by five 'principles' which include the 'fair sharing of the net value of matrimonial property' (fair presumptively meaning equal); taking fair account of the economic advantages or disadvantages experienced by either partner as a result of the marriage, the fair sharing of the economic burden of caring for children under the age of 16 after divorce; relief for a dependent spouse from temporary financial hardship over a period of up to three years to allow for adjustment to the divorce; and relief from serious hardship over a period of up to three years to allow for adjustment to the divorce; and relief over a reasonable period from serious financial hardship arising from the divorce. This assertion of principle has attracted support from some in England (see the speech by Lady Young in the Third Reading debate on the Family Law Act 1996, *Official Report* (HL) 11 March 1996, vol. 570, col. 717); and Scottish lawyers find that this legislation provides a satisfactory basis for negotiation about the financial consequences of divorce: see notably *The Impact of the Family Law (Scotland) Act 1985 on Solicitors' Divorce Practice* (1990). But the *Report to the Lord Chancellor of the Ancillary Relief Advisory Group* (chaired by Lord Justice Thorpe) (1998) whilst recognising that the Scottish law embodied a 'skilfully crafted modification of presumptive equal division' concluded that it would not be appropriate for England and Wales. Amongst criticisms made of the Scottish system were its failure to give any priority to the interests of children, the fact that it is only exceptionally that the court may order periodical payments in favour of a divorced spouse for a period in excess of three years; the belief that the definition of the 'matrimonial property' which falls to be divided necessitates costly valuations and sometimes leads to bizarre results (as for instance where one husband retains a valuable shareholding acquired before marriage and another actively trades, the result being that the first husband's shares are not matrimonial property whilst the second husband's are).

[231] *The Financial Consequences of Divorce* (Law Com. No. 112, 1981).

necessity to make such financial provision as would safeguard the maintenance and welfare of the children;[232] greater weight should be given to a divorced wife's earning capacity and to the desirability of both parties becoming self sufficient, and the courts should be more clearly directed to the desirability of promoting a smooth transition from the status of marriage to the status of independence and to the ultimate severance of financial obligations between the parties.[233]

Eventually, after lengthy parliamentary debate and enquiry,[234] the Matrimonial and Family Proceedings Act 1984 gave effect to the Law Commission's recommendations.[235] The Act[236] was not a fundamental restructuring of the law, and retained the requirement that the court considering making an ancillary relief order should consider all the circumstances, including a number of specified matters which required particular attention. It directed the court to give first consideration to the welfare while a minor of any child of the family. It contained provisions directing the court's attention to the desirability of limited term periodical payments and once-for-all settlements in appropriate cases (the so-called 'clean break').[237] It removed the direction requiring the court to seek to place the parties in the financial position they would have been in had the marriage continued without replacement.[238] Detailed analyses of the law will be found in family law textbooks;[239] but the following three general points are significant for the historical evolution of the law.

Law continues to be based on wide discretion

First, the law remains firmly based on a preference for discretion over formula and rule. It can be argued that the 1984 Act, by removing the direction to the courts to seek to place the parties in the financial position they would have been in had the marriage not broken down without substituting any alternative, has increased the ambit of the discretion. But, apparently, those administering the

---

[232] Paras. 24, 46(5)(a).   [233] Paras. 26–30; 46(5)(b).

[234] The Committee stage was taken in a Special Standing Committee which heard evidence from a number of witnesses including the then President of the Family Division: see *Official Report* (HC) 15 February 1984, vol. 54, col. 356.

[235] The Lord Chancellor stated that the Bill did what the Law Commission recommended, 'neither more nor less': *Official Report* (HL) 2 February 1984, vol. 447, col. 769.

[236] s. 3, substituting a new s. 25 Matrimonial Causes Act 1973.

[237] s. 3, substituting a new s. 25A Matrimonial Causes Act 1973.

[238] This had 'proved quite impossible of practical attainment': *Cowan v. Cowan* [2002] Fam 97, 110 *per* Thorpe LJ.

[239] Although the Law Commission insisted on the need for legislation to be the subject of systematic monitoring and regular reports to Parliament, there is little empirical data available. Some general information about the impact of the law on the financial position of families can be found in research carried out in the context of the introduction of a statutory scheme of child support: see J Bradshaw and J Millar, *Lone Parent Families in the United Kingdom* (1991); whilst the development of policy is analysed by J Eekelaar and M Maclean in SN Katz, J Eekelaar and M Maclean, *Cross Currents* (2000) Chapters 18 and 24. R Bird, *Ancillary Relief Handbook* (3rd ed., 2002) is a particularly useful guide reflecting an experienced District Judge's view of considerations relevant to the exercise of the court's powers.

law[240] (an increasingly specialist practising profession and judiciary)[241] believed they had been able to use this statutory framework to develop principles on the basis of which[242] bespoke solutions to fit the infinite variety of individual cases and to do fairness between the parties were tailored.[243] And according to the District Judges who deal with more than 85% of all the cases these principles were 'well-known to family lawyers' who could accordingly advise clients 'in the confident knowledge that the litigation is likely to be disposed of fairly'.

There can be no dispute that the existence of a wide discretion has enabled the court to deal with cases against the background of changing social and economic facts (such as the inflation of house prices in the 1970s and 1980s, the emergence of negative equity in the late 1980s, the transformation of the United Kingdom from a country in which income taxes were amongst the highest in the world into one which ranks as a tax haven in respect of such taxes, and the consequences of membership of the European Union including such arcane matters as the effect of 'milk quotas' on a financial relief application).

Considerations of misconduct rarely relevant

Although the legislation[244] directs the court to have regard (as one of the relevant circumstances) to the 'conduct of each of the parties, if that conduct is such that it would . . . be inequitable to disregard it' the courts seem still to discourage attempts to rely on allegations of misconduct.[245] Equally clearly, there is some popular discontent about the way in which the courts and legal advisers have in this way given a restrictive interpretation to those provisions which direct the court. In 1996 backbench MPs forced onto an unwilling Government

---

[240] But others were less so: Mr Geoff Hoon, at the time Parliamentary Secretary in the Lord Chancellor's Office had, in an address to the Solicitors' Family Law Association on 21 February 1998, announced the government's intention to seek change which would 'deliver a greater sense of certainty for the parties, without preventing the courts from ensuring that the outcome of cases is, as far as possible, fair and just to all concerned'. However, no action seems to have been taken: see the summary of events provided by Thorpe LJ in his judgment in *Cowan v. Cowan* [2002] Fam 97, 112.

[241] The increasing specialisation of the judiciary (scarcely noticed by most commentators) is one of the most significant developments in the history of the ancillary relief jurisdiction.

[242] The Association of District Judges Memorandum (above, para. 2.3) states the principles as follows: '(1) The first priority is housing for minor children and the parent with care. (2) The second priority is housing for the non-caring parent. (3) Once housing has been dealt with, the reasonable requirements of the parties must be considered and, if possible, met. (3) The need for self-sufficiency is an important principle to be observed at all time. (4) Subject to the above, and to any other s. 25 considerations [*sic*] once housing and the reasonable requirements of both parties have been met, jointly owned capital is divided equally and the parties retain any separate capital which they hold.

[243] The one significant gap in the court's powers to deal with the whole of a couple's financially valuable assets was filled by the Welfare Reform and Pensions Act 1999, which empowers the court to make pension sharing orders in respect of benefits under Occupational and other pensions.

[244] Matrimonial Causes Act 1973, s. 25(2)(g)—a provision consequential on the removal of the statutory hypothesis which included a reference to conduct. It does not appear that the revised wording was intended to change the law in this respect.

[245] See eg R Bird, *Ancillary Relief Handbook* (3rd ed., 2002) para. 1.34 ff.

an amendment of the law which was intended to give greater prominence to considerations of conduct; but that provision (along with the other provisions relating to divorce contained in that Act) has not been brought into force. It can be argued that the law as it is currently administered does not adequately reflect the community's perceptions of what is fair and just.

'Clean break' solution favoured

Finally, the complex and interrelated provisions[246] imposing a general duty on the court to consider terminating the parties' mutual financial relationships on the divorce or as soon thereafter as the court considers just and reasonable do seem to have encouraged the legal profession and the judiciary to think in terms of a so-called clean break in many cases. In effect, the objective is to make provision once for all by way of reallocation of capital on divorce thereby enabling the parties to 'go their separate ways without the running irritant of financial interdependence or dispute'.[247] Even in the case of the less affluent, this objective might be achieved by allowing the wife and children at least the right to occupy the former matrimonial home for the rest of the wife's life,[248] relieving the husband of any obligation to make ongoing payments to the wife.[249] In the case of the affluent, the courts adopted sophisticated actuarial techniques[250] to calculate the once for all capital sum which, if invested on certain assumptions about yields and tax rates, would provide a fund sufficient to meet the wife's 'requirements' for the rest of her life but would not leave any substantial surplus on her death.

THE COST OF LITIGATION: THE LEGAL AID STATUTORY CHARGE

The fact that the court had wide discretionary powers to reallocate the parties' funds inevitably led to a great deal of expertise being devoted to influencing the decisions on how those powers were to be exercised. The pre-World War II situation of financial orders being usually limited to orders for periodical payments the amount of which was largely determined by reference to the simple question of who had 'won' the divorce suit could not survive in a world in which

---

[246] For an explanation, see SM Cretney and JM Masson, *Principles of Family Law* (6th ed., 1997) p. 454.

[247] *per* Waite J, *Tandy v. Tandy* (1986) October 24, as cited in *Whiting v. Whiting* [1988] 2 FLR 189, 199.

[248] Various techniques were used, ranging from the simplicity of an outright transfer of the home to the wife to settlements of various kinds: see SM Cretney and JM Masson, *Principles of Family Law* (6th ed., 1997) p. 482, ff.

[249] The law does not permit a parent to contract out of obligations to support children, although it appears that this was not always appreciated before the introduction of the statutory child support scheme by Child Support Act 1991: see *Crozier v. Crozier* [1994] 1 FLR 126; SM Cretney and JM Masson, *Principles of Family Law* (6th ed., 1997) pp. 529–538.

[250] The most common was the so-called 'Duxbury' calculation, as explained in *F v. F (Duxbury Calculation: Rate of Return)* [1996] 1 FLR 833 and in *B v. B (Financial Provision)* [1990] 1 FLR 20.

the form of the decree was largely irrelevant, and in which the court had to take into account a large number of circumstances in deciding on the orders which should be made. Cases came before the courts in which the parties' financial affairs were extremely complex. For example, Baron Thyssen-Bornemisza, one of the wealthiest men in the world, admitted he had an annual income of ten million pounds and assets—including interests in a tanker fleet and shipyard, a collection of pictures and other works of art, houses (some owned through companies) in Switzerland, Spain, Jamaica and Sardinia, a yacht and a private jet aeroplane—together worth some four hundred million pounds; and the courts had to decide what investigations should be ordered in the light of suggestions that in reality his assets might be worth as much as one thousand million pounds.[251] In such cases a great deal of financial expertise from the parties' advisers was required; and not surprisingly specialist accountants and lawyers emerged to supply what was required. The necessary investigations and analyses[252] could prove extremely (and sometimes disproportionately) expensive. For example:

In *H v. H (Financial Relief: Costs)*[253] a middle-class husband and wife living (in the judge's words) comfortably but not luxuriously had incurred costs of £175,000 in seeking resolution of their financial disputes. Part of this was said to be attributable to 'innumerable, unnecessary and repetitive requests for questions to be answered and unnecessary, or unnecessarily expensive, resort to experts'; and the case generated seven lever-arch files containing about 1,750 pages, most of which were not looked at or even opened during the hearing of the case. The parties had only comparatively modest means; and the judge said that the burden of costs made it impossible to achieve a fair resolution of the case because the burden of costs was likely to be penurious to one or other or both of them.

It is true that husbands and wives involved in disputes about the financial consequences of divorce should have been made aware of the amount of costs being incurred;[254] and it could be said that if they chose to spend money on litigation that was their right as a free citizen. But when the litigation was financed by

---

[251] See *Thyssen-Bornemisza v. Thyssen-Bornemisza* [1986] Fam 1; and *Thyssen-Bornemisza v. Thyssen-Bornemisza (No. 2)* [1985] FLR 1069. The courts in fact ruled that the scale of the Baron's wealth was such that it would be only an academic exercise to seek to find whether his own estimate of his wealth was accurate or not.

[252] The legal costs of negotiation and advocacy could also often be disproportionate to any benefit to the parties: in *Piglowska v. Piglowski* [1999] 1 WLR 1360 husband and wife had a home worth some £100,000 and other assets worth £27,400. The total legal costs incurred—there were three appeals—were estimated to exceed £128,000, ie more than the total value of all the couple's assets. Even in cases of more substantial means, expenditure on legal costs might not always seem justified in the light of the outcome: in *White v. White* [2001] 1 AC 596 the couple had between them assets worth some £4.6 million; each appealed to the House of Lords incurring further costs of half a million pounds in doing so. The House dismissed both appeals.

[253] [1997] 2 FLR 57.

[254] It is the duty of solicitors and counsel to keep clients informed at all stages of the proceedings: see eg the *Solicitors' Family Law Association Code of Practice*, para. 10.

legal aid—and the wife might well be eligible for support even when her husband had very substantial assets—it was tempting for those concerned to think that the State would be responsible for any legal costs. This was not true: the legal aid legislation[255] imposed a first charge on all property 'recovered or preserved' for the assisted person. In a typical personal injuries case (for example) this would not make any difference to the claimant. The court would make an award of damages and order the defendant to pay the plaintiff's costs. All the money due under that order would be paid over to the Legal Aid Board, which would recoup the net expenditure it had incurred (taking account of the plaintiff's own contributions) in financing the claim, and then pay the balance over to the claimant.[256] The successful claimant would thus end up with the damages the court had awarded, and all or most of his costs would have been paid. The crucial factor which distinguished such a case from a claim for financial relief in divorce is that in ordinary civil litigation the costs would be paid by the defendant (or, very often, his insurers); but in divorce any order for costs would simply reduce the total of assets available to be distributed.

It is true that in the early days of the legal aid scheme[257] the existence of the statutory charge probably did not cause any particular problem in divorce cases:[258] the divorce court had no power to make orders that one party transfer property to the other and accordingly there would be no property 'recovered or preserved'[259] in the proceedings to which the statutory charge would apply. But when the Divorce Court was given (and began to exercise) extensive powers to make property adjustment orders it soon[260] became apparent that the impact of the statutory charge was often, in effect, to make a legally aided party pay the costs out of the property the court had awarded. Of course, this could be avoided if the court made an order for costs against the other party; but that might not be practicable even if it were just. For example:

[255] Legal Aid and Advice Act 1949, s. 3(4).

[256] The decision to impose a charge on property recovered or preserved was presumably primarily directed at situations in which which property other than cash—perhaps a house or farmland, for example—was in issue: see above.

[257] See Chapter 8, above; and on the history of the legislation governing the charge *Hanlon v. The Law Society* [1981] AC 124, HL.

[258] The papers do not indicate that the potential significance of the statutory charge was appreciated: the first draft note on clauses (PRO LCO2/4621, 20 October) states that the provision was aimed at an assisted person gaining or preserving a valuable asset since it would be inequitable to incur public expense in such cases. The provision creating the statutory charge was included as Item 18 in a departmental list of 'main deviations' from the Rushcliffe proposals but it appears that this related to the decision that the sums in question be paid to the Law Society rather than the Area Committee: *Rushcliffe Report*, para. 173.

[259] Periodical payments by way of maintenance were excluded from the operation of the charge: see Civil Legal Aid (General) Regulations 1989, reg. 94(c).

[260] Until 1976 all sums ordered to be paid by way of ancillary relief in divorce proceedings were exempt from the charge. It was the removal—presumably prompted by the realisation that the courts were increasingly making property adjustment orders in divorce—of that blanket exemption which made the problems acute.

In *Evans v. Evans*[261] the legally aided wife's costs amounted to £25,000. Although she wanted to remain in the former matrimonial home with her children the need to pay off this amount from any property transferred to her made it impossible for her to do so since her husband (whose own legal costs amounted to £35,000) did not have sufficient funds to support an order of the size which would be needed.

Particular hardship was caused if the most practicable solution would have been for the former matrimonial home to be sold and the proceeds divided so that each could purchase a substitute property:

In *Simmons v. Simmons*[262] the President of the Family Division made an order that the former matrimonial home be sold and that £26,750 be paid out of the proceeds to the wife. It was intended that, with the aid of a £7,000 mortgage, she would buy another house for herself and the children. The order took no account of the fact that the statutory charge would attach to the sale proceeds, leaving the wife with insufficient funds for rehousing.

The same result would follow if the house were transferred to the husband[263] on his paying a sum to the wife in respect of her share.[264] Following much criticism a scheme was devised[265] under which the enforcement of the charge could be postponed (although interest accrued on the amount outstanding) in cases in which money or property was required for a home in which the assisted person or his dependants would live. This enabled many families to keep their home; but it also highlighted the fact that legal aid is in reality only a loan, and that eventually the loan (and interest) has to be repaid. The official view appears to be that the legally aided should, just like the fee paying, be made to appreciate that litigation is an expensive luxury which has to be paid for,[266] and that it is generally in everyone's interest that the distribution of the family assets on divorce should be dealt with by negotiated settlement rather than by contested litigation.

---

[261] [1990] 1 FLR 319, Booth J.   [262] [1984] Fam 17.

[263] It had been accepted that enforcement of the charge could be postponed until the property was sold, so that the husband (assuming that he too was legally aided) would in contrast be able to stay in the property for as long as he wished, in effect financed by an interest free loan from the legal aid fund. This situation was described as 'surely grotesque' by the House of Lords in *Simpson v. The Law Society* [1987] AC 861.

[264] See *Simpson v. The Law Society* [1987] AC 861, where the Law Lords strongly criticised the anomalies and injustice to which these rules gave rise.

[265] See Civil Legal Aid (General) Regulations 1989, regs 96–99. The effect of the regulations is clearly explained in the *Legal Aid Handbook 1996/7*, prepared by The Legal Aid Board (1996), Sweet & Maxwell, paras. 16-01 to 16-23. For a detailed account of the background and a critical analysis of the provisions for deferment, see S Shute, 'The Effect of the Statutory Charge on Legally Aided Matrimonial Litigation' (1993) 109 LQR 636.

[266] The legally aided litigant did enjoy other advantages, not least that it was unlikely that a substantial order for costs would be enforced against him or her but again this depended on the circumstances and there were cases in which it was considered reasonable for the assisted person to be made to pay the other party's costs: see *Chaggar v. Chaggar* [1997] 1 FLR 566; *Parr v. Smith* [1996] 1 FLR 490, CA; and *R v. R (Costs: Child Case)* [1997] 2 FLR 95, CA.

The scheme for deferring enforcement of the statutory charge did remove one particular source of difficulty and grievance; but the underlying problems of the expense (and acrimony) engendered by litigation about the financial consequences of divorce remained. The judges accepted that there was a pressing need for reform.[267] The first attempt to encourage settlement in preference to the expense of contested litigation was found by adapting the principles governing the exercise of the courts' discretion to decide how the burden of costs should be divided between the parties. It was made quite clear that this discretion would be exercised in such a way as to penalise those who rejected a reasonable offer of settlement.[268] Towards the end of the century a new procedural regime was introduced in an attempt to streamline procedures and in particular to reduce delay, facilitate settlements, and limit the parties' costs. It was also expected that the court would have greater and more effective control over the process, and that this would increase efficiency.[269]

But search for principle unsuccessful

Such reforms might improve the routine processing of many divorce cases. But procedural change could have little if any impact on the question of principle: what was the objective of the law governing the financial consequences of divorce. As the century moved to its close it became increasingly apparent that, although the divorce related legislation of 1970 to 1984 had greatly improved the position of wife and children in respect of housing needs, the law in those cases in which large sums of capital were available still did little more than the divorce court had done (albeit through the medium of income payments alone) a century earlier. A wife's contributions to the welfare of the family might give her a claim to the house and other 'family assets'; and if she could show that her contributions had in some way specifically increased the family capital the court would take account of that fact and make an award to take account of it. Apart from that, however, the principle applied by the courts remained essentially

---

[267] *Evans v. Evans* [1990] 1 WLR 575 (Booth J); *H v. H (Financial Relief: Costs)* [1997] 2 FLR 57 (Holman J); *Piglowska v. Piglowski* [1999] 1 WLR 1360 (Lord Hoffmann).

[268] Ie under the so-called *Calderbank* principle: *Calderbank v. Calderbank* [1976] Fam 93. One party would make an offer to settle 'without prejudice save as to costs'. If accepted, the court would be invited to make a consent order to give effect to the parties' agreement, which would include terms as to the allocation of costs. If the offer were rejected, the case would proceed to trial and no reference would be made to the offer until the judge announced his decision about financial orders. If that award were more than the amount offered in settlement the successful party would normally be awarded costs, but if it were less—effectively implying that the costs of the hearing had been incurred unecessarily—the court would usually order that the person who had rejected the offer should pay all the costs incurred by both sides after the time when the offer was made: see *Gojkovic v. Gojkovic (No. 2)* [1992] Fam 40.

[269] See notably the judgment of Booth J in *Evans v. Evans* [1990] 1 WLR 575; but the impact of this appears to have been transient: see *Piglowska v. Piglowski* [1999] 1 WLR 1360. At the end of the century Procedural Rules were introduced in an attempt to encourage openness and settlement and to limit costs: Family Proceedings (Amendment No. 2) Rules 1999, SI 1999/3491, and see *Practice Direction (Ancillary Relief Procedure)* [2000] 1 FLR 997, and p. 760.

unchanged: the wife's reasonable requirements in terms of 'homes, children and lifestyle' were to be satisfied. But the court would not go beyond that level. Specifically, the court would not apply any presumption that the parties' assets should be divided equally. For example:

In *Dart v. Dart*[270] the husband's family business making foam cups had greatly prospered and supported a lavish life style (at the level of some £400,000 a year). The marriage broke down after 14 years. The wife asked the court to order him to transfer the matrimonial home and investments worth £122 million to her. The Court of Appeal upheld the judge's decision that she should have the house and nine million pounds, that amount being sufficient to satisfy her 'reasonable requirements' for the rest of her life. The court unequivocally rejected the notion that the court's function was redistributive; and the court made it clear that in its view no fixed principle of equal division governed the allocation even of assets acquired by the parties' joint efforts.[271]

It was true that a wife who could be seen to have made real contributions to a business enterprise might expect to receive some financial compensation—for example, in *Conran v. Conran*[272] the judge assessed the 'reasonable requirements' of a wife who had made an outstanding contribution to the success of her husband's restaurant and other businesses at some eight million pounds but added a sum of two million pounds in recognition of the part she had played. But there was to be no presumption of equal division of assets. As the present author put it in a published lecture:[273]

'The courts . . . firmly drew the line at claims that contributions to the welfare of the family should as such give the wife an interest in the husband's business.[274] True, [a wife's] participation *in the business* was to receive tangible recognition;[275] . . . true the contributions of countless wives to providing a comfortable family home from which the husband could set out refreshed to jet in and out of the market places of the global economy would be recognised by ensuring that she had sufficient resources to preserve a comfortable and affluent life-style, this being encompassed in terms of her "reasonable requirements". But the wife who does not give active help to the business, who merely does what "a good wife does", giving moral support to her husband by looking after the home, encouraging him to keep going when he is depressed or in difficulty cannot (so Lord Denning held in 1972)[276] claim a share in those business assets as such, over and above

---

[270] [1996] 2 FLR 286, CA.   [271] *Burgess v. Burgess* [1996] 2 FLR 34, CA.

[272] [1997] 2 FLR 615.

[273] 'Trusting the Judges: Money after Divorce' (1999) 52 CLP 286.

[274] See notably *Page v. Page* (1981) 2 FLR 198, CA, in which the earlier case of *O'D v. O'D* [1976] Fam 83, CA (wife who had contributed to success of hotel business by working as receptionist, chamber maid, cook, waitress and clerk held properly awarded £70,000 out of total assets worth £215,000: the scale and speed of the business's development was largely attributable to capital supplied by husband's father) was distinguished on the basis that Mrs Page's contributions were not to the business. J Eekelaar, *Financial and Property Adjustment on Divorce* (1991) p. 30 reports a 'prevalent opinion' that a direct contribution to business assets would be required.

[275] *Gojkovic v. Gojkovic* [1990] 1 FLR 140, CA.

[276] *Trippas v. Trippas* [1973] Fam 134; and see *Preston v. Preston* [1982] Fam 17, 25, *per* Ormrod LJ. In contrast, in *Vicary v. Vicary* [1992] 2 FLR 271, 289, Purchas LJ refused to accept the supposed

what is necessary to preserve her standard of living. Husband and wife may indeed come to the judgment seat on a basis of complete equality;[277] but the courts for long consistently held that it does not follow that there should be an equal division of assets . . .'

However, the decision of the House of Lords in *White v. White*[278] (a case of a working partnership between husband and wife in their farming business) left it unclear whether this was still true. Whilst referring to a 'yardstick of equal division' the House did not on the facts alter the division of assets made below; and although apparently criticising the use of a criterion of 'reasonable requirements' did not condescend to explain what principle (other than that of 'fairness') should be applied.

In these circumstances, it is not surprising that some commentators have suggested that amending legislation, based on clear decisions about the principles to be applied, is required.[279] Certainly case law at the end of the twentieth century evidences the remarkable shift which had taken place: for many years, the courts and Parliament had regarded the question whether the marriage should continue as one of vital importance and issues of the consequences of divorce were hardly considered, but after the divorce reforms embodied in the Matrimonial Causes Act 1973 the issue of dissolution was rarely controversial while the financial consequences have become a dominant feature of the family justice system.

The underlying question is really one of interpreting the terms of the marital contract: it is certainly a partnership, but does the partnership extend to all the parties' activities (business as well as domestic) or is the partnership to be regarded as primarily to do with domestic life, business interests being relevant to the extent only that they provide the means to support the parties' common lifestyle? At the end of the century, the courts—with little real guidance from Parliament—had decisively rejected the notion that a divorced wife should expect only to be compensated to the extent that her performance of 'domestic chores' had enabled the couple to acquire 'family assets'[280] and the House of Lords[281] had firmly rejected the satisfaction of the wife's 'reasonable requirements'[282] as the criterion. The result is by no means clear[283] but may come close to the imposition by the judiciary of the community of property which neither Parliament nor any official advisory body had ever accepted as the basis of English matrimonial law.

---

distinction 'between those cases in which the wife makes an actual financial contribution to the assets of the family and those in which her contribution is indirect inasmuch as she supplied the infrastructure and support in the context of which the husband is able to work hard, prosper and accumulate his wealth'; but the Court's judgment is otherwise put entirely in terms of meeting needs and supporting a standard of living, and there is no suggestion that a transfer of wealth is the objective. The outcome in this as in many other cases (see the table of outcomes published each year in the Family Law Bar Association's invaluable *At a Glance*) was that the wife received sufficient to bring her assets up a third of the whole—£637,000 out of some £2 million.

[277] *Calderbank v. Calderbank* [1976] Fam 93, 103, CA.   [278] [2001] 1 AC 596.

[279] See the discussion in *Cowan v. Cowan* [2002] Fam 97, 112, *per* Thorpe LJ.

[280] See note 234, above.   [281] In *White v. White* [2001] 1 AC 596.

[282] See p. 432, above.

[283] See also *Cowan v. Cowan* [2002] Fam 97, CA; *Lambert v. Lambert* [2003] 1 FLR 139.

11

Maintenance, the Magistrates' Courts and the State

INTRODUCTION

By the beginning of the twentieth century, the magistrates' courts were making extensive use of their jurisdiction (codified in 1895)[1] to make separation and maintenance orders. Statistically this was for long more important than the matrimonial jurisdiction of the High Court. Even after legal aid became available[2] for divorce in 1950 and for the first time gave wage earners faced with marital breakdown a realistic possibility of opting for divorce, magistrates were still making[3] nearly 15,000 spouse maintenance orders each year;[4] and in 1958 the Maintenance Orders Act 1958 gave the magistrates' courts the power to vary many periodical payment orders originally made in divorce. In this way, the magistrates' courts came to play a large part in determining the ongoing financial arrangements for the divorced and their families, notwithstanding the fact that they never had power to grant divorces.

Magistrates had also traditionally been concerned with the obligations imposed by the Poor Law;[5] and the magistrates' courts continued to have an important role in dealing with the relationship between the Welfare State and private support after the abolition of the the Poor Law in 1948. But increasingly it came to be asked whether these matters might not be better dealt with by administrative (rather then judicial procedures) and the magistrates' jurisdic-

---

[1] Summary Jurisdiction (Married Women) Act 1895: see p. 201, above.

[2] The number of divorces overtook the number of magistrates' spouse maintenance orders for the first time during World War II, when a number of measures—for example, the Services Legal Aid scheme—were put in place to facilitate divorce by poorer citizens: see Chapter 8, above.

[3] To a significant extent the explanation for this is that magistrates' orders were used to obtain repayment from husbands of state benefits paid to their wives: see below.

[4] At this time, the number of divorces was running at around 30,000 per annum: see Appendix II, Table 2, to the *Report of the Royal Commission on Marriage and Divorce* (1956, Cmd. 9678). The best source of statistical and other information about this jurisdiction is OR McGregor, L Blom-Cooper, and C Gibson, *Separated Spouses, A Study of the matrimonial jurisdiction of magistrates' courts* (1970): see in particular Table 2.

[5] At the beginning of the twentieth century some 4,000 orders under the Poor Law and related legislation were made each year, in effect requiring relatives of those who had become a charge on the community to reimburse all or part of the costs so incurred: see OR McGregor, L Blom-Cooper, and C Gibson, *Separated Spouses, A Study of the matrimonial jurisdiction of magistrates' courts* (1970) Table 2. Magistrates also made some 6,000 orders each year under what was then called the bastardy legislation against putative fathers.

tion was scrutinised by three important official committees[6] between 1968 and 1974. The Domestic Proceedings and Magistrates' Courts Act 1978 eventually introduced many important changes in the substantive law (not least by ending the power to the magistrates to make separation orders) but did little if anything to alter the balance between judicial and administrative process. In 1991 however the Child Support Act challenged what was described as the common assumption that the State should assume financial responsibility for the family when a marriage or other family relationship broke down. In the result, the role of the magistrates in relation to the financial aspects of family law[7] remains at the turn of the century unclear and its future uncertain. But historically the development of the courts' powers to regulate the financial relationship between a couple whose marriage was in difficulties is important, and the present chapter seeks to trace the more important stages.

THE LEGISLATIVE FRAMEWORK: THE DEVELOPMENT OF THE SUBSTANTIVE LAW

The marginal notes to the Matrimonial Causes Act 1878 make it clear[8] that the Act was seen primarily as protecting the wives of men convicted of aggravated assault by providing that the wife victim should (at least if the court was satisfied[9] that her future safety was in peril) no longer be legally obliged to live with the guilty husband; but the Act also provided[10] that on making such a non-cohabitation order the court could in addition order the husband to pay the wife

'such weekly sum as the Court . . . may consider to be in accordance with his means, and with any means which the wife may have for her support . . . and the Court . . . shall have power from time to time to vary the same on the application of either the husband or the wife, upon proof that the means of the husband or wife have altered in amount since the original order' was made.

But no such order was to be made if the wife had committed uncondoned adultery; and the court could discharge the order if at any time the wife committed adultery.

In 1886 Parliament went much further by giving a deserted wife a direct financial remedy against her husband:[11] the Married Women (Maintenance in Cases

---

[6] *Report of the Departmental Committee on Statutory Maintenance Limits* (Chairman, Jean Graham Hall, 1968, Cmnd. 3587); *Report of the Committee on the Enforcement of Judgment Debts* (Chairman, the Hon Mr Justice Payne, 1969, Cmnd. 3909); *Report of the Committee on One-Parent Families* (Chairman, the Hon Sir M Finer, 1974, Cmnd. 5629).

[7] As distinct from administering the code of law established by the Children Act 1989: see below, Chapter 20.

[8] 'If husband convicted of aggravated assault, Court may order that wife be not bound to cohabit, etc.'

[9] This was a specific requirement imposed by Matrimonial Causes Act 1878, s. 1.

[10] s. 4(1).

[11] The Bill as introduced would have allowed the magistrates also to make separation and custody orders based solely on desertion, but the Government opposed this as going 'much too far': see *Official Report* (HC) 24 March 1886, vol. 303, col. 1770; 5 May 1886, vol. 305, col. 344; and 16 June

of Desertion) Act 1886 provided that the court could order the man to pay the deserted wife[12] a weekly sum not exceeding £2 provided he was able wholly or in part to maintain her but had wilfully refused or neglected to do so. In this way, the deserted wife was no longer forced into the workhouse until such time as the Poor Law authorities were able to take action against her husband.[13]

In 1895 the Summary Jurisdiction (Married Women) Act tidied up, and in one important respect extended the legislation.[14] As the Graham Hall Committee was to put it:[15]

The 1895 Act was 'significant because it conferred on magistrates' courts the general matrimonial jurisdiction which has been widely exercised in the twentieth century. In addition to consolidating the provisions of the 1878 and 1886 Acts, the Act enabled justices to make orders for separation and maintenance where the husband had wilfully neglected to maintain, a power not available to the High Court until 1949. Justices could also make orders on the grounds of desertion even though the desertion had not continued for two years'.

The Act[16] remained the basis for the magistrates' matrimonial jurisdiction[17] for more than 70 years.[18]

1886, vol. 306, col. 1672. Contrary to the statement in para. 32 of the *Report of the Departmental Committee on Statutory Maintenance Limits* (Chairman, Jean Graham Hall, 1968, Cmnd. 3587) the Act does not 'declare' that a wife was bound to give her husband consortium if she wished to re-establish cohabitation (although it is true that the husband could always terminate his desertion by making the wife a bona fide offer to return). A similar statement appears in p. 15 of OR McGregor, L Blom-Cooper, and C Gibson, *Separated Spouses, A Study of the matrimonial jurisdiction of magistrates' courts* (1970) with a footnote reference to *R v. Jackson* [1891] 1 QB 671, CA, which does not appear to be directly relevant.

[12] Provided the wife had not committed uncondoned adultery.

[13] As noted at p. 200, note 29, it appears that while a deserted working class woman in Bermondsey could 'sometimes drag along with the aid of friends' she would often be 'driven to the workhouse in a week or a fortnight'. The Poor Law authorities were reluctant to allow married women claiming to have been deserted so-called 'outdoor relief' for fear that they were acting in collusion with their husbands: see *Report of the Committee on One-Parent Families* (Chairman, the Hon. Sir M Finer, 1974, Cmnd. 5629) Appendix 5 paras. 68–69. In any event, the poor law authorities had a right to reimbursement from the husband of the cost of any relief given to a married woman or his children: see Poor Law Amendment Act 1868, s. 33 (the relevant provisions being subsequently consolidated in Poor Law Act 1927, ss. 41 and 43) and generally LN Brown (1955) 18 MLR 114, 110–116.

[14] The Bill's promoter (EW Byrne) stated that it was intended to get 'rid of some of the anomalies which exist in the civil law and the criminal law in cases of aggravated assaults on wives by husbands and . . . to give similar relief in cases of persistent cruelty by a husband towards a wife as now exists in cases of aggravated assault': *Official Report* (HC) (4th Series) 22 May 1895, vol. 34, col. 62. Apart from that the Bill (which had Home Office support) passed through both Houses of Parliament with little discussion.

[15] *Report of the Departmental Committee on Statutory Maintenance Limits* (Chairman, Jean Graham Hall, 1968, Cmnd. 3587), para. 34.

[16] The following were the grounds of complaint: (a) husband convicted of aggravated assault contrary to Offences against the Persons Act 1861, s. 43; (b) husband convicted on indictment of assault and sentenced to a fine of more than £5 or a prison term exceeding two months; (c) husband had deserted wife; (d) husband guilty of persistent cruelty, or wilful neglect to provide reasonable maintenance, provided that the cruelty or neglect had caused her to leave and live separately and

An inadequate remedy?

The National Union of Societies for Equal Citizenship[19] and the other women's groups which became particularly active at the end of World War I[20] did not think this legislation went anything like far enough. Their starting point was a belief in 'real equality of liberties, status and opportunities between men and women' and an equal moral standard between men and women;[21] and specifically they believed married women should be entitled to a reasonable share of the husband's earnings. But NUSEC realised that there was no prospect of getting radical legislation compelling husbands to share their incomes through Parliament. Instead, they seized on the fact that the magistrates could only order financial support for women who had been driven out of the home or had the courage to leave. And even if a wife got an order she could not enforce it at any time that she was living with the husband.[22] NUSEC demanded the abolition of these restrictions: the wife who was not being adequately maintained should be able to get an order if she could establish neglect or cruelty; there should be no financial limits on the orders which the court could make[23]; and the

apart from him: Summary Jurisdiction (Married Women) Act 1895, s. 4. However, the adulterous wife lost her rights unless the husband had condoned, connived at or by wilful neglect or misconduct conduced to the adultery: ss. 6, 7.

[17] The court had power to make a non-cohabitation order, a custody order giving the wife custody of children of the marriage so long as they were under 16, maintenance at a rate not exceeding £2 weekly, and costs: s. 5. The Act blurred the distinction between cases involving the wife's safety and those in which the sole issue was financial: see *Dodd v. Dodd* [1906] P 189, *per* Gorell J at p. 198.

[18] The evidence to the Gorell Committee gives a vivid picture of the realities of working class life at the beginning of the twentieth century: see in particular the evidence of the Metropolitan Police Magistrate at Tower Bridge court containing many examples of life for the carters and workers in warehouses, factories and docks in Bermondsey and Southwark. It appears that a typical order might be for the husband to pay 7/- (35 pence—possibly £20 in year 2000 values) on the principle that men would 'attempt to pay a small order, [but would] make no attempt to pay' an order truly sufficient to support the wife and children. In practice in these cases women had to 'eke out the difference with her own labour and the labour of her children': *Evidence taken before the Royal Commission*, 1912, Vol. I, Cd. 6478, and Vol. 2, Cd. 6479, q. 1973.

[19] Henceforth abbreviated as NUSEC.

[20] See generally SM Cretney, *Law, Law Reform and the Family* (1998) Chapter 7 and the sources relating to NUSEC and Mrs Eva Hubback (its Parliamentary Secretary) cited at pp. 158–160.

[21] Statement of the Objectives of NUSEC as appearing in its Annual Reports, eg for 1925–1926.

[22] Abolition of this rule (introduced in relation to applications founded on cruelty and neglect in 1895: see above) had been recommended in the *Report of the Royal Commission on Divorce and Matrimonial Causes* (1912, Cd. 6478), para. 152.

[23] Notwithstanding the fact that the 1878 Act had not restricted the amounts which the courts could order, a maximum of £2 weekly was imposed by the Married Women (Maintenance in Cases of Desertion) Act 1886 and was consistently defended as marking an appropriate dividing line between cases suitable for the magistrates and those requiring the attention of the superior courts: see eg the Home Secretary's memorandum to the Home Affairs Committee dated 24 July 1922, PRO LCO2/773—removal of limits would upset 'the whole of the existing arrangements for division of jurisdiction between the Divorce Court and the magistrates'. The policy of confining the use of the summary jurisdiction to the working classes seems to have been deliberate, and was in part founded on the perception of the magistrates offering a social service to working class communities: see Chapter 8, above and note eg the comments dated 9 June 1922 of Chief Magistrate Biron on PRO

grounds[24] upon which orders could be made should be extended. NUSEC also wanted an end to the rule under which a wife's adultery—even if the husband's failure to support had driven her onto the streets—was a bar to her enforcing the order.[25] They wanted more effective means of enforcement, and in particular they wanted the court to have power to order the husband's employer to deduct the amount due from his wages and pay it to the wife.

NUSEC drafted a Bill[26] which was introduced as a Private Member's Bill by Sir Robert Newman[27] in 1922. Not surprisingly this all proved highly controversial.[28] The Government conceded that the Bill would effect some useful changes; but it considered some of the proposals to be 'mischievous' and totally unacceptable. In particular, there was strong opposition to any proposal which

HO45/11936: removal of the limits would subvert the purpose of the summary matrimonial jurisdiction, which was largely concerned with preserving the working class home in the belief that in the then prevalent circumstances 'almost any domestic conditions are preferable to the disadvantages of a separate existence'. The view that a court should be specifically geared to the requirements of the working classes became unacceptable to informed opinion in the post World War II world, but there appears to be no justification for the 'conjecture' (made by the *Report of the Departmental Committee on Statutory Maintenance Limits* (Chairman, Jean Graham Hall, 1968, Cmnd. 3587, para. 179)) that the limit was influenced by a 'censorious attitude to bastardy' (admittedly an area in which the summary courts were experienced) and by the philosophy of the 1834 Poor Law Commission that the situation of recipients of relief should never be allowed to be 'really or apparently so eligible as the situation of the independent labourer of the lowest class'.

[24] The Licensing Act 1902 had added habitual drunkenness and the Summary Jurisdiction (Separation and Maintenance) Act 1925, s. 3 habitual taking of opium or other prescribed drugs to the grounds on which an order could be made. Either spouse could obtain an order on these grounds.

[25] The Home Office would not accept the amendment originally put forward which (it was claimed: see PRO LCO2/773, Home Secretary's Memorandum to the Home Affairs Committee, 24 July 1922) would have allowed a wife to commit adultery, get an order against her husband, and live with her paramour at her husband's expense.

[26] NUSEC Annual Report 1925–1926, p. 8.   [27] 1871–1947, MP for Finchley.

[28] The Chief Magistrate, Sir Chartres Biron, saw the Bill is an 'ill-considered and unfortunate piece of legislation, which . . . would have the most serious consequences' destroying 'the existing legislation on the subject and [substituting] for approved legal principles the theories of amateur experiment' (although Biron did concede the Bill did contain some good things). Parliamentary Counsel Hugh Godley saw the whole Bill introduced by NUSEC as 'preposterous' and 'like other Bills promoted by the Women's Societies under the pretence of removing slight inequalities between the sexes strike at the roots of domestic felicity': Godley to Blackwell 22 June 1922. The provision allowing the court to make orders whilst the couple were still residing together was a source of particular controversy: on the one hand the experienced Metropolitan Magistrate W Clarke Hall wrote to the Permanent Under Secretary of State at the Home Office in 1922 that there were 'many husbands who are not bad or cruel men, but who have an entirely misconceived opinion as to the proper amount to allow'—eg only £1.50 out of a £4 wage. He thought a provision empowering the court to fix maintenance for spouses who continued to live together could be supported: PRO HO45/11936. But a Home Office official recorded on 24 February 1922 the view that such a provision would be 'quite ludicrous' and entail a 'great deal of mischievous interference by probation officers and others between married persons and would do no good in practice'. The Summary Jurisdiction (Separation and Maintenance) Act 1925 eventually provided that an order could be made notwithstanding the fact that husband and wife were still living together but could not be enforced so long as they did so and would automatically come to an end if they lived together for as long as three months. This was a compromise intended to give a well-meaning husband an opportunity to become reconciled to his wife and to his family obligations; but it was strongly criticised: see note 32 below.

could be seen as giving the courts power to regulate the lives of a married couple who were still living together.[29] Eventually, a deal was done: Sir Robert Newman agreed to drop his Bill provided the Government would introduce legislation[30] but the Summary Jurisdiction (Separation and Maintenance) Act did not actually get onto the statute book until 1925.[31]

It did very little to meet the women's groups' demands. True, it was no longer necessary for a wife to leave her husband before seeking an order; but orders were not enforceable so long as the wife continued to reside with her husband. Orders were effectively in suspense so long as the parties remained together, and an order would automatically come to an end if the couple continued to reside together for three months or more.[32] It is true the courts were given powers to make orders against husbands who were on drugs, sent their wives onto the streets, or insisted on having intercourse notwithstanding the fact they had VD;[33]

---

[29] See note 32 below.

[30] Memorandum to Home Affairs Committee, 24 July 1922, PRO LCO2/773.

[31] In part the delay was caused by the volatile political situation. There were three General Elections in less than two years. The Lloyd George coalition which had agreed the compromise referred to above was brought to an end on his resignation on 19 October 1922, and the Bill was lost. After a General Election in November 1922, a Conservative administration under A Bonar Law took office. On Bonar Law's resignation, S Baldwin became Prime Minister but Parliament was again dissolved (in part because of Baldwin's reluctance to commit himself to a continuance of free trade) and the Conservatives lost their absolute majority at the General Election held on 6 December 1923. A Bill had been introduced by Sir R Newman with the collaboration of the Home Office, and passed through all its stages in the House of Commons, but was again lost on the dissolution. Ramsay Macdonald took office at the head of a minority Labour administration on 22 January 1924; and a Bill passed all its stages except for the Commons consideration of House of Lords amendments. But the Macdonald Government fell in October, and the Bill was again lost. The Conservatives under Baldwin gained a large majority at the election held on 29 October 1924 and the King's Speech contained a commitment to legislate, but even then there were problems, notably about the effect on court orders of husband and wife residing together, whilst the Government was determined to (and did) procure the defeat of an amendment which would have given magistrates the power to reallocate household furniture on separation.

[32] Summary Jurisdiction (Separation and Maintenance) Act 1925, s. 1(4). This provision satisfied neither the womens' groups nor those who attached importance to the privacy of the family unit. In the view of E Jenks the provision was 'calculated . . . to turn a working-class household into a hell for the wife and children' since a wife—especially a wife with nagging tongue or an undue desire to dominate—would apply for an order which she would then keep 'in her pocket, or on the mantelpiece, as a perpetual reminder to her husband that she has it in her power to leave him and reside at his expense elsewhere, extracting from him a substantial weekly sum through the . . . police court; he, in the meanwhile, like a convict on a ticket-of-leave, being required to notify each change of address in order that he may the more readily be tracked by the officers of the law': (1928) 44 LQR 314, 319.

[33] These new grounds were added to those created by the Summary Jurisdiction (Married Women) Act 1895: see Chapter 6, note 32, above; and the legislation was to be cited as the Summary Jurisdiction (Separation and Maintenance) Acts 1895 to 1925. The Government had not resisted implementation of the Gorell Commission's recommendation that a wife should be able to obtain an order if the husband's behaviour had compelled her to submit herself to prostitution, and this became s. 1(2)(c), Summary Jurisdiction (Separation and Maintenance) Act 1925. Campaigning groups also successfully urged that a husband who insisted on having sexual intercourse with his wife whilst knowingly suffering from a venereal disease should be liable to an order: Summary Jurisdiction (Separation and Maintenance) Act 1925, s. 1(2)(b). The addition of persistent cruelty to the children to the grounds was not controversial.

but in practice these grounds were rarely invoked.[34] The only provision
intended to improve enforcement was the obligation imposed on a husband to
notify changes of address.[35] It remained the law that a single casual act of adultery would deprive a wife of any right to a magistrates' order;[36] and the court's
powers were still restricted to an amount[37] which emphasised that the magistrates' courts were courts for the working classes.[38] There was no further significant change in the substantive law until 1978.[39]

The law in practice: exercising discretion

The only guidance given to magistrates about the exercise of their financial
powers was that they could order a husband to pay his wife[40] a weekly sum of
such an amount (up to the £2 weekly statutory maximum)[41] 'as the court . . .

[34] But the campaign that a husband's adultery should be a sufficient basis for an order (a proposal
rejected by the Gorell Barnes Commission in 1911) was unsuccessful, the Government arguing that
such a change should not be made without very careful thought, and the President of the Divorce
Court (Lord Merrivale) that such a provision would lead to wives breaking up the home and obtaining maintenance without discharging their matrimonial obligations: *Official Report* (HL) 18 June
1925, vol. 61, col. 665. The law was only amended by Matrimonial Causes Act 1937, s. 11(1) which
added adultery to the grounds on which an order could be made.
[35] Summary Jurisdiction (Separation and Maintenance) Act 1925, s. 4. Breach was punishable by
a fine of no more than £2.
[36] A compromise was reached in 1925 whereby a wife's uncondoned adultery remained a bar to
the making of an order; but the court could refuse to discharge an order in favour of a wife if the
husband's failure to make such payments as he was able to make under the order had conduced to
the adultery: Summary Jurisdiction (Separation and Maintenance) Act 1925, s. 2(1).
[37] £2 weekly (perhaps £50 in year 2000 values) for the wife and (as a result of the Married Women
(Maintenance) Act 1920) 10/- (ie 50p or perhaps £12 in year 2000 values) for each child.
[38] *Report of the Royal Commission on Divorce and Matrimonial Causes* (1912, Cd. 6478) para. 148.
[39] Domestic Proceedings and Magistrates' Courts Act 1978. The Morton Royal Commission
(*Royal Commission on Marriage and Divorce*, 1956, Cmd. 9678, paras. 1000–1065) did examine the
magistrates' jurisdiction and made a number of recommendations. These were mostly of a minor
nature (although the Commission recommended that the fact that a couple remained under the same
roof should not affect a maintenance order so long as they were living in separate households,
reversing the interpretation put on the law in *Evans v. Evans* [1948] 1 KB 175, and confirmed by the
Court of Appeal in *Wheatley v. Wheatley* [1950] 1 KB 39). It also recommended that an order on the
ground of wilful neglect to maintain should be enforceable even if the couple continued to cohabit;
that the relief available to a husband should be 'substantially the same as that available to a wife'
and that the court should accordingly have power to order a wife to maintain the children. The
Commission's recommendation that the law he codified was accepted by the Government but the
task proved more difficult than anticipated: see *Official Report* (HC) 6 February 1958, vol. 581, col.
193; and in 1958 an expert committee (chaired by a High Court judge, Sir William Arthian Davies)
was appointed to recommend how best to achieve a convenient, workable and up-to-date system of
law relating to matrimonial proceedings in magistrates' courts. The Committee took a restricted
view of its role; and although the Matrimonial Proceedings (Magistrates' Courts) Act 1960 enacted
on the basis of the Committee's recommendations made the legislation more accessible for the
courts and the professionals involved it made few significant changes of substance.
[40] In 1920 the Married Women (Maintenance) Act provided that maintenance orders could be
made in favour of children under 16 up to a maximum of 10/- (50 pence) weekly for each child.
[41] This remained unaltered until 1949 when the Law Reform (Miscellaneous Provisions) Act 1949
raised the maximum order to £5 for a wife and 30/- (ie £1.50) for each child. In 1960 the Matrimonial
Proceedings (Magistrates' Courts) Act raised these maxima to £7-10-0 (£7.50) and 50/- (£2.50)
respectively. The limits on the powers to award weekly periodical payments were removed by the

having regard to the means both of the husband and wife' considered to be 'reasonable'. For many years,[42] the fact that in practice those who came before the magistrates were poor meant that there was little discussion of the principles upon which the discretion should be exercised. Overwhelmingly, the question was simply how much could, somehow, be extracted from a husband. One magistrate,[43] asked in 1910 by the Gorell Committee what order he would make against a man earning 25/- weekly, replied:

'I make small orders, because it is impossible for him to pay a large sum. My orders seldom run to 10s. In a case of 25s[44] a week with regular employment, and . . . three or four children, it may be 10s a week, but that leaves him not very much when he has to pay another rent and his food, and so on . . . they will attempt to pay a small order, and they make no attempt to pay what you would call a sufficient order, and the woman ekes out the difference with her own labour and the labour of her children'.

Magistrates asked to explain the theoretical basis for the assessment of orders would often refer[45] to the so-called one-third test applied in the Divorce Court;[46] but both the actual practice of experienced magistrates and the various official committees which investigated the magistrates' jurisdiction over the years favoured a much more pragmatic and less doctrinaire approach. Thus, the Fischer Williams Committee[47] remarked in 1936 that

'Circumstances differ so widely that it is unwise to attempt to fetter the discretion of the Court by prescribing a definite scale of payments. We believe some Courts adopt the practice of the divorce court and grant the wife one-third of her husband's income, with some addition where there are children. While such a proportion may be just in the bulk of cases, it may be inadequate in the case of a man earning "good money" who after years

---

Maintenance Orders Act 1968, following the recommendations made in the *Report of the Departmental Committee on Statutory Maintenance Limits* (Chairman, Jean Graham Hall, 1968, Cmnd. 3587): see below.

[42] In 1961, legal aid became available for representation in matrimonial proceedings in magistrates' courts, and lawyers increasingly appeared: see OR McGregor, L Blom-Cooper, and C Gibson, *Separated Spouses, A Study of the matrimonial jurisdiction of magistrates' courts* (1970) p. 58. No doubt in consequence appellate courts began to address the principles upon which magistrates should exercise their discretion. In *Kershaw v. Kershaw* [1966] P 13 the Divisional Court asserted that if cohabitation was destroyed by the husband's wrongful conduct the wife's maintenance should be assessed so that her standard of living did not suffer more than was inherent in the circumstances of separation; and that she should not be relegated to a lower standard than that enjoyed by her husband; and see also *Northrop v. Northrop* [1968] P 74, on the inter-relationship between provision for the wife and provision for the children.

[43] Sitting mostly at the Tower Bridge Court which covered the population of Bermondsey and Southwark consisting largely of workers on the docks warehouses and in the large jam and sacking factories then providing much employment to both men and women. No doubt this approach was followed in other working class areas such as the South West London Court (on which see GK Behlmer, *Friends of the Family, The English Home and its Guardians. 1850–1940*, Chapter 4).

[44] Fifty pence and £1.25 (£30 and £75 in year 2000 values) respectively.

[45] Notwithstanding severe criticism in decisions of the appellate courts: see notably *Ward v. Ward* [1948] P 62.

[46] See above, Chapter 10.

[47] *Report of the Departmental Committee on Imprisonment by Courts of Summary Jurisdiction in Default of Payment of Fines and other Sums of Money* (1936, Cmd. 4649) para. 121.

of married life deserts a wife who has little prospect of obtaining employment. On the other hand, one-third of a man's wage may be too large a proportion in the case of a young and healthy woman in good employment or free from domestic ties and capable of obtaining such employment'.[48]

But not all courts behaved with the restraint evident in the testimony of experienced stipendiary magistrates. It is not surprising that men on low wages should resent being forced to hand over a significant part of their pay packet to the wives they had come to hate,[49] and should accordingly complain bitterly that the order was 'too much'; but there is little doubt that on occasion magistrates ignored the financial realities and made orders apparently calculated primarily to punish the husband:

In one reported case[50] magistrates had ordered a 66-year-old London railway porter earning £1.15 a week to make periodical payments to his wife of £1 a week. The husband, unsurprisingly, did not pay and was committed to prison. On appeal (financed by commuters who had learned of the porter's plight) the order was reduced to 40 pence.[51]

—and more than 30 years later the Fischer Williams Committee[52] drew attention to a case in which

'an unemployed man in receipt of Unemployment Benefit amounting to 15s. 3d. a week, with additional allowances of 8s. for his wife and 2s. for his child, was ordered to pay 15s. a week, and was expected to continue payment at that rate even when the additional allowance for the wife had been discontinued on her obtaining employment. There appeared to be no evidence that the man had any other means . . .'.

Only in the 1960s was a serious attempt made to gather information about the sums actually awarded as maintenance.[53] This demonstrated that the husbands

[48] Two decades (and a World War) later the practice seemed—notwithstanding criticism by superior courts: see notably *Ward v. Ward* [1948] P 62—unchanged. According to the Home Office evidence given to the *Royal Commission on Marriage and Divorce* para. 50, 'magistrates' courts probably generally follow this rough test within the statutory limit; but the test is only a rough one used as a matter of practice and it does not absolve the court from enquiring into the particular needs of the case': see *Morton Commission Evidence*.

[49] A survey of men imprisoned in the 1960s for failure to pay maintenance noted that they 'often claimed that their default was a matter of principle, although most of them rationalised the situation and said it was because their wives were living with other men, or the children they were asked to support were not theirs. In fact, they simply hated their wives and were stubbornly prepared to undergo an indefinite number of prison sentences rather than pay a penny': *Report of the Committee on the Enforcement of Judgment Debts* (Chairman, The Hon Mr Justice Payne, 1969, Cmnd. 3909) para. 1092, citing P Morris, *Prisoners and their Families* (1965) pp. 234–235.

[50] *Cobb v. Cobb* [1900] P 294.

[51] See *per* Sir FH Jeune P, at p. 295.

[52] *Report of the Departmental Committee on Imprisonment by Courts of Summary Jurisdiction in Default of Payment of Fines and other Sums of Money* (1936, Cmd. 4649) para. 123.

[53] See the *Report of the Departmental Committee on Statutory Maintenance Limits* (Chairman, Jean Graham Hall, 1968, Cmnd. 3587) Chapter 4, particularly at para. 121 ff. The Graham Hall Enquiry drew on research findings made by the Bedford College Research Project, subsequently published as OR McGregor, L Blom-Cooper, and C Gibson, *Separated Spouses, A Study of the matrimonial jurisdiction of magistrates' courts* (1970) Chapter 6, Table 14 of which contains a wealth of statistical information.

involved in magistrates' maintenance proceedings were within the lowest income groups, and that the average amounts payable under court orders were low. At a time when male workers in manufacturing industry earned an average of £18 weekly, the average order made for a wife's maintenance seems to have been around £2 weekly; and less than one in five of the orders made were for amounts which would keep the wife and her family at subsistence level as reflected in welfare benefit rates.

It seems that the magistrates' courts were for long not primarily concerned with the difficult questions of policy which troubled the superior courts but rather with obtaining reliable information about the means and circumstances of the parties. In 1936 the Fischer Williams Committee[54] accepted that the court should strike a balance between the needs of the husband and the needs of the wife, and urged courts first to consider the man's means and to decide the maximum he could reasonably be expected to pay, and then to go on to consider what sum within that maximum would be reasonable having regard to the means of the woman. But the Committee accepted that courts often lacked reliable information about the parties' finances[55] and deplored the fact that a court of law often had to act on less information than would be collected by a charitable organisation concerned with the relief of poverty. It accordingly made recommendations for the appointment of investigating officers (perhaps Probation Officers) to make the necessary enquiries,[56] and the Committee also recommended a number of minor improvements (for example, giving the courts power to request and act on employers' certificates of wages). In the event little was done,[57] and 30 years later the question of how the courts could best be provided with reliable information continued to exercise official committees.[58]

[54] *Report of the Departmental Committee on Imprisonment by Courts of Summary Jurisdiction in Default of Payment of Fines and other Sums of Money* (1936, Cmd. 4649) para. 124.

[55] 'The wife frequently does not know what is her husband's income. If she knows, or thinks she knows, and names a figure, and this is contradicted, there is no ready method of checking the conflicting statements. The difficulty is not so great in the case of a defendant in some regular occupation for which the rate of wages is known, but when the defendant is working irregularly or working on commission, or is working as a small tradesman or hawker, it is very serious': para. 124.

[56] Para. 260.

[57] The Money Payments (Justices Procedure) Act 1935, s. 12, did implement the recommendation relating to the admissibility of an employer's wage certificate; but the Bill had to be restricted to non-contentious matters in order to secure its speedy passage through Parliament: see the correspondence on PRO HO45/17094. The Summary Procedure (Domestic Proceedings) Act 1937 gave formal statutory recognition to the role of the probation service in carrying out enquiries (see ss. 5 and 7) but the courts discouraged the use of the probation service unless this was the only reasonable way of ascertaining the facts: see *Kershaw v. Kershaw* [1966] P 13. The Probation Service also became reluctant to become involved in such matters which might interfere with their work in promoting reconciliation: *Report of the Departmental Committee on Statutory Maintenance Limits* (Chairman, Jean Graham Hall, 1968, Cmnd. 3587) para. 218.

[58] Notably the *Departmental Committee on Statutory Maintenance Limits* (Chairman, Jean Graham Hall, 1968, Cmnd. 3587); see paras. 212–223. In 1974 the (Finer) *Report of the Committee on One-Parent Families* (Cmnd. 5629) rather wearily noted that 'departmental enquiries over a period which now covers some forty years have expressed anxieties over the adequacy of the methods used and the reliability of the results achieved in many magistrates' courts when fixing the amount of maintenance. Our own enquiries show that there is continuing good cause for these anxieties . . .': para. 4.117.

Enforcement of orders

It is one thing for the court to make an order but quite another to collect the payments due under it. Although the 1886 Act had given the married woman the right to a court order, and provided that it should be enforceable[59] the responsibility for taking steps to enforce the order if the husband did not pay was entirely the wife's. The court had no functions in this respect unless and until she issued a further summons against her husband. If she did so, the husband might well claim that he had in fact made payments, and it could be difficult to ascertain whether this was true or not. All this might be tolerable in the case of High Court orders for substantial amounts, but the legal enforcement procedures had not been adapted to take account of the realities of working class life.

In 1912 the Gorell Barnes Committee[60] suggested that it would 'relieve the wife of many difficulties' if payments due under maintenance orders were made to an officer of the court: payments would be made more regularly, and there would no longer be disputes about how much was owing;[61] and in 1914 legislation[62] required courts to appoint a so-called collecting officer and gave the courts the power to direct that payments due under maintenance orders should be paid through a third party (thus avoiding the difficulties 'liable to arise if the woman has to make personal application to the man for payment').[63]

It has been said[64] that this 'procedural device transformed the situation of separated wives attempting to enforce their declared rights to be maintained by their husbands'; and it is true that eventually[65] the justices' clerks office became the linch-pin of what was intended to be a quick, cheap and effective tribunal, able to keep a close and constant local surveillance over the enforcement of

---

[59] In the same manner as payments due under an affiliation order: Married Women (Maintenance in case of Desertion) Act 1886, s. 1(1).

[60] *Report of the Royal Commission on Divorce and Matrimonial Causes* (1912, Cd. 6478) para. 168(c).

[61] The Commission also thought that such a procedure would prevent undue pressure being put upon a wife who had obtained a separation order to compel her return to cohabitation (presumably by the husband saying that only on that basis would he support her).

[62] The Affiliation Orders Act 1914 required courts (other than metropolitan police courts) to appoint a collecting officer; and the Criminal Justice Administration Act 1914, s. 10, provided that the court could, if it thought fit, order that payment be made through an officer of the court or other third party.

[63] *Departmental Committee on Imprisonment by Courts of Summary Jurisdiction in Default of Payment of Fines and other Sums of Money* (1936, Cmd. 4649) para. 129.

[64] OR McGregor, L Blom-Cooper, and C Gibson, *Separated Spouses, A Study of the matrimonial jurisdiction of magistrates' courts* (1970) p. 21.

[65] In 1936 the (Fischer Williams) *Departmental Committee on Imprisonment by Courts of Summary Jurisdiction in Default of Payment of Fines and other Sums of Money* (1936, Cmd. 4649) para. 130 pointed out that there was no obligation on a court to direct payments to a collecting officer, and recommended that the court should be required to do so unless in any particular case the applicant objected and satisfied the court that there were good grounds for the objection: para. 130. But—notwithstanding protests from Eleanor Rathbone MP Claud Mullins and other campaigners—the Money Payments (Justices Procedure) Act 1935 did not implement the Committee's recommendation.

orders.[66] The clerk's office kept proper accounts[67] and in 1949 legislation[68] imposed a formal duty on justices' clerks to act as collecting officers, and to take any necessary enforcement proceedings. Formal procedures were also supplemented by a good deal of informal threat, exhortation and encouragement,[69] as well as liaison with other relevant agencies (such as local authority housing departments and the social service departments[70] which, after World War II, came to play a large part in supporting one-parent families). By the 1950s, the true centre for resolving family issues for the working classes had become the office of the justices' clerk: in evidence to the Morton Commission the Justices' Clerks Society pointed out that in Birmingham and other comparable cities the clerk's office collected as much as £230,000 (more than £4 million in year 2000 values), and in the course of this work received 98,000 letters and wrote some 5,000 letters each year.

Effectiveness of Justices' Clerks' Procedure prompts extension to enforcement of Divorce Court financial orders

In 1956 the *Royal Commission on Marriage and Divorce*[71] acknowledged that the magistrates' enforcement procedures had advantages (not least the

---

[66] *Departmental Committee on Statutory Maintenance Limits* (Chairman, Jean Graham Hall, 1968, Cmnd. 3587) para. 56.

[67] And this indirectly sometimes brought the parties together: the Justices' Clerks' Society claimed the clerk's work in keeping records made his office the centre of innumerable domestic enquiries, and the spirit in which it was performed did much to produce a more reasonable atmosphere between the parties, and even assist in a reconciliation: Evidence of the Justices' Clerks' Society to the Royal Commission on Marriage and Divorce (1956), para. 41(g).

[68] Justices of the Peace Act 1949, s. 19; Married Women (Maintenance) Act 1949, s. 4. In this way, belated effect was given to a recommendation of the (Fischer Williams) *Departmental Committee on Imprisonment by Courts of Summary Jurisdiction in Default of Payment of Fines and other Sums of Money* (1936, Cmd. 4649) paras. 131–132. The Committee had been particularly concerned that large arrears sometimes built up, and it was provided that the clerk should communicate with the wife if the order fell into arrears for four weeks or more 'with a view to obtaining her consent to his taking proceedings on her behalf for the recovery of arrears. Upon receiving such consent he should apply to the court immediately for a summons or warrant of arrest': *op. cit.* para. 132. But notwithstanding the mandatory character of the provision, the Graham Hall Committee reporting in 1968 recorded that some clerks were reluctant to undertake the duty of taking proceedings: *Departmental Committee on Statutory Maintenance Limits* (Chairman, Jean Graham Hall, 1968, Cmnd. 3587) para. 56; and the (Finer) *Report of the Committee on One-Parent Families*, Cmnd. 5629) noted not only some divergence of practice but also the difficulties with which justices' clerks might be faced.

[69] *Report of the Departmental Committee on Statutory Maintenance Limits* (Chairman, Jean Graham Hall, 1968, Cmnd. 3587) para. 57; and see also the *Departmental Committee on Imprisonment by Courts of Summary Jurisdiction in Default of Payment of Fines and other Sums of Money* (1936, Cmd. 4649) paras. 129–132. No action was taken on the Fischer Williams Committee's recommendation that a 'definite responsibility should be placed on the Collecting Officer to advise both the woman and the man . . .': para. 132.

[70] *Report of the Committee on the Enforcement of Judgment Debts* (Chairman, the Hon Mr Justice Payne, 1969, Cmnd. 3909) para. 1297; and note the claim in the Evidence of the Justices' Clerks' Society to the Royal Commission on Marriage and Divorce (1956) about the volume of correspondence undertaken from the clerks' office with public authorities on such matters as pensions, tax, welfare benefits, housing.

[71] The *Morton Report*.

availability of the facilities of justices' clerk's office) over the procedures available in the Divorce Court; and it recommended that Divorce Court orders should be registrable in the magistrates' court.[72] The effect of registration would be to enable collection of payments and enforcement of arrears to be dealt with in exactly the same way as if the order had originally been made by the magistrates' court.[73] The Royal Commission also recommended[74] that it should be for the magistrates to decide variation applications. The Maintenance Orders Act 1958 gave effect to these recommendations.[75]

The effect of these changes (which does not seem to have been foreseen) was effectively to transfer the power of dealing with much of the aftermath of marital breakdown to the magistrates' court. This had a profound impact on the enforcement of support obligations: the law officially recognised that the magistrates' courts had become the usual forum for dealing with default in the making of orders for periodical payments.[76] Paradoxically this occurred at a time when the availability of legal aid for divorce had reduced the number of applications to magistrates for matrimonial orders; and to some extent the role of the courts changed from making and enforcing orders for the support of separated wives to that of an enforcement agency for the divorced.[77] The fact that it was primarily the existence of a state-provided administrative collection machinery which had influenced the *Morton Report's* recommendations was also significant for the future: it was increasingly suggested that the attempt to deal with maintenance obligations by judicial process was outdated and that court procedures should be replaced by a system of administrative assessment and recovery. But before considering this argument we should note the enforcement procedures which the law did make available.

Sanctions for non-payment: committal to prison

Breach of a court order is traditionally visited with sanctions designed to compel obedience. The Matrimonial Causes Act 1878,[78] adopting the pattern which had in essence been in existence for some three centuries under the Poor Law, provided that a maintenance order was to be enforced in the same way as an affiliation order made against a putative father: if a man failed to pay within a fortnight of being notified of the outstanding arrears he would be either arrested on warrant or issued with a summons requiring him to attend court. If he then failed to pay the court could order that his goods be seized and sold. But in most cases this remedy was ineffective and the magistrates could commit him to prison for a period not exceeding three months.

---

[72] *Morton Report*, para. 582.   [73] *Ibid.*

[74] *Ibid.*, para. 586. This was because attempts to enforce orders often raised the question whether the order should be varied.

[75] Part I.   [76] See eg *Judicial Statistics Annual Report* (1993) p. 54.

[77] See C Gibson, 'Maintenance in the Magistrates' Courts in the 1980s' (1982) 12 Fam Law 138.

[78] s. 4(1), repealed and re-enacted by the Summary Jurisdiction (Married Women) Act 1895, s. 9.

A large and steadily increasing number of men were sent to prison in this way: in 1900 the courts made 6,583 orders, and 1,288 men were sent to prison; by 1930 the number of orders made had nearly doubled[79] but the number imprisoned each year multiplied by three and a half times. In the five years 1928–1932 an average of 4,062 committals were made each year. This may have been very unpleasant for the men committed but did the impoverished wives little good since imprisonment operated to extinguish all arrears due at the date of the committal, and generally no arrears accrued whilst the man was in prison.[80]

The prisons were becoming silted up[81] with maintenance and other defaulters;[82] and, at a time when mass unemployment was creating widespread distress and prompting a greater awareness of the economic problems of the working classes, pressure for reform grew. In 1932 Lord Snell[83] initiated a debate on the subject in the House of Lords;[84] and the Government responded[85] by appointing a Departmental Committee chaired by an eminent lawyer, John Fischer Williams KC,[86] to investigate the 'enforcement of wife maintenance and affiliation orders . . . and to consider whether by changes in the law or in the methods of administration it is possible to reduce the number of imprisonments in default of payment, due regard being given to the importance of securing compliance with orders made by the courts'.

The Fischer Williams Committee reported within a year, and one of its recommendations was that the court should inquire into the defendant's means and

---

[79] To 11,296. The statistical data is drawn from OR McGregor, L Blom-Cooper, and C Gibson, *Separated Spouses, A Study of the matrimonial jurisdiction of magistrates' courts* (1970) p. 22; and the Report of the (Fischer Williams) *Departmental Committee on Imprisonment by Courts of Summary Jurisdiction in Default of Payment of Fines and other Sums of Money* (1936, Cmd. 4649) para. 112.

[80] (Fischer Williams) *Departmental Committee on Imprisonment by Courts of Summary Jurisdiction in Default of Payment of Fines and other Sums of Money* (1936, Cmd. 4649) paras. 111, 155. The court had power to direct that the order should remain effective during the sentence, but this was rarely done.

[81] OR McGregor, L Blom-Cooper, and C Gibson, *Separated Spouses, A Study of the matrimonial jurisdiction of magistrates' courts* (1970) p. 22. In fact it appears that nearly 40% of all imprisonments at this time were for failure to pay rates, fines and maintenance: Home Secretary's Memorandum to Cabinet, PRO HO45/17094, 3 May 1935.

[82] Notably those imprisoned for non-payment of a fine or domestic rates. In addition the superior courts retained the power to make committal orders under s. 5, Debtors' Act 1869 against persons who failed to pay sums due under an order or judgment (eg for debt or breach of contract), but this power could only be exercised on proof that the person making default had since the judgment in question had the means to pay the sum due but refused or neglected to do so.

[83] See Biographical Notes.

[84] *Official Report* (HL) 6 December 1932, vol. 86, col. 201.

[85] See the papers on PRO LCO2/1145, which reveal (amongst other things) the concern of the Lord Chancellor's Permanent Secretary to repudiate any suggestion that the county courts were imprisoning debtors on a large scale, and emphasising the fact that the great majority of civil prisoners were committed for failing in one way or another to maintain their wives or children. Schuster was particularly irritated by a book entitled *The Gospel and the Law* written by Sir Edward Parry (a retired county court judge of 34 years' standing) and his letter to Parry dated 9 October 1928 is a masterpiece of invective. Schuster also tried to engineer publication of a letter in *The Times* criticising the author's lack of even a 'rudimentary understanding' of the realities of the position.

[86] See Biographical Notes.

circumstances and not commit unless the default was due to his wilful refusal or culpable neglect. This proposal was speedily implemented by the Money Payments (Justices' Procedure) Act 1935;[87] and the effect seems to have been immediate. In 1935, 2,271 maintenance defaulters were sent to prison, but in 1936 the number fell to 1,828.[88] But the effect seems to have been only short-term: after World War II the number[89] of committals rose to almost pre-1936 figures.

Attachment of wages instead of imprisonment?

The Fischer Williams Committee tried to produce a comprehensive and coherent package of proposals.[90] For example, the Committee also recommended[91] that the court be given the power to order the attachment of a maintenance defaulter's wages. But this attack on the 'sanctity of the pay packet'[92] was anathema to organised Labour[93] and not surprisingly was not immediately accepted. Only in 1957 (40 years later) did RA Butler,[94] impressed by the ineffectiveness of imprisonment as a means of securing payment and its harmful impact on the men concerned,[95] decide to try to overcome opposition from the Trade Union

---

[87] s. 8(1). The text reproduces the language of the statute rather than the Committee's recommendation. The Committee believed that the court could and should carry out a proper investigation (in appropriate circumstances using its own investigating officer) and satisfy itself that the man could have met his obligations by reasonable effort: para. 153. The recommendations for investigative machinery were never fully implemented.

[88] OR McGregor, L Blom-Cooper, and C Gibson, *Separated Spouses, A Study of the matrimonial jurisdiction of magistrates' courts* (1970) p. 23. The Prison Commissioners noted that the daily average prison population could be expected to fall by as much as 500 (ie that the great majority of maintenance and affiliation defaulters would no longer be imprisoned) but this expectation was not met: PRO PRI COM9/208.

[89] In the period 1950/54 a total of 3,430 committal orders were made to enforce magistrates' spouse maintenance orders; but that represented 23% of the maintenance orders made (whereas in the years between 1920 and 1934 the proportion was more than a third): OR McGregor, L Blom-Cooper, and C Gibson, *Separated Spouses, A Study of the matrimonial jurisdiction of magistrates' courts* (1970) Table 2.

[90] The Committee first considered ways in which (for example, by conciliation) the number of maintenance orders could be reduced; it then considered methods—notably, the appointment of investigating officers—designed to ensure that orders should be within the power of the husband to pay; and it then identified the fact that arrears were allowed to accumulate for long periods and the inadequacy of the arrangements for varying orders when a man's income was reduced as the main factors leading to recourse to imprisonment. To remedy that, it recommended that payments should have to be made through a collecting officer, and that the court's powers to remit arrears and vary orders should be extended (recommendations implemented by Money Payments (Justices' Procedure) Act 1935, ss. 8(2) and 9). Finally it recommended that there be power to attach wages.

[91] *Departmental Committee on Imprisonment by Courts of Summary Jurisdiction in Default of Payment of Fines and other Sums of Money* (1936, Cmd. 4649) paras. 194–196.

[92] For a critical history of this principle, see *Report of the Committee on the Enforcement of Judgment Debts* (Chairman, the Hon Mr Justice Payne, 1969, Cmnd. 3909) paras. 584–588.

[93] One member of the Fischer Williams Committee, the Trade Unionist member, Annie Loughlin, had dissented from the Committee's recommendation on the ground that it would be a dangerous innovation and was likely to be taken as a precedent.

[94] Home Secretary in the Macmillan administration.

[95] 'I hate in my soul the taint and the dour weight of prison upon a man's mind and future': *Official Report* (HC) 12 December 1957, vol. 579, col. 1543.

movement by emphasising the 'unique combination of circumstances' which made enforcement of maintenance different in principle from the enforcement of other court orders. To do so he gave an unequivocal assurance that the remedy of attachment would not be extended to other kinds of debt;[96] and the Government brought forward legislation[97] giving the court power to order that payment be taken from a defaulter's earnings.

The impact of the attachment provisions was immediate, and long lasting. More than 5,000 orders were made each year in the first five years;[98] but attachment did not provide a panacea:[99] many orders were ineffective at least in the long term. But even so the number of men committed to prison for failure to comply with a court maintenance order fell dramatically over the years[100] (notwithstanding the fact that magistrates still apparently sometimes committed men to prison without proper regard to the statutory requirements intended to ensure that committal be the last resort against a man guilty of deliberate defiance or reckless disregard of a court order).[101]

PUBLIC LAW AND PRIVATE LAW: THE STATE-PROVIDED SAFETY NET

No system for enforcing court orders can ever be completely effective; and the fact that a woman deserted by her husband and unable to get maintenance from him might become destitute and be driven to the workhouse to survive[102] created a link between the justices and the administration of the Poor Law. Giving the married woman a direct right to seek a magistrates' maintenance order[103]

---

[96] In fact attachment was made available as a means of enforcement of all civil debts by the Administration of Justice Act 1970 (giving effect to recommendations of the *Report of the Committee on the Enforcement of Judgment Debts* (Chairman, the Hon Mr Justice Payne, 1969, Cmnd. 3909).

[97] The Maintenance Orders Act 1958.

[98] See the *Report of the Committee on the Enforcement of Judgment Debts* (Chairman, the Hon Mr Justice Payne, 1969, Cmnd. 3909) paras. 594–601.

[99] A very high proportion of the orders made came quickly to an end, often because the husband gave up the employment: the Payne Committee (see above, para. 601(b)) conceded that the attachment procedure was 'virtually powerless against the defendant who is determined to avoid payment'.

[100] In 1991 only 240 persons were received into prison for non-payment of spousal maintenance: *Prison Statistics 1991*, Cm. 2157, Chapter 6.

[101] *R v. Luton Magistrates' Court ex parte Sullivan* [1992] 2 FLR 196 where (*per* Waite J at p. 201) a man was sent to prison by a bench which, 'with knowledge of his poor health and present lack of means, treated him as a defiant or culpably neglectful defaulter on the scantiest of evidence after denying him the opportunity of professional advice . . . and disregarding the alternatives which it was their statutory duty to consider'; and see also *R v. Slough Magistrates' Court ex parte Lindsay* [1997] 1 FLR 695.

[102] In theory a wife could pledge her husband's credit for the supply of necessary goods and services, and in this way middle and upper class women might be able to obtain the means to live: see eg *Sandilands v. Carus* [1945] 1 KB 27, CA (cost of wife's stay in boarding house—judgment for £651 against husband). But this remedy was of no assistance to working class women to whom tradesmen would not extend adequate credit.

[103] Married Women (Maintenance in Cases of Desertion) Act 1886.

reinforced the link between the family support machinery administered by the courts and that administered directly by the State;[104] but for many years[105] the way in which the two systems operated was not widely appreciated.

The Poor Law was based on the principle that no one should perish from want[106] but equally that the primary responsibility for support should lie with the family.[107] Hence, although relief (pitched at a level 'less eligible' than the standard of living of an 'independent labourer of the lowest class')[108] would be made available,[109] those whom the law declared to be responsible for the claimant would be required to reimburse the cost. There were two main procedures designed to this end. First, a person who wilfully refused or neglected to maintain his family was liable to be adjudged a 'rogue and vagabond' and imprisoned;[110] secondly, legislation[111] gave the Poor Law authorities the right to apply to the court for an order requiring the husband to maintain his wife.[112]

These powers were widely used, and over 4,000 orders requiring relatives to reimburse relief were made annually in the years leading up to the outbreak of World War I. It seems to have been thought that such orders were quickly obtained and that the procedure was effective;[113] but as the Finer *Committee on One-Parent Families* pointed out in 1974[114] the apparent success of the authorities was illusory because the result, 'in no less than half the cases . . . was not reimbursement but imprisonment'.

The basic structure established at the beginning of the twentieth century (a wife has the right to apply to magistrates' court for a periodical payment order

[104] Until 1948 through the Poor Law and subsequently by National Assistance, Supplementary Benefit and Income Support.

[105] The relationship only became widely understood with the publication in 1974 of the report of the Finer Committee *Report of the Committee on One-Parent Families*, Cmnd. 5629).

[106] *Report of the Royal Commission on the Poor Laws* (1834, ed. by SG and EOA Checkland, 1974) p. 335.

[107] Poor Relief Act 1601, s. 7. See generally the succinct account of the evolution of the law given by Lord Goddard CJ in *National Assistance Board v. Wilkinson* [1952] 2 QB 648, 656–657; and see also LN Brown, 'National Assistance and the Liability to Maintain One's Family' (1955) 18 MLR 113, 110–116.

[108] Poor Law Report (1834) p. 335.

[109] At the beginning of the twentieth century relief was dealt with by Boards of Guardians.

[110] Vagrancy Act 1824, s. 3.

[111] The Poor Law Amendment Act 1834, s. 56, treated relief given to a wife as being given to the husband. The Poor Law Amendment Act 1868 provided that when a married woman required relief without her husband, the guardians could apply to the justices to require the husband to show cause why an order should not be made on him to maintain his wife. (The Married Women's Property Act 1870, s.13 imposed a corresponding duty on any wife with separate property to maintain her husband.) The legislation was eventually codified by Poor Law Act 1927, s. 33 and consolidated by the Poor Law Act 1930, ss. 41, 43.

[112] The Poor Law obligation ended if the wife committed adultery, and was suspended for so long as she was in desertion: *R v. Flintan* (1830) 1 B&Ad 227; *Jones v. Newtown & Llanidloes Union* [1920] 3 KB 381; and see *National Assistance Board v. Wilkinson* [1952] 2 QB 648.

[113] See the evidence of the Metropolitan Magistrate J Rose, 1 March 1910, q. 2024 emphasising that the guardians could have the husband brought up for punishment under the Vagrancy Act as soon as the wife became chargeable (ie at the moment she went into the workhouse): *Evidence taken before the Royal Commission on Divorce*, 1912, Vol. I, Cd. 6478, and Vol. 2, Cd. 6479.

[114] *Report of the Committee on One-Parent Families*, Cmnd. 5629, 1974, Appendix 5, para. 70.

against a husband in breach of his obligation to support her; the State has right to reimbursement from the husband of the cost of supporting the wife and failure to support is a criminal offence) remained in place at the end of the twentieth century.[115] But the interrelationship between the participants has radically changed. The most important step was the change in administrative practice to reflect the policy evidenced in the abolition of the Poor Law and the substitution by the National Assistance Act 1948 of welfare benefits to which claimants had rights.[116] No longer did the deserted wife have to seek charity: the Welfare State gave her (and all her fellow citizens) entitlements. In the words of the Finer Report:[117]

'. . . it was the express intention of the poor law to impose a stigma upon those whom it relieved, and it was the express intention of the National Assistance Act . . . that the [National Assistance] Board . . . should not impose a stigma upon recipients of benefit. Accordingly, today the unsupported wife . . . both retains her legal right of maintenance which she may seek to enforce through an order of the court, and enjoys also, in her capacity as citizen, a right to support from the social security authorities which carries no stigma.'

The 1948 Act did not remove the obligation to support; but, reflecting the new entitlement based approach of the 1948 legislation, the benefit authorities changed their policy about seeking to recover payments from those who came to be called 'liable relatives'. The authorities would no longer themselves routinely pursue husbands.[118] Instead they would usually negotiate with the husband and accept any offer he made which was 'reasonable' having regard to his circumstances.[119] If legal proceedings were necessary the benefit authorities

---

[115] Ie the wife may bring proceedings in a magistrates' court under Domestic Proceedings and Magistrates' Courts Act 1978, s. 1 for failure to maintain; whilst the social security legislation provides that a man is liable to maintain his wife, and the Secretary of State may apply for an order against him on the ground that this obligation has not been met: Social Security Administration Act 1992, ss. 78(6)–(9), 105(3), 105(3) and 106(1). It is a criminal offence persistently to refuse or neglect to maintain a wife or other person whom one is legally liable to maintain: Social Security Administration Act 1992, s. 105(1). However, the Child Support Act 1991 had a considerable if indirect effect on the enforcement and assessment of support obligations: see below.

[116] Legislation consolidated by Supplementary Benefits Act 1976, s. 1(1) declared that every British resident aged 16 or over whose resources were insufficient to meet his requirements (as defined) was entitled to benefit; and the policy of the law was judicially asserted to be that supplementary benefits formed the subject of rights and entitlement, and that no shame attached to the receipt of them: *Reiterbund v. Reiterbund* [1974] 1 WLR 788, 797, *per* Finer J.

[117] *Report of the Committee on One-Parent Families* (1974, Cmnd. 5629) Appendix 5, para. 112.

[118] The number of cases in which the benefit authorities themselves sought a court order fell dramatically from more than 4,000 a year in the period just before World War II to some 300 annually in the early 1950s: OR McGregor, L Blom-Cooper, and C Gibson, *Separated Spouses, A Study of the matrimonial jurisdiction of magistrates' courts* (1970) Table 2.

[119] In deciding whether an offer was reasonable or not, the benefit authorities applied a formula under which the husband would be allowed to keep a quarter of his own take home pay plus the amount which he would receive for himself and his current family if he were a benefit claimant: *Report of the Committee on One-Parent Families* (the *Finer Report*) (1974, Cmnd. 5629) paras. 4.188–4.189. In contrast, the courts, when faced with maintenance applications by a woman on benefit, would not allow the husband any margin over subsistence level (as determined by Benefit rates): see *Barnes v. Barnes* [1972] 1 WLR 1381; *Ashley v. Ashley* [1968] P 582. As the *Finer Report* put it

would (rather than taking proceedings themselves) 'encourage and assist' a wife left without support to apply for her own order.[120]

This new approach had one very real disadvantage. Many women found themselves

'on a see-saw between the court collecting office and the [benefit office]. She would have to attend the collecting office to receive the maintenance payments, accommodating herself to the opening hours and to the company of people awaiting trial on criminal charges, or paying fines. But if, as so often was the case, the maintenance had not been remitted for her to collect . . . the [benefit] assessed on the basis that maintenance was in payment would be insufficient. Such women could be seen, often with children accompanying them, taking themselves back and forth between the two offices, as like as not at a considerable distance from each other, in harassed pursuit of the subsistence which each expected the other to produce'.[121]

Eventually—in what the *Finer Report*[122] aptly described as a victory of realism over bureaucracy—an administrative procedure was adopted under which a wife who got her own maintenance order from the court would[123] sign a certificate authorising the court's collecting office to pay over any sums received from the husband to the benefit authorities. In return, she would get an order book for payment of her full benefit entitlement, and in this way a large number of women[124] were relieved of any worry whether their maintenance orders were paid 'regularly, intermittently, or never'.[125]

So far, so good. But the relationship between the practices of the benefit system, the magistrates' courts and the Divorce Court was complicated; and in the 1970s the *Finer Report's* analysis[126] of what it described as the 'disorderly and anomalous tangle of relationship between the three systems of family law' involved led to the whole relationship between private obligation and State benefit and the respective functions of the courts and administrative agencies being brought into question. The Labour Government, returned at the October 1964 election, was committed to social reform; and its members had a traditional sympathy for the potential of the social sciences in helping to shape the agenda; and this was one of the factors reinforcing pressure for radical reform of the whole structure of family support. Over the next decade four separate enquiries

(at para. 4.205) the benefit authorities would divide whatever was available so as normally to leave the liable relative somewhat above subsistence level and bring up the claimant's income to her benefit entitlement, but the courts aimed merely to produce rough equality at benefit levels.

[120] It appears that many women were reluctant to do so, not least because obtaining an order would rarely be of any obvious benefit to the claimant. For a full discussion of the policy see the *Finer Report*, paras. 4.184–4.202.

[121] The *Finer Report*, para. 4.207.   [122] *Ibid.*, para. 4.209.

[123] The procedure was only applied in cases—the great majority: see the *Finer Report*, paras. 4.73–4.76—in which the order was for a smaller amount than the claimant's Benefit entitlement.

[124] In 1970, nearly three quarters of all maintenance orders were diverted in this way: *Finer Report*, Table 4.12.

[125] OR McGregor, L Blom-Cooper, and C Gibson, *Separated Spouses, A Study of the matrimonial jurisdiction of magistrates' courts* (1970) p. 157.

[126] At para. 4.190.

investigated aspects of the problem. First, the *Committee on Statutory Maintenance Limits*, chaired by a Metropolitan Stipendiary Magistrate, Jean Graham Hall,[127] was set up[128] to examine the financial limits prescribed by statute for magistrates' maintenance orders. It reported in 1968.[129] Secondly, a *Committee on the Enforcement of Judgment Debts* chaired by Mr Justice Payne[130] was set up, and the Committee reported in 1969. Thirdly, the *Committee on One-Parent Families*, chaired by Mr Justice Finer reported in 1974. Finally, the Law Commission examined the substantive law applied in magistrates' courts, and reported on this subject in 1976. Professor OR McGregor was a member of the Graham Hall, Payne, and Finer Committees and provided a wealth of statistical and other information derived in part from research which he had directed into the social results of the exercise of the matrimonial jurisdiction of magistrates' courts. His influence is manifest and pervasive.[131]

(i) The *Graham Hall Report*[132]

This report noted the history of the limits on the financial orders that magistrates could make; and, finding itself 'unable to find any criteria which would enable us to recommend the fixing of new limits',[133] recommended that all the

---

[127] For the Committee's membership, see Biographical Notes.

[128] The Committee was established on the recommendation of the Law Commission; but the correspondence on PRO BC3/428 (the Law Commission file on *Financial Limits on Magistrates' Orders in Domestic and Affiliation Proceedings*) reveals differences of opinion about the Committee's remit. The Law Commission envisaged terms of reference confining the Committee to the development of a machinery for changing the limits without the need for primary legislation. The terms of reference as eventually settled required the Committee to examine the financial limits for magistrates' wife and child maintenance orders and 'to consider the appropriate machinery for adjusting such limits to changing circumstances'; and the Committee was told that the omission of the question whether any limits were desirable was deliberate, it being the Government's view that this question could 'more appropriately . . . be considered as part of the general subject of family law to which the Law Commission intended to give further study': see *Report of the Departmental Committee on Statutory Maintenance Limits* (Chairman, Jean Graham Hall, 1968, Cmnd. 3587) para. 2. This restriction did not prevent the Committee from concluding that the retention of limits could not be defended and recommending that they should accordingly be abolished: para. 204; and see further below.

[129] It seems probable that the Government had been made aware of its intended recommendation some months previously: see the remarks of the Home Office Minister, Dick Taverne, *Official Report* (HC) 8 December 1967, vol. 755, col. 1867.

[130] 1969, Cmnd. 3909. This Committee appointed by the Lord Chancellor on 3 March 1965 was originally confined to the enforcement of orders made in the High Court and county court, but in June 1965 its terms of reference were extended to cover the maintenance and other civil jurisdiction of magistrates: see below.

[131] His personal views are stated with great clarity in the 31st series of Hamlyn Lectures, *Social History and Law Reform* (1981); and also emerge from *Separated Spouses, A Study of the matrimonial jurisdiction of magistrates' courts* (1970) (co-authored with L Blom-Cooper, and C Gibson) and reporting the findings of a major empirical research project.

[132] *Report of the Departmental Committee on Statutory Maintenance Limits* (Chairman, Jean Graham Hall, 1968, Cmnd. 3587).

[133] Para. 204.

existing limits be abolished.[134] By a fortunate coincidence, Quintin Hogg MP[135] had drawn a favourable place in the Ballot for Private Members and had already introduced a Bill intended to give power to alter the limits by delegated legislation. Hogg had declared himself personally opposed to the abolition of maxima[136] but the Bill had been drafted by Parliamentary counsel so as to be easily capable of amendment to achieve that objective,[137] and the Maintenance Orders Act 1968 in fact implemented the Committee's recommendation.

It had for some time been clear that in practice the existing limits were rarely relevant, and only 2% of the orders made were for the maximum amounts then permitted. But it would be wrong to draw the conclusion that the Graham Hall Committee's report and the legislation which gave effect to it were of little significance. The Committee took the view[138] that it could not sensibly proceed without undertaking a survey of

'the general working of this branch of law both in magistrates' and in higher courts. For want of any earlier review of this kind, we found it the more necessary to examine how magistrates determine the amount of maintenance in individual cases, the nature of the maintenance obligation, relations between magistrates' and other courts, the method of initiating proceedings and the subsequent enforcement and variation of orders, the circumstances of the parties and the social background against which these proceedings take place. Our report . . . gives our view of the whole pattern of the operation of this jurisdiction. The matter is complex because the interests and obligations of the State and the individual are often in competition; because many of those affected are without resources and in poverty; and because, set beside [state benefit provision] the financial arrangements secured through the courts inevitably appear cumbersome, inconvenient and much less assured'.[139]

—and in effect much of the Report seems to have been primarily designed to furnish the basis for a critique of the whole system of family support.

The Committee's review of the working of the magistrates' jurisdiction incorporated many of the findings[140] of the Bedford College research survey directed

---

[134] The Committee made a number of recommendations for improving the procedures followed in magistrates' courts, for example, that they use a standard questionnaire designed to elicit information about the parties' financial resources and commitments: para. 222. It also recommended that certain matters (eg whether the magistrates' courts should have power to order lump sum payments) be considered by the Law Commission.

[135] See Biographical Notes.

[136] *Official Report* (HC) 8 December 1967, vol. 755, col. 1840.

[137] *Official Report* (HC) 8 December 1967, vol. 755, cols. 1866–1870.

[138] 'The total information we collected about the amounts of orders, the resources of defendants and the contribution made by supplementary benefit gave us no ground for believing either that the existing limits are causing hardship in more than a minority of cases or that raising the limits would produce substantially increased amounts in more than a few orders . . . less than 2% of all orders for wives are for the maximum amounts permitted by law. We found it hard to believe that a committee had been appointed to ensure that the difficulties of a fraction as small as 2% should be remedied or that we had been given the task of making an even more refined adjustment . . .': paras. 165–166.

[139] Para. 8.

[140] But the Committee did not always see eye to eye with the Bedford College findings: for example, the Committee (at para. 181) recorded its view that '. . . the jurisdictions of the High Court and

by McGregor[141] who had already become convinced[142] that the magistrates' courts merely performed 'at great social cost and disadvantage for the lumpen proletariat what the high court achieves efficiently and finally for the better off and better informed'. For the next few years McGregor devoted much effort to attempts to eliminate what he believed to be the 'terrifyingly wide . . . abyss between reality and myth';[143] and the *Graham Hall Report* can be seen as the preliminary bombardment in a campaign which concluded with the publication in 1974 of the Report of the Finer Committee. Although the *Graham Hall Report* does not specifically refer to the issue whether the system of family law administered by magistrates' courts should survive, the Report makes it clear that it would soon become impossible to avoid confronting that issue.

The Committee also recorded its belief[144] that historically the working class family became a 'going concern only within the protective shelter of expanding social services . . .'; and, undeterred by the fact that the subject was manifestly not within its terms of reference devoted a (brief and tentative) chapter to the question 'How Far Ought Maintenance to be Based on Court Proceedings?' It did not answer[145] the question it had posed but did state its belief that re-organisation of the system required a new perspective of State and personal obligations to fatherless families and that a full study of possible change should be undertaken as soon as possible.[146] The Committee claimed that the evidence it had received would encourage 'those looking at the wider issues to strive for a more rational inter-relation of the roles of the State and the individual in the maintenance of "fatherless families"'. Far-reaching evolution of the maintenance system would be found necessary.[147] This reflected a view at the time widely held and stated with great clarity by Professor L Neville Brown[148] that the private law of maintenance would

'tend to wither away and its place assumed by social security legislation . . . [B]y the year 2000 the law will have abandoned as socially undesirable, frequently ineffectual and

---

of the magistrates in fact serve different, albeit overlapping, functions' and it asserted (para. 28) that 'the main concern of the magistrates' domestic court is to determine issues which will affect the wife's financial position, and only rarely now do justices make an order providing for the non-cohabitation of the spouses'. But *Separated Spouses* (p. 60) reported that 'the reality of what happens in magistrates' courts hardly bears out such a bald assertion. Separation orders still figure prominently in the exercise of Justices' matrimonial jurisdiction . . .'.

[141] The survey's findings were subsequently published as OR McGregor, L Blom-Cooper, and C Gibson, *Separated Spouses, A Study of the matrimonial jurisdiction of magistrates' courts* (1970).

[142] The quotation is taken from a letter dated 15 November 1966 to LCB Gower, commenting on the Law Commission's Working Paper No. 9 (*Matrimonial and Related Proceedings—Financial Relief*, 1967): PRO BC3/388.

[143] McGregor believed that there were 'really two systems; one in the books and in the accounts given by official bodies, and the other' what actually happened in the courts as demonstrated by empirical research: McGregor to Gower, *ibid*.

[144] Para. 37.

[145] The authors of the Bedford College Survey dealt very briefly with the issue (see p. 214) but explained this by saying that informed discussion would require further investigation: p. xvii.

[146] Para. 237.   [147] Para. 240.

[148] See Biographical Notes; and LN Brown, 'Maintenance and Esoterism' (1968) 31 MLR 121.

wholly uneconomic the hounding of spouses through the courts for non-support of their families. Non-support . . . will be ranged alongside those other vicissitudes of life— unemployment, sickness, industrial injury, child-birth, death itself—for which social insurance should make provision'.

(ii) The *Payne Report* on the enforcement of judgment debts[149]

This Committee was clearly not intended to have any part to play in these broad discussions of social policy; but the Committee's terms of reference were extended to cover enforcement of orders made by magistrates in their civil juris- diction, and this brought matrimonial and other maintenance orders[150] within the Committee's remit.[151] As the Committee's *Report* puts it[152] (perhaps with a slight note of weariness) the extension greatly added to its labours 'more, we confess, than we had imagined at the time'—and it is perhaps not surprising that although the Committee was appointed on 3 March 1965 its 455-page Report was not published until February 1969. The extension required the Committee to consider, not only the emotive issue[153] of whether imprisonment should be retained as the ultimate sanction for the enforcement of maintenance obliga- tions but also suggested to many that the Committee could be persuaded to rec- ommend a dramatic shift towards acceptance of an administrative model for determination and collection of maintenance assessments for separated wives and their children. In their deliberations, the Committee recorded[154] that

the 'most common and persistent proposal [was] that the entire responsibility for the maintenance of separated wives and their children should be taken over by the Ministry of Social Security. The details of the schemes advanced vary but the general aim is that the Ministry should pay to a separated wife the weekly sum which she requires for the proper maintenance of herself and her children, that she or the Ministry should wherever possible obtain an order against the husband, and that the Ministry should recover from the husband or, in appropriate cases, from his employer by means of attachment of wages, such sums as can be obtained in reduction of the amounts paid by the Ministry to the wife'.

The *Payne Report*[155] accepted that such a 'far-reaching scheme of social wel- fare' was outside its terms of reference, but recorded that it would be failing in

---

[149] *Report of the Committee on the Enforcement of Judgment Debts* (Chairman, the Hon Mr Justice Payne, 1969, Cmnd. 3909) (hereafter the *'Payne Report'*).

[150] Whether made by a magistrates' court, or made in the Divorce Court and registered in the magistrates' court for enforcement. The registration procedure, introduced with virtually no dis- cussion by the Maintenance Orders Act 1958, was of great importance in extending the magistrates' jurisdiction in family cases at a time when it was the subject of a great deal of informed criticism: see below.

[151] Professor OR McGregor was a member of the Committee, which thus had access to the find- ings of the Bedford College survey into the workings of the magistrates' family law jurisdiction. Professor McGregor's Report on the efficacy of Attachment of Earnings orders made under the Maintenance Orders Act 1958 is published as Appendix 2 to the Committee's Report.

[152] The *Payne Report*, para. 20.   [153] See below.
[154] The *Payne Report*, para. 1305.   [155] Para. 1306.

its duty if it did not draw attention to the importance of a scheme of this kind; and it also emphasised that the problem of providing for the financial consequences of marital breakdown stemmed from the fact that a man with a modest income could not make reasonable provision for the maintenance of two homes of the same standard, and that in these circumstances[156] there was 'likely to be an overall dependency on the state'. The problem, the Committee recorded, was

not one 'of enforcement but of economics, and we cannot too strongly or too often invite attention to the simple fact that no improvement which we can suggest in the machinery of the courts will put more money into the pockets of husbands . . . or enable them to meet commitments beyond their capacity to pay . . . Whatever may be done in the approval or implementation of our recommendations, the basic problem of providing adequately for many deserted or separated wives and their children would remain to be solved by other means'.

It was perhaps comparatively easy to obtain unanimity about a passage in the Committee's Report which did not commit its members to anything. In relation to many of the matters which did require a positive decision the Committee was evidently deeply divided.[157] It is true that the Committee did unanimously recommend that the enforcement of civil debts and court orders should be placed in the hands of an enforcement office, operating an integrated system of enforcement, based on proper enquiry into the means and circumstances of the debtor;[158] and the Committee did recommend that attachment of a debtor's earnings should be available as a means of enforcing all debts[159] (and not merely the maintenance orders to which attachment had been extended in 1958) and it did unanimously recommend that imprisonment should be abolished as a remedy for debts other than family maintenance obligations.[160] But the Committee was split on whether imprisonment should be retained in respect of failure to discharge maintenance obligations;[161] and there were significant differences of opinion about many other detailed recommendations. The Government (notwithstanding the fact that the existence of the Enforcement Office was clearly seen by many of the Committee's members as essential to its other recommendations)[162] refused to create such a

---

[156] In the absence of other wage earners in the families affected.

[157] Apart from the major split on the retention of imprisonment for maintenance defaulters (see below), the chairman and nine of the other members of the 12-strong Committee entered reservations to its Report as indeed did its Chairman. Many of these reservations related to fairly basic aspects of the enforcement process, particularly the extent to which it should properly come under the control of administrators employed in the Enforcement Office rather than the courts.

[158] Para. 316 ff.   [159] See para. 629.   [160] See para. 1007.

[161] Six of the 12 members (including Professor McGregor) favoured abolition; three favoured abolition in principle but considered the time not to be ripe; three (including the Chairman) favoured retention, the Chairman commenting (see p. 387) that the answer to those who thought it illogical to abolish imprisonment for civil debts whilst retaining it for maintenance default was 'that we are not concerned with logic but with men'.

[162] For example, improvements to the system of collecting maintenance were expected to flow from the fact that enforcement would be in the hands of the Enforcement Office; and the husband would be under the surveillance of the enforcement office which would assist the wife in securing payment: see para. 1331 (10)–(13).

system.[163] But it did extend attachment to all civil debts;[164] and did nothing to restrict (much less remove) the courts' power to imprison those who defied maintenance orders.

In terms of specific change in accordance with identifiable recommendations the Payne Committee made little impact on family law; and at a more general level the Payne Committee did nothing to minimise the feeling that the enforcement of maintenance obligations by private law means brought the law to the margins of its effectiveness. But the Committee's failure to agree on issues central to its terms of reference highlighted the difficulties of achieving consensus on major reform affecting the legal system, particularly in the face of opposition from those who could claim expertise in the administration of the existing law and who could point to difficulties likely to be experienced in the actual working of any new system. This might have served as a warning to the members of the Finer Committee, but it apparently did not.

(iii) The *Finer Report*

The Finer Committee[165] was appointed on 6 November 1969 with breathtakingly wide terms of reference: to consider 'the problems of one-parent families in our society'.[166] As Professor McGregor (an especially active member of the Committee)[167] subsequently[168] wrote:

The terms of reference 'involved an examination of some of the fundamental moral, social and economic issues of today . . . Most of the questions . . . which had to be answered focussed on the social status and economic situation of women in British society. Thus the Committee had to begin their work by searching for light and order among a welter of disparate issues. One route lay through family law. Since the law and the courts are prime agents in the regulation of marriage breakdown and unmarried parenthood, the state of the law and its administration has a direct bearing on everyone . . . in one parent families. This becomes even clearer given the fact that the law here includes the law of social security. The heavy dependence of poor one parent families on the law of supplementary benefit explains why the Committee paid a great deal of attention to the relationship between the private law of family maintenance and the public law of

---

[163] The *Finer Report* commented that in this way the legislation had 'shorn off the attachment process from an institutional reform that was intended both to civilise that process and to make it more successful': para. 4.161.

[164] Administration of Justice Act 1970.

[165] For Sir Morris Finer and the membership of the Finer Committee, see Biographical Notes.

[166] The Committee was specifically 'to examine the nature of any special difficulties which the parents . . . may encounter; the extent to which they can obtain financial support when they need it; and the ways in which other provisions and facilities are of help to them'. It was also 'to consider in what respects and to what extent it would be appropriate to give one-parent families further assistance' having regard to the provisions of a number of statutes and the 'need to maintain equity as between one-parent families and other families' and 'practical and economic limitations'.

[167] In particular, he and the chairman wrote a 600-page typescript of the History of the Obligation to Maintain (of which a 'very truncated' but still invaluable version is printed as Appendix 5 to the *Finer Report*).

[168] In *Social History and Law Reform, the 31st Series of Hamlyn Lectures* (1981) at p. 46.

social security and the institutions which manage them. The Committee quickly discovered[169] that the legal scene was a chaos of overlapping jurisdictions and conflicting philosophies, strewn with . . . much debris from earlier centuries . . .'.

The *Finer Report* is an outstanding piece of social and historical analysis. The Report noted[170] that 'nothing could exceed the confusion created by three modes of assessment of a liability, all different from each other, and two of them employed by courts of law acting in ignorance of the third mode which the [Benefit authority] use in making decisions which affect the very same group of people'; and the Report's recommendations were based on the belief that the lack of integration of the 'three systems of family law . . . administered respectively by the divorce courts, the magistrates' courts and the supplementary benefits authorities' was a 'major cause of the hardships from which many one-parent families suffer'.[171] 89 of the Committee's 230 recommendations (contained in a text which, with appendices, ran to 910 printed pages) dealt with reforms of the substantive and procedural law of maintenance, whilst a further 28 recommendations covered the Committee's proposal for a Guaranteed Maintenance Allowance (which would be a substitute for maintenance in the hands of lone parents).

The Committee proposed what Professor McGregor described as 'two fundamental changes in family law and its administration'.[172] First, the Committee believed that it had assembled 'compelling evidence to demonstrate that the very existence and persistence of the dual jurisdiction [with the High Court and County Court on the one hand and the summary jurisdiction of magistrates on the other], and of the attitudes and institutions stemming from it, account for the presence in magistrates' courts of many very poor folk who possess neither knowledge nor expectation of any other legal cure for their marital ills'.[173] The Committee accordingly recommended that the domestic jurisdiction of magistrates' courts[174] be abolished; and a system of family courts established. This proposal is considered in the last chapter of this book.

Secondly, the Committee recommended a major shift from judicial to administrative procedures in assessing the liabilities of relatives to support one another. There were three essential elements in the proposal:

---

[169] Anyone familiar with the previous writings of Professor McGregor (notably *Separated Spouses, A Study of the matrimonial jurisdiction of magistrates' courts* (1970)—co-authored with L Blom-Cooper, and C Gibson—the *Graham Hall Report* and the passages dealing with imprisonment and attachment in the *Payne Report*) would in fact have been well aware of these matters.

[170] At para. 4.190.   [171] *Finer Report*, para. 4.5.

[172] *Social History and Law Reform*, p. 50.   [173] *Finer Report*, para. 4.383.

[174] The Committee emphasised that lay justices (suitably trained) would play a 'vital role' in the work of the Family Court (para. 4.379(2)) and that the Committee's criticisms of the matrimonial jurisdiction of the courts were 'not intended to spill over to the magistracy, whose fate it has been to try to make that jurisdiction work. It is probable . . . that only the care which so many magistrates have devoted to this task has saved the jurisdiction from foundering long ago under the weight of its inherent defects': para. 4.348.

(i) The Supplementary Benefits Commission would assess the means of the husband[175] and determine what it would be proper for him to pay to the Commission in or towards satisfaction of the money they have paid out to the wife in welfare payments. The Commission would make an 'administrative order' requiring the husband to pay the amounts assessed. The amount of the administrative order would never exceed the amount of the wife's entitlement to supplementary benefit;[176] and it would be calculated 'in accordance with published criteria for assessment' (which would leave the husband an amount out of his own income exceeding the amount to which he and any dependants would be entitled if he were on supplementary benefit).

(ii) A woman who considered she had a claim for maintenance at a rate higher than her benefit entitlement would still be able to go to the court for a maintenance order; but in the great majority of cases there would be no need for the wife to have any dealings with the husband at all.

(iii) The Commission would never have to pass judgment on matrimonial conduct (although the husband would be entitled to apply to the court, which might in exceptional cases take the parties' conduct into account).

In addition the Committee recommended the creation of a special non-contributory social security benefit, to be known as the Guaranteed Maintenance Allowance pitched at a level substantially above the Supplementary Benefit level and only means tested to a restricted extent.

The *Finer Report* engendered a great deal of enthusiastic support, and pressure groups campaigned for implementation. But the Report was published at a time when a succession of economic crises had finally convinced Harold Wilson's Labour Government of the need to cut back dramatically on public expenditure. As one Cabinet Minister memorably put it: the party was over.[177] Within two years of the publication of the *Finer Report* the Government was compelled (as a condition of getting assistance from the International Monetary Fund) to impose drastic cut backs even on social services with much more obvious popular appeal than the plight of single parents.[178] Finer's plan for a Guaranteed Maintenance Payment, payable as of right at a generous level, was doomed;[179] and even the more modest proposals for administrative orders (involving as they did an apparent extension of

[175] Or other liable relative (eg a child's father).
[176] The successor to the National Assistance provided under the 1948 legislation and the predecessor of Income Support.
[177] A Crosland, at the time Secretary of State for the Environment: see K Jeffery, *Anthony Crosland, A New Biography* (1999) p. 184.
[178] It has been said that acceptance of the terms imposed by the IMF in 1976 marked a 'great watershed in British politics: the moment when the post-war welfare state finally hit the buffers': see K Jeffery, *Anthony Crosland, A New Biography* (1999) p. 215.
[179] The first indication of what many saw as inevitable was given in the debates on a Government motion to 'take note' of the Report on 20 October 1975 (*Official Report* (HC) vol. 898, col. 53) and on a motion calling for papers initiated in the House of Lords by Lord Simon of Glaisdale on 19 January 1977, *Official Report* (HL) vol. 379, col. 84.

public involvement in the collection of maintenance) aroused opposition. They were never implemented.[180]

(iv) The Law Commission and reform of the substantive law applied in magistrates' courts

All that the Wilson Government could do to placate its own supporters, outraged by the rejection of the main Finer proposals,[181] was to emphasise the beneficial results which would flow from the reformulation of the substantive law applied in the magistrates' courts following the recommendations expected to be made by the Law Commission.[182] In fact the Government knew perfectly well, first, that there was serious disagreement[183] about the extent to which the assessment of financial orders should be affected by considerations of the parties' culpability; and secondly that there could be no real compromise between the Finer approach (which would have abolished the domestic jurisdiction of magistrates) and the Law Commission's belief[184] that the magistrates' jurisdic-

---

[180] *Official Report* (HC) 20 October 1975, vol. 898, col. 53 (Mrs Barbara Castle). The policy of 'encouraging' women on benefit to seek court orders was, however, abandoned in 1975: see Appendix 1 to the Supplementary Benefits Commission's *Annual Report 1975*, and compare the explanation given by Mrs Castle (above) with the account given by Professor McGregor, *Social History and Law Reform* (The Hamlyn Lectures, 31st Series, 1981) p. 53.

[181] For some time, official policy was to claim that many Finer proposals had been accepted and were being implemented; but in reality all the major structural changes were rejected.

[182] See the speech by the Secretary of State, Mrs Barbara Castle, *Official Report* (HC) 20 October 1975, vol. 898, col. 53.

[183] The Law Commission had expressed the view that the availability of the courts' powers should not depend on whether the applicant was guilty or innocent; but the Home Office (which had departmental responsibility for the magistrates' courts) and some of the judges—including Sir Roger Ormrod whose decision in the *Wachtel* case was subsequently to be responsible for minimising the significance of conduct in assessing the financial consequences of divorce—had strong reservations about this approach. The Home Office noted that enforcement of maintenance orders already presented magistrates' courts with a serious problem 'and orders against "innocent" husbands would certainly prove an even greater problem': see PRO BC3/388. In an attempt to reach agreement it was decided in January 1971 to refer the whole matter to a Joint Law Commission/ Home Office Working Party, chaired by the Law Commission chairman Sir L Scarman and composed of the Law Commissioner primarily responsible for family law, LCB Gower, two members of the Law Commission's legal staff, and two Civil Servants. (It appears that this Working Party had first been set up in 1967, and that in August of that year Professor McGregor had become a Member: see PRO BC3/ 414, but he withdrew at some stage.) At the outset what the Law Commission's Secretary described as 'the split on conduct' (see PRO BC3/401, Cartwright Sharp to Beedle, 25 April 1967) caused difficulty; and the Working Party's Consultation Paper eventually published in 1973, whilst accepting that adultery should no longer be an absolute bar to the making of an order, discussed four possible approaches to the question of how far such conduct should affect the courts' decisions in relation to financial matters. For the compromise eventually adopted, see below.

[184] The Law Commission had first considered the magistrates' financial jurisdiction in the context of its work on divorce; and it had taken the view that there was a clear distinction between the divorce and the magistrates' jurisdiction: 'Procedure in magistrates' courts is summary; the issues must be readily ascertainable and clear cut so that cases can be disposed of rapidly. It would be quite inappropriate to require magistrates' courts to try complex issues which cannot be isolated without preliminary pleadings or to exercise far wider discretions than they do now': Published Working Paper No. 9, para. 3. The *Finer Report's* conclusions were based on a very different assessment of the courts' role. See *Report on Matrimonial Proceedings in Magistrates' Courts* (Law Com. No. 77, 1976, para. 1.12).

tion had a role in dealing with the consequences of any marital breakdown which was neither permanent nor irretrievable.[185] But the Secretary of State assured Parliament that reform of the substantive law would 'strike at the root of the main defects' in the law.[186]

Reform of the substantive law: the Domestic Proceedings and Magistrates' Courts Act 1978

In 1976 the Law Commission published its proposals for a codification of the law applied by magistrates' courts in domestic cases.[187] The Government speedily brought a Bill forward, and the Law Commission's proposals were embodied, with only minor addition and amendment, in the Domestic Proceedings and Magistrates' Courts Act 1978. The underlying policy of the Act was to harmonise the law administered in the magistrates' courts and the divorce law as reformed in 1969 administered in the superior courts. The 1968 Act simplified and rationalised the grounds upon which an order could be made and the orders which the court could make if the applicant established his or her case. The grounds were reduced to three: first, that the respondent had failed to provide reasonable maintenance for the applicant or a child of the family; secondly, that he or she had deserted the applicant; thirdly that he or she had been guilty of behaviour such that the applicant could not reasonably be expected to live with the respondent.[188] The court could on proof of any ground order periodical payments and/or a lump sum not exceeding £500[189] but the court could no longer make

---

[185] The Law Commission/Home Office working party believed magistrates' courts had a role as a 'casualty clearing station': 'all the casualties of marriage can be brought to the magistrates' court. Some are clearly mortal; they should go on to be laid to rest by proceedings in the divorce court; some are serious, being more likely than not to end in final breakdown; some however will respond to local treatment and may well recover completely; others are trivial, requiring no more than sympathetic handling and encouragement'. But the Finer Committee (see particularly paras. 4.383 ff.) believed the analogy to be fundamentally misconceived, pointing out that a large number of those involved in magistrates' proceedings were never 'cured' but remained for many years in a 'matrimonial limbo in which they are single in reality but married in law': para. 4.383.

[186] Mrs Barbara Castle, *Official Report* (HC) 20 October 1975, vol. 898, col. 58.

[187] *Report on Matrimonial Proceedings in Magistrates' Courts* (Law Com. No. 77, 1976). The Report also made recommendations for giving magistrates power to make orders dealing with the occupation of the family home and prohibiting molestation; and these were implemented by the Domestic Proceedings and Magistrates' Courts Act 1978. The Family Law Act 1996 Part IV made further changes and largely assimilated the magistrates' powers in these respects to those of the superior courts.

[188] Domestic Proceedings and Magistrates' Courts Act 1978, s. 1. The Act also empowers the court to make orders by consent (s. 6) but these were rarely made; whilst the provision (s. 7—inserted as a result of pressure from back benchers) giving the court power to make orders reflecting payments previously made voluntarily remained virtually a dead letter. Consistently with the policy of keeping the magistrates' jurisdiction in harmony with the ground for divorce, the Family Law Act 1996 would (had the relevant provisions had been brought into force) have repealed the 'desertion' and 'behaviour' grounds, leaving failure to provide maintenance as the sole ground on which a magistrates' court could make a financial order.

[189] Domestic Proceedings and Magistrates' Courts Act 1978, s. 2: the power to order a lump sum was intended to be used to cover comparatively small liabilities such as outstanding fuel bills or

separation orders.[190] In deciding whether to exercise its powers, and if so in what manner, the court was directed[191] to have regard to a number of specified matters and to any other matter it considered to be relevant 'including, so far as it is just to do so, the conduct of each of the parties in relation to the marriage'.

The retention of 'fault' grounds and of the conduct of the parties as a factor relevant to determining how the court's powers should be exercised gave substance to the claim made by Professor McGregor[192] and others that the 1978 Act was 'backward looking'. But the most important complaint made by those whose hopes of fundamental reform had been dashed was based on the refusal of Government to abolish the separate magistrates' jurisdiction and to shift the emphasis in providing financially for broken families away from the private law and towards accepting the provision of support as a legitimate and indeed inevitable function of the State.

The magistrates' financial jurisdiction in practice

Professor McGregor believed that the magistrates' jurisdiction in husband and wife financial issues was 'dying of inanition';[193] but unhappily it is impossible to make any informed judgment about the contemporary significance of the magistrates' jurisdiction in this area. The reason for this is that successive Governments have not only failed to take any effective action on the pleas made over the years by Finer and others[194] for an *improvement* in the published official statistics about how the courts' powers are exercised but have gradually almost abandoned the publication of *any* statistical information about the financial aspects[195] of the

removal expenses: *Report on Matrimonial Proceedings in Magistrates' Courts* (Law Com. No. 77, 1976, para. 2.34). The maximum sum can be increased by Order, and in 2000 the specified figure was £1,000.

[190] However, the court was given power to make personal protection and exclusion orders; and it was hoped that these would protect the victims of domestic violence more effectively than the old separation order: see Chapter 21 below.

[191] Domestic Proceedings and Magistrates' Courts Act 1978, s. 3. (These provisions were amended by the Matrimonial and Family Proceedings Act 1984 in pursuance of the policy of harmonisation with the divorce law.)

[192] *Social History and Law Reform*, p. 51.

[193] *Ibid.*, p. 53; and note the detailed critique in the *Finer Report* , recommendations 52–58.

[194] A Committee, *The Committee on Civil Judicial Statistics*, set up under the chairmanship of Chief Master Paul Adams had reported in 1968 (Cmnd. 1968) making detailed proposals for the content and form of the statistics required to give the detailed and comprehensive information about the working of the family jurisdiction of magistrates which the Committee rightly regarded as essential for effective law reform and indeed for the formation of informed public opinion, as well as to meet the needs of law teachers, social researchers and historians: see paras. 11–15. The sad history of decline in the course of the twentieth century is dispassionately analysed by the Committee; whilst reference should also be made to OR McGregor, 'The Statistical Contribution to Law Reform of Sir John Macdonell', Chapter 4 of *Social History and Law Reform*.

[195] Notwithstanding the fact that the Lord Chancellor's Department has, since 1992, had departmental responsibility for the administration of the magistrates' courts, the *Judicial Statistics* contain no information about the number of applications made to magistrates' courts for orders under the Domestic Proceedings and Magistrates' Courts Act 1978, or about the outcome of those applications. Figures relating to applications under Children Act 1989 were published by the Children Act Advisory Committee, but this Committee was wound up in 1996.

magistrates' domestic jurisdiction.[196] It is impossible even to say how many applications for financial provision under the Domestic Proceedings and Magistrates' Courts Act are made each year. But, notwithstanding the lack of statistical data it does seem clear that the involvement of the courts in maintenance issues has (at least in cases in which the applicant has a child) been greatly reduced.[197] Paradoxically, this is because legislation[198] (introduced by a right-wing Conservative Government, which emphatically denied that responsibility for the financial consequences of family breakdown was primarily a matter for the State much less for State support) brought about a radical shift away from judicial and towards administrative procedures for quantifying and enforcing the liabilities which arise. From one perspective the Labour Government's rejection of Finer may be seen as reflecting the ending of the post-war consensus on the need for collective and administrative remedies for family breakdown; yet it was under the right-wing Thatcher administration that schemes in some respects strikingly similar to Finer's proposals for administrative orders were introduced.

RADICAL REFORM AT LAST? MAINTENANCE ENFORCEMENT AND CHILD SUPPORT, 1990–2000

The Domestic Proceedings and Magistrates' Courts Act 1978 had little effect on the social problems identified by Finer. The words of a White Paper issued by the Thatcher Government in 1990[199] could easily have been taken from the pages of Finer published 16 years earlier:

'The present system of maintenance is unnecessarily fragmented, uncertain in its results, slow and ineffective. It is based largely on discretion. The system is operated through the High and county courts . . . and the offices of the Department of Social Security. The cumulative effect is uncertainty and inconsistent decisions about how much maintenance should be paid. In a great many instances, the maintenance awarded is not paid or the payments fall into arrears and take weeks to re-establish . . .'

This view of the ineffectiveness of the law was supported by research studies, one of which concluded[200] that the law was 'far from satisfactory' not least because

'not all divorced women with children receive awards, the awards made are low—often lower than the child scale rates in income support, . . . many awards are not paid or paid

---

[196] These matters do not appear to figure in the work of HM Magistrates' Courts Service Inspectorate (which aims to 'promote continuous improvement to the magistrates' courts service'); nor in the publications of the Court Service's Civil and Family Modernisation Division whose report *Modernising the Civil and Family Courts* (2002) does not appear to mention the (Magistrates') Family Proceedings Courts.
[197] CS Gibson, *Dissolving Wedlock* (1994) provides an excellent analysis: see in particular Chapters 13 and 14 and the sources cited.
[198] Child Support Act 1991.   [199] *Children Come First* (Cm. 1263).
[200] J Bradshaw and J Millar, *Lone Parent Families in the UK* (1991, HMSO) p. 221.

irregularly, awards are not increased over time and the arrangements for enforcing maintenance are often not used and unsatisfactory'.[201]

There had over the years been a massive increase in social security costs such as would have caused concern to any responsible government. Not only were the *numbers* of lone parents dependent on benefits rapidly increasing—in 1971 213,000 lone parents received supplementary benefit, but by 1987 649,000 did so[202]—but the *proportion* of lone-parent families claiming benefit had increased dramatically. In 1971 the proportion of all single parent families receiving benefit was just over a third, but by 1987 it was nearly 60%. Apart from considerations of public expenditure, the fact that so many men seemed not to support their former partners—only 15% of women received maintenance for their own support from their husbands, and only 30% of lone mothers received financial support of any kind from the fathers[203]—fostered the feeling that moral issues were at the forefront:

'. . . when one of the parents not only walks away from marriage but neither maintains nor shows any interest in the child, an enormous unfair burden is placed on the other. Nearly four out of five lone mothers claiming income support received no maintenance from the fathers. No father should be able to escape from his responsibility and that is why the Government is looking at ways of strengthening the system for tracing an absent father and making the arrangements for recovering maintenance more effective'.[204]

The eventual response was two-fold.[205] First, the Government introduced legislation dealing with Maintenance Enforcement[206] and intended to improve the effectiveness of court orders and thus indirectly reduce expenditure on welfare benefits. Historically the most significant change was the reversal of the rule (which reflected the belief that interference with the relationship between employer and employee could only be justified in exceptional circumstances) that an attachment of earnings order could only be made against a person proved to have failed to pay maintenance by wilful neglect or culpable default.[207] Under the Maintenance Enforcement Act 1991 the court could make such an order even against a person who had a proven record of scrupulous compliance with legal support obligations. The Act also gave the court power to order payment of maintenance by means of a standing order or direct debit

[201] The financial position of divorced women was the concern of magistrates' courts (notwithstanding the fact that they had no power to dissolve marriage) because of their role in enforcing and varying orders originally made by the Divorce Court. The most serious problems have usually arisen in the context of women *with children* and is therefore conceptualised as a problem of *child support*; but the source of the obligation to maintain is ignored in what follows.

[202] J Bradshaw and J Millar, *Lone Parent Families in the UK* (1991, HMSO) p. 64.

[203] Bradshaw and Millar, *Children Come First* (Cm. 1263) p. 78.

[204] Prime Minister Margaret Thatcher, National Children's Homes George Thomas Memorial Lecture, 17 January 1990, as quoted in Bradshaw and Millar, *op. cit.* p. 77.

[205] A stimulating account of the policy background is given by K Kiernan, H Land and J Lewis in *Lone Motherhood in Twentieth Century Britain* (1998).

[206] The Maintenance Enforcement Act 1991 received Royal Assent on 27 June 1991.

[207] Attachment of Earnings Act 1971, s. 3.

arrangement; and magistrates' courts making a maintenance order were directed to do so unless they ordered attachment.[208]

But these changes in the way in which the private law was administered could at best only have a marginal impact on the problem[209] which 'appalled' Prime Minister Thatcher[210]—that of men who

'fathered a child and then absconded, leaving the single mother and the taxpayer to foot the bill for their irresponsibility . . . I thought it scandalous that only one in three children entitled to receive maintenance actually benefited from regular payments. So—against considerable opposition from . . . the Social Security Secretary and the Lord Chancellor's department—I insisted that a new Child Support Agency be set up . . .'.

The Child Support Act 1991 gave effect to the Prime Minister's insistence. The Act involved a fundamental change in technique.[211] Instead of the courts determining the amount of periodical payments in respect of children on a discretionary case by case basis, the Child Support Agency would assess all child support maintenance by applying a sophisticated formula.[212] The Agency was also to provide a specialist service for tracing absent parents and investigating the family's circumstances and for enforcing support obligations. In many ways, the system thus created could claim to be founded on the assumptions about the relative efficiency of the court based legal system and of professionally managed administration on which the *Finer Report's* proposals for administrative orders had been founded;[213] but—notwithstanding the all-party support originally given to the Child Support Act—the system introduced in 1991 is now universally agreed to have been a disastrous failure.[214]

In response to widespread criticism, changes were made in the Child Support scheme so as to allow departures from the prescribed formulae in certain situations in which particular hardship had been experienced.[215] But the belief that

---

[208] Maintenance Enforcement Act 1991, s. 2. The Act exacerbates the confused relationship between the powers of the superior courts and the magistrates' court (the superior courts having for example power, denied to the magistrates, to order a party to open a bank account but giving them a discretion—in contrast to the mandatory obligation imposed on the magistrates: cf. ss. 1 and 2—whether or not to attach earnings or make a so-called means of payment order).

[209] The lack of even rudimentary statistical information, for example about the number of attachment and means of payment orders made, makes it impossible to assess the impact of the new powers contained in the 1991 Act.

[210] M Thatcher, *The Downing Street Years* (1995) p. 630.

[211] The policies were set out in a White Paper, *Children Come First* (1991, Cm. 1263).

[212] See eg SM Cretney and JM Masson, *Principles of Family Law* (6th ed., 1997) Chapter 16; R Bird, *Child Maintenance* (3rd ed., 2000).

[213] However, whereas Finer proposed that improved enforcement of parental obligation should be accompanied by a generous Guaranteed Maintenance Allowance for lone parent families, the 1991 legislation was intended to bring about a large saving in welfare benefit expenditure. It did not succeed in achieving this.

[214] See the numerous official enquiries referred to in Cretney and Masson, note 212 above; and see the material collected by G Davis, N Wilkeley, R Young et al, *Child Support in Action* (1998).

[215] For example, where the absent parent had to incur unusually high travelling expenses: Child Support Act 1995, and Regulations made thereunder: see Cretney and Masson, *op. cit.*, pp. 532–538.

the introduction of an administrative formula-based system would necessarily solve the problems proved to have been ill-founded; and shortly after taking office Prime Minister Blair declared[216] that

the 'system of child support we inherited is a mess. It is failing our children, 1.8 million of whom receive no maintenance from their fathers. It is failing parents—the mothers on Income Support who see every penny of maintenance go straight to the Exchequer—and the fathers who lose contact with their children. It is failing the taxpayer who is picking up the bill for the non-resident parents who don't support their children'.

The Blair Government produced a Consultation Paper, *Children First: a New Approach to Child Support*; and in 2000 the Child Support, Pensions and Social Security Act was enacted to provide the 'urgent reform' which the Prime Minister believed to be necessary. The Act will replace the 'unworkable' formula introduced in 1991 with 'a workable new system based on a simple method for deciding how much an absent father should pay'. In essence, the 'non-resident parent' is to pay a flat rate percentage of his take-home pay—15% for one child, 20% for two, and 25% for three or more—with no deductions for housing costs or other expenses, and irrespective of the other parent's income.[217] This is to be backed up with 'tough new measures' to 'deal with parents who side-step their responsibilities (such as making it a criminal offence not to provide the information the Agency requires; and even giving power to confiscate culpable defaulters' driving licences).[218]

It remains to be seen how far the rhetoric accompanying the introduction of this measure will be reflected in greater effectiveness. Many of the failings of the original child support scheme were attributable to administrative inefficiency on the part of the Child Support Agency: numerous examples of chronic maladministration were identified by official enquiries; and the Agency's Chief Executive candidly (if naively) admitted that it had not been fully appreciated that intervention into personal and sensitive areas of private life would be resented, and that many people would actively resist the Agency's attempts to prioritise family support obligations.[219] As the House of Commons Social Security Committee observed: the social change brought about by the 1991 Act would have been controversial 'even if the administrative performance of the Agency implementing the Act had been impeccable. In the event, the Agency's performance . . . was dire'.[220] Confidence in the ability of the Government to

---

[216] Introduction to the Consultation Paper, *Children First: a New Approach to Child Support* (1998, Cm. 3992). This was followed by a White Paper, *A New Contract for Welfare: Children's Rights and Parents' Responsibilities* (1999, Cm. 4349).

[217] It was originally intended that there should be no upper limit to the liability, but amendments were introduced so that a non-resident's income over £2,000 per week is ignored. Even so, it appears that a wealthy parent will be required to pay £15,600 annually for even the youngest child, irrespective of the other parent's means.

[218] Child Support, Pensions and Social Security Act, s. 16.

[219] *Investigation of complaints against the Child Support Agency* (1995–96, HC 20, para. 7).

[220] *The Performance and Operation of the Child Support Agency* (1995–96, HC 50, para. 2).

provide adequate administrative machinery is not increased by the announcement, made as this book is going to press, that implementation of the 2000 reforms has had to be deferred because of the failure of the Agency's computer systems to perform the calculations required.

12

The Ending of Relationships by Death: The Financial Consequences

INTRODUCTION

All civilised states have rules about how property should be dealt with on death. But at the beginning of the twentieth century English succession law was distinctive: it had accepted[1] the principle of absolute[2] freedom of testation: a person of full age and capacity could make a will leaving property to whomsoever he chose. It mattered not what (if any) legal relationship existed between the testator and beneficiary: a man could leave property equally to his wife or his mistress, and to his child whether legitimate or illegitimate. Conversely, neither a wife, a child, nor anyone else had any legal cause for complaint if a testator made no provision for him or her. Of course, many people fail to make wills,[3] and the law also has to provide rules to determine who is to inherit in the event of intestacy. This chapter seeks to outline the development of the law in these two areas.

Two particularly significant trends can be identified. First, the rules of intestate succession were modified over the years so as to favour the claims of a surviving spouse as against other members of the family. The law was also strongly influenced by the increase in the owner occupation of houses, and increasingly adopted the principle that a surviving spouse should on intestacy inherit the deceased's interest in the matrimonial home.

The second trend in the development of English succession law was the (initially reluctant) acceptance that in some cases dependants of the deceased should have a right to ask for more. In 1938 the Inheritance (Family Provision) Act restricted a testator's right to disinherit dependants; and the law (rather than giving a wife or other members of the family a right to inherit a certain proportion of the deceased's property) gave the court a discretion to override the terms of the will so as to make reasonable financial provision for surviving

---

[1] Local customs restricting this right had been progressively removed: see F Pollock and FW Maitland, *The History of English Law before the Time of Edward I* (revised ed. 1968) p. 350.

[2] Until 1891 (when the Mortmain and Charitable Uses Act was passed) the mortmain legislation had restricted the freedom to leave property to charity by will.

[3] Only a third of a sample of people interviewed for the Law Commission in 1988/89 had made wills (although almost two-thirds of people aged 60 or over had done so): see *Distribution on Intestacy* (Law Com. No. 187, 1989) App. C. On the significance of intestacy in relation to the transfer of wealth, see JM Masson, 'Making Wills, Making Clients' [1994] Conv. 267, 268–270, and generally J Finch, J Mason, J Masson, L Hayes and L Wallis, *Wills, Inheritance, Families* (1995).

dependants. Over the years, the court's powers were extended, the category of 'dependant' eligible to make a claim for provision under this legislation broadened, and the significance of marriage in determining eligibility reduced.

INTESTACY: THE COMMON LAW RULES

At the beginning of the twentieth century, the distribution of property not disposed of by a valid will[4] depended on whether it was classified as real or personal. Succession to real property (notably freehold land) was governed by the common law rules of descent[5] which identified the heir to whom the property passed automatically on the death. The outstanding feature of these complex rules was that the deceased's children and other issue[6] were preferred to other relatives, with male issue being preferred to females and the elder male[7] being preferred to the younger.[8]

The heir took the property subject to the rights of the deceased's surviving spouse: a widower was (subject to a number of conditions)[9] entitled to a life estate 'by the Curtesy of England' in the whole of his wife's realty while a widow was in theory[10] entitled to dower (ie a life interest in one-third of her husband's realty).

Intestate succession to personal property (which included leases as well as money and chattels) was governed by the Statute of Distributions 1670[11] the scheme of which was that a widower took the whole of his wife's personalty to the exclusion of other relatives, whilst a widow took one-third of the deceased's personal property absolutely, the balance going to the deceased's legitimate

---

[4] The effect of the Married Women's Property Act 1882 was to enable a woman who married after 1882 to dispose of property by will as if she were unmarried: see RE Megarry and HWR Wade, *The Law of Real Property* (3rd ed., 1966), pp. 986–987.

[5] Modified in some respects by the Inheritance Act 1833.

[6] But only a legitimate relation of the deceased could take as the heir at law: *Birtwhistle v. Vardill* (1840) 7 Cl & Fin 895, HL.

[7] However, the issue of a deceased child or other descendant stood in his place, so that (for example) a grandson would take the property which would otherwise have passed to his deceased father.

[8] However, females of the same degree took equally as 'coparceners'. The rules of descent are lucidly expounded in RE Megarry and HWR Wade, *The Law of Real Property* (3rd ed., 1966), p. 516.

[9] eg that issue of the marriage capable of inheriting the land had been born alive: see RE Megarry and HWR Wade, *The Law of Real Property* (3rd ed., 1966) pp. 522–524.

[10] Conveyancing techniques (see RE Megarry and HWR Wade, *The Law of Real Property* (3rd ed., 1966) pp. 526–527) had been developed enabling the widow's right to be barred *inter vivos*, whilst the Dower Act 1833 allowed the widow's right to dower to be barred by will. By the early nineteenth century dower was apparently rarely encountered save in cases of 'inadvertency or unskilfulness , or from short sighted economy': Real Property Commissioners, *First Report* (1829), BPP Vol. 10, p. 17.

[11] As amended by Statute of Frauds 1677 and Statute of Distributions 1685, and subject to any local custom preserved by s. 4 of the 1670 Act.

children and issue. If there were no issue, the widow's share was increased to one half, and the balance went to the next of kin.[12]

Providing for homeless widows

The effect of the common law rules would often be to deprive the widow of a clerk or workman of the family home; and in 1890 the Intestates' Estates Act provided that a widow (but not a widower) should be entitled to a legacy[13] of £500 (perhaps £30,000 in year 2000 values) if her husband left neither will nor issue. The 1890 Act marked a significant change in policy:[14] for the first time English law gave a widow preference over her husband's kin; and the Act created a precedent by giving the widow a right to a legacy sufficient to ensure that she would be able to inherit a modest family home.

The fact that real and personal property were governed by different legal regimes caused many complications; and it was the policy of what is usually described as 'the 1925 property legislation' to assimilate[15] the two. For this purpose, it was essential to have a uniform set of rules to govern the devolution of all forms of property on death: the content of the rules did not matter; what was important was that the same rules should apply to all the property which passed as part of a deceased person's estate. This may explain how it came about that what, in retrospect, can be clearly seen as a decisive change in the policy of the law was carried through with very little discussion or consideration.[16]

The 1925 legislation provided that the intestate's spouse should (save in the case of the largest estates) be preferred to other relatives; and the principle that spouse and children should share even the smallest estate was finally abandoned. Under the new regime the surviving spouse (husband and wife were put on an equal footing) was entitled to the personal chattels[17] absolutely, to a statutory legacy[18] of £1,000, and to a life interest in any residue.[19] The reason for fix-

---

[12]   Statute of Distributions 1670, s. 6.

[13]   The legacy was in addition to any right of dower, and was charged rateably on realty and personalty: see RE Megarry and HWR Wade, *The Law of Real Property* (3rd ed., 1966), p. 528.

[14]   Its significance does not seem to have been appreciated at the time: the Second Reading debate in the House of Lords on 8 July 1890 is extremely brief, and there was virtually no discussion in the House of Commons.

[15]   The Long Title of the Law of Property Act 1922 declared that it was an Act to 'assimilate and amend the law of Real and Personal Estate'. For the background, see A Offer, 'The Origins of the Law of Property Acts 1925 (1977) 40 MLR 505; A Offer, *Property and Politics 1870–1914* (1978); and JS Anderson, *Lawyers and the Making of English Land Law 1832–1940* (1992).

[16]   The legislation has its immediate origins in the *Report of the Acquisition and Valuation of Land Committee*, established in 1919 by the Minister of Reconstruction to consider Land Transfer in England and Wales and to advise on action to facilitate and cheapen the transfer of land.

[17]   The *Report from the Joint Select Committee on the Law of Property Bill* (1920) BPP Vol. 7, p. 131, had proposed that the personal representatives be empowered to allow a surviving spouse who did not take the whole estate absolutely the use and enjoyment of furniture and 'other like chattels (including consumable stores)' for life: amendment to clause 138 (1)(ii).

[18]   The origins of the statutory legacy are to be found in the Intestates Estates Act 1890: see above.

[19]   One-half if there were surviving issue. The legislation gave the personal representatives power to redeem any life interest with the consent of the life tenant or leave of the court; but this power was apparently little used.

ing the statutory legacy at £1,000[20] was because wills of small estates almost invariably gave the surviving spouse the whole estate and the £1,000 legacy would produce the same result in the great majority of intestacies.[21] Even with somewhat larger estates a £1,000 legacy would usually enable the deceased's house to be retained for occupation by the survivor.[22]

Policy of 1925 legislation defeated by inflation

The 1925 legislation thus gave clear expression to the related policies of allowing the whole of all but the largest estates to pass to the surviving spouse and of ensuring that the widow should be able to go on living in the family home after her husband's death. But the technique of quantifying the surviving spouse's entitlement as a fixed money sum meant that, in a period of inflation and rising property prices, those objectives were no longer attained. In the course of World War II, the value of money fell by a third or more; and in 1948 (according to official indices) £1,700 would be needed to buy goods which would have cost £1,000 when the amount of the statutory legacy was fixed in 1925. Eventually, a Parliamentary Question[23] led the Lord Chancellor[24] to appoint a Committee under Lord Morton of Henryton[25] to consider the rights of a surviving spouse in the residuary estate of an intestate and report whether change in the law was desirable.[26]

[20] It had originally been proposed that the statutory legacy should be fixed at £500 (in line with the recommendation of the Acquisition and Valuation of Land Committee and reflecting the sum in respect of which a widow had been given priority by the Intestates' Estates Act 1890): see the speech of Lord Birkenhead LC on the Second Reading of the Law of Property Bill 1920, *Official Report* (HL) 3 March 1920, vol. 39, col. 255. But in fact £1,000 in 1922 corresponded in purchasing power to £500 in 1890; and the lengthy gestation period of the Birkenhead legislation allowed time for further reflection on the amount of the legacy: see notably the *Report from the Joint Select Committee on the Law of Property Bill* (1920) BPP Vol. 7, p. 131, amendments to clause 138.

[21] According to the Lord Chancellor, in 97% of cases the surviving spouse 'either takes the whole or some substantial life or other interest': *Official Report* (HL) 17 March 1921, vol. 44, col. 650; and according to the Solicitor-General, about 98% of intestate estates were less than £1,000, so that in the great majority of cases the survivor would take the whole estate: *Official Report* (HC) vol. 154, col. 93.

[22] See *Official Report* (HC) 15 May 1922, vol. 154, col. 99.

[23] On 16 April 1950 the recently elected Iain Macleod (see Biographical Notes) asked the Attorney-General to set up a committee on intestacy 'particularly in relation to the widow's right to purchase the home where she and her deceased husband have lived'. He had earlier written to the Attorney-General, Sir Hartley Shawcross (1902–: see Biographical Notes) referring to a constituency case in which the deceased's daughter was insisting that the house be put up for auction 'which is, I believe, within her rights . . . although the widow's money contributed greatly to the buying of the house'.

[24] Viscount (subsequently Earl) Jowitt (1855–1957): see Biographical Notes.

[25] See Biographical Notes.

[26] The Committee's Terms of Reference were a matter of great importance—and difficulty—to the Lord Chancellor's officials not least because any increase in the provision for a surviving spouse on intestacy would inevitably also increase the number of cases in which hardship might be caused to others dependent on the deceased; yet the Lord Chancellor's officials had no wish to reopen discussion on what had proved the exceedingly controversial matter of allowing the court to override a testator's wishes or even to override the provisions laid down by law on intestacy in such cases. In

THE MORTON REPORT ON THE LAW OF INTESTATE SUCCESSION 1951

The Morton Committee worked with astonishing speed. It had no doubts about its ability to interpret what it described[27] as the spirit of the age; and the Committee accepted the philosophy (previously adopted in framing the 1925 legislation) that the provision in fact made in wills provided a sound basis upon which the rules of intestate distribution could be based.[28] To this end, the Committee drew on a survey of wills probated over a five-week period;[29] and it also received advice[30] on the law of intestacy in foreign countries and considered a large number of written suggestions (including a petition signed by 3,202 persons urging improvement in the widow's position).

The Committee did not even consider carrying out an attitude or other public opinion survey; but in spite of (or perhaps because of this) the Committee rapidly agreed on its policy. It accepted that there had been a considerable depreciation in the value of sterling since the 1925 reforms, that the matrimonial home was often worth a sum 'greatly in excess' of the statutory legacy, and that, in consequence, the home would often have to be sold to satisfy the claims of a deceased intestate's children. In contrast, the average testator's will would make better provision for the surviving spouse; and the Committee concluded that the surviving spouse's entitlement on intestacy should be increased. But deciding on the nature and scale of the increase was less easy.

The Committee drew a distinction between cases where the intestate left surviving issue and other cases. Where there were surviving issue, the Committee recommended a five-fold increase (to £5,000—substantially more than the increase to £2,000 which would have sufficed to take account of general inflation since 1925) in the amount of the statutory legacy payable to a surviving spouse.[31] In cases in which the deceased left no issue, the Committee recommended a compromise between those[32] who favoured giving the whole estate to the survivor;[33] and those who thought that the deceased's kin should also bene-

---

the end, pressure from within the Government machine made it impossible altogether to exclude this topic from the terms of reference; but they were skilfully crafted to confine the issues as narrowly as possible: see below.

[27] *Report of the Committee on the Law of Intestate Succession* (1951, Cmd. 8130) (hereafter referred to as '*Morton Intestacy Report*') para. 10.

[28] Contrast the cogent criticism of this approach by the Law Commission, *Distribution on Intestacy*, Law Com. No. 187 (1989) para. 4.

[29] *Morton Intestacy Report*, para. 18.

[30] Prepared by Sir David Hughes Parry (1893–1973), Director of the Institute of Advanced Legal Studies, London University, and author of a still widely used student's text: Parry and Clark, *The Law of Succession* (10th ed. by R Kerridge, 1996).

[31] The survivor's entitlement to the personal chattels and to a life interest in half the residue was to remain unchanged; but the survivor was to be given the right to claim the capital equivalent (calculated according to statutory tables) of the life interest: *Morton Intestacy Report*, para. 32.

[32] Notably, the Council of the Law Society: *Morton Intestacy Report*, para. 34.

[33] 'This seems rather a striking proposal. It means that the spouse would take the whole estate even if the intestate left a very large estate . . . We feel that under such circumstances a childless

fit. Where the deceased died without issue but left a spouse and a parent or sibling of the whole blood the spouse should take a legacy of £20,000 and half the residue absolutely.

The balance of the estate should go to the surviving parent or parents, or (if neither parent survived) to the brothers and sisters of the whole blood.[34] The Committee did not think the average individual would want relatives more remote than this to benefit from the estate at the expense of the surviving spouse[35] and accordingly recommended that brothers and sisters of the half blood and their issue, grandparents, uncles and aunts of the whole or half blood and their issue, should lose the right[36] to share in the estate of an intestate who died leaving a surviving spouse.[37]

The general tenor of the Committee's proposals was thus vividly to exemplify what has been described[38] as the amputation of the blood stock and the increased significance of claims based on marriage (as against claims based on genetic kinship).[39] But the Committee was well aware that making the increased provision proposed for the surviving spouse might well work injustice in many cases where there were step-children by a previous marriage; and after considerable debate the Committee decided to recommend that the Inheritance (Family Provision) Act should be made to apply to cases of intestacy.[40] In effect, the Committee accepted that the complexity of modern family structures required recourse to a judicial discretion to do what would be fair in all the circumstances.

person, dying intestate, would wish that close relatives . . . should take some benefit from the estate, subject always to adequate provision being made for the spouse. It often happens that a large portion of the intestate's estate has been derived from his family and it seems just, therefore, that the family should have an opportunity of sharing in it after the intestate's death.'(*Morton Intestacy Report*, para. 34).

[34] On the statutory trusts defined by Administration of Estates Act 1925, s. 47, which also provide for substitution of issue of deceased siblings.

[35] *Morton Intestacy Report*, para. 36. The surviving spouse was to take the whole estate absolutely if no relatives within the defined class survived.

[36] Administration of Estates Act 1925, s. 46.

[37] *Morton Intestacy Report*, para. 36. Such relatives were to retain the right to succeed if there were no surviving spouse.

[38] By Sundberg, cited by D Bradley, 'Marriage, family property and inheritance in Swedish law' (1990) 39 ICLQ 370.

[39] This thesis is persuasively developed by MA Glendon, *The New Family and the New Property* (1981).

[40] *Morton Intestacy Report*, paras. 41–51; and see further below.

The Intestates' Estates Act 1952

The Government accepted the Morton Committee's recommendations,[41] and the Intestates' Estates Act 1952[42] gave effect to them.[43] Notwithstanding the lack of parliamentary interest[44]—the Bill received almost no critical probing of legislative policy or detail—the Intestates' Estates Act 1952 is of major significance in the development of the law. Not only did it emphatically recognise the primacy to be accorded to the claims of a surviving spouse and (for the first time in English statute law) recognise the family home as an asset deserving special protection; it also accepted the principle that, since no general code for intestate distribution could achieve satisfactory results in every case, the court should be given power to vary the statutory provisions in cases in which those provisions failed to make reasonable provision for the deceased's dependants. However, as we shall see, the class of person qualifying as 'dependants' was defined rather narrowly.

[41] For an account of the extensive discussions within the government machine, see SM Cretney, *Law, Law Reform and the Family* (1998) pp. 259–264. It was soon pointed out that the Committee had not fully considered the implications of the rule that the younger of two persons who died in circumstances rendering it uncertain which had died first was to be deemed to have survived. The larger the surviving spouse's entitlement on intestacy the more likely it was (for example) that the family of a young bride killed with her husband in an air crash would inherit substantial wealth, perhaps derived from his family. The Lord Chancellor eventually agreed that legislation should nullify the statutory presumption for the purposes of intestate succession.

[42] The Bill was handed to a recently elected Private Member, Harry Hylton-Foster (see Biographical Notes). Hylton-Foster was evidently correct in his assessment that 'speed and joviality looked like the easiest way' of getting the Bill through; and the few members who attended the debates were regaled with accounts of 'elderly gentlemen who marry little blonde creatures much younger than themselves in the autumn of their days' and similar witticisms. In the House of Lords, a light-hearted speech by Lord Mancroft (see Biographical Notes) was evidently skilfully attuned to the mood of the House. The Administration of Estates Act had, he said, been drafted by the late Sir Benjamin Cherry, and contained a table of 'a complexity and confusion equal only to that in the Table of Affinity in the Prayer Book, concluding with certain nefarious characters which could have stepped only from the pages of Saki or PG Wodehouse—namely, aunts of the half-blood. I never met a case of a man being disinherited by a half-blooded aunt, but presumably Sir Benjamin Cherry did not want to take any risks!' (*Official Report* (HL) 29 July 1952, vol. 178, col. 390).

[43] The Government was seriously embarrassed only by the attempt made by Barnett Janner MP (a solicitor and himself the son of a shop-keeper) to give a surviving spouse the right to take the family business as well as the family home (*Official Report* (HC) 15 July 1952, vol. 503, col. 2106). The Government accepted an amendment (moved by Charles Fletcher-Cooke (1914–) the barrister Conservative MP for Darwen) to allow brothers and sisters (and uncles and aunts) of the half-blood to retain their right to succeed in default of any spouse, issue, or parent of the deceased, ranking after relatives of the whole blood in the same degree.

[44] See above; and note that civil servants recorded their concern about the unrepresentative nature of the debates: the House of Commons Second Reading Debate was 'a very thin house' with few speakers. (In fact the House was counted out on 28 March, but the Second Reading was carried 'on the nod' in the following week.) The Committee debate was 'very meagre'; and officials regretted that the Bill had had so little consideration because there were 'many questions of principle' on which any Government would want a free vote (eg the size of the statutory legacy).

JUDICIAL DISCRETION TO ORDER REASONABLE PROVISION FOR DEPENDANTS[45]

A person of sound mind, memory and understanding could make a will disinheriting his wife and children; and the disappointed relatives would have no legal redress. But the qualification that the testator be of sound mind is important. If the will were truly eccentric (as in one case where a man left his wife no more than the sum of five pounds and his pet parrot)[46] the disinherited relatives[47] might have a case for attacking the deceased's sanity, and it was said by lawyers[48] that very often compromises satisfactory to all concerned were negotiated without the publicity of a contested law suit. But it could be difficult and expensive to attack the validity of a will in this way and it was not sufficient to show that the testator was 'moved by capricious, frivolous, mean or even bad motives'.[49] A testator who hates all human beings[50] but satisfies the 'sound mind and understanding' test of testamentary capacity was entitled to leave the whole of his property to charities benefiting animals; whilst a testator could 'disinherit . . . his children, and leave his property to strangers to gratify his spite, or to charities to gratify his pride'.[51]

The National Union of Societies for Equal Citizenship campaign

In the 1920s the National Union of Societies for Equal Citizenship (hereafter 'NUSEC') (which had adopted the principle[52] that husband and wife should each have the right to an equal share of the couple's income) began to campaign for reform. The fact that a husband's obligation to maintain his wife did not

[45] There is an extensive literature. The (New Zealand) Testator's Family Maintenance Act 1900 was particularly influential: see Sir Benjamin Cherry's Memorandum of 7 May 1928 on *Probate Practice in Relation to the Provisions made for the Spouses, Issue and Dependants of Testators in Different Parts of the British Empire and in the United States of America*, PRO LCO2/1185.

[46] An example given by the chancery barrister WP Spens QC (1885–1973) Conservative MP for Ashford Kent, speaking against the Inheritance (Family Provision) Bill: *Official Report* (HC) 5 November 1937, vol. 328, col. 1317.

[47] On occasion a relative might seek to upset a will under which the relative would take less than on intestacy: see *Culross v. Park* (Unreported, 1 December 1949) in which the widow of a testator forgetful of the day of the week and given to sitting down to breakfast with shaving lather on his face convinced a jury that he had lacked the capacity to make a will immediately after going through a marriage ceremony with her. (The testator's relatives subsequently attempted, unsuccessfully, to establish that the deceased lacked the mental capacity to contract the marriage, in which event as the law then stood, it would have been void and the 'widow' not entitled to take on intestacy.)

[48] See, for example, the speech by WP Spens, note 46 above.

[49] R Kerridge, *Parry & Clark's Law of Succession* (10th ed., 1996) p. 59.

[50] As in *Re Satterthwaite's Will Trusts* [1966] 1 WLR 277, CA; and note that generally mere eccentricity does not deprive a person of testamentary capacity—see for a striking example *Barry v. Butlin* (1838) 2 Moo PC 480 where a will disinheriting the only son of the testator—a man of 'slender capacity . . . indolent habits . . . addicted to drinking . . . and . . . childish in his amusements'—in favour of the testator's butler, solicitor and a friend was upheld.

[51] *Boughton v. Knight* (1873) LR 3 P&D 64, 66, *per* Sir James Hannen.

[52] See the Union's *Immediate Programme* (*Annual Report, 1927*, para. 5(d)).

extend to an obligation to provide for his widow and children was a particular source of complaint. NUSEC's formidable President (Eleanor Rathbone)[53] and Parliamentary Secretary (Mrs Eva Hubback)[54] began a campaign to influence politicians and civil servants. Mrs Hubback did not seek any 'rash change in our law of testamentary freedom' but wanted something done to protect lower middle class widows left entirely without provision.[55] Lord Astor seems to have acted as NUSEC's spokesman; and the Lord Chancellor's Permanent Secretary, Sir Claud Schuster, evidently arranged for to him to consult Sir Benjamin Cherry[56] whose memorandum on the subject was (Schuster told Cherry) of great help, making Astor appreciate the difficulties:

'information and advice coming from you has a double advantage that it is obviously disinterested while he may suspect me of merely trying to make things easy for the government'.

Astor duly moved a resolution in the House of Lords[57] asking that a Select Committee be set up to consider 'whether a change is necessary in the laws governing testamentary provision for wives, husbands and children based on the experience of Scotland, Australia and the other portions of the Empire'. He had previously agreed with Schuster what he would say; and also that he would not press the motion to a division; and no one can have been surprised that the proposal was opposed by the Government and others. NUSEC claimed the opposition was on 'various and mutually destructive grounds'; but they had got what they wanted. Astor's speech had created 'an extraordinary amount of interest' amongst the general public, and press comment had been 'almost wholly favourable'. The publicity prompted revelations from those who had suffered from the law and been advised that they had no remedy; and NUSEC was able to produce a pamphlet, 'Unjust Wills' highlighting specific instances of hardship.

The imminence of the first General Election in which women were eligible for the vote on the same terms as men[58] gave politicians an especial interest in topics likely to gain (or lose) women's votes; and on 19 April 1929 Prime Minister Baldwin (accompanied by the Chancellor of the Exchequer, Winston Churchill) received a delegation organised by NUSEC and the Equal Rights General Election Campaign Committee. Baldwin did not give a specific response on the inheritance issue, but the leaders of the other two major political parties were less

---

[53] For Rathbone, Hubback, Schuster, Cherry and Astor, see Biographical Notes.

[54] Mrs Hubback had already established a cordial relationship with the Lord Chancellor's Permanent Secretary Sir Claud Schuster.

[55] Hubback to Lord Chancellor Hailsham, 11 May 1928, PRO LCO2/1185. In fact Hailsham was a strong and consistent opponent of legislation on this subject: see below.

[56] See Biographical Notes.

[57] See *Official Report* (HL) 16 May 1928, vol. 71, col. 37.

[58] Representation of the People (Equal Franchise) Act 1928.

hesitant.[59] Lloyd George[60] claimed to have seen cases in his career as a solicitor in which the 'monstrous' law had deprived[61] women of any share in the business which their own intelligence and skill had built up. For his part, Ramsay MacDonald[62] claimed the law frequently had poor women 'bundled out into the streets' after their husband's death, and agreed that something had to be done.

The defeat of the Conservatives in the 1929 General Election[63] no doubt encouraged Mrs Hubback, Miss Rathbone and others to think that there was now[64] a realistic prospect of getting a Bill through Parliament; and certainly the incoming Lord Chancellor[65] was sympathetic to reform.[66]

The search for an acceptable solution

It soon became apparent that there were very different notions as to how the problem should be tackled. On the one hand there were those who, for ideological[67] or

[59] See the Memorandum 'Answers of the Three Party Leaders to a question on Testamentary Provision when receiving deputations prior to the General Election 1929': LCO22/1185.

[60] Chairman of the Parliamentary Liberal Party and Leader of the Liberal Party.

[61] 'merely because [the husband] was an ill-conditioned fellow'.

[62] Chairman and Leader of the Parliamentary Labour Party. Prime Minister in the Labour administration 1929–31; subsequently Prime Minister 1931–1935 in the 'National Government'.

[63] Labour won 288 seats, Conservatives 260, and the Liberals 59. The fact that women had become entitled on the same terms as men to vote influenced the decision that the Conservative Prime Minister Baldwin should immediately resign (notwithstanding the fact that no party had an absolute majority in the House of Commons) rather than continuing in office until defeated: see H Nicolson, *King George V, His Life and Reign* (1952) p. 435.

[64] Although one of the most powerful speeches against reform of any kind in the debate on the May 1928 debate on the Astor motion was made by Viscount Haldane (1856–1928), Lord Chancellor in the first (1924) Labour Government: '. . . there are only two ways in this matter: either you leave people to make their wills and trust to their sense of justice, as you do in an infinite number of other matters, or you say it is better that some State authority should make their wills for them. Now, I am not averse from the intervention of the State in many cases, but when the State intervenes in matters of wills I have seen too much of what goes on in the Courts to think that the Judges are able to do it wisely . . . If there is to be a tribunal set up, I would much rather set it up out of the Bench of Bishops . . .': *Official Report* (HL) 16 May 1928, vol. 71, col. 47. It is no doubt true (as the Conservative peer Viscount Cecil of Chelwood was to put it) that Haldane had been 'on the extreme right of the discussion'. Home Office officials were also critical of what one of them described as 'this ridiculous Bill': PRO HO45/16479/176695.

[65] Viscount Sankey (1866–1948): see Biographical Notes.

[66] He wrote that he was 'sympathetic towards' the desires of NUSEC; and suggested that a reference of the proposal to a Select Committee would give 'general satisfaction to a number of women who think, and probably rightly think, that the English law causes some hardship, or even injustice, in certain cases . . .': Sankey to Parmoor, 14 October 1929, PRO LCO2/1185. The 77-year-old Parmoor (a highly successful barrister, brother-in-law of Beatrice Webb, and father of Sir Stafford Cripps, Chancellor of the Exchequer 1947–1950) was Lord President of the Council in the 1929 Macdonald administration.

[67] Mrs Hubback told the *Joint Select Committee of the House of Lords and the House of Commons on the Wills and Intestacies (Family Maintenance) Bill 1930–31* (HC 127) that NUSEC preferred a system under which 'it should be laid down as a right . . . that a certain share of the estate should be left' to the surviving spouse and dependent children; but the most remarkable exposition of the case for fixed entitlement was made in the debate on the 1928 Astor motion by Viscount Buckmaster (1861–1934, Lord Chancellor 1915–1916): '. . . men and women should be socially and economically equal, free and independent . . . When a woman is left a widow society ought to be so

practical[68] reasons, thought that the widow should have a legal entitlement to a definite share of the deceased's property. On the other hand, an impressive body of legal opinion (powerfully represented by Sir Benjamin Cherry)[69] considered that any restriction on the right of disposition by will would not only be unworkable[70] but was 'unsuitable to the genius of the people'.[71] But even Cherry agreed that a Bill 'somewhat on the lines of the New Zealand'[72] and Australian statutes[73] allowing the court to order maintenance for spouses and children left destitute would be workable and 'would probably be welcomed by all political parties'.[74]

Faced with this conflict, the reformers tried to find an acceptable compromise. The first Bill, introduced by Astor in 1928[75] gave the widow and children a right to apply to the court if (but only if) the will[76] did not give them a certain pro-

organised that she should be just as able to protect herself as a man when his wife dies . . . It is in enlarging . . . opportunities, in encouraging women in their work and in the development of their economic life, that I would like to see reform take place . . .': *Official Report* (HL) 16 May 1928, vol. 71, cols. 50–51. Buckmaster accepted that women were in fact in a condition of 'economic subjection' but rejected giving the courts discretionary powers to provide for dependants on the ground that the courts were reluctant to exercise such powers and that they would be unlikely to exercise such powers well.

[68] Amongst reasons put forward were the unwillingness and unsuitability of judges to administer a broad discretion, the difficulty facing testators who wanted to make proper provision but could not prejudge what that would be, and the fear that a broad discretion would encourage litigation and thus the dissipation of the estate in costs.

[69] Notwithstanding his own preference, Cherry appears to have been responsible for drafting Miss Rathbone's 1931 Bill (see Schuster to Bowker, 16 February 1931, PRO LCO2/1187: 'carefully drawn, I think by Cherry; and like most of Cherry's work it is probably rather over-elaborate').

[70] Conveyancers would be instructed, in the testator's lifetime, to devise schemes to defeat the legal rights conferred; the rigidity of such a scheme would generally work inequitably in practice; legal costs would be increased, and wills rendered more complicated: Cherry's 1928 Memorandum (see below) para. 1(8).

[71] Cherry's memorandum dated 7 May 1928 on *Probate Practice in Relation to the Provisions made for the Spouses, Issue and Dependants of Testators in Different Parts of the British Empire and in the United States of America* (see PRO LCO2/1185)was made available to the Lord Chancellor's Permanent Secretary: Cherry to Schuster, 10 May 1928. This document, in many ways impressively, marshals practical arguments against any interference with the freedom of disposition; but the writer's starting point is clearly ideological: property 'is power, but only in relation to the right which the country gives to dispose and make use of it. Directly the value of property, depending, in the main, on powers of disposition, is reduced in any country, that country would have no right to complain if its most useful citizens migrated . . . [T]he result would certainly be to reduce the desire for acquisition or saving . . . so essential for the well being of any State, and especially for Great Britain at a time when she has to meet immense liabilities . . . [Any] proposal, involving a restriction on powers of disposition, must *prima facie*, be regarded with grave suspicion, and its adoption can only be justified where the object in view is paramount to all other considerations, and cannot be achieved by means of any other expedient'.

[72] Family Provision Act 1909.

[73] Family Protection Act 1895. An editorial comment in the *Law Quarterly Review* commented that few parliamentary debates had been as interesting from the jurisprudential point of view as that on 16 May 1928: see (1928) 44 LQR 281; and an article by SA Wiren, 'Testator's Family Maintenance in New Zealand' (1929) 45 LQR 378 was published and became influential.

[74] Cherry's *Memorandum* dated 28 May 1928, para. 12.

[75] HL Bill No. 146, 1928.

[76] But provision made during the deceased's lifetime was to be taken into account in computing what provision had been made: see clause 2(1).

portion of the estate.[77] The reformers argued that the Bill would establish a benchmark for reasonable provision.[78] Testators would know that if they made a 'capricious or unreasonable' will the personal representatives would inevitably do a deal or 'in the last resort' the court would rectify the offending document'[79] and would accordingly ensure their wills contained proper provision.[80]

Other people tried their hands at drafting Bills, all with different emphases. The breakthrough came in 1931[81] when Eleanor Rathbone managed[82] to get a Bill[83] referred to a Joint Select Committee.[84] The Committee[85] took a great deal of evidence,[86] but this revealed little support for radical reform.[87] In particular,

[77] If a widow or child exercised the right to apply to the court, the court had extensive discretionary powers to make or refuse orders.

[78] In the case of a widow, the requirement was a provision of a third of the income of the estate or £3,000 per annum, whichever was the less. In the case of a child the requirement was a third of the amount to which the child would have been entitled on the deceased's intestacy or £10,000 whichever was the less: clause 4(1). In the case of small estates, therefore, the children would have been debarred from making a claim even if they were (for example, as a result of disability) wholly dependent on the deceased and destitute following his death.

[79] Explanatory Memorandum to the Astor 1928 Wills and Intestacies (Family Maintenance) Bill, Bill No. 146. The Bill provided that a marriage settlement could debar the parties from the right to apply for provision under a will; and that anyone could, for valuable consideration, release his own rights and the rights of his descendants: clause 7.

[80] The Bill provided that the court could refuse to make an order on account of the character or conduct of any person or for any other sufficient reason: clause 9(4).

[81] There had been extensive lobbying; and in particular Sir John Withers set up a meeting in 1930 between the Lord Chancellor's officials and 'a few people who would understand the effect of the limitation of testamentary powers': Withers to Schuster—'My dear Claud'—29 January 1930, PRO LCO2/1187.

[82] PRO HO 45/16479/176695, letter and memorandum by Miss Rathbone dated 13 February 1931. Schuster had also favoured reference to a Select Committee: Schuster to Bowker, 18 February 1931, PRO LCO2/1187 and the Lord Chancellor moved the necessary motion. Mrs Hubback wrote a fulsome letter to Schuster thanking him personally and asking that he convey NUSEC's thanks to the Lord Chancellor 'for the help you both gave to the Wills and Intestacies Bill . . . I felt very doubtful at the time as to what the issue would be, and was delighted that the efforts of the Lord Chancellor . . . prevailed': Hubback to Schuster, 4 March 1931, PRO LCO2/1187.

[83] The Wills and Intestacies (Family Maintenance) Bill, Bill No. 15, 1930. This Bill went much further in the direction of statutory entitlement than had the original Astor Bill: the surviving spouse was to be entitled to a 'priority payment' of £1,000 (or half the estate if less) and to a life interest in a third (or if there were no children a half) of the rest ('the surplus net estate'): clauses 1–3. The Bill would have allowed contracting out: clause 6; but the onus was on the personal representatives or other interested parties (eg the person to whom the deceased's will had bequeathed his entire estate) to ask the court to annul the stautory rights to priority payment and surplus net estate given to spouse and children: clauses 7–8.

[84] *Joint Select Committee of the House of Lords and the House of Commons on the Wills and Intestacies (Family Maintenance) Bill 1930–31* (HC 127).

[85] Miss Rathbone had put in amendments which she would make to meet criticisms in the House of Commons: see the Committee's *Report* para. 1 and App. C. These amendments illustrate the delicate balance between giving scope and encouragement to litigation and providing a remedy in cases of hardship: see eg the amendments proposed to the annulment provisions in clauses 7 and 8 of the Bill: *Report* p. 133.

[86] The evidence is printed only in the House of Lords version of the *Report*: HL 97, 1930–31.

[87] The Committee, notwithstanding Miss Rathbone's efforts to strike a balance, considered that the Bill would directly invade the right of disposal by will for so long a characteristic of English law and would affect 'every will—whether just or unjust—unless the parties in right of the provisions

several solicitor witnesses[88] were sceptical[89] about whether there really was a problem.[90] But the Committee came down in favour of reform: it accepted that there were cases in which widows or widowers and children, unable to support themselves, had been unjustifiably left unprovided for; and the Committee was not prepared to 'say that, absolutely, their number is negligible'.[91]

So the Committee accepted that there was a problem. But it unequivocally rejected the Rathbone Bill—'complicated and would undoubtedly lead to greater expenses'—as a remedy.[92] Rather, a surviving spouse or child left without adequate support should be allowed to apply to the court for maintenance of an amount 'measured by the amount of the estate and the circumstances in which the family had been living'. The Committee considered that 'a Measure on these lines would be worthy of serious consideration by Parliament'.[93] Mrs

under the Bill contract out by themselves, if qualified to do so, or with the leave of the Court in other cases': *Joint Select Committee of the House of Lords and the House of Commons on the Wills and Intestacies (Family Maintenance) Bill 1930–31* (HC 127) para. 4.

[88] However, Sir John Withers MP (see Biographical Notes) supported the general principles of the Bill and believed there to be a 'considerable number of cases in which husbands and wives have died leaving their money away from the surviving spouse and their families and leaving them penniless . . . the cases are sufficiently numerous and important as to warrant the making of a provision compelling a spouse . . . to leave a certain amount of money to the surviving spouse and the children': *Joint Select Committee Report* Evidence, qs. 111–114.

[89] For example, Charles G May (a member of the Law Society council) could not remember a single case of a testator improperly cutting out his wife and children. He believed that the testator usually had good grounds for his action: *Joint Select Committee Report* Evidence, q. 449. LS Holmes, a Liverpool solicitor, took the same view: q. 660. The Public Trustee also had a negative attitude to the Bill, and his reservations about the difficulties to which it would give rise carried weight with the Committee: *Joint Select Committee Report*, para. 6.

[90] NUSEC had produced a Second Edition of the pamphlet *Unjust Wills* (1931). This consisted partly of eloquently stated arguments of general principle; but the most effective part of the pamphlet seems to have been the summary of 'typical hard cases': the 'fairly rich' public house manager forced to maintain the wife he had deserted during his life, but free to give all his property by will to his mistress, leaving the widow to live on Poor Law relief; the woman who left her entire estate (mostly given to her by the husband) to her own relations, disinheriting the husband and their children; the husband who left his entire estate including furniture to the children of his first marriage, making his wife of 20 years destitute.

[91] *Joint Select Committee of the House of Lords and the House of Commons on the Wills and Intestacies (Family Maintenance) Bill 1930–31* (HC 127), para. 3.

[92] *Ibid.*, paras. 6, 7.

[93] *Joint Select Committee Report*, para. 7. The Committee in effect accepted the view put forward on behalf of the Judges of the Chancery Division, ie that there were 'so many grave objections to the Bill in its present form that they would regret to see it passed into law . . . the legal costs of carrying into effect the provisions of the Bill would . . . far exceed any benefits to be derived in exceptional cases to which the Bill is intended to apply'. The Judges conceded that there would not be any 'real objection to a Measure which enabled a Court in a case where no adequate provision had been made for a spouse or infant children to order proper provision to be made for them out of the deceased's estate having regard to all the circumstances': Bennet to Thankerton, 21 May 1931, reproduced in Appendix A of the *Joint Select Committee Report*. But subsequent events suggest that the judges had not fully considered the matter and they began to have serious reservations about being given *carte blanche* to override testamentary provisions: see the letter from Sir Thomas Inskip AG, 2 March 1934, PRO LCO2/1188: 'I find the Bill is regarded with great anxiety, I might almost say hostility, by such Chancery Judges as I have consulted informally'. Sir Claud Schuster acerbically commented that it was a pity the Judges had not thought before communicating with the Chairman of the Select Committee which would never have given approval to the idea of a

Hubback and her colleagues had won an important victory. The end was not yet in sight, but perhaps they could celebrate the end of the beginning.[94]

Attrition: 1931–1938

It was to be seven more years before the Inheritance (Family Provision) Act received the Royal Assent in 1938. It is true that at the 1931 election the Labour representation in Parliament (and thus the number of those with strong commitment to the policies advocated by NUSEC) was dramatically reduced[95] and it was not until 1933 that another Bill[96] was introduced by a Conservative. But the issue was never one of party politics,[97] and on the occasions when the House of Commons divided on family provision Bills there were never more than 30 votes against. Why then did it take so long for legislation to reach the statute book?

The answer lies in the existence of differences of opinion within the Government machine.[98] In particular, Lord Chancellor Hailsham[99] was

discretion had not the Judges appeared to encourage this solution: Schuster to Inskip, 3 March 1934, PRO LCO2/1188.

[94] As she put it to Schuster (evidently regarded by her as a fellow conspirator on this issue): Hubback to Schuster, 18 May 1928, PRO LCO2/1187.

[95] From 288 to 52 (with an additional 13 National Labour MPs, supporting the National Government formed by Ramsay Macdonald at the end of August.

[96] The Powers of Disinheritance Bill, an 'absolute discretion' Bill introduced by Sir John Wardlaw Milne was given an unopposed Second Reading (*Official Report* (HC) 18 December 1933, vol. 284, col. 1082) and emerged in substance without significant change from Standing Committee A (albeit the title was changed to 'Inheritance (Family Provision) Bill'). But with the connivance of the Government the Bill was then 'talked out' *Official Report* (HC) 27 April 1934, vol. 288, col. 2029. JFW Galbraith KC MP boasted that he had 'put down, or procured to be put down, a very large number of amendments for the purpose of putting an end to' the Bill and that only a quarter of them had been dealt with by the end of the time available for debate: Galbraith to Schuster, 30 April 1934, PRO LCO2/1188. But although Schuster replied the next day that he had 'worked the business with extraordinary guile and success' Galbraith was to be proved wrong in his prediction that he had succeeded in 'finally disposing' of the issue.

[97] It is not clear that any social class had a strong interest for or against the principle of the Bill: Mrs Hubback thought the main beneficiaries would be what 'may be called the lower middle class' since the wealthy made provision by marriage and other settlements and the working class were covered by the National Insurance scheme. Sir Claud Schuster agreed that the 'ordinary working woman' was not very interested, but thought the Bill excited 'a great deal of interest among that wing of the professional feminists who belong to the upper and middle classes': Schuster to Bowker, 16 February 1931, PRO LCO2/1187. The view that 'ordinary working women' were not very interested in such measures can be supported by reference to the speech and interventions of the Communist MP W Gallacher: *Official Report* (HC) 5 November 1937, vol. 328, col. 1347. Another MP, Rhys Davies, complained that the legislation only 'concerned with a quarrel between the rich people of this country': *Official Report* (HC) 27 April 1934, vol. 288, col. 2044.

[98] There is considerable evidence of opposition on the part of officials. Sir Claud Schuster was initially sympathetic to the reformers' objectives, but his attitude seems to have shifted. In particular, he considered that the 1931 Joint Select Committee had uncovered no evidence of any need for alteration in the present law; and he was 'very much impressed by the mass of litigation' which the New Zealand legislation—often relied on as a precedent—'would probably entail' and by the fact that the New Zealand legislation did not make it clear whether disinherited relations had 'a right to be protected against destitution or a right to the kind of maintenance to which they have been accustomed': Schuster to Gwyer 19 February 1934, PRO LCO2/1188. In 1937, Schuster's deputy (and

strongly[100] opposed to legislation; whilst the least equivocal supporter was the comparatively junior Law Officer Sir Donald Somervell KC.[101] Each made his position clear;[102] but eventually even Hailsham[103] had to admit[104] that whilst he remained strongly opposed to any legislation there would be 'a good deal of sentimental support' for it in both Houses of Parliament and 'that the Government could hardly oppose' it. The Whips reported that nearly all the opposition in Parliament had disappeared and that there was likely to be 'something like unanimous support' for the Bill which had been introduced.

successor) the Hon Sir Albert Napier described the 1937 Bill as 'obnoxious': Memorandum dated 22 November 1937, PRO LCO2/1189. Subsequently, Parliamentary Counsel recorded that he had never ceased 'to say at every opportunity throughout the time whilst I was dealing with it that it appeared to me to be wrong in both conception and in drafting': Ellis to Coldstream, 6 August 1941, PRO LCO2/1516.

[99] See Biographical Notes.

[100] Sir Claud Schuster made a rare misjudgment in assessing the political situation in his prediction that Hailsham did not feel such hostility to legislation that he 'would be inclined to fight hard' against the Wardlaw Milne bill: Schuster to Gwyer, 14 February 1934, PRO LCO2/1188. Hailsham immediately made it clear that he thought the Whips had blundered badly in allowing the Bill to get through its Second Reading and thereby causing embarrassment to the Government in which he now served as War Minister. (The embarrassment was all the more acute in that Lord Chancellor Sankey was known to support legislation: see note above.) Hailsham's wish that the Whips should 'not be caught napping again' was met: see above.

[101] See Biographical Notes.

[102] Somervell wrote to Hailsham on 25 March 1936 (ie within a week of becoming Attorney-General) that he felt there was 'support in the House for a measure of this kind in some form or other'—indeed, his letter was prompted by the number of enquiries he had from MPs seeking guidance—and that the report of the 1931 Joint Select Committee afforded 'a strong case in debate for adopting the form embodied in [a Bill introduced in 1936] which . . . is operative in New Zealand. If I am right, it seems probable that in some Session or other a Bill of this kind will get through, unless of course the Government definitely opposed it, and, speaking entirely from the point of view of the House of Commons, I feel it might be difficult to oppose it unless the Government were prepared to deal with the matter in some other way. If this is right, it clearly is desirable that the matter should be dealt with in the best way . . . I am sure you will appreciate the position in which I am placed when asked for information as to the Government's attitude to the Bill'. On 1 December 1936 he wrote in similar terms to Sir John Simon, then Home Secretary: see PRO LCO2/1189, HO 45 16479/176695.

[103] Hailsham had recorded his 'very great hesitancy in accepting the proposal to interfere with a man's free disposition of his own property after his death. There are, of course, hard cases which appeal to public sympathy and are very likely to make bad law. But I think that the difficulty and danger of the other course and the impossibility of proving in Court the reasons which may have induced the testator to adopt a certain course are very strong arguments against the provisions' of the Bills introduced in 1933 and 1934: Memorandum dated 20 March 1936, PRO LCO2/1189. In 1937 Hailsham urged his continued strong opposition to any legislation and his belief that a testator might have excellent reason for disinheriting his dependants which died with him, and that to discuss them in open court after his death, and therefore necessarily in his absence and without his testimony would be disastrous, that it would arouse forgotten scandals and embitter family life': Schuster to Simonds, 29 October 1937, PRO LCO2/1189.

[104] In 1937 Hailsham, whilst claiming that he was anxious rather to know [the Chancery judges'] views than to express his own, none the less made his own views quite clear. The response of the Judges (Clauson J dissenting) was that, whilst there would be no unresolvable difficulty in exercising a discretion to award maintenance the 'fundamental objection in principle to interference with a testamentary disposition outweighs any advantage which might be expected' from the Bill eventually enacted in 1938: Memorandum of the Judges, 2 November 1937, PRO LCO2/1189.

1937: the Government accepts the inevitable

In 1937 the Cabinet[105] accepted Prime Minister Neville Chamberlain's advice to assume an attitude of neutrality to the Bill, pointing out fully and frankly the difficulties which would arise. Eventually a deal was done: the promoters of the Bill made concessions,[106] and the Government agreed to make the assistance of Parliamentary Counsel available[107] and to give the Bill a safe passage.

There was some opposition to the Bill as it passed through its various parliamentary stages.[108] This ranged from the argument of principle denying the legislature any right to interfere with free disposition of property save in truly exceptional circumstances,[109] through the criticism that the lack of any guidance about the scale of provision to be expected of a reasonable testator would make the courts' task impossible[110] particularly since the testator would not be

[105] 2 November 1937. Hailsham continued to voice his opposition to the Bill, and Schuster took objection on Hailsham's behalf to the minutes which the Cabinet Secretary had prepared. Eventually an anodyne statement of the Cabinet's Conclusions was agreed: see Schuster to Somervell, 3 November 1937, PRO LCO2/1189.

[106] Hailsham agreed that the Bill should no longer be blocked provided (i) the court's powers were confined to what was necessary for maintenance; and there was an upper limit to the amount ordered; (ii) that any provision for a child should be restricted to the child's minority; and (iii) jurisdiction was confined to the High Court—Hailsham expressed 'unqualified hostility to County Court jurisdiction' since there could be no uniform principle of discretion among 60 County Court Judges': Agreed memorandum of Discussion between Solicitor-General Sir T O'Connor and Lord Chancellor, 18 November 1937, PRO LCO2/1189. Hailsham had suffered a stroke in late 1936; and his manuscript annotation 'I leave the handling to the L[aw] O[fficers]. I agree the SG's memo of our talk' manifest both the difficulty of a sick man in writing and his evident distaste for the subject. Hailsham's health led to his resignation in March 1938, and his successor Maugham was responsible for stating the Government view in its passage through the House of Lords.

[107] *Official Report*, Standing Committee B, 23 November 1937, cols. 6–8.

[108] The Bill was given a Second Reading after a division in the House of Commons in which 159 voted for the Bill and 29 against: *Official Report* (HC) 5 November 1937, vol. 328, col. 1372. (A particularly effective Second Reading speech was made by the London solicitor Sir John Withers who was able to draw on his professional experience in support of two propositions, first that the Bill was needed to meet a real evil, and secondly that the courts would not find difficulty in assessing what would be appropriate for maintenance since they already did so (presumably in divorce, wardship and other proceedings relating to the administration of the estates of persons under a disability): *Official Report* (HC) 5 November 1937, vol. 328, col. 1351.) The other stages of the Bill were uncontentious, although amendments were made: *Official Report* (HC) 29 April 1938, vol. 338, col. 488; and the Bill's passage through the House of Lords was not opposed: *Official Report* (HL) 31 May 1938, vol. 109, col. 803 (Second Reading). A significant number of amendments on matters of detail were made without opposition (or indeed much discussion) in the House of Lords Committee stage: *Official Report* (HL) 23 June 1938, vol. 109, col. 246.

[109] 'The Bill is ill-judged because it restricts individual liberty and, what is much more important, it invades the property and personal affairs of the family . . . [W]e should do well to remember that we are the guardians of the liberties of the people . . . [The Bill takes] away from a man or woman the right to do what they like with their own': Commander Sir A Southby (1886–1969, Conservative MP for Epsom 1928–1947, and sometime Conservative Whip), *Official Report* (HC) 5 November 1937, vol. 328, col. 1332.

[110] Those (such as Colonel AP Heneage (1881–1971), Conservative MP for Louth, 1924–1945)who objected to the lack of guidance were driven to express a preference for fixed share measures of the kind found in Scots and other civil law jurisdictions, and had to pass over in silence the difficulties in adapting this principle identified by the Joint Select Committee in May 1931: *Official Report* (HC) 5 November 1937, vol. 328, col. 1297.

there to explain why he had acted as he did,[111] to the more practical considerations of how a small farm or other business could be divided up amongst the testator's family without destroying it.[112] But the promoters and the Government[113] did their best to meet points of any substance.

The Inheritance (Family Provision) Act 1938

The Act[114] which eventually received Royal Assent gave the High Court[115] power to order 'reasonable provision for the maintenance' of applicants who fell within certain specified classes of 'dependant'—the testator's surviving spouse, an unmarried or disabled daughter, or a son under 21 or disabled.[116] The Act did not accept the principle that relatives should in principle be entitled to provision out of the deceased's estate;[117] and it was certainly not intended

[111] The Bill as introduced contained provision whereby the testator's statutory declaration as to his reasons for his actions had to be accepted by the court as *prima facie* evidence of the truth of the matters stated; but this was criticised because a testator would 'hesitate to put on record perhaps the very personal, perhaps the very private, or perhaps the very delicate reasons as to why he is disinheriting a certain person' and that considerations of family loyalty would inhibit relatives from speaking the truth about their kin: see Major A VG Dower (1898–1986, Conservative MP for Stockport and subsequently Penrith, 1931–1950), *Official Report* (HC) 5 November 1937, vol. 328, col. 1304.

[112] 'There is the case of a small-holding or a small farm producing an income which keeps the family going. The testator decides to leave it to one of his children, naturally the best in his opinion . . . The other children go to the court . . . How is the court to decide? Is it going to divide up the small-holding?' Colonel Heneage (who was also concerned that the Bill would lead to farms being split between large numbers of relatives on the pattern said to exist in France): *Official Report* (HC) 5 November 1937, vol. 328, cols. 1299–1300.

[113] The Attorney-General, Sir D Somervell (a long-standing but discreet supporter of legislation) paid tribute to those who starting 'with very divergent views on certain matters raised by this very important Bill, succeeded in approaching those questions in a spirit of compromise, and while not giving away any points or principle, concentrated on putting into a workable form, principles which most people, in the end, recognised as sound . . . [T]he Bill in its present form is a great improvement on the Bill as introduced, and a great improvement on previous measures of this kind which have been brought before the House': *Official Report* (HC) 29 April 1938, vol. 338, col. 484.

[114] Which applied to deaths occurring on or after 13 July 1939: s. 6(2).

[115] The Bill as introduced would have given the county court jurisdiction in cases where the net estate did not exceed £2,000. Lord Chancellor Hailsham was 'implacably opposed' to this but the Law Officers anticipated that the 'greatest difficulty might arise over the exclusion of the County Court Jurisdiction'. In the event the promoters accepted the inevitable without public fuss; and so High Court judges had to concern themselves with cases in which the net estate was as little as £600 (£18,000 in year 2000 values): see *Re Catmull* [1943] Ch 262 where Uthwatt J refused to make an order in favour of the widow, left nothing except a life interest in furniture valued at £15 (£450) on the basis that she would be entitled to a state pension of 10/- (£15) weekly and was a working woman who could fend for herself. The estate (depleted by no doubt considerable legal costs) thus fell to be divided between the testator's seven children.

[116] Inheritance (Family Provision) Act 1938, s. 1(1). The dependant had to be domiciled in this country—a qualification attributable to the concerns of parliamentary counsel: PRO LCO2/1189, 13 December 1937.

[117] In Standing Committee B a group of those opposing the Bill moved amendments which would have given spouses and infant children a right to a statutory maintenance allowance and children a statutory portion on attaining majority; but Hailsham insisted that fixed portions were 'wholly undesirable' and that the principle of maintenance only for infant children and spouses 'must be retained': Memorandum by Sir T O'Connor SG, 18 November 1937, PRO LCO2/1189.

that the court should seek to impose a fair or equitable redistribution of the testator's capital. It was a fundamental principle that provision be restricted to *maintenance* (and save in the case of very small estates[118] provision was to be made exclusively by ordering periodical payments). These periodical payments were to determine on the ending of the dependency—for example, on the widow's remarriage—or earlier if the court so ordered.[119] Moreover, there was a cap on the proportion of the testator's estate which could be allocated to those qualifying as 'dependants': they were not to get more than the income from two-thirds of the estate (leaving a third for the testator to dispose of as he wished).[120] The Act also accepted that testators might reasonably leave it to the widow or widower to decide what would be proper provision for their children; and no application by a child could succeed if the will left two-thirds of the estate's income to the deceased's surviving spouse.[121]

In an attempt to meet concerns that farms and other small businesses would have to be sold, the Act provided that the court should have regard to the nature of the testator's property and that it should not order any provision which would require an improvident[122] realisation of assets. There was also concern about the impact of the legislation on the routine administration of estates. How could executors safely distribute property if they were faced with the possibility that a subsequent successful application for provision would be made? The answer was found in a time bar:[123] the application had to be made within six months of the grant of probate (and prudent executors would not distribute during that time).

The Act also tried to meet concern that the court might not know the reasons which had influenced the testator in deciding on the terms of his will. The court was to be required to 'have regard' to the testator's reasons so far as ascertainable; and the Act expressly permitted the court to accept such evidence as it considered sufficient for that purpose.[124] Another provision evidently intended to

---

[118] Ie no more than £2,000 (£60,000 in year 2000 values): Inheritance (Family Provision) Act Family 1938, s. 1(4).

[119] Inheritance (Family Provision) Act 1938, s. 1(2).

[120] *Per* Farwell J, *Re Lidingon* [1940] Ch 927; and see also *Re Catmull* [1943] Ch 262 applying Inheritance (Family Provision) Act 1938, s. 1(3). The two-thirds proportion applied if the testator left a spouse surviving and one or more other 'dependants', otherwise it was one-half.

[121] See Lord Russell of Killowen *Official Report* (HL) 31 May 1938, vol. 109, col. 801; Inheritance (Family Provision) Act 1938, s. 1(1) proviso. But this bar did not apply to applications by a child of the deceased who was not also the child of the surviving spouse: see further below.

[122] 'Having regard to the interests of the testator's dependants and of the person who, apart from the order, would be entitled to that property': Inheritance (Family Provision) Act 1938, s. 1(5). The concern was that businesses yielding as much as £1,000 a year might only fetch £2,000 or £3,000 (yielding investment income of perhaps £150 a year): *Official Report* (HC) 29 April 1938, vol. 338, col. 462.

[123] Inheritance (Family Provision) Act 1938, s. 2.

[124] The Act specifically included 'any statement in writing signed by the testator and dated, so, however, that in estimating the weight, if any, to be attached to any such statement the court shall have regard to all the circumstances from which any inference can reasonably be drawn as to the accuracy or otherwise of the statement': Inheritance (Family Provision) Act 1938, s. 1(7).

prevent the undeserving[125] from benefiting directed the court to have regard, not only to the dependant's and testator's financial position but also to the 'conduct of that dependant in relation to the testator and otherwise, and to any other matter or thing which in the circumstances of the case the court may consider relevant or material.'[126]

The impact of the Inheritance (Family Provision) Act 1938

The Act gave the court powers which it had never had before; but, for that reason, the powers were strictly limited.[127] Mrs Hubback was characteristically up-beat about the likely impact of the legislation;[128] but Eleanor Rathbone forcefully expressed her regret[129] that it did not give the family any entitlements; and that the Act had put the interests of property 'above and beyond the interests of flesh and blood'. Nevertheless, modest as the Bill was there would (she said) be many widows and orphans who would have occasion to call its promoter blessed.

Fears voiced by the opponents of reform that it would precipitate a 'flood' of cases in the courts proved unfounded. In part, this may be because the judges gave very little encouragement to disappointed relatives. The general approach was one of great caution: it was precisely because the Act constituted an invasion (albeit only a limited invasion)[130] of the right of testamentary disposition that judges held the powers conferred by the Act should be 'exercised only with great circumspection and to a limited extent'.[131] For many years[132] applicants

[125] Eg the widow of a man gassed in World War I who had continued to maintain her during his life notwithstanding her telling him she had no further use for him: *Official Report* (HC) 5 November 1937, vol. 328, col. 1298 (Colonel Heneage).

[126] Inheritance (Family Provision) Act 1938, s. 1(7).

[127] *Re Bluston* [1967] Ch 615; and see *per* Lord Gardiner LC in the debates on the amending Family Provision Act 1966: *Official Report* (HL) 16 June 1966, vol. 275, col. 201.

[128] See her last Presidential Address to NUSEC, 16 March 1938. The *National Council for Equal Citizenship Annual Report* 1938/9 p. 8 accepted that as the price of getting the Bill onto the statute book it had been necessary to make concessions which would weaken its impact but asserted that the main principle of the Bill remained unimpaired, and that the Council had successfully vindicated the rights of disinherited spouses and their children.

[129] *Official Report* (HC) 29 April 1938, vol. 338, col. 483.

[130] The Act 'proceeds on the postulate that a testator should continue to have freedom of testamentary disposition, provided that his disposition as regards dependants should be capable, having regard to all the circumstances, of being regarded by the court as reasonable'. The Act was not designed to compel a man to make provision that his wife would be enabled to live in circumstances similar to those they had shared during their marriage: *Re Inns* [1947] Ch 576, *per* Wynn-Parry J.

[131] *Re Andrews* [1955] 1 WLR 1105, *per* Wynn-Parry J. The same principle was applied in the case of large estates: see eg *Re Inns* [1947] Ch 576 where the court refused to interfere with a will dealing with an estate of some £600,000 (£12 million in year 2000 values) notwithstanding the fact that the £3,000 (£60,000) life income given to the widow was insufficient to enable her to continue living (as the deceased had wished) in the matrimonial home. The situation was made even more difficult for the widow since the terms of the will made it practically impossible to sell the house during her lifetime.

[132] This was the view consistently taken down to the decision in *Re E* [1966] 1 WLR 709; but in *Re Goodwin* [1969] 1 Ch 283, 288, Megarry J held that the question was not whether the testator

had to show that the deceased had been 'unreasonable'[133] in not making more substantial provision, and judges reiterated that the Act was confined to making provision for the *maintenance* of dependants rather than providing legacies to relatives who might be thought to deserve recognition.[134] It is true that maintenance was not necessarily confined to mere subsistence: 'maintenance' extended beyond food to clothes, housing and spending money; and the wife of a wealthy man[135] was not to be restricted to 'just enough to put a little jam on her bread and butter'.[136] But where the deceased had only small means (and many of the reported cases involved tiny estates)[137] the court might well dismiss a claim on the basis that the funds available were simply not sufficient to make any realistic contribution to the applicant's maintenance so that it could not be said that the testator's failure to make provision for his wife was unreasonable.[138] And there was always the risk that the court would order an unmeritorious applicant to pay the costs[139] (which, in many small money cases, would otherwise absorb most if not all of the estate).

Reported cases are only a small proportion of those which come before the courts; and no doubt there are many cases in which claims (possibly even claims which deserve to be categorised as 'blackmailing') are settled out of court; but it

stood convicted of unreasonableness but whether the provision in fact made was, viewed objectively, reasonable, and this came to be accepted as correct.

[133] *Re Styler* [1942] Ch 387, *per* Morton J (where an application by a 68-year-old widower who had given up his job to be with the testatrix but was left with no money except his 10/- (£15 in year 2000) pension and the wages he could earn in a heavy labouring job was rejected).

[134] *Re Vrint* [1940] Ch 920.

[135] In *Re Borthwick (No. 2)* [1949] Ch 395 the deceased testator—at the time of separating from his wife a bankrupt hairdresser's assistant in Hull—bettered himself and (unknown to his wife) lived in considerable style in the Home Counties. For 25 years he had continued to pay his wife what the judge described as a 'miserable pittance' of £3 weekly, but when he died his estate was worth nearly £0.25 million (perhaps £5 million in year 2000 values). The court awarded her periodical payments of £1,000 (say, £20,000) per annum.

[136] *Re Borthwick (No. 2)* [1949] Ch 395, *per* Harman J.

[137] eg £134 *Re Vrint* [1940] Ch 920; £370 *Re Joslin* [1941] Ch 200; *Re Styler* [1942] Ch 387.

[138] See eg *Re Vrint* [1940] Ch 920 (where the court refused for this reason to order any provision out of a £134 estate for the testator's separated wife of 25 years) and *Re Joslin* [1941] Ch 200 (where the court refused to make any order in respect of the £370 estate of a man with moral obligations both to the applicant wife and to the woman with whom he lived and his children by her—the fact that the legal wife had some small means of her own being apparently the decisive factor influencing the decision that the testator had not been unreasonable). These decisions prompted criticism on the part of MPs to which the response of Parliamentary Counsel was that the court had misconstrued the statute: PRO LCO2/1516, Ellis to Coldstream, 6 August 1941.

[139] The Bill as introduced had included a provision debarring the court from making an order for costs against any beneficiary other than the applicant; but this was removed at the Report stage of the Bill's passage through the House of Commons on the basis that the court ought to have power to penalise spiteful beneficiaries acting improperly: see *Official Report* (HC) 29 April 1938, vol. 338, col. 476. The result was to leave the award of costs in the court's discretion; and it seems that there was no consistent approach: see RD Oughton, *Tyler's Family Provision* (3rd ed., 1997) p. 365; M Albery, *The Inheritance (Family Provision) Act 1938* (1950) p. 41. For cases in which costs were awarded against the applicant see *Re Vrint* [1940] Ch 920 (application should not have been made) and *Re Joslin* [1941] Ch 200; and note that even to make no order for costs might leave an impecunious applicant with a heavy burden in respect of his own legal costs: see eg *Re Styler* [1942] Ch 387.

appears that upwards of 2,000 applications were made between 1939 and 1951.[140] There was some criticism[141] of aspects of the legislation;[142] but generally the utility of the Act in preventing injustice was accepted, if only gradually. By 1950 the Lord Chancellor's Department recorded the view that the Act had 'certainly served a useful purpose'.[143]

Investigation of further reform: the Lord Chancellor's Department driven to action

This did not mean that the Act was perfect. On the contrary it had well-recognised technical defects, and the restrictions which in 1938 had been prudently accepted as the price of getting the Bill onto the statute book often seemed unnecessarily to deny justice to dependants. But the tensions aroused within the Lord Chancellor's department by the events leading up to the 1938 Act (and particularly Lord Chancellor Hailsham's bitter opposition to the legislation which the Law Officers favoured)[144] had left scars: suggestions that enquiries be made about the desirability of extending the principles underlying the 1938 Act were politely rejected.[145]

It was not so easy to deny the need for action about the effect of inflation on the surviving spouse's £1,500 'statutory legacy' on intestacy; and (as already noted) a committee on the law of intestate succession, chaired by Lord Morton of Henryton,[146] was appointed in 1950. The Lord Chancellor's officials at first tried to exclude any consideration of the 1938 Act from that committee's terms of reference;[147] but it was soon pointed out that to increase the size of the widow's entitlement would greatly increase the risk of doing injustice to other dependants (and especially to the deceased's children by an earlier marriage or

---

[140] PRO LCO2/6671, Intestates Estates Bill, Notes on Clauses, p. 33.

[141] See in particular, M Albery, *The Inheritance (Family Provision) Act 1938* (1950).

[142] In 1941 Mrs Mavis Tate MP (see Biographical Notes) sent a cogently argued memorandum to Sir William Jowitt (then Solicitor General) claiming that the Act was not operating satisfactorily—the first such complaint, so the Lord Chancellor's officials noted, to be made. Mrs Tate urged (i) that the County Court should be given jurisdiction to hear applications relating to estates of £2,000 or less; (ii) that legislation should reverse the ruling in *Re Vrint* (above) and make it clear that the fact that an estate was so small that it would be impossible to make *adequate* provision from it was not a justification for making *no* provision; (iii) extending the court's powers to award a lump sum so that estates of £1,000 (£20,000 in year 2000 values) could simply be paid over to the applicant, and making the six-month time limit for applications somewhat more flexible. In July 1941 Jowitt met Mrs Tate and Miss Colwill MP, and was sympathetic to the views they had put forward; but it was considered impossible to do anything until after the end of the War: see the papers on LCO2/1516.

[143] *Ibid.*   [144] See above.

[145] See REK Thesiger's memorandum commenting on correspondence between a solicitor and his MP: PRO LCO2/1516, 3 March 1948.

[146] See Biographical Notes.

[147] The draft terms of reference for the Committee on the Law of Intestate Succession put by H Boggis-Rolfe to the Treasury Solicitor (PRO LCO2/4440, 22 May 1950) were confined to a consideration of the rights of a surviving spouse on intestacy, and stated that colleagues had 'not been able to think of any other subject which could conveniently be considered simultaneously'.

to his step-children). As the Senior Chancery Judge[148] put it, 'the more the widow is to take, the more need there is to protect the children'. The Lord Chancellor's Department had to give way: the Morton Committee's terms of reference were amended (as narrowly as possible in the circumstances) to include consideration of 'whether, and if so to what extent and in what manner the provisions of the [1938 Act] ought to be made applicable to intestacies'.[149]

The Morton Committee goes too far

The Morton Committee had no problem in making recommendations about those technical matters which the Lord Chancellor's officials had been willing for them to consider. Should the 1938 Act apply to *partial* intestacies (where the will dealt only with the deceased's house, for example)?[150] The Committee had no difficulty in deciding that legislation should put it beyond doubt that the court was to look at the estate of a deceased testator as a whole, and not be 'arbitrarily limited to such part thereof as he may have chanced to dispose of by will'. After all, as the Committee put it,[151] the 'needs of a dependant remain just the same whether the testator's estate devolves under his Will or under his intestacy, or partly under both'. But once that had been conceded, how could the extension of the Act to cases of total intestacy be resisted? It made no sense for the court's powers to depend on whether the testator left a duly executed will irrespective of whether it made any effective disposition of his estate; and if the 1938 Act were to be applied to a 99% intestacy, why should it not apply equally to a 100% intestacy?

It is true that some commentators felt it would be invidious for the Court to declare provisions made by Parliament in a statute to be 'unreasonable'; but the Committee considered this argument rested on a

'confusion between what is reasonable as a general provision of the law suitable to meet the average case, and what is reasonable in the special circumstances of an exceptional case. This may be illustrated by an example. It might be reasonable for Parliament to provide as a matter of general law that a surviving spouse should take the first £5,000 of the estate of an intestate. But it would not be reasonable that a woman dying possessed of an estate of £5,000 and leaving two infant children by her first marriage wholly without means and a wealthy husband by a second marriage should leave all her estate to her husband. If in such a case she died intestate we venture to think that there would be no

---

[148] Vaisey J. The same point was also made vigorously by the Treasury Solicitor: PRO LCO2/4440, 22 May 1950.
[149] *Morton Intestacy Report*, para. 1.
[150] A will might even fail to dispose of any of the testator's property (for example, where the court held a gift to 'charitable or benevolent purposes' to be wholly void: see *Morton Intestacy Report*, para. 42, or where it merely appointed guardians for the deceased's child). There was considerable doubt about whether the 1938 Act applied in such a case: see *Morton Intestacy Report*, para. 44.
[151] *Ibid.*

embarrassment in a Court declaring that the deceased had failed to make reasonable provision for her infant children and rectifying the matter accordingly'.[152]

It followed that the provisions of the 1938 Act should be extended to cases of total intestacy; and the Committee had no hesitation in so recommending. To do so was clearly within the Committee's terms of reference. But what about the effect of increasing the surviving spouse's entitlement on others who might have had some sort of claim to be supported by the deceased? The majority of the Committee refused to negotiate for an extension of their terms of reference[153] to enable them to consider this aspect of the matter. But, by way of compensation, the minority were allowed to have written into the Report—'at the risk of travelling outside out terms of reference'[154]—some forceful criticism[155] of the fact that the terms of the 1938 Act prevented the courts from making provision for maintenance where the estate was small.[156] (The Report claimed that the courts were 'quite unable' to provide maintenance in 'at least half the cases' which came before them[157]). Even more daringly, the Report included a statement that the extension of the 1938 Act to intestacies would 'obviously' make it 'necessary for the whole of the Act to be closely reviewed'.[158]

The Government accepted the Committee's recommendation to allow applications where the deceased had died intestate and the Intestates' Estates Act 1952 duly provided that the court should not be bound to assume that the law relating to intestacy made reasonable provision in all cases.[159] The Government also agreed to remedy the worst technical defects identified by Morton in the 1938 Act.[160] But it shrank[161] from tackling the fundamental issue of how to pro-

---

[152] *Ibid.*, para. 46. £5,000 (£85,000 in year 2000 values) was the amount the Committee recommended the surviving spouse should take absolutely on an intestacy in a case where the deceased left issue, a parent, or a sibling. The surviving spouse would also take a life interest in half the rest of the estate: see above.

[153] Minutes of First Meeting, 9 November 1950, PRO LCO2/4448.

[154] *Morton Intestacy Report*, para. 43.

[155] M Albery, author of *The Inheritance (Family Provision) Act 1938* (1950)—the leading text on the Act available at the time—was a member of the Committee and the Report draws heavily on a memorandum which he drafted: Memorandum No. 16, PRO LCO2/4447. The book was regarded within the Department as severely critical of the Act, but GP Coldstream recorded on 27 February 1952 that a good many of his points had been dealt with and that Albery had indicated he would be content: Coldstream to Barnes, 27 February 1952, LCO2/4451.

[156] This was the effect of the 'extremely restricted scope' of the quantum of awards resulting from the terms of s. 1(3) and the limitations on capital awards imposed by s. 1(4): *Morton Intestacy Report*, para. 49.

[157] *Ibid.*, para. 49.   [158] *Ibid.*, para. 51.

[159] Inheritance (Family Provision) Act 1938, s. 1(8) as inserted by Intestates' Estates Act 1952, s. 7 and Sch. 3.

[160] Ie the restrictions imposed by Inheritance (Family Provision) Act 1938, s. 1(3) and (4). Unhappily, the changes were not wholly effective. Although the court was no longer restricted to awarding a maximum of two-thirds of the income but could award the whole of the annual income of the estate, and the limit on the amount of the lump sum which could be awarded for maintenance in estates of £5,000 or less was abolished, it was decided to retain the bar (s. 1, proviso) on applications in cases where the widow was given two-thirds of the income and the deceased's only other dependants were children of the surviving spouse. It appears that spiteful husbands were sometimes advised to leave their wives a life interest in two-thirds of the estate, thereby preventing

vide a remedy for the injustice sometimes caused by giving the widow an over-riding preference[162] on intestacy. No comprehensive review of the Act took place for a further 20 years; but piecemeal amendments to the law made in 1958 and 1966 in response to particular pressures were effective in suggesting the need for a much bolder approach to reform.

(i) Provision for the divorced wife out of the husband's estate

In all the discussion about potential injustice no one had mentioned the case of the divorced wife. But the rise in the number of divorces, coupled with the fact that the Divorce Court had extremely limited powers to order capital provision on divorce, began to cause problems on a significant scale. Orders for periodical payments[163] came to an end on the husband's death; and as Lord Merriman, the President of the Divorce Division,[164] put it[165] in characteristically vivid language:

The Morton Committee had remarked on the injustice such an increase in the amount going to the widow could do to the children of an intestate's first marriage, but often in these cases the widow would care for them and make provision for them. 'But what about the marriage which has been dissolved? Take the case of the husband who has broken up the marriage and has married the woman named in the petition, and by that fact has become intestate. He then dies. She cannot be relied upon to have any particular tenderness for the children of the first marriage. The petitioning wife, unless there is a secured provision for her for her life, which is extremely unlikely in the range of figures we are considering, automatically loses her maintenance on the death of the husband, and with it, pro tanto, the power to support her children, who are cut out of the intestate's estate in favour of the woman who has broken up their home. The reverse case of the co-respondent taking the statutory legacy at the expense of the children would be no less shocking.'

The fact that the Government had set up a Royal Commission on Marriage and Divorce[166] (also chaired by Lord Morton) in 1951 was happy coincidence;

the court from entertaining an application by her or any other dependant, whereas had they disinherited her the court would have been able to award her the whole income of the estate: see Lord Gardiner LC moving the Second Reading of the Family Provision Bill 1966, *Official Report* (HL) 16 June 1966, vol. 275, col. 203.

[161] Lord Chancellor Simonds was warned by officials that the 'greatest difficulty presented by the Morton Report' was in connection with the 1938 Act: PRO LCO2/4457, Dobson to Simonds, 26 November 1951.

[162] See in particular the comments of the President of the Probate Divorce and Admiralty Division to the Lord Chancellor's Office: PRO LCO2/4457, Merriman to Coldstream, 5 March 1952. The type of problem which could arise was soon to be demonstrated by the Court of Appeal's decision in *Re Howell* [1953] 1 WLR 1034.

[163] Unless secured (which was rarely done).   [164] See Biographical Notes.

[165] Merriman to Coldstream, 5 March 1952, PRO LCO2/4451.

[166] *Report of the Royal Commission on Marriage and Divorce* (1956, Cmd. 9678).

since the position of the divorced spouse was clearly within their terms of reference. The Commission was impressed by the hardship likely to be caused to divorced wives wholly dependent on unsecured periodical payments and left destitute on the husband's death; and recommended that the deceased's estate be made liable for the support of the divorced wife in such circumstances and that the court should be guided by the same general principles as under the 1938 Act 'in so far as such principles are appropriate'.[167]

This recommendation no doubt seemed technical and uncontroversial. It attracted little attention; and the Committee of Officials set up to consider implementation of the Royal Commission's recommendations regarded legislation as acceptable.[168] A Bill was prepared[169] to give effect to this and other apparently uncontentious recommendations of the Royal Commission; and, in the time honoured way, the Bill was handed to a back bencher who had a good position in the ballot for Private Members' Bills. But the very fact that the Bill was passing through the House of Commons without debate or even a statement of its content[170] prompted suspicion on the part of some MPs. A storm blew up. The Government was attacked for accepting the 'novel provision' that a guilty wife should be able to get her hands on her husband's assets after his death, and was accused of bringing forward a charter for adulterous wives. It took a considerable amount of emollient explanation from respected back benchers in the Commons[171] and from the President of the Divorce Division in

[167] *Ibid.*, para. 524.

[168] Undated notes (apparently made in January 1957) in the Lord Chancellor's Office files indicate that this proposal (Royal Commission recommendation No. 61) was regarded as one of the Commission's 'particularly valuable' recommendations which merited Government help and support and could be treated as a 'high priority': PRO LCO2/6140, Annex.

[169] Not without difficulty. The draftsman (Stanley Krusin) raised a number of fundamental and difficult points—for example, was an application by a divorced wife to be treated as a 'matrimonial' application (in which case it had been suggested that the court should proceed on the same basis as it would if the deceased husband were still alive, and would look to the interests of the divorced wife and children and 'not even take into account the provisions of the husband's will or the claims of the second wife and children') or (as Krusin preferred) as essentially a matter of extending the Chancery Division's jurisdiction under the 1938 Act?: Krusin to Dobson, 10 January 1958, PRO LCO2/6152. It was decided that the jurisdiction should be for the Divorce Court, but the scheme of the legislation was to be modelled on that of the 1938 Act. There was also difficulty about whether divorced husbands should have the right to apply for provision out of their former wife's estate. Sir Hugh Lucas Tooth (the MP selected by the Government to take the Bill as a Private Member's Bill) was opposed to this, but the Cabinet thought it would be more controversial to exclude husbands than to include them and Sir Hugh recorded that it would be 'churlish not to accept' this: Lucas-Tooth to Dobson, 20 February 1958, PRO LCO2/6152. The Lord Chancellor's officials briefed Lord Meston to take the Bill through the House of Lords. For Meston, Lucas-Tooth and Dobson, see Biographical Notes.

[170] The only debate in the House of Commons was on the Report stage: see *Official Report* (HC) 2 May 1958, vol. 587, col. 810. The refusal of some MPs to allow the debate on the Bill to be curtailed meant that there was an adjournment to 16 May, when the Bill passed (in spite of what may have been filibustering speeches by two opponents): see *Official Report* (HC) vol. 588, col. 785.

[171] Particularly by Graham Page, the solicitor MP for Crosby. The Solicitor General, Sir Frank Soskice, explained that the Bill would give no *right* to the guilty but merely the *possibility* of making a claim: *Official Report* (HC) 16 May 1958, vol. 588, col. 802.

the House of Lords[172] to get the Bill safely on the statute book as the Matrimonial Causes (Property and Maintenance) Act 1958.

The 1958 Act did not take the simple course of adding divorced spouses to the statutory list of qualifying 'dependants'. Instead, it created a parallel regime, administered in the Divorce Court and in some respects different[173] from that created in 1938. But in practice the court found little difficulty in deciding the small number of applications[174] made under the Act. The first reported case[175] demonstrates both the mischief at which the 1958 Act was primarily aimed[176] and also the fact that there would often be no dispute about the amount to be awarded:

Mr and Mrs Askew were divorced in 1944, and Mr Askew was ordered to make periodical maintenance payments to the wife of £377 per annum. He remarried in 1945 and died in 1959 leaving his estate of some £28,000 to his second wife for life with remainder to nephews and nieces. The first wife had no assets and (the maintenance payments having ceased) depended on National Assistance. The parties agreed that provision of £286 per annum[177] should be made for her out of the estate, and the only dispute was as to the date from which the payments should start.

In retrospect the 1958 Act can be seen as a significant landmark in the gradual extension of the courts' powers to reallocate family assets in the wake of divorce; and in the acceptance of the view that the courts could reasonably be entrusted with wide discretionary powers to readjust family finances.

---

[172] See his speech on the Second Reading debate in the House of Lords: *Official Report* (HL) 16 June 1958, vol. 209, col. 978. Merriman claimed that the number of applications for maintenance by guilty wives was 'negligible'; and the Act (see s. 3(4)(c)) would specifically direct the court to consider the reason why no application had been made by the wife at the time of the divorce.

[173] The test under the 1958 Act was whether it 'would have been reasonable for the deceased to make provision for' his former wife's maintenance: s. 3(2). Under the 1938 Act the court at that time was requiring an applicant to satisfy the somewhat more demanding test of showing that the deceased had been *unreasonable*: see *Re Howell* [1953] 1 WLR 1034, CA; *Re Clayton deceased* [1966] 1 WLR 969. But in 1968 Megarry J firmly denied that the test under the 1938 Act was subjective in this sense (see *Re Goodwin* [1969] 1 Ch 283) and his approach was finally endorsed by the Court of Appeal in *Millward v. Shenton* [1972] 1 WLR 711. In *Roberts v. Roberts* [1964] 3 All ER 503 Sir J Simon P pointed out that it could be *understandable* for a man to make no provision out of a small estate yet still not *reasonable* for him to act in this way; and this approach was taken a stage further in *Re Shanahan* [1973] Fam 1.

[174] In the first five years there were never more than 50 applications in any one year: see the figures extracted from the *Civil Judicial Statistics* helpfully tabulated in Appendix A to RD Oughton, *Tyler's Family Provision* (3rd ed., 1997).

[175] *Askew v. Askew* [1961] 1 WLR 725.

[176] Ie the fact that the termination of maintenance payments on the husband's death would often leave the wife destitute. But the courts did not regard remedies under the Act as being confined to such cases, and in *Re Eyre* [1968] 1 WLR 530 the court held that where the estate was large enough to meet the claims of all those concerned a testator should make provision such as would preserve the level of maintenance payable under the Divorce Court order. In particular, it was not to be assumed that a secured periodical payments order was intended to be the sole provision which a divorced wife could expect.

[177] Perhaps £3,700 in year 2000 values.

(ii) The Family Provision Act 1966 opens the floodgates?

Irritating technical defects in the 1938 Act kept on appearing. First, in 1966 the Court of Appeal decided that the Act did not permit the making of orders giving a dependant a proportion (such as a half or a quarter) of the estate's income.[178] Unfortunately, many such orders had been made. Secondly, the rule prohibiting the making of applications more than six months after the grant of probate continued[179] to cause well documented hardship.[180] Thirdly, the rule confining the court's powers (save in the case of very small estates)[181] to periodical payments of income caused real inconvenience and disproportionate expense in administering small trusts. Finally, the fact that, however small the estate, applications had to be made to the High Court seemed increasingly difficult to justify. As Ungoed-Thomas J judiciously put it in March 1966, to restrict the jurisdiction in this way

'was obviously a sensible arrangement when this novel and difficult jurisdiction was introduced; but it may well be that this arrangement has outlasted this particular justification for it'.

The judge's tactfully expressed hope that the rule might 'perhaps now be considered' was timely. The Law Commission (established in 1965) had, with the perhaps naive enthusiasm of the pioneer, set up an 'immediate remedial department';[182] and this department had already begun to consider some of the

---

[178] *Re Gale* [1966] Ch 236.

[179] The 1938 Act (s. 2) imposed an absolute bar on proceedings unless the application were lodged within six months of the grant of probate. That caused such indefensible hardship—for example, in cases in which the meaning of the will was unclear and was only resolved by court decision months or even years after probate—that the Intestates' Estates Act 1952, s. 7 and Sch. 3 gave the court a discretion to extend the time limit. But this could only be done in closely defined circumstances 'affecting the administration or distribution of the estate' and in *Re Kay deceased* [1965] 1 WLR 724 it was held that failures within the post office and on the part of the applicant's solicitors did not fall within the amended provision.

[180] Departmental files contain numerous examples of hardship—not least the plight of a Yugoslav landowner now penniless and reduced to working as a waitress because (as her MP put it to the Lord Chancellor in June 1947) 'the excellent Marshall Tito had expropriated all her estates without compensation' and her husband (under the belief that his wife was a woman of substantial means) had left his estate elsewhere. She had failed to file an application within six months because she could not leave Yugoslavia during the war; but the Government could find no solution to her problems: PRO LCO2/3588. In *Re Kay deceased* [1965] 1 WLR 724, Russell LJ (sitting at first instance) felt obliged to reject the claim of a widow whose application—in part because of the time taken to get legal aid, in part because a work to rule in the post office 'struck our system of communications and superimposed an additional delay on an already leisurely progress'—reached the court a day late.

[181] The 1938 Act confined the power to award a lump sum to cases where the net estate was £2,000 or less: s. 1(4), but even where there was power to award lump sums, the provisions of s. 1(3) of the 1938 Act often made it impossible to do so where the estate was small (see *Re Catmull* [1943] Ch 262; *Morton Intestacy Report*, para. 49).

[182] *Official Report* (HL) 16 June 1966, vol. 275, col. 205 (Lord Gardiner LC).

problems to which judicial decisions regularly drew attention.[183] This sufficed
to allow Lord Chancellor Gardiner to introduce a Bill (which the Lord
Chancellor and the Law Officers described as a technical and boring response to
a number of judicial requests for minor improvement on points of detail)[184]
without going through the traditional process of seeking advice from a committee of experts. The Bill prompted very little[185] parliamentary discussion,[186] and
received the Royal Assent as the Family Provision Act in November 1966.

The Family Provision Act 1966 empowered the court to award lump sums,
however large (or small) the estate.[187] The county court was to have jurisdiction
in cases where the estate was £5,000 or less.[188] The bar preventing applications
being made where two-thirds of the income had been given to the surviving
spouse[189] and the troublesome restrictions on the maximum amount of periodical payments were swept away;[190] and the court was given a general power to
allow applications to be made notwithstanding that six months or more had

[183] In the present context, the Commission's file PRO BC3/373 had noted the decision in *Re Kay*
[1965] 1 WLR 724, and on 27 July 1965 the Secretary (H Boggis-Rolfe) wrote to the Lord
Chancellor's Permanent Secretary Sir George Coldstream that the issue of the time limit raised by
that case would 'profitably be examined by the Commission without delay'. Enquiries were immediately made of the Bar Council and the Law Society; and after consultation with Russell LJ legislation was drafted to ensure that the time limit applicable to widows under the 1938 Act was no
more rigorous than that applied to the divorced under the 1958 Act. The Government was able to
answer Leo Abse's Parliamentary Question (*Official Report* (HC) 24 November 1965, vol. 721, col.
512) with the assurance that the necessary Bill would be introduced 'at an early date'. Then on 27
January 1966 *The Times* published its report of *Re Gale* [1966] Ch 236 (see above); and the
Commission (against the initial reluctance of the Lord Chancellor's officials) immediately moved to
consider measures to remedy the difficulty exposed in the Court of Appeal's judgment. It seems that
the whole project nearly foundered because of the multiplicity of points raised by those consulted
(should there be anti-avoidance provisions? should the court's power to award a lump sum be unrestricted, should the class of relatives be extended? and so on). It appears—the Commission's file contains little material after March 1966, and the Lord Chancellor's Office files have not been
traced—that eventually it was decided to bring forward the Law Commission's original Bill with
only minor amendment leaving the other topics to the comprehensive examination given in the Law
Commission's *Second Report on Family Property* (1974): see below.
[184] s. 1 increased the statutory legacy payable on intestacy and, in an attempt to minimise problems caused by continuing inflation, gave the Lord Chancellor power to increase the amounts of the
'fixed net sum' by order: see SM Cretney, *Law, Law Reform and the Family* (1998) pp. 264–266.
[185] The only matter of real debate—see for example *Official Report* (HL) 16 June 1966, vol. 275
col. 213, Viscount Colville of Culross, and col. 216, Baroness Summerskill—was whether illegitimate children should be made eligible to apply for provision on the same terms as the legitimate: see
Re Makein [1955] Ch 194 applying to the construction of the 1938 Act the normal rule whereby the
word 'child' in a statute did not extend to the illegitimate. The Government view was that reform
of this matter should await the report of the *Committee on the Law of Succession in Relation to
Illegitimate Persons* then sitting under the chairmanship of Lord Russell of Killowen. (The
Committee's Report (1966, Cmnd. 3051) para. 62(4) in fact recommended that illegitimate children
should be included in the class of 'dependants' and the Family Law Reform Act 1969, s. 18, eventually gave effect to that recommendation.)
[186] The only real objection to reform came from one Conservative back-bencher, Charles
Fletcher Cook, who protested against sweeping away what had been 'regarded as an important barrier [*sic*] to the freedom of testamentary bequest': *Official Report* (HC) 4 November 1966, vol. 735,
col. 922.
[187] s. 4.   [188] s. 7.   [189] s. 2.   [190] s. 3.

gone by since probate.[191] Finally, the court was given power to make interim payments to an applicant in immediate need of financial assistance[192] thus remedying a defect pointed out by Lord Denning[193] in the Second Reading debate.

Perhaps these changes could fairly be described as intrinsically narrow and technical, but the effect of the 1966 Act was to destroy all the careful restrictions which had been imposed in 1938. As one author[194] has pointed out, the 1966 Act 'represented a substantial extension of the jurisdiction and was an endorsement by Parliament of the principle of varying testamentary disposition by judicial discretion'.[195] In this way, the Act prepared the ground for the much more radical reforms carried through in 1975. In the meantime, the courts began to take advantage of the greater freedom given them by the 1966 Act (by, for example, directing that the whole of the estate should simply be transferred to the deceased's husband's widow).[196] The cautious (perhaps even suspicious) approach previously taken to the legislation seemed increasingly difficult to justify.

Discretion triumphant? The Inheritance (Provision for Family and Dependants) Act 1975

The Matrimonial Proceedings and Property Act 1970 had extended the discretionary powers of the Divorce Court in financial matters, but this extension was intended to be without prejudice to the introduction of community of property and fixed rights of inheritance (for which there was a great deal of support). The question whether a system of legal rights of inheritance (under which a surviving spouse would be entitled as of right to a fixed proportion of the estate of a

---

[191] s. 5. The fact that the court had, under the Matrimonial Causes (Property and Maintenance) Act 1958, an 'absolutely general' power to allow applications by divorced spouses provided the administration and distribution of the estate had not been completed was anomalous and had been a source of judicial comment: *Re Kay deceased* [1965] 1 WLR 724, *per* Russell LJ (sitting at first instance). The 1966 Act gave the court an unrestricted power in both cases.

[192] s. 6, inserting s. 4A into the Inheritance (Family Provision) Act 1938.

[193] In *Re Ferrar (deceased)* [1966] P 126, CA, a divorced wife was living with the children in the former matrimonial home. The husband fell into arrears with the mortgage instalments. The mortgagee obtained an order for possession and, after the husband's death, took steps to enforce it. On the divorced wife's application under the 1958 Act the court ordered the executor to pay the arrears of some £300 to the mortgagee in exercise of an inherent power to make orders for the preservation of property; but the Court of Appeal (Lord Denning MR dissenting) held that there was no power to make such an order and that the court (*per* Russell LJ) being a court of law and not a court of sentiment, the wife's application was bound to fail.

[194] RD Oughton, *Tyler's Family Provision* (3rd ed., 1997) p. 23.

[195] This aspect of the legislation was recognised by the opposition spokesman, Viscount Colville of Culross: the 'principle that runs through this Bill—and after the length of experience that the country has had in the administration of this type of jurisdiction by the courts I think we can but welcome it—is the principle of flexibility. The court is given wider powers still under this Bill to deal with matters on the justice of the case before it without the various statutory restrictions which previously fettered the way in which the court could deal with the case': *Official Report* (HL) 16 June 1966, vol. 275, col. 210.

[196] See eg *Re Carter* (1968) 112 SJ 136.

deceased spouse whether he died testate or intestate and regardless of the terms of the will)[197] should be introduced into English law was central to the debate. In 1971 the Law Commission published a Working Paper[198] which examined the 'fixed share' question, and the case for giving the court wide discretionary powers to 'rewrite the will' if this were necessary to ensure the surviving spouse a fair share of the family assets (rather than simply enough to provide for her maintenance).[199]

INHERITANCE RIGHTS: THE CASE FOR FIXED SHARES

Many legal systems (including the Scottish legal system)[200] give a wife a right to a fixed share (one-third if there are surviving children)[201] of her husband's movable property on his death. Another common method of ensuring that the deceased's family inherit a stipulated portion of a deceased's estate (used in many of the United States for example)[202] is to give surviving relatives the right to set aside the deceased's will if it does not give a fixed proportion of his assets to the wife or other claimant.

The 1971 Law Commission Working Paper considered the introduction of a system under which a surviving spouse would be entitled as of right to a fixed proportion of the deceased's estate (perhaps one-third). The Commission identified advantages in a system of legal rights of this kind, not least that there would be a fixed standard capable of application without resort to the court.[203] But as the Commission pointed out, legal rights could not take account of the circumstances of each case; and if a fixed rights regime were simply added to the discretionary system created in 1938, 'the advantage of certainty, which legal rights would otherwise secure, would be diminished'. Moreover, some dependants would do worse than they would have done under a discretionary regime, and a fixed rights regime would at best be an imprecise way of protecting the survivor's interest in family assets.[204] The Law Commission's consultation on these proposals revealed a 'marked lack of support among members of the legal profession (practising and academic) for the principle of legal rights of inheritance for a surviving spouse', whilst the Commission reported that 'the

[197] The Law Commission, *Family Property Law* (PWP No. 42, 1971) para. 0.36.
[198] *Family Property Law* (PWP No. 42, 1971).
[199] The Law Commission, *Family Property Law* (PWP No. 42, 1971) para. 0.34.
[200] See generally 'Wills and Succession' in *The Laws of Scotland, Stair Memorial Encyclopaedia* Vol. 25 (1989) by DB Walters and E Clive.
[201] The children are also entitled to one-third of the estate of a man who dies leaving a widow.
[202] The United States Uniform Probate Code (adopted in a number of the states of the Union) adopts such an approach: see generally WF Fratcher, 'Towards Uniform Succession Legislation' (1966) 41 NY Univ LR 1037; LH Averill, 'An Eclectic History and Analysis of the 1990 Uniform Probate Code' (1992) 55 Albany L R 891; LW Waggoner, 'Marital Property Rights in Transition' (1994) 59 Missouri LR 21.
[203] Law Commission, *Family Property Law* (PWP No. 42, 1971) para. 4.65.
[204] *Ibid.*, paras. 4.65–4.72.

preponderance of opinion among women's organisations and members of the public' was also opposed to the introduction of such a system.[205] In 1973, the Commission concluded[206] that 'a strengthened family provision law, with its greater flexibility' would be a better means of securing the survivor's interests than a system of legal rights. The addition of a system of fixed legal rights of inheritance to the system of family provision law would lead to uncertainty and confusion. Any advantage derived from the automatic operation of legal rights of inheritance would be offset by the disadvantage of rigidity and possible incompatibility with the new standards proposed for the Family Provision legislation.[207]

Since 1973 no official or professional body has suggested that a fixed-rights system be introduced into English law. In this way, the 50-year struggle for the introduction of definite entitlement to a husband's property came to an end, apparently with the agreement of the women's organisations which had at one time been such committed advocates of reform.

IMPROVING THE FAMILY PROVISION LEGISLATION

How, then, should the principles of a system of family provision be 'strengthened'? There were three obvious grounds for criticism of the existing law. First, the class of dependants who alone could apply for reasonable provision out of the deceased's estate was narrowly restricted. Secondly, the Inheritance (Family Provision) Act was concerned solely with making reasonable provision for the applicant's *maintenance*; and it seemed anomalous that since 1973 a wife whose marriage was ended by divorce could expect the Divorce Court to award her a larger share of the 'family assets'[208] than a wife whose marriage was ended by death could expect under the Inheritance (Family Provision) Act. Thirdly it was a comparatively easy matter for the well-informed[209] to evade the operation of the Act.[210]

The Law Commission made the following recommendations.

(i) Eligibility to apply. The class of 'dependant' eligible to make an application under the Act should be widened.[211] A child who had been treated by the

---

[205] Law Commission, *First Report on Family Property: A New Approach* (1973) Law Com. No. 52, para. 33.

[206] *Ibid.*, para. 44.

[207] The Commission's rejection of legal rights of inheritance was conditional on the legislative acceptance of its proposals for co-ownership of the matrimonial home. No such legislation has ever been enacted.

[208] As a result of the interpretation of the law given by the Court of Appeal in *Wachtel v. Wachtel* [1973] Fam 72.

[209] M Albery, *The Inheritance (Family Provision) Act 1938* (1950) p. 67 contained a precedent for a lifetime settlement intended to defeat any possible application under the Act.

[210] See ELG Tyler, *Family Provision* (1971) pp. 24–28; CH Sherrin, 'Defeating the Dependants' [1978] Conv. 13.

[211] Law Commission, *Second Report on Family Property: Family Provision on Death* (Law Com. No. 61, 1974) para. 70.

deceased as a child of the family in relation to any marriage to which the deceased was a party should be entitled to apply[212] (so that step-children who have lived in the deceased's home would usually be within the class). All restrictions of age in applications by children and children of the family should be abolished.[213] Finally (and most radically) the definition of 'dependant' should be extended to include any person wholly or partly maintained by the deceased immediately prior to his death.[214] This would allow not only an elderly parent supported by the deceased to apply for provision but also a so-called de facto spouse.

(ii) Standard of provision. The 1938 Act was solely concerned with the issue of reasonable provision for the applicant's *maintenance*; and the 1971 Working Paper proposed that this policy remain unchanged.[215] But—apparently because the decision in *Wachtel* made it clear that the provision of maintenance was no longer the principal consideration in determining the financial consequences of divorce and that the divorce legislation gave the courts the 'widest possible powers' to 'effect an equitable sharing of the family assets'—the Law Commission decided to recommend that the claim of a surviving spouse to the family assets should be at least equal to that of a divorced spouse. (In the case of other applicants the question should remain simply whether reasonable provision was made for maintenance.[216])

(iii) Extent of the court's powers. The Commission recommended that the court should have powers over the property of the deceased similar to those which it had been given in divorce and other matrimonial proceedings.[217] In addition to the powers to order periodical payments and lump sums, there should be power to order the transfer or settlement of property and to vary

[212] The court was to have in mind a number of special factors in cases where the application was based on the fact of treatment as a child of the family: see Law Com. No. 61, para. 83; and see generally *Re Leach* [1986] Ch 226, CA; *Re Callaghan* [1985] Fam 1.

[213] Law Com. No. 61, para. 79.

[214] The qualifying condition was to be economic dependence on the deceased; and in one sense the more deserving the applicant—such as a person who had moved in to care for the deceased gratuitously during a long terminal illness—the less likely he or she would be to come within the statutory definition. The difficulties experienced by the courts in interpreting the relevant provision of the Inheritance (Provision for Family and Dependants) Act 1975—see eg *Jelley v. Iliffe* [1981] Fam 128, CA, and compare *Bishop v. Plumley* [1991] 1 WLR 582, CA—are to some extent attributable to the policy that the Act is solely concerned with providing maintenance for the dependant: see generally RD Oughton, *Tyler's Family Provision* (3rd ed., 1997) pp. 78–79, and 84–104.

[215] The Commission thought that to change the law to give a surviving spouse a claim for a fair share of property would introduce great uncertainty into the administration of estates, and that it would still leave the applicant dependent on the exercise of a discretion. The Commission believed that a power to award a surviving spouse a fair share of the estate would make it possible for any survivor who had received less than would have been received on intestacy to claim that he or she had not had a fair share: Law Commission, *Family Property Law* (PWP No. 42, 1971) paras. 3.6–3.9.

[216] Law Commission, *Second Report on Family Property: Family Provision on Death* (Law Com. No. 61, 1974) para. 28. In exercising its discretion the legislation was to provide detailed guidelines (although note the view of RD Oughton, *Tyler's Family Provision* (3rd ed., 1997) p. 25 that the Commission had failed to 'set out any really useful criteria').

[217] Law Commission, *Second Report on Family Property: Family Provision on Death* (Law Com. No. 61, 1974) para. 111.

'nuptial' settlements;[218] and the Commission recommended that the court should have power to order that funds from the estate be used to acquire property (for example, a house,[219] possibly smaller than the former matrimonial home) for the applicant.

(iv) *The property over which the court's powers are exercisable.* The Commission made detailed recommendations intended to enable the court to make orders over all the deceased's economically valuable interests, even if the interest in question would not normally form part of his estate on death. (For example, the court should have power in effect to bring the deceased's share of jointly owned property into his estate although technically such an interest would automatically accrue to the other joint tenant.[220]) The Commission also recommended the enactment of a sophisticated range of anti-avoidance measures.[221]

The Government did not waste time in introducing as a Government Bill what was in all save matters of minor detail[222] the Bill annexed to the Law Commission's Report[223] dated 29 July 1974. The Inheritance (Provision for Family and Dependants) Act[224] received Royal Assent on 12 November 1975 and came into force on 1 April 1976.[225] The parliamentary debates were well-informed and many issues of principle—should the restrictions on applications by children be removed? was it right to allow a person whose only claim was based on the fact that he or she had been supported by the deceased during his lifetime to launch what might be a blackmailing application?—were discussed, for the most part in an atmosphere of calm rationality. So too was the vexed question of whether cases heard in the High Court[226] should be allotted (as

---

[218] *Ibid.*, paras. 110–126.

[219] See eg *Re Hogg* [1979] Law Soc Gaz 476 where the judge ordered the executors to buy a house to be settled on the applicant for life or until she became financially dependent on another.

[220] See now Inheritance (Provision for Family and Dependants) Act 1975, s. 9, as applied on the interesting facts of *Jessop v. Jessop* [1992] 1 FLR 591, CA. The Law Commission (unconvincingly, in the author's view) refused to recommend that insurance policies written in trust (whether under the Married Women's Property Act 1882 or otherwise) be brought within the deceased life assured's estate: *Second Report on Family Property: Family Provision on Death* (Law Com. No. 61, 1974) para. 143.

[221] *Ibid.*, pp. 76–77. The statutory provisions and the policies to which they seek to give effect are critically examined by RD Oughton, *Tyler's Family Provision* (3rd ed., 1997) Chapter 7.

[222] The Parliamentary Counsel (who jealously reserve the right to consider critically the drafting of Law Commission bills) did make one or two minor changes—for example, a provision (s. 24) was inserted making it clear beyond doubt that any order under the Act would be effective to override the rights to *bona vacantia* of the Crown, the Duchy of Lancaster and the Duke of Cornwall.

[223] *Second Report on Family Property: Family Provision on Death* (Law Com. No. 61, 1974) Appendix 1, pp. 80–148. The explanatory notes attached to the Bill are particularly detailed and informative.

[224] The Bill was introduced on 13 February 1975: *Official Report* (HL) vol. 356, col. 1423.

[225] Inheritance (Provision for Family and Dependants) Act 1975, s. 27(3).

[226] The Act preserved the existing rule under which the county court had jurisdiction in cases where the net estate was no more than £5,000 (perhaps £23,000 in year 2000 values) but the Lord Chancellor was given power to raise this limit by order. In 1981 the power was exercised to raise the limit to £30,000 (SI 1981 No. 1636); and since 1991 the county court's jurisdiction has been unlimited: Courts and Legal Services Act 1990, s. 1; SI 1991, No 724 No official information about the use made of the different jurisdictions is available but RD Oughton, *Tyler's Family Provision* (3rd ed., 1997) pp. 345–346 and Appendix A are helpful.

the Law Commission had proposed)[227] to the Family Division, or whether the Chancery Division (which had enjoyed a monopoly over applications under the 1938 Act) should continue to have concurrent jurisdiction. (The Government's compromise, whereby applicants would have a choice,[228] was accepted.) But the real significance of the 1975 Act is that, with very little opposition,[229] the principle of entrusting the court with a wide discretion to adjust property rights on death in favour of the defined class of dependants was finally accepted. The move from rule to discretion evident in the way in which the financial consequences of marital breakdown are resolved by the Divorce Court seemed complete. But in one respect (and quite deliberately)[230] the Act created what might come to be seen as an anomaly. In the case of applications by a surviving spouse, the court's discretion was virtually unrestricted, and the widow or widower could expect to have a level of provision similar to that which would have been ordered on divorce. But in the case of all other applicants, the court's discretion was to be restricted to making provision for maintenance.

BUT HAS THE LAW KEPT PACE WITH SOCIAL AND ECONOMIC DEVELOPMENTS?

(i) Inflation and intestacy

Throughout the twentieth century, the consistent policy of reform to the law of intestate distribution has been to safeguard the position of the surviving spouse. But it soon became clear that this policy was in danger of being defeated by economic factors. Inflation eroded the real value of the amounts fixed by the Intestates' Estates Act 1952 for the surviving spouse's statutory legacy: between 1952 and 1966 the purchasing power of the statutory legacy fell by 50% (whilst the increase in the cost of housing over that period was somewhere between 60% and 80%).[231] In 1966 the £5,000 legacy was increased by 75% to £8,750 in line with the increase in house prices, while the £20,000 legacy was increased by only 50% to

---

[227] *Second Report on Family Property: Family Provision on Death* (Law Com. No. 61, 1974) paras. 251–257. The Family Division had had jurisdiction over applications by divorced spouses under what had been the Matrimonial Causes (Property and Maintenance) Act 1958; but when the allocation of jurisdiction had been debated in 1970 a proposal which would have transferred applications under the 1938 Act to the Family Division was rejected on a division: *Official Report* (HC) 4 May 1970, vol. 801, cols. 109–117.

[228] See the discussion in RD Oughton, *Tyler's Family Provision* (3rd ed., 1997) p. 347. This concludes that, notwithstanding the reputation enjoyed by the Family Division for greater generosity to applicants, reported cases show no significant difference between the two divisions in the making of awards.

[229] Note, however, the speech (drawing on his experience as a Chancery Division judge) made by Lord Wilberforce on the Second Reading of the 1975 Bill (*Official Report* (HL) 20 March 1975, vol. 358, col. 933): 'It is . . . a very difficult jurisdiction for the judge to exercise . . . when one is sitting there and trying to make up one's mind what is fair and right for a particular man, of whose life history one knows little, what is fair and right to do as regards his divorced wife, his widow, a possible mistress, illegitimate children—to decide how to distribute the merits and demerits between these people is painful and exceedingly difficult. I am by no means certain that one is able in many cases to reach the right result. . . . The difficulty of bringing about a good result remains intense'.

[230] See above, p. 509.   [231] Official Report (HL) 16 June 1966, vol. 275, col. 202.

£30,000 in line with the cost of living. But there was an obvious need to be able to respond speedily to changing money values; and in 1966 the Government took power[232] to increase the amount of the statutory legacy by order. This power was used five times between 1966 and 1993;[233] and in 1999 a surviving spouse was entitled to £125,000 if the deceased left issue and £200,000 if he or she did not. The policy remains that the surviving spouse should take the whole of all save the largest estates and be enabled to 'remain in the former matrimonial home'[234] and 'to have a sufficient surplus on which to live'.[235] It is true that there is something of a mystery surrounding the taking of decisions on the exercise of the power to increase the amount of the legacy;[236] and there are those who believe that the law still fails adequately to protect the needs of widows who, especially at a time of escalating property values, may find their entitlement on intestacy insufficient to permit them to stay in the former matrimonial home.[237] In 1989 the Law Commission recommended[238] that this problem be dealt with by giving a surviving spouse the whole of the deceased's estate whatever its size; but this simple solution attracted little support and has been rejected.[239] The problem of changing money values is thus dealt with after a fashion by the crude procedure of spasmodic (and unexplained) changes to the amount of the statutory legacy.

(ii) Demographic change

In 1952 there were 31,966 divorces in England and Wales; in 1999 there were 144,556.[240] In 1952, the possibility that a deceased's widow would have had

---

[232] Family Provision Act 1966, s. 1(1).

[233] The changes in the amount of the surviving spouse's statutory legacy are conveniently summarised in Sherrin and Bonehill, *Law and Practice of Intestate Succession* (2nd ed., 1994) pp. 217–218.

[234] The average price of a semi-detached house or bungalow in England and Wales in 2000 was £91,826; but there are significant regional variations. (In South East England, for example, the average was £132,132.) In deciding whether the statutory legacy will suffice to enable a surviving spouse to stay in the former matrimonial home the trend to joint ownership of property should be kept in mind: in many cases only 50% of the value of the house will be part of the deceased's estate, and the survivor will already own the other 50%.

[235] Official Report (HL) 1 July 1993, vol. 547, col. WA 38.

[236] 'Frankly, I have not yet settled a future policy. Wherever there is such a sum of money which can be altered by an order under an Act, it ought to be looked at once a year. Whether some other period would be better, I am not sure. Where you get the information from depends entirely, of course, on the nature of the sum of money. What has happened is that if it is a question of a fall in the value of money, I get the information from the Treasury, who know all about that; and if it is a question of the price of houses, there are various building societies which publish information . . .' (*Official Report* (HL) 16 June 1966, vol. 275, col. 220). It is not clear whether an annual review has in fact been carried out; changes in the prescribed amount were made at approximately five-yearly intervals, and they have been considerable.

[237] The Law Commission, *Family Law: Distribution on Intestacy* (Law Com. No. 187, 1989) para. 18.

[238] *Ibid.*, para. 33.

[239] See *Official Report* (HL) vol. 547, col. WA 38; and the debates on the Bill for the Law Reform (Succession) Act 1995, *Official Report* (HL) vol. 538, cols. 170–178, and vol. 561, col. 502; and see generally SM Cretney, 'Reform of Intestacy: The Best We Can Do?' (1995) 111 LQR 77 (on which the text draws).

[240] *Marriage and Divorce Statistics 1999*, Table 4.20.

little to do with the children of her husband's earlier marriage or marriages (and might indeed have been on distinctly unfriendly terms with them) had, as we have seen, already begun to worry those considering changes in the rules about intestate succession: the more the widow took, the less there would be for the children. With the increase in divorce, the problem has increased;[241] and it was this factor which largely accounted for the rejection[242] of the Law Commission's 1989 proposal[243] (itself made in defiance of public opinion)[244] that an intestate's widow should take the whole estate, leaving disappointed children to make a claim under the Inheritance (Provision for Family and Dependants) Act 1975.

A second demographic change of great importance in this context is the growth of long-term cohabitation. But in 1989 the Law Commission[245]— notwithstanding the views of a majority of the sample in a public opinion survey—rejected suggestions that a cohabitant should be entitled to share on a deceased partner's intestacy. The Commission pointed out that the rules dividing property between, for example, a surviving spouse and a surviving cohabitant would have to be very complex, and that any such rule would inevitably increase legal costs and delay the administration of estates since 'disputes could easily arise as to whether a particular individual was a cohabitant or not'. But the Commission favoured a more limited reform: it believed that justice could be achieved by including cohabitants within the class of 'dependants' entitled to apply for reasonable financial provision out of the estate of the deceased (whether testate or intestate) partner. The Law Reform (Succession) Act 1995 accordingly added people who had lived with the deceased in the same household as man and wife for the two years immediately preceding the death to the statutory list of those eligible to apply for reasonable provision out of the deceased's estate.[246]

---

[241] It has been estimated that half of all the children of divorcing parents live with the mother and her new husband and that one in fifteen live with their mother and the man with whom she is cohabiting: J Haskey, 'Children in Families Broken by Divorce' (1990) *Population Trends (No. 61)* (1990), p. 42. In those circumstances, it is all too easy for the children to lose contact with their father; and it is not surprising that the father's second wife should feel little obligation to transmit property she inherited from the deceased to his children. The problem may be exacerbated if the widow has had children by her marriage to the intestate: there are some 40,000 births to remarried women—about 5% of all births within marriage—each year: see *Population Trends (No. 70)* (1992) Table 11.

[242] *Official Report* (HL) 13 February 1995, vol. 561, col. 503 (Lord Mackay of Clashfern LC).

[243] The Law Commission: *Family Law: Distribution on Intestacy* (Law Com. No. 187, 1989) para. 33.

[244] At least in so far as reliance can be placed on the response to an attitude survey carried out for the Commission. This found that, faced with a hypothetical case of a man leaving a second wife, a former wife, and children, only 27% of the sample favoured the widow receiving the whole estate: The Law Commission: *Family Law: Distribution on Intestacy* (Law Com. No. 187, 1989) p. 11, note 73.

[245] *Ibid.*

[246] Inheritance (Provision for Family and Dependants) Act 1975, s. 1(1)(ba), as inserted by Law Reform (Succession) Act 1995. There is no need for such an applicant to establish any relationship of dependency on the deceased; and the relationship between this provision and that of Inheritance (Provision for Family and Dependants) Act 1975, s. 1(1)(e) may be one of some difficulty: see RD Oughton, *Tyler's Family Provision* (3rd ed., 1997) pp. 78–108.

Legal Consequences of Breakdown

This amendment by no means resolves all the difficulties[247] which the increase in second marriages and cohabitation outside marriage present. For example, the children of a divorced father may see all his estate pass to his wife of perhaps only a few days,[248] and if they are in reasonably prosperous circumstances it seems unlikely that they will be able to persuade the court that the financial provision made by the will or intestacy should be modified in their favour. Even more unfortunate is the fact that children have no right to claim provision out of the estate of the man with whom their mother has been living outside marriage,[249] however great their needs and however long the mother's relationship.

A particularly important question is whether it was right to restrict the court's function[250] to ordering the provision of maintenance. In a period of increasing affluence this rule may often mean that there is no prospect of an apparently deserving application succeeding. The decision of the Court of Appeal in *Re Jennings (deceased)*[251] demonstrates some of the problems:

The applicant was a 50-year-old who had been brought up from the age of four by his mother and step-father. There was no contact between father and son after the divorce and the only thing the father did for his son was to send him ten shillings in a birthday card on his second birthday. The father left the residue of his estate (which amounted to some £300,000 after payment of Inheritance Tax) to charities. The son had been successful in business; and the Court of Appeal held that accordingly no requirement for maintenance had been made out.[252]

There are difficult questions. Should the whole of a father's estate go to his (perhaps wealthy) wife of a few days leaving his children without any claim merely because they are in employment and cannot establish a need for maintenance? The textbook answer is quite clear and (up to a point) convincing: the court cannot be expected to re-write a deceased's will to provide legacies or

---

[247] See the fuller discussion in SM Cretney, *Law, Law Reform and the Family* (1998) pp. 267–279.

[248] Since marriage revokes a will.

[249] Although 'children of the family' are eligible to claim, the deceased must have been a party to a marriage and treated by the deceased as a child of the family *in relation to that marriage*: Inheritance (Provision for Family and Dependants) Act 1975, s. 1(1)(d); *J v. J (Property Transfer)* [1993] 2 FLR 56 (child had lived with mother and her cohabitant for ten years—no claim to apply for provision out of cohabitant's estate).

[250] Save in the case of applications by a surviving spouse: see Inheritance (Provision for Family and Dependants) Act 1975, s. 1(2)(a); p. 509 above.

[251] [1994] Ch 286, CA.

[252] The *ratio* of the case was that the applicant had not demonstrated that the deceased had been unreasonable in failing to make financial provision for the applicant, it being necessary for an adult child to demonstrate some special circumstance (typically a moral obligation) if he or she was to be eligible for consideration. The mere existence of the relationship of father and son was not a sufficient basis for the making of an order: see *per* Nourse LJ at [1994] Fam 286, 296. Insofar as the case seemed to suggest the necessity to establish a moral obligation on the part of the deceased it should be noted that more recent decisions have taken a flexible approach: see notably *Re Hancock (deceased)* [1998] 2 FLR 346; *Espinosa v. Bourke* [1999] 1 FLR 747.

awards for the deserving; and the ideology of freedom of testation—that 'an Englishman remains at liberty at his death to dispose of his own property in whatever way he pleases'[253]—may provide an adequate answer. But can that same approach be justified where it is not the deceased's will which controls the devolution of his property, but rather the default code of intestate succession, inevitably incapable of dealing adequately with the diversity of family circumstances for which the law now has to provide? Half way through the century, the Intestates' Estates Act recognised the need to allow the application of the intestacy rules to be questioned; and at the end of the century it is arguable that demographic changes have made it desirable to extend the scope of that questioning to the allocation of family assets, irrespective of whether those for whom a reasonable testator would have provided do or do not need maintenance. Essentially the question is whether there is a case for further extension of judicial discretion in order to allow the courts to achieve justice on the basis of factual relationships (rather than legal status); and it seems not to have been finally answered.

[253] *Re Coventry (deceased)* [1980] Ch 461 at p. 474, *per* Oliver J.

13

Unmarried Couples: The Legal Consequences of the Ending of the Relationship

INTRODUCTION

At the beginning of the twentieth century there were certainly unmarried couples—no doubt a significant number—who lived together in a factual relationship impossible to distinguish from matrimony.[1] In many cases, as we have seen, they may have been driven to do so because the earlier marriage of one or both partners could not be dissolved.[2] In others they may have had an ideological preference for legal independence.[3] But whatever the couple's motivation no one suggested that by living together the couple acquired the status of husband and wife or any of the rights which flowed from that status.[4] They could, of course, make their own private arrangements: the man might (and at certain levels of society often did)[5] enter into an enforceable[6] deed of covenant to make

---

[1] See K Kiernan, 'The Rise of Cohabitation and Childbearing . . .' (2001) 15 *International Journal of Law, Policy and the Family* 1, 2, and the sources cited.

[2] For example, Marian Evans (the writer 'George Eliot' 1819–1880) lived openly with George Henry Lewes for 25 years, and adopted the name Marian Evans Lewes. She apparently regarded their relationship as a true marriage, and it was ended only by Lewes's death. She was unable to marry Lewes: he was married, and could not divorce his wife because he had—by causing himself to be registered as the father of two of the four children she bore by another man—condoned her adultery. There were other cases—notoriously that of HRH the Duke of Cambridge (1819–1904)— where marriage was deemed socially impossible by reason of the couple's different family backgrounds.

[3] As advocated by a number of 'progressive' writers (such as HG Wells, Bertrand Russell and Bernard Shaw in the 1930s): see p. 251, note 12.

[4] As explained in Chapter 3, above.

[5] Not least because until 1965 (Finance Act 1965, s. 12) payments under a Deed of Covenant complying with certain requirements operated to transfer the amounts involved for tax purposes from the payer to the payee. To take a dramatic example, a payer liable to income taxes at 98% could put £1,000 into his partner's pocket at a net cost of only £20.

[6] The rule that a contract 'founded on an immoral consideration' was illegal and would not be enforced was not apparently regarded as a bar, and there is no reported twentieth century decision in which this issue has been raised in the circumstances envisaged in the text: compare, on the one hand *Pearce v. Brooks* (1866) LR 1 Ex 213 (rent due from prostitute for hire of carriage known by owner to be intended for use in her trade held not recoverable, as contract tainted with immorality); *Upfill v. Wright* [1911] 1 KB 506 (landlord debarred from recovering rent for flat used as residence for mistress, court refused to restrict application of rule to prostitutes) and *Walker v. Perkins* (1764) 1 WBl 517 (promise by man to pay woman money if she would become his mistress unenforceable) with, on the other *Heglibiston Establishment v. Heyman* (1978) 36 P&CR 351 (permitting cohabitants to reside not 'immoral user') and cases such as *Eves v. Eves* [1975] 1 WLR 1338 and *Tanner v.*

periodical payments to the other; *inter vivos* (ie lifetime) settlements of capital could be made,[7] as could wills;[8] whilst arrangements for children could be dealt with by the appointment of guardians.[9] But on the whole (and with one conspicuous exception) for much of the century family law was able simply to ignore the family outside marriage. (The conspicuous exception was the law of bastardy, under which a man could be ordered to provide a measure of financial support for the children of a relationship outside marriage; and this topic—the subject of substantial textbooks in the nineteenth and early twentieth centuries—is dealt with in Part IV of this work.)

Generally speaking, statisticians and demographers seem also to have given little attention to the existence of non-marital relationships, and there is little accessible information about the extent of the phenomenon of stable extra-marital relationships at the beginning of the twentieth century.[10] And if cases about the legal consequences of a relationship outside marriage came before the courts they gave no sign of wishing to erode the distinction between legal marriage and unmarried cohabitation: half way through the century the then Master of the Rolls[11] justified a decision denying a man any claim to succeed to his mistress's tenancy by asserting that it would be no bad thing to demonstrate that 'in the Christian society in which we live . . . the privileges which may be derived from marriage [are] not equally enjoyed by those living together as man and wife but who are not married'.

At the end of the twentieth century, things are very different. First, far more is known about the numbers of people living together outside marriage.[12] Since 1979 the official *General Household Survey* has routinely collected information

Tanner [1975] 1 WLR 1346 in which one cohabitant has successfully asserted a claim founded on agreement to an interest in property the legal title to which is vested in the other; and in *Tinsley v. Milligan* [1994] 1 AC 340 the House of Lords did not allow the fact that two women were living in a lesbian relationship to affect the rights arising in favour of one of them by way of resulting trust. However, it seems the courts are sometimes reluctant to find that an unmarried couple intended to make a binding arrangement: see *Layton v. Martin* [1986] 2 FLR 227, p. 521 below (claim by a woman to recover from the estate of a man whose mistress she had been for 13 years under an agreement promising her financial security on his death failed, because the judge held there had been no intention to create legal relations rather than on any ground of illegality); and also (for what appears to have been a particularly harsh decision on the facts) *Horrocks v. Foray* [1976] 1 WLR 230.

[7] Subject to the rule that provisions in favour of illegitimate children born after the date of the settlement would be void: see below, Chapter 15.

[8] Only after the enactment of the Inheritance (Family Provision) Act 1938 was a valid will vulnerable to claims by the deceased's legal wife and other 'dependants'.

[9] See below, Chapter 16.

[10] Analyses of parish registers have thrown light on the extent to which children were born in non-marital relationships at earlier periods: see P Laslett, K Oosterveen and RM Smith, *Bastardy and its Comparative History* (1980).

[11] Lord Evershed MR in *Gammans v. Ekins* [1950] 2 KB 328, 334.

[12] See J Haskey, 'Demographic Aspects of Cohabitation in Great Britain' (2001) 15 *International Journal of Law, Policy and the Family* 51, 56; K Kiernan, 'The Rise of Cohabitation and Childbearing outside Marriage in Western Europe' (2001) 15 *International Journal of Law, Policy and the Family* 1; J Haskey, 'Cohabitational and marital histories of adults in Great Britain' (1999) 96 *Population Trends* 13; K E Kiernan and V Estaugh, 'Cohabitation, Extra-Marital Childbearing and Social Policy' (*Family Policy Studies Centre, Occasional Paper 17*, 1993) Table 2.2.

about cohabitation; and it seems that by 1989 more than 10% of all men aged 25 to 34 and more than 12% of women aged 20 to 24 were cohabiting.[13] The proportion of men and women living together outside marriage grew rapidly in the last quarter of the century: the proportion of women of child-bearing age[14] not currently married who are cohabiting has more than trebled, from 9% in 1976 to 29% in 1998.[15]

For some time, the conventional view was that cohabitation was often a pre-lude to marriage, and that marriage was simply deferred whilst the couple assessed their compatibility. Statistics provided support for this view. Whereas in the mid-1960s only 5% of couples marrying had cohabited before doing so, by the mid-1990s the figure had risen to 70%. More than a fifth of couples who do marry give the same address when completing the registration particulars. But it now seems to be accepted that (leaving 'trial marriages' on one side) there has been a substantial increase in long-term cohabitation by couples who have no intention of marrying and never do so; and that the increase in cohabitation has taken place at the expense of the numbers marrying.[16]

Many unmarried couples have children together. More than a third of all live births in England and Wales are to unmarried parents, and in many of these cases the parents are in a cohabiting relationship of some stability: in 1996 nearly 60% of all extra-marital births were to parents living at the same address; and in nearly 80% of such cases the birth was registered jointly by both parents.

The pre-eminence of marriage for those first entering into a relationship seems to have disappeared within an interval of just over three decades. Cohabitation has been transformed from being statistically insignificant to a familiar and routine way of life chosen by three in every five couples for their first union.[17] The statement made by the Graham Hall Committee on Statutory Maintenance Limits[18] that it would be 'hard to envisage a society with a greater enthusiasm for marriage' coincided with the start of a steady and continuous decline, with marriage rates falling by three or four per cent each year;[19] and the predictions confidently made by official bodies in the 1960s that liberalising divorce would dramatically reduce the number of children born outside marriage have been dramatically falsified.

By the end of the century, these developments had been judicially acknowledged at the highest level;[20] and judicial attitudes seem to have reflected a

[13] K E Kiernan and V Estaugh, 'Cohabitation, Extra-Marital Childbearing and Social Policy' (*Family Policy Studies Centre, Occasional Paper 17*, 1993) Table 2.2.

[14] For this purpose taken as 18 to 49.

[15] See J Haskey, 'Demographic Aspects of Cohabitation in Great Britain'(2001) 15 *International Journal of Law, Policy and the Family* 51, 56.

[16] *Ibid.*   [17] Haskey, *op. cit.* at p. 59.

[18] (1968, Cmd. 5787) para. 22.   [19] See further pp. 33, 513, above.

[20] See *Barclays Bank plc v. O'Brien* [1994] 1 AC 180, 198; *Midland Bank plc v. Massey* [1994] 2 FLR 342. And in *Fitzpatrick v. Sterling Housing Association Ltd* [2001] 1 AC 27 the House of Lords, whilst denying that a homosexual couple can be regarded as living together 'as husband and wife' accepted that such a couple may (unlike two adults who share their home on the basis of asexual companionship and mutual support: *Carega Properties SA v. Sharratt* [1979] 1 WLR 928, HL) be

perception which would have seemed unthinkable in mid-century.[21] For example, in 1998 one Lord Justice of Appeal noted[22] that, as non-marital cohabitation became more open

'so attitudes towards it became less judgmental. That included the attitude of the courts, where notwithstanding that the encouragement of marriage as an institution remains a well-established head of public policy, the respect due to the sincerity of commitment involved in many such relationships is reflected in judicial terminology—terms like "partner" now being more generally used than the once-preferred references to "common-law spouse", "mistress" or even . . . "living in sin"'.

CHANGING ATTITUDES[23]

Although the change in approach was particularly dramatic in the 30 years following the 1969 divorce reforms (which have been judicially said to have made divorce available on demand thereby transforming marriage into a 'state into which and from which people choose to enter and exit')[24] it seems that it was the First World War which prompted some recognition of the hardship and injustice which might be caused by a rigid denial of any recognition of the claims of the unmarried couple to equality of treatment with the married. Men who responded to the call to serve their country were paid as little as seven shillings weekly (35 pence—around £10 in year 2000 values) at a time when the average industrial wage was perhaps six or seven times as much.[25] In those circumstances, it made little real sense for the soldier's wife to talk of enforcing her common law right to be maintained; but a system of separation allowances provided some support, and (subject to quite severe restrictions) it was decided that unmarried women who were being maintained by the soldier should be equally eligible for these allowances. In due course, provision was also made for the payment of pensions if the soldier were killed.[26]

But this somewhat grudging recognition of the needs of the soldier's family did not herald any general breakdown of the principle that rights and duties attached to the *status* of marriage, and that *factual* relationships were not to be equated with legal marriage. Indeed, although it is true that in 1921 the Unemployed Workers' Dependants (Temporary Provisions) Act allowed the

regarded as living together as members of the same family so that the tenant's lover qualified as successor to his deceased partner's tenancy.

[21] Cf. Lord Evershed's remarks in *Gammans v. Ekins* [1950] 2 KB 328, 334, quoted in the text to note 11, above.

[22] Waite LJ in *Fitzpatrick v. Sterling Housing Association Ltd* [1998] Ch 304, 308.

[23] This passage draws extensively on an unpublished Research Paper by Rebecca Probert, 'Cohabitation and the Law in the Twentieth Century'.

[24] *Bellinger v. Bellinger* [2001] 2 FLR 1046, 1082, *per* Thorpe LJ.

[25] See the uneasy debate in the House of Commons on 18 November 1914: *Official Report* (HC) vol. 68, col. 493 (A Steel-Maitland, Chairman of the Unionist Party and MP for East Birmingham).

[26] The significance of this was first recognised by S Parker, *Informal Marriage, Cohabitation and the Law* (1990). Relevant official papers are in PRO files PIN 15/907, 149, and 2573 and T161/213.

single insured unemployed worker an extra payment of 5/- in respect of a
'female person' dependent on him and living with him as his wife, the outraged
reaction to a backbench MP's suggestion that 'only the parson's fee' distinguished the married from the unmarried[27] made it clear that traditional values
were still strongly held. In 1927 the Conservative Government's Unemployment
Insurance Act removed the 'unmarried wife' from the list of those dependants
whom the legislation recognised:[28] the extension of benefit had (in the words of
the Blanesburgh Committee on Unemployment Insurance)[29] 'been a cause of
serious misgivings to many people and is . . . injurious to the credit of the system'. Thereafter, for almost half a century, 'living together as husband and wife'
was only equated with legal marriage when to do so would *reduce* entitlement
to state benefits[30] and it was only in the 1960s and 1970s that this principle[31]
began to be contested.

THE APPROACH TO REFORM: HESITANCY AND UNCERTAINTY

In one respect, the unmarried should have suffered no disadvantage as compared with the married. This was, paradoxically, because of the legal regime of
separation of property established for married couples by the Married Women's
Property Act 1882. It followed (so the House of Lords held in a series of cases in
the 1970s)[32] that any dispute about entitlement to property between husband
and wife had to be determined 'on the general principles of law applicable to the
settlement of claims between those not so related, whilst making full allowances
in view of that relationship'.[33] Husband and wife disputes about the ownership
of the family home—and virtually all the cases coming before the courts were

---

[27] *Official Report* (HC) 1 November 1921, vol. 147, col. 1579 (W Thorne).

[28] Women looking after the unemployed man's children were, however, still classed as 'dependants'.

[29] So the House of Commons was told: *Official Report* (HC) 1 November 1921, vol. 147, col.
1579.

[30] For example, the widow's pension payable under the Widows' Orphans' and Old Age
Contributory Pensions Act 1925 was not payable so long as she was living with a man as his wife:
see s. 21(1). The National Assistance Act 1948 followed this precedent; but the application of the
notorious 'cohabitation rule' provoked much criticism in the 1960s and later, whilst the investigations sometimes necessary aroused exceptional 'distress and resentment': see the *Finer Report*,
paras. 5.266–276; and the *Report of the Committee on Abuse of Social Security Benefits* (1973,
Cmnd. 5228).

[31] The *application* of the principle was inevitably difficult. The question whether a couple are or
are not 'married' does not require any investigation of their personal relationship or any question of
which of the traditional incidents of a marital relationship (for example, sexual relations: see *Re
Watson (deceased)* [1999] 1 FLR 878, where the judge emphasised the 'multifarious nature of marital relationships') are of the essence of a marriage; but in contrast the question whether a couple are
living together as man and wife does involve precisely that judgment, and great difficulty was found
in deciding (for example) whether a couple who rejected any notion of mutual financial dependence
could be regarded as living together 'as husband and wife'. For judicial interpretation see *Crake v.
Supplementary Benefits Commission* [1982] 1 All ER 498.

[32] See pp. 124–125, above.   [33] [1970] AC 777, 813, *per* Lord Upjohn.

about the home or other land—should therefore be decided by ordinary principles of property law. In principle, the question was: 'who owned the legal estate in the house?' and that could easily be answered because the law stipulated certain formalities for the creation and transfer of land and interests in land. The recorded legal ownership of the land only failed to provide the definitive answer if someone other than the legal owner could claim an interest under the equitable doctrines of implied resulting or constructive trusts. When could such a claim be successfully advanced? According to the House of Lords only when the 'full allowances' made for a couple's relationship indicated (for example) that they had intended to share the ownership. How would the court determine this? In principle by examining the *content* of the couple's relationship, not their legal status; and therefore the existence (or lack) of 'paperwork' should make no difference to the outcome, Two couples who had had a similar relationship should find that they had comparable property rights, irrespective of the fact that one couple was, and the other was not, legally married.

In practice, things did not quite work out in that way. The courts seemed much less reluctant to infer that a married couple must have intended to share ownership (as well as use) of their home than was the case with an unmarried couple. In *Burns v. Burns*,[34] for example, a couple lived together for 19 years and had two children. The mother gave up her job to look after the home and the family and she formally changed her name to 'Mrs Burns'. The court denied her any share in the proceeds of sale of the house. Similarly, in *Layton v. Martin*[35] a woman had lived with a man for five years (and been his lover for much longer). As the judge put it, the 'services she was expected to supply were, to all intents and purposes, those of a wife'. The man had offered to give her emotional security during his life and financial security on his death; and she had agreed to live with him on that basis. But—in a claim against her lover's executors—she got nothing. The judge held that the man's promise was not intended to create a legally binding contract.

It is true that decisions about property disputes between the married could also produce what seemed to be harsh results; but by the 1970s this was comparatively unimportant in practice. This was because the courts had, in the wake of the 1969 divorce reforms, been given wide statutory discretionary powers on divorce or after death to redistribute the couple's property.[36] A judge explained the effect when giving judgment in the case of an unmarried couple with assets of half a million pounds who lived together for 11 years and had two children.[37] Had they been married

'the issue of ownership would scarcely have been relevant because the law these days, when dealing with the financial consequences of divorce, adopts a forward-looking perspective in which questions of ownership yield to the higher demands of relating the means of both to the needs of each, the first consideration given to the welfare of children . . .'.

[34] [1984] Ch 317.   [35] [1986] 2 FLR 227.   [36] See Chapters 10 and 12, above.
[37] *H v. M (Property: Beneficial Interest)* [1992] 1 FLR 229.

Legal Consequences of Breakdown

But since they had not married, the issue of ownership was the only relevant consideration. And those who fail to establish an ownership claim will be left without remedy.[38] As the judge explained in another case:[39] 'If this were California, this would be a claim for palimony, but it is England and it is not. English law recognises neither the term nor the obligation to which it gives effect ... The courts possess neither a statutory nor an inherent jurisdiction to disturb existing rights of property on the termination of an extra-marital relationship however deserving the claimant.'

Such recognition as has been given to the claims of unmarried couples and their families has been exceptional and unsystematic. Attitudes have, it is true, changed: for example, in 1950[40] the courts refused to accept that a man who had for 20 years lived with a woman in a relationship which had all the incidents of a marriage short of the birth of a child could be regarded as a member of her family for the purpose of the Rent Acts; but a quarter of a century later the courts accepted that the meaning given to this expression had changed over the years,[41] and two decades later the House of Lords[42] was prepared to accept that a homosexual couple were entitled to the recognition denied in 1950 to a heterosexual couple. But legislation was needed to equate the legal position of a person 'living with the original tenant as his or her wife or husband' with that of the original tenant's spouse.[43]

Again, as already noted,[44] in 1975 the legislation allowing a deceased's 'dependant' to claim 'reasonable financial provision' from the estate was amended so that a person being maintained by the deceased at the time of death became eligible to apply to the court; and it was understood that this would often allow the survivor of a non-marital relationship to seek provision. But the need for an applicant relying on this provision to show that he had been economically dependent on the deceased marked a clear distinction between the widow or widower on the one hand (who qualified simply by virtue of marital status) and the unmarried partner on the other;[45] and only in 1995 was the legislation amended to allow the person living with the deceased as husband or wife to qualify on that basis alone.[46] Even then, there were differences: the

---

[38] Since the Law Reform (Succession) Act 1995 came into force, there may be a claim to meet a need for maintenance if the relationship has been ended by death.

[39] *Windeler v. Whitehall* [1990] 2 FLR 505.

[40] *Gammans v. Ekins* [1950] 2 328, CA.

[41] *Dyson Holdings Ltd. v. Fox* [1976] QB 503, CA.

[42] *Fitzpatrick v. Sterling Housing Association Ltd* [2001] 1 AC 27.

[43] Housing Act 1988, s. 39 and Sch. 4. The effect of so doing was to give the unmarried significantly more extensive rights of succession than those accorded to mere 'members of the family'.

[44] See Chapter 12, above.

[45] In effect, the greater the applicant's contribution to the partnership the less likely it was that he or she would qualify. However, in *Bishop v. Plumley and Another* [1991] 1 FLR 121 the Court of Appeal urged the application of common sense and criticised the use of 'fine balancing computations' to assess the balance between the parties' contributions.

[46] Law Reform (Succession) Act 1995, amending Inheritance (Provision for Family and Dependants) Act 1975. See above, p. 513.

unmarried (unlike the widow or widower) had not only to show that the relationship had continued for at least two years before the death, but (again unlike the widow or widower) were restricted to provision necessary for maintenance.

The first avowed legislative attempt to extend the law's protection to unmarried couples on a basis of equality with the married was made in 1976 by the Domestic Violence and Matrimonial Proceedings Act. Thereafter reform recognising the claims of the unmarried lost something of its novelty. In 1982 the Fatal Accidents Act was amended to give an unmarried spouse the right to recover compensation for the loss of financial support provided by a partner killed by the defendant's negligence; but the way in which this was done is of some significance. To succeed the claimant must, first, have been living in the same household as the deceased; secondly the claimant must have been living with the deceased 'as husband and wife'; and finally that relationship must have subsisted throughout the two years preceding the death.

It thus appeared to have become quite acceptable to give a measure of statutory protection to cohabitants who could to some extent be described as victims; but there was certainly no general principle of entitlement. And attempts to remedy injustice provoked opposition. In 1995 the Conservative Government was forced into a humiliating climb-down, withdrawing the Family Homes and Domestic Violence Bill in response to complaints that it eroded the distinction between marriage and other relationships. (It appears that a reference to the use of the Married Women's Property Act 1882 by the unmarried was—although in fact a narrow procedural provision—particularly inflammatory.) When the legislation was reintroduced the Government thought it prudent to include provisions emphasising that the unmarried had not demonstrated the commitment involved in marriage; and resisted attempts to reinstate the original provisions. And the legislation intended to reform the divorce law was liberally spiced with provisions asserting that the institution of marriage was to be supported and that all practicable steps should be taken to 'save' marriages which might have broken down.[47]

It is difficult to deny that, at the turn of the century, the law still fails to provide an adequate legal regime for couples who live together in a relationship which is factually similar to that of a married couple but do not have the legal status of husband and wife.[48] In 2002 the eminent lawyer peer, Lord Lester of Herne Hill QC[49] told the House of Lords that unmarried cohabiting couples 'face immense and distressing difficulties in securing legal recognition of their caring and enduring family lives', that they do not enjoy full rights to communal property, or the right to be treated as next of kin by state agencies such as

---

[47] Family Law Act 1996, s. 1.

[48] See C Gibson, 'Changing Family Patterns in England and Wales' in SN Katz, J Eekelaar, and M Maclean (eds.), *Cross Currents* (2000) pp. 32–34.

[49] Moving the Second Reading of the Civil Partnerships Bill, *Official Report* (HL) 25 January 2002, vol. 630, col. 1692.

hospitals in the event of serious illness, and that the survivor of a cohabiting couple cannot even register her partner's death or sign for his funeral. Each House of Parliament has given a Second Reading to Bills making provision for civil partnerships but neither is likely to make further progress in the immediate future. Officials are working on the problems of giving greater legal recognition to such marriage-like partnerships;[50] but the future remains uncertain. A telling indication of the sensitive state of opinion may be found in the work of the Law Commission: in 1993 the Commission undertook a review of the property rights of home-sharers, but although it appears that the legal research into this issue had long ago been completed[51] no Consultation Paper appeared.[52] Possibly the reason for this delay is to be found in the Commission's expressed awareness[53] that proposals which might be seen to support or encourage couples to enter into non-marital cohabitation arouse strong feelings which need to be taken into account. Perhaps (it seems to be thought) some injustice to the unmarried has to be accepted as the price of demonstrating that marriage is the only legal regime for cohabitation which the law will unequivocally recognise.

The Blair Government itself seems to speak with two voices on this issue: on the one hand marriage is to be supported, not least as 'the most reliable framework for raising young children';[54] but at the same time this is not to 'mean trying to make people marry, or criticising or penalising people who choose not to'.[55] In the circumstances it seems possible that anyone writing a history of family law in twenty-first century Britain will find that the struggle for legislative change is almost as long as that for reform of the divorce laws in the first 69 years of the twentieth century.

---

[50] See *per* Lord Williams of Mostyn: *Official Report* (HL) 25 January 2002, vol. 630, col. 1740.

[51] Law Commission, *Twenty-Ninth Annual Report 1994* (1995) Law Com. No. 232, para. 2.79.

[52] The Law Commission published a Discussion Paper, *Sharing Homes*, Law Com. No. 278 in July 2002. The Commission stated that the Paper was 'not a Consultation Paper in the usual format, nor was [the Commission] seeking responses'. The Paper emphasised that the Law Commission had not examined the issue of the rights and obligations of unmarried couples; and that the purpose of the Paper was confined to 'providing a legal framework for future public debate and consideration by the Government'.

[53] Law Commission, *Thirtieth Annual Report 1995* (1996) Law Com. No. 239, para. 6.10.

[54] *Supporting Families* (1998) para. 4.3.   [55] *Ibid.*

PART IV

CHILDREN, THE FAMILY AND THE STATE

One of the persistent images of Victorian family life is that of dutiful children willingly obeying their parents. As the Senior Judge of the Chancery Division put it in 1967,[1] the law and public opinion accorded respect to the husband as head of the family and it was 'thought to be the duty of wives to submit to their husbands and of children to obey their fathers—and, by and large, wives and children did what was expected of them'.

It is certainly true that the Law Reports contain striking illustrations of the principle that the law would uphold the rights of the paterfamilias, the father of the family. He was to be the master in his own house, and 'king and ruler in his own family'; and (save only in case of gross moral turpitude or abdication of his authority) not even the court had a right to interfere with the 'sacred right of a father over his own children'.[2] Thus:

Before their marriage Mr and Mrs Agar-Ellis had agreed that their children would be brought up as Roman Catholics. They separated; and Mrs Agar-Ellis continued to take the children to Roman Catholic services. The children went to confession and were confirmed by a Roman Catholic bishop. When the oldest child was aged 12 she and her sisters refused to go with their father to Anglican services. The father was displeased by the fact that his children were being 'indoctrinated' in Roman Catholic beliefs and practices and obtained an injunction to prevent the mother from defying his wishes.[3] He then took the children away from their mother and arranged for them to be looked after by clergymen and others. But when his daughter Harriet was 16 she asked to be allowed to spend her holidays with her mother instead of being moved around from one lodging to another. Mr Agar-Ellis refused; and an application was

---

[1] Sir Geoffrey Cross, 'Wards of Court' (1967) 83 LQR 200, 201.

[2] *Re Plomley* (1882) 47 LT (NS) 284; *Re Agar-Ellis* (1878) 10 Ch D 49, CA.

[3] *Re Agar-Ellis* (1878) 10 Ch D 49, the first round of the litigation about the children's religious education. Malins V-C held that a 'father is the head of his house, [that] he must have the control of his family, he must say how and by whom they are to be educated, and where they are to be educated . . . ' and indeed that 'principles of common sense and the principles of propriety . . .' dictated that no Court should interfere with the father's right: see *per* Malins V-C, at p. 57. The Court of Appeal refused to interfere.

made to the court. This was unsuccessful. The courts consistently refused to see or hear Harriet or the other children; and held that since the father had not been guilty of any wrong-doing[4] the court would not interfere with his legal right to control the education and upbringing of his children.[5]

Nor was this principle confined to the upper classes. A father had the right to inflict moderate and reasonable corporal punishment[6] on his children, and:

In 1908 the Home Secretary refused to take any action in a case where a magistrate told the father that the law did not allow him to order his 15-year-old son, convicted of indecent exposure, to be flogged and that there was only one alternative to the boy being sent to prison. This was for the father to exercise his parental right and within the court precincts administer 12 strokes of the birch to the boy who would—provided the gaoler reported that he had had a 'proper flogging'—then be set free. The father did as he was told.[7]

Almost by definition, issues or disputes about family life which come before the courts are untypical; but even so the law does seek to answer a number of important questions. Who is a child's parent, for example? What is the significance of the parents' legal status (whether they are married or not) on their relationship with the child and others? What in any event are the legal consequences of being a child's parent? What is to happen if a child's parents die, or for some other reason are not capable of providing the necessary care? Does the fact that

---

[4] For example, bringing up the children as 'infidels or atheists': *Shelley v. Westbrooke* (1817) Jac 266; or where the father has been guilty of gross immorality, as in *Wellesley v. Wellesley* (1828) 2 Bli (NS) 124 (where the main complaints about the father's conduct were that he was living in adultery and that he encouraged the children in the habit of profane swearing; and his unfitness to have the sole control of his children was evidenced by his having told their tutor that 'a man and his children ought to be allowed to go to the devil their own way if he pleases').

[5] *Re Agar-Ellis (No. 2)* (1883) 24 Ch D 317.

[6] These qualifications were important. In *R v. Hopley* (1860) 2 F&F 202 an Eastbourne schoolmaster, entrusted with the care of a 'dull' boy aged 13 or 14, obtained the father's written agreement to his subduing the boy's obstinacy by chastising him severely, if necessary 'again and again' even if the boy held out for hours. As a result of the beating, the boy died. Cockburn, C J directed the jury that 'by the law of England, a parent or a schoolmaster (who for this purpose represents the parent and has the parental authority delegated to him), may for the purpose of correcting what is evil in the child inflict moderate and reasonable corporal punishment, always, however, with this condition, that it is moderate and reasonable. If it be administered for the gratification of passion or of rage, or if it be immoderate and excessive in its nature or degree, or if it be protracted beyond the child's powers of endurance, or with an instrument unfitted for the purpose and calculated to produce danger to life or limb; in all such cases the punishment is excessive, the violence is unlawful, and if evil consequences to life or limb ensue, then the person inflicting it is answerable to the law, and if death ensue it will be manslaughter'. The schoolmaster was convicted of manslaughter and sentenced to four years' penal servitude.

[7] *Hansard's Parliamentary Debates* (4th Series) 12 October 1908, vol. 194, col. 34. Perhaps this practice was not uncommon: in 1931 the Home Office—seeking (unsuccessfully) to remove the remaining powers of magistrates to sentence juveniles to be whipped—noted that if a juvenile court 'thinks a child would be better for some corporal punishment it can, in most cases, secure that such chastisement is given by the parent': HO45/14715, Memorandum on Draft 1931 Children and Young Persons Bill. It also appears that in a number of cases children were whipped on the basis that their parents authorised the punishment and then the court discharged the boy.

the parents' own relationship breaks down affect matters? What is the role of the State in influencing how children are brought up and in taking action when things go wrong? And, overhanging all these matters, there is the question of the role of the courts: when and how should the courts be prepared to intervene in family life?

The twentieth century was a period of great change in social attitudes and political philosophy. Both case law and statute reflected those changes to a greater or lesser extent. There was what has aptly been described[8] as a 'cascade of legislation' dealing with the welfare and protection of children; and the commitment of the 1945 Labour Government to the creation of a welfare state also increased the flow of statute and other regulatory material. Scientific and medical developments (notably in the field of genetics and what has become known as 'Human Assisted Reproduction') necessitated responses from the courts and Parliament. The result is that the law relating to children and the family has become enormous in volume and exceedingly complex in nature. For these reasons, the account of the historical development of the law which is practicable in the context of a comprehensive study of the law and the family must necessarily be selective and in some respects abbreviated.

Chapter 14 deals with the question of parentage: who in law is the child's parent? Chapter 15 deals with the question of how far the parents' legal status affects the child: when is a child legitimate and when illegitimate, and what consequences flow from this distinction? Chapter 16 deals with the question of identifying the person entitled to take decisions and exercise parental authority over children, and the circumstances in which the extent of this authority may be questioned in divorce and wardship proceedings—and supplanted by the child acquiring legal authority to act for himself. Chapter 17 deals with the institution of legal adoption, as introduced into English law in 1926. The remaining three chapters of this part deal with the circumstances in which the State has the power or duty to intervene in a child's upbringing and the effect of such intervention.

---

[8] By Sachs LJ, *Hewer v. Bryant* [1970] 1 QB 357, 371, CA.

14

Parentage

INTRODUCTION

Legally, identifying a child's parents was important. Entitlement to property might depend on a claimant's relationship; and only a parent was under a legal liability to maintain a child and legally entitled to exercise parental authority over a child. But at the beginning of the twentieth century only the most rudimentary scientific evidence was available to resolve a dispute about parentage; and it was often said (only half-jokingly) that paternity was a matter of opinion rather than fact. In contrast, there was rarely any dispute about maternity: someone would usually have seen a woman giving birth and (provided the child could be identified as the baby she had borne)[1] there could be no real dispute. But even so there were still occasionally disputes.[2]

DISPUTED MATERNITY

The Slingsby family owned large settled estates in Yorkshire. The family did not approve of the life tenant's marriage to a widow. Mrs Slingsby suffered a number of miscarriages and the marriage was childless for more than nine years; but in the spring of 1910 (when she was 41) Mrs Slingsby became pregnant. She claimed that a son was subsequently born to her in San Francisco, California (whither she had gone, unaccompanied by her husband). The family uncovered many inconsistencies in Mrs Slingsby's accounts of what had happened and became convinced that Mrs Slingsby's pregnancy had ended in a miscarriage, that she had never borne a

---

[1] An important qualification as a number of notorious cases demonstrate. Of these the most celebrated is the so-called *Tichborne* case in which (so the courts held) one Arthur Orton, the son of a Wapping butcher, falsely claimed to be Sir Roger Charles Tichborne Bt. Legal proceedings lasting over seven years ended in the claimant's conviction for perjury and his being sentenced to 14 years' imprisonment: see D Woodruff, *The Tichborne Claimant* (1957) and M Gilbert, *The Claimant* (1957) and the works therein referred to. Another celebrated case was the claim by Anna Andersen to be the Grand Duchess Anastasia. However, DNA tests carried out in the 1990s excluded the possibility of her being a member of the Russian Imperial family, whilst further DNA tests provided a substantial amount of evidence about the fate of Tsar Nicholas and other members of his family murdered at Ekaterinburg in 1918: see J Klier and H Mingay, *The Search for Anastasia* (1995).

[2] The most notorious example is that of the birth in 1688 of a child, James Francis Edward Stuart, to the wife of King James II, Mary of Modena. Notwithstanding the fact that the birth took place in the presence of 30 witnesses (including the Lord Chancellor, the Lord Privy Seal, and the Lord President of the Council) rumours that the child was supposititious and had been smuggled into the royal bed in a warming pan were circulated by those who saw the birth of an heir to the Roman Catholic king as a serious blow to the prospects of re-establishing a protestant monarchy.

child at all, and that the child she claimed to have borne was in fact the illegitimate child of a chauffeur. The Court of Appeal and the House of Lords[3] held that Mrs Slingsby had perjured herself, that the whole case she had put forward was one of fraud, and accepted the evidence of private detectives employed by the family that the child had been handed over to her in response to her newspaper advertisement seeking a child for 'adoption'. The child was supposititious and not entitled to succeed to the family estates as a Slingsby.

DISPUTED PATERNITY: AFFILIATION PROCEEDINGS

In contrast, disputes about *paternity* were commonplace. Most of the litigation occurred in so-called affiliation proceedings, that is applications for maintenance made by unmarried mothers under the Bastardy Laws Amendment Act 1872.[4] The legislation provided[5] that a 'single woman'[6] could take out a summons against the man she alleged to be the father of her child, and that the magistrates (having heard the evidence) could adjudge the man to be the 'putative father' of the child and make an order[7] against him for the child's maintenance and education.

The mother was required to establish paternity only on the balance of probabilities rather than the stricter 'beyond reasonable doubt' basis required in the criminal law, but statute (unusually in civil proceedings)[8] imposed[9] a requirement that the mother's evidence be 'corroborated in some material particular by other evidence to the satisfaction of the . . . justices'. The rule requiring corroboration was intended to 'prevent men being at the mercy of profligate women'[10] or at least to provide some protection against 'wicked or unfounded charges which might so easily be made if the evidence of the woman without corroborative testimony were sufficient'.[11]

---

[3] The trial judge, Bargrave Dean J, had upheld the child's claim to be the legitimate child of Mrs Slingsby and her husband, but the appeal courts took the view that the judge's view of the evidence was (*per* Lord Loreburn) 'completely erroneous'.

[4] The main principles of this legislation remained in force until the coming into force of the Family Law Reform Act 1987.

[5] Bastardy Laws Amendment Act 1872, s. 4.

[6] The expression extended to a married woman (a) who has lost the common law right to be maintained by her husband (for example by committing uncondoned adultery or having deserted him), and (b) who was in fact separated from him.

[7] The amount could not exceed five shillings weekly: s. 4 (25 pence, perhaps £15 in year 2000 values). Although this monetary limit was raised from time to time the maximum sum the courts could award remained small: see *Report of the Departmental Committee on Statutory Maintenance Limits* (Chairman, Jean Graham Hall, 1968, Cmnd. 3587) p. 88. That Report led to the abolition of any statutory restriction on the amount which could be ordered: Maintenance Orders Act 1968.

[8] See the Law Commission's Report, *Blood Tests and Proof of Paternity in Civil Proceedings* (Law Com. No. 16, 1968) p. 5. It has been said that the requirement for corroboration carried overtones of the criminal law into affiliation proceedings: *Re A (A Minor) (Paternity: Refusal of Blood Test)* [1994] 2 FLR 463, 468, *per* Waite LJ.

[9] Bastardy Laws Amendment Act 1872, s. 4.

[10] *Mash v. Darley* [1914] 3 KB 1226, 1235, *per* Phillimore LJ.

[11] *Thomas v. Jones* [1920] 2 KB 399, 405, *per* Lord Reading CJ.

Corroborative evidence is evidence, independent of the applicant's own state-ment, which shows or tends to show that the applicant's story is true:[12] classic examples are letters written by the man admitting paternity expressly or impliedly or his having made financial provision for the child or that the defen-dant had given different accounts of his behaviour on different occasions.[13] Even evidence that the parties had been seen to behave with a degree of famil-iarity consistent with an intimate relationship was capable of constituting corroborative evidence. As Lord Chief Justice Goddard put it in 1947:[14]

'For many years . . . it has been the practice, and very often the only way of giving cor-roborative evidence in these cases, to prove that the two young people concerned were, perhaps, a courting couple or sweethearts or, at any rate, were associating together on terms . . . of intimacy . . . [In the case before the court, the magistrates] were satisfied on the evidence before them that these young people were, and had, for a long period of time, been associating together on the closest terms of intimacy and affection, visiting places of amusement and refreshment, and going to dances together, and being in the company of each other in the evenings and that the [defendant] visited the girl's home, which means, I suppose, that her parents were allowing [him] to go there because . . . the parties were obviously on courting terms. It should be added that there was no sugges-tion that the respondent was having an association with any other man, a very important matter in these cases . . .'

What was required was evidence that tended to make it probable that the appli-cant's story was true. Something more than evidence of opportunity was needed. Thus:

In *Burbury v. Jackson*[15] a 15-year-old girl, employed to do light jobs at Crew Farm Kenilworth, claimed that she had been seduced by the farmer's son and that he had frequently made love to her in a barn in the farmyard. She also said that she had never slept with anyone else. The justices held evidence from the girl's mother that she had on several occasions seen the two together in the barn to be sufficient corroboration of her story, and made an order. The Divisional Court held that they had been wrong: all that the mother's evidence did was to show that it was *possible* the couple had had intercourse at the relevant time, whereas corroborative evidence had to show that it was *probable* they had done so. If (said the Lord Chief Justice) the man and woman 'were seen in the neighbourhood of a wood or other dark place where they had no occasion to be' that might possibly be corroborative evidence.[16] But in the present case the parties' work required them to be in the barn; and they had a reason (other than

---

[12] *R v. Baskerville* [1916] 2 KB 658, 667, CCA; *Simpson v. Collinson* [1964] 2 QB 80, 94, *per* Sellers LJ.

[13] *Mash v. Darley* [1914] 3 KB 1226, CA.

[14] *Moore v. Hewitt* [1947] 1 KB 831; and for a later discussion of the authorities see *McVeigh v. Beattie* [1988] Fam 69.

[15] [1917] 1 KB 16, KBD. This case was distinguished in *Moore v. Hewitt* (above).

[16] As might be the fact that a man and woman of 'different social positions' had been seen together in country lanes: *Harvey v. Anning* (1902) 87 LT 687.

love-making) to be in the same place. There was thus no corroboration of the applicant's claim, and the case should have been dismissed.

But the fact that the supposedly corroborative evidence was consistent equally with action dictated by kind and humane considerations did not prevent the court from making a finding of paternity: provided there was evidence which was *capable* of constituting corroboration the question of the inference which should be drawn from the material before the court was one for the court to decide in the light of its assessment of the plausibility of the witnesses:

In *Thomas v. Jones*[17] Miriam Jones went to work for a 43-year-old bachelor as servant and housekeeper at his farm in Llwynbeadd. On 11 May 1919 (the day before her period of service ended) she was ill and moaning. The farmer made a fire and gave her some brandy and tea. A doctor was called and a baby girl was born. The farmer allowed Miriam and her child to stay at the farm for some five weeks thereafter. On 14 July she wrote to him: 'Dear sir, I just take the priviledge [*sic*] of writing these few lines to you hoping you are well as it leaves me at present. I should like to know what you intend doing in regard to the child, Do you intend paying or not . . . you know the child is yours . . . , Your's truly, Miriam Jones'. The farmer (who denied ever having had intercourse with Miriam) did not reply. The magistrates held that the farmer's actions on the morning of the birth, coupled with his actions in allowing her to stay on at the farm for a period (said by the Divisional Court to have far exceeded the 'usual period of recovery in such cases') and in not answering the letter were capable of corroborating her evidence. They made an order, and the Divisional Court (by a majority) accepted that the magistrates had been right to accept that the mother's evidence had been corroborated. That being so, the decision was for the magistrates: did they believe the man or the woman? The magistrates had believed the woman, and that decision had to stand.

The most effective way of destroying the mother's case was to establish that she had also had intercourse with another man at the relevant time[18] but the percentage of applications which were successful was high.[19] It is difficult to resist

---

[17] [1920] 2 KB 399.

[18] This was a common defence, not surprisingly since the fact that two or more men could have been the father of her child would have been fatal to a claim against either: *Re A (A Minor) (Paternity: Refusal of Blood Test)* [1994] 2 FLR 463, 476, *per* Sir Ralph Gibson. Hence (as the 9th)— 1882—edition of the authoritative *Stone's Practice for Justices of the Peace*, p. 469 put it, if 'the mother has fixed the time when the connection took place which resulted in the birth of the child, she may be cross-examined to the fact that another person had connection with her on or about the time fixed by her, from which connection the birth of the child might have resulted; and if she deny the fact, evidence is admissible to contradict her'. Not surprisingly this led to unedifying scenes in which women were subjected to hostile cross-examination intended to prove that they were promiscuous or at least had had intercourse with a man other than the man named in the application.

[19] There was a substantial number of applications: in the period 1900/1904 7,895 (of which nearly 80% were successful). The number of applications peaked at 11,862 (of which 82% were successful) in 1919: OR McGregor, L Blom-Cooper, and C Gibson, *Separated Spouses, A Study of the matrimonial jurisdiction of magistrates' courts* (1970) Table 1.

the feeling that if the mother's evidence that she had had intercourse with the man concerned at the relevant time remained unshaken and there was something which could be classified as corroboration an order would be made.[20]

In affiliation proceedings the mother was by definition a 'single woman'[21] and her child therefore necessarily illegitimate. These factors were no doubt thought to justify the Justices' comparatively undemanding approach to making a finding that a man was the child's putative father.[22] But things were very different in the superior courts where the outcome might be to 'bastardise a child' (as the expression was) who would otherwise be legitimate. Many[23] of the more sensational cases involving parentage were in the Divorce Court: the fact that the husband was not the father of a child born to his wife was the clearest evidence of adultery.

The husband had to overcome two obstacles. First, the common law applied a strong *presumption* that a married[24] woman's husband was the father of any child born or conceived during the marriage. Thus:

[20] There is evidence that a significant number of men refused to make payments under affiliation orders because they denied paternity: for example, in 1922 a memorandum to the Home Office from the Shrewsbury Prison Visiting Committee expressed concern at the number of men imprisoned for non-payment who denied paternity. But HB Simpson (see Biographical Notes) recorded his view that a man does not 'suffer great hardship by being made to pay for [a child] if he has had immoral relations with the mother . . . Anyone who indulges in irregular sexual relations takes this risk . . . . Many of them may well have been seduced by the women, but it would be totally impossible in a very large proportion of bastardy cases to judge which of the parents is most culpable . . . '. In any event (Simpson thought) imprisonment might 'at least serve as a warning to others': PRO HO 45 11190/37149, 30 November 1922.

[21] This expression had a technical meaning: see note 6, above.

[22] It appears that by the mid-1960s the issue of paternity was only contested in some 25% of affiliation cases: *Separated Spouses, A Study of the matrimonial jurisdiction of magistrates' courts*, by OR McGregor, L Blom-Cooper, and C Gibson; *Report of the Departmental Committee on Statutory Maintenance Limits* (Chairman, Jean Graham Hall, 1968, Cmnd. 3587) para. 185.

[23] But not all: see eg the Scottish case of *Gardner v. Gardner* (1877) 2 App Cas 723, HL, a man and woman who had been courting for some years married when she was some eight months pregnant. The wife had told the husband that she had been raped; but she later told him that she had had intercourse with a shepherd employed by her brother. Husband and wife went to a hotel in Edinburgh for the delivery of the child Mary. Two days after her birth, Mary was handed over to a nurse. The husband provided funds to maintain Mary until she was 16 or 17; but for 22 years neither he nor the wife saw her. The husband (apparently influenced by the belief that an adverse finding would be inconsistent with his remaining an elder of the Kirk) denied paternity and instituted proceedings to prevent Mary from claiming otherwise. Husband and wife had consistently denied having had intercourse before the marriage. But the House of Lords refused to upset a decision of the Court of Session in Mary's favour. Although the presumption that the husband is the father of a child born to a married woman was weaker in Scotland than in England and Wales, the couple had had the opportunity to have intercourse at the relevant time, and the wife's statements about the circumstances leading up to her pregnancy had been inconsistent.

[24] At the time of the child's birth or conception. The common law allowed those fearful that a widow would falsely claim to have been pregnant at the date of her husband's death to have the matter determined by the writ *de ventre inspiciendo*: see Blackstone, *Commentaries on the Laws of England* (4th ed., 1770, Vol. 1) p. 456.

In *Watson v. Watson*[25] the wife had been committing adultery with a lodger over a period of years and had herself claimed that the lodger was the father of her child. But she refused to allow scientific paternity tests[26] to be carried out. The judge held that if he had been able to decide the case on the usual civil basis of 'balance of probabilities' he would have found the lodger to be the father. But the presumption of law meant that the judge had to be satisfied beyond all reasonable doubt; and for that reason the husband must be held to be the child's father. As another judge had put it[27] at the beginning of the century, the fact that a wife 'had committed adultery with one, two, or twenty other men' was insufficient to displace the presumption of the husband's parentage.

Secondly (and specifically) although this presumption that the husband was the father of his wife's child could be rebutted by evidence[28] establishing beyond reasonable doubt[29] that the husband could not be so, the law for many years[30] refused in the interests of public decency to allow either party to give evidence that they had not had intercourse at the relevant time.[31] Thus:

In *Russell v. Russell*[32] the husband convinced a jury that he had never had intercourse with his wife. She had borne a child, and must therefore have committed adultery. The House of Lords held that the husband's evidence about the

---

[25] [1954] P 48.   [26] See below.
[27] *Gordon v. Gordon and Granville Gordon* [1903] P 141.
[28] If a decree of judicial separation was in force the court would presume from that fact that the parties had not had intercourse at the relevant time; but this did not apply where there was merely a separation agreement: *see Ettenfiled v. Ettenfield* [1940] P 96, CA; *Parishes of St. George's v. St. Margaret's Westminster* (1706) 1 Salk 123.
[29] Not merely evidence establishing this on a balance of probabilities: see *Gordon v. Gordon and Granville Gordon* [1903] P 141. Contrast the view of Lord Denning in *Re L* [1968] P 119 but note that the other two Lords Justice expressly disagreed. Yet, whatever the theory, the courts' attitudes to what would suffice to rebut the presumption changed over the years. As Sir John Leach V-C put it in *Head v. Head* (1823) 1 Sim and St 151 the 'ancient policy of the law of England remains unaltered. A child born of a married woman is to be presumed to be the child of the husband, unless there is evidence, which excludes all doubt, that the husband could not be the father. But, in modern times, *the rule of evidence* has varied. Formerly it was considered that all doubt could not be excluded unless the husband were *extra quatuor maria* [beyond the four seas]. But, as it is obvious that all doubt may be excluded from other circumstances, although the husband be within the four seas, the modern practice permits the introduction of every species of legal evidence tending to the same conclusion. But still the evidence must be of a character to exclude all doubt . . .'. The courts first of all accepted evidence of physical impossibility (as where it was proved that the husband was impotent or sterile); and then, more controversially, they allowed themselves to draw the inference that it was *morally* impossible for the couple to have had intercourse: see below, and the extraordinary case of *Morris v. Davies* (1837) 5 Cl & F 163 where proceedings started in 1812 were only disposed of after three trials by jury, and the proceedings in the House of Lords cover more than 130 pages in the Law Reports.
[30] Ie from 1924 to 1949, the period between the House of Lord's decision in the *Russell* case and the statutory abolition of the so-called rule in *Russell v. Russell* by the Law Reform (Miscellaneous Provisions) Act 1949.
[31] *Ettenfield v. Ettenfield* [1940] P 96, CA. The rule in *Russell* was justified on the basis that evidence of access was 'irrelevant as proving that which the law presumes; and where it tends to show non-access it offends against public morality, decency, and policy': SL Phipson, *The Law of Evidence* (2nd ed., 1898).
[32] [1924] AC 687.

parties' sexual relationship should not have been admitted. There was no other evidence sufficient to justify a finding of adultery against the wife. The decree nisi obtained by the husband was accordingly rescinded, and in 1926 the High Court made a declaration that the child was the legitimate child of the marriage.[33]

The law thus prevented the courts from hearing evidence from those best qualified to say what had actually happened; but it apparently allowed judges to decide that the circumstances were such as to make it a moral impossibility that husband and wife should have had intercourse at the relevant time:

In *The Aylesford Peerage*[34] the question was whether a child, born five years after his parents' separation, was entitled to succeed to the husband's peerage. Lord Bramwell explained the facts and the inference he drew from them as follows:

'The wife, under the influence of a strong passion . . . for Lord Blandford, had left her husband's house to live in a state of adultery with Lord Blandford. The husband, knowing of that, had taken his children from her, had given up all intercourse with her, had entered into a deed of separation by which he and she were to live separate, and had endeavoured to free himself from the marriage that bound them together . . . [F]or your Lordships to entertain a doubt as to the case would be to suppose it possible that this unhappy lady while living in a state of adultery with Lord Blandford, for whom she had this passion, could permit her husband, what one may call her nominal husband, to have sexual intercourse with her, and that he himself, insulted as he must have felt himself to be . . . could have intercourse with her which he knew he was sharing with Lord Blandford. People will commit immoral actions, but they would never, I think, do anything so nauseous as what I have suggested as possible; and the very feeling, the very passion that caused the immoral action to be done, almost precludes the possibility of such a course of conduct as I have supposed.'

It is true (as explained elsewhere in this book) that during the two World Wars[35] the fact that the wife of a soldier serving overseas had given birth to a child could and often did form the basis of many divorce petitions. But that was because the husband's service records provided virtually irrefutable evidence that he could not possibly be the father of the wife's child and it was not necessary to rely on evidence from the parties that they had not had intercourse at the relevant time. But in other cases the courts, lacking any reliable scientific evidence, were faced with an impossibly difficult task[36] and were driven to rely

---

[33] *Russell (GDE)(By his guardian) v. The Attorney-General* (1926) *The Times*, 29 July. Fifty years later the Committee of Privileges of the House of Lords refused to allow this issue to be reopened even though scientific techniques for determining parentage had greatly improved over the years: see *The Ampthill Peerage* [1977] AC 547.

[34] (1885) 11 App Cas 1.   [35] See eg *Fearn v. Fearn* [1948] 1 All ER 459.

[36] In the *Russell* case the jury failed to agree after an eight-day trial in 1922: *The Times*, 22 July 1922; and see generally SM Cretney, *Law, Law Reform and the Family* (1998) Chapter 4. In the second trial (lasting 11 days) the jury found that the husband was not the child's father: *Russell v. Russell and Mayer* (1923) *The Times*, 17 March; but the House of Lords held that the evidence on which that verdict was based should not have been admitted: see below.

on such doubtful material as the resemblance[37] between the child and the alleged father.[38]

THE DEVELOPMENT OF SCIENTIFIC TESTING

(i) Blood groups

In 1900 a crucial scientific breakthrough was made: the Austrian scientist Karl Landsteiner[39] demonstrated that the red blood cells of some individuals contained different chemical substances from the blood cells of others; and all blood could be classified into a small number of groups. These characteristics are transmitted from one generation to another in accordance with recognised principles of genetics:

'[A] comparison of the characteristics of a child's blood with that of his mother and a particular man may show that the man *cannot* be the father ... [and] if it is known that at the material times the mother had had intercourse only with H (her husband) and X. and the blood test excludes H but not X, then X must be the father.'[40]

The courts began to accept such evidence in cases where paternity was relevant. The first reported case appears to be *Wilson v. Wilson otherwise Jennings* in 1942:[41]

A husband petitioned to have his marriage annulled on the ground that the wife was, at the time of the marriage, pregnant by another man; and an expert witness gave evidence that the parties' blood groups established that the husband could not be the father of the child the wife had born. The evidence was not disputed, and the judge granted a decree of nullity.

[37] In each of the two *Russell* trials the child was produced for inspection by the jury in support of the wife's belief that he looked like the husband. The husband was invited by the wife's counsel to move his head so that his ears (the formation of which was evidently thought to be strikingly similar to the child's) were clearly visible to the jury. The child's grandmother Lady Ampthill was called to assert that there was 'no resemblance at all' between the husband and the child. See generally SM Cretney, *Law, Law Reform and the Family* (1998) p. 101.

[38] See also *Burnaby v. Baillie* (1889) 42 Ch D 282, 290, where there 'was evidence that the child bore a strong resemblance to [the alleged adulterer], but other witnesses said there was no such likeness'.

[39] See Biographical Notes.

[40] Law Commission Report on *Illegitimacy* (Law Com. No. 118, para. 5.2). For further information on the medico-legal background see GW Bartholomew, 'The Nature and Use of Blood-Group Evidence' (1961) 24 MLR 313 and Appendix B to the Law Commission's Report on *Proof of Paternity in Civil Proceedings* (Law Com. No. 16, 1968).

[41] (1942) LJ 129, 226. The first case in which blood test evidence was led in a divorce case to establish that the husband could not be the father of a child born to the wife (and that she must therefore have committed adultery) appears to be *Liff v. Liff (orse Rigby)* [1948] WN 128. Blood group evidence had been received in criminal cases (for example, to prove that blood stains on the accused's clothing were not those of the victim) some years previously: see *R v. Blakeman* (1932) 76 SJ 138.

But there were many problems in making wide use of blood tests as a means of determining parentage in legal proceedings. Of these the most obvious lay in the fact that for a satisfactory result it was essential to have samples not only from the child but also from the adults involved. What was to happen if an adult refused to provide a sample, or if a parent refused to allow samples to be taken from the child? These problems began to be widely appreciated in the 1960s;[42] and in 1966 the judges of the Probate Divorce and Admiralty Division suggested that the Law Commission undertake a review. The recommendations in the Commission's Report, *Blood Tests and Proof of Paternity in Civil Proceedings*[43] were given statutory effect by the Family Law Reform Act 1969.

The 1969 Act was skilfully drafted to make blood testing available to establish parentage[44] whilst at the same time recognising concerns about the undesirability of compelling people to submit to the invasive procedure of taking a blood sample. The Act[45] provided that in any civil proceedings[46] in which the paternity of any person has to be decided the court could give a direction for the use of tests.[47] But failure to comply with such a direction (unlike failure to comply with a court *order*) does not constitute a contempt of court punishable by fine or imprisonment. Indeed, the Act specifically provides that in general a sample shall not be taken without the consent of the person concerned.[48] But the

---

[42] In 1963 the Court of Appeal held that the court had no power to order an adult to submit to blood tests: *W v. W (No. 4)* [1964] P 67. In *Re L* [1968] P 119 the Court of Appeal held that the court had power, in the exercise of its inherent jurisdiction over children, to order a blood sample to be taken from a child for testing in cases where the child's future custody was in issue. On 23 July 1970, however (ie after publication of the Law Commission's *Report* No. 16, but before the Family Law Reform Act 1969 came into force on 1 March 1971) the House of Lords rejected the view that the power to direct a test on a child should only be exercised when the child's future custody might be affected by the outcome, and held that it was generally in a child's interests for the truth to be determined and that it would be wrong to suppress evidence which could be made available unless the court was satisfied that in the particular circumstances of the case blood testing would be against the child's interests: *S v. S; W v. Official Solicitor* [1972] AC 24.

[43] Law Com. No. 16, 1968.

[44] The Act did not prevent blood test evidence being put before the court even if no direction had been given and the procedures laid down in the Act had not been complied with: see the remarkable case of *Re Moynihan* [2000] 1 FLR 113, HL, in which the mother received Human Assisted Reproduction treatment at a clinic in Los Angeles and thereafter bore a child. Some years later the husband had attended a Harley Street clinic and blood samples were taken. The House admitted evidence based on the testing of those samples that the husband could not be the father of the child concerned, and the child's claim to the peerage therefore failed.

[45] s. 20.

[46] The Child Support Act 1991—an ambitious statutory scheme intended to facilitate the enforcement of maintenance obligations against absent parents—provided that no assessment should be made against a person who denied parentage unless a finding of parentage had been made in certain specified proceedings; and it appears that in many cases—some 3,000 in the Act's first year of operation: *Child Support Agency Annual Report, The First Two Years*, p. 11—parentage was an issue. The Act provided a procedure for application to the court to determine the issue, and such an application constituted 'civil proceedings' for the purpose of making a blood test direction: Child Support Act 1991, s. 27; and see *F v. Child Support Agency* [1999] 2 FLR 244.

[47] The Act and regulations made under it established procedures to ensure that tests were properly carried out with appropriate safeguards against personation etc.

[48] s. 21(1).

court is empowered to draw such inferences from a refusal as it thinks fit;[49] and in *Re A (A Minor) (Paternity: Refusal of Blood Test)*[50] the Court of Appeal held that if a claim were made against someone who could possibly be the father, and that person chose to exercise his right not to submit to be tested, the inference that he was the father would (in the absence of very clear and cogent reasons for the refusal) be 'virtually inescapable'. In that case:

A prosperous businessman refused to undergo a test because the mother had been working as a prostitute and there were known to be two other men who might on the facts equally be the father. He claimed it would be unreasonable and unjust to put him alone at risk of having paternity conclusively established against him.[51] But Waite LJ said that any man who is unsure of his own paternity and harboured the least doubt as to whether the child he is alleged to have fathered may be that of another man now has it within his power to set all doubt at rest by submitting to a test. The accuracy of scientific testing made it impossible for any man in such circumstances to be forced against his will to accept paternity of a child whom he does not believe to be his.[52]

The 1969 Act also adopted the philosophy that it is generally in a child's interests to have the truth determined:

In *Re H (Paternity: Blood Test)*[53] the child's mother was adamantly opposed to samples being taken because she regretted the association she had had with another man after her husband's vasectomy. It was said that the mother wanted to expunge and treat the relationship almost as if it did not exist. But the Court considered that it would be better for the child to know that he had two 'fathers' rather than to 'leave a time-bomb ticking away'.

---

[49] s. 23(3).   [50] [1994] 2 FLR 463, 473, CA.

[51] In affiliation proceedings, at a time 'when scientific knowledge did not enable proof, based upon blood tests, to be given as to which of two men, both of whom had sexual intercourse with the woman at the relevant time, was the father, the woman's acknowledgment that two or more men could have been the father would have been fatal to the claim against either': *Re A (A Minor)(Paternity: Refusal of Blood Test)*[1994] 2 FLR 463, 476, *per* Sir Ralph Gibson. For this reason the courts had not allowed a woman to choose between two or more men with whom she had had intercourse, much less take successive proceedings: see eg the Scottish case of *Robertson v. Hutchison* (1935) SC 708. In contrast (so Sir Ralph Gibson thought) there was no reason after the 1969 Act had made blood test evidence available why a woman should not be free to take proceedings against 'any number of men against whom the evidence [such as that she had had intercourse with him at the relevant time] would justify the making of a direction for use of blood tests': *ibid.*

[52] A similar approach was taken in cases in which parentage was an issue under the Child Support Act 1991: see *F v. Child Support Agency* [1999] 2 FLR 244.

[53] [1996] 2 FLR 65. Contrast *Re F (A Minor) (Blood Tests: Parental rights)* [1993] Fam 314, a man applied for a direction that tests be carried out in an attempt to establish that he was the father of a child born to a woman with whom he had had a brief affair. The mother and her husband were reconciled, and were bringing the child up as the child of their marriage. The Court of Appeal held that the application had been rightly rejected because the stability of the family unit on which the child's security depended might be disturbed by the outcome of tests.

The 1969 Act provided[54] not only that samples could be taken from a consenting person aged 16 or over[55] but also from a child under that age provided that 'the person who has the care and control of him consents'. But this seemed to give a parent with care and control the right to refuse to permit a sample being taken from the child; and some judges were tempted to use procedures of doubtful validity[56] in the interests of settling parentage issues. The matter was resolved by legislation:[57] a child may be tested wherever the court considered it to be in the child's interests for this to be done.

(ii) DNA testing

The 1969 Act was passed at a time when blood group testing worked negatively and could only prove directly that the child could not possibly be the son or daughter of a particular person (although increasingly sophisticated analyses of blood samples would often in fact provide positive evidence that it was *possible* and sometimes indeed *highly probable* that the two were parent and child).[58] Moreover, the Act only allowed directions to be given in respect of blood samples. At much the same time research[59] into deoxyribonucleic acid or DNA (which carries genetic information from generation to generation) enabled tests on any human sample containing DNA (and not only blood) to establish a person's parentage positively in many cases and, provided that the tests have been carried out under proper conditions, without doubt. In 1987, the legislation was amended[60] to empower the courts[61] to give appropriate directions for the taking of bodily samples in order to obtain reports of the scientific evidence about an individual's parentage; and the function of testing was redefined. No longer were the tests to be directed primarily[62] to ascertain whether a man was or was

---

[54] s. 21(3).

[55] Ie rather than restricting the power to give a valid consent to adults—those of 18 or more.

[56] Contrast *Re R (Blood Test: Constraint)* [1996] 1 FLR 312, Hale J (where the court, purporting to exercise its inherent jurisdiction directed the child be handed over to the Official Solicitor who would then give the necessary consent) with *Re O and J (Paternity: Blood tests)* [2000] 1 FLR 418 where Wall J expressed the view that reform was a matter for Parliament).

[57] Child Support Social Security and Pensions Act 2000, s. 83.

[58] See eg *Turner v. Blunden* [1986] Fam 120 (where the respondent was not excluded, but the Report stated that 99.8% of men in a random sample would be excluded). Such evidence pointed to the respondent as the parent on far more than a balance of probabilities and was thus capable of corroborating the applicant's evidence for the purpose of affiliation proceedings.

[59] JD Watson, *The Double Helix: A Personal Account of the Discovery of DNA* (1968) gives an absorbing account of some of the research.

[60] Family Law Reform Act 1987, s. 23; Children Act 1989, s. 89; Child Support Social Security and Pensions Act 2000, s. 82.

[61] Whether on the application of a party or on the court's own initiative.

[62] The Law Commission had noted that if a large number of individual characteristics were found to be common to the child and the man alleged to be the father this could justify the court in making a finding: see *Report on Illegitimacy* (Law Com. No. 118, para. 5.2); and the 1969 Act required the Report, in cases in which tests did not exclude the person concerned from being the father, to assess the 'value, if any, of the results in determining' whether he was in fact the father: Family Law Reform Act 1969, s. 20(2)(c).

not excluded from being the child's father. Instead, the question was to be whether the tests showed that the person concerned was or was not the child's father or mother. In short, the legislation now recognises that, where the necessary samples are available, genetic testing will usually enable parentage to be established with positive certainty.[63] This is a profound revolution in forensic practice.

ARTIFICIAL INSEMINATION AND OTHER TECHNIQUES OF HUMAN ASSISTED REPRODUCTION

So far, it has been assumed that a child's legal parents are his or her *genetic* parents, that is, the man and woman who provided the genetic material (the egg and sperm, or 'gametes') which led to the child's conception and birth. It is true that the procedure of legal adoption has, since 1926, recognised that the *legal* parents of a child may in certain circumstances not be the genetic parents, but that recognition was both hesitant and exceptional. Lawyers knew perfectly well that men or women might well think of the foster parents who had cared for them from infancy as their 'real' parents; but for the common law it remained true that parentage concerned genetics. The law would not recognise social or psychological parentage as sufficient to constitute the legal relationship of parent and child: genetic factors alone determined the identity of a child's legal parents.[64]

But what was the position if the child's conception had occurred, not as a result of sexual intercourse, but by artificial insemination, that is by the manual introduction of sperm into the mother's cervix?[65] Did the common law rule apply (in which case the donor of the sperm—occasionally the husband but more often an anonymous third party donor—would be the child's legal father)? If so, the child born as the result of donor insemination (AID)[66] would have the

---

[63] *Re A (A Minor) (Paternity: Refusal of Blood Test)* [1994] 2 FLR 463, 472, *per* Waite LJ. Blood testing will make recourse to legal presumptions about parentage in cases of dispute much less frequent than in the past. In addition to the presumption that the husband is the father of a married woman's child (see above) it is rebuttably presumed that the man whose name is entered as being the child's father in the Register of Births is in fact the father, whilst the fact that a person has been found to be the father of a child in proceedings under the Children Act 1989 (and certain other statutes) creates a rebuttable presumption that he is indeed the child's father: Civil Evidence Act 1986, as amended by Courts and Legal Services Act 1990, Sch. 16, para. 2.

[64] *Re B (Parentage)* [1996] 2 FLR 15, 21, *per* Bracewell J. It does not follow that social or psychological parentage is not often determinative in determining who should have the care of a child: see *J v. C* [1970] AC 668, HL; and Chapter 16 below.

[65] *Ibid.* The *Report of the Departmental Committee on Human Artificial Insemination* (Chairman, The Earl of Feversham DSO: see Biographical Notes) (1960, Cmnd. 1105)—hereafter cited as the *Feversham Report*—paras. 12–13 states that the first reported case of successful human artificial insemination (in that case of a woman with the semen of her husband who was not able to have sexual intercourse) took place in 1790; and that the first successful insemination of a woman with semen taken from a donor took place in Philadelphia USA in 1884.

[66] In contrast, the child born as the result of insemination by the husband would be the legitimate child of the marriage.

same legal status as a child conceived in adultery and would be illegitimate and subject to the legal disadvantages to which illegitimacy for long gave rise.

Only after World War II did this and the other legal consequences of artificial insemination begin to attract much attention. It is true that in the 1930s there had been some discussion in this country of the possibility of using artificial insemination as a means of 'improving the race';[67] but the practice remained virtually unknown to the British public.[68] Things were different in the United States, however, where artificial insemination had become quite widely practised and apparently a large number of children had been conceived as a result of this treatment.[69] In the 1940s a small number of infertility specialists in England began to use donor semen to bring about a wife's pregnancy in cases in which prolonged investigation had proved the wife to be fertile and the husband infertile;[70] and apparently by the late 1950s some 100 children a year were being conceived in this country in this way. It also appeared that the practice was becoming more widespread.[71]

The Churches and other groups, drawing at first on accounts of the American experience, began to interest themselves in the moral and legal problems[72] to which artificial insemination gave rise;[73] and it appears that estimates (mostly

[67] *Feversham Report*, para. 19. The fact that eugenics was at this time a matter of public discussion in this country seems often to be overlooked. Note that in 1934 the *Report of the Departmental Committee on Sterilisation* Cmd. 4485 accepted that there was an 'overwhelming preponderance of evidence' in favour of some measure of sterilisation (albeit not to be compulsory) and the Committee accepted the utility of sterilisation as a 'measure of social hygiene' (para. 71). Equally, in the years immediately following World War II, progressive and liberal commentators advocated measures designed to discourage the 'breeding of children by certain sub-normal categories of parents' whilst also expressing concern that the 'future happiness and greatness of our people could not be assured if we were to continue to draw as large a proportion of our children as at present from parents less well endowed than are their fellows as regards health ability and uprightness of character': Eva M Hubback, *The Population of Britain* (1947) pp. 14–15. In 1944 the Government had set up a *Royal Commission on Population*, whose *Report* (1949, Cmd. 7695) criticised the 'cult of childlessness and the vogue of the one child family' as 'symptoms of something profoundly unsatisfactory in the Zeitgeist of the inter-war period' which might be connected with the 'sophistications and complacencies which contributed to the catastrophe of the second world war': para. 362.

[68] *Feversham Report*, para. 20.

[69] The *Feversham Report* suggested that as many as 10,000 AID children had been born in the United States: para. 14.

[70] *Feversham Report*, paras. 19–23. It appears that 'very occasionally' AID was used in cases where the husband suffered from severe hereditary disease, likely to be transmitted to children.

[71] *Feversham Report*, paras. 22, 23.

[72] These included whether the fact that a wife underwent AID treatment without her husband's consent constituted adultery or otherwise gave him grounds for divorce. The *Royal Commission on Marriage and Divorce* (1956, Cmd. 9678) thought it inappropriate to deem such conduct 'adultery' but unanimously recommended that acceptance by a wife of artificial insemination by a donor without the consent of her husband should become a new and separate ground for divorce': para. 90. The question whether acceptance of artificial insemination by a wife could constitute adultery was given further prominence by the decision of the Scottish courts in *Maclennan v. Maclennan* 1958 SLT 12, and it was this which influenced the Government to set up the Feversham Committee: see para. 1.

[73] See E Carpenter, *Archbishop Fisher, His Life and Times* (1991) p. 391; *Artificial Insemination: the Report of a Commission appointed by His Grace the Archbishop of Canterbury* (1948). The Commission considered that artificial insemination with donated semen 'involves a breach of the marriage. It violates the exclusive union set up between husband and wife. It defrauds the child

greatly exaggerated) of the number of AID children gave rise to considerable public anxiety.[74] Eventually,[75] in 1958, the Government set up a Departmental Committee, chaired by the Earl of Feversham, to enquire into the practice and its legal consequences and 'to consider whether, taking account of the interests of individuals involved and of society as a whole', any change in the law was necessary or desirable.[76]

The Feversham Committee[77] viewed the practice of AID with something approaching repugnance. It considered that the practice was in the interests neither of the individuals concerned nor of society as a whole, and concluded that society would be better off without AID. The Committee was concerned that publicity for the practice was likely to stimulate demand, and considered that AID treatment should be discouraged.[78] But the Committee stopped short of recommending that the State should seek to regulate the practice or even that it should be criminalised. In fact demand for AID increased[79] and the supply of the necessary genetic material was greatly increased by the development of techniques for freezing donated sperm and retaining it in sperm banks.[80] In 1968 the Labour Government decided that AID treatment should in principle be available within the National Health Service.[81]

---

begotten, and deceives both his putative kinsmen and society at large. . . . For the child there must always be the risk of disclosure . . . of the circumstances of his conception.': p. 58. The Commission accordingly judged AID to be wrong in principle and contrary to Christian standards; and it recommended that the practice of AID should become a criminal offence.

[74] *Feversham Report*, para. 2.

[75] The issue of human artificial insemination was first raised in the United Kingdom Parliament by Lord Brabazon of Tara on 28 July 1943: see *Official Report* (HL) vol. 128, col. 817. The Government spokesman (evidently taken somewhat by surprise that the debate extended to insemination of humans as well as animals) said that the issues were being 'closely watched': col. 833. There were further debates on 16 March 1949: *Official Report* (HL) vol. 161, col. 386 (when the Government, whilst undertaking to keep the matter under review, refused to set up an official enquiry) and on 26 February 1958: *Official Report* (HL) vol. 207, col. 926.

[76] *Feversham Report*, para. 1.

[77] See *Feversham Report* Part II, and especially para. 223.

[78] It specifically recommended that there should be no amendment of the laws relating to legitimacy or birth registration such as might improve the legal position of the AID child: para. 187. It recommended that a husband who had not agreed to his wife receiving AID treatment should be entitled to take divorce or other matrimonial proceedings: para. 117 (although the Committee did not believe a wife should be entitled to take such proceedings on the ground that her husband had donated semen for AID treatment without her consent): para. 195.

[79] By 1982 there were apparently more than 1,000 AID conceptions each year: see *Report of the Committee of Inquiry into Human Fertilisation and Embryology* (Chairman, Dame Mary Warnock, 1984, Cmnd. 9314) (hereafter cited as the '*Warnock Report*') paras. 4.7–4.8.

[80] In 1960 (when the Feversham Committee reported) no method had yet been developed for preserving human semen without impairing its fertilising power; and, as the Committee noted, the discovery of satisfactory cyropreservation techniques would make the task of obtaining donated semen very much easier. However, the Committee had reservations about the implications of such developments: they 'would mean that the practitioner was no longer personally responsible for ensuring that the donor was suited to the couple. He would not be acquainted with the donor, and the "bank" would not be acquainted with the couple': *Feversham Report*, para. 41.

[81] *Warnock Report*, para. 4.7.

Science did not stand still in other respects. Research into the possibility of creating live human embryos outside the human body had dramatic successes; and in 1978 a child (Louise Brown) was born as the result of such *in vitro* (ie in a glass test tube or other vessel) fertilisation.[82] But other techniques for alleviating the problems of infertility did not necessarily involve any advanced or novel scientific procedures. In particular, in the 1980s commercial enterprises sought to exploit the making of surrogacy arrangements for profit and the practice of surrogacy[83] was widely publicised.

The rapid development of scientific techniques for what is conveniently described as Human Assisted Reproduction and the publicity given to both 'test-tube babies' and to surrogacy led the Thatcher Government to establish a Committee, chaired by Dame Mary Warnock,[84] to consider the 'social, ethical and legal implications of recent, and potential developments' in this field. The Committee reported in 1984; and although the relevant professional medical bodies had done a great deal to regulate practice[85] it was clear that legislation was necessary. After a 'difficult, emotional and delayed passage' through Parliament,[86] the Human Fertilisation and Embryology Act 1990 established an Authority with extensive powers to control by licensing and otherwise the provision of treatment and services.[87]

For present purposes, the Act[88] is significant because it codified the law about parentage and created some exceptions to the common law principle that legal parentage means genetic parentage. It is true that the woman who bears a child will, at the child's birth, always be regarded as the child's legal mother[89] and

---

[82] *Warnock Report*, para. 1.1.

[83] 'Surrogacy is the practice whereby one woman (the *surrogate mother*) becomes pregnant, carries and gives birth to a child for another person(s) (*the commissioning couple*) as the result of an agreement prior to conception that the child should be handed over to that person after birth. The woman who carries and gives birth to the child is the surrogate mother, or "surrogate". She may be the genetic mother ("partial" surrogacy—ie using her own egg) or she may have an embryo—which may be provided by the *commissioning couple*—implanted in her womb using *in-vitro fertilisation* (IVF) techniques ("host" or "full" surrogacy)'. The commissioning couple 'are the people who wish to bring up the child . . . They may both be the genetic parents, or one of them may be, or neither of them may be genetically related to the child'. The commissioning mother may provide the egg; the genetic father may be the husband or partner of the commissioning mother, or he may be an anonymous donor, or he may even be the husband or partner of the carrying mother': *Surrogacy: Review for Health Ministers . . .* (Chairman, Professor Margaret Brazier, 1998, Cm. 4068) Annex A.

[84] See Biographical Notes.

[85] See 'The Legal Regulation of Infertility Treatment in Britain' by Ruth Deech, Chairman of the Human Fertilisation and Embryology Authority: see Biographical Notes, in SN Katz, J Eekelaar and M Maclean, *Cross Currents* (2000) p. 165.

[86] Deech, *op. cit.* p. 167.

[87] For an excellent succinct account of the regulatory framework and of the issues to which it gives rise see 'The Legal Regulation of Infertility Treatment in Britain' by Ruth Deech in SN Katz, J Eekelaar and M Maclean, *Cross Currents* (2000) p. 165.

[88] The Law Commission had investigated the issue of legal parentage of children born following artificial insemination in its Report *Illegitimacy* (Law Com. No. 118, 1982) Part XII. The Commission's recommendations about legal parentage were implemented in the Family Law Reform Act 1967, s. 27. The *Warnock Report* adopted the same policy: see below.

[89] Human Fertilisation and Embryology Act 1990, s. 27; *The Ampthill Peerage* [1977] AC 457.

that the Act adopts the general principle that the father of a child is in principle the person who provides the sperm which results in conception.[90] But this principle for identifying the legal father is subject to an important exception: the husband of a woman who is artificially inseminated (or had been implanted with an embryo not created from the husband's sperm) will be treated as the father of a child, unless it is proved that he did not consent to the treatment;[91] and a similar principle applies to an unmarried couple where sperm has been used in the course of 'treatment services' provided for a man and woman together under the licensing regime established by the 1990 Act 1990.[92]

It seems that at the turn of the century there were 7,000 or so births each year as a result of some officially recorded form of human assisted reproduction, but the majority of those do not involve the gametes of any third person.[93] The legislation clarifies the issue of legal parentage; whilst experience has shown that the regulatory system dealing with (the often exceedingly difficult)[94] issues which raise public fears and affect the family and personal safety has been said[95] to have 'been more of a success than a failure'. None the less, difficult issues—not least the question whether the child conceived as a result of AID should have rights comparable with those given to an adopted child to information about his or her genetic parentage—remained unresolved.

[90] *Re Q (Parental Order)* [1996] 1 FLR 369, 370, *per* Johnson J; *Re B (Parentage)* [1996] 2 FLR 15, 21, *per* Bracewell J.

[91] Human Fertilisation and Embryology Act 1990, s. 28(2).

[92] Human Fertilisation and Embryology Act 1990, s. 28(3). Conversely the legislation (in an attempt to protect donors participating in recognised infertility treatment from the legal responsibility which they would otherwise bear as father of a child at common law) provides that a man who donates sperm at an officially licensed centre is not to be treated as the child's father: s. 28(6)(a).

[93] Figures given in *Human Fertilisation and Embryology Authority Seventh Annual Report, 1998*, Tables 3.14–3.16, 3.20, suggest that less than 10% of the children born following Assisted Reproduction treatment (AID and IVF) have third-party genetic parents.

[94] For an informative account, see Ruth Deech, 'The Legal Regulation of Infertility Treatment in Britain' in SN Katz, J Eekelaar and M Maclean, *Cross Currents* (2000) pp. 168–186.

[95] By Deech, *op. cit.* p. 186.

15

Children's Legal Status: Legitimate or Illegitimate?

INTRODUCTION

The common law of England (like virtually all other legal systems) distinguished between *legitimate* children, recognised as full members of the family, and *illegitimate* children or *bastards*.[1] But the common law was, in one respect, much more severe than the canon and civil laws: those laws recognised that a child, born illegitimate, could acquire the status of legitimacy if his parents married; whereas for the common law it was an 'indispensable condition'[2] that a child could only be legitimate if he were born[3] after his parents' marriage.

An illegitimate child was not necessarily[4] *socially* disadvantaged:[5] it has been said[6] that countless 'children of the mist played happily in Whig and Tory

---

[1]   'Why bastard? Wherefore base?
      When my dimensions are as well compact,
      My mind as generous, and my shape as true,
      As honest madam's issue? Why brand they us
      With base? with baseness? bastardy, base, base?'

(Shakespeare, *King Lear*, Act 1, Scene 2.). Notwithstanding such eloquent pleas, the term 'bastard' with its disparaging overtones of being spurious or base-born was used in the legislation dealing with the financial consequences of illegitimacy down to the Bastardy Act 1923; whilst even in 1966 the *Report of the Committee on the Law of Succession in Relation to Illegitimate Persons* (1966, Cmnd. 3051) used the term 'bastard' to refer to an illegitimate person believing that this 'correct legal description' would avoid 'confusion in eye or ear between legitimate and illegitimate' as well as tending to brevity: para. 9.

[2] Blackstone's *Commentaries on the Laws of England* (4th ed., 1770) Book 1, p. 454. There were certain limited exceptions to this principle: see J Jackson, *Formation and Annulment of Marriage* (2nd ed., 1969) p. 42.

[3] The crucial date was that of the marriage: it did not matter that the child must have been conceived before the marriage: *Birtwhistle v. Vardill* (1834) 2 Cl & F 571, 591, *per* Lord Brougham.

[4] For example, HRH Field Marshal the Duke of Cambridge (1819–1904, Commander in Chief of the British Army 1856–1895) lived for 50 years with 'Mrs Fitzgeorge' and had three children by her. Their 'marriage' was (as all concerned well knew) absolutely void by reason of the provisions of the Royal Marriages Act 1772: see G StAubyn, *The Royal George 1819–1914* (1963). But the children appear to have had a happy upbringing, and they all had successful careers in the public service (which, in the case of Admiral Sir Adolphus Fitzgeorge and Colonel Sir Augustus Fitzgeorge, are recorded in *Who's Who*). OR McGregor, L Blom-Cooper, and C Gibson in *Separated Spouses, A Study of the matrimonial jurisdiction of magistrates' courts* (1970) p. 169 give other examples and conclude with the reminder that at the end of the nineteenth century 'Keir Hardie had made his way to the political leadership of the sternly respectable labour movement despite his illegitimate birth' and that the public revelation of Ramsay MacDonald's illegitimacy did not damage MacDonald's political career. By 1970 85% of those interviewed in an attitude survey agreed that 'illegitimate children are not social outcasts these days': Law Commission Report, *Illegitimacy* (1982, Law Com. No. 118) p. 6.

nurseries where they presented no threat to the property or interest of heirs'. But the majority of illegitimate children did suffer poverty and the administration of the Poor Law (upon which many such children were dependent for survival) was often harsh. Even for the favoured few not affected by poverty, the legal disadvantages of illegitimacy were considerable; and the fact that the illegitimate child was legally different may have reinforced the 'stain and stigma' of illegitimate birth.[7] In effect, the illegitimate child was legally an outcast.[8] As Blackstone put it:

The rights which appertain to a bastard 'are very few, being only such as he can *acquire*; for he can *inherit* nothing, being looked upon as the son of nobody, and sometimes called *filius nullius*, sometimes *filius populi*[9] . . . The incapacity of a bastard consists principally in this, that he cannot be heir to any one, neither can he have heirs, but of his own body; for being *nullius filius*, he is therefore of kin to nobody, and has no ancestor from whom any inheritable blood can be derived.'[10]

From the beginning of the twentieth century there was general agreement about the need for reform of the law affecting children born outside marriage; and the establishment of the National Council for the Unmarried Mother and Her Child in 1918[11] evidenced the strong feelings held by many people about the plight of such women and children.[12] Over the years the legal position of children born to parents not married to one another has been greatly improved. First, the Legitimacy Act 1926 allowed a child, in certain circumstances, to be legitimated by the marriage of the parents. Secondly, legislation gradually removed many of the legal disadvantages formerly associated with illegitimacy in respect of matters such as maintenance and succession rights. Finally, the Family Law Reform Act 1987 sought to remove the 'label' illegitimate from the statute book. But no legislation has been wholly effective in remedying the eco-

---

[5] See M Pinchbeck, 'Social Attitudes to Illegitimacy', *British Journal of Sociology,* Vol. 5, No. 4, 1954, p. 315.

[6] By M Finer and OR McGregor, 'The History of the Obligation to Maintain', Appendix 5 to the *Report of the Committee on One-Parent Families* (1974, Cmnd. 5629, 1974, Vol. II, p. 117) citing Lord David Cecil's *The Young Melbourne* (1939) pp. 1–7.

[7] See Lord Buckmaster's speech in *Official Report* (HL) 21 February 1924, vol. 56, col. 253: 'No law that we can pass can help amend the lot of the unhappy mother, but at least it is possible to do something to place the child in a position in which the law of the land does not exclude him from consideration as an ordinary legitimate child . . .'.

[8] Neville Chamberlain MP moving the Second Reading of the Bastardy Bill, *Official Report* (HC) 7 May 1920, vol. 128, col. 2396.

[9] In English 'nobody's child' and 'the child of the people' respectively.

[10] Blackstone's *Commentaries on the Laws of England* (4th ed., 1770) Book 1, p. 459.

[11] The Council was chaired at the crucial period by Mrs Lettice Fisher (see Biographical Notes) and her political contacts stood the Council in good stead: see eg PRO/LCO2 751, 23 February 1924.

[12] *The Times*, 8 May 1920, claimed that the debate on the 1920 Chamberlain Bill would 'furnish a notable paragraph to the future historian of English morals, for the broad charity shown on all sides to' reform and 'for the complete disappearance of the argument . . . that the hardship to the mother and injustice to the child are necessary pillars of moral society. The idea underlying the debate was that it is the parents who are illegitimate and not the child . . .'.

nomic hardship and social deprivation which often characterise lone parent households.

The issues of legal status, property rights and entitlement to financial and other support are, of course, all inter-related; and this was recognised in the ambitious Bastardy Bill[13] introduced into the House of Commons by Neville Chamberlain[14] in 1920. But it soon became apparent that there were strong feelings about how far the law should go in seeking to remove the legal discrimination between legitimate and illegitimate children. It seems best to deal separately with the three main issues: legitimation by subsequent marriage, improved property and maintenance rights, and finally the attempt to remove the legal distinction between legitimate and illegitimate from the statute book.

LEGITIMATION BY SUBSEQUENT MARRIAGE[15]

The common law rule

As long ago as the twelfth century, there were debates about whether English law should accept the doctrine propounded by the Church allowing children born *before* their parents' marriage the same legitimate status as those born *after* the marriage. But in 1236 all the Earls and Barons, assembled at Merton, 'with one voice answered that they would not change the laws of the realm which hitherto had been used and obeyed'.[16] It was 690 years before the Westminster Parliament (and then only grudgingly and partially) followed the example of the rest of Western Christendom and recognised legitimation by subsequent marriage.

---

[13] The Bill attempted greatly to improve the prospects of identifying the child's father and giving him some legal recognition; but Home Office officials believed the proposals for an investigation into parentage were 'so iniquitous as not to require detailed discussion': PRO HO45 11190/37149. Chamberlain's Bill would not only have improved the legal procedures for compelling the parents to make proper financial provision but contained other far reaching provisions (for example, providing that every bastard under the age of 16 should become a ward of the Juvenile Court which would have had power to appoint guardians and otherwise to promote the child's welfare) designed to provide protection for illegitimate children. These provisions provoked opposition even from those (such as the Women's Freedom League and the Labour Party) who were strongly in favour of the principle of reform but were concerned (for example) about the implications of the requirement to disclose the identity of the child's father, the degree of State interference implicit in the 'wardship' provisions, and the continued use of the expression 'bastard'. The Bill was given a Second Reading in the House of Commons on 7 May 1920 (see *Official Report* (HC) vol. 128, col. 2395). Renamed Children of Unmarried Parents Bill it was (as substantially amended by Standing Committee D) reintroduced the following year and passed the House of Commons on 16 August 1921 but made no further progress.

[14] See Biographical Notes.

[15] Children born illegitimate might also acquire the status of legitimacy by adoption: see below.

[16] *Re Goodman's Trusts* (1881) 17 Ch D 266, 271, *per* Lush LJ; and see JH Baker, *An Introduction to Legal History* (4th ed., 2002, p. 490).

The problems of achieving reform: 1920–1926

Although, as the Home Office Legal Adviser, Sir Ernley Blackwell[17] noted in 1920, the *principle* of legitimation *per subsequens matrimonium*[18] was generally conceded,[19] and legislation was 'desired by all parties and especially by women', the fluid and confused political situation in the early 1920s hampered progress.[20] There were two highly controversial points which caused particular difficulty.[21]

The problem of the 'adulterine bastard'

The first (and most emotive) issue was whether children born in adultery ('adulterine bastards') should be eligible for legitimation *per subsequens matrimonium*. To put the matter in plain English, should the fact that either or both the child's parents was married to a third party make it impossible for their child ever to be legitimated? As Blackwell noted

the 'argument in favour of giving such children the benefit . . . is that the interest of the child should be paramount and that it should not suffer from a parent's adultery. On the other hand it is urged (1) that it is in the interest of the children generally to preserve family life, and that the interest of children generally is more important than the interest of a comparatively few bastard children. (2) A wife should be protected otherwise she will be subjected to much pressure to divorce her husband in order that the bastard child may become legitimated and she will be told that she ought not to be an obstacle to an innocent child's future. (3) The fact that such a child may become legitimated will remove a deterrent against adulterous intercourse . . . [and finally] inclusion will be prejudicial to family life, increase divorce, and make it more difficult for a wife to restrain an erring husband or to regain his affection'.

The problem of filiation: determining parentage

It was all very well to say that a child should be legitimated by the subsequent marriage of the parents but how was the fact of parentage to be established? This would be a particularly difficult issue where the mother was married at

---

[17] See Biographical Notes. [18] Ie legitimation by subsequent marriage.

[19] On 8 May 1920 *The Times* stated that the clause in the Chamberlain Bill legitimising a child whose parents married after his birth 'was supported on all sides almost without dissent' and considered that if a single-clause Bill were introduced it would have a good chance of being passed in that Session of Parliament. The *Departmental Committee on Adoption of Children* (1921) published an interim report strongly supporting legitimation by subsequent marriage on the ground that this would give the child 'a proper legal status' and would help maintain the link between parent and child.

[20] Some 11 Bills were introduced in the period 1920–1924 (and some had been extensively debated: see the Home Office Note on PRO HO4655/12259). This led Sir William Joynson-Hicks (Home Secretary in Baldwin's 1924 administration) to describe Legitimacy Bills as 'hardy annuals': *Official Report* (HC) vol. 197, col. 318. The battle for reform was only conclusively won when the King's Speech on 9 December 1924 promised legislation. Even so more than two years went by before the Legitimacy Act 1926 eventually came into force on 1 January 1927. As an official noted, with considerable restraint, there were 'points connected with [the Bill] which lead to discussion and the difficulty has been to find time for the Bill': PRO LCO2/753, 5 February 1926.

[21] Home Office Note, PRO HO4655/12259, p. 2, 'Observations'.

the time of the child's birth: the common law would presume that the husband was the father of her child, so what was to happen when she married another man and claimed that he was in reality the child's father? But even if legitimation were confined to cases in which the father and mother would have been free at the time of the child's birth to marry, were there not risks that the child would make a bogus claim to be the offspring of the man she subsequently married?

These were difficult issues (particularly at a time when there were no effective and reliable scientific means for determining parentage) and the civil law systems which recognised legitimation *per subsequens matrimonium* had adopted different approaches. One suggestion was that the law should require some formal act of recognition of the child's parentage; but on this issue the Home Office formed a clear view. In the words of Blackwell's Memorandum:[22]

'The object of an avowal is to prevent bogus claims from arising in connection with an intestacy or under an instrument in the future after the death of the parents. Various clauses have been proposed but they are all open to objection . . . [and] to require an avowal would to a large measure defeat [the Reform] since the parents of the majority of bastard children would be unaware of the requirement. Sudden death would sometimes intervene before a contemplated avowal were made, and in some cases the parents might be abroad'. For these reasons, the Home Office was clearly of the view that legitimation 'should follow directly from the subsequent marriage, and should not be dependent upon a further act of the parents. . . . The onus of establishing the legitimation will always be upon the claimant and there is no reason to think that the Courts will not be able to deal with any disputed claim . . . on the evidence adduced'.

But in the absence of a formal system of recognition, the procedure for establishing legitimation became of crucial importance. There was a powerful movement which would have denied legitimation unless the court made a declaration of parentage;[23] but the majority felt this would be too onerous.[24] All that was left, then, was to rely on the birth certificate. And everyone agreed that it should be possible for a legitimated person's birth to be re-registered and that re-registration would be valuable evidence in support of a claim. But what criteria were to govern the decision on whether to re-register or to refuse re-registration? Should this—Blackwell asked—'be entirely a matter for the discretion of the Registrar-General, or should there be an appeal to a Court against his decision either way, or should he have power to refer an application to a Court'?

---

[22] See PRO HO45/4655/12259.

[23] See eg the remarks of Lords Middleton and Phillimore: *Official Report* (HL) 27 April 1926, vol. 63, cols. 936 ff. The 1926 Act did provide for a person claiming to have been legitimated to apply for a declaration under the Legitimacy Declaration Act 1858, which would be effectively conclusive: see *The Ampthill Peerage* [1977] AC 547, HL. But that was merely one (albeit particularly effective) method for obtaining a finding of parentage.

[24] See eg the debates in the House of Lords on 25 March 1924 and 26 March 1925: *Official Report* (HL) vol. 56, col. 1006 and vol. 60, col. 473 respectively.

The notion that a bureaucrat should have the apparent power to settle such matters was clearly anathema to some;[25] whilst the technicality of the subject (of which the Registrar-General, Sir Sylvanus Vivian[26] was a master) caused many problems.[27] In the end, the Government managed to avoid further controversy by the time-honoured device of getting the draftsman to put the relevant provisions (which did indeed give the Registrar-General a substantial measure of discretion) into a Schedule to the Act.[28]

The compromise: the Legitimacy Act 1926

It was not possible to use such tactics to avoid the question whether or not to exclude the adulterine bastard; and six years of parliamentary discussion did not add much to the arguments summarised above. The issue was one on which emotions were strong.[29] Lord Buckmaster devoted his considerable oratorical

[25] See eg the debates on the Children of Unmarried Parents Bill, *Official Report* (HC) 16 August 1921, vol. 146, col. 1375.

[26] Sylvanus P Vivian (1880–1958): see Biographical Notes.

[27] PRO LCO2/752 evidences that a great many amendments of a technical kind were put down at the instance of the Registrar-General. But the technicalities tended to obscure the principle; and at least one peer (Lord Raglan) tried to preserve the principle that registration should not of itself confer legal capacity or alter legal status. Eventually Lord Chancellor Cave settled the policy (embodied in Legitimacy Act 1926, Sch. para. 1, proviso): re-registration could only take place on the information of both the child's parents unless the father's name had already been entered in the Births Register or a court had determined the issue. The Registrar-General (who was in favour of a wide discretion to re-register) noted that this decision would cause 'great disappointment (perhaps unavoidable) to many people' and instanced the case of a father seeking to have the register amended after the mother's death as one example of possible hardship.

[28] Legitimacy Act 1926. The drafting of the legislation gave rise to considerable difficulty, not least because Sir Benjamin Cherry (see Biographical Notes), who had been responsible for some earlier versions, strongly objected to revisions made by the First Parliamentary Counsel Sir Eric Liddell: see Biographical Notes. Describing Liddell's Bill as a 'thing of shreds and patches', 'devoid of any intelligible principle' and as likely 'to give rise to unnecessary trouble, if not actual injustice', Cherry claimed that his fears were such that he hoped his name would not be associated with the Bill to be presented to Parliament 'in any way. I'm not [he rather unconvincingly added] a bit hurt only I don't want to see a mess and be told afterwards that it was my fault': Cherry to Liddell, 17 February 1926, PRO LCO2/753. Liddell for his part referring to 'the maze into which he [Cherry] has converted the Bill'. Eventually, the Lord Chancellor referred the drafts to an informal Committee chaired by Tomlin J which succeeded in settling a draft Bill of 'almost engaging simplicity' and proved to be acceptable to both parties. Schuster told Tomlin that 'any more annoying and harassing piece of work could hardly be imagined, and to have reduced it even to comparative simplicity is a great feat . . .': Schuster to Tomlin, 12 March 1926, PRO LCO2/753. Much of the difficulty centred on the provisions necessary to deal with the legitimated person's rights to succeed to property. (The point of principle which concerned some Peers was that the marriage which legitimated the child would also revoke the father's will, with the consequence that the child would be able to 'take the bread out of the mouths of brothers and sisters who are not base born': Middleton to Schuster, 16 April 1926, PRO LCO2/753.) The most important provisions were those restricting a legitimated person's claims to cases in which the operative event occurred after legitimation, and providing that a legitimated person's seniority as against other children should date from the legitimation rather than the date of birth.

[29] The Home Office file reflects the differing views: see PRO HO45/12259/40558. On the one hand, Sybil Lady Rhondda, in a letter to *The Times* 3 July 1924 claims that to legitimise children born in adultery 'must weaken the marriage tie and encourage a state of affairs which practically

talents to promoting reform. He urged[30] that it was 'inconceivable' that a distinction be drawn between the child 'born of a union that is both irregular and adulterous' and the child 'merely born out of wedlock by the irregular relations of unmarried people'. But the Archbishop of Canterbury was not the only one to believe that legitimation of the adulterine bastard would 'gravely imperil' the happiness and security of domestic life;[31] and (even though the majority of parents who married after the birth of a child had not been free to marry at the time of the birth)[32] the reformers eventually had to concede[33] that there was no likelihood of a Legitimation Bill becoming law unless the adulterine bastard were excluded from its scope.[34] The Legitimacy Act 1926[35] duly provided that nothing in the Act should operate to legitimate a person whose father or mother was married to a third person when the illegitimate person was born. Even so, a large number of children were, over the years, legitimated under the provisions of the Act.[36]

amounts to bigamy'; but compare the Divorce Law Reform Union pamphlet quoted at p. 126, note 123, above. But some progressive opinion—for example The National Union of Societies for Equal Citizenship: see Hubback to MacDonald, 1 August 1924—supported the exclusion of the adulterine bastard; and even the National Council for the Unmarried Mother and her Child had to accept that the only chance of getting legitimation by subsequent marriage onto the statute book was to accept the exclusion of such children. A conference of Officials decided that the adulterine bastard should be excluded from the scope of the legislation: PRO HO45/12259/40558, 17 December 1924.

[30] *Official Report* (HL) 21 February 1924, vol. 56, col. 256.
[31] *Official Report* (HL) 21 February 1924, vol. 56, col. 259.
[32] As the Chairman reminded the Home Affairs Committee at its meeting on 27 June 1922, PRO CAB 26/4, para. 6. In fact ministers in successive Governments took markedly different approaches to the issues of reform.
[33] The final debates in 1926 suggested that the tide might have turned in favour of extending the possibility of legitimation to the adulterine bastard; but Lord Cave (Lord Chancellor in Baldwin's Conservative administration) rejected suggestions that the Bill be amended arguing that the House of Lords had twice decided the issue and the matter should be regarded as closed. In the event an amendment was moved and rejected by 208 votes to 101: *Official Report* (HC) 13 December 1926, vol. 200, col. 2616.
[34] See Blackwell's note dated 14 July 1926, PRO file HO45/12259. The reformers had to fall back on the argument that 'the clause, by taking as the critical date the date of birth and not the date of conception, fails in its object' since it would permit children conceived in adultery to be legitimated. The Home Office agreed that the date of conception would indeed be the more logical date, and there would be no 'insuperable obstacle or objection' to accepting an amendment which would have confined legitimation to cases where the father and mother could lawfully have married one another either at the date of the birth or at any time within the preceding ten months. But the conclusion was that it would be better 'at this stage' to retain the principle that the date of birth was crucial.
[35] s. 1(2).
[36] Figures published by the Registrar-General suggest that somewhere between 5% and 9% of children born illegitimate between 1921 and 1959 (and surviving for four or more years from birth) were legitimated by their parents' subsequent marriage: see the Table reproduced in OR McGregor, L Blom-Cooper, and C Gibson, *Separated Spouses, A Study of the matrimonial jurisdiction of magistrates' courts* (1970) p. 175. (A much larger percentage acquired the status of legitimacy by adoption: *ibid.*)

Thirty years on: reform achieved

After the end of World War II[37] (and the associated large increase in the numbers of adulterine illegitimacies) there was increasing pressure to improve the legal position of the significant number[38] of children who could not be legitimated because one or both parents had been married to third parties when the child was born. There were Private Members' Bills, and in 1956, the *Royal Commission on Marriage and Divorce*[39] considered whether legitimation by the parents' subsequent marriage should be extended to all children born out of wedlock. A majority[40] of the Commissioners rejected this proposal. The majority thought the proposal wrong in principle:

'Legitimacy is the status held by a lawful child of the family. Any departure from that conception can only be made by ignoring the essential moral principle that a man cannot, during the subsistence of his marriage, beget lawful children by another woman. It is unthinkable that the State should lend its sanction to such a step for it could not fail to result in a blurring of moral values in the public mind. A powerful deterrent to illicit relationships would be removed, with disastrous results for the status of marriage as at present understood. The issue is fundamental but perfectly plain. If children born in adultery may subsequently acquire the status of legitimate children, an essential distinction between lawful marriages and illicit unions disappears.'[41]

The majority supported this argument of principle by one of pragmatism: it was perfectly possible for an illegitimate child to be legally adopted by the birth parents, and so an illegitimate child need not be 'at any serious material disadvantage. It is right that it should be possible to mitigate the material consequences

---

[37] The Lord Chancellor's Office file on the Legitimacy Bill 1955 opens with a Parliamentary Question asking for the Government's response to a joint report produced by the British Medical Association and the Magistrates' Association on *The Law in Relation to the Illegitimate Child* (1952); and the case for reform was also made in a 1952 *Memorandum by the Marriage Law Reform Society*. The minute by Lord Chancellor Simonds dated 26 October 1953 ('I am not, I imagine, required to do anything about this at this stage. That suits me.') suggests the Memorandum's immediate impact was not great. There were a number of other attempts to exert pressure through Parliamentary Questions: see most dramatically Mr Hector Hughes to Prime Minister Churchill, 18 March 1952 *Official Report* (HC) vol. 497, col. 2090. The fact that many children born to unmarried parents could not be legitimated because their parents (being already married) were not free to marry one another was a factor put at the forefront of the campaign for reform of the divorce laws in the 1950s and 1960s: see above, Chapter 9.

[38] There appears to be no reliable estimate. In 1956 the Registrar-General's office rejected 169 applications for re-registration as a legitimated child on the ground that the parent was not free to marry at the date of the birth: see PRO LCO2/6896A, 14 July 1959. But as the Registrar-General pointed out this figure presumably underestimates the total number of children affected because many potential applicants would have known that the 1926 Act precluded legitimation in such a case.

[39] 1956, Cmd. 9678.

[40] Twelve (including the Chairman) opposed such a change, seven were in favour: *Morton Report*, para. 1182.

[41] *Ibid.*, para. 1180.

for the child. It is quite another thing to suggest that no distinction should be made between the lawful children of the marriage and children who were born of an adulterous union'.[42]

The minority would have none of this:

They considered that there was no evidence that the law did deter couples from forming illicit unions. Even if the law did have this effect, the hypothetical risk of promoting immorality had to be weighed against the real benefits which legitimation conferred on a child. It was difficult to see why parents should be allowed to confer the consequences of legitimacy by the 'circuitous and somewhat absurd process' of adopting their own children rather than achieving the same result by marrying. Moreover, it would be wrong to allow an adulterous cohabiting couple to regularise their position by marriage as and when they became free whilst denying any possibility of such regularisation to the innocent offspring of the cohabitation.[43]

In 1959 John Parker MP[44] introduced a Private Member's Bill into the House of Commons. The arguments over legitimation had (he said) been 'repetitive and a very big waste of time' with the same points being made over and over again.[45] The simple truth, evidenced by MPs' constituency postbags, was that the law caused 'grievous hardship and mental suffering to people at all social levels'; and this 'helpless and unfortunate section of the community' relied on Parliament to rectify injustice.[46] The Government was advised by the Treasury Solicitor[47] that drafting a satisfactory Bill would be 'extremely difficult', but none the less it decided not to oppose the Bill either on principle or on the basis of its manifest drafting imperfections.[48] There was little resistance to the Bill in the House of Commons;[49] and the Government agreed to make the services of Parliamentary Counsel available. There were indeed formidable drafting difficulties;[50] but the only sustained opposition on the merits of the Bill came in the

[42] *Ibid.*, para. 1181.   [43] *Morton Report*, paras. 1182, 1174–78.
[44] See Biographical Notes.
[45] *Official Report* (HC) 30 January 1959, vol. 598, col. 1403.
[46] WA Wilkins MP, *Official Report* (HC) 30 January 1959, vol. 598, col. 1437.
[47] Sir Harold Kent, PRO LCO2/6895, 9 January 1959.
[48] PRO LCO2/6895: Meeting of Legislation Committee 15 January 1959.
[49] The Bill was given a Second Reading on 30 January 1959 by 45 votes to 4.
[50] The correspondence between the First Parliamentary Counsel, Sir Noel Hutton (1907–1984) and the Home Office and Lord Chancellor's Office officials is of great interest and demonstrates the extent of the influence which a skilled and experienced draftsman may have on the content of legislation. In 1959 officials were greatly concerned about the problem they believed would arise in cases in which a child born to a married woman had to be presumed to be the legitimate child of her marriage when in fact the child was the illegitimate child of X whom the mother married. Eventually Hutton succeeded, not only in demonstrating that there were endless variations on this situation but in convincing the Attorney-General and others that any provision seeking to deal with hypothetical problems (which did not seem to arise in practice) would not be worth the complications which it entailed: see eg Hutton to Barr, 2 March 1959, and Hutton to Manningham-Buller AG, 11 March 1959, PRO LCO2/6895.

House of Lords. Lord Salisbury[51] (at the time a prominent figure in the
Conservative Party) objected that the legislation would sanction a fiction,[52] the
Bishop of Exeter claimed that it would be totally inconsistent with the Christian
concept of marriage,[53] whilst the former Lord Chancellor, Lord Simonds,
claimed[54] that the proposal was 'bad in principle and in law . . . likely to undermine the Christian ideal of marriage and to lead to grave confusion in the
administration of the law'. But although the legitimation provision was struck
out in the House of Lords Committee[55] wiser counsels[56] eventually prevailed[57]
and the Bill received Royal Assent on 29 July 1959. The number of birth re-
registrations for people who had been legitimated[58] increased substantially.[59]

The putative marriage

It is perhaps surprising that the notoriously conservative 1956 *Royal
Commission on Marriage and Divorce*[60] should—with 'rare unanimity' as a
Home Office official rightly remarked[61]—have recommended that the canon
law doctrine of the *putative marriage*[62] (that is, that a child born of a void mar-

[51] See Biographical Notes.

[52] '. . . some lawyers always seem to think that by adding the adjective "legal" to the word
"fiction" it makes it much more respectable, just as in politics when a Government wants to do
something which is manifestly unjust to some section of the community it thinks it makes it sound
better by calling it "social" justice. . . . But to the ordinary man, such as most of us in this House are,
a fiction remains a fiction, whatever adjective is attached to it; a lie remains a lie even though it is
condoned by the law': *Official Report* (HL) 21 July 1959, vol. 218, col. 338.

[53] *Official Report* (HL) 2 July 1959, vol. 217, col. 689. But the Church of England did not oppose
legitimation as vigorously as it had done in 1926; and Archbishop Fisher (whilst objecting to 'playing about with the truth and the facts' and expressing concern that society would be deceived about
the nature of a child's parentage) eventually accepted the Bill as being in the best interests of the children affected: *Official Report* (HL) 21 July 1959, vol. 218, col. 321.

[54] *Official Report* (HL) 2 July 1959, vol. 217, col. 701.

[55] Provoking some MPs to claim that the House of Lords had broken the convention that it did
not seek to overturn considered decisions of the House of Commons: see *The Times*, 13 July 1959.

[56] Attempts were made to find some compromise acceptable to the opponents of extending legitimation, but in the event it was not necessary to consider such proposals.

[57] The House of Lords reinstated the legitimation provision on the Report stage by a majority of
83 to 64: *Official Report* (HL) 21 July 1959, vol. 218, col. 352. Further (unsuccessful) attempts to
restrict the scope of legitimation were made by Sir Hugh Lucas-Tooth and Ronald Bell at the last
stage of the Bill's progress through the House of Commons: *Official Report* (HC), 28 July 1959, vol.
610, col. 459. The fact that the courts were increasingly ready to expedite the divorce process to
enable a child to be legitimated by the parents' marriage was a telling argument used against those
who founded their objections to legitimation on the importance of truth and the avoidance of artificial fictions.

[58] There were 6,506 such re-registrations in 1960 (the first full year in which the 1959 Act was in
force) and 13,043 in 1967: Legitimation by subsequent marriage seems to have become less frequent
in the 1970s: see the Law Commission Report, *Illegitimacy* (1982, Law Com. No. 118, para. 2.2).

[59] See OR McGregor, L Blom-Cooper, and C Gibson, *Separated Spouses, A Study of the matrimonial jurisdiction of magistrates' courts* (1970) p. 176.

[60] *The Morton Report*; see p. 328 above.

[61] Memorandum to Sir Austin Strutt, PRO LCO2/6895, 24 April 1959, para. 2.

[62] For the history of this doctrine, see J Jackson, *Formation and Annulment of Marriage* (2nd ed.,
1969) p. 50 and the sources cited.

riage[63] should be held to be legitimate where it is shown that one or both of the parents was or were ignorant of the impediment to the marriage)[64] be reintroduced into English law.

The version of the 1959 Parker Bill originally debated in the House of Commons did not deal with this issue, but Parker moved an amendment at the Committee stage which was accepted without much discussion. Although the amendment was not originally well received by the officials dealing with the Bill[65] the Government[66] eventually decided not to oppose the inclusion of a suitably re-drafted clause.[67] Surprisingly, the House of Lords agreed that a child of a void marriage who was thus to be treated as legitimate should[68] (unlike the child legitimated[69] or adopted)[70] be entitled to succeed to dignities and titles of honour on the same basis as a child born to a married couple.[71] The child of a 'marriage' which has never existed[72] was thus to be treated more favourably[73]

---

[63] At common law, the effect of the court annulling a *voidable* marriage was retrospectively to declare that the marriage had never existed, thereby bastardising any children. Legislation—the Matrimonial Causes Act 1937 and the Law Reform (Miscellaneous Provisions) Act 1949—provided that any child of a voidable marriage who would have been legitimate had the marriage been dissolved (rather than annulled) should be deemed to be the legitimate child of the parents.

[64] *The Morton Report*, para. 1186.

[65] DW Dobson (Assistant Permanent Secretary in the Lord Chancellor's Department) thought the proposal was 'thoroughly bad' and 'should not be allowed to proceed'. The Solicitor-General had vigorously criticised the proposal, as had his predecessor when a similar proposal had been brought forward in 1949: see *Official Report* (HC) December 5, 1949, vol. 470, col. 1654; while the Lord Chancellor (Kilmuir) disagreed 'profoundly' with what was proposed (see his manuscript note on Dobson's minute of 7 May 1959: PRO LCO2/6895) and warned the Home Affairs Committee that the implications of the proposed change in the law were far-reaching and could lead to much legal uncertainty and difficulty. The issues are dispassionately set out in a Home Office memorandum: Memorandum to Sir Austin Strutt, PRO LCO2/6895, 24 April 1959.

[66] In deciding that the Government should not seek to remove the relevant clause from the Bill the Home Affairs Committee was influenced by the fact that 'it was by no means certain that a majority could be secured for . . . removal in the House of Commons' Bill: HA(59) 7th Meeting, 29 April 1959, conclusion 4. In the end, the Government advised acceptance of the provision: *Official Report* (HC) 28 July 1959, vol. 610, col. 457.

[67] The clause originally proposed by Parker was extensively redrafted by Parliamentary Counsel at a late stage. Opponents of the principle of legitimation in the House of Commons mounted a lengthy, but eventually unsuccessful, attack on the clause: *Official Report* (HL) 28 July 1959, vol. 610, col. 474.

[68] If born after 28 October 1959 (the commencement date).

[69] See Legitimacy Act 1926, s. 10; and the consolidating Legitimacy Act 1976, Sch. 1, para. 4(2).

[70] See now Adoption Act 1976, s. 44(1).

[71] The argument which seemed to have been most influential was that (by reason of the provisions of Matrimonial Causes Act 1950, s. 9) the child of a voidable marriage subsequently annulled (and thus, under the law then in force, retrospectively treated as having been void *ab initio*) was not debarred from inheriting. This argument was put by Kilmuir in a notably dispassionate speech in the House of Lords, and had also evidently been influential in the formation of departmental policy: see Dobson's Minute to the Lord Chancellor dated 7 May 1959.

[72] However, the child must have been born *before* the date on which the void 'marriage' took place: *Spence v. Dennis* [1990] Ch 652, CA.

[73] As demonstrated by Sir Nicolas Browne-Wilkinson VC in *Spence v. Dennis* [1990] Ch 652, CA, there are curious differences between the legal position of children of a void marriage on the one hand and pre-marriage children legitimated by the subsequent valid marriage of their parents on the other.

than the child of parents who had not married at the date of birth but did marry as soon as they were free to do so, perhaps only weeks after the birth.[74]

MITIGATING THE LEGAL DISADVANTAGES OF ILLEGITIMACY

(a) Maintenance

Legitimation was an important reform. But it did nothing to improve the legal position of the large number of children born illegitimate whose parents had no prospects of marrying. In some cases this was because the mother or father was in fact married to someone else who refused a divorce; and the plight of these children of so-called stable illicit unions was a major factor in the campaign which eventually led to the introduction by the Divorce Reform Act 1969 of divorce for irretrievable breakdown. But in many other cases—the maidservant seduced by her employer's son, the young girl led astray by the blandishments of a soldier on leave, for example—there was no realistic prospect of the parents ever marrying; and the plight of mother and child in such cases was unenviable. As witnesses told a House of Commons Select Committee in 1909[75] 'any servant girl who is pregnant is thrown absolutely out of employment' whilst none of the 'better class of factory' would keep a woman known to be pregnant on its staff.[76] Such 'fallen' women and their children were almost inevitably left to such help as could be provided under the Poor Law unless the man concerned could be induced to provide support.

Statute[77] had (as we have seen) given the mother of an illegitimate child the right to obtain a summons[78] against the man she claimed to be the father. If the magistrates hearing her case adjudged the man to be the putative father they

---

[74] It was evidently not at first appreciated that, by requiring the child of a void marriage to be treated as legitimate, the Act might confer rights of succession to the throne of the United Kingdom on members of the Royal Family who had not complied with the requirements of the Royal Marriages Act 1772. The problem caused Ministers and Officials much anxiety in the final stages of the Bill's passage not least because it was decided that it would be best if Parliament were given no explanation of the problem caused by the existence of the 1772 Act and of the reason for the amendment ultimately made to the Bill (which simply provided that nothing in the Legitimacy Act 1959 affected the succession to the throne: see s. 6(4)): see for a full account SM Cretney, 'The Royal Marriages Act 1772: A Footnote' (1995) 16 *Statute Law Review* 195.

[75] *Report of the Select Committee on Bastardy Orders*, 1909 HC 236, BPP 1909, vol. 6, p. 717.

[76] Evidence of Miss MEE James (amongst others).

[77] The Bastardy Laws Amendment Act 1872. For changes of policy in the nineteenth century (and especially on whether to allow the mother the right to bring proceedings against the father would encourage immorality) see M Finer and OR McGregor, 'The History of the Obligation to Maintain', Appendix 5 to the *Report of the Committee on One-Parent Families* (1974, Cmnd. 5629, Vol. II) p. 114 (paras. 54–65 contain an admirable and succinct account of the law governing financial provision for illegitimate children) and the sources there cited.

[78] There were a number of restrictions on this right, notably that the mother had to be a 'single woman' (a term which could include a married woman separated from her husband), whilst the application had normally to be made within 12 months of the birth: see Bastardy Laws Amendment Act 1872, s. 3.

could order him[79] to pay a sum not exceeding 5/- weekly[80] to the mother[81] for the child's maintenance[82] and education[83] until the child was 13.[84]

A mother whose neglect to maintain her illegitimate child led to his being maintained by the Poor Law was liable to be punished as an idle and disorderly person or a rogue and vagabond under the provisions of the Vagrancy Act 1824.[85] And if there was no application for a Bastardy Order[86] the Poor Law authorities were entitled to apply to the court for an order against the father to recover the amount of relief they were paying in respect of the child.[87]

There was (the 1909 Select Committee reported)[88] a 'general and well founded consensus' that the object of the law should be, firstly, 'to secure the adequate care and maintenance of the child until it reaches the age when it can be expected to earn something for itself' and secondly 'to facilitate the process by which mothers . . . and others can recover from the male parent expenses incurred in the child's birth or maintenance'. Equally there was little doubt that the law failed in these objectives.[89] Pressure for reform[90] before World War I achieved little.[91] The decade following the end of the War was characterised by

---

[79] The obligation to make the payments was enforceable by levying distress against the father's property, and in default by committal to prison for three months: Bastardy Laws Amendment Act 1872, s. 4.

[80] Ie 25 pence, perhaps £15 in year 2000 values.

[81] In some circumstances the payments might be diverted to a third party with custody of the child: Bastardy Laws Amendment Act 1872, s. 5, or to the Poor Law authorities: s. 7.

[82] There was also power in some circumstances to order the putative father to make payments in respect of the expenses incidental to the child's birth and to meet funeral expenses: Bastardy Laws Amendment Act 1872, s. 4.

[83] *Ibid.*, s. 4.

[84] *Ibid.*, s. 5. The magistrates could direct that the period be extended to the child's sixteenth birthday.

[85] Poor Law Amendment Act 1844, s. 7.

[86] But the general practice was for the Poor Law authorities to assist a mother to obtain an order herself (which would continue to be enforceable even if she ceased to be in receipt of Relief): *Report of the Select Committee on Bastardy Orders*, 1909 HC 236, BPP 1909, vol. 6, p. 717.

[87] Bastardy Laws Amendment Act 1872, s. 8.

[88] *Report of the Select Committee on Bastardy Orders*, 1909 HC 236, BPP 1909, vol. 6, p. 717.

[89] See the evidence given to the *Select Committee on Bastardy Orders*, 1909 HC 236, BPP 1909, vol. 6, p. 717; and the treatment of bastardy in both Majority and Minority Reports of the *Royal Commission on the Poor Laws and the Relief of Distress* (1909, Cd. 4499). Evidence to the Select Committee focussed on the desirability of increasing the 5/- limit on orders and on the desirability of the courts having power to increase orders in the light of the father's increased means.

[90] In 1909 Arnold Herbert MP presented a Bastardy Bill (the chief objective of which was to enable liability to be enforced against the estate of a deceased father); and the Affiliation Proceedings Act 1914 made some limited improvements in the law (notably, establishing the principle that a Collecting Officer be appointed to supervise the collection of payments due from the father).

[91] But the fact that the title of the 1914 Act for the first time used the expression 'affiliation' (rather than the traditional 'bastardy') order is of some significance (even if the next Act to reach the statute book reverted to Bastardy Act 1923). Home Office officials had pointed out in 1921 that the various 'Bastard's charters' were so drafted that any child who had recourse to them would be 'saddled more tightly than before with the name Bastard' since the drafts 'reeked with the word'. However, it apparently sufficed to note that the point was 'for the Ministry of Health (Maternity and Child Welfare Department) not the Home Office': PRO HO 45/11190/37149.

the formation of pressure groups[92] which campaigned vigorously[93] for reforms in the law intended to improve the social conditions and status of women and children. But so far as financial provision for the illegitimate child was concerned the outcome was, in legislative terms, not great.[94] Neville Chamberlain's ambitious 1920 Bastardy Bill[95] (with its provisions requiring a speedy investigation into the issue of paternity, encouraging putative fathers to enter into binding court-approved maintenance agreements[96] and giving juvenile courts a supervisory jurisdiction over illegitimate children as well as considerably extending the courts' powers to make financial orders) was opposed by the Government;[97] and only a seven-clause Bill of limited scope eventually passed the Commons.[98] Even in that form the Chamberlain Bill made no further progress, and all that eventually reached the statute book was an increase of the maximum maintenance order which magistrates could make in affiliation proceedings to £1 weekly (perhaps £30 in year 2000 values). A Bill intended to make both parents liable according to their means for the maintenance of all their children, whether legitimate or illegitimate, got nowhere. Parliament

[92] Notably the National Council for the Unmarried Mother and her Child (see above) which persuaded the Home Office to receive a deputation in November 1918. The Council's expressed concern was to provide additional facilities to expectant mothers. Translated into law reform, that meant allowing pre-birth applications for affiliation orders, allowing orders to accrue from two months prior to birth, and improving the Collection Officer procedure: PRO HO 45/11190/37149. Other groups were also active: for example, in June 1918 the National Union of Women Workers of Great Britain and Ireland urged the Home Office to abolish the limit on affiliation orders and the court fees charged on issuing a summons, to extend the provision for enforcement through Collecting Officers, and to allow orders originally obtained by the Poor Law Authorities to be transferred to the mother when she stopped receiving relief. But the Union adopted a more cautious attitude than other Groups to the notion that public funds be used to support the illegitimate child. The Salvation Army, concerned especially about enforcing orders against the men who had 'ruined the mother's life', also urged far-reaching reforms—including removal of the requirements that the mother give evidence in support of an application for an affiliation order and that her evidence be corroborated: PRO HO 45/11190/37149, 14 November 1919.

[93] A Home Office official complained in 1920 that these groups made 'so many proposals and change their substance and form so frequently that it is impossible and useless to do more than indicate briefly the nature of the suggestions made' in the marshalled list of reform suggestions then being constructed: *ibid*.

[94] Even within this restricted sphere the pressure groups faced a dilemma. In 1918 the National Council had to tell the Home Office that they believed increasing the maximum for affiliation payments would in fact be 'extremely prejudicial' to their work because this reform would 'take the ground from under their feet': PRO HO 45/11190/37149.

[95] Bill No. 15, 1920.

[96] The Home Office noted that 'agreements may be entered into out of weakness or fear, or may be sheer regularized blackmail': see PRO HO45 11190/37149.

[97] The Home Secretary, E Shortt, persuaded the Home Affairs Committee that Chamberlain's Bill was 'fundamentally wrong and confused the question of the protection of illegitimate children with that of their adoption'. Shortt told the House of Commons that this was 'bad bill' 'founded on wrong principles', that it carried out those principles 'in a wrong way' and warned that the Government would give no help to it—although they would support legitimation and increasing the top limit on orders to 15/- (75 pence): *Official Report* (HC), 7 May 1920, vol. 128, col. 2397.

[98] Ie as the Bastardy Act 1923, which increased the top limit for affiliation orders from the ten shillings to which it had been raised by the Affiliation Orders (Increase of Maintenance Payments) Act 1918 to one pound.

insisted on keeping a clear division between the legal rights of the legitimate and the illegitimate.

The main structure[99] of the distinctive regime for enforcing parental support for the illegitimate child remained, essentially unchanged, for 70 years.[100] This was not because the law achieved the objectives set out by the 1909 Select Committee. More than 70 years later the Law Commission, noting the view that affiliation proceedings were 'not a particularly effective way of obtaining financial provision for the illegitimate' and the fact that the number of applications seemed to be falling, commented:[101]

'This may be because many mothers of illegitimate children are already receiving adequate support from the child's father, or from some other source; but it has been claimed that there is a significant number of mothers who "cannot or will not complain to the court". Hence, affiliation proceedings do not play as important a role in securing financial provision for non-marital children as they might. Explanations for this may include the nature of the proceedings themselves, and the low level of orders that are actually made. There is now no formal limit on the amount of periodical payments orders made in affiliation proceedings, but in practice orders rarely exceed the level of the mother's [welfare benefits] in respect of herself and her child. The result is that because in many cases the mother is receiving [welfare benefits] any sum that is awarded by the court will often merely go towards reducing the amount of that benefit. . . . For many mothers . . . the prospect of being involved in perhaps unpleasant proceedings outweighs any advantage which may be derived from obtaining an affiliation order.'

Research seemed to support the view that mothers preferred to rely on the comparatively generous level of social security provision available from the Welfare State rather than seeking an order against the father and that many refused to institute proceedings. It was pointed out[102] that

If the mother 'dislikes the prospect of subjecting herself and her lover to unpleasant proceedings in a criminal atmosphere, she can easily decline to complain. It is all the more

---

[99] Changes in detail were made over the years: the Affiliation Orders Act 1952 raised the limit to £1.50 weekly and the Matrimonial Proceedings (Magistrates' Courts) Act 1960 further raised it to £2.50. The Maintenance Orders Act 1968 (following the *Report of the Committee on Statutory Maintenance Limits*, 1968, Cmnd. 3587) removed the limit altogether. The Affiliation Proceedings (Amendment) Act 1972 and the Domestic Proceedings and Magistrates' Courts Act 1978 made many changes mostly of procedural detail (although the 1972 Act did extend the time limits within which proceedings had to be started and the 1978 Act gave the court power to order the putative father to pay a lump sum of up to £500). For problems to which the time limits had given rise see PRO HO45 19730/651784.

[100] The Family Law Reform Act 1987 repealed the Affiliation Proceedings Act 1957 (which had consolidated the earlier legislation, going back to the Poor Law Amendment Act 1844): see below. The recommendations of the (Finer) *Committee on One-Parent Families* (1974, Cmnd. 5629) for a Guaranteed Maintenance Allowance for one-parent families and an administrative procedure for determining the extent of a liable relative's contribution in cases of dependence on means tested benefits envisaged the assimilation of illegitimate and other children; but—as explained elsewhere in this book—those recommendations were never implemented.

[101] Law Commission Report, *Illegitimacy* (1982, Law Com. No. 118) (subsequently cited as *Law Commission Illegitimacy Report*) para. 3.24.

[102] OR McGregor, L Blom-Cooper, and C Gibson, *Separated Spouses, A Study of the matrimonial jurisdiction of magistrates' courts* (1970) p. 187.

likely that she will act in this way if she hopes to establish a permanent relationship with the father of her child'.

Eventually, the Family Law Reform Act 1987 did away with distinctive affiliation procedure[103] with its apparently gratuitous offensiveness. The law no longer discriminated against a child claiming financial support merely because the parents were unmarried: the illegitimate child was to be able to make a claim for all kinds of financial support in the same way and to the same extent as the legitimate child.

It proved easier to change the law than to change behaviour. There was increasing concern that men did not support the children they had fathered; and it seems that it came to be widely believed that the State would assume financial responsibility for the children of a failed relationship.[104] The Child Support scheme was introduced in 1991[105] in a deliberate attempt to change the culture in which such attitudes flourished.

(b) Property rights

The common law principle that the illegitimate child was 'the son of nobody' meant that he could not inherit real property as heir; whilst the same principle prevented an illegitimate child inheriting personal property under the Statute of Distributions. For these reasons, an illegitimate child had no right to succeed on the intestacy of a parent, grandparent, brother or sister; whilst neither of the child's parents was entitled on his intestacy.

The fact that a person was illegitimate did not, of course, disqualify him from taking benefits as a beneficiary under a will or settlement; but in practice there were obstacles in the way of his doing so. First, there was a rule of construction under which words in a will or other disposition denoting family relationships were construed as referring only to legitimate relations, excluding anyone tracing the relationship through an illegitimate link. Thus:

In *Dorin v. Dorin*[106] the testator married the mother of his two children and made a will leaving his property to 'our children'. The court held that the chil-

---

[103] It should be mentioned that, where the child's mother married, the Matrimonial Proceedings (Children) Act 1958, s. 1, empowered the Divorce Court to make financial and other orders on divorce etc against the husband if he had 'accepted' the child as 'one of the family'; and the Domestic Proceedings (Magistrates' Courts) Act 1978 extended this principle to domestic proceedings. The requirement that the child be 'accepted' proved somewhat restrictive, and the Matrimonial Proceedings and Property Act 1970 substituted the objective criterion of whether a child had been 'treated' by both spouses as a 'child of the family'.

[104] House of Commons Social Security Committee, *The Operation of the Child Support Act*, First Report, Session 1993–4, HC 69, para. 3.

[105] See p. 475, above.

[106] (1875) LR 7 HL 568. The rule was still applied in the second half of the twentieth century, the courts being unreceptive to arguments that changed social attitudes required a different approach: see *Sydall v. Castings* [1967] 1 QB 302 where it was held that the illegitimate daughter of a pension scheme member did not qualify for benefits as his 'descendant'.

dren were debarred by this rule of construction from taking under the will, notwithstanding the fact that there were no other children, legitimate or illegitimate, and that the deceased had always treated the illegitimate children as his children for all purposes.

Secondly, there was a rule of evidence that the court would not, in this context, allow any enquiry into the paternity of an illegitimate child. Thus:

In *Re Homer*[107] a man who had been living with a woman for many years made a will naming their children as beneficiaries. Knowing that his partner was pregnant he made a codicil to his will shortly before his death and this gave property to any other child he and his partner might have. It was held that the child born shortly after his death could not benefit. To do so it would have to be proved that the deceased was her father, and the law prevented any enquiry being made into that issue.

Thirdly, there was a rule of public policy whereby an illegitimate child conceived after the making of a disposition could not take, however clear it was that the donor intended them to share. For example, if a man made a settlement for the benefit of his children, expressly extending the definition to children born out of wedlock, his illegitimate children born after the date of the settlement could not take. This rule was justified on the basis that to allow such children to benefit would encourage immorality.[108]

Fourthly, the definition of 'dependants' in the Inheritance (Family Provision) Act 1938 did not extend to the deceased's illegitimate children[109] even if the deceased's estate was substantial, the children had been totally dependent on him during his lifetime, and were left destitute on his death.

REFORM

The first breach of the principle that the illegitimate child had, for the purposes of succession, no relatives was made by the Legitimacy Act 1926. This provided (almost as an afterthought) that the mother was entitled to succeed on her illegitimate child's intestacy as if the child had been born legitimate and she was the only surviving parent.[110] The same Act gave the child[111] the right to take on his mother's intestacy if (but only if) the mother left no legitimate issue surviving.[112]

---

[107] (1916) 115 LT 703.

[108] *Crook v. Hill* (1876) 3 Ch D 773; *Re Hyde* [1932] 1 Ch 95; *Report of the Committee on the Law of Succession in Relation to Illegitimate Persons* (1966) (subsequently cited as the '*Russell Report*') para. 18. Of course, in many cases the operation of the rule against enquiring into the paternity of an illegitimate child—see above—would lead to the same result.

[109] *Re Makein* [1955] Ch 194.   [110] Legitimacy Act 1926, s. 9(2).

[111] Or, if he was dead, his issue: Legitimacy Act 1926, s. 9(1).

[112] Legitimacy Act 1926, s. 9(1).

The 1926 Act thereby removed the anomaly that all the property of an unmarried childless illegitimate intestate would necessarily pass to the Crown as property without an owner;[113] but the scope of this reform was deliberately narrow. Forty years were to go by before the subject of the illegitimate child's succession rights was fully examined;[114] and the *Report of the Committee on the Law of Succession in Relation to Illegitimate Persons*[115] adopted a cautious approach[116] to the issue whether any alteration was desirable in the law. But the Family Law Act 1969, modelled on the *Russell Report's* recommendations,[117] did make significant improvements in the illegitimate child's succession rights. In particular, the right of a child to share in his mother's intestacy was extended on the basis of equality to cases in which she also left legitimate issue; the illegitimate child[118] was given the same right to succeed on the father's intestacy as if the child had been born legitimate; while the father of an illegitimate child was given the right to succeed on his child's intestacy on equal terms with the child's mother.[119] The illegitimate child was also given the right to apply to the court under the Inheritance (Family Provision) Act 1938 on the same basis as a legitimate child.[120]

These changes substantially improved the succession rights of illegitimate persons under both intestacies and wills.[121] It is true that in strictness the Act did no more than to 'create limited and carefully defined rights in favour of [illegitimate] persons, which fall far short of the rights which would arise if legitimate relationship and illegitimate relationship were given exactly the same legal status'.[122] It remained true that an illegitimate child could not inherit on the intes-

---

[113] *Bona vacantia.* The Crown in practice would often make some provision out of the property for the deceased's dependants and for other persons for whom the intestate might reasonably have been expected to make provision (such as his siblings: see the *Russell Report*, para. 32); and this practice was given statutory force by the Administration of Estates Act 1925, s. 46.

[114] In 1959 the Government strongly resisted even allowing an illegitimate child the right to apply for reasonable financial provision out of the deceased person's estate, officials commenting that this would be illogical when there was no suggestion that the illegitimate child should be included amongst those entitled to share on intestacy: PRO LCO2/6895, notes on clauses, clause 5. The general stance of the Lord Chancellor's officials was that no change should be made in succession laws without much fuller enquiry: see Dobson to Kilmuir, 10 January 1959.

[115] Ie the *Russell Report* (see above). See Biographical Notes.

[116] Even so, the Report was not unanimous: Sir Hugh Munro Lucas-Tooth (believing not only that proving paternity would give rise to problems but also that the nature of the familial relationship between the child and its father would often be very different from that with the child's mother) considered that an illegitimate child should only be entitled to share in the father's intestacy if the father had recognised his parentage in certain specified ways: see the *Russell Report*, pp. 16–18.

[117] In some respects—notably in abolishing the rules of construction and public policy referred to above—the Act went further than the *Russell Report* had proposed.

[118] If the illegitimate child predeceased his mother or father the child's own legitimate issue would be entitled to stand in his shoes: Family Law Reform Act 1969, s. 14(1).

[119] Family Law Reform Act 1969, s. 14(2). The *Russell Report* decided not to recommend that any special provision be made in relation to the proof of paternity: see para. 44.

[120] Family Law Reform Act 1969, s. 18.

[121] *Law Commission Illegitimacy Report* (Law Com. No. 118, 1982) (subsequently referred to as *Law Commission Illegitimacy Report*) para. 8.5.

[122] EC Ryder, [1971] CLP 157, 161.

tacy of his grandparents, sisters, uncles or aunts, whether or not such relatives were themselves legitimate or illegitimate[123] and that those relatives were not entitled to inherit on the intestacy of the child. But the Act gave clear statutory effect to the principle (on which the *Russell Report* was founded) that to allot the illegitimate child an 'inferior, or indeed unrecognised, status in succession [would be] to punish him for a wrong of which he was not guilty'.[124] And experience of the working of the 1969 Act also demonstrated[125] that it caused neither difficulty in the practical administration of the law nor scandal by giving the neglectful fathers of wealthy illegitimate pop-stars the right to inherit their child's fortunes. The 1969 Act helped create a climate in which there was virtually no reasoned opposition to the enactment of the Family Law Reform Act 1987 which was intended to remove virtually all the disadvantages of birth outside wedlock so far as they related to the child's own legal entitlements.

RADICAL REFORM: THE FAMILY LAW REFORM ACT 1987, 'ABOLISHING ILLEGITIMACY'?

In spite of the reforms effected over the years, the fact that the law continued to distinguish between children on the basis of their parents' marital status increasingly became a matter of criticism in the 1960s. Apart from anything else, international conventions to which the United Kingdom had acceded,[126] were difficult to reconcile with some aspects of English domestic law. The Law Commission had committed itself to an examination of the law governing the legal position of what the Commission described as 'non-marital' children; and a Consultation Paper published in 1979[127] proposed not only that all legal disadvantages of illegitimate birth should be removed but that the concepts of 'legitimacy' and 'illegitimacy' should be removed from English law.

Consultation revealed anxiety (especially on the part of organisations such as the National Council for One-Parent Families)[128] about the legal consequences of complete assimilation. In particular, no one had previously given much thought to the fact that the illegitimate child's father did not have legal parental authority.[129] But the Law Commission pointed out that complete assimilation would result in even a completely unmeritorious father (for example a man who

---

[123] *Law Commission Illegitimacy Report*, para. 8.6.

[124] The *Russell Report*, para. 19.

[125] See the discussion in the *Law Commission Illegitimacy Report* pp. 108–115.

[126] Notably the European Convention on Human Rights and Fundamental Freedoms and the European Convention on the Legal Status of Children born out of Wedlock. The decision of the European Court of Human Rights in the case of *Marckx v. Belgium* (1979–80) 2 EHRR 330 was particularly influential in demonstrating the potential of the Human Rights Convention.

[127] Law Commission Working Paper No. 74.

[128] Formerly the National Council for the Unmarried Mother and Her Child.

[129] Parental authority in respect of an illegitimate child was vested solely in the mother: *Barnado v. McHugh* [1891] AC 388; see Chapter 16, below.

had raped the mother)[130] having parental authority[131] over the child unless and until steps were taken to remove this from him. Because of this concern,[132] the Law Commission decided to confine its recommendations to the removal of all the legal incidents of illegitimacy so far as they discriminated against the child. The Commission did not think that legal parental authority should vest in the fathers of non-marital children 'without prior scrutiny of the child's interests by the courts'.[133]

The Law Commission's recommendations were substantially implemented by the Family Law Reform Act 1987.[134] The distinctive affiliation procedure, with all its associations with the Poor Law and criminality, was abolished,[135] and for most purposes a child was to have the same legal rights irrespective of whether the parents ever married or not. However, the illegitimate child remained disadvantaged in relation to entitlement to British Citizenship;[136] and this must be accounted a serious and real disadvantage. Probably less significant is the fact that the illegitimate child also remains ineligible to succeed to a hereditary peerage;[137] and there seems to be no enthusiasm for the removal of this historic disability. At the end of the twentieth century, there were moves to remove some of the remaining distinctions affecting the fathers of illegitimate children: the Lord Chancellor's Department issued a consultation paper on the subject;[138]

---

[130] See *per* Balcombe LJ, *Re H (Minors) (Local Authority: Parental Rights) (No. 3)* [1991] Fam 151.

[131] Since the coming into force of the Children Act 1989 the term 'parental responsibility' is used to describe the rights, powers and authority which by law a child's parent has in relation to the child and his property: Children Act 1989, s. 3(1).

[132] See *Law Commission Illegitimacy Report*, Part IV.

[133] *Law Commission Illegitimacy Report,* para. 4.50. But the Children Act 1989, s. 4 provided that a child's mother and father could, by making an agreement in accordance with specified formalities, vest 'parental responsibility' in the father jointly with the mother. There is accordingly no requirement for judicial scrutiny of such agreements. No doubt it was considered that the formal requirements would deter fathers from obtaining parental rights agreements by exercising emotional or other pressure on an unwilling mother.

[134] The Law Commission (differently constituted) in a *Second Report* (Law Com. No. 157) recommended a somewhat different drafting technique from that adopted in the *Law Commission Illegitimacy Report*; and the Family Law Reform Act 1967 draws a distinction between children whose parents were married to each other at the time of the child's birth and other children, whereas the original *Report* had made the distinction depend on whether the child fell within the proposed definition of a 'marital' or a 'non-marital' child. There is no difference of substance in the outcome: the formula used in the Act is defined so that, for example, a child legitimated by his parents' marriage many years after his birth is deemed (contrary to the truth) to have been born to parents married at that time.

[135] A procedure for seeking financial support against parents is available under the Children Act 1989, Sch. 1. The fact that parentage can now usually be conclusively determined by scientific tests has dramatically changed the court's role.

[136] Which remains governed by the provisions of the British Nationality Act 1981.

[137] See *Re Moynihan* [2000] 1 FLR 113 in which the Committee for Privileges of the House of Lords refused to hold that denying an illegitimate child the right to succeed to a hereditary peerage would be incompatible with the provisions of the European Convention on Human Rights and Fundamental Freedoms.

[138] *The Law on Parental Responsibility*.

and the Adoption and Children Act 2002[139] provided that a man recorded on the Births Register as the child's father is entitled to parental authority over the child in the same way as is the father of a child born in wedlock.[140] But the Act carefully restricts this to cases in which the mother and father have jointly registered or re-registered the birth[141] and thus in theory at least preserves the right of the mother to retain sole authority unless and until the court orders otherwise.[142]

'Illegitimacy' as a legal concept may not have been formally abolished, but the fact that a child's parents are unmarried no longer stamps the child as legally fundamentally different from the child whose parents were in truth married at the time of his birth. As a Lord Justice of Appeal put it shortly after the end of the century:[143] illegitimacy 'with its stigma has been legislated away'.

---

[139] Adoption and Children Act 2002, s. 111.

[140] *Ibid.*

[141] Adoption and Children Act 2002, s. 111. The effect is not automatically to give the father parental authority if he is registered as the father following a court order determining parentage: see Cretney, Masson and Bailey-Harris, *Principles of Family Law* (7th ed., 2002) p. 530.

[142] The father cannot (without a court order) obtain registration of his parentage without the mother's agreement: see above. It has been suggested that mothers may be vulnerable to pressure from the man concerned.

[143] Thorpe LJ, *Bellinger v. Bellinger* [2001] 2 FLR 1048, 1082.

16

Parents and Children: Legal Authority in the Family[1]

This chapter first deals with the question: who is entitled to take decisions and exercise parental authority over children? It also deals with court procedures which sometimes allow the exercise of that authority to be questioned—for example, when the parents divorce, or by making a child a 'ward of court'. Finally it gives a brief account of the increasing recognition given to the claims of a mature child to take his or her own decisions, and the consequent erosion of parental authority as traditionally understood by the legal system.

PARENTAL POWER IS PATERNAL POWER: THE MONSTROUS LEGAL FICTION[2]

Who was entitled to exercise the authority to decide how a child should be educated, what religion he or she should observe, and so on? As we have already seen, the answer at the beginning of the twentieth century was clear and simple. The father of a legitimate child[3] was exclusively entitled to exercise parental authority over the child;[4] and the child's mother had no legal right to custody or care and control.[5] Of course, in this as in other respects, the law does not nec-

---

[1] This part of the text draws on material published under the title ' *"What will the Women want next?"* . . .' in (1996) 112 LQR 110.

[2] The quotation is from Eleanor Rathbone's *The Disinherited Family* (1924) p. 92. As President of the National Union of Societies for Equal Citizenship ('NUSEC') Miss Rathbone played a major part in the campaign to bring about legal equality for women and men: see Biographical Notes.

[3] Parental authority in respect of an illegitimate child was vested in the mother: *Barnado v. McHugh* [1891] AC 388. The paradox that the mother of an illegitimate child did have sole legal authority (and that a divorced wife might acquire sole legal authority by court order) was highlighted by Mrs Margaret Wintringham MP (see Biographical Notes) in the crucial 1924 parliamentary debates on the issue of reform: see *Official Report* (HC) 4 April 1924, vol. 171, col. 2260: and see below.

[4] And the father could by will appoint a guardian for the child: Tenures Abolition Act 1660. The testamentary guardian stepped into the shoes of the father, and the mother had no right to interfere with decisions taken by him: see *Wellesley v. Wellesley* (1828) 2 Bl (NS) 124, 145–146; *Talbot v. Earl of Shrewsbury* (1840) 4 My&Cr 672, 683.

[5] Nineteenth century legislation had made some limited inroads into the father's common law rights. (i) The Custody of Children Act 1839 gave the court power to award custody of a child to the mother (provided she had not been found guilty of adultery) until the child reached the age of seven; (ii) the Custody of Infants Act 1873 extended this power: the court could award a mother (adulterous or not) custody of a child up to the age of 16 (raised to 21 by the Guardianship of Infants Act 1886); (iii) the Matrimonial Causes Act 1857 had given the Divorce Court power to make custody orders in respect of the parties' children up to the age of 21; whilst the Matrimonial Causes Act 1878 empowered magistrates to include a provision giving the wife custody of children up to the age of

essarily reflect everyday life. No doubt the future Lord Chancellor, Sir John Simon,[6] spoke for many when he told the House of Commons in 1924 that his own father (a nonconformist Minister in Manchester) would have been 'greatly astonished' to learn that he alone had the right to decide not only such comparatively trivial issues as whether a young child should be allowed to go to watch the Lancashire cricket team but much more important and difficult matters such as whether a child suffering from an inflamed throat should be subjected to fashionable but dangerous tonsillectomy, and that the child's mother had 'nothing to do' with such matters.[7]

The fact that the law denied to a wife any legal right to the custody or care and control of her children may not have been important in daily life to most couples living together in modest contentment; but even so a law which denied the mother the legal status of being the parent of her own child[8] could hardly be regarded as satisfactory by the women's groups committed to achieving 'real equality of liberties status and opportunities between men and women'.[9] These groups became increasingly influential after 1918 (when women won the right to vote in general elections[10]) and the law seemed dramatically to underline the concept of the wife as a mere chattel whose identity merged in that of her husband.[11] It seemed intolerable that this principle should be allowed to govern the legal structure supporting the most basic of human relationships. Of course, men of a conservative disposition[12] could and did claim that these grievances

ten in a non-cohabitation order (and this power was subsequently broadened); (iv) the Guardianship of Infants Act 1886 made the mother guardian of the infant children after the husband's death (although she had to act jointly with any guardian he had appointed). The 1886 Act, s. 5, also required the court to 'have regard' to the welfare of the child when deciding a mother's custody application; and the Court of Chancery in the exercise of its inherent jurisdiction over wards of court would attach weight to the children's welfare. But none of these affected the basic principle. See generally PH Pettit, 'Parental Control and Guardianship' in RH Graveson and FR Crane (eds.), *A Century of Family Law 1857–1957* (1957).

   [6] See Biographical Notes.
   [7] *Official Report* (HC) 4 April 1924, vol. 171, col. 2968.
   [8] Notwithstanding the fact that she would be criminally responsible if the child were neglected: see the remarkable case of the mother of 20 children who, unable out of the £2 weekly allowed her by the husband to provide the footwear they needed to attend school, was fined under the Education legislation for failing to secure their attendance: evidence of Miss Chrystal Macmillan, Joint Select Committee on the Guardianship of Infants Bill, Minutes of Evidence 19 July 1922, p. 17.
   [9] Rule II of the Constitution of the National Union of Societies for Equal Citizenship.
   [10] The Representation of the People Act 1918 conceded the vote to women, but only to householders aged 30 or more; full equality between the sexes was only attained by the Representation of the People (Equal Franchise) Act 1928. In 1922 the Lord Chancellor's Permanent Secretary, Sir Claud Schuster explained that the Government's agreement to referring a NUSEC equal authority Bill to a Select Committee was influenced by the consideration that it was 'very undesirable to annoy the women who are the main backers of the Bill': Schuster to Birkenhead, 1 March 1922, PRO LCO2/757. Minutes by Blackwell, the Permanent Secretary, and the Home Secretary (E Shortt) are to the same effect: PRO HO 45/11566/404730, 20 February 1922.
   [11] *Per* Lord Upjohn, *J v. C* [1970] AC 668, 720.
   [12] Such as the Chief Magistrate Sir Chartres Biron (1863–1940): see Biographical Notes. Biron assured the Joint Select Committee on the Guardianship of Infants Bill that 'in the enormous number of cases I have had' to deal with as a Magistrate 'I do not remember any case in which a woman made a grievance of that kind': *Minutes of Evidence*, 19 July 1922, pp. 2, 8.

were a pre-occupation of the middle-class intelligentsia; and that sensible work-ing class wives were totally indifferent on the matter. But the women's groups were able to demonstrate that the law had serious, and adverse, practical con-sequences:

'The father may use his power over the children as a means to induce the mother to do what he wishes, by the threat of removing them from her. He can take the children away from her entirely, and entrust them to the custody of a third party without her consent. . . . The mother may apply to the High Court or to the County Court, but the costs are prohibitive to the poorer classes.'[13]

For example in one case taken from the files of NUSEC:

A 'perfectly sober, respectable woman' whose husband insisted on sending her six-year-old son to live in Canada with an aunt was 'broken hearted' but had no effective redress against an adamant father.[14]

It was not difficult to present a case which to the year 2000 reader seems over-whelming. As the President of NUSEC, Eleanor Rathbone, wrote:[15]

'It is surely . . . a great positive disability that a wife, so long as she nominally lives with her husband, has no legal right to any say or part whatever in the management of their children, nor any remedy (so far as those over five are concerned) against being totally separated from them . . . [The father's exclusive rights are not even] dissolved by death, since even when he leaves his children entirely unprovided for, he has the power of direct-ing by will the religion and manner in which they are to be brought up and of appointing a guardian who, acting jointly with the wife, must see to it that so far as possible the father's wishes are carried out . . . If comparatively few husbands abuse their power in this respect, it is because the sense of justice of the ordinary man refuses to let him take seriously the monstrous legal fiction that a man has a primary right to the sole control of the children whom a woman has borne with great suffering and at the risk of her life and to whose care nature and custom require her to devote herself as the chief work of the best years of her life.'

NUSEC (probably the leading women's group) put a commitment to legislation giving wives equal rights to the legal guardianship of their children in the fore-front of its programme; the leaders[16] of the political groups dominating the post-World War I coalition Government gave an election pledge[17] to remove 'all existing inequalities of law as between men and women'; and Bills giving wives

---

[13] Summary of the views of those witnesses who supported the principle of conferring equal rights on the mother before the Joint Committee of Lords and Commons to consider the Guardianship of Infants Bill introduced into the House of Lords by Lord Askwith and given a Second Reading on 26 March 1923, taken from a draft Report: PRO LCO2/757.

[14] 'Effect of Women's Franchise on Legislation', Hubback papers, NUSEC/X3/3, Fawcett Library, London Guildhall University.

[15] *The Disinherited Family* (1924) pp. 91–2.

[16] Andrew Bonar Law (Conservative) and David Lloyd George (Liberal).

[17] In the so-called 'coupon election' in November 1918—a fact of which they were reminded by Sir James Greig (1859–1934) Liberal MP for West Lothian introducing the first equal parental authority Bill to be debated in Parliament: *Official Report* (HC) 29 June 1921, vol. 143, col. 1400.

equal parental authority over the children were introduced into Parliament.[18] Yet no legislation dealing with the matter was enacted until 1925; and in fact the Guardianship of Infants Act of that year did not create the legal equality which NUSEC had claimed to be the 'keystone'[19] of its proposals. Another half century went by before a Conservative Government in 1973 eventually brought forward legislation giving a mother the same rights and authority as the law allowed to a father and stipulating that the rights and authority of mother and father should be equal.[20] What accounts for this long delay and what implications did this have for the law and the family?

THE GUARDIANSHIP OF INFANTS ACT 1925

Leaving on one side the view (still held by some in the 1920s) that men and women were 'not equal, they never will be equal, and you cannot make them equal'[21] there were those who believed that 'duality of control' militated against the child's interests: children should be in no doubt where authority lay.[22] Officials in the Lord Chancellor's Office, the Home Office, the Ministry of Health and even from the Parliamentary Counsel were also strongly opposed to conceding equal parental authority, and this opposition from within the Government machine was particularly effective. It was based on the belief that, 'from the purely administrative point of view', it was essential there be a single identifiable person in a household who could take the decisions required by (for example) the Poor Law and the legislation dealing with vaccination and birth registration. As Sir Claude Schuster advised the Lord Chancellor: the principle which equal authority legislation embodied was 'nonsense', because if two persons have equal rights there will be a deadlock 'whenever there is a difference between them'.[23]

The Lord Chancellor's officials gave particular weight to a second and more general argument against conceding equal authority. This was that there would be no real alternative to referring disputes between the parents about how

---

[18] For details, see SM Cretney, *Law, Law Reform and the Family* (1998) p. 167, note 64.

[19] Mrs E Hubback, in a letter of 29 April 1922 to the Attorney-General, Sir E Pollock (and, at the time, chairman of a Cabinet Committee established to consider the Bills): HO45/11566/14797.

[20] Guardianship Act 1973, s. 1(1): see further below, p. 574.

[21] Lord Banbury of Southam, *Official Report* (HL) 9 July 1924, vol. 58, col. 368.

[22] This argument was given a nautical flavour by Lord Askwith, the author of the (in the event never finalised) draft *Report from the Joint Committee of Lords and Commons to consider the Guardianship of Infants Bill given a second reading on 26 March 1923*: 'What is at stake . . . is the well-being of the child itself, and any duality of control must militate against that. The mate of a ship may be as good or better seaman than the captain, but he must either take his place and act in his stead, or else remain the second in command. No ship-owner would contemplate giving him equal authority and power. One man alone must dictate the course and prescribe the speed. Divided counsels in bad weather would make for ship-wreck, even though both parties aspired to save the ship. [We] hold no brief against equality in status between man and woman. It is on practical grounds alone' that the proposal is objectionable.

[23] Schuster to Birkenhead, 1 March 1922, PRO LCO2/752.

authority should be exercised to the court; and that this would be unacceptable for two slightly different reasons. First, it was said that intervention by a court (and especially by the magistrates' court) into the private realm of family life was intrinsically undesirable and would inevitably introduce an element of discord, never thereafter to be eradicated, into the family. Secondly, it was said that the issues involved were not really justiciable. Courts (said[24] Sir Claud Schuster) are

'concerned . . . with the definite ascertainment of the rights of the parties, a party on one side and a party on the other, and if they can ascertain what the right is then the court is inevitably led to its decision. There are no rights here. It is a question of discretion. To take a ridiculous instance, a dispute whether a child is to go to one school, or to another school—how on earth is the Court going to deal with that?'

In this view, the judge would in the end simply have to let his own personal inclinations determine the outcome,[25] and this would be wholly unacceptable.[26]

The two opposing positions seemed difficult to reconcile. From the Government's point of view, Sir Claud Schuster declared[27] that 'no compromise is possible'; whilst NUSEC had publicly committed itself to the proposition that it was 'absolutely impossible' to give up the principle of equal guardianship for joint rights and responsibilities. But Ministers and officials, faced with the possibility that the women's groups would succeed in humiliating the Government by carrying legislation against opposition, produced draft legislation which was accepted by NUSEC as embodying the 'main principles' for which the women's organisations had fought. In reality, the draft Bill still denied married woman the equal parental authority which it had been NUSEC's objective to achieve.[28] But the Bill was enacted as the Guardianship of Infants Act 1925; and it seems that many were satisfied that this brought to an end the hundred year long campaign by putting fathers and mothers[29] into an equal position in regard to their rights and powers over their offspring.[30] They were deceived.

---

[24] *Joint Select Committee on the Guardianship of Infants Bill, Minutes of Evidence* 25 July 1922, at p. 28; and note the similar objection of the Minister of Health to giving a court the impossible task of resolving a dispute between parents about vaccination: see his memorandum dated 16 February 1922 to the Home Affairs Committee: PRO LCO2/757.

[25] PO Lawrence J in evidence to the *Joint Select Committee on the Guardianship of Infants Bill, Minutes of Evidence* 25 July 1922, p. 65.

[26] In addition to these matters of juristic theory, officials were concerned with the practical question of the additional judicial resources necessary if the Court were to be 'imported into every family difference in every household in which perhaps some temporary contest of will or misunderstanding may arise': Schuster to Sir L Scott SG, 24 March 1922, PRO LCO2/752.

[27] Schuster to Birkenhead, 1 March 1922, PRO LCO2/752.

[28] For a detailed account of the complex chain of events, see SM Cretney, *Law, Law Reform and the Family* (1998) pp. 168–174.

[29] Provided they were married. Only in 1959 was the 1925 Act extended to give the parent of an illegitimate child the right to seek custody orders: see Legitimacy Act 1959, s. 3, reversing the effect of the decision in *Re CT (An Infant)* [1957] Ch 48. PRO file LCO2/5641 contains interesting material on this issue.

[30] See eg R Strachey, *The Cause* (1928) p. 383. Even lawyers seem to have taken the view that the 1925 Act effectively remedied women's grievances in this field: see E Reiss, *Rights and Duties of*

The Act did (unusually)[31] contain a preamble stating that it was expedient for the principle of equality in law between the sexes, as embodied in the Sex Disqualification (Removal) Act 1919 and other legislation to 'obtain with respect to the guardianship of infants and the rights and responsibilities conferred thereby'.[32] But the substantive provisions of the Act still denied a wife any legal authority over her child during marriage: she could only obtain such authority by seeking a court order. It is true that the Act provided for applications to be dealt with in the magistrates' court as well as in the High Court and county court[33] (a provision intended to make it possible for working-class families to have the access to justice which would have been denied them by the cost of proceedings in the superior courts) and that the Act provided for the child's mother to have the same powers as the father to apply to the court in respect of any matter affecting the child.[34] It is also true that the Act provided[35] that in reaching decisions about a child's custody or upbringing[36] the court was to regard the child's welfare as the first and paramount consideration, and 'should not take into consideration whether from any other point of view the claim of the father' was superior to that of the mother or the claim of the mother was superior to that of the father. But in only one respect did the Act give the mother a measure of equality not dependent on her making application to the court: the Act gave

Englishwomen (1934), Chapter III 'Woman as Mother 1837–1933' (1925 Act 'swept away the remaining vestiges of inequality' at p. 103) and the same author's statement in *Our Freedom and its Results* by five women (ed. R Strachey, 1936) Chapter 2, 'Changes in Law' p. 91 'another long fight which had begun as far back as 1839 came to an end'. As recently as 1982 the Act was said to have made spouses 'equal as guardians of their children': see DM Stetson, *A Woman's Issue: the Politics of Family Law Reform in England* (1982) p. 112.

[31] The 'Agreed Memorandum by members of the Committee appointed by the Home Secretary on the Guardianship of Infants negotiations' (Annex to CP 287 (24), 6 May 1924) states that the womens' groups 'attach great importance' to this statement of principle.

[32] In *J v. C* [1970] AC 668 the House of Lords (following the principle laid down in *A-G v. HRH Prince Ernest Augustus of Hanover* [1957] AC 436, 463, HL that the preamble to a statute cannot be allowed to override the statute's plain words) refused to accept that any guidance about the interpretation of the 1925 Act's substantive provisions was to be derived from the wording of the preamble.

[33] Guardianship of Infants Act 1925, s. 7.

[34] s. 2. The Act also gave the court power to make a maintenance order to the mother with a custody order and allowed orders to be made (albeit not enforced) even if mother and father were still residing together. This was a controversial matter: see pp. 447–448, above.

[35] Guardianship of Infants Act, 1925, s. 1. The text of the Bill agreed by the women's groups in 1924 had provided that in deciding such questions the court should have regard to the child's welfare as the *sole* consideration; but in the course of debate Lord Cave successfully proposed the (rather curiously drafted) 'first and paramount' formulation. He explained that he believed that matters such as the conduct and wishes of the parents were 'surely material in considering what is to become of their children' and that other matters 'such as the responsibility of the father for his children, the special suitability of a mother to have charge of young children, questions of religion, and matters of that kind' were relevant, and that the Judge should be entitled to take everything into consideration. In *Re Carroll (No 2)* [1931] 1 KB 317 the Court of Appeal gave effect to this view of the law; but subsequently the House of Lords in apparent ignorance of the legislative history effectively held that the child's welfare was the sole relevant consideration: see *J v. C* [1970] AC 668, and see further p. 572 below and SM Cretney, *Law, Law Reform and the Family* (1998) pp. 168–174.

[36] Or the administration of any property belonging to or held in trust for him or the application of the income thereof.

each parent the right to appoint a testamentary guardian to act jointly with the surviving parent and thus removed a husband's right to control the child's upbringing beyond the grave.[37] This was of largely symbolic importance.

The Guardianship of Infants Act 1925 did not give mothers the legal rights which they had demanded; but the provisions of section 1 of the Act—requiring the court to regard the child's welfare as the 'first and paramount' consideration—did greatly increase the potential role of the courts in resolving issues about children's upbringing; and the scope for judicial activism was further increased by a decision of the House of Lords in 1969.

In *J v. C*[38] the question for decision was whether a 10-year-old child should be returned to his 'unimpeachable' natural parents in Spain or continue to be in the care of the English foster parents who had looked after him for most of his life. The House of Lords held that section 1 of the Guardianship of Infants Act 1925 required that the child's welfare determine the outcome; and the Law Lords believed that to return a child who had been brought up as an English boy with English ways to a strange environment and to parents who would inevitably have difficulty in coping with his problems of readjustment would be incompatible with the statutory directive to regard the welfare of the child as the 'first and paramount' consideration. Surprisingly to anyone knowing the background to the 1925 Act, the House of Lords overruled a 1931 Court of Appeal decision[39] that the wishes of the child's parents about his or her upbringing were to be decisive unless the parents had in some way neglected their duties. The Law Lords gave no weight at all to the fact that in the course of the five-year gestation of the 1925 Act no one had suggested (whether in parliamentary debate, in the extensive proceedings of the Joint Select Committee, in the departmental papers, or indeed in the claims made by the Bill's sponsors) that the legislation could be pressed into service to justify a claim by an outsider—whether an individual, or one of the organisations concerned with child welfare—to the upbringing of a child merely on the basis that the claimant could better promote the child's welfare than the parents. Nor did the Law Lords seem aware that Slesser LJ[40] (who had delivered the leading judgment in the 1931 case) was particularly well-informed about the intentions underlying the guardianship legis-

[37] s. 4. Under the Guardianship of Infants Act 1886 the mother had only restricted rights in relation to the appointment of a guardian.

[38] [1970] AC 668.

[39] *Re Carroll (No 2)* [1931] 1 KB 317; see particularly the discussion of the effect of the 1925 Act by Slesser LJ at pp. 355–356. The headnote states that save 'as regards the respective claims of married parents as against one another, there has been no change of attitude on the part of the legislature between the years 1891 and 1926 in respect of the wishes of the parents with regard to the custody of infant children. Notwithstanding that the Guardianship of Infants Act 1925 has provided that the welfare of the infant is the first and paramount consideration for the Court . . . [it] cannot disregard the desire of [the child's] . . . parent unless that parent has so neglected his or her duty as no longer to deserve consideration'.

[40] Slesser's autobiography, *Judgment Reserved* (1941) at pp. 254–5 confirms that he had no doubt at all about the principle that the rights of the parent to the custody and religious education of the child were paramount, notwithstanding the fact that the result of applying that principle was that a child was taken from a good home with foster-parents and handed over to an institution.

lation, since it was he who (as Solicitor-General in the 1924 Labour Government) had chaired the meetings at which the compromise between the women's organisations and the Government had been worked out and translated into statutory form, and it was he who had procured the approval of the Home Affairs Committee and of the Cabinet to that compromise.[41]

Taken to a logical conclusion *J v. C*[42] would have authorised a major breach in the legal autonomy of the family unit; but subsequently the Children Act 1989 greatly restricted[43] the power of the court to authorise a child's removal from the family 'simply on the basis that the state could do better for the child' than the family. The fear—apparently live in the 1920s[44]—that the State would 'steal your children' was thus to some extent allayed.

The 1925 Act thus clearly had the potential to encourage recourse to the courts to resolve issues about the upbringing of children, but how far did it in fact do so? The fact that the Act allowed proceedings relating to child custody access and maintenance to be brought in magistrates' courts (which, in contrast to the High Court, were open to the unrepresented poor)[45] was certainly intended to make 'the benefits of the Bill open to all classes';[46] and (although the statistics are notoriously unreliable) it does seem that the number of cases involving children's upbringing became significant.[47] Those who had opposed the women's groups would have seen this as a confirmation of the fears which they had expressed; and by the middle of the century it had become part of the conventional orthodoxy that the courts should play an important role in supervising the arrangements made for children, at least in cases in which the parents' marriage had broken down.

[41] The opinions of the Law Lords also misinterpret the position of Lord Cave, and of the significance of his Opinion in the case of *Ward v. Laverty* [1925] AC 101: see SM Cretney, *Law, Law Reform and the Family* (1998) pp. 175–179.

[42] [1970] AC 668.

[43] In effect, by requiring proof of 'significant harm' as a precondition to the making of orders in favour of a local authority.

[44] In the General Election held in October 1924 the (successful) Conservative campaign concentrated heavily on the supposed threat of left-wing policies and claimed that in a Communistic Britain the 'home will be destroyed . . . Children will be taken away from their mothers and made the property of the State': RW Lyman, *The First Labour Government 1924* (1957) p. 252.

[45] In theory it had for long been open to a mother or other person to institute wardship proceedings and thereby have a court resolve questions about a child's upbringing by reference to the principle that the welfare of the child was the paramount consideration. But in practice the absence of public funding barred all but the affluent from recourse to the wardship jurisdiction at least for the first 50 years of the twentieth century. Legal aid became available for wardship proceedings under the Legal Aid and Advice Act 1949, and there was a substantial increase in the number of applications: see below p. 583 and NV Lowe and R White, *Wards of Court* (2nd ed., 1986) Chapter 1.

[46] See the NUSEC pamphlet *The Government's Guardianship of Infants Bill, 1924.* In the House of Lords Lord Askwith (*Official Report* (HL) 3 June 1924) claimed that giving the magistrates' jurisdiction was the key to giving to the 'masses of the women of this country . . . for the first time . . . the power to have something to say in regard to the welfare of their children'.

[47] In 1928 629 Guardianship of Infants applications were made in magistrates' courts, and thereafter the number rose steadily—to 1,169 in 1938, and 6,066 in 1948. In contrast only a handful of applications were made in the county court until the late 1960s: see below.

EQUALITY ATTAINED: THE GUARDIANSHIP ACT 1973

The law thus came to tolerate or even to welcome the involvement of the courts in resolving issues about children's upbringing; yet the wife was still denied legal parental authority over her own children unless and until a court gave her rights to custody, care and control or access on the breakdown of her marriage. Not until 1965 was there any further legislative initiative on this subject. In that year, Dame Joan Vickers[48] obtained leave[49] under the ten minute rule to bring in a Bill to remove this manifestation of continued discrimination against women. She claimed that to deny any legal right to a mother in the upbringing of her children was not only wrong in principle but also created a host of more mundane practical problems. For example, the mother had no legal right to permit her child to marry, no legal right to authorise withdrawals from the child's Post Office Savings Bank, and she had no legal right to consent to surgery on the child. In particular, the requirement of the Passport Office that any application for a passport in the name of a child should be accompanied by the explicit consent of the child's legal guardian caused resentment, since it prevented a separated mother from independently obtaining a passport for her child.

The grievance about the issue of passports could be (and was soon) dealt with by administrative action;[50] but more fundamental reform was needed. In sharp contrast to the situation in the 1920s, there was no real disagreement; and both Labour[51] and Conservative[52] parties published reports urging that the legal inequality of wives in this respect be remedied. In 1973 the Conservative Government introduced legislation providing that a mother should have the same rights and authority as the law allowed to a father and that the rights and authority of mother and father should be equal.[53] The Act did not require both parents to agree on a particular course of action; instead it empowered mother or father to act alone[54] but provided that the court could resolve any specific

---

[48] See Biographical Notes.   [49] *Official Report* (HC) 7 April 1965, vol. 710, col. 486.

[50] See *Official Report* (HC) *Written Answer* 27 January 1966, vol. 723, cols. 137–8: the Minister of State at the Foreign Office stated that the prior and explicit consent of the child's legal guardian would no longer be required for the issue of a passport; but it would remain open to the legal guardian or to any person awarded the custody or the care and control of a minor to enter a *caveat* against the grant of passport facilities and a decision would then be taken in the light of all the available information. Precautions were also to be taken against the danger that minors would be enabled to travel anywhere in the world without the knowledge of their parents.

[51] In its report on *Discrimination against Women*: see *per* Baroness Bacon *Official Report* (HL) 20 February 1973, vol. 339, col. 28.

[52] *Fair Shares for the Fair Sex*: see *per* Viscount Colville of Culross, *Official Report* (HL) 20 February 1973, vol. 339, col. 19.

[53] Guardianship Act 1973, s. 1(1).

[54] Guardianship Act 1973, s. 1(1). Subsequently, the Children Act 1975, s. 85(3) provided that where two or more persons had a parental right jointly either might exercise it without the other if the other had not 'signified disapproval' of such exercise; and the Children Act 1989, s. 2(4) provides that where more than one person has parental responsibility for a child, each of them may act alone and without the other in meeting that responsibility.

issue[55] on which the parents did not agree.[56] Mrs Hubback's view that the 1925 compromise would provide a firm foundation for the passage of legislation giving full equality was at last vindicated.[57]

Significance of equal authority legislation

From the perspective of the twenty-first century it may seem astonishing that anyone should ever have questioned the principle that both parents of a child ought to have legal authority to take decisions about their child's future. And yet as recently as 1987 Parliament denied legal parental authority to the father of an illegitimate child precisely because of fears that a man who had never had any real commitment to the child or involvement in the child's upbringing might abuse any authority which the law accorded him.[58] The fact that having legal authority is regarded as at least symbolically important[59] is evidenced by the large number of applications[60] made in each of the closing years of the twentieth century by fathers of illegitimate children for orders giving them parental authority,[61] by the willingness of the courts to accept that to make such an order will often be in the child's interests even if the father has no immediate prospect of exercising that authority or having any factual relationship with the child,[62] and perhaps most of all by the readiness of the Blair Government to promote legislation attributing such authority at least to a father who is registered as such.[63]

---

[55] The draftsman was careful to limit the court's powers in proceedings under the Guardianship Act 1973 to resolution of the particular matter in issue. The court had no power to make custody or access orders: see Guardianship Act 1973, s. 1(4); and for illustrations of the effect of this restriction SM Cretney, *Principles of Family Law* (4th ed., 1984) p. 366.

[56] Guardianship Act 1973, s. 1(3).

[57] See Eva M Hubback, *The Government's Guardianship of Infants Bill, 1924.*

[58] Note the view of Balcombe LJ expressed some years after that decision had been taken: '. . . the position of the natural father can be infinitely variable; at one end of the spectrum his connection with the child may be only the single act of intercourse (possibly even rape) which led to conception . . . Considerable social evils might have resulted if the father at the bottom end of the spectrum had been automatically granted full parental rights and duties . . .': *Re H (Minors) (Local Authority Parental Rights)(No 3)* [1991] Fam 151, 158.

[59] It has been said that entitlement to parental authority has 'real and tangible value, not only as something [the parent] can cherish to the sake of his own peace of mind, but also as a status carrying with it rights in waiting'; and that to give a father parental authority gives him an appropriate legal status: see *Re C (Minors) (Parental Rights)* [1992] 1 FLR 1, 3, 8, *per* Waite J.

[60] The Judicial Statistics Annual Report 2001, Table 5.3 states that 8,151 orders were made and only 374 refused. A large number of applications (1,194) were withdrawn.

[61] Ie parental responsibility orders under Children Act 1989, s. 4(1)(a). 'Parental responsibility' is defined by s. 3 of that Act as meaning all the rights, duties, powers, responsibilities and authority which by law a parent of a child has in relation to the child and his property.

[62] See eg *Re H (A Minor) (Parental Responsibility)* [1993] 1 FLR 484, CA (Judge correctly denied father contact with his child, but wrong to refuse to make parental responsibility order in his favour); and *Re S (A Minor) (Stay of Proceedings)* [1993] 2 FLR 912, 917–91 (father who has no prospect of being able to exercise parental rights in the immediate future entitled to ask court to 'recognise his position as the father of the child, irrespective of any question of maintenance or contact. It is a matter to which the father may well attach importance for its own sake').

[63] See the Adoption and Children Act 2002, s. 111 see p. 565, above.

With the benefit of hindsight, Sir Claud Schuster's fear[64] that to give both parents authority over their children would be 'to substitute a legal for a domestic forum in every household; to multiply causes of strife, and to bring into the courts, to the encumbrance of their proper business, a multitude of trivial disputes' can be seen to have been unfounded. The Guardianship Act 1973 did provide[65] machinery for a parent to ask the court to resolve an issue about which there was disagreement, but parents who are not separating do not in practice ask the court to resolve a disagreement[66] about their children's upbringing. There has been no reported example of an application having been made.

CHILDREN OF DIVORCE

The opposition to equal parental authority legislation reflects a more general reluctance to encourage or even allow the courts or other agents of the State to intervene in the private realm of family life;[67] but if parents split up it is obvious that someone may have to resolve disputes about what is to happen to the children. No one therefore questioned the need for the Divorce Court to have power to make orders about the children's upbringing, and the Matrimonial Causes Act 1857 provided that in judicial separation nullity and divorce proceedings the court could make such orders[68] with respect to the custody maintenance and education of the couple's children as it deemed 'just and proper'.[69]

For many years the existence of this power did not give rise to much discussion. The issue of 'custody' was secondary to the question whether the court would grant the decree or not; and if it did do so it would usually refuse to grant custody to a mother found to have committed adultery. In this way, Victorian judges gave effect[70] to the belief that it would 'have a salutary effect in the interests of public morality that it should be known that a woman, if found guilty of adultery, will forfeit . . . all right to the custody of or access to her children'.[71]

Gradually a somewhat more charitable view was taken, at least in relation to allowing the adulterous mother access to children who were in the legal custody

[64] He admitted that his view was expressed 'with somewhat more freedom than is usual in an official memorandum' in response to a request (presumably from the Lord Chancellor) for his personal view on the 1923 Bill: see LCO2/757, 24 March 1923.

[65] s. 1(3); see above.

[66] The Law Commission, *Review of Child Law: Custody* (Working Paper No. 96, para. 2.3).

[67] For the debate about the circumstances in which welfare agencies should be allowed to take compulsory measures about a child's upbringing, see Chapter 20 below.

[68] Interim orders could be made before the decree was granted.

[69] Matrimonial Causes Act 1857, s. 35; Matrimonial Causes Act 1859, s. 4. The court could also direct that proper proceedings be taken for placing the children as wards under the protection of the Court of Chancery. Magistrates exercising their domestic jurisdiction also had powers to make custody orders.

[70] See eg *Clout v. Clout* (1861) 2 Sw&Tr 391; *Bent v. Bent* (1861) 2 Sw&Tr 391, 394; *Handley v. Handley* [1891] P 124, 128.

[71] *Seddon v. Seddon* (1862) 2 Sw&Tr 640, 642, *per* Sir Cresswell Cresswell.

of the father.[72] But not until the end of World War II did it become fairly generally accepted[73] that the fact that a mother had committed adultery was not necessarily inconsistent with her being a good parent to her children.[74] Only then did the courts begin to emphasise[75] that since 1925[76] the welfare of the child had been statutorily declared to be the 'first and paramount' consideration in determining questions about a child's upbringing.[77] But it remained true that the question of who 'won' the divorce case could (and often would) also have an influence on the orders made about children, and this seems to have led to behind-the-scenes bargaining:[78] a mother who did not want a divorce might agree to drop her defence and even herself petition on terms that the husband would not seek care and control of the children but would be allowed ample access to them.[79]

[72] In 1936 AP Herbert had felt it necessary to include in his Divorce Bill a specific provision (Clause 8) that the court apply the welfare principle 'whichever party to the marriage may be the guilty party' but this was, after some discussion, dropped as being unnecessary: *Standing Committee A, Official Report*, 2 February 1937.

[73] But not universally: in 1948 a High Court judge (believing that a woman who had once committed adultery was likely to do so again) ordered a mother (divorced on the ground of adultery committed during her husband's four-year absence on war service with the man she subsequently married) to hand over the eight-year-old girl who had lived with her since birth to the care of her father. The Court of Appeal held that he had been wrong to apply the principle that the child's *moral* welfare was the paramount consideration. Even then, there was no appeal against the decision that custody (as distinct from care and control) of the child should remain with the father. In 1962 one Lord Justice of Appeal thought it necessary to declare that a woman guilty of deserting the husband might be deprived of the care of the children: 'If a wife chooses to leave her husband, for no ground which she chooses to put forward, but because she has a fancy or passion for another man, as this woman has, she must be prepared to take the consequences. She is a curious woman in that she seems to have no consciousness that she has duties as well as rights': *Re L* [1962] 1 WLR 886, 890, *per* Harman LJ. Fifteen years later the Court of Appeal expressed its disagreement with this approach in *Re K (Minors) (Children: Care and Control)* [1977] Fam 179 (where the Court refused to deny care and control of children to the wife of an Anglican clergyman who wanted an order so that she could set up home with her lover. The father argued that being brought up in an adulterous home would damage the children's spiritual welfare).

[74] See eg *Allen v. Allen* [1948] 2 All ER 413; *Willoughby v. Willoughby* [1951] P 184, 192, *per* Singleton LJ.

[75] *S(BD) v. S(DJ)* [1977] Fam 109, 116, *per* Ormrod LJ.

[76] Guardianship of Infants Act 1925, s. 1.

[77] This trend developed so far that in *Richards v. Richards* [1984] 1 AC 174 a county court judge felt the law compelled him to make an order excluding the husband from the matrimonial home notwithstanding the fact that this would be 'thoroughly unjust' on the grounds that otherwise the children's welfare would be prejudiced. The House of Lords held he had been wrong to do so, in part because the welfare principle embodied in the 1925 Act was only applicable in cases in which the child's upbringing was the central issue for decision.

[78] The *Report of the Royal Commission on Marriage and Divorce* (1956, Cmd. 9678) para. 231 accepted that it was natural for the parties to wish to make early arrangements for the upbringing of the children, but was concerned that the legal procedures did not necessarily allow the court properly to scrutinise what was proposed.

[79] It came to be accepted that a Divorce Court order granting an individual 'custody' of the child conferred on that person the 'bundle of rights and powers' which included not only the right to have physical possession of the child but also authority to take decisions on such matters as choice of education, religious upbringing, consent to medical treatment and so on: see *Willis v. Willis* [1928] P 10; *Hewer v. Bryant* [1970] 1 QB 357; and generally JM Eekelaar, (1973) 89 LQR 211. The courts, in their efforts to promote the child's welfare, developed the practice of making so-called 'split' orders

The Divorce Court's role: protecting children against parental selfishness?

In 1947 the Denning *Committee on Procedure in Matrimonial Causes*[80] concluded that in practice the divorce process subordinated the welfare of the children 'to the interests of their parents'.[81] The Committee believed that divorced
parents had 'disabled themselves from fulfilling their joint responsibility' and
regretted that the courts' procedures were 'but poorly fitted' for safeguarding
the children's interests.

The Denning Committee made two recommendations intended to mitigate
the defects in procedures which it had identified. First, the Committee thought
that the judge should in all cases deal with the future of the children on the same
day as he dealt with the divorce. This proposal was never implemented.
Secondly, the Committee urged the appointment of Court welfare officers who
would have access to all petitions and be empowered to report to the court.

The immediate impact of these recommendations was not great;[82] but in the
long term the Report was influential: in particular, whilst the Committee was
careful to distinguish between the judicial role to be discharged by a court on the
one hand and the social work role of investigation to be carried out by welfare
officers on the other, the Committee envisaged a role[83] for the court in moni-

in which one parent would be given 'care and control' (ie the right to have physical possession of the
child) but the other—or sometimes the two jointly—would be given 'custody' (the right to take decisions about the child's general upbringing). The courts would also make orders for 'access', either in
general terms (eg father to have 'reasonable access') or specific and sometimes extremely detailed
terms. But the traditional understanding of this terminology did not survive close scrutiny: see *Dipper
v. Dipper* [1981] Fam 31, CA and generally M Booth, 'Child Legislation. Custody: Its Judicial
Interpretation and Statutory Definition' [1982] Statute Law Review, 71. The Children Act 1975
attempted to rationalise the concepts used in certain legal proceedings relating to children (but not in
divorce proceedings). The Children Act 1989 introduced more radical reform: it provided that the
court in divorce and other family proceedings could make orders relating to residence and contact,
make a specific issue order dealing with any particular issue which arose in relation to the child's
upbringing (for example, where the child should be educated) and make a prohibited steps order (for
example, prohibiting the removal of a child from the place where he is currently living): see below.

[80] Set up because of concern about the large increase in divorces associated with World War II.
For the Committee's consideration of the impact of divorce on children, see *Final Report*, Cmd.
7024, para. 30.

[81] *Denning Report*, para. 30.

[82] Coldstream told Hodson J on 14 October 1947 (file PRO LCO2/3959) that the prospect of
bringing forward the legislation necessary for the appointment of court welfare officers was 'exceedingly remote'; but see below.

[83] The Committee recommended that a divorce petition should contain a statement about the
children, giving their ages, their past present and proposed homes, maintenance and education. It
appears that effect was given to this recommendation in 1947, but that the relevant provision was
dropped from the Matrimonial Causes Rules 'because it was found that it did not achieve its object.
Details of the children's future home and education were often very sketchily filled in, or completed
in the absence of any precise information at all, since it was often impossible at the time of filing the
petition to provide definite answers to those questions. Moreover, since the arrangements for the
children were not an issue in the case, and since the court had no sanctions to impose, the matter
tended to be dealt with perfunctorily, and without careful investigation . . .' *Royal Commission on
Marriage and Divorce* (Chairman, Lord Morton of Henryton) *Report 1951–1955*, 1956, Cmd. 9678,
(subsequently cited as the *Morton Report*) para. 379.

toring parental decisions which would certainly have surprised Sir Claud Schuster and the others who had so forcefully argued against involving the courts in 'trivial disputes' about children's upbringing. Moreover, the notion that starting divorce proceedings automatically rendered the family liable to scrutiny and report went some way to making the civil justice system part of the machinery of state policing, to which some were strongly hostile.[84]

The 1956 *Royal Commission on Marriage and Divorce*[85] was even more out-spoken about the effects of divorce on children:

'There is a wealth of testimony as to the effects on children of the breakdown of normal family relationships. Where family life breaks down there is always the risk of a failure to meet fully the child's need for security and affection. If in fact there is such failure, the child may become so emotionally disturbed as to reject the influences of the family and this may result in anti-social-behaviour. . . . Where divorce takes place it is . . . essential that everything which is possible in the circumstances should be done to mitigate the effects upon the child of the disruption of family life.'

The *Morton Report's* recommendations were much more radical than Denning's. Its starting point was (in essence) that the parents could not be trusted to invoke the court's powers and processes. The 'root of the trouble' lay in the fact that divorce was regarded as a matter for the husband and the wife, and for this reason there were 'no adequate means of ensuring that someone is specially charged to look after the children's interests'. For the *Morton Report*, it was not cases in which the parties contested custody issues which gave rise to concern: the parties would be only too ready to tell the court of each other's fail-ings, and the court had the means of deciding where the truth lay.[86] The Morton Commission's concern lay in precisely the fact that custody was not, in the great majority of cases, contested. In those circumstances, even though the applicant would not always be the most suitable person to care for the children, the court would rarely be able to make any order other than that which the parties had agreed since the procedure was 'not such as to allow the judge to satisfy himself about the position of the children'.[87]

The Morton Commission heard a great deal of evidence about the divorce process and children, and recorded that the

'solution which received most support was that the responsibility should be placed clearly upon the court, which should consider the arrangements for the children in every case, whether the question of custody was raised by either or both parties or not'.[88]

The *Morton Report* accordingly recommended a procedure under which the court would have an inquisitorial duty to investigate the arrangements proposed

---

[84] See generally GK Behlmer, *Friends of the Family* (1998), especially Chapter 2.

[85] 1956, Cmd. 9678.

[86] Although the Commission noted concern that a parent might claim custody 'from spiteful or selfish motives', the children becoming 'pawns in the struggle of wills', with the judge sometimes being 'forced back to the test of which of the parents was the innocent party in the divorce suit': para. 366(iii).

[87] *Morton Report*, paras. 366(ii) and 370.   [88] *Morton Report*, para. 367.

for the children's upbringing, and satisfy itself that those arrangements were satisfactory or at least the best that could be devised in the circumstances;[89] and the
Matrimonial Proceedings (Children) Act 1958[90] gave effect to those recommendations.[91] Thenceforth, a parent seeking divorce had to file a statement of the
arrangements made for the care and upbringing of children, and the marriage
would not be ended unless and until the court had expressed its satisfaction.

The *Morton Report* also recognised that increasing divorce meant that to
define the class of children with whom the court was concerned by reference
solely to *children of the parties' marriage*[92] no longer reflected the realities of
family life; and that the courts' powers and duties should be exercisable over
children of either spouse (whether legitimate or illegitimate) living in the family
at the time of the break-up and also other children living in the family and maintained by one or both of the spouses. The Matrimonial Proceedings (Children)
Act 1958[93] provided that children of either party *accepted by* the other should
be subject to the courts' powers and duties; and the Matrimonial Proceedings
and Property Act 1970[94] further widened the class to extend to any child *treated
by* the spouses as a 'child of the family'. No longer was any biological or formal
legal link required to make a child a member of the divorcing parent's family.

The effect of the 1958 legislation[95] was extensively researched,[96] and detailed

---

[89] The *Morton Report's* recommendation was the inspiration for s. 2, Matrimonial Proceedings
(Children) Act 1958, summarised in the text.

[90] s. 2. Rules of court prescribed details of the procedure.

[91] The Denning Committee and the *Morton Report* both made recommendations for the involvement of welfare officers in divorce proceedings.

[92] Including the adopted, legitimated or illegitimate children of the two spouses: see *Galloway v.
Galloway* [1956] AC 299.

[93] s. 1. Children boarded out with a spouse as a foster-parent were excluded from the definition.

[94] Matrimonial Proceedings and Property Act 1970, s. 27(1) giving effect to recommendations
made by the Law Commission in its *Report on Financial Provision in Matrimonial Proceedings*
(1969), Law Com. No. 25, paras. 23–32. The expression 'treated as' a child of the family was substituted for 'accepted as' such a child in order to remove difficulties where one spouse had not
known that a third party was the child's genetic parent: see *W(RJ) v. W(SJ)* [1972] Fam 152. Minor
changes in the definition of the children affected were made by the Children Act 1989.

[95] The Law Commission (in its Report, the *Field of Choice*, which led to the Divorce Reform Act
1969) considered that the procedural changes made in the light of the *Denning* and *Morton
Reports*—and especially the rule that before making a decree absolute of divorce the court be satisfied that arrangements for the children's upbringing were satisfactory or the best that could be made
in the circumstances—had led to greater attention being given to the children's interests in divorce:
para. 47. However, it accepted that the effect of divorce on children remained one 'of the most serious and disturbing aspects of the' matter. The Commission's response to the 'major problem' (*Field
of Choice*, para. 120(3)(d)) of providing adequate protection for children was unspecific; but the
Commission had no hesitation in rejecting suggestions made by influential and knowledgeable persons (including Sir Jocelyn Simon, the President of the Probate, Divorce and Admiralty Division, in
a lecture, *Seven Pillars of Divorce Reform* (1965)) that the law should not allow divorce at all where
there were children of school age: apart from any consideration of the justice of discriminating
between childless and other marriages in this way, to draw such a distinction could not be in the
interests of the children themselves who would inevitably come to be regarded as the main obstacle
to their parents' happiness.

[96] Notably by JC Hall (*Arrangements for the Care and Upbringing of Children* . . . published by
the Commission as its Published Working Paper No. 15; E Elston, J Fuller and M Murch, 'Judicial
Hearings of Undefended Divorce Petitions' (1975) 38 MLR 609; G Davis, A MacLeod and M Murch,

changes were made over the years. The procedural changes made by the 1958 Act were generally thought to have done something to reinforce the concept that the Divorce Court had inquisitorial functions of a wholly different kind from those of the common law courts, and in that sense are of considerable conceptual importance. But in practice the role of the court under the 1958 procedure was somewhat ambivalent, and often the judicial investigation was restricted to a quick perusal of the petitioner's written statement (in reality, once again often not wholly accurate)[97] and his or her (usually monosyllabic) response to a single formal question put by counsel at the hearing of the petition.[98]

Significant modifications had to be made when the so-called 'special procedure' for dealing with undefended divorce cases was introduced.[99] It was politically necessary to do something to demonstrate the law's concern to protect the children of divorcing parents;[100] and an elaborate system of judicial 'children's appointments' was therefore created. Husband and wife no longer needed to go before any judicial officer to get a decree nisi, but they would still have to file a statement of the arrangements proposed for the children and the petitioner would have to attend before a judge sitting in private for the purpose of considering what was proposed. A research project found this system of Children's Appointments to be largely ineffective[101] and the consensus of opinion seemed to be[102] that the court's role was rarely more than symbolic. The Children Act 1989 abolished the appointment system;[103] and the Act also introduced substantial changes reflecting a much more restricted view of the practicability and

'Undefended Divorce: Should Section 41 of the Matrimonial Causes Act 1973 be Repealed?' (1983) 46 MLR 121; and see J Eekelaar and E Clive, *Custody after Divorce* (Centre for Socio-Legal Studies Oxford 1977).

[97] See the study carried out by JC Hall for the Law Commission, *Arrangements for the Care and Upbringing of Children* . . . published by the Commission as its Published Working Paper No. 15.

[98] See E Elston, J Fuller and M Murch, 'Judicial Hearings of Undefended Divorce Petitions' (1975) 38 MLR 609, 618–619.

[99] A judge in chambers would, in the presence of one or both parties, consider the proposed arrangements at a so-called 'Children's Appointment': see G Davis, A MacLeod and M Murch, 'Undefended Divorce: Should Section 41 of the Matrimonial Causes Act 1973 be Repealed?' (1983) 46 MLR 121.

[100] In introducing the extension of the Special Procedure Lord Chancellor Elwyn-Jones said: '. . . If I thought that there would be anything in my proposals which detracted from such protection as the law already gives to children in this unhappy situation I should not be putting it forward today': *Official Report* (HL) 15 June 1976, vol. 371, col. 1218.

[101] 'Undefended Divorce: Should Section 41 of the Matrimonial Causes Act 1973 be Repealed?' by G Davis, A MacLeod and M Murch (1983) 46 MLR 121. The issue is fully considered in the Law Commission's Working Paper No. 96, *Review of Child Law: Custody* (1986) pp. 86–110, which concluded at para. 4.10 that the procedure had 'not been successful in any of its declared aims'.

[102] See M Murch et al, 'Safeguarding Children's Welfare in Uncontentious Divorce: A Study of s. 41 of the Matrimonial Causes Act 1973', Lord Chancellor's Department, Research Series No. 7/99, London (1999); G Douglas, M Murch, L Scanlan and A Perry, 'Safeguarding Children's Welfare in Non-Contentious Divorce: Towards a New Conception of the Legal Process?' (2000) 63 MLR 177.

[103] Children Act 1989, s. 108(4) and Sch. 12, para. 31, provided that the court should consider whether it was necessary to exercise its powers to make orders under that Act in respect of children of the family; and in certain very restricted circumstances the court could direct that the making of the decree absolute be postponed.

even the desirability of the courts seeking to supervise and intervene in parental arrangements. Parents still had to produce a written statement of the arrangements to be made; but the court's task was no longer to consider whether the arrangements were 'satisfactory'. Rather the question was whether the facts indicated a need for the court to exercise its power in relation to the child.[104]

In conceptual terms, the *Morton Report* had tried to make divorce less a matter for the parties and more a matter for an investigation of public interest; and the Children Act 1989 reversed the trend. The underlying aspiration remained unchanged, however. The *Morton Report* had had high expectations for the 'positive and beneficial' effect of the legislation it proposed: the interests of children would become just as important as the question whether the marriage should be dissolved; and the Report assumed that the scheme it envisaged would encourage a sense of parental responsibility. At the turn of the century, the statute book declares Parliament's view that broken marriages should be brought to an end 'with minimum distress to . . . the children affected' and that questions should be dealt with 'in a manner designed to promote as good a continuing relationship between the parties and . . . [the] children . . . as is possible in the circumstances'[105] and a great deal of effort is being put into attempts to safeguard the welfare of divorcing parents' children.[106] But the effectiveness of such measures is difficult to evaluate; and it remains to be seen what impact they have on safeguarding children's interests.

It is certainly now easy to demonstrate that the *Morton Report's* belief that to make parents realise at the outset their obligations to their children would lead to some of them abandoning the idea of divorce for the sake of the children'[107] was almost certainly not well founded: it is manifestly clear that the outcome of the 1958 scheme and its subsequent modifications did not lead to any reduction in the number of children affected by divorce. In 1956 there were some 20,000 such children each year; by the end of the twentieth century the parents of some 150,000 children aged 16 or under divorced each year in England and Wales.

---

[104] See Law Com. No. 172, paras. 3.7–3.11; A Bainham, 'The Privatisation of the Public Interest in Children' (1990) 53 MLR 206; and SM Cretney, 'Defining the Limits of State Intervention: The Child and the Courts' in D Freestone (ed.), *Children and the Law, Essays in Honour of Professor HK Bevan* (1990). The feeling that the courts had an important role to play in safeguarding the welfare of the children of divorcing parents was forcefully put in the debates on the Bill for the Family Law Act 1996, and s. 11 of that Act would have made further modifications to the procedures which however remained based on those introduced in 1958.

[105] Family Law Act 1996, s. 1. This provision was brought into force, and although the failure to implement other parts of the Act greatly restricts the scope of s. 1 there seems little dispute that it states an objective which most of those involved in the family justice system would support. For the impact of some measures taken to improve professional practice in such cases, see G Douglas and M Murch, 'Taking account of children's needs in divorce . . .' [2002] CFLQ 57.

[106] A Children Act Advisory Committee exercised an oversight over the impact of the provisions of the Children Act 1989. The Advisory Committee was dissolved in 1997, but the Family Law Advisory Board continued to discharge some of these functions until it too ceased to exist in 2002. In particular, the Board published two important Reports on problems of securing satisfactory contact between parent and child after divorce: *Contact in Cases where there is Domestic Violence* (2000) and *Making Contact Work* (2002).

[107] *Morton Report*, para. 377.

Moreover, whatever the case for and against these attempts to demonstrate an effective commitment to mitigating the adverse impact of divorce on children[108] it seems that contested litigation about such matters as contact had (perhaps because such litigation provides an officially sanctioned procedure whereby the parties can seek the emotional release not otherwise available to them) escalated dramatically in the closing years of the century.[109] There were contested applications for contact in one in every five divorce cases in which there were children,[110] and the number of court orders had risen by more than 100% over a five-year period. Inevitably, these proceedings involved precisely the bitterness, distress and humiliation which it was the declared objective of the 1969 legislation to minimise. It must also be said that the belief that the new divorce law would reduce the illegitimacy rate has been dramatically falsified: in 1971, there were some 74,000 illegitimate births in the United Kingdom or about 8%; but by 1998 there were no less than 270,000 such births or not far short of 40%. (It is of course true that these statistics may reflect social change—not least a sharp decline in the proportion of couples who believe that marriage is the only appropriate basis for a long term sexual relationship—not foreseen at all in 1969.)

The 1958 legislation, by accepting the policy that courts and welfare officers should have a responsibility for monitoring arrangements which the parents have agreed for the upbringing of their children, accepted the potential for increased State intervention in family life. But the scope of that intervention in practice pales into insignificance when compared with the greatly increased role adopted, in the course of the twentieth century by the administrative agencies of the State. First, however, we need to outline the powers of the court to take decisions in the exercise of the so-called wardship jurisdiction; and to consider the question of how and when parental authority yields to the child's right to make his or her own decisions.

THE INHERENT JURISDICTION OF THE HIGH COURT OVER CHILDREN: WARDS OF COURT

It had long been accepted that the Crown, as *parens patriae*[111] had the right and duty to protect the person and property of children and others (for example

---

[108] The political importance of this factor was again demonstrated during the passage of the Family Law Act 1996, when changes (of uncertain effect) in the court's duties were made (see s. 11 of the Act) in an attempt to still criticism that the law did not provide adequately for children involved in divorce.

[109] See the findings (summarised in SM Cretney (ed.), *Family Law—Essays for the New Millennium* (2000) p. 127) of a research project conducted by G Davis and others.

[110] In 2000 some 76,000 of the 141,000 divorced couples had children of the family aged under 16 but the proportion of divorcing parents with such children has fallen somewhat over the years: Table 4.10, *Marriage Divorce and Adoption Statistics 2000* (National Statistics) Series FM2 No. 28, 2002.

[111] See J Seymour, 'Parens Patriae and wardship powers: their nature and origins' (1994) 14 OJLS 159 (suggesting that historical analysis of this paternal role revealed a process of 'benevolent opportunism' on the part of the judiciary).

those once described as 'lunatics' or 'idiots')[112] in need of such care. By
Victorian times, there was no dispute that these functions were delegated[113] to
the Lord Chancellor and the other judges of the Court of Chancery;[114] and (in
theory at least) they could do whatever needed to be done to protect the ward's
welfare.[115] Readers of Charles Dickens' novel *Bleak House* have a vivid picture
of how this so-called inherent jurisdiction was exercised over the children and
young people[116] who came to be called 'wards of court'.[117] But these children
were, at the beginning of the twentieth century, few in number. This was
because the court had no effective means of acting unless there was property
which could be ordered to be applied for the use and maintenance of the child.
As Lord Chancellor Eldon put it: the court could not take on itself the maintenance of all the children in the country.[118] Accordingly, the main function of the
wardship jurisdiction at the beginning of the twentieth century was restricted to
protecting wealthy orphans and their property. In the words of the Chancery
Division judges' evidence to the *Committee on the Age of Majority* in 1967:[119]

The typical Ward of Court in the nineteenth century was

'a wealthy orphan—the "pretty young ward in Chancery" of the Lord Chancellor's song
in *Iolanthe*. The chief function of the Court was to supervise the administration of the
ward's property by his or her guardian and, if she was a girl, to consider—and if thought

---

[112] See *Re F (Mental Patient: Sterilisation)* [1990] AC 1, *per* Lord Brandon of Oakbrook. In 1960
the inherent jurisdiction over those suffering from mental illness (which had apparently been formally delegated to the judges by Royal Warrant under the Sign Manual: see *Re F (Mental Patient:
Sterilisation)* [1990] AC 1, 12, *per* Lord Donaldson) was revoked and the treatment of such persons
is now governed by statute. But revocation did not affect the jurisdiction in respect of children.

[113] The guardianship of a ward was a profitable incident of feudal tenure, which benefited the
Crown on the death of the tenant in chief. The Court of Wards and Liveries was established in 1540
in an attempt to maximise this source of revenue; but the Tenures Abolition Act 1660 abolished that
court, and the development of the law in the context of taking decisions intended to promote the
child's welfare stems from subsequent developments. See *Falkland v. Bertie* (1698) 2 Vern 333, 342;
Wellesley v. Beaufort (1827) 2 Russ 1, 20; *Wellesley v.Wellesley* (1828) 2 Bli NS 124; *Johnstone v.
Beattie* (1843) 10 Cl & Fin 41, 120; *Re Spence* (1847) 2 Ph 247.

[114] The wardship jurisdiction was exercised by the judges of the Chancery Division of the High
Court; but the Administration of Justice Act 1970, s. 1(2) transferred jurisdiction to the newly created Family Division of the High Court: see Chapter 21.

[115] *Wellesley v.Wellesley* (1828) 2 Bli NS 124, 136, 142, *per* Lords Redesdale and Manners.

[116] The jurisdiction was exercisable over any 'infant' ie anyone under the age of majority which
was 21 until reduced to 18 by the Family Law Reform Act 1969: see below. The expressions 'child'
and 'children' in the text refer to those legally classified as 'infants'.

[117] In theory, wardship was the *result* of the exercise of the court's inherent jurisdiction; and it
has been said that 'even if there was no property and the child was not a ward of court, ... the Court
of Chancery had the power to interfere for the protection of the infant by making whatever order
was appropriate': *Re L (An Infant)* [1968] P 119, 156, *per* Lord Denning MR; and see *Re N (Infants)*
[1967] 1 Ch 512, 531, *per* Stamp J. The relationship between wardship and the inherent jurisdiction
is reviewed by Ward LJ in *Re Z (A Minor)(Identification: Restrictions on Publication)* [1997]
Fam 1.

[118] *Wellesley v. Beaufort* (1827) 2 Russ 1, 21. The Chancery court apparently had no inherent
power to order a parent to maintain his child; but it became the practice to join an application for
maintenance under the Guardianship of Infants Act 1925 to the wardship summons: see *Latey
Report*, para. 250. The Family Law Reform Act 1969 gave the court statutory power to order a parent to make periodical maintenance payments to the ward or to any person having care and control.

[119] 1967, Cmnd. 3342, para. 200. The Committee's report is henceforth cited as the *Latey Report*.

fit to approve—proposals for her marriage and to see that her property was safeguarded by a suitable marriage settlement'.

It is true that the Matrimonial Causes Act 1857[120] gave the Divorce Court power to direct that children of divorcing parents be made wards of court; but in practice it seems that this power was normally exercised only in cases in which substantial property was involved.[121] The wardship jurisdiction was thus for long only of concern to the wealthy; and even half way through the twentieth century there were only some 60 applications to make children wards each year.[122]

This association between property and wealth was originally reinforced by the procedure used for invoking the court's jurisdiction. The mere filing of a Bill in Chancery to which a child was a party immediately made the child a ward of court; and thenceforth no important step in the ward's life (such as marriage or going abroad) could be taken without leave of the court.[123] But by the beginning of the twentieth century it was realised that parents (or others) could invoke the judicial power of the State by the simple process of settling a nominal sum of money[124] on the child and then bringing proceedings, nominally for the administration of the trusts of the settlement but in practice to control aspects of the child's life. Later, it was realised that the law prescribed no minimum sum for the purpose of making a child a ward; and in 1949 Lord Merriman P told the House of Lords that children were being warded in this way by the 'settlement' of even a trifling sum of money—perhaps less than £5 in year 2000 values.[125]

At the beginning of the twentieth century there were still cases in which a parent invoked the wardship jurisdiction as a disciplinary measure, possibly all the more effective because defiance of the parent and the court could lead to the child's imprisonment:

In *Re H's Settlement*[126] a 17-year-old boy had been intended for the army, but 'gave so much trouble owing to his disregard of regulations, and in particular by staying away at night that the tutor with whom he was then placed declined to keep him any longer'. His mother made him a ward, but he persistently neglected to obey the directions about his education made by the judge. Worse, without seeking the necessary permission from the court, he married in church

---

[120] s. 35.
[121] See eg *Mozley Stark v. Mozley Stark* [1910] P 190 where the court declined to exercise the power over a 16-year-old girl, notwithstanding the fact that there would certainly have been advantages in doing so. She had assets of no more than £150 (perhaps £9,000 in year 2000 values).
[122] *Latey Report*, para. 200.
[123] See *Re Hodges* (1857) 3 K&J 213; *Brown v. Collins* (1883) 25 Ch D 56.
[124] See *Re Race* (1857) 1 H&M 420n (£21—possibly £1,200 in year 2000 values) and *Re H's Settlement* [1909] 2 Ch 260 (£100—perhaps £6,000).
[125] 'it used to be thought that the minimum tariff should be £5 . . . but this has recently become 2/6d': *Official Report* (HL) 28 July 1949, vol. 164, col. 671 (ie 12.5p or less than £3 in year 2000 values). The judges had become concerned at the abuse of the system: see also *Final Report* of the Denning Committee (1947, Cmd. 7024) para. 32. The Law Reform (Miscellaneous Provisions) Act dealt with this 'abuse' by providing that a child should become a ward only by the issue of a summons. Far from reducing recourse to the jurisdiction the introduction of this simple procedure was followed by a sharp increase in the number of wardships.
[126] [1909] 2 Ch 260.

after banns, giving false information about his age and address. The judge[127] committed him to Brixton Prison for contempt: 'if ever there was a case in which it is right to resort to the ultimate sanction, this is . . . such a case'. The judge hoped that this would be a 'salutary lesson to this boy and teach him that he, as well as the rest of us, must obey the orders of those who are in authority or run the risk of serious personal discomfort'. History does not reveal whether these hopes were fulfilled.[128]

Over the years, it may be that the emphasis of the wardship jurisdiction changed from protecting the rights of parents to seeking to ensure the welfare of the young people concerned.[129] The principle (so a Chancery judge[130] put it in 1967) was that the court took the child into its care, and decided how and with whom he or she was to be brought up and all other relevant matters. But parental concern about romantic attachments and marriage was still what fuelled many cases; and in 1967 the *Latey Report* noted[131] that wardship enabled the court to act 'to protect the young and inexperienced from folly and exploitation up to the age of 21'.[132] This protection was reinforced by the power of the court not only to decide who should have 'care and control' of the ward but also to make orders binding on the ward (for example, directing the ward to reside at a specified place) and also to order third parties to refrain from associating or communicating with the ward.[133] In the 1960s the potential of wardship as a means of attempting to control young peoples' behaviour became much more widely understood; and the fact that legal aid had been made available meant that even people of modest means could ward their children. The judges became concerned about the apparent increase in the number of applications[134] involving young people 'usually young women'[135] in their later teens who

---

[127] Warrington J.

[128] The wife escaped imprisonment because she did not know her husband was a ward of court, she was young, and 'did not expect to receive any sordid advantage from the marriage', *per* Warrington J at p. 264. Third parties who defied court orders prohibiting contact or marriage with a ward also faced imprisonment: see eg *Re Elwes (No. 1)* (1958) *The Times*, 30 July; Chapter 2 above.

[129] See *Re K (Infants)* [1963] Ch 381, 386, *per* Ungoed-Thomas J.

[130] Lord Cross of Chelsea (1973) 83 LQR 200, 207.   [131] At para. 202.

[132] The *Latey Report* specifically referred to the court's authority in respect of property and education, the power to 'curb [a ward's] rebellious and anti-social-behaviour' as well as its powers in respect of administration and protection of property, and the power to prohibit marriage and to prevent a ward from leaving the country: para. 202. It also drew attention to the use of wardship to protect a child in adoption proceedings (for example, where the mother had withdrawn her consent to the adoption or where the father was challenging the making of an order) and in divorce. Some insight into the nature of the court's detailed control over the life of a ward can be gained from the personal experience of N Mostyn QC as recorded in 'Why be a Family Lawyer' in SM Cretney (ed.), *Family Law—Essays for the New Millennium* (2000) pp. 110–111.

[133] Paras. 202–203; and for examples *Re Elwes (No. 1)* (1958) *The Times*, 30 July; *Re F (orse. A) (A Minor) (Publication of Information)* [1977] Fam 58, below.

[134] The judges told the Committee that such orders were virtually unknown before World War II but that applications became common in the late 1950s and were now 'increasing every year': PRO LCO17/10. But in fact it seems that the substantial increase in the number of wardship applications was concentrated in the under-18 age group: *Latey Minority Report*, para. 583.

[135] The judges commented that the young women in question 'do not regard the fact that they are having sexual intercourse with—or even are pregnant by—men to whom they are not married, and

'resent the fact that their parents have made them wards. The relationship between the girl and her parents is further embittered and the rift widened. The girl's determination to pursue the association is hardened and she may even deliberately become pregnant. Any attempt to control her from a distance by a "non-association" order is usually foredoomed to failure. Committal to prison leaves a scar; it can hardly do any good. The Court finds itself in a helpless and intolerable position; its orders flouted; the law and the administration of it by the Court brought into disrepute and the public confidence in the administration of justice undermined. The time, effort and expense are very heavy . . .'.

There were, no doubt, some cases in which the court's intervention was effective at least in the short term. For example:

In *Re F (orse. A) (A Minor) (Publication of Information)*[136] Lord Denning MR referred to an association between a girl of 15 and a man of 28—'a very bad character. He had a long criminal record with 18 convictions. He took drugs and wore long hair. He was one of a "hippy" gang who did no work but squatted in empty premises. He gave this young girl drugs. He had sexual intercourse with her, knowing that she was only 15'. The court ordered that the child should reside at her parents' home or such other place as the Official Solicitor should approve, and that the man should not harbour her.

But it was becoming part of the conventional wisdom that the law had little part to play in deterring young people from engaging in behaviour which their seniors considered unwise;[137] and it became apparent that the law could easily be made to appear ridiculous:

In *Re Dunhill*[138] a 20-year-old woman, living with her widowed mother whilst trying to establish a career as a fashion model, was made a ward on the application of a night club owner. He apparently intended to ward all the young women working in the club as disk jockeys in an attempt to stop their working for a rival entertainer operating from the Goodwin Sands. No doubt he was aware that this move would attract publicity. When he told Miss Dunhill what he had done she responded that he 'must be joking'; but she soon discovered she had to apply to the court for an order striking out the proceedings. The judge described the club owner's action as an abuse of process, and noted the potential for trouble implicit in the continuance of the existing procedures.

to whom they may never be able to be married, as a particularly serious or regrettable state of affairs. They often resent the fact that their parents have made them wards and at best regard their parents' views with mild contempt': PRO LCO17/10. The Senior Chancery Judge told the Committee in oral evidence that he doubted whether the court's orders were complied with or indeed whether the parties took much notice of what he had said once they had left the court: Notes of oral evidence, 4 July 1966.

[136] [1977] Fam 58.

[137] '. . . if the ward is really intent on maintaining the association at all costs, the court can achieve little or nothing. In the end it will either have to throw in its hand either by "dewarding" her or by giving its consent to the marriage assuming that the pair wish to get married and can legally do so': Sir Geoffrey Cross, 'Wards of Court' (1967) 83 LQR 200, 211.

[138] (1967) 111 SJ 113.

There was another, perhaps even more telling, factor. As the *Latey Report*[139] put it in 1967, the courts could deal with the small number of cases coming before them in the first half of the twentieth century 'exhaustively' and realistically try to offer 'all the protection of a parent'.[140] But the nature of the jurisdiction was such that it could 'only cope really thoroughly with a comparatively small number of wards';[141] and there had been an almost six-fold increase in the number of applications in the 15 years from 1950.[142] The system was not really capable of dealing with such a large number of cases in the traditional manner.

The Latey Committee in 1967, believing that the answer to the kind of problems presented by teenage wardships lay 'in good family relationships and persuasion and not in a restrictive law and its sanctions'[143] had recommended that the age of majority be reduced from 21 to 18, and it would not really have made sense to seek to preserve the wardship jurisdiction in respect of children over that age.[144] The Committee accordingly recommended that the wardship jurisdiction should cease at 18; and the Family Law Act 1969 ended the power of the courts to exercise the inherent jurisdiction[145] over persons aged 18 or over.[146]

The Wardship Jurisdiction 1969–1989

The 1969 Act, contrary to expectations (or hopes) had no effect on the increase in the number of applications to ward a child: in 1971 622 originating summonses were issued, in 1982 2,301, and in 1991 the number reached 4,791.[147] As the Law Commission put it in 1987[148] wardship had come to be regarded 'not so much as a refuge for orphaned heiresses and a bulwark against predatory adventurers but rather as a means of resolving all kinds of disputes over children . . .'.

The underlying reason for the increase in recourse to wardship seems to have been its great flexibility.[149] There was no need to establish any 'ground' before

---

[139] Para. 194.   [140] *Latey Report*, para. 193.   [141] *Ibid.*, para. 194.

[142] The Committee believed that one factor accounting for this increase was that the 'nature of modern life, with parental authority accepted far less unquestioningly than it used to be' made it 'obvious that more and more disputes will find their way to the wardship jurisdiction': *Latey Report*, para. 194. The other factor (in addition to the fact that legal aid had become available to finance representation in wardship) influencing the sharply upward trend seem to have been the simplification of the procedure effected by Law Reform (Miscellaneous Provisions) Act 1949 whereby an infant became a ward forthwith upon the making of an application under that Act, and it was no longer necessary to create a settlement.

[143] *Latey Report*, para. 237.

[144] See *ibid.*, paras. 233–240. The Committee did not accept suggestions that the court's jurisdiction should end when a child attained 16 (even though he remained legally a minor).

[145] From which wardship derived.

[146] See *Bolton v. Bolton* [1891] 3 Ch 270; *F v. West Berkshire Health Authority* [1990] 2 AC 1.

[147] The figures are taken from the annual *Judicial Statistics*, and from the judgment of Ward LJ in *Re Z (A Minor) (Identification: Restrictions on Publication)* [1997] Fam 1, 13. The use made of the jurisdiction in the 1970s and 1980s is analysed by the Law Commission in its Working Paper No. 101, *Wards of Court* (1987).

[148] *Wards of Court* (Working Paper No. 101, 1987) para. 3.2.

[149] For a full account reference should be made to NV Lowe and R White, *Wards of Court* (2nd ed., 1986); and see also the Law Commission's Working Paper cited above.

a child could be made a ward: the issue of a summons had the immediate effect that the child became a ward, and thereafter (so long as the wardship continued) making all important decisions about the child's life was a matter for the court. Moreover, in deciding questions relating to the child's upbringing the court would apply the principle that the child's welfare was paramount; and to that end the court had available to it a wide range of powers. For these reasons, wardship was still used in some cases in which parents disapproved of a teenager's mode of life; it was increasingly used where there was a dispute between estranged parents; it was used where a child had been taken abroad (or where abduction was feared); it was used by grandparents and others—especially foster-parents and potential adopters seeking to keep a child in their care—who were not eligible to apply for care and control or access to the child under any of the statutory provisions relating to children; and it was used in cases where the medical care of a child was disputed. A striking example of the flexibility of wardship is furnished by two cases concerned with medical treatment:

In *Re D (Sterilisation)*[150] an 11-year-old girl was seriously mentally and physically disabled. Her widowed mother, fearful that her daughter might become pregnant and bear a child who would inherit some of these disabilities, consulted a paediatrician and gynaecologist. They recommended that the girl should be sterilised (a procedure at the time irreversible). A woman social worker came to hear of the case, and made the girl a ward so as to bring the matter before the court. The court ruled against sterilisation: it was not in the girl's best interests to be deprived in this way of the 'basic human right to reproduce'.

In *Re B (A Minor) (Wardship: Medical Treatment)*[151] the parents of a new-born and severely handicapped Down's Syndrome child, believing that in all the circumstances it would be best to allow nature to take its course, refused consent to the surgical removal of a potentially fatal intestinal blockage. The Court of Appeal held that it was in the child's interests to be allowed to live. The court was unconvinced that the child's life was 'demonstrably going to be so awful that the child must be condemned to die'; and the necessary surgery was carried out notwithstanding the parent's opposition.[152]

But perhaps the largest growth was in the number of cases relating to local authority decisions on the care of children. On the one hand, some local authorities increasingly preferred to apply to the High Court to make a child a ward of

---

[150] [1976] Fam 185.   [151] (1981) 3 FLR 117.

[152] Compare *Re T (Wardship: Medical Treatment)* [1997] 1 FLR 502, where the court refused to order parents to hand a baby over for the liver transplant surgeons believed to be necessary to save the baby's live. The Court of Appeal, overruling the trial judge, held that it would not be in the child's interests in effect to compel her mother to take on a total commitment when she did not agree with what was proposed.

court[153] rather than seeking a care order under somewhat restrictive legislative provisions:[154]

The factors which might lead an authority to take this view can be seen from the decision in *Re C (A Minor) (Justices' Decision: Review)*.[155] In that case, the local authority were concerned that the mother had not been feeding her baby properly, that she had been leaving him alone at night, and that he had suffered certain unexplained injuries. But the local authority were unable to muster sufficient evidence to convince the magistrates hearing their application for a care order that the child was being ill-treated or that his proper development was being avoidably impaired or neglected.[156] The Court of Appeal held that the child had properly been made a ward of court: the interests of the child justified the High Court in acting and investigating the case in full, notwithstanding the fact that the local authority had failed to satisfy the Juvenile Court that there were grounds for making a care order under the statutory code.[157]

On the other hand, parents were using wardship in an attempt to question decisions taken by the local authority under the care legislation. For example:

In *A v. Liverpool City Council*[158] a mother made her child (who was the subject of a care order) a ward of court in an attempt to challenge the local authority's decision to reduce her access to him from once weekly to once monthly. She argued that the local authority's decision was incompatible with the child's welfare; and that accordingly the Court should in wardship proceedings examine the merits.

Cases such as these explain why it is that by 1991 local authorities started more than half of all wardship applications and were involved in perhaps more than two-thirds of them. But in *A v. Liverpool City Council*[159] the House of Lords held that the wardship jurisdiction should not be used to review the merits of the authority's decision:[160] in reaching this decision, the Law Lords applied traditional principles of administrative law and held that the statutory code marked out an area in which, subject to the enacted limitations and safeguards, decisions for the child's welfare were removed from the parents and from supervision by the courts.

That decision seemed yet further to increase the potential unfairness of the law: local authorities (it seemed) could still invoke wardship when it suited them

---

[153] For a full consideration of situations in which a local authority might reasonably prefer wardship to proceedings under the statutory provisions, see NV Lowe and R White, *Wards of Court* (2nd ed., 1986) pp. 284–290.

[154] These are described in Chapter 19, below.   [155] (1979) 2 FLR 62, CA.

[156] Children and Young Persons Act 1969, s. 1(2)(a).

[157] See also *Essex County Council v. TLR and KBR* (1979) 9 Fam Law 15.

[158] [1982] AC 363, HL.   [159] [1982] AC 363, HL.

[160] The Law Lords were influenced to some extent by the cost and delay caused by the excessive use being made of the wardship jurisdiction at the time.

to do so, whereas the parents were deprived of a similar choice. Eventually[161] the Children Act 1989 placed significant restrictions on the power of local authorities to invoke the court's inherent jurisdiction.

The Children Act did not in terms affect the rights of individuals to invoke the wardship jurisdiction but by rationalising the private law (for example, by creating a statutory framework whereby any person who obtained the consent of the court could seek orders relating to the child's residence, contact with the child, or on any other aspect of the child's upbringing) the circumstances in which it was necessary to invoke the wardship jurisdiction were greatly reduced. And the courts seem to have been reluctant to allow the wardship jurisdiction to be invoked unless the statutory procedures are for some reason manifestly not apt. It has been said[162] that:

the courts have a 'clear duty, in loyalty to the scheme and purpose of the Children Act legislation, to permit recourse to wardship only when it becomes apparent to the judge in any particular case that the question which the court is determining . . . cannot be resolved . . . in a way that secures the best interests of the child' under the statutory procedures permitting individuals to seek orders relating to the upbringing of a child under Part II of the Act; 'or where the minor's person is in a state of jeopardy from which he can only be protected by giving him the status of a ward of court, or where the court's functions need to be secured from the effects potentially injurious to the child, of external influences (intrusive publicity for example) and it is decided that conferring on the child the status of a ward will prove a more efficient deterrent' than the use of proceedings for contempt of court.

The effect of the Children Act on the number of applications was dramatic: there were only 492 wardship applications in 1992 compared with nearly 5,000 in the year before the Act came into force.[163] But the flexibility of wardship and the extensive powers available to the court mean that the ancient inherent jurisdiction still has its uses. In the unusual case of *Re KR (Abduction: Forcible Removal by Parent)*[164] for example:

A 16-year-old girl had been forcibly taken to India where her parents intended to force her into an arranged marriage. The girl was able to communicate with her elder sister who issued a wardship summons. Thereafter the court made a number of orders intended to encourage the relevant Indian authorities to give

---

[161] See Chapter 20 below. The relationship of statutory and wardship jurisdiction was considered in the *Second Report from the Social Services Committee, Session 1983–84, Children in Care,* Vol. 1 (HC 360—I, 1984, chairman: Mrs Renee Short MP), in the *Review of Child Care Law* (1985), and in the Law Commission's Working Paper No. 101, *Wards of Court* (1987). In 1988, the Law Commission (apparently impressed by the view that reform of the statutory code would reduce the need to resort to wardship proceedings 'save in the most unusual and complex cases': *Review of Child Law, Guardianship and Custody* (1988) Law Com. No. 172, para. 1.4) confined its recommendations to the statutory powers of the courts to deal with the care and upbringing of children.

[162] *Per* Waite LJ, *Re T (A Minor) (Child: Representation)* [1994] Fam 49, CA.

[163] *Re Z (A Minor) (Identification: Restrictions on Publication)* [1997] Fam 1, 13, *per* Ward LJ. The *Judicial Statistics Annual Reports* ceased to give statistics about wardship in 1992.

[164] [1999] 2 FLR 542, Singer J.

assistance. The orders were successful: the girl was put into contact with the British High Commission in India and flown to England, protected by injunctions.

It seems that the inherent jurisdiction is found especially suitable where issues of consent to medical treatment are involved. For example:

In Re M (Medical Treatment: Consent),[165] a healthy active 15½-year-old girl suffered heart failure without any prior warning. Doctors concluded that she would die within a week or so unless she had a heart transplant. But the patient said she 'would rather die than have the transplant and have someone else's heart'. The authorities contacted a High Court judge at his home on a Friday evening and told him that application was to be made to carry out the transplant notwithstanding the absence of consent. The judge organised representation by solicitor and counsel, the patient was interviewed, representations made, and on Saturday morning the judge (whilst accepting that the views of this intelligent young person should carry considerable weight) concluded that an assessment of her welfare required him to give authority for the transplant to be carried out.

PARENTAL AUTHORITY ERODED AS CHILDREN'S LEGAL AUTONOMY INCREASED

So far, it has been assumed that parents do have rights (or authority) over their children subject only to the possibility that the courts[166] might intervene; but the text has not sought to explain the extent of those rights, nor has it posed the question of whether the child has any countervailing rights which could be set up in opposition to those of the parent. Neither of these matters received any extended discussion in a legal context in this country in the first half of the twentieth century.

The question of the *content* of parental authority remains largely devoid of specific statutory[167] or case law discussion; but academic analysis has identified the rights which were vested in the father of a legitimate child at common law.[168] Cases coming before the courts have often been concerned with such

---

[165] [1999] 2 FLR 1097.

[166] Or other state agencies, notably local authorities: see Chapter 20, below.

[167] In Scotland, the Children (Scotland) Act 1995, s. 2 sets out a list of parental rights. English statutes are unhelpfully tautologous: the Children Act 1975, for example, defined the 'parental rights and duties' as meaning 'all the rights and duties which by law the mother and father have in relation to a legitimate child and his property'; and it is apparent that the definition was provided to facilitate elegant and concise drafting rather than to clarify what was included within this expression. Similarly, the 'key concept' of 'parental responsibility' in the Children Act 1989 is defined in terms of 'the rights, duties, powers, responsibilities and authority which by law a parent of a child has in relation to the child and his property' and again does not provide any explanation of what these might be.

[168] See JM Eekelaar, 'What are parental rights?' (1973) 89 LQR 210; HK Bevan, *Child Law* (2nd ed., 1989) para. 1.17 ff; A Bainham, *Child Law* (2nd ed., 1998) p. 95 ff; and M Freeman, 'Disputing Children' in SN Katz, JM Eekelaar and M Maclean (eds.), *Cross Currents* (2000) Chapter 20. For a comparative overview of the situation in the United States, see BB Woodhouse, 'The Status of Children: A Story of Emerging Rights', in Katz et al. *op. cit.* Chapter 19.

matters as the child's education, religious upbringing, and medical treatment; but commentators have generally taken the view[169] that precise definition is unimportant, given the readiness (and indeed the duty)[170] of the courts to decide matters relating to a child's upbringing by reference to the child's welfare rather than to any question of entitlement.

It is very different with the *duration* of parental authority. First, the Family Law Reform Act 1969[171] (following the recommendations of the *Latey Report*) reduced the age of majority from 21 to 18, with the inevitable corollary that parental authority over a child terminates at the beginning of the child's 18th birthday[172] unless it has ended previously. The same Act contained a provision[173] that the consent of a person aged 16 or more to any 'surgical medical or dental treatment' should be as effective as if he were of full age. Hence, a young person of 16 or over may give an effective consent to any treatment without it being necessary for him or her to obtain any consent from the parent or guardian. But the decision of the House of Lords[174] in the case of *Gillick v. West Norfolk and Wisbech Area Health Authority*[175] is of much greater conceptual significance:

Mrs Victoria Gillick, the mother of four daughters under the age of 16 (none of whom, so far as is known, had expressed any interest in seeking such treatment) sought an assurance from the Health Authority that her daughters would not be given contraceptive treatment without her prior knowledge and evidence of her consent. The authority refused to give such an assurance. Mrs Gillick therefore asked the court to declare that DHSS advice to the effect that young people could in some circumstances be given contraceptive advice and treatment without their parent's knowledge and consent was unlawful and wrong, and that it adversely affected Mrs Gillick's right as the children's parent. The House of Lords held that the court should decline to make any such declaration.

The principle underlying the decision had wide implications. It was that parental authority 'yields to the child's right to make his own decisions when he reaches a sufficient understanding and intelligence to be capable of making up his own mind on the matter requiring decision'.[176] The question whether a child had sufficient understanding and intelligence must be an issue of fact in each case, depending on the complexity of the issues involved, and the child's emotional and intellectual maturity. Some decisions (including the decision whether to seek contraceptive advice) require a very high level of maturity and understanding; but less complex issues would require a correspondingly less highly developed intellectual and moral understanding.

---

[169] See notably the Law Commission's *Report on Illegitimacy* (Law Com. No. 118) para. 4.18.

[170] Imposed by statute by the Guardianship of Infants Act 1925, s. 1.

[171] s. 1. For the *Latey Report's* deliberations, see Chapter 2, above, pp. 65–68.

[172] See Family Law Reform Act 1969, s. 9 for the rule that a person attains a particular age at 'the commencement of the relevant anniversary of the date of his birth'.

[173] s. 8.   [174] By a majority of 3–2, overruling the decision of the Court of Appeal.

[175] [1986] AC 112.   [176] *Per* Lord Scarman at p. 186.

The decision quite clearly overturned the common law principle that (although no wise parent would try to enforce his views against the wishes of a mature child and although the law would refuse to lend its aid to a parent who sought to impose his will on a minor above the 'age of discretion') the parent did retain his authority until the child reached the age of majority, and the fact that a particular child's intellectual or emotional development was advanced was irrelevant in deciding whether or not parental authority continued.[177]

The decision thus reflected views about children's rights which would have astonished the judges who had decided cases such as *Re Agar Ellis*[178] but was more in line with the views of many modern academic commentators.[179]

But it soon became clear that not all judges favoured extending the child's right to take decisions at the expense of the parents' right to have the final word. The House of Lords' decision that a 'mature minor' had the right to give his or her consent to medical or other treatment could not be overridden; and it might have been thought that the same principle would govern the situation in which a child refuses to agree to treatment. But the courts held this was not so: the parents (and the court acting in a *parens patriae* capacity) apparently retain the right to give a consent on the child's behalf even though the child has the maturity to make the decision for himself and does not agree with what is proposed. A number of commentators[180] find this situation anomalous. Again, legislation frequently lays down rules which seem incompatible with the *Gillick* principle: for example, no 17-year-old child can make a valid will, however competent and mature he may be; whilst legislation making a parent guilty of a criminal offence if the child does not regularly attend school[181] seems to envisage that it is for the parent not only to take decisions about a child's education but also that the parent has the means of compelling a child to do as he is told.

The closing years of the century saw a great deal of discussion about children's rights; and sometimes the issue was raised by those who thought that the legal system did not adequately protect the child whose parents divorced. The Children Act 1989[182] did provide machinery whereby a child might be allowed himself to start proceedings questioning decisions taken about his upbringing by his parents; and press reports suggested that by allowing a child to start proceedings the Act would allow a child to 'divorce' his parents. But in practice the

[177] See the judgment of Parker LJ in *Gillick v. West Norfolk and Wisbech Area Health Authority* [1986] AC 112, 118, CA.

[178] (1883) 24 Ch D 317.

[179] MDA Freeman, *The Rights and Wrongs of Children* (1983) has been particularly influential in this country. There had been (and continues to be) a great deal of comment on the subject in the United States: see on this (and generally) the excellent discussion in A Bainham, *Child Law* (2nd ed., 1998) Chapter 3 (the book also contains a full discussion of the relevance of the provisions of the United Nations Convention on the Rights of the Child, 1989).

[180] See the discussion in A Bainham, *Child Law* (2nd ed., 1998), pp. 270–281.

[181] Education Act 1996, s. 443.

[182] The Act envisages that children may obtain the court's leave to make applications for orders under the Act; and contains guidelines about the factors relevant to the exercise of this jurisdiction: Children Act 1989, s. 10(9).

courts exercised considerable caution in defining the circumstances in which children might be allowed to become directly involved in litigation.[183] Again, in the debates on the Conservative Government's 1996 divorce reforms, groups representing children's interests were particularly vocal and the Family Law Act 1996 contained provisions[184] (in the event never brought into force) which would have led to children being independently represented in some divorce and other proceedings. These provisions were regarded as somewhat radical; and it seems to have been overlooked that 40 years previously the far-from-radical *Morton Report* had insisted that children should be routinely separately represented in divorce proceedings. At the close of the twentieth century this particular issue remains unresolved. But it can confidently be said that, at the end of the twentieth century, the law was far more ready to recognise that children have a right to be heard when decisions about their future are being taken and that they have specific rights to take legally effective decisions for themselves than it had been at the beginning of the century.

[183] See eg *Re S (A Minor) (Independent Representation)* [1993] Fam 263, 276; *Re C (A Minor) (Leave to seek section 8 order)* [1994] 1 FLR 26; *Re SC (A Minor) (Leave to seek residence order)* [1994] 1 FLR 96; *Re C (Residence: Child's Application for Leave)* [1995] 1 FLR 927.
[184] Family Law Act 1996, s. 64.

17

Legal Adoption of Children, 1900–1973

INTRODUCTION

At the beginning of the twentieth century, the term 'adoption' in relation to children was used in three different senses. First, it was used to describe the situation in which a child was taken into the home of a person other than the child's parent, and brought up to a greater or lesser extent as the child of the adopter. Examples of this practice are to be found in fictional classics,[1] and there seems no reason to doubt that this kind of 'adoption' had been and remained a familiar social institution in all classes of society.[2] Secondly, there was the situation in which 'adoption' was simulated: an unmarried pregnant woman would arrange for her child to be delivered in a private lying-in house, the owner of which would be paid a lump sum in exchange for arranging the child's 'adoption'.[3] The child would then be removed to 'the worst class of baby-farming house' where it would usually be neglected and die.[4] Thirdly, there was the so-called Poor Law Adoption in which the Poor Law Guardians assumed by resolution all the child's parents' rights and powers in respect of the child's upbringing; and would arrange for the child to be 'adopted'.[5]

In 1926 the Adoption of Children Act created the institution of legal adoption in this country. For many years thereafter adoption under the Act was used primarily in the case of babies (usually illegitimate) placed with childless families

---

[1] See eg Anthony Trollope's *Dr Thorne* (1858) (where an unmarried man 'adopts' his deceased brother's illegitimate daughter); and (for examples in the work of Jane Austen) GH Treitel, 'Jane Austen and the Law' (1984) 100 LQR 549, 574.

[2] See, on the practice of charitably minded neighbours in working class areas bringing up an orphaned child as their own, Major CR Attlee in the debate on the Bill for the Adoption Act 1926, *Official Report* (HC) vol. 192, col. 932.

[3] See the *Report of the Select Committee on the Protection of Infant Life* (1871, BPP vii 607).

[4] It seems that at this time adoption was still often a cover for child trafficking—either for paedophiles or for financial gain. In 1923 the NSPCC claimed that 'a certain class of person' would 'readily undertake care of a child for the sake of immediate financial gain' and gave examples from its Inspectors' Reports. The same source revealed the 'terrible story' of a 'little girl of five who, when twenty two months old, was adopted by a man and woman of no repute living at Wigan. This child was outraged continuously from the age of four, was suffering from acute gonorrhoea and, but for the intelligent observation of a neighbour, would still be living in these appalling conditions': R Parr (Director of the NSPCC) to SW Harris, Home Office, 31 May 1923, PRO HO45/11540. Over the years, comprehensive child protection measures were put onto the statute book.

[5] This procedure continued (under the name 'assumption of parental rights') until 1991: see p. 727, below. The working of the Poor Law Adoption for long seemed to many commentators to be admirable in every respect: see pp. 641–642, 679, below.

who would thenceforth care for the child as if it had been born to the husband and wife; and in 1949 the Adoption Act accepted the principle that the law should treat the adopted child as legally the child of the adoptive parents. Adoption became very popular: in 1968 the number of adoption orders made rose to a peak of 24,831.[6]

The Children Act 1948 imposed extensive duties on local authorities to care for children, and local authorities had power in certain circumstances to assume parental rights over children in their care. This did not constitute legal adoption; but it began to be realised that adoption could be an effective long term solution for the child otherwise likely to remain in a children's home or in some other form of local authority care. Adoption also came to be used in a way certainly not foreseen in 1926: step-parents and relatives increasingly had recourse to adoption as a technique to make them in law the parents of the child who was in fact living in their household.

The last quarter of the century was a period of dramatic change in the perception of adoption. The ready availability of contraception and legal abortion meant that very few healthy babies, born in this country, were available for adoption. Adoption accordingly ceased to be primarily concerned with babies: whereas in 1968 half the children adopted were less than a year old, by the end of the century the proportion had fallen to 4%.[7] And although step-parents continued to use adoption to make the legal family congruent with the social family and a significant number of babies were brought to the country from overseas to be adopted here, adoption became much more concerned with the provision of long-term care for children who had been in local authority care. In 1975, the Children Act marked the shift in emphasis; and at the end of the twentieth century about half of all adoptions were of children who had been in local authority care. Government policy focussed on increasing the use of adoption for children in care in a determined attempt to reduce the number of children cared for in institutions or by (possibly short-term) foster parents; and in February 2000 Prime Minister Blair personally headed a review to ensure the best use of adoption to meet the needs of children in care.[8]

The reader may well find these changes of emphasis difficult to understand; and it has to be admitted that there has traditionally been some difference between lawyers and lay people about the essence of adoption. For the lawyer, it is concerned above all with the legal rights of the birth and adoptive parents on the one hand and the adopted child on the other. Because the legal effect of adoption—in effect, an irrevocable transfer of a child from one family to another—is so dramatic lawyers have tended to regard it as a process necessarily different in

---

[6] *Report of the Departmental Committee on the Adoption of Children* (1972, Cmnd. 5107) Appendix B, Table 1.

[7] *Marriage, Divorce and Adoption Statistics 2000* (ONS, FM2).

[8] The *Prime Minister's Review, Adoption* (Cabinet Office, Performance and Innovation Unit, 2000) p. 3.

kind from other legal processes for dealing with the care of children. Social workers tend to be less impressed by these legal matters.

THE ADOPTION OF CHILDREN ACT 1926

'Adoption' in the sense of providing a home for a child who would be cared for as a member of the adopters' family certainly existed as a social institution at the beginning of the century, but the law made no provision for it. Whatever the facts of the relationship between adoptive parent and adopted child they remained legally strangers, and in particular there was no effective machinery[9] to prevent the natural parents exercising the common law right to remove the child—sometimes when the child became capable of earning a wage. Children's societies arranging adoption might make the parties sign formal agreements in an attempt to regulate the relationship,[10] but these agreements were legally ineffective.[11]

---

[9] Although the Custody of Children Act 1891 did give the court in *habeas corpus* proceedings a discretion to refuse to enforce the natural parents' legal right to recover a child the parent had abandoned or deserted. There is no evidence that this legislation had any significant impact in the present context. In 1921, the Salvation Army and Dr Barnado's Homes gave evidence of the birth parents reclaiming adopted children. They argued that potential foster parents were often deterred from taking children because of the lack of security: see *Report of a Conference of Officials held on 28 November 1921 to consider whether to advise the Home Secretary to introduce legislation*: PRO HO45/11540. For nineteenth century attempts to legislate in this area see NV Lowe, 'English Adoption Law: Past, Present and Future' in SN Katz, J Eekelaar and M Maclean, *Cross Currents* (2000) at pp. 308–309.

[10] For example, the National Children's Home and Orphanage required the mother to sign an 'Adoption Agreement' agreeing to the adoption of the child 'by foster parents selected by the Rev W Hodson Smith, Principal of the National Children's Home' and undertaking not to interfere with the child in any way or make any further claim on the child. Those who wrote applying to adopt a child were sent a discouraging letter stating that as a rule the Home did not have many children suitable for adoption, that children could only be sent to Christian families, and that provision must be made for the child's regular attendance at Divine Worship and for receiving 'careful religious instruction'. Applicants were required to submit a one-page questionnaire (asking eg whether the family kept a domestic servant, and whether they were total abstainers) and to name three referees, (one of whom had to be a Minister) and were warned that children were placed on a three-or six-month trial and that the Society reserved the right and power to remove the child if this proved necessary. But at the conclusion of the probationary period it was to be for the applicants to say whether or not the child suited them: see the form in PRO HO45/11540/14797.

[11] See eg *Re JM Caroll (an Infant)* [1931] 1 KB 317, CA, where a domestic servant, anxious to be released from the Workhouse signed an agreement for the adoption of her child. The agreement did not name the adopters, but the child was placed with a respectable couple. The mother subsequently changed her mind and wanted the child handed over to the Crusade of Rescue and Homes for Destitute Catholic Children which would foster the child until she was old enough to move to a home staffed by Sisters of Charity, and later opportunities would be given for her emigration. The Court of Appeal held that the agreement was ineffective and that effect should be given to the mother's present wishes.

Pressure for legal adoption

The War of 1914–1918 encouraged the activities of organisations aiming to 'place' children with adopters and also prompted the growth of pressure groups concerned to secure legislation.[12] (In fact[13] it seems doubtful whether the War had resulted in any significant increase in recourse to 'adoption'.) In 1920 the Coalition Government yielded to these expressions of demand and appointed a committee chaired by Sir Alfred Hopkinson KC[14] to consider the desirability of making legal provision for the adoption of children and, if so, the form which such legislation should take.

The two Committees

The Hopkinson Committee found that the adoption of children was legally recognised in 'almost all civilised states';[15] and believed that it would be better for children who could not be cared for by their birth parents to be placed in some other home as members of a family 'under the care of a suitable and

[12] Home Office officials believed that the situation was being exploited by organisations which had 'sprung up in the last year or two', one of which was 'run by rather doubtful people' (although another was said to place out 'vast numbers of babies'): *Report of a Conference of Officials . . . 28 November 1921* PRO HO45/11540, p. 2. In fact the National Children's Home claimed that, although it had arranged for the care and education of more than 15,000 children 'adoption' was only found relevant in 26 of them: PRO HO45/11540/14797.

[13] The Hopkinson Committee had no doubt that there had been an increase in adoptions and that the demand was likely to continue: it attributed this (see para. 62) to the preference for the 'family home' as the most suitable environment for young children when the alternative would be institutional care; the 'increasing tendency to value child life and to desire association with and the companionship of children on the part of those who have no children of their own or desire another child'; and the 'fact that some women are without the mother sense, or for some other reason, such as economic pressure or a desire for greater personal liberty, are unable or unwilling to carry out the obligations they should feel towards their children'. But the Home Office ascertained that the only statistics the Hopkinson Committee had obtained were from two adoption societies founded during the War with the specific objective of placing children; and the Home Office itself had no figures showing how far adoption 'in the proper sense' was practised (although enquiries of the Registrar-General revealed that applications were being received daily from people anxious to have their adopted child's name changed: *Report of a Conference of Officials . . . 28 November 1921* PRO HO45/11540, pp. 1–2). Some years later the *Report of the (Tomlin) Child Adoption Committee* (1924–1925, Cmd. 2401) hereafter the '*Tomlin Report*' para. 4 asserted that the 1914–1918 War led to 'an increase in the number of de facto adoptions but that increase has not been wholly maintained'; and the Tomlin Committee not only found itself 'unable to satisfy [itself] as to the extent of the effective demand for a legal system of adoption' by potential or actual adoptive parents but also thought that the 'activities in recent years of societies arranging systematically for the adoption of children' were not altogether commendable: see p. 601, below.

[14] Neville Chamberlain MP (1869–1940) was also a member of the Hopkinson Committee. See Biographical Notes.

[15] *Report of the Committee on Child Adoption* (1921, Cmd. 1254) (hereafter 'the *Hopkinson Report*') para. 4. The Hopkinson Committee was particularly impressed by experience in the British Dominions (eg New Zealand, where not only did legal adoption benefit adoptive parent and adopted child but the State also gained since the aid provided by private persons reduced the burden on the State of maintaining the destitute and educating the unfortunate child): para. 7.

responsible person' than to be 'gathered together in an institution with a number of others'.[16] But the Committee accepted the warnings of the NSPCC that adoption could easily become a cover for child trafficking. It claimed that the 'practice of adoption without definite legal sanction [had] already been accompanied in many cases by serious evils' and that if it became more frequent those evils might, in the absence of proper safeguards, become more serious.[17] But the Committee believed that, in the absence of appropriate legal machinery, adoption would still take place[18] 'under agreements entered into sometimes unwisely and without due premeditation';[19] and that the absence of proper control over the 'adoption' of children led inevitably to a situation in which children could be kept in institutions neither inspected nor controlled and that children might be 'handed from one person to another with or without payment, advertised for disposal, and even sent out of the country without any record being kept'.[20] Legislation should therefore provide the means for eliminating bad homes and agencies using 'unsatisfactory methods' in undertaking or furthering the 'adoption' of children;[21] and the Hopkinson Committee recommended that binding legal effect should be given to agreements for the adoption of children, provided that—in order to protect the welfare of the child concerned—the 'sanction of some responsible judicial or other public authority' were given to the adoption.[22]

The Hopkinson Committee's Report was not well received within the Home Office[23] or the Lord Chancellor's Office.[24] But that did not make it any easier to

---

[16] *Hopkinson Report*, para. 10.   [17] *Hopkinson Report*, para. 16.

[18] Particularly where the mother lacked maternal feeling: persons would always be found (the Committee considered, see para. 63) 'willing and anxious to transfer the custody of their children to others for reasons which are in fact inadequate or improper . . .' and this evil could best be minimised by proper regulation.

[19] *Hopkinson Report*, para. 11.   [20] *Hopkinson Report*, para. 61.

[21] *Hopkinson Report*, para. 60. The Committee thought the Infant Life Protection provisions of the Children Act 1908 provided an appropriate precedent: para. 64.

[22] *Hopkinson Report*, para. 19.

[23] Sir E Blackwell (see Biographical Notes) told the conference of officials held on 28 November 1921 that although the Hopkinson Committee had 'regarded the legalisation of adoption as an urgent matter' it had given 'little or no information in support of their recommendation'. On 7 April an official had minuted that the Report was 'not a very good one' not least because it made recommendations which were outside its terms of reference—possibly a reference to the Committee's recommendation that assisting necessitous mothers in the bringing up of their children by some form of allowance be actively considered—and had also advocated other reforms (including consolidation of the legislation relating to children) which would 'never have been made if [the Committee] had examined any witness from the administrative staff of the Home Office . . .'.

[24] Sir Claud Schuster 'strongly opposed the [Hopkinson] Committee's recommendation that sanction for adoption should be given by the County Courts. The Lord Chancellor was not at all disposed to agree to administrative work of this kind being placed on the County Courts. Besides, the County Court Judge was as a rule neither qualified to form an opinion on the merits of these applications, nor had he any staff at his disposal for making the necessary enquiries. It was quite a mistake to suggest that the . . . Judge or his officials were closely acquainted with the conditions of people living in the district'. (A manuscript note by a Home Office official points out that the evidence of the county court judges to the Committee was inconsistent with Schuster's contention: *Report of a Conference of Officials . . . 28 November 1921* PRO HO45/11540, p. 2.)

resist demands from inside Parliament and outside for something to be done. In 1922 a private member introduced what a Home Office official described as a 'delightfully simple' Bill which would have empowered parents to transfer, with the approval of the court, their rights and duties over a child under seven to a named individual. The Home Office concluded that it would be 'disastrous' to allow the enactment of a Bill which 'ignores all the difficulties',[25] and the Government declined to give facilities for that or other Bills.[26]

But something had to be done to deal with the pressures on ministers and MPs; and in 1924 Arthur Henderson (Home Secretary in the 1924 Labour Administration) appointed a Committee chaired by Tomlin J[27] (a Chancery Division judge who enjoyed the confidence of the Lord Chancellor's Permanent Secretary)[28] 'to examine the problem of child adoption from the point of view of possible legislation and to report upon the main provisions' to be included in any Bill. In fact the Tomlin Committee was less than enthusiastic about the need for legislation: it doubted whether people who wanted to 'adopt' children had in practice been deterred from doing so by the absence of any recognition by the law of the status of adoption; and it believed that in reality the number of people 'wishing to get rid of children are far more numerous than those wishing to receive them' and that 'the activities in recent years of societies arranging systematically for the adoption of children would appear to have given to adoption a prominence which is somewhat artificial and may not be in all respects wholesome'.[29] But, albeit somewhat grudgingly, the Committee did accept that people who cared for children as if they were their own ought to be able to have some legal security for the relationship; and the Committee took the unusual course of drafting the Bill which (with remarkably few amendments)[30] became the Adoption of Children Act 1926. This governed the substantive[31] law of adoption until 1949.

---

[25] The comments are those of SW Harris, then the Assistant Secretary in charge of the Children's Branch: for his career see Biographical Notes.

[26] See notes of Home Secretary's conference with sponsors of Adoption Bill, 14 July 1922; Locker Lampson to Brassey, 23 April 1923; and minute of 5 June 1923, PRO HO 45/11540. The Home Office was concerned that the Bills made no provision about succession to property, and that they would enable baby farmers to use the legislation as a cloak for their activities.

[27] (1867–1935); see Biographical Notes.

[28] Sir Claud Schuster.

[29] *Tomlin Report* (1924–1925, Cmd. 2401) para. 4. The Committee also rejected suggestions that institutionalising adoption would curb the practice of trafficking in children: '. . . some of those who have given evidence . . . suggested that a legal system of adoption should be supplemented by a prohibition of all transactions involving the bringing up of other people's children unless they are legalised by the forms prescribed by the Adoption Acts. This is a proposal the mere statement of which is sufficient to disclose its impracticability': *ibid.*, para. 7. (The Committee obtained a further reference on 13 March 1925 to deal with extensions to the child protection legislation; and its *Third and Final Report* (1926, Cmd. 2711) made proposals on this subject.)

[30] Although some of those amendments—particularly that dealing with the circumstances in which the court could dispense with the requirement of parental consent: see the provisos to Adoption of Children Act 1926, s. 2(3)(4)—are significant in the long-term development of the law.

[31] But the Adoption of Children (Regulation) Act 1939 made changes of great importance relating to the activities of adoption agencies and the making of arrangements for adoption: see below.

For the Tomlin Committee, the underlying principle was that it should be possible, under proper safeguards, for a person irrevocably[32] to transfer parental rights and duties to another.[33] The transaction was essentially contractual and dependent on the informed consent of the birth parents and the adopters; but the Committee recommended that judicial sanction should be required. This was to meet the Committee's concern to provide an effective safeguard against the possibility that social and economic pressures might compel a mother to 'make a surrender of her child final in character though she may herself, if a free agent, desire nothing more than a temporary provision for it'.[34] It is true that the Court was to have to have power to dispense with a parent's consent[35] (for example, if the parent could not be found) but that power was only to be exercised in the most exceptional circumstances.[36]

Once the court had been satisfied the parent's consent[37] was indeed real and informed[38] the court would be guided by the criterion that an adoption order

[32] *Tomlin Report*, para. 26. The Committee considered that it would 'be well that before the final order of adoption is made there should always be a probationary period of such length, not exceeding in any case two years, as the tribunal shall fix'; and the Committee drafted a provision (which became Adoption Act 1926, s. 6) empowering the court to make interim orders giving the applicants custody of the child for such a period 'on such terms as regards provision for the maintenance and education and supervision of the welfare of the infant and otherwise as the Court may think fit'. In fact such orders were rarely made, provision to ensure that parent and child were mutually suited was made in other ways, the law required no probationary period (although adoption agencies might insist on this: see *Report of the Departmental Committee on Adoption Societies and Agencies* (1937, Cmd. 5499) para. 12) and the purpose of the interim order provision was little understood.

[33] *Tomlin Report*, para. 9.   [34] *Ibid.*, para. 11.

[35] Adoption Act 1926, s. 2(3) in fact required the consent not only of 'any parent or guardian' of the child but also that of anyone with actual custody of the child and anyone liable to contribute to the support of the child. The court equally had power to dispense with the consent of any such person. In this context, therefore, the word 'parent' in the text must be understood in this extended sense. The Poor Law Act 1930 provided that for the purpose of that Act a local authority was deemed to be maintaining children in their care; and it appears that in such cases the authority's consent to an adoption would be required: see the *Report of Departmental Committee on Adoption Societies and Agencies* (1937, Cmd. 5499) (which does not however appear always to distinguish clearly between adoption under the 1926 Act and the 'poor law' adoption, ie the assumption of parental rights by resolution).

[36] The Tomlin Committee's draft Bill (see *Child Adoption Committee. Second Report* (1925, Cmd. 2469)) would have given the court power to dispense with any agreement required on the part of a parent, guardian, person with actual custody, or person liable to contribute to the support of the child if satisfied 'that the person whose consent is to be dispensed with has abandoned or deserted the infant or cannot be found or is incapable of giving such consent, or, being a person liable to contribute to the support of the infant, either has persistently neglected or refused to contribute to such support'. Those terms largely reflected the grounds upon which the Poor Law Guardians could put a child out for adoption. It is true that the Adoption Act 1926, s. 2(3) extended the dispensing power to cases in which the court considered that the parent was someone 'whose consent ought, in all the circumstances, to be dispensed with' but it seems possible that that addition was intended for example to empower the court to dispense with consent where a child had been kidnapped or where the child's mother refused agreement to adoption by a relative of her husband 'purely to annoy her husband' (see *H v. H* [1947] KB 463, *per* Lord Goddard). It is certainly true that only in 1947 did the Divisional Court unexpectedly hold that the power thus conferred was entirely at large: see below.

[37] Required by Adoption of Children Act 1926, s. 2(3).

[38] Evidence by the Hon AE Napier to the *Departmental Committee on Adoption Societies and Agencies* (1937, Cmd. 5499) as recorded in a note on PRO LCO2/1162.

should only be made if that would promote the child's welfare.[39] To achieve this, there would have to be a 'competent independent consideration of the matter from the point of view of the welfare of the child'[40] and this was to be achieved by requiring the appointment in every case of a *guardian ad litem* charged with the duty of protecting the interests of the child.[41]

Effect of adoption

What should be the effect of the transfer from birth to adoptive parent? The Tomlin Committee had no difficulty in recommending that adoption should effectively transfer the right to what can perhaps be described as the guardianship of the child to the adopters, and the 1926 Act provided for such a transfer in resounding language.[42] But the Committee[43] adopted a cautious

[39] As Adoption of Children Act 1926, s. 3(b) was to require. The Act adopted the principle that legislation should prescribe minimum conditions for eligibility—that the child be an unmarried person aged under 21, that joint adoption should only be allowed if the adopters were married, that there should be a substantial difference in age (21 years) between the adoptive parents and the child, and that whilst unmarried women should be able to adopt children of either sex, unmarried men should only be allowed to adopt girls in exceptional circumstances—leaving the general assessment of the impact of adoption on the child's welfare to the court's view of the facts of the individual case: see *Tomlin Report*, paras. 23–25, Adoption of Children Act 1926, s. 2.

[40] *Tomlin Report,* para. 11. The Committee insisted that there should be 'a real adjudication rather than a mere registration of the will of the parties seeking to part with and take over the child' or a rubber-stamping of the parties' agreement as it might be colloquially described: *Tomlin Report,* para. 15.

[41] *Tomlin Report,* para. 15. The Committee recommended that the High Court should have jurisdiction; and the notion of a *guardian ad litem* was familiar in the Court's wardship jurisdiction (para. 12). But the Bill as introduced also conferred jurisdiction on the magistrates' courts; and in response to parliamentary pressure—overcoming resistance from the Lord Chancellor's Department which had consistently 'tried to keep the County Court free' from what it regarded as the 'troublesome business' of adoption (see PRO LCO2/1120, Napier to Cann, 9 July 1926)—jurisdiction was also given to the county court. The lack of relevant resources and experience in county courts and magistrates' courts (where most adoption applications were dealt with) gave rise to difficulties, as can be seen from a series of articles by county court Registrars in *The County Court Officer* entitled 'How I do it'. The Director of the Local Education Authority was the choice apparently officially favoured to act as Guardian, but sometimes a clergyman or an official of the court was appointed. The question of the fees payable to Guardians was also discussed: a charge of fifteen shillings (75 pence or perhaps £20 in year 2000 values) was regarded as 'grossly excessive', perhaps suggesting that the Guardian's duties were not regarded as very onerous.

[42] The Act provided that upon the making of an adoption order, 'all rights, duties, obligations and liabilities of the parent or parents, guardian or guardians of the adopted child, in relation to the future custody, maintenance and education of the adopted child, including all rights to appoint a guardian or to consent or give notice of dissent to marriage shall be extinguished, and all such rights, duties, obligations and liabilities shall vest in and be exercisable by and enforceable against the adopter as though the adopted child was a child born to the adopter in lawful wedlock, and in respect of the same matters and in respect of the liability of a child to maintain its parents the adopted child shall stand to the adopter exclusively in the position of a child born to the adopter in lawful wedlock': s. 5(1).

[43] The Committee believed that there was no need to make special provision dealing with the adopted child's name: the Committee claimed that in law 'a surname is a matter of reputation and nothing else' and that there was no need for any statutory provision to enable the adopted child to be called by the surname of the adopting parent. But the Committee did accept that provision should be made for registering the child's adoption; and the Act provided that the Registrar-General should

approach[44] to the question of an adopted child's succession rights and to the effect of an adoption order on the prohibited degrees of marriage: an adoption order under the 1926 Act[45] left the adopted child's position in respect of these two matters unchanged.

Secrecy or informed consent?

The 1926 Act did not satisfy many of those professionally involved in arranging adoptions. In particular, the adoption societies tended to attach great importance to 'secrecy', meaning (as the Tomlin Committee put it)[46] 'not merely that the transaction itself should not be a matter of common notoriety but that the parties themselves should not become known to each other, that is to say, that the natural parent should not know where the child goes . . .'. The Committee[47] brushed these concerns aside; and when the Lord Chancellor's officials came to draft Rules they assumed that the court would, in order to satisfy itself that the birth parents' consent to the adoption was real and informed, need to see the

---

mark the original entry relating to an adopted child's birth with the word 'adopted' and record particulars of the adoption in an Adopted Children Register, a certified copy of which was given the force of an ordinary birth certificate but would not disclose the facts of the child's birth parentage. In practice these provisions gave rise to great difficulty: in particular, the High Court asserted a power to direct the entry in the Adopted Children's Register of a birth date for the child even if there were no English registration of the birth; and the High Court also directed the entry in that Register of the child's original surname (which would often make it easy, contrary to the policy adopted in 1926, to trace the original entry). County courts and magistrates' courts adopted a wide variety of practices: see in particular the letter of 1 August 1928, PRO LCO2/1159 from the Registrar General (SP Vivian) to Schuster, and the accompanying memorandum. To the annoyance of Sir Claud Schuster the Registrar-General believed high matters of constitutional principle to be involved: see Biographical Notes. Schuster was also reluctant to give the matter any publicity ('if we do, all the people who get excited on this subject (and they are many) will think they see an opportunity for airing their views' (Schuster to Luxmoore, 18 December 1929) while the prospect of legislation on the subject was unappealing 'both because the Government appear to have formed legislative plans which . . . are likely to occupy Parliament for the rest of our lifetime and because there is a risk lest, if the matter arises again in Parliament, it may be difficult to confine the amendments to those which you would consider necessary or desirable' (Schuster to Luxmoore, 29 July 1929).

[44] *Tomlin Report*, para. 18: no 'system of adoption, seeking as it does to reproduce artificially a natural relation, can hope to produce precisely the same result or to be otherwise than in many respects illogical, and this is made apparent in the diversity of provisions in relation to succession and marriage which appear in the adoption laws of other countries'.

[45] Adoption of Children Act 1926, s. 5(2) specifically provided that an adoption order should not affect the adopted child's rights under intestacies or dispositions of property and that, conversely, expressions such as 'child' and 'issue' should not (in the absence of an apparent contrary intention) extend to adoptive relationships.

[46] *Tomlin Report*, para. 28.

[47] So did Ministers in the course of the parliamentary debates and the Lord Chancellor's Permanent Secretary: see Schuster's response to Mrs E Hubback's letter of 4 August 1926, PRO LCO2/1120. (She had pointed out that depriving the birth parent of any legal claim to custody would not adequately meet adopters' concerns, and that adopters would 'not want to expose the child to any social intercourse with a parent who, in later years, might play on its feelings, attempt to get money, etc. I happen to know several people, some in my own family, who have adopted children, but who would not do so unless the complete secrecy . . . can be observed. Unless . . . the Rules . . . allow for this, such people would not take advantage of the Act, and unregulated adoptions would continue'.) This prophecy was correct.

birth parent and equally that the birth parent should know what was to happen to his or her child.[48] Would not a mother proposing to hand over her child to a stranger wish to be satisfied about the character and personality of the adopters? Would she not wish to know something about the home in which her child was to be brought up? For these reasons the Adoption Rules[49] provided that not only the name but also the address of the adoptive parents should be inserted on the form prescribed for the giving of parental consent.

This all no doubt seemed eminently reasonable to the officials in the House of Lords,[50] but many prospective adopters were concerned that a mother who found out where they lived might interfere in the child's upbringing or even blackmail them;[51] and apparently because of this some adopters[52] simply ignored the procedures laid down in the 1926 Act. They would simply take over the care of a child placed with them by an adoption society and rely on the society to keep the child's whereabouts and assumed identity secret.

It is certainly true that a significant number of *de facto* 'adoptions'[53] remained unsanctioned by the formality of an adoption order: ten years after the coming into force of the 1926 Act only a third of the 'adoptions' organised by one of the three largest Adoption Agencies in the country had been given legal sanction under the 1926 Act.[54]

The significance of the Adoption of Children Act 1926

The real significance of the Adoption of Children Act 1926 is that it made 'adoption' of children a legally recognised and sanctioned institution, providing for the permanent and irrevocable transfer of parentage.[55] It may be that in

[48] Sir C Schuster, PRO LCO2/1120, 21 December 1926.

[49] There were differences of detail between the rules applicable to the High Court, county court, and magistrates' courts.

[50] There was also extended discussion in Parliament, see eg *Official Report* (HC) 26 February 1926, vol. 192, col. 925 ff. It should also be said that the *Departmental Committee on Adoption Societies and Agencies* (1937, Cmd. 5499) considered the issue at length and agreed that the child's mother should be placed in possession of information such as would enable her to decide whether to give consent to her child's adoption or not: pp. 18–22.

[51] Report of the *Departmental Committee on Adoption Societies and Agencies* (1937, Cmd. 5499) para. 17. The Rules about registration in the Adopted Children's Register also engendered fears that an adopted child's original birth details might be traced. This was inconsistent with the policy of many of the adoption societies that there should be a complete break between the child's past and future: *Tomlin Report*, para. 28; SM Cretney, *Law, Law Reform and the Family* (1998) pp. 197–198.

[52] But the extent to which legal adoption was used should not be underestimated: in 1936 more than 5,000 adoption orders were made: *Report of the Departmental Committee on Adoption Societies and Agencies* (1937, Cmd. 5499) para. 3.

[53] In contrast, the Adoption of Children Act 1926, s. 10, allowed the court to make an adoption order without obtaining any parental consent if the applicants had cared for the child as if it were their own for two years before the Act came into force.

[54] *Departmental Committee on Adoption Societies and Agencies* (1937, Cmd. 5499) paras. 3 and 16.

[55] NV Lowe, 'English Adoption Law: Past, Present and Future' in SN Katz, J Eekelaar and M Maclean (eds.), *Cross Currents* (2000) at p. 313. The common law insisted that the law did not permit a transference of a parent's rights and liabilities: see *Humphrys v. Polak* [1901] 2 KB 385, CA

strictness the 1926 Act did little more than provide machinery for the registration (under minimal safeguards supervised by the court) and recognition of a private civil contract.[56] The Act reflected a certain ambivalence about quite what was involved in the transfer of parentage;[57] and it is also true that the Act failed to provide machinery to meet the legitimate demands of many of those wishing to bring up a child in secure membership of their own family. But the 1926 Act laid the foundation upon which progress could be made; and its significance in the development of English family law cannot be questioned. Over the years ahead, adoption was to evolve from being essentially a private transaction dependent on contractual principle into a process, largely administered by State welfare agencies,[58] from which contractual elements almost disappeared.

THE ADOPTION OF CHILDREN (REGULATION) ACT 1939:
STATE REGULATION OF ADOPTION

The 1926 Act itself left adoption almost entirely uncontrolled by the State; and—as we have seen—the requirement that a court look into applications for adoption orders in an attempt to ensure that the making of an order would be beneficial for the child could be evaded by taking possession of a child placed for adoption, concealing its whereabouts, and refraining from applying for the *de facto* adoption to be legalised. The fact that the adoption process was so little regulated meant that newspaper advertisements (at best tasteless)[59] could freely offer children for adoption; and there were suggestions that adoption agencies took inadequate precautions in deciding whether to place children[60] (often the children of unmarried mothers whose chief anxiety might be to get rid of the child);[61] there were fears that British children were being exported to coun-

---

(where the defendants' repudiation of a covenant to maintain and bring up the plaintiff's illegitimate child as though she were their own, and 'for ever to relieve the mother of all liability' was held to give the plaintiff no cause of action in damages).

[56] G Rentoul MP in the Second Reading Debate on the Adoption of Children Bill, *Official Report* (HC) 26 February 1926, vol. 192, col. 930.

[57] It seems doubtful whether adoption under the 1926 Act was truly an 'act of civil status' in the strict sense. Note that even in 1954 the *Report of the Departmental Committee on the Adoption of Children* (Chairman: HH Sir Gerald Hurst, QC) (1954, Cmd. 9248) para. 196 described adoption under the 1926 Act as being properly the creation of a special kind of guardianship; and see SM Cretney, *Law, Law Reform and the Family* (1998) p. 197.

[58] See NV Lowe, 'English Adoption Law: Past, Present and Future' in SN Katz, J Eekelaar and M Maclean, *Cross Currents* (2000) Chapter 14.

[59] Eg 'I's a lovely baby boy. I'm lonely and sad without mummy or daddy to make me glad; will anyone adopt me'?: *Report of the Departmental Committee on Adoption Societies and Agencies* (1937, Cmd. 5499) p. 37.

[60] Eg applications were accepted by some Societies without a home visit and sometimes even without a personal interview with the applicants, and references were sometimes accepted without investigation: *Report of the Departmental Committee on Adoption Societies and Agencies* (1937, Cmd. 5499) pp. 11–12.

[61] *Ibid.*, para. 7. The Committee accepted that the unmarried mother usually lacked the necessary knowledge and experience and that the difficulties of her situation made it impossible for her—

tries whose laws did not provide for adoption;[62] and that money changed hands.[63]

The Home Office, with its overall responsibility for child protection, became concerned; and in the autumn of 1935 an 'influentially composed deputation'[64] of persons concerned with the welfare of children convinced the Home Secretary[65] of the need for an investigation into the 'evils associated with unlicensed, unregulated and unsupervised adoption'.[66] A Committee chaired by Miss Florence Horsburgh MP[67] was appointed[68] to inquire into the methods pursued by adoption societies or other agencies engaged in arranging for the adoption of children; and to report whether measures should be taken to supervise or control their activities. The Committee's Report,[69] published in 1937, led to the enactment of the Adoption of Children (Regulation) Act 1939.

The Horsburgh Committee reported a large growth in the number of adoption societies: it believed that more than 1,200 children each year were placed with adopters by bodies describing themselves as such.[70] Some societies arranged large numbers of adoptions[71] but many organisations (for example the Salvation Army) did so only occasionally, whilst a significant number of

however anxious she might be about her child's future—to exercise sufficient care over the disposal of her child: *ibid.*

[62] The Press published a number of sensational accounts suggesting that 'foreign baby traffickers' obtained babies from foster mothers of illegitimate children. Although a police investigation of the allegations made in an article published by *John Bull* on 13 March 1937 apparently had no result (see PRO HO45/17115) the sober prose of the *Report of the Departmental Committee on Adoption Societies and Agencies* (1937, Cmd. 5499) pp. 28–35 confirms that there were shocking cases.

[63] Adoption of Children Act 1926, s. 9 prohibited payments to the adoptive or birth parent, but did not prohibit payments to third parties in consideration of their arranging an adoption. In practice it appears that even reputable agencies found difficulty in making ends meet, and resorted to methods which could be considered objectionable.

[64] PRO LCO2/1162, Harris to Schuster, 26 November 1935.

[65] Sir John Simon: see Biographical Notes.

[66] Some years later an official in the Lord Chancellor's Office noted that the objective was to 'stop a wicked ramp which was going on in baby-farming': see below.

[67] (1889–1969): see Biographical Notes.

[68] The Home Office apparently failed to consult the Lord Chancellor's Office about the desirability of appointing a Committee; and Schuster protested that the Lord Chancellor considered it to be 'a strange proceeding to appoint a Departmental Committee to inquire into matters with which this Department has been closely concerned without any consultation with him'. Accordingly, the Lord Chancellor would 'not necessarily consider himself bound by any of its findings . . .': PRO LCO2/1162, Schuster to Harris, 26 November 1935. Schuster subsequently asserted that the problems with which the Home Office were concerned came about because of the Adoption Societies' obsession with the need—unsatisfied by the 1926 Act: see above—for secrecy in relation to adoption (Schuster to Harris, 3 December 1935); and he told a county court judge that any inquiry short of a consideration of the whole procedure under the legislation (which the Lord Chancellor would not favour unless set up in conjunction with him and containing persons in whom he had confidence) would 'probably prove a completely useless performance': Schuster to Snagge, *op. cit.* 9 June 1936. Schuster's prediction was incorrect.

[69] *Report of the Departmental Committee on Adoption Societies and Agencies* (1937, Cmd. 5499) (hereafter referred to as the '*Horsburgh Report*').

[70] *Horsburgh Report*, pp. 4–7.

[71] The two largest seem to have been the National Adoption Society (394 cases a year) and the National Children Adoption Association (333): see *Horsburgh Report*, para. 8(1).

adoptions were arranged (from various motives) by private individuals. A few local authorities (notably the London County Council) made a regular practice of arranging adoptions, whilst many public officials brought prospective adopters into touch with children as a 'friendly service'.[72]

The Committee accepted that generally adoption societies and other adoption agencies were performing a useful function but it found many instances of unsatisfactory practice; and it therefore recommended that no organisation should be allowed to make any arrangements for the adoption of a child unless it was registered with the local authority.[73] The Committee recommended that the conditions on which licences were to be granted should be prescribed by the Secretary of State; and the Act gave the Secretary of State wide powers to make regulations governing placement procedures and other matters.[74]

The Committee was especially critical of the practice of avoiding the requirement that the court approve adoptions and relying simply on the fact that the adopter had the child and the birth parent would not be able to trace him or her. It recommended that prospective adopters should be required[75] to make an application to the court for an adoption order within a specified time from the placement of the child by an agency.[76]

Although in these ways State control over adoption was increased, the Committee did not recommend that private individuals should be prohibited from arranging adoptions. The Committee did recommend, and the 1939 Act provided, for local authority supervision of children under the age of nine[77] who were 'placed' otherwise than by adoption agencies. It also recommended control of payments in connection with adoption, advertising, and adoption abroad.

In these respects, the Adoption of Children (Regulation) Act 1939[78] is an important landmark in the move towards State control of the adoption

---

[72] *Horsburgh Report*, para. 8(iii).

[73] *Horsburgh Report*, pp. 44–47; Adoption of Children (Regulation) Act 1939, s. 1.

[74] *Horsburgh Report*, pp. 47–50; Adoption of Children (Regulation) Act 1939, s. 4. The Act required the mother to be issued with a memorandum explaining in ordinary language what was involved in adoption: this led a Home Office official to complain about the difficulty of drafting a document which could make 'certain rather complicated legal points . . . intelligible to quite stupid women': see PRO LCO2/3020, 5 March 1943.

[75] Adoption of Children (Regulation) Act 1939, s. 6(3).

[76] Adoption of Children (Regulation) Act 1939, s. 6 provided for a probationary period of three months from the child being 'delivered' into the care of the prospective adopters. During that time no application for an adoption order could be made; but thereafter the prospective adopters had, on pain of prosecution, either formally to reject the child or make an application to the court for an adoption order.

[77] The *Horsburgh Report* (p. 51) recommended that this provision should extend to children placed under the age of 16; but the provisions of s. 7 of the 1939 Act are restricted to placements of children under nine.

[78] The draftsman and officials were evidently working under considerable pressure at the time. The Act may have received little attention from Home Office officials or lawyers, and the draftsman subsequently confessed that the Act was 'as full of holes as a tennis net': PRO LCO2/3020, 16 April 1944.

process.[79] But the approach remained cautious.[80] State regulation was increased, but adoption remained essentially the private contract between individuals, ratified by a court, which had been recognised in 1926. True, adoption societies had to be registered with the local authority but few local authorities were directly concerned in themselves arranging adoption. But the way ahead is perhaps apparent from the prominence which the Committee gave to the 'admirable' procedures of the London County Council:[81] there was 'much that adoption societies and other adoption agencies might learn' from the Council's methods. The 1939 Act was essentially conservative in its approach but ten years later the Adoption Act 1949 decisively changed the concept of legal adoption.

THE ADOPTION OF CHILDREN ACT 1949

The background

In 1939 the courts made 7,926 adoption orders; in 1946, the first year after the end of World War II, they made 23,564.[82] Of the children adopted, the majority were illegitimate.[83] In 1946, the *Care of Children Committee* concluded[84] that a successful adoption was 'the most completely satisfactory method of providing a substitute home' giving the child new parents with all the parents' rights and responsibilities who would, so far as human nature allowed, take the place of the 'real parents'. And it seemed that there was a strong demand for adoption: there were many more would-be adopters than suitable children available.[85]

But how best to ensure that an adoption was 'satisfactory'? The *Curtis Report* noted that, at the time, adoption was still usually a matter of private

---

[79] The Act also contained extensive rule-making powers, and these were used over the years greatly to extend regulation of the adoption process in respect of matters such as prescribing the enquiries to be made about the suitability of a proposed adoption, stipulating that prospective adopters be interviewed by the Placing Agency, and so on.

[80] The Committee was particularly cautious in dealing with the demand that the adoption process should be more effectively arranged to prevent disclosure of the adopters' identity to the parent: *Horsburgh Report*, pp. 17–22. The rules governing procedures in the magistrates' courts had in fact been changed to remove the necessity for disclosure of the adopters' address, but the Committee seem to have accepted the Lord Chancellor's officials views about the need to disclose the identity of the adopters. The solution eventually found was to disguise the applicant's identity by the use of a serial number: see below.

[81] *Horsburgh Report*, pp. 40–42.   [82] *Horsburgh Report*, Appendix B, Table 1.

[83] It seems that in 1950, 80% of the children adopted were illegitimate: *A Survey of Adoption in Great Britain* (Home Office, 1971) p. 33 (but compare Viscount Simon's speculative view in 1949 that the child was illegitimate in only two-thirds of the cases: *Official Report* (HL) 11 July 1949, vol. 163, col. 1060). No doubt in many cases the mother thought (or was persuaded that she thought) that 'the great thing is to get rid of my baby': Viscount Simon *Official Report* (HL) 21 July 1949, vol. 164, col. 363. But in fact in a significant number of cases the adopter was the mother (either alone or jointly with her husband) seeking by adoption to equate her child's legal status with that of his factual status as a child fully integrated into the family.

[84] *Report of the Care of Children Committee* (Cmd. 9622) (hereafter cited as the *Curtis Report*) para. 448. For the context of the Committee's work see Chapter 19, below.

[85] *Curtis Report*, para. 448.

arrangement: less than a quarter of adoptions in 1944 were arranged by an adoption society and thereby subject to the protective measures introduced by the Adoption of Children (Regulation) Act 1939. The *Curtis Report* thought it highly unsatisfactory that there should be no public supervision or investigation in a private placement unless and until an application was made to the court, and urged the need for 'rigorous investigation' if failures were to be avoided.[86] The Committee believed that the interests of the child required (firstly) that there should be a probationary period in all cases to 'enable the adopters to test their own inclinations and make certain they can really give a parent's care and affection to the child'; (secondly) some degree of public supervision during that period; and (thirdly) some provision for compelling the removal of the child from a home which proved unsatisfactory, whether during the probationary period or after refusal of an adoption order.[87]

At the same period, lawyers were analysing some of the legal issues which experience had highlighted. The first area of concern stemmed from the policy underlying the 1926 Act that the mother's informed consent should be the crucial part of the adoption process. In 1926 it was thought this necessarily entailed allowing the mother to know who was to adopt her child and the Act required her to give a specific consent to adoption by a named adopter.[88] But over the years those concerned with adoption practice increasingly urged that the adoptive parents should be allowed to conceal their identity from the child's mother; and if this was permitted why should the law not allow a mother simply to agree to any adoption which the court approved? And should a mother who had once given her consent to adoption be allowed subsequently to withdraw it, almost inevitably causing great distress to the prospective adopters?

Another area of concern was how far the court should be able to override a parental refusal to agree to adoption. The Adoption of Children Act 1926 had indeed given the court power to dispense with parental consent; but the courts had interpreted the dispensing power narrowly[89] and were reluctant to make an order except in cases where the child had been abandoned or the parent was mentally incapable. Then in 1947 the Divisional Court unexpectedly held[90] that

---

[86] *Curtis Report*, para. 448.   [87] *Curtis Report*, para. 450.

[88] *Re JM Caroll* [1931] 1 KB 317.

[89] In *Re JM Caroll* [1931] 1 KB 317, CA, for example, Slesser LJ held that the court's power to dispense with consent if that, in all the circumstances, ought to be done 'should be construed as one' with the other dispensing provisions and that 'such a serious invasion of parental rights—for the dispensation of consent by the Court would mean that the rights and obligations of a parent . . . would be taken away and vested in the adopter—cannot reasonably be assumed to be within the competence of the Court in the absence of abandonment or desertion . . .'.

[90] In *H v. H* [1947] KB 463, 466 the contest was between a man who had cared for the child for three days a week and the child's maternal grandmother (who did so for the rest of the week). The man unsuccessfully claimed that the court had no jurisdiction to dispense with his consent, since the general power to dispense with consent contained in the proviso to the Adoption of Children Act 1926, s. 2(3) applied only to empower the court to dispense with the requisite consent by someone liable to maintain the child. The Court held that the words gave the Court the 'widest possible discretion' to dispense with the consent of *any* person whose consent the statute required.

the court's discretion was unfettered: the Court should simply apply the words of the Act and dispense with consent if in all the circumstances it considered it appropriate to do so. There were some[91] who thought that to give such a power to a court (or to anyone else) was to go much too far.

Finally, the effect of an adoption order was a controversial matter. Under the 1926 Act adoption did irrevocably vest the right to the child's custody in the adoptive parent, but it did not effect a transfer of the child from birth to adoptive parent for the purposes of succession to property or for certain other purposes. For some this, comparatively restrictive, approach was unsatisfactory: the aim of adoption should be to create a legal link between the child and the adoptive parents which approximated as closely as possible to the relationship between a child and his birth parent.[92]

These matters had been considered by a Committee set up by the National Council of Social Service and chaired by Judge Gamon;[93] and the Home Office believed that legislation was necessary.[94] In 1949 Basil Neild[95] agreed to sponsor a Bill drafted by Parliamentary Counsel;[96] and the Government throughout gave support. But the Bill's passage through Parliament was not easy. For the first (and last) time legislation dealing with adoption was brought forward without any prior consideration by an official Committee. Policy on a number of important issues had not been settled, and in this fluid situation the debates in Parliament (and behind the scenes) resulted in significant developments.

The end of the requirement for 'informed consent'?

The 1949 Act significantly changed the rules about the requirement of parental[97] consent to adoption. The policy remained that the mother's consent should be free and informed. This was to be achieved by stipulating that, to be effective, the consent could not be given until the child was six weeks old, and that the consent be given in writing witnessed by a JP.[98] It was no longer to be possible for a mother to give a consent before the child's birth, and the mother was to have time to consider 'soberly and objectively' whether she really wished to give

---

[91] Notably Viscount Simon (who had the carriage of the Bill for the Adoption of Children Act 1949 in the House of Lords): see *Official Report* (HL) 11 July 1949, vol. 163, col. 1085.

[92] See the speech of Basil Neild QC, sponsor of the Adoption of Children 1949, *Official Report* (HC) 18 February 1949, vol. 461, col. 1480.

[93] See Biographical Notes.

[94] On 18 October 1949 (when the Bill was threatened by the intransigence of a small group of MPs) the Home Secretary told the Home Affairs Committee that the Bill 'would undoubtedly relieve the Home Office of the task of promoting new legislation on the subject'.

[95] See Biographical Notes.

[96] PRO LCO2/4483: Home Affairs Committee, 8 and 15 February 1949.

[97] The father of an illegitimate child was not, for this purpose, a parent. The Act removed the requirement imposed by Adoption of Children Act 1926, s. 2(3) that anyone with actual custody of the child consent, but it continued to require the consent of any guardian and of anyone liable to maintain the child: Adoption of Children Act 1949, s. 3(1). In the text, unless the contrary is indicated, 'parent' and 'mother' in this context means any person whose consent is requisite.

[98] Adoption of Children Act 1949, s. 3(3).

up her child for ever.[99] But the Act completely rejected the notion, implicit in the 1926 Act, that a mother could not reasonably consent to adoption unless she knew the identity of the adopter. It is true that the House of Lords rejected a provision contained in the Bill as introduced which would have allowed consent to be given to adoption in general terms (a provision favoured by some not least because a general consent would make it easier to ensure that the mother never discovered the identity of the adopters)[100] and that the Act continued to require that the mother consent to a specific adoption. But the Act allowed the identity of the adopters to be concealed behind a serial number;[101] and specifically provided that consent could be given notwithstanding the fact that the person concerned did not know the prospective adopter's identity.[102] The widespread use of serial number applications effectively destroyed the mother's right to know the identity of those who were to assume her role as a parent.

Preserving the mother's right to change her mind?

Issues of consent lay behind the debates on a seemingly uncontroversial provision in the Bill (giving effect to the *Curtis Report's* insistence that there be a probationary period to test the relationship between prospective adopters and the child)[103] which would require a prospective adopter to give the welfare authority three months' notice of his intention to apply for an adoption

[99] Viscount Simon, *Official Report* (HL) 11 July 1949, vol. 163, col. 1061. This provision demonstrates the fluidity of policy: it was not included in the Bill until after the Bill had completed its passage through the House of Commons and was in Committee in the House of Lords.

[100] Simon to Jowitt, 13 July 1949, PRO LCO2/4483. Viscount Simon told the Lord Chancellor that he regarded this point as the most difficult in the Bill, and—noting that the Court would of course be 'much more particular if the mother was simply wishing to give her child away to anybody'—he favoured allowing a general consent provided that such a consent could be subject to conditions, for example as to religion. Paradoxically, as enacted, the legislation did not allow a general consent but did allow a parent to impose conditions as to the religion in which the child was to be brought up: Adoption of Children Act 1949, s. 3(2).

[101] This statement requires some qualification. The Adoption of Children Act 1949, s. 3(3) provided that a 'document signifying . . . consent to the making' of an adoption order should be admissible as evidence of that consent 'if the person in whose favour the order is made is named or otherwise described in the document'; and the Lord Chancellor's officials believed that it would suffice for this purpose if the prospective adopter were 'described' by a serial number allotted by the court. Rules—eg the Adoption of Children (County Court) Rules 1949, r. 3—were drafted on that basis. But doubts were expressed in the Chancery Division about the correctness of this belief; and in 1950 the opportunity was taken to amend the legislation and make it clear that a 'description' of the applicant 'in the prescribed manner' would suffice: s. 1(4) Adoption Act 1950. Perhaps surprisingly, this was done under the power to make 'minor improvements' conferred by the Consolidation of Enactments (Procedure) Act 1949: *Official Report* (HL) 13 June 1950, vol. 167, col. 645.

[102] It was also provided that consent withdrawn 'on the ground only' that it had been given in ignorance of the adopters' identity was to be treated as unreasonably withheld: Adoption of Children Act 1949, s. 3(2). The court would then have power to dispense with the mother's consent: see below.

[103] Viscount Simon put the case for a probationary period in somewhat old-fashioned language: the 'adopters may find that the child is not, for physical and mental reasons, a child whom they can possibly take into the family, and they must be given a limited opportunity of showing that the experiment has not succeeded': *Official Report* (HL) 11 July 1949, vol. 163, col. 1065.

order.[104] Such a provision sounds eminently reasonable, but in fact it precipitated the most serious threat to the Bill. The problem was that anything which increased the time which had to elapse before the court made the adoption order inevitably gave the mother more time to change her mind. A forceful pressure group led by the Labour playwright MP Benn Levy[105] introduced amendments intended to make the mother's consent irrevocable after a specified period of time thus depriving her of any right to recover her child—even if the court had made no order and even if no one had applied for an adoption order. The Government[106] set itself against such a provision[107] and agreed to take the Bill over if necessary, putting the whips on to ensure that the Bill reached the statute book. At a desperately late stage, provisions were inserted into the Bill reflecting a—not altogether successful[108]—attempt to meet the Levy group's concerns.[109]

Dispensing with consent

The Act reformulated the grounds upon which the court could dispense with consent: henceforth the court could dispense with any requisite consent on the ground that the person concerned could not be found, was incapable of giving a

---

[104] 'That gives the welfare authority an opportunity in the interests of the community at large, of visiting the home and seeing how this experiment is working out and, therefore, of assisting in the ultimate solution': Viscount Simon, *Official Report* (HL) 11 July 1949, vol. 163, col. 1066.

[105] (1900–1973): see Biographical Notes.

[106] It would be more accurate to say that the Home Secretary, James Chuter Ede (see Biographical Notes) did so and managed to convince a majority of his colleagues. Lord Chancellor Jowitt (whilst accepting that on this, as on other issues, it was best to 'let Simon have his way throughout': Jowitt to Younger, 27 July 1949, PRO LCO2/4483) continued to believe that Levy was right and indeed went so far as to tell Younger that to allow a mother to go back on her agreement was a 'glaring defect' in the Act: Jowitt to Younger, 25 November 1949, PRO LCO2/4483.

[107] 'I cannot' (Ede told the Cabinet's Legislation Committee) 'support the principle that a mother should be unable to change her mind and to recover her child at any time as long as the potential adopters are entitled to change their minds and to return the child to her; and, while I sympathise with people who have taken a child with a view to adoption and had it arbitrarily reclaimed by the mother, there is no way of protecting them from this risk without depriving a mother of the right to her own child if later she is in a position to bring it up herself, or she marries and her husband is ready to accept the child'. In any event he thought courts would be unlikely to make an adoption order in the knowledge that the 'mother would have withdrawn her consent had she been allowed to': PRO2 LCO/4483, Home Secretary's Memorandum, 14 October 1949.

[108] The amendment was only moved (by the Lord Chancellor) on the Lords' consideration of the amendments made by the Commons, themselves disagreeing with earlier amendments made by the Lords: *Official Report* (HL) vol. 165, col. 1508. Lord Iddesleigh protested that the amendment tipped the scales too much against the parent, whilst Viscount Simon was concerned that the provision might be abused by an applicant starting proceedings solely in order to prevent the mother removing the child and then not pursuing them. (In practice the provision was found to be of little value: *Report of the Departmental Committee on the Adoption of Children* (Chairman, HH Sir Gerald Hurst QC, 1954, Cmd. 9248) para. 189; see below.)

[109] Adoption of Children 1949, s. 3(4) provided that once an application had been made for an adoption order, the leave of the court would be necessary for the removal of the child from the applicant's care and possession. In considering whether to grant or refuse leave the court was to have regard to the child's welfare.

consent, or that the 'consent is unreasonably withheld'.[110] The Act preserved the principle that the mother remained free to withdraw her consent at any time before the court had actually made the adoption order[111] but the extent to which a change of mind could be the basis for a successful application to dispense with the mother's consent remained a matter on which the courts would experience difficulty.[112]

Effect of adoption

By 1949 opinion had moved strongly towards accepting the principle that, once an adoption order was made, the adoptive child should pass for all purposes into the family of the adoptive parents.[113] There was (astonishing though it may seem to the twenty-first century reader) no problem in drafting, or getting parliamentary approval, to a clause[114] effectively conferring United Kingdom citizenship on a child adopted by a citizen. The question of the effect of adoption on the prohibited degrees was more difficult: it was decided that the law should prohibit marriages between the adopted child and the adoptive parent,[115] but (for pragmatic reasons)[116] the logical step of also prohibiting marriage between the adopted child and his adoptive sister (or brother) was not taken.[117] But it was succession rights which were in practice seen as the most important and here the formidable complexities of the law deterred Nield from including any

[110] Adoption of Children Act 1949, s. 3(1). 'Unreasonable withholding' etc were grounds on which the court could dispense with any of the consents required by the Act. In the case of parents and guardians the court could also dispense with the consent in cases of abandonment, neglect or persistent ill-treatment; in the case of a person liable to maintain, persistent neglect or refusal to contribute to the child's maintenance was a ground for dispensing.

[111] The fact that the Rules (and the 1949 Act, s. 3(3)) made provision for the procedure whereby consent could be given before the hearing did not mean that the person concerned was debarred from revoking it: *Re Hollyman* [1945] 1 All ER 290, CA.

[112] Cf *H v. H* [1947] KB 463, above p. 610. Experience soon demonstrated that the change of wording had been ineffective to eradicate divergent judicial approaches to the exercise of the dispensing power: see below.

[113] *Official Report* (HL) 11 July 1949, vol. 163, col. 1062 (Viscount Simon).

[114] Adoption of Children 1949, s. 8 (described by Viscount Simon as 'an interesting little clause': *Official Report* (HL) 11 July 1949, vol. 163, col. 1066).

[115] Adoption of Children 1949, s. 11(1).

[116] Jowitt had received a letter from a man happily married for 35 years to his adoptive sister: see PRO LCO2/4483. Simon wrote to Jowitt on 13 July 1949 doubting the wisdom of going 'the whole way in this matter. A step-brother can marry his step-sister. Moreover, if we go the whole way, the brother of the adopter could not marry the adopted child, for an uncle cannot marry his niece. . . . The Home Office are anxious about the proposed extension because it might increase cases of incest'.

[117] The adopted child remained within the prohibited degrees to all the members of his natural family: see Adoption Act 1976, s. 47(1). But the impact of this rule in cases of affinal relationships mentioned in Simon's letter (above) has been reduced by the Marriage (Prohibited Degrees of Relationship) Act 1986; and the likelihood that a person will go through a form of marriage with a person who (unknown to either of them) was within the prohibited degrees has been minimised by provisions enabling an adopted person aged 18 or over to have access to his birth records (and a person under that age may inquire whether his birth records suggest that he could be within the prohibited degrees to any person he intends to marry): Adoption Act 1976, s. 51(2).

provision in the Bill he introduced. Although the Lord Chancellor's officials had started from the position that the Bill would provide a useful opportunity to rationalise the law, and there was strong pressure in the House of Commons for recognising the adopted child as a child for all the purposes of property entitlement, the draftsman found his task extremely difficult. Judges consulted on the policy to be adopted expressed strong and not altogether consistent views. In the end, the difficulty experienced in drafting attempted compromise solutions[118] was one of the factors which led to acceptance of the principle[119] (stated in terms in the Adoption of Children Act 1949)[120] that 'adopted persons should be treated as children of the adopters for the purposes of the devolution or disposal of real and personal property'; but this principle was not to apply to dispositions of property made before the date of the adoption order.[121]

THE HURST COMMITTEE AND THE 1958 ADOPTION LEGISLATION[122]

The 1949 Adoption Act, which did not have the recommendations of any official committee as a guide, introduced reforms of substance evidencing a considerable shift in the policy of the law insofar as the mother's agreement and the effects of making an order were concerned. In contrast, the Children Act 1958 was preceded by an 88-page Report[123] (with 48 recommendations) from a Departmental Committee chaired by Sir Gerald Hurst QC[124] (a recently retired county court judge) yet the reforms of adoption law effected by the 1958 Act[125] were comparatively modest in scope and the Act can best be seen as mildly evolutionary in its approach. It is also notable that while the two Houses of

---

[118] See SM Cretney, *Law, Law Reform and the Family* (1998) pp. 198–199 and the sources there referred to.

[119] The adopted child still did not qualify as a child of the deceased under dispositions made before the date of the order: see the discussion in the *Report of the Departmental Committee on the Adoption of Children* (1954, Cmd. 9248) paras. 155–160. The Children Act 1958, s. 22, dealt with one problem by providing that a will was for this purpose to be treated as made on the date of the testator's death; but did not remove the inability of the adopted child to take as the adoptive parent's child under (for example) a settlement made before the adoption in favour of the settlor's grandchildren.

[120] s. 9(1).   [121] Adoption of Children Act 1949, s. 9(5).

[122] Somewhat confusingly, changes to adoption (and child protection) law were made by the Children Act 1958; the legislation relating to adoption was then consolidated in the Adoption Act 1958.

[123] *Report of the Departmental Committee on the Adoption of Children* (1954, Cmnd. 9248) hereafter referred to as the *Hurst Report*. The Committee was appointed by Sir David Maxwell Fyffe as Home Secretary in 1954 and it was he who in 1958 (as Lord Chancellor Kilmuir) introduced the Bill giving effect to its recommendations into the House of Lords.

[124] See Biographical Notes.

[125] Many detailed changes were made by Rule of Court; but Lord Chancellor Kilmuir (see Biographical Notes) was notably reluctant to specify which of the *Hurst Report's* recommendations had been rejected: see his response to questions raised on the Second Reading in the House of Lords, *Official Report* (HL) 11 March 1958, vol. 208, col. 4.

Parliament were the forum in which the terms of the 1949 Act were principally settled, the 1958 Act followed lengthy formal consultation with major interest groups[126] on the basis of impressively weighty documentation and many issues were effectively settled at that preliminary stage.[127]

The *Hurst Report* seems to have accepted that adoption should be seen primarily as an issue of social work, with the child's legal status changing as a consequence of a satisfactory placement. The Committee's recommendation[128] that local authorities should be specifically empowered to arrange adoptions for any child (irrespective of whether the child was in its care) can be seen as a significant step on the way towards local authorities assuming responsibility for the provision of a comprehensive adoption service.[129] But the Committee emphasised the value of the work done by voluntary agencies:[130] it was distinctly cool in its response to suggestions that agencies should not be allowed to employ 'untrained' adoption workers[131] and the Committee refused to fetter agencies' discretion in relation to such matters as carrying out of visits. Significantly, the Committee believed that to impose such restrictions on the activities of adoption societies would 'be to close down a number, perhaps a considerable number, of societies'.[132]

---

[126] Unfortunately the High Court judges were not at first included in the list of those to be consulted. The Senior Chancery Judge, Sir Harry Vaisey protested to the Lord Chancellor's Permanent Secretary Sir George Coldstream on 30 October 1957 that the judges had 'learnt with some surprise that an Amending Adoption Bill is likely to be introduced into Parliament in the near future, and that suggestions have been invited from Magistrates (and also, I understand, County Court judges) while no intimations of any kind have been made to ourselves. I think that the Lord Chancellor would wish us to be told something about this matter and to be given an early opportunity of expressing our views. But perhaps we have been misinformed'. Coldstream hastened to respond in the grovelling tones at the period considered appropriate: 'In fairness to those concerned I must say that it did not occur to them that the proposed legislation had yet reached the stage at which they could properly seek the advice of the Judiciary. However that may be, the Lord Chancellor now asks me to say that he would be most grateful if you and your brethren would be good enough to take the Home Office document into consideration . . . may I venture to add that in accordance with the practice followed by himself and his predecessors the Lord Chancellor would always wish to consult the Senior Chancery Judge on a Bill which makes an alteration in the law and procedure . . . of the Chancery Division. In this instance an error of judgment in timing has been made which I greatly regret'. It then transpired that the judges had not been given a copy of the *Hurst Report*.

[127] See the papers on PRO LCO2/4777 and 4781.

[128] *Hurst Report*, para. 24; implemented by Children Act 1958, s. 30.

[129] Under Children Act 1975, s. 1, see below.

[130] 'We . . . are greatly impressed with the value of the work they do. We are satisfied that the arrangements they make are carried out with great care . . .' (*Hurst Report*, para. 34); and 'we have no wish to see local authorities usurp . . . the functions of voluntary adoption societies' (*Hurst Report*, para. 24).

[131] 'It is clear that the staffs of many societies have not received any formal training, but we are nevertheless aware that some "untrained" workers have had experience which renders them highly skilled. It may be mentioned in passing that the methods of those who have academic qualifications have also sometimes been criticised'. (*Hurst Report*, para. 36). Contrast the approach of the 1972 *Departmental Committee on the Adoption of Children* (1972, Cmnd. 5107) p. 13 ff., see below.

[132] *Hurst Report*, para. 38.

The Committee, noting recent advances in medical knowledge emphasising the speed with which babies 'grew roots',[133] reiterated the need for great care in placing a child:

'This is the crucial stage in the process of adoption since, once the child has been placed, much harm and unhappiness may result if a change has to be made'[134] '. . . The initial placing . . . is even more important than the later investigation . . .'[135]

—and the Committee noted the risks inherent in 'direct' adoption placements (ie where the mother gave her child to a friend, fellow-worker, or even a land-lady) and in 'third party' adoptions (ie where the mother placed her child with prospective adopters through the agency of a private individual—perhaps a doctor[136] or other person concerned primarily to help either the mother or the prospective adopters).[137] The Committee had received a volume of evidence 'from many different quarters' urging that only skilled workers be allowed to arrange adoptions[138] and accepted that adoptions 'arranged by persons of special experience and training' were much more likely to succeed[139] than others; and it noted cases in which a mother had been 'induced to part with her child to people . . . grossly unsuitable to care for him'.[140] In these circumstances the Committee's conclusion that it would be neither wise nor practicable to prohibit either direct or third party placements[141] seems rather surprising.[142] But the Committee's insistence on the importance of satisfactory placement did lead it to propose an extension to the three months' probationary period: the child should have his home with the adopters for two months before they were eligible to apply for an adoption order (thereby starting the probationary period running) and no period before the child was six weeks old should count towards the probationary period.[143] The Act gave effect to the second, but not to the first, of these recommendations.[144] The Committee also proposed a number of

---

[133] *Ibid.*, para. 52.   [134] *Ibid.*, para. 43.   [135] *Ibid.*, para. 52.

[136] The *Hurst Report*, para. 43, noted 'deplorable cases' in which a doctor acted 'as a third party for the benefit of a patient whose neurotic condition he seeks to remedy or whose marriage he hopes to stabilise by this means' and quoted an egregious letter from doctor to voluntary worker: 'Mrs X tells me that her husband threatens to leave her unless another baby is forthcoming, and adoption is the only way. I feel myself that, although the home is not ideal, a baby might go a long way to settle down the whole family and without itself suffering in the process. With such a brisk seasonal trade in "illegits" I feel one might perhaps be spared'.

[137] *Hurst Report*, para. 43.   [138] *Ibid.*, para. 52.   [139] *Ibid.*, para. 20.

[140] *Ibid.*, para. 43.   [141] *Ibid.*, para. 52.

[142] The Committee noted that there had been no 'careful research' into the comparative results of adoptions effected by agency and other means; and it believed that restrictions on direct and third party placements would be evaded, perhaps by increased recourse to *de facto* 'adoptions'. The Committee also saw merit in allowing people to adopt the particular child they had chosen rather than 'a child selected for them by others, however competent'. *Hurst Report*, paras. 45–46. It may also have been impressed by the large number of cases which would be affected since perhaps a third of all adoptions were third party or direct.

[143] *Hurst Report*, paras. 66–69.

[144] See Children Act 1958, s. 19(3).

changes intended to increase and make effective the procedures for preventing a child being kept in unsatisfactory conditions.[145]

The Hurst Committee gave extensive consideration to the circumstances in which adoption orders could be made where there was a prospect of the child having his home abroad. There were particular difficulties with prospective adopters who, though domiciled in this country were resident abroad (for example, whilst serving in the Colonial Service) and with others who, though resident in this country for two or three years, were not domiciled here. (Coloured American servicemen who had 'befriended and wished to adopt . . . coloured British children . . . for whom there was little prospect of adoption in this country' were identified by the Home Office as a deserving group.[146]) The Act allowed non-resident English domiciliaries to adopt provided they were here long enough to meet the three-month probationary placement requirement[147] whilst foreign domiciliaries would (again, subject to the same probationary requirement) be allowed to take a child abroad under the authority of what it was eventually decided to call a 'provisional adoption order'.[148] The Act also did away with the requirement that an adopter be 21 years older than the child, accepting the Hurst Committee's view that the courts could be trusted not to make adoption orders where the relative ages of the parties would make this inappropriate.[149]

There was no dispute that adoption should normally be dependent on parental[150] agreement, and the Hurst Committee saw the protection of the natural parents from 'hurried or panic' decisions as one of the functions of adoption law. But equally it was clear that the court should have power to dis-

[145] See *Hurst Report*, paras. 48–51. Many of these (in particular those placing extended obligations on third parties to give notice of the part they had played in making the arrangements) seemed unrealistic: as a Home Office memorandum put it: 'the difficulties seem to be inherent in the situation . . . it must often be difficult to decide on the facts whether or not a third party has deliberately participated in the arrangements . . . the obligation on third parties [to give notice of their participation in an adoption arrangement] can never be known amongst the generality of people, and courts may well be reluctant to punish an unintentional omission by someone genuinely ignorant of the law': Memorandum para. 8, copied on PRO LCO2/4777.

[146] Memorandum to Home Affairs Committee, 16 September 1957, PRO LCO2/4778, para. 8. The Committee was evidently impressed by the argument that 'excessive numbers of Roman Catholics and coloured children' were being cared for in institutions, and thought that 'a measure of flexibility in the law would be in the interests of such children': Minutes, 18 October 1957, PRO LCO2/4778.

[147] Children Act 1958, s. 23.

[148] Children Act 1958, s. 24. The Horsburgh Committee's concern about child trafficking had led to restrictions on sending children abroad to be adopted; and the 1958 Act made it a criminal offence to take or send British children abroad for adoption (whether legal or *de facto*) save under a provisional adoption order: s. 33.

[149] Children Act 1958, s. 2; *Hurst Report*, para. 149.

[150] Much more radically, the Hurst Committee thought the child should consent to his or her own adoption; but the High Court judges thought that this would cut across 'a fundamental concept of English law that an infant cannot give a valid consent. They conceded there would be something to be said for giving a child of 16 or 18 the right to refuse to be adopted; but were concerned that a younger child, understanding the effect of an adoption order but not the reason for its being necessary, might refuse to consent "to the embarrassment of all concerned"': PRO LCO2/4788.

pense with parental consent in some circumstances. The Hurst Committee thought[151] that the provision empowering the court to dispense with consent on the ground that the consent was being unreasonably withheld had been expected to lead the courts to give greater weight to the child's welfare[152] but case law[153] falsified this expectation: the courts asked whether the parent was being unreasonable as a parent and not primarily whether the child's welfare was likely to be better promoted by adoption rather than by refusal 'with its consequence that the child either reverts to the care of the parent who may merely place him in an institution, or that he remains in the *de facto* adoptive home without the security of legal adoption'.[154] The Committee rejected suggestions that the child's welfare be made the first and paramount consideration in deciding the issue of dispensation;[155] yet it wanted to allow adoption orders to be made in cases in which the parent had made no attempt to discharge the responsibilities of a parent.[156] It therefore recommended the addition of a specific provision which would in terms allow the court to dispense with parental consent in such cases, but it declined to remove 'unreasonable withholding'. Eventually the Government agreed that the court should have power to dispense with parental agreement if the parent or guardian had 'persistently failed without reasonable cause to discharge the obligations of a parent or guardian'[157] but it declined to remove 'unreasonable withholding' from the list of grounds.[158]

---

[151] Possibly incorrectly: see above.   [152] *Hurst Report*, para. 117.

[153] The *Hurst Report* referred to 'two recent judgments', and it seems probable that the Committee had in mind *Hitchcock v. WB* [1952] 2 QB 561 and *Re Adoption Act 1950, Re K (An Infant)* [1953] 1 QB 117 both of which emphasised that it was *prima facie* reasonable for a parent to withhold consent and that in taking that decision the child's welfare was not the paramount consideration.

[154] *Hurst Report*, para. 117.

[155] The Committee thought the analogy with the provisions of the Guardianship of Infants Act 1925 was imperfect in cases where the issue was whether the parents' relationship was to be 'permanently cancelled by artificial means'; and the risk that a parent who gave up the care of his child for a time might be deprived permanently 'merely because adopters had been found for him who appeared to be more suitable or financially better able to bring him up than the natural parents' fortified the Committee in this view. Finally the Committee 'mentioned' the view 'strongly held in some quarters, that it is generally best for a child to be brought up by its natural . . . parent. Quite apart from the possible value of the blood tie, we think that the importance of preserving parental responsibility is such that the parents' claims should not be reduced for the sake of giving greater claims to prospective adopters': *Hurst Report*, para. 119.

[156] The Committee had in mind cases in which a parent ('usually, but by no means always, an unmarried mother') had for a long period of time 'shown no interest in the child, . . . never visited him or enquired after his welfare, . . . sent no symbol of love or affection, no birthday or Christmas present, nor even a letter, nor by any other action shown that her parenthood is a reality for her': *Hurst Report*, para. 119.

[157] Children Act 1958, s. 18(3). The Act also removed the ground (Adoption of Children Act 1949, s. 3(1) proviso (c)) empowering the court to dispense with the consent of a person who had persistently neglected or refused to maintain a child: Children Act 1958, s. 18(1).

[158] This gave rise to much inter-departmental discussion. At a late stage the Home Office changed its collective mind prompting a furious minute from an official in the Lord Chancellor's Department who minuted the Chancellor: 'This is July, but even so it is difficult not to feel angry after reading these papers. . . . It is the fact that the House of Lords has been told that you and the Government

The Hurst Committee had no doubt that an adoption order once made should be irrevocable. True, there were unfortunate cases in which people whose 'adopted child had developed a serious mental or physical defect were anxious to have the adoption order revoked'.[159] But adopters assume the responsibilities of natural parents and must not expect to be able to give the child back at will 'any more than they could relieve themselves of their responsibilities if the child had been born to them'.[160] Of course, the prospective adopters should know before filing their application 'all that can be told them about the physical and mental health of the child for whom they are assuming responsibility' and they should be warned that a child's mental and physical development cannot be predicted beyond all doubt. Quite how this was to be achieved was a matter on which opinions differed[161]—should there be a medical report to the court, and if so who should pay for it, for example?—and in the end much was deliberately left to delegated legislation.[162] But in one respect the Hurst Committee again signalled a change in attitude to the purposes which adoption should seek to serve. Some agencies were refusing to place (and some courts refusing to sanction adoption for) children 'not completely healthy in every way'.[163] But the Committee considered[164] it

'wrong to suppose that only the robustly healthy and highly intelligent are suitable for adoption. . . . It is probably much nearer the truth to say that almost any child is adoptable, or with care can become so. . . . There should be no discouragement of the adoption of handicapped children, for there are, happily, still people who will accept the extra burdens which a handicapped child may entail, and take an even greater pride and joy in bringing up such a child successfully than others take in rearing a more fortunate child'.

The principle that it was best to allow those concerned to know the facts and take their own decisions in the light of those facts also underlay the *Hurst Report's* insistence that the child be told that he had been adopted:

have made up your minds. Now you are asked to consider the matter again because (a) discussions have taken place between the Home Office and welfare officers, etc., and (b) further dialectical argument is adduced'. It is not altogether clear whether all those peers who spoke on this issue in the debates were aware that 'unreasonable withholding' was to be retained.

[159] *Hurst Report*, para. 139.   [160] *Ibid.*, para. 21.

[161] The question of ensuring that the court was aware of the prospective adopters' health was also a matter of concern, extensively discussed in the *Hurst Report*: see paras. 140–147. The Home Office persisted in advocating that prospective adopters should routinely submit to an independent examination notwithstanding opposition from the Lord Chancellor's Office: see Rieu to Kilmuir, 17 October 1957, PRO LCO2/4777; and the Home Affairs Committee expressed 'serious misgivings' on the ground that such a requirement would constitute 'an unwarranted interference with individual privacy': Minute of Meeting, 18 October 1957. Officials were much exercised by the question of cost: it would (thought one official in the Lord Chancellor's department) be 'scandalous if the Treasury agreed to the proposed expenditure on medical inspection while pressing us to produce more revenue by putting up court fees . . .': PRO LCO2/4777, 17 July 1957.

[162] Eventually, the Home Secretary put forward a compromise proposal that the applicant be required to furnish his own medical evidence; and provision expressly requiring the court, in cases to be prescribed by Rule, to have regard to a doctor's certificate in determining whether the adoption would be for the child's welfare became Children Act 1958, s. 19(5): on the factors influencing this decision see Rieu to Kilmuir, 17 July 1958, PRO LCO2/4780.

[163] *Hurst Report*, para. 21.   [164] *Ibid.*

It 'is still far too common for adopters to try to conceal the fact of adoption, both from the child and from the rest of the community. . . . We have been told of tragic cases where the child has learned the truth suddenly from strangers with disastrous psychological effects. In some cases children, especially in adolescence, have become mentally unbalanced by the shock . . .'.[165]

But (as the Committee recognised) it was not easy to deal with this problem by legislation, and the Committee recommended[166] that the Court be required to satisfy itself before making an adoption order that the adopters had told the child (or intended to tell him) about his adoption.[167]

Far more controversial was the question whether an adopted child should have any right of access to the birth records which might allow him to trace his parents. The *Hurst Report* seems to have favoured a solution under which the child would be able to apply to the court for a full copy of the adoption order[168] which would give him the means of getting information from the Registrar General's records.[169] This, not surprisingly, gave rise to much controversy and disagreement:[170] in the end,[171] the Act[172] gave the High Court and Westminster County Court[173] jurisdiction to make orders for disclosure, but in practice this

---

[165] *Ibid.*, para. 22.   [166] *Ibid.*, para. 153.

[167] The Lord Chancellor's officials regarded such a provision as unrealistic; and the High Court judges thought that what was appropriate to be said could be left to the discretion of the Official Solicitor, who would interview the child: see Vaisey to Coldstream, 5 December 1957, PRO LCO2/4778. The Act was silent on the matter, but a Home Office Circular advised adopters to tell the child the facts 'as soon as he can begin to understand or as soon as he begins to ask questions, which is normally at 4 or 5'.

[168] It seems that *the adopters* were entitled to a full copy of the adoption order made by the court (and this would reveal full details of the child's birth and parentage) but that in practice an 'abridged form' was normally supplied: Appendix to Home Office letter HO58/59 of 25 March 1959 as printed in *Clarke Hall and Morrison on Children and Young Persons* (6th ed., 1960, p. 633).

[169] *Hurst Report*, paras. 201–204. The Bill as drafted would have required the Registrar-General to supply a copy of the original order.

[170] 'Serious misgivings' were expressed about the proposal when the Bill first came to the Home Affairs Committee: the adoption societies, which disapproved of anything which broke the secrecy of the process 'would canvass vigorously against it' and it would be 'neither expedient nor necessary to oppose them on this particular issue': Minutes of Meeting, 18 October 1957, PRO LCO2/4447. Some Home Office officials, including the Permanent Secretary, continued to believe that the Hurst Committee had been right; and it was said that opposition to the proposal had been 'worked up' by one particular adoption society, whose opposition was not shared by the other 50 or more members of the Standing Conference of Societies Registered for Adoption. But Miss Patricia Hornsby-Smith was 'completely satisfied that the proposal would be unacceptable to the great majority of Government supporters, and that there would be no chance of getting it through', and the Home Secretary was apparently not informed of his officials' views: Whittick to Rieu, 10 March 1958 enclosing Draft Home Office Minute dated December 1957, PRO LCO2/4779. Lord McNair— Professor of Comparative Law at Cambridge, Judge of the International Court of Justice, and (subsequently) first President of the European Court of Human Rights—wrote to the Lord Chancellor expressing concern at the Hurst Committee's proposal: McNair to Kilmuir, 3 February 1958, PRO LCO2/4779.

[171] The Home Affairs Committee had agreed to further consideration of the issue if there were 'strong Parliamentary pressure': *ibid.*

[172] Children Act 1958, s. 25.

[173] That court was selected because Somerset House (where the Records were at that time preserved) was within its geographical area: see PRO LCO2/6424.

power was rarely exercised and the issue was only firmly grasped two decades later.

The Hurst Committee wanted to reinforce the duty of the *guardian ad litem*—ever since 1926 appointed to safeguard the interests of the child[174]—to make enquiries and report the facts to the court (of which he was an officer).[175] But again, the recommendation that the Act should expressly provide that the guardian be independent[176] and suitably qualified and experienced[177] were left to delegated legislation.[178]

The *Hurst Report* took the position that adoption should be effective to integrate the adopted child into the adoptive family for all legal purposes, and it therefore recommended that an adopted child should qualify as the child of the adoptive parents for the purpose of determining entitlement under wills or settlements. This once again gave rise to difficulties: the draftsman and some of the Lord Chancellor's officials objected on the grounds that the *Hurst* proposal did not reflect either public opinion or the intention of the average settlor or testator, while the Chancery judges did not object to a rule that an adoptive parent should be presumed to include the adopted child as one of his children but thought very different considerations applied to dispositions by grandparents or other ancestors and collateral relatives. Eventually the Lord Chancellor agreed to a compromise;[179] and the Act[180] allowed the child to take as the adopters' child under a will if the testator died after the date of the adoption order, irrespective of when he had made the will. Quite deliberately, this did not completely equate the position of an adopted child with that of the adopters' natural born children: it did not affect lifetime settlements, whilst relatives who did not like the idea of an adopted child inheriting their property could (at least if they

---

[174] See above, p. 603.

[175] Since 1948 the Local Authority Children's Officer had often been appointed in the county court and Juvenile Court; but this was not always the case, and the *Hurst Report* expressed unease about 'the practice of certain courts, which regularly appoint persons such as solicitors, clergymen and others who, however willing and however admirable as individuals . . . are neither by training nor even by experience really competent to do work of this specialised nature on the efficiency of which the future happiness of the child must very largely depend': para. 75. The Committee thought the High Court practice of appointing the Official Solicitor as guardian was based on an obsolete principle, but the Judges believed that the *Hurst* recommendation had been made in ignorance of the way in which the Official Solicitor carried out his duties and strongly asserted their belief that the Official Solicitor was a 'skilled worker'. They considered there were many advantages to preserving his role (for example, that the Official Solicitor's report usually made it unnecessary for the parties or the welfare authority to attend the hearing): see Vaisey to Coldstream, 3 December 1957, PRO LCO2/4777.

[176] *Hurst Report*, para. 73.   [177] *Ibid.*, para. 76.

[178] The Act (s. 18(1)) did remove the requirement that a person liable to maintain the child (often the putative father of an illegitimate child) should consent; but provision for him to be notified of the proceedings were again—after a good deal of official discussion: see Whittick to Rieu, 16 July 1957, PRO LCO2/4777—left to Rules.

[179] See Dobson to Kilmuir, 7 January 1958, PRO LCO2/4778.

[180] Children Act 1958, s. 22(1).

knew about the adoption order) make a fresh will restricting the definition of 'child'.[181]

ADOPTION AS A LOCAL AUTHORITY SOCIAL SERVICE:
THE *HOUGHTON REPORT*

In 1958 the courts in England and Wales made 13,303 adoption orders. Ten years later the number had soared to 24,831[182]—a figure never since equalled. Many of these adoptions matched the traditional image: more than 9,000 of the adopted children were under two years old[183] and illegitimate[184] and the majority of adoption placements were made by adoption societies.[185] These societies, not surprisingly, found their resources 'stretched to the limit'.[186] The reorganisation of local authority services under the Local Authority Social Services Act 1970,[187] the publication of research findings into the working of adoption,[188] and publicity given to so-called 'tug-of love' cases and to the problem of children in institutions who were said to need permanent homes were also factors which increased concern and interest. In July 1969 the Home Secretary, James Callaghan (who had a long-standing interest in the problems of disadvantaged children and was proud of the work of the Home Office Children's Department)[189] set up a Committee, chaired by a distinguished educationalist Sir William Houghton,[190] to consider the law, policy and procedure

[181] Although there were difficult policy issues involved it seems that the problems of drafting provisions which would deal with all the consequences of seeking to equate adopted and natural children were at least in part responsible for the Government's reluctance. What for example was to be done where the testator's will left his estate to A for life with remainder to A's eldest child living at his death, and (as the draftsman Sir Noel Hutton put it to Viscount Simon in 1949 when the issue was under discussion: see his letter to Simon dated 13 July 1949, PRO LCO2/4483) A was 'sufficiently inconsiderate to die leaving surviving him a natural child aged 20' born in 1950 and an adopted child aged 25 adopted in 1951. It was left to the draftsman of the Children Act 1975, required to give effect to the recommendations of the (Houghton) *Departmental Committee on the Adoption of Children* (1972, Cmnd. 5107, para. 328) (hereafter referred to as the '*Houghton Report*'), to settle the provisions of Sch. 1, para. 6 to deal with the seniority of adopted children in such situations.
[182] *Houghton Report*, Appendix B, Table 1.
[183] The majority were young babies—7,446 of the total were adopted when under eight months old (*ibid.*, Table 2), and must therefore have been placed at or shortly after birth.
[184] *Ibid.* Neither of the adopters was the child's parent in these cases.
[185] In 1968, adoption societies made 8,482 placements in England and Wales; whilst 3,384 placements were made by local authorities: *ibid.*, Table 4.
[186] *Permanent Family Placement* (BAAF) p. 8.
[187] Following the *Report of the Committee on Local Authority and Allied Personal Social Services* (1968, Cmnd. 3703) (the '*Seebohm Report*').
[188] The Home Office Research Unit had carried out a detailed statistical analysis: E Grey and RM Blunden, *A Survey of Adoption in Great Britain* (1971). A study of a sample of children adopted in 1958 had been undertaken by J Seglow, ML Kellmer-Pringle, and PL Wedge, and findings were published as *Growing Up Adopted* in 1972. The Advisory Council on Child Care considered adoption practice, and *A Guide to Adoption Practice* was published by HMSO in 1970.
[189] See Biographical Notes.
[190] For Sir William Houghton, see Biographical Notes. The Committee's Report (Cmnd. 5107, 1972) is cited as the *Houghton Report*.

on the adoption of children. The Committee (on which social work and adoption interests were strongly represented)[191] was invited to (and did) interpret these terms of reference broadly. In particular, the problem of the position of long-term foster-parents who wanted (against the will of the parents) to keep a child permanently was seen as a central issue.[192]

The Committee's Report, published in 1972, is an impressive document, not least because it marked (for the first time in an official inquiry) an awareness that adoption could not sensibly be kept in isolation. In reality, adoption was merely one legal technique for dealing with the future of children whose birth parents were not going to provide their homes throughout their childhood. Again, the Committee was quick to perceive demographic changes which had significant implications. There were two particularly striking features. On the one hand, the number of illegitimate babies available for adoption had begun to fall[193] (and this trend was to accelerate over the following decade).[194] On the other hand, adoption was increasingly being used by step-parents (especially to create the legal relationship of parent and child after divorce and remarriage).[195] The Houghton Committee was also conscious that adoption had increasingly been suggested as suitable for older children, and especially for those who had spent long periods in residential care. Although local authorities had increasingly come to act as adoption agencies (and 8.7% of the children adopted in 1968 had come from local authority care, compared to 3.2% in 1952)[196] the Committee believed that coloured and handicapped children were being denied the permanency to which an adoption placement could lead.[197]

The *Houghton Report's* central recommendations focussed on the need for a comprehensive nationwide adoption service. Local authorities should have a statutory duty to ensure (in co-operation with voluntary societies) that such a service was available throughout their area.[198] Such a service would:

'Comprise a social work service to natural parents, whether married or unmarried, seeking placement for a child . . .; skills and facilities for the assessment of the parents' emotional resource, and their personal and social situation; short term accommodation for

---

[191] For the membership, see Biographical Notes, Part B.　　　[192] *Houghton Report*, para. 1.

[193] The *Houghton Report* attributed the fall to the increasing use of legal abortion (the Abortion Act 1968 came into force on 27 April 1968), more use of contraception, and a changing attitude to illegitimacy allowing more unmarried mothers to care for their babies: *Houghton Report*, para. 20.

[194] The statistics are helpfully analysed by NV Lowe, 'English Adoption Law: Past, Present and Future' in SN Katz, JM Eekelaar and M Maclean (eds.), *Cross Currents* (2000) pp. 314–320; whilst R Leete, 'Adoption Trends and Illegitimate Births 1951–77' (1978) 14 *Population Trends* 9–16 is a detailed examination of the period.

[195] There were 4,369 adoptions (the great majority jointly with his or her spouse) by a natural parent of his own child in England and Wales in 1962, and 10,751 in 1971. These represent 26% and 50% respectively of all adoptions in those years: *Houghton Report*, para. 19 and Appendix B Table 3; and see further Lowe, *op. cit.* and J Masson, D Norbury and SG Chatterton, *Mine, Yours or Ours?* (HMSO, 1983), pp. 12–14.

[196] Lowe, *op. cit.* p. 318. Local authorities were also active in arranging adoptions of other children; 19% of British adoptions in 1966 were arranged by local authorities, as against 40% by societies: *Houghton Report*, para. 82.

[197] See *Houghton Report*, paras. 22–25.　　　[198] *Ibid.*, paras. 40–43.

unsupported mothers; general child care resources, including short-term placement facilities for children pending adoption placement; assessment facilities; adoption placement services; after-care for natural parents who need it; counselling for adoptive families. In addition, it should have access to a range of specialised services, such as medical services (including genetic, psychiatric and psychological assessment services, arrangements for the examination of children and adoptive applicants, and a medical adviser) and legal advisory services'.

The Committee clearly saw making arrangements for adoption as something for the skilled and trained professional; but it saw a continuing place for voluntary societies (albeit they would have to be registered by Central Government, and registration could be refused or cancelled if the 'scope of the society's activities, the nature of its resources and the effectiveness of its organisation' were found to be such that the society was unlikely 'to make an effective contribution' to the adoption service in its area of operation).[199]

The Committee's belief that placement decisions should be taken by skilled social work professionals made it almost inevitable that it would recommend[200] that placements[201] be made exclusively by adoption agencies:[202] only in this way could the law give assurance of adequate safeguards for the welfare of the child. In fact, the proportion of independent placements had fallen sharply (from more than a third of all adoptions at the time of the *Hurst Report* to less than a tenth in 1966) but the Committee pointed out that the numbers involved were still considerable.[203] It also highlighted the activities of doctors and maternity home matrons, and hinted that the motivation of such people was often to provide a remunerative service to adults rather than serving the interests of the child.[204] The Committee therefore held firm to its view, discounting arguments based on concern for the personal liberties of the parties.[205]

The Committee insisted that the child's welfare should always be the first consideration when decisions had to be taken about adoption;[206] but the Committee held back from proposing that the court be empowered to make an adoption order against the will of the natural parent merely because that would best promote the child's welfare.[207] It did, however, make recommendations intended to improve the lot of the:

---

[199] *Ibid.*, para. 56.   [200] *Ibid.*, para. 92.   [201] With non-relatives.
[202] Ie local authorities and registered voluntary societies.
[203] Ie approximately 1,500 each year: *Houghton Report*, para. 83.
[204] See *ibid.*, para. 87.   [205] *Ibid.*, para. 85.   [206] *Houghton Report*, para. 17.
[207] The Committee recommended that the court should have power to dispense with parental consent if the parent were, judged objectively, unreasonably withholding that consent; and in deciding that issue the court should have regard to all the circumstances, first consideration being given to the effect of the parent's decision on the child's long-term welfare: *Houghton Report*, paras. 205–218. The Committee's 1970 *Working Paper* had provisionally recommended that in determining the question whether consent was being unreasonably withheld the court should apply the principle that the child's welfare was the paramount consideration (ie overriding all other considerations): see para. 173. The final recommendation has the marks of a compromise: see below.

'sizeable number of children in the care of local authorities and voluntary societies for whom no permanent future can be arranged for a variety of reasons, for example, because the parents cannot bring themselves to make a plan, or do not want their child adopted but are unable to look after him themselves. Some of these children may have no contact with their parents and would benefit from adoption, but the parents will not agree to it. In other cases a parent may have her child received into care shortly after birth and then vacillate for months or even years over the question of adoption, thus depriving her child of the security of a settled family home life'.[208]

The Committee believed the law contributed to the problems of arranging adoptions for these 'children who wait' in institutions or foster homes. In particular, a child had to be placed before the mother could give the formal consent to a specific adoption which the law required, and the possibility that a mother might eventually refuse to agree seems often to have deterred agencies from starting the process. In an attempt to minimise the problem the Committee recommended a 'relinquishment' procedure (under which, subject to court approval, the mother would irrevocably agree to a transfer of her rights to the agency with a view to it arranging an adoption);[209] it also recommended that local authorities and other agencies should be able to apply to the court, prior to placement, to dispense with the mother's consent to adoption.[210]

The Committee was prepared to be radical when it came to consider the effects of adoption: an adopted child should have 'exactly the same' rights under wills and other instruments as if he were the adopters' natural born child,[211] and (somewhat more hesitantly)[212] an adult who had been adopted should have a statutory right of access to his birth records. But the Committee did not carry logic to extremes: the Committee recognised the logic of denying any kind of financial subsidy to people willing to adopt handicapped children or several siblings—after all, no special allowance would be given to birth parents—but accepted that if allowances were payable more homes might be found for children with special needs. Again a compromise was found: pilot schemes for paying allowances to some adopters should be established.[213]

The Committee saw adoption as an institution which could enable a child to 'achieve permanent security in a substitute home with a couple fully committed to fulfilling parental responsibilities'.[214] But it was equally insistent that adoption was often only one of several possible solutions. In particular, the

[208] *Houghton Report*, para. 221.
[209] *Ibid.*, paras. 173–191. The Committee believed that the procedure would be used to minimise the stress arising from the mother's right to change her mind up to the moment when the adoption order was made: para. 187.
[210] *Ibid.*, paras. 221–225. These recommendations emerged in the Children Act 1975 as the 'freeing for adoption' procedure: see below.
[211] *Houghton Report*, para. 328.
[212] *Ibid.*, paras. 300–305—suggesting that counselling be available to those seeking access to birth records. Note also that the Committee did not favour allowing the adopted person an automatic right to see the court records of the adoption proceedings: para. 305.
[213] *Houghton Report*, paras. 93–95.   [214] *Ibid.*, para. 14.

Committee observed[215] that adoption might be used to sever strong bonds with the birth family (or some members of it), and it was especially concerned by the increased use of adoption by parents, step-parents[216] and other relatives:

'Adoption by relatives severs in law, but not in fact, an existing relationship of blood or of affinity, and creates an adoptive relationship in place of the natural relationship which in fact, though not in law, continues unchanged. In most cases the adopting relatives are already caring for the child and will continue to do so whether or not they adopt him; and adoption by relatives can be particularly harmful when it is used to conceal the natural relationship.'[217]

The Committee recommended procedures to discourage the routine use of adoption in such cases, and the extension of guardianship law to provide a legal institution more consonant with the factual situation.[218]

Overall the Committee's report can be seen as evidencing an approach[219] which would have seemed inconceivable at the time when adoption was first introduced into English law. The assessment of the Report as marking a 'final break with the old legal concept of children as chattels of their parents'[220] seems (the Committee's cautious approach to making the child's welfare the *paramount* consideration in decisions notwithstanding) fair. But the Houghton Committee's major achievement was to see adoption as an integral part of the legal framework for dealing with children in need; and consideration of how the Committee's recommendations on adoption were implemented in the Children Act 1975 must be deferred until the evolution of the State's powers and responsibilities in that respect have been outlined.

---

[215] *Ibid.*, para. 16.

[216] The great majority of step-parent adoptions were by a natural mother and the man she had married. In 1970 5,054 illegitimate children and 5,202 legitimate children were adopted by a parent and step-parent (*Houghton Report*, para. 103, footnote) ie 46% of all adoptions. The numbers and proportions continued to rise after 1970: see NV Lowe, 'English Adoption Law: Past, Present and Future' in SN Katz, JM Eekelaar and M Maclean (eds.), *Cross Currents* (2000) p. 320.

[217] *Houghton Report*, para. 97.

[218] *Houghton Report*, paras. 106–115 and Chapter 6. The Committee considered guardianship might also be appropriate for foster parents in some circumstances: see paras. 120–122.

[219] Note that the Committee recommended that local authorities be empowered to assume the parents' rights by passing a resolution to that effect if the child had been in their care for three years. The Committee also recommended that the law require 28 days' notice of removal of a child who had been in local authority care for 12 months: *Houghton Report*, paras. 152, 156, and see below, Chapter 20. These recommendations are not directly related to adoption, but greatly increased the opportunity for the local authority to make plans for a permanent placement for children in care: see below.

[220] J Heywood, *Children in Care: the development of the service for the deprived child* (1978) pp. 204–205.

18

The State, Parent and Child: (1) Before the Welfare State

INTRODUCTION[1]

The nineteenth century had been a time of concern about the welfare of the country's children. The attention of reformers first focussed on the plight of children employed, often for very long hours and in harsh conditions, in the factories and mines of the Industrial Revolution.[2] Legislation, starting with an Act of 1802 restricting the hours which Poor Law 'apprentices'[3] were allowed to work in factories,[4] was enacted piecemeal over the years.[5] In 1862 a Royal Commission was appointed to enquire into the employment of children and young persons in trades and manufactures not previously regulated by law. Its Reports provided a wealth of evidence of the appalling conditions in many

---

[1] For a comprehensive historical account of policy and its application, see H Hendrick, *Child Welfare, England 1872–1989* (1994). GK Behlmer, *Child Abuse and Moral Reform in England, 1870–1908* (1982) and *Friends of the Family, The English Home and Its Guardians, 1850–1940* (1998) are excellent historical treatments of major themes.

[2] W Clarke Hall, *The State and the Child* (1917) p. 132, claims that illegitimate children—and the same was presumably true of orphans dependent on the Poor Law—'were shipped by boards of guardians in barge loads to the great factories of the North, and, as the supply was almost inexhaustible, their health and limbs and lives were of little or no concern to the employers to whom they were consigned. . . . At the age of five and upwards they were sold like cattle as "apprentices" in the factories, where bad food, foetid atmosphere, and overwork brought them too often painful diseases and lingering death'.

[3] George Crabbe's *Peter Grimes* (1810) had told the story of a fisherman who obtained three apprentices (all of whom were beaten and died in his care before anyone asked whether he was suitable) and gave some notoriety to the process:

> 'Peter had heard there were in London then,—
> Still have they being!—workhouse clearing men,
> Who, undisturb'd by feelings just or kind,
> Would parish-boys to needy tradesmen bind:
> They in their want a trifling sum would take,
> And toiling slaves of piteous orphans make.'

Subsequently Charles Dickens' *Oliver Twist* and Charles Kingsley's *Water Babies* further raised public consciousness.

[4] The Parish Apprentices Act 1802 stipulated that 'apprentices' working in cotton mills should work no more than a 12-hour day. The Cotton Mills Act 1819 applied this restriction to all children under 16 working in such mills, and also prohibited nightwork.

[5] See generally BL Hutchins and A Harrison, *A History of Factory Legislation* (3rd ed., 1936); NW Thomas, *The Early Factory Legislation* (1951). The most notable individual associated with the campaigns for improved conditions of children working in factories and in trades such as chimney sweeping was the Earl of Shaftesbury (1801–1885): see JL and B Hammond, *Lord Shaftesbury* (1936); and GBAM Finlayson, *The Seventh Earl of Shaftesbury* (1981).

trades and industries; and the Commission made detailed recommendations for reform. In 1878 the Factory and Workshop Act consolidated the statutes and made comprehensive provision for regulating hours of employment and for control and inspection of the premises in which the young were employed as well as for the education of child employees.[6]

Central Government's direct formal involvement with child welfare issues (which was greatly to increase in the course of the twentieth century) can be said to have started with the Home Office being made responsible for supervising the factories legislation.[7] But it was one thing to inspect factories, quite another to dictate to parents how they should behave in the privacy of their homes. For long it was accepted that 'to patrol industry on behalf of the young was England's Christian duty' but 'to patrol the home was a sacrilege'.[8]

Protection or control?

Later generations may find difficulty in understanding how there could be any opposition to legislation which would prevent children of four or five years of age being dragged from bed at four in the morning and made to toil in the dark for perhaps 18 hours a day, sometimes chained to trucks which they had to drag on all-fours through mine shafts.[9] But at the time there were many people who thought it better for children to be employed in a cotton mill or factory than to be running uncontrolled in the streets of the large industrial cities; and certainly there was a general concern (mingled no doubt with a measure of fear) about 'the hordes of neglected and destitute children who frequented the streets begging and thieving, without homes or teaching or indeed anyone apparently to care for them'.[10]

One response to this nightmare was by philanthropists and religious bodies who sought to provide educational facilities ranging from the often primitive 'ragged school'[11] (intended to give children 'some knowledge of the commonest

---

[6] 'Children' were those aged under 14; the Act also made provision for 'young persons' aged between 14 and 18. Employment of children in street trading etc was dealt with by the cruelty legislation.

[7] *Home Office Note to the Machinery of Government Committee on Home Office Functions in relation to Child Welfare*, December 1944, PRO MH102/1379, para. 1.

[8] GK Behlmer, *Child Abuse and Moral Reform in England, 1870–1908* (1982).

[9] Memoir of Anthony Ashley Cooper, Seventh Earl of Shaftesbury: *Dictionary of National Biography* (1886).

[10] *Home Office Note to the Machinery of Government Committee on Home Office Functions in relation to Child Welfare*, December 1944, PRO MH102/1379, para. 1.

[11] It appears that John Pounds, a Portsmouth shoemaker, was responsible for the first ragged school. 'In 1818 he took some of the poorest children in Portsmouth and taught them cooking, cobbling and their ABC': *Report of the Departmental Committee on the Treatment of Young Offenders* (1927, Cmd. 2831) p. 9. Not surprisingly, standards were often very low; and the *Report of the Select Committee on the Education of Destitute Children* (1861) HC 460, BPP 1861, vii, 395 recommended that no child should attend such a school if educational provision could be made elsewhere. But the nineteenth century industrial school (and thus the twentieth century Approved School) have their origins in the Ragged School movement—'a rescue movement for the destitute and neglected children of the streets'. For a brief account see JS Heywood, *Children in Care* (2nd ed., 1964) pp. 39–47.

principles of morality and religion' and the elements of literacy and numeracy)[12] to more ambitious establishments in which some kind of industrial training was given to vagrant children and others. But where did the boundary lie between providing facilities which children and their families could use if they wished, and those which should be imposed on them?

In 1854 statute allowed certain 'Reformatory Schools' to be given official recognition,[13] and empowered magistrates to commit young offenders to schools which had been certified; and in 1857 the Industrial Schools Act was passed to give unconvicted children in moral danger the same 'advantages' as children in reformatory schools.[14] Magistrates were given power[15] to commit children found begging or wandering without means of subsistence (and even a child whose parent claimed to be unable to control him) to an Industrial School[16] where girls would be trained in the domestic duties to fit them for a life in service and boys would be taught the rudiments of tailoring or shoe-making or some other useful trade.[17] In theory there was a clear distinction between the Industrial School and the Reformatory School (specifically intended for the training of youthful *offenders*)[18] but in practice this was often blurred[19] both in relation to the regime imposed on inmates and the functions of the institution;[20]

[12] C Seymour, *Ragged Schools, Ragged Children* (1995).

[13] The Home Secretary was given power to issue certificates to private reformatory schools and to contribute to the maintenance of convicted children, and the parents could be ordered to make a contribution to the costs. This pattern of collaboration between private philanthropy and the State was followed in the Industrial Schools Act 1857: see generally L Radzinowicz and R Hood, *A History of English Criminal Law* (1986) vol. 5, Chap. 7 'The Reformatory System' which (although focussing on the treatment of the delinquent) is invaluable.

[14] L Radzinowicz and R Hood, *A History of English Criminal Law* (1986) vol. 5, p. 177.

[15] Industrial Schools Act 1857: the legislation was amended and then consolidated in the Industrial Schools Act 1866. The courts could only commit a child to a school which had been certified as fit for the purpose: see below.

[16] The grounds upon which a committal could be founded were extensive: the legislation allowed, for example, the committal of a child who frequented 'the company of any reputed thief or of any common or reputed prostitute', a child who had no parent or guardian to exercise proper control, the child of a parent imprisoned or sent to penal servitude, a child whose mother had been twice convicted of crime, and a child declared 'refractory' by the Poor Law Guardians (see below): Industrial Schools Act 1861, s. 17; Prevention of Crimes Act 1871, s.14.

[17] In practice, the 'training' might be merely in wood-chopping or match-box making or even oakum picking (the tearing apart of the fibres of old ropes, an occupation—invariably causing bleeding and laceration of the hands—traditional in convict prisons): *Report of the Royal Commission on Reformatories and Industrial Schools* (1884, C. 3876).

[18] The Reformatory Schools Act 1866, consolidating legislation dating back to the Parkhurst Prison Act 1838, was in principle entirely penal: children under 16 convicted of an offence punishable by imprisonment could be committed to a reformatory school for a period of not less than two nor more than five years. The punitive element was emphasised by the requirement that the offender first serve ten days in prison.

[19] See the dissenting memorandum of Lord Norton to the *Report of the Royal Commission on Reformatories and Industrial Schools* (1884, C. 3876). Eventually, in 1927 the *Departmental Committee on the Treatment of Young Offenders* urged the assimilation eventually brought about by the Children and Young Persons Act 1932 (which substituted the term 'Approved School' for both categories): see below.

[20] As the *Report of the Departmental Committee on the Treatment of Young Offenders* (1927, Cmd. 2831) p. 9 put it: legislation since 1857 'has tended to remove the original differences between

and the introduction of compulsory elementary education by the 1870 Education Act tended to emphasise the 'disciplinary' element in any kind of training dependent on the making of a magistrates' order.

Children's homes: the problem of parental rights

Industrial Schools may often have been founded by philanthropically or evangelistically minded individuals or groups, but committal by magistrates' order (and the fact that the schools in question had to be 'certified' by the Home Office) inevitably suggested a link with the coercive mechanisms of the State. This link was not present in the children's homes[21] set up (often with a religious motivation) on a large scale[22] in the last 30 years of the nineteenth century to provide the care which parents either could not or would not provide.

At the end of the nineteenth century Dr Thomas Barnado,[23] the most well-known person engaged in this work, had more than 4,700 children[24] under his charge.[25] But Barnado soon discovered that the parents of the children he had 'rescued' were not always grateful. Sometimes they came to believe that a child should not be brought up in Barnado's brand of evangelical Protestantism, and (almost always with the financial and other support of a rival denomination) instituted *habeas corpus* proceedings[26] so that the child could be moved to an institution controlled by the rival. In other cases, the parents' motive was mercenary: they simply wanted a child returned so that he or she could earn a wage. As Karl Marx had pointed out, children sometimes needed protection from their

the two classes of schools'. In the twentieth century the Home Office further blurred the distinction by describing all schools which it certified as 'Home Office Schools'.

[21] An early example of such a charity is the Foundling Hospital founded by Captain Thomas Coram and opened in 1747 in Lamb's Conduit Fields in London.

[22] Some homes were founded by individuals such as Dr Barnado and George Muller (see below). The main organisations were the National Children's Homes (whose first home opened in 1869) the Waifs and Strays (subsequently the Church of England Children's Society) and the Roman Catholic Crusade of Rescue (founded in 1899).

[23] But other philanthropists were also active, sometimes on a large scale, in the same field—for example George Muller who, inspired by his Evangelical beliefs, started an Orphan House in Bristol in 1835. In 1845 the first of Muller's purpose built houses was opened on Ashley Down in Bristol, and by 1870 there was a group of five houses, accommodating over 2,000 young people. A hagiographical biography, *George Muller of Bristol*, by AT Pierson (1899) states (at p. 214) that cleanliness, 'neatness, method and order . . . everywhere reign, and honest labour has always had . . . a certain dignity' the male orphans working in vegetable gardens, thereby getting wholesome exercise and also training them in self-support.

[24] Barnado had opened a small home for destitute boys in Stepney in 1870 and there was a rapid expansion. The commitment 'No destitute child ever refused admission' was prominently displayed.

[25] Barnado's evidence to the *Departmental Committee on Poor Law Schools* (Chairman AJ Mundella MP) (1896, C. 8027).

[26] The cases (*R v. Barnado* (1889) 23 QBD 305; *R v. Barnado* [1891] 1 QB 194; *Barnado v. McHugh* [1891] AC 388; *Barnado v. Ford* [1892] AC 326) resulted from a 'clash between the zeal of Dr Barnado and the increasingly organized work of the Roman Catholic Crusade of Rescue': JS Heywood, *Children in Care* (2nd ed., 1964) p. 63. For an excellent account of the background to this litigation see G Wagner, *Barnado* (1979).

parents[27] as much as from their employers. The problem was that even a cruel father has a

'legal and almost indefeasible right to retain possession and control of his victim. In such cases, to remove the child beyond the range of the father's influence may be the only means of saving it from a life of misery or destruction. Yet to do this . . . will require knowledge of the law, great care, and in some cases a considerable expenditure of time and money'.[28]

In 1891, in response to pressure, Parliament passed the Custody of Children Act which gave the court a discretion to refuse to enforce the parent's right[29] to custody if the parent had abandoned or deserted the child or otherwise so conducted himself as to make it inappropriate to enforce the parental right; but the problem of how to balance a parent's natural right to care for his children against the child's right to be protected from harm remained a source of concern well into the twentieth century.

The baby farm: Infant Life Preservation legislation

In contrast, there was no need for any balancing exercise where a baby's life was at risk. All too often, the desperate woman who found herself pregnant gave up the baby she lacked the means to support for what was then often called 'adoption'. The mother would hand the child over to a 'baby-farming house' which would agree to care for the child, perhaps in return for a small single payment (possibly as little as £5, or £300 in year 2000 values). These children were often starved, or neglected in other ways, with the result that 'with rare exceptions they all of them die in a very short time'. Sensational publicity was given to the trial and execution of Margaret Waters, a woman baby-farmer convicted of murdering the children in her care.[30] Pressure built up[31] for something to be done.

A Select Committee on the Protection of Infant Life[32] reported, giving horrifying details; and the Infant Life Preservation Acts 1872 and 1897 were enacted.[33]

[27] The *First Report* of the 1862 Royal Commission into the Employment of Children found evidence of parents 'selling' their young children (often for trifling sums of money) into the notorious chimney sweeping trade.

[28] Advice to the London Society for the Prevention of Cruelty to Children, as quoted in GK Behlmer, *Child Abuse and Moral Reform in England, 1870–1908* (1982) p. 79.

[29] Enforceable by *habeas corpus*. The Act was passed after a number of parents—often under pressure from sectarian organisations—had successfully brought *habeas corpus* proceedings against Dr Thomas Barnado to recover a child placed in one of Barnado's 'Homes': see above.

[30] See GK Behlmer, *Friends of the Family, The English Home and Its Guardians, 1850–1940* (1998) pp. 276–285. There were other sensational trials: see H Hendrick, *Child Welfare, England 1872–1989* (1994) pp. 45–49.

[31] An Infant Life Protection Society had been established under distinguished patronage and the British Medical Association was also active: see Hendrick, *op.cit.* above, Behlmer, *op. cit.* above, and Behlmer, *Child Abuse and Moral Reform in England, 1870–1908* (1982) p. 38.

[32] BPP 1871, vol. 7, 607.

[33] The Birth and Death Registration Act 1874 was also intended to guard against concealment of births and deaths: see Hendrick, *op. cit.* above, pp. 47–48.

These Acts required paid carers to register with the local authority and thereby made the conditions in which the children were kept open to scrutiny in certain circumstances. But the legislation fell short of what was required for effective protection of the very young[34] against those who fostered them for profit, not least because the Poor Law authorities responsible[35] for the inspection of premises in which children were cared for lacked the resources necessary to detect abuse.[36]

The child victim: the work of the National Society for the Prevention of Cruelty to Children

The evils of baby-farming provided much sensational copy for newspapers towards the turn of the nineteenth century; and this helped create a more general concern about the ill-treatment of children by their parents. A number of organisations were founded. In 1889 the London Society for the Prevention of Cruelty to Children[37] was reconstituted as the National Society for the Prevention of Cruelty to Children. In 1890 the NSPCC came under Royal patronage[38] and soon took the lead in campaigning for reforms.[39] Its most notable success was the campaign which led to the enactment in 1889 of the Prevention of Cruelty to, and Protection of, Children Act. The Act created both a general offence of ill-treating, neglecting, abandoning or exposing a child[40] in a manner likely to cause the child unnecessary suffering or injury to health and more specific offences of involving children in begging and street-trading or singing.[41] The Act also gave the courts useful ancillary powers (for example, to issue search warrants in cases where child abuse was suspected)[42] and relaxed the common law rules about the circumstances in which the courts could hear children's evidence.[43]

The Act not only dealt with cruelty by provisions for punishing guilty parents. In a provision of great significance for the future development of the law,

---

[34] The legislation was amended by the Children Act 1908.

[35] Outside London. The London County Council, in contrast, had established a Public Control Department which acted vigorously to seek out badly run foster homes: GK Behlmer, *Friends of the Family, The English Home and Its Guardians, 1850–1940* (1998) p. 282.

[36] GK Behlmer, *Friends of the Family, The English Home and Its Guardians, 1850–1940* (1998) p. 282.

[37] See generally GK Behlmer, *Child Abuse and Moral Reform in England, 1870–1908* (1982).

[38] The Society has, in spite of occasional controversy about its role, been officially regarded as having done 'a most valuable work for the welfare of children': *Home Office Note to the Machinery of Government Committee on Home Office Functions in relation to Child Welfare*, December 1944, PRO MH102/1379, para. (2).

[39] The NSPCC (and the other 'child-saving' organisations) depended for their success on creating a 'moral fervour' pointing to the need for urgent reform. These campaigns were often associated with specific scandals which had attracted attention. See for example the Criminal Law Amendment Act 1885 passed in an attempt to protect children from the brothel keeper and child trafficker.

[40] Ie a boy under 14 or a girl under 16.

[41] Prevention of Cruelty to, and Protection of, Children Act, 1889, s. 3.

[42] The child could be taken to a 'place of safety' and kept there: s. 6.

[43] s. 8. The legislation was amended and consolidated in 1894 and 1904.

the Act gave the court power to commit the child of a parent convicted of cruelty or ill-treatment to the care of a 'fit person'[44] or relative; and the 'fit person' could retain the child notwithstanding any claim by the parent.[45]

The 1889 Act gave the courts significant powers to investigate what had happened within the privacy of the home, and it has been described[46] as the 'first attempt to deal comprehensively with the domestic relationship of parent and child'. But the Act did not take away all parental prerogatives: in order to overcome opposition from school teachers (who feared the Act would affect their right to use corporal punishment) the Act specifically provided[47] that it did not affect the right of any parent, teacher or other person having the lawful control or charge of a child to administer punishment to the child.

Victims of misfortune

The campaigns for legislation aimed at cruelty attracted widespread interest and may perhaps have distracted attention from the fact that it was only a comparatively small number of children who were damaged by deliberate abuse, neglect[48] or cruelty on the part of their parents. In Victorian England disease and poverty[49] damaged many more. But the nineteenth century was a period of great concern for public health; and there had been a number of measures primarily directed to protecting children from disease. In particular, vaccination against small-pox had—controversially[50]—been made compulsory: the parent was required to have his child vaccinated within three months of the birth.[51]

---

[44] This expression seems to have its legislative origin in the provisions of the Infant Felons Act 1840 which empowered the Court of Chancery to assign the care and custody of any infant convicted of felony to any person willing to take charge of him. The 1840 Act appears to have been vigorously opposed as an interference with the rights of parents; but it proved to be 'almost entirely inoperative, as suitable persons willing to undertake such responsibilities did not come forward': *Report of the Departmental Committee on the Treatment of Young Offenders* (1927, Cmd. 2831) p. 10. The same problem was experienced after the power of the courts to make such orders was extended by the Children Act 1908: see below.

[45] s. 5(2). The Act also allowed a 'fit person' order to be made in circumstances in which the court could have committed the child to an Industrial School. The Act gave the court power to make a maintenance order against the parent.

[46] By GK Behlmer, *Child Abuse and Moral Reform in England, 1870–1908* (1982).   [47] s. 14.

[48] The Poor Law Amendment Act 1868 empowered the Poor Law Guardians to prosecute neglectful parents, but it appears that this power was little exercised: see H Hendrick, *Child Welfare, England 1872–1989* (1994) p. 53.

[49] Orphans and abandoned children might of course be taken into Barnado's or other children's homes: see above.

[50] The issue was investigated at length by the *Royal Commission . . . [on] Vaccination*, set up in 1889. The Commission published seven reports, the last in 1896: C. 8270 (BPP, vol. 33, p. 889). On the vaccination controversy, see generally GK Behlmer, *Friends of the Family, The English Home and Its Guardians, 1850–1940* (1998) pp. 79–92.

[51] Vaccination Act 1867, s. 16. The penalty for non-compliance was a fine of £1; but in practice parents who objected on principle were often committed to prison for non-payment of the fine. Following the Royal Commission, the Vaccination Act 1898 allowed a parent to reject vaccination of his child if he satisfied the magistrates that he conscientiously believed vaccination would be prejudicial to the child's health; and under the Vaccination Act 1907 a parent's statutory declaration that he held such a conscientious belief was conclusive.

Gradually, other public health measures[52] directed primarily at children (and sometimes associated with the compulsory education introduced by the Education Act of 1870) were introduced.[53] But it was the Poor Law which represented, however inadequately, the State's main response to the special problems of the orphan and the destitute; and this involvement had a profound impact on the development of child law. As Lord Scarman was to put it in the 1980s:

The 'poor law was the historic base from which Parliament advanced to meet the needs of the orphan, the deserted and the abandoned child'.[54]

THE POOR LAW: BENTHAMITE RATIONALITY

The 1601 Poor Law had envisaged that the unemployed poor should be 'set to work'—children being 'apprenticed'[55]—but it also provided that necessary relief should be given to the impotent poor. The 1834 *Report of the Royal Commission on the Poor Law*[56] painted a gloomy picture of how the system worked in practice. The 1834 Commissioners claimed that in reality poor relief was 'applied to purposes opposed to the letter, and still more to the spirit of the law, and destructive to the morals of the most numerous class of [the poor] and to the welfare of all'.[57] In this view, the great abuse was that payments in cash or kind were made to the able-bodied. And even when the poor were compelled to enter the workhouse (as the Commissioners thought they should) this was often a laxly administered establishment in which

'the young are trained in idleness, ignorance, and vice; the able-bodied maintained in sluggish sensual indolence; the aged and more respectable exposed to all the misery that

[52] These were amongst the factors which contributed to a massive fall in infant mortality over the course of the twentieth century. In 1899 163 children per thousand live births died before the age of one; and in 1917 for every nine soldiers killed at the front 12 babies died at home. By 1921 the death rate per thousand live births had fallen to 84, and there was a sharp fall after World War II from 48.8 per thousand in 1945 to 24.4 in 1956. The decline continued and in 2000 the rate was 5.6: see *Social Trends* (2002) p. 124.

[53] H Hendrick, *Child Welfare, England 1872–1989* (1994) contains a useful account.

[54] *Leeds City Council v. West Yorkshire Metropolitan Police* [1983] 1 AC 29, 41, *per* Lord Scarman. F Crompton, *Workhouse Children* (1997) is a comprehensive account drawing on the records of workhouses in Worcestershire of the reality of the Poor Law's impact on the lives of children.

[55] There was always a danger that the apprentice would be seen simply as a source of cheap unskilled labour rather than being taught a useful skilled trade; and in the early nineteenth century the demands of mills, situated in remote parts of the country because of their need to be close to a mill stream, were met by large numbers of so-called apprentices bound in effect as mill-hands by Overseers primarily concerned to minimise expenditure on poor relief. See pp. 628–629 above; and the account in JS Heywood, *Children in Care* (2nd ed. 1964) p. 20.

[56] The Report was reprinted by HM Stationery Office in 1905 when another Royal Commission was appointed. An edited and annotated edition by SG and OEA Checkland was published by Penguin Books in 1974, and it is this which is cited (as '1834 Poor Law Report') in the text.

[57] 1834 Poor Law Report, p. 82.

is incident to dwelling in such a society, without government or classification; and the whole body of inmates subsisted on food far exceeding both in kind and amount, not merely the diet of the independent labourer, but that of the majority of the persons who contribute to their support'.[58]

The 1834 Commissioners, apparently inspired with Benthamite zeal, proposed radical change; and the Poor Law Amendment Act 1834 gave effect to their proposals. The underlying principle was to be that of 'less eligibility'.[59] Relief should be refused save by admission to the workhouse; and the workhouse would 'impose severely deterrent conditions upon its inmates'.[60] Thus, husband and wife were to be separated from one another and from their children, inmates were confined to 'the House' and subjected to strict discipline, and amenities such as tobacco or even tea were not permitted. It is true that, in theory, education was provided for the children but practice was often different.[61]

'Outdoor relief' and children

The insistence of the 1834 Act on the principle that relief be given in the workhouse and nowhere but the workhouse gave rise to an immediate problem for it meant that children could no longer be apprenticed but had to be held in the House. This difficulty had to be dealt with by Statute: the Poor Law Amendment Act 1844 allowed children to be bound as apprentices but also sought to ensure that the child would indeed learn a useful skill. In other respects the 1834 Act did not in practice work quite as had been originally envisaged.[62] True, the Poor Law Commission in Somerset House had wide powers and duties to ensure the efficient working of the system, but in practice the law was administered locally by the Boards of Guardians of the country's 648 Poor Law Unions;[63] and different Boards of Guardians had very different views about how their powers and duties should be exercised.[64] In particular, well before the end of the nineteenth

---

[58] 1834 Poor Law Report, p. 127.

[59] *Report from . . . Commissioners for Inquiring into the Administration and Practical Operation of the Poor Laws* (1834) p. 228.

[60] M Finer and OR McGregor, 'The History of the Obligation to Maintain', App. 5 to the *Finer Report*, para. 55.

[61] See JS Heywood, *Children in Care* (2nd ed., 1964) p. 68; but compare F Crompton, *Workhouse Children* (1997) Chapter 6.

[62] H Hendrick, *Child Welfare, England 1872–1989* (1994) pp. 74–83 gives a succinct account of the treatment of Poor Law children in the period 1872–1908. For a fuller account of educational and other provision, see S and B Webb, *English Poor Law History* (1929) Vol. II, Chapter 8.

[63] E G Woodward, *Archbold's Poor Law* (16th ed., 1930), p. xxxii. Guardians were elected; and the Parish and District Councils Act 1894 broadened the franchise and women (as well as working men) were increasingly elected: in 1895 there were 875 women guardians. It appears that they often brought a fresh approach to the problems of providing for pauper children, and were particularly influential in organising the boarding out of children and subsequently visiting them: see P Hollis, *Ladies Elect* (1987), particularly at pp. 251–267.

[64] After 1871 the Local Government Board made orders for the administration of the Poor Law, but in practice there still appears to have been a wide divergence of practice.

century, many Boards had come to accept that children should be kept out of the workhouse.[65] This was most frequently done by allowing the parent the 'outdoor relief' which the 1834 Commissioners would have denied.[66]

The practice of supporting poor children by giving the parent outdoor relief remained controversial, but the underlying assumptions implicit in this criticism had changed by the beginning of the twentieth century. It began to be said that, far from providing a lavish standard of living, the amounts paid out as outdoor relief were usually not adequate to support a child to a reasonable standard as judged by contemporaries whilst the fact that the scales of benefit and the conditions subject to which relief was made available were fixed by the 650 or so Boards of Guardians led to anomalies.[67] A Report made for the 1909 *Royal Commission on the Poor Laws*[68] stated that most children at home and supported by outdoor relief were

'Under-nourished, many of them . . . poorly dressed, and many barefooted. The houses are bare of furniture, for there is not money to buy sufficient food or boots, and any extra expense has to be met by selling or pawning furniture . . .'.

Again, it was said that many mothers, condemned to keep house on an 'almost impossibly small sum',[69] broke down in 'health and courage [and had become] ineffective colourless and whining'.[70] The result was that a almost a third of them were ranked as 'slovenly and slipshod mothers' or even 'really bad mothers' guilty of wilful neglect, drunkenness or immorality.

[65] In the course of the nineteenth century a bewildering variety of provision was made for 'workhouse' children, some—such as the 'Cottage Homes' which became popular towards the end of the century—involving the provision of accommodation. There were, for example, workhouse schools (although it seems that little or no formal education was to be expected), 'farm schools' (which were not in fact agricultural schools but simply establishments to which pauper children could be 'farmed out') and separate Poor Law Schools, whilst some children were sent to 'certified schools' dealing with particular religious denominations: see generally *Departmental Committee on Poor Law Schools* (Chairman, AJ Mundella MP) (1896, C. 8027); JS Heywood, *Children in Care* (2nd ed., 1964) Chap. 5.

[66] It is true that there was no such easy solution if the child was orphaned or abandoned (as probably more than half of the Poor Law children were); and a different solution had to be found for them.

[67] See M Finer and OR McGregor, 'The History of the Obligation to Maintain', App. 5 to the *Finer Report*, para. 64.

[68] Cd. 4499; the quotations are from S and B Webb, *English Poor Law History* (1929) Vol. II, p. 507 ff.

[69] An indication of what poverty meant for the single parent family in nineteenth century Britain can be gleaned from the recorded history of WJ Thorne (1857–1946), Labour MP for Plaistow, 1918–1945. Orphaned, at the age of seven he worked a 12-hour day for a weekly wage of half-a-crown (£7.50 in year 2000 values). His mother supported him and her three daughters by sewing hooks and eyes onto cards. Outdoor relief from the Poor Law supplemented her income by a weekly payment of four shillings (£12) and provision of four bread loaves: see his autobiography, *My Life's Battles* (1925); and the entry by DE Martin in JM Belllamy and J Saville (eds.), *Dictionary of Labour Biography* (1972) Vol. 1.

[70] See S and B Webb, *English Poor Law History* (1929) Vol. II, p. 509.

A better future for the child? Emigration?

But what was the alternative to keeping a child on a bare subsistence in this way? One apparently attractive possibility was that the child should be sent to make his way in one of the British territories overseas. Legislation[71] had given guardians specific power to arrange for the emigration of paupers and emigration certainly had the merit of being the 'most economical method of providing for the children of the state'.[72] But the move towards arranging for pauper children to emigrate was not motivated entirely by financial considerations. At a time when large numbers of adults were opting to make a fresh start by taking advantage of the apparently boundless opportunities afforded in Australia, New Zealand and North America[73] there seemed to be positive advantages in encouraging young pauper children to share these prospects. In 1896, the *Departmental Committee on Poor Law Schools*[74] concluded that emigration opened out for the children 'a happy and successful career'. The Committee was impressed by the fact that emigration removed children from 'pauper surroundings and from bad relatives, who so often interfere with their well-being'; and noted that life in Canada (the country which attracted the greatest number of Poor Law child immigrants) was

'Healthy, the food abundant, the air . . . bracing, and the energy and industrious habits which characterise the people are specially beneficial in stimulating children descended from the pauper and thriftless classes. The openings for employment are more numerous and remunerative than those which can be obtained for Poor Law children in England, and the grant of land . . . enables lads with the necessary qualifications to become farmers and householders.'

Faced with this endorsement, it is not surprising that in 1910 the Liberal President of the Local Government Board said that he 'wished it were possible' to transplant some 15,000 or 20,000 such children to the Colonies 'where there are homes waiting for them, not as drudges or as servants, but rather as companions'.[75] But whether or not these favourable assessments were valid[76]

---

[71] Poor Law Amendment Acts 1848, s. 5, 1849, s. 20.

[72] *Report of the Departmental Committee on Poor Law Schools* (Chairman, AJ Mundella MP) (1896, C. 8027) para. 526.

[73] The *Royal Commission on Population* (1949, Cmd. 7695) para. 322 estimated that the United Kingdom lost on average 56,000 persons per annum during the nineteenth and early twentieth century.

[74] (1896, C. 8027) p. 137.

[75] John Burns (see Biographical Notes) who regretted the fact that it was the need to obtain the consent of the child's parents to emigration which made it practically impossible to do as he wished: *Official Report* (HC) 8 April 1910, vol. 16, col. 848. Burns reflected the conventional wisdom of the time: see for example the discussion in the *Report of the Departmental Committee on Reformatory and Industrial Schools* (1913, Cd. 6838) concluding that emigration was one of the 'best means of disposal' of the delinquent child.

[76] For a strongly hostile view ('We can only speculate as to the misery endured by these boys and girls, taken from their parents, brothers and sisters, families, communities and friends, and put to

emigration could only be used for a tiny proportion of the Poor Law children. A much more widely available solution was to board the children out with foster-parents.

Boarding out: the best (and cheapest) way of providing for children of the State?

In the latter part of the nineteenth century[77] the practice of boarding children out with foster-parents had attracted strong support and official approval.[78] The principle was that boarded-out children (who had to be orphans or children deserted by their parents) were 'placed with cottagers'[79] who were obliged to provide the child with proper food, lodging and washing and to endeavour to train the child in habits of truthfulness, obedience, personal cleanliness and industry, give the child suitable domestic and out-door work, and ensure that the child attended church and school regularly. The foster parents were required to give a formal undertaking to bring up the child as their own.[80]

The fact that the boarded out child would no longer be brought into contact with the criminals and other undesirables likely to be encountered in the work-house was a clear advantage; but there was more to it than that. The emphasis was to be on the 'home training' which one witness[81] to the 1896 Mundella

work in often Spartan environments where they were subjected to exploitation and violence') see H Hendrick, *Child Welfare, England 1872–1989* (1994) p. 80 ff. ; and note also the critical view taken by J Eekelaar, ' "The Chief Glory": the Export of Children from the United Kingdom' in N Lowe and G Douglas (eds.), *Families across Frontiers* (1996).

[77] A consequence of the 1834 Act's insistence that children be accommodated in the workhouse was that boarding out (which had had a long history: see J Heywood, *Children in Care* (2nd ed., 1965) Chapter 5) had to be classified as 'outdoor relief'. The effect was that a child could only be boarded out in the Poor Law District from which the family came. In 1870 the Poor Law Board's General Order of 25 November 1870 (printed as Appendix V to Heywood, *op. cit.*) for the first time allowed guardians to board children out 'beyond the Union'—ie in another district. This made boarding out much more attractive to guardians in industrial cities.

[78] The emergence of articulate and vocal women concerned about the public care of children may have been a special influence; but there were also objections based on the ease with which fostering could very easily be used to conceal baby farming: see V George, *Foster Care: Theory and Practice* (1970) p. 11.

[79] *Report of the Departmental Committee on Poor Law Schools* (Chairman, AJ Mundella MP) (1896, C. 8027) para. 25. Poor Law Boards had to establish a Boarding Out Committee, and a member of the Committee was to visit the child every six weeks.

[80] The terms of the undertaking (which required the foster parents to undertake to return the child when the Board required) were eventually settled by the Boarding Out Order made in 1889 by the Local Government Board. These terms remained little changed until the Children Act 1989 swept away the concept of boarding out (but not its practice under a different name): see below. Boarding out with foster-parents was also widely used by children's charities such as the Church of England Society for Waifs and Strays and Dr Barnado's; and Dr Barnado told the *Departmental Committee on Poor Law Schools* (1896, see above) that he believed boarding out to be greatly superior to providing for children in his own Institutions. Children were not subject to the provisions of the Boarding Out Order so long as their care was the responsibility of the Charity (rather than of the Boarding Out Committees appointed by Boards of Guardians).

[81] Miss Brodie Hall, *Report of the Departmental Committee on Poor Law Schools* (Chairman, AJ Mundella MP) (1896, C. 8027) p. 91.

Committee claimed had 'made an English Working Class as good as they are'. The Committee itself concluded[82] that

the boarded out child 'lives a natural life. Deprived by misfortune of its own parents, it finds substitutes in its foster mother and father, who are often not only kindly disposed, but affectionate and devoted to their young charges. Although dependent upon the rates, no stigma of pauperism attaches to the child, who takes his or her place among the ordinary children of the village, attends the ordinary elementary school, sits among others in the church or chapel, and shares with them the pleasures and experiences of childhood. . . . The child's experience of the foster mother's love, effort and anxiety on its behalf, and the time she is able to devote to its individual training, are influences of the highest importance in the formation of its character. The child brought up under the ordinary conditions of family and village life is in a position to see the results which follow conduct. He realises that drunkenness is succeeded by poverty, and that indigence is the offspring of thriftlessness . . .'.

The fact that boarding out was much the cheapest method of bringing up the children of the State (costing no more than £13 or something over £800 annually in year 2000 values) was an additional consideration in favour of the practice.[83] But boarding out could never be a panacea: the restrictions on the age of children[84] who could be dealt with in this way, and the fact that boarded-out children had to be placed with foster-parents of the same religious denomination had a restrictive effect. In spite of the emphasis placed by the authorities on the merits of boarding out, in 1907 only 8,659 out of the 69,030[85] Poor Law children were boarded out.[86]

Security for foster parents and the child

There were problems with boarding out. For example, how were the guardians to ensure that the children were properly accommodated and that adequate arrangements were in place for their supervision?[87] But perhaps the most seri-

---

[82] *Report of the Departmental Committee on Poor Law Schools* (Chairman, AJ Mundella MP) (1896, C. 8027) p. 99.
[83] *Ibid.*, para. 378. There was something of an ideological debate about whether the allowance (which was fixed locally but subject to a permitted maximum of four shillings, £12 in year 2000 values) should be such as to allow the foster-parents to make a profit. The fear was that foster-parents might be motivated solely by financial considerations, and that the system might degenerated into what was known as 'baby farming'. But the 1907 Committee thought it reasonable to allow foster-parents some 'small advantage' for the trouble and anxiety of caring for the children, and recommended that the maximum be increased. It was noted that the Voluntary Societies paid more than the Poor Law maximum: *ibid.*, para. 393.
[84] No Poor Law child could be boarded out for the first time at an earlier age than two years nor at a later age than ten; and no foster-parent was allowed to take more than two children: *ibid.*, p. 98. The Committee pointed out that these restrictions were disadvantageous.
[85] Ie 12.5%.
[86] Cf. 21,498 children in workhouses or infirmaries; 27,698 in 'separate establishments' such as Cottage Homes or Schools; while 9,319 were in 'other establishments' (including the Training Ships which enjoyed a certain vogue at the time). See *Report to the President of the Local Government Board* by TJ Macnamara (1908, Cd. 3899).
[87] *The Departmental Committee on Poor Law Schools* recommended that a Central Authority should undertake inspections: see para. 403.

ous problem for those administering the system was that all too often[88] the child's parent would exercise the common law right to have possession of the child (whether boarded out or being cared for in some other way) as soon as he was old enough to work and earn wages. The Poor Law Acts of 1889 and 1899 were passed to deal with this problem.

The 1889[89] Act gave the guardians power to assume by resolution all the 'powers and rights' of a parent who had deserted[90] the child. The 1899 Act (which was exclusively concerned with the assumption of parental rights) greatly extended the scope of this power. Under the 1899 Act a resolution could be founded not only on parental desertion, but on the ground[91] that a parent:

(i)   was unfit to have control of the child by reason of mental deficiency, vicious habits or mode of life;
(ii)   was unable to perform the parental duties by reason of being under sentence of penal servitude;[92]
(iii) had been sentenced to imprisonment in respect of any offence against the child;
(iv)   was permanently bedridden disabled, was an inmate of a workhouse, and consented to the passing of the resolution;
(v)   of the child had died.

Once the guardians had passed the resolution, they could allow the child to be 'adopted' by foster-parents.[93] This was not legal adoption in the modern sense of that word: the child's legal parentage remained unaffected, and indeed the guardians were obliged to arrange for the child to be visited at least twice a year for the next three years, and the guardians could if they thought fit revoke the 'adoption' and require the foster-parents to return the child. But so long as the resolution assuming parental rights remained in force the child's parents had no right to remove him.

It appears that this procedure of so-called 'poor law adoptions' was originally intended to be used only for the children of persons sentenced to long terms of imprisonment 'or demonstrably of vicious life or habits'; but 'poor law

---

[88] Notwithstanding the provisions of the Custody of Children Act 1891 which provided that the court should not make an order to deliver up a child to a parent who had allowed the child to be brought up by the guardians or others 'for such length of time and under such circumstances as to satisfy the court that the parent was unmindful of his parental duties': s. 3. It seems that in practice parents did not bother to apply to the court but simply retook the child.

[89] s. 1.

[90] Desertion was defined so as to extend to cases in which the parent was imprisoned for an offence against the child.

[91] Magistrates were given the power to determine a parental rights resolution if they believed there had been no ground to justify it, or if they considered that it would benefit the child to be permanently or temporarily under the parent's control: Poor Law Amendment Act 1899, s. 1(2).

[92] Or detention under the Inebriates Act 1898.

[93] 'Adoption' under the procedure should be distinguished from adoption under the Adoption Act 1926: the Poor Law procedure merely gave the foster-parents some security against the child's being removed and did not affect the child's legal status: see p. 596, and generally Chapter 17, above.

adoptions' came to be extensively used by some Boards of Guardians in other cases.[94] This system of Poor Law adoption was found 'very valuable in practice'[95] and it seems that many thousands of children (the majority deserted by their parents)[96] were 'adopted' in this way. But very little is known about the social reality of such 'adoptions'.

THE 'CHILDREN'S CHARTER': THE CHILDREN ACT 1908

The South African War of 1899 to 1902 was in a number of ways a shock to a complacent society. In particular, the poor physical condition of many of the young men who offered themselves for military service was a source of concern. It is true that the *Inter-Departmental Committee on Physical Deterioration*[97] rejected the more apocalyptic evidence presented to it and set out to 'allay apprehensions' about alleged deterioration of the national stock;[98] but the feeling that the young needed better provision seems to have become widespread. The landslide victory of the Liberals in the 1906 General Election[99] engendered expectations that something positive would be done; and Herbert Gladstone, the incoming Home Secretary[100] was quick to offer a 'children's charter'.[101] Home Office officials used much less emotive language: for them, the intention was simply to consolidate the existing law with minor amendments to remedy perceived defects.[102] Subsequent comment has tended to reflect similar differences of outlook. Some think an avowedly reforming Government should have been more imaginative and far-sighted: the Government should have done much more to shift the emphasis of child-protection legislation from punishing

[94] But by no means all: S and B Webb, *English Poor Law History* (1929) Vol. II, p. 730. There seem in fact to be no reliable statistics about the scale on which guardians exercised these powers. The *Molony Report* (1927, p. 116) stated that in '1908 there were 12,417 children so adopted. Figures for later years are not available'; but the Webbs state that 'in the course of a couple of decades, no fewer than 15,000 children' had been adopted in this way: *op. cit.*, Vol. I p. 282. *The Report of the Royal Commission on the Poor Law* (1909, Cd. 4499), believing that children rescued from indigent parents were often reclaimed and again 'subjected to evil influences and degrading surroundings', recommended that the Poor Law authorities should make greater use of their powers: see paras. 394–396.

[95] *Report of the Departmental Committee on the Treatment of Young Offenders* (1927, Cmd. 2831) p. 64.

[96] S and B Webb, *English Poor Law History* (1929) Vol. II, p. 282.

[97] (1904, Cd. 2175) (Chairman, Almeric Fitzroy).

[98] The Committee seems to have placed most of the blame for recruitment problems on the military authorities who were thought not to have recruited the best or even the tolerable. However, the Committee made a large number of recommendations for improved recreational activity. From the present perspective the recommendation that specially selected magistrates deal with cases involving children is significant.

[99] The Liberals held 400 out of the 670 seats in the new House of Commons.

[100] See Biographical Notes.

[101] Gladstone to the Prime Minister, Sir Henry Campbell-Bannerman, 18 November 1907, as quoted in B Wasserstein, *Herbert Samuel, A Political Life* (1992) p. 103. The Prevention of Cruelty to, and Protection of, Children Act, 1889 had also been described as a 'children's charter'; see above.

[102] See B Wasserstein, *Herbert Samuel, A Political Life* (1992).

offenders towards establishing preventive mechanisms.[103] Others celebrate the fact that the Act did establish the principle that juvenile delinquency should be dealt with in courts distinct from those dealing with adult criminals; and the fact that a 'host of amending laws and piecemeal legislation'[104] would be gathered together into a single statute publicly emphasised 'the social rights of children' and demonstrated the importance which the law and law-makers attached to these matters.[105] In this view it is no exaggeration to describe the Act as a 'great and fundamental step in child protection'.[106]

The truth is that the Government's hands were to some extent tied. There was a massive Government majority; but the fact that the Bill was intended to consolidate all the existing child cruelty and protection legislation meant that the Bill was also massive—the first version had 119 clauses and covered 72 pages; and it became a 134 section Act. There was, at the time, no special procedure to deal with Consolidation Bills;[107] and hence every clause was open to debate and amendment. The exigencies of the parliamentary timetable meant (as Gladstone told the King)[108] that the Opposition had it in their power to 'wreck the Bill'. To avoid this, the Bill was drafted so as to avoid controversial topics so far as possible; and the Government was ready to compromise whenever a serious conflict of attitudes seemed likely to cause difficulty. For example, the Government compromised between those who were anxious to remove children from immoral surroundings and those who thought the parental right should not be interfered with at all:[109] the court's power to intervene if a child 'frequented the company of any . . . common or reputed prostitute' was not to apply where the prostitute in question was the child's mother and she could show that she was exercising 'proper guardianship and due care to protect the child from contamination'.[110]

The emphasis of the 31 sections of the Act[111] intended to strengthen the law relating to cruelty was very clearly on the imposition of criminal sanctions as the

---

[103] S and B Webb, *English Poor Law History* (1929), p. 614; and see GK Behlmer, *Child Abuse and Moral Reform in England* (1982) pp. 220–223.

[104] W Clarke Hall, the magistrate and author of the leading textbook on the legislation (see below, and Biographical Notes) described the Act as 'a splendid piece of legislation' and claimed that Herbert Samuel (to whom he gave most of the credit for securing the 1908 Bill's enactment) had 'spared no pains to make it as comprehensive as possible': *The State and the Child* (1917) p. xiii.

[105] J Heywood, *Children in Care* (1978), p. 108. A similar approach was taken by a government insider more than a decade later: see Sir A Newsholme, *The Ministry of Health* (1925) p. 130. The fact that the 1908 Act had to be available and comprehensible to lawyers and those involved in public administration led to the publication of a number of important texts, notably William Clarke Hall's *The Children Act 1908* (new editions of which continued to be published, under the title *The Law Relating to Children* throughout the twentieth century). In this way the 1908 Act played a significant part in the recognition of the law relating to children as a proper object of study and scholarship.

[106] Heywood, *op. cit.*

[107] Compare the provisions of the Consolidation of Enactments (Procedure) Act 1949 allowing corrections and minor amendments to be made (subject to certain conditions).

[108] In the Home Secretary's Report to the Sovereign following the Report stage on 24 March 1908 (during which there had been strong criticism of some of the provisions relating to under-age tobacco smoking): see Wasserstein, *Herbert Samuel, A Political Life* (1992) p. 106.

[109] *Official Report* (4th Series), 4 November 1908, vol. 195, col. 1162, Earl Beauchamp.
[110] s. 58.   [111] ss. 12–38, forming Part II of the Act.

644 *Children, Family and the State*

means of protecting children's welfare. For example, the Act[112] attempted to
deal with the problem of the children—as many as 1,600 each year—burned to
death because they had been left unsupervised in reach of fire, by creating an
offence of leaving a child under seven 'in any room containing an open fire grate
not sufficiently protected to guard against the child being burned or scalded'.
The Act also made it a criminal offence to allow under 16s to beg[113] or to allow
anyone aged between four and 16 to 'reside in or frequent a brothel'.[114] But,
again, some proposals of this kind proved controversial. For example some MPs
were sceptical about the need for a specific criminal offence to penalise the adult
guilty of 'overlying'. True, a large number of child deaths were recorded as
being caused in this way; but some MPs claimed that 'overlying' was no more
than a 'generic term used by medical officers to cover many cases where children
were found dead in bed and a diagnosis proved somewhat difficult', and the
innuendo that death in many of those cases was really caused by the parent
going to bed drunk seemed to be based on no firmer evidence than the fact that
a high proportion of these deaths occurred on Saturday night or Sunday morning.[115] After long debate, the Government's original clause was greatly
restricted in scope: to get a conviction the prosecution would have to prove that
the death of a child under three was caused by suffocation whilst the child was
in bed with a person over 16 who 'was at the time of going to bed under the
influence of drink'.[116]

The Act also contained a number of other measures seen primarily as protecting children from damaging habits (notably smoking and drinking) but
inevitably enforced by criminal sanctions. But any provision about Public
Houses could be guaranteed to provoke fierce debate between temperance and
brewing interests;[117] whilst the provisions[118] prohibiting the sale of tobacco to
the under-16s (not to say imposing a duty on the police and on park-keepers
'being in uniform' to seize cigarettes from youths caught smoking in a public
place)[119] attracted scornful comment from the Conservative opposition about
the folly of 'grandmotherly legislation' likely to 'lead to a good many laughable

[112] s. 15. The offence was a summary one, punishable by fine of no more than £10 (perhaps £600
in year 2000 values).
[113] s. 14.   [114] s. 16.
[115] *Official Report* (HL), 28 October 1908, vol. 195, col. 211.
[116] Children Act 1908, s. 13. If these matters could be proved, the accused was deemed to have
neglected the child, and could be imprisoned for up to two years: s. 12.
[117] The Act eventually prohibited children under 14 from being in bars during permitted opening
hours (with exceptions, for example in the case of railway refreshment rooms where the sale of alcohol was merely auxiliary to other purposes): s. 120.
[118] ss. 39–43, together constituting a separate Part of the Act. The legislation was based on recommendations of the *Inter-Departmental Committee on Physical Deterioration* (1904, Cd. 2175) see
above. Possibly the draftsman of the Children Bill made a tactical mistake in grouping the provisions
relating to juvenile smoking in a separate Part of the Act, thereby giving them greater prominence.
[119] s. 40. The Act did not make smoking in public an offence, but it required the police and park-
keepers to search boys (but not girls) found smoking.

scenes of constables pursuing small boys who would drop their cigarettes in running away'.[120]

Industrial and reformatory schools[121]

The provisions consolidating and amending the 19 statutes relating to industrial and reformatory schools constitute, in terms of sheer bulk,[122] the major part of the 1908 Act; but these did not provoke any great controversy. As explained above, the distinction between the two types of institution had been that the reformatory was exclusively concerned with the delinquent, and (although the specifically punitive function of the reformatory had been perhaps reduced by legislation[123] removing the requirement that a youth spend the first weeks of the sentence in prison) the distinction was largely preserved by the 1908 Act. But it was far from rigid: in some cases magistrates could order a child offender[124] to be committed to an industrial school instead of a reformatory, and there were provisions for the transfer of reformatory children to industrial schools. Whatever euphemism was used there was likely to be a 'prison taint' about any school which admitted convicted children;[125] and in any event, the child sent to an industrial school under provisions[126] designed for his protection would, whatever the school's regime, not be under any illusions. He could be given 12 strokes of the birch for indiscipline; and if he was guilty of 'serious and wilful' breach of the rules[127] or escaped he was liable to be convicted of a criminal offence and sent to a reformatory;[128] whilst the overtones of delinquency were often reinforced by the retention of provisions[129] allowing magistrates to

---

[120] *Official Report* (HC), 24 March 1908, vol. 186, cols. 1266–70. On the Report stage there was 'a determined but unexpected resistance to the proposals, in which [the Conservative leader] Mr Balfour took part' and Samuel felt obliged to give up the provision making it an offence for boys to smoke in public places: see *Official Report* (HC), 12 October 1908, vol. 194, cols. 1266–70. The result is that the police had powers of search and confiscation even though no criminal offence had been committed. But the controversy prolonged debate and endangered the Bill: Gladstone to King Edward VII, 13 October 1908, see Wasserstein, *Herbert Samuel, A Political Life* (1992) p. 106.

[121] The great majority of industrial and reformatory schools were private institutions, kept under State control only by Home Office inspection and by the need to obtain a certificate (given after a Home Office inspection) that the school in question was 'fit for the reception of youthful offenders or children . . . sent there' under the provisions of the Act: Children Act 1908, s. 45. The magistrate, William Clarke Hall's *The State and the Child* (1917) pp. 65–73 cast doubt on the effectiveness of this kind of control, and—drawing on Chief Inspectors' Reports—Clarke Hall had harsh things to say about the training provided in some certified schools. Even so, in his *Children's Courts* (1926) he claimed that the 'best chance that can possibly be given to many neglected children is to send them to a good certified school': p. 54.

[122] Part IV of the Act, ss. 44 to 93.   [123] Reformatory Schools Act 1899.

[124] The Act (s. 58(2)) provided that a child under 12 charged with an imprisonable offence could be committed to an industrial school by magistrates if this was expedient; slightly older delinquent children could be sent to an industrial school if there were 'special circumstances' justifying such a course and the Bench was satisfied that the child's character and antecedents were such that he would not exercise an evil influence over the other children: s. 58(3).

[125] See L Radzinowicz and R Hood, *A History of English Criminal Law* (1986) vol. 5, p. 207.

[126] See below.   [127] Children Act 1908, s. 71(2).

[128] Children Act 1908, s. 72(2).   [129] See above.

commit children who had caused trouble to the workhouse authorities[130] to an industrial school.[131] Although the industrial school had been conceived as a preventive[132] and protective agency; the 1908 Act did nothing to meet the arguments of those who claimed that school staff were in danger of assuming the same attitude to the children in their charge as gaolers adopted to convicted prisoners.[133] As a senior civil servant[134] had put it nearly half a century previously, once the decision had been taken to commit a child to an industrial school there could be 'no substantial difference' between the treatment and discipline required by the child who had broken the law by 'positive crime' and those who were guilty of nothing worse than vagrancy (or, he might have added, of being the victim of his father or mother's cruelty). The question whether the social control of harmful and perhaps damaging behaviour by the young and the social measures necessary to help and protect the deprived are essentially separate and distinct processes or are better seen as complementary[135] was controversial for much of the twentieth century; but the impact of accepting the view that there should be no distinction between the 'treatment and discipline' of the young thief on the one hand and the child abused by his parents on the other obviously bore hardly on the needy child, especially at a time when few people had any doubt that harsh measures were necessary to deter the offender.

The creation of the juvenile court

The view of the 1908 Act as a 'children's charter' can best be justified by the fact that it included provisions to some extent[136] humanising the application of the criminal law to young people and making the courts agencies for the 'rescue as well as the punishment' of young offenders. For example, the Act required a person under 16 charged with an offence to be given bail;[137] it prohibited the imprisonment of children under 14 and provided that a young person aged between 14 and 16 was only to be imprisoned if the court certified that he was

---

[130] If the guardians satisfied the court that a child was 'refractory'.

[131] Similarly, child truants could be committed to an industrial school as could a child whose parents were unable to control him: Children Act 1908, s. 58(4).

[132] See Radzinowicz and Hood, *A History of English Criminal Law* (1986) vol. 5, p. 206.

[133] *Ibid.*

[134] Sir Ralph Lindgren, arguing successfully in 1860 that control for the schools should be a matter for the Home Office (rather than the education authorities): see Radzinowicz and Hood, *op. cit.*, p. 206.

[135] The debate came to a head with the publication of *Children in Trouble* (1968, Cmnd. 1191).

[136] The extent should not be exaggerated: for example, the Act allowed the court to order children to be whipped: s. 107(g). But it has to be remembered that at the time whipping was considered to be more humane than committing a young person to prison, and the 1908 Act did greatly reduce the circumstances in which sentences of imprisonment could be passed: see generally Radzinowicz and Hood, *op. cit.* p. 711 ff.

[137] s. 94: there were exceptions to the general principle, eg where the offence charged was homicide or 'other grave crime'. If detained the accused was not to be sent to prison but to a special establishment for the provision of which the police were responsible: ss. 97, 108.

of 'so unruly a character' that he could not be detained elsewhere[138] (or that he was of 'so depraved a character' that he was not a fit person to be so detained) and the Act allowed a delinquent under 16 to be placed under the supervision of a probation officer[139] (rather than being whipped or sent to a reformatory).

The Act also contained provisions intended to make it clear that the family was responsible for its young:[140] parents were to be required to attend the court hearing[141] and parents had to pay the fine imposed on their child unless the court was satisfied that the parent had not 'conduced to the commission of the offence by neglecting to exercise due care' of the offender[142] whilst a parent (broadly defined to extend to a step-parent, the mother's cohabitant, and the putative father of an illegitimate child)[143] could be ordered to pay the cost of maintaining the child in an industrial school or reformatory.[144]

All these provisions were important, but it was the apparent success of the campaign[145] to establish special juvenile courts to deal with delinquents which has attracted most comment both at the time and subsequently, and allows the Act to be seen as an important step in promoting the welfare of children who had offended. In reality, the innovation was exceedingly modest in scope. All that the Act did[146] was to provide that magistrates' courts should deal with under 16s in a different room from that used for other cases (or at least hear child delinquency cases at a different time from adult cases).[147] The Act did not even give effect to the recommendation of the *Inter-Departmental Committee*

---

[138] s. 102. The Act also provided that those under 16 should not be sentenced to death but rather to be detained during His Majesty's Pleasure (s. 103) and a sentence of detention for such period as the court thought fit could be passed on those convicted of attempted murder, manslaughter, or wounding with intent to do grievous bodily harm if the court considered no other punishment adequate: s. 104.

[139] s. 102(3): the Probation Service had been put onto a statutory basis by the Probation of Offenders Act 1907.

[140] These provisions were enthusiastically supported by both Government and Opposition speakers in the debates on the 1908 legislation. The Lord Advocate told the Commons that having to pay fines imposed on the child would ensure that the 'parents or guardians should know in future that their responsibility is not ended when they send their children into the streets or leave them to follow their own devices': *Official Report* (HC), 24 March 1908, vol. 186, col. 1258; whilst the Conservative opposition spokesman Mr Akers-Douglas supported 'the wider enforcement of parental authority' claiming that to penalise a parent for neglecting to train the child was 'rightly at variance with the socialist doctrine . . . that the moment a child comes into the world the State is to be responsible for it . . .': col. 1263.

[141] s. 98.   [142] s. 99.   [143] Children Act 1908, s. 125.   [144] s. 75.

[145] See the accounts in GK Behlmer, *Friends of the Family, The English Home and Its Guardians, 1850–1940* (1998) pp. 232–247; L Radzinowicz and R Hood, *A History of English Criminal Law* (1986) vol. 5, pp. 629–33; HK Bevan, *Child Law* (1989) paras. 12.01–03.

[146] The version presented to Parliament was much less radical than the first Home Office draft which, firmly embodying the principle that 'a child is not a criminal in the eyes of the law', would have raised the age of criminal responsibility to 16, and given the court a parental jurisdiction to exercise such powers over the delinquent as a parent could or use its powers under the industrial and reformatory schools legislation: see Radzinowicz and Hood, *op. cit.*, drawing on PRO HO 45/10364/15482/4A.

[147] s. 111. The Act did provide for the exclusion of members of the public (but not the press) from the court: s. 111(4).

on *Physical Deterioration*[148] that magistrates dealing with children should be specially selected for the purpose (although there was some talk of achieving this by administrative action, at least in the London area).

Removing the child from unsatisfactory parents

The industrial schools legislation[149] had given magistrates powers to deal with refractory Poor Law children, children beyond their parents' control and so on, but the 1908 Act very considerably extended the circumstances in which the juvenile court[150] could take action in respect of neglected, ill-treated and abused children. The Act provided that 'any person'[151] could bring before the court a child:

(a) found begging;
(b) found wandering and not having any home or settled place of abode, or visible means of support, or lacking adequate parental guardianship;
(c) found destitute, with the parents in prison;
(d) under the care of a parent or guardian unfit to have care of the child by reason of 'criminal or drunken habits';
(e) who was the daughter of a man convicted of sexual offences;
(f) frequenting the company of any 'reputed thief, or of any common or reputed prostitute';[152]
(g) living in a place used for prostitution or otherwise in circumstances calculated to 'cause, encourage, or favour the seduction or prostitution of the child'.

The court was to inquire into the matter, and if satisfied that one of the relevant conditions was satisfied and that to do so would be expedient,[153] could commit the child to an industrial school.[154] Alternatively it could commit the child to the care of a 'fit person'.[155] These provisions (of course, modified in a number of respects, some important) remained the basis for compulsory State intervention in a child's upbringing until the coming into force of the Children Act 1989; and the 1908 Act deserves to be remembered as marking the decisive

---

[148] (1904, Cd. 2175) (Chairman, Almeric Fitzroy).

[149] And also the Elementary Education Act 1876.

[150] The juvenile court was the forum because the Act (s. 111(1)) required that applications for orders relating to young people at which the young person's attendance was mandatory be heard by a court constituted as a juvenile court.

[151] The police were given a specific duty to take proceedings in respect of children in their district appearing to come within one of the specified categories: Children Act 1908, s. 58(8).

[152] An exception was made when the prostitute was the child's mother.

[153] Children Act 1908, s. 58(1)). The Act did not in terms require the court to consider the child's welfare: see below.

[154] The child committed to an industrial school could in some circumstances be transferred to the care of a fit person or be boarded out.

[155] It appears that few fit person orders were made—apparently only 13 committals to the care of a relative were made in 36,929 cases dealt with in the juvenile courts in 1914.

rejection of the view[156] that the 'enormous and indisputable' evil of child abuse was of 'so private internal and domestic a character as to be beyond the reach of legislation'. Parliament had given the police and others concerned with children's welfare potentially wide powers to intervene to protect children. But these provisions were inserted into legislation primarily focussed on the young delinquent (so that, for example, the child of a parent unfit to care for him is ordered to be 'detained' in an industrial school 'for such time as the court thinks appropriate for the teaching and training of the child').[157] This must have made it difficult for the young people concerned and their families not to feel that the victim of misfortune was in fact being treated in the same way as a young criminal. For all the good intentions the juvenile court remained primarily a place in which the young were accused of wrongdoing and punished for having broken the criminal law. The fact the same courts had, until the coming into force of the Children Act 1989, to discharge a welfare function for other children may have given rise to considerable tensions. Nevertheless, Acts of Parliament can often have a more substantial effect than could be predicted from a mere analysis of the statutory provisions, and the fact that the Home Office minister[158] could claim that the Children Act 1908 was 'saturated with the rising spirit of humanism' indicated the mood in which it was enacted and the expectations held for the future.

Other provisions intended to protect children

The Act contained four additional groups of provision intended to safeguard and protect children.

(i) Powers of search and removal

The 1908 Act gave the juvenile court powers to make orders for the future of neglected and abused children; but there was often need for immediate action. The 1908 Act codified and amended the child cruelty legislation in an attempt to protect, by direct State intervention, the child victim. Search warrants could authorise searches for children;[159] there were powers of arrest[160] and police officers were empowered to remove to a 'place of safety' children whose parents were suspected of having committed an offence.[161] If anyone with 'the custody charge or care' of someone under 16 was convicted[162] of abuse the court could order that the child be committed to the care of a relative 'or some other fit

---

[156] Expressed in 1881 by Lord Shaftesbury, the great advocate of the necessity of child protection measures: see GK Behlmer, *Child Abuse and Moral Reform in England* (1982) p. 52.

[157] Not extending beyond the child's 16th birthday: Children Act 1908, s. 65.

[158] *Official Report* (HC), 24 March 1908, vol. 186, cols. 1275 and 1284 (Herbert Samuel: see Biographical Notes).

[159] s. 24.   [160] s. 19.   [161] ss. 20 and 24.

[162] Or committed for trial or bound over to keep the peace: s. 21(1).

person'[163] who would then have the 'like control over the young person as if he were the child's parent'.[164]

(ii) More effective protection against baby farming

The Infant Life Preservation Acts of 1872 and 1897 had been intended to protect the child handed over to paid foster-parents or 'adopters'[165] but the regime of local authority[166] registration and inspection left 'many holes through which evil-disposed persons may escape its control'.[167] There had been continuing pressure to make the legislation more effective. But there was also opposition.[168] Why should the law intrude into the homes of respectable working class widows caring devotedly for a foster child? And 'if kindly nurse mothers became the objects of registration and inspection'[169] what would happen to the small-scale fostering on which many children's charities depended as way of carrying out the duty of care they had assumed?

After a great deal of discussion the 1908 Act was drafted to extend the scope of the legislation in three ways. First, the registration requirement was extended so as to apply to anyone who for reward undertook the nursing and maintenance of even a single child.[170] But the local authority could exempt any particular premises from inspection by an infant protection visitor if the premises were 'so conducted that it is unnecessary that they should be visited';[171] and the concerns of the major children's charities were allayed by allowing local authorities to delegate inspection[172] to the organisation responsible for the place-

[163] s. 21. But no such order could be made if the child had a parent or legal guardian who was not involved in the offence: s. 21(2). The court was directed to seek a person of the child's religious persuasion to be the 'fit person': s. 23.

[164] s. 22(1). The powers of the 'fit person' extended (provided the Home Secretary granted his licence) to procuring the child's emigration: s. 21(6): see J Eekelaar, ' "The Chief Glory": the Export of Children from the United Kingdom' in N Lowe and G Douglas (eds.), *Families across Frontiers* (1996). The 'fit person' was obliged to maintain the child, but the court could make a contribution order against the parent: s. 22(2).

[165] The Act was intended to apply only to cases where the transaction was in essence 'commercial'. Hence the Act was not to apply to the child's legal guardian or to a 'relative' (broadly defined, whether the child was legitimate or illegitimate, to extend to grandparents, brothers, sisters, uncles, and aunts, whether by consanguinity or affinity). Nor was it to apply to hospitals, convalescent homes or institutions established for the protection and care of infants, and conducted in good faith for religious or charitable purposes, or boarding schools at which efficient elementary education was provided: s. 11.

[166] Outside London, the Poor Law guardians were the responsible authority.

[167] *Official Report* (4th Series) 10 February 1908, vol. 183, col. 1433 (Herbert Samuel).

[168] See eg the speech by Mr Guinness *Official Report* (4th Series) 1 April 1908, vol. 187, col. 561.

[169] GK Behlmer, *Friends of the Family, The English Home and Its Guardians, 1850–1940* (1998) p. 284.

[170] Children Act 1908, s. 1(1). It was said that the exclusion of one-child 'homes' had meant that the 'majority of child-minders were beyond regulation and inspection': H Hendrick, *Child Welfare, England 1872–1989* (1994) p. 49.

[171] s. 2(5).

[172] It was the duty of every local authority to appoint infant protection visitors, required to visit the infants registered as the Act required: s. 2(2), and magistrates had power to grant search warrants in cases of suspected non-compliance, and place of safety orders in cases in which children were being cared for by a person unfit by reason of 'negligence, ignorance, inebriety, immorality,

ment.[173] Secondly, the legislation was extended to cover the care of children up to the age of seven. Thirdly, the Act did away with earlier provisions which had exempted from the reporting requirement of earlier legislation cases where the consideration for undertaking the care of a child up to two years old had been a lump sum of £20 (£1,000 or so in year 2000 values)[174] or more.

The effect of the extensions of the law made by the Infant Life Protection provisions of the 1908 Act[175] is difficult to evaluate: the Child Adoption Committee in 1925 was sufficiently alarmed by the potential for abuse left open by the legislation that it sought and obtained an extension of its terms of reference in order to make recommendation for further statutory control.[176]

(iii) Central Government's inspection powers increased

The Infant Life Preservation legislation had recognised the need for supervision of child care in the case of the very young being cared for by paid foster-parents; industrial and reformatory schools had been subject to inspection by officials appointed by the Home Secretary;[177] and Poor Law Institutions were subject to Inspection by the Local Government Board. But the inspections may well have been often spasmodic and ineffective;[178] and the 1908 Act extended the powers of the Central Government by a provision apparently giving officials appointed by the Home Secretary the right to visit and inspect any voluntarily funded institution not otherwise subject to Government supervised inspection.[179] This and other provisions of the 'children's charter' encouraged the Home Office to set up a distinct Children's Branch to supervise and control the various functions of the Home Office in relation to children;[180] and this Department had an

---

criminal conduct or other similar cause' and where children were found in insanitary overcrowded or dangerous premises: s. 5. Local authorities had power to fix the maximum number of infants who could be kept in particular premises: s. 4. It has to be remembered that the term 'local authority' meant (outside London) the Poor Law guardians: Children Act 1908, s. 10.

[173] s. 2(2), proviso.

[174] It appears that the original justification for the exemption was the belief that payment of a substantial sum indicated that the child would be well cared for by the recipient. The 1908 Act provided that any lump sum payment made for the child's nursing or maintenance was liable to be forfeited and applied for the benefit of the child in accordance with the court's directions: Children Act 1908, s. 1(7).

[175] Part I of the Act. There were a number of provisions directed against child homicide: a person caring for a child subject to the Act was not allowed to insure the child's life (s. 7) whilst the death of any such child was to be notified to the coroner within 24 hours: s. 6.

[176] See the Committee's *Third and Final Report* (1926, Cmd. 2711) p. 601, n. 29 above.

[177] The provisions were consolidated in Children Act 1908, s. 46, which provided for the appointment of a Chief Inspector of Reformatory and Industrial Schools.

[178] See, in relation to Reformatories and Industrial schools, L Radzinowicz and R Hood, *A History of English Criminal Law* (1986) vol. 5, p. 208.

[179] s. 25. In fact, whether by accident or design, the provision was not all embracing: it applied to 'institutions . . . supported wholly or partly by voluntary contributions' and thus did not extend to institutions which had a permanent endowment or were otherwise financially independent (for example, many Roman Catholic orphanages): see *Report of the Care of Children Committee* (1946, Cmd. 6922), paras. 69, 429.

[180] *Home Office Note to the Machinery of Government Committee on Home Office Functions in relation to Child Welfare*, December 1944, PRO MH102/1379, para. 4.

important and humanising influence on policy towards children until its functions were transferred to the Department of Health in 1971.

(iv) Illegal transactions

Finally, the 1908 Act[181] criminalised certain transactions (taking pawns from children under 14,[182] buying scrap metal from a person under 16)[183] which might expose a child to temptation or damage the child's health.[184]

CONSOLIDATION AND PROGRESS: FROM THE CHILDREN ACT 1908 TO THE
CHILDREN AND YOUNG PERSONS ACT 1933

The Children Act 1908 had clearly identified child cruelty and neglect as problems with which the legal system should seek to deal and, by providing a rudimentary legal framework for juvenile courts, stimulated thought about how best the legal system should deal with children in need. The Poor Law continued to provide a measure of support for children affected by their parents' poverty, but there appears to have been increasing dissatisfaction about its effectiveness and reform became a major concern of progressive opinion. The 1914–1918 War is associated with significant changes in social attitudes,[185] and in the aftermath of war pressure for change increased. (For example, the NSPCC drafted a Bill in 1919 seeking to provide better protection for foster children.) However, major legislation dealing specifically with children had to wait until 1932, when the 90-section-long Children and Young Persons Act (consolidated in the following year) provided a legislative framework which survived for more than half a century. Other legislation (notably the Local Government Act of 1929 and the Poor Law Act of 1930) vitally affected the role of the State and the law in relation to children; and as we have already seen[186] the Adoption of Children Act 1926 introduced into English law for the first time a procedure intended to satisfy the desire for formal legal recognition of the role of men and women who had assumed the responsibilities of parenthood. The period

---

[181] In many cases the 1908 Act merely consolidated previous statutory provisions sometimes with minor amendments: see the following footnote for one example.

[182] Children Act 1908, s. 117 (reproducing a provision of the Pawnbrokers Act 1872, but raising the age of the children affected from 14—outside the Metropolitan Police District—to 16: see Children Act 1908, Sch. 3).

[183] s. 116.

[184] For example, the provisions relating to juvenile smoking (see Children Act 1908, Part III) the prohibition on giving intoxicating liquor to a child under five or allowing a child under 14 to be in a licensed bar (ss. 119, 120) and the requirement to provide supervision for children in crowded places of entertainment: Children Act 1908, s. 121. Perhaps the provisions imposing penalties on travellers who in the result prevented their children from receiving a proper education (s. 118) should be classified under this head, as also the power given to local education authorities to enforce the parent's duty to keep his child and clothing free from vermin: s. 122.

[185] See for example the attitudes to illegitimacy manifested in the moves towards the Legitimacy Act 1926: see Chapter 15, above.

[186] Chapter 17.

between 1908 and 1932 also saw many important changes in public and judicial administration which had a sometimes considerable impact on the legal system's treatment of children and their families.

Lawyers inevitably tend to give most attention to the courts and their role; but in terms of the numbers of children whose upbringing was directly affected by the law it was at this period the Poor Law which had the greatest impact. The statistics are revealing: in the seven years from 1920 to 1926 the courts made on average 332 orders each year committing neglected or abused children to residential schools[187] under the legislation dealing with neglect and cruelty, but over the same period no fewer than 69,000 children removed from their families were in the care of the Poor Law authorities.[188]

The Poor Law, children and the family 1906–1929

In 1905, the Government set up a Royal Commission to enquire into the operation of the Poor Law and to make recommendations. The Commission was not unanimous and produced both Minority and Majority Reports. Neither found much to say in favour of the way in which the Poor Law impacted on the life of the children who came under its provisions; and even the conservative Majority Report[189] recommended the abolition of Boards of Guardians and accepted that children should not be kept in the workhouse. But the eloquent and well documented 716 pages of the Minority Report (to which Mrs Beatrice Webb[190] evidently made an important contribution) went much further.

The Minority Report highlighted shocking defects in the way in which children were treated, for example their being kept in the 'demoralising atmosphere of the General Mixed Workhouse'; and it claimed that poor supervision coupled with the inadequate scale of outdoor relief allowed for pauper children meant that the health and character of probably one hundred thousand child 'wards of the State' were seriously compromised. The Minority claimed that whilst lip service was given to progressive measures such as boarding out and better education, in reality little progress was made because the guardians could not provide adequate supervision. For the same reason, the powers of guardians to

[187] See the Home Office's *Report on the Work of the Children's Department* (1928) p. 74. The reason why there were few committals to the care of a fit person was said to be that suitable persons were often not available and it was no one's business to seek them out: *Home Office Circular to Magistrates*, 9 August 1933; *Report of the Departmental Committee on the Treatment of Young Offenders* (1927, Cmd. 2831) p. 119. W Clarke Hall in *The State and the Child* (1917) p. 19 had put the problem slightly more emotively: the poor—especially in London—'so quickly lose sight of their relatives and make few intimate friends'.

[188] Home Office's *Fourth Report on the Work of the Children's Department* (1928) p. 75. 15% of these were boarded out; 26% were in workhouses and infirmaries; 59% were in Poor Law Schools or other institutions. A large number of children were also being cared for by voluntary organisations but their homes were not usually required to register at this time and accordingly no statistics are available.

[189] *Royal Commission on the Poor Law* (1909, Cd. 4488) p. 259.

[190] See Biographical Notes.

prosecute cruel or neglectful parents were 'hardly ever' put into force. As a result many thousands of children were, for lack of the necessities of life, growing up stunted, debilitated and diseased.

The Minority believed the underlying problem was institutional: the Poor Law authorities' function was merely to 'relieve' those who voluntarily came forward and proved themselves. There was a simple, if radical, remedy. Social problems could only be cured by a proactive approach. There should be one authority in each district responsible for the whole of the provision made by the State for children of school age; and that authority should be the Local Education Authority under the supervision of the Central Government's Board of Education. No longer should 'the poor' be treated differently from others. The Poor Law should be broken up, and the functions of the Poor Law authorities transferred to specialist agencies of the local authorities.

In many ways the Minority Report presaged the development of the concept of the Welfare State. The Minority was insistent that bureaucracy should be efficient: there were simply too many bodies involved in providing for needy children. But the Minority[191] (in passages which became very influential) wanted the State to establish social machinery which would 'bring automatically to light . . . whatever child destitution exists' and take the action necessary to remedy the problem. And this required 'the steady and continuous guidance of a friend, able to suggest in what directions effective help can be obtained where help is really needed'. Again, this pointed to the Education Authorities as the responsible agent of public help.

The Royal Commission's report engendered heated controversy. Mrs Beatrice Webb[192] was a formidable publicist; a National Committee for the Break-up of the Poor Law was formed; and the Labour Party pressed strongly for implementation of the Minority Report. But there was also opposition to reform. In particular, many Board members (justifiably priding themselves on their commitment to providing the individual case work which the Minority Report had favoured)[193] did not take the prospect of extinction without protest.[194] And, inevitably, there were many controversial matters of financial policy and ideology to be resolved. The Liberal Government was not prepared to act precipitately; and, although Fabian Socialists drafted a 50-page Prevention of Destitution Bill (prompting an important and notably well informed Parliamentary Debate in 1910)[195] there seemed no prospect of legislation (and in fact there was no comprehensive legislation until 1929).[196]

[191] *Separate Report of the Royal Commission on the Poor Laws* (1909, Cd. 4488) pp. 163–169.
[192] See above.
[193] For an account of the work of women guardians see P Hollis, *Ladies Elect, Women in English Local Government 1865–1914* (1987).
[194] In fact, both Majority and Minority Reports agreed that Boards of Guardians should go.
[195] *Official Report* (HC) 8 April 1910, vol. 16, col. 780.
[196] For the reasons for delay see below.

The absence of primary legislation did not mean there was no progress. The Local Government Board had wide powers to legislate by order[197] and began to exercise them to bring about change, sometimes important. For example in 1910 the Board declared that 'in the case of children . . . pauperism is always due to misfortune'[198] and expressly renounced the application to children of the philosophy of 'less eligibility' on which the 1834 Act had been based. Keeping children in the workhouse could no longer be recognised as a legitimate way of dealing with the young; and children over the age of three[199] were no longer to be accommodated in that way. The Guardians were to take effective steps (notably by arranging systematic inspection by women inspectors) to safeguard the welfare of boarded out children; and Boards of Guardians were to be encouraged to assume parental authority[200] over the children of unfit parents.

Even so, the delay in bringing in primary legislation to deal with the defects in the Poor Law seems at first difficult to understand. The explanation is that what might have been seen as comparatively simple issues became part of a much more complex debate about the machinery appropriate for administering the public health, unemployment insurance, widows' and old age pensions,[201] schooling and other forms of welfare provision initiated[202] by the 1906 Liberal Government; and the social upheaval associated with the 1914–1918 war inevitably directed attention to the further development of social service provision.

Central Government control (and the formation of administrative and legislative policy) over these services was poorly co-ordinated. Particular difficulty was caused by the fact that the Local Government Board had many responsibilities in these areas, as well as responsibility for the central administration of the Poor Law; and there seems some force in the view[203] that its 'dominant tradition [was] that of the old Poor Law Board—a tradition of cramping the local authorities and preventing things from being done.' Certainly the Local Government Board set its face against any radical reform of the Poor Law.[204] But in spite of this opposition, it became clear that something had to be done'. Administrative confusion grew as popular feeling against the Poor Law led Parliament to

---

[197] The Poor Law Act 1834, had given the Minister power to 'make such rules . . . as he may think fit . . . for the management of the poor'.

[198] LGB Circular, *Children under the Poor Law*, 16 June 1910; LGB Fortieth Annual Report, 1911, p. xix.

[199] *Ibid*. By Order in 1913 the Board directed the removal of such children from the workhouse. Orders had set out detailed provisions for the improvement of the workhouse nurseries in which children under three were to be accommodated.

[200] Under the 'poor law adoption' provisions of the Poor Law Acts 1898 and 1898.

[201] Old Age Pensions Act 1908; National Insurance Act 1911.

[202] On this, see H Hendrick, *Child Welfare, England 1872–1989* (1994) Chapter 3.

[203] RCK Ensor, *England 1870–1914* (1936) p. 385.

[204] Sir Robert Ensor in his *England 1870–1914* (1936) p. 517 attributes the attitude of the Board in part to failings on the part of John Burns, the Board's President from 1905 until 1914: 'if any other member of the Liberal Government had held Burns's position, great and needed reforms would have become law. Burns single-handed fended them off . . .'.

entrust administration of new services to other local agencies.[205] In 1918 a powerful committee,[206] appointed to consider the better co-ordination of public assistance, emphasised the pressing need for reform. But what happened was simply that the Ministry of Health Act 1919 created a Ministry to take over the powers and duties relating to the Poor Law and otherwise of the Local Government Board and other health related functions (including housing).[207] The Act did give an indication that the Ministry of Health might be stripped of poor relief and other functions not relating to the health of the people, but it was left to Neville Chamberlain's Local Government Act of 1929 to abolish Boards of Guardians and to transfer the administration of the Poor Law to local authorities.[208]

The Chamberlain legislation was intended to make local authorities co-ordinate their various welfare facilities; and councils were encouraged[209] to provide assistance under legislation other than the Poor Law (for example the Education Act 1921[210] or the Maternity and Child Welfare Act 1918)[211] wher-

---

[205] 'There are, at this moment, a large number of different bodies giving various forms of public assistance. . . . Many of these bodies deal on different lines, and for different reasons, with members of the same family. There are, for instance, seven different public authorities giving money in the home. . . . These public bodies . . . have . . . no common system of registration of cases; so that even the names of persons receiving assistance from one or more of the bodies may be unknown to some other body which may be considering their case . . .': Ministry of Reconstruction, Local Government Committee, *Report on Transfer of Functions of Poor Law Authorities* (1918, Cd. 8917) para. 5.

[206] The Ministry of Reconstruction, Local Government Committee, *Report on Transfer of Functions of Poor Law Authorities* (1918, Cd. 8917) chaired by the Liberal statesman, Sir Donald Maclean, and with a significant representation of those who were known to favour poor law reform (not least Beatrice Webb) was said to 'represent a reasoned attempt to secure reforms in harmony with those indicated by the [Royal Commission on the Poor Law] without reviving the controversies which then centred around' the Commission's Minority and Majority Reports: *Prefatory Note* by the Minister of Reconstruction, Christopher Addison.

[207] The Act (s. 2) imposed a duty on the Minister to 'take all such steps as may be desirable to secure the preparation, effective carrying out and co-ordination of measures conducive to the health of the people, including measures for the prevention and cure of diseases, the avoidance of fraud in connection with alleged remedies . . ., the treatment of physical and mental defects, the treatment and care of the blind, the initiation and direction of research, the collection, preparation, publication and dissemination of information and statistics relating thereto, and the training of persons for health services'.

[208] Chamberlain, Minister of Health in the Conservative administration of 1924 to 1929, was an enthusiast for reform of local government: see Biographical Notes. As a preliminary to the major reforms made by the 1929 Act the Poor Law legislation was consolidated by the Poor Law Act 1927. In an attempt to make the Poor Law more accessible to those who had to administer it, the incoming 1929–1931 Labour Government decided to consolidate the Poor Law provisions once again, and they are to be found in the Poor Law Act 1930.

[209] s. 5.

[210] This Act had consolidated the provisions relating to education in a major Act of 173 sections and 7 schedules: the powers which local authorities had under the Act included the provision of school meals and school medical services: see generally H Hendrick, *Child Welfare, England 1872–1989* (1994) Chapters 3 and 4.

[211] This Act gave local authorities power to make arrangements for the health care of children under five (although the draftsman was careful to provide that this provision should not extend to general domiciliary health care).

ever this was possible. But there was force in the criticism[212] that the 1929 Chamberlain Act still retained the underlying principles of the Poor Law, not least in the provision[213] that local authorities had a duty 'to set to work' those who lacked the means to maintain themselves, and to 'put out as apprentices all children whose parents are not . . . able to keep and maintain' them.

It may be that some local authorities were able to rationalise and humanise the management of the Poor Law; but this was not how it appeared to the large numbers of unemployed whose families were driven to depend on the system in the 1930s. The Poor Law had to go; and it was the recognition of this fact which led (albeit indirectly) to the enactment of the Children Act 1948 and another attempt to bring about fundamental change in Society's provision for children in need.[214]

The juvenile court 1908–1933

The Poor Law may have been statistically the more significant of the State's mechanisms for dealing with problem children, but enthusiasts and propagandists[215] were attracted by the message that the creation of juvenile courts had been a truly 'revolutionary' step.[216] They had to admit that all the Act actually provided was that cases involving children should be dealt with separately from others; but it was claimed that much greater progress could be based on this secure foundation. What was presented as a bold experiment became (it seems) almost compulsory viewing for those—both from this country and overseas— interested in social problems, to the extent that (in defiance of the policy clearly underlying the legislation that children cases needed privacy)[217] the more accessible juvenile courts were thronged by crowds of 'observers'.[218]

---

[212] Made forcefully, for example by the Labour spokesman Sir Henry Slesser: see *Official Report* (HC) 26 November 1928, vol. 223, col. 178, and Biographical Notes.

[213] Poor Law Act 1930, s. 15.　　　　　[214] See below, Chapter 19.

[215] Not least the Metropolitan Police Magistrate William Clarke Hall. It is possible that the Chief Magistrate, Sir Chartres Biron, may have (albeit in characteristically colourful language) made a fair assessment of the situation. He believed that juvenile courts had 'thoroughly justified their existence' but also recorded his view that they had become the 'happy hunting ground of all the cranks, male and female. Psycho-analysts, psychiatrists, Christian scientists, all got to work, and it was not too easy to keep them in order'. *Without Prejudice* (1936) p. 259.

[216] *Official Report* (HC) 12 February 1932, vol. 262, col. 1171. For an excellent account of the controversy and its context, see GK Behlmer, *Friends of the Family, The English Home and Its Guardians, 1850–1940* (1998) Chapter 5.

[217] Children Act 1908, s. 111(4) provided that no person other than the members and officers of the court and the parties to the case, their solicitors and counsel, other persons directly concerned in the case, and journalists, should be allowed to attend hearings save with the leave of the court. Some magistrates encouraged the attendance of observers.

[218] The *Report of the Departmental Committee on the Treatment of Young Offenders* (1927, Cmd. 2831) found cases of crowds of 50 observing proceedings.

A specialist magistracy?

The Sex Disqualification (Removal) Act 1919 made it possible for women to be appointed as Justices of the Peace; and the newly appointed women JPs could thus bring their 'sympathy, experience and maternal instincts' to bear on cases (for which it was thought women were 'specially suited')[219] involving the young. But in London the summary courts were manned by stipendiary Metropolitan Police Magistrates, and if JPs—male or female—were to sit special legislation would be needed. The Government could have done nothing, leaving it to the Metropolitan magistrates to run the courts as they had since 1908, or they could have introduced a Bill simply providing that JPs could sit in London juvenile courts. But it was decided to go further: the proposal was that juvenile courts in the Metropolis should consist of three magistrates of whom two (one a woman) were to be JPs drawn from a special panel nominated by the Home Secretary. Moreover, in making nominations to the panel from which the Presiding magistrates would be drawn, the Secretary of State was required to 'have regard to [the magistrate's] previous experience and special qualifications for dealing with cases of juvenile offenders'.[220]

These proposals were disliked by the majority of the stipendiary Metropolitan Police Magistrates[221] (who apparently thought that the role of women in the juvenile court should be confined to acting as assessors); and there was a lot of publicity and debate. The Government was obliged to make a number of concessions, but the principle that juvenile justice was a matter for specialists survived and was embodied in the Act. Not surprisingly, people asked why this principle of a specialist bench should be confined to London; and it appears that special rotas for selecting magistrates to sit in juvenile cases were 'not infrequently' found, without statutory authority, outside London.[222] The publicity resulting from the Metropolitan magistrates' opposition to any change thus led to an outcome as unwelcome to men of a conservative outlook as it was welcome to the more radical reformers.

[219] The quotations are from the speech of Lord Chancellor Birkenhead on the Second Reading of the Juvenile Courts (Metropolis) Bill, *Official Report*, 15 June 1920, vol. 40, col. 591.

[220] This formulation betrays the fact that the draftsman did not have the magistrates' jurisdiction over deprived children in the forefront of his mind.

[221] Although the Chief Magistrate, Sir Chartres Biron, apparently accepted the Government's proposals, the Parliamentary Debates make it clear that he was in a minority: see *Official Report*, 15 June 1920, vol. 40, col. 608. It also seems that there was some opposition amongst London Probation Officers to the notion of women being on the bench, apparently because the Probation Officers (or at least some women amongst them) preferred the direct relationship with a single Metropolitan Police Magistrate which they had previously enjoyed.

[222] *Report of the Departmental Committee on the Treatment of Young Offenders* (1927, Cmd. 2831) p. 11.

The (Molony) Committee on the Treatment of Young Offenders

In 1925 the Home Secretary—against the background of widespread discussion of, and interest in, the role of the courts in relation to juveniles and the fact that juvenile crime seemed to be on the decrease, so that 'progressive' ideas were more acceptable than at some other periods in history—appointed a Committee[223] to inquire into the 'treatment of young offenders and young people who, owing to bad associations or surroundings, require protection and training'. These terms of reference are significant as indicating the extent to which delinquency and neglect were by that time associated in the official mind: the delinquent child needed treatment, whilst the neglected child might become delinquent if appropriate protective measures were not taken. As the Molony Committee's Report put it:[224]

'Our enquiry . . . is not concerned only with the young offender. There is also the problem of the neglected boy or girl who has not committed offences but who, owing to want of parental control, bad associations or other reasons, needs protection and training. The two problems are closely connected . . ., because neglect and delinquency often go hand in hand and experience shows that the young offender is only too often recruited from the ranks of those whose home life has been unsatisfactory. The legislature draws a distinction between the two classes, but in many cases the tendency to commit offences is only an outcome of the conditions of neglect, and there is little room for discrimination either in the character of the young person concerned or in the appropriate method of treatment. There are also young people who are the victims of cruelty or other offences committed by adults and whose natural guardianship having proved insufficient or unworthy of trust must be replaced.'

The Committee was enthusiastic[225] about the role of the juvenile court:

The court 'performs very important functions which are not generally realised by the public and not always appreciated at their full value by the Magistrates themselves. Before it appear boys and girls . . . who are often wayward or mischievous and in some cases serious offenders; who are sometimes dull of mind or undeveloped, but more often full of vitality and intelligence, though misdirected; who are all by virtue of their youthfulness hopeful subjects for care and training. The decision of the Magistrates with regard to the immediate future of these boys and girls must to a large extent influence their whole lives. . . . The importance of [the court's] functions lies not only in safeguarding the right of the less fortunate child to such protection and training as it has failed to receive or in assisting those parents who, from poverty or other circumstances, have not succeeded in keeping their children from bad influences or associations; there is also the duty of restraining those who commit offences from recruiting the ranks of hardened criminals at a later stage and becoming a serious menace and public burden . . .'.

---

[223] *The Departmental Committee on the Treatment of Young Offenders* (1927, Cmd. 2831), chaired by Sir Thomas Molony (see Biographical Notes). Other members of the Committee (hereafter referred to as 'the Molony Committee') included RF Graham-Campbell and the Home Office Official SW Harris (who, internal evidence suggests, played a considerable part in drafting the Committee's Report).

[224] At p. 6.   [225] *Molony Report*, pp. 15–16.

In a revealing aside, the Committee declared the 'main function' of the juvenile courts to be to 'consider the welfare of the young persons who come before it'[226] and the Committee had no doubt about the benefits to be derived from 'treatment' whether of the delinquent or the neglected child. An appropriate institution[227] 'constructed on the right principles can absorb and transmute bad characters with wonderful success', it declared.[228] In 1908 the legislation establishing the juvenile court had been largely experimental, but the court had 'long passed the experimental stage'. In any future legislation greater prominence should be given to the juvenile court, its constitution should be placed on a better footing and its functions enlarged.[229]

But how far were these changes to go? Some reformers in England (represented by the Metropolitan Police Magistrate William Clarke Hall) wanted not only simplification of court procedures, the creation of a special children's branch of the police force (composed largely of women) and the provision of expert medical advice, but also advocated that the court should have the power to make all delinquent, neglected or ill-treated children wards of court under the supervision of a probation officer.[230] The *Molony Report* noted that in a number of American States the jurisdiction exercised over children was said to be 'chancery or equity in nature', with emphasis laid not on any act done by the child 'but on the social facts and circumstances that are really the inducing causes of the child's appearance in court'. Even in cases of delinquency the purpose of the proceedings was 'not punishment but correction of conditions, care and protection of the child and prevention of a recurrence through the constructive work of the court'. In this view, there was fundamentally no distinction between the results desired with reference to children before the court because of a delinquent act and those who were simply neglected, dependent or destitute.[231]

The Molony Committee did not altogether accept the validity of this approach, and believed there would be dangers in adopting a principle which might lead to ignoring the offence on which the action of a juvenile court dealing with a delinquent could alone properly be based.[232] But the Committee recorded its view that the main defect in the English system was that it did not 'carry the principle of guardianship far enough'.[233] The 1908 Act 'marked a considerable advance' on the procedures previously available for dealing with the neglected or abused child but experience demonstrated that the law was defective in many respects and that it failed to afford 'anything like a complete solution of the problem'.[234]

---

[226] *Molony Report,* p. 34.   [227] A 'Home Office School'.
[228] *Molony Report,* p. 73.   [229] *Ibid.,* p. 16.
[230] W Clarke Hall, *Children's Courts* (1926) pp. 266–277 and *passim*. Clarke Hall also wanted the juvenile court to take over affiliation and husband and wife separation cases in which the welfare of children was involved.
[231] *Molony Report,* pp. 15–16 (drawing substantially on B Flexner and R Baldwin, *Juvenile Courts and Probation* (1915)).
[232] *Molony Report,* pp. 18–19.   [233] *Ibid.,* p. 21.   [234] *Ibid.,* p. 118.

The Committee identified three main gaps in the law. First, the legislation did not provide for many cases in which a child's physical or moral welfare was at risk. Secondly, the available 'methods of treatment' were unsatisfactory: too often the only course open to the court was to commit the child to the care of a relative or fit person, 'but such persons may not be readily available and it is no one's business to find them. A busy court cannot be expected to do so'.[235] Thirdly—although the NSPCC had 'performed a remarkable public service in discovering cases of cruelty and neglect, and in bringing such cases before the courts when necessary'—there was no authority whose duty it was to see that all suitable cases were considered and properly dealt with.[236]

To remedy these defects, the Molony Committee recommended:

(1) The grounds for making orders should be extended to cover cases in which children and young persons under 17 either had no parents or guardians or had parents or guardians who were unfit to care for them or who were not exercising proper guardianship. But the court would have to be satisfied that the children or young persons concerned were falling into bad associations, were exposed to moral danger, or were beyond control.[237]

(2) The local education authority should be specially charged with the duty of enquiring into cases coming into these categories and of bringing appropriate cases before the court.[238]

(3) The court should have wide powers to deal with neglected young people.[239] These would extend not only to power to commit the child to the care of a relative or fit person[240] but also to the guardianship of the local education authority,[241] to place the child under the supervision of a probation officer,[242] or commit him to an approved[243] school.

---

[235] *Ibid.*, p. 119. [236] *Ibid.*

[237] The court would also be empowered to act if specified offences had been committed against the child or other children living in the same household.

[238] *Molony Report*, p. 120. The Committee recommended that temporary accommodation be provided pursuant to a magistrate's warrant in a 'place of safety' (preferably not in a police station).

[239] The *Molony Report* was able to point to the similar philosophy adopted by the *Departmental Committee on Sexual Offences against Young Persons* (1925, Cmd. 2561).

[240] Although very few fit person orders were made by the courts, they were sometimes able to arrange foster-care for a child by committing him to an industrial school which would in theory be responsible for arranging his being boarded out. In practice the child would usually go directly to the foster family. The London County Council had 'adopted the method with considerable success and usually have about 300 children boarded out': *Molony Report*, p. 63.

[241] The Committee had noted the apparently successful use of 'poor law adoptions' and thought that a similar procedure should be available for young people who, although in need of protection, had not actually come within the Poor Law. It endorsed the view that local authorities should take children into their care, and be responsible for their boarding out supervision: see *Molony Report*, p. 64.

[242] 'Supervision in the home seems particularly appropriate in some . . . cases, as it is often found that a bad parent mends his ways when his responsibility is brought home to him': *Molony Report*, p. 120.

[243] This was the term proposed for all 'Home Office Schools' (ie those previously described as certified reformatory or industrial schools).

These recommendations are significant not least as foreshadowing the policy that ensuring proper care and treatment for neglected, abused and delinquent children was a task best entrusted to the local authority.

The Children's Charter re-defined: the Children and Young Persons Act 1932

The Molony Committee's report reinforced the pressure for an expansion in the role of the juvenile court; whilst the NSPCC was constantly active in seeking what it believed to be improvements in the child protection legislation.[244] In 1925 the *Report of the Committee on Sexual Offences against Young Persons*[245] had reported on the prevalence of sexual offences against young persons; and has the distinction of being the first official body to identify the problem of child sexual abuse.[246] After years of delay, the administration of the Poor Law had been reformed:[247] Boards of Guardians were abolished, the Ministry of Health was given overall direction and control of the administration of poor relief—which, as we have seen, included in effect the care of orphans and other children in need—whilst local authorities, acting through Public Assistance Committees, were responsible for day to day administration. The enactment of the Adoption of Children Act in 1926 had revealed gaps in the legislation intended to protect children living away from their families, but recommendations in this respect of the Tomlin Report remained unimplemented.

The case for further primary legislation was strong; and officials in the Home Office Children's Department prepared a massively detailed section by section list of the amendments regarded as desirable (and politically acceptable).[248] In 1927 the Home Office was given the necessary permission to instruct Parliamentary Counsel to settle the terms of a Bill which would consolidate and reform the law; but serious political and economic problems prevented a speedy introduction and in fact the Bill was not even shown to the Home Secretary[249]

[244] As early as 1919 the NSPCC had drafted its own Bill and submitted it to the Home Office. The Howard League was also active, as were a number of other organisations interested in general social issues—for example, the National Union of Societies for Equal Citizenship sent a deputation to see Herbert Samuel (now Home Secretary in the National Government) in January 1932, and wished to discuss with him not only sexual offences against children, but also divorce, inheritance, and the appointment of women police and a woman Prison Commissioner: see PRO HO45/14715.

[245] 1925, Cmd. 2561.

[246] The Committee found that there were many more sexual offences against the young than are reported to the police, and that only in a small proportion of those cases did any legal proceedings follow.

[247] And consolidated in the Poor Law Act 1930: see above.

[248] Herbert Samuel, Home Secretary in the National Government, opposed extension of the restrictions against juvenile employment (which might have been thought to harass the poor), and decided that the Bill should 'not touch' the law relating to supplying alcoholic drink to the young. He stood firm against the proposal made by the Molony Committee to extend the courts' powers to order corporal punishment of juvenile offenders guilty of any offence (and not merely an indictable offence): see notes of Ministerial Conference, 7 December 1931, PRO HO 45/14716, but as might be expected this subject was controversial, particularly during the Bill's passage through the House of Lords. The end result was that the law remained unchanged.

[249] JR Clynes, Home Secretary in Ramsay MacDonald's 1929–1931 Labour administration.

until January 1931.[250] But when the National Government decided to legislate in 1932[251] there was (with the predictable exception of the corporal punishment issue) little real opposition. The Bill received Royal Assent in July 1932; and the legislation was then consolidated in the Children and Young Persons Act 1933. That Act became, for many years,[252] the primary source of the law governing what the 1932 Act's long title described as the 'protection and welfare of the young'.

The ideology of the Children and Young Persons Act 1932

In many ways, the focus of the 1932 Act is on the treatment of young offenders; but in retrospect it can be seen as marking the legislative high water-mark of the view that there is no real distinction between 'treating' the young offender and providing for the young person in need. The Act was based on the belief[253] that the habitual criminal was often 'created by a mistake in early treatment rather than inherent vice' and that young offenders and their individual circumstances needed to be studied to devise the treatment[254] which would most effectively prevent their 'following the path of anti-social conduct'.[255] Bad surroundings led to delinquency; and 'in many cases the tendency to commit offences' was no more than an outcome of the conditions of neglect.[256] It followed that there was 'little room for discrimination either in the character of the young person concerned or in the appropriate method of treatment' between the child offender and young victims of cruelty or neglect; and for this reason the Act 'closely assimilated' the methods available to a court for dealing with a child or young person charged with an offence on the one hand and a child brought before a court as needing care or protection.[257]

---

[250] Clynes tried to get Treasury approval to the introduction of the Bill in February 1931, arguing that it would not only place the whole system of dealing with neglected and delinquent children on a much sounder footing, but that it would 'serve to prevent a considerable number of young people from becoming a burden to the State in later years'. However, these arguments were not sufficient to secure a place for the Bill in the legislative programme, and in August 1931 a serious economic crisis led to the collapse of the Labour Government. A so-called National Government (led by MacDonald with Conservative, some Liberal, and one or two Labour members) took office. In the October 1931 General Election only 52 Labour MPs were returned, and Labour MPs who had anything to do with MacDonald and others who were thought to have betrayed their party were ostracised. However, the fact that the National Government had such a massive majority—and that its leaders were anxious to show a commitment to progressive measures—seems to have contributed to the decision speedily to introduce the Children and Young Persons Bill in February 1932.

[251] The Home Secretary at the time was Herbert Samuel who had been primarily responsible for the 1908 Act: see Biographical Notes. On this occasion Samuel delegated the conduct of the Bill to his Under-Secretary, Oliver Stanley (1896–1950).

[252] Some fragments of the Act (albeit often significantly amended) remained on the statute book at the millennium.

[253] *Official Report* (HC) 12 February 1932, vol. 261, col. 1168 (Oliver Stanley, moving the Second Reading of the Bill).

[254] Symbolically, the Act provided (s. 22) that the words 'conviction' and 'sentence' were not to be used in relation to children and young persons dealt with by magistrates.

[255] *Home Office Circular* 9 August 1933, p. 2. [256] *Ibid.* [257] *Ibid.*

In pursuance of this philosophy, Part I of the Act made many important changes to the structure and powers of the juvenile courts[258] and the significance of this creation of a separate system of juvenile justice, with a strong emphasis on 'treatment', was deliberately highlighted by placing the relevant clauses at the very beginning of the Act.[259] The 'welfarist' policy was further highlighted by including a provision[260] directing every court dealing with a child or young person[261] (whether as an offender or as someone who needed care and protection or otherwise) to

'have regard to the welfare of the child or young person and . . . in a proper case take steps for removing him from undesirable surroundings, and for securing that proper provision is made for his education and training'.

It is true that this provision gives no indication of the *weight* to be attached to the delinquent child's welfare (as distinct from, for example, considerations of deterrence and retribution) yet the Home Office circular[262] explaining the Act makes it quite clear that it was intended to give effect to the policy that, even in cases in which 'stern measures' were necessary, the child's reclamation should remain the objective.

---

[258] Magistrates were to be chosen from a special panel 'specially qualified for dealing with juvenile cases' (Children and Young Persons Act 1932, s. 2(2)), and the Explanatory *Home Office Circular* expressed the Home Secretary's hope that justices would 'do their best to give effect to the spirit of this requirement by placing on the panel those men and women who by their knowledge and sympathetic understanding of young people or by their experience of dealing with them in various forms of social work . . . appear to be most suited for this important work of the juvenile court'. It was also the intention to involve younger magistrates who were 'normally in closer touch with young people and therefore better able to understand their point of view and sympathise with their interests'. Other significant changes were that (a) power was given to the Lord Chancellor to make rules intended to simplify the courts' procedure, making it 'more intelligible and less frightening' to the child; (b) a juvenile court was to sit in a different building or room from other courts (or at least on different days); (c) the right of attending court hearings was restricted (s. 6(2)) whilst the press—who were to be allowed to attend hearings—were in principle debarred from publishing identifying material (s. 81); (d) offenders could be committed to the care of a 'fit person' (an expression including a local authority) until they were 18.

[259] In contrast, the 1908 Act had placed them in s. 111, almost at the end: see the Memorandum on the 1931 draft on PRO HO45/14715, which makes the point that the re-ordering would reflect the fact that the juvenile court was to be the 'starting point of the treatment of neglected and delinquent young people'.

[260] Children and Young Persons Act 1932, s. 21.

[261] A 'child' was a person under 14 whilst a 'young person' was anyone under the age of 17 (and the extension of the definition was somewhat controversial): Children and Young Persons Act 1932, s. 70(1). For most purposes of the present text the distinction between child and young person is not material.

[262] In 'some cases offences by young people old enough to appreciate the nature of their actions may call for stern measures' but even so 'reclamation' should remain the objective, and the court's powers should be 'applied for the future welfare of the young people with appreciation of their temptations and difficulties': 1933 Home Office Circular. That the legislation embodied this policy, and that the Home Secretary in exercising discretions in respect of juvenile offenders was bound by the same considerations, was apparently accepted by the Home Secretary's counsel in *R v. Secretary of State for the Home Department ex parte Thompson and Venables* [1998] AC 407, 499; and their Lordships accepted that the statutory provision remained 'one of the basic principles applicable to dealing with child offenders': *per* Lord Browne-Wilkinson, at p. 496.

Extended powers where child in need of care and protection

The role of the juvenile courts in relation to children 'in need of care and protection'[263] was greatly extended. As the *Molony Report* had noted, there were considerable gaps in the powers of the court to take effective action in respect of such children; and Home Office experience confirmed that the 1908 provisions[264] were too restricted[265]—indeed it was said that in some cases necessary intervention was only brought about by the courts' readiness 'greatly to strain' the law.[266] The 1932 Act was intended to substitute 'general and wide' provision for the narrowly defined categories of the 1908 Act; but respect was still to be accorded to the principle of family autonomy.

Grounds for protective intervention

The grounds upon which the court could make an order were carefully defined,[267] as follows.[268]

(a) Lack of proper parenting

The first ground was that the child[269] either had no parent guardian, or that the parent or guardian was 'unfit to exercise proper care and guardianship'; and that the child was 'falling into bad associations or [was] exposed to moral danger or [was] beyond control'.[270]

(b) Victim of criminal abuse

The second ground was that the child (or another child in the same household) was the victim of certain specified offences;[271] or that a person convicted of any of those offences was a member of the same household; or that a girl was living in the same household as the victim of incest perpetrated by a member of the household. In all these cases it was also necessary for the court to find the child required care and protection.[272]

---

[263] This expression—the invention of the draftsman of the 1932 Act—remained an essential and central part of the definition of young people liable to State intervention in their upbringing until the Children Act 1989 substituted a somewhat more sophisticated 'threshold requirement'. According to Claud Mullins (see Biographical Notes) as cited in GK Behlmer, *Friends of the Family, The English Home and Its Guardians, 1850–1940* (1998) p. 265, the legislative formulae were 'a step toward the psycho-analytical conception of the needs of both individuals and the community'.

[264] ie Children Act 1908, s. 58.   [265] PRO HO45/14715.

[266] *Official Report* (HC) 12 February 1932, vol. 261, col. 1178.

[267] Contrast the view that the Act introduced 'sweeping terms of reference', founded on the view that the 'care and protection' formula 'now covered everyone under age 17 who had no parent or guardian, had an "unfit" parent or guardian, or had grown "out of control", not to mention all those children found wandering, begging or loitering': GK Behlmer, *Friends of the Family, The English Home and Its Guardians, 1850–1940* (1998) pp. 265–6.

[268] Children and Young Persons Act 1932, s. 9.   [269] Or young person.

[270] Children and Young Persons Act 1932, s. 9(1)(i). In this case (alone) it was necessary to show as a separate matter that the child required care or protection.

[271] Ie those referred to in Children Act 1908, Part II or Sch. 1.

[272] Children and Young Persons Act 1932, s. 9(1)(ii).

(c) Travellers' and vagrants' children

The fate of the children of vagrants had long been a preoccupation of the Poor Law and education authorities; and the Act allowed intervention on the ground[273] that the child was being prevented from receiving efficient elementary education by a person who habitually wandered from place to place.

(d) Children beyond parental control

The Act retained the provision[274] allowing a parent to bring a child he was unable to control before the court.[275]

A threat to the child's rights? The courts' powers

Ministers were careful to emphasise that the extension of the provisions allowing courts 'to entertain and consider cases in which no offence had been committed, but in which the circumstances made it desirable that the child should receive protection' did not entail any erosion of respect for the integrity of the family. There was to be[276] no attempt to

substitute 'the State for the parents, or [to break] up family life, because the fundamental basis in a matter of this kind is that parental control should be adequate, and that [State intervention is] legitimate when the proper parents or guardians are either unwilling or unable to exercise that parental control which we . . . recognise to be the best guide for the upbringing of children . . .'.

Hence, the answer to the Tory peer[277] who unsuccessfully sought to deny the Bill a Second Reading on the ground that allowing the courts to commit children innocent of crime to a reformatory (albeit now re-branded as an 'approved school')[278] would constitute a gross injustice[279] was, in part, that the Home Office would classify these establishments and thereby ensure that children went only to an institution appropriate to their needs. In any event committal to an approved school was only one of the powers the court could exercise:[280] the

---

[273] Children and Young Persons Act 1932, s. 9(1)(iii).   [274] Children Act 1908, s. 58(4).

[275] Children and Young Persons Act 1932, s. 10.

[276] *Official Report* (HC) 12 February 1932, vol. 261, cols. 1178–9.

[277] Viscount Bertie of Thame. The approach of some modern critics, approaching the legislation from a different perspective, has led to a similar conclusion. Note, for example, the view that the outcome was an 'all-permeating program of family regulation dressed as friendship': GK Behlmer, *Friends of the Family, The English Home and Its Guardians, 1850–1940* (1998) p. 266.

[278] The 1932 Act gave effect to the Molony recommendation whereby the reformatory and industrial schools 'certified by the Home Office were to be known as 'Approved Schools'.

[279] Lord Bertie was also unsuccessful in seeking to prevent the court from sending a child in need of care and protection to an approved school unless his character was such that he required exceptional control: *Official Report* (HL) 9 June 1932, vol. 84, col. 711.

[280] And in any event the court was required to have regard to the child's welfare: Children and Young Persons Act 1932, s. 21.

court could[281] alternatively commit the child to the care of a fit person (including a local authority) or order his parent or guardian to enter into a recognisance to exercise proper care and guardianship[282] (thus, in theory at least, providing some kind of financial incentive—or sanction—to improve their parenting). Even more to the point, perhaps, was the provision that the court could[283] place the child under the supervision of a probation officer[284] for up to three years;[285] and the probation officer was put under an obligation to 'visit, advise and befriend'[286] the child and when necessary try to find suitable employment for him.[287] Even so, the acceptance of the notion that a child guilty of no offence could in theory at least be sent to an approved school and thus be subjected to one of the most serious sanctions applied to the delinquent does demonstrate the extent to which the denial of any real distinction between the delinquent and the victim of misfortune had become part of the conventional wisdom.[288]

Local authorities primarily responsible: but to collaborate with other agencies

The 1932 Act marked a further step on the road to making local authorities responsible for child welfare. The primary responsibility for bringing children in need of care and protection before the court[289] was placed on local authorities (rather than on the police, as under the 1908 Act);[290] and the 1932 Act[291] confined the right to initiate proceedings[292] to local authorities, the police and

[281] Having regard to the child's welfare: Children and Young Persons Act 1932, s. 21, see above, p. 664.
[282] Children and Young Persons Act 1932, s. 9(1)(c).
[283] Whether or not it made any of these other orders.   [284] Or other person.
[285] Children and Young Persons Act 1932, s. 9(2).
[286] Children and Young Persons Act 1932, s. 13(1); but once again, sanctions were available if the child failed to collaborate: the supervisor was empowered to bring him before the court, which could send him to an approved school (or commit him to the care of a 'fit person') if the court considered that this would be desirable in the child's interests: Children and Young Persons Act 1932, s. 13(1).
[287] As the Home Office was to put it in 1944, the Probation Service had developed far beyond the original conception of the Probation of Offenders Act 1907; and by the beginning of World War II the policy had become that every court should have a trained social worker attached to it. These probation officers would not only supervise the young offenders placed on probation but undertake a 'substantial amount of work closely connected with other forms of child welfare'—not only the supervision of 'care and protection' children but also advising and helping parents and teachers in handling 'difficult or maladjusted children', and also acting as 'conciliators' in matrimonial cases. The Home Office claimed not only that successful conciliation work prevented the break up of the home and thus had an important bearing on the welfare of the children concerned, but also that probation officers helped in local youth activities and kept in close touch with the 'social work and social organisations of the neighbourhood'.
[288] The legislation adopted a policy of removing the normal language of the criminal trial from proceedings in respect of juvenile delinquents—for example, the terms 'conviction' and 'sentence' were no longer to be used.
[289] Unless satisfied that this would be undesirable in the interests of the child or that some other person—see below—was about to take proceedings: Children and Young Persons Act 1932, s. 9(4).
[290] Children Act 1908, s. 58(8).
[291] Action under Children Act 1908 could be initiated by any person: s. 58(1).
[292] Children and Young Persons Act 1932, s. 9(1) and (6).

'any society authorised for the purpose by the Home Secretary'. In this way, the Home Office recognised the historical claims of the NSPCC; and the Home Office circular[293] explaining the impact of the legislation stated that the Home Secretary presumed local authorities would 'not wish to deal with cases which they are satisfied are being dealt with effectively' by the NSPCC. The Home Office claimed that the Act was based on the principle that in this area 'the co-operation of many agencies is necessary. The Justices . . . education authorities, police authorities, probation officers and other social workers are all concerned'; and in particular the 'closer association of education authorities with the work of the juvenile courts is likely to assist the Justices in carrying out their functions'. But although the local authority had the primary responsibility the emphasis was to be on collaboration. Local authorities should consult with the police authority and any other relevant local agencies 'so as to ensure the co-operation of all concerned in the question of the care or protection of young people'.

Courts to make greater use of boarding out

The Children Act 1908 Act had given the court power to commit a needy child to the care of a relative or other fit person; but this was not often done. The Home Office's explanatory circular emphasised that the 1932 Act 'enlarged' the potential to use boarding out. The child who had no suitable 'relative or friend' to whom he could be intrusted could be committed to the care of a local authority; and the Home Office circular stated the 'intention of parliament'[294] to be that the children so committed should be boarded out with suitable foster-parents.

Increased supervision of 'voluntary' homes

The Children and Young Persons Act[295] enlarged the responsibilities of the Home Office in respect of 'homes' provided by a Children's Society or other philanthropic organisation. For the first time, managers were required to make an annual return to the Home Office, and the Home Office powers of inspection and control were increased. The Home Office took pride in its work in this respect: the inspections were carried out 'by the same trained and experienced staff of inspectors who inspect approved schools' some of whom (it was claimed) gave 'most of their time to the inspection of voluntary homes'. The

---

[293] Home Office Circular of 9 August 1933.

[294] The Home Office Circular to Local Authorities emphasised that 'wherever it appears that a child . . . can be suitably boarded out, the Local Authority should be prepared to accept responsibility. Boarding Out was particularly suitable for the younger children but the possibility of boarding out older children should always be considered'.

[295] Part III. The Act gave effect to recommendations made in the *Third and Final Report* of the Tomlin Committee into the adoption of children (1926, Cmd. 2711).

effectiveness of such inspection (and the role of the agencies providing such homes) was however soon to become a matter of controversy.[296]

IMPACT OF THE CHILDREN AND YOUNG PERSONS ACTS

The Home Office officials,[297] reporting in 1938 on the work of the Children's Department, claimed that public interest in the welfare of the 'less fortunate children in the community' was growing. It seemed eminently reasonable to expect the efforts of those concerned with the application of the law[298] would 'lead to a reduction in the amount of youthful delinquency and so to an increase in the well-being of the community'.[299] Of course, there were some disappointments.[300] For all the good intentions about youthful and sympathetic magistrates relating to those who came before them, the great majority of magistrates on juvenile court panels were aged between 50 and 70.[301] (In 1936 at least one 90-year-old male remained a panel member.[302]) But it appears—proper statistics were not collected[303]—that the courts were increasingly asked to exercise the 'care and protection' jurisdiction. In 1936 juvenile courts made 1,689 'care and protection' orders;[304] and the Home Office recorded with satisfaction that a significant number of children who would have fallen outside the provisions of the 1908 Act were dealt with under the reformed law.[305] But it is clear that some courts found difficulty in assessing the degree of care and guardianship to be regarded as 'normal'. The Home Office commented:

---

[296] See Chapter 19, below.

[297] Dr AH Norris, the Chief Inspector, and JF Hargreaves, an Assistant Secretary.

[298] The drafting of the legislation involved a massive commitment of resources by the Home Office and other departments of Central Government; but coming to terms with the new legislation also involved a great deal of activity at local level. For one example, note the concern expressed by a Director of Education that the provisions dealing with the employment of children (which had been controversial during the 1932 Act's passage through Parliament) had made it illegal for children under 12 to participate in school concerts and plays. The draftsman disabused him: Rowlatt to Brook, 8 May 1933, PRO ED/31 278.

[299] *Fifth Report on the Working of the Children's Department* (1938) p. iii. It is necessary to bear in mind that the reality of what was done under the Act may not always have reflected the ideology of Whitehall officials: see the critical appraisal in H Hendrick, *Child Welfare England 1872–1989* (1994) Chapter 6.

[300] On the contrast between theory and practice, see also GK Behlmer, *Friends of the Family, The English Home and Its Guardians, 1850–1940* (1998), particularly at p. 263 ff.

[301] In 1936 it appears that 4,726 out of a total of 7,005 justices on panels were aged between 50 and 69, whilst there remained 66 panels to which not a single woman had been appointed. The figures however should be treated with some caution: some justices 'exhibited a reluctance, shy, indignant or coy', to disclose their ages; and one justices' clerk 'begged to be excused from the delicate task of asking . . . women justices their age': *Fifth Report on the Working of the Children's Department* (1938) p. 4.

[302] *Fifth Report on the Working of the Children's Department* (1938) p. 5.

[303] *Fifth Report on the Working of the Children's Department* (1938) p. 38.

[304] 490 supervision orders, 596 fit person orders, and 603 approved school orders: *Fifth Report on the Working of the Children's Department* (1938) p. 38.

[305] *Ibid.*, p. 39.

'This degree obviously varies with the age of the boy or girl. The degree of care which the average parent may be expected to give to a child of 10 is obviously greater than the degree of care ordinarily to be given to a boy or girl of 16. There have been cases before the courts in which it has been represented by an anxious mother that her daughter of 16 was beyond her control and in which it has been found by the court that the mother was attempting to enforce a degree of control over her daughter which was quite unreasonable. The not unnatural disinclination of a daughter to submit to what she regards as excessive parental domination is sometimes hotly and bitterly resented by the mother as unnatural filial disobedience. A case occurred, for example, in which a girl of nearly 17 working as a shop assistant was only allowed to retain a minute fraction of her wages, and was expected to economise on lunch if she took a bus to work and was never allowed to go to a cinema except when she was chaperoned.'

There could be no magical answer to such problems:[306] it was (said the Home Office) 'no easy matter for the court in such cases to decide where the balance lies between parental autocracy and filial autonomy'. And of course no court order, however 'flexible',[307] could provide a 'cure' for the severely disturbed child who, so far as the law was concerned, came within the 'innocent description of being "in need of care or protection"'.[308]

But these issues soon seemed almost irrelevant: on the outbreak of World War II in September 1939 a 'large number of children of all ages were suddenly taken from their homes in London and the other great cities of England and put to live with strangers in country towns and villages'[309] in what a psychiatrist described as the biggest disturbance to family life in British history. The evacuation of children and other incidents of twentieth century warfare presented a huge challenge to those responsible for dealing with children in need; but it also created a climate of opinion in which far-reaching reform seemed not only desirable but possible.

[306] The case referred to was one in which a parent brought the child before the court as being beyond parental control.

[307] A key element of the legislation: *Fifth Report on the Working of the Children's Department* (1938) p. 3.

[308] *Fifth Report on the Working of the Children's Department* (1938) p. 41, giving a horrifying account of the plight of a 14-year-old girl, committed to prison and mental hospital in attempts to control her behaviour.

[309] Susan Isaacs (Head of the Department of Child Development, Institute of Education, London University) 'The Uprooted Child' in J Rickman (ed.), *Children in Wartime* (1940)—a collection of contemporary papers dealing with the problems associated with the evacuation of children from major cities in the early days of World War II. I am grateful to Professor Mervyn Murch for drawing my attention to this collection.

19

The State, Parent and Child: (2) The Welfare State and Child Care Legislation

INTRODUCTION[1]

In 1943, the Ministry of Health set up an informal committee[2] to consider what arrangements should be made for children left homeless when the wartime evacuation schemes were finally wound up. The Committee concluded that an 'urgent examination' should be undertaken of the machinery needed for the 'general care of children and adolescents'. Another Committee was considering the impact of the recommendations made in the 1942 Beveridge Report for the abolition of the Poor Law; and that Committee eventually produced detailed proposals for legislation intended to bring under a 'single well-qualified and sympathetic administration'[3] all provision for children in need.

These proposals were not quite as uncontroversial as they might seem: in particular, the Ministry of Health considered that there should be no association of any kind between the provision made for orphans and children whose parents were unable or unwilling to look after them properly and the authorities responsible for the police and the prevention and punishment of crime. This view was not welcome in the Home Office (which was the Department responsible not only for the administration of the Children and Young Persons Act 1933 but also for the police, and prisons and other penal establishments). The ground had been prepared for a grand battle between Departments of State.

---

[1] For a fuller account of the background to the enactment of the Children Act 1948, see SM Cretney, 'The State as a Parent . . .' in *Law, Law Reform and the Family* (1988) Chapter 9; and RA Parker, 'The gestation of reform: the Children Act 1948', in Philip Bean and Stuart Macpherson (eds.), *Approaches to Welfare* (1983).

[2] PRO MH102/1157 *Report of Informal Committee on consequences of ending wartime evacuation scheme*. The main concern was for children who fell outside the scope of both the Poor Law and the 'care and control' provisions of the Children and Young Persons Act 1933. The Appendix to the Committee's report gives examples of the sort of problems which would arise; and there was particular concern about the effect the uncertainty was having on the voluntary organisations caring for children.

[3] Falling 'readily and without overlap into the pattern formed by the [Education Act 1944], the proposals in the White Paper on a National Health Service, and the Social Insurance Plan, when these come into operation': *The Break Up of the Poor Law and the Care of Children and Old People*, see PRO MH102/1378.

THE CURTIS COMMITTEE

There was a bureaucratic need for reform of the administrative machinery; but there was also strong public pressure (associated in particular with a campaign initiated and led by Lady Allen of Hurtwood)[4] for improvements in the arrangements for care of the needy and neglected; and on this occasion the public pressure overbore any institutional opposition (or inertia). In March 1945, the Government set up a Committee of Inquiry, chaired by Miss Myra Curtis (a former civil servant, at the time Principal of Newnham College Cambridge).[5] The Committee was to

'inquire into existing methods of providing for children who from loss of parents or from any cause whatever are deprived of a normal home life with their own parents or relatives; and to consider what further measures should be taken to ensure that these children are brought up under conditions best calculated to compensate them for the lack of parental care'.

The Committee's Report, published in 1946, led directly to the enactment of the Children Act 1948 which remained the foundation of State provision for children in need for the next quarter of a century and can properly be regarded as an integral and important part of machinery of the post-World War II Welfare State.

More than two-thirds of the Committee's 182-page Report was given over to a detailed descriptive analysis of the existing arrangements, and (as the *Finer Report*[6] put it more than a quarter of a century later) the account of the physical emotional and intellectual deprivation suffered by some of the children in care 'shocked public opinion'. For example:[7]

in the children's ward of one workhouse, 'was an eight year old mentally defective girl . . . she could not use her arms or legs, There were two babies with rickets clothed in cotton frocks, cotton vests and dilapidated napkins, no more than discoloured cotton rags. The smell in this room was dreadful. A premature baby lay in an opposite ward alone. . . . The healthy children were housed in the ground floor corrugated hutment which had been once the old union casual ward. . . . The children fed, played and used their pots in this room. They ate from cracked enamel plates, using the same mug for milk and soup. They slept in another corrugated hutment in old broken black iron cots some of which had their sides tied up with cord. The mattresses were fouled and stained. . . . The children wore ankle length calico or flannelette frocks and petticoats and had no knickers. . . . Most of [the children] had lost their shoes; those who possessed shoes had either

---

[4] See Biographical Notes. Lady Allen was especially concerned by the Government's apparent failure to consider child care in planning for post-war reconstruction and in particular with the poor provision often made for children in residential children's homes. For an account of the campaign and its impact, see SM Cretney, *Law, Law Reform and the Family* (1998) pp. 208–216.

[5] See Biographical Notes.

[6] *Report of the Committee on One-Parent Families* (1974, Cmnd. 5629) para. 8.21.

[7] *Report of the Care of Children Committee* (1946, Cmd. 6922) (hereinafter referred to as the *Curtis Report*) para. 144.

taken them off to play with or were wearing them tied to their feet with dirty string. Their faces were clean; their bodies in some cases were unwashed and stained'.

The death of Dennis O'Neill

The public had already been prepared for shocks by the publicity given to the case of Dennis O'Neill, a 12-year-old boy in local authority care who had been boarded out with foster-parents at Bank Farm Minsterley Shropshire. He died there in January 1945 from acute cardiac failure following (as the coroner's jury recorded) violence applied to the front of the chest and being beaten with a stick. The jury added a rider that there had been a serious lack of supervision by the local authority. It was certainly true that the local authority placing official's statement that 'the lad has gone to a very good home and will be brought up well'[8] was sadly over optimistic. It is often thought that it was the publicity given to the O'Neill case which prompted the establishment of the Curtis Committee, but in fact the decision had been announced a month before Dennis O'Neill's death. However, the case (and the Report into it carried out by Sir Walter Monckton)[9] is repeatedly referred to in the *Curtis Report* and seems to have served as the justification for the new and positive ideology and the radical restructuring of child care services advocated by the Committee, whilst the decision to legislate was strongly influenced by politicians' perception of the climate of opinion which the O'Neill case had done much to create. Dennis O'Neill can fairly be described as the victim whose death put reform onto the urgent agenda of practical politics.

The Curtis Committee's recommendations

The *Curtis Report* contained 62 recommendations. The underlying themes can be summarised as follows.[10]

(1) The need for personal care

Public child care arrangements completely failed 'to provide any kind of individual interest or notice'[11] for a child. Substitute homes should compensate to the greatest possible extent for the psychological and material advantages derived by the ordinary child from a family background;[12] and the comprehensive scheme

---

[8] *Daily Mail*, 13 February 1945.

[9] *Report by Sir Walter Monckton KCMG, KCVO, MC, KC on the circumstances which led to the boarding out of Dennis and Terence O'Neill* . . . (1945, Cmd. 6636). For Monckton, see Biographical Notes.

[10] The summary draws substantially on Chapter 9 of SM Cretney, *Law, Law Reform and the Family* (1998).

[11] *Curtis Report*, para. 155.

[12] *per* Lord Listowel, *Official Report* (HL) 12 December 1946, vol. 144, col. 901. Evidence given to the Committee by prominent (and pioneering) workers in the child care field—including John Bowlby (then a Lieutenant Colonel in the Royal Army Medical Corps; subsequently the author of

recommended by the Committee was intended to achieve this objective so far as it was possible to do so.

(2) Local involvement

Central Government responsibility for child care should be vested in a single department which would have the important responsibility[13] of defining requirements, maintaining standards, advising and assisting those immediately responsible for the care of children, and acting as a clearing house for progressive ideas. Central Government would make rules governing such matters as boarding out procedures, and a central inspectorate would inspect children's homes. But the Curtis Report rejected any suggestion that children in need of care should be the direct responsibility of a department of the Central Government. Constant 'local interest in the children of a locality' was a very important element in ensuring the children's welfare.[14] To this end, every local authority should be required to appoint a single Children's Committee responsible for all the Council's child care functions.[15] This rationalisation would also avoid the dangerous confusion of the existing system.

(3) Appointment of Local Authority Children's Officers

The belief that no office staff dealing with children simply as 'cases' could establish this vital personal link was the foundation on which the *Curtis Report* based its central conclusion that every local authority should be required to appoint a Children's Officer of high standing and qualifications

'. . . highly qualified academically, if possible a graduate who has also a social science diploma. She[16] should not be under thirty at the time of appointment and should have had some experience of work with children. She should have marked administrative capacity. . . . Her essential qualifications, however, would be on the personal side. She should be genial and friendly in manner and able to set both children and adults at their ease. She should have a strong interest in the welfare of children and enough faith and enthusiasm to be ready to try methods new and old of compensating by care and affection those who have had a bad start in life. She should have very high standards of physical and moral welfare, but should be flexible enough in temperament to avoid a sterile institutional correctness.'[17]

This paragon was to be the pivot[18] of the whole organisation of child care:

many works on attachment theory and the effects of deprivation of maternal care); Dr Susan Isaacs (author of *The Cambridge Evacuation Survey*); Dr Donald Winnicott (an eminent child psychiatrist); and Clare Britton (subsequently in charge of the child care training course at the London School of Economics) was evidently influential.

[13] To use the language of the *Curtis Report,* para. 432.
[14] *Curtis Report,* para. 431.   [15] As enumerated in *Curtis Report,* para. 440.
[16] The Committee did not wish to exclude men from consideration, but thought that women would fill most of the vacancies: *Curtis Report,* para. 443.
[17] *Ibid.,* para. 446.   [18] *Ibid.,* para. 443.

'She . . . will be a specialist in child care as the Medical Officer of Health is a specialist in his own province and the Director of Education is in his; and she will have no other duties to distract her interests'.[19]

The Committee saw the Children's Officer as solving problems by personal contact and direct methods (such as talking to people rather than writing official memoranda).[20] In this way all the persons who dealt with the child would be known personally to the 'officer of the authority to whom the care of that particular child has been assigned'.[21]

(4) Preferred means of caring for children

The Committee had no doubt[22] that every effort should be made to keep a child in the family home.[23] But if this was not possible, the aim of the local authority had to be to 'find something better—indeed much better . . .'.[24] In order of preference, the Committee favoured adoption, then boarding out with foster-parents, and last, residential care in a children's home.[25]

Curtis's preference for adoption is often overlooked. But the reason why adoption does not figure in the Children Act 1948 (and was thus for long not regarded as a central part of the child care system) had nothing to do with the merits. It is rather that adoption was regarded as primarily concerned with legal status and thus not within the scope of a child welfare Bill[26]—a remarkable illustration of the way in which policy may effectively be determined by considerations of legal classification and departmental responsibility. It was to be nearly 30 years before the Children Act 1975 recognised that adoption constituted a technique vital to the provision of public care for the needy child.

The Curtis Committee's preference for boarding out was based on the belief 'that in the free conditions of ordinary family life with its opportunities for varied human contacts and experiences, the child's nature develops and his confidence in life and ease in society are established in a way that can hardly be achieved in a larger establishment living as it must a more strictly regulated existence'.[27] But this would only be true if the foster home were entirely satisfactory: under no circumstances should sub-standard homes be accepted (as was said to have been done in the O'Neill case).[28] The Committee had considerable faith in what could be achieved by administrative measures in ensuring good standards; but even so it was a bold step to commend the principle of boarding out when that had so disastrously failed Dennis O'Neill.

---

[19] *Ibid.*, para. 443.   [20] *Ibid.*, para. 421.
[21] *Ibid.* The Committee accepted that it would not be practicable for the Children's Officer in a large authority to know and keep in personal touch with all the children under her care, and she should therefore aim at allocating a group of children definitely to each of her subordinates. These subordinates would 'be the friend of those particular children through their childhood and adolescence': para. 445.
[22] *Ibid.*, para. 447.   [23] 'Or with its mother if it is illegitimate': para. 447.
[24] *Curtis Report*, para. 447.   [25] *Ibid.*
[26] See further p. 685, below.   [27] *Ibid.*, para. 461.
[28] *Ibid.*, para. 461.

The Committee accepted that institutional (or 'residential community' care) would necessarily still have a continuing role in the child care system. The Committee made detailed recommendations about the general principles to be adopted (and enforced by inspection) in such homes. It also emphasised the need for effective inspection, supervision and enforcement of proper standards in all aspects of child care.

(5) Training

The Committee noted that staff caring for children were often without any special training for the task; and identified this as a factor in part responsible for unsatisfactory standards.[29] A Central Training Council in Child Care should be established; and proper training should be given to the staff of children's homes and to Boarding Out Officers.

(6) Voluntary homes

'Voluntary homes', often with a religious inspiration and management, cared for large numbers of children, and some (such as Dr Barnado's) had established a favourable public image[30] as doing good to the disadvantaged at a time when State provision was not developed.

But had such institutions outlived their usefulness? There were certainly some who associated voluntary homes (which were only subject to Government inspection if they solicited contributions from the public or received Poor Law children)[31] with low standards of care, whilst the fact that many voluntary homes were exempt from inspection was a source of disquiet. There was also a more general conflict of ideology (particularly noticeable at a time when a Labour Government espousing socialist principles was in office with a large parliamentary majority) between those favouring the principle of centralised state planning and control on the one hand and those taking a more traditional attitude towards the proper function of government on the other. Lady Allen, for example, believed that since the State was to be responsible for the sick, the old and the unemployed it should equally assume direct responsibility for children in voluntary homes: all children deprived of a normal home life should become

[29] The Committee presented an *Interim Report on Training in Child Care* (Cmd. 6760) on 6 January 1946. Although the Interim Report was primarily concerned with the training of 'residential staff of the House Mother type in charge of groups of children in small cottage or independent . . . homes', it summarised the training available for child care workers of all kinds, and emphasised as a matter 'of great importance and urgency' the need to attract suitable recruits from the men and women then leaving the armed forces.

[30] '. . . the Curtis Committee's Report does not recommend the extinction of the great voluntary services which, indeed, they most strongly commend', *per* Viscount Simon, *Official Report* (HL) 12 December 1946, vol. 144, col. 904. Nevertheless, Barnado's (like other voluntary agencies, at a low ebb after World War II) was equivocal in its approach to Curtis, particularly since the possibility of state interference by inspectors threatened their historic 'freedom of action': see J Rose, *For the Sake of the Children* (1987) p. 199.

[31] See note 179, p. 651, above.

'wards of the state', albeit the direct responsibility of the an identified individual.[32]

The Curtis Committee was not sparing in its criticisms of some voluntary homes;[33] but concluded that 'as a group' the voluntary homes did not fall below 'the general level of child care now obtaining throughout the country' and indeed that in 'many instances they were well above it'.[34] Hence the Committee adopted one of those compromises which have for long characterised the provision of welfare services in this country: such homes (whatever their status) should be required to comply with Regulations made by the responsible Minister, and they should be registered with and inspected by the relevant department of Central Government; but, provided that they could be brought up to the appropriate standard, they should be allowed to continue their activities in the care of children.[35] If not, they should be closed down.

(7) Child neglect: compulsion

The Curtis Committee's Terms of Reference required it to deal with children who had in fact been deprived of a normal home life with their own parents and not with the circumstances in which a child might be removed from home. The Committee accepted that children suffering from neglect, malnutrition or other evils might well be said to be deprived of a 'normal' home life, yet 'the difficulty of drawing the line among children in their own homes is obvious'; and the Committee concluded that it was not its function to consider how to provide for children still in their own homes under their parents' care but suffering from neglect, malnutrition or other evils.[36] The Curtis Committee did regard the question of providing for the neglected child as one 'of the utmost importance' which it hoped would be given 'serious consideration'. But the Committee was clear that this was not the problem with which it had been asked to deal; and accordingly it did not consider the basis upon which the courts could order that a child be removed[37] from his parents against their will, nor did it consider how to improve the lot of disadvantaged children in their parents' homes. The Curtis Committee was clear that it was exclusively concerned with what should

---

[32] See *Memoirs of an Uneducated Lady*, by Marjory Allen and Mary Nicholson (1975) (subsequently cited as Allen, *Memoirs*) Chapter 14.

[33] See *Curtis Report*, para. 225 ff.   [34] *Ibid.*, para. 227.   [35] *Ibid.*, para. 433.

[36] The Bishop of Sheffield pointed out in the House of Lords debate on the Committee's Report that there were a 'very considerable number of children living with parents who are vicious or mentally deficient, under conditions of bestial squalor which are quite shocking'. Parents might be prosecuted and imprisoned, and their children lodged in the Poor Law Institution; but the parents received no psychiatric treatment and no education in parentcraft. At the end of the parents' sentence, the family would return to the 'previous conditions unchanged'. He considered that legislation as well as vigorous administration was needed *Official Report* (HL) 12 December 1946, vol. 144, col. 892.

[37] The Committee did however recommend that if a court wished to commit a child to the care of a local authority as a fit person the local authority should be obliged to undertake the child's care: *Curtis Report*, para. 425.

happen once a child was in the care of the State,[38] not with defining the circumstances in which the State should be entitled to intervene in the family and take a child into its care. In short, the Committee was concerned with the world of social administration rather than legal action.[39] Another 20 years would elapse before a government was prepared to bring forward legislation seeking to remedy the defects in the statutory provisions governing the circumstances in which a child could be removed from the home;[40] and statutory provision specifically focussing on preventive work also had to wait for another committee[41] and other legislation.[42]

(8) Guardians for the orphan?

Although the Curtis Committee was not concerned with the circumstances which might justify removing a child from the family, it was concerned with the question of legal authority in respect of the child who had in fact come into care. It followed from its view that an identifiable person should be (and be seen to be) responsible for the child's care that it recommended that every orphan or deserted child maintained or supervised by a local authority should have a legal guardian—preferably a relative, but otherwise the Head of an approved voluntary home, or the local authority itself[43]—able to take the major decisions in the child's life and 'to feel full responsibility' for the child's welfare.

The Committee accordingly recommended that county courts and magistrates' courts should be empowered to appoint a guardian for any child who had no natural or testamentary guardian, and it considered that the authority should ensure the question of guardianship was addressed in all cases in which it took responsibility for a child's welfare.[44] The Committee thought that its proposed guardianship procedure would help to give foster-parents a measure of security: 'if this simple procedure were available it might often make possible a stable

---

[38] The Committee accepted the Home Office view that was that it 'was often an accident' whether a child came before the court as a delinquent or as a neglected child; and for this reason the Committee concluded that *once a child was in the care of the community* 'the same methods of treatment should be equally available' in the two cases: *Curtis Report*, para. 38.

[39] *Lewisham London Borough Council v. Lewisham Juvenile Court Justices* [1980] AC 273, 306, *per* Lord Scarman.

[40] Amendment of the relevant 'care and protection' provisions of the Children and Young Persons Act 1933 was recommended by the Ingleby *Committee on Children and Young Persons* (1960, Cmnd. 1191): see paras. 83–94 and Appendix III. But the relationship between prosecution of the delinquent and care of the neglected became the subject of much discussion in the 1960s (see below, p. 688); and it was not until 1969 that the Children and Young Persons Act reformulated the principles upon which compulsory protective measures might be taken in respect of children.

[41] *Report of the Committee on Children and Young Persons* (The Ingleby Committee) (1960, Cmnd. 1191).

[42] Children and Young Persons Act 1963, s. 1.   [43] *Curtis Report*, para. 425(ii).

[44] The Committee contemplated that 'failing a suitable relative, for whom enquiry should be made, or the Head of an approved voluntary Home which has the child under care, the local authority itself should apply for appointment as a guardian'. This recommendation prompted some modification to the powers of local authorities under Poor Law Act 1930, s. 52, to assume parental rights over a child by resolution: see below.

relation short of adoption between a good foster parent and a child'.[45] But as we shall see, the implementation of this policy gave rise to difficulty; and the question of how best to create a secure legal status for the long-term foster-parent still remained troublesome at the end of the century.[46]

(9) Assumption of parental rights: 'Poor Law adoptions'

The Committee, in a somewhat confused passage in its Report[47] seemed to suggest that the appointment of a guardian by the court under the procedure it recommended would also supplant the 'poor law adoption' procedure derived from the Poor Law[48] whereby local authorities could by administrative means assume the parents' rights over a child[49] in their care in certain circumstances.

This procedure for dealing with the children of the poor may have been acceptable at the beginning of the twentieth century[50] and had (as we have seen) been viewed favourably by various official bodies. The *Curtis Report* found that authorities in fact used their power 'with discretion and a proper sense of responsibility';[51] but in the post-1945 world complaints by parents about the use of the power had become 'not uncommon', and the *Curtis Report* accepted that public opinion was critical of interference with parental rights and personal liberty. The Committee believed that any additional publicity and work involved in court proceedings to deprive a parent of his rights 'would be more than counterbalanced by the value of an impartial and detached judicial inquiry at the outset directed to the paramount welfare of the child'[52] and concluded that to

---

[45] *Curtis Report*, para. 425(ii).

[46] See below. On 23 April 1948 Lord Chancellor Jowitt wrote to the Home Secretary expressing concern about the position of small children deserted by their natural parents and boarded out with foster-parents: 'it frequently happens—and God be praised that it does—that these foster-parents become really attached to the children and would, if they could, be only too ready to adopt them so that they might have them "for keeps" and give them the benefit of a real home life. . . . Would it not be possible to provide in the case of a child deserted by its parents that, after a certain time and of course with the approval of the Home Office . . . an adoption might be allowed?' The response, as Jowitt had expected, was that such a proposal was not within the scope of the Bill.

[47] Para. 425(iii).

[48] Poor Law Act 1899, s. 2, see Chapter 17, above. Such 'adoptions' did not affect the child's legal status and did not protect the foster-parents against a decision by the authorities to remove the child, but they did give the 'adopters' a measure of protection against claims by the natural parents to resume the care of the child once he was able to earn wages.

[49] For these purposes a 'child' was a person under 18; and the assumption was that the years between 16 to 18 were critical 'because during them the young people's earnings will usually need to be supplemented, friendly advice is of special importance to them, and undesirable relatives attempt to resume control of them, either to claim their earnings or to corrupt their morals': *The Break Up of the Poor Law and the Care of Children and Old People*, PRO MH102/1378, para. 23.

[50] SW Harris's Memorandum dated 13 June 1944, PRO MH 102/1378, para. 8 stated that it was a 'subject for wonder how [this procedure] ever passed the scrutiny of Parliament'; but the short answer may be that Parliament gave the matter almost no scrutiny: see *Hansard's Parliamentary Debates* (4th Series) 29 June 1899, vol. 73, col. 951. In any event, the procedure was—notwithstanding its incompatibility with later notions of fairness and justice—commended by official enquiries, and even by left-wing commentators such as Mrs Beatrice Webb.

[51] *The Break Up of the Poor Law and the Care of Children and Old People*, see PRO MH102/1378, para. 24.

[52] *Curtis Report*, para. 425(ii).

extinguish the rights of a parent or other guardian by a mere resolution of a Council was fundamentally objectionable. But unfortunately the Committee's views on court-appointed guardians and Parental Rights Resolutions were not fully worked out;[53] and the procedure whereby parental rights could be assumed by administrative action not only survived until 1991[54] but was given an extended application by the Children Act 1975.[55]

THE CHILDREN ACT 1948

The *Curtis Report* was signed in August 1946[56] and there was strong press and parliamentary[57] pressure for legislation. Government ministers described the report as a 'landmark in the history of the collective care of children'[58] and gave assurances that the Report would not 'languish indefinitely' in Whitehall pigeon-holes.[59] Although many of the *Curtis Report's* recommendations could be implemented by administrative action[60] it was clear that there would have to be legislation if only to deal with the consequences for child care of the ending of the Poor Law.[61] But there was in fact considerable disagreement about the scope of the projected legislation and in consequence significant delay in bringing a Bill forward. The reason was that Curtis had recommended that a single Government Department should be responsible for child care but had—in response to some Whitehall pressure[62]—deliberately not recommended whether

[53] See below. The Committee seems not to have appreciated that its proposal for court-appointed guardians would not cover all the cases in which parental rights resolutions were available (eg cases in which the child had been deserted but still had a 'natural guardian'); nor did the Committee consider the difficulties (highlighted in SW Harris's Memorandum dated 13 June 1944, PRO MH 102/1378, paras. 8–9) arising from the interrelationship of the resolution procedure (and any substitute for it) and the powers of the court under Children and Young Persons Act 1933 to commit a child to the care of a fit person.

[54] With the coming into force of the Children Act 1989.   [55] See below, Chapter 20.

[56] Six members of the Committee signed a note of Reservation dissenting from the majority view recommending abolition of the Poor Law rule which prohibited the boarding out of a child with foster-parents of a different religious persuasion: see *Curtis Report*, para. 472, and p. 183.

[57] See notably the remarks by Wilson Harris MP in the debate on the King's Speech (*Official Report* (HC) 19 November 1946, vol. 430, col. 763) and a full debate was initiated in the House of Lords by the Earl of Iddesleigh: *Official Report* (HL) 12 December 1946, vol. 144, col. 884.

[58] *Official Report* (HL) 12 December 1946, vol. 144, col. 900 (Lord Listowel).   [59] *Ibid.*

[60] See for example the Prime Minister's statement in the House of Commons, *Official Report* (HC) 28 November 1946, vol. 430, col. 329; whilst in the House of Lords debate (*Official Report* (HL) 12 December 1946, vol. 144, cols. 903–907) Lord Listowel was able to point to a substantial number of administrative measures: (1) Publication of a Circular to local authorities requiring them to review arrangements in the light of recommendations and criticisms in the Curtis Report; (2) Strengthening of the Home Office and Ministry of Health Inspectorates; (3) Establishing training courses for house mothers and senior staff; and the creation of a Central Council on Training and Child Care; (4) Making of new Rules on Boarding out and fostering, and publication of detailed directions and guidance about the procedures to be followed; (5) Publication of Guidance on improved administrative procedures including placing responsibility for finding foster-homes and the supervision of foster-homes on a single officer.

[61] To which the Government was committed.

[62] See SM Cretney, *Law, Law Reform and the Family* (1998) p. 230, note 206.

this Department should be the Home Office, the Ministry of Health, or the Department of Education. A bitter Whitehall battle was fought behind closed doors,[63] and was only resolved (in favour of the Home Office) in March 1947. Until the issue of departmental responsibility had been settled there was little serious discussion of the contents of the legislation to be introduced. Even then, there was a strong (albeit in the end not effective) body of Official and Ministerial pressure to restrict the legislation to provisions essential in light of the abolition of the Poor Law.[64]

In spite of all this, and the many difficulties which had preoccupied the drafts-man,[65] the 62-clause Bill had a generally trouble-free passage through Parliament.[66] It would, after all, be politically unappealing to attack provisions intended to ensure that children cared for by the State should get the personal sympathy and human understanding necessary to the well-being of children who lacked the love and affection of parents;[67] and, although there might be reservations about the growth of State activity in this as in other areas, the Labour Government could point to a clear principle: the State was going to ensure, through the centralised administration of the National Assistance Board, that adequate financial resources were available to wipe out poverty as it had been known; and local authorities would bring 'warmth and humanity'[68] to caring for needy children.[69] Only the question[70] of the religious upbringing of children in care gave rise to much debate.[71]

---

[63] For a detailed account of the 'machinery of government' issue, see SM Cretney, *Law, Law Reform and the Family* (1998) pp. 228–234.

[64] The proposal was that 42 out of Curtis's 62 recommendations should not be included in the Bill. See on this the sources cited in SM Cretney, *Law, Law Reform and the Family* (1998) p. 234, note 229.

[65] See the account given in SM Cretney, *Law, Law Reform and the Family* (1998) p. 235.

[66] For parliamentary debates see (House of Lords) *Official Report* 10 February 1948, vol. 153, col. 913 (2nd Reading); 9 March 1948, vol. 154, col. 531 (Committee); 13 April 1948, vol. 155, col. 3 (Report); 20 April 1948, vol. 155, col. 156 (3rd Reading); 30 June 1948, vol. 157, col. 92, Consideration of Commons Amendments. (House of Commons) *Official Report* 7 May 1948, vol. 450, col. 1609 (2nd Reading); 28 June 1948, vol. 452, col. 1844 (Report); 28 June 1948, vol. 452, col. 1858 (3rd Reading); *House of Commons Standing Committee Session 1947/1948 Official Reports* vol. 111.

[67] Kenneth Younger, Parliamentary Under-Secretary of State at the Home Office, *Official Report* (HC) 7 May 1948, vol. 450, col. 1611.

[68] Aneurin Bevan, Minister of Health, *Official Report* (HC) 24 November 1947, vol. 444, col. 1604.

[69] Central supervision was exercised through the Home Office's inspectorial role; and by the obligation imposed on local authorities to exercise the relevant functions 'under the general guidance of the Secretary of State': Children Act 1948, s. 45(1) (subsequently repealed and replaced by Local Authority Social Services Act 1970, s. 7). This provision (in fact weaker than Curtis's recommendation that *mandamus* be available as the sanction for default, para. 432) has over the years proved an effective means whereby Central Government formulates standards and determines general policy—notably in the context of the volumes of Guidance relating to the Children Act 1989: see below, p. 732.

[70] Which had divided the Curtis Committee: see note 56, p. 680, above.

[71] The Archbishop of Canterbury had written to the Lord Chancellor urging that that Act make it clear that children in care should attend church: see PRO LCO2/4473. In the event, the Act referred to arrangements being made for children to 'receive a religious upbringing appropriate to

The Bill was attractively drafted to make the policy clear. Part I imposed a duty on local authorities to provide for children in need;[72] and Part II dealt with the treatment of children who were in the care of a local authority. The Act[73] provided that it was the duty of a local authority to 'exercise their powers so as to further the child's best interests, and to afford him opportunities for the proper development of his character and abilities';[74] and it expressly embodied the Curtis preference for boarding out with foster-parents (rather than institutional care). Only where boarding out was not practicable or desirable was the local authority to place the child in a home (either one provided by the authority itself[75] or a suitably approved and inspected home provided by a voluntary organisation).

The Act also tried to eradicate the stigma of 'being in a home', for example by a provision that local authorities make use of facilities and services available to children in the care of their own parents so far as appeared reasonable,[76] and by empowering authorities to pay for the further education and training of young people who had been in their care.[77] These provisions seemed to justify the claim that if a child in local authority care wished and had the aptitude to become a doctor, a lawyer, or a musician, or to pursue any other career of his choice, 'the local authority would see him through . . .';[78] and certainly the Act seemed to be inspired by a radically different philosophy from the provision which had previously required the authorities to 'set to work' orphans and destitute children.[79] In short, the Children Act not only greatly widened the circumstances which justified providing public help for a child;[80] it also greatly extended the kind of provision which could be made.

The Act also embodied (albeit under the unpromising heading of 'Administrative and Financial Provisions')[81] what was in ideological grounds perhaps the most striking of the Curtis recommendations—the requirement

---

the persuasion to which they belong': see eg s. 15(4). It was also thought necessary to prohibit the cremation of deceased children where cremation was not in accordance with the practice of the child's religious persuasion: s. 18(1) proviso.

[72] The duty applied to children under 17 who had no parent or guardian, and children whose parents were (either temporarily or permanently) prevented by illness or other incapacity from providing for them, but only if local authority intervention was necessary in the interests of the child's welfare: s. 1.

[73] s. 12(1).   [74] Children Act 1948, s. 12(1).

[75] The Act gave authorities the power to provide Children's Homes (and imposed an obligation on them to do so if the Secretary of State so required): s. 15.

[76] s. 12(2).   [77] s. 20.

[78] Lady Allen, in an article in the *News of the World* 25 January 1948, headlined 'A Triumph for Public Opinion—Blameless Children Get a New Charter'.

[79] This provision of the Elizabethan Poor Law was embodied in the Poor Law Act 1930, s. 15(1)(c).

[80] The extension of local authority responsibility far beyond destitution (the only basis for intervention under the Poor Law) was not in terms envisaged by the Curtis Committee: cf. *Curtis Report*, para. 424.

[81] Part VI. This Part of the Act also contained the important provisions requiring local authorities to appoint specialist children's committees (of which persons with relevant experience or training could be members even though they were not members of the authority): s. 39.

(giving effect to the policy that children's care should be in the hands of an identified human being) that each local authority should appoint a properly qualified children's officer.[82] Finally, the Act[83] included provisions greatly extending the provisions for registration and inspection of children's homes on which the *Curtis Report* relied as the best way to ensure good standards without inhibiting charitable organisations from continuing to play a full part in child welfare work; and it made important provision[84] for the training of social workers and for the establishment of an Advisory Council on Child Care to advise the Government about child care issues.[85]

The 1948 Act was (as already emphasised) primarily concerned with the provision of help for children in need. It was no doubt sensible for the Lord Chancellor to reassure Parliament that the Act would not permit children to be removed from parents against the parents' will;[86] but questions of legal status and authority played little part in the public discussion. However, they had occupied a great deal of attention whilst Parliamentary Counsel was seeking to translate the Curtis recommendations into statutory form. How, for example, could a local authority care properly for a child unless it had parental authority? The answer was found in a delicate compromise: a local authority which had received a child into care was under a duty to keep the child in care for so long as the child's welfare required,[87] and the local authority's statutory powers and duties then applied;[88] but the legislation specifically provided that this provision was not to authorise a local authority to keep a child in care against the wishes of a parent or guardian.[89]

The legislation could in this way be presented as intended to safeguard the rights of parents against the encroachments of the State.[90] But what was to

[82] s. 41. Local authorities were required to submit the short-list of candidates to the Home Secretary who had power to prohibit the appointment of anyone considered not to be a fit person: Children Act 1948, s. 41(2). It appears that some local authorities sought the Home Secretary's consent under Children Act 1948, s. 41(3) to the Children's Officer performing other functions; but the official view was that 'we shall have to maintain a firm front if we are to ensure that the children's officers posts are filled by suitable people possessing the requisite qualifications, and devoting their whole time to the work in those areas where there is a full-time job': Ross to Mayell, 20 April 1948, PRO LCO2/4473.

[83] Part IV.

[84] Children Act 1948, s. 45, empowered the Government to fund the cost of training child care workers. Although the Government was criticised for delay in providing training it seems that at least some staff specifically qualified in residential care and as boarding out officers were available when the Children Act 1948 came into force: see J Packman, *The Child's Generation* (2nd ed., 1981) p. 10.

[85] Children Act 1948, s. 43.

[86] *Official Report* (HL) 10 February 1948, vol. 153, col. 918.

[87] Children Act 1948, s. 1(2).   [88] Children Act 1948, Part II.

[89] Children Act 1948, s. 1(3) (which also imposed a duty on the local authority to endeavour to secure that care of the child be assumed by a parent, guardian, relative or friend if that would be consistent with the child's welfare).

[90] See *per* Lord Jowitt LC, *Official Report* (HL) 10 February 1948, vol. 153, col. 918; and note *Lewisham London Borough Council v. Lewisham Juvenile Court Justices* [1980] AC 273, 306, *per* Lord Scarman.

happen if a parent insisted on exercising the right to remove a child from care in circumstances which the local authority judged to be inconsistent with the child's welfare? The solution which finally[91] emerged[92] from the drafting process was a reformulation of the power which Curtis had wanted to scrap: the local authority was to be empowered to assume parental rights over a child in care[93] by resolution.[94] But something approaching a right of appeal to the court was introduced: the authority was required to inform the person whose rights[95] were to be acquired in this way of the fact that the resolution had been passed;[96] and that person could then apply to the juvenile court. If such an application was made, the resolution would lapse[97] unless the local authority satisfied the

[91] The Children Act 1948 (which had been under active consideration for four years) provides a striking illustration both of the close attention to detail necessary in drafting legislation in this country and of the fact that issues of policy are often to be found secreted in the details. No fewer than eight drafts of the Bill were printed before the Bill was introduced; and the policy on this issue was only finally settled with the circulation of the fifth draft (which gave rise to nine pages of drafting points) of the Bill on 24 December 1947: see MH102/1524; and even on the sixth draft vital points about funding the education of children in care were raised as well as four pages of minor drafting points.

[92] Ministers (notably Herbert Morrison: see his letter to Ede, 1 September 1947, MH102/1510; and see Biographical Notes) had been concerned at the initial decision not to give effect to the Curtis recommendation—which seems to have been based on a misapprehension about the likely scope and effect of the proposed provision—that all orphans and deserted children should have court-appointed guardians. The retention of the resolution procedure to some extent met that concern; but it was eventually decided also to give the courts a general power to appoint a guardian for any child who had no parent, no guardian of the person, and no other person having parental rights over him: Children Act 1948, s. 50, inserting s. 4(2A) into the Guardianship of Infants Act 1925. (In practice this provision was most often used to confer a legal status on a relative or other person taking over the care of an orphaned child, and seems to have been largely irrelevant in the local authority context.)

[93] The fact that a resolution could only be passed with respect to a child in the local authority's care under s. 1 of the Act meant that there was no power under this provision to *remove* a child from the parents: see *Lewisham London Borough Council v. Lewisham Juvenile Court Justices* [1980] AC 273, HL. A child could be removed under the 'care and protection' provisions of Children and Young Persons Act 1933 which the *Curtis Report* regarded as being outside its terms of reference; see above.

[94] The grounds upon which such a resolution could be passed were that the child's parents were dead and he had no guardian, or that a parent or guardian of his had abandoned him or suffered from some permanent disability rendering him incapable of caring for the child, or was of such habits or mode of life as to be unfit to have the care of the child: Children Act 1948, s. 2(1).

[95] It had originally been envisaged that all parental rights over the child would pass to the local authority, but s. 2(1) of the Children Act 1948 as enacted provided that 'all the rights and powers of the person on whose account the resolution was passed' should vest in the local authority. Hence it might be that one of the child's parents would retain parental rights in respect of a child subject to a resolution: see *R v. Oxford City Justices, ex parte H* [1975] QB 1, and for an account of the difficulties to which this could give rise, SM Cretney, *Principles of Family Law* (4th ed., 1984) pp. 516–517.

[96] Unless that person had consented in writing to the resolution being passed: Children Act 1948, s. 2(2). The comparable provision of Poor Law Act 1930, s. 52 allowed a juvenile court to revoke a parental rights resolution, but contained no provision for notifying the parent or other person concerned that a resolution had been passed.

[97] The Act also provided for the local authority to rescind a resolution if that would be for the child's benefit; and for the parent to apply to the court for the resolution to be determined: Children Act 1948, s. 4(2), (3). Otherwise a resolution would remain in force until the child attained 18—this age eventually being preferred to 16 because it was thought the years 16 to 18 were of especial importance in young peoples' personal development: see above.

court that the applicant had abandoned the child or was 'unfit to have the care of the child by reason of unsoundness of mind or mental deficiency or by reason of his habits or mode of life'.[98] In this way (it could be said) the legislation carefully preserved the principle that a parent was not to be deprived of his rights without having the opportunity to bring the matter before a court;[99] and the Children Act tried to set a happy mean between interfering with legitimate parental rights[100] and ensuring that local authorities were able to act effectively against neglect. But some years later, as parents (often supported by legal aid) became readier to challenge local authority decision taking,[101] the issue returned to prominence.

CHILD CARE AFTER CURTIS: SOCIAL WORK VALUES AND THE LEGAL FRAMEWORK

The Children Act 1948 gave statutory recognition to the principle that it was the State's duty to provide for children in need (and not merely, as had been the case under the old law, for children who were in need because they were destitute). But the fact that the administrative machinery which the Act created made the care of such children the concern of professional social workers and that over the years practice increasingly came to be seen as a matter for professional expertise[102] exposed some tensions between what was recognised as good social work on the one hand and a legal system which in part continued to reflect the values of an earlier period on the other. The most obvious of those tensions was in relation to adoption, traditionally viewed by lawyers as primarily a matter of legal status rather than as a means of providing care for needy children;[103] and

---

[98] Children Act 1948, s. 2(3).

[99] *Lewisham London Borough Council v. Lewisham Juvenile Court Justices* [1980] AC 273, 307, *per* Lord Scarman; and see *per* Lord Jowitt LC, *Official Report* (HL) 10 February 1948, vol. 153, col. 918.

[100] Lord Chancellor Jowitt subsequently told the House of Lords that his experience convinced him such interference would very seldom be justified: *Official Report* (HL) 10 February 1948, vol. 153, col. 918.

[101] See SM Cretney, *Principles of Family Law* (4th ed., 1984), pp. 518–522.

[102] On the impact of the Committee's approach see 'The gestation of reform: the Children Act 1948', by RA Parker, in Philip Bean and Stuart Macpherson (eds.), *Approaches to Welfare* (1983), at p. 212; and J Heywood, *Children in Care: the development of the service for the deprived child* (3rd ed., 1978) Chapters 9 to 12 (a perceptive account of the impact of the 1948 Act on social work practice). For judicial recognition of the trend towards professionalisation of welfare, see *R v. City of Birmingham District Council, ex parte O* [1982] 2 All ER 356, 361, *per* Donaldson LJ.

[103] The 'social work' element in adoption was implicit in the recommendations of the Horsburgh Committee and the changes made by the Adoption of Children (Regulation) Act 1939. Important changes in adoption law were made by the Adoption of Children Act 1949, and by the Adoption Act 1958, but (although after 1952 there was a significant increase in the adoption of children from local authority care) neither Act saw adoption as primarily concerned with children in need. The Children Act 1975 took some steps towards a more integrated approach, but the Children Act 1989 left adoption on one side. See NV Lowe, 'English Adoption Law: Past, Present, and Future' in SN Katz, J Eekelaar and M Maclean (eds.), *Cross Currents* (2000) and generally Chapters 17 and 20.

these different approaches were evidenced by the fact that adoption law, travel-ling in a compartment of its own marked 'legal status', was departmentally the concern of a different department of state[104] from the department concerned with providing care for needy children.[105]

Helping families: preventive social work

One of the consequences of professionalising child care and recognising its prac-titioners as professionals with a specific expertise was to encourage the emer-gence of interest groups of various kinds; and it was not long before some of the pressure groups began to chafe at the restrictions of the legal system within which they had to operate. For example, although the Home Office[106] had urged local authorities to 'keep in mind the desirability of doing anything that may be possible' to rehabilitate and educate neglectful parents the Children Act 1948 did not give authorities any power to give financial help, and the extent to which they could properly employ staff in Children's Departments simply to help fam-ilies was doubtful.[107] Again, the grounds upon which a court order could be made in respect of a child neglected in its parents' home remained as formulated in 1932[108] and were thought by some inadequate.

In 1949 some of these concerns were raised in the House of Commons by Mrs Ayrton Gould[109] who claimed that local authorities were unable to act in most cases of parental neglect unless the neglect could be shown to have caused a degree of suffering such as would justify prosecution of the parent;[110] and a number of other MPs made it clear that they had absorbed the message that emotional deprivation could be as damaging for children as physical abuse. The Home Office made valiant efforts to improve the situation by encouraging greater co-ordination between voluntary agencies and local authorities;[111] but the effectiveness of these attempts was questionable.

In 1952 a Conservative MP drew a favourable place in the ballot for Private Members' Bills; and the Children and Young Persons Act 1933 was amended[112]

---

[104] The Lord Chancellor's Department (which had, in the pre-1939 period, displayed some reluc-tance to become involved in social work issues).

[105] The Home Office until 1971, and thereafter the Department of Health and Social Security.

[106] *Home Office Circular 160/1948.*

[107] *Report of the (Ingleby) Committee on Children and Young Persons* (1960, Cmnd. 1191) para. 20; see further below.

[108] The Curtis Committee had deliberately refrained from making recommendations in this area: see above. Children and Young Persons Act 1932, s. 9(1)(i) provided that the court could make an order if his parent or guardian was 'unfit to exercise care and guardianship' or was 'not exercising proper care and guardianship'; and that the child was 'falling into bad associations or [was] exposed to moral danger or [was] beyond control'.

[109] See Biographical Notes.

[110] See *Official Report* (HC) 22 July 1949, vol. 467, col. 1740.

[111] See J Heywood, *Children in Care: the development of the service for the deprived child* (3rd ed., 1978) p. 177.

[112] With the collaboration of the Home Office.

in two main[113] respects. First, the grounds upon which the court could make a 'care and protection' order were slightly extended;[114] secondly (and potentially of much greater significance) the Act placed a specific duty on the local authority to make enquiries if it received information suggesting that a child was in need of care and protection.[115]

These changes in the law did not do much to meet the demands of increasingly vocal, committed and organised social workers for wider powers to undertake preventive work. In this view, the main need was to make 'skilled help' available to prevent the breakdown of the family and the reception of children into local authority care.[116] But the Government was under pressure from other interests too. In particular, the apparent increase in juvenile delinquency (which could no longer plausibly be attributed to the disruptions of World War II) made the authorities confront the question whether the juvenile courts had been as effective as had once been believed and whether anything could be done to *prevent* juvenile offending. In 1956 the Conservative Government responded in the (at the time almost inevitable) way. The Committee on Children and Young Persons, chaired by Lord Ingleby,[117] was to inquire into the working of the law relating to juveniles brought before the courts as delinquent or as being in need of care and protection, the functioning of the juvenile courts, the remand home and approved school systems, the prevention of cruelty to children and whether local authorities should be 'given new powers and duties to prevent or forestall the suffering of children through neglect in their own homes'.

THE 1960 INGLEBY REPORT

(i) Prevention better than cure

The Ingleby Committee reported in 1960;[118] and it was immediately clear[119] that it had been strongly influenced by the belief that the problems of the delin-

---

[113] The Act also made a number of comparatively minor changes, ranging from requiring the probation service and local authority to be notified of the fact that a parent had started 'beyond control' proceedings (thereby presumably prompting the offer of help in appropriate cases) to amending the definition of 'fire' in the provision dealing with exposing children to the risk of burning so as to extend to any heating appliance: s. 8.

[114] The court was empowered to make an order if the child's parent was not exercising 'proper care and guardianship' and the child was '... ill-treated or neglected in a manner likely to cause him unnecessary suffering or injury to health': Children and Young Persons (Amendment) Act 1952, s. 1.

[115] Unless satisfied that to do so was unnecessary.

[116] J Heywood, *Children in Care: the development of the service for the deprived child* (3rd ed., 1978) pp. 179–180.

[117] See Biographical Notes.

[118] *Report of the Committee on Children and Young Persons* (1960, Cmnd. 1191) (hereafter the *Ingleby Report*).

[119] See in particular Chapter 1 of the *Ingleby Report*. This accepted that the problem of the neglected and of the delinquent child was 'more often than not the problem of the family', that the need for prevention had become 'clearer than ever', that positive action was needed to this end and

quent and deprived child were similar, and that skilled community services could prevent much damage. It was because of this belief in the potential of preventive measures that the Committee's report (in contrast to its terms of reference)[120] gave first place to a lengthy consideration of the need for local authorities to have new powers and duties to prevent or forestall the suffering of children through neglect in their own homes. The *Ingleby Report*, noting that there was a 'certain amount of inter-departmental rivalry' in this field,[121] concluded that something could be achieved by improved administration and co-ordination of services; and that to this end all local authorities should be obliged by statute to submit for ministerial approval schemes for the prevention of suffering of children through neglect in their own homes.[122] But in terms of impact on the delivery of social service effort the Committee's most important recommendation was that local authorities should have a general duty to prevent or forestall the suffering of children through neglect in their own homes and should therefore have power not only to do preventive case work but also to provide in 'cash or kind' for material needs that could not be met from other sources.[123]

(ii) A sceptical approach to the role of the juvenile court

The Committee immediately identified the ambiguities inherent in the juvenile court's dual role. The historical evolution of the courts' jurisdiction (and espe-

---

that 'everything within reason' should be done to ensure 'not only that children are not neglected but that they get the best upbringing possible'. The Committee considered that whilst the primary responsibility for children belonged to the parents—it was often the parents as much as the child who needed to alter their ways, and that the State's principal duty was 'to assist the family in carrying out its proper functions'. Whilst the 'element of compulsion' could not be altogether eliminated the 'first and main line of defence' was the provision of positive measures for prevention and the building up of community services. If, in a particular instance, those measures failed it would 'always be possible to fall back on legal sanctions but the more effective and successful the social services become, the less often will it be necessary to bring either parents or child before the court'.

[120] See above.
[121] The Committee noted a tendency for the agency which first made contact with a family at risk to continue to deal with the case for as long as possible, rather than calling in further help: *Ingleby Report*, para. 37.
[122] The Committee noted that 'it should be made clear to which government department a local authority should look for advice or approval on matters of co-ordination': *Ingleby Report*, para. 51. There was influential pressure for reorganisation of the various services concerned with the family into a 'unified family service' and the Committee accepted that this would 'possibly' be the long-term solution, and (whilst accepting that such a proposal was 'well outside' its terms of reference) urged the importance of 'further study by the Government and by the local interests involved': para. 47. It seems the Committee was impressed by the activities of Family Service Units operating from centres conveniently placed to the areas in which they worked and making a 'concentrated attack on a family's problems by frequent, sometimes daily visits, manual and domestic help in the home, help with the children and assistance with material needs (furniture and other necessities), always with the underlying intention, through persuasion and education, of encouraging people to help themselves, with any necessary aid from other local social services': para. 30.
[123] *Ingleby Report*, para. 48. The Committee had identified the inability to provide 'help in cash or kind' as one of the impediments to the development of preventive social work, and this phrase was adopted in the Children and Young Persons Act 1963: see below.

cially the statutory directive introduced in 1932 that the court should have regard to the child's welfare) had been

'to produce a jurisdiction that rests, at least in appearance, on principles that are hardly consistent. The court remains a criminal court in the sense that it is a magistrates' court, that it is principally concerned with trying offences, that its procedure is a modified form of ordinary criminal procedure and that, with a few special provisions, it is governed by the law of evidence in criminal cases. Yet the requirement to have regard to the welfare of the child, and the various ways in which the court may deal with an offender, suggest a jurisdiction that is not criminal. It is not easy to see how the two principles can be reconciled: criminal responsibility is focussed on an allegation about some particular act isolated from the character and needs of the defendant, whereas welfare depends on a complex of personal, family and social considerations'.[124]

The Committee favoured retaining the basic principle that the court should have no power to intervene unless 'specific and definable matters [were] alleged and . . . adequately proved';[125] and it firmly rejected suggestions that the juvenile court should be replaced by some alternative non-judicial or quasi-judicial tribunal.[126] Yet members of the Committee clearly had some sympathy with those who wanted the courts to have an avowedly welfarist role, whether the child was alleged to have committed an offence or merely to be in need of care and protection; and the outcome was the unanimous acceptance of a compromise: the age of criminal responsibility should be raised to 12 (and possibly to 13 or 14 at some future date) and children under 12 who committed offences[127] should be brought to court as 'being in need of protection or discipline'.[128] The Committee thought that in this way the juvenile court would move 'still further away' from the notion that it was considered an essentially criminal jurisdiction.[129]

But what should be the 'specific and definable matters' proof of which was to be necessary to justify the court's intervention? It was easy enough if the child had acted in a manner which would render an older person guilty of a criminal offence, but what of the neglected or deprived child who had done no wrong? The Committee was told that under the existing law[130] 'some children who would be the better for treatment of the kind that the juvenile court could prescribe' were deprived of it;[131] and the Committee agreed that the 1933 definition

---

[124] *Ingleby Report*, para. 60.

[125] The *Ingleby Report* insisted that this was 'essential if State intervention is to be fitted into our general system of government and be acceptable to the community': para. 66.

[126] *Ingleby Report*, para. 77. (The cynical may note how well represented were the magistrates' courts on the Committee, which did however make a number of proposals about the constitution and procedure of the courts: see *Ingleby Report*, pp. 156–159.)

[127] As well as children of whatever age said to be in need of care and control or beyond the control of their parents.

[128] *Ingleby Report*, paras. 83–86.   [129] *Ibid.*, para. 77.

[130] Ie as set out in Children and Young Persons Act 1933, s. 61(1).

[131] Eg because although it could be established that the parents were not caring adequately for a very young child there was no evidence that the child was falling into bad associations etc. as the 1933 Act required.

of 'care and protection' was 'too restrictive'.[132] But it rejected the argument that parental unfitness should of itself justify court intervention: many children of unfit parents were capable of looking after themselves.[133] The Committee's solution was that the court be required to satisfy itself, first that the child was exposed to physical, mental or moral danger or was in need of control, and secondly that the child needed 'care, protection, treatment, control or discipline' which was 'likely to be rejected or unobtainable except by order of the court'.[134]

In this way the Ingleby Committee tried to compromise between the two perhaps irreconcilable positions in what became known as the 'deprived or depraved' debate. Like many compromises its Report satisfied few of those interested in the subject: the distinguished social scientist Barbara Wootton,[135] for example, denounced[136] the Committee's failure to recommend a 'bold and imaginative reconstruction of the whole system' for dealing with young people in trouble or need and its preference for 'minor reforms in a system . . . already outmoded'. Harold Macmillan's Conservative Government had (in this view) an even dimmer vision; and the Children and Young Persons Act 1963 appeared (notably in its refusal to accept any reduction in the age of criminal responsibility) to be a timid measure. The Act did, however, seek to meet the difficulty identified by Ingleby that the grounds for making a 'care and protection' order were too narrow. It did this, not by following the recommendation of the Committee, but by reformulating the dual criterion. The first question was intended to be purely objective:[137] was the child in fact not receiving 'such care, protection and guidance as a good parent' might 'reasonably be expected to give'; and the parent's culpability was no longer to be relevant in answering this question. The second question was whether the child was in fact being damaged or at risk in certain specified (but broadly defined)[138] ways. Thus, the court would have no power to remove a self-reliant child from its neglectful parents; but it would have power over the child prostitute. In this way, the Act achieved a modest change of emphasis.

---

[132] *Ingleby Report*, Appendix III, para. 3.

[133] Conversely the Committee refused to accept that a parent should be at risk of losing custody of a child because (for example) the child was engaging in prostitution unless there was also evidence of parental neglect or irresponsibility: *Ingleby Report*, Appendix III, para. 3.

[134] *Ingleby Report*, para. 86. The Committee thought that such a definition would avoid the need to refer expressly to the *parent's* not having provided care, but whether this is consistent with the Committee's concerns (see above) about unfairness to a parent anxious and willing to exercise responsibility but unable to do so perhaps because of the child's intransigence is not clear.

[135] See Biographical Notes.

[136] Speaking in the House of Lords debate on the Bill for the Children and Young Persons Act 1963: *Official Report* (HL) 20 November 1962, vol. 244, col. 803.

[137] Children and Young Persons Act 1963, s. 2(1)(a).

[138] For example, that the lack of 'care, protection or guidance' was likely to cause him unnecessary suffering or seriously to affect his health or proper development: Children and Young Persons Act 1963, s. 2(2)(b). Other secondary conditions mirrored the existing provisions relating to the child falling into bad associations, being exposed to moral danger, and so on: Children and Young Persons Act 1963, s. 2(2)(a)(c)(d) and (e).

The Children and Young Persons Act 1963 also (symbolically at least) emphasised the move towards regarding issues of family life as being a matter for
professional social work judgment rather than parental decision:[139] it abolished
the right of a parent or guardian to bring his child before the court on the ground
that the parent was unable to control him, but substituted a provision whereby
the parent or guardian could formally request the local authority to take proceedings on that ground. If the local authority did not do so[140] the parent or
guardian was to have a right of appeal to the juvenile court. The situations in
which a local authority could by administrative action assume parental rights
over a child in its care were also extended in a number of minor respects.[141]

In respect of the role of the courts, therefore, the 1963 Act was not of great
significance. In contrast, the Government's acceptance of Ingleby's recommendation for focussing on preventive work marked a breakthrough for the social
services; and s. 1 of the Children and Young Persons Act 1963 imposed a specific
duty on local authorities to

'make available such advice, guidance and assistance as may promote the welfare of children by diminishing the need to receive children into or keep them in care . . . or to bring
children before a juvenile court . . .'.

The Act went further. Borrowing the words of the *Ingleby Report* it gave local
authorities power to give such assistance 'in kind or, in exceptional circumstances, in cash'. This provision was both wide and flexible. The Home Office
Minister[142] introducing the Bill said that this would enable local authorities to
undertake extensive social case work, give or lend basic household equipment,
or even pay the travelling expenses of a relative to care for the family whilst a
parent was in hospital; and that the Bill would encourage local authorities to
work in partnership with voluntary agencies (such as the Family Service Units[143]
or Save the Children Fund). It appears that these expectations were more than
fulfilled: in 1967 nearly 110,000 applications or referrals calling for action or
investigation involving nearly a quarter of a million children were made to children's departments; and two years later the figures were 136,000 and 308,000
respectively.[144] The amount disbursed in 'exceptional circumstances' cash
grants (mostly, it seems, spent on help with fuel debts and payment of rent and

[139] But the Government refused to give effect to Ingleby's recommendation (*Ingleby Report*,
para. 88) that the NSPCC should no longer have the right to initiate care and protection proceedings.
[140] Children and Young Persons Act 1963, s. 3.
[141] For the purposes of Children Act 1948, s. 2(1) a child in the care of a local authority could be
deemed to have been abandoned if the whereabouts of the parents remained unknown; and a parent suffering from mental disorder could be deemed unfit to have the care of the child, as could a
parent who had persistently failed to discharge his parental obligations: Children and Young
Persons Act 1963, s. 48.
[142] Earl Jellicoe, *Official Report* (HL) 20 November 1962, vol. 244, col. 803.
[143] See note 122, above.
[144] *Report on the Work of the Children's Department*, Home Office (1970) paras. 11–12. (The
figures have been rounded.)

rate arrears)[145] was £88,000 in 1965–6 and £261,000 three years later;[146] and (largely because of the volume of preventive work) the number of child care officers employed in children's departments rose from 2,341 in 1966 to 3,082 in 1969.[147] It can be assumed that much suffering was mitigated in this way, but it is less clear that there was any significant reduction in the number of children received into local authority care.[148] Moreover, there remained doubt and confusion,[149] no doubt inevitable in a situation where so much was left to local discretion particularly about the giving of financial assistance.[150] But although the 1963 Act did not go anything like as far as some (including those social workers and others who had begun to have 'profound misgivings about the nature of society and about its so-called progress after the setting up of the welfare state')[151] would have wished, its impact was considerable.

THE RADICAL DAWN 1965: FAMILY COUNCILS, FAMILY SERVICES AND THE
TRIUMPH OF SOCIAL WORK PROFESSIONALISM?

The return of a Labour Government in 1964 engendered expectations of a much more radical approach to social issues. The publication in that year of the report of a group chaired by Lord Longford[152] (*Crime—A Challenge to us All*) was at first strongly influential in government circles. In 1965, the Government published a White Paper, *The Child, the Family and the Young Offender*[153] which accepted both the need for a comprehensive 'family service' and the principle that the future of young people (whether classified as offenders or as needing care and protection) should be removed so far as possible from the courts and instead entrusted to 'family councils' charged with bringing about an agreement on the best arrangements to be made. Only if the family council failed would a court be involved and then it would be a 'family court'.

But it soon became clear that these proposals were far in advance of what public opinion would accept; and in 1968 the Government published a second

---

[145] *Social Services for Children in England and Wales 1973–75* (HC 68, 1976) pp. 25–26.

[146] *Ibid.*

[147] *Report on the Work of the Children's Department*, Home Office (1970) paras. 13, 43.

[148] The Home Office *Report on the Work of the Children's Department*, Home Office (1970) para. 13 rather lamely states that the development of preventive work, whilst not leading to a reduction in the proportion of the child population in care 'was no doubt one of the factors operating to prevent an increase' over the period 1967 to 1969.

[149] Reflected in case law: *Attorney General ex rel Tilley v. Wandsworth LBC* (1980) 78 LGR 677; *R v. Local Commissioner for Administration . . . ex parte Bradford Metropolitan City Council* [1977] 2 QB 287.

[150] The *Report of the Committee on One-Parent Families* (1974, Cmnd. 5629) para. 8.24 gives an illuminating and sympathetic account of the operation of these provisions in the context of single parent families.

[151] J Heywood, *Children in Care: the development of the service for the deprived child* (3rd ed., 1978) p. 196 (this passage gives a remarkably vivid impression of the mood of the 'angry young man' generation of the 1960s).

[152] See Biographical Notes.   [153] Cmnd. 2742.

White Paper, *Children in Trouble*.[154] This claimed that the 'objectives and strategy' of the earlier document had been 'widely welcomed' but also admitted that there had been less agreement about the machinery whereby those objectives might be attained, and especially about the proposals to establish family councils in place of juvenile courts.[155] On that point, the Government backed down completely: juvenile courts were to be retained. But the prosecution of children under 14 was to cease. The statutory criteria for making 'care and protection' orders were to be amended to include the fact that the child had committed an offence[156] so that although action would wherever possible be taken on a voluntary basis, if need be a troublesome child could be taken before a juvenile court as a 'care and protection' case.

Finally the Government decided on a further shift in decision-taking away from the courts and towards the local authority social services departments. No longer would the courts have power to commit delinquents or others to approved schools. Instead, any order for the compulsory removal of a child from home was to take the form of a 'care order', ie the committal of the child to the care of the local authority.[157] In this way, the treatment of delinquency was to be made 'a matter of professional expertise by the child care workers, who were to concentrate on the family deprivation rather than the delinquency'.[158]

THE COLD LIGHT OF DAY: 1970

The Children and Young Persons Act 1969 was enacted[159] to give effect to the policies summarised above. But before the key provisions dealing with delinquency had been brought into force the Labour Government was defeated at a General Election;[160] and the incoming Conservative Government soon decided to abandon the policy of using 'care' proceedings in respect of young offenders. The technique adopted was simply to refrain from bringing the relevant provisions of the 1969 Act into force. Prosecution continued to be the usual way of dealing with delinquent children brought to court; and the last 30 years of the twentieth century saw the notion of regarding the youthful offender primarily as a victim of adverse circumstances rejected as sentimental nonsense.[161] The

---

[154] Cmnd. 3601.

[155] *Children in Trouble* (1968, Cmnd. 3601) para. 1.

[156] It was also intended to make what was described as a 'minor change' to the criteria for finding a child to be in need of care and protection: *Children in Trouble* (1968, Cmnd. 3601) para. 14 and Appendix B, para. 5: see further below. In fact the changes effected by the Children and Young Persons Act 1969 were substantial: see below.

[157] *Children in Trouble* (1968, Cmnd. 3601) para. 20.

[158] J Heywood, *Children in Care: the development of the service for the deprived child* (3rd edn., 1978) p. 198.

[159] For the Act's provisions, see p. 695, below.   [160] 18 June 1970.

[161] For the evolution of policy, see A Ashworth, *Sentencing and Criminal Justice* (3rd ed., 2000) Chapter 12.

principal aim of the youth justice system (as defined by the Crime and Disorder Act 1998)[162] became to prevent offending and this was often[163] done by avowedly punitive means rather than by 'treating' the delinquent. In this way, the assumptions which had influenced the development of policy for the 60 years since 1908 were decisively rejected. After the changes made by the Children Act 1989 and the Criminal Justice Act 1991 the court structure reflected this: delinquents charged with an offence[164] were dealt with by magistrates sitting in a so-called 'youth court'[165] whilst children whose welfare were thought to require court sanctioned action by the local authority would have their case considered by a 'family proceedings court'.[166] The remaining part of this book also reflects this change: it does not seek to deal with the way in which the law deals with children who have committed offences.

[162] s. 37(1).

[163] But there are procedures (such as providing for formal reprimands and warnings: s. 65(1)) intended to keep young people out of the penal system, whilst the youth court has at its disposal a wide range of non-custodial orders (including, for example, an order that the offender make reparations to the victim: s. 67). Significant reductions in the number of juveniles sentenced to custody were recorded in the 1980s; and the Youth Justice Board (established by the Crime and Disorder Act 1998) to promote good practice is committed to reducing the number of custodial disposals.

[164] An important qualification: in 1992 no less than 91% of boys and 97% of girls aged 10 to 14 were cautioned rather than prosecuted. But subsequently there was some reduction in the proportion of offenders cautioned.

[165] Criminal Justice Act 1991, s. 70 provides that juvenile courts should be renamed in this way.

[166] Children Act 1989, s. 92: see below, p. 766.

20

The State, Parent and Child: (3) Child Care Legislation at a Time of Transition, 1969–1989

THE CHILDREN AND YOUNG PERSONS ACT 1969: THE LEGACY OF IDEOLOGICAL CONFUSION

The 1969 Act had been intended to provide a comprehensive code apt to deal with all children, whether delinquent or in need of care and protection. The court had first to be satisfied that any one of a number of primary conditions was proved. If so, the court could make a care order[1] if (but only if) it was satisfied that the child was in need of care and control which he was unlikely to receive unless the court did exercise its powers. The primary conditions[2] were in part modelled on the provisions of the amended Children and Young Persons Act 1933[3] but some were new;[4] and broadly the 1969 Act can be seen as extending the circumstances in which the court could take action. However, the Act stopped short of empowering the court to make an order simply because the child was at risk of harm[5] much less on the ground that it would be in the child's interests to make an order.[6]

The Conservative Government's decision to retain prosecution of young delinquents[7] had consequences for the law governing the treatment of other

---

[1] Or certain other orders (including a so-called supervision order): Children and Young Persons Act 1969 (hereafter 'C&YPA 1969') s. 1(3).

[2] The primary conditions were (a) that the child's 'proper development is being avoidably prevented or neglected or his health is being avoidably impaired or neglected or he is being ill-treated; (b) it is probable that the condition set out [in (a) above] will be satisfied in his case, having regard to the fact that the court . . . has found that that condition is or was satisfied in the case of another child . . . who is or was a member of the household to which he belongs; (c) he is exposed to moral danger; (d) he is beyond the control of his parent or guardian'; (e) he is not receiving efficient full time education; (f) he is guilty of an offence, excluding homicide. Comparison with the grounds as formulated in 1932 (even as widened in 1963) suggests a shift towards protecting not only the child who has been harmed but the child who is at risk (see eg grounds (b) and (c)) but in fact this appearance is misleading: see below.

[3] s. 62(1).

[4] The reformulation of the grounds upon which the court could make an order was in fact somewhat more extensive than might have been anticipated from the indication of minor change given in the White Paper *Children in Trouble* (1968, Cmnd. 3601).

[5] *Essex County Council v. TLR and KBR* (1978) 9 Fam Law 208.

[6] *Re D (A Minor) (Justices' Decision: Review)* [1977] Fam 158, 163.

[7] The means by which the Conservative Government's decision to abandon this policy was simple and apparently ingenious: the provisions of the Act prohibiting the institution of criminal

children in need which may not have been appreciated at the time. In essence, the difficulty was that the draftsman's assumption that care proceedings would replace prosecution was reflected in the structure and drafting of the legislation; and the consequences were sometimes unfortunate for the child victim (however appropriate the policy might have been in its application to the delinquent). For example, it was assumed that the child accused of delinquency would still be entitled to be protected by strict rules of evidence and a high standard of proof was required. Little thought seems to have been given to the fact that the application of those same principles to the child at risk could easily put him further at risk. Again, the fact that the Act was drafted in terms of *the child* being brought before the court—the natural way of dealing with someone accused of an offence—could have unfortunate consequences where the child was a victim and not the offender. For example, only the child was given the right of appeal, and he could only appeal against the *making* of an order. Nobody accused of crime would want a right to appeal against an acquittal; but it did not seem to have been appreciated that a child might well be advised to appeal against a refusal to make a care order founded on his parents' failings. Again, in many cases in reality the contest was between the local authority and the parents, yet the rules did not reflect that fact. Finally, in practice the legal process contemplated by the Act seemed to be largely accusatorial and thus inapt to provide the objective examination of all the facts which was really needed; whilst the legislation seemed to sanction the view that the court should return a child to its birth parent once the court was satisfied that the parent was fit unless return could clearly be shown not to be in the child's best interests.[8]

The accusation that the 1969 Act failed adequately to protect children at risk seemed to be supported by the facts of the Maria Colwell case in 1973.

Maria Colwell was the youngest of the five children of her mother's first marriage. After her husband's death, the mother 'went completely to pieces', and the children were frequently left alone and were found to be neglected and dirty. Maria was cared for by her sister-in-law for some years, but in 1966 her mother (who had married an 'Irishman with quite a wild reputation') removed her. The local authority obtained a care order in 1966 but allowed Maria to remain with the sister-in-law. The authority believed that it was inevitable that sooner or later the court would order that she be returned to her mother whose circumstances seemed to have improved; and the social workers tried to build up contact between Maria and the mother notwithstanding the fact that Maria physically resisted their attempts. The mother was advised by her solicitor to make an application to revoke the care order. This forced the hand of the local

proceedings against those aged 14 or less were simply not brought into force. The provision of the Act whereby commission of a criminal offence (other than homicide) satisfied one of the primary conditions for the making of a care order did come into force; but in practice was rarely used.

[8] *Report of the Committee of Enquiry into the Care and Supervision provided in Relation to Maria Colwell* (Chairman, TG Field-Fisher QC, 1974) para. 42 (hereafter cited as the *Maria Colwell Inquiry*).

authority: a social worker made a report to the court which did say that the authority's decision not to oppose the discharge of the care order but to accept a supervision order in its place had been neither easy nor clear cut but did not indicate the extent of the concern. The sister-in-law was not informed about the hearing of the mother's application which she would have opposed had she been able to do so. No one spoke for Maria. There was therefore no probing of the case which went through 'virtually on the nod'.[9] Maria was returned to her home; and the supervision which should have taken place was ineffective. Her step-father killed her. Had the court been fully informed the outcome might have been different.[10] The 'accusatorial' tradition of magisterial justice was made to appear quite inapt to protect children at risk of harm.[11]

This case provoked a 'highly emotional and angry' public reaction.[12] It seemed to demonstrate that the law failed to protect children in danger. But equally, from a different perspective, the law seemed to be unfair to parents who were at risk of having their child taken away from them. In particular, local authorities could (and increasingly did) invoke the inherent wardship jurisdiction of the High Court[13] to remove a child believed to be at risk and on such an application the court would be guided simply by the question of what would best promote the child's welfare.[14] Judges sometimes urged local authorities to use wardship precisely to avoid having to 'take unpleasant awkward decisions themselves'—decisions which could cause 'great pain and anguish'.[15] There were even cases in which local authorities, failing to make out their case for a care order in the juvenile court, simply applied to the High Court to ward the child. This procedure may well have been effective in assessing risk rather than allocating blame but could hardly seem fair to the parents.[16] Moreover, once a juvenile court had made a care order the local authority seemed to have virtually unrestricted and unchallengeable powers to decide on how the child should be treated (and, crucially, on what contact the parents should be allowed). These grievances, as we shall see, did not go away.

[9] *Maria Colwell Inquiry*, para. 226.

[10] If the mother's application had been opposed there would have been 'a very full hearing with evidence and argument on both sides and the Court would have made its decision after every possible point had been taken and fully canvassed' and the local authority would itself have sought out evidence of risk (which would probably have been forthcoming): *Maria Colwell Inquiry*, para. 226.

[11] *Maria Colwell Inquiry*, para. 241.

[12] The view that care proceedings were essentially non-adversarial, non-party proceedings (see Lord Widgery CJ, *Humberside County Council v. DPR* [1977] 1 WLR 1251, 1254) was not easy to reconcile with the rules.

[13] See Chapter 16, above.

[14] The Family Law Reform Act 1969, s. 7(2) gave the court an express statutory power to commit a ward to the care of a local authority if there were exceptional circumstances making it impracticable or undesirable for the ward to continue to be under the care of any individual: see NV Lowe and RAH White, *Wards of Court* (1979) p. 87 ff. and Chapter 11.

[15] *Re Y (A Minor) (child in care: access)* [1976] Fam 125, 138; and see *Re B (a minor) (wardship: child in care)* [1975] Fam 36, 44.

[16] *Re D (a minor) (justices' decision: review)* [1977] Fam 158; *Re C (a minor) (justices' decision: review)* (1979) 2 FLR 62.

THE ORGANISATION OF SOCIAL SERVICES FOR CHILDREN:
PERSONAL INVOLVEMENT AS AGAINST RESOURCE MANAGEMENT

The Children and Young Persons Act 1969 may, in the emasculated form in which it was brought into force, have embodied an ambiguous approach to the relationship between the State and the family; but there was nothing ambiguous about the provisions of the Local Authority Social Services Act 1970 which came to govern the provision of social work services. It had been fundamental to the *Curtis Report* that the State should provide care for children in need through the medium of identifiable individuals dedicated to the welfare of those whose interests they served; and over the years children's officers acquired a status comparing favourably with any other social service professional.[17] But the increasing professionalisation of social work was one of the factors which brought about a change of approach. No longer would anyone claim that 'a good character and a little domestic experience'[18] was sufficient qualification (at least for residential care staff). The need for training in what had become a complex discipline became well understood; and it was increasingly appreciated that ensuring children received the most appropriate form of help available from the social services was much more difficult than had been appreciated by the *Curtis Report* in the immediate aftermath of World War II.

In 1968 the Report of the (Seebohm) Committee on *Local Authority and Allied Personal Social Services*[19] flatly rejected the assumption underlying the 1948 Act that catering for the needs of the elderly on the one hand and children on the other were fundamentally different tasks and that accordingly organisationally distinct structures were necessary to ensure proper arrangements for such different groups.[20] The Seebohm Committee recommended the creation of a new local authority department, providing a community based and family oriented service available to all; and the Local Authority Social Services Act 1970 gave effect to this philosophy. The Act provided for the unification under one committee and one chief officer of the social services responsibilities previously divided between children's, welfare and health services; and accordingly children's committees and children's officers were supplanted by Social Services Committees and the specialist children's officer and boarding out officer by the generic social worker.[21] The day of the children's officer, with a personal knowledge of all her charges, was unceremoniously despatched into history.

---

[17] This is the assessment made in the far from uncritical analysis by JAG Griffith, *Central Departments and Local Authorities* (1966) pp. 430–431.

[18] As Lord Listowel put it: *Official Report* (HL) 12 December 1946, vol. 144, col. 905.

[19] 1968, Cmnd. 3703.

[20] *The Break Up of the Poor Law and the Care of Children and Old People* (PRO MH102/1378) para. 20.

[21] But the reorganisation did not resolve all the administrative problems of catering for families in need, not least because housing decisions were not within the remit of the social services committee: see *R. v. Northavon District Council, ex parte Smith* [1994] 2 AC 402, HL.

The Seebohm Committee also recommended that a single Central Government department should be responsible for providing the overall national planning of social services, social intelligence and social research;[22] and it was axiomatic that Central Government should play a decisive role in deciding policy and that it should assume responsibility for ensuring the availability of trained personnel.[23] The Committee's approach was consistent with both the 1964–1970 Wilson Labour Governments'[24] belief in the planned economy and with the business inspired management philosophy of the 1970–1974 Heath Conservative administration.[25] It was clear that the Ministry of Health was in a strong position to claim responsibility for the social services,[26] and (notwithstanding a determined fight by Wilson's Home Secretary, James Callaghan[27] to preserve the Home Office Children's Department) those functions were transferred to the enlarged Department of Health and Social Security in 1971. Subsequent experience refutes the post-World War II Home Office fears that child-related work would be given low priority in so large a department. On the other hand, it seems that the implications at the local level of the extensive reorganisation recommended by Seebohm were not fully appreciated. Many social

---

[22] *Seebohm Report*, para. 637.   [23] *Seebohm Report*, paras. 646–647.

[24] The Local Authority Social Services Act 1970 was rushed through its final parliamentary stages because of Prime Minister Harold Wilson's decision to call an election on 18 June 1970. Royal Assent was given on 29 May 1970, the day on which Parliament was dissolved.

[25] The White Paper *The Reorganisation of Central Government* (1970, Cmnd. 4506) took as its starting point the belief that Government had been 'attempting to do too much', asserted that the outcome of the review would be 'less government, and better government carried out by fewer people', and adopted the principle that functions should be grouped together in departments with a wide span, so as to provide a series of fields of unified policy. Consistently with this approach, it considered that the 'effective development of a new, broadly based service to deal with family needs in accordance with the objectives of the Seebohm Committee [already being carried out at local level under the provisions of the Local Authority Social Services Act 1970] calls for the support, encouragement and guidance of a single minister'; and concluded that the Home Secretary's child care responsibilities should be transferred to the Secretary of State for Social Services (although the Home Secretary was to retain his existing responsibilities in relation to the juvenile courts and the problems of juvenile delinquency 'since these are integral to his overriding responsibility for protecting the public and ensuring the rights and liberties of the individual': para. 35).

[26] A full account of the negotiations, making use of documents not yet in the public domain, is given by C Webster, in the official history of *The Health Services since the War* Vol. 2 (1996) pp. 304–310. Reference may also be made to P Hall, *Reforming the Welfare. The politics of change in the Personal Social Services* (1976) and J Cooper, *The Creation of the British Personal Social Services 1962–1974* (1983).

[27] Callaghan not only got an undertaking from Wilson that the Children's Department would not be transferred so long as Callaghan remained Home Secretary (RHS Crossman, *The Diaries of a Cabinet Minister, Vol. 3, Secretary of State for Social Services, 1968–1970* (1977) pp. 147, 150, 160, 553) but also subsequently made 'private representations' (unsuccessfully) to R Maudling, his Conservative successor at the Home Office: see J Callaghan, *Time and Chance* (1987) p. 235. Callaghan (whose views on this issue were shared by the long-serving Permanent Under-Secretary of State Sir P Allen) wrote that 'After many years spent building up one of the best services of its kind, the work has to my everlasting regret been swallowed up by the Department of Health and Social Security. One of the brightest jewels in the Home Office crown is now submerged in the general work of the DHSS, without any improvement that I can detect' (see 'Cumber and Variableness' in *The Home Office, Perspectives on Policy and Administration, Bicentenary Lectures 1982*, Royal Institute of Public Administration (1982) pp. 10, 24, 33).

service departments suffered chronic overload; and this caused practical difficulties over the years ahead. It is at least arguable that the children's officers appointed under the 1948 Act were able better to protect the welfare of individual children than the social work teams created after 1970.[28]

THE WANING OF PARENTAL RIGHTS

The 1948 Act had been careful to protect the legal rights of parents: they were to be entitled to allow children to take advantage of the child care service without running the risk that their child would be taken from them. For this reason, the 1948 Act had provided that nothing in the provision imposing the duty to *receive* needy children into care was to authorise a local authority to *keep* a child in their care if any parent or guardian wished to take over the care of the child. Indeed the Act[29] imposed a duty on the authority, in all cases where it would be consistent with the child's welfare, to 'endeavour to secure' that the care of the child be taken over by a parent or guardian or even by a relative or friend.[30]

In the late 1960s and early 1970s it began to be questioned whether this continued respect for parental rights was consistent with the protection of children's interests' and a Home Office survey[31] confirmed that the problem of parents exercising their legal right to withdraw children from care in circumstances giving rise to concern was a real one. (In a single year[32] 455 children were reclaimed by their parents against the local authority's strong advice.) Sometimes the fact that the parents were asked to contribute to their child's maintenance, sometimes their being asked to agree to adoption, and in a few cases the fact that the child had reached working age, precipitated the request; but in many cases a change in the natural family's circumstances—often a solution of the problem which led to the child being in care—accounted for the parents wishing to have their child back in their own care. Given that there were nearly 70,000 children in care at the time, this evidence might not have been thought of itself sufficient to suggest the need for urgent action to protect chil-

<hr>

[28] It seems that for many years after 1970 generic field social workers were inadequately trained in the special problems of child care: see the discussion in *A Child in Trust, The Report of the Panel of Inquiry into the Circumstances surrounding the Death of Jasmine Beckford* (London Borough of Brent, 1985), chapter 20. The Panel's chairman, Louis Blom-Cooper QC, subsequently pointed out that child deaths from abusing carers did not register as a significant problem until the Maria Colwell case (see below) and suggested that perhaps 'children's officers did at least prevent the fatalities, if not serious abuse'. Subsequent cases evidenced the lack of focus by social workers on the specialisation of child care: 'Colwell to North Wales: A Journey through Public Inquiries' by Sir L Blom-Cooper QC in *Cleveland Ten Years On* (1997) National Council for Family Proceedings.

[29] Children Act 1948, s. 1(3).

[30] Where possible, a person of the same religious persuasion as the child or at least a person who would undertake to bring the child up in the same religious persuasion: s. 1(3)(b).

[31] See *Report of the Departmental Committee on the Adoption of Children* (1972, Cmnd. 5107) (subsequently cited as the *Houghton Report*) Appendix D, para. 3.

[32] The year ended 31 March 1968: *Houghton Report*, Appendix D, para. 3.

dren against arbitrary exercise of the parental authority which the 1948 Act had been careful not to disturb. But there were other, much more powerful, factors. The press frequently ran stories of so-called 'tug-of-love' cases in which birth and foster-parents were seen to be in conflict about the upbringing of a child, and these tended to suggest that the law was too solicitous of the parents' rights. Both popular journalists and academic writers increasingly urged greater recognition of children's rights and of the claims of psychological parents—those, such as foster-parents, who had actually cared for the child—as against those of the birth parents.

In 1969 the Government had set up the Houghton Committee on the Adoption of Children.[33] The Committee was asked to interpret its terms of reference broadly and in particular to consider the position of long-term foster-parents who wanted to keep the child for whom they were caring against the will of the natural parent.[34] The Committee duly recommended that local authorities should have power to assume parental rights over any child who had been in their care for a period of three years; but this was only one of a large number of recommendations intended to create a comprehensive institutional framework giving priority to the long-term welfare of children who could not be brought up by their own parents. In particular, the *Houghton Report* highlighted the potential of legal adoption as a technique (albeit only one of the techniques) available to social work professionals as part of a comprehensive social service for children.[35] The Committee's recommendations were the basis for the Children Act 1975.

THE CHILDREN ACT 1975: THE END OF PARENTAL RIGHTS?

The *Houghton Report* was published at a time of intellectual and political ferment about the issues of child care and protection. *Beyond the Best Interests of the Child* (a book written by an American lawyer, an American child development specialist and a British child psychiatrist[36] published in 1973) was widely publicised, as was its emphasis on the need for *continuity* in children's relationships with their social (as distinct from their genetic) families. (The authors' belief in the policy of minimum State intervention in family life was less frequently noted.) Research in this country evidenced the devastating impact of family and social deprivation on children and supported the *Houghton Report's* view of adoption as a means of providing substitute families where there had

---

[33] The Committee is usually known as the Houghton Committee, in recognition of the chairmanship of Sir William Houghton (see Biographical Notes) who served until his death some eight months before the Committee (then under the chairmanship of Judge Stockdale) reported.

[34] *Houghton Report*, para. 1.

[35] See Chapter 17, above.

[36] Joseph Goldstein, of the Yale Law School; Albert J Solnit of the Child Study Unit at Yale University; and Anna Freud (a child psychiatrist practising in London; daughter of Sigmund Freud).

been a total breakdown.[37] The fact that a child who had been in the care of a local authority for six months seemed in practice to have little chance of returning to his birth parents (and that children in care often had little actual contact with their parents)[38] coupled with an increased realisation that the child's concept of time was notably different from the adult's[39] reinforced the belief in the need for what was sometimes called permanency planning.[40] Judges who had suggested that there was a 'blood tie'[41] (ie a strong instinctual link between a birth parent and the child) were subjected to withering scorn by some commentators. The Finer Committee on One-Parent Families[42] drew attention not only to the inadequacies of the contemporary court system as a framework for resolving family matters[43] but also to the need for a more co-ordinated relationship between the legal framework and the needs of families.

The reorganisation of local authority social services into social services departments managed by Directors of Social Services[44] led to considerable expansion of the numbers of those employed;[45] but field social work loads remained heavy, and the reorganisation (which coincided with a reorganisation of the structure of local government) caused a considerable upheaval.[46] It was

[37] See notably J Seglow, ML Kellmer Pringle and P Wedge, *Growing up Adopted* (1972); J Rowe and L Lambert, *Children who Wait* (1973); ML Kellmer Pringle, *The Needs of Children* (1975).

[38] J Rowe and L Lambert, *Children who Wait* (1973), Chapter 4.

[39] J Goldstein, A Freud and AJ Solnit, *Beyond the Best Interests of the Child* (1973) and see also the *Justice* report *Parental Rights and Duties and Custody Suits* (note 43 below).

[40] The *Prime Minister's Review, Adoption* (Cabinet Office, Performance and Innovation Unit, 2000) p. 15 points out that 'permanency aimed to provide children with stable homes, whether with their birth families or with substitute families. This approach included the successful use of adoption for a much wider range of children, older with more complex needs, than had previously been thought possible. The new emphasis, especially on adoption, was taken on board enthusiastically . . . in the UK'.

[41] The Court of Appeal's decision in the case of *Re W (An Infant)* [1970] 2 QB 589 (and especially the judgment of Sachs LJ) were seen as betraying an outdated approach. But subsequently the House of Lords, in judgments emphasising the significance of the child's welfare in determining whether consent to adoption had been unreasonably withheld, reversed this decision: see [1971] AC 682, HL, and note 88, below. Note also the comment of Dr Olive Stevenson in her dissenting report in the *Colwell* enquiry that the phrase 'blood tie' 'may trip off the tongues of lawyers much more readily than those of social workers. If the phrase means that an emotional relationship . . . exists simply because of consanguinity, then this is not generally accepted by social workers [who see it as much more a question] of the development in a child of a good self image and sound sense of identity': *Report of the Committee of Inquiry into the Care and Supervision Provided in Relation to Maria Colwell* (1974) para. 315.

[42] 1974, Cmnd. 5629.

[43] The 1975 report *Parental Rights and Duties and Custody Suits* by *Justice* (the British section of the International Commission of Jurists) was also influential in directing lawyers' attention to procedural and other issues arising in disputes involving children.

[44] By the Local Authority Social Services Act 1970, following the recommendations of the (Seebohm) *Report of the Committee on Local Authority and allied Personal Social Services* (1968, Cmnd. 3703).

[45] See the account of the dilemma facing the Secretary of State in A Denham and M Garnett, *Keith Joseph* (2001) pp. 212–217. For Joseph, see Biographical Notes.

[46] The Secretary of State had acknowledged that reorganisation meant that the 'average social worker . . . has inevitably less experience of child care than her predecessor in Children's Departments': Statement by Mrs Barbara Castle, 4 September 1974. See also Lord Wells-Pestell, Government spokesman on the 1975 Children Act: *Official Report (HL)* 21 January 1975, vol. 356, col. 93.

certainly not clear that the problem of bureaucratic failure of communication (which had been a theme common to the 1945 Monckton Inquiry into the O'Neill case and the Maria Colwell case nearly three decades later)[47] had disappeared with a wave of managerial wands.[48] However, the political controversy helped to raise public interest in social service issues; and the finding of the *Maria Colwell Inquiry* (published in 1974)[49] that 'the system' had failed the child in that case aroused strong public feeling.[50] The press gave the Colwell case 'prodigious exposure'[51] and even broadsheets[52] launched emotive campaigns for reform.

In November 1973 the Labour MP Dr David Owen,[53] disappointed by the failure of the (Heath) Conservative government to announce legislation implementing the Houghton Report, decided to use his favourable place in the ballot for Private Members' Bills to introduce a Bill intended to give effect to the main Houghton recommendations but also including further protection against what was coming to be called child abuse. Refusing to be bought[54] off by the offer of Government support for a 'short bill to implement the findings of' the Colwell enquiry[55] he and a team of helpers produced a 64-clause draft.[56] This was never

---

[47] As the Secretary of State said when releasing the *Colwell Report*, its 'main lesson' is to underline the 'vital need for members of all the professions concerned with the welfare of children to work together and exchange information': Statement by Mrs Barbara Castle, 4 September 1974.

[48] The view that Maria Colwell would not have been killed if all the social service and other local authority agencies had been aware of the actions of others was strongly urged by Lord Elton in the debate on the Bill for the Children Act 1975: *Official Report*, 20 February 1975, vol. 375, col. 463. But his proposal that a court dealing with a child in need should have a responsibility for notifying the police, and education and health authorities, was not well received by the Government.

[49] *Maria Colwell Inquiry*, para. 242. Two of the Committee's three members identified specific failings on the part of individuals and departments; but note that on this issue Dr Olive Stevenson (who was much more understanding of the difficulties faced by social workers in attempting to cope with an 'extraordinarily complex, rapidly changing situation') did not think a 'hierarchy of censure' appropriate, and disassociated herself from her colleagues' conclusions in this area: paras. 312–334.

[50] The actual content of the *Colwell Report* did not in fact justify the media reaction; and the *Sunday Times* noted correctly that the Report proposed little legal change. But the impact of the case and the Report on it was considerable: N Parton, *The Politics of Child Abuse* (1985) p. x records that, as a generic social worker in a social services department 'undergoing various traumas and readjustments resulting' from Seebohm and the contemporaneous reorganisation of local government, it seemed rather that social workers were being 'pilloried—particularly in the media' and asked to take responsibility for child abuse which was 'qualitatively different from anything that social workers had dealt with before. . . . There was a pervasive fear that the circumstances surrounding the death of Maria Colwell could have happened to any of us. It was as if the optimism . . . so evident at the beginning of the [1970s] was dealt a fatal blow by one dramatic event . . .'.

[51] N Parton, *The Politics of Child Abuse* (1985) p. 94; and see generally Chapter 4 for a detailed survey and analysis of press coverage at the time.

[52] The *Sunday Times* was particularly active: see Parton, *op. cit.*

[53] See Biographical Notes.

[54] Owen rightly saw that acceptance of this offer would be dangerous: 'if the Government could take the heat off reforming the law of adoption in this way, the Houghton Report could well be pigeon-holed indefinitely. Its recommendations were meant to be taken as a whole and I had become convinced that legislation should not be piecemeal': D Owen, *Time to Declare* (1992) p. 219.

[55] Presumably a Bill providing representation for the child in certain court cases. In fact the *Colwell Report* was not published until the following year.

[56] Bill No. 20, 1973/1974.

debated because the Heath Government faced with a major economic and political crisis resigned and Parliament was dissolved. Polling in the General Election (often said to have been fought on the issue whether Government or Trade Unions governed Britain) took place on the day which had been allotted to the Owen Bill's Second Reading.[57] But the draft Bill (a remarkable achievement for a Private Member without official assistance) was to form the basis for the Children Act 1975. Possibly more to the point, the publicity given to the Bill increased the pressure for Government action; and in March 1974 the incoming Labour Government announced that it intended to introduce a comprehensive Bill dealing with adoption, guardianship, and fostering of children on the basis of the *Houghton Report*.[58] Moreover, in response to the strong feelings[59] engendered by the Colwell case, the Government decided to add to the Bill provisions (said to be 'carefully circumscribed' to avoid a mere diversion of resources from field social work to lawyers) for the separate representation of children. Where there was or might be a conflict of interest in care proceedings between the child and his parents the court was to have power to order that the parent was not to be treated as representing the child, that an independent guardian ad litem[60] should do so, and in these circumstances the parents would become eligible for legal aid in order to help the presentation of their case. These provisions were to prove exceptionally significant for the future development of the family justice system.[61]

THE CHILDREN ACT 1975 ON THE STATUTE BOOK[62]

The key provision of the 1975 Act was to be found in its first section. This provided that local authorities should either provide an adoption service[63] themselves or secure that it was provided by others. The Act defined the functions of this service very broadly: it was to include the provision of accommodation for pregnant women and mothers and children, making arrangements for the plac-

---

[57] Polling started on Thursday 28 February 1974.

[58] See the Queen's Speech: *Official Report* (HL) 12 March 1974, vol. 350, col. 10.

[59] The Lord Chancellor, Elwyn Jones, introducing the Bill for the Children Act 1975, said that the case had 'shocked the nation': *Official Report* (HL) 21 January 1975, vol. 356, col. 17.

[60] The Act provided for Panels of Independent Guardians to be established in accordance with Regulations.

[61] But at the time there was strong pressure for a far greater measure of separate representation for the child in legal proceedings affecting its future: see eg the article by M Kellmer Pringle, *The Observer*, 19 January 1975.

[62] The Act was not a codifying measure; but the draftsman—apparently almost as an afterthought—inserted provisions seeking to 'explain' the concepts (such as 'the parental rights and duties' and 'legal custody') not only in the Children Act 1975 but when such terms were used in other legislation. This attempt at clarifying concepts was carried further by Children Act 1989: see below.

[63] References henceforth are to the legislation as eventually enacted. Children Act 1975, s. 1(1) defined the adoption service as a service designed to meet the needs in relation to adoption of children who have been or may be adopted, parents and guardians of such children, and persons who have adopted or may adopt a child.

ing of children and the provision of counselling about adoption for prospective adopters, birth parents, and children;[64] and the Act also required the adoption service[65] to act in conjunction with the other social services provided by local authorities, such as those relating to children in care and foster children. In this way the Act would have integrated adoption with other services relating to children in need; and the fundamental aspiration[66] was that help should 'be given in a co-ordinated manner without duplication, omission or avoidable delay'.

The 1975 Act also sought to shift the balance by giving greater prominence to the child's welfare when decisions had to be made about adoption: the legislation required courts and adoption agencies to give 'first consideration'[67] amongst all the circumstances of the case to the need to 'safeguard and promote the welfare of the child throughout his childhood', and so far as practicable ascertain the child's wishes and feelings and give 'due consideration' to them.[68] At a practical level, the Act sought to reduce the stress to parents and adopters (and also to encourage adoption being seen as a possible option even in cases in which it was known that the parents would not agree) by creating the framework for a procedure ('freeing for adoption') whereby all issues relating to parental consent to adoption would be dealt with before the child was placed for adoption.[69] In this way, no additional harm would be done to the child if the court upheld the parental refusal, whilst adopters could be more secure in the knowledge that the child placed with them was 'free' for adoption and that their plans could not be upset by a parental change of mind.

The professionalisation of the adoption process was to be underlined by prohibiting independent placements for adoption[70] and the Act also contained provisions discouraging adoption by parents, step-parents or other relatives of the child.[71] The legislation provided the statutory framework for an alternative legal institution ('custodianship') to provide legal security for those providing

[64] Children Act 1975, s. 1(2)(c).

[65] The Act envisaged that local authorities should act in conjunction with voluntary adoption agencies: s. 1(3).

[66] Children Act 1975, s. 1(3).

[67] This formulation replaced the requirement in the Bill as introduced to 'take full account' of the child's welfare: see *Official Report* (HL) vol. 356, col. 782. For an interesting account of the difficulties experienced by the draftsman in giving effect to the desired policy, see F Bennion, 'First Consideration: A Cautionary Tale' (1976) 126 New LJ 1237.

[68] A similar duty was laid on local authorities in respect of children in their care: Children Act 1975, s. 59.

[69] Children Act 1975, ss. 14–16.

[70] The Government adopted the strategy of imposing criminal sanctions for breach of the rules against non-agency placements, whilst recognising that such placements would still take place and that it might in such a case be in the child's interest to make an adoption order: see *Standing Committee A Official Report*, col. 133 (Dr David Owen). The prohibition did not extend to placements with a relative.

[71] See p. 627, above. The Act also significantly extended the 'probationary period' applicable to applications to adopt a child who (contrary to the general policy of the Act) was not placed by an agency (or a relative): Children Act 1975, s. 9. Such applications might (entirely properly) be made by foster-parents, for example, or by those who brought a child into this country and applied to adopt him here.

long-term family care for a child.[72] Not only foster-parents[73] but step-parents and relatives who might otherwise have opted for adoption were amongst those at whom this new procedure was targeted.

A foster-parents' charter?[74]

The Children Act 1975 shifted the balance against the birth parents in a number of other ways; and the new custodianship legislation was only one provision intended to give those caring for a child greater legal security as against a claim by the birth parents. First, the Act provided that once a child had been in local authority care for six months anyone wishing to remove him had to give 28 days' notice of his intention. Secondly, the grounds upon which a parental rights resolution[75] could be based were extended, notably to cover the situation in which the child had been in the care of a local authority or voluntary organisation for three years or more.[76] Thirdly, foster-parents who had cared for a child for five years and wanted to seek a permanent adoptive relationship were given a measure of protection by a new rule prohibiting the birth parents from removing the child until the court had dealt with the foster-parents' adoption application.[77] These new provisions did not please some (who thought they went too far)[78] but others thought they did not give sufficient weight to the primacy of the child's interests.[79] In practice, it was foster parents, and especially those who had cared for a child for some time, who most clearly had their legal position strengthened by the Act.

Adoption remains different

Although the 1975 Act was intended to remove obstacles to adoption and to encourage its use in long term planning for a child's future it also contained pro-

---

[72] These provisions are elaborate: see Children Act 1975, Part II. They were little used: see E Bullard and E Malos, with RA Parker, *Custodianship* (1990).

[73] The Act expanded the statutory provisions dealing with private fostering in an attempt to improve local authority control and supervision: Children Act 1975, ss. 95–97.

[74] MDA Freeman, *The Children Act 1975*; but contrast HK Bevan and ML Parry, *The Children Act 1975* (who reject criticisms of the Act as anti-parent).

[75] Ie the administrative procedure, replacing the old Poor Law Adoption, established by the Children Act 1948: see pp. 596, 679, above.

[76] Local authorities were given power to vest the parental rights in a voluntary organisation: ss. 60–62.

[77] Children Act 1975, s. 29. The Act also conferred powers to approve schemes for the payment of allowances to adopters and prospective adopters: s. 32. The provisions of Children Act 1975, ss. 56 and 57 (empowering local authorities to assume parental rights over children who had been in care for three years and restricting the parental right to remove without notice a child who had been in care for six months) were also seen as part of a strategy to make foster-parents more secure in their relationship with the child): see below.

[78] The principal concern was that parents might be reluctant to allow their children to be cared for by the local authority if their doing so could lead to the parents permanently losing the right to contact.

[79] There was a movement to extend the grounds for assuming parental rights to the situation where the child's emotional needs and development so required.

visions which emphasised the difference between adoption (which effected a change of legal status) and other procedures for dealing with the care of a child (which did not have that effect). Thus, adoption was to put the adopted child in virtually the same position as the adopters' birth child for purposes of entitlement to property.[80] In this way, the fact that adoption severed the legal relationship between the birth parent and the child was emphasised; but the legislation accepted that the genetic facts could not be altered and it had increasingly been realised that many adopted children felt a strong need to find out the truth about their origins and genetic identity. The Act therefore gave effect to the Houghton Report's recommendation that people who had been adopted should have the right of access to their original birth records.[81] These provisions—surrounded by conditions and qualifications as they were—prompted a great deal of concern, but that did not surprise those familiar with the history of the adoption agencies' concern for secrecy.[82]

Problems of implementing the Children Act 1975

Had the provisions of the 1975 Act actually been brought into force with only the delay necessary to allow appropriate administrative structures to be set up it is possible that it would have been seen as a landmark in the history of child law. But the enactment of the Children Act coincided with a period of severe economic difficulties and the Government had made it plain from the outset that those parts of the Act which involved public expenditure could only be implemented as funds became available. No less that ten years went by before the provisions relating to custodianship were brought into force on 1 December 1985; and there was an even longer delay in bringing into force the statutory requirement that local authorities secure the provision of a comprehensive adoption service. These did not become law until 1988.[83] Of course, this did not mean that practice remained unchanged. The Department of Health issued Circulars to local authorities exhorting the various agencies concerned to follow good practice; and the Department took full advantage of the power to make delegated legislation—for example, the Adoption Agencies Regulations, made in 1983, laid down very detailed procedures intended to ensure so far as possible

---

[80] In contrast to earlier moves in this direction the change attracted little comment The provisions were inserted into the Bill at its Third Reading in the House of Lords: *Official Report* (HL) 17 April 1975.

[81] This, not surprisingly, prompted much discussion and amendments were made to the text of the Bill originally introduced in an attempt to meet concerns. In particular, local authorities and others concerned were to provide counselling for adopted persons seeking information, and those adopted before 12 November 1975 were to attend a counselling interview as a condition of being given the information they sought: see the debate in *Standing Committee A, Official Report*, col. 330 and Children Act 1975, s. 26.

[82] See above, Chapter 17.

[83] Children Act 1975 and Adoption Act 1976 (Commencement No. 2) Order 1987, SI No. 1242.

that the child's interests were properly assessed and met—whilst a great deal could be and was done by purely administrative means.[84]

The decade following the enactment of the 1975 Act increased public and academic interest in child law and led to calls for further reform;[85] but at the same time the different interests tended to become polarised. As the House of Commons Social Services Committee[86] put it in 1984:

'There has recently come into discussion of child care issues a new and disturbing stridency in the advocacy of [the respective rights of the child, his parents and the state] on behalf of one group or another . . .'.

The emphasis of the 1975 Act had been on the position of the children and those who were caring for them; and it was not difficult to rouse support for birth parents faced with intervention by local authority social workers. First, once a care order had been made under the Children and Young Persons Act 1969 it seemed that the local authority was in a position to prevent a parent having any significant contact with the child; and the parent was legally powerless to do anything about it. Thus:

In *A v. Liverpool City Council* the local authority proposed restricting the mother's access to her 2½-year-old son to a supervised visit once a month to his day nursery. The House of Lords held that the child care legislation had marked out an area in which decisions about what would serve the child's welfare had been removed from the parents and from any supervision by the courts.

The consequences for the parents could be devastating. It is true that an adoption order could not be made unless the parents either gave their consent or the court dispensed with it on specified grounds.[87] But it would be open to the local authority to argue (with some prospects of success) that since the parents' contact with their child had been so limited a refusal by them to agree to the child's

---

[84] For example, the *First Report to Parliament on the Children Act 1975* (HC 268, 1979) claimed that in this way adoption was 'beginning to take its place in local authority child care services, and there is an ever increasing area of over-lap between long-term fostering and adoption'.

[85] Groups devoted to a wide range of problems affecting needy children such as the Child Poverty Action Group (founded in 1965) and Gingerbread (founded in 1970) were joined by organisations (such as the Family Rights Group, founded in 1974) the Children's Legal Centre (founded in 1981) and Kidscape (founded in 1984) with somewhat more specific interests. Other organisations (such as the British Association of Social Workers) continued to represent the views and experience of their members.

[86] *Children in Care* (Second Report from the Social Services Committee, Session 1983–84) HC 360–1 para. 15. The Committee thought that if more consideration were given to the respective *responsibilities* of those concerned the issues 'might be seen in more positive and less divisive terms'.

[87] See Chapter 17, above.

adoption was unreasonable;[88] with the result that the court would dispense with consent and the link between parent and child would be conclusively, permanently, and irrevocably severed.

Secondly, it could be argued that the parents were at a serious disadvantage when a local authority decided to apply to the court for a care order. The juvenile court might find that the authority had not established one of the grounds specified in the Children and Young Persons Act 1969; but the local authority could then invoke the wardship jurisdiction of the High Court and seek to have the child entrusted to its care simply on the ground that the child's welfare would be best served in this way. Apart from that, the fact that the child's parents were not parties to care proceedings sometimes made it difficult for them to put their side of the story as they would wish.

It was all very well for the Government to repeat that the 1975 Act did not disregard the interests of parents; but it was also compelled to admit that some parents 'understandably' felt themselves to be at a disadvantage.[89] It was easy enough for the Government to claim that the child's welfare was 'central to the thinking underlying the Act'. But local authorities, urged to plan the future of children in care 'more vigorously',[90] may have made a different assessment than did the families involved not only of how the balance between their rights and interests and those of the child should be struck but also of where the child's welfare lay. It has been said[91] that the 1975 legislation 'came to be viewed by some as unhelpfully tipping the balance away from "conciliation" with birth parents towards "confrontation"'.

It was not only parents who complained. Groups representing children in care had emerged; whilst the view that the law failed to give effect to the child's own rights as an autonomous individual began to be urged in academic and other literature.[92] The belief that establishing 'family courts' would solve

[88] See *Re W (An Infant)* [1971] AC 682, HL. This case established that a parent might properly be held unreasonable if he or she failed to give proper weight to the advantages of adoption to the child: '. . . the fact that a reasonable parent does pay regard to the welfare of his child must (said Lord Hailsham) enter into the question of reasonableness as a relevant factor. It is relevant in all cases if and to the extent that a reasonable parent would take it into account. It is decisive in those cases where a reasonable parent must so regard it.' Thus, in *Re El-G (Minors) (Wardship and Adoption)* (1982) 4 FLR 589, CA, where the mother had been struck down by 'a series of terrible blows which destroyed her health and prevented her from fulfilling her maternal role in spite of her desire to do so' the court dispensed with her agreement notwithstanding the fact that it was entirely misfortune which made it impossible for her to care for the child.

[89] The Children Act 1975, s. 105, required Ministers to report periodically to Parliament on its operation; and the Reports published in 1978 and 1984 (HC 268, 1978–79 and HC 20, 1984–5 respectively) provide much valuable information. The DHSS also commissioned research on the working of the Act: see the list in the *Second Report to Parliament on the Children Act 1975* pp. 35–37. Para. 3 of this Report is the source for the statement in the text.

[90] *Second Report to Parliament on the Children Act 1975*, para. 2.

[91] The *Prime Minister's Review, Adoption* (Cabinet Office, Performance and Innovation Unit, 2000) p. 15.

[92] MDA Freeman, *The Rights and the Wrongs of Children* (1983) was a particularly influential analysis. In the United States scholarly articles by (amongst others) Hillary Rodham (better known as Mrs—and subsequently Senator—Hillary Clinton) sought to give content to what had become a

many of the difficulties was—at least outside the Government machine—widespread.[93]

Child abuse: social work failures

Parental grievances often seemed to suggest that social workers had been given too much power; but it was the publicity given to cases in which the child care system had nevertheless failed adequately to protect children which made the greatest contribution to keeping the topic on the political agenda. The names of John George Auckland, Richard Clark, Stephen Menheniott, Darryn James Clark and Paul Steven Brown[94] should be added to those of Dennis O'Neill and Maria Colwell in any memorial to those whose sufferings created the climate of opinion requiring that something be done.

Those cases were perhaps only the most dramatic. The 1970s saw an upsurge of interest in the phenomenon of domestic violence; and in 1977 a House of Commons Select Committee[95] estimated that as many as 40,000 children each year were victims of abuse[96] causing injury. The catalyst for further reform was the Inquiry carried out by the House of Commons Social Services Committee chaired by Mrs Renee Short,[97] between 1982 and 1984 into the whole subject of children in care.[98]

The Short Inquiry did consider the substantive and procedural law, and made a number of recommendations. But historically its most important recommendation was this:

'The time has arrived—indeed it arrived some time ago—for a thorough-going review of the body of statute law, regulation and judicial decisions relating to children, with a view to the production of a simplified and coherent body of law comprehensible not only to those operating it but also to those affected by its operation. It is not just to make life easier for practitioners that the law must be sorted out; it is for the sake of justice that the legal framework of the child care system must be rationalised. Such a review goes well

slogan, and popularised the concept: see 'Children under the Law' (1973) 43 Harvard Education Journal 487.

[93] *Second Report to Parliament on the Children Act 1975*, para. 3.

[94] Official inquiries into the cases of these children were published in 1975, 1975, 1978, 1979, and 1980 respectively. The list does not purport to be complete. For a full survey (and a valiant attempt to derive lessons for professional practice from the inquiry findings) see *Child Abuse: Study of Inquiry Reports 1973–1981* (DHSS, 1981).

[95] *First Report from the Select Committee on Violence in the Family, Violence to Children*, Session 1976–77 (1977, HC 329–i) para. 24; (and see also the Government's White Paper *Response*, 'Violence to Children', 1978, Cmnd. 7123). The Committee—whose Report Proceedings and Record of Evidence cover 689 pages—discussed some aspects of the relevant legislation designed to protect children but it did not recommend any change in the substantive law.

[96] At this period interest focussed on what was called the 'battered child'; public concern about child sexual abuse seems to have developed rather later: see below.

[97] See Biographical Notes.

[98] *Second Report from the Social Services Committee, Session 1983–84, Children in Care*, Vol. 1 (HC 360-I, 1984). The Evidence given to the Committee is also published as Volumes 2 and 3 of the Report.

beyond questions of legal technicalities but falls short of a fundamental examination of family courts, which must of necessity take longer, or of child care practices as such. We consider that such a review would be best carried out under the Department [of Health's] policy direction, by a Working Party of lawyers, social work practitioners and others . . . It should work to a tight timetable, and should be expected to produce a draft codified child care law within nine months of its establishment.'

The Second Thatcher Government reacted speedily. In July 1984 it set up an Interdepartmental Working Party 'to set out options for codification and amendment of child care law'.[99]

THE 1985 REVIEW OF CHILD CARE LAW

The Group worked speedily and with great thoroughness, publishing no fewer than 12 detailed interim discussion papers and considering a mass of evidence (including specially commissioned research).[100] Its task was eased by the fact that the Government excluded the way in which the law treated juvenile offenders from the scope of the enquiry thereby, almost casually, destroying the belief (axiomatic for more than half a century in informed circles both within Government and outside it) that delinquency on the one hand and deprivation on the other were merely two sides of the same coin. The Working Party itself decided to exclude adoption from detailed consideration. This greatly simplified the Working Party's task, but at the price of reversing the progress made by the *Houghton Report* and the 1975 Act towards viewing the legal structure for children in need as a whole.

The Working Party's Report, published in October 1985,[101] contained no fewer than 223 recommendations; and the members of the Working Party—all but one[102] Civil Servants—evidently did not share the traditional reluctance of the Civil Servant to abstain from making firm and public recommendations about future policy.[103] The Government treated the Report as a Consultative Document, and in 1987 published a White Paper[104] setting out the policy which it had adopted in the light of the reactions of professional and other groups' responses to the Working Party's Report.

---

[99] See *Review of Child Care Law* (1985) para. 1.1. The *Second Report to Parliament on the Children Act 1975*, para. 6, states that the codification was to 'provide a framework for developing the best child care practice and meeting more effectively the needs of children and their families'.
[100] *Review of Child Care Law* (1985), paras. 1.4–1.5.
[101] *Review of Child Care Law* (1985).
[102] Mrs Brenda Hoggett, at the time a Law Commissioner: see Biographical Notes.
[103] The Working Party's terms of reference were to 'make proposals and set out options for codification and amendment of child care law', but very few 'options' were in fact presented.
[104] *The Law on Child Care and Family Services* (1987, Cm. 62).

The Law Commission's Review of the Private Law

At much the same time the Law Commission was carrying out a review of the law[105] allocating responsibility for caring for children to individuals (for example, parents involved in divorce proceedings or guardians). Between 1985 and 1987 the Commission published four impressive scholarly and comprehensive Working Papers as a basis for consultation;[106] and both the Working Party's *Review of Child Care Law* (to which one of the Law Commissioners[107] had been a prominent and evidently influential contributor) and the Government's response to the *Review* were available as the Commission deliberated on the recommendations for reform of the private law it would make in its final report.[108] The Commission, like the *Review* Working Party, did not consider adoption law.[109]

A bold vision: the Law Commission demonstrates the need for joined-up legislation

The Law Commission's starting point[110] was that the private law was confusing and unintelligible, but it also expressed its belief that the public law examined by the *Review* was not only 'complicated, confusing and unclear' but also in places unjust. The Commission concluded that 'consistency, clarity and simplicity' in the courts' powers could best be achieved by a single set of statutory provisions dealing with all powers to put children into local authority care; and it believed that those provisions could be combined with the provisions necessary to deal with local authority provision of services for families and children.[111] But the Commission went further than merely pointing out the desirability of change. Rather than paying excessive respect to a rigorous interpretation of its terms of reference, the Commission boldly seized what Lord Chancellor Mackay had described[112] as the 'historic opportunity to reform the English law into a single rationalised system as it applies to the care and upbringing of children' and published draft clauses for legislation giving effect not only to its own proposals for the private law relating to the upbringing of children but also to the Government's proposals for the public law dealing with

---

[105] Under Item XIX of the Law Commission's *Second Programme of Law Reform* (1968) Law Com. No. 14.

[106] *Guardianship* (1985) WP 91; *Custody* (1986) WP 96, *Care, Supervision* . . . (1987) WP 100; *Wards of court* (1987) WP 101.

[107] Mrs Brenda Hoggett: see above.

[108] *Review of Child Law Guardianship and Custody*, Law Com. No. 172, published in July 1988 and subsequently cited as the *Law Commission Review*.

[109] Notwithstanding the fact that it would have been within its programme of Law Reform: see note 104 above.

[110] *Law Commission Review*, paras. 1.2–1.3.   [111] *Law Commission Review*, para. 1.10.

[112] In the Child & Co lecture delivered on 27 April 1988 and published as *The Child and the Law: A view across the Tweed*.

State intervention in the family. This demonstrated how a complete legislative code could be achieved, and the advantages which such a code would bring.[113]

There is always strong competition for space in the Government's legislative programme, and legislation (especially legislation dealing with controversial matters, perhaps cutting across traditional party boundaries) will not be brought forward unless the case for doing so seems strong to the Government and the ruling political party. The mere fact that a body of legal experts such as the Law Commission found child law 'confusing and unclear' would of itself not seem a compelling ground for taking action. But there were other events which did have a decisive impact on the course of events.

The first was the death of a four-year-old girl, Jasmine Beckford, at her home in Kensal Rise in the London Borough of Brent (as it happened, in July 1984 as the Inter-Departmental Working Party was being established) at the hands of her step-father. Jasmine was in the care of the London Borough of Brent under a care order, but for two years prior to her death Brent had allowed her to be physically in the care of her mother and step-father. A Panel of Inquiry chaired

---

[113] *Law Commission Review*, para. 1.11. The draft Bill appended to the Review as Appendix 1 is incomplete. It was nevertheless influential in the preparation of the Bill for the Children Act 1989 even in the public law areas outside the scope of the Law Commission's Review. The Commission did not simply follow the recommendations of the *Review of Child Care Law*; but in turn the Bill which the Government introduced differed in some respects from the Commission's draft, whilst Parliament made numerous amendments, often tipping the balance in one direction or another. For example, the *Review* had recommended that a court could only make a 'care order' (a term which it did not favour: see para. 8.4) if satisfied that 'there is or is likely to be a substantial deficit in the standard of health, development or well-being that can reasonably be expected for the child; and that that deficit or likely deficit is the result either of the child not receiving or being unlikely to receive the care that a reasonable parent can be expected to provide . . .'. The Commission's draft clause provided that the court was to be satisfied 'that the child concerned has suffered significant harm, or that there is a real risk of his suffering such harm; and that the harm, or risk of harm, is attributable to . . . the standard of care given to the child, or likely to be given to the child if the order were not made, being below that which it would be reasonable to expect a parent to give to a similar child . . .'. Children Act 1989, s. 31 provides that the court must be satisfied that 'the child concerned is suffering, or is likely to suffer, significant harm; and . . . that the harm, or likelihood of harm, is attributable to . . . the care given to the child, or likely to be given to him if the order were not made, not being what it would be reasonable to expect a parent to give to him . . .'. Many points would emerge from a detailed comparison of these three versions. A few are: (i) the Law Commission's formulation of 'significant harm'—a concept itself the subject of further statutory explanation—which became one of the key concepts in the legislation; (ii) the degree of risk of harm being suffered in the future which will satisfy the criteria; (iii) the standard to be applied in deciding whether there has been a 'deficit'—that of a 'reasonable parent' or that which 'a parent' would give 'a similar child'? Such verbal niceties often reflect real issues of policy: reference may be made to J Masson, *The Children Act 1989, Text and Commentary* (1990) or R White, P Carr and N Lowe, *A Guide to the Children Act 1989* (1990) for detailed comments on the legislative text (including the parliamentary history of its various provisions) whilst textbooks on family law reveal the approaches adopted by the courts in subsequently seeking to ascertain the policy of the legislation.

by the prominent reforming lawyer Louis Blom-Cooper QC[114] was appointed to investigate. The Panel decided that the Inquiry should go beyond an examination of the events surrounding the fatality of a particular child in care and into 'some of the broader issues that provide the framework . . . of the law of child care.'[115] It heard 93 witnesses (and the 18 lawyers who represented some of them).

The Report of the Beckford Inquiry was completed in 1985 and covers more than 300 pages. It examines not only the facts of the Beckford case[116] but also considers the underlying principles governing the State's duty to protect children from abuse. The Panel stated[117]—

'. . . we have identified and isolated one fundamental aspect of professional response to child abuse that has been overlooked or discarded by modern social work training and practice. It is that the making of a Care Order invests Social Services with pervasive parental powers. By such a judicial act society expects that a child at risk of abuse from its parents will be protected by Social Services personnel exercising parental powers effectively and authoritatively on behalf of society. Such a child is a child in trust.'

The Panel made a number of detailed recommendations for the improvement of law and practice based on that premise.[118] Of these, the recommendations dealing with court procedures were of particular significance. But the *Beckford Report* (in this respect like the *O'Neill Report* 40 years previously) was perhaps of most significance not for its detailed recommendations but for the contribution it made to the climate of opinion. There was much public criticism of social workers for failing to act promptly and decisively; and more generally a feeling that something needed to be done.[119] In particular, the Report was seized on as ammunition supporting the case for a so-called family court,[120] and for a Private Member's Bill which would have required applica-

---

[114] See Biographical Notes.

[115] *A Child in Trust, The Report of the Panel of Inquiry into the Circumstances surrounding the Death of Jasmine Beckford* (London Borough of Brent, 1985) subsequently cited as *Beckford Report*.

[116] The *Beckford Report* concluded that none of the statutory agencies involved was blameless, but that it would be 'crude and simplistic' to focus exclusively on failings of the Social Service Department and of one particular social worker: p. 296. The Report does criticise the conduct of the magistrates hearing the authority's application for a care order ('From almost every point of view, the forensic process was little short of disastrous': p. 103) on the ground that they should not have seemed to give support to the view that a physically abused child would soon be returned to the care of its parents, whilst comments made by the Judge presiding at the parents' trial are also severely criticised: pp. 38–39.

[117] *Beckford Report*, p. 297 and, on the concept of the local authority as trustee, see p. 21.

[118] They are collected in the *Beckford Report*, Chapter 32.

[119] The *Beckford Report* was also influential in leading local authority social services departments to review their practices and it added impetus to the development of training programmes: see for experience in the County of Cleveland the *Report of the Inquiry into Child Abuse in Cleveland 1987* (1988, Cm. 412) para. 4.15.

[120] In December 1985 *The Times* reported that MPs were backing a Family Courts Campaign; and claimed that Louis Blom-Cooper had said the failure of the legal system in the Beckford case highlighted the need for a move towards establishing family courts.

tion to the court before a child in care under a care order could be allowed home 'on trial' to its parents.[121]

The second event which seems to have added to the pressure for 'something to be done' was the death of another four-year-old girl, Kimberley Carlile, on 8 June 1986. The immediate cause of death was a blow to the head inflicted by her step-father; but the Commission of Inquiry—again chaired by Louis Blom-Cooper QC—found that Kimberley had been 'tortured and starved for many weeks before her death'.[122] The Inquiry detected failings in the conduct of a number of those professionally involved; and made more than 50 detailed recommendations.[123] But the *Kimberley Carlile Inquiry* was especially notable for seeking to explain the reasons for the public response to cases in which a child died whilst in the care of a local authority or when social service departments seemed to have failed to protect a child from abuse or neglect:

'Verbal abuse of social workers, bordering on the hysterical, abounds in the popular press; threats of violence have not been uncommon. Social workers have not found it easy to cope with such saturating media coverage devoted to each child abuse case'.[124]

—and the Commission pointed out that

those who undermined 'the confidence and morale of the people that society is sending out in its name to protect our children should realise that what they are thereby doing is, unwittingly, to put at risk the children whom they wish devoutly to protect'.[125]

Reform of the system was necessary to make the child protection system effective in safeguarding children and providing the necessary support for those professionally involved.

In the 15 years following the death of Maria Colwell there had been more than 30 major child abuse inquiries[126] yet the subject refused to go away. It is possible that (as the *Kimberley Carlile Inquiry* suggested)[127] there had 'at last' emerged some 'glimmerings of public awareness that the problems of protecting children from abusing parents do not yield readily to simplistic situations'. But events in the North East of England in the summer of 1987 were to demonstrate the fragility of rationality in this area. They were also, however, to lead directly to legislation which could be shown to be based on a rational appraisal of the balance between the interests of children and the interests of their parents and other adults and the end of what the *Kimberley Carlile Inquiry* called the

---

[121] *The Times* reported that support for Mr Dennis Walter's Bill (which in a much amended form became the Children and Young Persons (Amendment) Act 1986: see below) had 'further increased' immediately after the publication of the *Beckford Report*.

[122] *A Child in Mind: Protection of Children in a Responsible Society (The Report of the Commission of Inquiry into the circumstances surrounding the death of Kimberley Carlile)* (London Borough of Greenwich, 1987) (subsequently cited as the *Kimberley Carlile Inquiry*) p. 209.

[123] *Kimberley Carlile Inquiry*, Chapter 34.

[124] *Ibid.*, p. 134.   [125] *Ibid.*, p. 210.

[126] *Ibid.*, p. 209; and for details see Appendix H thereto.

[127] *Kimberley Carlile Inquiry*, p. 134.

'constant pendulum-swinging' which had characterised legislative policy over the previous 30 years.

The Cleveland crisis: child sexual abuse

Three months after the London Borough of Greenwich had set up the *Kimberley Carlile Inquiry* the Government ordered a statutory enquiry,[128] to be chaired by Dame Elizabeth Butler-Sloss[129] (a Judge of the High Court, Family Division) 'to examine the arrangements for dealing with suspected cases of child abuse in Cleveland since 1 January 1987, including in particular cases of child sexual abuse, and to make recommendations'.[130] The background was that between February and July 1987 two paediatricians in Cleveland had diagnosed 121 children as the victims of sexual abuse.[131] At the height of the crisis prompted by this unprecedented rise in the diagnosis of child sexual abuse,[132] the paediatricians told the Director of Social Services that the detection of abuse was a breakthrough in the care of children and could explain many problems of child health which had not previously responded to treatment.[133] The number of cases brought to court threatened to overwhelm the system, not least because applications by the local authority were often opposed and the medical evidence hotly disputed.[134] The events of the summer brought about a 'fundamental breakdown in communication with and co-operation between' the professional disciplines involved which had impeded the proper approach to the care and protection of children in the area.[135] They also aroused deep passions[136] and prompted huge media coverage and public controversy.[137] One local Member of

[128] Under the provisions of Child Care Act 1980, s. 76 and other legislation.
[129] See Biographical Notes.
[130] *Report of the Inquiry into Child Abuse in Cleveland 1987* (1988, Cm. 412) (subsequently cited as the *Cleveland Report*), para. 4.
[131] *Cleveland Report*, para. 64.   [132] *Ibid.*, para. 2.
[133] *Ibid.*, para. 52.   [134] *Ibid.*, para. 52.
[135] *Ibid.*, para. 7.
[136] And opinion became to some extent polarised: see for example the intervention by the Labour MP Clare Short suggesting that the problem of child sexual abuse had been understated, and that 10% of children (two-thirds of them female) had been subjected to such abuse, overwhelmingly perpetrated by the father: *Official Report* (HC) 29 June 1987, vol. 118, col. 255. The basis for this belief was not stated (and see note 151, below). Ms Short also claimed it was a mistake to have a judge chairing the inquiry apparently because of the unsatisfactory record of the judiciary in such matters: *Official Report* (HC) 9 July 1987, vol. 119, col. 532.
[137] Stuart Bell, in *When Salem came to the Boro, The True Story of the Cleveland Child Abuse Crisis* (1988) p. 11, describes the background in language which vividly conveys the feelings of some of those involved: 'children who had never been abused had been taken away from their parents, siblings had followed suit, and families had been broken up. One father suffered a heart attack, a mother decided upon an abortion rather than have another child taken from her, there was one arson attack on a home, windows were smashed, one family had to be evacuated. The children's casualty ward at Middlesborough General Hospital filled up with well children and their mothers slept on campbeds or cots by their beds. The tension thus generated eventually created a near riot and hands were laid on a consultant paediatrician, who called the police. Nurses were horrified at midnight checks on their wards for sexual abuse and complained to the South Tees Health Authority. In the end, the parents, out of fear and frustration, took to the streets.' The Conservative

Parliament made allegations of serious misconduct against the paediatricians who had diagnosed sexual abuse of young children,[138] another local Member (from a different party) urged that the paediatricians concerned be suspended pending the outcome of an inquiry,[139] whilst a third local Member of Parliament[140] compared the conduct of the Social Services to that of the war-time German SS. The decision to set up an Inquiry was the least response that the Government could take[141] to the 'enormous concern' voiced by nurses, the police, Members of Parliament and others;[142] and, a decade later, it is clear that public concern about the effectiveness and fairness of the family justice system in protecting the interests of those concerned, both parents and children, was indeed justified. But whereas previous inquiries had in general provided ammunition to those critical of social workers for failing to intervene many of the complaints giving rise to the Cleveland Inquiry were of ideologically motivated and wholly unjustified intrusion by social workers into family life.

The *Cleveland Report* was in many respects unlike other child abuse inquiries. In particular, it was concerned to provide a working solution to a crisis and to restore confidence in the working of the agencies concerned with the care and protection of children; and it did not make specific findings about the truth of the allegations which had given rise to the crisis. But it was the fact that

---

MP Mrs Virginia Bottomley (subsequently to be Secretary of State for Health) may have been correct in describing the public reaction to what she believed to be a professional over-reaction as 'near hysterical' (see *Official Report* (HC) 9 July 1987, vol. 119, col. 532) but such hysteria can easily have disastrous consequences.

[138] Mr Stuart Bell, who on 29 June 1987 put a private notice question to the Secretary of State and claimed that Dr Marietta Higgs (one of the two paediatricians at the centre of the controversy) and Mrs Sue Richardson (the Social Services' Child Abuse Consultant) had 'colluded and conspired to keep the police out of allegations of sexual abuse whereby Dr Higgs made the diagnosis, a social worker made out a place of safety order and a justice of the peace signed it without the intervention of the police, other agencies or any counselling procedures or corroboration': *Official Report* (HC) 29 June 1987, vol. 118, col. 255. The *Cleveland Report* subsequently found there to be no evidence of any collusion or conspiracy between Mrs Richardson and Dr Higgs: para. 9.3.22 3(a); but one of the recommendations of the Report was to reduce the period of time for which a child could be kept from the parents without their having the opportunity to challenge the decision: see p. 252.

[139] Mr Richard Holt, Conservative Member for Langbaugh, urged the suspension of the two doctors until there had been a 'cooling off period': *Official Report* (HC) 29 June 1987, vol. 118, col. 256.

[140] Mr Tim Devlin, Conservative MP for Stockton South: *Official Report* (HC) 29 June 1987, vol. 118, col. 257.

[141] Subsequently, other inquiries were commissioned by the responsible agencies into the handling of the crisis by the Social Services and the Health Authority. It is also understood that some of the parents affected brought actions for damages in the civil courts.

[142] *Cleveland Report*, para. 2. A vivid account of the background to the events examined in the *Cleveland Report*, is given by Stuart Bell, the Member of Parliament for Middlesborough, in *When Salem came to the Boro, The True Story of the Cleveland Child Abuse Crisis* (1988). (The title reflects the author's belief that—in his publishers' words—the events bore 'comparison with the Salem witch hunts of the 17th century'; and the book is said to reveal the 'chilling truth behind the horrifying events of May and June, 1987'. The *Cleveland Report*, paras. 9.3.28–30, makes critical comments about Mr Bell's communications with the media during the crisis which should be noted; although Mr Bell would probably say that in the modern world MPs concerned about constituents' grievances almost necessarily seek press coverage. A different perspective is provided by Beatrix Campbell, *Unofficial Secrets, Child Sexual Abuse—The Cleveland Case* (1988).)

the inquiry was (in contrast with the other post-World War II abuse inquiries which were concerned with neglect and what was at one time called 'battering') largely concerned with *sexual* abuse[143] which seems to have heightened media interest.

Sexual abuse of children is nothing new[144] and both the Punishment of Incest Act 1908 and the Age of Marriage Act 1929[145] were (at least in part) responses to this phenomenon. The work of Sigmund Freud had given prominence in literary circles to issues of infant sexuality, and latterly prompted controversy about the extent of child molestation.[146] Nor could this particular crime be regarded as the preserve of the traditional delinquent classes. There is, for example, compelling evidence that the distinguished British sculptor and typographer Eric Gill had habitually had sexual relations with his own daughters;[147] whilst Virginia Woolf has left her own account[148] of an incident with her half-brother:

'Once when I was very small Gerald Duckworth lifted me onto [a slab outside the family dining room used for storing dishes]. I can remember the feel of his hand going under my clothes; going firmly and steadily lower and lower. I remember how I hoped that he would stop; how I stiffened and wriggled as his hand approached my private parts. But it did not stop. His hand explored my private parts too. I remember resenting, disliking it—what is the word for so dumb and mixed a feeling? It must have been strong, since I still recall it . . .'.

But recognition that such behaviour did take place seems only to have become widespread in the 1970s; and then, as the distinguished clinician Dr Hamish Cameron told the Cleveland Inquiry:[149]

'Whenever a "new" illness or treatment is described a flurry of excitement develops amongst professionals. This has certainly been the case with child sex abuse. However, in addition to the normal excitement generated by any "new" condition, there is an added voyeuristic component arising from the universality of interest in sexual matters . . . [It is] well to bear in mind the complex forces which can affect judgment and action in dealing with emotionally powerful material'.

Amongst the factors which made the topic particularly emotive were the suggestions that such abuse was common *within the family*.[150] Increasing numbers of adults complain that they were sexually abused as children, and statistical

---

[143] The *Cleveland Report*, para. 4, accepted a definition of sexual abuse as 'the involvement of dependent, developmentally immature children and adolescents in sexual activities that they do not fully comprehend and to which they are unable to give informed consent or that violate the social taboos of family roles'. The Report summarised this as 'the use of children by adults for sexual gratification' and pointed out that the term could properly be applied to a wide range of activity—ranging from exhibitionism and exposing children to pornography or sexual activity to rape, oral vaginal or anal, of the victim.
[144] See the *Report of the Committee on Sexual Offences against Young Persons* (1925, Cmd. 2561).
[145] See Chapter 2, above.
[146] See J Masson, *The Assault on Truth: Freud and Child Sex Abuse* (1992).
[147] See F MacCarthy, *Eric Gill* (1990).   [148] V Woolf, *Moments of Being* (1978) pp. 79–80.
[149] *Cleveland Report*, para. 36.   [150] *Cleveland Report*, para. 6.

material examined by the Cleveland Inquiry confirmed that there had been a significant increase in investigations of the possibility that a child had been the victim of such abuse.[151] An eminent child psychiatrist[152] told the Cleveland Inquiry[153] that the reason for this increase was

'increased diagnosis, the recognition that children who described abusive experience were not fantasising, and an increasing awareness of the pattern of physical and behavioural disorders of children' who had been abused.

The question of diagnosis was crucial in the unfolding of events in Cleveland. A child who has been battered will usually have symptoms which will often be visible to the casual observer and almost always comprehensible by laymen on the basis of a medical examination. Moreover, battered children will sometimes complain about their injuries and can be asked about them; and their attitudes and behaviour will change in a way frequently apparent to a sensitive observer. In contrast, children who have been sexually abused often do not display symptoms apparent to the uninformed, and one of the striking features of the Cleveland cases was that the children generally said nothing, and there was often nothing in their behaviour which suggested to families or teachers that anything untoward had occurred.

Against this background, the main controversy centred on the reliance to be placed on comparatively novel diagnostic techniques used by the paediatricians involved in Cleveland. The senior police surgeon in Cleveland disagreed with the paediatricians, and became convinced that families whose children were removed on no other basis than the paediatrician's diagnosis were suffering a grave injustice.[154] Because of this, there was a breakdown of relationships between the police (responsible for investigating allegations of criminal behaviour) and the social workers concerned, the police advising officers to treat diagnoses by one consultant paediatrician with caution and not to take any positive steps based on those diagnoses unless there were substantial corroboration from other sources.[155]

The *Cleveland Report* concluded that because child sexual abuse has characteristics different from physical abuse it had been wrong for social workers to

---

[151] *Cleveland Report*, para. 6. The Report notes that some people have suggested that as many as 10% of all children suffer serious sexual abuse, but urged the need for 'great caution' in accepting percentages as to the prevalence and incidence of such abuse. The Report stated that there was no evidence before the Inquiry to support the 10% estimate.

[152] Dr Arnold Bentovim, Great Ormond Street Children's Hospital.

[153] *Cleveland Report*, para. 6.

[154] *Cleveland Report*, para. 7.23. The police surgeon appeared on television and gave press interviews in which he asserted that there was no evidence of abuse on the children of a particular family, and he believed that abuse had not taken place in the great majority of cases in which it had been diagnosed: paras. 7.24–7.30. The Inquiry found him to be an efficient and conscientious police surgeon who had however got out of his depth, and become emotionally and personally involved in a way which compromised his professional position. He thus bore a share of responsibility for the troubled relationships between the Police and the Social Services Department: see paras. 3.37–3.39.

[155] *Cleveland Report*, paras. 4.61 and 4.87.

'suspend disbelief' and automatically to initiate compulsory intervention procedures solely on the basis of a paediatrician's diagnosis. What was required in such cases (but had not been provided in Cleveland) was

'cautious measured intervention which will allow the risks of a false positive finding to be balanced against those of a false negative and which will produce the evidence required by the court to secure the future welfare of the child concerned'.[156]

The Cleveland Inquiry lasted for 78 days; and the *Cleveland Report* was delivered on 6 June 1988. The Report's 320 pages contain a full description of events and an analysis of the issues arising from them. It concluded that the authorities in Cleveland had made an honest attempt to address the problems of child sexual abuse; but that in the spring of 1987 things 'went wrong'.[157] The Report made careful findings about the conduct of the principal figures and the practices of the professional groups involved; and it made many recommendations for improvement (ranging from the establishment of specialist inter-agency assessment teams to the proper conduct of interviews with children thought to have been abused).[158]

In relation to the working of the legal system,[159] the Report highlighted the importance of the initial stages when Place of Safety Orders[160] were used to authorise the removal of children from their parents and parents denied access

[156] *Cleveland Report*, para. 4.189. The Report was critical of the conduct of the Cleveland Council Social Services Department's 'Child Abuse Consultant' for failing to exercise the management skills and foresight to control or contain the escalation of problems that eventually overwhelmed the Department. It noted that there was much in the Consultant's 'attitude and approach which would have been commendable' if she had been acting as advocate for a child's rights organisation; but as someone holding a position of importance and influence in a public authority her duty had been to 'weigh any advice she gave not only with the interest of children but also with the rights and responsibilities of parents, the proper consideration of the use of statutory authority, the good name of Cleveland Social Services Department and the wider public interest': para. 4.187. However, the *Cleveland Report* found 'not . . . a shred of evidence to support' suggestions of conspiracy, collusion, conspiracy, bad faith or impropriety on the part of the Child Abuse Consultant and one of the paediatricians involved: para. 4.188.

[157] *Cleveland Report*, p. 243.

[158] The use of 'disclosure interviews' in which children were invited to say what had happened to them had been particularly controversial, particularly when these involved the use of so-called 'anatomically correct dolls'.

[159] The *Cleveland Report* pp. 238–239 also considered evidence about the Scottish system of children's hearings and panels established by the Social Work (Scotland) Act 1968. This was in response to claims that such a system had advantages in dividing responsibility for taking decisions on contested issues of fact from questions of what should be done in the light of those decisions. The Report concluded that the relative advantages and disadvantages of the two systems 'would not be easy to evaluate'; and in 1990 the accuracy of that cautious statement was demonstrated by the judicial inquiry, *Report of the Inquiry into the Removal of Children from Orkney* (1992). This covered more than 360 pages and made 194 recommendations—including 47 about the working of the Scottish children's panel system. Perhaps the influence of legal structures should not be exaggerated.

[160] Made under the Children and Young Persons Act 1969, s. 28 and authorising a child's detention in a place of safety (defined to include a community home, police station, hospital, or surgery). Such orders could be made by a magistrate if the applicant had reasonable cause to believe that one of the primary conditions specified in s. 1(2)(a) to (e) of the 1969 Act was satisfied. The procedure (somewhat akin to that for obtaining a search or arrest warrant) could be markedly informal: see further below.

to their children; and it highlighted the difficulties of magistrates' courts faced with cases involving complex and disputed issues of fact. The Report also recorded the way in which the wardship jurisdiction of the High Court could be invoked.[161] But the Report disappointed those from both ends of what had become a highly politicised spectrum who looked to it to establish the extent of child abuse in general and the question whether the paediatricians' diagnosis (which had led to most of the 121 children concerned being separated for longer or shorter periods from their families) had been correct in particular. Instead the Report merely recorded the facts: at the time of the Inquiry 98 of those 121 children were at home with their parents (albeit some of them on terms which included requirements for supervision, medical examination and so on).[162] This was consistent with different interpretations about the extent of the problem.[163]

Nonetheless the Report, with its underlying assertion that the 'voices of the children were not heard' in Cleveland,[164] and the philosophy it adopted that the 'child is a person and not an object of concern'[165] were warmly welcomed.[166] But although the Report's recommendations for practice on such matters as interviewing techniques and on the proper exercise of agencies' discretion to invoke the legal system to remove children from their homes were widely disseminated and highly influential they were evidently not always immediately followed in practice. In 1989, for example, it seemed for a time that so called ritual or satanic abuse (a topic publicised especially by some North American sources) was set to replace sexual abuse as a topic for social work concern and media publicity, and in at least one case[167] it became clear that the lessons of Cleveland had been widely ignored:

A schoolteacher in Rochdale Greater Manchester became concerned about the emotional and psychological state of a six-year-old boy who 'seemed to live in another world' and talked about a 'family of ghosties' and of flying and being given special drinks which made him fly. Later he said that he had been digging in a cemetery and had had to bury people and ghosts there. Social workers became involved, interviewed the boy, and (believing that there had been horrifying and frightening organised ritual abuse) decided to seek a place of safety order in respect of the boy and the three other children in his family. The police

---

[161] See above; and see the full account of local authorities' invocation of wardship by local authorities 'conscious of their responsibilities and fuelled with the panic in the 1970s' in N Parton, *The Politics of Child Abuse* (1985) p. 122 ff. 67 of the 121 children diagnosed by the two paediatricians were made wards of court: *Cleveland Report*, p. 64.

[162] *Cleveland Report*, p. 21 and p. 244.

[163] 'After many months of bitter challenge in the courts, 26 of those children from twelve families were deemed by the judges to have been wrongly diagnosed . . . Contrary to media myth that most cases were "cleared" by the courts, most of the children became the subjects of some form of state support or protection': Beatrix Campbell, *Unofficial Secrets, Child Sexual Abuse—The Cleveland Case* (1988) p. 1.

[164] *Cleveland Report*, p. 25.   [165] *Cleveland Report*, p. 245.

[166] *Official Report* (HC) 6 July 1988, vol. 136, col. 1061.

[167] *Rochdale Borough Council v. A and Others* [1991] 2 FLR 192.

searched the family home and arrested the father, subsequently releasing him without charge. The boy and his sister had claimed other children were involved. The local authority instituted wardship proceedings in respect of the children in three families; and in a 'dawn raid' the police and social workers removed them from their homes. After a 47-day hearing the judge held there was no evidence that any of the children had been ritually or satanically abused. Whilst accepting that the social workers involved were dedicated and warm-hearted, devoted to the children's welfare and skilled at dealing with children in a sympathetic way, the judge was highly critical of the procedures adopted by the local authority in handling the case, not least for traumatising the children by removing them from home when they were scarcely awake and in failing to apply the *Cleveland Report's* guidelines for interviewing children.

THE GOVERNMENT'S RESPONSE TO PRESSURE: THE CHILDREN ACT 1989

As the Secretary of State had said in welcoming the *Cleveland Report* there is no 'single, simple answer' to the problem of child neglect and abuse; and it is certainly true that it takes time to change institutional cultures. The Secretary of State had given undertakings about the steps which were to be taken to deal with the administrative and other failings identified in the Report—in particular, specific guidance was published about inter-agency collaboration—but these took time to become effective.

In contrast, the substantive law can be changed immediately by statute, and the Secretary of State had come close to giving an undertaking that the Government would introduce comprehensive legislation. The Government had published a White Paper[168] setting out proposals intended to provide a 'clearer and fairer' framework for the provision of child care services and the protection of children at risk before the events in Cleveland had been publicised. The relevant sections had been considered in the *Cleveland Report*, and the Secretary of State was able to claim that the Report had accepted that the White Paper would 'strengthen the rights of parents and children'.[169] But the Bill which the Government eventually introduced (and which became the Children Act 1989) went much further than the White Paper, for it dealt not only with the public law of child care but also substantially integrated the public law and the private law (dealing with procedures not directly involving the State but regulating the up-bringing of children). The Law Commission had demonstrated that this was possible, and the fact that Professor Brenda Hoggett[170] had been able to formu-

---

[168] *The Law on Child Care and Family Services* (1987, Cm. 62).

[169] *Official Report* (HC) 6 July 1988, vol. 136, col. 1062.

[170] See Biographical Notes. EG Caldwell (see Biographical Notes) was at this time attached to the Law Commission and was primarily responsible for drafting the clauses included in the Law Commission's *Report*, and eventually he (together with Dr H Beynon) was responsible for settling the terms of the Children Bill as it was introduced and passed through Parliament (see P Mayhew, [1990] 11 *Statute Law Review* 1, 2).

late the Government's public law proposals in the context of a comprehensive codification seems to have been particularly significant.[171] Lord Mackay's description of the Children Act 1989 as the 'most comprehensive and far reaching' piece of reforming legislation in the area 'in living memory' was not a significant exaggeration.[172]

The Children Act 1989: a model of legislative codification

The Children Act 1989 demonstrably meets its sponsors' objective of providing a comprehensive clear and consistent statement of child law, based on clearly articulated principles. It remains in force at the turn of the century, and seems likely to continue to provide the foundation of the legal structure for resolving issues about children's upbringing for many years ahead. The reader must refer to other books for an account of the Act's provisions and of how they have been interpreted in the courts. All that the present text seeks to do is to indicate the major historical shifts of legislative policy and legal procedure.

Creation of a flexible and specialised court system for dealing with litigation about the care and upbringing of children

The Children Act 1989 confers jurisdiction in what are broadly defined as 'family proceedings' on the High Court, county courts, and magistrates' courts. It enables cases to be transferred between different courts so that (for example) cases involving children in the same family are dealt with together. It also permits transfers between the three tiers of court, and an attempt has been made to ensure that cases are allotted to the appropriate level in the judicial hierarchy. Judicial specialisation has, by administrative means, been encouraged: the professional judges are 'ticketed' to deal with different types of case whilst special training has been established for the lay magistrates sitting in what is now called the 'family proceedings court'.[173] Procedural measures have been taken to enable the courts to take an active and inquiring role into the facts of a case (rather than acting simply as umpires assessing the facts which the parties choose to put before them). At the same time, the legal profession, influenced to some extent by government decisions about the level of public funding for legal services, has come to recognise that family work in general (and work involving children and local authorities in particular) requires special interest, training and experience.

---

[171] See Lord Mackay of Clashfern LC, *Official Report* (HL) vol. 502, col. 489.

[172] *Official Report* (HL) vol. 502, col. 488. The regrettable if understandable failure to integrate the law of adoption into the scheme of the Children Act means that it cannot wholly accurately be described as 'comprehensive'.

[173] See the Lord Chancellor's Department's *Scoping Study On Delay In Children Act Cases, Findings & Action Taken* (2002) for a discussion of the working of these provisions.

Non-lawyers may doubt the significance of what may easily seem to be low-level management of the court system; but one remarkable (and rarely noticed) fact suggests that there has indeed been an important change. This is that right down to the debates on the 1989 Act no discussion on family law was complete without the invocation of the so-called 'family court' as a necessary (and often sufficient) response to the problem under review. Yet a decade later (whilst court structure and procedures remain a matter for debate) this simplistic response has become rare.

Integration and harmonisation of public and private law relating to children

The Act uses simple language intended to be non-technical: instead of referring to 'custody' it talks of residence orders, 'contact' is preferred to 'access', a child is 'looked after' by a local authority. There is an ideological intention behind some of the changes: for example, the Act talks of 'parental responsibility' (rather than parental rights or even parental authority) intending thereby to emphasise that responsibility rather than right is the main attribute of parenthood. But the same terminology is used throughout, and the effect of the orders the court can make is clearer than it was previously. More important is the fact that the Act created a single code, whether the proceedings directly involve the State ('public law') or are initiated by a private individual. The key definition is that of 'family proceedings': the Act brings a wide range of 'family' related litigation (for example, divorce, domestic violence, cases dealing with the family home, applications for an adoption order as well as applications under the Children Act itself for an order under the provisions of that Act) within the definition of this term, and confers power to make orders about where the child is to live, who is to have contact with him, and also to make orders dealing with specific issues relating to the child's upbringing (where is the child to go to school? by what surname should he be known?) in such proceedings. No doubt in most cases there will be an application for an order by one of those before the court, but the Act permits the court (once 'family proceedings' have been started) to make such orders if it considers that to do so would be in the child's interests even though no one has applied for the order. In this way, the Act enables the court to deal flexibly with a wide range of circumstances:

For example, the court hearing an adoption application could make a residence order in favour of the child's grandparent (if it considered the child's welfare would be best be promoted in this way) instead of making the adoption order; or it could make a contact order in favour of the birth parent as well as the adoption order for which the applicant has applied. The court hearing an application by a local authority for compulsory powers over the child's upbringing (a 'care order') could if it considers that to do so would better promote the child's welfare instead make a 'residence order' in favour of a relative (or, indeed, anyone else).

The child's welfare paramount

The Children Act 1989 asserts[174] the principle that where a court determines any question with respect to a child's upbringing the court is to apply the principle that the child's welfare is the court's paramount consideration. But this only applies where the court has power to determine the issue, and two important restrictions need to be kept in mind. First, there is no power to make an order authorising a local authority to take compulsory measures in respect of the child unless the court has first found as a fact that the child is suffering or is likely to suffer significant harm attributable to the standard of care available not being what it would be reasonable for a parent to give the child. These provisions (dealt with below) are intended to ensure that children are not at risk of being taken from their parents simply on the basis that the court believed the State would do better for the child than the child's own family. Secondly, although the Act adopts the so-called 'open door' principle of allowing (subject to narrow exceptions) anyone the right of access to the court to seek an order dealing with the child's upbringing, the applicant must—unless he or she is the child's parent or has had certain other kinds of family relationship with the child—first obtain the court's leave to make the application for an order. This is intended to protect the child against unwarranted disturbance; and in dealing with an application for leave the court is required to consider certain specific factors such as the risk that the proposed application would disrupt the child's life to such an extent as to cause harm.

In deciding the question of what is in the child's interests the court is directed to a check list of relevant factors intended to structure its decision (what, for example, are the child's wishes and feelings, what are his needs, and so on) but it also—more controversially—incorporates a so-called 'no-order presumption': the court is not to make an order relating to children unless it considers that doing so would be better for the child than making no order at all.[175] Non-intervention is thus elevated to the status of a guiding principle.

Striking a balance: children best cared for in the family

The Children Act was not drafted as a response to the Cleveland Inquiry or as a reaction to any of the other child abuse inquiries of the last third of the twentieth century. But it is impossible to leave out of account the impact which these inquiries had on creating the climate of opinion favouring reform of the law and the fact that broadly speaking the climate of opinion was not well disposed to unnecessary social work intervention in family life.[176] The notion of social work

---

[174] s. 1(1). [175] s. 1(5).

[176] However, one of the striking features of this period is the emergence of pressure groups representing a wide range of differing interests: thus the Family Rights Group had a special concern for the parents and other adults, whilst the Children's Legal Centre was primarily concerned to ensure that the child's point of view was fully represented.

professionalism enthusiastically espoused by the Seebohm Report in the 1970s had suffered a number of serious knocks thereafter. Moreover, the legislation was sponsored by a Conservative Government led for a decade by Mrs Margaret Thatcher and with a strong commitment to what were called 'family values' and individual responsibility. In the circumstances, it is not surprising that some of those who commented on the 1984 *Review of Child Law* believed that the Review proposals would 'shift the balance too far towards the interests of the parents and away from the interests of the child',[177] nor is it surprising that the Government (rejecting that view) stated that the Act rested on the belief that children were generally best looked after within the family and with both parents playing a full part and without resort to legal proceedings.[178] It is certainly true that a number of provisions in the Act were clearly intended to shift the balance somewhat towards protecting the legitimate claims of parents, but this was no crude response to political pressures: the Act can indeed claim to have struck a balance between the claims of family autonomy and those of child protection.[179] This balance is most clearly exemplified by the provisions dealing with the circumstances in which compulsory State intervention is justified.

Justification for compulsory State intervention

The Conservative Government took a deliberate decision to reject the notion that State intervention was justified simply on the basis of evidence that the child's welfare so required. In the Government's view, there was a crucial distinction between the criteria upon which the court could resolve disputes between members of a family (where a broad discretion guided by the principle of the child's best interests would be appropriate and defensible) and cases in which State intervention could be justified. Hence (as Lord Chancellor Mackay put it in explaining the policy to which the Children Act 1989 seeks to give effect)[180]

'Unless there is evidence that a child is being, or is likely to be, positively harmed because of a failure in the family, the State, whether in the guise of a local authority or a court, should not interfere'. Certain minimum criteria should always be satisfied 'before it can ever be justified for a court even to begin to contemplate whether the State should be enabled to intervene compulsorily in family life. . . . The integrity and independence of

---

[177] *The Law on Child Care and Family Services* (1987, Cm. 62) para. 11.

[178] The *Prime Minister's Review, Adoption* (Cabinet Office, Performance and Innovation Unit, 2000) p. 15 suggested that the Act 'responded to the growing disillusionment with the previous approach' under the Children Act 1975, that it was based on the assumption that the family would in most cases provide the best place for children, and that it sought to emphasise the importance of partnership with parents, support to families and strong child protection. The *Review* suggested that the 'focus on "permanence" was reduced, and the emphasis placed on adoption decreased'.

[179] The Act also requires local authorities to promote the upbringing of children by their own families so far as is consistent with their welfare: see Children Act 1979, s. 17(1)(b) and the discussion of the 'partnership' principle, below.

[180] (1989) 139 New LJ 505, 507 (and see also the citations from Lord Mackay's parliamentary speeches in the opinion of Lord Nicholls, *Lancashire County Council v. A* [2000] 2 AC 147, 164–165.

the family is the basic building block of a free and democratic society and the need to defend it should be clearly perceivable in the law . . . to provide otherwise would make it lawful for children to be removed from their families simply on the basis that a court considered that the state could do better for the child than his family. The threat to the poor and to minority groups, whose views of what is good for a child may not coincide closely with that of the majority, is all too apparent . . .'

Hence, the Act provided that before a court could begin to consider whether a care (or supervision) order would be in the child's interests there must be before the court a properly constituted application by a local authority,[181] and the court must be satisfied on the evidence before it that the 'threshold criteria' set out in s. 31 of the Children Act are met.[182] But that was not to be the end of the matter: if those conditions were satisfied the court would have jurisdiction to make an order, but it should only do so if satisfied that the making of an order would promote the child's welfare and would be better for the child than making no order at all.[183]

Court sanction required to justify State intervention

The principle that State intervention can only be justified if a court has made a finding that clearly formulated conditions are satisfied is reflected in other provisions of the 1989 Act. Of these the most striking in historical terms is the abolition of the parental rights resolution procedure: only a court order can vest a local authority[184] with the legal authority of a parent. But in practical terms it may be that the restrictions on the powers of the authorities to remove a child for a short time to protect him in an emergency are more important as a demonstration of the way in which the Act carefully balances the need for protection against the need to avoid injustice to parents (and indeed to the child himself). The *Cleveland Report* had confirmed that there were many disturbing features about the use made of the powers to make so-called 'place of safety orders'. For example, applications had been made ex parte without any notification to the parents, applications were made to a single magistrate sometimes sitting in his own home (even though the hearing took place during court hours), record keeping was defective, access by the parents to their child was often improperly

---

[181] The Act allows the NSPCC or other authorised persons to make application, but the NSPCC no longer initiates proceedings and no other person has been authorised.

[182] The provisions of s. 31 of the Act are complex: the main requirement is to show that the child concerned is 'suffering, or is likely to suffer, significant harm' attributable to a failure to provide care.

[183] Children Act 1989, s. 1(5). The fact that a care order is made does not necessarily mean that the child will be removed from the parents' physical care: see *Re T (A Minor) (Care or Supervision Order)* [1994] 1 WLR 103; Placement of Children with Parents etc. Regulations 1991.

[184] And the fact that the local authority acquires parental responsibility does not deprive the parents of their own parental responsibility: Children Act 1989, s. 2(6). It is true that the local authority may ultimately take decisions: s. 33(4); but the Act provides machinery whereby decisions on the—often crucial—issue of contact between parent and child are in effect subject to a right of appeal to the court: s. 34.

denied, medical examinations were carried out without the consent of parent or child, and, generally, the procedure seemed to be used in an attempt to obtain control over the situation for the local authority. The 1989 Act[185] embodies a clear principle: 'the application of emergency powers to remove a child at serious risk, which necessarily cannot be preceded by a full court hearing, must be of short duration and subject to court review if the parent wishes to challenge' the order.[186]

The limits of legislation

The House of Lords has had to decide a number of cases on the interpretation of those parts of the Children Act which govern the powers of local authorities to intervene in the family. For example,

In *Re H and R (Child Sexual Abuse: Standard of Proof)*[187] a 15-year-old girl alleged that her step-father had sexually abused her over a period of seven years, and that on four occasions he had raped her. The father was prosecuted for rape but acquitted. Subsequently, the judge hearing an application made by the local authority for care orders under the Children Act 1989 in respect of the 15-year-old's sisters said that he was 'more than a little suspicious' that the girl's account of what had happened was true and that the step-father had indeed done what was alleged. But the House of Lords held that since no allegation of maltreatment had been *proved* it was impossible (in the absence of other evidence) for the court to make a finding that the children were 'likely to suffer' significant harm. The Law Lords did accept that other evidence might, by establishing 'a combination of profoundly worrying features affecting the care of the child

---

[185] A court may make an 'emergency protection order' in specified circumstances, and this may include directions about medical examination and other assessment procedures. Such an order is not to continue beyond eight days (although it may be extended for one period of no more than seven days): s. 45. Thereafter a court may make Interim Orders if satisfied that there are reasonable grounds for believing the threshold criteria set out in s. 31 are met; and such orders may be for a period of eight weeks and may be extended for four weekly periods. However, the court is effectively in charge of decisions on the examinations or assessment which may be conducted during the currency of an Interim Care Order: s. 38.

[186] The White Paper, *The Law on Child Care and Family Services* (1987, Cm. 62) para. 6(e) had stated this as the Government's policy at a time when the *Beckford Inquiry* had highlighted the difficulty facing local authorities in providing adequate protection to the children of unco-operative parents. By the time the Bill for the Children Act came to be settled it was the circumstances in which local authorities had used the so-called 'place of safety orders' in Cleveland which had come to prominence; but the principle stated in the text was endorsed by the *Cleveland Report* and is reflected in the (albeit somewhat complex) provisions of the Children Act.

[187] [1996] AC 563. The fact that the court had no power under the Children and Young Persons Act 1969 to make a care order merely because there were well justified fears for the future (see eg *Essex County Council v. TLR and KBR* (1978) 9 Fam Law 18) was widely seen as a serious defect particularly in cases where the threat to the child's welfare was presented by parents seeking to remove the child from foster parents: *The Law on Child Care and Family Services* (1987, Cm. 62) para. 59. In such cases, local authorities would often invoke the High Court's wardship jurisdiction (and would merely have to show that the child's welfare would be promoted by his remaining away from his parents and that there were exceptional circumstances justifying this course).

within the family' allow a court to find 'on the basis of such facts as are proved' that the child was indeed likely to suffer significant harm if no order were made. But the possibility that a child at risk may remain exposed to serious damage because of the impossibility of satisfying requirements of legal proof has concerned some commentators.

In contrast, in *Lancashire County Council v. B*[188] there was no direct evidence of wrongdoing by the parents at all, but it was held that the court was justified in making a care order:

A seven-month-old baby was found to have suffered at least two episodes of violent shaking which resulted in subdural haemorrhages, retinal haemorrhages and cerebral atrophy. It was impossible to decide whether this harm—undoubtedly significant—had been caused by the child's mother or father or by the child minder who looked after the child while the child's parents were at work. The House of Lords rejected an argument that the threshold criterion could only be satisfied if it were shown that this harm suffered by the child was attributable to the care or absence of care given by the parent against whom the order was sought.

These cases may suggest that it is impossible to draft a statutory formula which will both do justice to the parents and protect the child in all cases. Certainly no legal formula can provide complete protection against the human fallibility not only of social workers but also of judges:

In *Re M (A Minor)(Care Order: Threshold Conditions)*[189] a husband brutally murdered his wife in the presence of their four-month-old son. The local authority applied for a care order with a view to the child being placed for adoption outside the family and the judge made the order. But there was a successful appeal: the Court of Appeal held that no court could say the child (who was at the time in foster care) was actually suffering harm at the date of the hearing. Hence the Act's 'is suffering' criterion[190] had not been satisfied. Nor could it be said the baby was 'likely' to suffer harm if no order were made: the child's aunt wished to care for him and was able to do so. Accordingly the Court of Appeal discharged the care order and made a residence order in the aunt's favour. There was a further appeal and the House of Lords held the Court of Appeal to have wrongly interpreted the legislation in a way which would make it impossible for a local authority removing a child under emergency powers subsequently to seek a care order. But in the present context what is most interesting is how fallible the High Court judge (and the expert evidence on which she relied) was shown by events to have been. She accepted that the child's welfare required a placement totally severing all his ties with his birth family. As a result of the Court of Appeal's (erroneous) view of the law, however, the child had in fact been in the aunt's care; and—notwithstanding the social workers' view that the aunt lacked

---

[188] [2000] 2 AC 147.   [189] [1994] 2 AC 424.   [190] See Children Act 1989, s. 31(2)(a).

the ability to provide the special quality of care the child needed—he had become a boisterous healthy and happy child. The child would never have had the chance of the upbringing within his family which it was supposedly the policy of the Children Act to favour had the Lords Justices in the Court of Appeal not, by misinterpreting the law, given the aunt the chance to prove herself and demonstrate that the social workers and the trial judge had been wrong in their assessment of her parenting skills.

The truth is that the law must be an imperfect instrument and it is certainly not easy to suggest how the wording of the statute could be significantly improved. Whatever the theoretical difficulties in the way of local authorities seeking a care order, an increasing number of such orders were made in the closing years of the twentieth century.[191]

Listening to the child

Although the *Cleveland Report* had highlighted the fact that the voices of the children concerned had not been heard the notion that children's own wishes and concerns were insufficiently regarded in cases about their upbringing did not at the time seem to have entered very much into official thinking. However, the Government (in its concern to ensure that courts taking decisions about a child's future should have all relevant information available to them and should hear all the competing arguments) did accept that an independent *guardian ad litem* be appointed to safeguard and protect the child's interests in all care proceedings[192] unless the court was satisfied that such an appointment was unnecessary for the purpose.[193] The Children Act 1989 so provided,[194] and guardians soon became a central feature in care cases, attending all hearings, making a full report to the court and giving advice on a wide range of matters.[195] The guardian also had to ensure that the child had a solicitor. But although the guardian is bound to put forward the child's views he is not bound to support them. The child's solicitor, in contrast, is required to represent the child (rather

---

[191] 3,221 care orders were made in 1993; 6,298 in 2000: *Children Act Report 2000*, figure 12.2.

[192] This did not satisfy those who thought that children should be entitled to put forward their own views in proceedings (for example, the parents' divorce) which could affect their future. The Government accepted amendments to the Family Law Act 1996 see s. 64, p. 595, above. This would have allowed separate representation in some cases to be specified in Regulations; but the Lord Chancellor emphasised the need to avoid putting children at risk or exacerbating conflict between spouses 'by unnecessarily dragging children into disputes between their parents': *Official Report*, 27 June 1996, col. 1075. The decision not to implement the 1996 Act's divorce reforms makes it difficult to predict the future of these provisions.

[193] *The Law on Child Care and Family Services* (1987, Cm. 62) para. 57.   [194] s. 41.

[195] But note that the Lord Chancellor's Department's *Scoping Study On Delay In Children Act Cases, Findings & Action Taken* (2002) p. 27 suggests that there 'are considerable frustrations between Guardians ad Litem and judges on the one hand and social workers on the other about the progress of care proceedings, and that the efforts of Guardians (particularly in seeking additional evidence and in arguing that the Local Authority has failed to make sufficient efforts at rehabilitating the child with the family) lead to unnecessary delay'.

than the guardian) and must (assuming that the child is capable of understanding the matter) conduct the case in accordance with the child's instructions if they conflict with the *guardian ad litem's* views.

The Children Act 1989, even more remarkably, envisaged that a child might be allowed to institute proceedings (for example, for a residence order—perhaps allowing the child to live with a friend rather than a parent—or for a contact or specific issue order) but the child must first obtain leave of the court to do so.[196] The courts have shown themselves well aware of the difficulties in exercising this discretion. As Sir Thomas Bingham MR put it:[197]

'The 1989 Act enables and requires a judicious balance to be struck between two considerations. First is the principle . . . that children are human beings with individual minds and wills, views and emotions, which should command serious attention. A child's wishes are not to be discounted or dismissed simply because he is a child. He should be free to express them and decision makers should listen. Secondly is the fact that a child is, after all, a child. The reason why the law is particularly solicitous in protecting the interests of children is because they are liable to be vulnerable and impressionable, lacking the maturity to weigh the longer term against the shorter, lacking the insight to know how they will react and the imagination to know how others will react in certain situations, lacking the experience to measure the probable against the possible . . . [Accordingly] where any sound judgment on the issues calls for insight and imagination which only maturity and experience can bring, . . . the court . . . will be slow to conclude that the child's understanding is sufficient.'

In particular, the courts are well aware of the destructive potential of family litigation[198] and experience suggests that the courts adopt a cautious approach to allowing children to bring family disputes to court, at least in cases which can be regarded as trivial[199] by the adults who decide these matters. But at the turn of the century there were clearly some who thought that the rights of children were still insufficiently recognised by the legal system.[200]

---

[196] Children Act 1989, s. 10(1)(a)(ii). The only explicit statutory guidance in deciding whether to grant leave is the provision that the court shall only do so if the child has 'sufficient understanding' to make the proposed application: s. 10(8).

[197] In *Re S (A Minor)(Independent Representation)* [1993] Fam 263, 276.

[198] See eg *Re C (Residence: Child's Application for Leave)* [1995] 1 FLR 927, Stuart-White J, where a 14-year-old girl who had been living with her father sought leave to apply for a residence order in favour of her mother. The judge pointed out that 'once a child is a party to proceedings between warring parents, that leads the child to be in a position in which the child is likely to be present hearing the evidence of those parents, hearing the parent cross-examined, hearing perhaps of many matters which at the tender age of the child, it would be better for her not to hear' and the child herself might be subjected to cross-examination. However, in the event the judge granted the child leave. In contrast, in *Re H (Residence Order: Child's Application for leave)* [2000] 1 FLR 780 the court refused a 12-year-old boy leave to apply in his parents' divorce proceedings for a residence order in part because the child's views would be adequately represented in any event.

[199] See *Re C (A Minor)(Leave to seek section 8 order)* [1994] 1 FLR 26 (15-year-old girl refused leave to seek a specific issue order authorising her to go on holiday to Bulgaria with a family other than her own not only because of the triviality of the issue but also because the judge considered it wrong to give the girl the impression that she had won a victory against her parents).

[200] See eg the analysis by H Hendrick, *Child Welfare, England 1872–1989* (1994). The organisation IRCHIN (Independent Representation for the Child in Need) has been particularly active.

Administration and collaboration: working together

'Working Together' and 'Partnership' were words often heard in the approach to the coming into force of the Children Act in October 1991. They tended to be invoked in two different contexts. One was in describing the relationship between the authorities on the one hand and families on the other: local authorities (it was said) must work in partnership with parents, seeking court orders only when compulsory action would be better for the child than 'working with the parents under voluntary arrangements'.[201] But equally important was the need for the professionals involved—local authorities, lawyers, the police, education services—to collaborate and co-operate so as to avoid the failings identified in the *Colwell* and *Beckford* cases. The basis of an effective child protection service was (so the Government asserted) that:

'professionals and individual agencies work together on a multi-disciplinary basis, with a shared mutual understanding of aims, of objectives and of what is good practice. This should take into account the sensitive issues associated with gender, race, culture and disability . . .'[202]

Administrative procedures—Child Protection Conferences, Child Protection Registers, and so on—were developed and supported by training and the publication of a vast quantity of guidance.[203]

The court system was, for the first time, directly involved in collaborative training and other ventures. A Children Act Advisory Committee was established under the chairmanship of a High Court judge and kept the working of the Act under detailed review.[204] Detailed reports on matters of special concern—notably on 'Avoiding Delay in Public Law Children Act Cases'[205] as well

[201] *Working Together Under the Children Act 1989* (HMSO, 1991) para. 1.4; and see also *Promoting Inter-Agency Working in the Family Justice System* (Lord Chancellor's Department, 2002). In fact the so-called 'partnership' principle is not mentioned in terms in the Act. But, by imposing a duty on local authorities to safeguard and promote the welfare of children in the authority's area who are 'in need' and to provide a range and level of services appropriate to the needs of children in their area so as to safeguard and promote the welfare of such children; and, so far as consistent with that duty, to promote their upbringing by their families—the Act implicitly recognises that support should be provided 'in partnership' with the parents. The view that family upbringing is best for children in most circumstances is reinforced by the imposition of a statutory duty on local authorities to make appropriate provision for services (ranging from advice, through home help, to travel and holiday facilities or assistance) to be available for children in need while they are living with their families.
[202] *Working Together Under the Children Act 1989* (HMSO, 1991) para. 5.2.
[203] For example, the Government published nine volumes of 'Guidance and Regulations' on aspects of the 1989 Act. Under the Local Authority Social Services Act 1970 local authorities exercising their social service function are required to act under such general guidance issued by the Secretary of State.
[204] The Committee ceased operations in June 1997, but the Lord Chancellor's Advisory Board on Family Law was to maintain an overview of the working of the policy embodied in the Children Act 1989 within the family court system. The Board's Children Act Sub-Committee published influential Reports and Consultation Papers on *Questions of Parental Contact in Cases where there is Domestic Violence* and on *Making Contact Work*.
[205] By Dame Margaret Booth (1996).

as Annual Surveys collecting and disseminating information and making rec-ommendations about good practice—were published. Eventually in 1997 the Committee published what was regarded as a definitive statement of good prac-tice[206] on matters ranging from the use of expert witnesses and guidance to mag-istrates on the preparation of the written findings and statement of reasons for decisions required by the Act to the compilation of dossiers for use in the courts. Networks of Family Court Business Committees and Family Court Forums were established and there were numerous local initiatives. Throughout, the emphasis was on the need for inter-disciplinary co-operation. Although inevitably there was some falling off in some areas and a reversion to the 'work-ing in isolation'[207] which preceded the 1989 Act, the benefits to be derived from interdisciplinary practice have (according to one senior member of the judiciary)[208] been proved 'beyond question'.

THE IMPACT OF THE CHILDREN ACT 1989

The 1989 Act unquestionably provides a far better framework for the adminis-tration of the law than anything that had gone before. But this is not to say that all is for the best in the best of possible worlds. Leaving on one side such issues as whether the courts can really determine what action will best promote a child's welfare,[209] there remain serious practical problems. Of these, delay is certainly one of the most serious. The Children Act[210] specifically directs courts to 'have regard to the general principle that any delay' in determining issues about a child's upbringing is likely to prejudice the child's welfare. Yet attempts to reduce delays seem to have been of only limited effectiveness. To take the par-ticularly striking example of cases about whether a child should be in care or not, it seems that in the more difficult cases at the turn of the century it was tak-ing almost a year from the start of the proceedings to get an actual decision.[211] There can be little doubt that such delays are seriously harmful.[212] Again, a con-sistent theme of Inquiries into child abuse cases has been that the prosecution of the abuser should not delay decisions about the child's future; yet such delays

[206] *Handbook of Best Practice in Children Act cases* (CAAC, 1997).

[207] Dame Margaret Booth, *Avoiding Delay in Public Law Children Act Cases*, Chapter 4.

[208] Lord Justice Thorpe, 'The Role of the Judiciary in Interdisciplinary Co-operation before and since Cleveland' in *Cleveland Ten Years On* (National Council for Family Proceedings, 1997) p. 30. For an assessment of the position at the end of the century, see *Promoting Inter-Agency Working in the Family Justice System* (Lord Chancellor's Department, 2002).

[209] See M King and C Piper, *How the Law thinks about Children* (1990).   [210] s. 1(2).

[211] Ie those which are transferred from the Magistrates' Family Proceedings Court to the Superior courts: see N Fricker, 'Family Law in the New Millennium . . .' in SM Cretney (ed.), *Family Law, Essays for the new Millennium* (2000) 89, 94. The Lord Chancellor's Department carried out a *Scoping Study On Delay In Children Act Cases, Findings & Action Taken* (2002) which suggested that by 1996 care cases were taking on average 46 weeks from start to finish, and that by the end of 2000 the average time had increased to 50 weeks. The target established when the Children Act came into force was 13 weeks.

[212] *Ibid.*

still seem to occur.[213] The contrast between the 1945 case of Dennis O'Neill (where the prosecution of the foster-parents was dealt with within six weeks) and the case of Jasmine Beckford some 40 years later (where there was a gap of nearly nine months) is striking; and it seems that at the turn of the century serious delays in dealing with the child's future were not unusual.[214]

Finally there must also be doubt about the effectiveness of the Children Act in diverting disagreements about children away from the courts and adversarial litigation.[215] It appears that the number of disputes about children presented to the courts has risen significantly over the years: some 20% of divorces in which the couple have a child are subject to a contest of some kind.[216] It has been suggested that the 'legislative framework'[217] is now 'extremely receptive to contested legal proceedings' and that the Children Act—by creating a 'seductive menu of orders for which the parties can apply' has played a part in fuelling this appetite for litigation.[218]

The limitations of the law

The Children Act 1989 created a superb piece of legal machinery. But how far has it truly improved the lives of children in need? The publicity given to child abuse cases helped create the climate of opinion in which the Children Act 1989 (like the earlier Acts of 1948 and 1975) was brought forward and enacted; and no doubt many people hoped that the more effective court and welfare structure created by the 1989 Act would reduce the incidence of such scandals. There is, of course, no way of determining with any reliability what impact the legislation has had; and it may well be that the protection which the legal system provides to children has improved.[219] No one could reasonably have believed that the

[213] The Home Office commissioned research which throws light on difficulties encountered in the investigation of suspected abuse and the decision taking process: G Davis et al, *An assessment of the admissibility and sufficiency of evidence in child abuse cases* (1999).

[214] The fact that both children were killed does not affect the validity of the general point that prosecutions seem to take more and more time; whilst investigations into whether an allegation of abuse can be substantiated may also in practice delay the resolution of questions about contact: see *Handbook of Best Practice in Children Act cases* (CAAC, 1997) p. 22. The question whether prosecution should be a weapon used with much more discrimination—delicately raised in the *Cleveland Report* p. 214, paras. 4 and 5—does not seem to have been addressed in any systematic way although the *Code for Crown Prosecutors* directs prosecutors, in considering whether a prosecution for which evidence is available would be 'in the public interest' to consider the welfare of the child as their primary, but not paramount, concern.

[215] See eg SM Cretney, 'Defining the limits of state intervention . . .' in D Freestone (ed.), *Children and the Law* . . . (1990).

[216] See the major research project undertaken by G Davis and others the findings of which (summarised in various issues of *Family Law* in 1988 and 1999) are discussed in G Davis, 'Love in a Cold Climate . . .' in SM Cretney (ed.), *Family Law—Essays for the New Millennium* (2000) 127.

[217] See Davis, *op. cit.* pp. 128–129.   [218] *Ibid.*

[219] The Department of Health published research findings on the effectiveness of child protection procedures: *Child Protection: Messages from Research* (1995).

problem of child abuse would go away.[220] But a particularly disturbing development was the increasing[221] evidence that children who were supposedly under the protection of the State were still being abused and were even at especial risk of abuse. Disquiet about continuing revelations of child abuse within children's homes led to a major review (conducted by Sir William Utting)[222] into the measures taken to protect children living away from home, particularly in children's residential homes, foster care and boarding schools. The Utting Report *People Like Us*[223] was followed by the publication in February 2000 of the Report of a judicial inquiry, conducted by Sir Ronald Waterhouse, into sexual abuse in children's residential homes in North Wales.[224] As the Secretary of State[225] put it the Utting Report

painted a 'woeful tale of failure. Many children who had been "taken into care" to protect and help them had not been protected and helped. Instead some had suffered abuse at the hands of those who were meant to help them. Many more had been let down, never given the attention they needed, shifted from place to place, school to school and then turned out when they reached 16 . . . The whole system had failed'.

It is all too clear that the confident expectations inspired by the *Curtis Report* 50 years earlier that the State could act as a good parent to the country's deprived and needy children were unrealistic. At the turn of the century there are almost a quarter of a million children receiving some kind of care from social services departments, and it is simply unrealistic to imagine that hard pressed staff can create a personal paternal link with all the children for whom they are responsible.[226] Instead, the Government is seeking to promote better standards by the use of inspections, monitoring, and modern management techniques.[227] Above all, the Government looks to adoption as the instrument whereby 'secure, permanent relationships' can be provided for 'some of society's most vulnerable children'.[228]

[220] There is little reliable evidence about the incidence of child abuse; and the *Cleveland Report* was careful to avoid making findings. A random survey undertaken at the end of the twentieth century amongst teenagers aged 18 to 24 revealed that 7% of them claimed to have suffered serious physical abuse by a parent, but only 1% to have suffered sexual abuse by a parent. 3% claimed that they had been subjected to sexual abuse by another relative, especially brothers and step-brothers: *Children Act Report 2000* (DOH, 2001), para. 2.20.

[221] An indication that all was not well was given by the Report of the Staffordshire Child Care Inquiry 1990, *The Pindown Experience and the Protection of Children* (1991). This dealt primarily with techniques used to control children in a residential home, but had broader implications.

[222] See Biographical Notes.   [223] (1997) HMSO.

[224] *Lost in Care: Report of the tribunal of inquiry into the abuse of children in care in . . . Gwynedd and Clwyd since 1974* (HC 201, 1999–2000).

[225] Frank Dobson, Foreword to *The Government's Response to the Children's Safeguards Review* (1998, Cm. 4105).

[226] Compare the role that the *Curtis Report* envisaged for the Children's Officer under the scheme created in 1948.

[227] See the Care Standards Act 2000 (which established a National Care Standards Commission); and generally the *Children Act Report 2000* (Department of Health, 2001). Efforts to improve the poor life chances of children in care were also to be made under the Children (Leaving Care) Act 2000.

[228] The *Prime Minister's Review, Adoption* (Cabinet Office, Performance and Innovation Unit, 2000) p. 5, para. 4.

Integrating adoption

As already noted the Children Act 1989 made no attempt to integrate the law of adoption into the supposedly comprehensive legal framework which it established.[229] It is true that by defining adoption proceedings as 'family proceedings' it did give the courts dealing with an adoption application a certain flexibility to make Children Act orders in addition to, or as an alternative to the adoption order; but it made no attempt to deal with major issues of policy—whether a degree of openness should be introduced into the adoption procedure, whether the 'total transplant' concept of adoption was still appropriate, whether the secrecy which 'engulfs the adoption process' was still necessary—which had come into prominence since the 1975 Act or with the major changes in demographic and other social factors influencing recourse to adoption.[230] Few commentators seemed to realise that to omit adoption from the 1989 reforms was to ignore the message convincingly given by the Houghton Committee that adoption should be regarded primarily as one of the various techniques available to deal with children in need. But the fact that reform of adoption law was not only technically a complex matter but also potentially a highly controversial one was soon to be convincingly demonstrated; and yet again it seems to have been the scandals which came to surround local authority care (and especially institutional care) in the last decade of the twentieth century which served as the catalyst necessary to prompt legislative activity.

The complexity of the issues was demonstrated by an impressively thorough review of Adoption Law and Practice carried out by the Department of Health; and the Conservative (Major) Governments issued two White Papers[231] on the subject, the latter of which incorporated a 104-clause draft Adoption Bill. Although Ministers stated that the Bill would be introduced into Parliament 'at the earliest opportunity' the excited debates on the 1996 divorce reforms[232] may have made the Government's business managers aware that debate on such matters as adoption by homosexuals might cause severe embarrassment with little compensating advantage. In the event, no legislation was introduced by the Conservative Government.[233]

In 1997, after the election of the Blair government, a Private Member was encouraged to introduce the Bill which became the Adoption (Intercountry

---

[229] See p. 711. The Lord Chancellor's statement that adoption is a 'specialized subject' (*Official Report* (HL) vol. 502, col. 488) cannot be regarded as a convincing justification.

[230] For example, the fact that few healthy infants were available for adoption in this country led many prospective adoptive parents to seek to adopt a child born abroad; and the economic problems following the collapse of East European communist regimes may have had an influence on this trend.

[231] *Adoption: The Future* (1993); and *Adoption—A Service for Children* (1976).

[232] Eventually embodied in Family Law Act 1996: see above.

[233] The *Prime Minister's Review, Adoption*, (Cabinet Office, Performance and Innovation Unit, 2000) p. 16 suggests that 'the failure to legislate after raising expectations signalled . . . the relative lack of significance the Government accorded to adoption, and left the legal position unclear'; but this seems somewhat unfair.

Aspects) Act 1999; but this limited (albeit valuable) measure deals with only a small part of adoption law. In February 2000 the Prime Minister announced that he would personally lead a thorough review of adoption policy; and in July 2000 a report by the Cabinet Office Performance and Innovation Unit[234] concluded that the Government should promote an increase in adoption for children who were in the care of local authorities. The Prime Minister stated that 'we know that adoption works for children. . . . we also know that many children wait in care for far too long', and regretted that 'too often in the past adoption has been seen as a last resort'. Eventually[235] a 145-clause Bill was brought forward to 'restate and amend' the law. The Bill once again proved controversial (not least on the issue whether unmarried couples, whether of the same or different sexes, should be allowed to adopt a child). But there seemed to be wide agreement on many of the proposed changes, of which two are particularly significant:

(i) *Child's welfare paramount.* The Bill makes the child's welfare the *paramount* consideration for courts and adoption agencies in all decisions relating to adoption, including whether to dispense with the agreement of a birth parent. Procedurally, the Bill provides for issues about consent to be dealt with before the child is placed for adoption.

(ii) *Facilitating adoption of children in care.* At the turn of the century about half of all adoptions were of children in local authority care.[236] The Government has set a target of a 40% increase in adoptions of such children. To this end, adoption support services are to be improved, and intending adopters rejected by adoption agencies are to have a right to an independent review of the decision; whilst a national register is to be established to assist in recruiting adopters and matching them with suitable children.

The new legislation[237] will go a long way to integrate adoption with other procedures for dealing with children in need. But the impression that greater use of adoption will follow and have the beneficial results which the Government anticipates remains to be tested.

---

[234] *Prime Minister's Review, Adoption* (2000).

[235] The Bill was introduced into the House of Commons in October 2001. It built on and incorporated many of the provisions in the Major Government's 1996 Bill, but also took account of the Blair government's White Paper, *Adoption, A New Approach* (2000, Cm. 5017). A similar Bill had been introduced in March 2001 and received a Second Reading but fell at the dissolution of Parliament in April.

[236] It appears that the others are mostly adoptions by step-parents or relatives or adoptions of children brought from abroad. There are now very few adoptions of the once traditional kind, ie adoptions by strangers of children under two.

[237] The Adoption and Children Act 2002 is intended to be brought into force in 2004.

PART V

THE FAMILY JUSTICE SYSTEM
AT THE MILLENNIUM

21

The Family and the Law: Reform of the English Family Justice System Towards the End of the Twentieth Century

INTRODUCTION

The debates leading to the enactment of the Divorce Reform Act 1969 had led to much renewed questioning of the role of the courts in relation to divorce; but the legal system, fuelled to a significant extent by legal aid, had increasingly come to be involved in other family issues. There were for example disputes about money and property, whether between a couple (married or unmarried) whose relationship had broken down or after a death, and there were issues about children. At the same time, many people claimed that cases involving the family required a different approach from commercial disputes or criminal prosecutions, and that the court system of 1969 did not encourage the development of the specialist expertise which was required.

The Administration of Justice Act 1970 created a Family Division of the High Court. But increasingly there was agitation for the creation of a specialist system of family courts, which would not only adjudicate on family disputes but which would also harness the skills of the social sciences to situations of family dysfunction. Publication in 1974 of the report of the *Committee on One-Parent Families*[1] (the Finer Report) gave powerful support to critics of the family justice system and advocates of family courts; and the Report's analysis of the concept of the family court came to dominate discussion for many years. But the Finer Report paid little attention to what came to be seen to be a major failing of the legal system: how women and others could most effectively be protected against violence and molestation. Here the problem was not so much that the law did not in theory offer protection but that the complexity of the law and the lack of effective enforcement procedures often meant that the legal right not to be beaten or abused was in practice illusory. Concern about the ineffectiveness of the law had an important impact on the formation of legal policy, whilst the suggestion that legal processes sometimes exacerbated family differences led to

---

[1] Chaired by Sir Morris Finer: see Biographical Notes. The Committee's Report (Cmnd. 5629) is hereafter referred to as 'the *Finer Report*'.

renewed interest in alternatives to litigation and notably to the possibilities of mediation and other forms of dispute resolution.

This chapter therefore:

(i) outlines the new court structure established by the Administration of Justice Act 1970;

(ii) analyses the Finer Report's recommendation for the creation of a system of family courts; and describes the campaign to which publication of the Report added momentum;

(iii) sketches the process by which new legislative procedures intended more effectively to deal with the phenomenon of domestic violence were introduced;

(iii) notes the influence of the pervasive belief that conciliation (or mediation) should have a greater role in the family justice system, and especially on the thinking which gave rise to the attempt made by the Family Law Act 1996 to translate the concept of divorce as a 'process over time' into legislative form.

Finally, we seek to assess the impact of the legislative and procedural changes in the last years of the twentieth century on the family justice system with particular reference to the question of how far the Finer Report's prescription has become a reality.

THE CREATION OF THE FAMILY DIVISION OF THE HIGH COURT, 1970: SPECIALISATION REVIVED

Divorce was originally a matter for specialists; and for half a century or more after the Matrimonial Causes Act 1857 made judicial divorce available in this country the judges of the 'Divorce Court' (as we have seen) repeatedly asserted that the jurisdiction they exercised required a high degree of specialist expertise. They claimed that to extend jurisdiction to other High Court judges or (even worse) to the county court would have the most serious and detrimental consequences for the administration of the law. But these claims could not be sustained in the world of mass divorce which emerged from the two World Wars when divorce cases were increasingly tried by common law judges at Assize and by Divorce Commissioners (including county court judges) both in London and the provinces. Finally it had to be accepted that the 400 or so county court judges could safely be entrusted with jurisdiction to grant at least those divorces which were undefended.[2] These changes made it difficult to sustain any notion that trying divorce cases was work for judicial specialists.

---

[2] See Chapter 8, above. By the year 2002 the number of circuit judges (formerly county court judges) had risen to 605: *Judicial Statistics Annual Report 2001* Table 9.1.

But the breakdown of marriage did not only affect the husband and wife. It is true that for many years the question of who was to have custody of the children and how they were to be supported was dealt with as an incident (and often only a minor incident) of the granting of a divorce, in practice usually following virtually automatically from the decision about who had succeeded in the divorce suit. But the end of World War II saw a considerable increase in litigation about the upbringing of children. In part this stemmed from increasing acceptance of the view that questions about the upbringing of the children of divorced parents should be resolved by an assessment of the children's welfare in which the question of the matrimonial guilt or innocence of the parents was not the dominant factor;[3] and this acceptance was underlined by recommendations in both the *Denning* and *Morton Reports* for distinctive procedures to ensure that the courts were properly informed about relevant considerations. But in part the question of how to provide for children arose in other cases, especially those in which (following the Children Act 1948) local authorities had become involved by reason of concerns about children's welfare. And disputes about property could arise between unmarried as well as between married (or formerly married) couples.

No rational general principle governed the allocation of cases involving family issues to different courts and different judges. Some (for example, the affiliation proceedings in which the court could adjudge a man the putative father of an illegitimate child and order him to make financial provision for the child, and proceedings involving a local authority's decision to assume parental rights over a child) were the preserve of the magistrates' courts, but in other areas (for example, applications by married women for financial support orders against a husband) applications could be made to either the High Court the county court or to the magistrates.[4] Even within the High Court by no means all cases concerning the family were allotted to the Probate Divorce and Admiralty Division. For example, the burgeoning[5] wardship jurisdiction of the High Court—often invoked in disputes about children, even in cases where a divorce petition had been filed—was, for historical reasons, dealt with exclusively in the Chancery Division of the High Court, as were applications for reasonable provision out of a deceased person's estate and many applications relating to property rights; whilst the Queen's Bench Division handled some appeals from decisions taken by magistrates in the exercise of their family jurisdiction.

---

[3] See Chapter 16, above.

[4] But the relevant statutory provisions were markedly different, and generally the magistrates had only restricted powers: see Chapter 11, above.

[5] See Chapter 16, above.

The situation obviously called for rationalisation;[6] and in 1969 Lord Chancellor Gardiner introduced legislation creating[7] a Family Division of the High Court (to which, for present purposes, it suffices to say 'almost every jurisdiction of a family kind'[8] was allotted). The Probate Divorce and Admiralty Division was no more; and since the coming into force of the Administration of Justice Act 1970 there has once again been a specialist High Court judiciary exclusively responsible for the greatly increased range of family litigation in the High Court.[9] As Lord Gardiner put it:[10]

'. . . we are not simply striving for something that would be tidier and look better on an organisational chart. This is a matter that concerns human feelings and it is most important that all family matters . . . should be dealt with in the most sympathetic atmosphere and by Judges and officials who really understand family problems and how to grapple with them. More and more emphasis is now laid on the importance of welfare: the welfare of every member of the family who may be concerned in any domestic case that comes before the courts. So long as the jurisdiction in family matters is scattered . . . and often dealt with by Judges and others in between other totally dissimilar kinds of business, it must surely be so much harder for those who are concerned to be familiar with welfare matters and keep an eye constantly on them'.

---

[6] Proposals for rationalisation along the lines ultimately taken by the Administration of Justice Act 1970 seem first to have been made by JES Simon (subsequently Lord Simon of Glaisdale and President of the Probate Divorce and Admiralty Division: see Biographical Notes) in evidence to the *Royal Commission on Marriage and Divorce* (Chairman, Lord Morton of Henryton: *Minutes of Evidence* (7th day, 29 May 1952) pp. 202–203. See also the material cited in the *Report of the Committee on the Age of Majority* (Chairman: the Hon. Mr Justice Latey) (1967, Cmnd. 3342) paras. 241–248. The Latey Committee recommended that the divorce division be invested with wardship (and some other child-related) jurisdiction; and that the Law Commission should consider the desirability of establishing a Family Division of the High Court and giving the magistrates' courts jurisdiction in all children's cases (including wardship). In the event no public investigation of this subject (extremely sensitive insofar as it contemplated an extension of the magistrates' jurisdiction) took place.

[7] In strict accuracy, the Act simply re-named the Probate Divorce and Admiralty Division the Family Division: Administration of Justice Act 1970, s. 1(1).

[8] *Per* Lord Gardiner LC, *Official Report* (HL) 4 December 1969, vol. 306, col. 196. The business allocated to the Family Division was specified in detail in Schedule 1 of the Administration of Justice Act 1970. There was a certain amount of what might be described as horse-trading between different groups of practitioners (see SM Cretney, 'New Courts for Old' (1970) 114 SJ 579): thus, the Chancery Division had to be compensated for the loss of the wardship jurisdiction, so contentious probate business was assigned to the Chancery Division of the High Court (Administration of Justice Act 1970, s. 1(4)(b)) whilst the Chancery Division retained jurisdiction to deal with applications under the Inheritance (Family Provision) Act 1938. (An attempt to transfer this jurisdiction to the Family Division was defeated: see *Official Report* (HC) 4 May 1970, vol. 801, col. 109, although subsequently the Inheritance (Provision for Family and Dependants) Act gave the Family Division concurrent jurisdiction, the Government rejecting the Law Commission's proposal that such jurisdiction should be exclusive.)

[9] Over the years other members of the judicial hierarchy have also become specialists; whilst specialist barristers and solicitors have come to dominate the administration of family law.

[10] *Official Report* (HL) 4 December 1969, vol. 306, col. 198.

[11] By, amongst others, SM Cretney, 'New Courts for Old' (1970) 114 SJ 579.

The creation of the Family Division can be seen in retrospect to have had considerable significance, not least in confirming the separate identity and intellectual respectability of family law. But the legislation was strongly criticised at the time[11] for its limited scope.[12] In particular, the legislation dealt only with the arrangement of business at the highest level in the court hierarchy, and did nothing to reform or integrate the extensive family jurisdiction exercised by magistrates. There were many who believed that much more radical reform was necessary: the creation of the Family Division of the High Court did little to still criticism of such matters as the random distribution[13] of family business between the High Court the county court and the magistrates,[14] the supposedly criminal atmosphere of the magistrates' courts, and the fact that the basis of matrimonial relief differed according to the court in which proceedings were instituted.[15]

[12] See eg the Bishop of Leicester's comments on the Second Reading debate: *Official Report* (HL) 4 December 1969, vol. 306, col. 226: it would have been 'more natural to begin at the bottom, and to bring in family courts at local level, able to absorb much of the work now done in juvenile courts and in the domestic procedures which take place in magistrates' courts . . . appeals from decisions in magistrates' courts on findings of fact in bastardy cases will continue to go . . . to quarter sessions where they lose that degree of privacy which is afforded to such cases in magistrates' courts, and where they enter a more or less criminal atmosphere. Similarly, appeals arising out of orders in magistrates' juvenile courts, orders concerning [local authority] care for the most part, continue to go to quarter sessions . . .'.

[13] See J Eekelaar, *Family Security and Family Breakdown* (1971) pp. 278–279; and note the view expressed by Sir Jack Jacob (sometime Senior Master of the Queen's Bench Division and an acknowledged authority on procedures) in 'The Reform of Civil Procedural Law' (1980) 14 L Teach 13–14 that the two systems of jurisdiction, two sets of procedures, two ranges of remedies and two different kinds of justice being administered in the magistrates' courts on the one hand and the superior courts on the other led to 'difference, anomalies and evils . . . as indefensible as was the co-existence of the Courts of Common Law and the Court of Chancery before 1875 . . .'.

[14] For example, the High Court and County Court could commit a child to the care of a local authority if it considered there were exceptional circumstances rendering that course desirable for the child's welfare, whereas a magistrates' court could only make such an order if one of the grounds specified in the Children and Young Persons Act 1969 was made out; and whereas most family work in the magistrates' courts was handled by specialist domestic courts the making of care orders was entrusted to the juvenile court (the great bulk of whose business was concerned with delinquency). For a full analysis of the procedural and structural complexities of the court system see *Report of the Committee on Statutory Maintenance Limits* (Chairman, Miss Jean Graham Hall) (1968, Cmnd. 3587) Chapter 2; and for a remarkable (albeit mercifully hypothetical) illustration of how the system could create unnecessary confusion, inconvenience, extra costs and delays, see B Hoggett, 'Family courts or family law reform—which should come first?' (1986) 6 *Legal Studies* 1, 3–5.

[15] In particular, in order to obtain financial relief or a separation order in a magistrates' court under Matrimonial Proceedings (Magistrates' Courts) Act 1960 it was necessary to prove the commission of a matrimonial offence, whereas relief in the High Court or county court was (after the coming into force of the Divorce Reform Act 1969) based on the fact that the marriage had irretrievably broken down.

[16] For the appointment of the Committee and its terms of reference, see p. 467, above.

THE *FINER REPORT*:[16] FAMILY COURTS

The background

The *Finer Report* was not the first official body in this country to suggest the creation of a system of 'family courts'. In 1965[17] the White Paper *The Child The Family and the Young Offender*,[18] heavily influenced by the notion that protecting society from juvenile delinquency and helping and protecting deprived children were complementary rather than contradictory,[19] had made a proposal for the creation of 'family courts'[20] to work in partnership with 'family councils'. Those proposals were never accepted, and reforms of the law relating to children made by the Children and Young Persons Act 1969[21] did not extend to any radical restructuring of the court system. But the notion of a 'family court' remained the subject of favourable if loosely structured comment and discussion:[22] there was little if any analysis of what exactly was meant. As the *Finer Report* noted, the notion of a 'family court' had come to be canvassed amongst social workers and family lawyers but submissions on the subject made to the Committee offered, for the most part, 'more by way of enthusiasm than elucidation'; and the Report found it difficult to 'extract from the discussion precisely what [were] the attributes and advantages of the institution which those who praise it have in mind'.[23]

The Committee proceeded to fill this vacuum with a detailed prescription for what it believed to be required. This dominated discussion for the next two decades and still forms the basis for any discussion of the structure of the English family justice system.

---

[17] In the same year, the Law Commission's *First Programme of Law Reform* (1965) Item X(c) envisaged an examination of the 'jurisdiction of the courts dealing with family matters; . . . in particular as to how such jurisdiction should be allocated between the courts, and whether or not any new courts should be constituted to deal with such matters'. These developments may have prompted the first comprehensive analysis from an English perspective of the concepts of a family court: see LN Brown, 'The Legal Background to the Family Court' (1966) *British Journal of Criminology* 139.

[18] 1965, Cmnd. 2742.   [19] *Children in Trouble* (1968, Cmnd. 3601) para. 7.

[20] The statement in the *Finer Report*, para. 4.279, that this was the 'first official use of the term' is incorrect.

[21] See Chapter 20, above.

[22] For example, the Government's proposals in 1974 to allow undefended divorces to be tried in the county court were attacked on the basis that they were insufficiently radical and that the creation of a family court would be the only satisfactory solution to the problem of dealing with the consequences of marital breakdown: see eg *Official Report* (HC) 4 April 1967, vol. 744, col. 82; and there was similar criticism in 1970. M Murch and D Hooper, *The Family Justice System* (1992) is a stimulating, well-informed and thoughtful analysis of developments.

[23] *Finer Report*, para. 4.280. However, note J Graham Hall, 'Outline of a Proposal for a Family Court' [1971] Fam Law 6.

The *Finer Report's* concept of a family court: a judicial institution doing justice according to law[24]

The philosophical starting point of the Finer Committee's *Report* was conservative. The Committee rejected out of hand the notion founded in a 'social work philosophy which regards family breakdown as a phenomenon to be dealt with primarily by diagnosis and treatment'.[25] It followed that the Committee rejected models (of the kind the Committee believed to be common in the United States)[26] of the family court as an essentially therapeutic institution concerned to diagnose and cure the underlying cause of family disorder.[27] Rather, the Committee accepted the distinction[28] previously drawn by the Harris and Denning Committees between adjudication (which was the proper role of the courts) and treatment (which, in this context, was not).[29] Whilst the courts should certainly encourage reconciliation, make orders designed to promote the welfare of those affected, and in suitable cases refer questions of reconciliation and welfare to other more appropriate agencies they should not assume responsibility for either reconciliation or welfare.[30] As Lord Mackay of Clashfern was subsequently to say: the primary role of courts is to resolve disputes 'where an authoritative judicial decision has something positive to contribute to a family's well being'.[31]

---

[24] *Finer Report*, para. 4.285. [25] *Ibid.*, para. 4.281.

[26] The Committee emphasised that its approach owed 'little to American experience or writings', and recorded its view that some manifestations of the family court in the United States 'might be regarded as verging on the bizarre': see paras. 4.281–4.282.

[27] 'Americans preach that the procedure of the family court must be therapeutic. This means no more (but no less) than that, just as the juvenile court seeks to do what is best for the child, so the family court should approach its wider jurisdiction inspired by a similar philosophy. In every case it would seek to diagnose and cure the underlying cause of the family disorder. Thus, in divorce it would think first of marriage-mending before marriage-ending. For this remedial function it would need to be buttressed with adequate expert assistance, whether within the court or in the local community. Where, however, cure proved impossible, the family court would perform its legal operation (such as divorce) with the least traumatic effect upon the personalities involved': LN Brown, 'The Legal Background to the Family Court' (1966) *British Journal of Criminology* 139, 149.

[28] Note also the view, expressed with characteristic vigour by Sir Claud Schuster to the Joint Select Committee on the Guardianship of Infants Bill (Minutes of Evidence 25 July 1922 at p. 28) cited at p. 571, above that courts are not equipped to resolve differences of opinion or questions where no actual legal right or wrong was involved; and that a court must be concerned with the definite ascertainment of the rights of the parties, a party on one side and a party on the other. But in practice, the family courts now routinely decide issues such as the school to be attended by a child: see eg *Re P (A Minor)(Education)* [1992] 1 FLR 316, CA.

[29] The validity of this distinction has become so widely accepted that it seems pointless to question it. But it is perhaps worth pointing out that three successive Presidents of the High Court family division (ie Lord Merrivale, Lord Merriman, and Lord Simon of Glaisdale) seem to have had doubts about its validity (and Lord Simon believed that to accept a rigid distinction between adjudication and social services was based on the erroneous belief that this country's constitution was based on Montesquieu's doctrine of the separation of powers: see Simon to Scarman, PRO BC3/387, 22 June 1966).

[30] Sir L Scarman, 'Achievements and the Way Ahead' (1971) 121 New LJ 671, 672.

[31] *Official Report* (HL) 31 January 1991, vol. 925, col. 799.

In accordance with this philosophy, the first of the *Finer Report's* 'major criteria' for a family court was that it should be an 'impartial judicial institution, regulating the rights of citizens and settling their disputes according to law'.[32] But if the family court was to satisfy consumer expectations, it would have to be efficient; and it would take account of the need to 'service problems of different orders of complexity at different levels'[33] by deploying the different levels in the judicial hierarchy (including lay magistrates) to the appropriate kind of case.

The family court would also be a 'unified institution applying a uniform set of legal rules'.[34] No longer would the rules for deciding whether a spouse was under an obligation to maintain or whether he or she should be excluded from the family home, for example, differ depending on the court to which the application was made. Moreover, the court should be what is now described as 'user friendly': it should 'organise its procedures, sittings and administrative services and arrangements with a view to gaining the confidence and maximising the convenience of the citizens who appear before it',[35] perhaps (for example) having sittings in the evenings or at weekends. Finally, although it would not be the court's function itself to provide therapy[36] it would 'organise its work in such a way as to provide the best possible facilities for conciliation'[37] between the parties to matrimonial disputes; and to this end the court would have 'professionally trained staff to assist both the court and the parties appearing before it in all matters requiring social work services and advice, and work in close relationship with the social security authorities in the assessment both of need and liability in cases involving financial provision'.[38]

The campaign for a family court

The Finer Committee's advocacy convinced many of those professionally involved in the family justice system[39] as well as many[40] other commentators;

---

[32] The court was to be a civil court with no criminal jurisdiction (eg over delinquents or parents alleged to have abused their children): see *Finer Report*, paras. 4.360–4.363. In this respect too the Committee rejected American models.

[33] *Finer Report*, para. 4.353.   [34] *Ibid.*, para. 4.282.   [35] *Ibid.*, para. 4.283(6).

[36] This was not to say that those involved in the family justice system might not need special skills and training to deal appropriately with parties caught up in emotional conflicts: see British Agencies for Adoption and Fostering and Association of Directors of Social Services, *Family Justice—a Structure for the Family Court* (1986).

[37] A term to which the *Finer Report* gave a distinctive meaning: see below.

[38] *Finer Report*, para. 4.283(3), (4) and (5).

[39] See notably J Graham Hall and DF Martin, 'Towards a Unified Family Court—the Cost Factor' [1983] CJQ 223; and note that the *Finer Report's* analysis was echoed in other Commonwealth jurisdictions: see notably the Law Reform Commission of Canada's Working Paper on *The Family Court* (1974). But for an analysis of some of the difficulties see M Murch, *Justice and Welfare in Divorce* (1980); and E Szwed, 'The Family Court' in MDA Freeman (ed.), *State, Law, and the Family* (1984).

[40] There were those who favoured a different approach, for example, B Mortlock (the pseudonym of a distinguished London solicitor) argued in *The Inside of Divorce* (1972) that the 'atmosphere and ethos' of courts—'places where trials take place, legal rights are established, damages awarded and people sent to prison'—are 'inconsistent with, if not hostile to, the needs of people in

and political pressures during the 1970s for the creation of a family court were unrelenting.[41] Pressure groups[42] dedicated to the creation of family courts were established, and various official and quasi-official bodies voiced their support[43] (albeit there were still often significant differences in what was meant by a 'family court').[44]

Finer prescription rejected as too costly

Successive Governments followed the example of the Secretary of State for Social Services in the Labour Government, Mrs Barbara Castle,[45] who told Parliament, in 1975[46] that there was 'no prospect' of implementing the Finer proposals. The mid-1970s were a time of serious economic difficulty;[47] and it was evidently felt that creation of family courts would be costly both in terms of building and providing the support services to which Finer had attached great

family difficulties'; and suggested the establishment of tribunals which would 'discuss the particular family matter in a friendly relaxed atmosphere in order to decide how best to effect the reorganisation with the smallest disadvantage to anybody'. In contrast, MDA Freeman, 'The Settlement of Disputes—Historical and Theoretical Perspectives', in J Eekelaar and S Katz (eds.), *The Resolution of Family Conflicts* (1984) cautioned against the risks of excessive delegalisation of family dispute resolution which he saw as permitting rampant interventionism by supposedly expert professionals.

[41] See E Szwed, 'The Family Court' in MDA Freeman (ed.), *State, Law, and the Family* (1984). Stimulus to the campaign for the introduction of family courts was also provided by favourable accounts of the experience of Commonwealth countries. In Australia the Family Law Act 1975 had set up a court well-resourced with counselling and welfare services and devoid of the traditional trappings of the common law court system (such as wigs and gowns). However, it appears that by the early 1980s criticism of the Australian court was being voiced with increasing frequency—it was said that the court was a 'Star Chamber, a secret court whose transactions were closed to the public, with the result that there was little or no public scrutiny of its work': HA Finlay, RJ Bailey-Harris and MFA Otlowski, *Family Law in Australia* (5th ed., 1997) p. 28. The image of the court certainly became somewhat tarnished when one judge of the court (and also the wife of another) were murdered by dissatisfied litigants.

[42] Eg the *Family Courts Campaign* (which in 1986 published *A Court fit for Families*).

[43] Support was given by organisations representing lawyers (the Law Society's Family Law Committee published three papers supporting the creation of a family court: *A Better Way Out* (1979); *A Better Way Out Reviewed* (1982); *A Family Court, Consultation Paper* (1985)); local authorities (Association of County Councils Working Party, *Juvenile Courts* (1984)); and social workers (Association of Directors of Social Services, *Children still in Trouble* (1985) and British Association of Social Workers, *Family courts, A Discussion Document* (1984)); whilst the Conservative Party also published a pamphlet favouring family courts: see *The Case for Family Courts* (Conservative Political Centre, 1978). The *Select Committee on Violence in the Family*, 1977 HC 329 i–iii had urged the creation of family courts, whilst the *Social Services Committee Report on Children in Care*, HC 360, 1983–84, paras. 83–93 had favoured family courts although recognising that this was a project for the longer term. It was repeatedly urged upon the 1985 *Review of Child Law* that reform of the substantive law could not be contemplated in isolation from reform of the courts: B Hoggett, 'Family courts or family law reform—which should come first?' (1986) 6 *Legal Studies* 1, 3.

[44] MDA Freeman, 'The Settlement of Disputes—Historical and Theoretical Perspectives', in J Eekelaar and S Katz (eds.), *The Resolution of Family Conflicts* (1984) p. 8.

[45] See Biographical Notes.

[46] *Official Report* (HC) 20 October 1975, vol. 898, col. 60. Further negative responses are collected in SM Cretney, *Principles of Family Law* (4th ed., 1984) p. 979.

[47] See p. 469, above.

importance. But whilst the need to keep public expenditure in check[48] was clearly an important consideration for the government;[49] it has been suggested that some professionals' and officials' opposition to reform reflected more deep-seated concerns.[50]

The magistrates: *Finer Report* prompts successful counter-attack

There was certainly one source of opposition to the Finer proposals. Finer had made an eloquent and well-documented denunciation[51] of the magistrates' domestic[52] jurisdiction.[53] It was not only that the substantive law which the magistrates administered was different from that of the other courts. For Finer,[54] the magistrates' courts were essentially criminal courts; and the magis-

---

[48] See p. 469, above and note Mrs Castle's statement in *Official Report* (HC) 20 October 1975, vol. 898, col. 59. In her published diary (B Castle, *The Castle Diaries 1974–1976* (1980) p. 523) Mrs Castle records that the then Lord Chancellor (Elwyn Jones), albeit 'as charming as usual' had convinced her that 'the elaborate new machinery Finer proposes is just not on'.

[49] See the Law Commission's *Fourteenth Annual Report 1978–1979* (1980) Law Com. No. 97, para. 2.27: in the light of discussions between the Law Commission and the Lord Chancellor's Department it became 'clear that this matter is so much governed by considerations of public finance that it would not be practicable for the Commission to seek to review it at this time. Further consideration of this issue must therefore be left to departmental channels of law reform, at any rate for the time being'.

[50] See M Murch, *Justice and Welfare in Divorce* (1980) Chapter 15, for the view that the ambiguity and confusion of the existing system 'allows all kinds of conflicting interests to be served—at the cost of consumer satisfaction'; and that many of the widely criticised attributes of forensic activity—such as procedures which 'depersonalise, create delays and which fragment the handling of [consumers'] affairs by parcelling them up so that different parts are dealt with by different people in different places, at different times'—reflect defence mechanisms against judges, lawyers and others professionally involved becoming overwhelmed by 'intense and unmanageable anxiety' stemming from their own psychological and emotional background.

[51] The *Finer Report* was particularly critical of the inadequacy of the assessment of financial matters made by the magistrates, and by the alleged tendency of the magistrates to seek to enforce financial obligations by imprisonment: see Chapter 11, above.

[52] It had been widely assumed that the availability of legal aid for divorce had transformed the magistrates' jurisdiction to one concerned primarily with regulating financial matters: see eg the *Report of the Committee on Statutory Maintenance Limits* (Chairman, Miss Jean Graham Hall) (1968, Cmnd. 3587) para. 28; and note that the Law Commission in its Working Paper No. 53 *Matrimonial Proceedings in Magistrates' Courts* (1973) at para. 24 had even suggested that the magistrates' jurisdiction was invoked to deal with marital difficulties which had not become irretrievable. The *Finer Report* convincingly refuted the view that the magistrates provided a 'casualty clearing station' for the victims of marital breakdown (see p. 471, note 185, above) whilst research established that non-cohabitation orders were in practice still made in many cases, and that such orders often remained in force for many years: see the *Finer Report*, particularly at para. 4.383; OR McGregor, L Blom-Cooper and C Gibson, *Separated Spouses* (1970) p. 60 ff.

[53] An increasing proportion of spouses taking court action preferred to seek a divorce (for which legal aid had been available since 1950). Whereas in 1935 there had been 480 complaints for matrimonial orders to the magistrates' courts for every 100 divorce petitions by wives, in 1970 the ratio was 66 magistrates' applications to 100 divorce petitions. But even so more than 30,000 applications for magistrates' orders were still made each year: the *Finer Report*, para. 4.71.

[54] And others. The magistrates' domestic jurisdiction had a bad press in the 1970s: there were a number of widely publicised (and often misunderstood) cases—for example, the *Desramault* case: see T Skyrme, *The Changing Face of the Magistracy* (2nd ed., 1983) pp. 169–170; whilst magistrates' courts were usually the judicial organ involved in various child care scandals of the period.

trates' matrimonial jurisdiction did no more than provide inferior legal remedies for 'many very poor folk who possess neither knowledge nor expectation of any other legal cures for their marital ills'.[55] For Finer, there was only one solution: the distinctive domestic jurisdiction of the magistrates' courts[56] should be abolished. Finer did emphasise the 'vital role' which lay magistrates would play in the new family court,[57] but that did little to make extinction more palatable.

Faced with this challenge, in the 1970s the magistrates—particularly through the Magistrates' Association[58] and the increasingly articulate and progressive Justices' Clerks Society[59]—began (evidently with the support of the Home Office)[60] to fight back.

The counter-attack seems to have been largely successful. In 1974, the Law Commission effectively abandoned the enquiry which it had started into court structures in 1971;[61] and in 1975 the Government rejected a proposal[62] that the magistrates should give up their family (and other civil) jurisdiction in order to allow them to develop to the full the skills required in their primary role of administering the criminal law. As already noted,[63] in 1978 the Government speedily brought forward the Domestic Proceedings and Magistrates' Courts Bill, based on recommendations from a Home Office/Law Commission Working Party[64] and intended to enable magistrates' courts the better to

---

[55] *Finer Report*, para. 4.383.

[56] *Finer Report*, para. 4.379(1); and the participation of magistrates in Finer's family court would be restricted to sitting with a professional circuit judge in the lowest tier of the family court. *Finer Report*, para. 4. 379(1).

[57] *Finer Report*, para. 4.379(2). The Committee also recorded that the 'inclusion of the magistrates in the family court would for us be a matter of choice even if [the need to provide an adequate number of family court judges had not made it] a matter of necessity': para. 4.348.

[58] See T Skyrme, *History of the Justices of the Peace* (1994) p. 694 ff, p. 794 ff, and p. 880 ff.

[59] *Ibid.*, p. 827 ff. Justices' clerks play a crucial role in the system of Family Proceedings Courts established under the Children Act 1989 and have power to exercise certain judicial functions in family cases: see the Justices' Clerks Rules 1970 as amended; and the discussion of the Clerks' role in case management in *The Children Act Advisory Committee Annual Report 1994/95*, p. 55.

[60] Which at that time had departmental responsibility for the magistrates' courts.

[61] The decision to set up the Working Party (on which the Home Office was represented) was prompted by the restructuring of the High Court in 1970. Its remit was to consider the structure, composition and jurisdiction of courts below High Court level which dealt with family matters: *Seventh Annual Report* (1972) Law Com. No. 50, para. 46. Publication of the Finer proposals made the future of the magistrates' jurisdiction largely a political matter, and the Working Party's operations were accordingly 'suspended indefinitely': Law Commission *Ninth Annual Report* (1974), Law Com. No. 64, para. 31. Some account of the activities of the Working Party is given by J Neville Turner (1974) 4 Fam Law 39.

[62] Made by the *Committee on the Distribution of Criminal Business between the Crown Court and Magistrates' Courts* (1975, Cmnd. 6323).

[63] See Chapter 11, above.

[64] The Working Party seems to have been in existence since 1967: see PRO BC3/414, and p. 470, note 183, above but its remit was evidently reviewed in 1971 and became to consider 'what changes in the matrimonial law administered by magistrates' courts may be desirable as a result of the coming into operation of the Divorce Reform Act 1969 and the Matrimonial Proceedings and Property Act 1970, and any other changes which may appear to be called for in related legislation to avoid the creation of anomalies'. At this stage, the Working Party consisted of two Law Commissioners, two members of the Commission's staff, and four Whitehall officials. Its provisional proposals were published as Law Commission Working Paper No. 53, *Matrimonial Proceedings in Magistrates'*

perform the function of providing 'first aid in a marital casualty clearing station'.[65] All this was quite inconsistent with any notion that the magistrates' family jurisdiction should wither away. On the contrary: a decade later, in 1989, the Children Act gave the magistrates' courts (under the guise of 'Family Proceedings Courts') jurisdiction to make orders in both public and private law cases under that Act; and in practice many applications for care orders are dealt with by the magistrates.[66] Although statistical information about the family related case load of magistrates' courts is sparse, government policy has been to meet Finer's criticisms by harmonising the substantive law which they apply and treating them as the lowest of three tiers of a family justice system consisting of the High Court, the County Court and the Family Proceedings Court.

The significance of Finer

The fact that Finer's family court recommendations were not implemented does not mean that the Committee's work was wasted. On the contrary, it has been highly influential in many ways, not least in giving further momentum to the notion of conciliation as an objective of the family justice system and in its analysis of the objectives which such a system should serve. Indeed, as we shall see, it is at least arguable that at the end of the twentieth century a 'family court' had been created in this country, albeit in a somewhat modified form. But before dealing with those issues, it is necessary to highlight a puzzling omission from the *Finer Report*. This is that the Report contains no significant discussion of the effectiveness of the legal system in protecting families against violence—an omission all the more surprising since it was the need to protect women against violent husbands which in 1878 had prompted the creation of the magistrates' 'domestic' jurisdiction.[67]

THE LAW'S RESPONSE TO DOMESTIC VIOLENCE:
CIVIL AND CRIMINAL PROCEDURES

Possibly the reason why the *Finer Report* largely ignored the question of the effectiveness of the court system in protecting one-parent families was that, in

Courts (1973); and the Law Commission published its final recommendations and draft legislation in 1976: *Report on Matrimonial Proceedings in Magistrates' Courts* (Law Com. No. 77).

[65] The *Finer Report* had strongly criticised this analogy: see *Finer Report,* paras. 4.365–4.378; but the Law Commission's *Report on Matrimonial Proceedings in Magistrates' Courts* (Law Com. No. 77, at para. 1.12) asserted that it was 'realistic to expect that the function of the magistrates' courts in a dual system will to an increasing extent be that' which the Working Party had envisaged.

[66] In 2001, 14,130 of the 24,134 'public law' applications were made to magistrates' Family Proceedings Courts (as against 9,864 to the county court and 140 to the High Court): *Judicial Statistics Annual Report 2001*, Cm. 5551, Table 5.1.

[67] In the Matrimonial Causes Act 1878; see Chapter 11, above. Remarkably, the *Report of the (Graham Hall) Committee on Statutory Maintenance Limits*, 1968, Cmnd. 3587, para. 29, asserted that 'wives today rarely need the law's protection against cruel husbands'.

theory, the law provided ample redress. Magistrates had power to make a 'separation order' against a man guilty of cruelty, the Divorce Court had power to grant a divorce on that ground, it was well settled that the High Court and the county court had power to grant injunctions restraining the husband (on pain of imprisonment for breach) from molesting the wife and in some circumstances even requiring him to leave the family home, while most 'wife battering' would constitute a criminal offence in respect of which the perpetrator could be prosecuted and imprisoned.[68] But that was theory. The publication in 1974—coincidentally the year in which the *Finer Report* was published—of Erin Pizzey's *Scream Quietly or the Neighbours will Hear* drew attention to the reality, which was that the law often failed to provide any effective redress to victims of what became known as domestic violence. The House of Commons set up a *Select Committee on Violence in Marriage*;[69] and a great deal of attention was given to the subject by scholars and commentators in this country and elsewhere (particularly in the United States).[70]

The Select Committee accepted that the law was inadequate to protect victims. Some of the problems—the apparent reluctance of the police to intervene in what were classified as 'domestic' incidents, at least in the absence of serious physical injury and the reluctance of women to pursue legal proceedings which could result in the punishment of a partner, for example—transcended the imperfections of the legal framework; but that framework was itself shown to be defective. For example, although a woman might obtain an injunction restraining her husband from 'molesting' her, enforcement of its terms was a matter for the civil (rather than the criminal) law. The police had no power to arrest the husband even if they were aware that he was in breach of the injunction. It was up to the wife to apply to the court for a committal order, and if such an order were granted it would be up to the officers of the court (the tipstaff in

---

[68] On the limits of a husband's legal right to control his wife, see *R v. Jackson* [1891] 1 QB 671, p. 146 above. The common law was traditionally said to allow a husband to beat his wife provided he used a stick no bigger than his thumb; and although the existence of such a power began to be doubted in the seventeenth century Blackstone (writing a century later) stated that the 'lower rank of people, who were always fond of the old common law, still claim and exert their ancient privilege': W Blackstone, *Commentaries on the Laws of England* (4th ed., 1770) p. 445; and it appears that this belief remained prevalent: see ME Doggett, *Marriage, Wife-Beating and the Law in Victorian England* (1992). In 1978 the courts affirmed that such a right no longer existed if indeed it ever had: see *Davis v. Johnson* [1979] AC 264, 270. The belief that a man could not be convicted of rape against his wife was widely held until the House of Lords decision in *R v. R* [1992] 1 AC 599: see JL Barton, 'The Story of Marital Rape' (1992) 108 LQR 260 for a provocative historical account.

[69] See Reports of the *Select Committee on Violence in Marriage*, Session 1974–1975, HC 553, i and ii; *Second Report of the Select Committee on Violence in Marriage*, Session 1976–77, HC 431, and *Government Observations on Report from the Select Committee on Violence in Marriage*, (1976, Cmnd. 6690). In 1977 a Select Committee examined the somewhat broader topic of *Violence in the Family*, Session 1976–77, HC 1977 HC 329 i–iii.

[70] The most useful comparative account is by S Maidment, 'The Law's Response to Marital Violence in England and the USA' (1977) 26 ICLQ 403; whilst the contributions to M Borland (ed.), *Violence in the Family* (1976) and JM Eekelaar and SN Katz (eds.), *Family Violence* (1979) put the issues in a somewhat broader context. LJF Smith, *Domestic Violence: an overview of the literature* (Home Office Research Study No. 107, 1989) provides an accessible guide.

the High Court, the bailiffs in the county court) to execute it. And if the husband happened to be the owner of the family home the court (so the House of Lords had held in 1972)[71] had no power under the Matrimonial Homes Act 1967 to order him to leave it (although it could require him to occupy only a part of the house).

The Domestic Violence and Matrimonial Proceedings Act 1976 was intended to remedy some of the defects in the law. It empowered a county court to grant orders forbidding molestation of the other spouse or a child and excluding a spouse from the family home (or part of it); and also extended these powers to cases where a couple were not married but had been living together on a stable basis.[72] But the most significant innovation made by the Act was to bring the police and the criminal justice system into the protective scheme provided in the civil courts: provided there was evidence that the defendant had caused actual bodily harm to the applicant or to a child, the court was given a discretion to attach a *power of arrest* to what were commonly called ouster and non-molestation orders.[73] Such on order would be registered with the police; and the police were empowered to arrest without warrant a person reasonably suspected of being in breach 'by reason of that person's use of violence or . . . his entry into any premises or area'.[74] A person arrested under this provision would be brought before a court and could then be punished for breaking the terms of the order.[75]

The 1976 Act did not extend to the magistrates' courts; but the Domestic Proceedings and Magistrates' Courts Act 1978[76] gave magistrates' courts powers to make personal protection orders and exclusion orders and sought to establish more effective enforcement procedures including a power of arrest.

The 1978 Act was formidably complex; it was also, when compared with the powers of the superior courts under the 1976 Act, in many ways restricted. There was no protection for unmarried couples, the magistrates were not to be allowed to make orders protecting against molestation which did not extend to threatened violence, whilst the magistrates' powers to make orders excluding a spouse from the family home were much narrower than those available in the superior courts. Far from creating the uniform code of law which Finer had envisaged for the family court the 1978 Act, in its application to situations of

---

[71] *Tarr v. Tarr* [1973] AC 254.

[72] The interpretation of this provision caused difficulties only resolved by the House of Lords: *Davis v. Johnson* [1979] AC 264. The Act (s. 1) also abrogated the rule that the wide power to grant injunctions apparently conferred by Supreme Court Act 1981, s. 37 (consolidating earlier legislation) was in fact restricted to cases in which a wife had started (or was prepared to undertake to start) divorce or other proceedings: see *Montgomery v. Montgomery* [1965] P 46.

[73] s. 2(1). A non-molestation order only qualified if its terms restrained the respondent from using violence.

[74] s. 2(3).

[75] It was imperative to comply with the somewhat complex statutory requirements, otherwise a committal order would be set aside: see eg *Williams v. Fawcett* [1985] 1 WLR 501.

[76] The Act was based on recommendations in the Law Commission's *Report on Matrimonial Proceedings in Magistrates' Courts* (Law Com. No 77): see p. 752 above.

domestic violence, seemed to reflect Lord Scarman's telling description[77] of a 'hotchpotch of enactments of limited scope passed into law to meet specific situations or to strengthen the powers of specified courts'; whilst experience of the working of the law[78] demonstrated that it still failed to provide protection on the scale which justice seemed to require. No doubt some of the problems were not apt for a purely legislative solution[79] but the legal framework was still seriously defective.

In 1992 the Law Commission recommended reform so that the law would provide adequate protection for the adults and children involved whilst avoiding unnecessarily exacerbating hostilities. The Commission also proposed synthesising the legal remedies available to deal with domestic violence into a clear, simple and comprehensive code.[80] But there were some who thought that the Law Commission had gone too far in equating the legal position of unmarried and married couples,[81] whilst the question of what qualifications should be required of an applicant wanting to seek legal protection against being 'molested'—the Law Commission had sought to give such protection to those who had had a genuine 'family' relationship rather than, for example, the relationship of householder and lodger—aroused some controversy.[82]

---

[77] *Richards v. Richards* [1984] 1 AC 174, 206–207.

[78] For example, in *Richards v. Richards* [1984] 1 AC 174 the House of Lords emphasised that the conduct of the parties was a relevant consideration in deciding whether a spouse should be excluded from the family home; and the application of this principle (and in particular of the corollary that it was insufficient to show that the welfare of the children would be promoted by excluding a parent) was thought by some to be unsatisfactory. The decision of the House of Lords in *Ainsbury v. Millington* [1987] 1 WLR 379 demonstrated that the protection available to unmarried couples was restricted.

[79] See LJF Smith, *Domestic Violence: an overview of the literature* (Home Office Research Study No. 107, 1989); G Hague and E Malos, *Domestic Violence, Action for Change* (1993); *Report of the Home Affairs Committee, Domestic Violence* (and accompanying Evidence) (1992–3) HC 245. Changing the law so that women became compellable (as distinct from merely competent) witnesses did not seem to have much influence on the high proportion of prosecutions which failed because the victim withdrew or failed to give evidence: see *Hoskyn v. Metropolitan Police Commissioner* [1979] AC 474, Police and Criminal Evidence Act 1984, s. 80; A Cretney and G Davis, 'Prosecuting "Domestic Assault"' [1996] Crim LR 162. But although legislation is only one of the factors influencing (for example) the attitude of the police to cases of domestic violence, changes do occur: it appears that Domestic Violence Units are now universal and that evaluation of police response amongst abused women has improved: see 'Violence against Women in the Family', by R and R Dobash in SN Katz, J Eekelaar and M Maclean (eds.), *Cross Currents . . . (2000)* p. 495.

[80] *Domestic Violence and Occupation of the Family Home* (Law Com. No. 207).

[81] See for an example of the attacks made on the Law Commission and its approach the Memorandum by East London Families need Fathers to the House of Lords Special Public Committee on the Family Homes and Domestic Violence Bill (HL Paper 55, 1994–95) p. 24. Similar views were expressed by some MPs and in a press campaign (notably in the *Daily Mail*): see the Law Commission's *Thirtieth Annual Report 1995* (Law Com. No 239, 1996) para. 1.20.

[82] The Government rejected the Law Commission's proposal that persons who have or have had a 'sexual relationship with each other (whether or not including sexual intercourse)' should thereby be entitled to seek redress. Such a provision might have posed a serious threat to the burgeoning 'kiss and tell' market. The Government also at first resisted a proposal to allow the betrothed (or formerly betrothed) to bring proceedings, but it was eventually decided that such persons should qualify provided there were specified evidence of the agreement.

In 1995, the (Major) Conservative Government introduced a Family Homes and Domestic Violence Bill to give effect to the Law Commission's main proposals. The Bill was carefully examined by the House of Lords Special Public Bill Committee and did not attract much public notice or interest, much less any significant opposition on grounds of principle. But, faced with a sudden storm of opposition from 'pro-marriage' groups amongst its own supporters in the House of Commons, the Government decided to withdraw the Bill. In the following session, the relevant clauses with some additions intended to emphasise the importance of the question whether or not a couple had (or had not) given each other 'the commitment involved in marriage'[83] were reintroduced and became Part IV of the Family Law Act 1996.[84]

The 1996 Act sweeps away the earlier legislation, replacing it with a single consistent set of remedies available in all the courts having jurisdiction in family matters[85] (although it seems that the great bulk of applications for protection against domestic violence are made to the county court).[86] On one view,[87] the combined effect of the 1996 Act and the Children Act 1989 is to create what can properly be called a 'family court'; but before discussing that claim we need to consider in the light of subsequent developments Finer's concept of 'conciliation' as a part of the process for dealing with family breakdown.

FINER'S CONCEPT OF CONCILIATION: A NEW MEANING FOR A NEW ERA

We have seen that for many years it had generally been assumed that the function of 'conciliation' had been primarily (albeit not exclusively) to bring together a couple whose marriage seemed to have broken down. But the *Finer Report* (building, it must be said, on the slenderest of foundations)[88] drew a

[83] See eg Family Law Act 1996, ss. 36, 41; and generally SM Cretney and JM Masson, *Principles of Family Law*, (6th ed., 1997) pp. 255–256.

[84] This part of the Act (unlike the provisions dealing with divorce) was brought into force in 1997: see Family Law Act 1996 (Commencement No. 2) Order, SI No. 1892.

[85] The Protection from Harassment Act 1997—a Private Member's Bill rushed through the House of Commons in two days in the belief that urgent measures were needed against the phenomenon of 'stalking'—effectively creates a tort of harassment, and may be invoked by those who do not qualify to apply under Part IV of the Family Law Act 1996. This episode raises many interesting questions—in the present context, for example, as to what are the boundaries of 'family law' and thus of the 'family court'. For a study of the impact of the 1997 Act see E Finch, *The Criminalisation of Stalking: Constructing the Problem and Evaluating the Solution* (2001).

[86] *Judicial Statistics Annual Report 2000*, Table 5.9: in that year more than 15,000 applications for non-molestation orders were made in the county court (as against 419 in the magistrates' courts).

[87] In the Second Reading Debate on the Family Homes and Domestic Violence Bill (see *Official Report* (HL) 23 February 1995, vol. 561) Lord Chancellor Mackay said (at cols. 1269–1270) that he believed the Children Act 1989 'in effect set up a family court' since it allowed proceedings to be taken either in the family proceedings court at the magistrates' level or in the county court, presided over by judges who have made special studies, and, finally, the Family Division.

[88] The main basis for the distinction was a Report from the National Marriage Guidance Council of New Zealand which (Finer considered) made the 'pragmatic, working distinction' between the concepts of reconciliation and conciliation: see *Finer Report*, paras. 4.304–4.305.

sharp distinction between *reconciliation*, which it defined as 'reuniting persons who are estranged',[89] on the one hand and *conciliation* on the other. For Finer, conciliation was not (or at least not primarily) concerned to bring about a reconciliation, but was rather 'the process of engendering common sense, reasonableness and agreement in dealing with the consequences of estrangement'.[90] The Committee accepted[91] that the judge and the welfare services associated with the court should be alive to any sign that a reconciliation was possible, and in such a case would take the steps ('usually involving referral to an outside agency') most likely to procure it. But the Committee shared the scepticism (common amongst many who had previously studied the issue) about the prospects for securing reconciliation once the parties had presented themselves to formalise the breakdown of the relationship;[92] and urged the 'fundamental importance' of empowering families 'to make the best decisions and reach the best solutions over the whole range of problems' which breakdown involved, placing primary emphasis on the 'practical needs of the family at the time when the court assumes control over the relationship between its members and their affairs'. The message of Finer was that the victims of family breakdown should be encouraged to 'wind up their failure with the least possible recrimination, and to make the most rational and efficient arrangements possible for their own and their children's future'. The Committee believed couples could be helped in this by the provision of conciliation services, notwithstanding the fact that their marriage had broken down, and broken down irretrievably.

The *Finer Report's* eloquent insistence that achieving reconciliation[93] was *not* directly a function for the court system at all, whilst conciliation[94] in the sense in which the Finer Committee defined[95] it was in contrast a service which should be encouraged in the context of the family justice system may, viewed negatively, be no more than the final confirmation of the traditional view put

---

[89] *Finer Report*, para. 4.305.   [90] *Ibid.*   [91] See para. 4.313.   [92] See para. 4.298 ff.

[93] The Committee expressed the conventional view that courts should be alive to any possibility of reconciliation but courts should also bear in mind the policy of the law that dead marriages should be decently buried: para. 4.313. The Finer Committee favoured a procedure under which a family court conference would be held two years after the making of any financial order to encourage the parties to consider their matrimonial future. The Committee clearly considered that many couples, if properly advised, would favour divorce rather than the preservation of the empty legal shell of a broken marriage.

[94] See p. 758, below. The Law Commission's Report *The Ground for Divorce* (Law Com. No. 192, 1990) regarded the terms 'mediation' and 'conciliation' as being 'interchangeable' in the context of the types of activity available to people facing marital breakdown; but those responsible for the Government's Consultation Paper, *Looking to the Future: Mediation and the Ground for Divorce* (1993, Cm. 2424) and the White Paper, *Looking to the Future: Mediation and the Ground for Divorce, The Government's Proposals* (1995, Cm. 2799) on reform use the term 'mediation' rather than conciliation, as does the Family Law Act 1996.

[95] Assisting the parties 'to deal with the consequences of the established breakdown of their marriage . . . by reaching agreements or giving consents in reducing the area of conflict upon custody, support, access to the education of the children, financial provision, the disposition of the matrimonial home, lawyers' fees, and every other matter arising from the breakdown which calls for a decision on future arrangements': *Finer Report*, para. 4.288.

forward in the 1930s by Lord Chancellor Sankey, upheld by the Harris Committee, and accepted by Denning. But the positive side of Finer lies in the influence which its analysis had on the subsequent development of the family justice system. In particular, the enthusiastic support given by the *Finer Report* to conciliation in the context of a family court structure seems to have been influential in shaping opinion.

Finer's distinction between conciliation and reconciliation was almost immediately accepted by the Law Commission's *Report on Matrimonial Proceedings in Magistrates' Courts*;[96] and it was soon realised that although the Finer proposals were made in the context of the creation of a new family court structure[97] 'conciliation' could be practised without this innovation. The notion that conciliation (or—in another interesting verbal change—'mediation') had the potential to help bring failed relationships to an end with the minimum of bitterness and in such a way as to promote a good continuing relationship between the parties and their children[98] was highly influential in developments over the last quarter of the twentieth century. In contrast, although reconciliation remained part of the rhetoric of divorce reform—the Divorce Reform Act 1969[99] had proclaimed that its purpose was to facilitate reconciliation and references to reconciliation as an object of policy continued to be embodied in the family justice legislation[100]—the Finer Report's emphasis on what appeared to be the more attainable objectives of *conciliation* found a ready response. As an Inter-Departmental Committee on Conciliation[101] reported in 1983, there had been an 'enormous growth' of interest in conciliation and great enthusiasm 'both in terms of the numbers of those who freely give their services, and in the strength of their commitment to it'.[102] A vast literature—apparently out of all proportion to the amount of conciliation work actually being undertaken—was published.[103]

The *Finer Report's* enthusiasm for conciliation was influenced primarily by concern for civilising the consequences of marital breakdown. But there was

[96] Law Com. No. 77, 1976, para. 4.11.

[97] Finer claimed that in the family court adjudication and welfare would 'march hand in hand' but without any blurring of the edges, either in principle or in administration. The result would be 'a new and highly beneficial synthesis between law and social welfare, and the respective skills, experience and efforts of lawyers and social workers; but the individual in the family court must in the last resort remain the subject of rights, not the object of assistance': *Finer Report*, para. 4.285.

[98] Family Law Act 1996, s. 1(c).

[99] In this respect following the precedent of the 1937 Matrimonial Causes Act ('the true support of marriage') and the Matrimonial Causes Act 1963 (an 'Act to facilitate reconciliation').

[100] The Domestic Proceedings and Magistrates' Courts Act 1978, s. 26, required magistrates hearing an application for a matrimonial financial order to consider whether there was any possibility of reconciliation between the parties whilst the Probation Rules 1984 r. 26(3) made it clear that attempting to effect a reconciliation under this provision was a part of the probation officer's duties. The Divorce Reform Act 1969 contained a number of procedural measures intended to make reconciliation procedures an institutionalised feature of the divorce process: see Matrimonial Causes Act 1973, s. 6; SM Cretney and JM Masson, *Principles of Family Law* (5th ed., 1990) pp. 146–148.

[101] Chairman, PD Robinson (Lord Chancellor's Department, 1983).   [102] Para. 1.4.

[103] See eg the Bibliography in L Parkinson, *Family Mediation* (1997).

another factor which made the concept attractive to Government. This was that encouraging recourse to conciliation rather than litigation might be an effective technique for reducing the ever increasing pressure on publicly funded legal aid. For this reason, the desirability of encouraging and assisting husband and wife to 'settle their differences without recourse to formal court procedures'[104] became a recurrent and insistent theme[105] of Government pronouncements. The Lord Chancellor's Advisory Committee[106] in particular took an active and supportive interest in the development of facilities for conciliation[107] which (it was hoped) would make divorce less 'adversarial' and thereby not only benefit the parties but also achieve a saving in legal aid expenditure and court time.[108] Conciliation would also minimise the cost of other services—such as health care and education—which were often increased as a result of emotional trauma in divorce.

Much of the public interest and enthusiasm was directed to establishing agencies[109] *outside* the court system intended to assist couples to resolve their problems without litigation. But, although a number of Inquiries were established,[110] Governments concerned to minimise expenditure for long refused to provide any significant assured funding to support what came to be called

[104] As the Lord Chancellor's Advisory Committee on Legal Aid put it in the 39th *Annual Reports*, para. 43. The Advisory Committee (which was dissolved in 1995: see Legal Aid Advisory Committee (Dissolution) Order 1995, SI No. 162 for reasons given in *Official Report* (HL) 30 November 1994, vol. 559, col. 693) believed that if proceedings were necessary the issues should be dealt with 'fairly, expeditiously and inexpensively' and that 'the only way in which this objective can properly be achieved is by the establishment of a unified family court with an emphasis on conciliation and agreement rather than adversarial argument concluded by judgment': para. 43.

[105] See eg *Legal Aid—Targeting Need* (1995, Cm. 2854) paras. 3.29–3.32; and the (Conservative) Government's White Paper, *Striking the Balance* (1996, Cm. 3306) which envisaged holding back legal aid expenditure by measures such as allocating the Legal Aid Board a specific budget for different categories of work (eg family law). The provision of services would not be confined to lawyers, and there would be strong incentives to avoid litigation.

[106] The Reports of the Advisory Committee—certainly down to the 35th *Annual Report 1984–85*—are of great interest for the study of developments in the family justice system.

[107] See in particular the discussion of the services then available in the *30th Legal Aid Annual Reports 1979/80*, Appendix D to which contains a Report on the Bristol Courts Family Conciliation Service in its first year of operation, whilst Appendix E briefly describes other schemes of which the Committee was aware.

[108] Notably by defining the issues between the parties which really required judicial time: see *31st Legal Aid Annual Reports 1980/81*, para. 60. However, in the same report The Law Society noted the lack of a 'coherent policy to ascertain precisely what sort of conciliation service would be most effective in the long term' and in particular to make a choice between so called 'in-court' and 'out of court' schemes. This remains a contentious issue.

[109] It appears that the first service was established in Bristol in 1978: see on this (and generally) L Parkinson, *Family Mediation* (1997) p. 7(and *passim*) and the references there cited.

[110] The *Inter-Departmental Committee on Conciliation* (1983); the *Matrimonial Causes Procedure Committee* (Chairman, Mrs Justice Booth DBE) (1985) and *Report to the Lord Chancellor on the Costs and Effectiveness of Conciliation in England and Wales* (Conciliation Project Unit, University of Newcastle upon Tyne, 1989). Originally most of the Conciliation Services were primarily concerned with issues relating to the upbringing of children, but latterly attempts were made to stimulate comprehensive or all-issues mediation: see J Walker, O McCarthy and N Timms, *Mediation: the Making and Remaking of Co-operative Relationships* (Relate Centre for Family Studies, Newcastle-upon-Tyne 1994).

'out-of-court' conciliation. In direct[111] practical terms, the most that the legal aid authorities could do to support out of court conciliation was to authorise payment by solicitors of modest fees to recognised professionals offering conciliation services and to include that disbursement in the bill which legal aid would pay.[112] But a great deal of work was done *within* the publicly funded court system, in part by the probation service in the Family Court Welfare Service,[113] and in part by District Judges adapting a pre-trial review procedure—sometimes to the extent of giving the parties an indication of what the particular District Judge involved would regard as the likely outcome if the case were litigated—in attempts to encourage the settlement of the financial consequences of their divorce. In the year 2000 this practice—which at one time would have seemed totally inconsistent with traditional notions of the judicial function—was officially adopted, and Rules provided a comprehensive new procedure for dealing with the financial consequences of divorce.[114] This scheme, intended to reduce delay, facilitate settlements, limit costs and provide the court with greater control over the management of the proceedings, was based in essence, on the practices developed over the years by progressively minded District Judges (including the practice of a District Judge giving an indication of the level of provision which he would think appropriate on the basis of the information before him). One form of conciliation was thus formally incorporated into the family justice system.[115]

But there remains one strongly voiced reservation[116] about excessive reliance on conciliation (and even more if the concept is taken to extend to reconcilia-

[111] The legal aid authorities had sanctions available to encourage the parties to reach a settlement rather than pursuing a case to a contested hearing. Although the principle of the legal aid scheme was that the relationship of solicitor and client should be the same for the legally aided as it was for the fee-paying, solicitors owed duties to the Legal Aid Board. In particular, a solicitor had to inform the Legal Aid Board if the client required his case to be conducted so as to involve 'unjustifiable expense'; and the solicitor had to report all reasonable settlement offers to the Board, which would withdraw legal aid if a reasonable offer was rejected: Civil Legal Aid (General) Regulations, regs 1989 regs 70, 77.

[112] See *33rd Legal Aid Annual Reports, 1982/83*, p. 21: the persons producing the Report for which payment was made had to be qualified social workers or probation officers or acceptable substitutes such as suitably trained marriage guidance counsellors. The maximum amount payable under the Green Form scheme was £15 for the Report and £5 for the solicitor (it being a condition that the client should obtain legal advice about the report).

[113] The scale of conciliation work done by the Family Court Welfare Service is often over-looked in the publicity given to services offered by the voluntary sector: in 1992/3 family court welfare officers undertook child-related conciliation in nearly 20,000 cases (whereas the voluntary sector dealt with only a third of this number): *Looking to the future: mediation and the ground for divorce* (1993, Cm. 2424) paras. 7.13–7.14.

[114] Family Proceedings (Amendment No. 2) Rules 1999, SI 1999/3491. The effect of the Rules was stated in a *Practice Direction (Ancillary Relief Procedure)* [2000] 1 FLR 997.

[115] The *Practice Direction (Ancillary Relief Procedure)* also incorporates a *Pre-Application Protocol* which is intended in part to facilitate early and well informed settlement of financial issues. The *Protocol* emphasises the duty on solicitors of keeping under review whether it would be appropriate to suggest mediation to the client as an alternative to solicitor negotiation or court based litigation: para. 2.3.

[116] There also seems to be a measure of scepticism in some quarters about the effectiveness of mediation even in the context of difficulties over contact: see Advisory Board on Family Law: Children Act Sub-Committee *Making Contact Work* (2002) Chapter 7.

tion). This is that an 'amicable settlement' may in fact represent an abuse of bargaining power by the physically and emotionally stronger party—usually the man—and may thus even become an instrument for further damaging a vulnerable woman. It was for this reason that the 'general principles' laid down in the Family Law Act 1996[117] included—albeit only after prolonged opposition from the Government—a directive that any risk to one of the parties to a marriage, and to any children, should 'so far as reasonably practicable, be removed or diminished'.[118]

Marriage saving revived: the Family Law Act 1996

Following the publication in 1990 of the Law Commission's Report on *The Ground for Divorce*[119] the Government accepted[120] that mediation (as 'conciliation' was described, apparently to avoid confusion between the process of dispute resolution and the process of reconciling the parties and saving their marriage)[121] should have a central part in resolving disputes. A White Paper[122] stated:

'Family mediation is a process in which an impartial third person, the mediator, assists couples considering separation or divorce to meet together to deal with the arrangements which need to be made for the future. Because the parties discuss these matters face to face, family mediation is much better able to identify marriages which might be capable of being saved than is the legal process . . . [It] has as its primary objectives: to help separating and divorcing couples to reach their own agreed joint decisions about future arrangements; to improve communications between them; and to help couples work together on the practical consequences of divorce with particular emphasis on their joint responsibilities to co-operate as parents in bringing up their children.'

---

[117] s. 1, brought into force in 1997 and applicable to Legal Aid functions (as well as to the divorce and separation procedures, in the event never brought into force). For the Government's opposition see *per* Mr Jonathan Evans, *Official Report, Standing Committee E*, 4th Sitting, 7 May 1966.

[118] At the end of the twentieth century there was considerable concern about the incidence of violence associated with fathers' contact visits to children: see the Advisory Board on Family Law: Children Act Sub-Committee *Report to the Lord Chancellor on the Question of Contact where there is Domestic Violence* (2000).

[119] Law Com. No 192.

[120] See the Consultation Paper *Looking to the future: mediation and the ground for divorce* (1993, Cm. 2424), and the subsequent White Paper *Looking to the future: mediation and the ground for divorce: the Government's Proposals* (1995, Cm. 2799).

[121] See p. 758 above: there appears to be no difference of substance between 'mediation' and 'conciliation', the former being preferred by reason of its more extensive use in other jurisdictions (particularly in North America) and the minimisation of confusion with 'reconciliation': see eg L Parkinson, *Family Mediation* (1997) p. 7. But the reader should be warned that the vast literature on the subject contains much (sometimes polemical) discussion of the practice and theoretical basis of mediation and conciliation, and it may still be true (as Parkinson says in relation to 'conciliation') that the word became a 'fashionable portmanteau word which increasingly carried whatever bundle of meanings and values its users decided to pack into it').

The Family Law Act 1996 was based on an unequivocal acceptance of the view that mediation had 'enormous potential' to minimise the adverse consequences of marital breakdown. The Act contained a number of provisions to encourage mediation in divorce proceedings. But for the first time the Government went beyond words: public funding was made available through the Legal Aid Board for the provision of mediation. (Conversely, there was to be no funding of legal representation in divorce unless the applicant had first attended a meeting with a mediator and intended to determine whether mediation was suitable in all the circumstances.[123]) Although the provisions relating to the substantive law of divorce were never brought into force, the provisions for funding mediation were implemented;[124] and thus mediation has become a statutorily recognised part of the divorce process.

The 1996 Act also, dramatically, marked a revival of the belief (long scorned by 'informed opinion') that marriages can be 'saved' even after the parties have decided to start the divorce process: the Act required[125] courts and others to have regard to the general principle that the parties to a marriage should be 'encouraged to take all practicable steps, whether by marriage counselling or otherwise, to save the marriage'.[126] Departmental responsibility for marriage support was transferred to the Lord Chancellor's Department; and the 1996 Act[127] gave the Lord Chancellor power to make grants in connection with the provision of marriage support services.[128] Lord Chancellor Mackay believed

---

[122] *Looking to the Future* (1995, Cm. 2799) paras. 5.4–6.

[123] Family Law Act 1996, s. 26. This provision was brought into force in 1997: SI 1997/1897.

[124] Under the Access to Justice Act 1999, 'community Legal Services' administered by the Legal Services Commission replaced legal aid. The principles to be applied in relation to 'Legal Help' and 'Family Mediation' are set out in a Funding Code.

[125] Family Law Act 1996, s. 1(b). This (and the other 'general principles' embodied in the Act) only apply to the exercise of functions under Part II and III of the Act (dealing respectively with divorce and legal aid). Although Part II is not to be brought into force it can be assumed that this assertion of policy will have some influence on the administration of the substantive law embodied in Matrimonial Causes Act 1973.

[126] The Government's 1995 *Divorce White Paper* had asserted (in language which might have been used by Claud Mullins in the 1930s) that people contemplating divorce should have to 'face up to the consequences of their actions and make arrangements to meet their responsibilities' and it was clearly expected that imposing a requirement of a period for 'reflection and consideration' (ie for the parties 'to reflect' on whether the marriage could be saved and to 'have an opportunity to effect a reconciliation intended) before the parties could divorce would make the parties contemplate the practical consequences of divorce and might deter some from opting for it as a solution to their problems.

[127] s. 22. This provision was brought into force in 1997.

[128] See *The Funding of Marriage Support, Report by Sir Graham Hart* (1999). Since 1997 the Lord Chancellor's Department has (in addition to funding for core organisations, for example nearly £2 million for *Relate* in 1998/9) funded research and a number of pilot projects intended to reduce the incidence of marriage breakdown—ranging from a media campaign to change the culture of marriage, through marriage preparation for couples not marrying in church, to various telephone helplines. The 1999 Hart Review recommended that the Lord Chancellor's Department should play a more active role in these matters, and that government should substantially increase the level of funding and also provide leadership on policy matters. The Lord Chancellor's Department has also launched a research programme to investigate the causes of marriage breakdown and ways of preventing breakdown.

that the reconciliation part of the divorce process was 'as important as the mediation proposals, if not more so',[129] but once again it is too early to assess the impact of the legislative support given by the 1996 Act for marriage support; whilst the Blair Government's decision to repeal the new divorce law makes the future difficult to predict.

THE COURT SYSTEM ESTABLISHED BY THE CHILDREN ACT 1989 AND THE FAMILY LAW ACT 1996: A FAMILY COURT FOR THE MILLENNIUM?

What of Lord Mackay's claim that the English legal system now provides what can fairly be described as a family court system?[130] The main features of structural reform since Finer have been:

(i) the creation of a single coherent legislative framework under which—with certain exceptions[131]—all courts in the family justice system administer the same law and have the same remedies available to them;

(ii) the creation of procedures whereby, in an attempt to ensure that cases are heard by the most appropriate court, cases are initially allocated to different levels of court in accordance with specified criteria and can thereafter be transferred either vertically between the three tiers of courts or horizontally within the same tier; and

(iii) the establishment of a comprehensive liaison network intended to improve the management of the court system. How far do these changes satisfy the criteria laid down by Finer?

(1) Harmonisation of the law

The first major step in reform was the enactment of the Children Act 1989, which swept away the confused mass of legislation which made court intervention into children's lives depend on the court in which proceedings were started.[132] The Act created a single comprehensive, practical and clear code, for the first time integrating the law relating to private individuals and public authorities; and that code is applicable in all three levels of court—the Family

---

[129] *Official Report* (HL) 25 March 1996, vol. 561, col. 741.

[130] See *Official Report* (HL) 23 February 1995, vol. 560, cols. 1269–1270, cited at p.756, note 87 above.

[131] Most obviously the fact that the magistrates' courts have no jurisdiction to make divorce, nullity or separation orders: Matrimonial and Family Proceedings Act 1984, s. 33, and the fact that only the High Court can exercise that court's inherent jurisdiction over children. There are a number of other specific provisions—for example, a magistrate's court is not to exercise jurisdiction to make occupation orders under Family Law Act 1996 Part IV if to do so would involve disputed questions of title to property: FLA 1996, s. 59(1).

[132] See B Hoggett, 'Family courts or family law reform—which should come first?' (1986) 6 *Legal Studies* 1.

At the Millennium

Division of the High Court, the County Court and the (magistrates') Family Proceedings Court—in the family justice system.[133]

The Children Act thus demonstrated what could be achieved by way of harmonisation in one of the most complex and apparently intractable areas of the law; and the provisions governing the availability of remedies against domestic violence and molestation embodied in Part IV of the Family Law Act 1996 were clearly inspired[134] by the same philosophy. As a staging-post on the route to the Law Commission's declared objective of comprehensive codification of the law, the legislation now makes use of the same terms[135] and concepts[136] as are used in other relevant areas of the law wherever that is appropriate.[137] The substantive law has now been comprehensively rationalised, and a single consistent set of remedies, founded on identical principle and available in all three levels of the family justice system, established.[138] In the result, the objective of establishing a 'uniform set of legal rules' (seen by the *Finer Report* as a necessary attribute of the family court) has been largely[139] achieved.

---

[133] Exceptionally, the inherent jurisdiction of the High Court over children remains vested exclusively in the High Court: see R White, P Carr and N Lowe, *The Children Act in Practice* (2nd ed., 1995) Chapter 12.

[134] In the course of debates on the Children Act and apparently in part in response to continued pressure for the creation of a family court the Government established an inter-departmental working party to oversee a rolling programme of work directed at improving family law and business. As part of the review of the family justice system which the working party undertook, attention was to be given to (amongst other topics) the extension of the concurrent jurisdiction of the magistrates' and county courts and the High Court under the Children Act 1989 to other family proceedings, other reforms appropriate and necessary to the creation of a unified jurisdiction, and the functions and organisation of the support services in family proceedings: *Official Report* (HL) 4 March 1992, vol. 536, col. WA 25–26.

[135] For example, 'significant harm'—a key concept in the Children Act 1989 and in that context the subject of judicial exegesis is also used in the provisions structuring the exercise of the courts' discretion to make occupation orders under the 1996 Act: see eg Family Law Act 1996, s. 36(8).

[136] For example, the term 'family proceedings' is a key concept in the Children Act 1989 where (in broad terms) the fact that such proceedings are in being is sufficient to give the court power to make orders (such as residence or contact orders) of its own motion under the Act if it considers that a question arises in those proceedings relating to the welfare of a child: s. 10(1)(b). Similarly, the Family Law Act 1996, s. 62(3)(g) provides that persons who are parties to the same 'family proceedings' are to be treated as 'associated with one another' for the purpose of the Act (and thus have, in effect, the necessary standing to seek occupation and non-molestation orders).

[137] See generally B Hale, 'Family Law Reform: Whither or Whether?' (1995) 48 CLP 217.

[138] Cf. Lord Scarman's description of the law as 'a hotchpotch of enactments of limited scope passed into law to meet specific situations or to strengthen the powers of particular courts': *Richards v. Richards* [1984] 1 AC 174, 206–207.

[139] But not wholly. For example, the availability of financial relief in the magistrates' court is still governed by a separate Act—the Domestic Proceedings and Magistrates' Courts Act—which has a number of distinctive provisions; whilst the creation of a tort and criminal offence of harassment by the Protection from Harassment Act 1997 not only intermingles civil and criminal law in an unusual way but fails to relate the new provisions to the well-established procedures (now incorporated in the Family Law Act 1996) for dealing with domestic violence within the family justice system. Again, the provisions of the Crime and Disorder Act 1998 giving the Youth Court power to make a care order where a child has broken the terms (intended to deal with anti-social behaviour) of a 'child safety order' seem difficult to reconcile with the general policy of the Children Act 1989.

(2) 'Servicing problems of different orders of complexity at different levels'

(a) A specialist, trained, judiciary

The English legal system has traditionally been hierarchical, with the High Court at the summit of the civil trial court system and the magistrates' courts at the bottom; but the question whether judges at any particular level in the hierarchy should be permitted or even encouraged to specialise was for long controversial.[140] In 1990, however, the Courts and Legal Services Act 1990 marked a decisive shift in favour of judicial specialisation. The Lord Chancellor was given power[141] to direct that family proceedings[142] should be allocated to 'specified judges or specified descriptions of judge'; and that power was exercised[143] to create an elaborate system[144] designed, first, to allocate particular types of case to particular classes of judge, and secondly to nominate selected individuals within a class so that those nominated will be qualified to hear cases of the 'order of complexity' deemed to be appropriate to their background, aptitude, training[145] and experience. (For example, although the county court has jurisdiction to make a care order, only those circuit judges who have been 'ticketed' for public law children cases are eligible to sit in care cases.) The policy has been explained by the Children Act Advisory Committee[146] in these words:

'All the judiciary involved in Children Act proceedings . . . have been chosen for their special interest in family proceedings. They must have received special training designed for the Act before undertaking any of the work. They have the critical task of ensuring that

[140] But the judges of the Probate, Divorce and Admiralty Division had for many years claimed that the exercise of discretion in matrimonial cases made it essential for the judges of the Division to be specialists; but as shown above this claim could not realistically survive the great expansion of matrimonial jurisdiction after World War I.

[141] Courts and Legal Services Act 1990, s. 9(1).

[142] In the county court. For specialisation in the magistrates' courts see p. 766, below. It is still assumed that all judges of the High Court are competent to try all classes of family business; but it had become the official policy only to appoint to the High Court bench persons who had had training in, and substantial experience of, family work as a Recorder or Deputy High Court judge. It is not clear whether this policy was consistently followed in the closing years of the century.

[143] By the Family Proceedings (Allocation to Judiciary) Directions 1997 [1997] 2 FLR 780 (replacing earlier Directions).

[144] There are three categories of nominated family circuit judges: *designated family judges* (who have full jurisdiction in all Children Act cases, chair the Family Court Business Committee for the county court care centre at which they are based and are expected to establish close personal liaison not only with other judges but also with everyone involved in the administration of family justice, being 'seen throughout the [court] building and . . . aware of all that is going on': *Avoiding Delay in Children Act Cases*, by Dame Margaret Booth DBE, 1996, para 2.2.1); *nominated care judges*, who have full jurisdiction in public and private law care proceedings; and *circuit family judges* who have full private law family jurisdiction. District Judges (whose jurisdiction was extended by the Family Proceedings (Allocation to Judiciary) Directions 1997 [1997] 2 FLR 780) may also be nominated as care district judges. A clear and accessible (albeit now in some detailed respects outdated) summary is given in the *Children Act Advisory Committee Annual Report 1991/2*, Chapter 2 and Annexes 1–2; and see the *Judicial Statistics Annual Report 2000* pp. 50–51.

[145] The Judicial Studies Board conducts an intensive programme of training for all levels of the professional judiciary: the Board's *Annual Reports* give details.

[146] *Annual Report 1991/92*, p. 10.

any decision as to the upbringing of a child . . . maintains the paramountcy of the welfare of the child. In order to achieve this, it is essential that all levels of the judiciary
involved in family proceedings have a firm commitment to the ideals and philosophy of
the [Children] Act . . .'

The mere idea that the professional judiciary should have to be trained and
assessed for their suitability in handling particular kinds of work would, until
very recently, have astonished most judges and lawyers; and the changes made
to the administration of family justice in the wake of the Children Act are in this
and other respects revolutionary.[147]

In the case of the lay magistracy, it is true that the principle that special skills
may be required for cases involving the young dates back a long way;[148] and a
requirement that magistrates handling domestic cases should be specially
selected and trained was embodied in the Domestic Proceedings and
Magistrates' Courts Act 1978.[149] But the schemes established in the wake of the
Children Act 1989[150] are much more demanding. It is provided[151] that a magistrate is not qualified to sit in a 'family proceedings court'[152] unless he or she is
a member of a 'family panel'.[153] Rules[154] provide for training courses; and the
Judicial Studies Board has published details of the demanding[155] training
syllabus.[156] It appears that in relation to training and otherwise magistrates
display enthusiasm and commitment to family work, and many members of

---

[147] There is also increasing specialisation amongst practitioners. As Sir Stephen Brown P put it in *Re
Pelling (Rights of Audience)* [1997] 2 FLR 458, 470: 'The courts of this country are particularly anxious
that in children cases those who represent them and who are representing the parties in children cases
should be specially experienced. In the case of solicitors the Law Society carries out serious education
and operates panels of solicitors who can appear in those cases. The Family Law Bar Association also
carries out education of the judiciary. The whole ethos . . . is that these cases must not be carried out
as battles in the old adversarial system, but should be carried out much more discreetly having regard
to the overriding interests of the children. It is not in their interests that battles should be fought'.

[148] To the creation of the Juvenile Court by the Children Act 1908.

[149] Domestic Proceedings and Magistrates' Courts Act 1978, s. 80.

[150] Children Act 1989, s. 92(1).

[151] Magistrates' Courts Act 1980, s. 67(2), as amended.

[152] Ie a court dealing with any of a wide range of family business: see Magistrates' Courts Act
1980, s. 65(1), as amended.

[153] Ie a 'panel of justices specially appointed to deal with family proceedings': Magistrates'
Courts Act 1980, s. 67(2).

[154] The Family Proceedings Courts (Constitution) Rules 1991, SI No. 1405.

[155] 'Many [magistrates] have devoted many hours of their time, without remuneration of any
kind and sometimes at considerable financial loss . . . in training to deal with such cases': *per* Lord
Mackay of Clashfern, LC, *Official Report* (HL) 23 February 1995, vol. 561, col. 1270.

[156] This consists of a foundation programme lasting 12 hours to be completed before a magistrate
first sits and also a basic programme (eight hours) to be completed between six and 18 months after
first sitting. There are in addition 12 hour refresher courses to be completed every three years.
Special programmes of chairmanship training are also provided. The training courses are not
restricted to narrowly legal matters—for example, the basic programme includes the nature of
attachment and the effect of separation and divorce on children, approaches to child rearing in families of varying ethnic origin, signs of emotional, physical and sexual abuse and the treatment of children who have been abused, and the services available to assist families and children in need:
Children Act Advisory Committee, Final Report June 1997, Annex B.

family panels would prefer to do nothing but family work.[157] At the turn of the century the criticisms of the magistrates' courts so mordantly made by the *Finer Report* seem no longer to be heard.[158]

(b) Allocation to appropriate court; transfers between courts

The Matrimonial and Family Proceedings Act 1984,[159] accepting the principle that cases started in one level of the family justice system might more appropriately be dealt with at another, established[160] a procedure permitting family cases[161] started in the county court[162] to be transferred to the High Court, and *vice versa*. The Children Act 1989 built on this modest foundation, and provides for the allocation and transfer[163] of cases either vertically between the various tiers of court (for example, from magistrates' Family Proceedings Court to the county court) or horizontally between different courts in the same tier.[164] A similar regime was created for proceedings for occupation and non-molestation orders under the Family Law Act 1996, Part IV.[165] Far from withering away the

---

[157] See *Avoiding Delay in Children Act Cases*, by Dame Margaret Booth DBE, 1996, para. 3.2.2. Note, however, that the demands in terms of commitment of time are such that it is often difficult to achieve a proper balance on the bench (which sometimes consists of three women) and that the length of hearings of child cases often led to their being transferred to the county court.

[158] Lord Chancellor Mackay believed that, notwithstanding its involvement in the criminal justice system, magistrates sitting in a family proceedings court were 'an extremely effective way of dealing with family matters'. He went on: 'I believe that in many matters, particularly those concerned with children, the law books and technical knowledge of the law, although helpful, have only limited value. I feel that the practical decisions about where a child should live and so on are just as well taken by the magistrates . . . I take this opportunity to say how well . . . the magistrates have responded to the challenge of the family proceedings court': *Official Report* (HL) 23 February 1995, vol. 561, col. 1270.

[159] ss. 37–39.

[160] Following consideration of the response to the Lord Chancellor's Consultation Paper, *Family Jurisdiction of the High Court and County Courts* (1983).

[161] For example, a difficult case concerned with the financial consequences of divorce could be transferred to the High Court although the divorce petition had been filed in the county court, whilst proceedings relating to a ward of court could be transferred from the High Court to the county court: Matrimonial and Family Proceedings Act 1984, s. 38(2)(b).

[162] Over the years the county courts had become the work horse of the civil judicial system, but their physical and other amenities (including the availability of welfare support services) differed widely. For that and other reasons there are now three different categories of 'specialist' county court concerned with family cases: (a) Divorce County Courts, in which divorce petitions must be filed and which can deal with uncontested applications under the Children Act; (b) Family Hearing Centres which can deal with all matters within the family jurisdiction of the county court *except* applications for a care order and other 'public law' business; and (c) Care Centres, which have full jurisdiction in all public and private law children matters. For a map showing the location of Care Centres and Family Hearing Centres see Annexes B and C to the *Final Report of the Children Act Advisory Committee* (1997).

[163] For a schematic portrayal of the transfer structure as originally created see *The Children Act Advisory Committee Annual Report 1991/92*, Annex 1.

[164] Such a transfer might be made for example from one county court to another if there are proceedings pending in that court relating to a child of a family involved in divorce proceedings.

[165] See the Family Law Act 1996 (Part IV)(Allocation of Proceedings) Order 1997, SI No. 1896. This—in common with the other allocation directives—provides that certain applications (eg for an occupation or non-molestation order by an applicant aged under 18) must be made to the High Court.

magistrates have been given a new lease of life in dealing with a large number of applications for care orders: in 1996 there were 13,809 such applications, and—even though 2,473 of these were transferred to the county court, the contrast with the 2,601 applications to the county court (and even more with the 141 to the High Court) is striking.[166] At the end of the twentieth century, the complaint was not that parties were stigmatised by the fact that their disputes are dealt with exclusively in the lowest court in the judicial hierarchy but rather that cases are too readily transferred from the magistrates' Family Proceedings Court to the county court.[167]

The criteria governing decisions on transfer are prescribed in Rules;[168] but the question of what qualifications best suit a person to handle family cases—possibly caricatured as whether 'common sense' is better than legal or social work qualification—remains controversial.[169]

(3) A comprehensive liaison network

The enactment of the Children Act 1989 also prompted the creation of a comprehensive liaison network intended to ensure (amongst other things) 'commonality of administrative practice and procedure in the family proceedings courts and the county courts'.[170] At the summit of this network was the Children Act Advisory Committee,[171] and it was supported by 52 Family Court Business Committees (each chaired by the Designated Family Judge)[172] and by

---

[166] The statistics are taken from the last *Annual Report of the Children Act Advisory Committee, June 1977*, Tables 1A and 1B.

[167] See *Avoiding Delay in Children Act Cases*, by Dame Margaret Booth DBE, 1996, paras. 3.2.17–24; 3.8.5.

[168] The Children (Allocation of Proceedings) Order 1991 and the Family Law Act 1996 (Part IV)(Allocation of Proceedings) Order 1997, SI No. 1896 set out the principles to be applied and provide detailed rules and guidelines.

[169] 'I know that more than one of your Lordships believed that a family court had to be based at least at the county court level. I did not share that view.' (Lord Mackay of Clashfern LC, *Official Report* (HL) 23 February 1995, vol. 561, col. 1270); see further note 158, above.

[170] See the terms of reference as set out in *The Children Act Advisory Committee Annual Report 1994/95*, p. 7.

[171] The Committee ceased to exist in July 1997, when the Lord Chancellor's Advisory Board on Family Law—established primarily to advise on the implementation and operation of the Family Law Act 1996 but also charged with considering the overall impact of Children Act work within the family court system—was established under the chairmanship of Lieutenant General Sir Thomas Boyd-Carpenter, sometime Deputy Chief of the Defence Staff. It is intended that the network of Family Court Business Committees and Family Court Forums described in the text will continue to deal with operational aspects of Children Act work: *The Children Act Advisory Committee Final Report 1997*, p. 8. For a description of the mechanisms in place at the end of the twentieth century to encourage inter-agency working in the family justice system, and a discussion of possible improvements, see the Lord Chancellor's Department's Consultation Paper, *Promoting inter-agency working in the family justice system* (2002).

[172] The Committees' functions include ensuring that allocation and transfer arrangements are working properly at local level: *The Children Act Advisory Committee Annual Report 1994/95*, p. 8.

Family Court Forums (intended to represent the interests of consumers, and charged with recommending action to improve the service provided to the parties to family proceedings).[173] There are also Court User Groups intended to obtain customer feedback on their services.[174]

Important management functions were also allotted to the judiciary;[175] and in particular a Family Division Judge was appointed in each of the seven circuits in England and Wales as the Liaison Judge. The Liaison Judge in each circuit is responsible for a wide range of functions, including the operation of a flexible system whereby 'standby judges' go to different parts of the country to deal immediately with urgent cases,[176] presiding over annual regional circuit conferences and bringing together magistrates and others to discuss matters of concern.

(4) Other aspects of a family court

(a) The physical environment

Campaigners for a family court drew attention to the depressing physical amenities of many court buildings, and the fact that courtrooms used by magistrates were often only too clearly primarily adapted for the trial of criminal cases. There seems little doubt that these factors contributed to the feeling of stigmatisation reported by researchers.[177] But in recent years, there have been many major building schemes,[178] and a large number of new courtrooms have been provided.[179] Even so, it has been estimated[180] that it would take

---

[173] See *The Children Act Advisory Committee Annual Report 1994/95*, pp. 7–10. (The diagram of the supporting committee structure set out at p. 8 will be found particularly helpful.)

[174] See the Lord Chancellor's Department's Consultation Paper, *Promoting inter-agency working in the family justice system* (2002) para. 10.

[175] The judiciary has taken a leading part in encouraging inter-disciplinary collaboration, notably through the President's Interdisciplinary Committee (which has a special interest in education, training and research) and also through other more specialist groups: see the Lord Chancellor's Department's Consultation Paper, *Promoting inter-agency working in the family justice system* (2002) paras. 16–18.

[176] See *Children Act Advisory Committee Annual Report 1992/93*, pp. 53–54.

[177] See in particular *The Overlapping Family Jurisdiction of Magistrates' and County Courts*, by M Murch (with M Borkowski, R Copner and M Griew), University of Bristol (1987).

[178] A conspicuous example is the opening in 1997 of the refurbished Inner London and City Family Proceedings Court situated at Wells Street in the West End of London and serving the 12 Inner London Boroughs and the City of London. No criminal cases are heard in the seven courtrooms, which were refurbished to provide what the court service described as 'a light and relaxed atmosphere consistent with the informal approach taken in family proceedings'. It is said that magistrates (stipendiary and lay) and the legally qualified clerks who advise them, all work closely together to ensure that cases are considered with minimum delay.

[179] *The Children Act Advisory Committee Annual Report 1992/93*, p. 55 (which also gives a description of a particularly good example of imaginative refurbishment at the Havant Family Court Centre, resulting in a 'less formal and intimidating' environment, with a 'user friendly' reception area and 'soft pastel colours and fabrics' used in the decor throughout. Ancillary accommodation includes a creche area, baby changing facilities, private interview rooms for welfare officers and additional facilities for disabled people and for video links).

[180] *The Children Act Advisory Committee Annual Report 1992/93*, p. 55.

'well into the next century' to bring all magistrates' courthouses up to modern standards.[181]

(b) Availability of social work input: welfare reports

Over the years[182] it was increasingly thought that adjudication and welfare should 'march hand in hand'[183] in the family justice system; and it followed from this view of family justice that the contribution of what is called 'black letter law' was to be necessarily limited,[184] and that the work of all those involved—whether as judges, social workers or as lawyers and advocates—should have common perspectives and a mutual understanding of all the relevant professional disciplines. As we have seen, after the end of World War II the long-standing and substantial involvement of the probation service in the domestic jurisdiction of magistrates' courts began to be mirrored in the provision of welfare officers in the divorce court. The courts increasingly saw the need for welfare reports and made extensive use of their powers to direct what came to be called the Divorce Court Welfare Service[185] to investigate and make recommendations.[186] In 1960 some 880 reports were commissioned;[187] in 1995 there were 627 main grade welfare officers in post and 34,697 written reports were completed.[188]

Welfare Officers' reports were not the only source of information for the courts. The Children Act 1948 required local authorities to appoint children's officers whose duties often brought them into contact with dysfunctional families, with the result that the courts often had recourse to reports from local authority social workers for information and for assessments of children whose

---

[181] This problem is not confined to the Family Proceedings Courts: notwithstanding many improvements, by no means all county court care centres have facilities—such as separate waiting rooms for parties to contested cases, separate offices for welfare officers, children's waiting rooms, sufficient and accessible toilet and refreshment services—now recognised as desirable: *The Children Act Advisory Committee Annual Report 1991/92,* para. 13.

[182] For a succinct account of the history of the various services' involvement, see M Murch and D Hooper, *The Family Justice System* (1992) Chapter 7.

[183] *Finer Report*, para. 4.285.

[184] Lord Mackay of Clashfern, *The Upjohn Lecture* (1991); and see the extract from Lord Mackay's speech on the second reading of the Family Homes and Domestic Violence Bill, note 87 above.

[185] Rules (the Probation Rules 1984, as amended) made under the consolidating Probation Services Act 1993 imposed duties on the probation service to discharge these functions; but—although in recent years the Government tried to restrict the involvement of the probation service in civil work: see M Murch (with D Hooper), *The Family Justice System* (1992) p. 57, not least by confining its budget to 10% of the expenditure on criminal work—the commitment of individuals to family work was and evidently remained strong.

[186] 'A welfare report is prepared by the divorce court welfare officer to help the court to come to a decision on a matter in which children are involved. In essence it is evidence obtained for the court by someone who is impartial . . .': *Report of the Matrimonial Causes Procedure Committee* (Chairman, the Hon Mrs Justice Booth DBE) 1985.

[187] M Murch with D Hooper, *The Family Justice System* (1992) p. 67.

[188] *Children Act Advisory Committee, Annual Report 1994/1995,* p. 72. In 1983 the *Matrimonial Causes Procedure Committee* (Chairman, the Hon Mrs Justice Booth DBE) *Consultation Paper* (1983) para. 1.9(d), reported that some 150 officers produced some 21,870 reports.

future the courts had to determine (particularly those already in care or who had for one reason or another come to the attention of the social services).[189]

The *Finer Report*[190] had no doubt that the family court's needs for information and supportive family services entailed it having 'an arm to the court itself' to perform these functions; but it rejected continued reliance on the probation service because it feared contamination of the welfare function by the 'ancient criminal taint' of the work with which the probation service was primarily concerned. Instead it favoured the creation of a service of specialised welfare workers, perhaps provided by local authorities, or perhaps a specially created and distinct court welfare service.

(c) Representing the child's point of view

The Children Act 1975, in an attempt to meet the problem that the child's own interests and wishes might be overlooked,[191] introduced a procedure whereby in certain cases an independent *guardian ad litem*[192] was appointed to act as an independent voice speaking for the child. The *guardian ad litem* procedure was much expanded under the Children Act 1989,[193] and although it is crucially important to appreciate that such a guardian is primarily a representative of the child[194] (rather

---

[189] The involvement of local authority social workers might have been increased by reason of a number of provisions in the Children Act 1989, notably s. 37 (court may direct local authority to undertake investigation of circumstances of child and consider whether to apply for care or supervision order).

[190] Para. 4.315 ff.

[191] The *Report of a Committee of Enquiry into the Care and Supervision provided in relation to Maria Colwell* (Chairman, G Field-Fisher, 1974) stated that it would have been of assistance to the court to have had the views of a social worker independent of the local authority and the parents; and the *Colwell* and other cases were thought to demonstrate the need for the child's case to be put forward by someone wholly committed to the child's interests (and not tempted to put forward what may seem to be a reasonable compromise taking account of all the various competing interests).

[192] The High Court had power to appoint a *guardian ad litem*—an expression literally meaning a guardian for the purpose of the litigation—and this power was habitually exercised in wardship cases: and see further note 202, below. The Adoption Act 1926 made a guardian an essential component in dealing with adoption applications: see Chapter 17, p. 603. Guardians under the Children Act 1975 were appointed from panels established by local authorities; but the courts emphasised the need for the independence of guardians to be safeguarded: *R v. Cornwall County Council, ex parte G* [1992] 1 FLR 270, Sir Stephen Brown P.

[193] In 1993/4 there were 937 guardians: *The Guardian ad Litem and Reporting Officer Service, Annual Reports 1993–1994, An Overview* (1994, p. 1) and more than 8,000 appointments, involving more than 19,000 children, were requested annually: *Children Act Advisory Committee, Final Report 1997*, p. 51. A wealth of guidance was available to guardians (see eg *Manual of Practice Guidance for Guardians ad Litem* . . . prepared for the Department of Health by the director of the charity, Independent Representation for Children in Need, J Timms); and the Department of Health introduced 'National Standards' with the aim of improving the delivery of a professionally competent service: *Children Act Advisory Committee, Final Report 1997*, p. 52.

[194] It has been said that the distinction between welfare officer and guardian was that the guardian has the added duty of representing the child in court and if necessary instructing legal representation for the child: *Re S (A Minor)(Guardian ad Litem: Welfare Officer)* [1993] 1 FLR 110, CA, *per* Butler-Sloss LJ.

than an agent of the court)[195] the guardian's role clearly combined elements of the social worker making enquiries, the advocate[196] protecting the child's interests, and also the independent expert presenting an informed view to the court.[197] Both welfare officers and guardian had a duty to report to the court;[198] both had a duty to consider the welfare of the interests of the child; both could be cross-examined on any report which they gave; and both had a similar duty to advise the court as to what was best for the child independently of the other parties to the proceedings.[199]

There was some judicial criticism of what was seen as over-representation in cases involving children;[200] whilst researchers[201] claimed that separate representation added to the complexity of proceedings and significantly increased the length of proceedings. This is a controversial issue; but whether or not the incremental growth of reporting and other welfare services improved outcomes for those involved or not it was impossible to deny that the organisational structure had for long remained confused.[202]

Paradoxically it was the Government's decision to change the role of the probation service in the criminal justice system which made it necessary to end the link between family court welfare services and the probation service. At a time when welfare and treatment played a significant part in dealing with young

[195] Even so it has been held that the court should give clear reasons if it decided not to adopt a guardian's recommendation: see *Re W (A Minor)(Secure Accommodation Order)* [1993] 1 FLR 962; and the same is true of recommendations made in a welfare officer's report: *Re CB (Access: Attendance of Court Welfare Officer)* [1995] 1 FLR 622, CA.

[196] However, the guardian was required to appoint a solicitor to represent the child; but the solicitor could conduct the case in accordance with the child's instructions if those instructions conflicted with the *guardian ad litem's*.

[197] The Guardian would attend all directions appointments and all hearings, and advise the court on a wide range of matters including the wishes of the child, the appropriate forum for the hearing (eg Family Proceedings Court or County Court Care Centre), the appropriate timing for the proceedings, the options available to the court, and any other matter concerning which the court seeks the guardian's advice or concerning which the guardian considers the court should be informed: the Family Proceedings Courts (Children Act 1989) Rules 1991, r. 11. Guardians often instructed expert witnesses and co-ordinate and chair meetings of expert witnesses: *Children Act Advisory Committee, Annual Report 1994/1995*, p. 70.

[198] It was on the basis that the courts were 'the principal commissioner' of guardians' work that they were (controversially) asked to participate in the assessment of guardians' performance: *Children Act Advisory Committee, Final Report 1997*, p. 53.

[199] *Re S (A Minor)(Guardian ad Litem: Welfare Officer)* [1993] 1 FLR 110, CA, *per* Butler-Sloss LJ.

[200] See notably *Birmingham City Council v. H (A Minor)* [1994] 2 AC 212, 217, *per* Lord Keith of Kinkel. But equally there have been pressures for more separate representation especially in private law cases, and these were influential during parliamentary debates on the reformed divorce process to be created by the Family Law Act 1996.

[201] M Murch with D Hooper, *The Family Justice System* (1992) p. 72.

[202] Mention should also be made of the Official Solicitor who acted as a *guardian ad litem* in family proceedings in the High Court and the county court: see D Venables, 'The Official Solicitor' (1990) 20 Fam Law 53, and SM Cretney and JM Masson, *Principles of Family Law* (6th ed., 1997) pp. 667–668. High Court judges traditionally had great confidence in the work of the Official Solicitor notwithstanding (or perhaps because of) the fact that the Official Solicitor's staff are qualified neither as social workers nor lawyers: see (1989) 105 LQR 188.

offenders the involvement of probation officers in family issues was possible to justify; but the move of the criminal justice system to a more overtly punitive role and the consequent redefinition of the role formerly played by the probation service in the criminal courts made the involvement of the service in family cases no longer tenable. Eventually the Criminal Justice and Court Services Act 2000 established a *Children and Family Court Advisory and Support Service* (CAFCASS) as a non-departmental public body accountable to the Lord Chancellor. The Act[203] defines CAFCASS's function as including safeguarding and promoting the welfare of children, giving advice to the court, and making provision for representation of children in family proceedings in High Court, county court or magistrates' court. CAFCASS was to take over the functions of the Family Court Welfare Service (formerly provided by the probation service and tracing its history back to the efforts of probation officers to reconcile couples) as well as those of *guardians ad litem* and Reporting Officers. It was claimed[204] that amalgamation would provide an improved service to the courts, better safeguards for the interests of children, as well as reducing 'wasteful overlap and so increase efficiency'; and there were great expectations that this would provide the opportunity for a great expansion of services for children and their parents.[205]

The text of the Act suggests that CAFCASS might satisfy Finer's criterion for a specialised family court welfare service; and there were high hopes that CAFCASS would provide a coherent and integrated service for children and families involved in relationship breakdown and family proceedings.[206] But administrative and other difficulties were experienced,[207] and it would be premature to make any judgment on the new service. At the turn of the century, the relationship between the courts and the family, and between adjudication and private bargaining, remains in some respects uneasy.

CONCLUSION

The family justice system changed radically in the course of the twentieth century. In the year 2000 there was in place a system constructed on rational principles, and for the most part staffed by men and women who had an informed

---

[203] s. 12.

[204] *Judicial Statistics Annual Report 2001*, p. 54. But it had to be admitted that for users of the courts the most notable change would be in job titles: a *guardian ad litem* became a Children's Guardian, and in cases where the court asks for a report about a child the official would be designated a Children and Family Reporter: *ibid*.

[205] Advisory Board on Family Law: Children Act Sub-Committee *Making Contact Work* (2002) para. 6.3.

[206] *Advisory Board on Family Law, 2000/2001*.

[207] For a brief summary, see *Making Contact Work* (Advisory Board on Family Law, Children Act Sub-Committee, 2002) Chapter 6.

commitment not only to seeking an efficient and humane judicial process but also to the distinctive values—promoting the welfare of children, and minimising the cost (emotional as well as financial) to all those involved in family disputes, for example—which had come to be generally accepted as appropriate in the year 2000. And it is not only the judiciary who have become specialist. The emergence of strong specialist groups of solicitors and barristers—the Solicitors Family Law Association (formed in 1982, and with some 5,000 members at the turn of the century) and the Family Law Bar Association—committed to a conciliatory role in situations of family breakdown—has transformed the atmosphere in many courts. The once fashionable overtly hostile and provocative approach to advocacy[208] is now not often found and is never encouraged. Although there is (and will always be) room for improvement it would be difficult to deny that the system had become both more efficient and more humane than at the beginning of the twentieth century. Yet there remain fundamental difficulties. The twentieth century saw a remarkable withdrawal of the State and the law from the private relationship between man and wife. Although legislation[209] continued to emphasise the importance of supporting the institution of marriage it seemed more and more to be accepted that only the couple concerned could decide whether or not a particular marriage was viable; and the extent to which courts could sensibly supervise the arrangements to be made (about financial matters and the children's upbringing, for example) came increasingly to be questioned.[210] Yet the fact that the courts provide a forum—even a theatre—in which men and women who have suffered often severe emotional damage can not only have their feelings ventilated but can also invoke the judicial power of the State to impose solutions, makes it difficult to believe that any court system can keep 'bitterness, distress and humiliation' at bay. The proliferation of contests observed towards the close of the century about the arrangements for contact between parent and child would certainly seem to suggest that there is an apparently insatiable demand for institutionalised dispute procedures; and that the law's attempts to retreat to the sidelines have been only partially successful.

Where compulsory State intervention in children's upbringing is the issue, the trend has been in the opposite direction. Far from withdrawing, the law now provides not only a closely regulated system governing the conduct of the Agencies concerned but also a highly sophisticated legal structure to resolve

---

[208] See T Frisby, *Outrageous Fortune* (1998) for an account of one husband's experience.

[209] Family Law Act 1996, s. 1.

[210] There are also (at least in theory) significant tensions between the traditional inquisitorial role of the family courts and the modern 'settlement culture' favouring private negotiation between the parties over financial and child-upbringing arrangements in preference to court adjudication. However, techniques have been developed—notably the process of submitting a privately negotiated financial settlement to the court for embodiment in a formal court order—which seem broadly satisfactory in practice: see generally SM Cretney and JM Masson, *Principles of Family Law* (6th ed. 1997) pp 397–403; and compare *Hyman v. Hyman* [1929] AC 601 *Pounds v. Pounds* [1994] 1 WLR 775 and *Xydhias v. Xydhias* [1999] 1 FLR 683.

the conflict between the right of the family to determine its own affairs and the interests of society in protecting the vulnerable against harm. Here the question seems to be whether the demands made of Agencies (not only in resolving the human problems which confront them on such a large scale but also by the requirements of the legal system for information and representation of the different interests involved) are really capable of being met. Certainly in the year 2000 the Curtis Report's noble vision of the State discharging the role of a deprived child's parent through the medium of an individual local authority official seems distinctly naive. It remains to be seen whether the belief, underlying the Adoption and Children Act 2002, that encouraging recourse to legal adoption will improve the life chances of deprived children and help to avoid the child care scandals which have been such a feature of the second half of the twentieth century, was well founded. Certainly the procedures applied by the courts hearing adoption applications at the beginning of the twenty-first century are infinitely more complex and demanding than those established in 1926; but experience may suggest that there are still questions to be answered about the relationship between court process on the one hand and administrative and social work decision-taking on the other.

Biographical Notes

Part A contains biographical notes about individuals. The length of entries is intended to bear some relationship to the subject's contribution to the topics dealt with in this book (so that, for example, the entry for Sir Claud Schuster, Permanent Secretary to the Lord Chancellor, is longer than that for any of the Ministers he served). Those (notably peers and married women) who have been commonly known by more than one name are recorded primarily under that by which they were best known at the time of their involvement in the events dealt with in this book, but some cross-references are supplied.

Part B lists membership of a number of the Commissions and Committees whose recommendations are dealt with in the text. Some entries contain brief biographical notes about members.

Part C lists chronologically the Presidents of the Probate Divorce and Admiralty Division and the Family Division of the High Court.

A. Individuals

Abse, Leo (1917–) Solicitor, Labour MP for Welsh constituencies 1958–1987. A brilliantly skilled master of parliamentary procedures, he probably had a greater influence on the development of law relating to family matters than any other MP in the twentieth century. The moving force behind the parliamentary proceedings eventually leading to the enactment of the Divorce Reform Act 1969 he also successfully sponsored legislation on adoption, homosexuality, legitimacy, congenital disabilities and family planning. Member of Departmental Committee on the Adoption of Children (1972). Interested in psycho-analysis, his autobiography *Private Member* (1973) gives an invaluable and detailed (if not always objective) account of the background to divorce reform, whilst *Margaret, daughter of Beatrice: a politician's psychobiography of Margaret Thatcher* (1989) and *The Man behind the Smile, Tony Blair and the Politics of Perversion* (1996) also seek to make use of psychoanalytical perceptions.

Allen, Marjory, Lady Allen of Hurtwood (1897–1976) Widow of the Labour MP and conscientious objector Clifford Allen. A life-long interest in education and child welfare matters led her to launch a highly effective campaign, initiated by a letter published in *The Times* on 15 July 1944 and carried on by public and private pressure brought to bear on the Home Secretary Herbert Morrison, for a

full inquiry into the plight of children in public or voluntary care and in particular into whether the organisations concerned were 'enabling these children to
lead full and happy lives' and into the means whereby the community could
'compensate them for the family life they have lost'. Her memoirs vividly reveal
her impressions of the 'fat, flabby and listless appearance' of the children in Poor
Law institutions and their 'heavy, ill-fitting clothes and boots so clumsy they
could only shuffle along' and her belief that defective administration was at the
root of the problem: *Memoirs of an Uneducated Lady,* by Marjory Allen and
Mary Nicholson (1975) p. 170.

Alverstone, Viscount (1842–1915), born Richard Everard Webster. Conservative
MP for the Isle of Wight, Attorney-General for 12 years in the period 1885 to
1900; subsequently (as Lord Alverstone) Master of the Rolls (1900) and Lord
Chief Justice of England (1900–1913). Opposed divorce reform. The subject of
an entertaining but notably hostile memorial (written by FD MacKinnon, see
below) in the *Dictionary of National Biography.*

Anderson, J N D (1908–1994) Professor of Oriental Laws in the University of
London and a leader of the Evangelical wing of the Church of England.
A prominent and influential member of the Archbishop of Canterbury's Group
whose report *Putting Asunder* led to the enactment of the Divorce Reform Act
1969, he was also particularly effective in the negotiations which took place
between that Group and the Law Commission. D McClean (1995) 90
Proceedings of the British Academy 251 gives a sympathetic account of his life.

Anson, Sir William Reynell, Bart (1843–1914) Barrister, Warden of All Souls
College Oxford, Unionist MP for Oxford University 1899–1914: Parliamentary
Secretary to the Board of Education 1902–1905. A committed Anglican
(Chancellor of the Diocese of Oxford 1899–1912) he was one of the three
authors of the minority Report of the 1912 *Royal Commission on Divorce and
Matrimonial Causes.* Also author of standard legal texts including *Law and
Custom of the Constitution* and *Principles of the English Law of Contract* (in its
28th edition, 2002).

Appelbe, Ambrose Erle Fuller (1903–1999) Solicitor, pacifist, helped to found
National Marriage Guidance Council, Help the Aged, War on Want, the Anti-
Noise Society, and the Smell Society ('devoted to the elimination of foul
odours'). Co-founder of the Married Women's Society and prominent advocate
of improved rights for married women. As his obituarist in *The Times* notes,
Appelbe 'conformed neither to the cautious legal establishment nor to the north
London socialist set'. The solicitors' practice he established in Lincoln's Inn in
1935 prospered, and in the twenty-first century sponsors the Orchestra of the
Age of Enlightenment and other cultural activities.

Astor, Baron (1879–1952) born Waldorf Astor. Proprietor of the *Observer*
newspaper and founder of Observer Trust, MP for Plymouth 1910–1919,

agriculturalist, and influential as member of Round Table group committed to imperial unity. A junior minister 1918–1921. Succeeded to father's peerage in 1919 (when his wife Nancy was elected to her husband's seat in the House of Commons and became the first woman MP). The house at Cliveden, Berkshire, given to him by his father as a wedding present, was the rendezvous for what was (sometimes pejoratively) called the Cliveden Set which was thought to play a significant role in fostering the British Government's appeasement policy. Astor played an influential role in the debates leading to the Inheritance (Family Provision) Act 1938.

Bacon, Baroness (1909–1993) born Alice Martha Bacon, daughter of a miner. Worked as schoolmistress before entering Parliament in 1945. MP for Leeds constituencies 1945–1970 and held ministerial office 1964–70. Chairman of Labour Party 1950–51. Created a Life Peer in 1970 she played an active part in the debates on the 1975 Children Act.

Barnes, John Gorell, see **Gorell of Brampton.**

Barnes, Sir Thomas James (1888–1964) Solicitor and civil servant, became Treasury Solicitor (effectively head of the Government's Legal Service) and King's Proctor in 1934 (the first solicitor to hold those offices). As Treasury Solicitor and King's Proctor at the time of the passage of AP Herbert's 1937 Matrimonial Causes Act he gave much effective assistance to those seeking reform. Played important role in 1936 abdication crisis, since he had responsibility for determining whether to intervene in Mrs WW Simpson's divorce suit.

Bell, Stuart (1938–) Labour MP for Middlesborough 1983– and Second Church Estates Commissioner since 1997. Formerly a colliery clerk, reporter and writer. Called to the Bar in 1970. His concern about the events in Cleveland in 1987 evidently had a significant influence on the Government's decision to establish a judicial inquiry into *Child Abuse in Cleveland* (1987). Author of *When Salem Came to the Boro, The True Story of the Cleveland Child Abuse Crisis* (1988).

Beloe, Robert (1905–1984) Wykehamist son of a clergyman public school head, brother of an admiral, and for a time an Assistant Master at Eton. Became Educational Administrator (latterly Chief Education Officer for Surrey). Member of Royal Commission on Marriage and Divorce, 1956, and took a stance notably conservative even by the generally conservative standards set by his colleagues. Appointed Lay Secretary to Archbishop of Canterbury 1959 and skilfully organised opposition to Abse 1963 separation divorce Bill. However, five years later he was instrumental in gathering support for reform eventually leading to Divorce Reform Act 1969.

Bethell, Sir Richard (1800–1873) Barrister, called 1823, outstanding draftsman and advocate. Liberal MP from 1851, his sarcastic brilliance did not make him widely popular with colleagues. Active reforming Attorney-General (1856), in which capacity he had the carriage of the Matrimonial Causes Act 1857 and

Court of Probate Act 1857 proving himself (almost) a match for WE Gladstone (see below). Created Baron Westbury and appointed Lord Chancellor 1863 but resigned in 1865 following vote of censure in House of Commons relating to the appointment of his son to the office of Registrar.

Betterton, Henry Bucknall, see **Rushcliffe, Baron.**

Birkenhead, Earl of (1872–1930) born Frederick Edwin Smith. Barrister and Conservative politician: Lord Chancellor 1919–1922 in Lloyd George coalition. Outstanding advocate and committed supporter of divorce reform. Birkenhead is said to have regarded his speech on the 1920 Buckmaster Divorce Bill as 'one of the greatest—perhaps the greatest—of his life': J Campbell, *FE Smith, First Earl of Birkenhead* (1983) p. 517; and his opinion was shared by *The Times* which said the speech revealed him as a 'true modern' and a man of sincerity passion and even a strain of fine democratic idealism.

Biron, Sir Chartres (1863–1940) Chief Magistrate, Bow Street, 1920–1933. Son of a QC, educated at Eton and Trinity College Cambridge, a member of Brooks's, the Garrick, the Beefsteak, Princes and the Royal Yacht Squadron. Recorded his recreation as travel but also had taste for letters: author of collection of essays (*Pious Opinions* 1923) on literary subjects, including a sympathetic piece on 'Dickens and the Law'. His autobiography, *Without Prejudice* (1936) does not shrink from pungent observations on the legal system: for example, although he thought the juvenile courts created under the Children Act 1908 had 'thoroughly justified their existence' he also recorded his view that they had become the 'happy hunting ground of all the cranks, male and female. Psychoanalysts, psychiatrists, Christian scientists, all got to work, and it was not too easy to keep them in order'. Biron thought that plans for a special domestic court to deal with the matrimonial cases of the poor were 'foolish' apparently because 'as a body the working classes are too busy for domestic differences. It is the idle rich who crowd the corridors of the divorce court . . .'. Biron was not one of nature's radicals, and there was a painful tension between him and the reforming Claud Mullins (see below) who recorded that he had 'never heard such deep-dyed Toryism in my life . . . Biron's idea of a magistrate is one who does his three days a week and plays the rest of the time' and Mullins recorded that at both ends of his life Biron 'had a strong distaste for work': C Mullins, *Fifteen Years Hard Labour* (1948) pp. 163, 168.

Bishop, Edward (1920–1984) Labour MP for Newark, Assistant Government Whip, held junior ministerial office 1974–1979, ennobled as Baron Bishopston, 1981. Promoted Matrimonial Property Bill, 1969.

Bishopston, Baron, see **Bishop, Edward.**

Blackwell, Sir Ernley Robertson Hay (1868–1941) Barrister, entered Home Office and served as Legal Assistant Under-Secretary of State, 1913–1933. Notably prominent in advising on post-World War I legislation relating to magistrates and children. It has been alleged he took a prominent part in seeking to blacken character of Sir Roger Casement by circulating diaries containing accounts of Casement's homosexual proclivities as part of Government's public relations exercise intended to justify refusal to grant reprieve following conviction for treason.

Blom-Cooper, Sir Louis (Jacques) (1926–) Barrister (QC), Law Reformer and Author. Director of Legal Research Insitute Bedford College London 1967–1982, and joint author of *Separated Spouses* (1970) and *Final Appeal: a study of the House of Lords in its judicial capacity* (1972). Chairman of Panel of Inquiry into the circumstances surrounding the death of Jasmine Beckford (1985), and of Commission of Inquiry into the circumstances surrounding the death of Kimberley Carlile (1987).

Bramall, Margaret Elaine (1916–) Social worker and writer, Director of National Council for the Unmarried Mother and her Child 1962–1979; member of Departmental Committee on the Adoption of Children (1972), JP.

Braye, Baron (1849–1928) born Alfred Thomas Townshend Verney-Cave. Soldier, Roman Catholic convert, the main spokesman on the divorce issue for Roman Catholic opinion in the House of Lords down to 1924. His speeches on the subject are collected in Braye, *A Life in Two Centuries* (1927): the book contains a strong attack on allowing divorce for adultery which he believed constituted a 'legal and accepted stimulus to commit crime in order that a plea for getting a decree may be substantiated' (p. 350). Braye particularly deplored the 'intimate proofs' presented in 'degraded and degrading reports'.

Bridgeman, William Clive (1864–1935) Conservative MP for North Shropshire 1906–1929 (in which year he was raised to the peerage as a Viscount). Home Secretary 1922–1924. Resisted extension of ground for divorce and unsympathetic to claims for equal rights for women in family matters. Bridgeman took the controversial decision not to recommend the exercise of the prerogative of mercy in the case of Mrs Edith Thompson (convicted of the murder of her husband although the killing was actually effected by her lover) and recorded his view that in this respect the law admitted of no distinction between men and women. See P Williamson, *The Modernisation of Conservative Politics: the diaries and letters of W Bridgeman* (1988).

Brown, Professor Lionel Neville (1923–) Solicitor, Professor of Comparative Law, University of Birmingham, 1966–1990, author of powerful and influential scholarly papers on family maintenance.

Buckmaster, Viscount (1861–1934) born Stanley Owen Buckmaster. Liberal MP 1906–1915 Appointed Lord Chancellor, 1915. Regarded by CP Scott (the influential editor of *The Manchester Guardian*) as 'the best and strongest of the Liberal ex-ministers' he lost office after only 18 months when Prime Minister Asquith was supplanted by David Lloyd-George. He was never again to hold political or judicial office. An active—indeed, by his own admission (see *Official*

Report (HL) 26 June 1923, vol. 54, col. 579) an obsessive—supporter of divorce reform. No reader of Buckmaster's speeches in the House of Lords on this subject would wish to dispute the assessment made by Sir John Simon in a note of condolence to Buckmaster's daughter: 'It was not enough to say [of him] that he had a passion for justice, it was a burning flame fed by his hatred of everything that was cruel or unfair': see RFV Heuston, *Lives of the Lord Chancellors 1885–1940* (1964) p. 268. It may be that there were aspects of his own home life which made divorce a subject of especial interest to him (see Heuston, *op. cit.* p. 263, and the autobiography of his son and heir Viscount Buckmaster, *Roundabout* (1969)) but his concern to remedy what he believed to be manifest injustice was not confined to divorce law. He displayed an almost Churchillian refusal to accept defeat (notably on his proposal to make child marriages illegal). His oratorical style may seem 'to a modern generation . . . almost embarrassingly high flown and melodramatic' but his audiences by 'universal testimony' appreciated and 'found [it] persuasive': Heuston, *op. cit.* p. 296. Sir John Simon noted in his autobiography, *Retrospect* (1952) p. 87 that Buckmaster was almost the only one of his contemporaries who 'could venture to climb to the real heights of eloquence' and recorded HH Asquith's assessment of Buckmaster as the finest speaker of his time. It is thus unfortunate that Buckmaster is today remembered mainly for his sometimes mordant opinion in *Donoghue v. Stevenson* [1932] AC 562, 577–578, HL, dissenting from the view of the majority that the manufacturer of products owed a duty of care to the ultimate consumer who could accordingly bring an action in negligence for breach of that duty.

Burns, John (1858–1943) Self educated politician and writer: According to *Who's Who* entry, educated in Battersea 'and at night schools and still learning'. Liberal MP 1892–1918. President of Local Government Board 1905–1914. Resigned from Cabinet in August 1914 in protest against British involvement in World War I. Career at Local Government Board gave him opportunity to carry through reforms but his approach judged insufficiently radical by his critics.

Butler-Sloss, The Rt. Hon Dame (Ann) Elizabeth (Oldfield) (1933–) Daughter of High Court judge Sir Cecil Havers (and sister of Attorney-General and—for four months in 1987, Lord Chancellor—Havers (1923–1992)). Called to Bar 1955, Registrar of the Principal Registry 1970–1979 when appointed to High Court bench (Family Division). Subsequently first woman Lord Justice of Appeal (1988), President of the Family Division 1999. Chaired Inquiry into Child Abuse in Cleveland (1987).

Caldwell, Edward George (1941–) Lawyer on staff of Law Commission 1967–1969 when joined Office of Parliamentary Counsel. One of the Parliamentary Counsel attached to the Law Commisssion 1975–1977 and 1986–1988. Involved in drafting provisions put forward by Commission to demonstrate possibility of codification of child law, eventually achieved in

Children Act 1989 (for which he was lead draftsman). Believed to have played significant part in ensuring that both 'public' and 'private' law provisions were included in a single Bill. Subsequently First Parliamentary Counsel, QC, KBE.

Callaghan, (Leonard) James (1912–) Labour Politician, Prime Minister 1976–1979. Home Secretary 1967–70. Keenly interested in child welfare issues he was responsible for setting up Departmental Committee on the Adoption of Children (the Houghton Committee) and remained a strong supporter of the Home Office's record in the administration of state provision for child care.

Campbell, Baron (1779–1861) born John Campbell. Barrister called 1806. Entered Parliament as MP for Stafford and active in promoting legislation on a wide range of important subjects (not least Lord Campbell's Act, allowing Personal Representatives to sue for damages in respect of the deceased's death). Chaired Royal Commission on Divorce (1853); appointed Lord Chancellor 1859 in his 80th year. Author of *Lives of the Lord Chancellors*.

Campbell, Keith Bruce (1916–) Conservative MP for Oldham 1968–1970 and effective opponent of Divorce Reform Act 1969. Appointed a circuit judge in 1976 Campbell has his own place in history as the only English judge in modern times to be removed from office on the grounds of misconduct. He was—notwithstanding his plea that the goods were intended for personal consumption—convicted of smuggling 125 litres of whisky and 9,460 cigarettes in his yacht *Papyrus* and was removed from office on 5 December 1983. He was apparently allowed to retain his pension: *The Times*, 6 December 1983.

Cave, Viscount (1856–1928) born George Cave. Barrister, Conservative MP 1906–1918, Lord Chancellor 1922–4, and 1924–1928. Defeated HH Asquith in election for chancellorship of Oxford University, 1925. Firm opponent of divorce reform, but eventually conceded principle of Guardianship of Infants Act 1925.

Chamberlain, (Arthur) Neville (1869–1940) Member of influential Birmingham political and industrial family. Lord Mayor of Birmingham, Unionist MP, Prime Minister 1937–1940. The failure of the policy of appeasement he unsuccessfully pursued has obscured Chamberlain's considerable achievements as an effective social reformer. His first parliamentary initiative was to introduce the Bastardy Bill 1920 intended to make sweeping reforms in the law affecting those born outside marriage, and he served as a member of the Hopkinson Committee on the Adoption of Children. A highly effective Minister for Health, he masterminded the massive Local Government Act 1929 making major reforms to the Poor Law and improvements to child welfare services.

Chelmsford, Baron (1794–1878) born Frederic Thesiger, saw action as 13 year old Midshipman at the Battle of Copenhagen. Called to the bar (Gray's Inn 1818), elected MP (Conservative) in 1840, solicitor-general 1844, subsequently attorney-general. Lord Chancellor 1858–1859, 1866–1868. Chelmsford chaired the Royal Commission on the Laws of Marriage (1968) which recommended radical reforms.

Cherry, Sir Benjamin (1869–1932) Barrister, chief architect of 1925 property legislation. Played significant role in discussions of succession and legitimacy reforms in 1920s; but evidently found a difficult colleague by some officials: see further under **Tomlin**.

Chuter-Ede, Baron, see **Ede, James Chuter.**

Clynes, John Robert (1869–1949) Trade Unionist and Labour Politician. As Lord Privy Seal in the 1924 MacDonald administration played an active part in reform of Guardianship legislation. As Home Secretary in the 1929–1931 Labour government he was influential in bringing forward the Bill for the Children and Young Persons Act 1932.

Coldstream, Sir George (1907–2004) Barrister, called 1930, entered office of Parliamentary Counsel 1934, but after five years transferred to Lord Chancellor's office. As Deputy to Permanent Secretary for ten years from 1944 played major part in post-World War II reforms of family justice system (notably in aftermath of *Reports of Committee on Procedure in Matrimonial Causes*, 1946). As Permanent Secretary 1954–1968 played important part in negotiations eventually leading to 1969 divorce reforms.

Cole, Norman (1909–1979) Conservative MP for Bedford South, served with Royal Navy throughout World War II, a member of numerous Committees concerned with youth, health and welfare issues, sponsor of the Children and Young Persons (Amendment) Act 1952 extending the grounds upon which a child could be found 'in need of care and protection' and subjected to fit person and other orders.

Colville of Culross, Viscount (1933–) Barrister, served as member of Archbishop's Group on Divorce Reform 1963–1965; and, as hereditary peer, promoted Guardianship Act 1973. Circuit judge 1993–1999.

Cranworth, Baron (1790–1868) born Robert Monsey Rolfe. Barrister, called 1816, MP for Penryn and Falmouth, Lord Chancellor 1852–1858. Much involved in events leading up to 1857 divorce legislation.

Curtis, Dame Myra (1886–1971) After working for seven years as an Assistant Editor of the *Victoria County History*, entered the Civil Service in 1915 and served as Superintendent of the Post Office Savings Bank, Director of Women Establishments in the Treasury, and Principal Assistant Secretary in the War Damage Commission. In 1942 she retired from the civil service to become Principal of Newnham College, Cambridge. In 1944 she served as one of the two members of a Committee of Enquiry into allegations relating to the accommodation of a seven-year-old girl in an LCC Remand Home; and the fact that the *London County Council Remand Homes, Report of a Committee of Enquiry* (1945, Cmd. 6594) was thought by some to be a 'white-washing' inquiry nearly led to her being supplanted as Chairman of the *Care of Children Committee*

(1946, Cmd. 6922). In the event that Report can be regarded as one of the foundations of post-World War II social services for children. As Chairman of the Committee appointed by Cambridge University to investigate the case for a third women's college she played a major part in the establishment of New Hall (which received its first undergraduates in the year she retired from Newnham); but it seems questionable whether she ever reconciled herself to the indecisiveness of much academic administration whilst she found young peoples' changes of mind 'somewhat exasperating': *Newnham College Roll Letter 1972*, p. 55. The judgment that she was at work 'certainly a formidable figure' is corroborated by Lady Allen of Hurtwood's experience giving evidence to the Curtis Committee in 1946: *Memoirs of an Uneducated Lady,* by M Allen and M Nicholson (1975) pp. 190–191.

Davidson, Archbishop Randall (1848–1930) Clergyman with somewhat conservative outlook on social issues. Skilful and committed opponent of divorce and marriage law reforms. See GKA *Bell, Randall Davidson, Archbishop of Canterbury* (3rd ed., 1952) pp. 996–1002.

Deech, Ruth Lynn (1943–) born Ruth Lynn Fraenkel. Academic lawyer (barrister 1967), member of the Law Commission's legal staff 1966–1967, latterly Principal of St. Anne's College Oxford and Chairman of the Human Fertilisation and Embryology Authority. DBE 2002.

De la Bere, Rupert (1893–1978) Conservative MP for Evesham 1935–1950 and for South Worcestershire 1950–1955. Nominal sponsor of AP Herbert's Matrimonial Causes Bill. Impeccable credentials: in 1936 had been married for 18 years to the daughter of a Knight and was the father of four children, had served in the Forces throughout World War I, and became a powerful figure in the City of London (Lord Mayor 1952), knighted in 1952, appointed KCVO and created a baronet in 1953.

Denning, Baron (1899–1999) born Alfred Thompson Denning. Probably the best known lawyer of the twentieth century, apparently not embarrassed by fame. Barrister (called 1923), appointed Judge of High Court Probate Divorce and Admiralty Division 1943, but found divorce work 'sordid in the extreme' and transferred to King's Bench Division in 1945. Chaired *Committee on Procedure in Matrimonial Causes* (1946) which opposed transfer of divorce jurisdiction to county court. As Master of the Rolls 1962–1982—he had served five unhappy years as a Lord of Appeal in Ordinary 1957–1962—gave important judgments in family matters, especially *Wachtel v. Wachtel* (1973). Presented radical image, but apparently conservative in social attitudes. Author of autobiographical and other works. Did not succeed in examination for Prize Fellowship All Souls College Oxford (1922).

Dilhorne, Viscount (1905–1980) born Reginald Edward Manningham-Buller. Barrister and Conservative MP (1943–1962); Lord Chancellor 1962–1964 (and subsequently Lord of Appeal in Ordinary, 1969–1980). Poor public image of unintelligent reactionary difficult to reconcile with record as significant contributor to divorce and other law reform.

Dobson, Sir Dennis (1908–1995) Solicitor, in practice 1933–1940; after war service, joined Lord Chancellor's Office in 1947. Transferred to Bar in 1951 with a view to becoming Permanent Secretary (which he did in 1968). Saw through Courts Act 1971 (which abolished Assize system, and created new court structure in which influence of civil service administrators much more apparent than previously). Skilled draftsman with somewhat cautious approach to law reform—his obituarist in *The Times* claims that Lord Chancellors Gardiner, Hailsham and Elwyn-Jones 'might well have been more adventurous . . . but for his influence'.

Duke, Henry Edward (1855–1939) created Baron Merrivale in 1925. Son of a clerk in a Devonshire granite works, Duke began his career as a journalist on the *Western Morning News*, but was called to the Bar in 1885. He is said by Lord Sankey (see below) to have been 'one of the finest . . . advocates of his time' who 'understood well the outlook and reactions of the ordinary juryman'. Elected a Unionist MP for Plymouth he held West Country seats until 1918, and in the wake of the 1916 Easter Rising in Ireland was appointed Chief Secretary. After following a conciliatory policy there, he resigned, and was appointed a Lord Justice of Appeal. According to Sir Claud Schuster, he only accepted appointment as President of the Probate Divorce and Admiralty Division of the High Court in 1919 in response to 'direct and vehement' pressure, since it required him to engage in an 'extremely laborious and, in many respects, repulsive occupation'. Even so he served until 1933, and thereafter made informed contributions to debates in the House of Lords (especially on improving procedures for dealing with domestic cases in the magistrates' courts, a cause in which he had long believed).

Eadie, Ellice Aylmer (1912–2001) Daughter of Bishop of Cork and Dr MET Hearn. Called to Bar 1936. After War Service, served in office of Parliamentary Counsel 1949–1972, and (whilst attached to Law Commission) drafted Matrimonial Homes Act 1967 and Divorce Reform Act 1969. Subsequently Standing Counsel to General Synod of the Church of England. Lady Summerskill, sponsor of the 1967 Act, described Eadie as 'a wonderful draftswoman': *Official Report* (HL) 14 June 1967, vol. 273, col. 20.

Ede, James Chuter (1882–1965) Labour MP 1923, 1929–1931 and 1935–1964, formerly schoolteacher and NCO in Army during World War I. In Cabinet as Home Secretary 1945–1951 and as such involved in passage of Children Act 1948.

Entwistle, Cyril Fullard (1877–1974) Barrister, called 1919 after war service. Liberal MP 1918–1924; Unionist MP 1931–1945. Introduced Matrimonial Causes Act 1923.

Ernle, Baron (1851–1937) born Rowland Edmund Prothero. Fellow of All Souls College Oxford 1875–1891, Conservative MP for the University of Oxford 1914–1919, Chief Land Agent to the Duke of Bedford 1898–1918 and a distinguished agriculturalist, author of *Pioneers and Progress of English Farming* (1887), President of the Board of Agriculture 1916–1919. Chaired Select Committee on Age of Marriage Bill (1929).

Feversham, Earl of (1906–1963) born Charles William Slingsby Duncombe. Yorkshire landowner. Parliamentary Secretary to Minister of Agriculture and Fisheries 1936–1939; war service 1939–1945. Chaired *Departmental Committee on Human Artificial Insemination* (1960).

Finer, Sir Morris (1917–1974) High Court judge. Won scholarships from Elementary School in Bethnal Green to Kilburn Grammar School and London School of Economics. Built up a heavy commercial practice at the Bar, but was a committed democratic socialist believing in the law as a purposive instrument of social reform. Chaired the influential *Committee on One-Parent Families* (1974). Appointed Judge of the High Court (Family Division) 1972.

Fischer Williams, Sir John (1870–1947) Barrister and public servant, chaired *Departmental Committee on Imprisonment by Courts of Summary Jurisdiction in Default of Payment of Fines and Other Sums of Money*, 1936.

Fisher, Lettice (1875–1956) daughter of Sir Courtenay Ilbert, the Parliamentary Counsel and Clerk to the House of Commons. Married her Oxford tutor the distinguished historian HAL Fisher (Education Minister in the Coalition Government 1916–1922). She wrote on social and other issues (*Mothers and families*, 1932) and was Chairman of National Council for Unmarried Mother and Her Child at an important period in the development of child law. Even after the fall of the Coalition, Mrs Fisher's contacts with Ministers stood her and the causes she represented in good stead.

Fletcher, Sir Eric (1903–1990) Solicitor, Labour MP 1945–1970, served on *Committee on the Law of Intestate Succession* (1951). The Prime Minister having been advised that it would be constitutionally impossible for a solicitor to be appointed to the office of Solicitor-General (or even Queen's Solicitor: see RFV Heuston, *Lives of the Lord Chancellors 1940–1970* (1987) p. 231) Fletcher became from 1964 to 1966 Minister without Portfolio in Harold Wilson's administration. In that capacity, he was responsible for law reform. A committed Anglican, his enthusiasm for reform of divorce law was not great. Life peer 1970. See generally his autobiography *Random Reflections* (1968).

Foster, Sir John Galway (1904–1982) Barrister, Conservative MP for Northwich 1945–1974 and a junior minister in Sir Winston Churchill's last administration. Highly regarded by the Lord Chancellor's Department he served on the Denning *Committee on Procedure in Matrimonial Causes* (1946) the Morton *Committee* *on the Law of Intestate Succession* (1951) and other government committees. Fellow of All Souls College, Oxford, 1925–1982.

Gamon, Hugh Reeve Percival (1880–1953) Chancery barrister, appointed County Court judge 1936. Chaired unofficial Committee established by National Conference of Social Service. Its Report was influential in demonstrating the need for the legislation which became the Adoption of Children Act 1949.

Gardiner, Gerald (1900–1990) Reforming barrister, edited (jointly with Andrew Martin: see below) *Law Reform NOW* (1963); Lord Chancellor in Harold Wilson's administrations, 1964–1970 and it is a law reformer that he 'will live in English history': RFV Heuston, *Lives of the Lord Chancellors 1940—1970* (1987) p. 226. Responsible for creation of Law Commissions by the Law Commissions Act 1965, for conferring divorce jurisdiction on County Courts and for creation of the Family Division of the High Court, the Matrimonial Homes Act 1967, and for the Divorce Reform Act 1969. His second wife, Muriel Box, in her biography *Rebel Advocate, A Biography of Gerald Gardiner* (1983) states that his first wife refused to divorce him so that he could marry the woman with whom he had fallen in love.

Gladstone, Herbert (1854–1930) son of the Liberal Leader WE Gladstone. Home Secretary from 1905 to 1910 in Liberal Administrations and responsible for the Probation of Offenders Act 1907 and the Children Act 1908. Gladstone subsequently became Governor-General of South Africa, and was raised to the peerage as a Viscount in 1910. For a sensitive memoir, see J Grigg, in A Horne (ed.), *Telling Lives, from WB Yeats to Bruce Chatwin* (2000).

Gladstone, William Ewart (1809–1898) Statesman (four times Prime Minister), committed Anglican, Liberal Leader; vigorous opponent of Matrimonial Causes Act 1857 and of amendment of prohibited degrees of marriage.

Gorell of Brampton, 1st Baron Gorell (1848–1913) born John Gorell Barnes. Son of a Liverpool shipowner, called to the Bar 1876 and built up substantial commercial practice before his appointment as a Judge of the Probate Divorce and Admiralty Division in 1892. He became President in 1905, and in the case of *Dodd v. Dodd* [1906] P 189 delivered a remarkable attack on the law administered in the Division. In 1908 he chaired the *Committee appointed by the Lord Chancellor to inquire into certain matters relating to County Court Procedure*; and in 1909 was made a hereditary peer: see p. 209, above. His appointment to chair the Royal Commission on Divorce and Matrimonial Causes suggested that there would be proposals for reform, and in fact that Royal Commission's 1912 Report was the basis for the Matrimonial Causes Act a quarter of a century later. See JEG de Montmorency, *John Gorell Barnes, First Lord Gorell (1848–1913)* (1920).

Gorell of Brampton, 2nd Baron Gorell (1882–1917) born Henry Gorell Barnes, succeeded to the title of his father, the 1st Baron. Had acted as Secretary to the Royal Commission on Matrimonial Causes, 1912 and introduced Bill to give effect to its recommendations into the House of Lords in July 1914. Killed in action, 1917.

Gorell of Brampton, 3rd Baron Gorell (1884–1963) born Ronald Gorell Barnes and succeeded to the peerage on his brother's death. Played active part in promoting legislation to give effect to recommendations of Royal Commission on Divorce and Matrimonial Causes; but also (after successful career in Army during World War I, culminating in founding Royal Army Education Corps) active in many other spheres of public life not least in chairing official committees concerned with the preservation of Carlton House Terrace and the terraces in Regent's Park. His unpublished diaries are a valuable resource.

Gould, Barbara Ayrton (died 1950) Labour politician. Her first public activity was as Organising Secretary of the National Society for Lunacy Reform. Having stood unsuccessfully as Labour candidate in several elections she became Chairman of the Labour Party in 1939–40, and was returned as MP for Hendon North in the 1945–50 Parliament. By raising the issue of child neglect in the House of Commons in July 1949 she gave publicity to an issue which eventually led to the appointment of the (Ingleby) Committee on Children and Young Persons (1960) and the enactment of the Children and Young Persons Act 1963.

Gower, Lawrence Cecil Bartlett (1913–1997) Solicitor; effective and enthusiastic law reformer. First came to public attention with evidence about collusive divorce given to the Royal Commission on Marriage and Divorce, 1956. Gower had practised as a solicitor before his appointment in 1948 to the Cassel Chair of Commercial Law in the University of London, and he continued to have links with the practising profession. His practice and academic interests were primarily in Commercial Law, but specialisation was not at the time as intense as it was subsequently to become, and Gower had had experience of handling divorce cases. In 1965 he was appointed one of the first Commissioners under the Law Commissions Act, and it is apparent from archival sources that he was primarily responsible for the Law Commission's work in divorce and family law until his retirement from the Commission in 1971: see generally the Memoir by SM Cretney in (1998) 101 *Proceedings of the British Academy* 379.

Graham-Campbell, Rollo F (1868–1946) Succeeded Sir Chartres Biron (see above) as Chief Metropolitan Police Magistrate in 1933. A member of the influential Molony *Departmental Committee on the Treatment of Young Offenders* (1927, Cmd. 2831) he was by no means unique in attracting the somewhat pitying scorn of the avowedly progressive Magistrate Claud Mullins (who described Graham-Campbell as 'Eton all through, with all its excellent qualities and its limitations . . . courtesy personified . . . deeply religious . . . hard working even to the detriment of his own health . . . [but] completely out of touch with modern movements . . . doubtful if [he] realised the necessity for any reforms in the courts: . . . this lovable old man really belonged to the world of aspidistras, heavy curtains and red-papered dining rooms . . .': C Mullins, *Fifteen Years Hard Labour* (1948) pp. 171–172).

Graham Hall, Jean (1917–) Social worker 1937–1944, subsequently Probation Officer 1945–1951. Called to the Bar, 1951; appointed Metropolitan Stipendiary Magistrate 1965, and Circuit Judge 1971. Author of biographies and other works. Chaired *Departmental Committee on Statutory Maintenance Limits* (1968).

Gurdon, Sir Brampton (1840–1919) MP for North Norfolk 1899–1910, owner of some 3,000 acres and married to the daughter of an Earl, he had become a civil servant by competitive examination at the age of 23 and had acted as Private Secretary to Mr Gladstone as Chancellor of the Exchequer and Prime Minister before entering Parliament. Promoter of Deceased Wife's Sister's Marriage Act 1907 which resolved the question whether a man should be allowed to marry his deceased wife's sister.

Gwyer, Sir Maurice Linford (1878–1952) Barrister and public servant. Called to the Bar 1903, but entered public service during World War I. As Solicitor and Legal Adviser to the Ministry of Health 1919–1926 he was a member of the Tomlin Child Adoption Committee (1924–1925) whose Report was the foundation for the Adoption Act 1926. Gwyer was deeply concerned by the potential of adoption as a cloak for child abuse; but the recommendations of the Tomlin Committee on that subject were not implemented for some years. Served as Treasury Solicitor 1926–1933 and as First Parliamentary Counsel 1934–1937. In that capacity he played an important part in the passage of the Matrimonial Causes Act 1937 and in the legal formalities incidental to the abdication of King Edward VIII. Appointed Chief Justice of India and President of the Federal Court, 1937. Fellow of All Souls College Oxford, 1902–1916.

Hailsham, 1st Viscount (1872–1950) born Douglas McGarel Hogg. For eight years West India merchant; then served with Yeomanry in South African War before being called to the Bar in 1902. Conservative MP for St. Marylebone, 1922–1928; Lord Chancellor 1928–1929 and 1935–1938. Suffered disabling stroke in 1936, but continued to support principle of freedom of testation which he saw as threatened by Inheritance legislation. An opponent of changes made by Matrimonial Causes Act 1937 he refrained from opposing the legislation in public.

Hailsham of St. Marylebone, Baron (1907–2001) born Quintin McGarel Hogg. Lawyer (called to the Bar 1932, QC) and Conservative politician, MP for Oxford City 1938–1950, when succeeded father as Viscount Hailsham. Disclaiming that peerage in 1963 in unsuccessful attempt to succeed Harold Macmillan as Prime Minister he was elected MP for St. Marlylebone and gave loyal support to Sir Alec Douglas Home's administration. Introduced Maintenance Orders Act 1968 as private member. Appointed Lord Chancellor in 1970, he served in that office from 1970 to 1974 and from 1979 to 1987. A progressive conservative in his approach to legal reform in general and family law in particular. Responsible for the Matrimonial and Family Proceedings Act 1984 but was unenthusiastic about proposals for community of property. His daughter became a judge of the High Court (Family Division) in 1995.

Haldane, Viscount Haldane of Cloan (1856–1928) Secretary of State for War 1905–1912 in Asquith's Liberal administration and subsequently described by Field Marshall Haig as 'the greatest Secretary for War England has ever had': see RFV Heuston, *Lives of the Lord Chancellors 1885–1940* (1964) p. 212. From 1912 to 1915 Lord Chancellor but resigned 1915 in large part because of a press campaign based on his supposedly pro-German sympathies. An active worker for the Labour Party in the 1923 election campaign, he became Lord Chancellor in Ramsay MacDonald's 1924 administration. Supporter of divorce reform as a Liberal MP but not as Lord Chancellor in the Labour government.

Hale, Brenda Marjorie, see **Hoggett**.

Hall, William Clarke (1866–1932) Barrister (called 1899) Metropolitan Police Magistrate and author. A close associate of the Reverend Benjamin Waugh (the crusading founding Secretary of the NSPCC) whose artist daughter Edna he married, Hall had developed a strong interest in the plight of deprived and delinquent children and the law. In 1894 wrote a detailed commentary on the law, *The Law relating to Children*. The third edition published in 1909 became the standard work; and new editions continued to be published after his death (the 10th in 1991). Clarke Hall wrote a vigorous polemic, *The Queen's Reign for Children*, published in 1897 urging much greater State involvement. In 1913 the Liberal Home Secretary Reginald McKenna appointed him as a stipendiary magistrate, and for the rest of his life he was enthusiastically committed to reform: in 1926 he published *Children's Courts* which contained telling criticism of the law's treatment of children under the 1908 Act, and advocated radical reforms (for example, giving the juvenile court 'control over all children and young persons under 18 who have fallen or were likely to fall into delinquency', and power to place such children and any neglected child and any child associating with 'bad companions' under the care of a probation officer and to make them wards of the juvenile court). But although progressive in outlook he was prepared to accept the force of some traditional views, at one time even being prepared to accept that there were arguments justifying judicially ordered corporal punishment of children. However, study of the evidence convinced him that the case for abolition was overwhelming: see *The State and the Child* (1917) a book containing measured criticism of the law embodied in the Children Act 1908. He became an influential figure, chairing the Magistrates' Association, the National Association of Probation Officers, and was well regarded by Home Office officials serving on the Home Office Advisory Committee on Probation. GK Behlmer *Friends of the Family, The English Home and Its Guardians, 1850–1940* (1998) p. 245 gives a full account of his life and work.

792   *Biographical Notes*

Hanworth, Viscount (1861–1936) born Ernest Murray Pollock. Barrister (called 1885), Unionist MP 1910–1923, Law Officer 1919–1922, Master of the Rolls, 1923–1935. Chaired Business of the Courts Committee, 1933.

Harris, Sidney West (1876–1962) Served for 48 years in the Home Office, and was Head of the Children Department from 1919 to 1934. Harris acted as Secretary to the Tomlin Committee on Adoption in 1924, was an influential member of the Molony *Departmental Committee on the Treatment of Young Offenders* (1927, Cmd. 2831) and chaired the *Committee on the Social Services in the Courts of Summary Jurisdiction* in 1936. After his retirement from the civil service he chaired the British Board of Film Censors, but for the development of the family justice system his role as Chairman of the *Departmental Committee on Grants for the Development of Marriage Guidance* is more significant since the Committee's Report (1948, Cmd. 7566) led to the provision of Government funding for a number of marriage guidance organisations. Described by John Watson JP as 'sweet and unwarlike' and by *The Times* (10 July 1962) as 'of a somewhat shy and retiring nature'—a colleague wrote that he would bid you good morning and then wonder if he had gone too far: CP Hill, *The Times* 27 July 1962—his personality may explain why he failed to reach the heights to be expected of his abilities. But 'no one in his generation better upheld the best traditions of the civil service' whilst the modern observer must note with admiration the effectiveness of his concern for securing the public good in general and the welfare of children in particular.

Haynes, Edmund Sydney Pollock (1877–1949) Solicitor, man of letters and divorce reformer. A leading figure in Divorce Law Reform Union, he drafted reforming Bills in 1908 and 1915. AP Herbert dedicated his autobiographical account of how the Matrimonial Causes Act 1937 eventually became law to 'ESP Haynes and all the veterans'. Haynes firmly believed in divorce by consent and was incensed by the elaborate machinery of espionage at the time maintained by the King's Proctor to prevent couples colluding in divorce proceedings.

Herbert, Sir Alan (Patrick) (1890–1971) Author and MP. Gained first class honours degree in Law at New College, Oxford, and read for the Bar in the chambers of Sir Leslie Scott (subsequently a Lord Justice of Appeal). Although he preferred writing musicals and humourous and satirical pieces for *Punch* to following a legal career, his *Misleading Cases* (1927) could only have been written by someone with an insider's knowledge of the law. *Holy Deadlock* (1934), a satirical account of the divorce process, was influential in creating an atmosphere favourable to reform. Elected Independent MP for Oxford University, serving from 1935 to 1950, he sponsored the Matrimonial Causes Act 1937: see his own account *The Ayes Have It* (1937) and Chapter 6 above. See also Herbert's autobiography, *Independent Member* (1950) and R Pound, *AP Herbert, A Biography* (1976).

Hogg, Quintin, see **Hailsham.**

Hoggett, Brenda Marjorie (1945–) Barrister 1969. From 1966 to 1989 on staff of Law Faculty Manchester University (Professor 1986). Appointed a Law Commissioner in 1984 and served to 1993. Also a member of Government's group carrying out *Review of Child Care Law* (1985). Responsible for Law Commission's work in Family Law (notably the *Review of Child Law Guardianship and Custody*, 1988, Reports on *Domestic Violence and Occupation of the Family Home* (1992—recommendations implemented by Family Law Act 1996—and *The Ground for Divorce* (1990)). One of main architects of Children Act 1989. Reverted to maiden surname of Hale on leaving Law Commission and taking appointment as Judge of High Court Family Division. Lord Justice of Appeal 1999.

Hopkinson, Alfred (1851–1939) Lawyer, educationalist and Unionist MP (1926–1929 for the Combined English Universities). Chairman of the *Committee on Child Adoption* (1921, Cmd. 1254). For some years Hopkinson combined the duties of Professor of Law at Manchester with practice at the bar; and he served as Vice-Chancellor of the Victoria University of Manchester from 1900–1913.

Horsburgh, Miss Florence Gertrude (1889–1969) Chairman of the *Departmental Committee on Adoption Societies and Agencies* (1937, Cmd. 5499). Conservative MP (at the time, for Dundee) she was able to introduce as a private member the Bill for the Adoption of Children (Regulation) Act 1939 giving effect to many of the Committee's recommendations. In 1951 she became Minister of Education in Winston Churchill's administration; and in 1953 she became (in that capacity) the first woman to hold Cabinet Office in a Conservative Government. Created a life peer in 1959.

Houghton, Sir William Frederick (1909–1971) Teacher 1932–1936 and thereafter Educational Administrator (latterly Education Officer of the London County Council and Inner London Education Authority, 1956–1971). Chairman of Departmental Committee on the Adoption of Children (1969–71).

Hubback, Mrs Eva (1886–1949) Parliamentary Secretary of NUSEC 1919–1927, and thereafter Principal of Morley College. Daughter of the banker, Sir Meyer Spielman, she graduated from Newnham College Cambridge in 1908, worked as a voluntary social worker for the LCC, married FW Hubback (lecturer at Manchester University) 1911 by whom she had three children. To the lawyer, her skill in mastering complex legal issues and securing the confidence—if not always the agreement—of influential civil servants (and in particular that of the Lord Chancellor's Permanent Secretary, Sir Claude Schuster) is remarkable. The Lord Chancellor's Department's continuing respect for her abilities is evidenced by its suggestion (not in the event accepted) that she should serve on the

(Denning) Committee on *Procedure in Matrimonial Causes* in 1946. It may (as suggested by M Pugh, *Women and the Women's Movement in Britain 1914–1959*) be true that Hubback's writings—and notably *The Population of Britain* (Pelican 1948) in which she urged that the bearing and rearing of children was the finest of all professions for women—reflect a 'highly conventional concern with finding means of encouraging women to have more children'; but it is impossible to deny her contribution to the development of English family law between the two World Wars. NUSEC was largely responsible for the passing of the Guardianship of Infants Act and other family legislation in 1925, and Hubback remained active in the cause of reform to the time of her death. A tribute to her work, and in particular her contribution to a Report on the *Neglected Child and the Family* was paid by the Under Secretary of State at the Home Office in May 1952. There is an informative memoir by Gillian Sutherland in DNB *Missing Persons* and biographical writings by her daughter, Diana Hopkinson (*Family Inheritance, a Life of Eva Hubback* (1954); *The Incense Tree* (1968)); but the most accessible account is now to be found in Chapter 10 of B Harrison's *Prudent Revolutionaries, Portraits of British Feminists between the Wars* (1987).

Hunter, William Alexander (1844–1898) Liberal MP for Aberdeen North 1885–1896, sometime Professor of Roman Law University College London, and author of *Roman Law in the Order of a Code*, promoter in 1892 of first parliamentary attempt to widen ground for divorce after Matrimonial Causes Act 1857.

Hurst, Gerald Berkeley (1877–1957) Chancery Barrister, QC, Treasurer of Lincoln's Inn, Commanded Battalion of Manchester Regiment World War I, Conservative MP for Manchester Moss Side 1918–1923, 1924–1925, County Court Judge 1938–1952. His autobiography, *Closed Chapters* (1942) reveals him to have been a long standing enthusiast for adoption (which he saw as 'bringing the homeless child to the childless home'). Appropriately, Chaired Departmental Committee on the Adoption of Children (Report, 1954, Cmd. 9248). Son in law of A Hopkinson (see above).

Hutton, Sir Noel (Kilpatrick) (1907–1984) Barrister (called 1932); entered office of the Parliamentary Counsel 1938; First Parliamentary Counsel 1956–1968. Heavily involved in drafting of Law Commissions Act 1965.

Hylton-Foster, Sir Harry Braustyn (1905–1965) Barrister (called 1928) Conservative MP 1950 onwards, Solicitor-General, 1954–1959, Speaker of the House of Commons) 1959 onwards. Introduced Intestates' Estates Act 1952.

Iddesleigh, Viscount (1901–1970) born Henry Stafford Northcote. Served Welsh Guards World War I, succeeded uncle 1927, active in child-related issues in House of Lords.

Ingleby, Viscount (1897–1966) born Osbert Peake. Educated Eton, Sandhurst and Christ Church, served in Coldstream Guards 1916–1919, called to Bar, Conservative MP for North Leeds 1929–1955, held office as Under-Secretary of State at the Home Office, Financial Secretary to the Treasury and Minister of Pensions and National Insurance. Chaired Committee on Children and Young Persons 1956–60.

Jackson, Joseph (1924–1987) Barrister (called 1947, QC) and scholar. Formidable and successful advocate who dominated divorce bar for many years. Author of fifth to fourteenth editions of leading practitioner's text, *Rayden on Divorce*. Jackson's *Formation and Annulment of Marriage* (1951, second edition 1969) is a major contribution to legal history. Committed reformer.

Jones, (Trevor) Alec (1924–1983) Schoolteacher, subsequently Labour MP for Rhondda West, sponsor of Bill for Divorce Reform Act 1969. Held junior ministerial office 1974–1979.

Jones, Sir David Brynmor (1852–1921) Barrister (called 1876), County Court judge (1885–1892), resigned and sat as Liberal MP 1892–1914. Active supporter of divorce reform.

Joseph, Keith Sinjohn (1918–1994) created Baron Joseph of Portsoken 1987. Fellow of All Souls College Oxford 1946–60 and 1972–1994. Active Service in World War II 1939–1946. Barrister and Conservative MP for Leeds NE 1956–1987. Cabinet Minister in governments between 1962 and 1986. Strongly influential in development of conservative philosophies applied during Thatcher administrations. As Secretary of State for Social Services developed and publicised concept of 'cycle of deprivation' and responsible for commissioning much social science research. See A Denham and M Garnett, *Keith Joseph* (2001).

Jowitt, Earl (1885–1957) born William Allen Jowitt. Successful lawyer (called to Bar 1909), Lord Chancellor in Attlee Labour Government 1945–1951. Did not have high reputation for consistency, in part because of his conduct in accepting office as Attorney-General in MacDonald Labour government, June 1929, only days after being returned as Liberal MP for Preston, then continued in office in the MacDonald National Government which was shunned by most Labour MPs.

Joynson-Hicks, William (1865–1932) Solicitor (1887) built up large practice. Unionist MP 1908–1929, and strong Evangelical churchman. Home Secretary 1924–1929. Created Viscount Brentford 1929.

Kahn-Freund, Sir Otto (1900–1979) German lawyer, judge 1928–1933. Called to English bar 1936, and became distinguished comparative lawyer holding chairs at London School of Economics and Oxford.

Kent, Sir Harold (Simcox) (1903–1998) Barrister (called 1928, QC). Entered office of Parliamentary Counsel and largely responsible for providing the assistance promised by Government to Sir Alan Herbert's 1937 Matrimonial Causes Act. Subsequently Treasury Solicitor and Queen's Proctor 1953–1963; Dean of the Arches Court of Canterbury 1972; Standing Counsel to the Church Assembly and General Synod of the Church of England. Author of an informative and entertaining account of the drafting of the 1937 legislation and other matters, *In on the Act* (1979).

Kilbracken, Lord (1877–1950) born Hugh John Godley. Barrister, called 1902. Assistant Parliamentary Counsel (in which capacity concerned with the Summary Jurisdiction (Separation and Maintenance) Bills). Appointed Counsel to the Chairman of Committees, House of Lords 1923 and served to 1944. Produced initial draft of AP Herbert's 1936 Marriage Bill (and was also apparently the draftsman of 'Buckmaster's Bill of 1912': Kilbracken to Schuster, 4 December 1936, PRO LCO2/1195). A close friend of the Asquith family and for some ten years prior to her marriage a persistent suitor of the Prime Minister's daughter, Violet. The letters and diaries of Violet Bonham Carter, *Lantern Slides* (ed. M Bonham Carter and M Pottle, 1996) and *Daring to Hope* (ed. M Pottle, 2000) cast much light on his personality and character.

Kilmuir, Earl (1900–1967) born David Patrick Maxwell Fyffe. Barrister practising in Liverpool, QC 1934, Conservative MP for Liverpool West Derby 1934–1954. Highly effective as prosecuting counsel at 1945 Nuremberg trial of major German war criminals. Enthusiastic supporter of European movement and strong supporter of European Convention on Human Rights, doing much of the drafting. As Home Secretary (1951–1954) advised against a reprieve for the 19-year-old Derek Bentley. As Lord Chancellor 1954–1962 opposed any extension of ground for divorce but was responsible for carrying Children Act 1958 and Law Reform (Husband and Wife) Act 1962 through House of Lords. Meticulous in discharging his duties (as evidenced by his copious notes and annotations for debates in the House of Lords) but dismissed from office in July 1962 by Prime Minister Macmillan in the so-called 'night of the long knives'. Compensated with Earldom.

Knight, GW Holford (1877–1936) Barrister, Labour MP for South Nottingham 1929–1935. Strong advocate of women's rights (especially at Bar): author of *Advancing Woman*. Introduced divorce reform Bills (which would have allowed divorce of an incurably insane spouse) into House of Commons 1930. See also Helena Normanton.

Landsteiner, Karl (1868–1943) Scientist, born in Vienna, emigrated to the United States, became an American citizen, and in 1930 was awarded the Nobel Prize in Physiology and Medicine for his work in identifying blood groups.

Lang, Cosmo Gordon (1864–1935) Archbishop of York 1908–1928 (and signatory of Minority Report, *Royal Commission on Matrimonial Causes*, 1912); Archbishop of Canterbury (1928–1942) and prominent in denouncing failings of

King Edward VIII, 1936. Although opposed to marriage and divorce reform he came to accept that the rules of the Church should not necessarily constitute a guide to those imposed by the legislature. Fellow of All Souls College, Oxford, 1889.

Latey, John Brinsmead (1914–1999) Served in World War II and established scheme for 'conciliation' for servicemen seeking divorce. Successful practitioner at divorce bar, appointed to High Court bench by Lord Chancellor Gardiner and served for nearly 25 years. His most significant achievement was in chairing the *Committee on the Age of Majority* established by Lord Chancellor Gardiner in 1965. Latey approached this task with an open mind and urged the need for such an approach on the other members.

Levy, Benn Wolfe (1900–1973) Playwright, served RAF 1918, Royal Navy 1939–1945, Labour MP for Eton and Slough 1945–1950. Played significant role in debates on Bill for Adoption of Children Act 1949.

Liddell, Sir (Fred)eric Francis (1865–1950) Brother of Alice Liddell (of *Wonderland* and *Looking Glass* fame). Barrister (called 1894, QC); First Parliamentary Counsel 1917–1928, and as such heavily involved in 1925 Guardianship, Property and Succession legislation. Fellow of All Souls College, Oxford, 1891. See further under **Tomlin**.

Lipton, Lieutenant Colonel Marcus (1900–1978) Barrister (called 1926), Labour MP 1945 onwards. Strongly active in parliamentary campaign for divorce reform.

Listowel, Earl of (1906–1997) born William ('Billy') Hare. He became the fifth Earl of Listowel in the peerage of Ireland and the sixth Baron Hare in the peerage of the United Kingdom on his father's death in 1931. In an attempt to shield his son from left-wing influences the Fourth Earl had removed him from Balliol College Oxford and sent him to Magdalene College Cambridge; but the fifth Earl none the less remained a lifelong socialist and advocate of progressive causes. In 1934 he introduced into the House of Lords a Bill (drafted by Claud Mullins, see below) intended to reform procedures in magistrates' courts domestic cases but was apparently at this period rather unpopular with the more traditionally minded members of the House of Lords and it was thought prudent to find another peer 'more acceptable to the House generally' to pilot the Bill for the Summary Procedure (Domestic Proceedings) Act 1937 through the House of Lords. Listowel expressed an interest in Law Reform on other occasions (eg in the debates on the Law Reform (Married Women and Tortfeasors) Act 1935) and served as a Minister throughout the post-World War II Attlee administration (briefly from April 1947 to January 1948 in the cabinet as the last Secretary of State at the India office). As Postmaster General, involved in putting the Government case on the 1946 *Curtis Report*. Subsequently, at Dr Kwame Nkrumah's personal request, Listowel served as Governor-General (1957–1960) of the newly independent Ghana. Listowel's Autobiography, published on the Internet, does not refer to his law reform interests.

Longford, Lord (1905–2001) born Francis ('Frank') Aungier Pakenham. Minister in Labour administrations 1945–1968, keenly interested in social and especially penal matters. Author of many books and pamphlets: chaired influential committee on *Crime, A Challenge to us All* (1964).

Lucas-Tooth, Sir Hugh (1903–1985) Barrister, Conservative MP 1924–1929 and 1945–1970; held junior ministerial office 1952–1955. Dissented from recommendations of *Committee on the Law of Succession in Relation to Illegitimate Persons* (1966).

Lyndhurst, Baron (1772–1863) born John Singleton Copley, son of celebrated American painter. Tory Lord Chancellor 1826–1830, 1834–1835, 1841–1845. 'Lord Lyndhurst's Act' 1835 prompted long battle about prohibited degrees for marriage. Also active in debates on Matrimonial Causes Act 1857.

McCardie, Sir Henry Alfred (1869–1933) King's Bench Division Judge, noted for scholarly judgments particularly on the more esoteric aspects of the law. Was a man who repudiated an engagement to marry entitled to a return of the engagement ring, for example? For McCardie this required a lengthy and erudite review of Roman and Civilian systems of law: *Cohen v. Sellar* [1926] 1 KB 536. McCardie was greatly interested in the legal position of married women; and was rebuked by Scrutton LJ for considering sociological issues in his judgment in an action for enticement: *Place v. Searle* [1932] 2 KB 497. Had personal problems and committed suicide.

McGregor, Oliver Ross (1921–1997) Social historian and Public Servant; Professor of Social Institutions, London University 1964–1985; Director of Bedford College Socio-Legal Research Unit; member of Finer Committee on One-Parent Families and many other official committees. Had a huge influence on the development of attitudes to the relationship between the law and social problems. Author of *Divorce in England* (1957) and joint author of *Separated Spouses* (1970). Subsequently chaired Royal Commission on Press, and Press Complaints Commission. Life Peer 1981.

MacKinnon, Sir Frank Douglas (1871–1946) King's Bench judge 1924–1937; Lord Justice of Appeal 1937–1946. Outspoken and often critical. His *On Circuit* (1940) gives a vivid picture of his life and attitudes.

Macleod, Iain Norman (1913–1970) Conservative MP and Cabinet Minister. Parliamentary question prompted reform of Intestacy laws, 1952.

Mancroft, Baron (1914–1987) born Stormont Mancroft Samuel Mancroft. Served in 1939–1945 War as Colonel in Royal Artillery, subsequently held junior Ministerial Office, but resigned and pursued business interests (including Director of Great Universal Stores and the Horserace Totalisator Board). Influential in procuring reform of law relating to prohibited degrees of marriage, Intestate's Estates Act 1952 and in 1951 active in House of Lords in seeking appointment of Royal Commission into law of marriage and divorce.

Martin, Andrew (1906–1985) born Andras Neugroschel in Hungary. Barrister, called 1940, QC. Held Chair of International and Comparative Law, Southampton, 1963–1977. Jointly edited *Law Reform Now* (1963) and played influential part in proposals for a Law Commission. Appointed one of the foundation Commissioners under the Law Commissions Act 1965.

Maxwell, Sir Alexander (1880–1963) Son of congregational Minister and Quaker GP. Civil Servant, Permanent Under-Secretary of State, Home Office 1938–1948 and in that capacity played significant role in dealings with magistrates' courts (and with individual magistrates, not least the uneasy colleague Claud Mullins). Said by Jennifer Hart (his Private Secretary from 1939) to have fervent belief that the Home Office had important duty to safeguard liberty: see her *Ask Me No More* (1998) Chapter 6.

Merriman, Baron (1880–1962) born Frank Boyd Merriman. After education at Winchester was articled to a Manchester solicitor but was called to Bar in 1904. He served in the Manchester Regiment throughout World War I. In 1924 he was elected Conservative MP for Manchester, Rusholme, became Solicitor-General in 1928, and in 1933 was appointed from that office to be President of the Probate, Divorce and Admiralty Division. Merriman's handling of commercial cases was not well regarded by the shipping community, but (as the text of this work demontrates) he was extremely conscientious in the discharge of his duties as President and took a close and careful interest in policy matters. Although strongly opposed to divorce by consent, and concerned that collusion was all too often said to be common in divorce proceedings, he was not opposed to reform, and the scheme he formulated in 1946 for Conciliation and Inquiry Tribunals was in many ways far-sighted. But a man of Merriman's somewhat choleric disposition could not be expected to, and did not, accept the manner in which his proposals were treated by the 1946 Denning Committee on Procedure in Matrimonial Causes and the attitude of that Committee's chairman clearly irritated him. Equally his fiercely expressed opinions did not always find a sympathetic ear in the Lord Chancellor's Department, and concern was expressed within the Department about his mental health. But Merriman continued to serve until his death at the age of 81. He remained active to the end; and his carefully written Opinion in the House of Lords' case of *Ross-Smith* ([1963] AC 280) was delivered by a colleague.

Merrivale, First Baron, see **Duke**.

Meston, Second Baron (1894–1984) born Dougall Meston. Soldier, 1914–1922; barrister (called 1924) and writer on legal subjects. Active in affairs of Divorce Law Reform Union.

Meston, Third Baron (1950–) born James Meston. Barrister, prominent practitioner at Family Law Bar (QC). Active in law reform initiatives in House of Lords, notably the Bill which became the Marriage (Prohibited Degrees of Relationship) Act 1986. Subsequently a circuit judge (1999).

Molony, The Rt. Hon Sir Thomas Francis (1865–1949) Irish lawyer with a distinguished academic record, became Lord Chief Justice of Ireland in 1918. Resigned in 1924, when the Irish Free State judicature was established, and devoted the rest of his life to public service. A committed Roman Catholic, he became Vice-Chancellor of the University of Dublin in 1931. Chairman of the Departmental Committee on the Treatment of Young Offenders 1925–1927.

Monckton, Walter Turner (1891–1965) QC One of the most highly regarded lawyers and negotiators of his day, Attorney-General to the Prince of Wales 1932–1936 (and thereafter deeply involved in the negotiations surrounding King Edward's abdication in December 1936). Subsequently acted for the Nizam of Hyderabad in relation to constitutional issues arising from Indian independence. Conducted influential Inquiry into *Circumstances which led to the boarding out of Dennis and Terence O'Neill . . .*, 1945, Cmd. 6636. Entered Parliament 1951; Cabinet minister in Conservative administrations 1951–1957 (resigning as Minister of Defence in October 1956 because of disagreement about the Eden government's policy of armed intervention in the Middle East, but retaining Cabinet Office apparently to preserve the appearance of ministerial solidarity). It is often said that Churchill offered Monckton the reversion to the office of Lord Chief Justice of England when it was vacated by Lord Goddard (1877–1971) and that Goddard—disapproving of the fact that Monckton was divorced—refused to retire so long as there was any possibility of Monckton succeeding him in office. There is an excellent biography of Monckton by the Second Earl of Birkenhead (*Walter Monckton: the life of Viscount Monckton of Brenchley 1891–1965*) in which, however, there is no mention of Monckton's involvement in the O'Neill case.

de Montmorency, James Edward Geoffrey (1866–1934) Assistant Secretary to the 1909 *Royal Commission on Divorce and Matrimonial Causes* and biographer of its Chairman, Lord Gorell: see *John Gorell Barnes, First Lord Gorell (1848–1913)* (1920). Subsequently Quain Professor of Comparative Law and Dean of the Faculty of Law University College London.

Morrison, Herbert Stanley (1888–1965) Labour politician, Leader of London County Council 1939–40, MP for many years, Home Secretary 1940–1945 in World War II coalition government, and a powerful figure in Attlee's 1945 administration. His political skills are evidenced by his skilful fight to retain departmental responsibility for the care of children in the Home Office.

Mortimer, Robert (1902–1976) Bishop of Exeter 1949, formerly University Lecturer in Early Canon Law and Regius Professor of Moral and Pastoral Theology at Oxford, had edited and substantially revised TA Lacey's *Marriage in Church and State* (1947). Regarded as a learned moral theologian of conservative outlook: O Chadwick, *Michael Ramsey, A Life* (1990). Appointed to chair group established by Archbishop Ramsey to investigate ground for divorce; the group's Report, *Putting Asunder* was a catalyst for the Divorce Reform Act 1969.

Morton, Baron (1887–1973) born Fergus Dunlop Morton. Scotsman, committed member of Church of Scotland to the end of his life. Called to English Bar 1912 and practised in Chancery Division after active service in Highland Light Infantry in World War I (in which his two brothers were killed). Appointed High Court judge (Chancery Division) 1938, promoted to Court of Appeal 1944, appointed Lord of Appeal in Ordinary 1947. Thought to have demonstrated sound judgment in role as chairman of *Committee on the Law of Intestate Succession* (1951); and subsequently appointed to chair *Royal Commission on Marriage and Divorce* (1956). The conservative approach of the Commission has been much criticised, and Morton has been given little credit for the Commission's thorough and painstaking review of the law which resulted in many reforms.

Mullins, Claud (1887–1968) Metropolitan police magistrate, publicist and law reformer. He had strong views about the treatment of disputes between husbands and wives under the Summary Jurisdiction (Separation and Maintenance) Act 1925, and believed magistrates should be trained in the causes of marital disharmony and thus enabled to dispense social help to those who came before them. Mullins drafted a Summary Jurisdiction (Domestic Procedure) Bill which was debated in 1934 and generated sufficient support to persuade the Government that the magistrates' domestic jurisdiction ought to be investigated by a Departmental Committee. He was also largely instrumental in drawing public attention to the excessive use of imprisonment for debt and thus in influencing the decision to appoint the (Fischer Williams) Departmental Committee on Imprisonment by Courts of Summary Jurisdiction (1934) which led to the Money Payment (Justices' Procedure) Act 1935. However, his attempts to secure for the magistrates an enhanced role in the administration of the reformed divorce law brought about by AP Herbert's Matrimonial Causes Act 1937 were unsuccessful. He had an uneasy relationship with his magisterial brethren; and in 1942 was publicly rebuked for his conduct by the Home Secretary, Herbert Morrison (see above). Retiring from the bench on grounds of ill-health in 1942 he devoted the rest of his life to writing, lecturing and voluntary work. As Sir Alexander Maxwell, the Permanent Under-Secretary at the Home Office, put it to the Home Secretary on Mullins' retirement, '. . . with his egoism and assertiveness, [Mullins] has combined a very genuine zeal for improving the work of the Courts and for helping the numerous classes of unfortunate people with whom the Summary courts come into contact'. His significance in the history of law reform has for long been underrated, but see now GK Behlmer, *Friends of the Family, The English Home and its Guardians, 1850–1940* (1998) pp. 213–229; and SM Cretney, 'Marriage Saving and the Role of the Courts, Claud Mullins and the Early Days of Conciliation' in *Law, Law Reform and the Family* (1988).

Neild, Basil Edward (1903–1996) Educated Harrow and Magdalen College Oxford, Barrister 1925, QC, Conservative MP for Chester 1940–1956, served

War 1940–1945. Appointed first permanent judge of Crown Court Manchester 1956–1960 (when he was appointed to the High Court bench, serving until 1978). Claimed to have been the only judge to have presided at all the 61 Assize towns in England and Wales before the abolition of the Assize system in 1972. As Private Member, introduced the Bill which became Adoption of Children Act 1949.

Newsholme, Sir Arthur (1857–1943) Had a long and successful career in public health administration. Born and brought up in Haworth Yorkshire (home of the Bronte sisters) he qualified as a doctor, served as a Medical Officer of Health, and was appointed Medical Officer to the Local Government Board in 1908 (the year in which the so called 'children's charter' was enacted), and held strong views on the relationship between public health and other state welfare functions: see his *The Ministry of Health* (1925) and *Fifty Years in Public Health* (1935).

Normanton, Mrs Helena Florence (died 1957) One of first women called to bar (1922) and appointed King's Counsel, 1949. Encountered much discrimination at Bar, as revealed in her Papers (held in the Women's Library, London Guildhall University). President of the Council of Married Women 1952–3, and active in law reform movements. Gave much assistance to Holford Knight MP, standing in for him at public meetings as early as 1919.

Ormrod, Sir Roger (Fray Greenwood) (1911–1992) Judge of the High Court (Probate Divorce and Admiralty Division and Family Division) 1961–1974 and Lord Justice of Appeal 1974–1982. A qualified doctor as well as a barrister, his judgment in the *Corbett* case (see Chapter 2) settled for nearly 30 years the law relating to the status of transsexuals. Ormrod had a successful practice as an advocate, but his main contribution to the development of family law was in the 1970s. A judicial colleague (Sir Robin Dunn, *Sword and Wig, Memoirs of a Lord Justice*, 1993) has written that Ormrod 'practically single-handed . . . revolutionised the whole approach to divorce law' refusing to regard the Divorce Court as a court of morals but rather as a forum for resolving the practical consequences of divorce. Thus, Ormrod strongly discouraged seeking to resolve issues about the upbringing of children by invoking what he regarded as the myth of the 'unimpeachable parent'; and he played a decisive part in re-asserting the view that the court should exercise its wide discretionary powers in financial matters by looking to the circumstances of the particular case and not (as the Court of Appeal had suggested in the *Wachtel* case) by applying guidelines or fractional presumptions. Ormrod contributed a number of penetrating studies to scholarly journals.

Owen, Dr David Anthony Llewellyn (1938–) Neurologist psychiatrist and medical researcher, Labour MP 1966–1981, Foreign Secretary 1977–79, co-founder of Social Democratic Party 1981. Sponsored Children Bill 1973 and ministerially responsible for passage of Children Act 1975. Remained MP for Plymouth constituencies to 1992 when created a life peer.

Parker, John (1906–1987) Fabian socialist, Labour MP for Essex constituencies 1935–1983. An eventually successful campaigner for reform of the law relating to illegitimacy (including Legitimacy Act 1959 providing for a child to be legitimated by the parents' subsequent marriage notwithstanding their inability to marry at the date of birth) and divorce.

Percy, Lord Eustace (1887–1958) Conservative educationalist, seventh son of the seventh Duke of Northumberland, Rector of King's College Newcastle. Formerly Unionist MP 1921–37, President of the Board of Education 1924–29. Offered chairmanship of Royal Commission on Marriage and Divorce in 1951, but the invitation was withdrawn when Percy told officials of his strong belief in the indissolubility of marriage. Created Baron, 1958.

Perry, Sir (Thomas) Erskine (1806–1882) Barrister 1834, but (having lost money in the failure of a Bank) was compelled to seek preferment from Lord Chancellor. In the event he became a Judge (latterly Chief Justice) of the Supreme Court of Bombay, but returned to England and was elected Liberal MP for Plymouth Devenport in 1854. In 1856 he presented a petition urging reform of the law governing the property rights of married women, and deplored the Government's decision to reform divorce law rather than property law. He remained active in the cause of property law reform until his death.

Ramsey, Archbishop (Arthur) Michael (1904–1988) Professor of Divinity, Cambridge, 1950–1952; Archbishop of York 1956–1961; Archbishop of Canterbury 1961–1974. Responsible for setting up Group to consider divorce reform (*Putting Asunder*, 1965) but distanced himself from Group's recommendations and did not support Divorce Reform Act 1969.

Rathbone, Eleanor Florence (1872–1946) President of NUSEC and MP (Independent) for Combined English Universities from 1929 until her death. Daughter of a prominent and wealthy Liverpool family. Social Reformer, educated at Somerville College, Oxford, she became perhaps the leading Parliamentary proponent of women's interests, especially (but by no means exclusively) in her campaign for family maintenance (note in particular *The Disinherited Family, A Plea for the Endowment of the Family*, 1924). She fought and won her last feminist battle on the issue of paying family allowances to mothers—a matter on which the Ministry of National Insurance had strong views based on 'departmental legalism connected with the law of maintenance'. See M Stocks, *Eleanor Rathbone, a biography* (1949) and B Harrison, *Prudent Revolutionaries, Portrait of British Feminists between the Wars* (1987) Chapter 4.

Rayner, Sir Derek (1926–1998) subsequently Lord Rayner of Crowborough, Adviser to the Prime Minister on improving efficiency and eliminating waste in government, 1979–1983 and in this capacity responsible for Efficiency Scrutiny of Registration Service (1985). Joint Managing Director Marks and Spencer plc 1973–1991, Chairman 1984–1991.

Rendall, Athelstan (1871–1948) Solicitor, MP (Liberal) for Thornbury 1906–1922 and 1923–1924. Joined Labour Party 1925. Sponsored Deceased Brother's Widow's Marriage Act 1921; spoke in interests of Divorce Law Reform Union in House of Commons, and sought to introduce divorce reform legislation 1920.

Rushcliffe, Baron (1872–1949) born Henry Bucknall Betterton. Barrister, MP (Conservative) 1918–1934, Minister of Labour in 1931 National Government, Chairman Unemployment Assistance Board 1934–41. Chaired Committee on Legal Aid and Legal Advice in England and Wales, 1945. Evidently a man of considerable ability (although like Lord Gardiner, see above, he had been placed in the 4th Class by Oxford University examiners). R Stevens (*The Independence of the Judiciary* (1993)) claims that 'it is clear from the Lord Chancellor's Office Papers that Rushcliffe owed his appointment as Chair [of the Legal Aid Committee] to the feeling that he could be controlled by the office . . .'.

Russell, 2nd Earl, of Kingston Russell (1865–1931) born John Francis Stanley Russell. Promoter of first twentieth century divorce reform Bill (1902) and founder of Society for Promoting Reforms in Marriage and Divorce Laws in England (eventually merged into Divorce Law Reform Union). Grandson of Lord John Russell, Prime Minister 1846–1852. His own colourful matrimonial career included being convicted by his peers (probably incorrectly) of bigamy. Notwithstanding this conviction of felony, Grays Inn allowed him to be called to the Bar in 1905 and he practised as a barrister for some years. In 1911 Prime Minister Asquith secured a free pardon for him. The Earl held junior ministerial office in the 1929–31 Labour government; and was succeeded by his brother, the celebrated mathematician philosopher and publicist Bertrand Russell.

Russell of Killowen, Lord (1908–1986) Lawyer, son of Law Lord, grandson of Lord Chief Justice of England. Called to Bar 1931. Served in Airborne Forces in World War II. Chancery Division judge 1960–1962; Lord Justice of Appeal 1962–1975, subsequently a Lord of Appeal in Ordinary. Chaired *Committee on the Law of Succession in Relation to Illegitimate Persons*, 1966.

Salisbury, Robert Arthur James, fifth Marquess of Salisbury (1893–1972) Held ministerial office in Conservative-led administrations until, on 29 March 1957, he resigned from Harold Macmillan's cabinet over the decision to release the Greek Cypriot leader Archbishop Makarios from detention. Thereafter he concentrated on bitter opposition to the Government's 'wind of change' policy in Africa, notoriously accusing the Colonial Secretary (Iain Macleod: see above) of being 'too clever by half'. Fierce opponent of legislation extending legitimation by the parents' subsequent marriage.

Samuel, Herbert Louis (1870–1965) Statesman with life long interest in social problems. Entering the House of Commons (as Liberal MP for Cleveland, Yorkshire) in 1902 he became Under-Secretary of State at the Home Office in

1905 and, in that capacity, was the Minister primarily responsible for the Children Act 1908. The split in the Liberal Party associated with the formation of a coalition under David Lloyd George in 1916 damaged Samuel's political career, but from 1919 to 1925 he was High Commissioner under the United Kingdom's mandate for Palestine; and he became Home Secretary in Ramsay MacDonald's 1931 National Government. He was thus the Minister with primary departmental responsibility for the Children and Young Persons Act 1932. Resigning from the Cabinet at the end of 1932 he was defeated at the 1935 General Election but was leader of the Liberals in the House of Lords. B Wasserstein, *Herbert Samuel, A Political Life* (1992) provides a full account of Samuel's life and his deep philosophical interests.

Sankey, Viscount (1866–1948) born John Sankey. Barrister, King's Bench judge 1914–1928, and appointed Lord Justice of Appeal, 1928. Lord Chancellor in the 1929 Labour Government, and continued to serve in the National Government formed in 1931 by Ramsay MacDonald of whom Sankey remained a 'devoted supporter': RFV Heuston, *Lives of the Lord Chancellors 1885–1940* (1964) p. 511. Sankey, a zealous believer in the need to improve the institutional machinery for law reform, had established the Law Revision Committee in 1934 to consider how far legal doctrines required 'revision in modern conditions': see further MC Blair, 'The Law Reform Committee: the First Thirty Years' [1982] CJQ 64.

Scarman, Sir Leslie George (1911–) Barrister 1936, QC; War Service RAFVR. Judge, Probate Divorce and Admiralty Division 1961. First Chairman of Law Commission, 1965. Involved in many high profile public inquiries. Ultimately Lord of Appeal in Ordinary 1977–1986. Generally regarded as man of strongly progressive outlook the Law Commission archives reveal that he often had a more cautious approach to family law reform than some of his colleagues.

Schuster, Sir Claud (1869–1956) Permanent Secretary in the Lord Chancellor's office and Clerk to the Crown in Chancery 1915–1944. A powerful figure in Whitehall and a superbly competent administrator who played a central role in the formation of Government policy on such matters dealt with in this book as legitimacy, adoption, the guardianship legislation, divorce reform, and (as a member of the Rushcliffe Committee on Legal Aid and Advice (1945, Cmd. 6641) access to legal services. Schuster was rewarded with a peerage on his retirement in 1944, and after the end of World War II played an active part in debates in the House of Lords on matters connected with the administration of justice. Schuster's successor as Permanent Secretary, Sir A Napier, wrote in the *Dictionary of National Biography* that Schuster 'had many of the prejudices common amongst Englishmen of his class, and he often gave pungent expression to his dislikes'. Departmental papers certainly bear out that assessment; but equally they demonstrate Schuster's readiness to form close working relationships with people—such as Mrs Eva Hubback—with whom he might not have been expected to have much in common. Schuster also fostered close relationship between the Lord Chancellor's office and the Judiciary; but in December 1934 Lord Chief Justice Hewart made a bitter attack on Schuster in the House of Lords debate on the Law Reform (Miscellaneous Provisions) Bill—which he mistakenly believed to be intended to make the judiciary subservient to the administration. Oral tradition has it that mutual antipathy between Schuster and Lord Chancellor Simon was such that each avoided being in the same room as the other so far as possible. Schuster was an enthusiastic alpinist and wrote extensively about mountains and mountaineering: see his *Men, Women and Mountains, Days in the Alps and Pyrenees* and the Romanes lecture, *Mountaineering*, delivered by Schuster in the Sheldonian Theatre, Oxford, on 21 May 1948. He also wrote a romantic historical adventure novel, *Sweet Enemy* (1934). The only person recorded as having comprehensively floored Schuster was the Duke of York (subsequently King George VI): see J W Wheeler-Bennett, *King George VI, His Life and Reign* (1958) p. 295. R Stevens, *The Independence of the Judiciary, The View from the Lord Chancellor's Office* (1993) is a useful study.

Seaton-Tiedeman, Mrs May Louise (1858–1948) Campaigner for divorce reform. Particularly active in speaking and other activities to the extent that it could be said that she was for many in reality the Divorce Law Reform Union. An attempt to get Mrs Seaton-Tiedeman sponsored as a Parliamentary Candidate in the 1918 general election failed.

Service, Alastair Stanley Douglas (1933–) Writer (particularly on architectural topics) publisher and campaigner. Gained considerable experience between 1964 and 1967 in organising what *The Times* described as 'the most sophisticated pressure group of modern times' in support of the Abortion Law Reform Association and the Abortion Act 1967. Thereafter he became the Divorce Law Reform Union's Honorary Parliamentary Officer and devoted himself to intensive work in support of the Watson and Jones Bills both at Westminster and in obtaining favourable press publicity. Subsequently Chairman of Health Authorities.

Shawcross, Sir Hartley William (1902–) An outstandingly successful advocate, QC, Labour MP 1945–1958, Attorney-General 1945–1951, Chief Prosecutor for United Kingdom at Nuremberg Trial of Major German War Criminals, 1945. More radical in approach to law reform than many of his colleagues in government.

Short, Renee (1919–2003) Labour MP for Wolverhampton 1964–1987. Interested in social issues and penal reform. Chaired House of Commons Social Services Committee, which reported on *Children in Care* (1984).

Shortt, Edward (1862–1935) Barrister, Liberal MP 1910–1922; Home Secretary 1919–1922. Sympathetic to divorce reform, had represented interests of Divorce Law Reform Union in House of Commons.

Simon of Glaisdale, Baron (1911–) born Jocelyn Edward Salis Simon. Barrister, Conservative MP 1951–1962; Solicitor-General 1959–1962 and opposed 1951 White Divorce Bill. President of the Probate Divorce and Admiralty Division in 1962 he became a firm supporter of divorce reform and also of improving the property rights of married women.

Simon, John Alsebrooke (1873–1954) Statesman and Lawyer. Attorney-General 1913–1915, Home Secretary 1915–1916 (resigned as opponent of conscription); Foreign Secretary 1931–1935, Home Secretary 1935–1937, Chancellor of the Exchequer 1937–1940; Lord Chancellor (created Viscount Simon, 1940) 1940–1945. One of the most successful advocates of his day he held the unfashionable view that an advocate should not specialise in any one field of law, and apparently made a point of appearing once a year in the Divorce Court. In the context of this book, his involvement as Home Secretary in dealing with reforms of the magistrates' domestic jurisdiction, the assistance he gave to the promoters of the AP Herbert 1937 divorce legislation, as Lord Chancellor his Opinion in the case of *Blunt v. Blunt* greatly increasing the likelihood that an adulterous spouse would none the less be successful in petitioning for divorce, and (after retirement) his involvement in promoting reform of adoption legislation are particularly notable. A man of great gifts and achievements (see generally D Dutton, *Simon, A Political Biography of Sir John Simon* (1992)) he has been maligned for his association with appeasement in the 1930s.

Simpson, Harry Butler (1861–1940) Educated Winchester and Magdalen College, Oxford (Double First in Classical Moderations and 'Greats'); Home Office official 1884–1925 (Assistant Secretary).

Skyrme, Sir Thomas (1913–2002) Public Servant and author, Secretary to Denning Committee on Procedure in Matrimonial Causes (1947); thereafter as Secretary of Commissions responsible for recommendations for appointment and training of magistrates. His *History of the Justices of the Peace* (1990) is a major work of scholarship. After retirement, became Chairman of Magistrates' Association.

Slesser, Henry Herman (1883–1979) born Henry Herman Schloesser but changed name by deed poll on outbreak of war in 1914. Barrister and Fabian Socialist, appointed Standing Counsel to the Labour Party in 1912, and Solicitor-General in 1924 Ramsay MacDonald government. Prominent as employment lawyer; but held strongly conservative views on social issues and law governing marriage and divorce. Appointed Lord Justice of Appeal in 1929. His erudite judgment in *Re Carroll (No 2)*, holding that the Guardianship of Infants Act 1925 (which he had helped to draft) did not affect the rights of a parent to determine his child's upbringing was overruled 40 years later by a House of Lords apparently unimpressed by Slesser's invocation of the views of St Thomas Aquinas and unaware of his involvement in settling the policy of the 1925 Act. Retired from judicial office on the ground of ill-health in 1940 but continued to write extensively on social and religious issues and survived to the age of 96.

Snell, Lord (1865–1944) born Henry Snell. Overcame the handicaps of illegitimate birth and a schooling which ended when he was eight to become a Labour MP, Chairman of the London County Council, and finally Deputy Leader of the House of Lords during World War II. Prominent in campaigns for improvement of procedures for dealing with domestic cases in magistrates' courts. See his autobiography, *Men, Movements, and Myself* (1936) and SM Cretney, 'Marriage Saving and the Role of the Courts, Claud Mullins and the Early Days of Conciliation' in *Law, Law Reform and the Family* (1988).

Somervell, Sir Donald Bradley (1889–1960) Conservative MP for Crewe, 1931–1945, Solicitor-General 1933–1936; Attorney-General 1936–1945. A diplomatic progressive in law reform issues: favoured reform of married women's property law and divorce law. Lord of Appeal in Ordinary 1954–1960. Fellow of All Souls College, Oxford.

Spens, William Patrick (1885–1973) Barrister, called 1910, QC. Served World War I. Conservative MP 1933–1943; 1956–1959. Rational opponent of 1938 inheritance legislation, eventually compromising.

Spicer, Eulalie (1906–1997) Solicitor. After completing doctoral thesis on Aristotle's conception of the soul took charge of Law Society's Services Divorce Department, 1942. Played an important part in formulating the plans for the 1949 legal aid and advice scheme; became Secretary of London Area Committee 1950–1966. Her obituary in *The Times*, 30 April 1997, stated that under pressure to prove herself she 'developed a tough, somewhat masculine exterior. Not even close colleagues addressed her by her Christian name. She wore her hair in an Eton crop, never used make-up and occasionally dressed in a suit and tie. At various stages in life she played saxophone in her older brother's dance band, and was reckoned a handy shot with a rifle. Until she was 80, she smoked cigarettes through a long amber holder'. Committed Anglican.

Stonham, Baron (1903–1971) born Victor John Collins. Labour MP 1945–1958, Minister of State Home Office 1967–1969 and in that capacity involved in legislation on Children and Young Persons.

Summerskill, Edith Clara (1901–1980) Qualified as doctor, 1924. Entered Labour politics: MP 1938–1950; chairman of Labour Party 1954–1955; Life Peer 1961. Strong and active supporter of improving rights for women: responsible for Matrimonial Homes Act 1967; and opposed 1969 divorce reforms as 'Casanova's charter'.

Tate, Mavis Constance (died 1947) MP (National and National Conservative) 1931–1945. Discreetly active in support of 1937 divorce reforms and in seeking to protect women inadequately provided for on husband's death. Described by Sir Harold Kent (see above) as 'one of those enlightened, humane and able women who contribute a good deal to public life, out of all proportion to their numbers' (HS Kent, *In on the Act*, p. 83).

Tomlin, Thomas James Chesshyre (1867–1935) Chairman of the *Committee on Child Adoption* (1924–1926); Judge of the High Court, Chancery Division, 1925. Tomlin was said by his memorialist in the *Dictionary of National Biography* (1949) to have had a mind which was the 'incarnation of pure common sense, an uncommon quality'. Possibly for that reason, the Lord Chancellor's Permanent Secretary Sir Claud Schuster relied heavily on Tomlin's advice, for example in connection with proposals (eventually coming to fruition in the Legitimacy Act 1926) to introduce legitimation by subsequent marriage into English law. On occasion Tomlin was called in to mediate between Benjamin Cherry (the freelance draftsman of much of the 1925 property legislation) and Sir FJ Liddell, the First Parliamentary Counsel. In 1929 Tomlin was promoted direct to the House of Lords.

Utting, Sir William (**Benjamin**) (1931–) Social worker (probation officer 1956–1968; Director of Social Services, Kensington and Chelsea 1970–1976) and public servant (DHSS 1976–1991). Author of influential report *People like Us* (1997).

Van Straubenzee, Sir William Radcliffe (1924–1999) Served in Army throughout World War II. Admitted solicitor 1952. Conservative MP 1959 onwards. One of leaders of parliamentary opposition to Abse 1963 divorce reform Bill. Member General Synod of Church of England 1975 and much involved in affairs of Church of England.

Vickers, Dame Joan (1907–1994) Conservative MP for Plymouth Devonport, subsequently a life peer. Campaigned for women's rights, believing (according to *The Times* obituary, 25 May 1994) that anti-feminism was as serious a problem as racialism or any other prejudice. Prompted by the Conservative Government's decision to legislate against race discrimination she was influential in securing the enactment of the Guardianship Act 1973.

Vivian, Sir Sylvanus Percival (1880–1958) Registrar-General 1921–45, insistent (particularly in the context of adoption and legitimation) on the need to preserve the accuracy of the Registers as a record of historical fact. Vivian was a remarkable example of the scholar civil servant, editing the *Collected Works of Thomas Campion* (1909) contributing to the *Cambridge History of English Literature* and the *Dictionary of Literary Terms* and (after his retirement) completing *The Manor of Etchingham* (1953) for the Sussex Record Society. But his apparent pedantry irritated the Lord Chancellor's Permanent Secretary Sir Claud Schuster who (when the question of registering adoption was under discussion in 1929) expressed his unwillingness to stimulate Vivian into 'any further correspondence, principally for the reason that, being a very conscientious man and a very ingenious man, he usually writes at enormous length and I find it very difficult to follow what he writes': Schuster to Luxmoore, 15 March 1929, PRO LCO2/1159.

Walters, Sir Dennis (1928–) Long time Personal Assistant to Lord Hailsham of St. Marylebone, Conservative MP for Westbury Wiltshire 1964–1992. As Private Member introduced Bill for Children and Young Persons (Amendment) Act 1986. Knighted 1988. His autobiography, *Not always with the Pack* (1989) is always interesting (especially on his war-time experiences behind enemy lines in Italy and in the events leading up to the appointment of Sir Alec Douglas Home as Prime Minister in October 1963) and revealing but does not refer to his part in promoting the 1986 Act.

Ward, Irene (Mary Bewick) (1895–1980) Conservative MP 1931–1945 and 1950–1974; life peer 1974. Tireless campaigner on women's issues.

Warnock, Dame Mary (1924–) Educationalist and philosopher, Senior Research Fellow of St. Hugh's College Oxford, chaired *Committee of Inquiry into Human Fertilisation and Embryology*, 1984 which led to enactment of Human Fertilisation and Embryology Act 1990 and creation of Human Fertilisation and Embryology Authority.

Webb, Beatrice (1858–1943) Scholar, campaigner, Fabian socialist. First achieved prominence as Member of Royal Commission on Poor Law; joint author of influential Minority Report, 1909. Author of massive works of social history, including *English Local Government* (7 volumes) and *English Poor Law History* (3 volumes); also of *Soviet Communism—A New Civilisation?* and a revealing autobiographical sketch, *My Apprenticeship* (1926).

Webster, Richard, see **Alverstone (Lord)**.

Wells Pestell, Baron (1910–1991) born Reginald Alfred Wells Pestell. Worked as Probation Officer, served as JP chairing Domestic Courts. Active in Labour politics, contesting various parliamentary seats 1950–1956; Life Peer 1965 and, as DHSS spokesman in House of Lords 1973–1979, had effectively the carriage of Children Act 1975. Parliamentary Under Secretary DHSS 1979.

White, Dame Eirene (1909–1999) born Eirene Lloyd Jones. Daughter of Dr Thomas Jones CH, for many years Deputy Secretary of the Cabinet and closely associated with his fellow Welshman David Lloyd-George. Returned at the 1950 General Election as MP for East Flint. A powerful debater and former journalist, she wrote many articles in the popular press putting forward the case for her Bill. Remained prominent in Labour politics (becoming in 1966 the first woman to hold ministerial office in the Foreign Office) and public life for many years. Appointed Dame (and subsequently Baroness) White. Her papers preserved at the National Library of Wales, Aberystwyth, contain much material of interest on the subject of marriage and divorce, including numbers of moving letters from members of the public prevented from remarrying by the divorce law as it existed in 1950.

Wilson, William (1913–) Solicitor (in practice 1939–1969). War Service 1941–1945. MP (Labour) for Coventry South 1964–1974. Sponsor of the 1967 Divorce Reform Bill.

Wintringham, Margaret (died 1955, aged 76) Formerly a Headmistress in Grimsby and active in social work amongst refugees during World War I; stood as an Independent Liberal for the Louth, Lincolnshire, seat vacated by the death of her husband in 1921. According to Sarah Baxter, *The Times* 5 February 1994, Mrs Wintringham did not utter a word in public during the campaign out of respect for her husband's memory; but she was successful and became the second woman to sit as an MP. Made a strongly positive personal impression: her obituary in *The Times,* 23 March 1955 states that she 'remained until her death the same bright helpful and generous being whose presence so captivated the House of Commons'; and Mary Stocks records that Mrs Wintringham was one of those MPs cherished and taken to the heart of the House 'with a kind of paternal personal affection': *Eleanor Rathbone* (1949) p. 142. After effectively campaigning for equality of parental rights, she lost her seat in the 1924 General Election but continued to play an active part in public affairs not least as President of the Women's National Liberal Federation. Professor Brian Harrison (who interviewed her) considers that the premature termination of her career in Parliament symbolizes the loss to British public life (and to feminism) that resulted for the inter-war split between Liberals and Labour: *Prudent Revolutionaries, Portraits of British Feminists between the Wars* (1987) p. 13.

Withers, Sir John (James) (1863–1939) Solicitor, founded firm of Withers & Co. 1896, established what he correctly described as a 'very considerable' practice 'in family matters and particularly in matters relating to the relations between husbands and wives'. Unionist MP for Cambridge University 1926 onwards. Prominent as progressive reformer in debates on succession and divorce laws. On close terms with Sir Claud Schuster (with whom he shared an active interest in Alpinism).

Wootton, Baroness (1897–1988) born Barbara Frances Adams. Economist, later keenly interested in criminology and social sciences, Professor of Social Studies London University 1943–1952, member of many government enquiries and author of influential works on justice and social matters. Promoted legislation to allow marriage between relatives.

Young, Baroness (1926–2002) born Janet Mary Baker. Conservative Councillor Oxford City Council 1957 (and subsequently Leader of Conservative Group and Alderman). Created Life Peer 1971; Government Whip 1972–1973 and subsequently Minister (Leader of the House of Lords 1981–1983). Strong and effective opponent of changes to divorce law embodied in Family Law Act 1996.

B. Membership of selected committees and commissions

Archbishop's Group on Affinity, Report of a Group Appointed by the Archbishop of Canterbury, *No Just Cause, The Law of Affinity in England and Wales: Some Suggestions for Change* (1984).

Chairman: Baroness Seear (1913–1997) sometime Reader in Personnel Management, London School of Economics; Leader of the Liberal Peers, House of Lords, 1984–1988. *Members*: Sir George Baker (formerly President of the Family Division of the High Court); the Reverend Professor GR Dunstan; Dr Ruth Finnegan, Reader in Comparative Social Institutions at the Open University; Dr RJC Hart, Consultant Medical Microbiologist; Mrs Ruth Hook, Parent and Author; Janet Mattinson, psychiatrist; the Reverend Professor OMT O'Donovan; Joan Rubinstein, a practising Methodist, partner in a London firm of solicitors with a substantial divorce practice and a practising psychotherapist.

Archbishop's Group on Divorce (*Putting Asunder*, 1965)

Chairman: Robert Mortimer, Bishop of Exeter (see above).

Members: Professor JND Anderson, Viscount Colville of Culross and Joan Rubinstein (see entries above), GB Bentley (1909–), Canon of Windsor; Lord Devlin (1905–1992), Lord of Appeal in Ordinary and Roman Catholic, much interested in relationship between law and morality; GR Dunstan (1917–), Minor Canon of Westminster Abbey, heavily involved in the work of the Church of England's Board for Social Responsibility and subsequently FD Maurice Professor of Moral and Social Theology, King's College, London; Quentin Edwards (1925–) Barrister (subsequently a Circuit Judge and Chancellor of Blackburn and Chichester); Professor Donald MacRae (1921–1997) Martin Wise Professor of Sociology, London School of Economics; Lady Helen Oppenheimer (1926–) writer on moral and philosophical theology and subsequently Lecturer in Ethics, Cuddesdon Theological College; Sir Henry Josceline Phillimore, Queen's Bench (formerly Probate Divorce and Admiralty) judge; Dr Desmond Pond (1919–1986), Consultant Psychiatrist (subsequently Sir Desmond Pond, Chief Scientist DHSS). Edward W Short (1912–) MP (Labour) for Newcastle upon Tyne Central was also appointed to the Group but resigned on appointment as Labour Chief Whip in November 1964.

The Booth Committee, the *Matrimonial Causes Procedure Committee* (1985).

Chairman: Dame Margaret Booth, Family Division judge.

Members: Major-General JGR Allen CB (the Lay Observer); JL Barratt, a practising solicitor; DHC Lewis, a Registrar; Mrs AB Macfarlane, the Master of the Court of Protection (formerly a Registrar); Mrs JG Marsh, a lay magistrate; RB Rowe, a Registrar of the Principal Registry of the Family Division; PKJ Thompson, an official in the Lord Chancellor's Department; HH Judge Tibber, a circuit judge; Mr Alan H Ward, a practising barrister; and AB Wells, an Assistant Chief Probation Officer.

The Chelmsford Royal Commission, *Report of the Royal Commission on the Laws of Marriage* (1868, BPP 1867–1868 vol. 32) chaired by Lord Chelmsford (1794–1878): see above.

Members included three future Lord Chancellors: Sir W Page Wood (1801–1888) at the time Vice Chancellor, as Lord Hatherley Lord Chancellor 1868–1872; Roundell Palmer (1812–1895) subsequently as Lord Selborne Lord Chancellor 1872–1874, 1880–1885 and Sir Hugh Cairns (1819–1885) as Lord Cairns Lord Chancellor (1874–1880). Other lawyer members were Sir James Wilde (1816–1899) (at the time judge of the Court of Probate, subsequently raised to the peerage as Lord Penzance); and Sir Travers Twiss QC, Professor of Civil Law at Oxford. Three MPs—Spencer Walpole, William Monsell and A M Dunlop—served on the Commission; while Irish and Scottish interests were represented by Judges and others from those jurisdictions. JF Macqueen QC (1803–1881) a noted authority on the law of marriage—acted as the Commission's Secretary.

The County Court Committee, The *Committee appointed by the Lord Chancellor to inquire into certain matters relating to County Court Procedure* (1909).

Chairman: Sir John Gorell Barnes (see above).

The Denning Committee, The *Committee on Procedure in Matrimonial Causes* (1946).

Chairman: the Hon Mr Justice Denning (see above).

Membership: Notwithstanding the fact that the Government's Committee on Legal Procedure had considered the question of membership and recorded that it did not wish the Committee to be 'dominated by lawyers' six of the ten members of the Committee were practising lawyers: His Honour Judge Collingwood was a county court judge; Terence Donovan KC MP, John Foster MP (see above) and Ethel Lloyd Lane were barristers; whilst Sir Edwin Herbert and Eric Davies were solicitors. However, none was a divorce specialist. The two other male members were both peers: Major-General Viscount Bridgeman was the son of the conservative Home Secretary (see above); Lord Rusholme was a businessman with strong roots in the Co-operative movement. The Committee on Legal Procedure wanted 'working class women' to be appointed, believing that whilst such a person 'would be unable to contribute much if anything' on legal matters she could be expected to make a valuable contribution to discussion of the social issues involved. In the event three women became members of the Committee: Dr Grace Calver (who had a substantial psychiatric practice of referrals from the Tavistock Clinic, and this experience led to her being preferred to Mrs Geoffrey Fisher—wife of the Archbishop of Canterbury—who had seven children and was active in the affairs of the Mother's Union); Mrs Cressall and Mrs Jessie Smith.

The Feversham Committee, The *Departmental Committee on Human Artificial Insemination* (1960).

Chairman: The Earl of Feversham DSO, see above.

The Finer Report, the *Report of the Committee on One-Parent Families* (1974) *Chairman*: the Hon Mr Justice Finer (1917–1974).

Members: DCH Abbott CB (formerly Assistant Under Secretary of State at the Department of Health and Social Security), Mrs JM Scott-Batey (wife of the Chairman of the Newcastle City Labour Party); WB Harbert; S Isaacs; Mrs BJ Kahan (Deputy Chief Inspector, Home Office Children's Department); Professor OR McGregor (see above), Eve Macleod JP (wife of Iain Macleod MP, see above, subsequently a life peer as Baroness Maclean of Borve, resigned from the Committee in 1972); N Murchison OBE; Mrs CM Patterson CBE (an official in the Transport and General Workers' Union, and Member of the TUC General Council); Mrs Marjorie Proops OBE (a journalist with the *Daily Mirror* she had established a reputation as an 'Agony Aunt'); HG Simpson OBE (Director of Housing and Property Services, London Borough of Lambeth); and Professor RM Titmuss (1907–1973, Professor of Social Administration at the London School of Economics, official historian of *Problems of Social Policy* (1950), Deputy Chairman of the Supplementary Benefits Commission, often regarded as the 'high priest of the welfare state').

The Gorell Commission, The *Royal Commission on Divorce and Matrimonial Causes*, 1912.

Chairman: Lord Gorell (see above).

Members: This Commission was avowedly intended to be representative of specific 'interests'.

The *Legal Profession* was represented by Rufus Isaacs KC (at the time of appointment Liberal MP for Reading and a prominent advocate; he resigned from the Commission in March 1910 on appointment as Solicitor General); Judge Henry Tindal Atkinson (a County Court Judge and JP for Hertfordshire); and Edgar Brierley, Stipendiary Magistrate for the City of Manchester); whilst the Hon Lord Guthrie, a Senator of the College of Justice in Scotland, repre-sented the *Scottish legal system*.

The Rt Hon Thomas Burt, Liberal MP for Morpeth since 1874 was well qualified to represent the interests of the *industrial working classes* having begun his working life at age ten in the coal mines after only two years' atten-dance at village schools. After 18 years' underground work he became Secretary of the Northumberland Miners' Mutual Confident Association, and had been President of the TUC in 1891.

In contrast, the seventeenth Earl of Derby (Conservative MP for the West Houghton Division of Lancashire 1892–1906) was a model of the paternalistic Tory *landed aristocracy*, but he resigned from the Commission on the grounds of pressure of work—possibly associated with his opposition to the 1909 Lloyd George budget.

J Alfred Spender, editor of the Westminster Gazette 1896–1922, was a distin-guished *liberal journalist* and author.

The opportunity presented by Isaacs' resignation was taken to appoint a *doctor* to the Commission: Sir Frederick Treves Bt had had a distinguished career which included academic appointments and service in the South African War but most notably carrying out, in the course of his duties as Serjeant Surgeon to the King, the removal of Edward VII's appendix on 24 June 1902.

The *Church of England* was represented by Cosmo Gordon Lang (Archbishop of York from 1908; subsequently Archbishop of Canterbury 1928–1942), Sir Lewis Dibdin, a distinguished canon lawyer who was at the time Dean of the Arches and First Church Estates Commissioner and Sir William Anson Bt (see above).

Sir George White, an Industrialist, Liberal MP for North West Norfolk and sometime President of the Baptist Union must be taken to reflect the need to have the *non-conformist interest* represented.

Finally, although it has been said that King Edward VII objected to the appointment of women on the ground that divorce was not a subject on which their opinions could be 'conveniently expressed' (*Ne Obliviscaris*, by Lady Frances Balfour (1930) Vol I) two ladies were appointed. They were Lady Frances Balfour (daughter of the Duke of Argyll, married to Colonel Eustace Balfour and thus sister in law of AJ Balfour, Prime Minister 1902–1905, mother of five children, a leading figure—albeit a firm constitutionalist—in the women's suffrage movement, a prominent figure in Edwardian society, and an author) and Mrs HJ (May) Tennant (formerly—before her marriage to the Liberal MP and Minister HJ Tennant—HM Superintending Inspector of Factories, an Assistant Commissioner on the Royal Commission on Labour 1891, author of *The Law Relating to Factories and Workshops* and long interested in social problems particularly those affecting women working outside the home).

Graham Hall Committee The *Departmental Committee on Statutory Maintenance Limits*, 1968.

Chairman: Jean Graham Hall (see above).

Members: Professor OR McGregor (see above); Lady (Barbara) Littlewood (a Solicitor, sometime President of the West Surrey Law Society, wife of Sir Sydney Littlewood, sometime President of the Law Society); P Beedle (An Assistant Secretary in the Home Office); LA Edgar (a Justices' Clerk); F Jackson (A Principal Executive Officer in the division of the Department of Health and Social Security concerned with liability to maintain and legal aid); JG Collins (replacing JG Lewis—both of the Inland Revenue).

Houghton Committee, The *Departmental Committee on the Adoption of Children*, 1972.

Chairman: Sir William Houghton (see above). On Sir William's death (some eight months before the Committee reported) Judge Stockdale became Chairman.

Members: There were 16 signatories to the Report. Disregarding those with primarily Scottish affiliations, five of the signatories had strong social work connections (including Mrs Margaret Bramall, see above) and three (including Jane Rowe, Director of the British Agencies for Adoption and Fostering) may be seen as representing adoption agency interests. There were two doctors; and the law was represented by Judge Stockdale, a Justices' clerk, and the solicitor Labour MP and law reformer Leo Abse (see above). Dame Joan Vickers MP (see above) was also a member.

Latey Committee, *Report of the Committee on the Age of Majority*, 1967.

Chairman: the Hon. Mr Justice Latey (see above).

Members: Professor AL Diamond (1923–) Professor of Law at the London School of Economics, subsequently a Law Commissioner; Dr Barbara Grey JP, Reader in Sociology, Birmingham University; Mrs Marjorie Hume, one of the founders of the Marriage Guidance Council; Dick Taverne QC, MP (1928–) replaced in 1966, on his appointment to ministerial office, by Robert Maclennan MP (1936–); Mrs Rosemary Makhulu, (formerly a Youth Leader working in the South Poplar Youth Club); The Revd. John Perry, an Anglican clergyman "with a large family of his own"; Mrs Beatrice Serota JP (1919–2000) Chairman of the LCC Children's Committee 1958–1965, (as Baroness Serota, and a Government Whip in the House of Lords she introduced the Bill for the Family Law Reform Act 1969 which gave effect to the Committee's recommendations: *Official Report* (HL) 26 November 1968, vol. 297, col. 1132) ; and Miss Katharine Whitehorn, journalist and columnist. It appears that Miss Whitehorn was responsible for drafting much of the Report (see G Howe, *Conflict of Loyalty* (1995) p. 42) which is universally agreed to be unusually and indeed delightfully readable: see eg Lord Brooke of Cumnor, *Official Report* (HL) 26 November 1968, vol. 297, col. 1058. Two members of the Committee—JC Stebbings (1924–1998) a practising solicitor, subsequently President of The Law Society 1979 and Geoffrey Howe QC (1926–) subsequently a Conservative MP and Cabinet Minister whose speech on resigning as Deputy Prime Minister and Lord President in November 1990 playing a significant part in the erosion of support for the leadership of Mrs Margaret Thatcher—declined to sign the Report, and wrote a Dissenting Report (apparently drafted by Howe: *Conflict of Loyalty* p. 42) based on a 'fundamental difference of approach' from that of their colleagues.

The Law Commission, established by the Law Commissions Act 1965. In the period 1965–1996 the following held office:

Chairmen: Lord Scarman (1965–1973); the Hon Mr Justice Cooke (1973–1978); the Hon Mr Justice Kerr (1978–1981); the Hon Mr Justice (Ralph) Gibson (1981–1985); the Hon Mr Justice Beldam (1985–1989); the Hon Mr Justice Peter Gibson (1990–1992); the Hon Mr Justice Brooke (1993–1995); the Hon Mrs Justice Arden DBE (1996–1999). With the exception of Cooke J (who died in office) all were appointed Lords Justice of Appeal on, or immediately after, the end of their service as Chairman.

Commisioners: During this period, a settled practice developed: one of the four Commissioners would be a practising Queen's Counsel (and it seems that he could expect to be offered appointment to the High Court bench at the end of his Law Commission service); one would be a practising solicitor; and two would be primarily academic lawyers (although some of these had also had significant experience of legal practice). The Commissioners were:

LCB Gower (1965–1971) (see above); Neil Lawson QC (1965–1971); Norman Marsh (1965–1978); Andrew Martin QC (see above) (1965–1970); Claud Bicknell (1970–1975); Derek Hodgson QC (1971–1977); Professor Aubrey Diamond (1971–1976); William Forbes QC (1977–1981); Stephen Edell (1975–1983); Dr Peter North (1976–1984); Stephen Cretney (1978–1983); Brian Davenport QC (1981–1988); Trevor Aldridge (1984–1993); Brenda Hoggett (1984–1993); Professor Julian Farrand (1984–1988); Richard Buxton QC (1989–1993); Jack Beatson (1989–1994); Diana Faber (1994–2000); Charles Harpum (1994–2001); Andrew Burrows (1994–1999); Stephen Silber QC (1994–1999).

Marriage Guidance Funding, *Departmental Committee on Grants for the Development of Marriage Guidance*, 1948.

Chairman: Sir Sidney Harris: see above.

The Molony Committee, *The Departmental Committee on the Treatment of Young Offenders* (1927).

Chairman: Sir Thomas Molony (see above).

The Morton Committee, *The Report of the Committee on the Law of Intestate Succession* (1951).

Chairman: Lord Morton of Henryton (see above).

Members: Michael Albery (1910–1975) barrister author of a work, evidently admired within the Lord Chancellor's Office, on the Inheritance (Provision for Family and Dependants) Act 1938; Sir Hugh Chance (1896–1981), chairman of a family glass manufacturers; Eric Fletcher (see above); Sir John Foster KC (see above); Mrs Dorothy Rees (1898–)Labour MP and former school teacher; Lord Kershaw (1881–1961)(appointed to represent Trade Union interests; had served as Chairman of Courts of Referees under the Unemployment Insurance Acts).

The (Morton) Royal Commission on Marriage and Divorce (1956).

Chairman: Lord Morton of Henryton (see above).

Members: The following were appointed: Viscountess Portal, Lord Keith, Holroyd Pearce J, Sir Frederick Burrows, Lady Bragg, HLO Flecker, Dr Violet Roberton, Kate Jones–Roberts, Thomas Young, Dr May Baird, Robert Beloe, Mrs Ethel Brace, George Brown, Geoffrey Lawrence QC, Darrell Mace, Mrs Mabel Ridehalgh, and James Walker QC. Some died or resigned before the Commission had completed its work; and Mrs Margaret Allen, Colonel Sir Wilfrid Bennett, Sir William Russell Brain and HH Maddocks were appointed as replacements. The membership is analysed at p. 330, above.

The Payne Committee, *The Committee on the Enforcement of Judgment Debts,* 1969.

Chairman: The Hon Mr Justice Payne.

The Rushcliffe Committee, The *Report of the Committee on Legal Aid and Legal Advice in England and Wales,* 1945.
Chairman: Baron Rushcliffe (see above).
Membership: The Committee had a powerful membership, including both Claud Schuster and his successor as Permanent Secretary in the Lord Chancellor's Office (Sir Albert Napier) two High Court judges (one the future Law Lord, Hodson, who had been appointed to chair the aborted pre-war enquiry into legal aid and advice) and one future Lord Chancellor, then Major RE Manningham-Buller.

C. The Judges Ordinary of the Court for Divorce and Matrimonial Causes and the Presidents of the Probate Divorce and Admiralty Division and the Family Division of the High Court

The Judge Ordinary:

1857–1863: Sir Cresswell Cresswell[1]
1863–1872: Sir James Plaistead Wilde[2]
1872–1875: Sir James Hannen[3]

Presidents of the Probate, Divorce and Admiralty Division of the High Court of Justice:

1875–1891: Sir James Hannen[4]
1891–1892: Sir Charles Parker Butt
1892–1905: Sir Francis Henry Jeune[5]
1905–1909: Sir John Gorell Barnes[6]

---

[1] Formerly a judge of the Court of Common Pleas.
[2] Formerly a Baron of the Exchequer, created Lord Penzance, 1869, resigned on health grounds.
[3] Formerly a judge of the Court of Queen's Bench.
[4] Became President by virtue of the provisions of the Judicature Acts. Appointed Lord of Appeal in Ordinary, 1891.
[5] Jeune had practised at the bar mostly in ecclesiastical cases, but had had a short period (18 months) as a puisne judge of the Division before appointment as President. He was highly regarded in that capacity, as is evidenced by his being raised to the peerage as Lord St Helier on his retirement on health grounds in 1905.
[6] See Section A, above. Candid assessments by Lord Phillimore of the Presidents who held office in the early part of the twentieth century can to be found in a Memorandum (written in support of the abolition of the Probate Divorce and Admiralty) dated 11 June 1920, LCO2/460.

1909–1910: Sir John C Bigham[7]
1910–1918: Sir Samuel Evans[8]
1918–1919: Lord Sterndale[9]
1919–1933: Sir Henry Duke[10]
1933–1962: Sir (Frank) Boyd Merriman[11]
1962–1971: Sir Jocelyn Simon[12]
1971   Sir George Baker

Presidents of the Family Division of the High Court of Justice, 1972–2000:

1972–1979: Sir George Baker
1979–1988: Sir John Arnold
1988–1999: Sir Stephen Brown[13]
1999–   Dame Elizabeth Butler-Sloss

---

[7] Retired on health grounds in 1910. According to Clement Davies KC (in a speech urging the transfer of divorce to the King's Bench division *Official Report* (HC) 8 November 1937, vol. 328, col. 1445) Bigham (in common with most of his predecessors and successors) 'had never been inside a divorce court and never heard a divorce case' prior to his appointment.

[8] As his memorialist (Professor JL Brierly) comments, Evans had 'few apparent qualifications for his new post' and the appointment was perhaps made primarily on political grounds. However, World War I brought a vast quantity of Admiralty work; and Evans made a formidable reputation. Clement Davies KC described him as 'one of the greatest judges that ever sat in that Division'; and note also the eulogy by Lord Chancellor Birkenhead: *Points of View* (1922) p. 83.

[9] For candid comments by Sir Claud Schuster on the appointment of Lord Sterndale and some of his successors, see p. 199, note 22, above.

[10] Created Baron Merrivale, 1925; see Section A, above.

[11] Created Baron Merriman, 1941; see Section A, above.

[12] Created Baron Simon of Glaisdale, 1971; see Section A, above.

[13] Appointed GBE, 1999.

Sources and Select Bibliography

The place of publication is London unless otherwise stated.

Private Papers

Abse Papers (Leo Abse, National Library of Wales, Aberystwyth)

Denning Papers (Lord Denning of Whitchurch, Hampshire Record Office Winchester)

Diaries of the Third Lord Gorell (Bodleian Library, Oxford)

Diary of Ramsay MacDonald (Public Record Office 36/69/175)[1]

Divorce Law Reform Union (Millicent Fawcett Library, London)

Hubback Papers (Eva Hubback, Married Women's Association)

Married Women's Association (Papers and Minutes, Millicent Fawcett Library,[2] London)

Monckton Papers (The First Viscount Monckton of Brenchley, Bodleian Library Oxford)

Normanton Papers (Helena Normanton KC, Millicent Fawcett Library,[3] London Guildhall University)

NUSEC Papers (National Council of Societies for Equal Citizenship, Millicent Fawcett Library,[4] London Guildhall University)

Nutting Papers (Lady Helen Nutting, Millicent Fawcett Library, London Guildhall University)

'Putting Asunder' Papers (Minutes and other papers of the Archbishop's Group on the Reform of Divorce, 1963–1966, Lambeth Palace Library)

Ramsey Papers (Archbishop Ramsey, Archbishop of Canterbury, 1961–1974, Lambeth Palace Library)

Service Papers (Private archive of Alastair SD Service)

Simon Papers (The First Viscount Simon, Bodleian Library Oxford, MS Simon)

Somervell Papers (Lord Somervell of Harrow, Bodleian Library Oxford, MS Eng c 6565)

White Papers (Baroness (Eirene) White, National Library of Wales, Aberystwyth)

---

[1] The diaries bear the statement that 'published work must contain a note to the following effect: "The contents of these diaries were in Ramsay MacDonald's words 'meant as notes to guide and revive memory as regards happenings and must on no account be published as they are'." '

[2] Now Women's Library.   [3] Now Women's Library.

[4] Now Women's Library.

OFFICIAL RECORDS IN THE PUBLIC RECORD OFFICE, KEW, SURREY[5]

The papers are grouped primarily by reference to the originating department:

LORD CHANCELLOR'S DEPARTMENT FILES

LCO33/23	Lord Schuster—Personal file

Marriage:

LCO2/6674	Marriage Bill—Consolidation of Enactments relating to Marriage, 1949
LCO2/120	Ecclesiastical General, Marriage of Divorced Persons in Parish Churches

Children:

LCO1/47	Guardianship of Infants Act 1886
LCO2/751	Legitimacy Bill 1.1.1924–21.12.24
LCO2/752	Continuation of above 20.12.24–1925
LCO2/753	Further continuation 1926
LCO2/757	Guardianship of Infants Bill 1920, 1921, 1922, and 1923
LCO2/758	Guardianship of Infants Bill 1.1.1924–21.12.1924
LCO2/754	Legitimacy Bill, re provisions as regards Scotland, 1925
LCO2/759	Continuation of above
LCO2/812	Administration of Justice Bill, 1928, Legitimacy Act, 1926, Amendment of section 2
LCO2/5608	Guardianship of Infants Act 1886; re *R v. Sandbach Justices* 1951/2—Guardianship and Maintenance of Infants Act, 1951, 14 & 15 Geo 6, Chap. 6
LCO2/ 1828	Passports after divorce
LCO2/1619, 20	Administration of Justice Bill 1937—Variation of Maintenance Orders
LCO2 3824	Summary Jurisdiction (C&YP) Rules 1950
LCO2 4119	Tribunals under Children Act 1948
LCO2 4485	Married Women (Maintenance Bill) 1949
LCO2/5626	Illegitimate Children: Report of a Joint Committee of the British Medical Association and the Magistrates' Association on the law in relation to (1952)
LCO2/5641	Guardianship of Infants Acts, 1886 and 1925, Application to illegitimate children (1956)
LCO2/3600	Law Society suggestion about construction of 'father'

[5] There are helpful reference books, notably the *Guide to the Records of the Lord Chancellor's Department* by P Polden (1988) HMSO; *The Development of the Welfare State, 1939–51, A Guide to Documents in the Public Record Office*, by A Land, R Lowe and N Whiteside (1992) HMSO; and *Law and Society, An Introduction to Sources for Criminal and Legal History from 1800* by Michelle Cale, PRO Publications 1996. In addition, reference should be made to R Stevens, *The Independence of the Judiciary, The View from the Lord Chancellor's Office* (1993).

LCO2/4877	Legitimation (Re-registration of Birth) Bill
LCO2/6895	Legitimacy Bill 1959—correspondence 12.11.58–26 5.1959
LCO2/6896A[6]	Legitimacy Bill 1959
LCO2/6897	Legitimacy Bill 1959—Notes on Amendments
LCO2/6898	Legitimacy Bill 1959— Notes on Clauses
LCO2/4473	Children Bill 1948
LCO2/1159	Adopted Children Register
LCO2/6421	Adoption (County Court) Rules 1959: Explanatory Memorandum to County Court Registrars
LCO2/6422	Adoption (High Court) Rules 1959[7]
LCO2 1120	Adoption of Children (County Court) Rules 1926
LCO2/1162	Adoption of Children—Home Office Committee of Enquiry into the activities of adoption societies
LCO2/1276	Adoption Order: Form of Consent (No 2) (1933)
LCO2/4483	Adoption of Children Bill 1949
LCO2 3020	Legal points on The Adoption of Children (Regulation) Act 1939
LCO2/3021	Solicitors' charges—whether Adoption of Children (Regulation) Act 1939 prevents solicitors charging in respect of ordinary professional charges
LCO2 4777–81 A,B	Children Bill 1958
LCO2/6418	Adoption Bill 1958—Consolidation
LCO2/6419	Appointments of Guardians ad Litem in cases where mother under 21.
LCO2/6424	Adoption Orders—production in Divorce cases,1959

The Latey Committee on the Age of Majority:[8]

LCO17/1–2	Committee Documents—Minutes and Papers
LCO17/3	Minutes of Meetings
LCO17/8,10, 11 and 12	Evidence
LCO17/5	Report of Attitude Survey conducted by National Opinion Polls Limited

Inheritance:

The 1938 Inheritance Legislation

LCO2/1185	Testamentary Provision for Husbands, Wife and Children; Inheritance Bills 1928–9
LCO2/1186	Wills and Intestacies (Family Maintenance) Bill 1928
LCO2/1187–8	Wills and Intestacies (Family Maintenance) Bill 1930, 1931
LCO2/1189	Inheritance (Family Provision) No 2 Bill 1936 and similar Bills to 1938
LCO2/1516	Inheritance (Family Provision) Act 1938, suggested amendments
LCO2/3588	Time limit on applications under 1938 Act: hardship case.
LCO2/6152	Matrimonial Causes (Property and Maintenance) Bill 1958

---

[6] File 6896B remains closed.   [7] LCO2 6423 is closed until 2004.
[8] The following remain closed: LCO17/7, 9, 14, 15, 16, 17, 18 (until 1.1.2042); LCO17/ 23 until 2003.

Intestacy and other Inheritance Issues

LCO2/4440	Law of Intestacy—Committee: terms of reference (1950)
LCO2/4441, 4443, 4445, 4446, 4447[9]	Committee on the Law of Intestacy, Evidence, Correspondence with Members
LCO2/4448	Committee on the Law of Intestacy, Minutes of Meetings
LCO2/4449	Committee on the Law of Intestacy, Publication of Report etc
LCO2/4450	Committee on the Law of Intestacy—as to carrying out Report
LCO2/4451	The Intestates Estates Bill 1951, Correspondence 1951–2
LCO2/4452	The Intestates' Estates Bill, further correspondence
LCO2/6671	The Intestates Estates Bill 1951, Notes on Clauses

Property:

Aspects of the 1925 property legislation:

Correspondence re Law of Property Bill 1921/2:

LCO2 443	Correspondence to 11 March 1920
LCO2 444	Correspondence to 26 July 1920
LCO2 445	Further Correspondence
LCO2 446	Correspondence to 15 March 1921
LCO2 449	Correspondence from 1 October 1921 to end

Matrimonial property; legal effects of marriage:

LCO2/1969	Liability of Husband for Wife's Torts (Law Revision Committee)
LCO2/1977	Law Revision Committee 3rd Report
LCO2/1978	Law Reform (Married Women and Tortfeasors) Bill 1935, Parliamentary Proceedings
LCO2/7383	Liability in Tort of one spouse to another (Law Reform Committee, Correspondence)
LCO2/7384	Liability in Tort of one spouse to another (Law Reform Committee, Memoranda
LCO2/7385–8	Liability in Tort of one spouse to another, further papers (including passage through Parliament)
LCO2/2777	Wife's Housekeeping Allowances
LCO2/3204	Mountbatten Estates Bill
LCO2/3601	Law Reform (Married Women and Tortfeasors) Act 1935, Restraint on Anticipation
LCO2/4851	Deserted Wives Bill 1951
LCO2/3558	English law as to property of married women

Divorce:

LCO2/460	Matrimonial Causes Bill 1920
LCO2/775	Judicial Proceedings (Regulation of Reports) Act 1926
LCO2/1194	Matrimonial Causes Bill 1933
LCO2/1195 and 1196	Marriage Bill 1936 (AP Herbert); Similar Bill (Mr de la Bere) 1936–7

[9] Files 4442 and 4444 remain closed.

LCO2/1619	Administration of Justice Bill 1937—Alimony—power to vary
LCO2/1842	The Matrimonial Causes Rules 1937
LCO2/ 4189	Scottish Reception Orders etc. under MCA 1937
LCO2/4190	same topic
LCO2/5341	Divorce as a bar to appointment as silk
LCO2/3828	Probate Divorce and Admiralty: Suggested Amalgamation with KBD
LCO2/5639	Deeds Poll—Use of by Married Women to conceal adultery

The Denning Committee:

LCO2/3831	State of Divorce Lists, 1947
LCO2/3927	Committee on Reform of Legal Procedure
LCO2/3946	Denning Committee: appointment etc.
LCO2/3947	Denning Committee—Minutes
LCO2/3948	Denning Committee—Evidence and Notes of Proceedings
LCO2/3949	Denning Committee—1st Interim Report: Reduction of Period between Decree Nisi and Absolute
LCO2/4201	Correspondence with the Law Society on the Matrimonial Causes (Decree Absolute) General Order 1946
LCO2/4202	The Matrimonial Causes (Decree Absolute) General Order 1946
LCO2/3950	Divorce Committee (Denning J)—2nd Interim Report: Recommendation that jurisdiction be confined to the High Court but exercised by County court judges sitting as special commissioners . . .
LCO2/3951, 3952, 3953, 3954 and 3955	Procedure (and responses to Denning Report)
LCO2/3956	Denning Committee, Second Interim Report, Replies to Circular letters sent to Provincial County Court judges
LCO2/3957	Matrimonial Causes Rules: President's Written Objections to certain Alterations recommended in Part II of Denning Committee's Second Interim Report
LCO2/3958	Matrimonial Causes Rules—Prayer for Annulment
LCO2/3959	Denning Committee, Second Interim Report, Recommendations not dealt with in Matrimonial Causes Rules 1947, including substituted service by advertisement
LCO2/3962	Denning Committee, Second and Final Report, Printing and Publication, General Discussion on carrying out the recommendations including reconciliation
LCO2/3963	Financial Assistance to enable the Marriage Guidance Council to carry on their work until the new Welfare Service as recommended by the Denning Committee is set in motion
LCO2/3964	Denning Committee, Second and Final Reports, Consideration of outstanding recommendations
LCO2/3965	Privilege for information obtained by social workers
LCO2/4617	'Freedom under the Law' by Lord Denning
LCO2/5481	Divorce: Costs
LCO2/6163	Trial of Divorce in the Provinces, Memorandum by Lord Chief Justice for consideration by Royal Commission (1951)

LCO2/4197	State of Business generally in the Divorce Court (1945); Matrimonial Causes (Divorce Commissioners) Bill 1945
LCO2/4198	Proposed appointment of additional judges, etc.
LCO2/4228	Appointment of Catholic judges

The Royal Commission on Marriage and Divorce:

LCO2/4854	Matrimonial Causes Bill 1951
LCO2/6131	Royal Commission on Divorce, Appointment of members and terms of reference
LCO2/6132	Continuation of above
LCO2/6135	Home Office Memorandum to Morton Commission on Law and Practice of Magistrates' Courts
LCO2/6136	Memorandum on International Recognition
LCO2/6139	Report of the Royal Commission on Marriage and Divorce, Implementation and correspondence to 31.12.1956
LCO2/6140	Report of the Royal Commission on Marriage and Divorce, Implementation. Correspondence 1.1.57–17.6.57
LCO2/6157	Matrimonial Causes (Breakdown of Marriage) Bill 196–
LCO2/6180	Reconciliation between parties to impending divorce

Maintenance issues:

LCO2/1145	Imprisonment for Debt[10]
LCO2/1594	Rules consequent on Money Payments (Justices Procedure) Act 1935
LCO2/6173	Maintenance Deeds—effect of decision in Bennett v. Bennett; Maintenance Agreements Bill
LCO2/6174	Maintenance Agreements Bill 195—Correspondence
LCO2/773	The Summary Jurisdiction (Separation and Maintenance) Bill 1925

Legal Aid:

LCO2/3899, 3900	Committee on Legal Aid and Advice in England and Wales, Report—Written Evidence and Analysis of Divergent Views
LCO2/4098	Proposed amendment to enable the Services Divorce Department to take *all* Poor Persons matrimonial causes
LCO2/4255	Amendments to Legal Aid Rules regarding Security for costs

Home Office Files

Marriage—The Prohibited Degrees

HO45/10064/B2853	Deceased Wife's Sisters Bill
HO45/1035/152169	Punishment of Incest
HO45 /15651	Marriage (Degrees of Relationship) Bill 1930
HO45/22820	Marriage (Enabling) Bill 1949

---

[10] File PRI COM 9/208: Effect of Money Payments (Justices Procedure) Act 1935 on Prisons is also relevant.

Marriage—General

| HO45/15078 | Validity of Soviet etc divorces, 1920–33 |

The Summary Jurisdiction (Separation and Maintenance) Bill 1925
HO45/11936

Conciliation in Magistrates' Courts:

HO45/21034	Claud Mullins
HO45/24151	Metropolitan Magistrates' Courts
HO45/25146	Matrimonial Conciliation: Improvement of Technique
HO45/15719	Proposals for Domestic Courts, 1919–1934
HO45/17152	Summary Proceedings (Domestic Procedures) Bill 1937
HO45/25034	Domestic Proceedings in London

Divorce:

HO45/10696	Divorce etc.
HO45/15006	Home Office files on projected divorce legislation 1891–1933
HO45/17102	Home Office file on AP Herbert Bill

Children:

HO45/11566/404730	On the 1920s guardianship legislation
HO45/11540	Adoption of children
HO45/12642	Adoption of Children Bills 1924/6
HO45/11982/456799	The Guardianship of Infants Bill 1925
HO45/12054/474998	The Guardianship of Infants Bill 1925 (second file)
HO45/22931	Guardianship of Infants Act
HO45/12259/405558	(in two parts) on Legitimacy Legislation 1924–6
HO45/ 25303	1950 Adoption Bill
HO45/16479/176695	Maintenance Orders Bills, 1909; Wills and Intestacies (Family Maintenance) Bill 1929
HO45 11936/429604	Summary Jurisdiction (Separation and Maintenance Bills) 1922–1925
HO45 17152/ 695967	Summary Procedure (Domestic Proceedings) Bill 1937
HO45 11190/ 371349	Bastardy Bills 1920 and 1923
HO45 19730/651784	Maintenance and Affiliation Orders: time limit for proceedings
HO45 11031/421028	Summary Jurisdiction (Married Persons) Bill 1921
HO45 15722/523880	Continuance of Maintenance Orders after husband's death
HO45 23095	Non-cohabitation orders etc
HO45/17094	Committee on Imprisonment for Non-Payment (Fischer Williams)

The Children and Young Persons Acts 1932/1933:

HO45/14714	Children Act 1908—Notes on Suggested Amendments
HO45/14715	Children and Young Persons Bill 1931
HO45/14716	Children and Young Persons Bill 1932

Marriage Guidance:

HO45/25202   The departmental committee on funding marriage guidance

Ministry of Health[11] and other central goverment files

The Children and Young Persons Acts 1932/1933:

CAB26/15	Home Affairs Committee, Children and Young Persons Bill 1932
ED31/275	Children's employment—Children and Young Persons Bill 1932
ED31/278	Children and Young Persons Bill 1933—Consolidation
MH 102/1483	Shortened form of Birth Certificate (1947)

The Ground for Divorce:

Prem1/38	Prime Minister's Meeting with Buckmaster and Divorce Law Reform Union (1924)
Prem11/1783	Papers on the Royal Commission on Marriage and Divorce
CAB 23/23.63(2)	
CAB 23/86 66(36)	
J85/70	Somerset House comments on reform
T 163/109/4	Treasury Comments
MEPOL2/4300	Divorce Proceedings: Application by King's Proctor for information in possession of police

The Curtis Committee and the Children Act 1948:

CAB 124/780	Conditions in Public Assistance Homes for Children
CAB 124/781	Report of the Care of Children Committee
CAB 128/6	Minutes of Cabinet Meetings 1946
CAB 128/9	Minutes of Cabinet Meetings 1947
CAB 129/17	Cabinet Papers 1947
MH102/1157	Report of Informal Committee on consequences of ending of evacuation schemes
MH102/1158	Post-War Provision for the care and education of children under eight
MH102/1161	Lady Allen of Hurtwood, Children in Homes, correspondence with Lord Woolton urging Public Enquiry
MH102/1293	Residential Homes for Children
MH102/1295	Voluntary Homes—Annual Returns 1945
MH102/1378	Children in Need of Care
MH102/1379	Children in Need of Care
MH102/1380	Care of Children deprived of normal home life: memorandum in opposition to Home Office's memorandum
MH102/1382	Machinery of Government Committee (Sir Alan Barlow), Care of Homeless Children, Which Government Department is Responsible?
MH102/1385	Machinery of Government: transfer of administration of Public Assistance Institutions

[11] Many of the files relating to children are in reality Home Office files, redesignated after departmental responsibility was transferred to the Ministry of Health.

MH102/1386	Care of homeless children—responsibility of Home Office as opposed to Ministry of Education
MH102/1390	Report of the Official Inter-Departmental Committee on the Break-up of the Poor Law—the position of children
MH102/1393	Care of Homeless Children: Appointment of Ministerial Committee to consider main recommendations of Curtis and Clyde Reports
MH102/1396	Designation of a Central Authority: Memoranda and Press cuttings
MH102/1412	Care of Children Committee, First Interim Report.
MH102/1413	Interim Report of the Curtis Committee: Inter-Departmental Meeting of 13 February 1946
MH102/1490	Recommendations of the Care of Children Committee; Note for legislation and administrative action
MH102/1491	Implementation of the recommendations of the Care of Children Committee; The break up of the Poor Law, Instructions for Parliamentary Counsel
MH102/1504	Children Bill 1947/1948: Essential Legislation
MH102/1506	Children Bill 1947–48, Scope of the Bill
MH102/1508	Children Bill: Memorandum for the Lord President's Committee
MH102/1510	Children Bill: Implementation of recommendation 4 of Curtis Report; and no new voluntary home to be opened without consent of Secretary of State
MH102/1513	Children Bill: Drafts—consideration of points arising between submission of Instructions . . . and receipt of first draft
MH102/1518	Children Bill: Consideration of First Draft
MH102/1519	Children Bill: Consideration of Second Draft
MH102/1520	Children Bill 1947–1948, Memorandum on submission to legislation committee
MH102/1521	Children Bill: Consideration of Third Draft
MH102/1522	Children Bill: Consideration of Fourth Draft
MH102/1523	Children Bill 1947–1948, Issue of a White Paper—Memo by the Secretary of State
MH102/1524	Children Bill: Consideration of Fifth Draft
MH102/1525	Children Bill: Consideration of Sixth Draft
MH102/1528	Children Bill: Second Reading Debate: Speeches in the House of Lords
ED136/718	Evidence prepared by the Ministry of Education for the Care of Children Committee
ED136/719	Care of Homeless Children—Departmental Response by the Ministry of Education
ED136/720	Care of Homeless Children—Consideration by the Ministry of Education of Ministerial Committee
ED136/721	Care of Homeless Children—Consideration by Cabinet
ED136/722	Care of Homeless Children—Debate in House of Commons on 19 November 1946 on Motion to amend address in reply to King's speech

Property:

Prem8/1055	Mountbatten Estate Bill
BT37/227	Married Women (Restraint upon Anticipation) Act: Effect

Registration of marriages etc:

RG48/139	Notice of Marriage Irregularly accepted
RG48/141	Publicity for Marriage Notices
RG48/253	Purported Marriage by person not in holy orders
RG48/2327	Marriage Acts—Suggested Amendments

Records of Matrimonial Proceedings (Court files):

J78/11	Divorce division: index to petitions 1921–1923
J77/1839	Divorce division: divorce proceedings 1921–1923
J77/2742/5029	

Probate Divorce and Admiralty Division, Boswell v. Boswell (Poor Person) 1930

J77/3689	Probate Divorce and Admiralty division: Davis v. Davis and Pinto (1936)
J77/3695	Probate Divorce and Admiralty division: Cavendish-Bentinck v. Cavendish-Bentinck (1942)
J77/3896	Probate Divorce and Admiralty division: Pilgrim v. Pilgrim (1939)

Law Commission files

BC3/1	Meetings of the Law Commissioners to December 1965
BC3/2	Meetings of the Law Commissioners to December 1966
BC3/3	Minutes of Commissioners' Meetings 1967
BC3/4	Minutes of Commissioners' Meetings 1968
BC3/5	Minutes of Commissioners' Meetings 1969

Solemnisation of Marriage:

BC3/374	Solemnisation of Marriages
BC3/375	Solemnisation of Marriages
BC3/376	Kilbrandon Committee on the Marriage Law of Scotland

Restitution of Conjugal Rights:

BC3/422	Restitution of Conjugal Rights

Nullity of Marriage:

BC3/415	Nullity of Marriage
BC3/417	Nullity of Marriage
BC3/418	Nullity of Marriage
BC3/419	Nullity of Marriage

The Matrimonial Homes Act 1967:

BC3/424	Matrimonial Homes Bill Part 1
BC3/425	Matrimonial Homes Bill Part 2

Divorce:

BC3/375–83	The Ground for Divorce
BC3/592	Oxford Seminars on Family Law 8th and 9th July 1966
BC3/387	Reconciliation Procedures
BC3/389	s. 33 of the MCA 1965, Cambridge Law Faculty
BC3/420	Divorce Bill (Scotland)

Financial Matters:

BC3/385	Wife's Right to Maintenance—Arrears of Maintenance-Financial Relief
BC3/386	Wife's Right to Maintenance—Financial Relief
BC3/388	Replies to Paper on Financial Provision and Related proceedings
BC3/399	Costs in Legally aided Matrimonial Proceedings, Security for Costs
BC3/400	Revised Paper on Financial Relief
BC3/401	Matrimonial Causes and Related Procedures, Financial Relief, Published Working Paper No 9
BC3/402	Replies to Published Working Paper No 9
BC3/403–5	Replies to Paper on Financial Provision and Related proceedings
BC3/414	Working Party on Financial Provision in Magistrates' Courts
BC3/428	Financial Limits on Magistrates' Orders in Domestic and Affiliation Proceedings

Matrimonial Property:

BC3/600	Seminar on Matrimonial Property, Manchester, September 1970

Succession:

BC3/373	Family Provision Act 1966

OFFICIAL AND OTHER REPORTS

Aarvold (1962): *Report of the Inter Departmental Committee on Magistrates' Courts in London*, Chairman: HH Judge Aarvold, Cmnd. 1606, 1962

Adams (1968): *Report of The Committee on Civil Judicial Statistics*, Chairman: Chief Master Paul Adams, Cmnd 3684, 1968

Administration of Child Support Act: *Child Support Agency's 1993/4 Annual Report and 1994/5 Business Plan*; *Child Support Agency 1994/5 Annual Report and Accounts*, HC 596, 1995. Parliamentary Commissioner for Administration's *Third Report— Session 1994–5, Investigation of complaints against the Child Support Agency*, HC 135

Admiralty Courts (1833): *Report of the Select Committee on Admiralty Courts*, BPP 1833, vol 7, p. 379

Adoption: Prime Minister's Review (2000): *Prime Minister's Review, Adoption*, Cabinet Office, Performance and Innovation Unit, 2000

Adoption Practice (1970): *A Guide to Adoption Practice*, Advisory Council on Child Care, HMSO, 1970

Adoption Survey (1950): *A Survey of Adoption in Great Britain*, Home Office, 1971

Advisory Board Children Reports: *Contact in Cases where there is Domestic Violence* (2000) and *Making Contact Work* (2002) (Advisory Board on Family Law)

Advisory Board Reports: *Annual Reports* of the Advisory Board on Family Law 1998–

Age of Marriage Select Committee (1929): *Report of the Select Committee on the Age of Marriage Bill* (HL 90, 66, BPP 1928–29) vol. 5

Bastardy Orders Select Committee (1909): *Report of the Select Committee on Bastardy Orders*, 1909 HC 236, BPP 1909, vol. 6

Beckford Inquiry: *A Child in Trust, The Report of the Panel of Inquiry into the Circumstances surrounding the Death of Jasmine Beckford*, Chairman: Louis Blom Cooper QC, (London Borough of Brent, 1985)

Beveridge (1942): *Social Insurance and Allied Services: Report . . . November 1942*, 1942, Cmd. 6404

Booth Report (1985): *Report of the Matrimonial Causes Procedure Committee* (Chairman: The Hon Mrs Justice Booth DBE, 1985)

Booth Report (1996): *Avoiding Delay in Children Act Cases*, by Dame Margaret Booth DBE, 1996

Butler-Sloss Report: *Report of the Enquiry into Child Abuse in Cleveland 1987*, 1988, Cm. 412

Campbell Report (1853): *First Report of the Commissioners . . . into the Law of Divorce and more particularly into the mode of obtaining Divorces a vinculo matrimonii* BPP 1852–3 vol. 40, p. 249

Carlile Inquiry (1987): *A Child in Mind: Protection of Children in a Responsible Society (The Report of the Commission of Inquiry into the circumstances surrounding the death of Kimberley Carlile)* (London Borough of Greenwich, 1987)

Central Government (1970): *The Reorganisation of Central Government*, (1970, Cmnd. 4506)

Chelmsford Royal Commission (1868): *Report of the Royal Commission on the Laws of Marriage* (1868, BPP 1867–1868 vol. 32). Chairman: Lord Chelmsford

Child Care Review: *Review of Child Care Law*, Report to Ministers of an interdepartmental working party, published by the Government as a Consultative Document, September 1985

Child Care White Paper (1987): *The Law on Child Care and Family Services* (1987, Cm. 62)

Child Life Protection Select Committee: *Report of the Select Committee on the Protection of Infant Life*, 1871, BPP vii

The Child, The Family, and the Young Offender (1965, Cmnd. 2742)

Child Support: *Children Come First* (1990, Cm. 1263)

Improving child support (1995, Cm. 2745)

Child Support Act Enquiries: Reports by *House of Commons Social Security Committee*: First Report Session 1993–4, *The Operation of the Child Support Act* HC 69; Fifth Report Session 1993–4, *The Operation of the Child Support Act: Proposals for Change* HC 470

Children Act 1975 Reports: *First and Second Reports to Parliament on the Children Act 1975*

Children Act Advisory Committee Best Practice: *Handbook of Best Practice in Children Act cases*, 1997

Children Act Advisory Committee Reports: *Reports of the Children Act Advisory Committee*, 1991/92 to *Final Report* June 1997

Children Act White Paper (1948): *Summary of the Main Provisions of the Children Bill*, 1948, Cmd. 7306, BPP 1947/48 xxii, 717

Children First: *Children First: a New Approach to Child Support* (1998, Cm. 3992) (A White Paper, *A New Contract for Welfare: Children's Rights and Parents' Responsibilities* (1999, Cm. 4349) followed)

Children in Trouble (1968, Cmnd. 3601)

Children Looked after Report: Report of the House of Commons Health Committee on *Children Looked After by Local Authorities*, 1997/8 HC 319–1

Child Support Agency Annual Report: *The First Two Years*

Child Support Select Committee (1994): House of Commons Social Security Committee, *The Operation of the Child Support Act,* First Report, Session 1993–4, HC 69

Church and State (1970): *Report of the Archbishop's Committee*, 1970 reprinted 1984

Church Artificial Insemination Report: *Artificial Insemination: the Report of a Commission appointed by His Grace the Archbishop of Canterbury* (1948)

Church Nullity Report (1955): *The Church and the Law of Nullity of Marriage, the report of a Commission appointed by the Archbishops of Canterbury and York in 1949,* 1955

Colwell Inquiry: *Report of the Committee of Enquiry into the Care and Supervision provided in Relation to Maria Colwell* (Chairman: TG Field-Fisher QC, 1974)

Conciliation: Newcastle Report (1989): *Report to the Lord Chancellor on the Costs and Effectiveness of Conciliation in England and Wales* (Conciliation Project Unit, University of Newcastle upon Tyne, 1989)

Conciliation Report (1983): *Report of the Inter-Departmental Committee on Conciliation* (Chairman: PD Robinson) (Lord Chancellor's Department, 1983)

Consolidation Committee (1949): *Joint Select Committee on Consolidation Bills*, 1949, BPP 1948/49, vol. 6 (Marriage Bill)

County Court Report (1909): *Report of the Committee appointed by the Lord Chancellor to inquire into certain matters relating to County Court Procedure,* Chairman: Sir John Gorell Barnes, (1909) BPP vol. 72, p. 311

Court Welfare Services: *Support Services in Family Proceedings—Future Organisation of Court Welfare Services*, A Consultation Paper, Department of Health and others (1998)

Curtis Report (1946): *Interim Report of the Child Care Committee*, 1946, Cmd. 6760; *Report of the Care of Children Committee* (1946, Cmd. 6922)

Denning Committee (1946–1947): *Committee on Procedure in Matrimonial Causes*, (Chairman: The Hon. Mr Justice Denning), *First Interim Report* (1946, Cmd. 6881); *Second Interim Report* (1946, Cmd. 6945);*Final Report of the Committee on Procedure in Matrimonial Causes* (1947, Cmd. 7024)

Destitute Children: *Report of the Select Committee on the Education of Destitute Children* (1861) HC 460, BPP 1861, vii

Divorce 1995 White Paper: *Looking to the future: mediation and the ground for divorce: the Government's Proposals* (1995, Cm. 2799)

Divorce Consultation Paper: *Looking to the future: mediation and the ground for divorce* (1993, Cm. 2424)

Divorce: Scotland: *Divorce, The Grounds Considered*, Scottish Law Commission (1967, Cmnd. 3256)

Domestic Employment: *Report on Post-War Organisation of Private Domestic Employment* (1945, Cmd. 6650)

Domicile: Private International Law Committee's *First Report* on *Domicile* (1954, Cmd. 9068)

Ecclesiastical Courts (1832): *Reports of the Commissioners . . . into the . . . Ecclesiastical Courts . . .* (HL Sessional Papers 1801–33 vol. 302, p. 48

Family Jurisdiction Paper: *Family Jurisdiction of the High Court and County Courts* (Lord Chancellor's Consultation Paper 1983)

Feversham Report (1960): *Report of the Departmental Committee on Human Artificial Insemination* (Chairman: The Earl of Feversham DSO) (1960, Cmnd. 1105)

Field of Choice: *Reform of the Grounds for Divorce, the Field of Choice*, Law Com. No. 15 (1966, Cmnd. 3123)

Finer Report: *Report of the Committee on One-Parent Families* (1974, Cmnd. 5629)

Finlay Report (1926): *First Report of the Committee on Legal Aid for the Poor*, (Chairman, The Hon Mr Justice Finlay, Cmd. 2638, BPP 1926 xiii, 195)

Finlay Report (1928): *Final Report of the Committee on Legal Aid for the Poor*, (Chairman, The Hon Mr Justice Finlay, Cmd. 3016 BPP 1928 xi, 243)

Fischer Williams Report: *Report of the Departmental Committee on Imprisonment by Courts of Summary Jurisdiction in default of payment of fines and other sums of money* (Chairman, Sir J Fischer Williams), 1934, Cmd. 4649, BPP 1933–34, xi, 69

Gorell Barnes Commission: *Report of the Royal Commission on Divorce and Matrimonial Causes*, 1912, Cd. 6478. *Evidence taken before the Royal Commission*, 1912, Vols I–III, Cd. 6479–82. BPP 1912–13, vols. 18–20

Gorell Committee (1909): see County Courts Committee (1909)

Graham Hall Report: *Report of the Committee on Statutory Maintenance Limits* (1968, Cmnd. 3587)

Guardian ad litem Annual Reports: *The Guardian ad Litem and Reporting Officer Service, Annual Reports 1993–1994, An Overview* (1994)

Guardian ad Litem Practice: *Manual of Practice Guidance for Guardians ad Litem . . .* (prepared for the Department of Health by J Timms, director of Independent Representation for Children in Need)

Guardianship Bill Select Committee: *Joint Select Committee on the Guardianship of Infants Bill, Minutes of Evidence,* 1922

Hanworth Committee: *The Business of the Courts Committee* (Chairman, Lord Hanworth MR), *Interim Report* (1933, Cmd. 4265, BPP 1932/3 x. 561; *Second Interim Report* (1933, Cmd. 4471, BPP 1933/4, xi. 1); *Third and Final Report* (1936, Cmd. 5066, BPP 1935/6, viii. 81)

Harris Report: *Report of the Departmental Committee on the Social Services in Courts of Summary Jurisdiction* (1936, Cmd. 5122)

Honourable Estate: *An Honourable Estate,* the institution of marriage according to English Law and the obligation of the church to marry all parishioners who are not divorced. The report of a Working Party established by the Standing Committee of the General Synod of the Church of England, 1988

Hopkinson Report: *Committee on Child Adoption* (1921, Cmd. 1254)

Horsburgh Report: *Report of the Departmental Committee on Adoption Societies and Agencies* (1937, Cmd. 5499)

Houghton Committee Report: *Report of the Departmental Committee on the Adoption of Children* (Chairman: HH Judge Stockdale) (1972, Cmnd. 5107)

Human Fertilisation and Embryology Authority: *Annual Reports and Accounts,* annually to 2000

Hurst Report (1954): *Report of the Departmental Committee on Adoption of Children,* Cmd. 9240

Ingleby Report: Report of the Committee on Children and Young Persons (Chairman: Viscount Ingleby) (1960, Cmnd. 1191)

Inter-Agency Working: *Promoting Inter-Agency Working in the Family Justice System* (Lord Chancellor's Department, 2002)

James Report: *Committee on the Distribution of Criminal Business between the Crown Court and Magistrates' Courts* (Chairman: The Hon Mr Justice James) (1975, Cmnd. 6323)

Judicature Commission: *First Report of the Commissioners* (with Minutes of Evidence) (1869) BPP 1868–1869 Vol. 25; *Second Report of the Commissioners* (with Minutes of Evidence) (1872) C. 631, BPP 1872 Vol. 20; *Third Report of the Commissioners* (with Minutes of Evidence) (1874) C. 957, BPP 1874 Vol. 24

Judicial Statistics Annual Reports

Judicial Studies Board, Annual Reports

Justice Report (1975): *Parental Rights and Duties and Custody Suits* (Justice, 1975)

Kilbrandon Report: *Report of the Departmental Committee appointed to inquire into the Law of Scotland relating to the Constitution of Marriage. The Marriage Law of Scotland* (1969, Cmnd. 4011)

Land Transfer: *Fourth Report of the Acquisition and Valuation of Land Committee* (1919, Cmd. 424)

Lang Prohibited Degrees Commission: *Kindred and Affinity as Impediments to Marriage* (1940)

Latey Report: *Report of the Committee on the Age of Majority* (1967, Cmnd. 3342)

Law Commission Reports and Working Papers:
  Annual Reports of the Law Commission 1965–
    Published Working Paper No. 9: Matrimonial and Related Proceedings—Financial Relief (1967)

Law Commission Reports and Working Papers (cont.):

Published Working Paper No. 15: Arrangements for the Care and Upbringing of Children . . . (by JC Hall)

Published Working Paper No. 19: The Action for Loss of Services, Loss of Consortium, Seduction and Enticement (1968)

Published Working Paper No. 35: Solemnisation of Marriage (1971)

Published Working Paper No. 42: Family Property Law (1971)

Published Working Paper No. 53: Matrimonial Proceedings in Magistrates' Courts (1973)

Published Working Paper No. 74: Illegitimacy (1979)

Published Working Paper No. 76: Time Restrictions on Presentation of Divorce and Nullity Petitions (1980)

Published Working Paper No. 90: Transfer of Money between Spouses (1985)

Published Working Paper No. 96: Review of Child Law: Custody (1986)

Published Working Paper No. 100: Review of Child Law: Care and Supervision (1987)

Published Working Paper No. 101: Review of Child Law: Wards of Court (1987)

Report on Blood Tests and Proof of Paternity in Civil Proceedings, Law Com. No. 16, 1968

Proposal for the Abolition of the Matrimonial Remedy of Restitution of Conjugal Rights, Law Com. No. 23 (1969)

Report on Financial Provision in Matrimonial Proceedings, Law Com. No. 25, 1969

Report on Breach of Promise of Marriage, Law Com. No. 26, 1969

Report on Nullity of Marriage, Law Com. No. 33, 1970

First Report on Family Property: A New Approach, Law Com. No. 52, 1973

Report on Solemnisation of Marriage in England and Wales, Law Com. No. 53, 1973

Report on Matrimonial Proceedings in Magistrates' Courts, Law Com. No. 77, 1976

Third Report on Family Property: The Matrimonial Home (Co-ownership and Occupation Rights) and Household Goods, Law Com. No. 86, 1978

The Financial Consequences of Divorce: The Basic Policy, A Discussion Paper, Law Com. No. 103, 1980

The Financial Consequences of Divorce: The Response to the Law Commission's Discussion Paper . . ., Law Com. No. 112, 1981

Report on Time Restrictions on Presentation of Divorce and Nullity Petitions, Law Com. No. 116, 1982

Illegitimacy, Law Com. No. 118, 1982

Report on Declarations in Family Matters, Law Com. No. 132, 1984

Illegitimacy, Second Report, Law Com. No. 157, 1986

Facing the Future, A Discussion Paper on the Ground for Divorce, Law Com. No. 170, 1988

Review of Child Law, Guardianship and Custody, Law Com. No. 172, 1988

Report on Family Law: Matrimonial Property, Law Com. No. 175, 1988

Report on Distribution on Intestacy, Law Com. No. 187, 1989

Report on the Ground for Divorce, Law Com. No. 192, 1990

Law of Property Bill Committee: *Report from the Joint Select Committee on the Law of Property Bill* (1920) BPP Vol. 7, p. 131

Law Reform Committee (1961): *Ninth Report of the Law Refom Committee* (Liability of Spouses in Tort) (1961, Cmnd. 1268)

Law Revision Committee (1934): *Fourth Interim Report of the Law Revision Committee* (Married Women) (1934, Cmd. 4770)

Lawrence Report (1919): *Report of the Committee to Enquire into the Poor Persons Rules, RSC 1883 Ord. 16, rr 22–31* (Chairman: The Hon Mr Justice PO Lawrence), Cmd. 430, BPP 1919, xxvii, 743

Lawrence Report (1925): *Report of the Poor Persons Rules Committee*, (Chairman, The Hon Mr Justice PO Lawrence), Cmd. 2358, BPP 1924–1925 xv, 313)

Lay Observer's Report: *Fifth Annual Report of the Lay Observer appointed under the provisions of the Solicitors Act 1974*, 1980

Legal Aid Advisory Committee Reports: *40th and 41st Annual Reports of the Lord Chancellor's Advisory Committee on Legal Aid 1992–93 and 1993–4* (HC 759 and 462) (Previous Reports of the Advisory Committee are published in the same volumes as the Law Society's Reports)

Legal Aid Board Franchising (1995): *Franchising Specification* issued by the Legal Aid Board (2nd ed., 1995)

Legal Aid Board Reports: *Reports to the Lord Chancellor on the Operation and Finance of the Legal Aid Act 1988*, 1989–90 Cm. 688 HC 489, to 1995–96 (1996) HC 505

Legal Aid Reports: *Annual Reports of the Law Society on the Operation and Finance of the Legal Aid Acts with comments of the Lord Chancellor's Advisory Committee* 1951–1989

Legal Aid White Paper (1987): *Legal Aid in England and Wales: A New Framework*, Lord Chancellor's Department (1987, Cm. 118)

Legal Education Advisory Committee: *Lord Chancellor's Advisory committee on Legal Education and Conduct, Annual Report 1996–1997* (HC 375, 1997)

London County Council Remand Homes, *Report of a Committee of Enquiry*, (Chairman: Godfrey Russell Vick KC, 1945, Cmd. 6594)

Lost in Care Inquiry: *Lost in Care: Report of the tribunal of inquiry into the abuse of children in care in . . . Gwynedd and Clwyd since 1974* (HC 201, 1999–2000)

Maclean Committee: *Report on Transfer of Functions of Poor Law Authorities in England and Wales* (Chairman: Sir Donald Maclean KBE MP) (1918, Cd. 8917)

Marriage and Divorce Statistics (OPCS, and subsequently Office for National Statistics, annually)

Marriage, Divorce and the Church: *the report of a Commission appointed by the Archbishop of Canterbury to prepare a statement . . .*, SPCK, 1971

Marriage Guidance: *Report of the Departmental Committee on Grants for the Development of Marriage Guidance* (Chairman: Sir Sidney Harris) (1948, Cmd. 7566)

Marriage Matters: a consultative document issued in 1979 by the Working Party on Marriage Guidance set up by the Home Office in consultation with the DHSS

Marriage Support: *The Funding of Marriage Support*, Report by Sir Graham Hart, Lord Chancellor's Department, 1999

Married Women's Property Bill Report: *Report of the Married Women's Property Bill Committee*, BPP 1867–1868, vii, 365

Married Women's Property Bill Report(1869): *Report of the Married Women's Property Bill Committee*, BPP 1868–1869, viii, 769

Married Women's Property Bill, House of Lords Report: *Report of the House of Lords Select Committee on the Married Women's Property Bill*: BPP 1870, HL No. 196, vol. 8, p. 1

Maud Report: *Report of the Royal Commission on Local Government in England* (Chairman: the Rt Hon Lord Redcliffe-Maud) (1969, Cmnd. 4040)

Maxwell Report: *Report of the Departmental Committee on Courts of Summary Jurisdiction in the Metropolitan Area* (Chairman: Sir A Maxwell) (1937) HMSO

Millard Tucker Report: *Report of the Committee on the Taxation Treatment of Provision for Pensions for Retirement* (Chairman: J Millard Tucker QC) (1954, Cmd. 9063)

Monckton Report: *Report by Sir Walter Monckton . . . on the circumstances which led to the boarding out of Dennis and Terence O'Neill . . .* (1945, Cmd. 6636)

Morton Commission Evidence: *Minutes of Evidence taken before the Royal Commission on Marriage and Divorce*, 1952–1954

Morton Committee: *Report of the Committee on the Law of Intestate Succession,* Chairman Lord Morton of Henryton (1951, Cmd. 8130)

Morton Commission: *Report of the Royal Commission on Marriage and Divorce* (1956, Cmd. 9678)

No Just Cause: *No Just Cause, The Law of Affinity in England and Wales: Some Suggestions for Change.* A Report by a Group Appointed by the Archbishop of Canterbury, 1984

Nonconformist marriages Committee (1893): *Report of the Select Committee on Nonconformist Marriages (Attendance of Registrars)* (HC 368, 1893)

Orkney Inquiry (1992): Report of the Inquiry into the Removal of Children from Orkney in February 1991 HC 195 (Edinburgh: HMSO, 1992)

Parental Responsibility Consultation Paper: Lord Chancellor's Department, *Determination of Paternity & Parental Responsibility for Unmarried Fathers* (1997)

Payne Committee Report: *Report of the Committee on the Enforcement of Judgment Debts* (1969, Cmnd. 3909)

Peel Report: *Report of the Royal Commission on the Despatch of Business at Common Law 1934–6* (Chairman: Earl Peel) (1936, Cmd. 5065) BPP 1935–6, xi, 105

Pension Law Review Committee (Chairman: Professor Roy Goode) *Consultation Document on the Law and Regulation of Occupational Pension Schemes* (1992); and *Pension Law Reform: The Report of the Pension Law Review Committee* (1993, Cm. 2342)

Pension White Paper: *Pension Rights on Divorce* (1997, Cm. 3564)

Pensions Management Institute: *Pensions And Divorce*, The report of the independent Working Group on Pensions and Divorce appointed by the Pensions Management Institute in agreement with the Law Society (1993)

Physical Deterioration Committee: *Report of the Inter-Departmental Committee on Physical Deterioration* (1904, Cd. 2175)

Pindown Report (1992): *The Pindown Experience and the Protection of Children*, the report of the Staffordshire Child Care Inquiry 1990, Members: Allan Levy QC and Barbara Kahan (Staffordshire County Council, 1991)

Population Commission: *Report of the Royal Commission on Population* (Chairman: Professor Sir Hubert Henderson FBA) (1949, Cmd. 7695)

Poor Law Report: see Checkland (1974): *The Poor Law Report of 1834* (The *Report of the Royal Commission on the Poor Laws* edited with an introduction by SG and EOA Checkland, 1974), Penguin Books Ltd. Harmondsworth

Poor Law Royal Commission (1909): *Report of the Royal Commission on the Poor Laws and the Relief of Distress* (1909, Cd. 4499)

Poor Law Schools: *Report of the Departmental Committee on Poor Law Schools* (Chairman: AJ Mundella MP) (1896) C. 8027

Population Trends (National Statistics, The Stationery Office) issued periodically

Press Reporting Committee (1923): *Select Committee on the Matrimonial Causes (Regulation of Reports) Bill* (1923) HC 118, BPP 1923, vii

Privacy Consultation Paper (1993): *Infringement of Privacy*, A Consultation Paper issued by the Lord Chancellor's Department and the Scottish Office

Probation Officers' Report (1922): *Report of the Departmental Committee on the Training, Appointment and Payment of Probation Officers* (1922, Cmd. 1601)

Probation Service Report (1962): *Report of the Departmental Committee on the Probation Service* (1962, Cmnd. 1650)

Prohibited Degrees Royal Commission (1848): The *Royal Commission into the Law of Marriage as relating to the Prohibited Degrees of Affinity . . .* (1848) BPP 1847–8, Vol. 28

Putting Asunder: *Putting Asunder, A Divorce Law for Contemporary Society*. The Report of a group appointed by the Archbishop of Canterbury in January 1964, SPCK 1966

Rayner Scrutiny (1985): *Report of the Efficiency Scrutiny of the Registration Service* (1985)

Reformatories Commission: *Report of the Royal Commission on Reformatories and Industrial Schools* (1884, C. 3876)

Reformatories: *Report of the Departmental Committee on Reformatory and Industrial Schools* (1913, Cd. 6838)

Registrar-General Annual Report: *Sixty-Second Annual Report of the Registrar-General* (1900, Cd. 323)

Registration Green Paper (1988): *Registration: A Modern Service* (1988, Cm. 531)

Registration Proposals (2002): *Civil Registration: Vital Change* (2002, Cm. 5355)

Registration White Paper (1990): *Registration: Proposals for Change* (1990, Cm. 939)

Rushcliffe Report (1945): *Report of the Committee on Legal Aid and Legal Advice in England and Wales*, (Chairman, Lord Rushcliffe) (1945, Cmd. 6641) BPP 1944–45, v. 187

Russell Committee (1966): *Report of the Committee on the Law of Succession in Relation to Illegitimate Persons* (Chairman: Lord Russell of Killowen) (1966, Cmnd. 3051)

Safeguards Review: *The Government's Response to the Children's Safeguards Review* (1998, Cm. 4105)

Schuster Report: *Report of the Poor Persons (Divorce Jurisdiction) Committee* (1929, Cmd. 3375) Chairman: Sir Claud Schuster

Scottish Law Commission Reports:
  Report on Aliment and Financial Provision (Scot. Law Com. No. 67, 1981)
  Report on Matrimonial Property (Scot. Law Com. No. 86, 1984)

Seebohm Report: *Report of the Committee on Local Authority and Allied Personal Social Services* (1968, Cmnd. 3703) (Chairman: Frederick Seebohm Esq)

Sexual Offences Report (1925): *Report of the Committee on Sexual Offences against Young Persons* (1925, Cmd. 2561)

Short Report: *Second Report from the Social Services Committee* Session 1983–4, Children in Care, Vol. I (H.C. 360-I). (Evidence given to this Committee is collected in *ibid*. Vols. II and III)

Social Security Abuse: *Report of the Committee on Abuse of Social Security Benefits*, (1973, Cmnd. 5228)

Social Trends Annual Reports by Central Statistical Office (and latterly by the Office for National Statistics) to No. 32 (2002)

Statistics, Historical (1990): *Marriage and Divorce Statistics 1873–1983*, Series FM2 No. 16, OPCS, 1990

Statistics: *Marriage and Divorce Statistics,* Government Statistical Service, Series FM2 (1978 and other years). Subsequently *Marriage, divorce and Adoption Statistics*

Sterlisation Committee (1934): *Report of the Departmental Committee on Sterilisation,* (1934, Cmd. 4485)

Stockdale Report: see Houghton Committee Report

Summary Jurisdiction Committee: House of Commons Standing Committee on Law, and Courts of Justice and Legal Procedure, *Report from the Committee on the Summary Jurisdiction (Married Women) Bill,* HC 307, 1895 (BPP 1895, xiii, 13)

Supporting Families (1998): *Supporting Families, a Consultation Document*, 1998

Taxation Commission (1956): *Royal Commission on the Taxation of Profits and Income,* Second Report, Cmd. 9105; Final Report, Cmd. 9474 (1955–6)

Taxation Consultation Paper (1980): *The Taxation of Husband and Wife*, 1980

Teenage Pregnancy (1999): Report of the Social Exclusion Unit on *Teenage Pregnancies* (1999)

The Thorpe Report: *Report to the Lord Chancellor of the Ancillary Relief Advisory Group* (July 1998)

Tomlin Report: *Reports of the Child Adoption Committee* (Cmd. 2401, Cmd. 2469, Cmd. 2711) 1924–1926

Transfer of Functions Committee: Ministry of Reconstruction, Local Government Committee, *Report on Transfer of Functions of Poor Law Authorities* (1918, Cd. 8917)

Transsexuals Working Group (2000): *Report of the Interdepartmental Working Group on Transsexual People,* Home Office, 2000

Utting Report: *People Like Us, The Report of the Review of the Safeguards for Children Living Away from Home,* a Report commissioned by the Secretary of State for Health (1997, HMSO)

Vaccination Commission: *Reports of the Royal Commission . . . [on] Vaccination,* Seven Reports, the seventh C. 8270, 1896

Violence in Marriage: *Report of the Select Committee on Violence in Marriage,* Session 1974–1975, HC 553, i and ii

— *Second Report of the Select Committee on Violence in Marriage,* Session 1976–77, HC 431

— *Government Observations on Report from the Select Committee on Violence in Marriage*(1976, Cmnd. 6690)

Violence in the Family: *First Report from the Select Committee on Violence in the Family, Violence to Children,* Session 1976–77 (1977, HC 329-i)

Violence to Children: '*Violence to Children', The Government's Response,* White Paper, (1978, Cmnd. 7123)

Warnock Report: *Report of the Committee of inquiry into Human Fertilization and Embryology,* chaired by Mary Warnock (1984, Cmnd. 9314)

Wedgewood Report: *Report of the Matrimonial Causes (Trial in the Provinces) Committee* (Chairman: Sir R Wedgewood, Bart. (1943, Cmd. 6480)

Wills and Intestacies Committee: *Joint Select Committee of the House of Lords and the House of Commons on the Wills and Intestacies (Family Maintenance) Bill 1930–31* (HC 127)

Wolfenden Report: *Report of the Committee on Homosexual Offences and Prostitution,* Chairman: Sir J Wolfenden (1957, Cmnd. 247)

Young Offenders: *Report of the Committee on the Treatment of Young Offenders*, Chairman: Sir TF Molony, Bart. (1927, Cmd. 2831)

Younghusband: *Report of the Working Party on Social Workers in the Local Authority Health and Welfare Services*, Chairman: Miss EL Younghusband (1959) Ministry of Health

STATUTES

The Statutes at Large, 1225–1869, vols 1–29, Eyre and Spottiswoode

The Public General Acts 1882 onwards, published by Eyre and Spottiswoode until 1938–9, and thereafter by HMSO

Current Law Statutes, published annually from 1948 by Stevens and Sons, Sweet and Maxwell Ltd

LAW REPORTS

The English Reports 1220–1865, as published by Stevens & Sons Ltd

The Law Reports as published by the Incorporated Council of Law Reporting, 1860–

The All England Law Reports, 1936–, Butterworths

Family Law Reports, 1980–, Jordan Publishing Ltd, Bristol

The Law Journal (1831–1949)

The Law Times (1859–1947)

PARLIAMENTARY DEBATES

Hansard's Parliamentary Debates, 1803–2000, 1st to 6th Series. For years subsequent to 1908 these are referred to in the text as the *Official Report* for House of Commons and House of Lords respectively.

NEWSPAPERS

The Times
The Sunday Times
The News of the World
The Daily Express
The Daily Mail

PUBLISHED BOOKS

Reference Works

Bellamy and Saville, *Dictionary of Labour Biography*, by J Bellamy and J Saville (Nine volumes), 1972–

Butler (2000): *Twentieth Century British Political Facts*, by DE and G Butler (8th ed. 2000), Macmillan Press Ltd

The Columbia Encyclopedia, by BA Chernow and GA Vallasi (eds), Columbia University Press, New York, USA

The Dictionary of National Biography, 1900–1990 (Ten Volumes) Oxford University Press, Oxford, and *The Dictionary of National Biography, Missing Persons*, Oxford University Press, Oxford (1993)

Dod's Parliamentary Companion (published annually since 1865) Dod's Parliamentary Companion Ltd, Hailsham, E Sussex and latterly Vacher Dod Publishing Ltd

Erskine May (1997): *Erskine May's Treatise on the law . . . and usages of Parliament*, 22nd ed. by WR McKay and others, Butterworths, 1997

Halsbury's Laws of England, Editor in Chief, Lord Hailsham of St. Marylebone, 4th ed.

The *Imperial Calendar and Civil Service Lists* (1900–1973); subsequently the *Civil Service Year Book*, The Stationery Office

Index to the Statutes 1235–; Chronological Table of the Statutes 1235–, Published Annually since 1870 by Her Majesty's Stationery Office

The Law List (published annually until 1977 by The Law Society)

Official Index to The Times (1906–)

OR McGregor, 'The Social Position of Women in England 1850–1914' A Bibliography (1955) *British Journal of Sociology*, vol. 6

Ramsden (2002): *The Oxford Companion to Twentieth-Century British Politics*, by J Ramsden (ed.) Oxford University Press, Oxford, 2002

Rosen (2001): *Dictionary of Labour Biography*, by G Rosen (ed.) Politico's Publishing, 2001

Simpson (1984): *Biographical Dictionary of the Common Law*, by AWB Simpson (ed.) Butterworths, 1984

Whitaker: *Whitaker's Almanack*, Annual Volumes, latterly published by The Stationery Office

Who was Who, 1897–1995 (Nine volumes) and *Who's Who 1996–2002,* Annual Volumes, A & C Black

Williams (1996): *Chronology of the Modern World, 1763 to the Present Time*, by N Williams, Barrie and Rockliff, 1966

Unpublished theses and other material

Buttner (1996): *The Deceased Wife's Sister Debate (1835–1907)* by E Buttner (unpublished M Juris dissertation, Oxford, 1996)

Herbert (1956): *The Birth of an Act*, by AP Herbert (Sterling Library, University of London)

Moyse (1996): *Reform of Marriage and Divorce Law in England and Wales 1909–37* (Cambridge University PhD thesis)

Other books

Abel-Smith and Stevens (1967): *Lawyers and the Courts*, by B Abel-Smith and R Stevens (Heinemann, 1967)

Abel-Smith and Stevens (1968): *In Search of Justice*, by B Abel-Smith and R Stevens (Allen Lane, The Penguin Press, 1968)

Abse (1973): *Private Member*, by L Abse (Macdonald and Co (Publishers), 1973)

Abse (1996): *The Man behind the Smile, Tony Blair and the Politics of Perversion*, by L Abse (Robson Books, 1996)

Albery (1950): *The Inheritance (Family Provision) Act 1938*, by M Albery (Sweet & Maxwell, 1950)

Allen (1944): *Whose Children?*, by Lady Allen of Hurtwood (Simpkin Marshall (1941) Ltd, 1944)

Allen and Nicholson (1975): *Memoirs of an Uneducated Lady*, by Marjorie Allen and Mary Nicholson (Thames and Hudson, 1975)

Anderson (1984): 'Legislative Divorce: Law for the Aristocracy', by S Anderson, in GR Rubin and D Sugarman (eds) *Law, Economy and Society, 1750–1914: Essays in the History of English Law* (Abingdon: Professional Books, 1984)

Anderson (1992): *Lawyers and the Making of English Land Law 1832–1940*, by JS Anderson (Oxford: Oxford University Press, 1992)

Anderson (1995): *Approaches to the History of the Western Family*, by M Anderson (Cambridge, Cambridge University Press, 1995)

Archbold (1930): *Archbold's Poor Law*, 16th ed. by EG Woodward (Butterworth & Co, 1930)

Arens (1986): *The Original Sin Incest and its meaning*, by W Arens (Oxford: Oxford University Press, 1986)

Aries (1973): *Centuries of Childhood*, by P Aries (Harmondsworth, Penguin Books, 1973)

Ashworth (2000): *Sentencing and Criminal Justice*, by A Ashworth (3rd ed., Butterworths, 2000)

Asquith and Stafford (1995): *Families and the Future*, ed. by S Asquith and A Stafford (Edinburgh: HMSO, 1995)

Atkinson (1975): The Economics of Inequality, by AB Atkinson (Oxford: Oxford University Press, 1975)

Atlay (1908): *The Victorian Chancellors*, by JB Atlay (Smith, Elder, & Co., 1908)

Aylett (1978): *Under the Wigs*, by S Aylett (Eyre Methuen, 1978)

Bainham (1998): *Child Law*, by A Bainham, 2nd ed. (Bristol: Jordan Publishing Limited, 1998)

Baker (1964): *Children in Chancery*, by J Baker (Hutchinson, 1964)

Baker (2002): *Introduction to English Legal History*, by JH Baker, 4th ed. (Sweet & Maxwell, 2002)

Balfour (1930): *Ne Obliviscaris. Dinna Forget*, by Lady F Balfour, Vol. 1 (Hodder & Stoughton, 1930)

Barker and Drake (1982): *Population and Society in Britain 1850–1950*, ed. by T Barker and M Drake (Batsford, 1982)

Barrington Baker (1977): *The Matrimonial Jurisdiction of Registrars*, by W Barrington Baker, J Eekelaar, C Gibson, and S Raikes (SSRC, 1977)

Barton and Douglas (1995): *Law and Parenthood*, by C Barton and G Douglas (Butterworths, 1995)

Bartrip (1984): 'County Court and Superior Court Registrars, 1820–1875: the Making of a Judicial Official', by P Bartrip, in GR Rubin and D Sugarman (eds.) *Law, Economy and Society, 1750–1914: Essays in the History of English Law* (Abingdon: Professional Books, 1984)

Bean (1984): *Adoption: Essays in Social Policy, Law and Sociology*, ed. by P Bean (Tavistock, 1984)

Bean & Macpherson (1983): *Approaches to Welfare*, ed. by P Bean and S Macpherson (Routledge & Kegan Paul, 1983)

Bean & Melville (1989): *Lost children of the Empire*, by P Bean and J Melville (Unwin Hyman, 1989)

Beatson (2002): *Anson's Law of Contract*, 28th ed. by J Beatson (Oxford: Oxford University Press, 2002)

Beaumont and McEleavy (1999): *The Hague Convention on International Child Abduction*, by P Beaumont and P McEleavy (Oxford: Oxford University Press, 1999)

Bechman (1923): *'Married Misery' and its Scandinavian Solution: a Reprint of Lord Buckmaster's Articles . . .*, by HG Bechman (Gyldendal, 1923)

Bechover Roberts (1938): *Sir John Simon*, by Bechover Roberts (Robert Hale Ltd, 1938)

Bedingfield (1998): *The Child in Need, Children, the State and the Law*, by D Bedingfield, (Bristol: Jordan Publishing Limited, 1998)

Behlmer (1982): *Child Abuse and Moral Reform in England, 1870–1908* by GK Behlmer (Stanford, California: Stanford University Press, 1982)

Behlmer (1998): *Friends of the Family, The English Home and its Guardians. 1850–1940*, by George K Behlmer (Stanford, California: Stanford University Press, 1998)

Bell (1952): *Randall Davidson, Archbishop of Canterbury*, 3rd ed., by GKA Bell, (Geoffrey Cumberledge: Oxford University Press, 1952)

Bell (1988): *When Salem came to the Boro, The True Story of the Cleveland Child Abuse Crisis*, by S Bell (Pan, 1988)

Berger (1983): *The War over the Family, Capturing the Middle Ground*, by B and P Berger (Garden City, New York: Anchor Books, 1983)

Bevan (1989): *Child Law*, by HK Bevan (Butterworths 1989)

Bevan and Parry (1978): *Children Act 1975*, by HK Bevan and ML Parry (Butterworths, 1978)

Biggs (1962): *The Concept of Matrimonial Cruelty*, by JM Biggs (The Athlone Press, 1962)

Binney (1957): *The Divorce Court*, by C Binney (Herbert Jenkins, 1957)

Bird (2000): *Child Maintenance*, 3rd ed., by R Bird (Bristol, Jordan Publishing Limited, 2000)

Bird (2002): *Ancillary Relief Handbook*, by R Bird (Bristol, Jordan Publishing Limited, 2002)

Birkenhead (1922): *Points of View*, by Viscount Birkenhead, Lord High Chancellor of Great Britain (Vols. 1 and 2) (Hodder and Stoughton, 1922)

Birkenhead (1929): *The Speeches of Lord Birkenhead* (with a preface by Lord Hugh Cecil) (Cassell and Co Ltd., 1929)

Birkenhead (1969): *Walter Monckton, The Life of Viscount Monckton of Brenchley*, by Lord Birkenhead (the 2nd Earl) (Weidenfeld and Nicolson, 1969)

Blackstone (1770): *Commentaries on the Laws of England*, 4th ed. by William Blackstone (Oxford: the Clarendon Press, 1770)

Bochel (1976): *Probation and After-Care: its development in England and Wales*, by D Bochel (Edinburgh: Scottish Academic Press, 1976)

Boden (1932): *Mischiefs of the Marriage Law, An Essay in Reform*, by JF Wesley-Boden (Williams and Norgate, 1932)

Bogdanor (1995): *The Monarchy and the Constitution*, by V Bogdanor (Oxford: Oxford University Press, Oxford, 1995)

Bonfield (1983): *Marriage Settlements, 1601–1740: The Adoption of the Strict Settlement*, by L Bonfield, (Cambridge: Cambridge University Press, 1983)

Bonham Carter (1996): *Lantern Slides: The Diaries and Letters of Violet Bonham Carter 1904–1914*, ed. by M Bonham Carter and M Pottle (Weidenfeld & Nicolson, 1996)

Bonham Carter (1998): *Champion Redoubtable: The Diaries and Letters of Violet Bonham Carter 1914–1945*, ed. by M Pottle (Weidenfeld & Nicolson, 1998)

Bonham Carter (2000): *Daring to Hope: The Diaries and Letters of Violet Bonham Carter 1946–1969*, ed. by M Pottle (Weidenfeld & Nicolson, 2000)

Borland (1976): *Violence in the Family*, by M Borland (Manchester: Manchester University Press, 1976)

Bourguignon (1987): *Sir William Scott, Lord Stowell*, by HJ Bourguignon (Cambridge, Cambridge University Press, 1987)

Boswell (1995): *The Marriage of Likeness, Same-sex Unions in Pre-Modern Europe*, by J Boswell (HarperCollins, 1995)

Bott (1971): *Family and Social Networks*, by E Bott, 2nd ed. (Tavistock Publications, 1971)

Bradshaw and Millar (1991): *Lone Parent Families in the UK* by J Bradshaw and J Millar (HMSO, 1991)

Brandreth (1999): *Breaking the Code: Westminster Diaries May 1990–May 1997*, by GD Brandreth (Weidenfeld and Nicolson, 1999)

Brasnett (1964): *The Story of the Citizens' Advice Bureaux*, by ME Brasnett (National Council of Social Service, 1964)

Brasnett (1969): *Voluntary Social Administation: a History of the National Council for Social Service 1919–1969*, by ME Brasnett (National Council of Social Service, 1969)

Braye (1927): *Fewness of my Days, A Life in Two Centuries*, by Lord Braye (Sands, 1927)

Bridge (1997): *Family Law towards the Millenium, Essays for PM Bromley*, ed. by C Bridge (Butterworths, 1997)

Bridgeman and Millns (1998): *Feminist Perspectives on Law*, by J Bridgeman and S Millns (Sweet & Maxwell, 1998)

Bright and Dewar (1998): *Land Law, Themes and Perspectives*, by S Bright and J Dewar (Oxford: Oxford University Press, 1998)

Brivati (1999): *Lord Goodman*, by Brian Brivati (Richard Cohen Books, 1999)

Bromhead (1956): *Private Members' Bills in the British Parliament*, by PA Bromhead (Routledge and Kegan Paul, 1956)

Bromley (1998): *Bromley's Family Law*, 9th ed. by N Lowe and G Douglas, (Butterworths, 1998)

Brook and Lobban (1997): *Communities and Courts in Britain 1150–1900*, ed. by C Brooks and M Lobban (Hambledon Press, 1997)

Brown et al (1985); 'Marriage and the Family' by J Brown, M Comber, K Gibson, and S Howard, in *Values and Social Change in Britain* (ed. by M Abrams, D Gerard, and N Timms) (Macmillan, 1985)

Brundage (1987): *Law, Sex and Christian Society in Medieval Europe*, by JA Brundage, (Chicago and London: Chicago University Press, 1987)

Brundage (1991): *The Crusades, Holy War and Canon Law*, by JA Brundage (Variorum, 1991)

Bryant (1997): *Stafford Cripps, The First Modern Chancellor*, by C Bryant (Hodder and Stoughton, 1997)

Buckmaster (1923): see Bechman (1923)

Buckmaster (1932): *An Orator of Justice, A Speech Biography of Viscount Buckmaster*, ed. by JFSS Johnson (Nicholson & Watson, Ltd, 1932)

Sources and Select Bibliography

Bullard and Malos (1990): *Custodianship—A Report to the Department of Health on the implementation of Part II of the Children Act 1975 in England and Wales from December 1985 to December 1988*, by E Bullard and E Malos, with RA Parker (Bristol: Department of Social Policy, University of Bristol, 1990)

Bullock Little and Milham (1993): *Residential Care for Children—A Review of the Research* by S Bullock, M Little and S Milham (HMSO, 1993)

Burrows (1995): *Family Law Legal Aid Guide 1995/96*, by D Burrows (Bristol: Jordan Publishing Ltd, 1995)

Bursell (1996): *Liturgy Order and the Law*, by RDH Bursell (Oxford: Oxford University Press, 1996)

Burton and Drewry (1981): *Legislation and Public Policy: Public Bills in the 1970–1974 Parliament*, by I Burton and G Drewry (Macmillan, 1981)

Butler et al (1994): *Failure in British Government: the Politics of the Poll Tax*, by D Butler, A Adonis and T Travers (Oxford: Oxford University Press, 1994)

Byatt (1997): *Babel Tower*, by AS Byatt (Vintage, 1997)

Callaghan (1987): *Time and Chance*, by J Callaghan (Collins, 1987)

Cambridge (1990): *The Cambridge Social History of Britain*, ed. by FM Longstreth, (Cambridge: Cambridge University Press, 1990)

Campbell (1983): *FE Smith, First Earl of Birkenhead*, by J Campbell (Jonathan Cape, 1983)

Campbell (1997): *Unofficial Secrets, Child Sexual Abuse—The Cleveland Case,* by B Campbell, revised ed. (Virago, 1997)

Carpenter (1991): *Archbishop Fisher—His Life and Times*, by E Carpenter (Norwich: Canterbury Press, 1991)

Casey (1989): *The History of the Family*, by J Casey (Oxford: Basil Blackwell, 1989)

Castle (1980): *The Castle Diaries 1974–1976*, by B Castle (Weidenfeld and Nicolson, 1980)

Chadwick (1971): *The Victorian Church*, 3rd ed. by O Chadwick (Adam and Charles Black, 1971)

Chadwick (1983): *Hensley Henson, A Study in the friction between Church and State*, by O Chadwick (Oxford: Oxford University Press, 1983)

Chadwick (1990): *Michael Ramsey, A Life*, by O Chadwick (Oxford: Oxford University Press, 1990)

Chafe (1991): *The Paradox of Change: American Women in the 20th Century*, by WH Chafe (Oxford: Oxford University Press, 1991)

Chapman (1925): *The Poor Man's Court of Justice: Twenty five Years as a Metropolitan Magistrate*, by C Chapman (Hodder and Stoughton Ltd, 1925)

Checkland (1974): *The Poor Law Report of 1834* (The *Report of the Royal Commission on the Poor Laws* edited with an introduction by SG and EOA Checkland, (Harmondsworth: Penguin Books Ltd, 1974)

Cheshire and North (1999): Cheshire and North's *Private International Law*, 13th ed. by P North and JJ Fawcett (Butterworths, 1999)

Chester and Wilson (1957): *The Organisation of British Central Government 1914–1956*, by DN Chester and FMG Wilson (Geo Allen & Unwin, 1957)

Chuter Ede (1987): *Labour and the Wartime Coalition: from the diaries of James Chuter Ede, 1941–1945*, ed. by K Jefferys (Historian's Press, 1987)

Clarke (2002): *The Cripps Version: The Life of Sir Stafford Cripps*, by P Clarke (Allen Lane, The Penguin Press, 2002)

Clarke Hall (1897): *The Queen's Reign for Children*, by W Clarke Hall (1897)

Clarke Hall (1909): *The Law relating to Children*, by W Clarke Hall, 3rd ed. 1909 (subsequent editions as Clarke Hall and Morrison's Law Relating to Children, under various editors, down to 10th ed., Butterworths, 1991)

Clarke Hall (1917): *State and the Child*, by W Clarke Hall (1917)

Clarke Hall (1926): *Children's Courts* (George Allen & Unwin, 1926)

Clulow and Vincent (1987): *In the Child's Best Interests*, by CF Clulow and C Vincent (Tavistock, Sweet & Maxwell, 1987)

Cobbe (1869): *Criminals, Idiots, Women and Minors. Is the Classification sound?* by Francis Power Cobbe (A Ireland and Co, Pall Mall, Manchester, 1869)

Cockburn (1995): *Child Abuse and Protection: The Manchester Boys and Girls Refuges . . . 1884–1894*, by T Cockburn (Manchester: Manchester University Press, 1995)

Comyn (1991): *Summing it up: memoirs of an Irishman at law in England*, by J Comyn (Dublin: Round Hall Press, 1991)

Comyn (1993): *Watching Brief: Further memoirs of an Irishman at law in England*, by J Comyn (Dublin: Round Hall Press, 1993)

Comyn (1994): *Leave to Appeal: Further legal memoirs* by J Comyn (Dublin: Round Hall Press, 1994)

Cook (1997): *Priestley*, by J Cook (Bloomsbury, 1997)

Cook (1999): *A Slight and Delicate Creature*, by M Cook (Weidenfeld and Nicolson, 1999)

Cooper (1971): *The Death of the Family*, by D Cooper (Allen Lane, 1991)

Cooper (1983): *The Creation of the British personal social services 1962–1974*, by Joan Cooper (Heinemann Educational Books, 1983)

Cornish and Clark (1989): *Law and Society in England 1750–1950* by WR Cornish and G de N Clark (1989, Sweet & Maxwell)

Craffe (1971): *La Puissance Paternelle en Droit Anglais*, by Mauricette Craffe (Paris: Librairie Generale de Droit et Jurisprudence, 1971)

Cranston (1985): *Legal Foundations of the Welfare State*, by Ross Cranston (Weidenfeld and Nicolson, 1985)

Cressy (1997): *Birth, Marriage, and Death*, by D Cressy (Oxford: Oxford University Press, 1997)

Cretney (1984): *Principles of Family Law*, 4th ed. by SM Cretney (Sweet & Maxwell Ltd, 1984)

Cretney (1998): *Law, Law Reform and the Family*, by SM Cretney (Oxford: Oxford University Press, 1998)

Cretney (2000): *Family Law—Essays for the New Millennium*, ed. by SM Cretney, (Bristol: Jordan Publishing Limited, 2000)

Cretney and Masson (1997): *Principles of Family Law* (6th ed. by SM Cretney and JM Masson, Sweet & Maxwell Ltd, 1997)

Cretney, Bailey-Harris and Masson (2002): *Principles of Family Law*, 7th ed. by SM Cretney, JM Masson and R Bailey-Harris (Sweet & Maxwell Ltd, 2002)

Cross (1991): *The English Doctrine of Precedent*, 4th ed. by R Cross and JW Harris (Oxford: Oxford University Press, 1991)

Crossman (1973): *The Role of the Volunteer in the Modern Social Services*, by RHS Crossman (Sydney Ball Memorial Lecture, 1973, Oxford)

Crossman (1977): *The Diaries of a Cabinet Minister, Vol. 3, Secretary of State for Social Services, 1968–1970* (Hamish Hamilton and Jonathan Cape, 1977)

Crowther (1981): *The Workhouse System 1834–1929*, by MA Crowther (Batsford, 1981)

Dangerfield (1997): *The Strange Death of Liberal England*, by George Dangerfield (Serif, 1997)

Davidson (1929): *The Six Lambeth Conferences 1867–1920*, ed. RT Davidson and H Thomas (SPCK, 1929)

Davie (1976): *The Diaries of Evelyn Waugh*, M Davie (ed.) (Weidenfeld and Nicolson, 1976)

Davies (1993): *How to apply for a Legal Aid Franchise*, by M Davies (Blackstone Press Ltd, 1993)

Davin (1996): *Growing up Poor, Home School and Street in London 1870–1914*, by A Davin (Rivers Oram Press, 1996)

Davis, (1988): *Partisans and Mediators: The Resolution of Divorce Disputes*, by G Davis (Oxford: Clarendon Press, 1988)

Davis and Murch (1988): *Grounds for Divorce*, by G Davis and M Murch (Oxford: Clarendon Press, 1988)

Davis, Cretney and Collins (1994): *Simple Quarrels, Negotiating Money and Property Disputes on Divorce*, by G Davis, SM Cretney and J Collins (Oxford: Clarendon Press, 1994)

Davis, Wikeley and Young (1998): *Child Support in Action*, by G Davis, N Wikeley, R Young (with others) (Oxford: Hart Publishing, 1998)

de Mause (1991): *The History of Childhood: the untold story of child abuse*, by L de Mause (Bellew, 1991)

de Montmorency (1920): *John Gorell Barnes, First Lord Gorell (1848–1913)* by JEG de Montmorency with an introduction by Ronald, Third Lord Gorell (John Murray, 1920)

Denham and Garnett (2001): *Keith Joseph*, by A Denham and M Garnett (Chesham: Acumen, 2001)

Denning (1980): *The Due Process of Law*, by Lord Denning (Butterworths, 1980)

Devlin (1963): 'Morals and the Law of Marriage', by P Devlin, The Earl Grey Memorial Lecture, University of Durham, 15 March 1963, reprinted in *The Enforcement of Morals* (1965)

Dewey (1997): *War and Progress, Britain 1914–1945*, by Peter Dewey (Longman, 1997)

DHSS (1985): *Social Work Decisions in Child Care: Recent Research Findings and Their Implications*, Department of Health and Social Security (HMSO, 1985)

Dibdin and Healey (1912): English Church Law and Divorce, by L Dibdin and CEH Chadwyck Healey (John Murray, 1912)

Dicey (1914): *Lectures on the Relation between Law and Public Opinion in England During the Nineteenth Century* by AV Dicey, 2nd ed. (Macmillan, 1914)

Digby (1978): *Pauper Palaces*, by A Digby (Routledge & Kegan Paul, 1978)

Dilks (1984): *Neville Chamberlain, Vol. 1, Pioneering and Reforms 1865–1929*, by D Dilks (Cambridge: Cambridge University Press, 1984)

Dingwall and Eekelaar (1988): *Divorce Mediation and the Legal Process*, ed. by R Dingwall and J Eekelaar (Oxford: Oxford University Press, 1988)

Dingwall, Eekelaar and Murray (1995): *The Protection of Children: State Intervention and Family Life*, by R Dingwall, JM Eekelaar and T Murray, 2nd ed. (Aldershot, Avebury, 1995)

Dinnage (1986): *Annie Besant*, by Rosemary Dinnage (Harmondsworth, Penguin, 1986)

Doggett (1992): *Marriage, Wife-Beating and the Law in Victorian England*, by ME Doggett (Weidenfeld and Nicolson, 1992)

DoH (1988): *Protecting Children*, Department of Health (HMSO, 1988)

DoH (1989): *An Introduction to the Children Act 1989* (HMSO, 1989)

DoH (1991): Guidance: *The Children Act 1989, Guidance and Regulations*, Vols. 1–9, Department of Health (HMSO, 1991)

DoH (1991): *Working Together under the Children Act 1989,* Department of Health, (HMSO, 1991)

DoH (1991): *Patterns and Outcomes in Child Placement*, Department of Health (HMSO, 1991)

DoH (1991): *Child Abuse, A study of Inquiry Reports 1980–89*, Department of Health (HMSO, 1991)

DoH (1992): *Manual of Practice Guidance for Guardians ad Litem and Reporting Officers*, Department of Health (HMSO, 1992)

DoH (1994): *The Child, The Court and the Video,* Department of Health (HMSO, 1994)

DoH (1995): Child Protection: *Messages from Research,* Department of Health (HMSO, 1995)

DoH (1995): *Guide for Guardians ad litem in Public Law Proceedings under the Children Act 1989,* Department of Health (HMSO, 1995)

DoH (1995): *The Challenge of Partnership,* Department of Health (HMSO, 1995)

Donaldson (1986): *Edward VIII*, by F Donaldson (Weidenfeld and Nicolson, 1986)

Donoghue and Jones (1973): *Herbert Morrison, Portrait of a Politician*, by B Donoghue and GW Jones (Weidenfeld and Nicolson, 1973)

Donzelot (1980): *The Policing of Families*, by J Donzelot translated by R Hurley (Hutchinson University Library, 1980)

Douglas (1991): *Law, Fertility and Reproduction*, by G Douglas (Sweet & Maxwell, 1991)

Drewry and Butcher (1988): *The Civil Service Today*, by G Drewry and T Butcher, 2nd ed. (Oxford: Blackwell Publishers, 1988)

Driver (1993): *Power and Pauperism, The Workhouse System, 1834–1884*, by F Driver, (Cambridge: Cambridge University Press, 1993)

Dunn (1993): *Sword and Wig, Memoirs of a Lord Justice*, by R Dunn (Quiller Press, 1993)

Dutton (1992): *Simon, A Political Biography of Sir John Simon*, by D Dutton (Aurum Press Ltd, 1992)

Dyhouse (1989): *Feminism and the Family in England 1880–1939*, by C Dyhouse (Oxford: Oxford University Press, 1989)

Edwards (1964): *Law Officers of the Crown*, by J Ll J Edwards (Sweet & Maxwell, 1964)

Eekelaar (1991): *Regulating Divorce*, by J Eekelaar (Oxford: Oxford University Press, 1991)

Eekelaar (1998): *Financial and Property Adjustment on Divorce* (Centre for Socio-Legal Studies, Oxford, 1998)

Eekelaar and Clive (1977): *Custody after Divorce. The Disposition of Custody in Divorce Cases in Great Britain*, by John Eekelaar and Eric Clive with Karen Clarke and Susan Raikes (Family Law Studies No. 1 (1977), Centre for Socio-Legal Studies, Wolfson College, Oxford)

Eekelaar and Dingwall (1988): *Divorce Mediation and the Legal Process*, by J Eekelaar and R Dingwall (Oxford: Clarendon Press, 1988)

Eekelaar and Dingwall (1990): *The Reform of Child Care Law*, by J Eekelaar and R Dingwall (Tavistock, Routledge, 1990)

Eekelaar and Dingwall (1995): *The Protection of Children: State Intervention and Family Life*, by J Eekelaar and R Dingwall (Aldershot: Avebury, 1995)

Eekelaar and Katz (1979): *Family Violence*, ed. by J Eekelaar and S Katz (Toronto, Canada: Butterworths, 1979)

Eekelaar and Katz (1984): *The Resolution of Family Conflicts* ed. by J Eekelaar and S Katz (Toronto, Canada: Butterworths, 1984)

Eekelaar and Maclean (1986): *Maintenance after Divorce*, by J Eekelaar and M Maclean (Oxford: Oxford University Press, 1986)

Eekelaar and Maclean (1991): *Regulating Divorce*, by J Eekelaar and M Maclean, (Oxford: Oxford University Press, 1991)

Eekelaar and Nhlapo (1998): *The Changing Family, International Perspectives on the Family and Family Law,* by J Eekelaar and T Nhlapo (eds.) (Oxford: Oxford University Press, 1998)

Eekelaar and Sarcevic (1993): *Parenthood in Modern Society*, ed. by J Eekelaar and P Sarcevic (Dordrecht and London: Martinus Nijhoff, 1993)

Eekelaar, Maclean and Beinart (2000): *Family Lawyers. The Divorce Work of Solicitors*, by J Eekelaar, M Maclean and S Beinart (Oxford: Hart Publishing, 2000)

Egerton (1945): *Legal Aid*, by RE Egerton (Kegan Paul, Trend, Trubner & Co, 1945)

El Alami (1992): *The Marriage Contract in Islamic Law*, by DS El Alami (Graham and Trotman, 1992)

Elliot (1986): *The Family: Change or Continuity*, by F Robertson Elliot (Basingstoke: Macmillan Education Ltd, 1996)

Elliot (1996): *Gender, Family and Society*, by F Robertson Elliot (Basingstoke: Macmillan Education Ltd, 1996)

Ellis (1992): *TJ, A Life of Dr Thomas Jones, CH*, by EL Ellis (University of Wales Press, Cardiff, 1992)

Engels (1940): *The Origin of the Family, Private Property and the State . . .,* by F Engels (Lawrence and Wisheart, 1940)

Ensor (1936): *England 1870–1914* by RCK Ensor (Oxford: Oxford University Press, 1936)

Erikson (1993): *Women and Property in Early Modern England* by AL Erikson (Routledge and Kegan Paul, 1993)

Esmein (1929): *Le Mariage en droit canonique*, by A Esmein, 2nd ed. (Paris: Librairie de Recueil Sirey, 1929)

Eversley (1906): *The Law of Domestic Relations*, 3rd ed. by WP Eversley (Stevens & Haynes, 1906)

Ewens (1924): *Thirty Years at Bow Street Police Court*, by WT Ewens (T Werner Laurie, 1924)

Fallon (1991): *Billionaire, The Life and Times of Sir James Goldsmith*, by I Fallon (Hutchinson, 1991)

Faulks (1977): *No Mitigating Circumstances* by N Faulks (William Kimber, 1977)

Faulks (1978): *A Law unto Myself* by N Faulks (William Kimber, 1978)

Fehlberg (1997): *Sexually Transmitted Debt, Surety Experience and English Law*, by B Fehlberg (Oxford: Oxford University Press, 1997)

Feiling (1970): *The Life of Neville Chamberlain*, by K Feiling (Macmillan, 1970)

Ferguson (1996): *Henrik Ibsen, A New Biography*, by R Ferguson (Richard Cohen Books, 1996)

Ferri (1984): *Step-Children: A National Study*, by E Ferri (Windsor: NFER-Nelson, 1984)

Fildes (1988): *Wet Nursing from Antiquity to the Present*, by V Fildes (Oxford: Basil Blackwell, 1988)

Finch (1989): *Family Obligations and Social change* by J Finch (Cambridge: Polity, 1989)

Finch (2002): *The Criminalisation of Stalking: Constructing the Problem and Evaluating the Solution*, by E Finch (Cavendish, 2001)

Finch (1996): *Wills, Inheritance and Families* by J Finch and others (Oxford: Oxford University Press, 1996)

Finch and Mason (1993): *Negotiating Family Responsibilities* by J Finch and J Mason (London and New York: Tavistock, Routledge, 1993)

Finlay (1983): *Family Law in Australia*, by HA Finlay, 3rd ed. (Sydney: Butterworths, 1983)

Finlay (1997): *Family Law in Australia*, by HA Finlay, RJ Bailey Harris and S Otlowski, 5th ed. (Sydney: Butterworths, 1997)

Finlayson (1981): *The Seventh Earl of Shaftesbury*, by GBAM Finlayson (Eyre Methuen, 1981)

Fisher et al. (1986): *In and out of care,* by M Fisher, P Marsh with D Phillips and E Sainsbury (Batsford, 1986)

Fisher (1992): *Family Conciliation within the United Kingdom, Policy and Practice* Revised ed. by T Fisher (Bristol: Jordan Publishing Ltd, 1992)

Fletcher (1968): *Random Reminiscences*, by (Lord) Eric GM Fletcher (Bishopsgate Press, 1968)

Fletcher (1988): *The Abolitionists: The Family and Marriage under Attack*, by R Fletcher (Routledge, 1988)

Fletcher (1988a): *The Shaking of the Foundations: Family and Society*, by R Fletcher (Routledge, 1988)

Fletcher (1996): *The Law of Insolvency*, by IF Fletcher, 2nd ed. (Sweet & Maxwell, 1996)

Flinn and Smout (1974): *Essays in Social History*, MW Flinn and TC Smout (eds.) (Oxford: Clarendon Press, 1974)

Foakes (1984): *Family Violence*, by J Foakes (Hemstal Press, 1984)

Foote, Levy and Sander (1966): *Cases and Materials on Family Law* by C Foote, RJ Levy and FEA Sander (Boston and Toronto: Little Brown & Co, 1966)

Fortin (1998): *Children's Rights and the Developing Law*, by J Fortin (Butterworths, 1998)

Foster (1986): 'Caroline Norton' in *Significant Sisters, Active Feminism 1839–1939*, by M Foster (Harmondsworth: Penguin, 1986)

Foucault (1988) *The Care of the Self*, Volume 3, The History of Sexuality, by M Foucault (trans. R Hurley) (Allen Lane, 1988)

Fratter (1991): *Permanent Family Placement, A Decade of Experience*, ed. by J Fratter (British Agencies for Adoption and Fostering, 1991)

Freedman, Hammond, Masson and Morris (1988): *Property and Marriage: An Integrated Approach, Property, Tax, Pensions and Benefits in the Family*, by J Freedman, E Hammond, J Masson and N Morris, Institute for Fiscal Studies Report Series No. 29 (1988)

Freeman (1983): *The Rights and Wrongs of Children*, by MDA Freeman (London and Dover New Hampshire: Frances Pinter (Publishers) 1983)

Freeman (1984): *State, Law, and the Family, Critical Perspectives*, ed. by MDA Freeman (Sweet & Maxwell Ltd, 1984)

Freeman (1996): *Divorce: Where Next?*, ed. by MDA Freeman (Aldershot: Dartmouth, 1996)

Freeman & Lyon (1983): *Cohabitation Without Marriage*, by MDA Freeman and C M Lyon (Aldershot: Gower, 1983)

Freeman & Veerman (1992): *The Ideologies of Children's Rights*, by MDA Freeman and P Veerman (Dordrecht and London: Martinus Nijhoff, 1992)

Freestone (1990): *Children and the Law, Essays in Honour of Professor H K Bevan*, ed. by D Freestone (Hull: Hull University Press, 1990)

Fricker (1997): *Emergency Remedies in the Family Courts*, by N Fricker and others (Bristol: Jordan Publishing Ltd, 1997)

Fricker and Bean (1991): *Enforcement of Injunctions and Undertakings*, by N Fricker and D Bean (Bristol: Jordan Publishing Ltd, 1991)

Frisby (1998): *Outrageous Fortune*, by T Frisby (First Thing Publications, 1998)

Furstenburg and Cherlin (1991): *Divided Families: what happens to children when parents part*, by FJ Furstenburg and AJ Cherlin (Cambridge, Mass: Harvard University Press, 1991)

Ganghofer (1993): *Le Droit de la Famille en Europe, Son Évolution depuis l'Antiquité à nos Jours* (ed. by R Ganghofer, 1993, Strasbourg)

Gardiner and Martin (1963): *Law Reform NOW*, ed. by G Gardiner and A Martin (Gollancz, 1963)

Garland (1986): *Punishment and Welfare: a history of penal strategies* by D Garland (Aldershot: Gower, 1986)

Garnham and Knights (1994): *Putting the Treasury First, The truth about child support*, by A Garnham and E Knights (Child Poverty Action Group, 1994)

Gay (1984): *The Bourgeois Experience, Victoria to Freud*, Volume 1 (Education of the Senses) and Volume 2 (The Tender Passion) by Peter Gay (Oxford: Oxford Univeristy Press, 1984)

Geach and Szwed (1983): *Providing Civil Justice for Children*, ed. by H Geach and E Szwed (E Arnold, 1983)

Genn and Genn (1989): *The Effectiveness of Representation at Tribunals*, reports to the Lord Chancellor by H Genn and Y Genn (HMSO, 1989)

Gibson (1994): *Dissolving Wedlock*, by CS Gibson (Routledge, 1994)

Gies (1989): *Marriage and the family in the Middle Ages*, by FJ Gies (New York: Harper and Row, 1989)

Gilbert (1957): *The Claimant,* by M Gilbert (Constable, 1957)

Gilbert (1965): *Plough my own Furrow, The Story of Lord Allen of Hurtwood . . .,* by M Gilbert (Longmans, 1965)

Gilbert (1986): *Road to Victory, Winston S Churchill 1941–1945,* by M Gilbert (Heineman, 1986)

Gillis (1985): *For Better, for Worse: British Marriages, 1600 to the Present* (New York: Oxford University Press, 1985)

Gillis (1996): *A World of their own Making, A History of Myth and Ritual in Family Life*, by JR Gillis (Oxford: Oxford University Press, 1997)

Glendon (1977): *State, Law and Family*, by MA Glendon (Amsterdam: North Holland Publishing, 1977)

Glendon (1981): *The New Family and the New Property*, by MA Glendon (Toronto: Butterworths, 1981)

Glendon (1987): *Abortion and Divorce in Western Law: American Failures European Challenges*, by MA Glendon (Cambridge, Mass: Harvard University Press, 1987)

Goldstein, Freud and Solnit (1973): *Beyond the Best Interests of the Child*, by J Goldstein, A Freud and AJ Solnit (New York: Free Press, 1973)

Goldstein, Freud & Solnit (1980): *Before the Best interests of the child*, by J Goldstein, A Freud and AJ Solnit (Burnett, 1980)

Goldthorpe (1987): *Family Life in Western Societies: a historical sociology of family relationship in Britain and North America*, by JE Goldthorpe (Cambridge: Cambridge University Press, 1987)

Goodacre (1966): *Adoption policy and practice*, by I Goodacre (Allen and Unwin, 1966)

Goode (1963): *World Resolution and Family Patterns*, by WJ Goode (New York: Free Press, 1963)

Goodman (1997): *The State of the Nation: the Political Legacy of Aneurin Bevan* (ed. by G Goodman (Victor Gollancz, 1997)

Goodman (1993): *Tell them I'm on my Way*, by A Goodman (Chapmans, 1993)

Goody (1983): *The Development of the Family and Marriage in Europe*, by J Goody, (Cambridge: Cambridge University Press)

Gottlieb (1993): *The Family in the Western World, From the Black Death to the Industrial Age*, by B Gottlieb (Oxford: Oxford University Press, 1993)

Graveson and Crane (1957): *A Century of Family Law 1857–1957*, ed. by RH Graveson and FR Crane (Sweet & Maxwell, 1957)

Gray (1977): *Reallocation of Property on Divorce*, by KJ Gray (Abingdon: Professional Books, 1977)

Gray and Symes (1981): *Real Property for Real People*, by Kevin J Gray and P Symes (Butterworths, 1981)

Gregory and Foster (1990): *The Consequences of Divorce*, The Report of the 1984 OPCS Consequences of Divorce Survey carried out on behalf of the Lord Chancellor's Department, by J Gregory and K Foster (HMSO, 1990)

Gribble (1932): *The Fight for Divorce*, by FH Gribble (Hurst & Blackett Ltd, 1932)

Grierson (1959): *Storm Bird, The Strange Life of Georgina Weldon*, by E Grierson (Chatto, 1959)

Griffith (1966): *Central Departments and Local Authorities*, by JAG Griffith (George Allen & Unwin, 1966)

Griffith (1993): J Griffith, *Judicial Politics since 1920, A Chronicle* (Oxford: Blackwell Publishers, 1993)

Griffith, Ryle and Wheeler-Booth (1989): *Parliament, Functions, Practice and Procedures*, by J Griffith and M Ryle with MAJ Wheeler-Booth (Sweet & Maxwell, 1989)

Groner (1991): *Hilary's Trial, The Elizabeth Morgan Case: A Child's Ordeal in America's Legal System*, by J Groner (New York: Simon and Schuster, 1991)

Grubb and Pearl (1990): *Blood Testing Aids and DNA Profiling, Law and Policy*, by A Grubb and D Pearl (Bristol: Jordan Publishing Ltd, 1990)

Hale (1996): *From the Test Tube to the Coffin, Choice and Regulation in Private Life*, by B Hale (Sweet & Maxwell Ltd, 1996)

Hall (1975): *Social Services of Modern England* (10th ed. 1975, by J Mays with A Forder and O Keidan) (Routledge and Kegan Paul, 1975)

Hall (1976): *Reforming the Welfare. The politics of change in the Personal Social Services*, by P Hall (Heineman Educational, 1976)

Halsey (1988): *Trends in British Society since 1900: A Guide to the Changing Social Structure of Britain*, 2nd ed., by AH Halsey (Macmillan, 1988)

Halsey (1996): *No Discouragement: An Autobiography*, by AH Halsey (Macmillan Press Ltd, 1996)

Hamilton (1995): *Family, Law and Religion* by C Hamilton (Sweet & Maxwell, 1995)

Hamilton (1999): *The Warwickshire Scandal*, by E Hamilton (Michael Russell, 1999)

Hamilton and Standley (1995): *Family Law in Europe* by C Hamilton and K Standley (Butterworths, 1995)

Hammerton (1992): *Cruelty and Companionship: Conflict in nineteenth-century married life*, by AJ Hammerton (Routledge, 1992)

Hammond (1936): *Lord Shaftesbury*, by JL and B Hammond (Longmans, Green, 1936)

Harris (1977): *William Beveridge: A Biography*, by J Harris (Oxford: Oxford University Press, 1977)

Harris (1993): *Private Lives, Public Spirit, A Social History of Britain 1870–1914*, by J Harris (Oxford: Oxford University Press, 1993)

Harrison (1982): *Peaceable Kingdom: stability and change in modern Britain*, by BH Harrison (Oxford: Oxford University Press, 1982)

Harrison (1987): *Prudent Revolutionaries, Portraits of British Feminists between the Wars*, by BH Harrison (Oxford: Clarendon Press, 1987)

Harrison (1996): *The Transformation of British Politics 1860–1995*, by BH Harrison (Oxford: Oxford University Press, 1996)

Hart (1959): 'Immorality and Treason' reprinted from *The Listener*, 30 July 1959, in *The Law as Literature* (LJ Blom-Cooper, ed.) (Bodley Head, 1961)

Hart (1998): *Ask me No More, An Autobiography*, by J Hart (Peter Halban Publishers Ltd, 1998)

Hawkins (1997): *The Human Face of Law, Essays in Honour of Donald Harris*, ed. by K Hawkins (Oxford: Oxford University Press, 1997)

Hay (1967): *William Hay's Lectures on Marriage* ed. by John C Barry (Stair Society, Edinburgh, 1967)

Haynes (1912): *Divorce Problems of Today* by ESP Haynes (W Heffer & Sons Ltd, Cambridge, 1912)

Haynes (1915): *Divorce as it might be*, by ESP Haynes (W Heffer & Sons Ltd, Cambridge, 1915)

Haynes (1916): *The Decline of Liberty in England*, by ESP Haynes (Grant Richards Ltd, 1916)

Haynes (1926): *Lycurgus or The Future of Law* by ESP Haynes (Kegan Paul, Trench, Trubner & Co Ltd, 1926)

Haynes (1927): *Much ado about women* by ESP Haynes (The Cayme Press, Kensington, 1927)

Haynes (1936): *Life Law and Letters* by ESP Haynes (William Heinemann Ltd, 1936)

Haynes (1936b): *A Lawyer's Notebook* by ESP Haynes (with an Introduction by Alec Waugh) (Martin Secker & Warburg Ltd, 1936)

Haynes (1951): *The Lawyer, A Conversation Piece*, selected from the Lawyer's Notebooks and other writings by ESP Haynes 1877–1949, with an autobiographical introduction and memoir by Renee Haynes (Eyre & Spottiswoode (Publishers) Ltd 1951)

Haynes and Walker-Smith (1935): *Divorce and its Problems* by ESP Haynes and D Walker-Smith (Methuen & Co Ltd, 1935)

Hayward (1845): *Remarks regarding marriage with the sister of a deceased wife*, by A Hayward (W Benning, 1845)

Helmholz (1974): *Marriage Litigation in Medieval England*, by RH Helmholz (Cambridge: Cambridge University Press, 1974)

Helmholz (1987): *Canon Law and the Law of England*, by RH Helmholz (London, Hambledon, 1987)

Hendrick (1994): *Child Welfare, England 1872–1989*, by H Hendrick (Routledge, 1994)

Henriques (1950): *The Indiscretions of a Magistrate*, by BLQ Henriques (George G Harrap & Co, 1950)

Henson (1920): *A Memoir of the Right Honourable Sir William Anson*, by HH Henson (Oxford: Oxford University Press, 1920)

Herbert (1934): *Holy Deadlock*, by AP Herbert (Methuen, 1934)

Herbert (1935): *Letter to the Electors of Oxford University from AP Herbert, New College 1910–1914, Independent National Candidate* (published by the author, 1935)

Herbert (1937): *The Ayes Have it, The Story of the Marriage Bill*, by AP Herbert (Methuen, 1937)

Herbert (1950): *Independent Member*, by AP Herbert (Methuen, 1950)

Herbert (1954): *The Right to Marry*, by AP Herbert (Methuen, 1954)

Hershman and McFarlane (2000): *Children Law and Practice*, 2 Vols, by D Hershman and A McFarlane QC (with Consultant Editors) (Bristol: Jordan Publishing Limited, 2000, with subsequent loose leaf supplements)

Heuston (1964): *Lives of the Lord Chancellors 1885–1940*, by RFV Heuston (Oxford: Clarendon Press, 1964)

Heuston (1987): *Lives of the Lord Chancellors 1940–1970*, by RFV Heuston (Oxford: Clarendon Press, Oxford, 1987)

Heywood (1965): *Children in Care: the development of the service for the deprived child*, 2nd ed. 1965, by JS Heywood (Routledge and Kegan Paul, 1965)

Heywood (1978): *Children in Care: the development of the service for the deprived child*, 3rd ed. 1978 by JS Heywood (Routledge and Kegan Paul, 1978)

Hilgendorf (1981): *Social workers & solicitors in child care cases*, by L Hilgendorf (HMSO, 1981)

Hoggett (1993): *Parents and Children: The Law of Parental Responsibility*, by BM Hoggett (Sweet & Maxwell, 1993)

Hoggett and Pearl (1991): *The Family, Law and Society*, by BM Hale and others (5th ed. 2002)

Holcombe (1983); *Wives and Property; Reform of the Married Women's Property Law in 19th–Century England*, by L Holcombe (Oxford: Martin Robertson, 1983)

Hollis (1974): *Pressure from Without*, by P Hollis (E Arnold, 1974)

Hollis (1979): *Women in Public Life: The Women's Movement 1850–1900*, by P Hollis (George Allen and Unwin, 1979)

Hollis (1987): *Ladies Elect, Women in English Local Government 1865–1914*, by P Hollis (Oxford: Oxford University Press, 1987)

Hollis (1997): *Jennie Lee, A Life*, by P Hollis (Oxford: Oxford University Press, 1997)

Holmes (1900): *Pictures and Problems from London Police Courts*, by T Holmes, (E Arnold, 1900)

Home Office (1983): *The Home Office, Perspectives on Policy and Administration, Bicentenary Lectures 1982* (Royal Institute of Public Administration, 1982)

Home Office (1984): *Magistrates' Domestic Courts: New Perspectives*, ed. by JF Marshall (Home Office Research and Planning Unit, 1984)

Honoré (1978): *Sex Law*, by T Honoré (Duckworth, 1978)

Hooper and Murch (1990): *The Family Justice System and its Support Services*, a Concluding Report to the Nuffield Trustees, by D Hooper and M Murch (1990)

Hopkinson (1954): *Family Inheritance, a Life of Eva Hubback,* by D Hopkinson (Staples Press, 1954)

Hopkinson (1968): *The Incense Tree,* by D Hopkinson (Routledge and Kegan Paul, 1968)

Hoppen (1998): *The Mid-Victorian Generation 1846–1886,* by KT Hoppen (Oxford: Oxford University Press, 1998)

Horne (2000): *Telling Lives, from WB Yeats to Bruce Chatwin,* ed. by A Horne (Macmillan, 2000)

Horstman (1985): *Victorian Divorce*, by A Horstman (Croom Helm, 1985)

Houlbrooke (1984): *The English Family 1450–1700*, by R A Houlbrooke (Longmans, 1984)

Howard (1904): *A History of Matrimonial Institutions, chiefly in England and the United States*, by GE Howard (Chicago, 1904)

Howarth (1986): *Intelligence Chief Extraordinary, The Life of the Ninth Duke of Portland*, by P Howarth (Bodley Head, 1986)

Hubback (1924): *The Government's Guardianship of Infants Bill, 1924*, by E Hubback (National Union of Societies for Equal Citizenship, 1924)

Hubback (1948): *The Population of Britain,* by E Hubback (Pelican, 1948)

Hutchins and Harrison (1936): *A History of Factory Legislation*, by BL Hutchins and A Harrison (3rd ed., 1936)

Ingleby (1992): *Solicitors and Divorce,* by R Ingleby (Oxford: Oxford University Press, 1992)

Ingram (1988): *Church Courts, Sex and Marriage in England 1570–1640*, by M Ingram (Cambridge: Cambridge University Press, 1988)

Jackson (1969): *The Formation and Annulment of Marriage*, by Joseph Jackson, 2nd ed., Butterworths, 1969)

Jackson (1992): *Jackson's Matrimonial Finance and Taxation*, by R Hayward Smith, CR Newton, and DTA Davies 5th ed., 1992; subsequently to 7th ed. 2002 by R Hayward Smith and CR Newton (Buttterworths, 1992)

Jalland (1988): *Women, Marriage and Politics 1860–1940*, by P Jalland (Oxford: Oxford University Press, 1988)

Jeffery (1999): *Anthony Crosland, A New Biography*, by K Jeffery (Richard Cohen Books, 1999)

Jenkins (1965): *Sir Charles Dilke: A Victorian Tragedy*, by R Jenkins (Collins, 1965)

Jenks (1909): *Husband and Wife in the Law*, by E Jenks (JM Dent, 1909)

Jones (1984): *Eileen Younghusband, A Biography*, by K Jones (Bedford Square Press, 1984)

Jones and Miller (1996): *The Politics of the Family*, by H Jones and K Miller (Aldershot: Avebury, 1996)

Jordan (1959): *Philanthropy in England 1480–1660*, by WK Jordan (George Allen and Unwin, 1959)

Jowell and Oliver (2000): *The Changing Constitution*, ed. by J Jowell and D Oliver, 4th ed. (Oxford: Oxford University Press, 2000)

Juxon (1983): *Lewis and Lewis*, by J Juxon (Collins, 1983)

Katz, Eekelaar and Maclean (2000): *Cross Currents, Family Law and Policy in the US and England* ed. by SN Katz, JM Eekelaar and M Maclean (Oxford: Oxford University Press, 2000)

Kellmer-Pringle (1975): *The Needs of Children*, by ML Kellmer-Pringle (Hutchinson, 1975)

Kenny (1879): *The History of the Law of England as to the Effects of Marriage on Property and on the Wife's Legal Capacity*, by CS Kenny (London, 1879)

Kent (1979): *In on the Act: Memoirs of a Lawmaker*, by Sir HS Kent (Macmillan, 1979)

Kevles (1995): *In the name of Eugenics*, by DJ Kevles, 3rd ed. (Cambridge, Mass.: Harvard University Press, 1995)

Kiernan, Land and Lewis (1998): *Lone Motherhood in Twentieth Century Britain*, by K Kiernan, H Land and J Lewis (Oxford: Oxford University Press, 1998)

Kilmuir (1964): *Political Adventure, The Memoirs of the Earl of Kilmuir* (David Maxwell-Fyffe) (Weidenfeld and Nicolson, 1964)

King and Piper (1995): *How the Law Thinks About Children*, by M King and C Piper, 2nd ed. (Aldershot: Arena, 1995)

Kirk (1948): *Marriage and Divorce*, by KE Kirk, 2nd ed.(Hodder and Stoughton, 1948)

Klein (1965): *Britain's Married Women Workers*, by V Klein (Routledge and Kegan Paul, 1965)

Klier and Mingay (1995): *The Search for Anastasia,* by JD Klier and H Mingay (Smith Gryphon, 1995)

Krause (1971): *Illegitimacy: Law and Social Policy*, by HD Krause (Bobbs-Merrill, Indianapolis, 1971)

Krause (1988): *Family Law*, by HD Krause (Black Letter Series, West Publishing & Co, 1988)

Krause (1992): *Family Law* (International Library of Essays in Law and Legal Theory) ed. by HD Krause (Dartmouth Publishing Co Ltd, Aldershot, 1992)

Krause (1992b): *Child Law: Parent, Child and State*, by HD Krause (Vols 1 and 2, Dartmouth Publishing Co Ltd, Aldershot, 1992)

Krause (1995): *Family Law in a Nutshell* by HD Krause (St. Paul Minn, 1995)

La Fontaine (1990): *Child Sexual Abuse*, by JS La Fontaine (Cambridge: Polity, 1990)

Laing (1960): *The Divided Self*, by RD Laing (Tavistock, 1960)

Laing (1971): *The Politics of the Family and other Essays*, by RD Laing (Tavistock Publications, 1971)

Lambert & Seglow (1988): *Report for Department of Health and Welsh Office, Adoption Allowances in England & Wales: The early years*, by L Lambert & J Seglow (1988)

Laslett and Wall (1972): *Household and Family in Past Times*, by P Laslett and R Wall (Cambridge: Cambridge University Press, 1972)

Laslett et al. (1980): *Bastardy and its Comparative History*, by P Laslett, K Oosterveen and RM Smith (E Arnold, 1980)

Latey (1973): *Latey on Divorce: the Law and Practice in Divorce and Matrimonial Causes*, 15th ed. by W Latey (editor in chief) and others (Longman, 1973) (This work was originally an adaptation of *A Treatise on the Principles and Practice of the Court for Divorce and Matrimonial Causes*, by G Browne (1863))

Law Society (1979): *A Better Way Out*, a discussion paper prepared by the Family Law Sub-Committee of The Law Society (The Law Society, 1979)

Leckie (1999): *Culture and Adultery, The Novel, the Newspaper and the Law*, by B Leckie (Philadelphia: University of Pennsylvania Press, 1999)

Lee (1974): *Divorce Law Reform in England* by BH Lee (Peter Owen Limited, 1974)

Lees (1998): *The Solidarities of Strangers. The English Poor Law and the People 1700–1948*, by LH Lees (Cambridge: Cambridge University Press, 1998)

Legal Aid Board (1996): *Legal Aid Handbook 1996/7*, prepared by The Legal Aid Board (Sweet & Maxwell, 1996)

Lewis (1980): *The Politics of Motherhood* by J Lewis (Croom Helm, 1980)

Lewis (1984) *Women in England, 1870–1950* by J Lewis (Brighton: Wheatsheaf, 1984)

Lewis (1986): *Labour and Love, Women's Experience of Home and Family, 1850–1946* by J Lewis (Oxford: Blackwell Publishing, 1986)

Lewis (1993): *Lord Atkin,* by G Lewis (Butterworths, 1993)

Lewis (1997): *Lord Hailsham, A Life,* by G Lewis (Random House, 1997)

Lewis, Clark and Morgan (1992): *Whom God hath Joined Together, The Work of Marriage Guidance,* by J Lewis, D Clark and D Morgan (Tavistock, Routledge, 1992)

Lockhart (1949): *Cosmo Gordon Lang,* by JG Lockhart (Hodder and Stoughton, 1949)

Lowe (1999): *The Welfare State in Britain since 1945* by R Lowe, 2nd ed. (Basingstoke: Macmillan, 1999)

Lowe and White (1986): *Wards of Court,* by NV Lowe and RAH White, 2nd ed. (Butterworths, 1986)

Lush (1933): *Lush on the Law of Husband and Wife,* 4th ed. by SN Grant-Bailey (Stevens & Sons Ltd, 1933)

Lutyens (1965): *Effie in Venice,* by M Lutyens (John Murray, 1965)

Lutyens (1967): *Millais and the Ruskins,* by M Lutyens (John Murray, 1967)

Lyman (1957): *The First Labour Government 1924* (Chapman and Hall, 1957)

McCarthy (1989): *Eric Gill,* by F McCarthy (Faber, 1989)

Macfarlane (1978): *The Origins of English Individualism: the Family, Property and Social Transition,* by A Macfarlane (Oxford: Oxford University Press, 1978)

Macfarlane (1986): *Marriage and Love in England, Modes of Reproduction 1300–1840,* by A Macfarlane (Oxford: Blackwell, 1986)

McGregor (1957): *Divorce in England, A Centenary Study,* by OR McGregor (Heinemann, 1957)

McGregor (1981): *Social History and Law Reform* (The Hamlyn Lectures, 31st Series, 1981) by OR McGregor, Baron McGregor of Durris (Sweet and Maxwell, 1981)

McGregor et al. (1970): *Separated Spouses, A Study of the matrimonial jurisdiction of magistrates' courts* by OR McGregor, L Blom-Cooper, and C Gibson (Duckworth, 1970)

Machin (1998): *Churches and Social Issues in Twentieth-Century Britain,* by GIT Machin (Oxford: Oxford University Press, 1998)

McKibbin (1998): *Classes and Cultures: England 1918–1951,* by R McKibbin (Oxford: Oxford University Press, 1998)

MacKinnon (1940): *On Circuit 1924–1937,* by Sir FD MacKinnon (Cambridge: Cambridge University Press, 1940)

Maclean and Eekelaar (1997): *The Parental Obligation, A Study of parenthood across households* (Oxford: Hart Publishing, 1997)

Macpherson (1841): *Law Relating to Infants,* by W Macpherson (1841)

Macqueen (1842): *A Practical Treatise on the Appellate Jurisdiction of the House of Lords and Privy Council together with the Practice of Parliamentary Divorce,* by J Macqueen (A Maxwell & Son, 1842)

Macqueen (1849): *The Rights and Liabilities of Husband and Wife,* by JF Macqueen (S Sweet, 1849)

Macqueen (1860): *A Practical Treatise on the Law of Marriage, Divorce, and Legitimacy,* by JF Macqueen, 2nd ed. (W Maxwell, H Sweet and V&R Stevens, 1860)

Maidment (1982): *Judicial Separation: A Research Study,* by S Maidment (Oxford, Centre for Socio-Legal Studies, Wolfson College, 1982)

Maidment (1984): *Child Custody and Divorce*, by S Maidment (Croom Helm, 1984)

Manchester (1980): *A Modern Legal History of England and Wales 1750–1950*, by AH Manchester (Butterworths, 1980)

Manchester (1984): *Sources of English Legal History, Law History and Society in England and Wales 1750–1950* by AH Manchester (Butterworths, 1984)

Marjoribanks (1929): *The Life of Sir Edward Marshall Hall*, by E Marjoribanks (Victor Gollancz, 1929)

Marsden (1973): *Mothers Alone*, by Dennis Marsden, revised ed. 1973 (Penguin, 1973)

Marsh (1998): *The changing social structure of England and Wales 1871–1961*, by DC Marsh (Routledge, 1998)

Marwick (1998): *The Sixties, Cultural Revolution in Britain, France, Italy and the United States, 1958–1974*, by A Marwick (Oxford: Oxford University Press, 1998)

Masson (1983): *Mine, Yours or Ours? A study of step-parent adoption*, by J Masson, D Norbury and SG Chatterton (HMSO, 1983)

Masson (1990): *The Children Act 1989, Text and Commentary*, by J Masson (Sweet & Maxwell, 1990)

Masson (1992): *The Assault on Truth: Freud and Child Sex Abuse*, by J Masson, (Fontana, 1992)

Matthew (1994): *The Gladstone Diaries* ed. by HCG Matthew, vols. 5 and 12 (Oxford: Oxford University Press, 1998)

Matthews and Oulton (1971): *Legal Aid and Advice under the Legal Aid Acts 1949 to 1964*, by EJT Matthews and ADM Oulton (Butterworths, 1971)

Megarry and Wade (1966): *The Law of Real Property*, by RE Megarry and HWR Wade, 3rd ed. (Stevens and Sons Ltd, 1966)

Menefee (1981): *Wives for Sale*, by SP Menefee (Oxford: Blackwells, 1981)

Meulders-Klein (1997): *Familles et Justice* ed. by MT Meulders-Klein (Brussels: Editions Bruylant, 1997)

Mill (1869): *The Subjection of Women*, by JS Mill (First edition, 1869; reprinted Everyman's Library, JM Dent & Son Ltd, 1929 and subsequently)

Millham et al. (1986): *Lost in Care*, by S Millham, R Bullock, K Hosie and M Haak (Aldershot: Gower, 1986)

Morgan (1984); *Labour in Power 1945–1951*, by KO Morgan (Oxford: Oxford University Press, 1984)

Morgan (1991): *Edwina Mountbatten, A Life of Her Own*, by J Morgan (Harper Collins, 1991)

Morgan (1997): *Callaghan: A Life*, by KO Morgan (Oxford: Oxford University Press, 1997)

Morgan (1998): *Adoption and the Care of Children: The British and American Experience*, by P Morgan (IEA Health and Welfare Trust, 1998)

Morgan (1999): *Farewell to the Family?*, by P Morgan, 2nd revised edition, Institute of Economic Affairs (1999)

Morris et al. (1980): *Justice for Children*, by A Morris, H Giller, E Szwed and H Geach (Macmillan, 1980)

Morrison (1960): *Herbert Morrison, An Autobiography*, by Lord Morrison of Lambeth (Odhams Press, 1960)

Morrison (1964): *Government and Parliament: A Survey from the Inside*, by Lord Morrison of Lambeth, 3rd ed. (Oxford: Oxford University Press, 1964)

Mortimer (1947): *Marriage in Church and State*, by TA Lacey, 1st edition 1912, revised by R Mortimer (SPCK, 1947)

Mortlock (1972): *The Inside of Divorce*, by B Mortlock (Constable, 1972)

Mount (1982): *The Subversive Family*, by F Mount (Jonathan Cape, 1982)

Mullins (1921): *The Leipzig Trials, An Account of the War Criminals' Trials and a Study of German Mentality*, by C Mullins (HF&G Witherby, 1921)

Mullins (1931): *In Quest of Justice*, by C Mullins (John Murray, 1931)

Mullins (1935): *Wife v. Husband in the Courts*, by C Mullins (George Allen & Unwin, 1935)

Mullins (1948): *Fifteen Years Hard Labour*, by C Mullins (Victor Gollancz Ltd, 1948)

Mullins (1954): *Marriage Failures and the Children*, by C Mullins (Epworth Press, 1954)

Mullins (1963): *One Man's Furrow*, by C Mullins (Johnson, 1963)

Mullins (1957): *The Sentence on the Guilty*, by C Mullins (Chichester: Justice of the Peace Ltd, Chichester, 1957)

Murch (1980): *Justice and Welfare in Divorce*, by M Murch (Sweet & Maxwell, 1980)

Murch (1987): *The Overlapping Family Jurisdiction of Magistrates' and County Courts*, by M Murch (with M Borkowski, R Copner and M Griew) (Bristol: University of Bristol, 1987)

Murch (1992): *The Family Justice System*, by M Murch (with D Hooper), (Bristol: Jordan Publishing Ltd, 1992)

Murch and Hooper (1988): *The Family Justice System*, by M Murch and D Hooper (Bristol: Bristol University Socio-Legal Centre for Family Studies, 1988)

Murch et al. (1992): *Management information and the family jurisdictions . . .*, by M Murch, and K Griew with R Copner (Bristol: Jordan Publishing Ltd, 1992)

Murch et al. (1996): *Safeguarding Children's Welfare in Uncontentious Divorce: A Study of s 41 of the Matrimonial Causes Act 1973*, by M Murch and others (Lord Chancellor's Department, Research Series No 7/99, 1999)

Murch, Hunt and Macleod (1990): *Representation of the Child in Civil Proceedings*, by M Murch, J Hunt and A Macleod (Bristol: Bristol University Socio-Legal Centre for Family Studies, 1990)

Murch, Lowe, Borkowski et al. (1993): *Pathways to Adoption: Research Project*, by M Murch, N Lowe, M Borkowski, R Copner and K Griew (HMSO, 1993)

Nacro (1992): *Criminal Justice and the Prevention of Child Sexual Abuse*, the report of a Committee set up by the National Association for the Care and Resettlement of Offenders (NACRO, 1992)

Napley (1982): *Not Without Prejudice, The memoirs of Sir David Napley* (Harrap, 1992)

Newburn (1992): *Permission and Regulation: law and morals in post-war Britain*, by T Newburn (Routledge, 1992)

Newell (1989): *Children are people too: the case against physical punishment*, by P Newell (Bedford Square Press, 1989)

Newsam (1954): *The Home Office*, by Sir Frank Newsam (George Allen & Unwin Ltd, 1954)

Nicolson (1952): *George V, His Life and Reign*, by H Nicolson (Constable, 1952)

Nissel (1987): *People Count, A History of the General Register Office*, by M Nissel (HMSO, 1987)

Oakley (1974): *Housewife*, by A Oakley (Allen Lane, 1974)

Offer (1981): *Property and Politics 1870–1914 . . .*, by A Offer (Cambridge, Cambridge University Press, 1981)

O'Neill (1981): *A Place Called Hope*, by Tom O'Neill (Oxford: Basil Blackwell, 1981)

Oughton (1997): *Tyler's Family Provision*, 3rd ed. by R Oughton (Butterworths, 1997)

Outhwaite (1981): *Marriage and society, Studies in the Social History of Marriage*, by RB Outhwaite (Europa, 1981)

Outhwaite (1995): *Clandestine Marriage in England, 1500–1850*, by RB Outhwaite (Hambledon, 1995)

Owen (1992): *Time to Declare*, by D Owen (Revised ed., Penguin Books, 1992)

Packman (1981): *The Child's Generation, Child Care Policy in Britain*, by J Packman, 2nd ed. (Oxford: Blackwell, 1981)

Packman (1986): *Who Needs Care?* by J Packman (Oxford: Blackwell, 1986)

Pahl (1989): *Money and Marriage*, by J Pahl (Basingstoke, Macmillan Education, 1989)

Pannick (1987): *Judges*, by D Pannick (Oxford: Oxford University Press, 1987)

Pannick (1992): *Advocates*, by D Pannick (Oxford: Oxford University Press, 1992)

Parker (1965): *Local Health and Welfare Services*, by J Parker (Allen & Unwin, 1965)

Parker (1990): *Informal Marriage, Cohabitation and the Law, 1750–1989*, by S Parker (Basingstoke: Macmillan Education, 1990)

Parker (1991): *Cohabitees*, by S Parker, 3rd ed. (Longman, 1991)

Parkinson (1997): *Family Mediation*, by L Parkinson (Sweet & Maxwell, 1997)

Parry and Clark, *The Law of Succession*, 10th ed., by R Kerridge (Sweet & Maxwell, 1996)

Parton (1985): *The Politics of Child Abuse,* by N Parton (Basingstoke, Macmillan Education, 1985)

Parton (1991): *Governing the Family*, by N Parton (Basingstoke, Macmillan Education 1991)

Paton (1935): *Proletarian Pilgrimage*, by J Paton (G Routledge & Sons Ltd, 1935)

Paton (1936): *Left Turn* by J Paton (M Secker & Warburg Ltd, 1936)

Pedersen (1993): *Family, Dependence and the Origins of the Welfare State: Britain and France 1914–1945* by S Pedersen (Cambridge: Cambridge University Press, 1993)

Pellew (1982): *The Home Office 1848–1914: from clerks to bureaucrats*, by J Pellew (Heinemann Educational Books, 1982)

Perkin (1989): *Women and Marriage in Nineteenth-Century England*, by J Perkin, (Routledge, 1989)

Phillips (1988): *Putting Asunder, A History of Divorce in Western Society*, by R Phillips (Cambridge, Cambridge University Press, 1988)

Phipson (1898): *The Law of Evidence*, by SL Phipson (2nd ed., 1898)

Pierson (1899): *George Muller of Bristol*, by AT Pierson (5th ed. 1899, James Nisbet & Co)

Pinchbeck & Hewitt (1968)(1973): *Children in English Society*, by I Pinchbeck and M Hewitt (Routledge & Kegan Paul, vol. I 1968, vol II 1973)

Platt (1969): *The Child Savers*, by AM Platt (Chicago: University of Chicago Press, 1969)

Polden (1988): Guide to the Records of The Lord Chancellor's Department (HMSO, 1988)

Polden (1999): *A History of the County Court, 1846–1971*, by P Polden (Cambridge: University Press, 1999)

Pollock (1983): *Forgotten Children: parent child relations from 1500–1900* by L Pollock (Cambridge, Cambridge University Press, 1983)

Pollock (1987): *A Lasting Relationship: Parents and Children over Three Centuries*, by L Pollock (University Press of New England, 1987)

Pollock and Maitland (1898): *The History of English Law*, by Sir Frederick Pollock and Frederic William Maitland (Cambridge: Cambridge University Press, 2nd ed., 1898, reissued 1968)

Porter and Hall (1995): *The Facts of Life: The creation of Sexual Knowledge in Britain, 1650–1950*, by R Porter and L Hall (Yale University Press, 1995)

Posner (1992): *Sex and Reason*, by RA Posner (Cambridge, Mass.: Harvard University Press, 1992)

Poster (1978): *Critical Theory of the Family*, by M Poster (Pluto Press, 1978)

Potter and Monroe (1956): *Potter and Monroe's Tax Planning with Precedents*, 2nd ed. by DC Potter and HH Monroe (Sweet & Maxwell, 1956)

Poulter (1986): *English Law and Ethnic Minority Customs*, by S Poulter (Butterworths, 1986)

Pound (1976): *AP Herbert, A Biography,* by R Pound (Joseph, 1976)

Poynter (1824): *A concise view of the doctrine and practice of the ecclesiastical courts in Doctors commons, on various points relative to the subject of marriage and divorce*, by Thomas Poynter (2nd ed., 1824)

Prochaska (1980): *Women and Philanthropy in Nineteenth-Century England*, by FK Prochaska (Oxford: Oxford University Press, 1980)

Pugh (1981): *Pugh's Matrimonial Proceedings before Magistrates,* by JB Horsman, 4th ed. (Butterworths, 1981)

Pugh (2000): *Women and the Women's Movement in Britain 1914–1999*, by M Pugh (Basingstoke, Macmillan Education, 2000)

Radzinowicz and Hood (1986): *A History of the English Criminal Law and its Administration from 1750* by Sir L Radzinowicz and R Hood, 5 volumes (Stevens, 1948–86)

Rathbone (1924): *The Disinherited Family, A Plea for the Endowment of the Family*, by EF Rathbone (E Arnold, 1924)

Rayden (1910): *Practice and Law in the Divorce Division*, by W Rayden (Butterworths, 1910)

Rayden (1926): *Rayden's Practice and Law in the Divorce Division*, 2nd ed. 1926, by C Mortimer and CTA Wilkinson (Butterworths, 1926)

Rayden (1932): *Rayden's Practice and Law in the Divorce Division*, 3rd ed. 1932, by C Mortimer and HHH Coates (Butterworths, 1932)

Rayden (1942): *Rayden's Practice and Law in the Divorce Division*, 4th ed. 1942, by N Middleton, CTA Wilkinson, JF Compton Miller, and FC Ottway (Butterworths, 1942)

Rayden (1967): *Rayden's Practice and Law in the Divorce Division*, 10th ed. 1967, by J Jackson, RB Rowe, and M Booth, with WDS Caird (Butterworths, 1967)

Rayden (1971): *Rayden's Practice and Law in Divorce and Family Matters*, 11th ed. 1971, by J Jackson, CF Turner, M Booth and EW Morris, with WDS Caird (Butterworths, 1971)

Rayden and Jackson (1997): *Rayden & Jackson's Law and Practice in Divorce and Family Matters*, 17th ed. by N Wall and others (Butterworths, 1997)

Redlich (1903): *Local Government in England*, by J Redlich, ed. by FW Hirst (1903)(Book 1 was reissued in 1958 under the title *The History of Local Government in England*, and a second edition with introduction and epilogue by B Keith-Lucas was published by Macmillan in 1970)

Reiss (1934): *The Rights and Duties of English Women*, by E Reiss (Manchester, Sherratt & Hughes, 1934)

Rheinstein (1972): *Marriage Stability, Divorce and the Law* by M Rheinstein (Chicago University Press, 1972)

Richards (1964): *Honourable Members: A Study of the British Backbencher*, by PG Richards, 2nd ed. (Faber and Faber, 1964)

Richards (1970): *Parliament and Conscience*, by PG Richards (George Allen & Unwin, 1970)

Richards (1983): *The Local Government System*, by PG Richards (George Allen & Unwin, 1983)

Richards and Light (1986): *Children of Social Worlds: Development in a Social Context*, ed. by M Richards and P Light (Cambridge: Polity, 1986)

Riley (1991): *Divorce: An American Tradition*, by G Riley (Oxford: Oxford University Press, 1991)

Roberts (1979): *Order and Dispute*, by S Roberts (Oxford: Martin Robertson, 1979)

Roberts (1997): *Mediation in Family Disputes* by M Roberts, 2nd ed. (Arena, 1997)

Rose (1986): *The Relief of Poverty 1834–1914*, by ME Rose, 2nd ed. (Macmillan, 1986)

Rose (1989): *For the Sake of the Children: Inside Dr Barnado's, 120 years of caring for children,* by J Rose (Fuutura, 1989)

Rosen (1975): *Matrimonial Offences*, by L Rosen, 3rd ed. (Oyez, 1975)

Rowe and Lambert (1973): *Children who Wait*, by J Rowe and L Lambert (Association of British Adoption Societies, 1973)

Rowe et al. (1984): *Long-term Foster Care*, by J Rowe, H Kane, M Hundleby and A Keene (Batsford, British Agencies for Adoption and Fostering, 1984)

Rowe et al. (1989): *Child Care Now*, by J Rowe, M Hindleby and L Garnett (British Agencies for Adoption and Fostering, 1989)

Royle (1987) *Modern Britain: a social history 1750–1985*, by E Royle (E Arnold, 1987)

Rubin and Sugarman (1984): *Law Economy and Society, Essays in the History of English Law 1750 1914*, ed. by GR Rubin and D Sugarman (Abingdon: Professional Books, 1984)

Rubinstein (1986): *Before the Suffragettes: Women's Emancipation in the 1890s*, by D Rubinstein (Brighton: Harvester, 1986)

Ruskin (1865): *Sesame and Lilies*, by J Ruskin (1864), two lectures delivered in Manchester in 1864, ed. by S Wragge (T Nelson and Sons Ltd, 1937)

Russell (1923): *My Life and Adventures*, by Earl Russell (Cassel and Co Ltd, 1923)

Russell (1930): *Divorce as I see It* (Noel Douglas, 1930)

Russell (1966): *Divorce*, by B Russell and others (New York: Johns Day Co, 1966)

St Aubyn (1963): *The Royal George 1819–1904, The Life of HRH Prince George, Duke of Cambridge* by G St. Aubyn (Constable & Co, 1963)

Scarisbrick (1997): *Henry VIII*, by J Scarisbrick, 2nd ed. (Yale University Press, New Haven and London, 1997)

Scarman (1971): *Women and Equality before the Law* (Bristol: Bristol University, 1971)

Scottish Office (1990): *The Resolution of Financial Disputes in Divorce* (Scottish Office, Central Research Unit Papers)

Segalen (1986): *Historical Anthropology of the Family*, by Martine Segalen, (translated from *Sociologie de la Famille*, 1981, Paris) (Cambridge: Cambridge University Press, 1986)

Seglow et al. (1972): *Growing Up Adopted,* by J Seglow, ML Kellmer-Pringle, and PL Wedge (National Council for Education and Research in England and Wales, 1972)

Seymour (1995): *Ragged Schools, Ragged Children,* by C Seymour (Ragged School Museum Trust, 1995)

Shanley (1989): *Feminism, Marriage, and the Law in Victorian England 1850–1895*, by ML Shanley (Princeton: Princeton University Press)

Shannon (1999): *Gladstone, Peel's Inheritor 1809–1865*, by R Shannon (Allen Lane, The Penguin Press, 1999)

Shapiro and Garry (1998): *Trial and Error, An Oxford Anthology of Legal Stories*, ed. by FR Shapiro and J Garry (New York: Oxford University Press, 1998)

Shelford, *A Practical Treatise of the Law of Marriage and Divorce and Registration*, by L Shelford (C Sweet, 1841)

Sheppard (1957): *George, Duke of Cambridge, A Memoir of his Private Life*, ed. by E Sheppard, vol 2 (George Allen and Unwin, 1957)

Shorter (1977): *The Making of the Modern Family*, by E Shorter (New York: Basic Books, 1977)

Simon (1926): *A City Council from Within*, by ED Simon (Longmans, Green and Co. Ltd, 1926)

Simpson (1925): *A Treatise on the Law and Practice Relating to Infants,* by AH Simpson 1st ed., 1875; 4th ed. (Stevens & Haynes, 1925)

Skyrme (1983): *The Changing Face of the Magistracy*, by T Skyrme, 2nd ed. (Macmillan, 1983)

Skyrme (1994): *History of the Justices of the Peace*, by Sir T Skyrme, 2nd ed. (Chichester: B Rose, 1994)

Slesser (1941): *Judgment Reserved*, by Sir H Slesser (Hutchinson, 1941)

Smart (1984): *The Ties That Bind: Law, Marriage and the Reproduction of Patriarchal Relations*, by C Smart (Routledge & Kegan Paul, 1984)

Smart (1989): *Feminism and the Power of Law*, by C Smart (Routledge, 1989)

Smart and Sevenhuijsen (1989): *Child Custody and the Politics of Gender*, by C Smart and S Sevenhuijsen (Routledge, 1989)

Smith (1989): *Domestic Violence: An overview of the literature*, by LJF Smith (Home Office Research Study No. 107)

Smith (1993): *A Queen on Trial: the affair of Queen Caroline, 1820–1821*, by EA Smith (Stroud, Glos.: Alan Sutton Publishing, 1993)

Smith Bailey and Gunn (2002): *The Modern English Legal System*, 4th ed. by SH Bailey J Ching, MJ Gunn and D Ormerod (Sweet & Maxwell, 2002)

Snell (1929): *Will Democracy Last?*, by H Snell, MP, The First Horace Seal Memorial Lecture given before the Ethical Union of London on 21 March 1929 (The Ethical Union, 1929)

Snell (1930): *Daily Life in Parliament*, by H Snell, MP (Routledge, 1930)

Snell (1935): *The Ethical Movement Explained*, by Lord Snell, CBE (The Ethical Union, 1935)

Snell (1936): *Men, Movements and Myself*, by Lord Snell, CBE, LLD (JM Dent and Sons Ltd, 1936)

Snell (1940): *Britain, America, and World Leadership*, by Lord Snell, PC, CBE, LLD, The Conway Memorial Lecture delivered at Conway Hall, Red Lion Square, WC1, on March 17, 1940 (1940)

Snell (1947): *The New World*, by Lord Snell, CBE, LLD (London: Watts, 1947)

Snell (1990): *Snell's Principles of Equity*, 27th ed. by RE Megarry and PV Baker (Sweet and Maxwell, 1990)

Snell (2000): *Snell's Principles of Equity*, 30th ed. by J McGhee (Sweet and Maxwell, 2000)

Squibb (1977): *Doctors' Commons*, by GD Squibb (Oxford: Oxford University Press, 1977)

Star (1996): *Counsel of Perfection, The Family Court in Australia*, by L Star (Oxford: Oxford University Press, 1996)

Staves (1990): *Married Women's Separate Property in England, 1660–1833*, by S Staves (Cambridge, Mass.: Harvard University Press, 1990)

Stead (1885): *The Maiden Tribute of Modern Babylon—the Report of the Pall Mall Gazette's Secret Commission* (1885)

Stenton (1927): *The English Woman in History*, by DM Stenton (1927)

Stephen (1873): *Liberty, Equality and Fraternity*, by L Stephen (1873)

Stetson (1982): *The Politics of Family Law Reform*, by DM Stetson (Westport, USA: Greenwood Press, 1982)

Stevens (1993): *The Independence of the Judiciary. The View from the Lord Chancellor's Office*, by R Stevens (Oxford: Oxford University Press, 1993)

Stocks (1949): *Eleanor Rathbone. A Biography*, by M Stocks (Gollancz, 1949)

Stone (1882): *Stone's Practice for Justices of the Peace*, 9th ed. (Stevens, 1882)

Stone (1977): *The Family, Sex and Marriage in England, 1500–1800*, by L Stone, (Weidenfeld & Nicolson, 1977)

Stone (1990): *Road to Divorce, England 1530–1987*, by L Stone (Oxford: Oxford University Press, 1990)

Stone (1992): *Uncertain Unions, Marriage in England 1660–1753*, by L Stone (Oxford: Oxford University Press, 1992)

Stone (1993): *Broken Lives, Separation and Divorce in England, 1660–1857*, by L Stone (Oxford: Oxford University Press, 1993)

Strachey (1936): *Our Freedom and its Results*, by Five Women, ed. R Strachey (Hogarth Press, 1936)

Sugarman and Kay (1991): *Divorce Reform at the Crossroads*, ed. by SD Sugarman and HH Kay (Yale University Press, 1991)

Summerskill (1967): *A Woman's World*, by E Summerskill (Heinemann, 1967)

Swinburne (1686): *A Treatise of Spousals or Matrimonial Contracts . . .*, by H Swinburne (Robert Clavell, 1686)

Sykes (1975): *Evelyn Waugh, A Biography*, by C Sykes (Collins, 1975)

Taylor (1965): *English History 1914–1945*, by AJP Taylor (Oxford: Oxford University Press, 1965)

Taylor (1999): *Falling, The Story of One Marriage*, by J Taylor (V Gollancz, 1999)

Temkin (1987): *Rape and the Legal Process*, by J Temkin (Sweet and Maxwell, 1987)

Terrot (1959): *The Maiden Tribute*, by C Terrot (Muller, 1959)

Thane (2000): *Old Age in English History*, by P Thane (Oxford: Oxford University Press, 2000)

Thane and Sutcliffe (1986): *Essays in Social History, Volume 2*, ed. by P Thane and A Sutcliffe (Oxford: Oxford University Press, 1986)

Thatcher (1995): *The Downing Street Years*, by M Thatcher (Harper Collins, 1995)

Thatcher (2001): *Celebrating Christian Marriage*, ed. by A Thatcher (T T Clark Ltd, 2001)

Thoburn (1990): *Review of Research Relating to Adoption*—Interdepartmental Review of Adoption, Background paper No. 2, by J Thoburn (1990)

Thompson (1990): *The Cambridge Social History of Britain* ed. by FML Thompson (Cambridge: Cambridge University Press, 1990)

Thompson (1991): *The Making of the English Working Class*, by EP Thompson (Harmondsworth: Penguin Books, 1991)

Thompson (2000): *A Monkey among Crocodiles, The Lives, Loves and Lawsuits of Mrs Georgina Weldon*, by B Thompson (Harper Collins, 2000)

Thorpe (2000): *No Fault or Flaw: The Future of the Family Law Act 1996*, by M Thorpe and others (Bristol: Jordan Publishing Ltd, 2000)

Thring (1902): *Practical Legislation*, by Lord Thring (John Murray, 1902)

Titmuss (1950): *History of the Second World War, Problems of Social Policy*, by RM Titmuss (1950, revised 1976, HMSO and Kraus Reprint)

Tizard (1977) *Adoption, a second chance*, by B Tizard (Open Books, 1977)

Todd and Jones (1972): *Matrimonial Property*, by JE Todd and LM Jones (Office of Population Censuses and Surveys, 1972)

Townsend (1970): *The Concept of Poverty*, ed. by P Townsend (Heinemann Education, 1970)

Tranter (1985): *Population and Society 1750–1940*, Contrasts in Population Growth, by NL Tranter (Longman, 1985)

Treherne (1923): *A Plaintiff in Person*, by P Treherne (Heinemann, 1923)

Triseliotis (1973): *In search of Origins*, by J Triseliotis (Routledge & Kegan Paul, 1973)

Underhill (1936): *The Law Reform (Married Women & Tortfeasors) Act, 1935* by Sir A Underhill (Butterworths, 1936)

Underhill (1938): *Change and Decay, The Recollections and Reflections of an Octogenarian Bencher*, by Sir A Underhill (Butterworths, 1938)

van Bueren (1994): *International Law on the rights of the child*, by G van Bueren (The Hague: Martinus Nijhoff, 1994)

Verhellen (1996): *Monitoring Children's Rights*, ed. by E Verhellen (Kluwer Law International, 1996)

Vernon (1982): *Ellen Wilkinson*, by BD Vernon (Croom Helm, 1982)

Waddams (1992): *Law Politics and the Church of England, The Career of Stephen Lushington 1782–1873*, by SM Waddams (Cambridge: Cambridge University Press, 1992)

Wagner (1979): *Barnado*, by G Wagner (Weidenfeld and Nicolson, 1979)

Wagner (1982): *Children of the Empire*, by G Wagner (Weidenfeld and Nicolson, 1982)

Wagner (1988): *Residential Care, The Research Reviewed*, Literature Surveys commissioned by the Independent Review of Residential Care Chaired by G Wagner OBE PhD. Ed. by I Sinclair (HMSO 1988)

Walker McCarthy and Timms (1994): *Mediation: the Making and Remaking of Co-operative Relationships* by J Walker, O McCarthy and N Timms (Newcastle-upon-Tyne: Relate Centre for Family Studies, 1994)

Walkowitz (1992): *City of Dreadful Delight: narratives of sexual danger in late-Victorian London*, by JR Walkowitz (Virago, 1992)

Wall (1997): *Rooted Sorrows, Psychoanalytic Perspectives on Child Protection . . .* ed. by the Hon Mr Justice Wall (Bristol: Jordan Publishing Ltd, 1997)

Wallerstein and Kelly (1980): *Surviving the Breakup*, by J Wallerstein and JB Kelly (Grant McIntyre, 1980)

Wallerstein and Blakeslee (1989): *Second Chances: Men Women and Children a decade after divorce*, by JS Wallerstein and S Blakeslee (Bantam, 1989)

Walls and Bergin (1997): *The Law of Divorce in Ireland*, by M Walls and D Bergin (Bristol: Jordan Publishing Ltd, 1997)

Walters and Clive (1989): *Wills and Succession* by DB Walters and E Clive in *The Laws of Scotland, Stair Memorial Encyclopaedia* Vol. 25 (The Law Society of Scotland; Butterworths, 1989)

Walvin (1982): *A Child's World: A Social History of English Childhood, 1800–1914* by J Walvin (Penguin Books Ltd, Harmondsworth, 1982)

Wasserstein (1992): *Herbert Samuel, A Political Life*, by B Wasserstein (Oxford: Oxford University Press, 1992)

Watson (1968): *The Double Helix: A Personal Account of the Discovery of DNA*, by JD Watson (Weidenfeld and Nicolson, 1968)

Watson (1969): *Which is the Justice?*, by JAF Watson (George Allen & Unwin Ltd, 1969)

Waugh (1934): *A Handful of Dust*, by E Waugh (Chapman and Hall, 1934)

Weaver (1998): *The Hammonds: A Marriage in History*, by SA Weaver (Stanford, Calif.: Stanford University Press, 1998)

Webb (1929): *English Local Government*, Vols 7–10: English Poor Law History, Part II: The Last Hundred Years, Vols I and II, by S and B Webb (Longmans, Green and Co, 1929)

Webster (1996): *The Health Services since the War, Vol II*, by C Webster (HMSO, 1996)

Webster (1998): *The National Health Service, A Political History*, by C Webster (Oxford: Oxford University Press, 1998)

Weitzman (1985): *The Divorce Revolution*, by LJ Weitzman (Collier Macmillan, 1985)

Weitzman and Maclean (1991): *The Economic Consequences of Divorce*, by L Weitzman and M Maclean (Oxford: Oxford University Press, 1991)

Welsby (1984): *A History of the Church of England*, by PA Welsby (Oxford: Oxford University Press, 1984)

Weeks (1981): *Sex Politics and Society, The regulation of sexuality since 1800*, by J Weeks (Longman, 1981)

White (1990): *Tax Planning on Marriage Breakdown*, by P White, 5th ed. (Longman, 1987)

White, Carr and Lowe (1990): *A Guide to the Children Act 1989*, by RAH White, NV Lowe and P Carr (Butterworths, 1990)

R White, P Carr and N Lowe (1995): *The Children Act in Practice*, 2nd ed. (Butterworths, 1995)

Wicks (1993): *Yesterday They Took My Baby, True Stories of Adoption*, by B Wicks (Mandarin, 1993)

Wieacker (1995): *A History of Private Law in Europe (with particular reference to Germany)*, by F Wieacker, trans. by T Weir (Oxford: Oxford University Press, 1995)

Williamson (1988): *The Modernisation of Conservative Politics: the diaries and letters of W Bridgeman*, ed by P Williamson (Historians' Press, 1988)

Wilson (1977): *Women and the Welfare State*, by E Wilson (Tavistock, 1977)

Winfield (1954): *Textbook of the Law of Tort*, by PM Winfield (6th ed. by T Ellis Lewis, Sweet & Maxwell, 1954)

Wintermute and Andrenas (2001): *Legal Recognition of Same Sex Relationships*, by R Wintermute and M Andenas (Oxford: Hart Publishing, 2001)

Wise (1991): *Child Abuse: the NSPCC Version*, by S Wise (Feminist Praxis, 1991)

Wolfram (1987): *In Laws and Out-laws: kinship and marriage in England*, by S Wolfram (Croom Helm, 1987)

Woodruff (1957): *The Tichborne Claimant*, by D Woodruff (Hollis and Carter, 1957)

Woodward (1962): *The Age of Reform*, 2nd ed. by Sir L Woodward (Oxford: Oxford University Press, 1962)

Woolf (1985): *Moments of Being*, by V Woolf, 2nd ed. (Hogarth Press, 1985)

Wrigley and Schofield (1989): *The Population History of England 1541–1871, A Reconstruction*, by EA Wrigley and RS Schofield (Cambridge: Cambridge University Press, 1989)

Young and Rao (1998): *Local Government since 1945*, by K Young and N Rao (Oxford: Blackwell Publishers Ltd, 1998)

Ziegler (1985): *Mountbatten*, by P Ziegler (Fontana Collins, 1985)

Ziegler (1990): *King Edward VIII, The Official Biography*, by P Ziegler (Collins, 1990)

Index

Index